intel

P9-EBZ-877

U.S. and CANADA LITERATURE ORDER FORM

NAME: _____

COMPANY: _____

ADDRESS: _____

CITY: _____ STATE: _____ ZIP: _____

COUNTRY: _____

PHONE NO.: (_____) _____

ORDER NO.	TITLE	QTY.		PRICE		TOTAL
☐☐☐☐☐☐☐	_____	____	×	_____	=	_____
☐☐☐☐☐☐☐	_____	____	×	_____	=	_____
☐☐☐☐☐☐☐	_____	____	×	_____	=	_____
☐☐☐☐☐☐☐	_____	____	×	_____	=	_____
☐☐☐☐☐☐☐	_____	____	×	_____	=	_____
☐☐☐☐☐☐☐	_____	____	×	_____	=	_____
☐☐☐☐☐☐☐	_____	____	×	_____	=	_____
☐☐☐☐☐☐☐	_____	____	×	_____	=	_____
☐☐☐☐☐☐☐	_____	____	×	_____	=	_____
☐☐☐☐☐☐☐	_____	____	×	_____	=	_____

Subtotal _____

Must Add Your
Local Sales Tax _____

Postage: add 10% of subtotal	⟶ Postage _____

Total _____

Pay by check, money order, or include company purchase order with this form ($100 minimum). We also accept VISA, MasterCard or American Express. Make payment to Intel Literature Sales. Allow 2-4 weeks for delivery.

☐ VISA ☐ MasterCard ☐ American Express Expiration Date _____

Account No. _____

Signature _____

Mail To: Intel Literature Sales
P.O. Box 7641
Mt. Prospect, Il 60056-7641

International Customers outside the U.S. and Canada should use the International order form or contact their local Sales Office or Distributor.

**For phone orders in the U.S. and Canada
Call Toll Free: (800) 548-4725**

Prices good until 12/31/90.

Source HB

INTERNATIONAL LITERATURE ORDER FORM

NAME: _____

COMPANY: _____

ADDRESS: _____

CITY: _____ STATE: _____ ZIP: _____

COUNTRY: _____

PHONE NO.: ( ) _____

ORDER NO.	TITLE	QTY.	PRICE	TOTAL
☐☐☐☐☐☐	_____	____ ×	_____ =	_____
☐☐☐☐☐☐	_____	____ ×	_____ =	_____
☐☐☐☐☐☐	_____	____ ×	_____ =	_____
☐☐☐☐☐☐	_____	____ ×	_____ =	_____
☐☐☐☐☐☐	_____	____ ×	_____ =	_____
☐☐☐☐☐☐	_____	____ ×	_____ =	_____
☐☐☐☐☐☐	_____	____ ×	_____ =	_____
☐☐☐☐☐☐	_____	____ ×	_____ =	_____
☐☐☐☐☐☐	_____	____ ×	_____ =	_____
☐☐☐☐☐☐	_____	____ ×	_____ =	_____

Subtotal _____

Must Add Your
Local Sales Tax _____

Total _____

PAYMENT

Cheques should be made payable to your local Intel Sales Office

Other forms of payment may be available in your country. Please contact the Literature Coordinator at your local Intel Sales Office for details.

The completed form should be marked to the attention of the LITERATURE COORDINATOR and returned to your local Intel Sales Office.

Intel the Microcomputer Company:
When Intel invented the microprocessor in 1971, it created the era of
microcomputers. Whether used in embedded applications such as automobiles
or microwave ovens, or as the CPU in personal computers or supercomputers,
Intel's microcomputers have always offered leading-edge technology. Intel continues
to strive for the highest standards in memory, microcomputer components, modules
and systems to give its customers the best possible competitive advantages.

16-/32-BIT
EMBEDDED PROCESSOR
HANDBOOK

1990

Intel Corporation makes no warranty for the use of its products and assumes no responsibility for any errors which may appear in this document nor does it make a commitment to update the information contained herein.

Intel retains the right to make changes to these specifications at any time, without notice.

Contact your local sales office to obtain the latest specifications before placing your order.

The following are trademarks of Intel Corporation and may only be used to identify Intel Products:

MDS is an ordering code only and is not used as a product name or trademark. MDS® is a registered trademark of Mohawk Data Sciences Corporation.

*MULTIBUS is a patented Intel bus.

CHMOS and HMOS are patented processes of Intel Corp.

Intel Corporation and Intel's FASTPATH are not affiliated with Kinetics, a division of Excelan, Inc. or its FASTPATH trademark or products.

Additional copies of this manual or other Intel literature may be obtained from:

Intel Corporation
Literature Sales
P.O. Box 7641
Mt. Prospect, IL 60056-7641

CUSTOMER SUPPORT

INTEL'S COMPLETE SUPPORT SOLUTION WORLDWIDE

Customer Support is Intel's complete support service that provides Intel customers with hardware support, software support, customer training, consulting services and network management services. For detailed information contact your local sales offices.

After a customer purchases any system hardware or software product, service and support become major factors in determining whether that product will continue to meet a customer's expectations. Such support requires an international support organization and a breadth of programs to meet a variety of customer needs. As you might expect, Intel's customer support is quite extensive. It can start with assistance during your development effort to network management. 100 Intel sales and service offices are located worldwide — in the U.S., Canada, Europe and the Far East. So wherever you're using Intel technology, our professional staff is within close reach.

HARDWARE SUPPORT SERVICES

Intel's hardware maintenance service, starting with complete on-site installation will boost your productivity from the start and keep you running at maximum efficiency. Support for system or board level products can be tailored to match your needs, from complete on-site repair and maintenance support to economical carry-in or mail-in factory service.

Intel can provide support service for not only Intel systems and emulators, but also support for equipment in your development lab or provide service on your product to your end-user/customer.

SOFTWARE SUPPORT SERVICES

Software products are supported by our Technical Information Service (TIPS) that has a special toll free number to provide you with direct, ready information on known, documented problems and deficiencies, as well as work-arounds, patches and other solutions.

Intel's software support consists of two levels of contracts. Standard support includes TIPS (Technical Information Phone Service), updates and subscription service (product-specific troubleshooting guides and; *COMMENTS Magazine*). Basic support consists of updates and the subscription service. Contracts are sold in environments which represent product groupings (e.g., iRMX® environment).

CONSULTING SERVICES

Intel provides field system engineering consulting services for any phase of your development or application effort. You can use our system engineers in a variety of ways ranging from assistance in using a new product, developing an application, personalizing training and customizing an Intel product to providing technical and management consulting. Systems Engineers are well versed in technical areas such as microcommunications, real-time applications, embedded microcontrollers, and network services. You know your application needs; we know our products. Working together we can help you get a successful product to market in the least possible time.

CUSTOMER TRAINING

Intel offers a wide range of instructional programs covering various aspects of system design and implementation. In just three to ten days a limited number of individuals learn more in a single workshop than in weeks of self-study. For optimum convenience, workshops are scheduled regularly at Training Centers worldwide or we can take our workshops to you for on-site instruction. Covering a wide variety of topics, Intel's major course categories include: architecture and assembly language, programming and operating systems, BITBUS™ and LAN applications.

NETWORK MANAGEMENT SERVICES

Today's networking products are powerful and extremely flexible. The return they can provide on your investment via increased productivity and reduced costs can be very substantial.

Intel offers complete network support, from definition of your network's physical and functional design, to implementation, installation and maintenance. Whether installing your first network or adding to an existing one, Intel's Networking Specialists can optimize network performance for you.

Table of Contents

Table of Contents (Continued)

Alphanumeric Index

80186/188/C186/C188
Data Sheets

80186
HIGH INTEGRATION 16-BIT MICROPROCESSOR

- **Integrated Feature Set**
  - Enhanced 8086-2 CPU
  - Clock Generator
  - 2 Independent DMA Channels
  - Programmable Interrupt Controller
  - 3 Programmable 16-bit Timers
  - Programmable Memory and Peripheral Chip-Select Logic
  - Programmable Wait State Generator
  - Local Bus Controller

- **Available in 10 MHz (80186-10) and 8 MHz (80186) Versions**

- **High-Performance Processor**
  - 4 MByte/Sec Bus Bandwidth Interface @ 8 MHz
  - 5 MByte/Sec Bus Bandwidth Interface @ 10 MHz

- **Direct Addressing Capability to 1 MByte of Memory and 64 KByte I/O**

- **Completely Object Code Compatible with All Existing 8086, 8088 Software**
  - 10 New Instruction Types

- **Complete System Development Support**
  - Development Software: ASM 86 Assembler, PL/M-86, Pascal-86, Fortran-86, C-86, and System Utilities
  - In-Circuit-Emulator (I²ICE™-186)

- **Numerics Coprocessing Capability Through 8087 Interface**

- **Available in 68 Pin:**
  - Plastic Leaded Chip Carrier (PLCC)
  - Ceramic Pin Grid Array (PGA)
  - Ceramic Leadless Chip Carrier (LCC)

  (See Packaging Outlines and Dimensions, Order # 231369)

- **Available in EXPRESS**
  - Standard Temperature with Burn-In
  - Extended Temperature Range ($-40°C$ to $+85°C$)

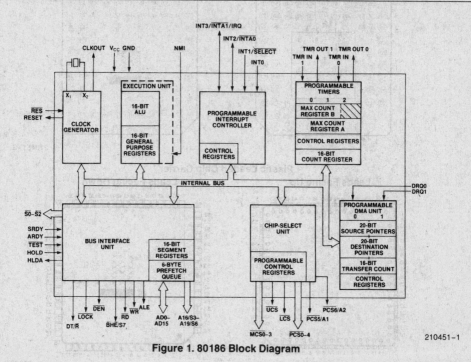

Figure 1. 80186 Block Diagram

210451–1

October 1989
Order Number: 210451-011

The Intel 80186 is a highly integrated 16-bit microprocessor. The 80186 effectively combines 15–20 of the most common 8086 system components onto one. The 80186 provides two times greater throughput than the standard 5 MHz 8086. The 80186 is upward compatible with 8086 and 8088 software and adds 10 new instruction types to the existing set.

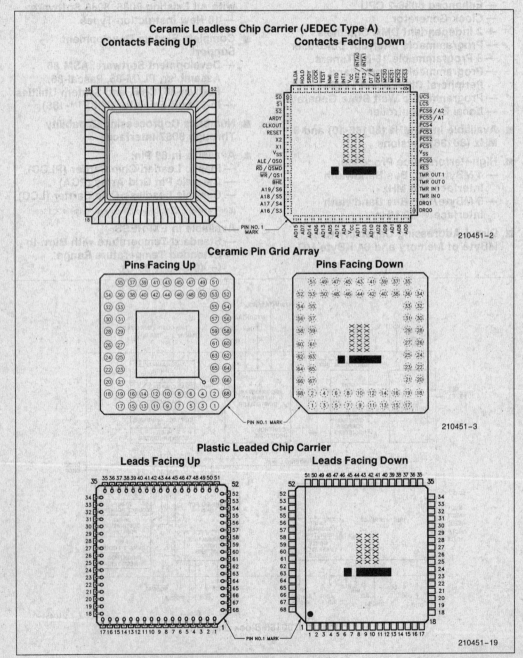

Figure 2. 80186 Pinout Diagrams

Table 1. 80186 Pin Description

Symbol	Pin No.	Type	Name and Function
V_{CC}	9 43	I	**System Power:** +5 volt power supply.
V_{SS}	26 60	I	System Ground.
RESET	57	O	Reset Output indicates that the 80186 CPU is being reset, and can be used as a system reset. It is active HIGH, synchronized with the processor clock, and lasts an integer number of clock periods corresponding to the length of the $\overline{\text{RES}}$ signal.
X1 X2	59 58	I O	Crystal Inputs X1 and X2 provide external connections for a fundamental mode parallel resonant crystal for the internal oscillator. Instead of using a crystal, an external clock may be applied to X1 while minimizing stray capacitance on X2. The input or oscillator frequency is internally divided by two to generate the clock signal (CLKOUT).
CLKOUT	56	O	Clock Output provides the system with a 50% duty cycle waveform. All device pin timings are specified relative to CLKOUT.
$\overline{\text{RES}}$	24	I	An active $\overline{\text{RES}}$ causes the 80186 to immediately terminate its present activity, clear the internal logic, and enter a dormant state. This signal may be asynchronous to the 80186 clock. The 80186 begins fetching instructions approximately 6½ clock cycles after $\overline{\text{RES}}$ is returned HIGH. For proper initialization, V_{CC} must be within specifications and the clock signal must be stable for more than 4 clocks with $\overline{\text{RES}}$ held LOW. $\overline{\text{RES}}$ is internally synchronized. This input is provided with a Schmitt-trigger to facilitate power-on $\overline{\text{RES}}$ generation via an RC network.
$\overline{\text{TEST}}$	47	I/O	$\overline{\text{TEST}}$ is examined by the WAIT instruction. If the $\overline{\text{TEST}}$ input is HIGH when "WAIT" execution begins, instruction execution will suspend. $\overline{\text{TEST}}$ will be resampled until it goes LOW, at which time execution will resume. If interrupts are enabled while the 80186 is waiting for $\overline{\text{TEST}}$, interrupts will be serviced. During power-up, active $\overline{\text{RES}}$ is required to configure $\overline{\text{TEST}}$ as an input. This pin is synchronized internally.
TMR IN 0 TMR IN 1	20 21	I I	Timer Inputs are used either as clock or control signals, depending upon the programmed timer mode. These inputs are active HIGH (or LOW-to-HIGH transitions are counted) and internally synchronized.
TMR OUT 0 TMR OUT 1	22 23	O O	Timer outputs are used to provide single pulse or continous waveform generation, depending upon the timer mode selected.
DRQ0 DRQ1	18 19	I I	DMA Request is asserted HIGH by an external device when it is ready for DMA Channel 0 or 1 to perform a transfer. These signals are level-triggered and internally synchronized.
NMI	46	I	The Non-Maskable Interrupt input causes a Type 2 interrupt. An NMI transition from LOW to HIGH is latched and synchronized internally, and initiates the interrupt at the next instruction boundary. NMI must be asserted for at least one clock. The Non-Maskable Interrupt cannot be avoided by programming.
INT0 INT1/$\overline{\text{SELECT}}$ INT2/$\overline{\text{INTA0}}$ INT3/$\overline{\text{INTA1}}$/IRQ	45 44 42 41	I I I/O I/O	Maskable Interrupt Requests can be requested by activating one of these pins. When configured as inputs, these pins are active HIGH. Interrupt Requests are synchronized internally. INT2 and INT3 may be configured to provide active-LOW interrupt-acknowledge output signals. All interrupt inputs may be configured to be either edge- or level-triggered. To ensure recognition, all interrupt requests must remain active until the interrupt is acknowledged. When Slave Mode is selected, the function of these pins changes (see Interrupt Controller section of this data sheet).

Table 1. 80186 Pin Description (Continued)

Symbol	Pin No.	Type	Name and Function
A19/S6 A18/S5 A17/S4 A16/S3	65 66 67 68	O O O O	Address Bus Outputs (16–19) and Bus Cycle Status (3–6) indicate the four most significant address bits during T_1. These signals are active HIGH. During T_2, T_3, T_W, and T_4, the S6 pin is LOW to indicate a CPU-initiated bus cycle or HIGH to indicate a DMA-initiated bus cycle. During the same T-states, S3, S4, and S5 are always LOW. The status pins float during bus HOLD or RESET.
AD15 AD14 AD13 AD12 AD11 AD10 AD9 AD8 AD7 AD6 AD5 AD4 AD3 AD2 AD1 AD0	1 3 5 7 10 12 14 16 2 4 6 8 11 13 15 17	I/O I/O I/O I/O I/O I/O I/O I/O I/O I/O I/O I/O I/O I/O I/O I/O	Address/Data Bus (0–15) signals constitute the time multiplexed memory or I/O address (T_1) and data (T_2, T_3, T_W, and T_4) bus. The bus is active HIGH. A_0 is analogous to $\overline{BHE}$ for the lower byte of the data bus, pins D_7 through D_0. It is LOW during T_1 when a byte is to be transferred onto the lower portion of the bus in memory or I/O operations.
$\overline{BHE}$/S7	64	O	During T_1 the Bus High Enable signal should be used to determine if data is to be enabled onto the most significant half of the data bus; pins D_{15}–D_8. $\overline{BHE}$ is LOW during T_1 for read, write, and interrupt acknowledge cycles when a byte is to be transferred on the higher half of the bus. The S_7 status information is available during T_2, T_3, and T_4. S_7 is logically equivalent to $\overline{BHE}$. $\overline{BHE}$/S7 floats during HOLD.

$\overline{BHE}$ and A0 Encodings

$\overline{BHE}$ Value	A0 Value	Function
0	0	Word Transfer
0	1	Byte Transfer on upper half of data bus (D15–D8)
1	0	Byte Transfer on lower half of data bus (D_7–D_0)
1	1	Reserved

Symbol	Pin No.	Type	Name and Function
ALE/QS0	61	O	Address Latch Enable/Queue Status 0 is provided by the 80186 to latch the address. ALE is active HIGH. Addresses are guaranteed to be valid on the trailing edge of ALE. The ALE rising edge is generated off the rising edge of the CLKOUT immediately preceding T_1 of the associated bus cycle, effectively one-half clock cycle earlier than in the 8086. The trailing edge is generated off the CLKOUT rising edge in T_1 as in the 8086. Note that ALE is never floated.
$\overline{WR}$/QS1	63	O	Write Strobe/Queue Status 1 indicates that the data on the bus is to be written into a memory or an I/O device. $\overline{WR}$ is active for T_2, T_3, and T_W of any write cycle. It is active LOW, and floats during HOLD. When the 80186 is in queue status mode, the ALE/QS0 and $\overline{WR}$/QS1 pins provide information about processor/instruction queue interaction.

QS1	QS0	Queue Operation
0	0	No queue operation
0	1	First opcode byte fetched from the queue
1	1	Subsequent byte fetched from the queue
1	0	Empty the queue

Table 1. 80186 Pin Description (Continued)

Symbol	Pin No.	Type	Name and Function
RD/QSMD	62	I/O	Read Strobe is an active LOW signal which indicates that the 80186 is performing a memory or I/O read cycle. It is guaranteed not to go LOW before the A/D bus is floated. An internal pull-up ensures that $\overline{RD}$ is HIGH during RESET. Following RESET the pin is sampled to determine whether the 80186 is to provide ALE, $\overline{RD}$, and $\overline{WR}$, or queue status information. To enable Queue Status Mode, $\overline{RD}$ must be connected to GND. $\overline{RD}$ will float during bus HOLD.
ARDY	55	I	Asynchronous Ready informs the 80186 that the addressed memory space or I/O device will complete a data transfer. The ARDY pin accepts a rising edge that is asynchronous to CLKOUT, and is active HIGH. The falling edge of ARDY must be synchronized to the 80186 clock. Connecting ARDY HIGH will always assert the ready condition to the CPU. If this line is unused, it should be tied LOW to yield control to the SRDY pin.
SRDY	49	I	Synchronous Ready informs the 80186 that the addressed memory space or I/O device will complete a data transfer. The SRDY pin accepts an active-HIGH input synchronized to CLKOUT. The use of SRDY allows a relaxed system timing over ARDY. This is accomplished by elimination of the one-half clock cycle required to internally synchronize the ARDY input signal. Connecting SRDY high will always assert the ready condition to the CPU. If this line is unused, it should be tied LOW to yield control to the ARDY pin.
LOCK	48	O	$\overline{LOCK}$ output indicates that other system bus masters are not to gain control of the system bus while $\overline{LOCK}$ is active LOW. The $\overline{LOCK}$ signal is requested by the LOCK prefix instruction and is activated at the beginning of the first data cycle associated with the instruction following the LOCK prefix. It remains active until the completion of that instruction. No instruction prefetching will occur while $\overline{LOCK}$ is asserted. When executing more than one LOCK instruction, always make sure there are 6 bytes of code between the end of the first LOCK instruction and the start of the second LOCK instruction. $\overline{LOCK}$ is driven HIGH for one clock during RESET and then floated.
$\overline{S0}$ $\overline{S1}$ $\overline{S2}$	52 53 54	O O O	Bus cycle status $\overline{S0}$–$\overline{S2}$ are encoded to provide bus-transaction information:

80186 Bus Cycle Status Information			
$\overline{S2}$	$\overline{S1}$	$\overline{S0}$	Bus Cycle Initiated
0	0	0	Interrupt Acknowledge
0	0	1	Read I/O
0	1	0	Write I/O
0	1	1	Halt
1	0	0	Instruction Fetch
1	0	1	Read Data from Memory
1	1	0	Write Data to Memory
1	1	1	Passive (no bus cycle)

The status pins float during HOLD.
$\overline{S2}$ may be used as a logical M/$\overline{IO}$ indicator, and $\overline{S1}$ as a DT/$\overline{R}$ indicator.

Table 1. 80186 Pin Description (Continued)

Symbol	Pin No.	Type	Name and Function
HOLD HLDA	50 51	I O	HOLD indicates that another bus master is requesting the local bus. The HOLD input is active HIGH. HOLD may be asynchronous with respect to the 80186 clock. The 80186 will issue a HLDA (HIGH) in response to a HOLD request at the end of T_4 or T_i. Simultaneous with the issuance of HLDA, the 80186 will float the local bus and control lines. After HOLD is detected as being LOW, the 80186 will lower HLDA. When the 80186 needs to run another bus cycle, it will again drive the local bus and control lines.
$\overline{UCS}$	34	O	Upper Memory Chip Select is an active LOW output whenever a memory reference is made to the defined upper portion (1K–256K block) of memory. This line is not floated during bus HOLD. The address range activating $\overline{UCS}$ is software programmable.
$\overline{LCS}$	33	O	Lower Memory Chip Select is active LOW whenever a memory reference is made to the defined lower portion (1K–256K) of memory. This line is not floated during bus HOLD. The address range activating $\overline{LCS}$ is software programmable.
$\overline{MCS0}$ $\overline{MCS1}$ $\overline{MCS2}$ $\overline{MCS3}$	38 37 36 35	O O O O	Mid-Range Memory Chip Select signals are active LOW when a memory reference is made to the defined mid-range portion of memory (8K–512K). These lines are not floated during bus HOLD. The address ranges activating $\overline{MCS0}$–3 are software programmable.
$\overline{PCS0}$ $\overline{PCS1}$ $\overline{PCS2}$ $\overline{PCS3}$ PCS4	25 27 28 29 30	O O O O O	Peripheral Chip Select signals 0–4 are active LOW when a reference is made to the defined peripheral area (64K byte I/O space). These lines are not floated during bus HOLD. The address ranges activating $\overline{PCS0}$–4 are software programmable.
$\overline{PCS5}$/A1	31	O	Peripheral Chip Select 5 or Latched A1 may be programmed to provide a sixth peripheral chip select, or to provide an internally latched A1 signal. The address range activating $\overline{PCS5}$ is software-programmable. $\overline{PCS5}$/A1 does not float during bus HOLD. When programmed to provide latched A1, this pin will retain the previously latched value during HOLD.
$\overline{PCS6}$/A2	32	O	Peripheral Chip Select 6 or Latched A2 may be programmed to provide a seventh peripheral chip select, or to provide an internally latched A2 signal. The address range activating $\overline{PCS6}$ is software programmable. $\overline{PCS6}$/A2 does not float during bus HOLD. When programmed to provide latched A2, this pin will retain the previously latched value during HOLD.
DT/$\overline{R}$	40	O	Data Transmit/Receive controls the direction of data flow through an external data bus transceiver. When LOW, data is transferred to the 80186. When HIGH the 80186 places write data on the data bus.
$\overline{DEN}$	39	O	Data Enable is provided as a data bus transceiver output enable. $\overline{DEN}$ is active LOW during each memory and I/O access. $\overline{DEN}$ is HIGH whenever DT/$\overline{R}$ changes state. During RESET, $\overline{DEN}$ is driven HIGH for one clock, then floated. $\overline{DEN}$ also floats during HOLD.

FUNCTIONAL DESCRIPTION

Introduction

The following Functional Description describes the base architecture of the 80186. The 80186 is a very high integration 16-bit microprocessor. It combines 15–20 of the most common microprocessor system components onto one chip while providing twice the performance of the standard 8086. The 80186 is object code compatible with the 8086/8088 microprocessors and adds 10 new instruction types to the 8086/8088 instruction set.

80186 BASE ARCHITECTURE

The 8086, 8088, 80186, and 80286 family all contain the same basic set of registers, instructions, and addressing modes.

Register Set

The 80186 base architecture has fourteen registers as shown in Figures 3a and 3b. These registers are grouped into the following categories.

General Registers

Eight 16-bit general purpose registers may be used for arithmetic and logical operands. Four of these (AX, BX, CX, and DX) can be used as 16-bit registers or split into pairs of separate 8-bit registers.

Segment Registers

Four 16-bit special purpose registers select, at any given time, the segments of memory that are immediately addressable for code, stack, and data. (For usage, refer to Memory Organization.)

Base and Index Registers

Four of the general purpose registers may also be used to determine offset addresses of operands in memory. These registers may contain base addresses or indexes to particular locations within a segment. The addressing mode selects the specific registers for operand and address calculations.

Status and Control Registers

Two 16-bit special purpose registers record or alter certain aspects of the 80186 processor state. These are the Instruction Pointer Register, which contains the offset address of the next sequential instruction to be executed, and the Status Word Register, which contains status and control flag bits (see Figures 3a and 3b).

Status Word Description

The Status Word records specific characteristics of the result of logical and arithmetic instructions (bits 0, 2, 4, 6, 7, and 11) and controls the operation of the 80186 within a given operating mode (bits 8, 9, and 10). The Status Word Register is 16-bits wide. The function of the Status Word bits is shown in Table 2.

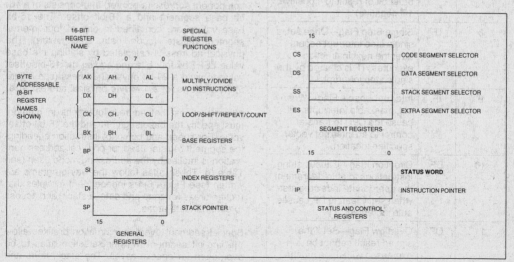

Figure 3a. 80186 Register Set

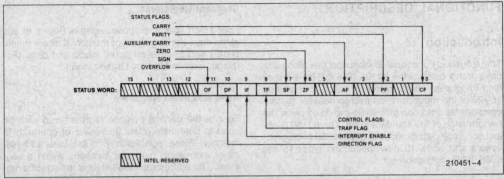

Figure 3b. Status Word Format

Table 2. Status Word Bit Functions

Bit Position	Name	Function
0	CF	Carry Flag—Set on high-order bit carry or borrow; cleared otherwise
2	PF	Parity Flag—Set if low-order 8 bits of result contain an even number of 1-bits; cleared otherwise
4	AF	Set on carry from or borrow to the low order four bits of AL; cleared otherwise
6	ZF	Zero Flag—Set if result is zero; cleared otherwise
7	SF	Sign Flag—Set equal to high-order bit of result (0 if positive, 1 if negative)
8	TF	Single Step Flag—Once set, a single step interrupt occurs after the next instruction executes. TF is cleared by the single step interrupt.
9	IF	Interrupt-enable Flag—When set, maskable interrupts will cause the CPU to transfer control to an interrupt vector specified location.
10	DF	Direction Flag—Causes string instructions to auto decrement the appropriate index register when set. Clearing DF causes auto increment.
11	OF	Overflow Flag—Set if the signed result cannot be expressed within the number of bits in the destination operand; cleared otherwise

Instruction Set

The instruction set is divided into seven categories: data transfer, arithmetic, shift/rotate/logical, string manipulation, control transfer, high-level instructions, and processor control. These categories are summarized in Figure 4.

An 80186 instruction can reference anywhere from zero to several operands. An operand can reside in a register, in the instruction itself, or in memory. Specific operand addressing modes are discussed later in this data sheet.

Memory Organization

Memory is organized in sets of segments. Each segment is a linear contiguous sequence of up to 64K (2^{16}) 8-bit bytes. Memory is addressed using a two-component address (a pointer) that consists of a 16-bit base segment and a 16-bit offset. The 16-bit base values are contained in one of four internal segment register (code, data, stack, extra). The physical address is calculated by shifting the base value LEFT by four bits and adding the 16-bit offset value to yield a 20-bit physical address (see Figure 5). This allows for a 1 MByte physical address size.

All instructions that address operands in memory must specify the base segment and the 16-bit offset value. For speed and compact instruction encoding, the segment register used for physical address generation is implied by the addressing mode used (see Table 3). These rules follow the way programs are written (see Figure 6) as independent modules that require areas for code and data, a stack, and access to external data areas.

Special segment override instruction prefixes allow the implicit segment register selection rules to be overridden for special cases. The stack, data, and extra segments may coincide for simple programs.

GENERAL PURPOSE	
MOV	Move byte or word
PUSH	Push word onto stack
POP	Pop word off stack
PUSHA	Push all registers on stack
POPA	Pop all registers from stack
XCHG	Exchange byte or word
XLAT	Translate byte
INPUT/OUTPUT	
IN	Input byte or word
OUT	Output byte or word
ADDRESS OBJECT	
LEA	Load effective address
LDS	Load pointer using DS
LES	Load pointer using ES
FLAG TRANSFER	
LAHF	Load AH register from flags
SAHF	Store AH register in flags
PUSHF	Push flags onto stack
POPF	Pop flags off stack
ADDITION	
ADD	Add byte or word
ADC	Add byte or word with carry
INC	Increment byte or word by 1
AAA	ASCII adjust for addition
DAA	Decimal adjust for addition
SUBTRACTION	
SUB	Subtract byte or word
SBB	Subtract byte or word with borrow
DEC	Decrement byte or word by 1
NEG	Negate byte or word
CMP	Compare byte or word
AAS	ASCII adjust for subtraction
DAS	Decimal adjust for subtraction
MULTIPLICATION	
MUL	Multiply byte or word unsigned
IMUL	Integer multiply byte or word
AAM	ASCII adjust for multiply
DIVISION	
DIV	Divide byte or word unsigned
IDIV	Integer divide byte or word
AAD	ASCII adjust for division
CBW	Convert byte to word
CWD	Convert word to doubleword

MOVS	Move byte or word string
INS	Input bytes or word string
OUTS	Output bytes or word string
CMPS	Compare byte or word string
SCAS	Scan byte or word string
LODS	Load byte or word string
STOS	Store byte or word string
REP	Repeat
REPE/REPZ	Repeat while equal/zero
REPNE/REPNZ	Repeat while not equal/not zero
LOGICALS	
NOT	"Not" byte or word
AND	"And" byte or word
OR	"Inclusive or" byte or word
XOR	"Exclusive or" byte or word
TEST	"Test" byte or word
SHIFTS	
SHL/SAL	Shift logical/arithmetic left byte or word
SHR	Shift logical right byte or word
SAR	Shift arithmetic right byte or word
ROTATES	
ROL	Rotate left byte or word
ROR	Rotate right byte or word
RCL	Rotate through carry left byte or word
RCR	Rotate through carry right byte or word
FLAG OPERATIONS	
STC	Set carry flag
CLC	Clear carry flag
CMC	Complement carry flag
STD	Set direction flag
CLD	Clear direction flag
STI	Set interrupt enable flag
CLI	Clear interrupt enable flag
EXTERNAL SYNCHRONIZATION	
HLT	Halt until interrupt or reset
WAIT	Wait for TEST pin active
ESC	Escape to extension processor
LOCK	Lock bus during next instruction
NO OPERATION	
NOP	No operation
HIGH LEVEL INSTRUCTIONS	
ENTER	Format stack for procedure entry
LEAVE	Restore stack for procedure exit
BOUND	Detects values outside prescribed range

Figure 4. 80186 Instruction Set

CONDITIONAL TRANSFERS	
JA/JNBE	Jump if above/not below nor equal
JAE/JNB	Jump if above or equal/not below
JB/JNAE	Jump if below/not above nor equal
JBE/JNA	Jump if below or equal/not above
JC	Jump if carry
JE/JZ	Jump if equal/zero
JG/JNLE	Jump if greater/not less nor equal
JGE/JNL	Jump if greater or equal/not less
JL/JNGE	Jump if less/not greater nor equal
JLE/JNG	Jump if less or equal/not greater
JNC	Jump if not carry
JNE/JNZ	Jump if not equal/not zero
JNO	Jump if not overflow
JNP/JPO	Jump if not parity/parity odd
JNS	Jump if not sign

JO	Jump if overflow
JP/JPE	Jump if parity/parity even
JS	Jump if sign
UNCONDITIONAL TRANSFERS	
CALL	Call procedure
RET	Return from procedure
JMP	Jump
ITERATION CONTROLS	
LOOP	Loop
LOOPE/LOOPZ	Loop if equal/zero
LOOPNE/LOOPNZ	Loop if not equal/not zero
JCXZ	Jump if register CX = 0
INTERRUPTS	
INT	Interrupt
INTO	Interrupt if overflow
IRET	Interrupt return

Figure 4. 80186 Instruction Set (Continued)

To access operands that do not reside in one of the four immediately available segments, a full 32-bit pointer can be used to reload both the base (segment) and offset values.

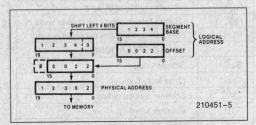

Figure 5. Two Component Address

Table 3. Segment Register Selection Rules

Memory Reference Needed	Segment Register Used	Implicit Segment Selection Rule
Instructions	Code (CS)	Instruction prefetch and immediate data.
Stack	Stack (SS)	All stack pushes and pops; any memory references which use BP Register as a base register.
External Data (Global)	Extra (ES)	All string instruction references which use the DI register as an index.
Local Data	Data (DS)	All other data references.

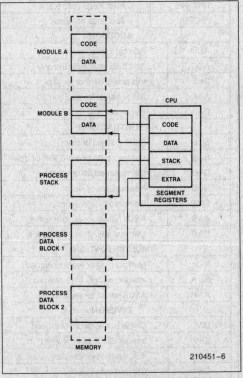

Figure 6. Segmented Memory Helps Structure Software

Addressing Modes

The 80186 provides eight categories of addressing modes to specify operands. Two addressing modes are provided for instructions that operate on register or immediate operands:

- *Register Operand Mode:* The operand is located in one of the 8- or 16-bit general registers.
- *Immediate Operand Mode:* The operand is included in the instruction.

Six modes are provided to specify the location of an operand in a memory segment. A memory operand address consists of two 16-bit components: a segment base and an offset. The segment base is supplied by a 16-bit segment register either implicitly chosen by the addressing mode or explicitly chosen by a segment override prefix. The offset, also called the effective address, is calculated by summing any combination of the following three address elements:

- the *displacement* (an 8- or 16-bit immediate value contained in the instruction);
- the *base* (contents of either the BX or BP base registers); and
- the *index* (contents of either the SI or DI index registers).

Any carry out from the 16-bit addition is ignored. Eight-bit displacements are sign extended to 16-bit values.

Combinations of these three address elements define the six memory addressing modes, described below.

- *Direct Mode:* The operand's offset is contained in the instruction as an 8- or 16-bit displacement element.
- *Register Indirect Mode:* The operand's offset is in one of the registers SI, DI, BX, or BP.
- *Based Mode:* The operand's offset is the sum of an 8- or 16-bit displacement and the contents of a base register (BX or BP).
- *Indexed Mode:* The operand's offset is the sum of an 8- or 16-bit displacement and the contents of an index register (SI or DI).
- *Based Indexed Mode:* The operand's offset is the sum of the contents of a base register and an Index register.
- *Based indexed Mode with Displacement:* The operand's offset is the sum of a base register's contents, an index register's contents, and an 8- or 16-bit displacement.

Data Types

The 80186 directly supports the following data types:

- *Integer:* A signed binary numeric value contained in an 8-bit byte or a 16-bit word. All operations assume a 2's complement representation. Signed 32- and 64-bit integers are supported using an 8087 Numeric Data Coprocessor with the 80186.
- *Ordinal:* An unsigned binary numeric value contained in an 8-bit byte or a 16-bit word.
- *Pointer:* A 16- or 32-bit quantity, composed of a 16-bit offset component or a 16-bit segment base component in addition to a 16-bit offset component.
- *String:* A contiguous sequence of bytes or words. A string may contain from 1 to 64K bytes.
- *ASCII:* A byte representation of alphanumeric and control characters using the ASCII standard of character representation.
- *BCD:* A byte (unpacked) representation of the decimal digits 0–9.
- *Packed BCD:* A byte (packed) representation of two decimal digits (0–9). One digit is stored in each nibble (4-bits) of the byte.
- *Floating Point:* A signed 32-, 64-, or 80-bit real number representation. (Floating point operands are supported using an 8087 Numeric Data Coprocessor with the 80186.)

In general, individual data elements must fit within defined segment limits. Figure 7 graphically represents the data types supported by the 80186.

I/O Space

The I/O space consists of 64K 8-bit or 32K 16-bit ports. Separate instructions address the I/O space with either an 8-bit port address, specified in the instruction, or a 16-bit port address in the DX register. 8-bit port addresses are zero extended such that $A_{15}-A_8$ are LOW. I/O port addresses 00F8(H) through 00FF(H) are reserved.

Interrupts

An interrupt transfers execution to a new program location. The old program address (CS:IP) and machine state (Status Word) are saved on the stack to allow resumption of the interrupted program. Interrupts fall into three classes: hardware initiated, INT instructions, and instruction exceptions. Hardware initiated interrupts occur in response to an external input and are classified as non-maskable or maskable.

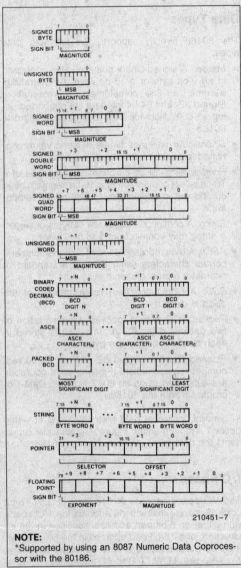

210451-7

NOTE:
*Supported by using an 8087 Numeric Data Coprocessor with the 80186.

Figure 7. 80186 Supported Data Types

Programs may cause an interrupt with an INT instruction. Instruction exceptions occur when an unusual condition, which prevents further instruction processing, is detected while attempting to execute an instruction. If the exception was caused by executing an ESC instruction with the ESC trap bit set in the relocation register, the return instruction will point to the ESC instruction, or to the segment override prefix immediately preceding the ESC instruction if the prefix was present. In all other cases, the return address from an exception will point at the instruction immediately following the instruction causing the exception.

A table containing up to 256 pointers defines the proper interrupt service routine for each interrupt. Interrupts 0–31, some of which are used for instruction exceptions, are reserved. Table 4 shows the 80186 predefined types and default priority levels. For each interrupt, an 8-bit vector must be supplied to the 80186 which identifies the appropriate table entry. Exceptions supply the interrupt vector internally. In addition, internal peripherals and noncascaded external interrupts will generate their own vectors through the internal interrupt controller. INT instructions contain or imply the vector and allow access to all 256 interrupts. Maskable hardware initiated interrupts supply the 8-bit vector to the CPU during an interrupt acknowledge bus sequence. Non-maskable hardware interrupts use a predefined internally supplied vector.

Interrupt Sources

The 80186 can service interrupts generated by software or hardware. The software interrupts are generated by specific instructions (INT, ESC, unused OP, etc.) or the results of conditions specified by instructions (array bounds check, INT0, DIV, IDIV, etc.). All interrupt sources are serviced by an indirect call through an element of a vector table. This vector table is indexed by using the interrupt vector type (Table 4), multiplied by four. All hardware-generated interrupts are sampled at the end of each instruction. Thus, the software interrupts will begin service first. Once the service routine is entered and interrupts are enabled, any hardware source of sufficient priority can interrupt the service routine in progress.

Those pre-defined 80186 interrupts which cannot be masked by programming are described below.

DIVIDE ERROR EXCEPTION (TYPE 0)

Generated when a DIV or IDIV instruction quotient cannot be expressed in the number of bits in the destination.

SINGLE-STEP INTERRUPT (TYPE 1)

Generated after most instructions if the TF flag is set. Interrupts will not be generated after prefix instructions (e.g., REP), instructions which modify segment registers (e.g., POP DS), or the WAIT instruction.

NON-MASKABLE INTERRUPT—NMI (TYPE 2)

An external interrupt source which cannot be masked.

Table 4. 80186 Interrupt Vectors

Interrupt Name	Vector Type	Vector Address	Default Priority	Related Instructions	Applicable Notes
Divide Error Exception	0	00H	1	DIV, IDIV	1
Single Step Interrupt	1	04H	1A	All	2
Non-Maskable Interrupt (NMI)	2	08H	1	All	
Breakpoint Interrupt	3	0CH	1	INT	1
INTO Detected Overflow Exception	4	10H	1	INTO	1
Array Bounds Exception	5	14H	1	BOUND	1
Unused Opcode Exception	6	18H	1	Undefined Opcodes	1
ESC Opcode Exception	7	1CH	1	ESC Opcodes (Coprocessor)	1, 3
Timer 0 Interrupt	8	20H	2A		4, 5
Timer 1 Interrupt	18	48H	2B		4, 5
Timer 2 Interrupt	19	4CH	2C		4, 5
Reserved	9	24H	3		
DMA 0 Interrupt	10	28H	4		5
DMA 1 Interrupt	11	2CH	5		
INT0 Interrupt	12	30H	6		
INT1 Interrupt	13	34H	7		
INT2 Interrupt	14	38H	8		
INT3 Interrupt	15	3CH	9		
Reserved	16, 17	40H, 44H			
Reserved	20–31	50H–7CH			

NOTES:

Default priorities for the interrupt sources are used only if the user does not program each source to a unique priority level.

1. Generated as a result of an instruction execution.
2. Performed in same manner as 8086.
3. An ESC (coprocessor) opcode will cause a trap only if the proper bit is set in the peripheral control block relocation register.
4. All three timers constitute one source of request to the interrupt controller. As such, they share the same priority level with respect to other interrupt sources. However, the timers have a defined priority order among themselves (2A > 2B > 2C).
5. The vector type numbers for these sources are programmable in Slave Mode.

BREAKPOINT INTERRUPT (TYPE 3)

A one-byte version of the INT instruction. It uses 12 as an index into the service routine address table (because it is a type 3 interrupt).

INTO DETECTED OVERFLOW EXCEPTION (TYPE4)

Generated during an INTO instruction if the OF bit is set.

ARRAY BOUNDS EXCEPTION (TYPE 5)

Generated during a BOUND instruction if the array index is outside the array bounds. The array bounds are located in memory at a location indicated by one of the instruction operands. The other operand indicates the value of the index to be checked.

UNUSED OPCODE EXCEPTION (TYPE 6)

Generated if execution is attempted on undefined opcodes.

ESCAPE OPCODE EXCEPTION (TYPE 7)

Generated if execution is attempted of ESC opcodes (D8H–DFH). This exception will only be generated if a bit in the relocation register is set. The return address of this exception will point to the ESC instruction causing the exception. If a segment override prefix preceded the ESC instruction, the return address will point to the segment override prefix.

Hardware-generated interrupts are divided into two groups: maskable interrupts and non-maskable interrupts. The 80186 provides maskable hardware interrupt request pins INT0–INT3. In addition, maskable interrupts may be generated by the 80186 integrated DMA controller and the integrated timer unit. The vector types for these interrupts is shown in Table 4. Software enables these inputs by setting the interrupt flag bit (IF) in the Status Word. The interrupt controller is discussed in the peripheral section of this data sheet.

Further maskable interrupts are disabled while servicing an interrupt because the IF bit is reset as part of the response to an interrupt or exception. The saved Status Word will reflect the enable status of the processor prior to the interrupt. The interrupt flag will remain zero unless specifically set. The interrupt return instruction restores the Status Word, thereby restoring the original status of IF bit. If the interrupt return re-enables interrupts, and another interrupt is pending, the 80186 will immediately service the highest-priority interrupt pending, i.e., no instructions of the main line program will be executed.

Non-Maskable Interrupt Request (NMI)

A non-maskable interrupt (NMI) is also provided. This interrupt is serviced regardless of the state of the IF bit. A typical use of NMI would be to activate a power failure routine. The activation of this input causes an interrupt with an internally supplied vector value of 2. No external interrupt acknowledge sequence is performed. The IF bit is cleared at the beginning of an NMI interrupt to prevent maskable interrupts from being serviced.

Single-Step Interrupt

The 80186 has an internal interrupt that allows programs to execute one instruction at a time. It is called the single-step interrupt and is controlled by the single-step flag bit (TF) in the Status Word. Once this bit is set, an internal single-step interrupt will occur after the next instruction has been executed. The interrupt clears the TF bit and uses an internally supplied vector of 1. The IRET instruction is used to set the TF bit and transfer control to the next instruction to be single-stepped.

Initialization and Processor Reset

Processor initialization is accomplished by driving the $\overline{RES}$ input pin LOW. $\overline{RES}$ must be LOW during power-up to ensure proper device initialization. $\overline{RES}$ forces the 80186 to terminate all execution and local bus activity. No instruction or bus activity will occur as long as $\overline{RES}$ is active. After $\overline{RES}$ becomes inactive and an internal processing interval elapses, the 80186 begins execution with the instruction at physical location FFFF0(H). $\overline{RES}$ also sets some registers to predefined values as shown in Table 5.

Table 5. 80186 Initial Register State after RESET

Status Word	F002(H)
Instruction Pointer	0000(H)
Code Segment	FFFF(H)
Data Segment	0000(H)
Extra Segment	0000(H)
Stack Segment	0000(H)
Relocation Register	20FF(H)
UMCS	FFFB(H)

80186 CLOCK GENERATOR

The 80186 provides an on-chip clock generator for both internal and external clock generation. The clock generator features a crystal oscillator, a divide-by-two counter, synchronous and asynchronous ready inputs, and reset circuitry.

Oscillator

The oscillator circuit of the 80186 is designed to be used with a parallel resonant fundamental mode crystal. This is used as the time base for the 80186. The crystal frequency selected will be double the CPU clock frequency. Use of an LC or RC circuit is not recommended with this oscillator. If an external oscillator is used, it can be connected directly to the input pin X1 in lieu of a crystal. The output of the oscillator is not directly available outside the 80186. The recommended crystal configuration is shown in Figure 8.

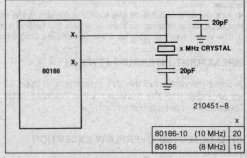

80186-10	(10 MHz)	20
80186	(8 MHz)	16

Figure 8. Recommended 80186 Crystal Configuration

Intel recommends the following values for crystal selection parameters:

Temperature Range:	0 to 70°C
ESR (Equivalent Series Resistance):	30Ω max
C_0 (Shunt Capacitance of Crystal):	7.0 pf max
C_1 (Load Capacitance):	20 pf ± 2 pf
Drive Level:	1 mW max

Clock Generator

The 80186 clock generator provides the 50% duty cycle processor clock for the 80186. It does this by dividing the oscillator output by 2 forming the symmetrical clock. If an external oscillator is used, the state of the clock generator will change on the falling edge of the oscillator signal. The CLKOUT pin provides the processor clock signal for use outside the 80186. This may be used to drive other system components. All timings are referenced to the output clock.

READY Synchronization

The 80186 provides both synchronous and asynchronous ready inputs. Asynchronous ready synchronization is accomplished by circuitry which samples ARDY in the middle of T_2, T_3, and again in the middle of each T_W until ARDY is sampled HIGH. One-half CLKOUT cycle of resolution time is used for full synchronization of a rising ARDY signal. A high-to-low transition on ARDY may be used as an indication of the not ready condition but it must be performed synchronously to CLKOUT **either** in the middle of T_2, T_3, or T_W, **or** at the falling edge of T_3 or T_W.

A second ready input (SRDY) is provided to interface with externally synchronized ready signals. This input is sampled at the end of T_2, T_3 and again at the end of each T_W until it is sampled HIGH. By using this input rather than the asynchronous ready input, the half-clock cycle resolution time penalty is eliminated. This input must satisfy set-up and hold times to guarantee proper operation of the circuit.

In addition, the 80186, as part of the integrated chip-select logic, has the capability to program WAIT states for memory and peripheral blocks. This is discussed in the Chip Select/Ready Logic description.

RESET Logic

The 80186 provides both a $\overline{\text{RES}}$ input pin and a synchronized RESET output pin for use with other system components. The $\overline{\text{RES}}$ input pin on the 80186 is provided with hysteresis in order to facilitate power-on Reset generation via an RC network. RESET output is guaranteed to remain active for at least five clocks given a $\overline{\text{RES}}$ input of at least six clocks. RESET may be delayed up to approximately two and one-half clocks behind $\overline{\text{RES}}$.

Multiple 80186 processors may be synchronized through the $\overline{\text{RES}}$ input pin, since this input resets both the processor and divide-by-two internal counter in the clock generator. In order to ensure that the divide-by-two counters all begin counting at the same time, the active going edge of $\overline{\text{RES}}$ must satisfy a 25 ns setup time before the falling edge of the 80186 clock input. In addition, in order to ensure that all CPUs begin executing in the same clock cycle, the reset must satisfy a 25 ns setup time before the rising edge of the CLKOUT signal of all the processors.

LOCAL BUS CONTROLLER

The 80186 provides a local bus controller to generate the local bus control signals. In addition, it employs a HOLD/HLDA protocol for relinquishing the local bus to other bus masters. It also provides outputs that can be used to enable external buffers and to direct the flow of data on and off the local bus.

Memory/Peripheral Control

The 80186 provides ALE, $\overline{\text{RD}}$, and $\overline{\text{WR}}$ bus control signals. The $\overline{\text{RD}}$ and $\overline{\text{WR}}$ signals are used to strobe data from memory or I/O to the 80186 or to strobe data from the 80186 to memory or I/O. The ALE line provides a strobe to latch the address when it is valid. The 80186 local bus controller does not provide a memory/$\overline{\text{I/O}}$ signal. If this is required, use the $\overline{\text{S2}}$ signal (which will require external latching), make the memory and I/O spaces nonoverlapping, or use only the integrated chip-select circuitry.

Transceiver Control

The 80186 generates two control signals to be connected to transceiver chips. This capability allows the addition of transceivers for extra buffering without adding external logic. These control lines, DT/$\overline{\text{R}}$ and $\overline{\text{DEN}}$, are generated to control the flow of data through the transceivers. The operation of these signals is shown in Table 6.

Table 6. Transceiver Control Signals Description

Pin Name	Function
$\overline{\text{DEN}}$ (Data Enable)	Enables the output drivers of the transceivers. It is active LOW during memory, I/O, or INTA cycles.
DT/$\overline{\text{R}}$ (Data Transmit/ Receive)	Determines the direction of travel through the transceivers. A HIGH level directs data away from the processor during write operations, while a LOW level directs data toward the processor during a read operation.

Local Bus Arbitration

The 80186 uses a HOLD/HLDA system of local bus exchange. This provides an asynchronous bus exchange mechanism. This means multiple masters utilizing the same bus can operate at separate clock frequencies. The 80186 provides a single HOLD/HLDA pair through which all other bus masters may gain control of the local bus. External circuitry must arbitrate which external device will gain control of the bus when there is more than one alternate local bus master. When the 80186 relinquishes control of the local bus, it floats $\overline{DEN}$, $\overline{RD}$, $\overline{WR}$, $\overline{S0}$–$\overline{S2}$, $\overline{LOCK}$, AD0–AD15, A16–A19, $\overline{BHE}$, and DT/$\overline{R}$ to allow another master to drive these lines directly.

The 80186 HOLD latency time, i.e., the time between HOLD request and HOLD acknowledge, is a function of the activity occurring in the processor when the HOLD request is received. A HOLD request is the highest-priority activity request which the processor may receive: higher than instruction fetching or internal DMA cycles. However, if a DMA cycle is in progress, the 80186 will complete the transfer before relinquishing the bus. This implies that if a HOLD request is received just as a DMA transfer begins, the HOLD latency time can be as great as 4 bus cycles. This will occur if a DMA word transfer operation is taking place from an odd address to an odd address. This is a total of 16 clocks or more, if WAIT states are required. In addition, if locked transfers are performed, the HOLD latency time will be increased by the length of the locked transfer.

Local Bus Controller and Reset

During RESET the local bus controller will perform the following action:

- Drive $\overline{DEN}$, $\overline{RD}$, and $\overline{WR}$ HIGH for one clock cycle, then float.

NOTE:
$\overline{RD}$ is also provided with an internal pull-up device to prevent the processor from inadvertently entering Queue Status Mode during RESET.

- Drive $\overline{S0}$–$\overline{S2}$ to the inactive state (all HIGH) and then float.
- Drive $\overline{LOCK}$ HIGH and then float.

- Float AD0–15, A16–19, $\overline{BHE}$, DT/$\overline{R}$.
- Drive ALE LOW (ALE is never floated).
- Drive HLDA LOW.

INTERNAL PERIPHERAL INTERFACE

All the 80186 integrated peripherals are controlled by 16-bit registers contained within an internal 256-byte control block. The control block may be mapped into either memory or I/O space. Internal logic will recognize control block addresses and respond to bus cycles. During bus cycles to internal registers, the bus controller will signal the operation externally (i.e., the $\overline{RD}$, $\overline{WR}$, status, address, data, etc., lines will be driven as in a normal bus cycle), but D_{15-0}, SRDY, and ARDY will be ignored. The base address of the control block must be on an even 256-byte boundary (i.e., the lower 8 bits of the base address are all zeros). All of the defined registers within this control block may be read or written by the 80186 CPU at any time.

The control block base address is programmed by a 16-bit relocation register contained within the control block at offset FEH from the base address of the control block (see Figure 9). It provides the upper 12 bits of the base address of the control block. The control block is effectively an internal chip select range and must abide by all the rules concerning chip selects (the chip select circuitry is discussed later in this data sheet). Any access to the 256 bytes of the control block activates an internal chip select. Other chip selects may overlap the control block only if they are programmed to zero wait states and ignore external ready. In addition, bit 12 of this register determines whether the control block will be mapped into I/O or memory space. If this bit is 1, the control block will be located in memory space. If the bit is 0, the control block will be located in I/O space. If the control register block is mapped into I/O space, the upper 4 bits of the base address must be programmed as 0 (since I/O addresses are only 16 bits wide).

In addition to providing relocation information for the control block, the relocation register contains bits which place the interrupt controller into Slave Mode, and cause the CPU to interrupt upon encountering ESC instructions. At RESET, the relocation register

	15	14	13	12	11	10	9	8	7	6	5	4	3	2	1	0
OFFSET: FEH	ET	SLAVE/MASTER	X	M/IO					Relocation Address Bits R19–R8							

ET = ESC Trap / No ESC Trap (1/0)
M/IO = Register block located in Memory / I/O Space (1/0)
SLAVE/$\overline{MASTER}$ = Configure interrupt controller for Slave/Master Mode (I/O)

Figure 9. Relocation Register

is set to 20FFH, which maps the control block to start at FF00H in I/O space. An offset map of the 256-byte control register block is shown in Figure 10.

CHIP-SELECT/READY GENERATION LOGIC

The 80186 contains logic which provides programmable chip-select generation for both memories and peripherals. In addition, it can be programmed to provide READY (or WAIT state) generation. It can also provide latched address bits A1 and A2. The chip-select lines are active for all memory and I/O cycles in their programmed areas, whether they be generated by the CPU or by the integrated DMA unit.

	OFFSET
Relocation Register	FEH
DMA Descriptors Channel 1	DAH
	D0H
DMA Descriptors Channel 0	CAH
	C0H
Chip-Select Control Registers	A8H
	A0H
Time 2 Control Registers	66H
	60H
Time 1 Control Registers	5EH
	58H
Time 0 Control Registers	56H
	50H
Interrupt Controller Registers	3EH
	20H

Figure 10. Internal Register Map

Memory Chip Selects

The 80186 provides 6 memory chip select outputs for 3 address areas; upper memory, lower memory, and midrange memory. One each is provided for upper memory and lower memory, while four are provided for midrange memory.

The range for each chip select is user-programmable and can be set to 2K, 4K, 8K, 16K, 32K, 64K, 128K (plus 1K and 256K for upper and lower chip selects). In addition, the beginning or base address of the midrange memory chip select may also be selected. Only one chip select may be programmed to be active for any memory location at a time. All chip select sizes are in bytes, whereas 80186 memory is arranged in words. This means that if, for example, 16 64K x 1 memories are used, the memory block size will be 128K, not 64K.

Upper Memory $\overline{\text{CS}}$

The 80186 provides a chip select, called $\overline{\text{UCS}}$, for the top of memory. The top of memory is usually used as the system memory because after reset the 80186 begins executing at memory location FFFF0H.

The upper limit of memory defined by this chip select is always FFFFFH, while the lower limit is programmable. By programming the lower limit, the size of the select block is also defined. Table 7 shows the relationship between the base address selected and the size of the memory block obtained.

Table 7. UMCS Programming Values

Starting Address (Base Address)	Memory Block Size	UMCS Value (Assuming R0 = R1 = R2 = 0)
FFC00	1K	FFF8H
FF800	2K	FFB8H
FF000	4K	FF38H
FE000	8K	FE38H
FC000	16K	FC38H
F8000	32K	F838H
F0000	64K	F038H
E0000	128K	E038H
C0000	256K	C038H

The lower limit of this memory block is defined in the UMCS register (see Figure 11). This register is at offset A0H in the internal control block. The legal values for bits 6–13 and the resulting starting address and memory block sizes are given in Table 7. Any combination of bits 6–13 not shown in Table 7 will result in undefined operation. After reset, the UMCS register is programmed for a 1K area. It must be reprogrammed if a larger upper memory area is desired.

The internal generation of any 20-bit address whose upper 16 bits are equal to or greater than the UMCS value (with bits 0–5 as "0") asserts $\overline{UCS}$. UMCS bits R2–R0 specify the ready mode for the area of memory defined by this chip select register, as explained later.

Lower Memory $\overline{CS}$

The 80186 provides a chip select for low memory called $\overline{LCS}$. The bottom of memory contains the interrupt vector table, starting at location 00000H.

The lower limit of memory defined by this chip select is always 0H, while the upper limit is programmable. By programming the upper limit, the size of the memory block is defined. Table 8 shows the relationship between the upper address selected and the size of the memory block obtained.

Table 8. LMCS Programming Values

Upper Address	Memory Block Size	LMCS Value (Assuming R0 = R1 = R2 = 0)
003FFH	1K	0038H
007FFH	2K	0078H
00FFFH	4K	00F8H
01FFFH	8K	01F8H
03FFFH	16K	03F8H
07FFFH	32K	07F8H
0FFFFH	64K	0FF8H
1FFFFH	128K	1FF8H
3FFFFH	256K	3FF8H

The upper limit of this memory block is defined in the LMCS register (see Figure 12) at offset A2H in the internal control block. The legal values for bits 6–15 and the resulting upper address and memory block sizes are given in Table 8. Any combination of bits 6–15 not shown in Table 8 will result in undefined operation. After RESET, the LMCS register value is undefined. However, the $\overline{LCS}$ chip-select line will not become active until the LMCS register is accessed.

Any internally generated 20-bit address whose upper 16 bits are less than or equal to LMCS (with bits 0–5 "1") will assert $\overline{LCS}$. LMCS register bits R2–R0 specify the READY mode for the area of memory defined by this chip-select register.

Mid-Range Memory $\overline{CS}$

The 80186 provides four $\overline{MCS}$ lines which are active within a user-locatable memory block. This block can be located within the 80186 1M byte memory address space exclusive of the areas defined by $\overline{UCS}$ and $\overline{LCS}$. Both the base address and size of this memory block are programmable.

The size of the memory block defined by the mid-range select lines, as shown in Table 9, is determined by bits 8–14 of the MPCS register (see Figure 13). This register is at location A8H in the internal control block. One and only one of bits 8–14 must be set at a time. Unpredictable operation of the $\overline{MCS}$ lines will otherwise occur. Each of the four chip-select lines is active for one of the four equal contiguous divisions of the mid-range block. If the total block size is 32K, each chip select is active for 8K of memory with $\overline{MCS0}$ being active for the first range and $\overline{MCS3}$ being active for the last range.

The EX and MS in MPCS relate to peripheral functionality as described in a later section.

Table 9. MPCS Programming Values

Total Block Size	Individual Select Size	MPCS Bits 14–8
8K	2K	0000001B
16K	4K	0000010B
32K	8K	0000100B
64K	16K	0001000B
128K	32K	0010000B
256K	64K	0100000B
512K	128K	1000000B

The base address of the mid-range memory block is defined by bits 15–9 of the MMCS register (see Figure 14). This register is at offset A6H in the internal

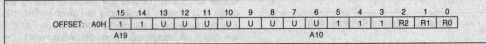

Figure 11. UMCS Register

Figure 12. LMCS Register

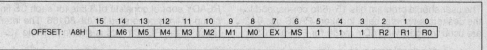

OFFSET: A8H	15	14	13	12	11	10	9	8	7	6	5	4	3	2	1	0
	1	M6	M5	M4	M3	M2	M1	M0	EX	MS	1	1	1	R2	R1	R0

Figure 13. MPCS Register

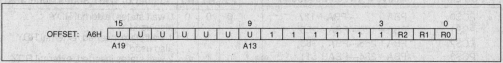

OFFSET: A6H	15						9						3			0
	U	U	U	U	U	U	U	1	1	1	1	1	1	R2	R1	R0
	A19						A13									

Figure 14. MMCS Register

control block. These bits correspond to bits A19–A13 of the 20-bit memory address. Bits A12–A0 of the base address are always 0. The base address may be set at any integer multiple of the size of the total memory block selected. For example, if the mid-range block size is 32K (or the size of the block for which each $\overline{MCS}$ line is active is 8K), the block could be located at 10000H or 18000H, but not at 14000H, since the first few integer multiples of a 32K memory block are 0H, 8000H, 10000H, 18000H, etc. After RESET, the contents of both of these registers are undefined. However, none of the $\overline{MCS}$ lines will be active until both the MMCS and MPCS registers are accessed.

MMCS bits R2–R0 specify READY mode of operation for all four mid-range chip selects.

The 512K block size for the mid-range memory chip selects is a special case. When using 512K, the base address would have to be at either locations 00000H or 80000H. If it were to be programmed at 00000H when the $\overline{LCS}$ line was programmed, there would be an internal conflict between the $\overline{LCS}$ ready generation logic and the $\overline{MCS}$ ready generation logic. Likewise, if the base address were programmed at 80000H, there would be a conflict with the $\overline{UCS}$ ready generation logic. Since the $\overline{LCS}$ chip-select line does not become active until programmed, while the $\overline{UCS}$ line is active at reset, the memory base can be set only at 00000H. If this base address is selected, however, the $\overline{LCS}$ range must not be programmed.

Peripheral Chip Selects

The 80186 can generate chip selects for up to seven peripheral devices. These chip selects are active for

seven contiguous blocks of 128 bytes above a programmable base address. The base address may be located in either memory or I/O space.

Seven $\overline{CS}$ lines called $\overline{PCS0}$–6 are generated by the 80186. The base address is user-programmable; however it can only be a multiple of 1K bytes, i.e., the least significant 10 bits of the starting address are always 0.

$\overline{PCS5}$ and $\overline{PCS6}$ can also be programmed to provide latched address bits A1 and A2. If so programmed, they cannot be used as peripheral selects. These outputs can be connected directly to the A0 and A1 pins used for selecting internal registers of 8-bit peripheral chips. This simplifies the external hardware because the peripheral registers can be located on even boundaries in I/O or memory space.

The starting address of the peripheral chip-select block is defined by the PACS register (see Figure 15). The register is located at offset A4H in the internal control block. Bits 15–6 of this register correspond to bits 19–10 of the 20-bit Programmable Base Address (PBA) of the peripheral chip-select block. Bits 9–0 of the PBA of the peripheral chip-select block are all zeros. If the chip-select block is located in I/O space, bits 12–15 must be programmed zero, since the I/O address is only 16 bits wide. Table 10 shows the address range of each peripheral chip select with respect to the PBA contained in PACS register.

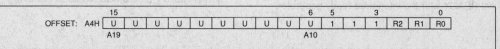

OFFSET: A4H	15								6	5		3			0
	U	U	U	U	U	U	U	U	U	U	1	1	1	R2	R1	R0
	A19								A10							

Figure 15. PACS Register

The user should program bits 15–6 to correspond to the desired peripheral base location. PACS bits 0–2 are used to specify READY mode for $\overline{PCS0}$–$\overline{PCS3}$.

Table 10. PCS Address Ranges

$\overline{PCS}$ Line	Active between Locations
$\overline{PCS0}$	PBA —PBA + 127
$\overline{PCS1}$	PBA + 128—PBA + 255
$\overline{PCS2}$	PBA + 256—PBA + 383
$\overline{PCS3}$	PBA + 384—PBA + 511
$\overline{PCS4}$	PBA + 512—PBA + 639
$\overline{PCS5}$	PBA + 640—PBA + 767
$\overline{PCS6}$	PBA + 768—PBA + 895

The mode of operation of the peripheral chip selects is defined by the MPCS register (which is also used to set the size of the mid-range memory chip-select block, see Figure 13). The register is located at offset A8H in the internal control block. Bit 7 is used to select the function of $\overline{PCS5}$ and $\overline{PCS6}$, while bit 6 is used to select whether the peripheral chip selects are mapped into memory or I/O space. Table 11 describes the programming of these bits. After RESET, the contents of both the MPCS and the PACS registers are undefined, however none of the PCS lines will be active until both of the MPCS and PACS registers are accessed.

Table 11. MS, EX Programming Values

Bit	Description
MS	1 = Peripherals mapped into memory space.
	0 = Peripherals mapped into I/O space.
EX	0 = 5 $\overline{PCS}$ lines. A1, A2 provided.
	1 = 7 $\overline{PCS}$ lines. A1, A2 are not provided.

MPCS bits 0–2 specify the READY mode for $\overline{PCS4}$–$\overline{PCS6}$ as outlined below.

READY Generation Logic

The 80186 can generate a READY signal internally for each of the memory or peripheral $\overline{CS}$ lines. The number of WAIT states to be inserted for each peripheral or memory is programmable to provide 0–3 wait states for all accesses to the area for which the chip select is active. In addition, the 80186 may be programmed to either ignore external READY for each chip-select range individually or to factor external READY with the integrated ready generator.

READY control consists of 3 bits for each $\overline{CS}$ line or group of lines generated by the 80186. The interpretation of the READY bits is shown in Table 12.

Table 12. READY Bits Programming

R2	R1	R0	Number of WAIT States Generated
0	0	0	0 wait states, external RDY also used.
0	0	1	1 wait state inserted, external RDY also used.
0	1	0	2 wait states inserted, external RDY also used.
0	1	1	3 wait states inserted, external RDY also used.
1	0	0	0 wait states, external RDY ignored.
1	0	1	1 wait state inserted, external RDY ignored.
1	1	0	2 wait states inserted, external RDY ignored.
1	1	1	3 wait states inserted, external RDY ignored.

The internal ready generator operates in parallel with external READY, not in series if the external READY is used (R2 = 0). For example, if the internal generator is set to insert two wait states, but activity on the external READY lines will insert four wait states, the processor will only insert four wait states, not six. This is because the two wait states generated by the internal generator overlapped the first two wait states generated by the external ready signal. Note that the external ARDY and SRDY lines are always ignored during cycles accessing internal peripherals.

R2–R0 of each control word specifies the READY mode for the corresponding block, with the exception of the peripheral chip selects: R2–R0 of PACS set the $\overline{PCS0}$–3 READY mode, R2–R0 of MPCS set the $\overline{PCS4}$–6 READY mode.

Chip Select/Ready Logic and Reset

Upon RESET, the Chip-Select/Ready Logic will perform the following actions:

- All chip-select outputs will be driven HIGH.
- Upon leaving RESET, the $\overline{UCS}$ line will be programmed to provide chip selects to a 1K block with the accompanying READY control bits set at 011 to insert 3 wait states in conjunction with external READY (i.e., UMCS resets to FFFBH).

- No other chip select or READY control registers have any predefined values after RESET. They will not become active until the CPU accesses their control registers. Both the PACS and MPCS registers must be accessed before the $\overline{\text{PCS}}$ lines will become active.

DMA CHANNELS

The 80186 DMA controller provides two independent DMA channels. Data transfers can occur between memory and I/O spaces (e.g., Memory to I/O) or within the same space (e.g., Memory to Memory or I/O to I/O). Data can be transferred either in bytes (8 bits) or in words (16 bits) to or from even or odd addresses. Each DMA channel maintains both a 20-bit source and destination pointer which can be optionally incremented or decremented after each data transfer (by one or two depending on byte or word transfers). Each data transfer consumes 2 bus cycles (a minimum of 8 clocks), one cycle to fetch data and the other to store data. This provides a maximum data transfer rate of 1.25 Mword/sec or 2.5 MBytes/sec at 10 MHz.

DMA Operation

Each channel has six registers in the control block which define each channel's operation. The control registers consist of a 20-bit Source pointer (2 words), a 20-bit destination pointer (2 words), a 16-bit Transfer Count Register, and a 16-bit Control Word. The format of the DMA Control Blocks is shown in Table 13. The Transfer Count Register (TC) specifies the number of DMA transfers to be performed. Up to 64K byte or word transfers can be performed with automatic termination. The Control Word defines the channel's operation (see Figure 17). All registers may be modified or altered during any DMA activity. Any changes made to these registers will be reflected immediately in DMA operation.

Table 13. DMA Control Block Format

Register Name	Register Address	
	Ch. 0	Ch. 1
Control Word	CAH	DAH
Transfer Count	C8H	D8H
Destination Pointer (upper 4 bits)	C6H	D6H
Destination Pointer	C4H	D4H
Source Pointer (upper 4 bits)	C2H	D2H
Source Pointer	C0H	D0H

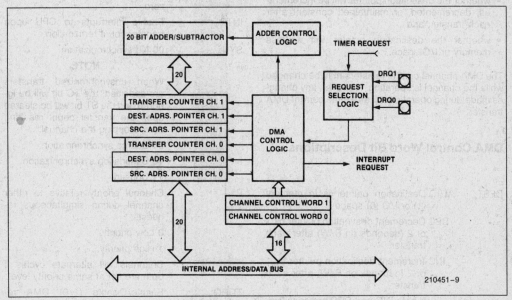

210451–9

Figure 16. DMA Unit Block Diagram

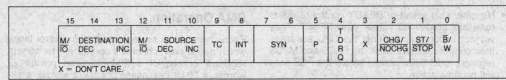

15	14	13	12	11	10	9	8	7	6	5	4	3	2	1	0
M/IO	DESTINATION DEC INC		M/IO	SOURCE DEC INC		TC	INT	SYN		P	T D R Q	X	CHG/NOCHG	ST/STOP	B/W

X = DON'T CARE.

Figure 17. DMA Control Register

DMA Channel Control Word Register

Each DMA Channel Control Word determines the mode of operation for the particular 81086 DMA channel. This register specifies:

- the mode of synchronization;
- whether bytes or words will be transferred;
- whether interrupts will be generated after the last transfer;
- whether DMA activity will cease after a programmed number of DMA cycles;
- the relative priority of the DMA channel with respect to the other DMA channel;
- whether the source pointer will be incremented, decremented, or maintained constant after each transfer;
- whether the source pointer addresses memory or I/O space;
- whether the destination pointer will be incremented, decremented, or maintained constant after each transfer; and
- whether the destination pointer will address memory or I/O space.

The DMA channel control registers may be changed while the channel is operating. However, any changes made during operation will affect the current DMA transfer.

DMA Control Word Bit Descriptions

DEST: M/IO Destination pointer is in memory (1) or I/O (0) space.

DEC Decrement destination pointer by 1 or 2 (depends on B/W) after each transfer.

INC Increment destination pointer by 1 or 2 (depends on B/W) after each transfer.

If both INC and DEC are specified, the pointer will not change after each cycle.

SOURCE: M/IO Source pointer is in memory (1) or I/O (0) space.

DEC Decrement source pointer by 1 or 2 (depends on B/W) after each transfer.

INC Increment source pointer by 1 or 2 (depends on B/W) after each transfer.

If both INC and DEC are specified, the pointer will not change after each cycle.

TC: If set, DMA will terminate when the contents of the transfer count register reach zero. The ST/STOP bit will also be reset at this point. If cleared, the DMA controller will decrement the transfer count register for each DMA cycle, but DMA transfers will not stop when the transfer count register reaches zero.

INT: Enable interrupts to CPU upon transfer count termination.

SYN: 00 No synchronization.

NOTE:

When unsynchronized transfers are specified, the TC bit will be ignored and the ST bit will be cleared upon the transfer count reaching zero, stopping the channel.

01 Source synchronization.

10 Destination synchronization.

11 Unused.

P: Channel priority relative to other channel during simultaneous requests.

0 Low priority.

1 High priority.

Channels will alternate cycles if both are set at same priority level.

TDRQ: Enable/Disable (1/0) DMA requests from timer 2.

CHG/NOCHG: Change/Do not change (1/0) ST/STOP bit. If this bit is set when writing the control word, the ST/STOP bit will be programmed by the write to the control word. If this bit is cleared when writing the control word, the ST/STOP bit will not be altered. This bit is not stored; it will always be read as 0.

ST/STOP: Start/Stop (1/0) channel.

B/W: Byte/Word (0/1) transfers.

DMA Destination and Source Pointer Registers

Each DMA channel maintains a 20-bit source and a 20-bit destination pointer. Each of these pointers takes up two full 16-bit registers in the peripheral control block. The lower four bits of the upper register contain the upper four bits of the 20-bit physical address (see Figure 18). These pointers may be individually incremented or decremented after each transfer. If word transfers are performed the pointer is incremented or decremented by two. Each pointer may point into either memory or I/O space. Since the DMA channels can perform transfers to or from odd addresses, there is no restriction on values for the pointer registers. Higher transfer rates can be obtained if all word transfers are performed to even addresses, since this will allow data to be accessed in a single bus cycle.

DMA Transfer Count Register

Each DMA channel maintains a 16-bit transfer count register (TC). The register is decremented after every DMA cycle, regardless of the state of the TC bit in the DMA Control Register. If the TC bit in the DMA control word is set or if unsynchronized transfers are programmed, however, DMA activity will terminate when the transfer count register reaches zero.

DMA Requests

Data transfers may be either source or destination synchronized, that is either the source of the data or the destination of the data may request the data transfer. In addition, DMA transfers may be unsynchronized; that is, the transfer will take place continually until the correct number of transfers has occurred. When source or unsynchronized transfers are performed, the DMA channel may begin another transfer immediately after the end of a previous DMA transfer. This allows a complete transfer to take place every 2 bus cycles or eight clock cycles (assuming no wait states). When destination synchronized transfers are performed, data will not be fetched from the source address until the destination device signals that it is ready to receive it. Also, the DMA controller will relinquish control of the bus after every transfer. If no other bus activity is initiated, another destination synchronized DMA cycle will begin after two processor clocks. This allows the destination device time to remove its request if another transfer is not desired. Since the DMA controller will relinquish the bus, the CPU can initiate a bus cycle. As a result, a complete bus cycle will often be inserted between destination synchronized transfers. Table 14 shows the maximum DMA transfer rates.

Table 14. Maximum DMA Transfer Rates @ CLKOUT = 10 MHz

Type of Synchronization Selected	CPU Running	CPU Halted
Unsynchronized	2.5MBytes/sec	2.5MBytes/sec
Source Synch.	2.5MBytes/sec	2.5MBytes/sec
Destination Synch.	1.7MBytes/sec	2.0MBytes/sec

HIGHER REGISTER ADDRESS	XXX	XXX	XXX	A19–A16
LOWER REGISTER ADDRESS	A15–A12	A11–A8	A7–A4	A3–A0

15   0

XXX = DON'T CARE

Figure 18. DMA Pointer Register Format

DMA Acknowledge

No explicit DMA acknowledge pulse is provided. Since both source and destination pointers are maintained, a read from a requesting source, or a write to a requesting destination, should be used as the DMA acknowledge signal. Since the chip-select lines can be programmed to be active for a given block of memory or I/O space, and the DMA pointers can be programmed to point to the same given block, a chip-select line could be used to indicate a DMA acknowledge.

DMA Priority

The DMA channels may be programmed to give one channel priority over the other, or they may be programmed to alternate cycles when both have DMA requests pending. DMA cycles always have priority over internal CPU cycles except between locked memory accesses or word accesses to odd memory locations; also, an external bus hold takes priority over an internal DMA cycle. Because an interrupt request cannot suspend a DMA operation and the CPU cannot access memory during a DMA cycle, interrupt latency time will suffer during sequences of continuous DMA cycles. An NMI request, however, will cause all internal DMA activity to halt. This allows the CPU to quickly respond to the NMI request.

DMA Programming

DMA cycles will occur whenever the ST/STOP bit of the Control Register is set. If synchronized transfers

are programmed, a DRQ must also be generated. Therefore the source and destination transfer pointers, and the transfer count register (if used) must be programmed before the ST/STOP bit is set.

Each DMA register may be modified while the channel is operating. If the CHG/NOCHG bit is cleared when the control register is written, the ST/STOP bit of the control register will not be modified by the write. If multiple channel registers are modified, it is recommended that a LOCKED string transfer be used to prevent a DMA transfer from occurring between updates to the channel registers.

DMA Channels and Reset

Upon RESET, the DMA channels will perform the following actions:

* The Start/Stop bit for each channel will be reset to STOP.
* Any transfer in progress is aborted.

TIMERS

The 80186 provides three internal 16-bit programmable timers (see Figure 19). Two of these are highly flexible and are connected to four external pins (2 per timer). They can be used to count external events, time external events, generate nonrepetitive waveforms, etc. The third timer is not connected to any external pins, and is useful for real-time coding and time delay applications. In addition, the third timer can be used as a prescaler to the other two, or as a DMA request source.

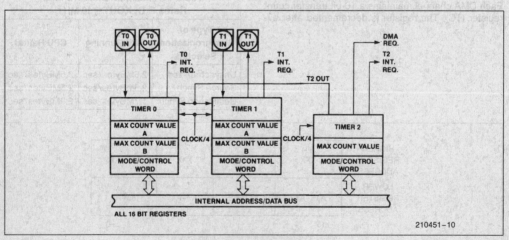

Figure 19. Timer Block Diagram

Timer Operation

The timers are controlled by 11 16-bit registers in the peripheral control block. The configuration of these registers is shown in Table 15. The count register contains the current value of the timer. It can be read or written at any time independent of whether the timer is running or not. The value of this register will be incremented for each timer event. Each of the timers is equipped with a MAX COUNT register, which defines the maximum count the timer will reach. After reaching the MAX COUNT register value, the timer count value will reset to zero during that same clock, i.e., the maximum count value is never stored in the count register itself. Timers 0 and 1 are, in addition, equipped with a second MAX COUNT register, which enables the timers to alternate their count between two different MAX COUNT values. If a single MAX COUNT register is used, the timer output pin will switch LOW for a single clock, 1 clock after the maximum count value has been reached. In the dual MAX COUNT register mode, the output pin will indicate which MAX COUNT register is currently in use, thus allowing nearly complete freedom in selecting waveform duty cycles. For the timers with two MAX COUNT registers, the RIU bit in the control register determines which is used for the comparison.

Each timer gets serviced every fourth CPU-clock cycle, and thus can operate at speeds up to one-quarter the internal clock frequency (one-eighth the crystal rate). External clocking of the timers may be done at up to a rate of one-quarter of the internal CPU-clock rate (2 MHz for an 8 MHz CPU clock). Due to internal synchronization and pipelining of the timer circuitry, a timer output may take up to 6 clocks to respond to any individual clock or gate input.

Since the count registers and the maximum count registers are all 16 bits wide, 16 bits of resolution are provided. Any Read or Write access to the timers will add one wait state to the minimum four-clock bus cycle, however. This is needed to synchronize and coordinate the internal data flows between the internal timers and the internal bus.

The timers have several programmable options.

- All three timers can be set to halt or continue on a terminal count.

- Timers 0 and 1 can select between internal and external clocks, alternate between MAX COUNT registers and be set to retrigger on external events.

- The timers may be programmed to cause an interrupt on terminal count.

These options are selectable via the timer mode/control word.

Timer Mode/Control Register

The mode/control register (see Figure 20) allows the user to program the specific mode of operation or check the current programmed status for any of the three integrated timers.

Table 15. Timer Control Block Format

Register Name	Register Offset		
	Tmr. 0	Tmr. 1	Tmr. 2
Mode/Control Word	56H	5EH	66H
Max Count B	54H	5CH	not present
Max Count A	52H	5AH	62H
Count Register	50H	58H	60H

15	14	13	12	11		5	4	3	2	1	0
EN	INH	INT	RIU	0	...	MC	RTG	P	EXT	ALT	CONT

Figure 20. Timer Mode/Control Register

EN:

The enable bit provides programmer control over the timer's RUN/HALT status. When set, the timer is enabled to increment subject to the input pin constraints in the internal clock mode (discussed previously). When cleared, the timer will be inhibited from counting. All input pin transistions during the time EN is zero will be ignored. If CONT is zero, the EN bit is automatically cleared upon maximum count.

INH:

The inhibit bit allows for selective updating of the enable (EN) bit. If INH is a one during the write to the mode/control word, then the state of the EN bit will be modified by the write. If INH is a zero during the write, the EN bit will be unaffected by the operation.This bit is not stored; it will always be a 0 on a read.

INT:

When set, the INT bit enables interrupts from the timer, which will be generated on every terminal count. If the timer is configured in dual MAX COUNT register mode, an interrupt will be generated each time the value in MAX COUNT register A is reached, and each time the value in MAX COUNT register B is reached. If this enable bit is cleared after the interrupt request has been generated, but before a pending interrupt is serviced, the interrupt request will still be in force. (The request is latched in the Interrupt Controller).

RIU:

The Register In Use bit indicates which MAX COUNT register is currently being used for comparison to the timer count value. A zero value indicates register A. The RIU bit cannot be written, i.e., its value is not affected when the control register is written. It is always cleared when the ALT bit is zero.

MC:

The Maximum Count bit is set whenever the timer reaches its final maximum count value. If the timer is configured in dual MAX COUNT register mode, this bit will be set each time the value in MAX COUNT register A is reached, and each time the value in MAX COUNT register B is reached. This bit is set regardless of the timer's interrupt-enable bit. The MC bit gives the user the ability to monitor timer status through software instead of through interrupts.

Programmer intervention is required to clear this bit.

RTG:

Retrigger bit is only active for internal clocking (EXT = 0). In this case it determines the control function provided by the input pin.

If RTG = 0, the input level gates the internal clock on and off. If the input pin is HIGH, the timer will count; if the input pin is LOW, the timer will hold its value. As indicated previously, the input signal may be asynchronous with respect to the 80186 clock.

When RTG = 1, the input pin detects LOW-to-HIGH transitions. The first such transition starts the timer running, clearing the timer value to zero on the first clock, and then incrementing thereafter. Further transitions on the input pin will again reset the timer to zero, from which it will start counting up again. If CONT = 0, when the timer has reached maximum count, the EN bit will be cleared, inhibiting further timer activity.

P:

The prescaler bit is ignored unless internal clocking has been selected (EXT = 0). If the P bit is a zero, the timer will count at one-fourth the internal CPU clock rate. If the P bit is a one, the output of timer 2 will be used as a clock for the timer. Note that the user must initialize and start timer 2 to obtain the prescaled clock.

EXT:

The external bit selects between internal and external clocking for the timer. The external signal may be asynchronous with respect to the 80186 clock. If this bit is set, the timer will count LOW-to-HIGH transitions on the input pin. If cleared, it will count an internal clock while using the input pin for control. In this mode, the function of the external pin is defined by the RTG bit. The maximum input to output transition latency time may be as much as 6 clocks. However, clock inputs may be pipelined as closely together as every 4 clocks without losing clock pulses.

ALT:

The ALT bit determines which of two MAX COUNT registers is used for count comparison. If ALT = 0, register A for that timer is always used, while if ALT = 1, the comparison will alternate between register A and register B when each maximum count is reached. This alternation allows the user to change one MAX COUNT register while the other is being used, and thus provides a method of generating non-repetitive waveforms. Square waves and pulse outputs of any duty cycle are a subset of available signals obtained by not changing the final count registers. The ALT bit also determines the function of the timer output pin. If ALT is zero, the output pin will go LOW for one clock, the clock after the maximum count is reached. If ALT is one, the output pin will reflect the current MAX COUNT register being used (0/1 for B/A).

CONT:

Setting the CONT bit causes the associated timer to run continuously, while resetting it causes the timer to halt upon maximum count. If CONT = 0 and ALT = 1, the timer will count to the MAX COUNT register A value, reset, count to the register B value, reset, and halt.

Not all mode bits are provided for timer 2. Certain bits are hardwired as indicated below:

ALT = 0, EXT = 0, P = 0, RTG = 0, RIU = 0

Count Registers

Each of the three timers has a 16-bit count register. The contents of this register may be read or written by the processor at any time. If the register is written while the timer is counting,the new value will take effect in the current count cycle.

Max Count Registers

Timers 0 and 1 have two MAX COUNT registers, while timer 2 has a single MAX COUNT register. These contain the number of events the timer will count. In timers 0 and 1, the MAX COUNT register used can alternate between the two max count values whenever the current maximum count is reached. A timer resets when the timer count register equals the max count value being used. If the timer count register or the max count register is changed so that the max count is less than the timer count, the timer does not immediately reset. Instead, the timer counts up to 0FFFFH, "wraps around" to zero, counts up to the max count value, and then resets.

Timers and Reset

Upon RESET, the Timers will perform the following actions:

- All EN (Enable) bits are reset preventing timer counting.
- For Timers 0 and 1, the RIU bits are reset to zero and the ALT bits are set to one. This results in the Timer Out pins going high.

INTERRUPT CONTROLLER

The 80186 can receive interrupts from a number of sources, both internal and external. The internal interrupt controller serves to merge these requests on a priority basis, for individual service by the CPU.

Internal interrupt sources (Timers and DMA channels) can be disabled by their own control registers or by mask bits within the interrupt controller. The 80186 interrupt controller has its own control register that sets the mode of operation for the controller.

The interrupt controller will resolve priority among requests that are pending simultaneously. Nesting is provided so interrupt service routines for lower priority interrupts may be interrupted by higher priority interrupts. A block diagram of the interrupt controller is shown in Figure 21.

The 80186 has a special Slave Mode in which the internal interrupt controller acts as a slave to an external master. The controller is programmed into this mode by setting bit 14 in the peripheral control block relocation register. (See Slave Mode section.)

MASTER MODE OPERATION

Interrupt Controller External Interface

Five pins are provided for external interrupt sources. One of these pins is NMI, the non-maskable interrupt. NMI is generally used for unusual events such as power-fail interrupts. The other four pins may be configured in any of the following ways:

- As four interrupt input lines with internally generated interrupt vectors.
- As an interrupt line and interrupt acknowledge line pair (Cascade Mode) with externally generated interrupt vectors plus two interrupt input lines with internally generated vectors.
- As two pairs of interrupt/interrupt acknowledge lines (Cascade Mode) with externally generated interrupt vectors.

External sources in the Cascade Mode use externally generated interrupt vectors. When an interrupt is acknowledged, two INTA cycles are initiated and the vector is read into the 80186 on the second cycle. The capability to interface to external 8259A programmable interrupt controllers is provided when the inputs are configured in Cascade Mode.

Interrupt Controller Modes of Operation

The basic modes of operation of the interrupt controller in Master Mode are similar to the 8259A. The interrupt controller responds identically to internal interrupts in all three modes: the difference is only in the interpretation of function of the four external interrupt pins. The interrupt controller is set into one of these three modes by programming the correct bits in the INT0 and INT1 control registers. The modes of interrupt controller operation are as follows:

Fully Nested Mode

When in the fully nested mode four pins are used as direct interrupt requests as in Figure 22. The vectors for these four inputs are generated internally. An in-service bit is provided for every interrupt source. If a lower-priority device requests an interrupt while the in service bit (IS) is set, no interrupt will be generated by the interrupt controller. In addition, if another interrupt request occurs from the same interrupt source while the in-service bit is set, no interrupt will be generated by the interrupt controller. This allows interrupt service routines to operate with interrupts enabled, yet be suspended only by interrupts of higher priority than the in-service interrupt.

When a service routine is completed, the proper IS bit must be reset by writing the proper pattern to the EOI register. This is required to allow subsequent interrupts from this interrupt source and to allow servicing of lower-priority interrupts. An EOI command is executed at the end of the service routine just before the return from interrupt instruction. If the fully nested structure has been upheld, the next highest-priority source with its IS bit set is then serviced.

Cascade Mode

The 80186 has four interrupt pins and two of them have dual functions. In the fully nested mode the four pins are used as direct interrupt inputs and the corresponding vectors are generated internally. In the Cascade Mode, the four pins are configured into interrupt input-dedicated acknowledge signal pairs. The interconnection is shown in Figure 23. INT0 is an interrupt input interfaced to an 8259A, while INT2/$\overline{\text{INTA0}}$ serves as the dedicated interrupt acknowledge signal to that peripheral. The same is true for INT1 and INT3/$\overline{\text{INTA1}}$. Each pair can selectively be placed in the Cascade Mode by programming the proper value into INT0 and INT1 control registers. The use of the dedicated acknowledge signals eliminates the need for the use of external logic to generate $\overline{\text{INTA}}$ and device select signals.

The primary Cascade Mode allows the capability to serve up to 128 external interrupt sources through the use of external master and slave 8259As. Three levels of priority are created, requiring priority resolution in the 80186 interrupt controller, the master 8259As, and the slave 8259As. If an external interrupt is serviced, one IS bit is set at each of these levels. When the interrupt service routine is completed, up to three end-of-interrupt commands must be issued by the programmer.

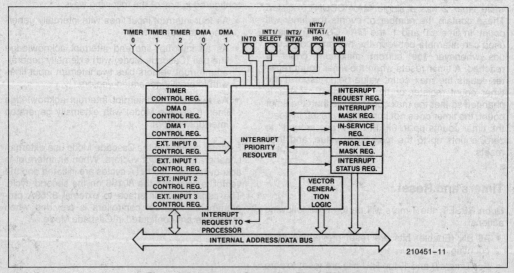

Figure 21. Interrupt Controller Block Diagram

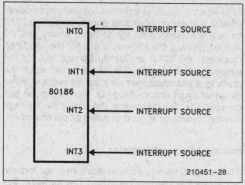

Figure 22. Fully Nested (Direct) Mode Interrupt Controller Connections

Special Fully Nested Mode

This mode is entered by setting the SFNM bit in INT0 or INT1 control register. It enables complete nestability with external 8259A masters. Normally, an interrupt request from an interrupt source will not be recognized unless the in-service bit for that source is reset. If more than one interrupt source is connected to an external interrupt controller, all of the interrupts will be funneled through the same 80186 interrupt request pin. As a result, if the external interrupt controller receives a higher-priority interrupt, its interrupt will not be recognized by the 80186 controller until the 80186 in-service bit is reset. In Special Fully Nested Mode, the 80186 interrupt controller will allow interrupts from an external pin regardless of the state of the in-service bit for an interrupt source in order to allow multiple interrupts from a single pin. An in-service bit will continue to be set, however, to inhibit interrupts from other lower-priority 80186 interrupt sources.

Special procedures should be followed when resetting IS bits at the end of interrupt service routines. Software polling of the IS register in the external master 8259A is required to determine if there is more than one bit set. If so, the IS bit in the 80186 remains active and the next interrupt service routine is entered.

Operation in a Polled Environment

The controller may be used in a polled mode if interrupts are undesirable. When polling, the processor disables interrupts and then polls the interrupt controller whenever it is convenient. Polling the interrupt controller is accomplished by reading the Poll Word (Figure 32). Bit 15 in the poll word indicates to the processor that an interrupt of high enough priority is requesting service. Bits 0–4 indicate to the processor the type vector of the highest-priority source requesting service. Reading the Poll Word causes the In-Service bit of the highest priority source to be set.

It is desirable to be able to read the Poll Word information without guaranteeing service of any pending interrupt, i.e., not set the indicated in-service bit. The 80186 provides a Poll Status Word in addition to the conventional Poll Word to allow this to be done. Poll Word information is duplicated in the Poll Status Word, but reading the Poll Status Word does not set the associated in-service bit. These words are located in two adjacent memory locations in the register file.

Master Mode Features

Programmable Priority

The user can program the interrupt sources into any of eight different priority levels. The programming is done by placing a 3-bit priority level (0–7) in the control register of each interrupt source. (A source with a priority level of 4 has higher priority over all priority levels from 5 to 7. Priority registers containing values lower than 4 have greater priority). All interrupt sources have preprogrammed default priority levels (see Table 4).

If two requests with the same programmed priority level are pending at once, the priority ordering scheme shown in Table 4 is used. If the serviced interrupt routine reenables interrupts, other interrupt requests can be serviced.

End-of-Interrupt Command

The end-of-interrupt (EOI) command is used by the programmer to reset the In-Service (IS) bit when an interrupt service routine is completed. The EOI command is issued by writing the proper pattern to the EOI register. There are two types of EOI commands, specific and nonspecific. The nonspecific command does not specify which IS bit is reset. When issued, the interrupt controller automatically resets the IS bit of the highest priority source with an active service routine. A specific EOI command requires that the programmer send the interrupt vector type to the interrupt controller indicating which source's IS bit is to be reset. This command is used when the fully nested structure has been disturbed or the highest priority IS bit that was set does not belong to the service routine in progress.

Trigger Mode

The four external interrupt pins can be programmed in either edge- or level-trigger mode. The control register for each external source has a level-trigger mode (LTM) bit. All interrupt inputs are active HIGH. In the edge sense mode or the level-trigger mode, the interrupt request must remain active (HIGH) until the interrupt request is acknowledged by the 80186 CPU. In the edge-sense mode, if the level remains high after the interrupt is acknowledged, the input is disabled and no further requests will be generated. The input level must go LOW for at least one clock cycle to re-enable the input. In the level-trigger mode, no such provision is made: holding the interrupt input HIGH will cause continuous interrupt requests.

Interrupt Vectoring

The 80186 Interrupt Controller will generate interrupt vectors for the integrated DMA channels and the integrated Timers. In addition, the Interrupt Controller will generate interrupt vectors for the external interrupt lines if they are not configured in Cascade or Special Fully Nested Mode. The interrupt vectors generated are fixed and cannot be changed (see Table 4).

Interrupt Controller Registers

The Interrupt Controller register model is shown in Figure 24. It contains 15 registers. All registers can both be read or written unless specified otherwise.

In-Service Register

This register can be read from or written into. The format is shown in Figure 25. It contains the In-Service bit for each of the interrupt sources. The In-Service bit is set to indicate that a source's service routine is in progress. When an In-Service bit is set, the interrupt controller will not generate interrupts to the CPU when it receives interrupt requests from devices with a lower programmed priority level. The TMR bit is the In-Service bit for all three timers; the D0 and D1 bits are the In-Service bits for the two DMA channels; the I0–I3 are the In-Service bits for the external interrupt pins. The IS bit is set when the processor acknowledges an interrupt request either by an interrupt acknowledge or by reading the poll register. The IS bit is reset at the end of the interrupt service routine by an end-of-interrupt command.

Interrupt Request Register

The internal interrupt sources have interrupt request bits inside the interrupt controller. The format of this register is shown in Figure 25. A read from this register yields the status of these bits. The TMR bit is the logical OR of all timer interrupt requests. D0 and D1 are the interrupt request bits for the DMA channels.

The state of the external interrupt input pins is also indicated. The state of the external interrupt pins is not a stored condition inside the interrupt controller, therefore the external interrupt bits cannot be written. The external interrupt request bits are set when an interrupt request is given to the interrupt controller, so if edge-triggered mode is selected, the bit in the register will be HIGH only after an inactive-to-active transition. For internal interrupt sources, the register bits are set when a request arrives and are reset when the processor acknowledges the requests.

Writes to the interrupt request register will affect the D0 and D1 interrupt request bits. Setting either bit will cause the corresponding interrupt request while clearing either bit will remove the corresponding interrupt request. All other bits in the register are read-only.

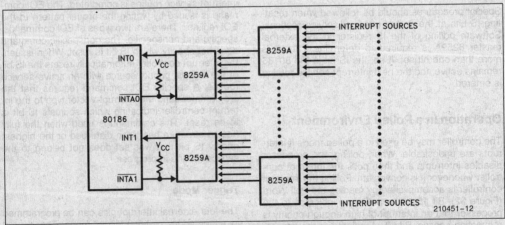

Figure 23. Cascade and Special Fully Nested Mode Interrupt Controller Connections

Mask Register

This is a 16-bit register that contains a mask bit for each interrupt source. The format for this register is shown in Figure 25. A one in a bit position corresponding to a particular source masks the source from generating interrupts. These mask bits are the exact same bits which are used in the individual control registers; programming a mask bit using the mask register will also change this bit in the individual control registers, and vice versa.

	OFFSET
INT3 CONTROL REGISTER	3EH
INT2 CONTROL REGISTER	3CH
INT1 CONTROL REGISTER	3AH
INT0 CONTROL REGISTER	38H
DMA 1 CONTROL REGISTER	36H
DMA 0 CONTROL REGISTER	34H
TIMER CONTROL REGISTER	32H
INTERRUPT STATUS REGISTER	30H
INTERRUPT REQUEST REGISTER	2EH
IN-SERVICE REGISTER	2CH
PRIORITY MASK REGISTER	2AH
MASK REGISTER	28H
POLL STATUS REGISTER	26H
POLL REGISTER	24H
EOI REGISTER	22H

**Figure 24. Interrupt Controller Registers
(Master Mode)**

Priority Mask Register

This register masks all interrupts below a particular interrupt priority level. The format of this register is shown in Figure 26. The code in the lower three bits of this register inhibits interrupts of priority lower (a higher priority number) than the code specified. For example, 100 written into this register masks interrupts of level five (101), six (110), and seven (111). The register is reset to seven (111) upon RESET so no interrupts are masked due to priority number.

Interrupt Status Register

This register contains general interrupt controller status information. The format of this register is shown in Figure 27. The bits in the status register have the following functions:

DHLT: DMA Halt Transfer; setting this bit halts all DMA transfers. It is automatically set whenever a non-maskable interrupt occurs, and it is reset when an IRET instruction is executed. This bit allows prompt service of all non-maskable interrupts. This bit may also be set by the programmer.

IRTx: These three bits represent the individual timer interrupt request bits. These bits differentiate between timer interrupts, since the timer IR bit in the interrupt request register is the "OR" function of all timer interrupt request. Note that setting any one of these three bits initiates an interrupt request to the interrupt controller.

15	14				10	9	8	7	6	5	4	3	2	1	0
0	0	•	•	•	0	0	0	I3	I2	I1	I0	D1	D0	0	TMR

Figure 25. In-Service, Interrupt Request, and Mask Register Formats

15	14											3	2	1	0
0	0	•	•	•	•	•	•	•	•	•		0	PRM2	PRM1	PRM0

Figure 26. Priority Mask Register Format

15	14						7	6	5	4	3	2	1	0
DHLT	0	•	•	•	•	•	0	0	0	0	0	IRT2	IRT1	IRT0

Figure 27. Interrupt Status Register Format (Master Mode)

Timer, DMA 0, 1; Control Register

These registers are the control words for all the internal interrupt sources. The format for these registers is shown in Figure 28. The three bit positions PR0, PR1, and PR2 represent the programmable priority level of the interrupt source. The MSK bit inhibits interrupt requests from the interrupt source. The MSK bits in the individual control registers are the exact same bits as are in the Mask Register; modifying them in the individual control registers will also modify them in the Mask Register, and vice versa.

INT0-INT3 Control Registers

These registers are the control words for the four external input pins. Figure 29 shows the format of the INT0 and INT1 Control registers; Figure 30 shows the format of the INT2 and INT3 Control registers. In Cascade Mode or Special Fully Nested Mode, the control words for INT2 and INT3 are not used.

The bits in the various control registers are encoded as follows:

PRO-2: Priority programming information. Highest Priority = 000, Lowest Priority = 111

LTM: Level-trigger mode bit. 1 = level-triggered; 0 = edge-triggered. Interrupt Input levels are active high. In level-triggered mode, an interrupt is generated whenever the external line is high. In edge-triggered mode, an interrupt will be generated only when this

level is preceded by an inactive-to-active transition on the line. In both cases, the level must remain active until the interrupt is acknowledged.

MSK: Mask bit, 1 = mask; 0 = non-mask.

C: Cascade mode bit, 1 = cascade; 0 = direct

SFNM: Special Fully Nested Mode bit, 1 = SFNM

EOI Register

The end of the interrupt register is a command register which can only be written into. The format of this register is shown in Figure 31. It initiates an EOI command when written to by the 80186 CPU.

The bits in the EOI register are encoded as follows:

S_x: Encoded information that specifies an interrupt source vector type as shown in Table 4. For example, to reset the In-Service bit for DMA channel 0, these bits should be set to 01010, since the vector type for DMA channel 0 is 10.

NOTE:

To reset the single In-Service bit for any of the three timers, the vector type for timer 0 (8) should be written in this register.

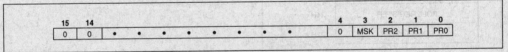

Figure 28. Timer/DMA Control Registers Formats

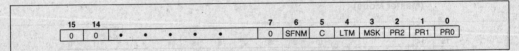

Figure 29. INT0/INT1 Control Register Formats

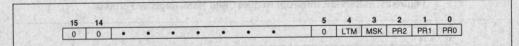

Figure 30. INT2/INT3 Control Register Formats

NSPEC/: A bit that determines the type of EOI command. Nonspecific = 1, Specific = 0.
SPEC

Poll and Poll Status Registers

These registers contain polling information. The format of these registers is shown in Figure 32. They can only be read. Reading the Poll register constitutes a software poll. This will set the IS bit of the highest priority pending interrupt. Reading the poll status register will not set the IS bit of the highest priority pending interrupt; only the status of pending interrupts will be provided.

Encoding of the Poll and Poll Status register bits are as follows:

S_x: Encoded information that indicates the vector type of the highest priority interrupting source. Valid only when INTREQ = 1.

INTREQ: This bit determines if an interrupt request is present. Interrupt Request = 1; no Interrupt Request = 0.

SLAVE MODE OPERATION

When Slave Mode is used, the internal 80186 interrupt controller will be used as a slave controller to an external master interrupt controller. The internal 80186 resources will be monitored by the internal interrupt controller, while the external controller functions as the system master interrupt controller. Upon reset, the 80186 will be in Master Mode. To provide for slave mode operation bit 14 of the relocation register should be set.

Because of pin limitations caused by the need to interface to an external 8259A master, the internal interrupt controller will no longer accept external inputs. There are however, enough 80186 interrupt controller inputs (internally) to dedicate one to each timer. In this mode, each timer interrupt source has its own mask bit, IS bit, and control word.

In Slave Mode each peripheral must be assigned a unique priority to ensure proper interrupt controller operation. Therefore, it is the programmer's responsibility to assign correct priorities and initialize interrupt control registers before enabling interrupts.

These level assignments must remain fixed in the Slave Mode of operation.

Slave Mode External Interface

The configuration of the 80186 with respect to an external 8259A master is shown in Figure 33. The INT0 (pin 45) input is used as the 80186 CPU interrupt input. IRQ (pin 41) functions as an output to send the 80186 slave-interrupt-request to one of the 8 master-PIC-inputs.

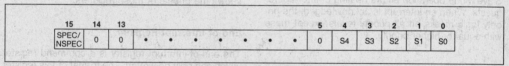

Figure 31. EOI Register Format

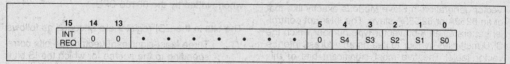

Figure 32. Poll and Poll Status Register Format

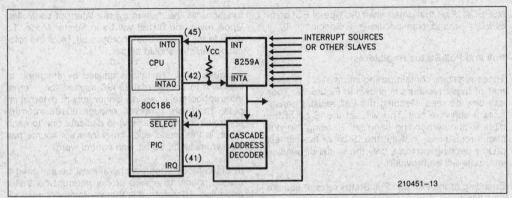

Figure 33. Slave Mode Interrupt Controller Connections

Correct master-slave interface requires decoding of the slave addresses (CAS0-2). Slave 8259As do this internally. Because of pin limitations, the 80186 slave address will have to be decoded externally. SELECT (pin 44) is used as a slave-select input. Note that the slave vector address is transferred internally, but the READY input must be supplied externally.

INTA0 (pin 42) is used as an acknowledge output, suitable to drive the INTA input of an 8259A.

Interrupt Nesting

Slave Mode operation allows nesting of interrupt requests. When an interrupt is acknowledged, the priority logic masks off all priority levels except those with equal or higher priority.

Vector Generation in the Slave Mode

Vector generation in Slave Mode is exactly like that of an 8259A or 82C59A slave. The interrupt controller generates an 8-bit vector type number which the CPU multiplies by four to use as an address into the vector table. The five most significant bits of this type number are user-programmable while the three least significant bits are defined according to Figure 34. The significant five bits of the vector are programmed by writing to the Interrupt Vector register at offset 20H.

Specific End-of-Interrupt

In Slave Mode the specific EOI command operates to reset an in-service bit of a specific priority. The user supplies a 3-bit priority-level value that points to an in-service bit to be reset. The command is executed by writing the correct value in the Specific EOI register at offset 22H.

Interrupt Controller Registers in the Slave Mode

All control and command registers are located inside the internal peripheral control block. Figure 34 shows the offsets of these registers.

End-of-Interrupt Register

The end-of-interrupt register is a command register which can only be written. The format of this register is shown in Figure 35. It initiates an EOI command when written by the 80186 CPU.

The bits in the EOI register are encoded as follows:

VT_x: Three least-significant vector type bits corresponding to the source for which the IS bit is to be reset. Figure 34 indicates these bits.

In-Service Register

This register can be read from or written into. It contains the in-service bit for each of the internal interrupt sources. The format for this register is shown in Figure 36. Bit positions 2 and 3 correspond to the DMA channels; positions 0, 4, and 5 correspond to the integral timers. The source's IS bit is set when the processor acknowledges its interrupt request.

Interrupt Request Register

This register indicates which internal peripherals have interrupt requests pending. The format of this register is shown in Figure 36. The interrupt request bits are set when a request arrives from an internal source, and are reset when the processor acknowledges the request. As in Master Mode, D0 and D1 are read/write; all other bits are read only.

Mask Register

This register contains a mask bit for each interrupt source. The format for this register is shown in Figure 36. If the bit in this register corresponding to a particular interrupt source is set, any interrupts from that source will be masked. These mask bits are exactly the same bits which are used in the individual control registers, i.e., changing the state of a mask bit in this register will also change the state of the mask bit in the individual interrupt control register corresponding to the bit.

Control Registers

These registers are the control words for all the internal interrupt sources. The format of these registers is shown in Figure 37. Each of the timers and both of the DMA channels have their own Control Register.

The bits of the Control Registers are encoded as follows:

pr_x: 3-bit encoded field indicating a priority level for the source.

msk: mask bit for the priority level indicated by pr_x bits.

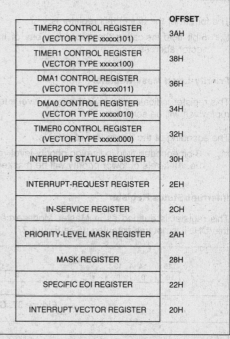

Figure 34. Interrupt Controller Registers (Slave Mode)

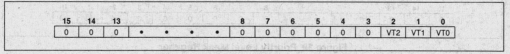

Figure 35. Specific EOI Register Format

Figure 36. In-Service, Interrupt Request, and Mask Register Format

Interrupt Vector Register

This register provides the upper five bits of the interrupt vector address. The format of this register is shown in Figure 38. The interrupt controller itself provides the lower three bits of the interrupt vector as determined by the priority level of the interrupt request.

The format of the bits in this register is:

t_x: 5-bit field indicating the upper five bits of the vector address.

Priority-Level Mask Register

This register indicates the lowest priority-level interrupt which will be serviced.

The encoding of the bits in this register is:

m_x: 3-bit encoded field indication priority-level value. All levels of lower priority will be masked.

Interrupt Status Register

This register is defined as in Master Mode except that DHLT is not implemented. (See Figure 27).

Interrupt Controller and Reset

Upon RESET, the interrupt controller will perform the following actions:

- All SFNM bits reset to 0, implying Fully Nested Mode.
- All PR bits in the various control registers set to 1. This places all sources at lowest priority (level 111).
- All LTM bits reset to 0, resulting in edge-sense mode.
- All Interrupt Service bits reset to 0.
- All Interrupt Request bits reset to 0.
- All MSK (Interrupt Mask) bits set to 1 (mask).
- All C (Cascade) bits reset to 0 (non-Cascade).
- All PRM (Priority Mask) bits set to 1, implying no levels masked.
- Initialized to Master Mode.

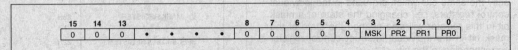

Figure 37. Control Word Format

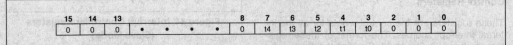

Figure 38. Interrupt Vector Register Format

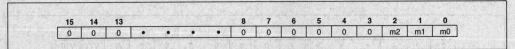

Figure 39. Priority Level Mask Register

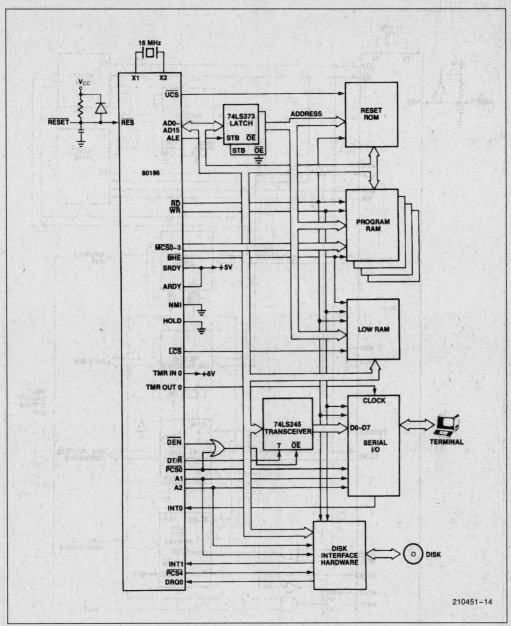

Figure 40. Typical 80186 Computer

210451–14

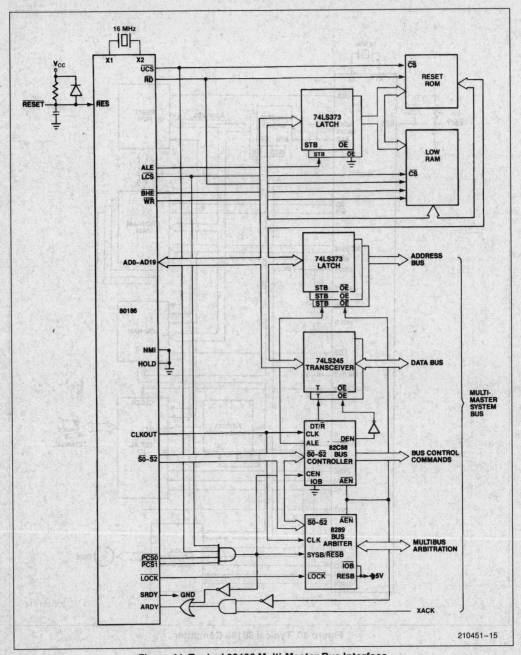

Figure 41. Typical 80186 Multi-Master Bus Interface

210451–15

ABSOLUTE MAXIMUM RATINGS*

Ambient Temperature under Bias ......0°C to 70°C

Storage Temperature ....−65°C to +150°C

Voltage on any Pin with
Respect to Ground..............−1.0V to +7V

Power Dissipation 3W

*Notice: Stresses above those listed under "Absolute Maximum Ratings" may cause permanent damage to the device. This is a stress rating only and functional operation of the device at these or any other conditions above those indicated in the operational sections of this specification is not implied. Exposure to absolute maximum rating conditions for extended periods may affect device reliability.

D.C. CHARACTERISTICS (T_A = 0°C to +70°C, V_{CC} = 5V ±10%)

Applicable to 80186 (8 MHz), 80186-10 (10 MHz).

Symbol	Parameter	Min	Max	Units	Test Conditions
V_{IL}	Input Low Voltage	−0.5	+0.8	V	
V_{IH}	Input High Voltage (All except X1 and ($\overline{RES}$))	2.0	V_{CC} + 0.5	V	
V_{IH1}	Input High Voltage ($\overline{RES}$)	3.0	V_{CC} + 0.5	V	
V_{OL}	Output Low Voltage		0.45	V	I_a = 2.5 mA for $\overline{S0}$–$\overline{S2}$ I_a = 2.0 mA for all other Outputs
V_{OH}	Output High Voltage	2.4		V	I_{oa} = −400 μA
I_{CC}	Power Supply Current		600*	mA	T_A = −40°C
			550	mA	T_A = 0°C
			415	mA	T_A = +70°C
I_{LI}	Input Leakage Current		±10	μA	0V < V_{IN} < V_{CC}
I_{LO}	Output Leakage Current		±10	μA	0.45V < V_{OUT} < V_{CC}
V_{CLO}	Clock Output Low		0.6	V	I_a = 4.0 mA
V_{CHO}	Clock Output High	4.0		V	I_{oa} = −200 μA
V_{CLI}	Clock Input Low Voltage	−0.5	0.6	V	
V_{CHI}	Clock Input High Voltage	3.9	V_{CC} + 1.0	V	
C_{IN}	Input Capacitance		10	pF	
C_{IO}	I/O Capacitance		20	pF	

*For extended temperature parts only.

PIN TIMINGS

A.C. CHARACTERISTICS (T_A = 0°C to +70°C, V_{CC} = 5V ±10%)

80186 Timing Requirements All Timings Measured At 1.5V Unless Otherwise Noted.

Symbol	Parameter	80186 (8 MHz) Min	80186 (8 MHz) Max	80186-10 (10 MHz) Min	80186-10 (10 MHz) Max	Units	Test Conditions
T_{DVCL}	Data in Setup (A/D)	20		15		ns	
T_{CLDX}	Data in Hold (A/D)	10		8		ns	
T_{ARYHCH}	Asynchronous Ready (ARDY) Active Setup Time [1]	20		15		ns	
T_{ARYLCL}	ARDY Inactive Setup Time	35		25		ns	
T_{CLARX}	ARDY Hold Time	15		15		ns	
T_{ARYCHL}	Asynchronous Ready Inactive Hold Time	15		15		ns	
T_{SRYCL}	Synchronous Ready (SRDY) Transition Setup Time [2]	20		20		ns	
T_{CLSRY}	SRDY Transition Hold Time [2]	15		15		ns	
T_{HVCL}	HOLD Setup [1]	25		20		ns	
T_{INVCH}	INTR, NMI, TEST, TIM IN, Setup [1]	25		25		ns	
T_{INVCL}	DRQ0, DRQ1, Setup [1]	25		20		ns	

80186 Master Interface Timing Responses

Symbol	Parameter	80186 (8 MHz) Min	80186 (8 MHz) Max	80186-10 (10 MHz) Min	80186-10 (10 MHz) Max	Units	Test Conditions
T_{CLAV}	Address Valid Delay	5	55	5	44	ns	C_L=20–200 pF all Outputs (Except T_{CLTMV}) @ 8 & 10 MHz
T_{CLAX}	Address Hold	10		10		ns	
T_{CLAZ}	Address Float Delay	T_{CLAX}	35	T_{CLAX}	30	ns	
T_{CHCZ}	Command Lines Float Delay		45		40	ns	
T_{CHCV}	Command Lines Valid Delay (after Float)		55		45	ns	
T_{LHLL}	ALE Width	T_{CLCL}−35		T_{CLCL}−30		ns	
T_{CHLH}	ALE Active Delay		35		30	ns	
T_{CHLL}	ALE Inactive Delay		35		30	ns	
T_{LLAX}	Address Hold from ALE Inactive	T_{CHCL}−25		T_{CHCL}−20		ns	
T_{CLDV}	Data Valid Delay	10	44	10	40	ns	
T_{CLDOX}	Data Hold Time	10		10		ns	
T_{WHDX}	Data Hold after WR	T_{CLCL}−40		T_{CLCL}−34		ns	
T_{CVCTV}	Control Active Delay 1	5	50	5	40	ns	
T_{CHCTV}	Control Active Delay 2	10	55	10	44	ns	
T_{CVCTX}	Control Inactive Delay	5	55	5	44	ns	
T_{CVDEX}	DEN Inactive Delay (Non-Write Cycle)	10	70	10	56	ns	

1. To guarantee recognition at next clock.
2. To guarantee proper operation.

80186

PIN TIMINGS (Continued)

A.C. CHARACTERISTICS ($T_A = 0°C$ to $+70°C$, $V_{CC} = 5V \pm 10\%$) (Continued)

80186 Master Interface Timing Responses (Continued)

Symbol	Parameter	80186 (8 MHz)		80186-10 (10 MHz)		Units	Test Conditions
		Min	Max	Min	Max		
T_{AZRL}	Address Float to $\overline{RD}$ Active	0		0		ns	
T_{CLRL}	$\overline{RD}$ Active Delay	10	70	10	56	ns	
T_{CLRH}	$\overline{RD}$ Inactive Delay	10	55	10	44	ns	
T_{RHAV}	$\overline{RD}$ Inactive to Address Active	$T_{CLCL}-40$		$T_{CLCL}-40$		ns	
T_{CLHAV}	HLDA Valid Delay	5	50	5	40	ns	
T_{RLRH}	$\overline{RD}$ Width	$2T_{CLCL}-50$		$2T_{CLCL}-46$		ns	
T_{WLWH}	$\overline{WR}$ Width	$2T_{CLCL}-40$		$2T_{CLCL}-34$		ns	
T_{AVLL}	Address Valid to ALE Low	$T_{CLCH}-25$		$T_{CLCH}-19$		ns	
T_{CHSV}	Status Active Delay	10	55	10	45	ns	
T_{CLSH}	Status Inactive Delay	10	65	10	50	ns	
T_{CLTMV}	Timer Output Delay		60		48	ns	100 pF max @ 8 & 10 MHz
T_{CLRO}	Reset Delay		60		48	ns	
T_{CHQSV}	Queue Status Delay		35		28	ns	
T_{CHDX}	Status Hold Time	10		10		ns	
T_{AVCH}	Address Valid to Clock High	10		10		ns	
T_{CLLV}	$\overline{LOCK}$ Valid/Invalid Delay	5	65	5	60	ns	

80186 Chip-Select Timing Responses

Symbol	Parameter	Min	Max	Min	Max	Units	Test Conditions
T_{CLCSV}	Chip-Select Active Delay		66		45	ns	
T_{CXCSX}	Chip-Select Hold from Command Inactive	35		35		ns	
T_{CHCSX}	Chip-Select Inactive Delay	5	35	5	32	ns	

80186 CLKIN Requirements

Symbol	Parameter	Min	Max	Min	Max	Units	Test Conditions
T_{CKIN}	CLKIN Period	62.5	250	50	250	ns	
T_{CKHL}	CLKIN Fall Time		10		10	ns	3.5 to 1.0V
T_{CKLH}	CLKIN Rise Time		10		10	ns	1.0 to 3.5V
T_{CLCK}	CLKIN Low Time	25		20		ns	1.5V
T_{CHCK}	CLKIN High Time	25		20		ns	1.5V

80186 CLKOUT Timing (200 pF load)

Symbol	Parameter	Min	Max	Min	Max	Units	Test Conditions
T_{CICO}	CLKIN to CLKOUT Skew		50		25	ns	
T_{CLCL}	CLKOUT Period	125	500	100	500	ns	
T_{CLCH}	CLKOUT Low Time	$\frac{1}{2}T_{CLCL}-7.5$		$\frac{1}{2}T_{CLCL}-6.0$		ns	1.5V
T_{CHCL}	CLKOUT High Time	$\frac{1}{2}T_{CLCL}-7.5$		$\frac{1}{2}T_{CLCL}-6.0$		ns	1.5V
T_{CH1CH2}	CLKOUT Rise Time		15		12	ns	1.0 to 3.5V
T_{CL2CL1}	CLKOUT Fall Time		15		12	ns	3.5 to 1.0V

EXPLANATION OF THE AC SYMBOLS

Each timing symbol has from 5 to 7 characters. The first character is always a "T" (stands for time). The other characters, depending on their positions, stand for the name of a signal or the logical status of that signal. The following is a list of all the characters and what they stand for.

A: Address
ARY: Asynchronous Ready Input
C: Clock Output
CK: Clock Input
CS: Chip Select
CT: Control (DT/$\overline{R}$, $\overline{DEN}$, . . .)
D: Data Input
DE: $\overline{DEN}$
H: Logic Level High

IN: Input (DRQ0, TIM0, . . .)
L: Logic Level Low or ALE
O: Output
QS: Queue Status (QS1, QS2)
R: $\overline{RD}$ signal, RESET signal
S: Status ($\overline{S0}$, $\overline{S1}$, $\overline{S2}$)
SRY: Synchronous Ready Input
V: Valid
W: WR Signal
X: No Longer a Valid Logic Level
Z: Float

Examples:

T_{CLAV} — Time from Clock low to Address valid
T_{CHLH} — Time from Clock high to ALE high
T_{CLCSV} — Time from Clock low to Chip Select valid

WAVEFORMS

MAJOR CYCLE TIMING

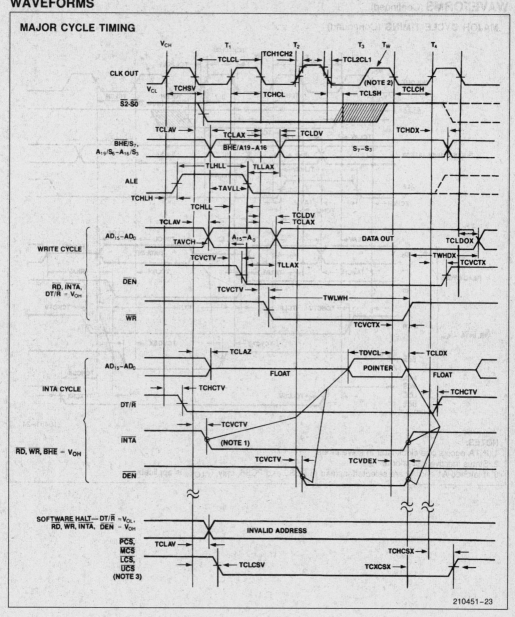

210451-23

WAVEFORMS (Continued)

MAJOR CYCLE TIMING (Continued)

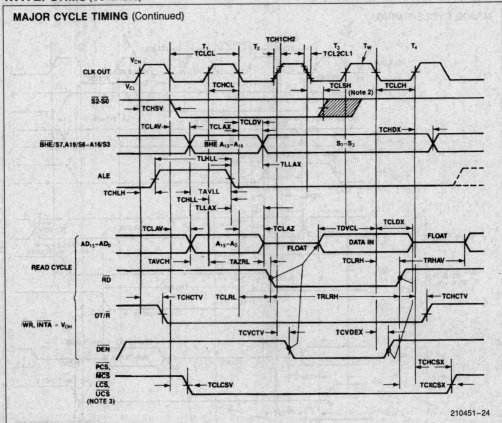

210451–24

NOTES:
1. INTA occurs one clock later in slave mode.
2. Status inactive just prior to T_4.
3. If latched A1 and A2 are selected instead of $\overline{PCS5}$ and $\overline{PCS6}$, only T_{CLCSV} is applicable.

WAVEFORMS (Continued)

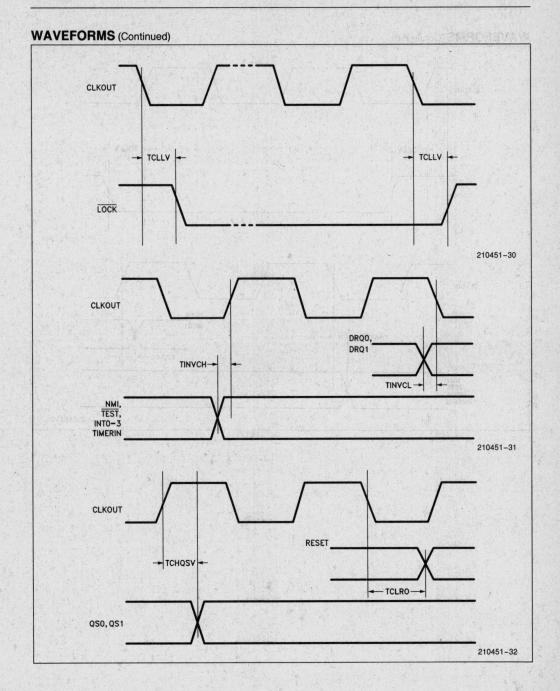

210451–30

210451–31

210451–32

WAVEFORMS (Continued)

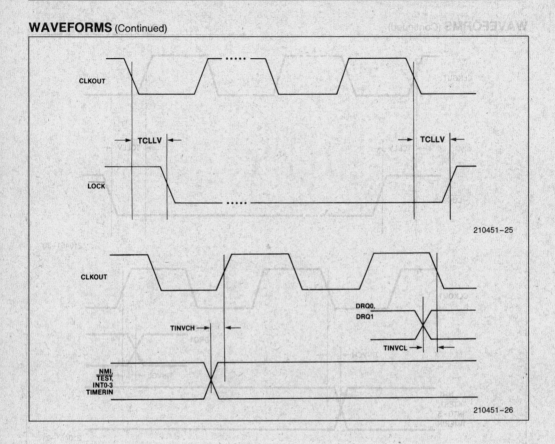

WAVEFORMS (Continued)

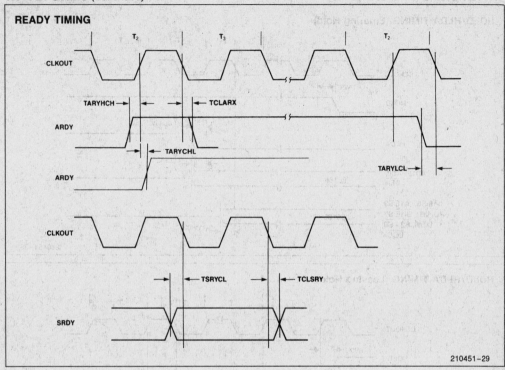

READY TIMING

210451–29

WAVEFORMS (Continued)

HOLD/HLDA TIMING (Entering Hold)

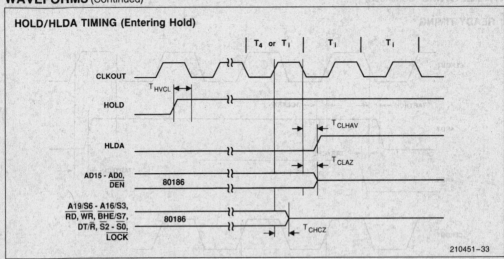

210451–33

HOLD/HLDA TIMING (Leaving Hold)

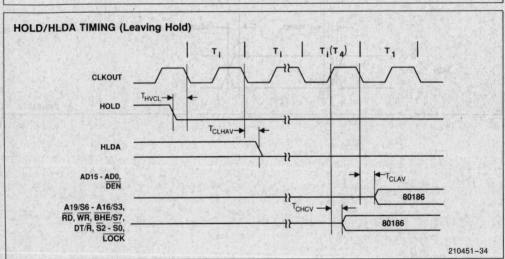

210451–34

WAVEFORMS (Continued)

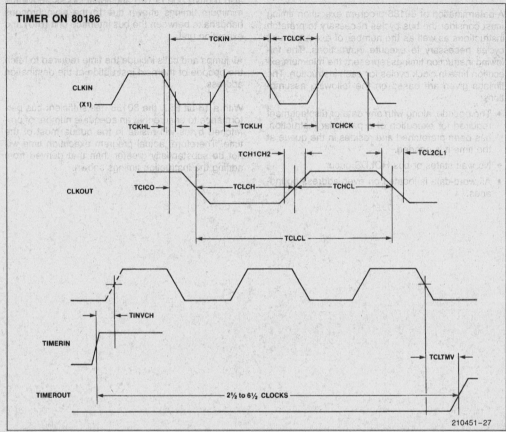

TIMER ON 80186

210451–27

80186 EXPRESS

The Intel EXPRESS system offers enhancements to the operational specifications of the 80186 microprocessor. EXPRESS products are designed to meet the needs of those applications whose operating requirements exceed commercial standards.

The EXPRESS program includes the commercial standard temperature range with burn-in and an extended temperature range without burn-in.

With the commercial standard temperature range operational characteristics are guaranteed over the temperature range of 0°C to +70°C. With the extended temperature range option, operational characteristics are guaranteed over the range of −40°C to +85°C.

The optional burn-in is dynamic, for a minimum time of 160 hours at +125°C with V_{CC} = 5.5V ±0.25V, following guidelines in MIL-STD-883, Method 1015.

Package types and EXPRESS versions are identified by a one- or two-letter prefix to the part number. The prefixes are listed in Table 16. All A.C. and D.C. specifications not mentioned in this section are the same for both commercial and EXPRESS parts.

Table 16. Prefix Identification

Prefix	Package Type	Temperature Range	Burn-In
A	PGA	Commercial	No
N	PLCC	Commercial	No
R	LCC	Commercial	No
TA	PGA	Extended	No
QA	PGA	Commercial	Yes
QR	LCC	Commercial	Yes

NOTE:
Not all package/temperature range/speed combinations are available.

80186 EXECUTION TIMINGS

A determination of 80186 program execution timing must consider the bus cycles necessary to prefetch instructions as well as the number of execution unit cycles necessary to execute instructions. The following instruction timings represent the minimum execution time in clock cycles for each instruction. The timings given are based on the following assumptions:

- The opcode, along with any data or displacement required for execution of a particular instruction, has been prefetched and resides in the queue at the time it is needed.
- No wait states or bus HOLDS occur.
- All word-data is located on even-address boundaries.

All instructions which involve memory accesses can also require one or two additional clocks above the minimum timings shown due to the asynchronous handshake between the bus interface unit (BIU) and execution unit.

All jumps and calls include the time required to fetch the opcode of the next instruction at the destination address.

With a 16-bit BIU, the 80186 has sufficient bus performance to ensure that an adequate number of prefetched bytes will reside in the queue most of the time. Therefore, actual program execution time will not be substantially greater than that derived from adding the instruction timings shown.

INSTRUCTION SET SUMMARY

Function	Format				Clock Cycles	Comments
DATA TRANSFER						
MOV = Move:						
Register to Register/Memory	`1000100w`	`mod reg r/m`			2/12	
Register/memory to register	`1000101w`	`mod reg r/m`			2/9	
Immediate to register/memory	`1100011w`	`mod 000 r/m`	data	data if w = 1	12–13	8/16-bit
Immediate to register	`1011w reg`	data	data if w = 1		3–4	8/16-bit
Memory to accumulator	`1010000w`	addr-low	addr-high		8	
Accumulator to memory	`1010001w`	addr-low	addr-high		9	
Register/memory to segment register	`10001110`	`mod 0 reg r/m`			2/9	
Segment register to register/memory	`10001100`	`mod 0 reg r/m`			2/11	
PUSH = Push:						
Memory	`11111111`	`mod 1 1 0 r/m`			16	
Register	`01010 reg`				10	
Segment register	`000 reg 110`				9	
Immediate	`011010s0`	data	data if s = 0		10	
PUSHA = Push All	`01100000`				36	
POP = Pop:						
Memory	`10001111`	`mod 000 r/m`			20	
Register	`01011 reg`				10	
Segment register	`000 reg 111`	(reg ≠ 01)			8	
POPA = Pop All	`01100001`				51	
XCHG = Exchange:						
Register/memory with register	`1000011w`	`mod reg r/m`			4/17	
Register with accumulator	`10010 reg`				3	
IN = Input from:						
Fixed port	`1110010w`	port			10	
Variable port	`1110110w`				8	
OUT = Output to:						
Fixed port	`1110011w`	port			9	
Variable port	`1110111w`				7	
XLAT = Translate byte to AL	`11010111`				11	
LEA = Load EA to register	`10001101`	`mod reg r/m`			6	
LDS = Load pointer to DS	`11000101`	`mod reg r/m`	(mod ≠ 11)		18	
LES = Load pointer to ES	`11000100`	`mod reg r/m`	(mod ≠ 11)		18	
LAHF = Load AH with flags	`10011111`				2	
SAHF = Store AH into flags	`10011110`				3	
PUSHF = Push flags	`10011100`				9	
POPF = Pop flags	`10011101`				8	

Shaded areas indicate instructions not available in 8086, 8088 microsystems.

INSTRUCTION SET SUMMARY (Continued)

Function	Format				Clock Cycles	Comments
DATA TRANSFER (Continued)						
SEGMENT = Segment Override:						
CS	`00101110`				2	
SS	`00110110`				2	
DS	`00111110`				2	
ES	`00100110`				2	
ARITHMETIC						
ADD = Add:						
Reg/memory with register to either	`000000dw`	`mod reg r/m`			3/10	
Immediate to register/memory	`100000sw`	`mod 000 r/m`	data	data if s w = 01	4/16	
Immediate to accumulator	`0000010w`	data	data if w = 1		3/4	8/16-bit
ADC = Add with carry:						
Reg/memory with register to either	`000100dw`	`mod reg r/m`			3/10	
Immediate to register/memory	`100000sw`	`mod 010 r/m`	data	data if s w = 01	4/16	
Immediate to accumulator	`0001010w`	data	data if w = 1		3/4	8/16-bit
INC = Increment:						
Register/memory	`1111111w`	`mod 000 r/m`			3/15	
Register	`01000 reg`				3	
SUB = Subtract:						
Reg/memory and register to either	`001010dw`	`mod reg r/m`			3/10	
Immediate from register/memory	`100000sw`	`mod 101 r/m`	data	data if s w = 01	4/16	
Immediate from accumulator	`0010110w`	data	data if w = 1		3/4	8/16-bit
SBB = Subtract with borrow:						
Reg/memory and register to either	`000110dw`	`mod reg r/m`			3/10	
Immediate from register/memory	`100000sw`	`mod 011 r/m`	data	data if s w = 01	4/16	
Immediate from accumulator	`0001110w`	data	data if w = 1		3/4	8/16-bit
DEC = Decrement						
Register/memory	`1111111w`	`mod 001 r/m`			3/15	
Register	`01001 reg`				3	
CMP = Compare:						
Register/memory with register	`0011101w`	`mod reg r/m`			3/10	
Register with register/memory	`0011100w`	`mod reg r/m`			3/10	
Immediate with register/memory	`100000sw`	`mod 111 r/m`	data	data if s w = 01	3/10	
Immediate with accumulator	`0011110w`	data	data if w = 1		3/4	8/16-bit
NEG = Change sign register/memory	`1111011w`	`mod 011 r/m`			3/10	
AAA = ASCII adjust for add	`00110111`				8	
DAA = Decimal adjust for add	`00100111`				4	
AAS = ASCII adjust for subtract	`00111111`				7	
DAS = Decimal adjust for subtract	`00101111`				4	
MUL = Multiply (unsigned):	`1111011w`	`mod 100 r/m`				
Register-Byte					26–28	
Register-Word					35–37	
Memory-Byte					32–34	
Memory-Word					41–43	

Shaded areas indicate instructions not available in 8086, 8088 microsystems.

INSTRUCTION SET SUMMARY (Continued)

Function	Format					Clock Cycles	Comments
ARITHMETIC (Continued)							
IMUL = Integer multiply (signed):	1 1 1 1 0 1 1 w	mod 1 0 1 r/m					
Register-Byte						25–28	
Register-Word						34–37	
Memory-Byte						31–34	
Memory-Word						40–43	
IMUL = Integer Immediate multiply (signed)	0 1 1 0 1 0 s 1	mod reg r/m	data	data if s=0		22–25/ 29–32	
DIV = Divide (unsigned):	1 1 1 1 0 1 1 w	mod 1 1 0 r/m					
Register-Byte						29	
Register-Word						38	
Memory-Byte						35	
Memory-Word						44	
IDIV = Integer divide (signed):	1 1 1 1 0 1 1 w	mod 1 1 1 r/m					
Register-Byte						44–52	
Register-Word						53–61	
Memory-Byte						50–58	
Memory-Word						59–67	
AAM = ASCII adjust for multiply	1 1 0 1 0 1 0 0	0 0 0 0 1 0 1 0				19	
AAD = ASCII adjust for divide	1 1 0 1 0 1 0 1	0 0 0 0 1 0 1 0				15	
CBW = Convert byte to word	1 0 0 1 1 0 0 0					2	
CWD = Convert word to double word	1 0 0 1 1 0 0 1					4	
LOGIC							
Shift/Rotate Instructions:							
Register/Memory by 1	1 1 0 1 0 0 0 w	mod TTT r/m				2/15	
Register/Memory by CL	1 1 0 1 0 0 1 w	mod TTT r/m				5+n/17+n	
Register/Memory by Count	1 1 0 0 0 0 0 w	mod TTT r/m	count			5+n/17+n	

TTT Instruction

TTT	Instruction
0 0 0	ROL
0 0 1	ROR
0 1 0	RCL
0 1 1	RCR
1 0 0	SHL/SAL
1 0 1	SHR
1 1 1	SAR

Function	Format				Clock Cycles	Comments
AND = And:						
Reg/memory and register to either	0 0 1 0 0 0 d w	mod reg r/m			3/10	
Immediate to register/memory	1 0 0 0 0 0 0 w	mod 1 0 0 r/m	data	data if w=1	4/16	
Immediate to accumulator	0 0 1 0 0 1 0 w	data	data if w=1		3/4	8/16-bit
TEST = And function to flags, no result:						
Register/memory and register	1 0 0 0 0 1 0 w	mod reg r/m			3/10	
Immediate data and register/memory	1 1 1 1 0 1 1 w	mod 0 0 0 r/m	data	data if w=1	4/10	
Immediate data and accumulator	1 0 1 0 1 0 0 w	data	data if w=1		3/4	8/16-bit
OR = Or:						
Reg/memory and register to either	0 0 0 0 1 0 d w	mod reg r/m			3/10	
Immediate to register/memory	1 0 0 0 0 0 0 w	mod 0 0 1 r/m	data	data if w=1	4/16	
Immediate to accumulator	0 0 0 0 1 1 0 w	data	data if w=1		3/4	8/16-bit

Shaded areas indicate instructions not available in 8086, 8088 microsystems.

INSTRUCTION SET SUMMARY (Continued)

Function	Format				Clock Cycles	Comments
LOGIC (Continued)						
XOR = Exclusive or:						
Reg/memory and register to either	`0 0 1 1 0 0 d w`	`mod reg r/m`			3/10	
Immediate to register/memory	`1 0 0 0 0 0 0 w`	`mod 1 1 0 r/m`	data	data if w = 1	4/16	
Immediate to accumulator	`0 0 1 1 0 1 0 w`	data	data if w = 1		3/4	8/16-bit
NOT = Invert register/memory	`1 1 1 1 0 1 1 w`	`mod 0 1 0 r/m`			3/10	
STRING MANIPULATION						
MOVS = Move byte/word	`1 0 1 0 0 1 0 w`				14	
CMPS = Compare byte/word	`1 0 1 0 0 1 1 w`				22	
SCAS = Scan byte/word	`1 0 1 0 1 1 1 w`				15	
LODS = Load byte/wd to AL/AX	`1 0 1 0 1 1 0 w`				12	
STOS = Store byte/wd from AL/AX	`1 0 1 0 1 0 1 w`				10	
INS = Input byte/wd from DX port	`0 1 1 0 1 1 0 w`				14	
OUTS = Output byte/wd to DX port	`0 1 1 0 1 1 1 w`				14	
Repeated by count in CX (REP/REPE/REPZ/REPNE/REPNZ)						
MOVS = Move string	`1 1 1 1 0 0 1 0`	`1 0 1 0 0 1 0 w`			8+8n	
CMPS = Compare string	`1 1 1 1 0 0 1 z`	`1 0 1 0 0 1 1 w`			5+22n	
SCAS = Scan string	`1 1 1 1 0 0 1 z`	`1 0 1 0 1 1 1 w`			5+15n	
LODS = Load string	`1 1 1 1 0 0 1 0`	`1 0 1 0 1 1 0 w`			6+11n	
STOS = Store string	`1 1 1 1 0 0 1 0`	`1 0 1 0 1 0 1 w`			6+9n	
INS = Input string	`1 1 1 1 0 0 1 0`	`0 1 1 0 1 1 0 w`			8+8n	
OUTS = Output string	`1 1 1 1 0 0 1 0`	`0 1 1 0 1 1 1 w`			8+8n	
CONTROL TRANSFER						
CALL = Call:						
Direct within segment	`1 1 1 0 1 0 0 0`	disp-low	disp-high		15	
Register/memory indirect within segment	`1 1 1 1 1 1 1 1`	`mod 0 1 0 r/m`			13/19	
Direct intersegment	`1 0 0 1 1 0 1 0`	segment offset			23	
		segment selector				
Indirect intersegment	`1 1 1 1 1 1 1 1`	`mod 0 1 1 r/m`	(mod ≠ 11)		38	
JMP = Unconditional jump:						
Short/long	`1 1 1 0 1 0 1 1`	disp-low			14	
Direct within segment	`1 1 1 0 1 0 0 1`	disp-low	disp-high		14	
Register/memory indirect within segment	`1 1 1 1 1 1 1 1`	`mod 1 0 0 r/m`			11/17	
Direct intersegment	`1 1 1 0 1 0 1 0`	segment offset			14	
		segment selector				
Indirect intersegment	`1 1 1 1 1 1 1 1`	`mod 1 0 1 r/m`	(mod ≠ 11)		26	

Shaded areas indicate instructions not available in 8086, 8088 microsystems.

INSTRUCTION SET SUMMARY (Continued)

Function	Format				Clock Cycles	Comments
CONTROL TRANSFER (Continued) **RET** = Return from CALL:						
Within segment	1 1 0 0 0 0 1 1				16	
Within seg adding immed to SP	1 1 0 0 0 0 1 0	data-low	data-high		18	
Intersegment	1 1 0 0 1 0 1 1				22	
Intersegment adding immediate to SP	1 1 0 0 1 0 1 0	data-low	data-high		25	
JE/JZ = Jump on equal/zero	0 1 1 1 0 1 0 0	disp			4/13	JMP not taken/JMP taken
JL/JNGE = Jump on less/not greater or equal	0 1 1 1 1 1 0 0	disp			4/13	
JLE/JNG = Jump on less or equal/not greater	0 1 1 1 1 1 1 0	disp			4/13	
JB/JNAE = Jump on below/not above or equal	0 1 1 1 0 0 1 0	disp			4/13	
JBE/JNA = Jump on below or equal/not above	0 1 1 1 0 1 1 0	disp			4/13	
JP/JPE = Jump on parity/parity even	0 1 1 1 1 0 1 0	disp			4/13	
JO = Jump on overflow	0 1 1 1 0 0 0 0	disp			4/13	
JS = Jump on sign	0 1 1 1 1 0 0 0	disp			4/13	
JNE/JNZ = Jump on not equal/not zero	0 1 1 1 0 1 0 1	disp			4/13	
JNL/JGE = Jump on not less/greater or equal	0 1 1 1 1 1 0 1	disp			4/13	
JNLE/JG = Jump on not less or equal/greater	0 1 1 1 1 1 1 1	disp			4/13	
JNB/JAE = Jump on not below/above or equal	0 1 1 1 0 0 1 1	disp			4/13	
JNBE/JA = Jump on not below or equal/above	0 1 1 1 0 1 1 1	disp			4/13	
JNP/JPO = Jump on not par/par odd	0 1 1 1 1 0 1 1	disp			4/13	
JNO = Jump on not overflow	0 1 1 1 0 0 0 1	disp			4/13	
JNS = Jump on not sign	0 1 1 1 1 0 0 1	disp			4/13	
JCXZ = Jump on CX zero	1 1 1 0 0 0 1 1	disp			5/15	
LOOP = Loop CX times	1 1 1 0 0 0 1 0	disp			6/16	LOOP not taken/LOOP taken
LOOPZ/LOOPE = Loop while zero/equal	1 1 1 0 0 0 0 1	disp			6/16	
LOOPNZ/LOOPNE = Loop while not zero/equal	1 1 1 0 0 0 0 0	disp			6/16	
ENTER = Enter Procedure	1 1 0 0 1 0 0 0	data-low	data-high	L		
L = 0					15	
L = 1					25	
L > 1					22 + 16(n − 1)	
LEAVE = Leave Procedure	1 1 0 0 1 0 0 1				8	
INT = Interrupt:						
Type specified	1 1 0 0 1 1 0 1	type			47	
Type 3	1 1 0 0 1 1 0 0				45	if INT. taken/ if INT. not taken
INTO = Interrupt on overflow	1 1 0 0 1 1 1 0				48/4	
IRET = Interrupt return	1 1 0 0 1 1 1 1				28	
BOUND = Detect value out of range	0 1 1 0 0 0 1 0	mod reg r/m			33–35	

Shaded areas indicate instructions not available in 8086, 8088 microsystems.

INSTRUCTION SET SUMMARY (Continued)

Function	Format		Clock Cycles	Comments
PROCESSOR CONTROL				
CLC = Clear carry	`1 1 1 1 1 0 0 0`		2	
CMC = Complement carry	`1 1 1 1 0 1 0 1`		2	
STC = Set carry	`1 1 1 1 1 0 0 1`		2	
CLD = Clear direction	`1 1 1 1 1 1 0 0`		2	
STD = Set direction	`1 1 1 1 1 1 0 1`		2	
CLI = Clear interrupt	`1 1 1 1 1 0 1 0`		2	
STI = Set interrupt	`1 1 1 1 1 0 1 1`		2	
HLT = Halt	`1 1 1 1 0 1 0 0`		2	
WAIT = Wait	`1 0 0 1 1 0 1 1`		6	if $\overline{TEST}$ = 0
LOCK = Bus lock prefix	`1 1 1 1 0 0 0 0`		2	
ESC = Processor Extension Escape	`1 1 0 1 1 T T T`	`mod LLL r/m`	6	
	(TTT LLL are opcode to processor extension)			
NOP = No Operation	`1 0 0 1 0 0 0 0`		3	

Shaded areas indicate instructions not available in 8086, 8088 microsystems.

FOOTNOTES

The Effective Address (EA) of the memory operand is computed according to the mod and r/m fields:

if mod = 11 then r/m is treated as REG field
if mod = 00 then DISP = 0*, disp-low and disp-high are absent
if mod = 01 then DISP = disp-low sign-extended to 16-bits, disp-high is absent
if mod = 10 then DISP = disp-high: disp-low
if r/m = 000 then EA = (BX) + (SI) + DISP
if r/m = 001 then EA = (BX) + (DI) + DISP
if r/m = 010 then EA = (BP) + (SI) + DISP
if r/m = 011 then EA = (BP) + (DI) + DISP
if r/m = 100 then EA = (SI) + DISP
if r/m = 101 then EA = (DI) + DISP
if r/m = 110 then EA = (BP) + DISP*
if r/m = 111 then EA = (BX) + DISP

DISP follows 2nd byte of instruction (before data if required)

*except if mod = 00 and r/m = 110 then EA = disp-high: disp-low.

EA calculation time is 4 clock cycles for all modes, and is included in the execution times given whenever appropriate.

Segment Override Prefix

0	0	1	reg	1	1	0

reg is assigned according to the following:

reg	Segment Register
00	ES
01	CS
10	SS
11	DS

REG is assigned according to the following table:

16-Bit (w = 1)	8-Bit (w = 0)
000 AX	000 AL
001 CX	001 CL
010 DX	010 DL
011 BX	011 BL
100 SP	100 AH
101 BP	101 CH
110 SI	110 DH
111 DI	111 BH

The physical addresses of all operands addressed by the BP register are computed using the SS segment register. The physical addresses of the destination operands of the string primitive operations (those addressed by the DI register) are computed using the ES segment, which may not be overridden.

REVISION HISTORY

The sections significantly revised since version -010 are:

Pin Description Table
Added note to $\overline{\text{TEST}}$ pin requiring proper RESET at power-up to configure pin as input.

Renamed pin 44 to INT1/$\overline{\text{SELECT}}$ and pin 41 to INT3/$\overline{\text{INTA1}}$/IRQ to better describe their functions in Slave Mode.

Initialization and Processor Reset
Added reminder to drive $\overline{\text{RES}}$ pin LOW during power-up.

Major Cycle Timing Waveform
Clarified applicability of T_{CLCSV} to latched A1 and A2 in footnote.

HOLD/HLDA Timing Waveforms
Redrawn to indicate correct relationship of HOLD inactive to HLDA inactive.

Slave Mode Operation
The three low order bits associated with vector generation and performing EOI are not alterable; however, the priority levels are programmable. This information is a clarification only.

The sections significantly revised since version -009 are:

Pin Description Table
Various descriptions rewritten for clarity.

Interrupt Vector Table
Redrawn for clarity.

A.C. Characteristics
Added reminder that T_{SRYCL} and T_{CLSRY} must be met.

Explanation of the A.C. Symbols
New section.

Major Cycle Timing Waveforms
T_{CLRO} indicated.

The sections significantly revised since version -008 are:

Pin Description Table
Noted $\overline{\text{RES}}$ to be low more than 4 clocks. Connections to X1 and X2 clarified.

DMA Control Bit Descriptions
Moved and clarified note concerning TC condition for ST/$\overline{\text{STOP}}$ clearing during unsynchronized transfers.

Interrupt Controller, etc.
Renamed iRMX Mode to Slave Mode.

Interrupt Request Register
Noted that D0 and D1 are read/write, others read-only.

Execution Timings
Effect of bus width clarified.

The sections significantly revised since the October, 1986 version -007 are:

A.C. Characteristics
Deleted column for 12.5 MHz devices. Intel never marketed a 12.5 MHz 80186.

The sections significantly revised since the February, 1986 version -007 are:

A.C. Characteristics
Several timings changed in anticipation of test change (all listed in ns): T_{CLAV} (min.) at 10 MHz from 50 to 44; T_{CVCTV} (min.) at 8 MHz from 10 to 5; T_{CVCTV} (max.) from 70 to 50 at 8 MHz and 56 to 40 at 10 MHz.

80C186
CHMOS HIGH INTEGRATION 16-BIT MICROPROCESSOR

- Operation Modes Include:
  - Enhanced Mode Which Has
    - DRAM Refresh Control Unit
    - Power-Save Mode
    - Direct Interface to New Numerics Coprocessor
  - Compatible Mode
    - NMOS 80186 Pin for Pin Replacement for Non-Numerics Applications

- Integrated Feature Set
  - Enhanced 80C86/C88 CPU
  - Clock Generator
  - 2 Independent DMA Channels
  - Programmable Interrupt Controller
  - 3 Programmable 16-Bit Timers
  - Dynamic RAM Refresh Control Unit
  - Programmable Memory and Peripheral Chip Select Logic
  - Programmable Wait State Generator
  - Local Bus Controller
  - Power Save Mode
  - System-Level Testing Support (High Impedance Test Mode)

- Available in 16 MHz (80C186-16), 12.5 MHz (80C186-12) and 10 MHz (80C186) Versions

- Direct Addressing Capability to 1 MByte Memory and 64 KByte I/O

- Completely Object Code Compatible with All Existing 8086/8088 Software and Also Has 10 Additional Instructions over 8086/8088

- Complete System Development Support
  - All 8086 and NMOS 80186 Software Development Tools Can Be Used for 80C186 System Development
    - ASM 86 Assembler, PL/M-86, Pascal-86, Fortran-86, C-86, and System Utilities
    - In-Circuit-Emulator (ICE™-186)

- High Performance Numeric Coprocessing Capability through 80C187 Interface

- Available in 68 Pin:
  - Plastic Leaded Chip Carrier (PLCC)
  - Ceramic Pin Grid Array (PGA)
  - Ceramic Leadless Chip Carrier (JEDEC A Package)

(See Packaging Outlines and Dimensions, Order Number 231369)

- Available in EXPRESS Extended Temperature Range ($-40°C$ to $+85°C$)

- Available in Military:
  - Different Specifications
  - 10 MHz (M80C186-10) and 12.5 MHz (M80C186-12) Versions

(See M80C186 data sheet, Order Number 270500 for specifications)

The Intel 80C186 is a CHMOS high integration microprocessor. It has features which are new to the 80186 family which include a DRAM refresh control unit, power-save mode and a direct numerics interface. When used in "compatible" mode, the 80C186 is 100% pin-for-pin compatible with the NMOS 80186 (except for 8087 applications). The "enhanced" mode of operation allows the full feature set of the 80C186 to be used. The 80C186 is upward compatible with 8086 and 8088 software and fully compatible with 80186 and 80188 software.

October 1989
Order Number: 270354-005

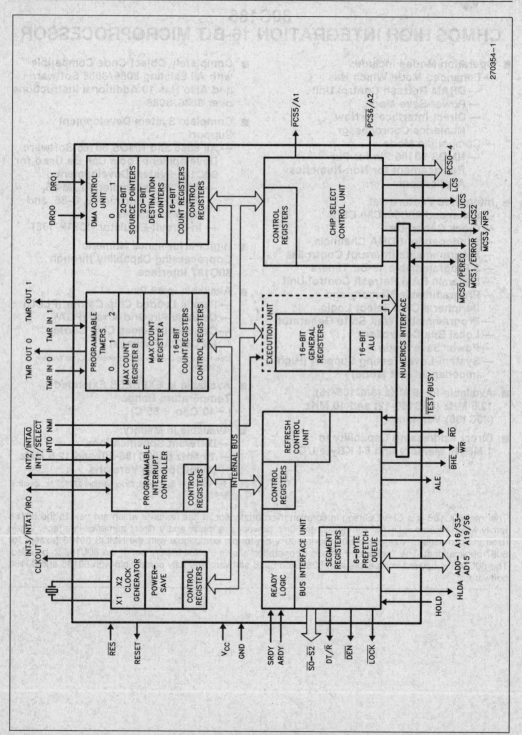

270354-1

Figure 1. 80C186 Block Diagram

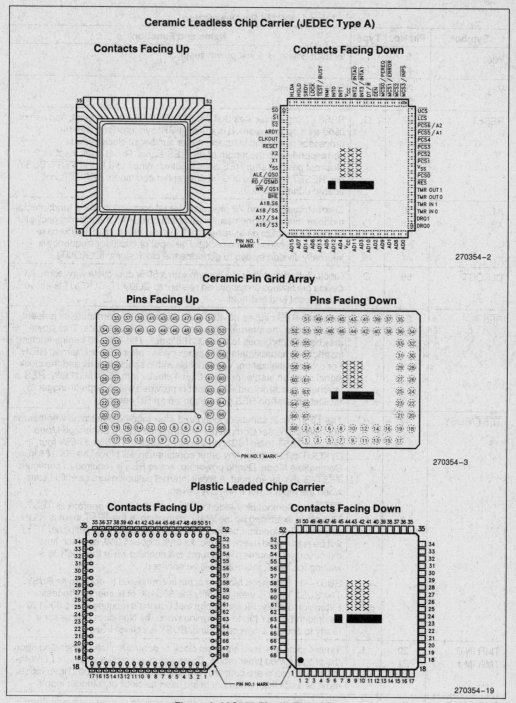

Figure 2. 80C186 Pinout Diagrams

Table 1. 80C186 Pin Description

Symbol	Pin No.	Type	Name and Function
V_{CC} V_{CC}	9 43	I I	System Power: +5 volt power supply.
V_{SS}	26 60	I I	System Ground.
RESET	57	O	RESET Output indicates that the 80C186 CPU is being reset, and can be used as a system reset. It is active HIGH, synchronized with the processor clock, and lasts an integer number of clock periods corresponding to the length of the $\overline{RES}$ signal. Reset goes inactive 2 clockout periods after $\overline{RES}$ goes inactive. When tied to the $\overline{TEST}$/BUSY pin, RESET forces the 80C186 into enhanced mode. RESET is not floated during bus hold.
X1 X2	59 58	I O	Crystal Inputs X1 and X2 provide external connections for a fundamental mode or third overtone parallel resonant crystal for the internal oscillator. X1 can connect to an external clock instead of a crystal. In this case, minimize the capacitance on X2. The input or oscillator frequency is internally divided by two to generate the clock signal (CLKOUT).
CLKOUT	56	O	Clock Output provides the system with a 50% duty cycle waveform. All device pin timings are specified relative to CLKOUT. CLKOUT is active during reset and bus hold.
$\overline{RES}$	24	I	An active $\overline{RES}$ causes the 80C186 to immediately terminate its present activity, clear the internal logic, and enter a dormant state. This signal may be asynchronous to the 80C186 clock. The 80C186 begins fetching instructions approximately $6\frac{1}{2}$ clock cycles after $\overline{RES}$ is returned HIGH. For proper initialization, V_{CC} must be within specifications and the clock signal must be stable for more than 4 clocks with $\overline{RES}$ held LOW. $\overline{RES}$ is internally synchronized. This input is provided with a Schmitt-trigger to facilitate power-on $\overline{RES}$ generation via an RC network.
$\overline{TEST}$/BUSY	47	I/O	The $\overline{TEST}$ pin is sampled during and after reset to determine whether the 80C186 is to enter Compatible or Enhanced Mode. Enhanced Mode requires $\overline{TEST}$ to be HIGH on the rising edge of $\overline{RES}$ and LOW four CLKOUT cycles later. Any other combination will place the 80C186 in Compatible Mode. During power-up, active $\overline{RES}$ is required to configure $\overline{TEST}$/BUSY as an input. A weak internal pullup ensures a HIGH state when the input is not externally driven. $\overline{TEST}$—In Compatible Mode this pin is configured to operate as $\overline{TEST}$. This pin is examined by the WAIT instruction. If the $\overline{TEST}$ input is HIGH when WAIT execution begins, instruction execution will suspend. $\overline{TEST}$ will be resampled every five clocks until it goes LOW, at which time execution will resume. If interrupts are enabled while the 80C186 is waiting for $\overline{TEST}$, interrupts will be serviced. BUSY—In Enhanced Mode, this pin is configured to operate as BUSY. The BUSY input is used to notify the 80C186 of Numerics Processor Extension activity. Floating point instructions executing in the 80C186 sample the BUSY pin to determine when the Numerics Processor is ready to accept a new command. BUSY is active HIGH.
TMR IN 0 TMR IN 1	20 21	I I	Timer Inputs are used either as clock or control signals, depending upon the programmed timer mode. These inputs are active HIGH (or LOW-to-HIGH transitions are counted) and internally synchronized. Timer Inputs must be tied HIGH when not being used as clock or retrigger inputs.
TMR OUT 0 TMR OUT 1	22 23	O O	Timer outputs are used to provide single pulse or continous waveform generation, depending upon the timer mode selected. These outputs are not floated during a bus hold.

Table 1. 80C186 Pin Description (Continued)

Symbol	Pin No.	Type	Name and Function
DRQ0 DRQ1	18 19	I I	DMA Request is asserted HIGH by an external device when it is ready for DMA Channel 0 or 1 to perform a transfer. These signals are level-triggered and internally synchronized.
NMI	46	I	The Non-Maskable Interrupt input causes a Type 2 interrupt. An NMI transition from LOW to HIGH is latched and synchronized internally, and initiates the interrupt at the next instruction boundary. NMI must be asserted for at least one CLKOUT period. The Non-Maskable Interrupt cannot be avoided by programming.
INT0 INT1/$\overline{\text{SELECT}}$ INT2/$\overline{\text{INTA0}}$ INT3/$\overline{\text{INTA1}}$/IRQ	45 44 42 41	I I I/O I/O	Maskable Interrupt Requests can be requested by activating one of these pins. When configured as inputs, these pins are active HIGH. Interrupt Requests are synchronized internally. INT2 and INT3 may be configured to provide active-LOW interrupt-acknowledge output signals. All interrupt inputs may be configured to be either edge- or level-triggered. To ensure recognition, all interrupt requests must remain active until the interrupt is acknowledged. When Slave Mode is selected, the function of these pins changes (see Interrupt Controller section of this data sheet).
A19/S6 A18/S5 A17/S4 A16/S3	65 66 67 68	O O O O	Address Bus Outputs (16–19) and Bus Cycle Status (3–6) indicate the four most significant address bits during T_1. These signals are active HIGH. During T_2, T_3, T_W, and T_4, the S6 pin is LOW to indicate a CPU-initiated bus cycle or HIGH to indicate a DMA-initiated bus cycle. During the same T-states, S3, S4, and S5 are always LOW. These outputs are floated during bus hold or reset.
AD15 AD14 AD13 AD12 AD11 AD10 AD9 AD8 AD7 AD6 AD5 AD4 AD3 AD2 AD1 AD0	1 3 5 7 10 12 14 16 2 4 6 8 11 13 15 17	I/O I/O I/O I/O I/O I/O I/O I/O I/O I/O I/O I/O I/O I/O I/O I/O	Address/Data Bus (0–15) signals constitute the time multiplexed memory or I/O address (T_1) and data (T_2, T_3, T_W, and T_4) bus. The bus is active HIGH. A_0 is analogous to $\overline{\text{BHE}}$ for the lower byte of the data bus, pins D_7 through D_0. It is LOW during T_1 when a byte is to be transferred onto the lower portion of the bus in memory or I/O operations. These pins are floated during a bus hold or reset.

Table 1. 80C186 Pin Description (Continued)

Symbol	Pin No.	Type	Name and Function
$\overline{BHE}$	64	O	The $\overline{BHE}$ (Bus High Enable) signal is analogous to A0 in that it is used to enable data on to the most significant half of the data bus, pins D15–D8. $\overline{BHE}$ will be LOW during T_1 when the upper byte is transferred and will remain LOW through T_3 AND T_W. $\overline{BHE}$ does not need to be latched. $\overline{BHE}$ will float during HOLD or RESET. In Enhanced Mode, $\overline{BHE}$ will also be used to signify DRAM refresh cycles. A refresh cycle is indicated by both $\overline{BHE}$ and A0 being HIGH.

$\overline{BHE}$ and A0 Encodings

$\overline{BHE}$ Value	A0 Value	Function
0	0	Word Transfer
0	1	Byte Transfer on upper half of data bus (D15–D8)
1	0	Byte Transfer on lower half of data bus (D_7–D_0)
1	1	Refresh

Symbol	Pin No.	Type	Name and Function
ALE/QS0	61	O	Address Latch Enable/Queue Status 0 is provided by the 80C186 to latch the address. ALE is active HIGH, with addresses guaranteed valid on the trailing edge.
$\overline{WR}$/QS1	63	O	Write Strobe/Queue Status 1 indicates that the data on the bus is to be written into a memory or an I/O device. It is active LOW, and floats during bus hold or reset. When the 80C186 is in queue status mode, the ALE/QS0 and $\overline{WR}$/QS1 pins provide information about processor/instruction queue interaction.

QS1	QS0	Queue Operation
0	0	No queue operation
0	1	First opcode byte fetched from the queue
1	1	Subsequent byte fetched from the queue
1	0	Empty the queue

Symbol	Pin No.	Type	Name and Function
$\overline{RD}$/QSMD	62	O/I	Read Strobe is an active LOW signal which indicates that the 80C186 is performing a memory or I/O read cycle. It is guaranteed not to go LOW before the A/D bus is floated. An internal pull-up ensures that $\overline{RD}$/QSMD is HIGH during RESET. Following RESET the pin is sampled to determine whether the 80C186 is to provide ALE, $\overline{RD}$, and $\overline{WR}$, or queue status information. To enable Queue Status Mode, $\overline{RD}$ must be connected to GND. $\overline{RD}$ will float during bus HOLD.
ARDY	55	I	Asynchronous Ready informs the 80C186 that the addressed memory space or I/O device will complete a data transfer. The ARDY pin accepts a rising edge that is asynchronous to CLKOUT and is active HIGH. The falling edge of ARDY must be synchronized to the 80C186 clock. Connecting ARDY HIGH will always assert the ready condition to the CPU. If this line is unused, it should be tied LOW to yield control to the SRDY pin.
SRDY	49	I	Synchronous Ready informs the 80C186 that the addressed memory space or I/O device will complete a data transfer. The SRDY pin accepts an active-HIGH input synchronized to CLKOUT. The use of SRDY allows a relaxed system timing over ARDY. This is accomplished by elimination of the one-half clock cycle required to internally synchonize the ARDY input signal. Connecting SRDY high will always assert the ready condition to the CPU. If this line is unused, it should be tied LOW to yield control to the ARDY pin.

Table 1. 80C186 Pin Description (Continued)

Symbol	Pin No.	Type	Name and Function
LOCK	48	O	LOCK output indicates that other system bus masters are not to gain control of the system bus. LOCK is active LOW. The LOCK signal is requested by the LOCK prefix instruction and is activated at the beginning of the first data cycle associated with the instruction immediately following the LOCK prefix. It remains active until the completion of that instruction. No instruction prefetching will occur while LOCK is asserted. LOCK floats during bus hold or reset.
$\overline{S0}$ $\overline{S1}$ $\overline{S2}$	52 53 54	O O O	Bus cycle status $\overline{S0}$–$\overline{S2}$ are encoded to provide bus-transaction information:

80C186 Bus Cycle Status Information

$\overline{S2}$	$\overline{S1}$	$\overline{S0}$	Bus Cycle Initiated
0	0	0	Interrupt Acknowledge
0	0	1	Read I/O
0	1	0	Write I/O
0	1	1	Halt
1	0	0	Instruction Fetch
1	0	1	Read Data from Memory
1	1	0	Write Data to Memory
1	1	1	Passive (no bus cycle)

The status pins float during HOLD.
$\overline{S2}$ may be used as a logical M/$\overline{IO}$ indicator, and $\overline{S1}$ as a DT/$\overline{R}$ indicator.

Symbol	Pin No.	Type	Name and Function
HOLD HLDA	50 51	I O	HOLD indicates that another bus master is requesting the local bus. The HOLD input is active HIGH. The 80C186 generates HLDA (HIGH) in response to a HOLD request. Simultaneous with the issuance of HLDA, the 80C186 will float the local bus and control lines. After HOLD is detected as being LOW, the 80C186 will lower HLDA. When the 80C186 needs to run another bus cycle, it will again drive the local bus and control lines. In Enhanced Mode, HLDA will go low when a DRAM refresh cycle is pending in the 80C186 and an external bus master has control of the bus. It will be up to the external master to relinquish the bus by lowering HOLD so that the 80C186 may execute the refresh cycle.
$\overline{UCS}$	34	O/I	Upper Memory Chip Select is an active LOW output whenever a memory reference is made to the defined upper portion (1K–256K block) of memory. $\overline{UCS}$ does not float during bus hold. The address range activating $\overline{UCS}$ is software programmable. $\overline{UCS}$ and $\overline{LCS}$ are sampled upon the rising edge of $\overline{RES}$. If both pins are held low, the 80C186 will enter ONCE Mode. In ONCE Mode all pins assume a high impedance state and remain so until a subsequent RESET. $\overline{UCS}$ has a weak internal pullup that is active during RESET to ensure that the 80C186 does not enter ONCE mode inadvertently.

Table 1. 80C186 Pin Description (Continued)

Symbol	Pin No.	Type	Name and Function
$\overline{\text{LCS}}$	33	O/I	Lower Memory Chip Select is active LOW whenever a memory reference is made to the defined lower portion (1K–256K) of memory. $\overline{\text{LCS}}$ does not float during bus HOLD. The address range activating $\overline{\text{LCS}}$ is software programmable. $\overline{\text{UCS}}$ and $\overline{\text{LCS}}$ are sampled upon the rising edge of $\overline{\text{RES}}$. If both pins are held low, the 80C186 will enter ONCE Mode. In ONCE Mode all pins assume a high impedance state and remain so until a subsequent RESET. $\overline{\text{LCS}}$ has a weak internal pullup that is active only during RESET to ensure that the 80C186 does not enter ONCE mode inadvertently.
$\overline{\text{MCS0}}$/PEREQ $\overline{\text{MCS1}}$/$\overline{\text{ERROR}}$ $\overline{\text{MCS2}}$ $\overline{\text{MCS3}}$/$\overline{\text{NPS}}$	38 37 36 35	O/I O/I O O	Mid-Range Memory Chip Select signals are active LOW when a memory reference is made to the defined mid-range portion of memory (8K–512K). These lines do not float during bus HOLD. The address ranges activating $\overline{\text{MCS0}}$–3 are software programmable. In Enhanced Mode, $\overline{\text{MCS0}}$ becomes a PEREQ input (Processor Extension Request). When connected to the Numerics Processor Extension, this input is used to signal the 80C186 when to make numeric data transfers to and from the NPX. $\overline{\text{MCS3}}$ becomes $\overline{\text{NPS}}$ (Numeric Processor Select) which may only be activated by communication to the Numerics Processor Extension. $\overline{\text{MCS1}}$ becomes $\overline{\text{ERROR}}$ in enhanced mode and is used to signal numerics coprocessor errors. $\overline{\text{MCS0}}$/PEREQ and $\overline{\text{MCS1}}$/$\overline{\text{ERROR}}$ have weak internal pullups which are active during reset.
$\overline{\text{PCS0}}$ $\overline{\text{PCS1}}$ $\overline{\text{PCS2}}$ $\overline{\text{PCS3}}$ $\overline{\text{PCS4}}$	25 27 28 29 30	O O O O O	Peripheral Chip Select signals 0–4 are active LOW when a reference is made to the defined peripheral area (64K byte I/O or 1 MByte memory space). These lines do not float during bus HOLD. The address ranges activating $\overline{\text{PCS0}}$–4 are software programmable.
$\overline{\text{PCS5}}$/A1	31	O	Peripheral Chip Select 5 or Latched A1 may be programmed to provide a sixth peripheral chip select, or to provide an internally latched A1 signal. The address range activating $\overline{\text{PCS5}}$ is software-programmable. PCS5/A1 does not float during bus HOLD. When programmed to provide latched A1, this pin will retain the previously latched value during HOLD.
$\overline{\text{PCS6}}$/A2	32	O	Peripheral Chip Select 6 or Latched A2 may be programmed to provide a seventh peripheral chip select, or to provide an internally latched A2 signal. The address range activating $\overline{\text{PCS6}}$ is software-programmable. PCS6/A2 does not float during bus HOLD. When programmed to provide latched A2, this pin will retain the previously latched value during HOLD.
DT/$\overline{\text{R}}$	40	O	Data Transmit/Receive controls the direction of data flow through an external data bus transceiver. When LOW, data is transferred to the 80C186. When HIGH the 80C186 places write data on the data bus. DT/$\overline{\text{R}}$ floats during a bus hold or reset.
$\overline{\text{DEN}}$	39	O	Data Enable is provided as a data bus transceiver output enable. $\overline{\text{DEN}}$ is active LOW during each memory and I/O access (including 80C187 access). $\overline{\text{DEN}}$ is HIGH whenever DT/$\overline{\text{R}}$ changes state. During RESET, $\overline{\text{DEN}}$ is driven HIGH for one clock, then floated. $\overline{\text{DEN}}$ also floats during HOLD.

FUNCTIONAL DESCRIPTION

Introduction

The following Functional Description describes the base architecture of the 80C186. The 80C186 is a very high integration 16-bit microprocessor. It combines 15–20 of the most common microprocessor system components onto one chip. The 80C186 is object code compatible with the 8086/8088 microprocessors and adds 10 new instruction types to the 8086/8088 instruction set.

The 80C186 has two major modes of operation, Compatible and Enhanced. In Compatible Mode the 80C186 is completely compatible with NMOS 80186, with the exception of 8087 support. The Enhanced mode adds three new features to the system design. These are Power-Save control, Dynamic RAM refresh, and an asynchronous Numerics Co-processor interface.

80C186 BASE ARCHITECTURE

The 8086, 8088, 80186, and 80188 family all contain the same basic set of registers, instructions, and addressing modes. The 80C186 processor is upward compatible with the 8086 and 8088 CPUs.

Register Set

The 80C186 base architecture has fourteen registers as shown in Figures 3a and 3b. These registers are grouped into the following categories.

General Registers

Eight 16-bit general purpose registers may be used for arithmetic and logical operands. Four of these (AX, BX, CX, and DX) can be used as 16-bit registers or split into pairs of separate 8-bit registers.

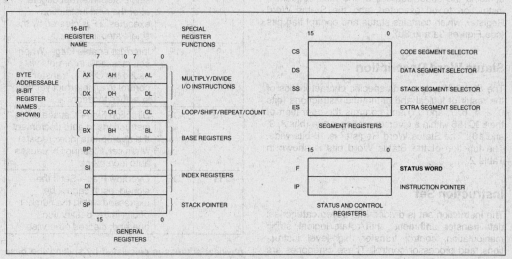

Figure 3a. 80C186 Register Set

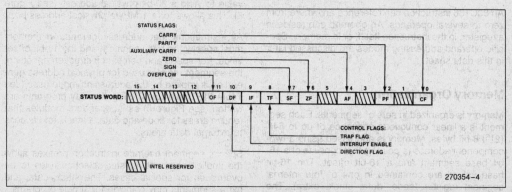

Figure 3b. Status Word Format

270354–4

Segment Registers

Four 16-bit special purpose registers select, at any given time, the segments of memory that are immediately addressable for code, stack, and data. (For usage, refer to Memory Organization.)

Base and Index Registers

Four of the general purpose registers may also be used to determine offset addresses of operands in memory. These registers may contain base addresses or indexes to particular locations within a segment. The addressing mode selects the specific registers for operand and address calculations.

Status and Control Registers

Two 16-bit special purpose registers record or alter certain aspects of the 80C186 processor state. These are the Instruction Pointer Register, which contains the offset address of the next sequential instruction to be executed, and the Status Word Register, which contains status and control flag bits (see Figures 3a and 3b).

Status Word Description

The Status Word records specific characteristics of the result of logical and arithmetic instructions (bits 0, 2, 4, 6, 7, and 11) and controls the operation of the 80C186 within a given operating mode (bits 8, 9, and 10). The Status Word Register is 16-bits wide. The function of the Status Word bits is shown in Table 2.

Instruction Set

The instruction set is divided into seven categories: data transfer, arithmetic, shift/rotate/logical, string manipulation, control transfer, high-level instructions, and processor control. These categories are summarized in Figure 4.

An 80C186 instruction can reference anywhere from zero to several operands. An operand can reside in a register, in the instruction itself, or in memory. Specific operand addressing modes are discussed later in this data sheet.

Memory Organization

Memory is organized in sets of segments. Each segment is a linear contiguous sequence of up to 64K (2^{16}) 8-bit bytes. Memory is addressed using a two-component address (a pointer) that consists of a 16-bit base segment and a 16-bit offset. The 16-bit base values are contained in one of four internal segment register (code, data, stack, extra). The

Table 2. Status Word Bit Functions

Bit Position	Name	Function
0	CF	Carry Flag—Set on high-order bit carry or borrow; cleared otherwise
2	PF	Parity Flag—Set if low-order 8 bits of result contain an even number of 1-bits; cleared otherwise
4	AF	Set on carry from or borrow to the low order four bits of AL; cleared otherwise
6	ZF	Zero Flag—Set if result is zero; cleared otherwise
7	SF	Sign Flag—Set equal to high-order bit of result (0 if positive, 1 if negative)
8	TF	Single Step Flag—Once set, a single step interrupt occurs after the next instruction executes. TF is cleared by the single step interrupt.
9	IF	Interrupt-enable Flag—When set, maskable interrupts will cause the CPU to transfer control to an interrupt vector specified location.
10	DF	Direction Flag—Causes string instructions to auto decrement the appropriate index register when set. Clearing DF causes auto increment.
11	OF	Overflow Flag—Set if the signed result cannot be expressed within the number of bits in the destination operand; cleared otherwise

physical address is calculated by shifting the base value LEFT by four bits and adding the 16-bit offset value to yield a 20-bit physical address (see Figure 5). This allows for a 1 MByte physical address size.

All instructions that address operands in memory must specify the base segment and the 16-bit offset value. For speed and compact instruction encoding, the segment register used for physical address generation is implied by the addressing mode used (see Table 3). These rules follow the way programs are written (see Figure 6) as independent modules that require areas for code and data, a stack, and access to external data areas.

Special segment override instruction prefixes allow the implicit segment register selection rules to be overridden for special cases. The stack, data, and extra segments may coincide for simple programs.

GENERAL PURPOSE	
MOV	Move byte or word
PUSH	Push word onto stack
POP	Pop word off stack
PUSHA	Push all registers on stack
POPA	Pop all registers from stack
XCHG	Exchange byte or word
XLAT	Translate byte
INPUT/OUTPUT	
IN	Input byte or word
OUT	Output byte or word
ADDRESS OBJECT	
LEA	Load effective address
LDS	Load pointer using DS
LES	Load pointer using ES
FLAG TRANSFER	
LAHF	Load AH register from flags
SAHF	Store AH register in flags
PUSHF	Push flags onto stack
POPF	Pop flags off stack
ADDITION	
ADD	Add byte or word
ADC	Add byte or word with carry
INC	Increment byte or word by 1
AAA	ASCII adjust for addition
DAA	Decimal adjust for addition
SUBTRACTION	
SUB	Subtract byte or word
SBB	Subtract byte or word with borrow
DEC	Decrement byte or word by 1
NEG	Negate byte or word
CMP	Compare byte or word
AAS	ASCII adjust for subtraction
DAS	Decimal adjust for subtraction
MULTIPLICATION	
MUL	Multiply byte or word unsigned
IMUL	Integer multiply byte or word
AAM	ASCII adjust for multiply
DIVISION	
DIV	Divide byte or word unsigned
IDIV	Integer divide byte or word
AAD	ASCII adjust for division
CBW	Convert byte to word
CWD	Convert word to doubleword

MOVS	Move byte or word string
INS	Input bytes or word string
OUTS	Output bytes or word string
CMPS	Compare byte or word string
SCAS	Scan byte or word string
LODS	Load byte or word string
STOS	Store byte or word string
REP	Repeat
REPE/REPZ	Repeat while equal/zero
REPNE/REPNZ	Repeat while not equal/not zero
LOGICALS	
NOT	"Not" byte or word
AND	"And" byte or word
OR	"Inclusive or" byte or word
XOR	"Exclusive or" byte or word
TEST	"Test" byte or word
SHIFTS	
SHL/SAL	Shift logical/arithmetic left byte or word
SHR	Shift logical right byte or word
SAR	Shift arithmetic right byte or word
ROTATES	
ROL	Rotate left byte or word
ROR	Rotate right byte or word
RCL	Rotate through carry left byte or word
RCR	Rotate through carry right byte or word
FLAG OPERATIONS	
STC	Set carry flag
CLC	Clear carry flag
CMC	Complement carry flag
STD	Set direction flag
CLD	Clear direction flag
STI	Set interrupt enable flag
CLI	Clear interrupt enable flag
EXTERNAL SYNCHRONIZATION	
HLT	Halt until interrupt or reset
WAIT	Wait for TEST pin active
ESC	Escape to extension processor
LOCK	Lock bus during next instruction
NO OPERATION	
NOP	No operation
HIGH LEVEL INSTRUCTIONS	
ENTER	Format stack for procedure entry
LEAVE	Restore stack for procedure exit
BOUND	Detects values outside prescribed range

Figure 4. 80C186 Instruction Set

CONDITIONAL TRANSFERS	
JA/JNBE	Jump if above/not below nor equal
JAE/JNB	Jump if above or equal/not below
JB/JNAE	Jump if below/not above nor equal
JBE/JNA	Jump if below or equal/not above
JC	Jump if carry
JE/JZ	Jump if equal/zero
JG/JNLE	Jump if greater/not less nor equal
JGE/JNL	Jump if greater or equal/not less
JL/JNGE	Jump if less/not greater nor equal
JLE/JNG	Jump if less or equal/not greater
JNC	Jump if not carry
JNE/JNZ	Jump if not equal/not zero
JNO	Jump if not overflow
JNP/JPO	Jump if not parity/parity odd
JNS	Jump if not sign

JO	Jump if overflow
JP/JPE	Jump if parity/parity even
JS	Jump if sign
UNCONDITIONAL TRANSFERS	
CALL	Call procedure
RET	Return from procedure
JMP	Jump
ITERATION CONTROLS	
LOOP	Loop
LOOPE/LOOPZ	Loop if equal/zero
LOOPNE/LOOPNZ	Loop if not equal/not zero
JCXZ	Jump if register CX = 0
INTERRUPTS	
INT	Interrupt
INTO	Interrupt if overflow
IRET	Interrupt return

Figure 4. 80C186 Instruction Set (Continued)

To access operands that do not reside in one of the four immediately available segments, a full 32-bit pointer can be used to reload both the base (segment) and offset values.

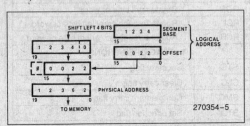

Figure 5. Two Component Address

Table 3. Segment Register Selection Rules

Memory Reference Needed	Segment Register Used	Implicit Segment Selection Rule
Instructions	Code (CS)	Instruction prefetch and immediate data.
Stack	Stack (SS)	All stack pushes and pops; any memory references which use BP Register as a base register.
External Data (Global)	Extra (ES)	All string instruction references which use the DI register as an index.
Local Data	Data (DS)	All other data references.

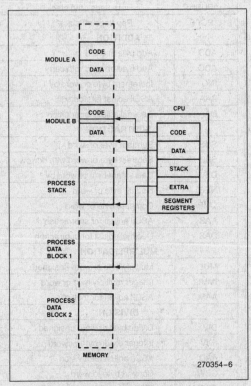

Figure 6. Segmented Memory Helps Structure Software

Addressing Modes

The 80C186 provides eight categories of addressing modes to specify operands. Two addressing modes are provided for instructions that operate on register or immediate operands:

- *Register Operand Mode:* The operand is located in one of the 8- or 16-bit general registers.
- *Immediate Operand Mode:* The operand is included in the instruction.

Six modes are provided to specify the location of an operand in a memory segment. A memory operand address consists of two 16-bit components: a segment base and an offset. The segment base is supplied by a 16-bit segment register either implicitly chosen by the addressing mode or explicitly chosen by a segment override prefix. The offset, also called the effective address, is calculated by summing any combination of the following three address elements:

- the *displacement* (an 8- or 16-bit immediate value contained in the instruction);
- the *base* (contents of either the BX or BP base registers); and
- the *index* (contents of either the SI or DI index registers).

Any carry out from the 16-bit addition is ignored. Eight-bit displacements are sign extended to 16-bit values.

Combinations of these three address elements define the six memory addressing modes, described below.

- *Direct Mode:* The operand's offset is contained in the instruction as an 8- or 16-bit displacement element.
- *Register Indirect Mode:* The operand's offset is in one of the registers SI, DI, BX, or BP.
- *Based Mode:* The operand's offset is the sum of an 8- or 16-bit displacement and the contents of a base register (BX or BP).
- *Indexed Mode:* The operand's offset is the sum of an 8- or 16-bit displacement and the contents of an index register (SI or DI).
- *Based Indexed Mode:* The operand's offset is the sum of the contents of a base register and an index register.
- *Based indexed Mode with Displacement:* The operand's offset is the sum of a base register's contents, an index register's contents, and an 8- or 16-bit displacement.

Data Types

The 80C186 directly supports the following data types:

- *Integer:* A signed binary numeric value contained in an 8-bit byte or a 16-bit word. All operations assume a 2's complement representation. Signed 32- and 64-bit integers are supported using a Numeric Data Coprocessor with the 80C186.
- *Ordinal:* An unsigned binary numeric value contained in an 8-bit byte or a 16-bit word.
- *Pointer:* A 16- or 32-bit quantity, composed of a 16-bit offset component or a 16-bit segment base component in addition to a 16-bit offset component.
- *String:* A contiguous sequence of bytes or words. A string may contain from 1 to 64K bytes.
- *ASCII:* A byte representation of alphanumeric and control characters using the ASCII standard of character representation.
- *BCD:* A byte (unpacked) representation of the decimal digits 0–9.
- *Packed BCD:* A byte (packed) representation of two decimal digits (0–9). One digit is stored in each nibble (4-bits) of the byte.
- *Floating Point:* A signed 32-, 64-, or 80-bit real number representation. (Floating point operands are supported using a Numeric Data Coprocessor with the 80C186.)

In general, individual data elements must fit within defined segment limits. Figure 7 graphically represents the data types supported by the 80C186.

I/O Space

The I/O space consists of 64K 8-bit or 32K 16-bit ports. Separate instructions address the I/O space with either an 8-bit port address, specified in the instruction, or a 16-bit port address in the DX register. 8-bit port addresses are zero extended such that A_{15}–A_8 are LOW. I/O port addresses 00F8(H) through 00FF(H) are reserved.

Interrupts

An interrupt transfers execution to a new program location. The old program address (CS:IP) and machine state (Status Word) are saved on the stack to allow resumption of the interrupted program. Interrupts fall into three classes: hardware initiated, INT instructions, and instruction exceptions. Hardware initiated interrupts occur in response to an external input and are classified as non-maskable or maskable.

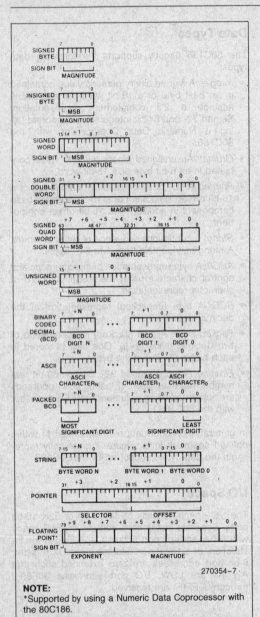

NOTE:
*Supported by using a Numeric Data Coprocessor with
the 80C186.

270354–7

Figure 7. 80C186 Supported Data Types

Programs may cause an interrupt with an INT instruction. Instruction exceptions occur when an unusual condition, which prevents further instruction processing, is detected while attempting to execute an instruction. If the exception was caused by executing an ESC instruction with the ESC trap bit set in the relocation register, the return instruction will point to the ESC instruction, or to the segment override prefix immediately preceding the ESC instruc-

tion if the prefix was present. In all other cases, the return address from an exception will point at the instruction immediately following the instruction causing the exception.

A table containing up to 256 pointers defines the proper interrupt service routine for each interrupt. Interrupts 0–31, some of which are used for instruction exceptions, are reserved. Table 4 shows the 80C186 predefined types and default priority levels. For each interrupt, an 8-bit vector must be supplied to the 80C186 which identifies the appropriate table entry. Exceptions supply the interrupt vector internally. In addition, internal peripherals and noncascaded external interrupts will generate their own vectors through the internal interrupt controller. INT instructions contain or imply the vector and allow access to all 256 interrupts. Maskable hardware initiated interrupts supply the 8-bit vector to the CPU during an interrupt acknowledge bus sequence. Non-maskable hardware interrupts use a predefined internally supplied vector.

Interrupt Sources

The 80C186 can service interrupts generated by software or hardware. The software interrupts are generated by specific instructions (INT, ESC, unused OP, etc.) or the results of conditions specified by instructions (array bounds check, INT0, DIV, IDIV, etc.). All interrupt sources are serviced by an indirect call through an element of a vector table. This vector table is indexed by using the interrupt vector type (Table 4), multiplied by four. All hardware-generated interrupts are sampled at the end of each instruction. Thus, the software interrupts will begin service first. Once the service routine is entered and interrupts are enabled, any hardware source of sufficient priority can interrupt the service routine in progress.

Those pre-defined 80C186 interrupts which cannot be masked by programming are described below.

DIVIDE ERROR EXCEPTION (TYPE 0)

Generated when a DIV or IDIV instruction quotient cannot be expressed in the number of bits in the destination.

SINGLE-STEP INTERRUPT (TYPE 1)

Generated after most instructions if the TF flag in the status word is set. This interrupt allows programs to execute one instruction at a time. Interrupts will not be generated after prefix instructions (e.g., REP), instructions which modify segment registers (e.g., POP DS), or the WAIT instruction. Vectoring to the single-step interrupt service routine clears the TF bit. An IRET instruction in the interrupt service routine

Table 4. 80C186 Interrupt Vectors

Interrupt Name	Vector Type	Vector Address	Default Priority	Related Instructions	Applicable Notes
Divide Error Exception	0	00H	1	DIV, IDIV	1
Single Step Interrupt	1	04H	1A	All	2
Non-Maskable Interrupt (NMI)	2	08H	1	All	
Breakpoint Interrupt	3	0CH	1	INT	1
INTO Detected Overflow Exception	4	10H	1	INTO	1
Array Bounds Exception	5	14H	1	BOUND	1
Unused Opcode Exception	6	18H	1	Undefined Opcodes	1
ESC Opcode Exception	7	1CH	1	ESC Opcodes (Coprocessor)	1, 3
Timer 0 Interrupt	8	20H	2A		4
Timer 1 Interrupt	18	48H	2B		4, 6
Timer 2 Interrupt	19	4CH	2C		4, 6
Reserved	9	24H	3		
DMA 0 Interrupt	10	28H	4		6
DMA 1 Interrupt	11	2CH	5		6
INT0 Interrupt	12	30H	6		
INT1 Interrupt	13	34H	7		
INT2 Interrupt	14	38H	8		
INT3 Interrupt	15	3CH	9		
Numerics Coprocessor Exception	16	40H	1	ESC Opcodes (Numerics Coprocessor)	1, 5
Reserved	17	44H			
Reserved	20–31	50H . . . 7CH			

NOTES:
Default priorities for the interrupt sources are used only if the user does not program each source to a unique priority level.
1. Generated as a result of an instruction execution.
2. Performed in the same manner as 8086.
3. An ESC (coprocessor) opcode will cause a trap if the 80C186 is in compatible mode or if the processor is in Enhanced Mode with the proper bit set in the peripheral control block relocation register. **The 80C186 is not directly compatible with the 80186 in this respect.**
4. All three timers constitute one source of request to the interrupt controller. As such, they share the same priority level with respect to other interrupt sources. However, the timers have a defined priority order among themselves (2A > 2B > 2C).
5. Numerics coprocessor exceptions are detected by the 80C186 upon execution of a subsequent numerics instruction.
6. The vector type numbers for these sources are programmable in Slave Mode.

restores the TF bit to logic "1" and transfers control to the next instruction to be single-stepped.

NON-MASKABLE INTERRUPT—NMI (TYPE 2)

An external interrupt source which is serviced regardless of the state of the IF bit. No external interrupt acknowledge sequence is performed. The IF bit is cleared at the beginning of an NMI interrupt to prevent maskable interrupts from being serviced. A typical use of NMI would be to activate a power failure routine.

BREAKPOINT INTERRUPT (TYPE 3)

A one-byte version of the INT instruction. It uses 12 as an index into the service routine address table (because it is a type 3 interrupt).

INTO DETECTED OVERFLOW EXCEPTION (TYPE4)

Generated during an INTO instruction if the 0F bit is set.

ARRAY BOUNDS EXCEPTION (TYPE 5)

Generated during a BOUND instruction if the array index is outside the array bounds. The array bounds are located in memory at a location indicated by one of the instruction operands. The other operand indicates the value of the index to be checked.

UNUSED OPCODE EXCEPTION (TYPE 6)

Generated if execution is attempted on undefined opcodes.

ESCAPE OPCODE EXCEPTION (TYPE 7)

Generated if execution is attempted of ESC opcodes (D8H–DFH). In compatible mode operation, ESC opcodes will always generate this exception. In enhanced mode operation, the exception will be generated only if a bit in the relocation register is set. The return address of this exception will point to the ESC instruction causing the exception. If a segment override prefix preceded the ESC instruction, the return address will point to the segment override prefix.

NOTE:
80C186 processing of ESC (numerics coprocessor) opcodes differs substantially from the 80186.

NUMERICS COPROCESSOR EXCEPTION (TYPE 16)

An interrupt generated in response to an unmasked error in the 80C187 Numerics Coprocessor Extension. In general, the 80C187 does not detect an error until the instruction after the error occurred. A numerics coprocessor error is signalled to the 80C187 on its ERROR input pin.

Hardware-generated interrupts are divided into two groups: maskable interrupts and non-maskable interrupts. The 80C186 provides maskable hardware interrupt request pins INT0–INT3. In addition, maskable interrupts may be generated by the 80C186 integrated DMA controller and the integrated timer unit. The vector types for these interrupts is shown in Table 4. Software enables these inputs by setting the interrupt flag bit (IF) in the Status Word. The interrupt controller is discussed in the peripheral section of this data sheet.

Further maskable interrupts are disabled while servicing an interrupt because the IF bit is reset as part of the response to an interrupt or exception. The saved Status Word will reflect the enable status of the processor prior to the interrupt. The interrupt flag will remain zero unless specifically set. The interrupt return instruction restores the Status Word, thereby restoring the original status of IF bit. If the interrupt return re-enables interrupts, and another interrupt is pending, the 80C186 will immediately service the highest-priority interrupt pending, i.e., no instructions of the main line program will be executed.

Initialization and Processor Reset

Processor initialization is accomplished by driving the RES input pin LOW. RES must be LOW during power-up to ensure proper device initialization. RES forces the 80C186 to terminate all execution and local bus activity. No instruction or bus activity will occur as long as RES is active. After RES becomes inactive and an internal processing interval elapses, the 80C186 begins execution with the instruction at physical location FFFF0(H). RES also sets some registers to predefined values as shown in Table 5.

Table 5. 80C186 Initial Register State after RESET

Status Word	F002(H)
Instruction Pointer	0000(H)
Code Segment	FFFF(H)
Data Segment	0000(H)
Extra Segment	0000(H)
Stack Segment	0000(H)
Relocation Register	20FF(H)
UMCS	FFFB(H)

80C186 CLOCK GENERATOR

The 80C186 provides an on-chip clock generator for both internal and external clock generation. The clock generator features a crystal oscillator, a divide-by-two counter, synchronous and asynchronous ready inputs, and reset circuitry.

Oscillator

The 80C186 oscillator circuit is designed to be used either with a parallel resonant fundamental or third-overtone mode crystal, depending upon the frequency range of the application as shown in Figure 8c. This is used as the time base for the 80C186. The crystal frequency chosen should be twice the required processor frequency. Use of an LC or RC circuit is not recommended.

The output of the oscillator is not directly available outside the 80C186. The two recommended crystal configurations are shown in Figures 8a and 8b. When used in third-overtone mode the tank circuit shown in Figure 8b is recommended for stable operation. The sum of the stray capacitances and load-

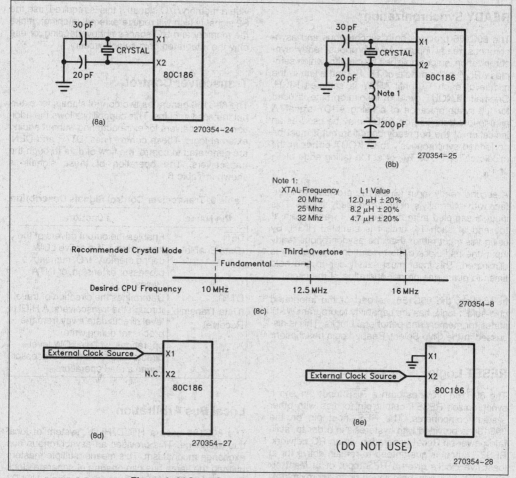

Note 1:

XTAL Frequency	L1 Value
20 Mhz	12.0 μH ±20%
25 Mhz	8.2 μH ±20%
32 Mhz	4.7 μH ±20%

Figure 8. 80C186 Oscillator Configurations (see text)

ing capacitors should equal the values shown. It is advisable to limit stray capacitance between the X1 and X2 pins to less than 10 pF. While a fundamental-mode circuit will require approximately 1 ms for start-up, the third-overtone arrangement may require 1 ms to 3 ms to stabilize.

Alternately, the oscillator may be driven from an external source as shown in Figure 8d. The configuration shown in Figure 8e is not recommended.

Intel recommends the following values for crystal selection parameters.

Temperature Range:	0 to 70°C
ESR (Equivalent Series Resistance):	40Ω max
C_0 (Shunt Capacitance of Crystal):	7.0 pF max
C_1 (Load Capacitance):	20 pF ± 2 pF
Drive Level:	1 mW max

Clock Generator

The 80C186 clock generator provides the 50% duty cycle processor clock for the 80C186. It does this by dividing the oscillator output by 2 forming the symmetrical clock. If an external oscillator is used, the state of the clock generator will change on the falling edge of the oscillator signal. The CLKOUT pin provides the processor clock signal for use outside the 80C186. This may be used to drive other system components. All timings are referenced to the output clock.

READY Synchronization

The 80C186 provides both synchronous and asynchronous ready inputs. Asynchronous ready synchronization is accomplished by circuitry which samples ARDY in the middle of T_2, T_3, and again in the middle of each T_W until ARDY is sampled HIGH. One-half CLKOUT cycle of resolution time is used for full synchronization of a rising ARDY signal. A high-to-low transition on ARDY may be used as an indication of the not ready condition but it must be performed synchronously to CLKOUT **either** in the middle of T_2, T_3, **or** T_W, or at the falling edge of T_3 or T_W.

A second ready input (SRDY) is provided to interface with externally synchronized ready signals. This input is sampled at the end of T_2, T_3 and again at the end of each T_W until it is sampled HIGH. By using this input rather than the asynchronous ready input, the half-clock cycle resolution time penalty is eliminated. This input must satisfy set-up and hold times to guarantee proper operation of the circuit.

In addition, the 80C186, as part of the integrated chip-select logic, has the capability to program WAIT states for memory and peripheral blocks. This is discussed in the Chip Select/Ready Logic description.

RESET Logic

The 80C186 provides both a $\overline{\text{RES}}$ input pin and a synchronized RESET output pin for use with other system components. The $\overline{\text{RES}}$ input pin on the 80C186 is provided with hysteresis in order to facilitate power-on Reset generation via an RC network. RESET output is guaranteed to remain active for at least five clocks given a $\overline{\text{RES}}$ input of at least six clocks. RESET may be delayed up to approximately two and one-half clocks behind $\overline{\text{RES}}$.

LOCAL BUS CONTROLLER

The 80C186 provides a local bus controller to generate the local bus control signals. In addition, it employs a HOLD/HLDA protocol for relinquishing the local bus to other bus masters. It also provides outputs that can be used to enable external buffers and to direct the flow of data on and off the local bus.

Memory/Peripheral Control

The 80C186 provides ALE, $\overline{\text{RD}}$, and $\overline{\text{WR}}$ bus control signals. The $\overline{\text{RD}}$ and $\overline{\text{WR}}$ signals are used to strobe data from memory or I/O to the 80C186 or to strobe data from the 80C186 to memory or I/O. The ALE line provides a strobe to latch the address when it is valid. The 80C186 local bus controller does not pro-

vide a memory/$\overline{\text{I/O}}$ signal. If this is required, use the $\overline{\text{S2}}$ signal (which will require external latching), make the memory and I/O spaces nonoverlapping, or use only the integrated chip-select circuitry.

Transceiver Control

The 80C186 generates two control signals for external transceiver chips. This capability allows the addition of transceivers for extra buffering without adding external logic. These control lines, DT/$\overline{\text{R}}$ and $\overline{\text{DEN}}$, are generated to control the flow of data through the transceivers. The operation of these signals is shown in Table 6.

Table 6. Transceiver Control Signals Description

Pin Name	Function
$\overline{\text{DEN}}$ (Data Enable)	Enables the output drivers of the transceivers. It is active LOW during memory, I/O, numeric processor extension, or INTA cycles.
DT/$\overline{\text{R}}$ (Data Transmit/ Receive)	Determines the direction of travel through the transceivers. A HIGH level directs data away from the processor during write operations, while a LOW level directs data toward the processor during a read operation.

Local Bus Arbitration

The 80C186 uses a HOLD/HLDA system of local bus exchange. This provides an asynchronous bus exchange mechanism. This means multiple masters utilizing the same bus can operate at separate clock frequencies. The 80C186 provides a single HOLD/HLDA pair through which all other bus masters may gain control of the local bus. External circuitry must arbitrate which external device will gain control of the bus when there is more than one alternate local bus master. When the 80C186 relinquishes control of the local bus, it floats $\overline{\text{DEN}}$, $\overline{\text{RD}}$, $\overline{\text{WR}}$, $\overline{\text{S0}}$–$\overline{\text{S2}}$, $\overline{\text{LOCK}}$, AD0–AD15, A16–A19, $\overline{\text{BHE}}$, and DT/$\overline{\text{R}}$ to allow another master to drive these lines directly.

The 80C186 HOLD latency time, i.e., the time between HOLD request and HOLD acknowledge, is a function of the activity occurring in the processor when the HOLD request is received. A HOLD request is second only to DRAM refresh requests in priority of activity requests the processor may receive. Any bus cycle in progress will be completed before the 80C186 relinquishes the bus. This implies that if a HOLD request is received just as a DMA transfer begins, the HOLD latency can be as great as 4 bus cycles. This will occur if a DMA word transfer operation is taking place from an odd address to an odd address. This is a total of 16 clock cycles or more if WAIT states are required. In addition, if locked transfers are performed, the HOLD latency time will be increased by the length of the locked transfer.

If the 80C186 has relinquished the bus and a refresh request is pending, HLDA is removed (driven low) to signal the remote processor that the 80C186 wishes to regain control of the bus. The 80C186 will wait until HOLD is removed before taking control of the bus to run the refresh cycle.

Local Bus Controller and Reset

During RESET the local bus controller will perform the following action:

- Drive $\overline{DEN}$, $\overline{RD}$, and $\overline{WR}$ HIGH for one clock cycle, then float them.
- Drive $\overline{S0}-\overline{S2}$ to the inactive state (all HIGH) and then float.
- Drive $\overline{LOCK}$ HIGH and then float.
- Float AD0–15, A16–19, $\overline{BHE}$, DT/$\overline{R}$.
- Drive ALE LOW
- Drive HLDA LOW.

$\overline{RD}$/QSMD, $\overline{UCS}$, $\overline{LCS}$, $\overline{MCS0}$/PEREQ, $\overline{MCS1}$/ERROR, and $\overline{TEST}$/BUSY pins have internal pullup devices which are active while $\overline{RES}$ is applied. Excessive loading or grounding certain of these pins causes the 80C186 to enter an alternative mode of operation:

- $\overline{RD}$/QSMD low results in Queue Status Mode.
- $\overline{UCS}$ and $\overline{LCS}$ low results in ONCE™ Mode.
- $\overline{TEST}$/BUSY low (and high later) results in Enhanced Mode.

INTERNAL PERIPHERAL INTERFACE

All the 80C186 integrated peripherals are controlled by 16-bit registers contained within an internal 256-byte control block. The control block may be mapped into either memory or I/O space. Internal logic will recognize control block addresses and respond to bus cycles. During bus cycles to internal registers, the bus controller will signal the operation externally (i.e., the $\overline{RD}$, $\overline{WR}$, status, address, data, etc., lines will be driven as in a normal bus cycle), but D_{15-0}, SRDY, and ARDY will be ignored. The base address of the control block must be on an even 256-byte boundary (i.e., the lower 8 bits of the base address are all zeros). All of the defined registers within this control block may be read or written by the 80C186 CPU at any time.

The control block base address is programmed by a 16-bit relocation register contained within the control block at offset FEH from the base address of the control block (see Figure 9). It provides the upper 12 bits of the base address of the control block. The control block is effectively an internal chip select range and must abide by all the rules concerning chip selects (the chip select circuitry is discussed later in this data sheet). Any access to the 256 bytes of the control block activates an internal chip select.

Other chip selects may overlap the control block only if they are programmed to zero wait states and ignore external ready. In addition, bit 12 of this register determines whether the control block will be mapped into I/O or memory space. If this bit is 1, the control block will be located in memory space. If the bit is 0, the control block will be located in I/O space. If the control register block is mapped into I/O space, the upper 4 bits of the base address must be programmed as 0 (since I/O addresses are only 16 bits wide).

In addition to providing relocation information for the control block, the relocation register contains bits which place the interrupt controller into Slave Mode, and cause the CPU to interrupt upon encountering ESC instructions. At RESET, the relocation register is set to 20FFH, which maps the control block to start at FF00H in I/O space. An offset map of the 256-byte control register block is shown in Figure 10.

CHIP-SELECT/READY GENERATION LOGIC

The 80C186 contains logic which provides programmable chip-select generation for both memories and peripherals. In addition, it can be programmed to provide READY (or WAIT state) generation. It can also provide latched address bits A1 and A2. The chip-select lines are active for all memory and I/O cycles in their programmed areas, whether they be generated by the CPU or by the integrated DMA unit.

Memory Chip Selects

The 80C186 provides 6 memory chip select outputs for 3 address areas; upper memory, lower memory, and midrange memory. One each is provided for upper memory and lower memory, while four are provided for midrange memory.

The range for each chip select is user-programmable and can be set to 2K, 4K, 8K, 16K, 32K, 64K, 128K (plus 1K and 256K for upper and lower chip selects). In addition, the beginning or base address

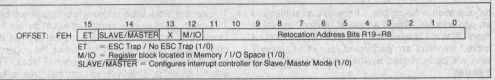

ET = ESC Trap / No ESC Trap (1/0)
M/IO = Register block located in Memory / I/O Space (1/0)
SLAVE/MASTER = Configures interrupt controller for Slave/Master Mode (1/0)

Figure 9. Relocation Register

	OFFSET
Relocation Register	FEH
DMA Descriptors Channel 1	DAH D0H
DMA Descriptors Channel 0	CAH C0H
Chip-Select Control Registers	A8H A0H
Time 2 Control Registers	66H 60H
Time 1 Control Registers	5EH 58H
Time 0 Control Registers	56H 50H
Interrupt Controller Registers	3EH 20H

Figure 10. Internal Register Map

of the midrange memory chip select may also be selected. Only one chip select may be programmed to be active for any memory location at a time. All chip select sizes are in bytes, whereas 80C186 memory is arranged in words. This means that if, for example, 16 64K x 1 memories are used, the memory block size will be 128K, not 64K.

Upper Memory $\overline{CS}$

The 80C186 provides a chip select, called $\overline{UCS}$, for the top of memory. The top of memory is usually used as the system memory because after reset the 80C186 begins executing at memory location FFFF0H.

The upper limit of memory defined by this chip select is always FFFFFH, while the lower limit is programmable. By programming the lower limit, the size of the select block is also defined. Table 7 shows the relationship between the base address selected and the size of the memory block obtained.

Table 7. UMCS Programming Values

Starting Address (Base Address)	Memory Block Size	UMCS Value (Assuming R0 = R1 = R2 = 0)
FFC00	1K	FFF8H
FF800	2K	FFB8H
FF000	4K	FF38H
FE000	8K	FE38H
FC000	16K	FC38H
F8000	32K	F838H
F0000	64K	F038H
E0000	128K	E038H
C0000	256K	C038H

The lower limit of this memory block is defined in the UMCS register (see Figure 11). This register is at offset A0H in the internal control block. The legal values for bits 6–13 and the resulting starting address and memory block sizes are given in Table 7. Any combination of bits 6–13 not shown in Table 7 will result in undefined operation. After reset, the UMCS register is programmed for a 1K area. It must be reprogrammed if a larger upper memory area is desired.

The internal generation of any 20-bit address whose upper 16 bits are equal to or greater than the UMCS value (with bits 0–5 as "0") asserts $\overline{UCS}$. UMCS bits R2–R0 specify the ready mode for the area of memory defined by the chip select register, as explained later.

Lower Memory $\overline{CS}$

The 80C186 provides a chip select for low memory called $\overline{LCS}$. The bottom of memory contains the interrupt vector table, starting at location 00000H.

The lower limit of memory defined by this chip select is always 0H, while the upper limit is programmable. By programming the upper limit, the size of the memory block is defined. Table 8 shows the relationship between the upper address selected and the size of the memory block obtained.

Table 8. LMCS Programming Values

Upper Address	Memory Block Size	LMCS Value (Assuming R0=R1=R2=0)
003FFH	1K	0038H
007FFH	2K	0078H
00FFFH	4K	00F8H
01FFFH	8K	01F8H
03FFFH	16K	03F8H
07FFFH	32K	07F8H
0FFFFH	64K	0FF8H
1FFFFH	128K	1FF8H
3FFFFH	256K	3FF8H

The upper limit of this memory block is defined in the LMCS register (see Figure 12) at offset A2H in the internal control block. The legal values for bits 6–15 and the resulting upper address and memory block sizes are given in Table 8. Any combination of bits 6–15 not shown in Table 8 will result in undefined operation. After RESET, the LMCS register value is undefined. However, the $\overline{LCS}$ chip-select line will not become active until the LMCS register is accessed.

Any internally generated 20-bit address whose upper 16 bits are less than or equal to LMCS (with bits 0–5 "1") will assert $\overline{LCS}$. LMCS register bits R2–R0 specify the READY mode for the area of memory defined by this chip-select register.

Mid-Range Memory $\overline{CS}$

The 80C186 provides four $\overline{MCS}$ lines which are active within a user-locatable memory block. This block can be located within the 80C186 1M byte memory address space exclusive of the areas defined by $\overline{UCS}$ and $\overline{LCS}$. Both the base address and size of this memory block are programmable.

The size of the memory block defined by the mid-range select lines, as shown in Table 9, is determined by bits 8–14 of the MPCS register (see Figure 13). This register is at location A8H in the internal control block. One and only one of bits 8–14 must be set at a time. Unpredictable operation of the $\overline{MCS}$ lines will otherwise occur. Each of the four chip-select lines is active for one of the four equal contiguous divisions of the mid-range block. If the total block size is 32K, each chip select is active for 8K of memory with $\overline{MCS0}$ being active for the first range and $\overline{MCS3}$ being active for the last range.

The EX and MS in MPCS relate to peripheral functionality as described in a later section.

Table 9. MPCS Programming Values

Total Block Size	Individual Select Size	MPCS Bits 14–8
8K	2K	0000001B
16K	4K	0000010B
32K	8K	0000100B
64K	16K	0001000B
128K	32K	0010000B
256K	64K	0100000B
512K	128K	1000000B

The base address of the mid-range memory block is defined by bits 15–9 of the MMCS register (see Figure 14). This register is at offset A6H in the internal control block. These bits correspond to bits A19–A13 of the 20-bit memory address. Bits A12–A0 of the base address are always 0. The base address may be set at any integer multiple of the size of the total memory block selected. For example, if the mid-range block size is 32K (or the size of the block for which each $\overline{MCS}$ line is active is 8K), the block could be located at 10000H or 18000H, but not at 14000H, since the first few integer multiples of a 32K memory block are 0H, 8000H, 10000H, 18000H, etc. After RESET, the contents of both registers are undefined. However, none of the $\overline{MCS}$ lines will be active until both the MMCS and MPCS registers are accessed.

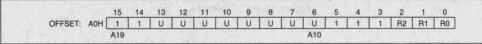

Figure 11. UMCS Register

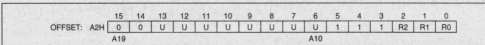

Figure 12. LMCS Register

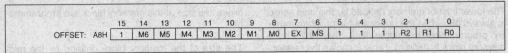

OFFSET: A8H	15	14	13	12	11	10	9	8	7	6	5	4	3	2	1	0
	1	M6	M5	M4	M3	M2	M1	M0	EX	MS	1	1	1	R2	R1	R0

Figure 13. MPCS Register

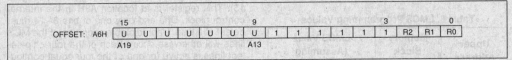

OFFSET: A6H	15						9					3		0
	U	U	U	U	U	U	U	1	1	1	1	1	1	R2	R1	R0
	A19						A13							

Figure 14. MMCS Register

MMCS bits R2–R0 specify READY mode of operation for all four mid-range chip selects.

The 512K block size for the mid-range memory chip selects is a special case. When using 512K, the base address would have to be at either locations 00000H or 80000H. If it were to be programmed at 00000H when the $\overline{LCS}$ line was programmed, there would be an internal conflict between the $\overline{LCS}$ ready generation logic and the $\overline{MCS}$ ready generation logic. Likewise, if the base address were programmed at 80000H, there would be a conflict with the $\overline{UCS}$ ready generation logic. Since the $\overline{LCS}$ chip-select line does not become active until programmed, while the $\overline{UCS}$ line is active at reset, the memory base can be set only at 00000H. If this base address is selected, however, the $\overline{LCS}$ range must not be programmed.

In Enhanced Mode, three of the four $\overline{MCS}$ pins become handshaking pins for the 80C187 Numerics Processor Extension. $\overline{MCS2}$ is still available as a chip select covering one-fourth the mid-range address block, subject to the usual programming of the MPCS and MMCS registers.

Peripheral Chip Selects

The 80C186 can generate chip selects for up to seven peripheral devices. These chip selects are active for seven contiguous blocks of 128 bytes above a programmable base address. The base address may be located in either memory or I/O space.

Seven $\overline{CS}$ lines called $\overline{PCS0}$–6 are generated by the 80C186. The base address is user-programmable; however it can only be a multiple of 1K bytes, i.e., the least significant 10 bits of the starting address are always 0.

$\overline{PCS5}$ and $\overline{PCS6}$ can also be programmed to provide latched address bits A1 and A2. If so programmed, they cannot be used as peripheral selects. These outputs can be connected directly to the A0 and A1 pins used for selecting internal registers of external 8-bit peripheral chips. This scheme simplifies the external hardware because the peripheral registers can be located on even boundaries in I/O or memory space.

The starting address of the peripheral chip-select block is defined by the PACS register (see Figure 15). The register is located at offset A4H in the internal control block. Bits 15–6 of this register correspond to bits 19–10 of the 20-bit Programmable Base Address (PBA) of the peripheral chip-select block. Bits 9–0 of the PBA of the peripheral chip-select block are all zeros. If the chip-select block is located in I/O space, bits 12–15 must be programmed zero, since the I/O address is only 16 bits wide. Table 10 shows the address range of each peripheral chip select with respect to the PBA contained in PACS register.

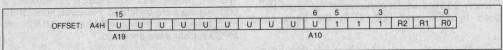

OFFSET: A4H	15							6	5	3			0
	U	U	U	U	U	U	U	U	U	U	1	1	1	R2	R1	R0
	A19								A10				

Figure 15. PACS Register

The user should program bits 15–6 to correspond to the desired peripheral base location. PACS bits 0–2 are used to specify READY mode for $\overline{PCS0}$–$\overline{PCS3}$.

Table 10. PCS Address Ranges

PCS Line	Active between Locations
$\overline{PCS0}$	PBA — PBA + 127
$\overline{PCS1}$	PBA + 128 — PBA + 255
$\overline{PCS2}$	PBA + 256 — PBA + 383
$\overline{PCS3}$	PBA + 384 — PBA + 511
$\overline{PCS4}$	PBA + 512 — PBA + 639
$\overline{PCS5}$	PBA + 640 — PBA + 767
$\overline{PCS6}$	PBA + 768 — PBA + 895

The mode of operation of the peripheral chip selects is defined by the MPCS register (which is also used to set the size of the mid-range memory chip-select block, see Figure 13). The register is located at offset A8H in the internal control block. Bit 7 is used to select the function of $\overline{PCS5}$ and $\overline{PCS6}$, while bit 6 is used to select whether the peripheral chip selects are mapped into memory or I/O space. Table 11 describes the programming of these bits. After RESET, the contents of both the MPCS and the PACS registers are undefined, however none of the PCS lines will be active until both of the MPCS and PACS registers are accessed.

Table 11. MS, EX Programming Values

Bit	Description
MS	1 = Peripherals mapped into memory space.
	0 = Peripherals mapped into I/O space.
EX	0 = 5 $\overline{PCS}$ lines. A1, A2 provided.
	1 = 7 $\overline{PCS}$ lines. A1, A2 are not provided.

MPCS bits 0–2 specify the READY mode for $\overline{PCS4}$–$\overline{PCS6}$ as outlined below.

READY Generation Logic

The 80C186 can generate a READY signal internally for each of the memory or peripheral $\overline{CS}$ lines. The number of WAIT states to be inserted for each peripheral or memory is programmable to provide 0–3 wait states for all accesses to the area for which the chip select is active. In addition, the 80C186 may be programmed to either ignore external READY for each chip-select range individually or to factor external READY with the integrated ready generator.

READY control consists of 3 bits for each $\overline{CS}$ line or group of lines generated by the 80C186. The interpretation of the READY bits is shown in Table 12.

Table 12. READY Bits Programming

R2	R1	R0	Number of WAIT States Generated
0	0	0	0 wait states, external RDY also used.
0	0	1	1 wait state inserted, external RDY also used.
0	1	0	2 wait states inserted, external RDY also used.
0	1	1	3 wait states inserted, external RDY also used.
1	0	0	0 wait states, external RDY ignored.
1	0	1	1 wait state inserted, external RDY ignored.
1	1	0	2 wait states inserted, external RDY ignored.
1	1	1	3 wait states inserted, external RDY ignored.

The internal ready generator operates in parallel with external READY, not in series if the external READY is used (R2 = 0). For example, if the internal generator is set to insert two wait states, but activity on the external READY lines will insert four wait states, the processor will only insert four wait states, not six. This is because the two wait states generated by the internal generator overlapped the first two wait states generated by the external ready signal. Note that the external ARDY and SRDY lines are always ignored during cycles accessing internal peripherals.

R2–R0 of each control word specifies the READY mode for the corresponding block, with the exception of the peripheral chip selects: R2–R0 of PACS set the $\overline{PCS0}$–3 READY mode, R2–R0 of MPCS set the PCS4–6 READY mode.

Chip Select/Ready Logic and Reset

Upon RESET, the Chip-Select/Ready Logic will perform the following actions:

- All chip-select outputs will be driven HIGH.
- Upon leaving RESET, the $\overline{UCS}$ line will be programmed to provide chip selects to a 1K block with the accompanying READY control bits set at 011 to insert 3 wait states in conjunction with external READY (i.e., UMCS resets to FFFBH).
- No other chip select or READY control registers have any predefined values after RESET. They will not become active until the CPU accesses their control registers. Both the PACS and MPCS registers must be accessed before the $\overline{PCS}$ lines will become active.

DMA CHANNELS

The 80C186 DMA controller provides two independent high-speed DMA channels. Data transfers can occur between memory and I/O spaces (e.g., Memory to I/O) or within the same space (e.g., Memory to Memory or I/O to I/O). Data can be transferred either in bytes (8 bits) or in words (16 bits) to or from even or odd addresses. Each DMA channel maintains both a 20-bit source and destination pointer which can be optionally incremented or decremented after each data transfer (by one or two depending on byte or word transfers). Each data transfer consumes 2 bus cycles (a minimum of 8 clocks), one cycle to fetch data and the other to store data.

DMA Operation

Each channel has six registers in the control block which define each channel's operation. The control registers consist of a 20-bit Source pointer (2 words), a 20-bit destination pointer (2 words), a

16-bit Transfer Count Register, and a 16-bit Control Word. The format of the DMA Control Blocks is shown in Table 13. The Transfer Count Register (TC) specifies the number of DMA transfers to be performed. Up to 64K byte or word transfers can be performed with automatic termination. The Control Word defines the channel's operation (see Figure 17). All registers may be modified or altered during any DMA activity. Any changes made to these registers will be reflected immediately in DMA operation.

Table 13. DMA Control Block Format

Register Name	Register Address	
	Ch. 0	Ch. 1
Control Word	CAH	DAH
Transfer Count	C8H	D8H
Destination Pointer (upper 4 bits)	C6H	D6H
Destination Pointer	C4H	D4H
Source Pointer (upper 4 bits)	C2H	D2H
Source Pointer	C0H	D0H

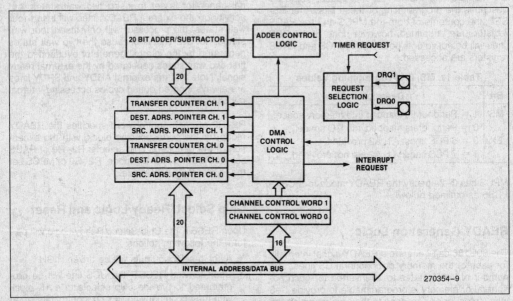

Figure 16. DMA Unit Block Diagram

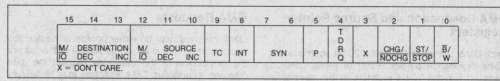

15	14	13	12	11	10	9	8	7	6	5	4	3	2	1	0
M/IO	DESTINATION DEC INC		M/IO	SOURCE DEC INC		TC	INT	SYN		P	T D R Q	X	CHG/ NOCHG	ST/ STOP	B/ W
X = DON'T CARE.															

Figure 17. DMA Control Register

DMA Channel Control Word Register

Each DMA Channel Control Word determines the mode of operation for the particular 80C186 DMA channel. This register specifies:

- the mode of synchronization;
- whether bytes or words will be transferred;
- whether interrupts will be generated after the last transfer;
- whether DMA activity will cease after a programmed number of DMA cycles;
- the relative priority of the DMA channel with respect to the other DMA channel;
- whether the source pointer will be incremented, decremented, or maintained constant after each transfer;
- whether the source pointer addresses memory or I/O space;
- whether the destination pointer will be incremented, decremented, or maintained constant after each transfer; and
- whether the destination pointer will address memory or I/O space.

The DMA channel control registers may be changed while the channel is operating. However, any changes made during operation will affect the current DMA transfer.

DMA Control Word Bit Descriptions

DEST: M/IO Destination pointer is in memory (1) or I/O (0) space.

DEC Decrement destination pointer by 1 or 2 (depends on B/W) after each transfer.

INC Increment destination pointer by 1 or 2 (depends on B/W) after each transfer.

If both INC and DEC are specified, the pointer will remain constant after each cycle.

SOURCE: M/IO Source pointer is in memory (1) or I/O (0) space.

DEC Decrement source pointer by 1 or 2 (depends on B/W) after each transfer.

INC Increment source pointer by 1 or 2 (depends on B/W) after each transfer.

If both INC and DEC are specified, the pointer will remain constant after each cycle.

TC: If set, DMA will terminate when the contents of the transfer count register reach zero. The ST/STOP bit will also be reset at this point. If cleared, the DMA controller will decrement the transfer count register for each DMA cycle, but DMA transfers will not stop when the transfer count register reaches zero.

INT: Enable interrupts to CPU upon transfer count termination.

SYN: 00 No synchronization.

NOTE:

When unsynchronized transfers are specified, the TC bit will be ignored and the ST/STOP bit will be cleared upon the transfer count reaching zero, stopping the channel.

01 Source synchronization.

10 Destination synchronization.

11 Unused.

P: Channel priority relative to other channel during simultaneous requests.

0 Low priority.

1 High priority.

Channels will alternate cycles if both are set at same priority level.

TDRQ: Enable/Disable (1/0) DMA requests from timer 2.

CHG/NOCHG: Change/Do not change (1/0) ST/STOP bit. If this bit is set when writing to the control word, the ST/STOP bit will be programmed by the write to the control word. If this bit is cleared when writing the control word, the ST/STOP bit will not be altered. This bit is not stored; it will always be read as 0.

ST/STOP: Start/Stop (1/0) channel.

B/W: Byte/Word (0/1) transfers.

DMA Destination and Source Pointer Registers

Each DMA channel maintains a 20-bit source and a 20-bit destination pointer. Each of these pointers takes up two full 16-bit registers in the peripheral control block. For each DMA channel to be used, all four pointer registers must be initialized. The lower four bits of the upper register contain the upper four bits of the 20-bit physical address (see Figure 18). These pointers may be individually incremented or decremented after each transfer. If word transfers are performed the pointer is incremented or decremented by two.

Each pointer may point into either memory or I/O space. Since the upper four bits of the address are not automatically programmed to zero, the user must program them in order to address the normal 64K I/O space. Since the DMA channels can perform transfers to or from odd addresses, there is no restriction on values for the pointer registers. Higher transfer rates can be achieved if all word transfers are performed to or from even addresses so that accesses will occur in single bus cycles.

DMA Transfer Count Register

Each DMA channel maintains a 16-bit transfer count register (TC). The register is decremented after every DMA cycle, regardless of the state of the TC bit in the DMA Control Register. If the TC bit in the DMA control word is set or if unsynchronized transfers are programmed, however, DMA activity will terminate when the transfer count register reaches zero.

DMA Requests

Data transfers may be either source or destination synchronized, that is either the source of the data or the destination of the data may request the data transfer. In addition, DMA transfers may be unsynchronized; that is, the transfer will take place continually until the correct number of transfers has occurred. When source or unsynchronized transfers are performed, the DMA channel may begin another transfer immediately after the end of a previous DMA transfer. This allows a complete transfer to take place every 2 bus cycles or eight clock cycles (assuming no wait states). When destination synchronization is performed, data will not be fetched from the source address until the destination device signals that it is ready to receive it. When destination synchronized transfers are requested, the DMA controller will relinquish control of the bus after every transfer. If no other bus activity is initiated, another DMA cycle will begin after two processor clocks. This allows the destination device time to remove its request if another transfer is not desired. Since the DMA controller will relinquish the bus, the CPU can initiate a bus cycle. As a result, a complete bus cycle will often be inserted between destination synchronized transfers. Table 14 shows the maximum DMA transfer rates.

Table 14. Maximum DMA Transfer Rates at CLKOUT = 16 MHz

Type of Synchronization Selected	CPU Running	CPU Halted
Unsynchronized	4.0MBytes/sec	4.0MBytes/sec
Source Synch	4.0MBytes/sec	4.0MBytes/sec
Destination Synch	2.7MBytes/sec	3.2MBytes/sec

HIGHER REGISTER ADDRESS	XXX	XXX	XXX	A19–A16
LOWER REGISTER ADDRESS	A15–A12	A11–A8	A7–A4	A3–A0
	15			0

XXX = DON'T CARE

Figure 18. DMA Pointer Register Format

DMA Acknowledge

No explicit DMA acknowledge pulse is provided. Since both source and destination pointers are maintained, a read from a requesting source, or a write to a requesting destination, should be used as the DMA acknowledge signal. Since the chip-select lines can be programmed to be active for a given block of memory or I/O space, and the DMA pointers can be programmed to point to the same given block, a chip-select line could be used to indicate a DMA acknowledge.

DMA Priority

The DMA channels may be programmed to give one channel priority over the other, or they may be programmed to alternate cycles when both have DMA requests pending. DMA cycles always have priority over internal CPU cycles except between locked memory accesses or word accesses to odd memory locations; also an external bus hold takes priority over an internal DMA cycle. Because an interrupt request cannot suspend a DMA operation and the CPU cannot access memory during a DMA cycle, interrupt latency time will suffer during sequences of continuous DMA cycles. An NMI request, however, will cause all internal DMA activity to halt. This allows the CPU to quickly respond to the NMI request.

DMA Programming

DMA cycles will occur whenever the ST/STOP bit of the Control Register is set. If synchronized transfers are programmed, a DRQ must also be generated.

Therefore the source and destination transfer pointers, and the transfer count register (if used) must be programmed before the ST/STOP bit is set.

Each DMA register may be modified while the channel is operating. If the CHG/NOCHG bit is cleared when the control register is written, the ST/STOP bit of the control register will not be modified by the write. If multiple channel registers are modified, it is recommended that a LOCKED string transfer be used to prevent a DMA transfer from occurring between updates to the channel registers.

DMA Channels and Reset

Upon RESET, the state of the DMA channels will be as follows:

- The ST/STOP bit for each channel will be reset to STOP.
- Any transfer in progress is aborted.
- The values of the transfer count registers, source pointers, and destination pointers are indeterminate.

TIMERS

The 80C186 provides three internal 16-bit programmable timers (see Figure 19). Two of these are highly flexible and are connected to four external pins (2 per timer). They can be used to count external events, time external events, generate nonrepetitive waveforms, etc. The third timer is not connected to any external pins, and is useful for real-time coding and time delay applications. In addition, the third timer can be used as a prescaler to the other two, or as a DMA request source.

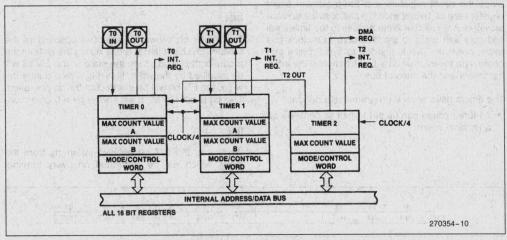

Figure 19. Timer Block Diagram

Timer Operation

The timers are controlled by 11 16-bit registers in the peripheral control block. The configuration of these registers is shown in Table 15. The count register contains the current value of the timer. It can be read or written at any time independent of whether the timer is running or not. The value of this register will be incremented for each timer event. Each of the timers is equipped with a MAX COUNT register, which defines the maximum count the timer will reach. After reaching the MAX COUNT register value, the timer count value will reset to zero during that same clock, i.e., the maximum count value is never stored in the count register itself. Timers 0 and 1 are, in addition, equipped with a second MAX COUNT register, which enables the timers to alternate their count between two different MAX COUNT values. If a single MAX COUNT register is used, the timer output pin will switch LOW for a single clock, 1 clock after the maximum count value has been reached. In the dual MAX COUNT register mode, the output pin will indicate which MAX COUNT register is currently in use, thus allowing nearly complete freedom in selecting waveform duty cycles. For the timers with two MAX COUNT registers, the RIU bit in the control register determines which is used for the comparison.

Each timer gets serviced every fourth CPU-clock cycle, and thus can operate at speeds up to one-quarter the internal clock frequency (one-eighth the crystal rate). External clocking of the timers may be done at up to a rate of one-quarter of the internal CPU-clock rate. Due to internal synchronization and pipelining of the timer circuitry, a timer output may take up to 6 clocks to respond to any individual clock or gate input.

Since the count registers and the maximum count registers are all 16 bits wide, 16 bits of resolution are provided. Any Read or Write access to the timers will add one wait state to the minimum four-clock bus cycle, however. This is needed to synchronize and coordinate the internal data flows between the internal timers and the internal bus.

The timers have several programmable options.

- All three timers can be set to halt or continue on a terminal count.

- Timers 0 and 1 can select between internal and external clocks, alternate between MAX COUNT registers and be set to retrigger on external events.

- The timers may be programmed to cause an interrupt on terminal count.

These options are selectable via the timer mode/control word.

Timer Mode/Control Register

The mode/control register (see Figure 20) allows the user to program the specific mode of operation or check the current programmed status for any of the three integrated timers.

Table 15. Timer Control Block Format

Register Name	Register Offset		
	Tmr. 0	Tmr. 1	Tmr. 2
Mode/Control Word	56H	5EH	66H
Max Count B	54H	5CH	not present
Max Count A	52H	5AH	62H
Count Register	50H	58H	60H

EN:

The enable bit provides programmer control over the timer's RUN/HALT status. When set, the timer is enabled to increment subject to the input pin constraints in the internal clock mode (discussed previously). When cleared, the timer will be inhibited from counting. All input pin transitions during the time EN is zero will be ignored. If CONT is zero, the EN bit is automatically cleared upon maximum count.

$\overline{INH}$:

The inhibit bit allows for selective updating of the enable (EN) bit. If $\overline{INH}$ is a one during the write to the mode/control word, then the state of the EN bit will be modified by the write. If $\overline{INH}$ is a zero during the write, the EN bit will be unaffected by the operation. This bit is not stored; it will always be a 0 on a read.

INT:

When set, the INT bit enables interrupts from the timer, which will be generated on every terminal

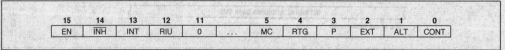

15	14	13	12	11		5	4	3	2	1	0
EN	$\overline{INH}$	INT	RIU	0	...	MC	RTG	P	EXT	ALT	CONT

Figure 20. Timer Mode/Control Register

count. If the timer is configured in dual MAX COUNT register mode, an interrupt will be generated each time the value in MAX COUNT register A is reached, and each time the value in MAX COUNT register B is reached. If this enable bit is cleared after the interrupt request has been generated, but before a pending interrupt is serviced, the interrupt request will still be in force. (The request is latched in the Interrupt Controller).

RIU:

The Register In Use bit indicates which MAX COUNT register is currently being used for comparison to the timer count value. A zero value indicates register A. The RIU bit cannot be written, i.e., its value is not affected when the control register is written. It is always cleared when the ALT bit is zero.

MC:

The Maximum Count bit is set whenever the timer reaches its final maximum count value. If the timer is configured in dual MAX COUNT register mode, this bit will be set each time the value in MAX COUNT register A is reached, and each time the value in MAX COUNT register B is reached. This bit is set regardless of the timer's interrupt-enable bit. The MC bit gives the user the ability to monitor timer status through software instead of through interrupts.

Programmer intervention is required to clear this bit.

RTG:

Retrigger bit is only active for internal clocking (EXT = 0). In this case it determines the control function provided by the input pin.

If RTG = 0, the input level gates the internal clock on and off. If the input pin is HIGH, the timer will count; if the input pin is LOW, the timer will hold its value. As indicated previously, the input signal may be asynchronous with respect to the 80C186 clock.

When RTG = 1, the input pin detects LOW-to-HIGH transitions. The first such transition starts the timer running, clearing the timer value to zero on the first clock, and then incrementing thereafter. Further transitions on the input pin will again reset the timer to zero, from which it will start counting up again. If CONT = 0, when the timer has reached maximum count, the EN bit will be cleared, inhibiting further timer activity.

P:

The prescaler bit is ignored unless internal clocking has been selected (EXT = 0). If the P bit is a zero, the timer will count at one-fourth the internal CPU clock rate. If the P bit is a one, the output of timer 2 will be used as a clock for the timer. Note that the user must initialize and start timer 2 to obtain the prescaled clock.

EXT:

The external bit selects between internal and external clocking for the timer. The external signal may be asynchronous with respect to the 80C186 clock.

If this bit is set, the timer will count LOW-to-HIGH transitions on the input pin. If cleared, it will count an internal clock while using the input pin for control. In this mode, the function of the external pin is defined by the RTG bit. The maximum input to output transition latency time may be as much as 6 clocks. However, clock inputs may be pipelined as closely together as every 4 clocks without losing clock pulses.

ALT:

The ALT bit determines which of two MAX COUNT registers is used for count comparison. If ALT = 0, register A for that timer is always used, while if ALT = 1, the comparison will alternate between register A and register B when each maximum count is reached. This alternation allows the user to change one MAX COUNT register while the other is being used, and thus provides a method of generating non-repetitive waveforms. Square waves and pulse outputs of any duty cycle are a subset of available signals obtained by not changing the final count registers. The ALT bit also determines the function of the timer output pin. If ALT is zero, the output pin will go LOW for one clock, the clock after the maximum count is reached. If ALT is one, the output pin will reflect the current MAX COUNT register being used (0/1 for B/A).

CONT:

Setting the CONT bit causes the associated timer to run continuously, while resetting it causes the timer to halt upon maximum count. If CONT = 0 and ALT = 1, the timer will count to the MAX COUNT register A value, reset, count to the register B value, reset, and halt.

Not all mode bits are provided for timer 2. Certain bits are hardwired as indicated below:

ALT = 0, EXT = 0, P = 0, RTG = 0, RIU = 0

Count Registers

Each of the three timers has a 16-bit count register. The contents of this register may be read or written by the processor at any time. If the register is written while the timer is counting, the new value will take effect in the current count cycle.

The count registers should be programmed before attempting to use the timers since they are not automatically initialized to zero.

Max Count Registers

Timers 0 and 1 have two MAX COUNT registers, while timer 2 has a single MAX COUNT register. These contain the number of events the timer will count. In timers 0 and 1, the MAX COUNT register used can alternate between the two max count values whenever the current maximum count is reached. A timer resets when the timer count register equals the max count value being used. If the timer count register or the max count register is changed so that the max count is less than the timer count, the timer does not immediately reset. Instead, the timer counts up to 0FFFFH, "wraps around" to zero, counts up to the max count value, and then resets.

Timers and Reset

Upon RESET, the state of the timers will be as follows:

- All EN (Enable) bits are reset preventing timer counting.
- For Timers 0 and 1, the RIU bits are reset to zero and the ALT bits are set to one. This results in the Timer Out pins going HIGH.
- The contents of the count registers are indeterminate.

INTERRUPT CONTROLLER

The 80C186 can receive interrupts from a number of sources, both internal and external. The internal interrupt controller serves to merge these requests on a priority basis, for individual service by the CPU.

Internal interrupt sources (Timers and DMA channels) can be disabled by their own control registers or by mask bits within the interrupt controller. The 80C186 interrupt controller has its own control register that sets the mode of operation for the controller.

The interrupt controller will resolve priority among requests that are pending simultaneously. Nesting is provided so interrupt service routines for lower priority interrupts may be interrupted by higher priority interrupts. A block diagram of the interrupt controller is shown in Figure 21.

The 80C186 has a special Slave Mode in which the internal interrupt controller acts as a slave to an external master. The controller is programmed into this mode by setting bit 14 in the peripheral control block relocation register. (See Slave Mode section.)

MASTER MODE OPERATION

Interrupt Controller External Interface

Five pins are provided for external interrupt sources. One of these pins is NMI, the non-maskable interrupt. NMI is generally used for unusual events such as power-fail interrupts. The other four pins may be configured in any of the following ways:

- As four interrupt lines with internally generated interrupt vectors.
- As an interrupt line and interrupt acknowledge line pair (Cascade Mode) with externally generated interrupt vectors plus two interrupt input lines with internally generated vectors.
- As two pairs of interrupt/interrupt acknowledge lines (Cascade Mode) with externally generated interrupt vectors.

External sources in the Cascade Mode use externally generated interrupt vectors. When an interrupt is acknowledged, two INTA cycles are initiated and the vector is read into the 80C186 on the second cycle. The capability to interface to external 82C59A programmable interrupt controllers is provided when the inputs are configured in Cascade Mode.

Interrupt Controller Modes of Operation

The basic modes of operation of the interrupt controller in Master Mde are similar to the 82C59A. The interrupt controller responds identically to internal interrupts in all three modes: the difference is only in the interpretation of function of the four external interrupt pins. The interrupt controller is set into one of these three modes by programming the correct bits in the INT0 and INT1 control registers. The modes of interrupt controller operation are as follows:

Fully Nested Mode

When in the fully nested mode four pins are used as direct interrupt requests as in Figure 22. The vectors for these four inputs are generated internally. An in-service bit is provided for every interrupt source. If a lower-priority device requests an interrupt while the in service bit (IS) is set, no interrupt will be generated by the interrupt controller. In addition, if another interrupt request occurs from the same interrupt source while the in-service bit is set, no interrupt will be generated by the interrupt controller. This allows interrupt service routines to operate with interrupts enabled, yet be suspended only by interrupts of higher priority than the in-service interrupt.

When a service routine is completed, the proper IS bit must be reset by writing the proper pattern to the EOI register. This is required to allow subsequent interrupts from this interrupt source and to allow servicing of lower-priority interrupts. An EOI command is executed at the end of the service routine just before the return from interrupt instruction. If the fully nested structure has been upheld, the next highest-priority source with its IS bit set is then serviced.

Cascade Mode

The 80C186 has four interrupt pins and two of them have dual functions. In the fully nested mode the four pins are used as direct interrupt inputs and the corresponding vectors are generated internally. In the Cascade Mode, the four pins are configured into interrupt input-dedicated acknowledge signal pairs. The interconnection is shown in Figure 23. INT0 is an interrupt input interfaced to an 82C59A, while INT2/$\overline{\text{INTA0}}$ serves as the dedicated interrupt acknowledge signal to that peripheral. The same is true for INT1 and INT3/$\overline{\text{INTA1}}$. Each pair can selectively be placed in the Cascade Mode by programming the proper value into INT0 and INT1 control registers. The use of the dedicated acknowledge signals eliminates the need for the use of external logic to generate $\overline{\text{INTA}}$ and device select signals.

The primary Cascade Mode allows the capability to serve up to 128 external interrupt sources through the use of external master and slave 82C59As. Three levels of priority are created, requiring priority resolution in the 80C186 interrupt controller, the master 82C59As, and the slave 82C59As. If an external interrupt is serviced, one IS bit is set at each of these levels. When the interrupt service routine is completed, up to three end-of-interrupt commands must be issued by the programmer.

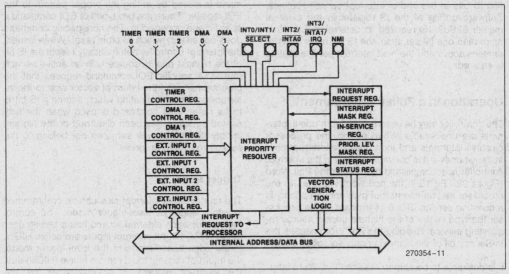

Figure 21. Interrupt Controller Block Diagram

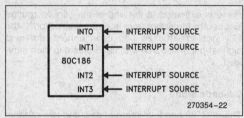

Figure 22. Fully Nested (Direct) Mode Interrupt Controller Connections

Special Fully Nested Mode

This mode is entered by setting the SFNM bit in INT0 or INT1 control register. It enables complete nestability with external 82C59A masters. Normally, an interrupt request from an interrupt source will not be recognized unless the in-service bit for that source is reset. If more than one interrupt source is connected to an external interrupt controller, all of the interrupts will be funneled through the same 80C186 interrupt request pin. As a result, if the external interrupt controller receives a higher-priority interrupt, its interrupt will not be recognized by the 80C186 controller until the 80C186 in-service bit is reset. In Special Fully Nested Mode, the 80C186 interrupt controller will allow interrupts from an external pin regardless of the state of the in-service bit for an interrupt source in order to allow multiple interrupts from a single pin. An in-service bit will continue to be set, however, to inhibit interrupts from other lower-priority 80C186 interrupt sources.

Special procedures should be followed when resetting IS bits at the end of interrupt service routines. Software polling of the IS register in the external master 82C59A is required to determine if there is more than one bit set. If so, the IS bit in the 80C186 remains active and the next interrupt service routine is entered.

Operation in a Polled Environment

The controller may be used in a polled mode if interrupts are undesirable. When polling, the processor disables interrupts and then polls the interrupt controller whenever it is convenient. Polling the interrupt controller is accomplished by reading the Poll Word (Figure 32). Bit 15 in the poll word indicates to the processor that an interrupt of high enough priority is requesting service. Bits 0–4 indicate to the processor the type vector of the highest-priority source requesting service. Reading the Poll Word causes the In-Service bit of the highest priority source to be set.

It is desirable to be able to read the Poll Word information without guaranteeing service of any pending interrupt, i.e., not set the indicated in-service bit. The 80C186 provides a Poll Status Word in addition to the conventional Poll Word to allow this to be done. Poll Word information is duplicated in the Poll Status Word, but reading the Poll Status Word does not set the associated in-service bit. These words are located in two adjacent memory locations in the register file.

Master Mode Features

Programmable Priority

The user can program the interrupt sources into any of eight different priority levels. The programming is done by placing a 3-bit priority level (0–7) in the control register of each interrupt source. (A source with a priority level of 4 has higher priority over all priority levels from 5 to 7. Priority registers containing values lower than 4 have greater priority). All interrupt sources have preprogrammed default priority levels (see Table 4).

If two requests with the same programmed priority level are pending at once, the priority ordering scheme shown in Table 4 is used. If the serviced interrupt routine reenables interrupts, other interrupt requests can be serviced.

End-of-Interrupt Command

The end-of-interrupt (EOI) command is used by the programmer to reset the In-Service (IS) bit when an interrupt service routine is completed. The EOI command is issued by writing the proper pattern to the EOI register. There are two types of EOI commands, specific and nonspecific. The nonspecific command does not specify which IS bit is reset. When issued, the interrupt controller automatically resets the IS bit of the highest priority source with an active service routine. A specific EOI command requires that the programmer send the interrupt vector type to the interrupt controller indicating which source's IS bit is to be reset. This command is used when the fully nested structure has been disturbed or the highest priority IS bit that was set does not belong to the service routine in progress.

Trigger Mode

The four external interrupt pins can be programmed in either edge- or level-trigger mode. The control register for each external source has a level-trigger mode (LTM) bit. All interrupt inputs are active HIGH. In the edge sense mode or the level-trigger mode, the interrupt request must remain active (HIGH) until the interrupt request is acknowledged by the

80C186 CPU. In the edge-sense mode, if the level remains high after the interrupt is acknowledged, the input is disabled and no further requests will be generated. The input level must go LOW for at least one clock cycle to re-enable the input. In the level-trigger mode, no such provision is made: holding the interrupt input HIGH will cause continuous interrupt requests.

Interrupt Vectoring

The 80C186 Interrupt Controller will generate interrupt vectors for the integrated DMA channels and the integrated Timers. In addition, the Interrupt Controller will generate interrupt vectors for the external interrupt lines if they are not configured in Cascade or Special Fully Nested Modes. The interrupt vectors generated are fixed and cannot be changed (see Table 4).

Interrupt Controller Registers

The Interrupt Controller register model is shown in Figure 24. It contains 15 registers. All registers can both be read or written unless specified otherwise.

In-Service Register

This register can be read from or written into. The format is shown in Figure 25. It contains the In-Service bit for each of the interrupt sources. The In-Service bit is set to indicate that a source's service routine is in progress. When an In-Service bit is set, the interrupt controller will not generate interrupts to the CPU when it receives interrupt requests from devices with a lower programmed priority level. The TMR bit is the In-Service bit for all three timers; the D0 and D1 bits are the In-Service bits for the two DMA channels; the I0–I3 are the In-Service bits for the external interrupt pins. The IS bit is set when the

processor acknowledges an interrupt request either by an interrupt acknowledge or by reading the poll register. The IS bit is reset at the end of the interrupt service routine by an end-of-interrupt command.

Interrupt Request Register

The internal interrupt sources have interrupt request bits inside the interrupt controller. The format of this register is shown in Figure 25. A read from this register yields the status of these bits. The TMR bit is the logical OR of all timer interrupt requests. D0 and D1 are the interrupt request bits for the DMA channels.

The state of the external interrupt input pins is also indicated. The state of the external interrupt pins is not a stored condition inside the interrupt controller, therefore the external interrupt bits cannot be written. The external interrupt request bits are set when an interrupt request is given to the interrupt controller, so if edge-triggered mode is selected, the bit in the register will be HIGH only after an inactive-to-active transition. For internal interrupt sources, the register bits are set when a request arrives and are reset when the processor acknowledges the requests.

Writes to the interrupt request register will affect the D0 and D1 interrupt request bits. Setting either bit will cause the corresponding interrupt request while clearing either bit will remove the corresponding interrupt request. All other bits in the register are read-only.

Mask Register

This is a 16-bit register that contains a mask bit for each interrupt source. The format for this register is shown in Figure 25. A one in a bit position corre-

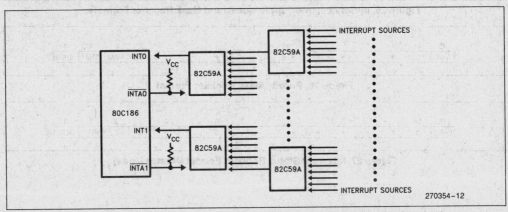

Figure 23. Cascade and Special Fully Nested Mode Interrupt Controller Connections

sponding to a particular source masks the source from generating interrupts. These mask bits are the exact same bits which are used in the individual control registers; programming a mask bit using the mask register will also change this bit in the individual control registers, and vice versa.

	OFFSET
INT3 CONTROL REGISTER	3EH
INT2 CONTROL REGISTER	3CH
INT1 CONTROL REGISTER	3AH
INT0 CONTROL REGISTER	38H
DMA 1 CONTROL REGISTER	36H
DMA 0 CONTROL REGISTER	34H
TIMER CONTROL REGISTER	32H
INTERRUPT STATUS REGISTER	30H
INTERRUPT REQUEST REGISTER	2EH
IN-SERVICE REGISTER	2CH
PRIORITY MASK REGISTER	2AH
MASK REGISTER	28H
POLL STATUS REGISTER	26H
POLL REGISTER	24H
EOI REGISTER	22H

Figure 24. Interrupt Controller Registers (Master Mode)

Priority Mask Register

This register masks all interrupts below a particular interrupt priority level. The format of this register is shown in Figure 26. The code in the lower three bits of this register inhibits interrupts of priority lower (a higher priority number) than the code specified. For example, 100 written into this register masks interrupts of level five (101), six (110), and seven (111). The register is reset to seven (111) upon RESET so no interrupts are masked due to priority number.

Interrupt Status Register

This register contains general interrupt controller status information. The format of this register is shown in Figure 27. The bits in the status register have the following functions:

DHLT: DMA Halt Transfer; setting this bit halts all DMA transfers. It is automatically set whenever a non-maskable interrupt occurs, and it is reset when an IRET instruction is executed. This bit allows prompt service of all non-maskable interrupts. This bit may also be set by the programmer.

IRTx: These three bits represent the individual timer interrupt request bits. These bits differentiate between timer interrupts, since the timer IR bit in the interrupt request register is the "OR" function of all timer interrupt request. Note that setting any one of these three bits initiates an interrupt request to the interrupt controller.

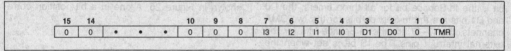

Figure 25. In-Service, Interrupt Request, and Mask Register Formats

15	14				10	9	8	7	6	5	4	3	2	1	0
0	0	•	•	•	0	0	0	I3	I2	I1	I0	D1	D0	0	TMR

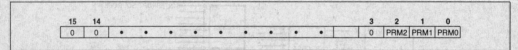

Figure 26. Priority Mask Register Format

15	14											3	2	1	0
0	0	•	•	•	•	•	•	•	•	•	•	0	PRM2	PRM1	PRM0

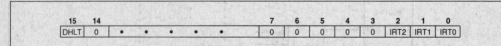

Figure 27. Interrupt Status Register Format (Master Mode)

15	14						7	6	5	4	3	2	1	0
DHLT	0	•	•	•	•	•	0	0	0	0	0	IRT2	IRT1	IRT0

Timer, DMA 0, 1; Control Register

These registers are the control words for all the internal interrupt sources. The format for these registers is shown in Figure 28. The three bit positions PR0, PR1, and PR2 represent the programmable priority level of the interrupt source. The MSK bit inhibits interrupt requests from the interrupt source. The MSK bits in the individual control registers are the exact same bits as are in the Mask Register; modifying them in the individual control registers will also modify them in the Mask Register, and vice versa.

INT0-INT3 Control Registers

These registers are the control words for the four external input pins. Figure 29 shows the format of the INT0 and INT1 Control registers; Figure 30 shows the format of the INT2 and INT3 Control registers. In Cascade Mode or Special Fully Nested Mode, the control words for INT2 and INT3 are not used.

The bits in the various control registers are encoded as follows:

PR0-2: Priority programming information. Highest Priority = 000, Lowest Priority = 111

LTM: Level-trigger mode bit. 1 = level-triggered; 0 = edge-triggered. Interrupt Input levels are active high. In level-triggered mode, an interrupt is generated whenever the external line is high. In edge-triggered mode, an interrupt will be generated only when this

level is preceded by an inactive-to-active transition on the line. In both cases, the level must remain active until the interrupt is acknowledged.

MSK: Mask bit, 1 = mask; 0 = non-mask.

C: Cascade mode bit, 1 = cascade; 0 = direct

SFNM: Special Fully Nested Mode bit, 1 = SFNM

EOI Register

The end of the interrupt register is a command register which can only be written into. The format of this register is shown in Figure 31. It initiates an EOI command when written to by the 80C186 CPU.

The bits in the EOI register are encoded as follows:

S_x: Encoded information that specifies an interrupt source vector type as shown in Table 4. For example, to reset the In-Service bit for DMA channel 0, these bits should be set to 01010, since the vector type for DMA channel 0 is 10.

NOTE:

To reset the single In-Service bit for any of the three timers, the vector type for timer 0 (8) should be written in this register.

NSPEC/: A bit that determines the type of EOI command. Nonspecific = 1, Specific = 0.
SPEC

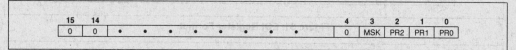

Figure 28. Timer/DMA Control Registers Formats

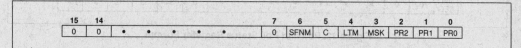

Figure 29. INT0/INT1 Control Register Formats

Figure 30. INT2/INT3 Control Register Formats

Poll and Poll Status Registers

These registers contain polling information. The format of these registers is shown in Figure 32. They can only be read. Reading the Poll register constitutes a software poll. This will set the IS bit of the highest priority pending interrupt. Reading the poll status register will not set the IS bit of the highest priority pending interrupt; only the status of pending interrupts will be provided.

Encoding of the Poll and Poll Status register bits are as follows:

S_x: Encoded information that indicates the vector type of the highest priority interrupting source. Valid only when INTREQ = 1.

INTREQ: This bit determines if an interrupt request is present. Interrupt Request = 1; no Interrupt Request = 0.

SLAVE MODE OPERATION

When Slave Mode is used, the internal 80C186 interrupt controller will be used as a slave controller to an external master interrupt controller. The internal 80C186 resources will be monitored by the internal interrupt controller, while the external controller functions as the system master interrupt controller.

Upon reset, the 80C186 will be in master mode. To provide for slave mode operation bit 14 of the relocation register should be set.

Because of pin limitations caused by the need to interface to an external 82C59A master, the internal interrupt controller will no longer accept external inputs. There are however, enough 80C186 interrupt controller inputs (internally) to dedicate one to each timer. In this mode, each timer interrupt source has its own mask bit, IS bit, and control word.

In Slave Mode each peripheral must be assigned a unique priority to ensure proper interrupt controller operation. Therefore, it is the programmer's responsibility to assign correct priorities and initialize interrupt control registers before enabling interrupts.

Slave Mode External Interface

The configuration of the 80C186 with respect to an external 82C59A master is shown in Figure 33. The INT0 (Pin 45) input is used as the 80C186 CPU interrupt input. IRQ (Pin 41) functions as an output to send the 80C186 slave-interrupt-request to one of the 8 master-PIC-inputs.

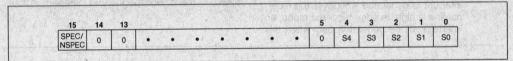

Figure 31. EOI Register Format

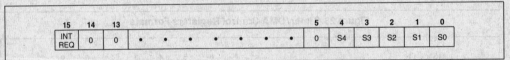

Figure 32. Poll and Poll Status Register Format

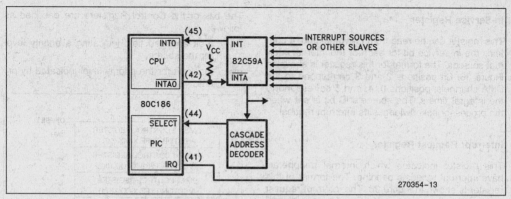

270354–13

Figure 33. Slave Mode Interrupt Controller Connections

Correct master-slave interface requires decoding of the slave addresses (CAS0-2). Slave 82C59As do this internally. Because of pin limitations, the 80C186 slave address will have to be decoded externally. SELECT (Pin 44) is used as a slave-select input. Note that the slave vector address is transferred internally, but the READY input must be supplied externally.

INTA0 (Pin 42) is used as an acknowledge output, suitable to drive the INTA input of an 82C59A.

Interrupt Nesting

Slave Mode operation allows nesting of interrupt requests. When an interrupt is acknowledged, the priority logic masks off all priority levels except those with equal or higher priority.

Vector Generation in the Slave Mode

Vector generation in Slave Mode is exactly like that of an 8259A or 82C59A slave. The interrupt controller generates an 8-bit vector type number which the CPU multiplies by four to use as an address into the vector table. The five most significant bits of this type number are user-programmable while the three least significant bits are defined according to Figure 34. The significant five bits of the vector are programmed by writing to the Interrupt Vector register at offset 20H.

Specific End-of-Interrupt

In Slave Mode the specific EOI command operates to reset an in-service bit of a specific priority. The user supplies a 3-bit priority-level value that points to an in-service bit to be reset. The command is executed by writing the correct value in the Specific EOI register at offset 22H.

Interrupt Controller Registers in the Slave Mode

All control and command registers are located inside the internal peripheral control block. Figure 34 shows the offsets of these registers.

End-of-Interrupt Register

The end-of-interrupt register is a command register which can only be written. The format of this register is shown in Figure 35. It initiates an EOI command when written by the 80C186 CPU.

The bits in the EOI register are encoded as follows:

VT_x: Three least-significant vector type bits corresponding to the source for which the IS bit is to be reset. Figure 34 indicates these bits.

In-Service Register

This register can be read from or written into. It contains the in-service bit for each of the internal interrupt sources. The format for this register is shown in Figure 36. Bit positions 2 and 3 correspond to the DMA channels; positions 0, 4, and 5 correspond to the integral timers. The source's IS bit is set when the processor acknowledges its interrupt request.

Interrupt Request Register

This register indicates which internal peripherals have interrupt requests pending. The format of this register is shown in Figure 36. The interrupt request bits are set when a request arrives from an internal source, and are reset when the processor acknowledges the request. As in Master Mode, D0 and D1 are read/write; all other bits are read only.

Mask Register

This register contains a mask bit for each interrupt source. The format for this register is shown in Figure 36. If the bit in this register corresponding to a particular interrupt source is set, any interrupts from that source will be masked. These mask bits are exactly the same bits which are used in the individual control registers, i.e., changing the state of a mask bit in this register will also change the state of the mask bit in the individual interrupt control register corresponding to the bit.

Control Registers

These registers are the control words for all the internal interrupt sources. The format of these registers is shown in Figure 37. Each of the timers and both of the DMA channels have their own Control Register.

The bits of the Control Registers are encoded as follows:

pr_x: 3-bit encoded field indicating a priority level for the source.

msk: mask bit for the priority level indicated by pr_x bits.

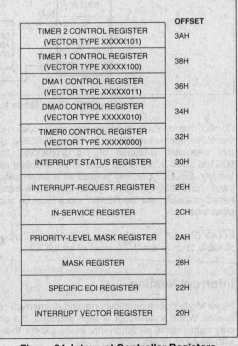

	OFFSET
TIMER 2 CONTROL REGISTER (VECTOR TYPE XXXXX101)	3AH
TIMER 1 CONTROL REGISTER (VECTOR TYPE XXXXX100)	38H
DMA1 CONTROL REGISTER (VECTOR TYPE XXXXX011)	36H
DMA0 CONTROL REGISTER (VECTOR TYPE XXXXX010)	34H
TIMER0 CONTROL REGISTER (VECTOR TYPE XXXXX000)	32H
INTERRUPT STATUS REGISTER	30H
INTERRUPT-REQUEST REGISTER	2EH
IN-SERVICE REGISTER	2CH
PRIORITY-LEVEL MASK REGISTER	2AH
MASK REGISTER	28H
SPECIFIC EOI REGISTER	22H
INTERRUPT VECTOR REGISTER	20H

Figure 34. Interrupt Controller Registers (Slave Mode)

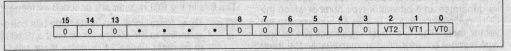

15	14	13					8	7	6	5	4	3	2	1	0
0	0	0	•	•	•	•	0	0	0	0	0	0	VT2	VT1	VT0

Figure 35. Specific EOI Register Format

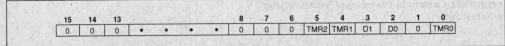

15	14	13					8	7	6	5	4	3	2	1	0
0	0	0	•	•	•	•	0	0	0	TMR2	TMR1	D1	D0	0	TMR0

Figure 36. In-Service, Interrupt Request, and Mask Register Format

Interrupt Vector Register

This register provides the upper five bits of the interrupt vector address. The format of this register is shown in Figure 38. The interrupt controller itself provides the lower three bits of the interrupt vector as determined by the priority level of the interrupt request.

The format of the bits in this register is:

t_X: 5-bit field indicating the upper five bits of the vector address.

Priority-Level Mask Register

This register indicates the lowest priority-level interrupt which will be serviced.

The encoding of the bits in this register is:

m_X: 3-bit encoded field indication priority-level value. All levels of lower priority will be masked.

Interrupt Status Register

This register is defined as in Master Mode except that DHLT is not implemented (see Figure 27).

Interrupt Controller and Reset

Upon RESET, the interrupt controller will perform the following actions:

- All SFNM bits reset to 0, implying Fully Nested Mode.
- All PR bits in the various control registers set to 1. This places all sources at lowest priority (level 111).
- All LTM bits reset to 0, resulting in edge-sense mode.
- All Interrupt Service bits reset to 0.
- All Interrupt Request bits reset to 0.
- All MSK (Interrupt Mask) bits set to 1 (mask).
- All C (Cascade) bits reset to 0 (non-Cascade).
- All PRM (Priority Mask) bits set to 1, implying no levels masked.
- Initialized to Master Mode.

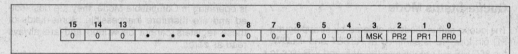

15	14	13					8	7	6	5	4	3	2	1	0
0	0	0	•	•	•	•	0	0	0	0	0	MSK	PR2	PR1	PR0

Figure 37. Control Word Format

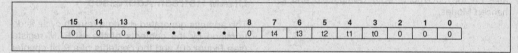

15	14	13					8	7	6	5	4	3	2	1	0
0	0	0	•	•	•	•	0	t4	t3	t2	t1	t0	0	0	0

Figure 38. Interrupt Vector Register Format

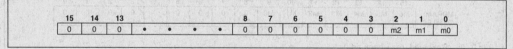

15	14	13					8	7	6	5	4	3	2	1	0
0	0	0	•	•	•	•	0	0	0	0	0	0	m2	m1	m0

Figure 39. Priority Level Mask Register

Enhanced Mode Operation

In Compatible Mode the 80C186 operates with all the features of the NMOS 80186, with the exception of 8087 support (i.e. no numeric coprocessing is possible in Compatible Mode). Queue-Status information is still available for design purposes other than 8087 support.

All the Enhanced Mode features are completely masked when in Compatible Mode. A write to any of the Enhanced Mode registers will have no effect, while a read will not return any valid data.

In Enhanced Mode, the 80C186 will operate with Power-Save, DRAM refresh, and numerics coprocessor support in addition to all the Compatible Mode features.

Entering Enhanced Mode

If connected to a numerics coprocessor, this mode will be invoked automatically. Without an NPX, this mode can be entered by tying the RESET output signal from the 80C186 to the TEST/BUSY input.

Queue-Status Mode

The queue-status mode is entered by strapping the RD pin low. RD is sampled at RESET and if LOW, the 80C186 will reconfigure the ALE and WR pins to be QS0 and QS1 respectively. This mode is available on the 80C186 in both Compatible and Enhanced Modes.

DRAM Refresh Control Unit Description

The Refresh Control Unit (RCU) automatically generates DRAM refresh bus cycles. The RCU operates only in Enhanced Mode. After a programmable period of time, the RCU generates a memory read request to the BIU. If the address generated during a refresh bus cycle is within the range of a properly programmed chip select, that chip select will be activated when the BIU executes the refresh bus cycle. The ready logic and wait states programmed for that region will also be in force. If no chip select is activated, then external ready is automatically required to terminate the refresh bus cycle.

If the HLDA pin is active when a DRAM refresh request is generated (indicating a bus hold condition), then the 80C186 will deactivate the HLDA pin in order to perform a refresh cycle. The circuit external to the 80C186 must remove the HOLD signal for at least one clock in order to execute the refresh cycle. The sequence of HLDA going inactive while HOLD is being held active can be used to signal a pending refresh request.

All registers controlling DRAM refresh may be read and written in Enhanced Mode. When the processor is operating in Compatible Mode, they are deselected and are therefore inaccessible. Some fields of these registers cannot be written and are always read as zeros.

DRAM Refresh Addresses

The address generated during a refresh cycle is determined by the contents of the MDRAM register (see Figure 40) and the contents of a 9-bit counter. Figure 41 illustrates the origin of each bit.

		15	14	13	12	11	10	9	8	7	6	5	4	3	2	1	0
MDRAM:	Offset E0H	M6	M5	M4	M3	M2	M1	M0	0	0	0	0	0	0	0	0	0

Bits 0–8: Reserved, read back as 0.

Bits 9–15: M0–M6, are address bits A13–A19 of the 20-bit memory refresh address. These bits should correspond to any chip select address to be activated for the DRAM partition. These bits are cleared to 0 on RESET.

Figure 40. Memory Partition Register

A19	A18	A17	A16	A15	A14	A13	A12	A11	A10	A9	A8	A7	A6	A5	A4	A3	A2	A1	A0
M6	M5	M4	M3	M2	M1	M0	0	0	0	CA8	CA7	CA6	CA5	CA4	CA3	CA2	CA1	CA0	1

M6–M0: Bits defined by MDRAM Register

CA8–CA0: Bits defined by refresh address counter. These bits change according to a linear/feedback shift register; they do not directly follow a binary count.

Figure 41. Addresses Generated by RCU

CDRAM: Offset E2H	15	14	13	12	11	10	9	8	7	6	5	4	3	2	1	0
	0	0	0	0	0	0	0	C8	C7	C6	C5	C4	C3	C2	C1	C0

Bits 0–8:   C0–C8, clock divisor register, holds the number of CLKOUT cycles between each refresh request.

Bits 9–15: Reserved, read back as 0.

Figure 42. Clock Pre-Scaler Register

EDRAM: Offset E4H	15	14	13	12	11	10	9	8	7	6	5	4	3	2	1	0
	E	0	0	0	0	0	0	T8	T7	T6	T5	T4	T3	T2	T1	T0

Bits 0–8:   T0–T8, refresh clock counter outputs. Read only.

Bits 9–14: Reserved, read back as 0.

Bit 15:   Enable RCU, set to 0 on RESET.

Figure 43. Enable RCU Register

Refresh Control Unit Programming and Operation

After programming the MDRAM and the CDRAM registers (Figures 40 and 42), the RCU is enabled by setting the "E" bit in the EDRAM register (Figure 43). The clock counter (T0–T8 of EDRAM) will be loaded from C0–C8 of CDRAM during T_3 of instruction cycle that sets the "E" bit. The clock counter is then decremented at each subsequent CLKOUT.

A refresh is requested when the value of the counter has reached 1 and the counter is reloaded from CDRAM. In order to avoid missing refresh requests, the value in the CDRAM register should always be at least 18 (12H). Clearing the "E" bit at anytime will clear the counter and stop refresh requests, but will not reset the refresh address counter.

POWER-SAVE CONTROL

Power Save Operation

The 80C186, when in Enhanced Mode, can enter a power saving state by internally dividing the processor clock frequency by a programmable factor. This divided frequency is also available at the CLKOUT pin. The PDCON register contains the two-bit fields for selecting the clock division factor and the enable bit.

All internal logic, including the Refresh Control Unit and the timers, will have their clocks slowed down by the division factor. To maintain a real time count or a fixed DRAM refresh rate, these peripherals must be re-programmed when entering and leaving the power-save mode.

The power-save mode is exited whenever an interrupt is processed by automatically resetting the enable bit. If the power-save mode is to be re-entered after serving the interrupt, the enable bit will need to be set in software before returning from the interrupt routine.

The internal clocks of the 80C186 will begin to be divided during the T_3 state of the instruction cycle that sets the enable bit. Clearing the enable bit will restore full speed in the T_3 state of that instruction.

At no time should the internal clock frequency be allowed to fall below 0.5 MHz. This is the minimum operational frequency of the 80C186. For example, an 80C186 running with a 12 MHz crystal (6 MHz CLOCKOUT) should never have a clock divisor greater than eight.

	15	14	13	12	11	10	9	8	7	6	5	4	3	2	1	0
PDCON: Offset F0H	E	0	0	0	0	0	0	0	0	0	0	0	0	0	F1	F0

Bits 0–1: Clock Divisor Select

F1	F0	Division Factor
0	0	divide by 1
0	1	divide by 4
1	0	divide by 8
1	1	divide by 16

Bits 2–14: Reserved, read back as zero.

Bit 15:   Enable Power Save Mode. Set to zero on RESET.

Figure 44. Power-Save Control Register

Interface for 80C187 Numeric Processor Extension

In Enhanced Mode, three of the mid-range memory chip selects are redefined according to Table 16 for use with the 80C187. The fourth chip select, $\overline{MCS2}$ functions as in compatible mode, and may be programmed for activity with ready logic and wait states accordingly. As in compatible mode, $\overline{MCS2}$ will function for one-fourth a programmed block size.

Table 16. $\overline{MCS}$ Assignments

Compatible Mode	Enhanced Mode	
$\overline{MCS0}$	$\overline{PEREQ}$	Processor Extension Request
$\overline{MCS1}$	$\overline{ERROR}$	NPX Error
$\overline{MCS2}$	$\overline{MCS2}$	Mid-Range Chip Select
$\overline{MCS3}$	$\overline{NPS}$	Numeric Processor Select

Four port addresses are assigned to the 80C186/80C187 interface for 16-bit reads and writes. Table 17 shows the port definitions. These ports are not accessible by using the 80C186 I/O instructions. However, numerics operations will cause a $\overline{PCS}$ line to be activated if it is properly programmed for this I/O range.

Table 17. Numerics Coprocessor I/O Port Assignments

I/O Address	Read Definition	Write Definition
00F8H	Status/Control	Opcode
00FAH	Data	Data
00FCH	reserved	CS:IP, DS:EA
00FEH	Opcode Status	reserved

ONCE™ Test Mode

To facilitate testing and inspection of devices when fixed into a target system, the 80C186 has a test mode available which allows all pins to be placed in a high-impedance state. ONCE stands for "ON Circuit Emulation". When placed in this mode, the 80C186 will put all pins in the high-impedance state until RESET.

The ONCE mode is selected by tying the $\overline{UCS}$ and the $\overline{LCS}$ LOW during RESET. These pins are sampled on the low-to-high transition of the $\overline{RES}$ pin. The $\overline{UCS}$ and the $\overline{LCS}$ pins have weak internal pull-up resistors similar to the $\overline{RD}$ and $\overline{TEST}/BUSY$ pins to guarantee normal operation.

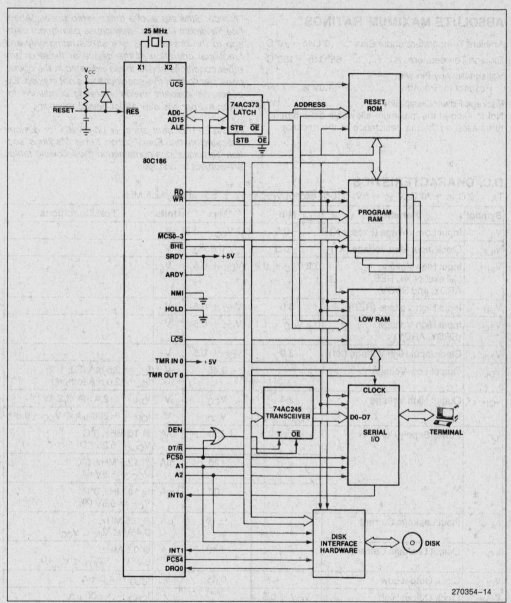

Figure 45. Typical 80C186 Computer

ABSOLUTE MAXIMUM RATINGS*

Ambient Temperature under Bias ....0°C to +70°C

Storage Temperature .... −65°C to +150°C

Voltage on Any Pin with
Respect to Ground .... −1.0V to +7.0V

Package Power Dissipation 1W
Not to exceed the maximum allowable die temperature based on thermal resistance of the package.

*Notice: Stresses above those listed under "Absolute Maximum Ratings" may cause permanent damage to the device. This is a stress rating only and functional operation of the device at these or any other conditions above those indicated in the operational sections of this specification is not implied. Exposure to absolute maximum rating conditions for extended periods may affect device reliability.

NOTICE: This data sheet is only valid for devices indicated in the Specification Level Markings section. Specifications contained in the following tables are subject to change.

D.C. CHARACTERISTICS

$T_A = 0°C$ to $+70°C$, $V_{CC} = 5V \pm 10\%$ except $V_{CC} = 5V \pm 5\%$ at f > 12.5 MHz

Symbol	Parameter	Min	Max	Units	Test Conditions
V_{IL}	Input Low Voltage (Except X1)	−0.5	$0.2 V_{CC} - 0.3$	V	
V_{IL1}	Clock Input Low Voltage (X1)	−0.5	0.6	V	
V_{IH}	Input High Voltage (All except X1, $\overline{RES}$, ARDY, and SRDY)	$0.2 V_{CC} + 0.9$	$V_{CC} + 0.5$	V	
V_{IH1}	Input High Voltage ($\overline{RES}$)	3.0	$V_{CC} + 0.5$	V	
V_{IH2}	Input High Voltage (SRDY, ARDY)	$0.2 V_{CC} + 1.1$	$V_{CC} + 0.5$	V	
V_{IH3}	Clock Input High Voltage (X1)	3.9	$V_{CC} + 0.5$	V	
V_{OL}	Output Low Voltage		0.45	V	$I_{OL} = 2.5$ mA (S0, 1, 2) $I_{OL} = 2.0$ mA (others)
V_{OH}	Output High Voltage	2.4	V_{CC}	V	$I_{OH} = -2.4$ mA @ 2.4V [4]
		$V_{CC} - 0.5$	V_{CC}	V	$I_{OH} = -200 \mu A$ @ $V_{CC} -0.5$ [4]
I_{CC}	Power Supply Current		150	mA	@ 16 MHz, 0°C $V_{CC} = 5.25V$ [3]
			120	mA	@ 12.5 MHz, 0°C $V_{CC} = 5.5V$ [3]
			100	mA	@ 10 MHz, 0°C $V_{CC} = 5.5V$ [3]
I_{LI}	Input Leakage Current		±10	μA	@ 0.5 MHz, $0.45V \leq V_{IN} \leq V_{CC}$
I_{LO}	Output Leakage Current		±10	μA	@ 0.5 MHz, $0.45V \leq V_{OUT} \leq V_{CC}$ [1]
V_{CLO}	Clock Output Low		0.45	V	$I_{CLO} = 4.0$ mA
V_{CHO}	Clock Output High	$V_{CC} - 0.5$		V	$I_{CHO} = -500 \mu A$
C_{IN}	Input Capacitance		10	pF	@ 1 MHz [2]
C_{IO}	Output or I/O Capacitance		20	pF	@ 1 MHz [2]

NOTES:
1. Pins being floated during HOLD or by invoking the ONCE Mode.
2. Characterization conditions are a) Frequency = 1 MHz; b) Unmeasured pins at GND; c) V_{IN} at + 5.0V or 0.45V. This parameter is not tested.
3. Current is measured with the device in RESET with X1 and X2 driven and all other non-power pins open.
4. $\overline{RD}$/QSMD, $\overline{UCS}$, $\overline{LCS}$, $\overline{MCS0}$/PEREQ, $\overline{MCS1}$/$\overline{ERROR}$, and $\overline{TEST}$/BUSY pins have internal pullup devices. Loading some of these pins above $I_{OH} = -200 \mu A$ can cause the 80C186 to go into alternative modes of operation. See the section on Local Bus Controller and Reset for details.

80C186

 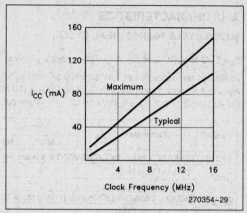

POWER SUPPLY CURRENT

Current is linearly proportional to clock frequency and is measured with the device in RESET with X1 and X2 driven and all other non-power pins open.

Maximum current is given by $I_{CC} = 8.4$ mA $\times$ freq. (MHz) $+ 15$ mA.

Typical current is given by I_{CC} (typical) $= 6.4$ mA $\times$ freq. (MHz) $+ 4.0$ mA. "Typicals" are based on a limited number of samples taken from early manufacturing lots measured at $V_{CC} = 5$V and room temperature. "Typicals" are not guaranteed.

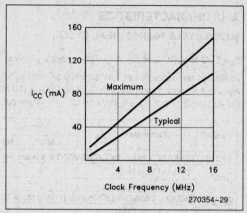

Figure 46. I_{CC} vs Frequency

80C186 PRELIMINARY

A. C. CHARACTERISTICS

MAJOR CYCLE TIMINGS (READ CYCLE)

$T_A = 0^\circ$ C to $+70^\circ$ C, V_{CC} = 5V ± 10% except V_{CC} = 5V ± 5% at f > 12.5 MHz

All timings are measured at 1.5V and 100 pF loading on CLKOUT unless otherwise noted.
All output test conditions are with C_L = 50-200 pF (10 MHz) and C_L = 50-100 pF (12.5-16 MHz).
For A.C. tests, input V_{IL} = 0.45V and V_{IH} = 2.4V except at X1 where $V_{IH} = V_{CC}$ - 0.5V.

Symbol	Parameter	80C186 Min	80C186 Max	80C186-12 Min	80C186-12 Max	80C186-16 Min	80C186-16 Max	Unit	Test Conditions
80C186 GENERAL TIMING REQUIREMENTS (Listed More Than Once)									
T_{DVCL}	Data in Setup (A/D)	15		15		15		ns	
T_{CLDX}	Data in Hold (A/D)	3		3		3		ns	
80C186 GENERAL TIMING RESPONSES (Listed More Than Once)									
T_{CHSV}	Status Active Delay	5	45	5	35	5	31	ns	
T_{CLSH}	Status Inactive Delay	5	46	5	35	5	30	ns	
T_{CLAV}	Address Valid Delay	5	44	5	36	5	33	ns	
T_{CLAX}	Address Hold	0		0		0		ns	
T_{CLDV}	Data Valid Delay	5	40	5	36	5	33	ns	
T_{CHDX}	Status Hold Time	10		10		10		ns	
T_{CHLH}	ALE Active Delay		30		25		20	ns	
T_{LHLL}	ALE Width	T_{CLCL} - 15		T_{CLCL} - 15		T_{CLCL} - 15		ns	
T_{CHLL}	ALE Inactive Delay		30		25		20	ns	
T_{AVLL}	Address Valid to ALE Low	T_{CLCH} - 18		T_{CLCH} - 15		T_{CLCH} - 15		ns	Equal Loading
T_{LLAX}	Address Hold from ALE Inactive	T_{CHCL} - 15		T_{CHCL} - 15		T_{CHCL} - 15		ns	Equal Loading
T_{AVCH}	Address Valid to Clock High	0		0		0		ns	
T_{CLAZ}	Address Float Delay	T_{CLAX}	30	T_{CLAX}	25	T_{CLAX}	20	ns	
T_{CLCSV}	Chip-Select Active Delay	3	42	3	33	3	30	ns	
T_{CXCSX}	Chip-Select Hold from Command Inactive	T_{CLCH} - 10		T_{CLCH} - 10		T_{CLCH} - 10		ns	Equal Loading
T_{CHCSX}	Chip-Select Inactive Delay	5	35	5	30	5	25	ns	
T_{DXDL}	DEN Inactive to DT/$\overline{R}$ Low	0		0		0		ns	Equal Loading
T_{CVCTV}	Control Active Delay 1	3	44	3	37	3	31	ns	
T_{CVDEX}	DEN Inctive Delay	5	44	5	37	5	31	ns	
T_{CHCTV}	Control Active Delay 2	5	44	5	37	5	31	ns	
T_{CLLV}	LOCK Valid/Invalid Delay	3	40	3	37	3	35	ns	
80C186 TIMING RESPONSES (Read Cycle)									
T_{AZRL}	Address Float to RD Active	0		0		0		ns	
T_{CLRL}	RD Active Delay	5	44	5	37	5	31	ns	
T_{RLRH}	RD Pulse Width	$2T_{CLCL}$ - 30		$2T_{CLCL}$ - 25		$2T_{CLCL}$ - 25		ns	
T_{CLRH}	RD Inactive Delay	5	44	5	37	5	31	ns	
T_{RHLH}	RD Inactive to ALE High	T_{CLCH} - 14		T_{CLCH} - 14		T_{CLCH} - 14		ns	Equal Loading
T_{RHAV}	RD Inactive to Address Active	T_{CLCL} - 15		T_{CLCL} - 15		T_{CLCL} - 15		ns	Equal Loading

270354-34

A. C. CHARACTERISTICS

READ CYCLE WAVEFORMS

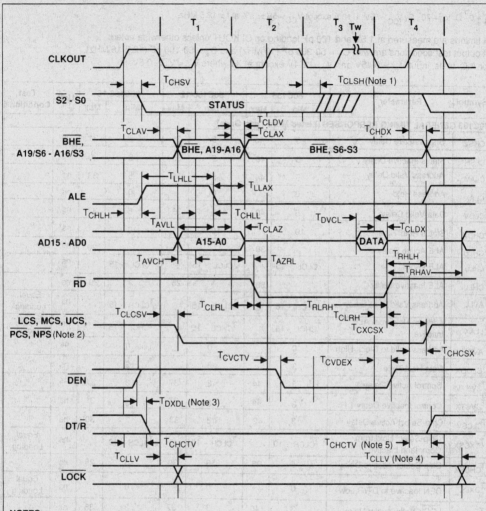

NOTES:
1. Status inactive in state preceding T$_4$.
3. For write cycle followed by read cycle.
4. T$_1$ of next bus cycle.
5. Changes in T-state preceding next bus cycle if followed by write.

270354–35

A. C. CHARACTERISTICS

MAJOR CYCLE TIMINGS (WRITE CYCLE)

$T_A = 0^\circ$ C to $+ 70^\circ$ C, $V_{CC} = 5V \pm 10\%$ except $V_{CC} = 5V \pm 5\%$ at $f > 12.5$ MHz

All timings are measured at 1.5V and 100 pF loading on CLKOUT unless otherwise noted.
All output test conditions are with $C_L = 50$-200 pF (10 MHz) and $C_L = 50$-100 pF (12.5-16 MHz).
For A.C. tests, input $V_{IL} = 0.45V$ and $V_{IH} = 2.4V$ except at X1 where $V_{IH} = V_{CC} - 0.5V$.

Symbol	Parameter	80C186 Min	80C186 Max	80C186-12 Min	80C186-12 Max	80C186-16 Min	80C186-16 Max	Unit	Test Conditions
80C186 GENERAL TIMING RESPONSES (Listed More Than Once)									
T_{CHSV}	Status Active Delay	5	45	5	35	5	31	ns	
T_{CLSH}	Status Inactive Delay	5	46	5	35	5	30	ns	
T_{CLAV}	Address Valid Delay	5	44	5	36	5	33	ns	
T_{CLAX}	Address Hold	0		0		0		ns	
T_{CLDV}	Data Valid Delay	5	40	5	36	5	33	ns	
T_{CHDX}	Status Hold Time	10		10		10		ns	
T_{CHLH}	ALE Active Delay		30		25		20	ns	
T_{LHLL}	ALE Width	$T_{CLCL} - 15$		$T_{CLCL} - 15$		$T_{CLCL} - 15$		ns	
T_{CHLL}	ALE Inactive Delay		30		25		20	ns	
T_{AVLL}	Address Valid to ALE Low	$T_{CLCH} - 18$		$T_{CLCH} - 15$		$T_{CLCH} - 15$		ns	Equal Loading
T_{LLAX}	Address Hold from ALE Inactive	$T_{CHCL} - 15$		$T_{CHCL} - 15$		$T_{CHCL} - 15$		ns	Equal Loading
T_{AVCH}	Address Valid to Clock High	0		0		0		ns	
T_{CLDOX}	Data Hold Time	3		3		3		ns	
T_{CVCTV}	Control Active Delay 1	3	44	3	37	3	31	ns	
T_{CVCTX}	Control Inactive Delay	3	44	3	37	3	31	ns	
T_{CLCSV}	Chip-Select Active Delay	3	42	3	33	3	30	ns	
T_{CXCSX}	Chip-Select Hold from Command Inactive	$T_{CLCH} - 10$		$T_{CLCH} - 10$		$T_{CLCH} - 10$		ns	Equal Loading
T_{CHCSX}	Chip-Select Inactive Delay	5	35	5	30	5	25	ns	
T_{DXDL}	$\overline{DEN}$ Inactive to DT/$\overline{R}$ Low	0		0		0		ns	Equal Loading
T_{CLLV}	$\overline{LOCK}$ Valid/Invalid Delay	3	40	3	37	3	35	ns	
80C186 TIMING RESPONSES (Write Cycle)									
T_{WLWH}	$\overline{WR}$ Pulse Width	$2T_{CLCL} - 30$		$2T_{CLCL} - 25$		$2T_{CLCL} - 25$		ns	
T_{WHLH}	$\overline{WR}$ Inactive to ALE High	$T_{CLCH} - 14$		$T_{CLCH} - 14$		$T_{CLCH} - 14$		ns	Equal Loading
T_{WHDX}	Data Hold After $\overline{WR}$	$T_{CLCL} - 34$		$T_{CLCL} - 20$		$T_{CLCL} - 20$		ns	Equal Loading
T_{WHDEX}	$\overline{WR}$ Inactive to $\overline{DEN}$ Inactive	$T_{CLCH} - 10$		$T_{CLCH} - 10$		$T_{CLCH} - 10$		ns	Equal Loading

270354–36

A. C. CHARACTERISTICS

WRITE CYCLE WAVEFORMS

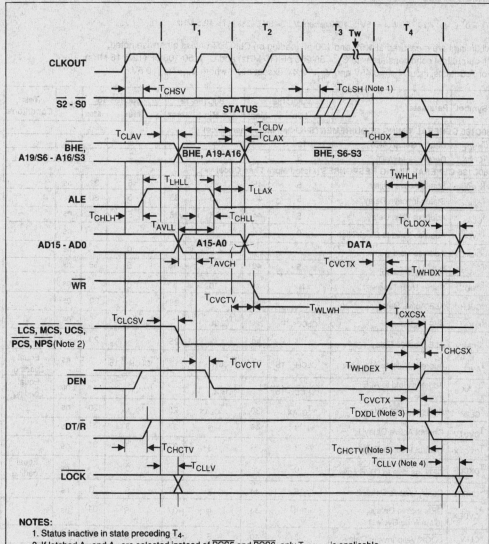

NOTES:
1. Status inactive in state preceding T4.
2. If latched A_1 and A_2 are selected instead of $\overline{PCS5}$ and $\overline{PCS6}$, only T_{CLCSV} is applicable.
3. For write cycle followed by read cycle.
4. T_1 of next bus cycle.
5. Changes in T-state preceding next bus cycle if followed by read, INTA, or halt.

270354–37

A. C. CHARACTERISTICS

MAJOR CYCLE TIMINGS (INTERRUPT ACKNOWLEDGE CYCLE)

$T_A = 0^{\circ}$ C to $+70^{\circ}$ C, $V_{CC} = 5V \pm 10\%$ except $V_{CC} = 5V \pm 5\%$ at f > 12.5 MHz

All timings are measured at 1.5V and 100 pF loading on CLKOUT unless otherwise noted.
All output test conditions are with C_L = 50-200 pF (10 MHz) and C_L = 50-100 pF (12.5-16 MHz).
For A.C. tests, input V_{IL} = 0.45V and V_{IH} = 2.4V except at X1 where $V_{IH} = V_{CC}$ - 0.5V.

Symbol	Parameter	80C186 Min	80C186 Max	80C186-12 Min	80C186-12 Max	80C186-16 Min	80C186-16 Max	Unit	Test Conditions
80C186 GENERAL TIMING REQUIREMENTS (Listed More Than Once)									
T_{DVCL}	Data in Setup (A/D)	15		15		15		ns	
T_{CLDX}	Data in Hold (A/D)	3		3		3		ns	
80C186 GENERAL TIMING RESPONSES (Listed More Than Once)									
T_{CHSV}	Status Active Delay	5	45	5	35	5	31	ns	
T_{CLSH}	Status Inactive Delay	5	46	5	35	5	30	ns	
T_{CLAV}	Address Valid Delay	5	44	5	36	5	33	ns	
T_{AVCH}	Address Valid to Clock High	0		0		0		ns	
T_{CLAX}	Address Hold	0		0		0		ns	
T_{CLDV}	Data Valid Delay	5	40	5	36	5	33	ns	
T_{CHDX}	Status Hold Time	10		10		10		ns	
T_{CHLH}	ALE Active Delay		30		25		20	ns	
T_{LHLL}	ALE Width	T_{CLCL} - 15		T_{CLCL} - 15		T_{CLCL} - 15		ns	
T_{CHLL}	ALE Inactive Delay		30		25		20	ns	
T_{AVLL}	Address Valid to ALE Low	T_{CLCH} - 18		T_{CLCH} - 15		T_{CLCH} - 15		ns	Equal Loading
T_{LLAX}	Address Hold to ALE Inactive	T_{CHCL} - 15		T_{CHCL} - 15		T_{CHCL} - 15		ns	Equal Loading
T_{CLAZ}	Address Float Delay	T_{CLAX}	30	T_{CLAX}	25	T_{CLAX}	20	ns	
T_{CVCTV}	Control Active Delay 1	3	44	3	37	3	31	ns	
T_{CVCTX}	Control Inactive Delay	3	44	3	37	3	31	ns	
T_{DXDL}	$\overline{DEN}$ Inactive to DT/$\overline{R}$ Low	0		0		0		ns	Equal Loading
T_{CHCTV}	Control Active Delay 2	5	44	5	37	5	31	ns	
T_{CVDEX}	$\overline{DEN}$ Inctive Delay (Non-Write Cycles)	5	44	5	37	5	31	ns	
T_{CLLV}	$\overline{LOCK}$ Valid/Invalid Delay	3	40	3	37	3	35	ns	

270354-38

A. C. CHARACTERISTICS

INTERRUPT ACKNOWLEDGE CYCLE WAVEFORMS

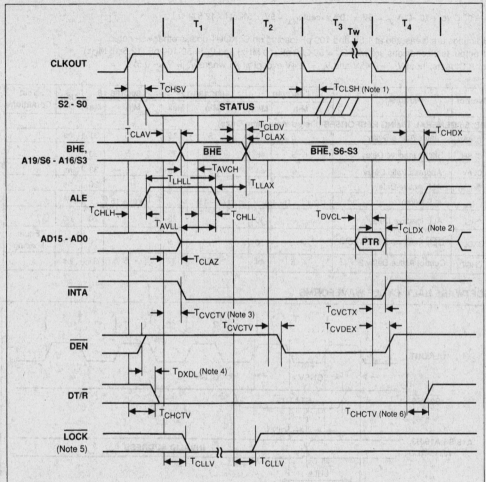

NOTES:

1. Status inactive in state preceding T_4.
2. The data hold time lasts only until $\overline{INTA}$ goes inactive, even if the $\overline{INTA}$ transition occurs prior to T_{CLDX} (min).
3. $\overline{INTA}$ occurs one clock later in Slave Mode.
4. For write cycle followed by interrupt acknowledge cycle.
5. $\overline{LOCK}$ is active upon T_1 of the first interrupt acknowledge cycle and inactive upon T_2 of the second interrupt acknowledge cycle.

270354–39

A. C. CHARACTERISTICS

SOFTWARE HALT CYCLE TIMINGS

$T_A = 0^\circ$ C to $+ 70^\circ$ C, $V_{CC} = 5V \pm 10\%$ except $V_{CC} = 5V \pm 5\%$ at f > 12.5 MHz

All timings are measured at 1.5V and 100 pF loading on CLKOUT unless otherwise noted.
All output test conditions are with C_L = 50-200 pF (10 MHz) and C_L = 50-100 pF (12.5-16 MHz).
For A.C. tests, input V_{IL} = 0.45V and V_{IH} = 2.4V except at X1 where $V_{IH} = V_{CC} - 0.5V$.

Symbol	Parameter	80C186 Min	80C186 Max	80C186-12 Min	80C186-12 Max	80C186-16 Min	80C186-16 Max	Unit	Test Conditions
\multicolumn{10}{l}{**80C186 GENERAL TIMING RESPONSES (Listed More Than Once)**}
T_{CHSV}	Status Active Delay	5	45	5	35	5	31	ns	
T_{CLSH}	Status Inactive Delay	5	46	5	35	5	30	ns	
T_{CLAV}	Address Valid Delay	5	44	5	36	5	33	ns	
T_{CHLH}	ALE Active Delay		30		25		20	ns	
T_{LHLL}	ALE Width	T_{CLCL} - 15		T_{CLCL} - 15		T_{CLCL} - 15		ns	
T_{CHLL}	ALE Inactive Delay		30		25		20	ns	
T_{DXDL}	$\overline{DEN}$ Inactive to DT/$\overline{R}$ Low		0		0		0	ns	Equal Loading
T_{CHCTV}	Control Active Delay 2	5	44	5	37	5	31	ns	

SOFTWARE HALT CYCLE WAVEFORMS

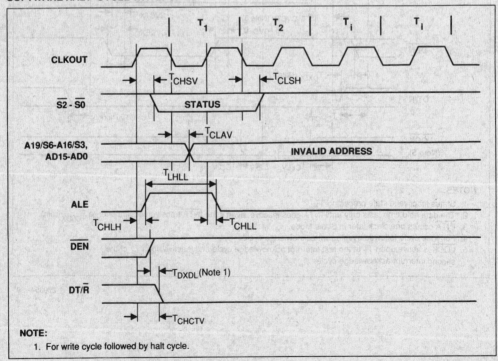

NOTE:
1. For write cycle followed by halt cycle.

270354-40

A. C. CHARACTERISTICS

CLOCK TIMINGS

$T_A = 0^{\circ}C$ to $+70^{\circ}C$, $V_{CC} = 5V \pm 10\%$ except $V_{CC} = 5V \pm 5\%$ at f > 12.5 MHz

All timings are measured at 1.5V and 100 pF loading on CLKOUT unless otherwise noted.
All output test conditions are with $C_L = 50\text{-}200$ pF (10 MHz) and $C_L = 50\text{-}100$ pF (12.5-16 MHz).
For A.C. tests, input $V_{IL} = 0.45V$ and $V_{IH} = 2.4V$ except at X1 where $V_{IH} = V_{CC} - 0.5V$.

Symbol	Parameter	80C186		80C186-12		80C186-16		Unit	Test Conditions
		Min	Max	Min	Max	Min	Max		
80C186 CLKIN REQUIREMENTS Measurements taken with following conditions: External clock input to X1 and X2 not connected (float)									
T_{CKIN}	CLKIN Period	50	1000	40	1000	31.25	1000	ns	
T_{CLCK}	CLKIN Low Time	20		16		13		ns	1.5 V [2]
T_{CHCK}	CLKIN High Time	20		16		13		ns	1.5 V [2]
T_{CKHL}	CLKIN Fall Time		5		5		5	ns	3.5 to 1.0V
T_{CKLH}	CLKIN Rise Time		5		5		5	ns	1.0 to 3.5V
80C186 CLKOUT TIMING									
T_{CICO}	CLKIN to CLKOUT Skew		25		21		17	ns	
T_{CLCL}	CLKOUT Period	100	2000	80	2000	62.5	2000	ns	
T_{CLCH}	CLKOUT Low Time	$0.5\ T_{CLCL}$ -8		$0.5\ T_{CLCL}$ -7		$0.5\ T_{CLCL}$ -7		ns	$C_L=100pF$ [2]
		$0.5\ T_{CLCL}$ -6		$0.5\ T_{CLCL}$ -5		$0.5\ T_{CLCL}$ -5		ns	$C_L=50pF$ [3]
T_{CHCL}	CLKOUT High Time	$0.5\ T_{CLCL}$ -8		$0.5\ T_{CLCL}$ -7		$0.5\ T_{CLCL}$ -7		ns	$C_L=100pF$ [4]
		$0.5\ T_{CLCL}$ -6		$0.5\ T_{CLCL}$ -5		$0.5\ T_{CLCL}$ -5		ns	$C_L=50pF$ [3]
T_{CH1CH2}	CLKOUT Rise Time		10		10		10	ns	1.0 to 3.5V
T_{CL2CL1}	CLKOUT Fall Time		10		10		10	ns	3.5 to 1.0V

NOTES:
1. T_{CLCK} and T_{CHCK} (CLKIN Low and High times) should not have a duration less than 40% of T_{CKIN}
2. Tested under worst case conditions: $V_{CC} = 5.5V$ (5.25V @ 16 MHz). $T_A = 70^{\circ}C$.
3. Not Tested.
4. Tested under worst case conditions: $V_{CC} = 4.5V$ (4.75V @ 16 MHz). $T_A = 0^{\circ}C$.

CLOCK WAVEFORMS

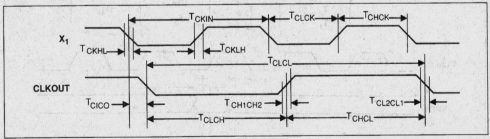

270354-41

A. C. CHARACTERISTICS

READY, PERIPHERAL, AND QUEUE STATUS TIMINGS

$T_A = 0^{\circ}C$ to $+70^{\circ}C$, $V_{CC} = 5V \pm 10\%$ except $V_{CC} = 5V \pm 5\%$ at $f > 12.5$ MHz

All timings are measured at 1.5V and 100 pF loading on CLKOUT unless otherwise noted.
All output test conditions are with C_L = 50-200 pF (10 MHz) and C_L = 50-100 pF (12.5-16 MHz).
For A.C. tests, input V_{IL} = 0.45V and V_{IH} = 2.4V except at X1 where V_{IH} = V_{CC} - 0.5V.

Symbol	Parameter	80C186		80C186-12		80C186-16		Unit	Test Conditions
		Min	Max	Min	Max	Min	Max		
80C186 READY AND PERIPHERAL TIMING REQUIREMENTS									
T_{SRYCL}	Synchronous Ready(SRDY) Transition Setup Time (1)	15		15		15		ns	
T_{CLSRY}	SRDY Transition Hold Time (1)	15		15		15		ns	
T_{ARYCH}	ARDY Resolution Transition Setup Time (2)	15		15		15		ns	
T_{CLARX}	ARDY Active Hold Time (1)	15		15		15		ns	
T_{ARYCHL}	ARDY Inactive Holding Time	15		15		15		ns	
T_{ARYLCL}	Asynchronous Ready (ARDY) Setup Time (1)	25		25		25		ns	
T_{INVCH}	INTx, NMI, $\overline{TEST}$/BUSY, TMR IN Setup Time (2)	15		15		15		ns	
T_{INVCL}	DRQ0, DRQ1 Setup Time (2)	15		15		15		ns	
80C186 PERIPHERAL AND QUEUE STATUS TIMING RESPONSES									
T_{CLTMV}	Timer Output Delay		40		33		27	ns	
T_{CHQSV}	Queue Status Delay		37		32		30	ns	

NOTES:

1. To guarantee proper operation.
2. To guarantee recognition at clock edge.

SYNCHRONOUS READY (SRDY) WAVEFORMS

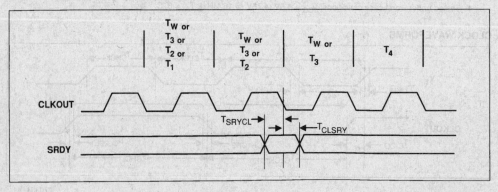

270354–42

80C186

A. C. CHARACTERISTICS

ASYNCHRONOUS READY (ARDY) WAVEFORMS

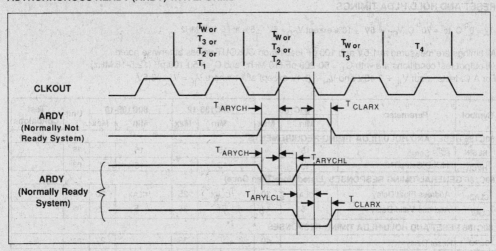

PERIPHERAL AND QUEUE STATUS WAVEFORMS

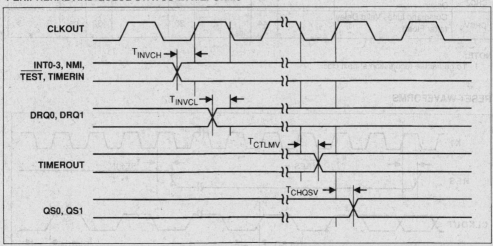

270354–43

1-113

A. C. CHARACTERISTICS

RESET AND HOLD/HLDA TIMINGS

$T_A = 0^\circ C$ to $+70^\circ C$, $V_{CC} = 5V \pm 10\%$ except $V_{CC} = 5V \pm 5\%$ at f > 12.5 MHz

All timings are measured at 1.5V and 100 pF loading on CLKOUT unless otherwise noted.
All output test conditions are with $C_L = 50\text{-}200$ pF (10 MHz) and $C_L = 50\text{-}100$ pF (12.5-16 MHz).
For A.C. tests, input $V_{IL} = 0.45V$ and $V_{IH} = 2.4V$ except at X1 where $V_{IH} = V_{CC}\text{-} 0.5V$.

Symbol	Parameter	80C186		80C186-12		80C186-16		Unit	Test Conditions
		Min	Max	Min	Max	Min	Max		
80C186 RESET AND HOLD/HLDA TIMING REQUIREMENTS									
T_{RESIN}	$\overline{RES}$ Setup	15		15		15		ns	
T_{HVCL}	HOLD Setup (1)	15		15		15		ns	
80C186 GENERAL TIMING RESPONSES (Listed More Than Once)									
T_{CLAZ}	Address Float Delay	T_{CLAX}	30	T_{CLAX}	25	T_{CLAX}	20	ns	
T_{CLAV}	Address Valid Delay	5	44	5	36	5	33	ns	
80C186 RESET AND HOLD/HLDA TIMING RESPONSES									
T_{CLRO}	Reset Delay		40		33		27	ns	
T_{CLHAV}	HLDA Valid Delay	3	40	3	33	3	25	ns	
T_{CHCZ}	Command Lines Float Delay		40		33		28	ns	
T_{CHCV}	Command Lines Valid Delay (after Float)		44		36		32	ns	

NOTE:
1. To guarantee recognition at next clock.

RESET WAVEFORMS

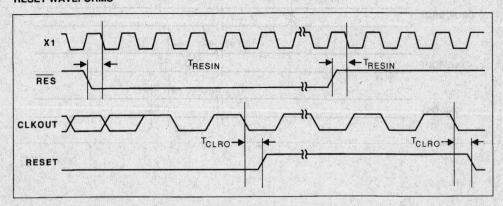

270354–44

A. C. CHARACTERISTICS

HOLD/HLDA WAVEFORMS (Entering Hold)

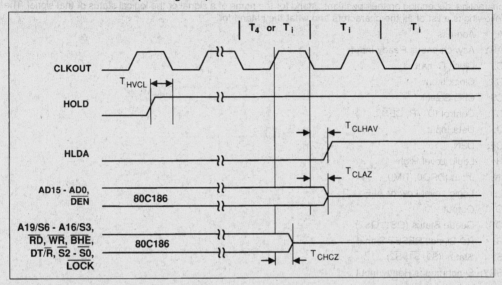

HOLD/HLDA WAVEFORMS (Leaving Hold)

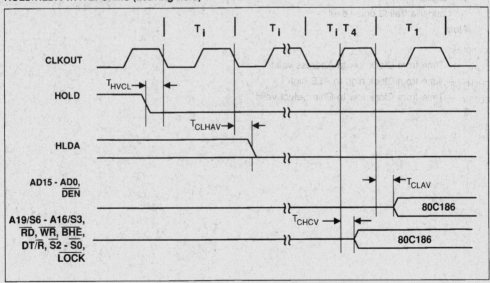

270354-45

EXPLANATION OF THE AC SYMBOLS

Each timing symbol has from 5 to 7 characters. The first character is always a 'T' (stands for time). The other characters, depending on their positions, stand for the name of a signal or the logical status of that signal. The following is a list of all the characters and what they stand for.

A: Address
ARY: Asynchronous Ready Input
C: Clock Output
CK: Clock Input
CS: Chip Select
CT: Control (DT/$\overline{R}$, $\overline{DEN}$, ...)
D: Data Input
DE: $\overline{DEN}$
H: Logic Level High
IN: Input (DRQ0, TIM0, ...)
L: Logic Level Low or ALE
O: Output
QS: Queue Status (QS1, QS2)
R: $\overline{RD}$ Signal, RESET Signal
S: Status ($\overline{S0}$, $\overline{S1}$, $\overline{S2}$)
SRY: Synchronous Ready Input
V: Valid
W: WR Signal
X: No Longer a Valid Logic Level
Z: Float

Examples:

T_{CLAV} — Time from Clock low to Address valid
T_{CHLH} — Time from Clock high to ALE high
T_{CLCSV} — Time from Clock low to Chip Select valid

WAVEFORMS (Continued)

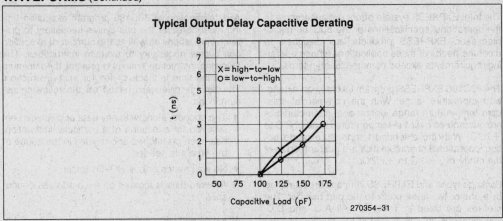

Figure 47. Capacitive Derating Curve

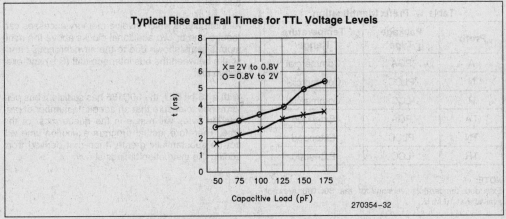

Figure 48. TTL Level Rise and Fall Times for Output Buffers

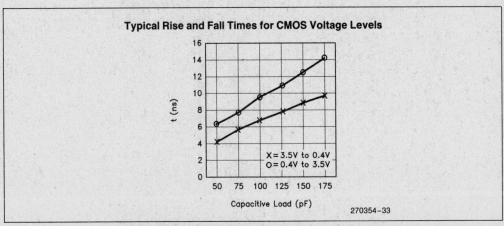

Figure 49. CMOS Level Rise and Fall Times for Output Buffers

80C186 EXPRESS

The Intel EXPRESS system offers enhancements to the operational specifications of the 80C186 microprocessor. EXPRESS products are designed to meet the needs of those applications whose operating requirements exceed commercial standards.

The 80C186 EXPRESS program includes an extended temperature range. With the commercial standard temperature range, operational characteristics are guaranteed over the temperature range of 0°C to +70°C. With the extended temperature range option, operational characteristics are guaranteed over the range of −40°C to +85°C.

Package types and EXPRESS versions are identified by a one or two-letter prefix to the part number. The prefixes are listed in Table 17. All A.C. and D.C. specifications not mentioned in this section are the same for both commercial and EXPRESS parts.

Table 17. Prefix Identification

Prefix	Package Type	Temperature Range
A	PGA	Commercial
N	PLCC	Commercial
R	LCC	Commercial
TA	PGA	Extended
TN	PLCC	Extended
TR	LCC	Extended

NOTE:
Extended temperature versions of the 80C186 are not available at 16 MHz.

80C186 EXECUTION TIMINGS

A determination of 80C186 program execution timing must consider the bus cycles necessary to prefetch instructions as well as the number of execution unit cycles necessary to execute instructions. The following instruction timings represent the minimum execution time in clock cycles for each instruction. The timings given are based on the following assumptions:

- The opcode, along with any data or displacement required for execution of a particular instruction, has been prefetched and resides in the queue at the time it is needed.
- No wait states or bus HOLDs occur.
- All word-data is located on even-address boundaries.

All jumps and calls include the time required to fetch the opcode of the next instruction at the destination address.

All instructions which involve memory accesses can require one or two additional clocks above the minimum timings shown due to the asynchronous handshake between the bus interface unit (BIU) and execution unit.

With a 16-bit BIU, the 80C186 has sufficient bus performance to ensure that an adequate number of prefetched bytes will reside in the queue most of the time. Therefore, actual program execution time will not be substantially greater than that derived from adding the instruction timings shown.

INSTRUCTION SET SUMMARY

Function	Format				Clock Cycles	Comments
DATA TRANSFER						
MOV = Move:						
Register to Register/Memory	1 0 0 0 1 0 0 w	mod reg r/m			2/12	
Register/memory to register	1 0 0 0 1 0 1 w	mod reg r/m			2/9	
Immediate to register/memory	1 1 0 0 0 1 1 w	mod 000 r/m	data	data if w = 1	12–13	8/16-bit
Immediate to register	1 0 1 1 w reg	data	data if w = 1		3–4	8/16-bit
Memory to accumulator	1 0 1 0 0 0 0 w	addr-low	addr-high		8	
Accumulator to memory	1 0 1 0 0 0 1 w	addr-low	addr-high		9	
Register/memory to segment register	1 0 0 0 1 1 1 0	mod 0 reg r/m			2/9	
Segment register to register/memory	1 0 0 0 1 1 0 0	mod 0 reg r/m			2/11	
PUSH = Push:						
Memory	1 1 1 1 1 1 1 1	mod 1 1 0 r/m			16	
Register	0 1 0 1 0 reg				10	
Segment register	0 0 0 reg 1 1 0				9	
Immediate	0 1 1 0 1 0 s 0	data	data if s = 0		10	
PUSHA = Push All	0 1 1 0 0 0 0 0				36	
POP = Pop:						
Memory	1 0 0 0 1 1 1 1	mod 0 0 0 r/m			20	
Register	0 1 0 1 1 reg				10	
Segment register	0 0 0 reg 1 1 1	(reg ≠ 01)			8	
POPA = Pop All	0 1 1 0 0 0 0 1				51	
XCHG = Exchange:						
Register/memory with register	1 0 0 0 0 1 1 w	mod reg r/m			4/17	
Register with accumulator	1 0 0 1 0 reg				3	
IN = Input from:						
Fixed port	1 1 1 0 0 1 0 w	port			10	
Variable port	1 1 1 0 1 1 0 w				8	
OUT = Output to:						
Fixed port	1 1 1 0 0 1 1 w	port			9	
Variable port	1 1 1 0 1 1 1 w				7	
XLAT = Translate byte to AL	1 1 0 1 0 1 1 1				11	
LEA = Load EA to register	1 0 0 0 1 1 0 1	mod reg r/m			6	
LDS = Load pointer to DS	1 1 0 0 0 1 0 1	mod reg r/m	(mod ≠ 11)		18	
LES = Load pointer to ES	1 1 0 0 0 1 0 0	mod reg r/m	(mod ≠ 11)		18	
LAHF = Load AH with flags	1 0 0 1 1 1 1 1				2	
SAHF = Store AH into flags	1 0 0 1 1 1 1 0				3	
PUSHF = Push flags	1 0 0 1 1 1 0 0				9	
POPF = Pop flags	1 0 0 1 1 1 0 1				8	

Shaded areas indicate instructions not available in 8086, 8088 microsystems.

INSTRUCTION SET SUMMARY (Continued)

Function	Format				Clock Cycles	Comments
DATA TRANSFER (Continued)						
SEGMENT = Segment Override:						
CS	`00101110`				2	
SS	`00110110`				2	
DS	`00111110`				2	
ES	`00100110`				2	
ARITHMETIC						
ADD = Add:						
Reg/memory with register to either	`000000dw`	mod reg r/m			3/10	
Immediate to register/memory	`100000sw`	mod 0 0 0 r/m	data	data if s w = 01	4/16	
Immediate to accumulator	`0000010w`	data	data if w = 1		3/4	8/16-bit
ADC = Add with carry:						
Reg/memory with register to either	`000100dw`	mod reg r/m			3/10	
Immediate to register/memory	`100000sw`	mod 0 1 0 r/m	data	data if s w = 01	4/16	
Immediate to accumulator	`0001010w`	data	data if w = 1		3/4	8/16-bit
INC = Increment:						
Register/memory	`1111111w`	mod 0 0 0 r/m			3/15	
Register	`01000 reg`				3	
SUB = Subtract:						
Reg/memory and register to either	`001010dw`	mod reg r/m			3/10	
Immediate from register/memory	`100000sw`	mod 1 0 1 r/m	data	data if s w = 01	4/16	
Immediate from accumulator	`0010110w`	data	data if w = 1		3/4	8/16-bit
SBB = Subtract with borrow:						
Reg/memory and register to either	`000110dw`	mod reg r/m			3/10	
Immediate from register/memory	`100000sw`	mod 0 1 1 r/m	data	data if s w = 01	4/16	
Immediate from accumulator	`0001110w`	data	data if w = 1		3/4	8/16-bit
DEC = Decrement						
Register/memory	`1111111w`	mod 0 0 1 r/m			3/15	
Register	`01001 reg`				3	
CMP = Compare:						
Register/memory with register	`0011101w`	mod reg r/m			3/10	
Register with register/memory	`0011100w`	mod reg r/m			3/10	
Immediate with register/memory	`100000sw`	mod 1 1 1 r/m	data	data if s w = 01	3/10	
Immediate with accumulator	`0011110w`	data	data if w = 1		3/4	8/16-bit
NEG = Change sign register/memory	`1111011w`	mod 0 1 1 r/m			3/10	
AAA = ASCII adjust for add	`00110111`				8	
DAA = Decimal adjust for add	`00100111`				4	
AAS = ASCII adjust for subtract	`00111111`				7	
DAS = Decimal adjust for subtract	`00101111`				4	
MUL = Multiply (unsigned):	`1111011w`	mod 100 r/m				
Register-Byte					26–28	
Register-Word					35–37	
Memory-Byte					32–34	
Memory-Word					41–43	

Shaded areas indicate instructions not available in 8086, 8088 microsystems.

INSTRUCTION SET SUMMARY (Continued)

Function	Format				Clock Cycles	Comments
ARITHMETIC (Continued)						
IMUL = Integer multiply (signed):	1 1 1 1 0 1 1 w	mod 1 0 1 r/m				
Register-Byte					25–28	
Register-Word					34–37	
Memory-Byte					31–34	
Memory-Word					40–43	
IMUL = Integer Immediate multiply (signed)	0 1 1 0 1 0 s 1	mod reg r/m	data	data if s = 0	22–25/ 29–32	
DIV = Divide (unsigned):	1 1 1 1 0 1 1 w	mod 1 1 0 r/m				
Register-Byte					29	
Register-Word					38	
Memory-Byte					35	
Memory-Word					44	
IDIV = Integer divide (signed):	1 1 1 1 0 1 1 w	mod 1 1 1 r/m				
Register-Byte					44–52	
Register-Word					53–61	
Memory-Byte					50–58	
Memory-Word					59–67	
AAM = ASCII adjust for multiply	1 1 0 1 0 1 0 0	0 0 0 0 1 0 1 0			19	
AAD = ASCII adjust for divide	1 1 0 1 0 1 0 1	0 0 0 0 1 0 1 0			15	
CBW = Convert byte to word	1 0 0 1 1 0 0 0				2	
CWD = Convert word to double word	1 0 0 1 1 0 0 1				4	
LOGIC						
Shift/Rotate Instructions:						
Register/Memory by 1	1 1 0 1 0 0 0 w	mod TTT r/m			2/15	
Register/Memory by CL	1 1 0 1 0 0 1 w	mod TTT r/m			5 + n/17 + n	
Register/Memory by Count	1 1 0 0 0 0 0 w	mod TTT r/m	count		5 + n/17 + n	

TTT Instruction

0 0 0	ROL
0 0 1	ROR
0 1 0	RCL
0 1 1	RCR
1 0 0	SHL/SAL
1 0 1	SHR
1 1 1	SAR

Function	Format				Clock Cycles	Comments
AND = And:						
Reg/memory and register to either	0 0 1 0 0 0 d w	mod reg r/m			3/10	
Immediate to register/memory	1 0 0 0 0 0 0 w	mod 1 0 0 r/m	data	data if w = 1	4/16	
Immediate to accumulator	0 0 1 0 0 1 0 w	data	data if w = 1		3/4	8/16-bit
TEST = And function to flags, no result:						
Register/memory and register	1 0 0 0 0 1 0 w	mod reg r/m			3/10	
Immediate data and register/memory	1 1 1 1 0 1 1 w	mod 0 0 0 r/m	data	data if w = 1	4/10	
Immediate data and accumulator	1 0 1 0 1 0 0 w	data	data if w = 1		3/4	8/16-bit
OR = Or:						
Reg/memory and register to either	0 0 0 0 1 0 d w	mod reg r/m			3/10	
Immediate to register/memory	1 0 0 0 0 0 0 w	mod 0 0 1 r/m	data	data if w = 1	4/16	
Immediate to accumulator	0 0 0 0 1 1 0 w	data	data if w = 1		3/4	8/16-bit

Shaded areas indicate instructions not available in 8086, 8088 microsystems.

INSTRUCTION SET SUMMARY (Continued)

Function	Format				Clock Cycles	Comments
LOGIC (Continued) **XOR** = Exclusive or:						
Reg/memory and register to either	0 0 1 1 0 0 d w	mod reg r/m			3/10	
Immediate to register/memory	1 0 0 0 0 0 0 w	mod 1 1 0 r/m	data	data if w = 1	4/16	
Immediate to accumulator	0 0 1 1 0 1 0 w	data	data if w = 1		3/4	8/16-bit
NOT = Invert register/memory	1 1 1 1 0 1 1 w	mod 0 1 0 r/m			3/10	
STRING MANIPULATION						
MOVS = Move byte/word	1 0 1 0 0 1 0 w				14	
CMPS = Compare byte/word	1 0 1 0 0 1 1 w				22	
SCAS = Scan byte/word	1 0 1 0 1 1 1 w				15	
LODS = Load byte/wd to AL/AX	1 0 1 0 1 1 0 w				12	
STOS = Store byte/wd from AL/AX	1 0 1 0 1 0 1 w				10	
INS = Input byte/wd from DX port	0 1 1 0 1 1 0 w				14	
OUTS = Output byte/wd to DX port	0 1 1 0 1 1 1 w				14	
Repeated by count in CX (REP/REPE/REPZ/REPNE/REPNZ)						
MOVS = Move string	1 1 1 1 0 0 1 0	1 0 1 0 0 1 0 w			8 + 8n	
CMPS = Compare string	1 1 1 1 0 0 1 z	1 0 1 0 0 1 1 w			5 + 22n	
SCAS = Scan string	1 1 1 1 0 0 1 z	1 0 1 0 1 1 1 w			5 + 15n	
LODS = Load string	1 1 1 1 0 0 1 0	1 0 1 0 1 1 0 w			6 + 11n	
STOS = Store string	1 1 1 1 0 0 1 0	1 0 1 0 1 0 1 w			6 + 9n	
INS = Input string	1 1 1 1 0 0 1 0	0 1 1 0 1 1 0 w			8 + 8n	
OUTS = Output string	1 1 1 1 0 0 1 0	0 1 1 0 1 1 1 w			8 + 8n	
CONTROL TRANSFER						
CALL = Call:						
Direct within segment	1 1 1 0 1 0 0 0	disp-low	disp-high		15	
Register/memory indirect within segment	1 1 1 1 1 1 1 1	mod 0 1 0 r/m			13/19	
Direct intersegment	1 0 0 1 1 0 1 0	segment offset			23	
		segment selector				
Indirect intersegment	1 1 1 1 1 1 1 1	mod 0 1 1 r/m	(mod ≠ 11)		38	
JMP = Unconditional jump:						
Short/long	1 1 1 0 1 0 1 1	disp-low			14	
Direct within segment	1 1 1 0 1 0 0 1	disp-low	disp-high		14	
Register/memory indirect within segment	1 1 1 1 1 1 1 1	mod 1 0 0 r/m			11/17	
Direct intersegment	1 1 1 0 1 0 1 0	segment offset			14	
		segment selector				
Indirect intersegment	1 1 1 1 1 1 1 1	mod 1 0 1 r/m	(mod ≠ 11)		26	

Shaded areas indicate instructions not available in 8086, 8088 microsystems.

INSTRUCTION SET SUMMARY (Continued)

Function	Format				Clock Cycles	Comments
CONTROL TRANSFER (Continued)						
RET = **Return from CALL:**						
Within segment	11000011				16	
Within seg adding immed to SP	11000010	data-low	data-high		18	
Intersegment	11001011				22	
Intersegment adding immediate to SP	11001010	data-low	data-high		25	
JE/JZ = Jump on equal/zero	01110100	disp			4/13	JMP not taken/JMP taken
JL/JNGE = Jump on less/not greater or equal	01111100	disp			4/13	
JLE/JNG = Jump on less or equal/not greater	01111110	disp			4/13	
JB/JNAE = Jump on below/not above or equal	01110010	disp			4/13	
JBE/JNA = Jump on below or equal/not above	01110110	disp			4/13	
JP/JPE = Jump on parity/parity even	01111010	disp			4/13	
JO = Jump on overflow	01110000	disp			4/13	
JS = Jump on sign	01111000	disp			4/13	
JNE/JNZ = Jump on not equal/not zero	01110101	disp			4/13	
JNL/JGE = Jump on not less/greater or equal	01111101	disp			4/13	
JNLE/JG = Jump on not less or equal/greater	01111111	disp			4/13	
JNB/JAE = Jump on not below/above or equal	01110011	disp			4/13	
JNBE/JA = Jump on not below or equal/above	01110111	disp			4/13	
JNP/JPO = Jump on not par/par odd	01111011	disp			4/13	
JNO = Jump on not overflow	01110001	disp			4/13	
JNS = Jump on not sign	01111001	disp			4/13	
JCXZ = Jump on CX zero	11100011	disp			5/15	
LOOP = Loop CX times	11100010	disp			6/16	LOOP not taken/LOOP taken
LOOPZ/LOOPE = Loop while zero/equal	11100001	disp			6/16	
LOOPNZ/LOOPNE = Loop while not zero/equal	11100000	disp			6/16	
ENTER = Enter Procedure	11001000	data-low	data-high	L		
L = 0					15	
L = 1					25	
L > 1					22 + 16(n − 1)	
LEAVE = Leave Procedure	11001001				8	
INT = **Interrupt:**						
Type specified	11001101	type			47	
Type 3	11001100				45	if INT. taken/ if INT. not taken
INTO = Interrupt on overflow	11001110				48/4	
IRET = Interrupt return	11001111				28	
BOUND = Detect value out of range	01100010	mod reg r/m			33–35	

Shaded areas indicate instructions not available in 8086, 8088 microsystems.

INSTRUCTION SET SUMMARY (Continued)

Function	Format	Clock Cycles	Comments
PROCESSOR CONTROL			
CLC = Clear carry	`1 1 1 1 1 0 0 0`	2	
CMC = Complement carry	`1 1 1 1 0 1 0 1`	2	
STC = Set carry	`1 1 1 1 1 0 0 1`	2	
CLD = Clear direction	`1 1 1 1 1 1 0 0`	2	
STD = Set direction	`1 1 1 1 1 1 0 1`	2	
CLI = Clear interrupt	`1 1 1 1 1 0 1 0`	2	
STI = Set interrupt	`1 1 1 1 1 0 1 1`	2	
HLT = Halt	`1 1 1 1 0 1 0 0`	2	
WAIT = Wait	`1 0 0 1 1 0 1 1`	6	if $\overline{TEST}$ = 0
LOCK = Bus lock prefix	`1 1 1 1 0 0 0 0`	2	
NOP = No Operation	`1 0 0 1 0 0 0 0`	3	

(TTT LLL are opcode to processor extension)

Shaded areas indicate instructions not available in 8086, 8088 microsystems.

FOOTNOTES

The Effective Address (EA) of the memory operand is computed according to the mod and r/m fields:

if mod	=	11 then r/m is treated as a REG field
if mod	=	00 then DISP = 0*, disp-low and disp-high are absent
if mod	=	01 then DISP = disp-low sign-extended to 16-bits, disp-high is absent
if mod	=	10 then DISP = disp-high: disp-low
if r/m	=	000 then EA = (BX) + (SI) + DISP
if r/m	=	001 then EA = (BX) + (DI) + DISP
if r/m	=	010 then EA = (BP) + (SI) + DISP
if r/m	=	011 then EA = (BP) + (DI) + DISP
if r/m	=	100 then EA = (SI) + DISP
if r/m	=	101 then EA = (DI) + DISP
if r/m	=	110 then EA = (BP) + DISP*
if r/m	=	111 then EA = (BX) + DISP

DISP follows 2nd byte of instruction (before data if required)

*except if mod = 00 and r/m = 110 then EA = disp-high: disp-low.

EA calculation time is 4 clock cycles for all modes, and is included in the execution times given whenever appropriate.

Segment Override Prefix

`0  0  1  reg  1  1  0`

reg is assigned according to the following:

reg	Segment Register
00	ES
01	CS
10	SS
11	DS

REG is assigned according to the following table:

16-Bit (w = 1)	8-Bit (w = 0)
000 AX	000 AL
001 CX	001 CL
010 DX	010 DL
011 BX	011 BL
100 SP	100 AH
101 BP	101 CH
110 SI	110 DH
111 DI	111 BH

The physical addresses of all operands addressed by the BP register are computed using the SS segment register. The physical addresses of the destination operands of the string primitive operations (those addressed by the DI register) are computed using the ES segment, which may not be overridden.

REVISION HISTORY

The sections significantly revised since version -004 are:

Pin Description Table
Added note to $\overline{\text{TEST}}$/BUSY pin requiring proper RESET at power-up to configure pin as input.
Renamed pin 44 to INT1/$\overline{\text{SELECT}}$ and pin 41 to INT3/$\overline{\text{INTA1}}$/IRQ to better describe their functions in Slave Mode.

Initialization and Processor Reset Added reminder to drive $\overline{\text{RES}}$ pin LOW during power-up.

Read and Write Cycle Waveforms Clarified applicability of T_{CLCSV} to latched A1 and A2 in footnotes.

Slave Mode Operation
The three low order bits associated with vector generation and performing EOI are not alterable; however, the priority levels are programmable. This information is a clarification only.

The sections significantly revised since version -003 are:

Front Page
Deleted references to burn-in devices.

Local Bus Controller and Reset Clarified effects of excessive loading on pins with internal pullup devices. Equivalent resistance no longer shown.

D.C. Characteristics
Renamed V_{CLI} to V_{IL1}. Renamed V_{CHI} to V_{IH3}. Changed V_{OH} (min.) from 0.8 V_{CC} to V_{CC} − 0.5V. Changed I_{CC} (max.) from 180 mA to 150 mA at 16 MHz, 150 mA to 120 mA at 12.5 mA, and 100 mA to 120 mA at 10 MHz. Changed V_{CLO} (max.) from 0.5V to 0.45V. Changed V_{CHO} (min.) from 0.8 V_{CC} to V_{CC} − 0.5V. Clarified effect of excessive loading on pins with internal pullup devices.

Power Supply Current
Added equation and graph for maximum current.

A.C. Characteristics
Many timings changed (all listed in ns): T_{DVCL} (min.) at 16 MHz from 10 to 15; T_{CLDX} (min.) from 5 to 3; T_{CLAV} (max.) at 10 MHz from 50 to 44; T_{CHCV} (max.) from 45 to 44 at 10 MHz, and from 37 to 36 at 12.5 MHz; T_{LHLL} (min.) from T_{CLCL} − 30 to T_{CLCL} − 15; T_{LLAX} (min.) at 10 MHz from T_{CHCL} − 20 to T_{CHCL} − 15; T_{CVCTV} (max.) from 56 to 44 at 10 MHz and from 47 to 37 at 12.5 MHz; T_{CVDEX} (max.) from 56 to 44 at 10 MHz, 47 to 37 at 12.5 MHz, and from 35 to 31 at 16 MHz; T_{RHAV} (min.) from T_{CLCL} − 40 at 10 MHz and T_{CLCL} − 20 at 12.5 MHz and 16 MHz to T_{CLCL} − 15 at all frequencies; T_{RLRH} (min.) from 2 T_{CLCL} − 46 to 2 T_{CLCL} − 30 at 10 MHz, from 2 T_{CLCL} − 40 to 2 T_{CLCL} − 25 at 12.5 MHz, and 2 T_{CLCL} − 30 to 2 T_{CLCL} − 25 at 16 MHz; T_{WLWH} (min.) from 2 T_{CLCL} − 34 to 2 T_{CLCL} − 30 at 10 MHz, and 2 T_{CLCL} − 30 to 2 T_{CLCL} − 25 at 12.5 MHz; T_{AVLL} (min.) from T_{CLCH} − 19 to T_{CLCH} − 18 at 10 MHz; T_{CLSH} (max.) at 10 MHz from 50 to 46; T_{CLTMV} (max.) from 48 to 40 at 10 MHz, 40 to 33 at 12.5 MHz, and 30 to 27 at 16 MHz; T_{CLRO} (max.) from 48 to 40 at 10 MHz, 40 to 33 at 12.5 MHz, and 30 to 27 at 16 MHz; T_{CHQSV} (max.) from 28 to 37 at 10 MHz, 28 to 32 at 12.5 MHz, and 25 to 30 at 16 MHz; T_{CHDX} (min.) from 5 to 10; T_{CLLV} (max.) at 10 MHz from 45 to 40 and at 12.5 MHz from 40 to 37; T_{CLCSV} (max.) from 45 to 42 at 10 MHz; T_{CHCSX} (max.) from 32 to 35 at 10 MHz, 28 to 30 at 12.5 MHz, and 23 to 25 at 16 MHz; and T_{CH1CH2} and T_{CL2CL1} (max.) at 16 MHz from 8 to 10. Added new timings for T_{WHDEX}, T_{RHLH}, and T_{WHLH}. Established min. timing for T_{CLCSV}.

Timing Waveforms
Section rearranged to show waveforms on same or facing page relative to corresponding tabular data. T_{CLSRY} drawn to same clock edge as T_{SRYCL}. Drawing changed to indicate one less clock between HOLD inactive and HLDA inactive.

Specification Level Markings
New Section.

The sections significantly revised since version -002 are:

Block Diagram	Redrawn to illustrate numerics coprocessor interface.
Pin Description Table	Various descriptions rewritten for clarity.
Interrupt Vector Table	Redrawn for clarity. Interrupt Type 16 listed.
ESC Opcode Exception Description	Note added concerning ESC trap.
Oscillator Configurations	Deleted drive of X2 with inverted X1.
RESET Logic	Deleted paragraph concerning setup times for synchronization of multiple processors.
Local Bus Arbitration	Added description of HLDA when a refresh cycle is pending.
Local Bus Controller and Reset	Added description of pullup devices for appropriate pins.
DMA Controller	Added reminder to initialize transfer count registers and pointer registers.
Timers	Added reminder to intialize count registers.
DRAM Refresh Addresses	Refresh address counter described in figure.
D.C. Characteristics	V_{IH2} indicated for SRDY, ARDY. I_{CC} (max.) now indicated for all devices.
Power Supply Current	Typical I_{CC} indicated.
A.C. Characteristics	Input V_{IH} test condition at X1 added. T_{CLDOX}, T_{CVCTV}, T_{CVCTX}, T_{CLHAV}, and T_{CLLV} minimums reduced from 5 ns to 3 ns. T_{CLCH} (min.) and T_{CHCL} (min.) relaxed by 2 ns. Added reminder that T_{SRYCL} and T_{CLSRY} must be met.
Explanation of the A.C. Symbols	New Section.
Major Cycle Timing Waveforms	T_{DXDL} indicated in Read Cycle. T_{CLRO} indicated.
Rise/Fall and Capacitive Derating Curves	New Figures added.
Instruction Set Summary	ESC instruction clock count deleted.

The sections significantly revised since version -001 are:

Pin Description Table	Noted $\overline{RES}$ to be low more than 4 clocks.
Oscillator Configurations	Added reminder not to drive X2.
DMA Transfer Rate Table	Corrected to reflect 16 MHz capability.
DMA Control Bit Descriptions	Moved and clarified note concerning TC condition for ST/$\overline{STOP}$ clearing during unsynchronized transfers.
Interrupt Controller, etc.	Renamed iRMX Mode to Slave Mode.
Interrupt Request Register	Noted that D0 and D1 are read/write, others read-only.
DRAM Refresh Addresses	Added figure to explain refresh address bits.
A.C. Characteristics	Many timings changed (all listed in ns): T_{CLDX} (min.) from 8 to 5; T_{SRYCL} (min.) from 20 to 15; T_{HVCL} (min.) from 20 to 15; T_{INVCH} (min.) from 25 to 15; T_{INVCL} (min.) from 20 to 15; T_{CLAV} at 12.5 MHz from 4–33 to 5–36; T_{CLAV} at 16 MHz from 4–30 to 5–33; T_{CLAX} (min.) to 0; T_{CLDV} (min.) at 10 MHz from 10 to 5; T_{CLDV} (min.) at 12.5 MHz from 10–33 to 5–36; T_{CLDV} (min.) at 16 MHz from 10–30 to 5–33; T_{CLDOX} (min.) from 10 at 10 MHz and 8 at 12.5 MHz to 5 at both frequencies; T_{CVCTV} (max.) and T_{CHCTV} (max.) at 16 MHz from 25 to 31; T_{CHCTV} (min.) and T_{CVDEX} (min.) both from 10 at 10 MHz and 8 at 12.5 MHz to 5 at both frequencies; T_{CVCTX} (max.) at 16 MHz from 25 to 33; T_{CLRL} at 10 MHz from 10–56 to 5–44; T_{CLRL} at 12.5 MHz from 8–47 to 5–35; T_{CLRL} (max.) at 16 MHz from 25 to 31; T_{CLRH} (min.) at 10 MHz from 10 to 5 and at 12.5 MHz from 8 to 5; T_{CHSV} (min.) at 10 MHz from 10 to 5 and at 12.5 MHz from 8 to 5; T_{CHSV} (max.) at 16 MHz from 25 to 31; T_{CLSH} (min.) at 10 MHz from 10 to 5 and at 12.5 MHz from 8 to 5; T_{CHQSV} (max.) at 12.5 MHz from 23 to 28 and at 16 MHz from 23 to 25; T_{CHDX} (min.) at 10 MHz from 10 to 5 and at 12.5 MHz from 8 to 5; T_{AVCH} (min.) to 0; T_{CLLV} (max.) at 10 MHz from 60 to 45 and at 12.5 MHz from 55 to 40 and at 16 MHz from 40 to 35; T_{DXDL} (min.) to 0; T_{CXCSX} (min.) from 35 at 10 MHz and 29 at 12.5 MHz and 25 at 16 MHz to T_{CLCH} − 10 at all frequencies; T_{CHCSX} (min.) at 12.5 MHz and 16 MHz from 4–23 to 5–28 and 5–23 respectively.
Execution Timings	Clarified effect of bus width.

SPECIFICATION LEVEL MARKINGS

Current 80C186 devices bear backside lot code information consisting of seven digits followed by letters. The second, third, and fourth digits comprise a manufacturing date code. This preliminary data sheet applies only to 80C186 devices with a date code corresponding to week 25 of 1989 (backside markings x925xxx XXX) or later.

80C187
80-BIT MATH COPROCESSOR

- **High Performance 80-Bit Internal Architecture**
- **Two to Three Times 8087 Performance at Equivalent Clock Speed**
- **Implements ANSI/IEEE Standard 754-1985 for Binary Floating-Point Arithmetic**
- **Upward Object-Code Compatible from 8087**
- **Fully Compatible with 387™DX and 387™SX Math Coprocessors. Implements all 387 Architectural Enhancements over 8087**
- **Directly Interfaces with 80C186 CPU**
- **80C186/80C187 Provide a Software/ Binary Compatible Upgrade from 80186/82188/8087 Systems**

- **Expands 80C186's Data Types to Include 32-, 64-, 80-Bit Floating-Point, 32-, 64-Bit Integers and 18-Digit BCD Operands**
- **Directly Extends 80C186's Instruction Set to Trigonometric, Logarithmic, Exponential, and Arithmetic Instructions for All Data Types**
- **Full-Range Transcendental Operations for SINE, COSINE, TANGENT, ARCTANGENT, and LOGARITHM**
- **Built-In Exception Handling**
- **Eight 80-Bit Numeric Registers, Usable as Individually Addressable General Registers or as a Register Stack**
- **Available in 40-Pin CERDIP and 44-Pin PLCC Package**

(See Packaging Outlines and Dimensions, Order #231369)

The Intel 80C187 is a high-performance math coprocessor that extends the architecture of the 80C186 with floating-point, extended integer, and BCD data types. A computing system that includes the 80C187 fully conforms to the IEEE Floating-Point Standard. The 80C187 adds over seventy mnemonics to the instruction set of the 80C186, including support for arithmetic, logarithmic, exponential, and trigonometric mathematical operations. The 80C187 is implemented with 1.5 micron, high-speed CHMOS III technology and packaged in both a 40-pin CERDIP and a 44-pin PLCC package. The 80C187 is upward object-code compatible from the 8087 math coprocessor and completely object-code compatible with the 80387DX and 80387SX math coprocessors.

September 1989
Order Number: 270640-003

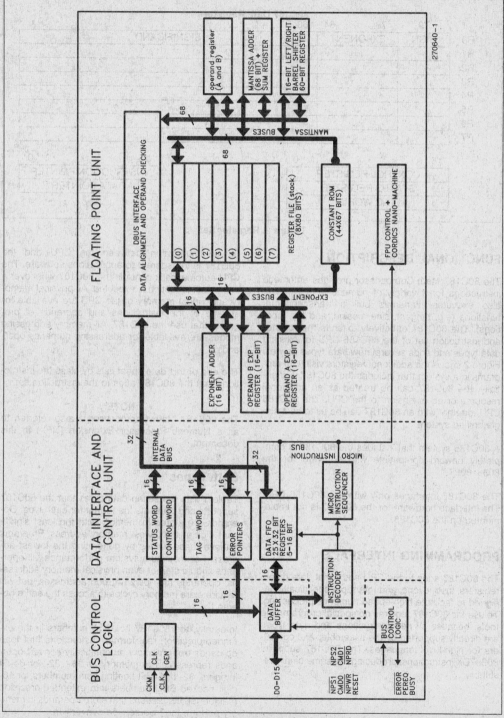

270640-1

Figure 1. 80C187 Block Diagram

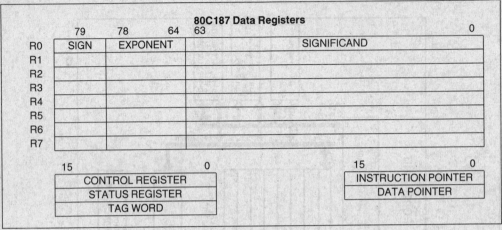

Figure 2. Register Set

FUNCTIONAL DESCRIPTION

The 80C187 Math Coprocessor provides arithmetic instructions for a variety of numeric data types. It also executes numerous built-in transcendental functions (e.g. tangent, sine, cosine, and log functions). The 80C187 effectively extends the register and instruction set of the 80C186 CPU for existing data types and adds several new data types as well. Figure 2 shows the additional registers visible to programs in a system that includes the 80C187. Essentially, the 80C187 can be treated as an additional resource or an extension to the CPU. The 80C186 CPU together with an 80C187 can be used as a single unified system.

A 80C186 system that includes the 80C187 is completely upward compatible with software for the 8086/8087.

The 80C187 interfaces only with the 80C186 CPU. The interface hardware for the 80C187 is not implemented on the 80C188.

PROGRAMMING INTERFACE

The 80C187 adds to the CPU additional data types, registers, instructions, and interrupts specifically designed to facilitate high-speed numerics processing. To use the 80C187 requires no special programming tools, because all new instructions and data types are directly supported by the assembler and compilers for high-level languages. The 80C187 supports 80387DX instructions, producing the same binary results.

All communication between the CPU and the 80C187 is transparent to applications software. The CPU automatically controls the 80C187 whenever a numerics instruction is executed. All physical memory and virtual memory of the CPU are available for storage of the instructions and operands of programs that use the 80C187. All memory addressing modes are available for addressing numerics operands.

The end of this data sheet lists by class the instructions that the 80C187 adds to the instruction set.

NOTE:
The 80C187 Math Coprocessor is also referred to as a Numeric Processor Extension (NPX) in this document.

Data Types

Table 1 lists the seven data types that the 80C187 supports and presents the format for each type. Operands are stored in memory with the least significant digit at the lowest memory address. Programs retrieve these values by generating the lowest address. For maximum system performance, all operands should start at even physical-memory addresses; operands may begin at odd addresses, but will require extra memory cycles to access the entire operand.

Internally, the 80C187 holds all numbers in the extended-precision real format. Instructions that load operands from memory automatically convert operands represented in memory as 16-, 32-, or 64-bit integers, 32- or 64-bit floating-point numbers, or 18-digit packed BCD numbers into extended-precision real format. Instructions that store operands in memory perform the inverse type conversion.

Numeric Operands

A typical NPX instruction accepts one or two operands and produces one (or sometimes two) results. In two-operand instructions, one operand is the contents of an NPX register, while the other may be a memory location. The operands of some instructions are predefined; for example, FSQRT always takes the square root of the number in the top stack element (refer to the section on Data Registers).

Register Set

Figure 2 shows the 80C187 register set. When an 80C187 is present in a system, programmers may use these registers in addition to the registers normally available on the CPU.

DATA REGISTERS

80C187 computations use the extended-precision real data type.

Table 1. Data Type Representation in Memory

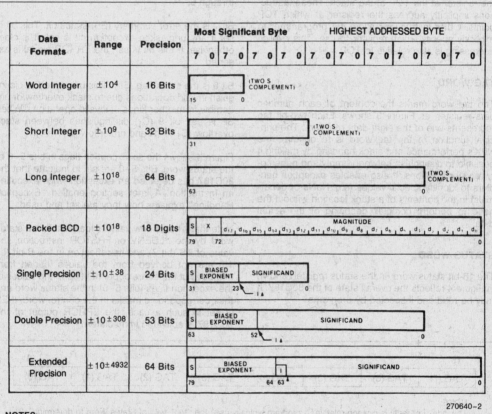

270640–2

NOTES:
1. S = Sign bit (0 = Positive, 1 = Negative)
2. d_n = Decimal digit (two per byte)
3. X = Bits have no significance; 80C187 ignores when loading, zeros when storing
4. ▲ = Position of implicit binary point
5. I = Integer bit of significand; stored in temporary real, implicit in single and double precision
6. Exponent Bias (normalized values):
   Single: 127 (7FH)
   Double: 1023 (3FFH)
   Extended Real: 16383 (3FFFH)
7. Packed BCD: $(-1)^S (D_{17} \ldots D_0)$
8. Real: $(-1)^S (2^{E-BIAS}) (F_0, F_1 \ldots)$

The 80C187 register set can be accessed either as a stack, with instructions operating on the top one or two stack elements, or as individually addressable registers. The TOP field in the status word identifies the current top-of-stack register. A "push" operation decrements TOP by one and loads a value into the new top register. A "pop" operation stores the value from the current top register and then increments TOP by one. The 80C187 register stack grows "down" toward lower-addressed registers.

Instructions may address the data registers either implicitly or explicitly. Many instructions operate on the register at the TOP of the stack. These instructions implicitly address the register at which TOP points. Other instructions allow the programmer to explicitly specify which register to use. This explicit addressing is also relative to TOP.

TAG WORD

The tag word marks the content of each numeric data register, as Figure 3 shows. Each two-bit tag represents one of the eight data registers. The principal function of the tag word is to optimize the NPX's performance and stack handling by making it possible to distinguish between empty and nonempty register locations. It also enables exception handlers to identify special values (e.g. NaNs or denormals) in the contents of a stack location without the need to perform complex decoding of the actual data.

STATUS WORD

The 16-bit status word (in the status register) shown in Figure 4 reflects the overall state of the 80C187. It may be read and inspected by programs.

Bit 15, the B-bit (busy bit) is included for 8087 compatibility only. It always has the same value as the ES bit (bit 7 of the status word); it does **not** indicate the status of the BUSY output of 80C187.

Bits 13–11 (TOP) point to the 80C187 register that is the current top-of-stack.

The four numeric condition code bits (C_3–C_0) are similar to the flags in a CPU; instructions that perform arithmetic operations update these bits to reflect the outcome. The effects of these instructions on the condition code are summarized in Tables 2 through 5.

Bit 7 is the error summary (ES) status bit. This bit is set if any unmasked exception bit is set; it is clear otherwise. If this bit is set, the $\overline{\text{ERROR}}$ signal is asserted.

Bit 6 is the stack flag (SF). This bit is used to distinguish invalid operations due to stack overflow or underflow from other kinds of invalid operations. When SF is set, bit 9 (C_1) distinguishes between stack overflow ($C_1 = 1$) and underflow ($C_1 = 0$).

Figure 4 shows the six exception flags in bits 5–0 of the status word. Bits 5–0 are set to indicate that the 80C187 has detected an exception while executing an instruction. A later section entitled "Exception Handling" explains how they are set and used.

Note that when a new value is loaded into the status word by the FLDENV or FRSTOR instruction, the value of ES (bit 7) and its reflection in the B-bit (bit 15) are not derived from the values loaded from memory but rather are dependent upon the values of the exception flags (bits 5–0) in the status word and their corresponding masks in the control word. If ES is set in such a case, the $\overline{\text{ERROR}}$ output of the 80C187 is activated immediately.

15							0
TAG (7)	TAG (6)	TAG (5)	TAG (4)	TAG (3)	TAG (2)	TAG (1)	TAG (0)

NOTE:
The index i of tag(i) is **not** top-relative. A program typically uses the "top" field of Status Word to determine which tag(i) field refers to logical top of stack.
TAG VALUES:
   00 = Valid
   01 = Zero
   10 = QNaN, SNaN, Infinity, Denormal and Unsupported Formats
   11 = Empty

Figure 3. Tag Word

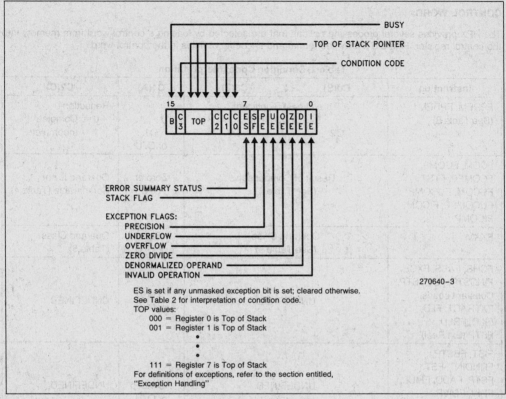

ERROR SUMMARY STATUS
STACK FLAG

EXCEPTION FLAGS:
PRECISION
UNDERFLOW
OVERFLOW
ZERO DIVIDE
DENORMALIZED OPERAND
INVALID OPERATION

270640–3

ES is set if any unmasked exception bit is set; cleared otherwise.
See Table 2 for interpretation of condition code.
TOP values:
    000 = Register 0 is Top of Stack
    001 = Register 1 is Top of Stack
        •
        •
        •
    111 = Register 7 is Top of Stack
For definitions of exceptions, refer to the section entitled,
"Exception Handling"

Figure 4. Status Word

CONTROL WORD

The NPX provides several processing options that are selected by loading a control word from memory into the control register. Figure 5 shows the format and encoding of fields in the control word.

Table 2. Condition Code Interpretation

Instruction	C0(S)	C3(Z)	C1(A)	C2(C)
FPREM, FPREM1 (See Table 3)	Three Least Significant Bits of Quotient Q2 Q0		Q1 or O/$\overline{U}$	Reduction 0 = Complete 1 = Incomplete
FCOM, FCOMP, FCOMPP, FTST FUCOM, FUCOMP, FUCOMPP, FICOM, FICOMP	Result of Comparison (See Table 4)		Zero or O/$\overline{U}$	Operand is not Comparable (Table 4)
FXAM	Operand Class (See Table 5)		Sign or O/$\overline{U}$	Operand Class (Table 5)
FCHS, FABS, FXCH, FINCSTP, FDECSTP, Constant Loads, FXTRACT, FLD, FILD, FBLD, FSTP (Ext Real)	UNDEFINED		Zero or O/$\overline{U}$	UNDEFINED
FIST, FBSTP, FRNDINT, FST, FSTP, FADD, FMUL, FDIV, FDIVR, FSUB, FSUBR, FSCALE, FSQRT, FPATAN, F2XM1, FYL2X, FYL2XP1	UNDEFINED		Roundup or O/$\overline{U}$	UNDEFINED
FPTAN, FSIN, FCOS, FSINCOS	UNDEFINED		Roundup or O/$\overline{U}$, Undefined if C2 = 1	Reduction 0 = Complete 1 = Incomplete
FLDENV, FRSTOR	Each Bit Loaded from Memory			
FLDCW, FSTENV, FSTCW, FSTSW, FCLEX, FINIT, FSAVE	UNDEFINED			

O/$\overline{U}$ When both IE and SF bits of status word are set, indicating a stack exception, this bit distinguishes between stack overflow (C1 = 1) and underflow (C1 = 0).

Reduction   If FPREM or FPREM1 produces a remainder that is less than the modulus, reduction is complete. When reduction is incomplete the value at the top of the stack is a partial remainder, which can be used as input to further reduction. For FPTAN, FSIN, FCOS, and FSINCOS, the reduction bit is set if the operand at the top of the stack is too large. In this case the original operand remains at the top of the stack.

Roundup   When the PE bit of the status word is set, this bit indicates whether one was added to the least significant bit of the result during the last rounding.

UNDEFINED   Do not rely on finding any specific value in these bits.

The low-order byte of this control word configures exception masking. Bits 5–0 of the control word contain individual masks for each of the six exceptions that the 80C187 recognizes.

The high-order byte of the control word configures the 80C187 operating mode, including precision, rounding, and infinity control.

- The "infinity control bit" (bit 12) is not meaningful to the 80C187, and programs must ignore its value. To maintain compatibility with the 8087, this bit can be programmed; however, regardless of its value, the 80C187 always treats infinity in the affine sense ($-\infty < +\infty$). This bit is initialized to zero both after a hardware reset and after the FINIT instruction.

- The rounding control (RC) bits (bits 11–10) provide for directed rounding and true chop, as well as the unbiased round to nearest even mode specified in the IEEE standard. Rounding control affects only those instructions that perform rounding at the end of the operation (and thus can generate a precision exception); namely, FST, FSTP, FIST, all arithmetic instructions (except FPREM, FPREM1, FXTRACT, FABS, and FCHS), and all transcendental instructions.

- The precision control (PC) bits (bits 9–8) can be used to set the 80C187 internal operating precision of the significand at less than the default of 64 bits (extended precision). This can be useful in providing compatibility with early generation arithmetic processors of smaller precision. PC affects only the instructions ADD, SUB, DIV, MUL, and SQRT. For all other instructions, either the precision is determined by the opcode or extended precision is used.

Table 3. Condition Code Interpretation after FPREM and FPREM1 Instructions

Condition Code				Interpretation after FPREM and FPREM1
C2	C3	C1	C0	
1	X	X	X	Incomplete Reduction: Further Iteration Required for Complete Reduction
	Q1	Q0	Q2	Q MOD 8	
0	0	0	0	0	Complete Reduction: C0, C3, C1 Contain Three Least Significant Bits of Quotient
	0	1	0	1	
	1	0	0	2	
	1	1	0	3	
	0	0	1	4	
	0	1	1	5	
	1	0	1	6	
	1	1	1	7	

Table 4. Condition Code Resulting from Comparison

Order	C3	C2	C0
TOP > Operand	0	0	0
TOP < Operand	0	0	1
TOP = Operand	1	0	0
Unordered	1	1	1

Table 5. Condition Code Defining Operand Class

C3	C2	C1	C0	Value at TOP
0	0	0	0	+ Unsupported
0	0	0	1	+ NaN
0	0	1	0	− Unsupported
0	0	1	1	− NaN
0	1	0	0	+ Normal
0	1	0	1	+ Infinity
0	1	1	0	− Normal
0	1	1	1	− Infinity
1	0	0	0	+ 0
1	0	0	1	+ Empty
1	0	1	0	− 0
1	0	1	1	− Empty
1	1	0	0	+ Denormal
1	1	1	1	− Denormal

INSTRUCTION AND DATA POINTERS

Because the NPX operates in parallel with the CPU, any exceptions detected by the NPX may be reported after the CPU has executed the ESC instruction which caused it. To allow identification of the failing numerics instruction, the 80C187 contains registers that aid in diagnosis. These registers supply the opcode of the failing numerics instruction, the address of the instruction, and the address of its numerics memory operand (if appropriate).

The instruction and data pointers are provided for user-written exception handlers. Whenever the 80C187 executes a new ESC instruction, it saves the address of the instruction (including any prefixes that may be present), the address of the operand (if present), and the opcode.

The instruction and data pointers appear in the format shown by Figure 6. The ESC instruction FLDENV, FSTENV, FSAVE and FRSTOR are used to transfer these values between the registers and memory. Note that the value of the data pointer is *undefined* if the prior ESC instruction did not have a memory operand.

Interrupt Description

CPU interrupt 16 is used to report exceptional conditions while executing numeric programs. Interrupt 16 indicates that the previous numerics instruction caused an unmasked exception. The address of the faulty instruction and the address of its operand are stored in the instruction pointer and data pointer registers. Only ESC instructions can cause this inter-

rupt. The CPU return address pushed onto the stack of the exception handler points to an ESC instruction (including prefixes). This instruction can be restarted after clearing the exception condition in the NPX. FNINIT, FNCLEX, FNSTSW, FNSTENV, and FNSAVE cannot cause this interrupt.

Exception Handling

The 80C187 detects six different exception conditions that can occur during instruction execution. Table 6 lists the exception conditions in order of precedence, showing for each the cause and the default action taken by the 80C187 if the exception is masked by its corresponding mask bit in the control word.

Any exception that is not masked by the control word sets the corresponding exception flag of the status word, sets the ES bit of the status word, and asserts the $\overline{ERROR}$ signal. When the CPU attempts to execute another ESC instruction, interrupt 16 occurs. The exception condition must be resolved via an interrupt service routine. The return address pushed onto the CPU stack upon entry to the service routine does not necessarily point to the failing instruction nor to the following instruction. The 80C187 saves the address of the floating-point instruction that caused the exception and the address of any memory operand required by that instruction.

If error trapping is required at the end of a series of numerics instructions (specifically, when the last ESC instruction modifies memory data and that data is used in subsequent nonnumerics instructions), it is necessary to insert the FNOP instruction to force the 80C187 to check its $\overline{ERROR}$ input.

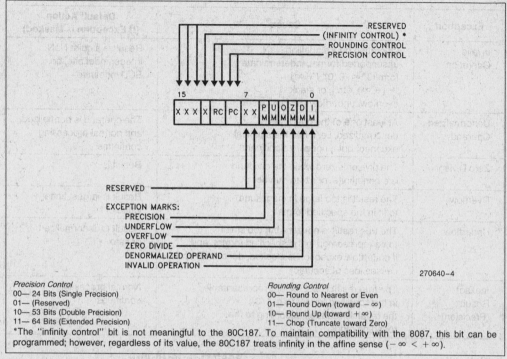

Precision Control
00— 24 Bits (Single Precision)
01— (Reserved)
10— 53 Bits (Double Precision)
11— 64 Bits (Extended Precision)

Rounding Control
00— Round to Nearest or Even
01— Round Down (toward $-\infty$)
10— Round Up (toward $+\infty$)
11— Chop (Truncate toward Zero)

270640–4

*The "infinity control" bit is not meaningful to the 80C187. To maintain compatibility with the 8087, this bit can be programmed; however, regardless of its value, the 80C187 treats infinity in the affine sense ($-\infty < +\infty$).

Figure 5. Control Word

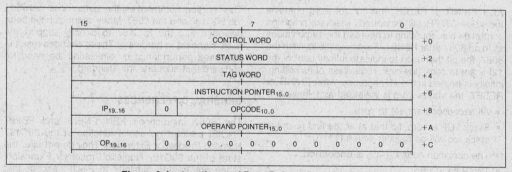

Figure 6. Instruction and Data Pointer Image in Memory

Table 6. Exceptions

Exception	Cause	Default Action (If Exception is Masked)
Invalid Operation	Operation on a signalling NaN, unsupported format, indeterminate form ($0^* \infty$, 0/0), ($+ \infty$) $+ (- \infty)$, etc.), or stack overflow/underflow (SF is also set)	Result is a quiet NaN, integer indefinite, or BCD indefinite
Denormalized Operand	At least one of the operands is denormalized, i.e. it has the smallest exponent but a nonzero significand	The operand is normalized, and normal processing continues
Zero Divisor	The divisor is zero while the dividend is a noninfinite, nonzero number	Result is ∞
Overflow	The result is too large in magnitude to fit in the specified format	Result is largest finite value or ∞
Underflow	The true result is nonzero but too small to be represented in the specified format, and, if underflow exception is masked, denormalization causes loss of accuracy	Result is denormalized or zero
Inexact Result (Precision)	The true result is not exactly representable in the specified format (e.g. 1/3); the result is rounded according to the rounding mode	Normal processing continues

Initialization

After FNINIT or RESET, the control word contains the value 037FH (all exceptions masked, precision control 64 bits, rounding to nearest) the same values as in an 8087 after RESET. For compatibility with the 8087, the bit that used to indicate infinity control (bit 12) is set to zero; however, regardless of its setting, infinity is treated in the affine sense. After FNINIT or RESET, the status word is initialized as follows:

- All exceptions are set to zero.
- Stack TOP is zero, so that after the first push the stack top will be register seven (111B).
- The condition code C_3–C_0 is **undefined**.
- The B-bit is zero.

The tag word contains FFFFH (all stack locations are empty).

80C186/80C187 initialization software should execute an FNINIT instruction (i.e. an FINIT without a preceding WAIT) after RESET. The FNINIT is not strictly required for 80C187 software, but Intel recommends its use to help ensure upward compatibility with other processors.

8087 Compatibility

This section summarizes the differences between the 80C187 and the 8087. Many changes have been designed into the 80C187 to directly support the IEEE standard in hardware. These changes result in increased performance by elminating the need for software that supports the standard.

GENERAL DIFFERENCES

The 8087 instructions FENI/FNENI and FDISI/FNDISI perform no useful function in the 80C187 Numeric Processor Extension. They do not alter the state of the 80C187 Numeric Processor Extension. (They are treated similarly to FNOP, except that ERROR is not checked.) While 8086/8087 code containing these instructions can be executed on the 80C186/80C187, it is unlikely that the exception-handling routines containing these instructions will be completely portable to the 80C187 Numeric Processor Extension.

The 80C187 differs from the 8087 with respect to instruction, data, and exception synchronization. Except for the processor control instructions, all of the 80C187 numeric instructions are automatically synchronized by the 80C186 CPU. When necessary, the

80C186 automatically tests the BUSY line from the 80C187 Numeric Processor Extension to ensure that the 80C187 Numeric Processor Extension has completed its previous instruction before executing the next ESC instruction. No explicit WAIT instructions are required to assure this synchronization. For the 8087 used with 8086 and 8088 CPUs, explicit WAITs are required before each numeric instruction to ensure synchronization. Although 8086/8087 programs having explicit WAIT instructions will execute on the 80C186/80C187, these WAIT instructions are unnecessary.

The 80C187 supports only affine closure for infinity arithmetic, not projective closure.

Operands for FSCALE and FPATAN are no longer restricted in range (except for $\pm \infty$); F2XM1 and FPTAN accept a wider range of operands.

Rounding control is in effect for FLD *constant*.

Software cannot change entries of the tag word to values (other than empty) that differ from actual register contents.

After reset, FINIT, and incomplete FPREM, the 80C187 resets to zero the condition code bits C_3–C_0 of the status word.

In conformance with the IEEE standard, the 80C187 does not support the special data formats pseudozero, pseudo-NaN, pseudoinfinity, and unnormal.

The denormal exception has a different purpose on the 80C187. A system that uses the denormal-exception handler solely to normalize the denormal operands, would better mask the denormal exception on the 80C187. The 80C187 automatically normalizes denormal operands when the denormal exception is masked.

EXCEPTIONS

A number of differences exist due to changes in the IEEE standard and to functional improvements to the architecture of the 80C186/80C187:

1. The 80C186/80C187 traps exceptions only on the next ESC instruction; i.e. the 80C186 does not notice unmasked 80C187 exceptions on the 80C186 ERROR input line until a later numerics instruction is executed. To force the 80C186 to sample its ERROR input, existing high-level compilers and assembly-language programmers typically insert WAIT and FWAIT for this purpose. Because the 80C186 does not sample ERROR on WAIT and FWAIT instructions, programmers

should place an FNOP instruction at the end of a sequence of numerics instructions to force the 80C187 to sample its ERROR input.

2. The 80C187 Numeric Processor Extension signals exceptions through a dedicated ERROR line to the CPU. The 80C187 error signal does not pass through an interrupt controller (the 8087 INT signal does). Therefore, any interrupt-controller-oriented instructions in numerics exception handlers for the 8086/8087 should be deleted.

3. Interrupt vector 16 must point to the numerics exception handling routine.

4. The ESC instruction address saved in the 80C187 Numeric Processor Extension includes any leading prefixes before the ESC opcode. The corresponding address saved in the 8087 does not include leading prefixes.

5. When the overflow or underflow exception is masked, the 80C187 differs from the 8087 in rounding when overflow or underflow occurs. The 80C187 produces results that are consistent with the rounding mode.

6. When the underflow exception is masked, the 80C187 sets its underflow flag only if there is also a loss of accuracy during denormalization.

7. Fewer invalid-operation exceptions due to denormal operands, because the instructions FSQRT, FDIV, FPREM, and conversions to BCD or to integer normalize denormal operands before proceeding.

8. The FSQRT, FBSTP, and FPREM instructions may cause underflow, because they support denormal operands.

9. The denormal exception can occur during the transcendental instructions and the FXTRACT instruction.

10. The denormal exception no longer takes precedence over all other exceptions.

11. When the denormal exception is masked, the 80C187 automatically normalizes denormal operands. The 8087 performs unnormal arithmetic, which might produce an unnormal result.

12. When the operand is zero, the FXTRACT instruction reports a zero-divide exception and leaves $-\infty$ in ST(1).

13. The status word has a new bit (SF) that signals when invalid-operation exceptions are due to stack underflow or overflow.

14. FLD *extended precision* no longer reports denormal exceptions, because the instruction is not numeric.

15. FLD *single/double precision* when the operand is denormal converts the number to extended precision and signals the denormalized oper-

and exception. When loading a signalling NaN, FLD *single/double precision* signals an invalid-operand exception.

16. The 80C187 only generates quiet NaNs (as on the 8087); however, the 80C187 distinguishes between quiet NaNs and signalling NaNs. Signalling NaNs trigger exceptions when they are used as operands; quiet NaNs do not (except for FCOM, FIST, and FBSTP which also raise IE for quiet NaNs).

17. When stack overflow occurs during FPTAN and overflow is masked, both ST(0) and ST(1) contain quiet NaNs. The 8087 leaves the original operand in ST(1) intact.

18. When the scaling factor is $\pm\infty$, the FSCALE (ST(0), ST(1)) instruction behaves as follows

(ST(0) and ST(1) contain the scaled and scaling operands respectively):

- FSCALE $(0, \infty)$ generates the invalid operation exception.
- FSCALE $(finite, -\infty)$ generates zero with the same sign as the scaled operand.
- FSCALE $(finite, +\infty)$ generates ∞ with the same sign as the scaled operand.

The 8087 returns zero in the first case and raises the invalid-operation exception in the other cases.

19. The 80C187 returns signed infinity/zero as the unmasked response to massive overflow/underflow. The 8087 supports a limited range for the scaling factor; within this range either massive overflow/underflow do not occur or undefined results are produced.

Table 7. Pin Summary

Pin Name	Function	Active State	Input/Output
CLK	CLocK		I
CKM	ClocKing Mode		I
RESET	System reset	High	I
PEREQ	Processor Extension REQuest	High	O
BUSY	Busy status	High	O
ERROR	Error status	Low	O
$D_{15}-D_0$	Data pins	High	I/O
NPRD	Numeric Processor ReaD	Low	I
NPWR	Numeric Processor WRite	Low	I
NPS1	NPX select #1	Low	I
NPS2	NPX select #2	High	I
CMD0	CoMmanD 0	High	I
CMD1	CoMmanD 1	High	I
V_{CC}	System power		I
V_{SS}	System ground		I

HARDWARE INTERFACE

In the following description of hardware interface, an overbar above a signal name indicates that the active or asserted state occurs when the signal is at a low voltage. When no overbar is present above the signal name, the signal is asserted when at the high voltage level.

Signal Description

In the following signal descriptions, the 80C187 pins are grouped by function as follows:

1. Execution Control— CLK, CKM, RESET
2. NPX Handshake— PEREQ, BUSY, $\overline{ERROR}$
3. Bus Interface Pins— D_{15}–D_0, $\overline{NPWR}$, $\overline{NPRD}$
4. Chip/Port Select— $\overline{NPS1}$, NPS2, CMD0, CMD1
5. Power Supplies— V_{CC}, V_{SS}

Table 7 lists every pin by its identifier, gives a brief description of its function, and lists some of its characteristics. Figure 7 shows the locations of pins on the CERDIP package, while Figure 8 shows the locations of pins on the PLCC package. Table 8 helps to locate pin identifiers in Figures 7 and 8.

Clock (CLK)

This input provides the basic timing for internal operation. This pin does not require MOS-level input; it will operate at either TTL or MOS levels up to the maximum allowed frequency. A minimum frequency must be provided to keep the internal logic properly functioning. Depending on the signal on CKM, the signal on CLK can be divided by two to produce the internal clock signal (in which case CLK may be up to 32 MHz in frequency), or can be used directly (in which case CLK may be up to 12.5 MHz).

Clocking Mode (CKM)

This pin is a strapping option. When it is strapped to V_{CC} (HIGH), the CLK input is used directly; when strapped to V_{SS} (LOW), the CLK input is divided by two to produce the internal clock signal. During the RESET sequence, this input must be stable at least four internal clock cycles (i.e. CLK clocks when CKM is HIGH; 2 × CLK clocks when CKM is LOW) before RESET goes LOW.

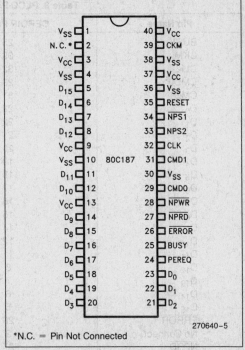

*N.C. = Pin Not Connected

Figure 7. CERDIP Pin Configuration

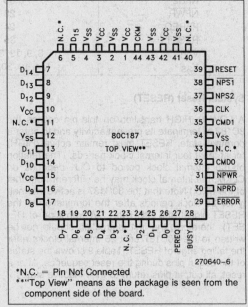

*N.C. = Pin Not Connected
**"Top View" means as the package is seen from the component side of the board.

Figure 8. PLCC Pin Configuration

Table 8. PLCC Pin Cross-Reference

Pin Name	CERDIP Package	PLCC Package
BUSY	25	28
CKM	39	44
CLK	32	36
CMD0	29	32
CMD1	31	35
D_0	23	26
D_1	22	25
D_2	21	24
D_3	20	22
D_4	19	21
D_5	18	20
D_6	17	19
D_7	16	18
D_8	15	17
D_9	14	16
D_{10}	12	14
D_{11}	11	13
D_{12}	8	9
D_{13}	7	8
D_{14}	6	7
D_{15}	5	5
$\overline{\text{ERROR}}$	26	29
No Connect	2	6, 11, 23, 33, 40
$\overline{\text{NPRD}}$	27	30
$\overline{\text{NPS1}}$	34	38
NPS2	33	37
$\overline{\text{NPWR}}$	28	31
PEREQ	24	27
RESET	35	39
V_{CC}	3, 9, 13, 37, 40	1, 3, 10, 15, 42
V_{SS}	1, 4, 10, 30, 36, 38	2, 4, 12, 34, 41, 43

System Reset (RESET)

A LOW to HIGH transition on this pin causes the 8C187 to terminate its present activity and to enter a dormant state. RESET must remain active (HIGH) for at least four internal clock periods. (The relation of the internal clock period to CLK depends on CLKM; the internal clock may be different from that of the CPU.) Note that the 80C187 is active internally for 25 clock periods after the termination of the RESET signal (the HIGH to LOW transition of RE-SET); therefore, the first instruction should not be written to the 80C187 until 25 internal clocks after the falling edge of RESET. Table 9 shows the status of the output pins during the reset sequence. After a reset, all output pins return to their inactive states.

Table 9. Output Pin Status during Reset

Output Pin Name	Value during Reset
BUSY	HIGH
$\overline{\text{ERROR}}$	HIGH
PEREQ	LOW
D_{15}–D_0	TRI-STATE OFF

Processor Extension Request (PEREQ)

When active, this pin signals to the CPU that the 80C187 is ready for data transfer to/from its data FIFO. When there are more than five data transfers,

PEREQ is deactivated after the first three transfers and subsequently after every four transfers. This signal always goes inactive before BUSY goes inactive.

Busy Status (BUSY)

When active, this pin signals to the CPU that the 80C187 is currently executing an instruction. This pin is active HIGH. It should be connected to the 80C186's TEST/BUSY pin. During the RESET sequence this pin is HIGH. The 80C186 uses this HIGH state to detect the presence of an 80C187.

Error Status (ERROR)

This pin reflects the ES bit of the status register. When active, it indicates that an unmasked exception has occurred. This signal can be changed to inactive state only by the following instructions (without a preceding WAIT): FNINIT, FNCLEX, FNSTENV, FNSAVE, FLDCW, FLDENV, and FRSTOR. This pin should be connected to the ERROR pin of the CPU. ERROR can change state only when BUSY is active.

Data Pins (D$_{15}$–D$_0$)

These bidirectional pins are used to transfer data and opcodes between the CPU and 80C187. They are normally connected directly to the corresponding CPU data pins. Other buffers/drivers driving the local data bus must be disabled when the CPU reads from the NPX. High state indicates a value of one. D$_0$ is the least significant data bit.

Numeric Processor Write (NPWR)

A signal on this pin enables transfers of data from the CPU to the NPX. This input is valid only when NPS1 and NPS2 are both active.

Numeric Processor Read (NPRD)

A signal on this pin enables transfers of data from the NPX to the CPU. This input is valid only when NPS1 and NPS2 are both active.

Numeric Processor Selects (NPS1 and NPS2)

Concurrent assertion of these signals indicates that the CPU is performing an escape instruction and enables the 80C187 to execute that instruction. No data transfer involving the 80C187 occurs unless the device is selected by these lines.

Command Selects (CMD0 and CMD1)

These pins along with the select pins allow the CPU to direct the operation of the 80C187.

System Power (V$_{CC}$)

System power provides the +5V ±10% DC supply input. All V$_{CC}$ pins should be tied together on the circuit board and local decoupling capacitors should be used between V$_{CC}$ and V$_{SS}$.

System Ground (V$_{SS}$)

All V$_{SS}$ pins should be tied together on the circuit board and local decoupling capacitors should be used between V$_{CC}$ and V$_{SS}$.

Processor Architecture

As shown by the block diagram (Figure 1), the 80C187 NPX is internally divided into three sections: the bus control logic (BCL), the data interface and control unit, and the floating-point unit (FPU). The FPU (with the support of the control unit which contains the sequencer and other support units) executes all numerics instructions. The data interface and control unit is responsible for the data flow to and from the FPU and the control registers, for receiving the instructions, decoding them, and sequencing the microinstructions, and for handling some of the administrative instructions. The BCL is responsible for CPU bus tracking and interface.

BUS CONTROL LOGIC

The BCL communicates solely with the CPU using I/O bus cycles. The BCL appears to the CPU as a special peripheral device. It is special in two respects: the CPU initiates I/O automatically when it encounters ESC instructions, and the CPU uses reserved I/O addresses to communicate with the BCL. The BCL does not communicate directly with memory. The CPU performs all memory access, transferring input operands from memory to the 80C187 and transferring outputs from the 80C187 to memory. A dedicated communication protocol makes possible high-speed transfer of opcodes and operands between the CPU and 80C187.

Table 10. Bus Cycles Definition

NPS1	NPS2	CMD0	CMD1	NPRD	NPWR	Bus Cycle Type
x	0	x	x	x	x	80C187 Not Selected
1	x	x	x	x	x	80C187 Not Selected
0	1	0	0	1	0	Opcode Write to 80C187
0	1	0	0	0	1	CW or SW Read from 80C187
0	1	1	0	0	1	Read Data from 80C187
0	1	1	0	1	0	Write Data to 80C187
0	1	0	1	1	0	Write Exception Pointers
0	1	0	1	0	1	Reserved
0	1	1	1	0	1	Read Opcode Status
0	1	1	1	1	0	Reserved

DATA INTERFACE AND CONTROL UNIT

The data interface and control unit latches the data and, subject to BCL control, directs the data to the FIFO or the instruction decoder. The instruction decoder decodes the ESC instructions sent to it by the CPU and generates controls that direct the data flow in the FIFO. It also triggers the microinstruction sequencer that controls execution of each instruction. If the ESC instruction is FINIT, FCLEX, FSTSW, FSTSW AX, FSTCW, FSETPM, or FRSTPM, the control executes it independently of the FPU and the sequencer. The data interface and control unit is the one that generates the BUSY, PEREQ, and ERROR signals that synchronize 80C187 activities with the CPU.

FLOATING-POINT UNIT

The FPU executes all instructions that involve the register stack, including arithmetic, logical, transcendental, constant, and data transfer instructions. The data path in the FPU is 84 bits wide (68 significant bits, 15 exponent bits, and a sign bit) which allows internal operand transfers to be performed at very high speeds.

Bus Cycles

The pins NPS1, NPS2, CMD0, CMD1, NPRD and NPWR identify bus cycles for the NPX. Table 10 defines the types of 80C187 bus cycles.

80C187 ADDRESSING

The NPS1, NPS2, CMD0, and CMD1 signals allow the NPX to identify which bus cycles are intended for the NPX. The NPX responds to I/O cycles when the I/O address is 00F8H, 00FAH, 00FCH, or 00FEH. The correspondence between I/O addresses and control signals is defined by Table 11. To guarantee correct operation of the NPX, programs must not perform any I/O operations to these reserved port addresses.

Table 11. I/O Address Decoding

I/O Address (Hexadecimal)	80C187 Select and Command Inputs			
	NPS2	NPS1	CMD1	CMD0
00F8	1	0	0	0
00FA	1	0	0	1
00FC	1	0	1	0
00FE	1	0	1	1

CPU/NPX SYNCHRONIZATION

The pins BUSY, PEREQ, and $\overline{ERROR}$ are used for various aspects of synchronization between the CPU and the NPX.

BUSY is used to synchronize instruction transfer from the CPU to the 80C187. When the 80C187 recognizes an ESC instruction, it asserts BUSY. For most ESC instructions, the CPU waits for the 80C187 to deassert BUSY before sending the new opcode.

The NPX uses the PEREQ pin of the CPU to signal that the NPX is ready for data transfer to or from its data FIFO. The NPX does not directly access memory; rather, the CPU provides memory access services for the NPX.

Once the CPU initiates an 80C187 instruction that has operands, the CPU waits for PEREQ signals that indicate when the 80C187 is ready for operand transfer. Once all operands have been transferred (or if the instruction has no operands) the CPU continues program execution while the 80C187 executes the ESC instruction.

In 8086/8087 systems, WAIT instructions are required to achieve synchronization of both commands and operands. The 80C187, however, does not require WAIT instructions. The WAIT or FWAIT instruction commonly inserted by high-level compilers and assembly-language programmers for exception synchronization is not treated as an instruction by the 80C186 and does not provide exception trapping. (Refer to the section "System Configuration for 8087-Compatible Exception Trapping".)

Once it has started to execute a numerics instruction and has transferred the operands from the CPU, the 80C187 can process the instruction in parallel with and independent of the host CPU. When the NPX detects an exception, it asserts the $\overline{ERROR}$ signal, which causes a CPU interrupt.

OPCODE INTERPRETATION

The CPU and the NPX use a bus protocol that adapts to the numerics opcode being executed. Only the NPX directly interprets the opcode. Some of the results of this interpretation are relevant to the CPU. The NPX records these results (opcode status information) in an internal 16-bit register. The 80C186 accesses this register only via reads from NPX port 00FEH. Tables 10 and 11 define the signal combinations that correspond to each of the following steps.

1. The CPU writes the opcode to NPX port 00F8H. This write can occur even when the NPX is busy or is signalling an exception. The NPX does not necessarily begin executing the opcode immediately.

2. The CPU reads the opcode status information from NPX port 00FEH.

3. The CPU initiates subsequent bus cycles according to the opcode status information. The opcode status information specifies whether to wait until the NPX is not busy, when to transfer exception pointers to port 00FCH, when to read or write operands and results at port 00FAH, etc.

For most instructions, the NPX does not start executing the previously transferred opcode until the CPU (guided by the opcode status information) first writes exception pointer information to port 00FCH of the NPX. This protocol is completely transparent to programmers.

Bus Operation

With respect to bus interface, the 80C187 is fully asynchronous with the CPU, even when it operates from the same clock source as the CPU. The CPU initiates a bus cycle for the NPX by activating both $\overline{NPS1}$ and NPS2, the NPX select signals. During the CLK period in which $\overline{NPS1}$ and NPS2 are activated, the 80C187 also examines the $\overline{NPRD}$ and $\overline{NPRW}$

input signals to determine whether the cycle is a read or a write cycle and examines the CMD0 and CMD1 inputs to determine whether an opcode, operand, or control/status register transfer is to occur. The 80C187 activates its BUSY output some time after the leading edge of the $\overline{NPRD}$ or $\overline{NPRW}$ signal. Input and ouput data are referenced to the trailing edges of the $\overline{NPRD}$ and $\overline{NPRW}$ signals.

The 80C187 activates the PEREQ signal when it is ready for data transfer. The 80C187 deactivates PEREQ automatically.

System Configuration

The 80C187 can be connected to the 80C186 CPU as shown by Figure 9. (Refer to the 80C186 Data Sheet for an explanation of the 80C186's signals.) This interface has the following characteristics:

- The 80C187's $\overline{NPS1}$, $\overline{ERROR}$, PEREQ, and BUSY pins are connected directly to the corresponding pins of the 80C186.

- The 80C186 pin $\overline{MCS3}/\overline{NPS}$ is connected to $\overline{NPS1}$; NPS2 is connected to V_{CC}. Note that if the 80C186 CPU's $\overline{DEN}$ signal is used to gate external data buffers, it must be combined with the $\overline{NPS}$ signal to insure numeric accesses will not activate these buffers.

- The $\overline{NPRD}$ and $\overline{NPRW}$ pins are connected to the $\overline{RD}$ and $\overline{WR}$ pins of the 80C186.

- CMD1 and CMD0 come from the latched A_2 and A_1 of the 80C186, respectively.

- The 80C187 BUSY output connects to the 80C186 $\overline{TEST}/BUSY$ input. During RESET, the signal at the 80C187 BUSY output automatically programs the 80C186 to use the 80C187.

- The 80C187 can use the CLKOUT signal of the 80C186 to conserve board space when operating at 12.5 MHz or less. In this case, the 80C187 CKM input must be pulled HIGH. For operation in excess of 12.5 MHz, a double-frequency external oscillator for CLK input is needed. In this case, CKM must be pulled LOW.

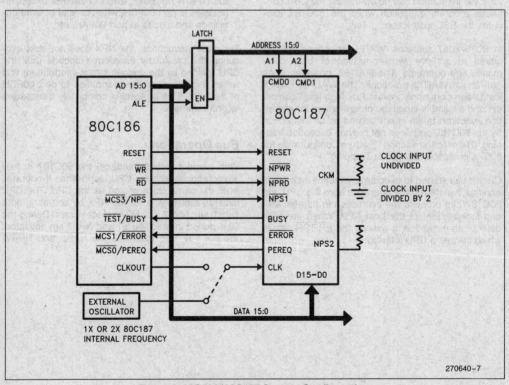

Figure 9. 80C186/80C187 System Configuration

270640–7

System Configuration for 80186/80187-Compatible Exception Trapping

When the 80C187 $\overline{\text{ERROR}}$ output signal is connected directly to the 80C186 $\overline{\text{ERROR}}$ input, floating-point exceptions cause interrupt #16. However, existing software may be programmed to expect floating-point exceptions to be signalled over an external interrupt pin via an interrupt controller.

For exception handling compatible with the 80186/82188/8087, the 80C186 can be wired to recognize exceptions through an external interrupt pin, as Figure 10 shows. (Refer to the 80C186 Data Sheet for an explanation of the 80C186's signals.) With this arrangement, a flip-flop is needed to latch BUSY upon assertion of $\overline{\text{ERROR}}$. The latch can then be cleared during the exception-handler routine by forcing a $\overline{\text{PCS}}$ pin active. The latch must also be cleared at RESET in order for the 80C186 to work with the 80C187.

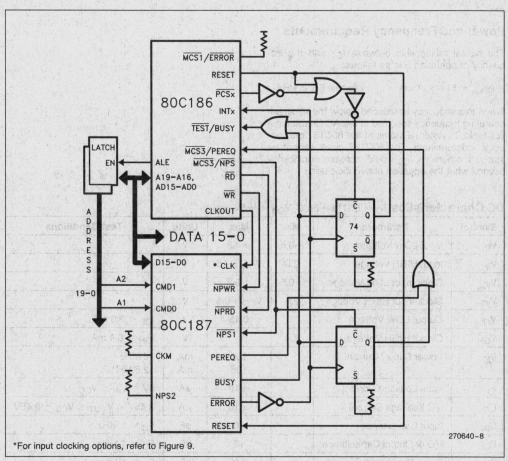

*For input clocking options, refer to Figure 9.

270640–8

Figure 10. System Configuration for 8087-Compatible Exception Trapping

ELECTRICAL DATA

Absolute Maximum Ratings*

Case Temperature Under Bias (T_C)...0°C to +85°C

Storage Temperature .... −65°C to +150°C

Voltage on Any Pin
  with Respect to Ground .... −0.5V to V_{CC} +0.5V

Power Dissipation.........................1.5W

*Notice: Stresses above those listed under "Absolute Maximum Ratings" may cause permanent damage to the device. This is a stress rating only and functional operation of the device at these or any other conditions above those indicated in the operational sections of this specification is not implied. Exposure to absolute maximum rating conditions for extended periods may affect device reliability.

Power and Frequency Requirements

The typical relationship between I_{CC} and the frequency of operation F is as follows:

$$I_{CC_{typ}} = 55 + 5 \cdot F \text{ mA} \qquad \text{where F is in MHz.}$$

When the frequency is reduced below the minimum operating frequency specified in the AC Characteristics table, the internal states of the 80C187 may become indeterminate. The 80C187 clock cannot be stopped; otherwise, I_{CC} would increase significantly beyond what the equation above indicates.

DC Characteristics $T_C = 0°C$ to $+85°C$, $V_{CC} = +5V \pm 10\%$

Symbol	Parameter	Min	Max	Units	Test Conditions
V_{IL}	Input LOW Voltage	−0.5	+0.8	V	
V_{IH}	Input HIGH Voltage	2.0	V_{CC} +0.5	V	
V_{ICL}	Clock Input LOW Voltage	−0.5	+0.8	V	
V_{ICH}	Clock Input HIGH Voltage	2.0	V_{CC} +0.5	V	
V_{OL}	Output LOW Voltage		0.45	V	$I_{OL} = 3.0$ mA
V_{OH}	Output HIGH Voltage	2.4		V	$I_{OH} = 0.4$ mA
I_{CC}	Power Supply Current		156 135	mA mA	16 MHz 12.5 MHz
I_{LI}	Input Leakage Current		±10	μA	$0V \leq V_{IN} \leq V_{CC}$
I_{LO}	I/O Leakage Current		±10	μA	$0.45V \leq V_{OUT} \leq V_{CC} - 0.45V$
C_{IN}	Input Capacitance		10	pF	$F_C = 1$ MHz
C_O	I/O or Output Capacitance		12	pF	$F_C = 1$ MHz
C_{CLK}	Clock Capacitance		20	pF	$F_C = 1$ MHz

AC Characteristics

T_C = 0°C to +85°C, V_{CC} = 5V ±10%

All timings are measured at 1.5V unless otherwise specified

Symbol	Parameter	12.5 MHz		16 MHz		Test Conditions
		Min (ns)	Max (ns)	Min (ns)	Max (ns)	
T_{dvwh} (t6)	Data Setup to $\overline{NPWR}$	43		33		
T_{whdx} (t7)	Data Hold from $\overline{NPWR}$	14		14		
T_{rlrh} (t8)	$\overline{NPRD}$ Active Time	59		54		
T_{wlwh} (t9)	$\overline{NPWR}$ Active Time	59		54		
T_{avwl} (t10)	Command Valid to $\overline{NPWR}$	0		0		
T_{avrl} (t11)	Command Valid to $\overline{NPRD}$	0		0		
T_{mhrl} (t12)	Min Delay from PEREQ Active to $\overline{NPRD}$ Active	40		30		
T_{whax} (t18)	Command Hold from $\overline{NPWR}$	12		8		
T_{rhax} (t19)	Command Hold from $\overline{NPRD}$	12		8		
T_{ivcl} (t20)	$\overline{NPRD}$, $\overline{NPWR}$, RESET to CLK Setup Time	46		38		Note 1
T_{clih} (t21)	$\overline{NPRD}$, $\overline{NPWR}$, RESET from CLK Hold Time	26		18		Note 1
T_{rscl} (t24)	RESET to CLK Setup	21		19		Note 1
T_{clrs} (t25)	RESET from CLK Hold	14		9		Note 1
T_{cmdi} (t26)	Command Inactive Time					
	Write to Write	69		59		
	Read to Read	69		59		
	Read to Write	69		59		
	Write to Read	69		59		

NOTE:

1. This is an asynchronous input. This specification is given for testing purposes only, to assure recognition at a specific CLK edge.

Timing Responses

All timings are measured at 1.5V unless otherwise specified

Symbol	Parameter	12.5 MHz		16 MHz		Test Conditions
		Min (ns)	Max (ns)	Min (ns)	Max (ns)	
T_{rhqz} (t27)	NPRD Inactive to Data Float*		18		18	Note 2
T_{rlqv} (t28)	NPRD Active to Data Valid		50		45	Note 3
T_{ilbh} (t29)	ERROR Active to Busy Inactive	104		104		Note 4
T_{wlbv} (t30)	NPWR Active to Busy Active		80		60	Note 4
T_{klml} (t31)	NPRD or NPWR Active to PEREQ Inactive		80		60	Note 5
T_{rhqh} (t32)	Data Hold from NPRD Inactive	2		2		Note 3
T_{rlbh} (t33)	RESET Inactive to BUSY Inactive		80		60	

NOTES:
*The data float delay is not tested.
2. The float condition occurs when the measured output current is less than I_{OL} on $D_{15}-D_0$.
3. $D_{15}-D_0$ loading: C1 = 100 pF.
4. BUSY loading: C1 = 100 pF.
5. On last data transfer of numeric instruction.

Clock Timings

Symbol		Parameter		12.5 MHz		16 MHz*		Test Conditions
				Min (ns)	Max (ns)	Min (ns)	Max (ns)	
T_{clcl}	(t1a)	CLK Period	CKM = 1	80	250	N/A	N/A	Note 6
	(t1B)		CKM = 0	40	125	31.25	125	Note 6
T_{clch}	(t2a)	CLK Low Time	CKM = 1	35		N/A		Note 6
	(t2b)		CKM = 0	9		7		Note 7
T_{chcl}	(t3a)	CLK High Time	CKM = 1	35		N/A		Note 6
	(t3b)		CKM = 0	13		9		Note 8
T_{ch2ch1} (t4)					10		8	Note 9
T_{ch1ch2} (t5)					10		8	Note 10

NOTES:
*16 MHz operation is available only in divide-by-2 mode (CKM strapped LOW).
6. At 1.5V
7. At 0.8V
8. At 2.0V
9. CKM = 1: 3.7V to 0.8V at 16 MHz, 3.5V to 1.0V at 12.5 MHz
10. CKM = 1: 0.8V to 3.7V at 16 MHz, 1.0V to 3.5V at 12.5 MHz

AC DRIVE AND MEASUREMENT
POINTS—CLK INPUT

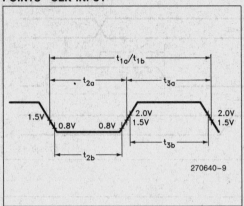

270640–9

AC SETUP, HOLD, AND DELAY TIME
MEASUREMENTS—GENERAL

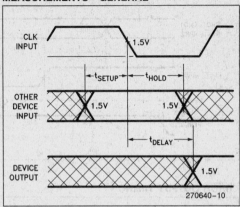

270640–10

AC TEST LOADING ON OUTPUTS

DEVICE
OUTPUT

C_L

270640–11

DATA TRANSFER TIMING (INITIATED BY CPU)

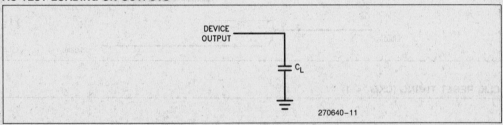

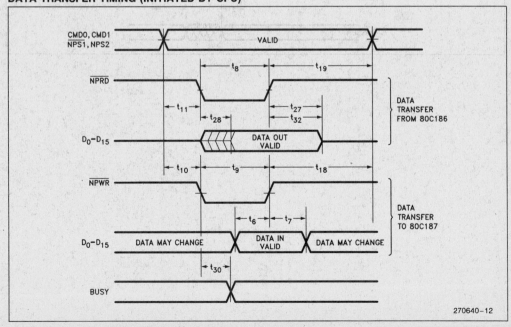

270640–12

DATA CHANNEL TIMING (INITIATED BY 80C187)

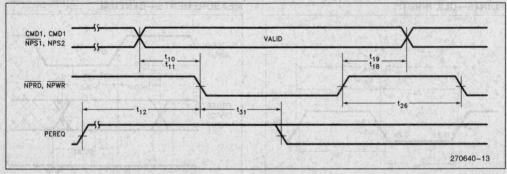

270640–13

ERROR OUTPUT TIMING

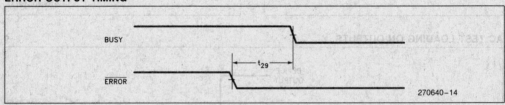

270640–14

CLK, RESET TIMING (CKM = 1)

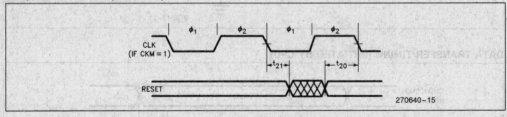

270640–15

CLK, NPRD, NPWR TIMING (CKM = 1)

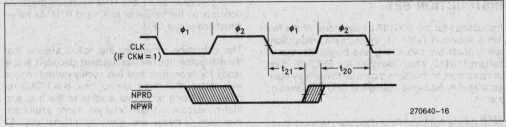

270640-16

CLK, RESET TIMING (CKM = 0)

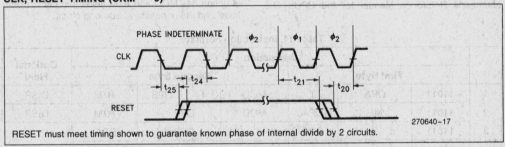

270640-17

RESET must meet timing shown to guarantee known phase of internal divide by 2 circuits.

NOTE:
RESET, NPWR, NPRD inputs are asynchronous to CLK. Timing requirements are given for testing purposes only, to assure recognition at a specific CLK edge.

CLK, NPRD, NPWR TIMING (CKM = 0)

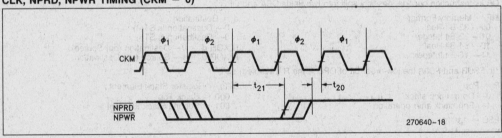

270640-18

RESET, BUSY TIMING

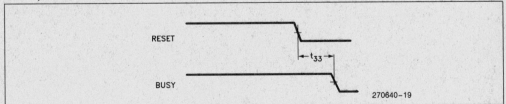

270640-19

80C187

80C187 EXTENSIONS TO THE CPU's INSTRUCTION SET

Instructions for the 80C187 assume one of the five forms shown in Table 11. In all cases, instructions are at least two bytes long and begin with the bit pattern 11011B, which identifies the ESCAPE class of instruction. Instructions that refer to memory operands specify addresses using the CPU's addressing modes.

MOD (Mode field) and R/M (Register/Memory specifier) have the same interpretation as the corresponding fields of CPU instructions (refer to Programmer's Reference Manual for the CPU). The

DISP (displacement) is optionally present in instructions that have MOD and R/M fields. Its presence depends on the values of MOD and R/M, as for instructions of the CPU.

The instruction summaries that follow assume that the instruction has been prefetched, decoded, and is ready for execution; that bus cycles do not require wait states; that there are no local bus HOLD requests delaying processor access to the bus; and that no exceptions are detected during instruction execution. Timings are given in internal 80C187 clocks and include the time for opcode and data transfer between the CPU and the NPX. If the instruction has MOD and R/M fields that call for both base and index registers, add one clock.

Table 11. Instruction Formats

	Instruction							Optional Field
	First Byte			Second Byte				
1	11011	OPA	1	MOD	1	OPB	R/M	DISP
2	11011	MF	OPA	MOD	OPB *		R/M	DISP
3	11011	d	P	OPA	1	1	OPB *	ST (i)
4	11011	0	0	1	1	1	1	OP
5	11011	0	1	1	1	1	1	OP
	15–11	10	9	8	7	6	5 4 3	2 1 0

NOTES:

OP = Instruction opcode, possibly split into two fields OPA and OPB

MF = Memory Format
00— 32-Bit Real
01— 32-Bit Integer
10— 64-Bit Real
11— 16-Bit Integer

d = Destination
0— Destination is ST(0)
0— Destination is ST(i)
R XOR d = 0— Destination (op) Source
R XOR d = 1— Source (op) Destination

*In FSUB and FDIV, the low-order bit of OPB is the R (reversed) bit

P = Pop
0— Do not pop stack
1— Pop stack after operation

ESC = 11011

ST(i) = Register Stack Element *i*
000 = Stack Top
001 = Second Stack Element
•
•
•
111 = Eighth Stack Element

80C187 Extensions to the 80C186 Instruction Set

Instruction	Encoding			Clock Count Range			
	Byte 0	Byte 1	Optional Bytes 2–3	32-Bit Real	32-Bit Integer	64-Bit Real	16-Bit Integer
DATA TRANSFER							
FLD = Load[a]							
Integer/real memory to ST(0)	ESC MF 1	MOD 000 R/M	DISP	40	65–72	59	67–71
Long integer memory to ST(0)	ESC 111	MOD 101 R/M	DISP		90–101		
Extended real memory to ST(0)	ESC 011	MOD 101 R/M	DISP		74		
BCD memory to ST(0)	ESC 111	MOD 100 R/M	DISP		296–305		
ST(i) to ST(0)	ESC 001	11000 ST(i)			16		
FST = Store							
ST(0) to integer/real memory	ESC MF 1	MOD 010 R/M	DISP	58	93–107	73	80–93
ST(0) to ST(i)	ESC 101	11010 ST(i)			13		
FSTP = Store and Pop							
ST(0) to integer/real memory	ESC MF 1	MOD 011 R/M	DISP	58	93–107	73	80–93
ST(0) to long integer memory	ESC 111	MOD 111 R/M	DISP		116–133		
ST(0) to extended real	ESC 011	MOD 111 R/M	DISP		83		
ST(0) to BCD memory	ESC 111	MOD 110 R/M	DISP		542–564		
ST(0) to ST(i)	ESC 101	11001 ST (i)			14		
FXCH = Exchange							
ST(i) and ST(0)	ESC 001	11001 ST(i)			20		
COMPARISON							
FCOM = Compare							
Integer/real memory to ST(0)	ESC MF 0	MOD 010 R/M	DISP	48	78–85	67	77–81
ST(i) to ST(0)	ESC 000	11010 ST(i)			26		
FCOMP = Compare and pop							
Integer/real memory to ST	ESC MF 0	MOD 011 R/M	DISP	48	78–85	67	77–81
ST(i) to ST(0)	ESC 000	11011 ST(i)			28		
FCOMPP = Compare and pop twice							
ST(1) to ST(0)	ESC 110	1101 1001			28		
FTST = Test ST(0)	ESC 001	1110 0100			30		
FUCOM = Unordered compare	ESC 101	11100 ST(i)			26		
FUCOMP = Unordered compare and pop	ESC 101	11101 ST(i)			28		
FUCOMPP = Unordered compare and pop twice	ESC 010	1110 1001			28		
FXAM = Examine ST(0)	ESC 001	11100101			32–40		
CONSTANTS							
FLDZ = Load + 0.0 into ST(0)	ESC 001	1110 1110			22		
FLD1 = Load + 1.0 into ST(0)	ESC 001	1110 1000			26		
FLDPI = Load pi into ST(0)	ESC 001	1110 1011			42		
FLDL2T = Load $\log_2(10)$ into ST(0)	ESC 001	1110 1001			42		

Shaded areas indicate instructions not available in 8087.

NOTE:
a. When loading single- or double-precision zero from memory, add 5 clocks.

80C187 Extensions to the 80C186 Instruction Set (Continued)

Instruction	Encoding			Clock Count Range			
	Byte 0	Byte 1	Optional Bytes 2–3	32-Bit Real	32-Bit Integer	64-Bit Real	16-Bit Integer
CONSTANTS (Continued)							
FLDL2E = Load $\log_2(e)$ into ST(0)	ESC 001	1110 1010			42		
FLDLG2 = Load $\log_{10}(2)$ into ST(0)	ESC 001	1110 1100			43		
FLDLN2 = Load $\log_e(2)$ into ST(0)	ESC 001	1110 1101			43		
ARITHMETIC							
FADD = Add							
Integer/real memory with ST(0)	ESC MF 0	MOD 000 R/M	DISP	44–52	77–92	65–73	77–91
ST(i) and ST(0)	ESC d P 0	11000 ST(i)			25–33[b]		
FSUB = Subtract							
Integer/real memory with ST(0)	ESC MF 0	MOD 10 R R/M	DISP	44–52	77–92	65–73	77–91[c]
ST(i) and ST(0)	ESC d P 0	1110 R R/M			28–36[d]		
FMUL = Multiply							
Integer/real memory with ST(0)	ESC MF 0	MOD 001 R/M	DISP	47–57	81–102	68–93	82–93
ST(i) and ST(0)	ESC d P 0	1100 1 R/M			31–59[e]		
FDIV = Divide							
Integer/real memory with ST(0)	ESC MF 0	MOD 11 R R/M	DISP	108	140–147[f]	128	142–146[g]
ST(i) and ST(0)	ESC d P 0	1111 R R/M			90[h]		
FSQRT[i] = Square root	ESC 001	1111 1010			124–131		
FSCALE = Scale ST(0) by ST(1)	ESC 001	1111 1101			69–88		
FPREM = Partial remainder of ST(0) ÷ ST(1)	ESC 001	1111 1000			76–157		
FPREM1 = Partial remainder (IEEE)	ESC 001	1111 0101			97–187		
FRNDINT = Round ST(0) to integer	ESC 001	1111 1100			68–82		
FXTRACT = Extract components of ST(0)	ESC 001	1111 0100			72–78		
FABS = Absolute value of ST(0)	ESC 001	1110 0001			24		
FCHS = Change sign of ST(0)	ESC 001	1110 0000			26–27		

Shaded areas indicate instructions not available in 8087.

NOTES:
b. Add 3 clocks to the range when d = 1.
c. Add 1 clock to **each** range when R = 1.
d. Add 3 clocks to the range when d = 0.
e. typical = 54 (When d = 0, 48–56, typical = 51).
f. Add 1 clock to the range when R = 1.
g. 153–159 when R = 1.
h. Add 3 clocks to the range when d = 1.
i. $-0 \le$ ST(0) $\le +\infty$.

80C187 Extensions to the 80C186 Instruction Set (Continued)

Instruction	Encoding			Clock Count Range
	Byte 0	Byte 1	Optional Bytes 2–3	
TRANSCENDENTAL				
FCOS = Cosine of ST(0)	ESC 001	1111 1111		125–774j
FPTANk = Partial tangent of ST(0)	ESC 001	1111 0010		193–499j
FPATAN = Partial arctangent	ESC 001	1111 0011		316–489
FSIN = Sine of ST(0)	ESC 001	1111 1110		124–773j
FSINCOS = Sine and cosine of ST(0)	ESC 001	1111 1011		196–811j
F2XM1l = $2^{ST(0)} - 1$	ESC 001	1111 0000		213–478
FYL2Xm = $ST(1) * \log_2(ST(0))$	ESC 001	1111 0001		122–540
FYL2XP1n = $ST(1) * \log_2(ST(0) + 1.0)$	ESC 001	1111 1001		259–549
PROCESSOR CONTROL				
FINIT = Initialize NPX	ESC 011	1110 0011		35
FSTSW AX = Store status word	ESC 111	1110 0000		17
FLDCW = Load control word	ESC 001	MOD 101 R/M	DISP	23
FSTCW = Store control word	ESC 001	MOD 111 R/M	DISP	21
FSTSW = Store status word	ESC 101	MOD 111 R/M	DISP	21
FCLEX = Clear exceptions	ESC 011	1110 0010		13
FSTENV = Store environment	ESC 001	MOD 110 R/M	DISP	146
FLDENV = Load environment	ESC 001	MOD 100 R/M	DISP	113
FSAVE = Save state	ESC 101	MOD 110 R/M	DISP	550
FRSTOR = Restore state	ESC 101	MOD 100 R/M	DISP	482
FINCSTP = Increment stack pointer	ESC 001	1111 0111		23
FDECSTP = Decrement stack pointer	ESC 001	1111 0110		24
FFREE = Free ST(i)	ESC 101	1100 0 ST(i)		20
FNOP = No operations	ESC 001	1101 0000		14

Shaded areas indicate instructions not available in 8087.

NOTES:
j. These timings hold for operands in the range $|x| < \pi/4$. For operands not in this range, up to 78 clocks may be needed to reduce the operand.
k. $0 \le |ST(0)| < 2^{63}$.
l. $-1.0 \le ST(0) \le 1.0$.
m. $0 \le ST(0) < \infty, -\infty < ST(1) < +\infty$.
n. $0 \le |ST(0)| < (2 - \sqrt{(2)})/2, -\infty < ST(1) < +\infty$.

DATA SHEET REVISION REVIEW

The following list represents the key differences between this and the -001 version of the 80C187 data sheet. Please review this summary carefully.

1. Figure 10, titled "System Configuration for 8087—Compatible Exception Trapping", was replaced with a revised schematic. The previous configuration was faulty. Updated timing diagrams on Data Transfer Timing, Error Output, and RESET/BUSY.

80188
HIGH INTEGRATION 8-BIT MICROPROCESSOR

- **Integrated Feature Set**
  - **Enhanced 8086-2 CPU**
  - **Clock Generator**
  - **2 Independent DMA Channels**
  - **Programmable Interrupt Controller**
  - **3 Programmable 16-Bit Timers**
  - **Programmable Memory and Peripheral Chip-Select Logic**
  - **Programmable Wait State Generator**
  - **Local Bus Controller**

- **16-Bit Internal Architecture with 8-Bit Data Bus Interface**

- **High-Performance 8 MHz Processor**
  - **2 MByte/Sec Bus Bandwidth Interface @8 MHz**

- **Direct Addressing Capability to 1 MByte of Memory and 64 KByte I/O**

- **Completely Object Code Compatible with All Existing 8086/8088 Software**
  - **10 New Instruction Types**

- **Complete System Development Support**
  - **Development Software: ASM86 Assembler, PL/M-86, Pascal-86, Fortran-86, C-86, and System Utilities**
  - **In-Circuit-Emulator (I²ICE™-186/188)**

- **Numeric Coprocessing Capability Through 8087 Interface**

- **Available in 68 Pin:**
  - **Ceramic Leadless Chip Carrier (LCC)**
  - **Ceramic Pin Grid Array (PGA)**
  - **Plastic Leaded Chip Carrier (PLCC)**

  (See Packaging Outlines and Dimensions, Order #231369)

- **Available in EXPRESS**
  - **Standard Temperature with Burn-In**
  - **Extended Temperature Range (−40°C to +85°C)**

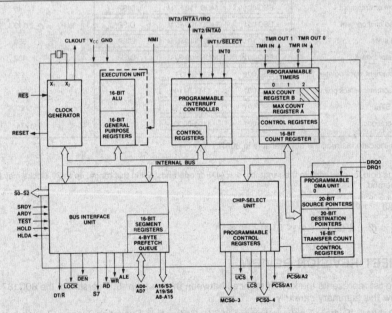

Figure 1. 80188 Block Diagram

210706–1

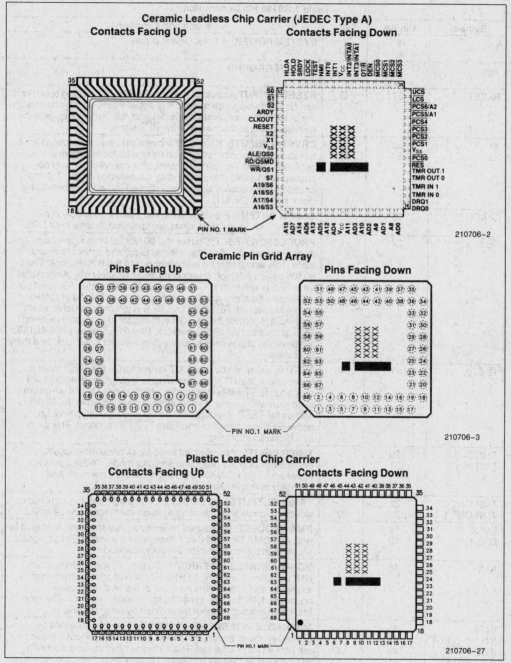

Figure 2. 80188 Pinout Diagram

Table 1. 80188 Pin Description

Symbol	Pin No.	Type	Name and Function
V$_{CC}$	9 43	I I	**SYSTEM POWER:** +5 volt power supply.
V$_{SS}$	26 60	I I	**SYSTEM GROUND**
RESET	57	O	**RESET OUTPUT:** Indicates that the 80188 CPU is being reset, and can be used as a system reset. It is active HIGH, synchronized with the processor clock, and lasts an integer number of clock periods corresponding to the length of the $\overline{RES}$ signal.
X1 X2	59 58	I O	**CRYSTAL INPUTS:** X1 and X2 provide external connections for a fundamental mode parallel resonant crystal for the internal oscillator. Instead of using a crystal, an external clock may be applied to X1 while minimizing stray capacitance on X2. The input or oscillator frequency is internally divided by two to generate the clock signal (CLKOUT).
CLKOUT	56	O	**CLOCK OUTPUT:** Provides the system with a 50% duty cycle waveform. All device pin timings are specified relative to CLKOUT.
$\overline{RES}$	24	I	**PROCESSOR RESET:** Causes the 80188 to immediately terminate its present activity, clear the internal logic, and enter a dormant state. This signal may be asynchronous to the 80188 clock. The 80188 begins fetching instructions approximately 6½ clock cycles after $\overline{RES}$ is returned HIGH. For proper initialization, V$_{CC}$ must be within specifications and the clock signal must be stable for more than 4 clocks with $\overline{RES}$ held low. $\overline{RES}$ is internally synchronized. This input is provided with a Schmitt-trigger to facilitate power-on $\overline{RES}$ generation via an RC network. When $\overline{RES}$ occurs, the 80188 will drive the status lines to an inactive level for one clock, and then float them.
$\overline{TEST}$	47	I/O	**TEST:** Is examined by the WAIT instruction. If the $\overline{TEST}$ input is HIGH when "WAIT" execution begins, instruction execution will suspend. $\overline{TEST}$ will be resampled until it goes LOW, at which time execution will resume. If interrupts are enabled while the 80188 is waiting for $\overline{TEST}$, interrupts will be serviced. During power-up, active $\overline{RES}$ is required to configure $\overline{TEST}$ as an input. This pin is synchronized internally.
TMR IN 0 TMR IN 1	20 21	I I	**TIMER INPUTS:** Are used either as clock or control signals, depending upon the programmed timer mode. These inputs are active HIGH (or LOW-to-HIGH transitions are counted) and internally synchronized.
TMR OUT 0 TMR OUT 1	22 23	O O	**TIMER OUTPUTS:** Are used to provide single pulse or continuous waveform generation, depending upon the timer mode selected.
DRQ0 DRQ1	18 19	I I	**DMA REQUEST:** Is asserted HIGH by an external device when it is ready for DMA Channel 0 or 1 to perform a transfer. These signals are level-triggered and internally synchronized.
NMI	46	I	**NON-MASKABLE INTERRUPT:** Causes a Type 2 interrupt. An NMI transition from LOW to HIGH is latched and synchronized internally, and initiates the interrupt at the next instruction boundary. NMI must be asserted for at least one clock. The Non-Maskable Interrupt cannot be avoided by programming.
INT0 INT1/SELECT INT2/$\overline{INTA0}$ INT3/$\overline{INTA1}$/ IRQ	45 44 42 41	I I I/O I/O	**MASKABLE INTERRUPT REQUESTS:** Can be requested by activating one of these pins. When configured as inputs, these pins are active HIGH. Interrupt Requests are synchronized internally. INT2 and INT3 may be configured to provide active-LOW interrupt-acknowledge output signals. All interrupt inputs may be configured to be either edge- or level-triggered. To ensure recognition, all interrupt requests must remain active until the interrupt is acknowledged. When Slave Mode is selected, the function of these pins changes (see Interrupt Controller section of this data sheet).

Table 1. 80188 Pin Description (Continued)

Symbol	Pin No.	Type	Name and Function
A19/S6 A18/S5 A17/S4 A16/S3	65 66 67 68	O O O O	**ADDRESS BUS OUTPUTS (16–19) and BUS CYCLE STATUS (3–6):** Indicate the four most significant address bits during T_1. These signals are active HIGH. During T_2, T_3, T_W, and T_4, the S6 pin is LOW to indicate a CPU-initiated bus cycle or HIGH to indicate a DMA-initiated bus cycle. During the same T-states, S3, S4, and S5 are always LOW. The status pins float during bus HOLD or RESET.
AD7 AD6 AD5 AD4 AD3 AD2 AD1 AD0	2 4 6 8 11 13 15 17	I/O I/O I/O I/O I/O I/O I/O I/O	**ADDRESS/DATA BUS (0-7):** Signals constitute the time multiplexed memory or I/O address (T_1) and data (T_2, T_3, T_W, and T_4) bus. The bus is active HIGH.
A15 A14 A13 A12 A11 A10 A9 A8	1 3 5 7 10 12 14 16	O O O O O O O O	**ADDRESS-ONLY BUS (8-15):** Containing valid address from T_1-T_4. The bus is active HIGH.
S7	64	O	This signal is HIGH to indicate that the 80188 has an 8-bit data bus. S7 floats during HOLD.
ALE/QS0	61	O	**ADDRESS LATCH ENABLE/QUEUE STATUS 0:** Is provided by the 80188 to latch the address. ALE is active HIGH. Addresses are guaranteed to be valid on the trailing edge of ALE. The ALE rising edge is generated off the rising edge of the CLKOUT immediately preceding T_1 of the associated bus cycle, effectively one-half clock cycle earlier than in the 8088. The trailing edge is generated off the CLKOUT rising edge in T_1 as in the 8088. Note that ALE is never floated.
W̄R̄/QS1	63	O	**WRITE STROBE/QUEUE STATUS 1:** Indicates that the data on the bus is to be written into a memory or an I/O device. W̄R̄ is active for T_2, T_3, and T_W of any write cycle. It is active LOW, and floats during HOLD. When the 80188 is in queue status mode, the ALE/QS0 and W̄R̄/QS1 pins provide information about processor/instruction queue interaction.

QS1	QS0	Queue Operation
0	0	No Queue Operation
0	1	First Opcode Byte Fetched from the Queue
1	1	Subsequent Byte Fetched from the Queue
1	0	Empty the Queue

Table 1. 80188 Pin Description (Continued)

Symbol	Pin No.	Type	Name and Function
RD/QSMD	62	I/O	**READ STROBE:** Is an active LOW signal which indicates that the 80188 is performing a memory or I/O read cycle. It is guaranteed not to go LOW before the A/D bus is floated. An internal pull-up ensures that RD is HIGH during RESET. Following RESET the pin is sampled to determine whether the 80188 is to provide ALE, RD, and WR, or queue status information. To enable Queue Status Mode, RD must be connected to GND. RD will float during bus HOLD.
ARDY	55	I	**ASYNCHRONOUS READY:** Informs the 80188 that the addressed memory space or I/O device will complete a data transfer. The ARDY pin accepts a rising edge that is asynchronous to CLKOUT and is active HIGH. The falling edge of ARDY must be synchronized to the 80188 clock. Connecting ARDY HIGH will always assert the ready condition to the CPU. If this line is unused, it should be tied LOW to yield control to the SRDY pin.
SRDY	49	I	**SYNCHRONOUS READY:** Informs the 80188 that the addressed memory space or I/O device will complete a data transfer. The SRDY pin accepts an active-HIGH input synchronized to CLKOUT. The use of SRDY allows a relaxed system timing over ARDY. This is accomplished by elimination of the one-half clock cycle required to internally synchronize the ARDY input signal. Connecting SRDY high will always assert the ready condition to the CPU. If this line is unused, it should be tied LOW to yield control to the ARDY pin.
LOCK	48	O	**LOCK:** Output indicates that other system bus masters are not to gain control of the system bus while LOCK is active LOW. The LOCK signal is requested by the LOCK prefix instruction and is activated at the beginning of the first data cycle associated with the instruction following the LOCK prefix. It remains active until the completion of that instruction. No instruction prefetching will occur while LOCK is asserted. When executing more than one LOCK instruction, always make sure there are 4 bytes of code between the end of the first LOCK instruction and the start of the second LOCK instruction. LOCK is active LOW, is driven HIGH for one clock during RESET, and then floated.
S̄0 S̄1 S̄2	52 53 54	O O O	**BUS CYCLE STATUS S̄0–S̄2:** Are encoded to provide bus-transaction information:

80188 Bus Cycle Status Information

S̄2	S̄1	S̄0	Bus Cycle Initiated
0	0	0	Interrupt Acknowledge
0	0	1	Read I/O
0	1	0	Write I/O
0	1	1	Halt
1	0	0	Instruction Fetch
1	0	1	Read Data from Memory
1	1	0	Write Data to Memory
1	1	1	Passive (no bus cycle)

The status pins float during HOLD.
S̄2 may be used as a logical M/ĪO indicator, and S̄1 as a DT/R̄ indicator.

Table 1. 80188 Pin Description (Continued)

Symbol	Pin No.	Type	Name and Function
HOLD (input) HLDA (output)	50 51	I O	**HOLD:** Indicates that another bus master is requesting the local bus. The HOLD input is active HIGH. HOLD may be asynchronous with respect to the 80188 clock. The 80188 will issue a HLDA in response to a HOLD request at the end of T_4 or T_i. Simultaneous with the issuance of HLDA, the 80188 will float the local bus and control lines. After HOLD is detected as being LOW, the 80188 will lower HLDA. When the 80188 needs to run another bus cycle, it will again drive the local bus and control lines.
$\overline{UCS}$	34	O	**UPPER MEMORY CHIP SELECT:** Is an active LOW output whenever a memory reference is made to the defined upper portion (1K–256K block) of memory. This line is not floated during bus HOLD. The address range activating $\overline{UCS}$ is software programmable.
$\overline{LCS}$	33	O	**LOWER MEMORY CHIP SELECT:** Is active LOW whenever a memory reference is made to the defined lower portion (1K–256K) of memory. This line is not floated during bus HOLD. The address range activating $\overline{LCS}$ is software programmable.
$\overline{MCS0}$ $\overline{MCS1}$ $\overline{MCS2}$ $\overline{MCS3}$	38 37 36 35	O O O O	**MID-RANGE MEMORY CHIP SELECT SIGNALS:** Are active LOW when a memory reference is made to the defined mid-range portion (8K–512K). These lines are not floated during bus HOLD. The address ranges activating $\overline{MCS0}$–3 are software programmable.
$\overline{PCS0}$ $\overline{PCS1}$ $\overline{PCS2}$ $\overline{PCS3}$ $\overline{PCS4}$	25 27 28 29 30	O O O O O	**PERIPHERAL CHIP SELECT SIGNALS 0–4:** Are active LOW when a reference is made to the defined peripheral area (64K byte I/O space). These lines are not floated during bus HOLD. The address ranges activating $\overline{PCS0}$–4 are software programmable.
$\overline{PCS5}$/A1	31	O	**PERIPHERAL CHIP SELECT 5 or LATCHED A1:** May be programmed to provide a sixth peripheral chip select, or to provide an internally latched A1 signal. The address range activating $\overline{PCS5}$ is software programmable. $\overline{PCS5}$/A1 does not float during bus HOLD. When programmed to provide latched A1, this pin will retain the previously latched value during HOLD.
$\overline{PCS6}$/A2	32	O	**PERIPHERAL CHIP SELECT 6 or LATCHED A2:** May be programmed to provide a seventh peripheral chip select, or to provide an internally latched A2 signal. The address range activating $\overline{PCS6}$ is software-programmable. $\overline{PCS6}$/A2 does not float during bus HOLD. When programmed to provide latched A2, this pin will retain the previously latched value during HOLD.
DT/$\overline{R}$	40	O	**DATA TRANSMIT/RECEIVE:** Controls the direction of data flow through an external data bus transceiver. When LOW, data is transferred to the 80188. When HIGH the 80188 places write data on the data bus.
$\overline{DEN}$	39	O	**DATA ENABLE:** Is provided as a data bus transceiver output enable. $\overline{DEN}$ is active LOW during each memory and I/O access. $\overline{DEN}$ is HIGH whenever DT/$\overline{R}$ changes state. During RESET, $\overline{DEN}$ is driven HIGH for one clock, then floated. $\overline{DEN}$ also floats during bus HOLD.

FUNCTIONAL DESCRIPTION

Introduction

The following Functional Description describes the base architecture of the 80188. The 80188 is a very high integration 8-bit microprocessor. It combines 15–20 of the most common microprocessor system components onto one chip while providing twice the performance of the standard 8088. The 80188 is object code compatible with the 8086, 8088 microprocessors and adds 10 new instruction types to the 8086, 8088 instruction set.

80188 BASE ARCHITECTURE

The 8086, 8088, 80186, 80188 and 80286 family all contain the same basic set of registers, instructions, and addressing modes. The 80188 processor is upward compatible with the 8086, 8088, 80186, and 80286 CPUs.

Register Set

The 80188 base architecture has fourteen registers as shown in Figures 3a and 3b. These registers are grouped into the following categories.

GENERAL REGISTERS

Eight 16-bit general purpose registers may be used for arithmetic and logical operands. Four of these (AX, BX, CX, and DX) can be used as 16-bit registers or split into pairs of separate 8-bit registers.

SEGMENT REGISTERS

Four 16-bit special purpose registers select, at any given time, the segments of memory that are immediately addressable for code, stack, and data. (For usage, refer to Memory Organization.)

BASE AND INDEX REGISTERS

Four of the general purpose registers may also be used to determine offset addresses of operands in memory. These registers may contain base addresses or indexes to particular locations within a segment. The addressing mode selects the specific registers for operand and address calculations.

STATUS AND CONTROL REGISTERS

Two 16-bit special purpose registers record or alter certain aspects of the 80188 processor state. These are the Instruction Pointer Register, which contains the offset address of the next sequential instruction to be executed, and the Status Word Register, which contains status and control flag bits (see Figures 3a and 3b).

STATUS WORD DESCRIPTION

The Status Word records specific characteristics of the result of logical and arithmetic instructions (bits 0, 2, 4, 6, 7, and 11) and controls the operation of the 80188 within a given operating mode (bits 8, 9, and 10). The Status Word Register is 16-bits wide. The function of the Status Word bits is shown in Table 2.

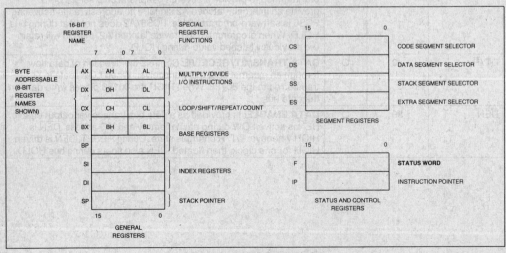

Figure 3a. 80188 Register Set

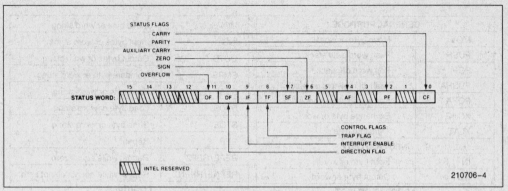

Figure 3b. Status Word Format

Table 2. Status Word Bit Functions

Bit Position	Name	Function
0	CF	Carry Flag—Set on high-order bit carry or borrow; cleared otherwise
2	PF	Parity Flag—Set if low-order 8 bits of result contain an even number of 1-bits; cleared otherwise
4	AF	Set on carry from or borrow to the low order four bits of AL; cleared otherwise
6	ZF	Zero Flag—Set if result is zero; cleared otherwise
7	SF	Sign Flag—Set equal to high-order bit of result (0 if positive, 1 if negative)
8	TF	Single Step Flag—Once set, a single step interrupt occurs after the next instruction executes. TF is cleared by the single step interrupt.
9	IF	Interrupt-Enable Flag—When set, maskable interrupts will cause the CPU to transfer control to an interrupt vector specified location.
10	DF	Direction Flag—Causes string instructions to auto decrement the appropriate index register when set. Clearing DF causes auto increment.
11	OF	Overflow Flag—Set if the signed result cannot be expressed within the number of bits in the destination operand; cleared otherwise

Instruction Set

The instruction set is divided into seven categories: data transfer, arithmetic, shift/rotate/logical, string manipulation, control transfer, high-level instructions, and processor control. These categories are summarized in Figure 4.

An 80188 instruction can reference anywhere from zero to several operands. An operand can reside in a register, in the instruction itself, or in memory. Specific operand addressing modes are discussed later in this data sheet.

Memory Organization

Memory is organized in sets of segments. Each segment is a linear contiguous sequence of up to 64K (2^{16}) 8-bit bytes. Memory is addressed using a two-component address (a pointer) that consists of a 16-bit base segment and a 16-bit offset. The 16-bit base values are contained in one of four internal segment registers (code, data, stack, extra). The physical address is calculated by shifting the base value LEFT by four bits and adding the 16-bit offset value to yield a 20-bit physical address (see Figure 5). This allows for a 1 MByte physical address size.

All instructions that address operands in memory must specify the base segment and the 16-bit offset value. For speed and compact instruction encoding, the segment register used for physical address generation is implied by the addressing mode used (see Table 3). These rules follow the way programs are written (see Figure 6) as independent modules that require areas for code and data, a stack, and access to external data areas.

Special segment override instruction prefixes allow the implicit segment register selection rules to be overridden for special cases. The stack, data, and extra segments may coincide for simple programs.

GENERAL PURPOSE	
MOV	Move byte or word
PUSH	Push word onto stack
POP	Pop word off stack
PUSHA	Push all registers on stack
POPA	Pop all registers from stack
XCHG	Exchange byte or word
XLAT	Translate byte
INPUT/OUTPUT	
IN	Input byte or word
OUT	Output byte or word
ADDRESS OBJECT	
LEA	Load effective address
LDS	Load pointer using DS
LES	Load pointer using ES
FLAG TRANSFER	
LAHF	Load AH register from flags
SAHF	Store AH register in flags
PUSHF	Push flags onto stack
POPF	Pop flags off stack
ADDITION	
ADD	Add byte or word
ADC	Add byte or word with carry
INC	Increment byte or word by 1
AAA	ASCII adjust for addition
DAA	Decimal adjust for addition
SUBTRACTION	
SUB	Subtract byte or word
SBB	Subtract byte or word with borrow
DEC	Decrement byte or word by 1
NEG	Negate byte or word
CMP	Compare byte or word
AAS	ASCII adjust for subtraction
DAS	Decimal adjust for subtraction
MULTIPLICATION	
MUL	Multiply byte or word unsigned
IMUL	Integer multiply byte or word
AAM	ASCII adjust for multiply
DIVISION	
DIV	Divide byte or word unsigned
IDIV	Integer divide byte or word
AAD	ASCII adjust for division
CBW	Convert byte to word
CWD	Convert word to doubleword

MOVS	Move byte or word string
INS	Input bytes or word string
OUTS	Output bytes or word string
CMPS	Compare byte or word string
SCAS	Scan byte or word string
LODS	Load byte or word string
STOS	Store byte or word string
REP	Repeat
REPE/REPZ	Repeat while equal/zero
REPNE/REPNZ	Repeat while not equal/not zero
LOGICALS	
NOT	"Not" byte or word
AND	"And" byte or word
OR	"Inclusive or" byte or word
XOR	"Exclusive or" byte or word
TEST	"Test" byte or word
SHIFTS	
SHL/SAL	Shift logical/arithmetic left byte or word
SHR	Shift logical right byte or word
SAR	Shift arithmetic right byte or word
ROTATES	
ROL	Rotate left byte or word
ROR	Rotate right byte or word
RCL	Rotate through carry left byte or word
RCR	Rotate through carry right byte or word
FLAG OPERATIONS	
STC	Set carry flag
CLC	Clear carry flag
CMC	Complement carry flag
STD	Set direction flag
CLD	Clear direction flag
STI	Set interrupt enable flag
CLI	Clear interrupt enable flag
EXTERNAL SYNCHRONIZATION	
HLT	Halt until interrupt or reset
WAIT	Wait for TEST pin active
ESC	Escape to extension processor
LOCK	Lock bus during next instruction
NO OPERATION	
NOP	No operation
HIGH LEVEL INSTRUCTIONS	
ENTER	Format stack for procedure entry
LEAVE	Restore stack for procedure exit
BOUND	Detects values outside prescribed range

Figure 4. 80188 Instruction Set

CONDITIONAL TRANSFERS	
JA/JNBE	Jump if above/not below nor equal
JAE/JNB	Jump if above or equal/not below
JB/JNAE	Jump if below/not above nor equal
JBE/JNA	Jump if below or equal/not above
JC	Jump if carry
JE/JZ	Jump if equal/zero
JG/JNLE	Jump if greater/not less nor equal
JGE/JNL	Jump if greater or equal/not less
JL/JNGE	Jump if less/not greater nor equal
JLE/JNG	Jump if less or equal/not greater
JNC	Jump if not carry
JNE/JNZ	Jump if not equal/not zero
JNO	Jump if not overflow
JNP/JPO	Jump if not parity/parity odd
JNS	Jump if not sign

JO	Jump if overflow
JP/JPE	Jump if parity/parity even
JS	Jump if sign
UNCONDITIONAL TRANSFERS	
CALL	Call procedure
RET	Return from procedure
JMP	Jump
ITERATION CONTROLS	
LOOP	Loop
LOOPE/LOOPZ	Loop if equal/zero
LOOPNE/LOOPNZ	Loop if not equal/not zero
JCXZ	Jump if register CX = 0
INTERRUPTS	
INT	Interrupt
INTO	Interrupt if overflow
IRET	Interrupt return

Figure 4. 80188 Instruction Set (Continued)

To access operands that do not reside in one of the four immediately available segments, a full 32-bit pointer can be used to reload both the base (segment) and offset values.

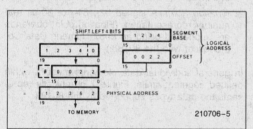

Figure 5. Two Component Address

Table 3. Segment Register Selection Rules

Memory Reference Needed	Segment Register Used	Implicit Segment Selection Rule
Instructions	Code (CS)	Instruction prefetch and immediate data.
Stack	Stack (SS)	All stack pushes and pops; any memory references which use BP Register as a base register.
External Data (Global)	Extra (ES)	All string instruction references which use the DI register as an index.
Local Data	Data (DS)	All other data references.

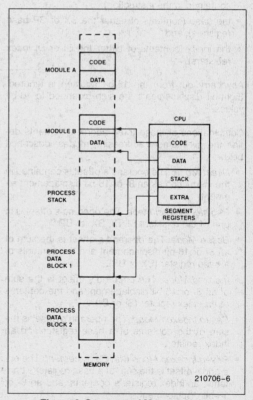

Figure 6. Segmented Memory Helps Structure Software

Addressing Modes

The 80188 provides eight categories of addressing modes to specify operands. Two addressing modes are provided for instructions that operate on register or immediate operands:

- *Register Operand Mode:* The operand is located in one of the 8- or 16-bit general registers.
- *Immediate Operand Mode:* The operand is included in the instruction.

Six modes are provided to specify the location of an operand in a memory segment. A memory operand address consists of two 16-bit components: a segment base and an offset. The segment base is supplied by a 16-bit segment register either implicitly chosen by the addressing mode or explicitly chosen by a segment override prefix. The offset, also called the effective address, is calculated by summing any combination of the following three address elements:

- the *displacement* (an 8- or 16-bit immediate value contained in the instruction);
- the *base* (contents of either the BX or BP base registers); and
- the *index* (contents of either the SI or DI index registers).

Any carry out from the 16-bit addition is ignored. Eight-bit displacements are sign extended to 16-bit values.

Combinations of these three address elements define the six memory addressing modes, described below.

- *Direct Mode:* The operand's offset is contained in the instruction as an 8- or 16-bit displacement element.
- *Register Indirect Mode:* The operand's offset is in one of the registers SI, DI, BX, or BP.
- *Based Mode:* The operand's offset is the sum of an 8- or 16-bit displacement and the contents of a base register (BX or BP).
- *Indexed Mode:* The operand's offset is the sum of an 8- or 16-bit displacement and the contents of an index register (SI or DI).
- *Based Indexed Mode:* The operand's offset is the sum of the contents of a base register and an index register.
- *Based Indexed Mode with Displacement:* The operand's offset is the sum of a base register's contents, an index register's contents, and an 8- or 16-bit displacement.

Data Types

The 80188 directly supports the following data types:

- *Integer:* A signed binary numeric value contained in an 8-bit byte or a 16-bit word. All operations assume a 2's complement representation. Signed 32- and 64-bit integers are supported using an 8087 Numeric Data Coprocessor with the 80188.
- *Ordinal:* An unsigned binary numeric value contained in an 8-bit byte or a 16-bit word.
- *Pointer:* A 16- or 32-bit quantity, composed of a 16-bit offset component or a 16-bit segment base component in addition to a 16-bit offset component.
- *String:* A contiguous sequence of bytes or words. A string may contain from 1 to 64K bytes.
- *ASCII:* A byte representation of alphanumeric and control characters using the ASCII standard of character representation.
- *BCD:* A byte (unpacked) representation of the decimal digits 0–9.
- *Packed BCD:* A byte (packed) representation of two decimal digits (0–9). One digit is stored in each nibble (4-bits) of the byte.
- *Floating Point:* A signed 32-, 64-, or 80-bit real number representation. (Floating point operands are supported using an 8087 Numeric Data Coprocessor with the 80188.)

In general, individual data elements must fit within defined segment limits. Figure 7 graphically represents the data types supported by the 80188.

I/O Space

The I/O space consists of 64K 8-bit or 32K 16-bit ports. Separate instructions address the I/O space with either an 8-bit port address, specified in the instruction, or a 16-bit port address in the DX register. 8-bit port addresses are zero extended such that A_{15}–A_8 are LOW. I/O port addresses 00F8(H) through 00FF(H) are reserved.

Interrupts

An interrupt transfers execution to a new program location. The old program address (CS:IP) and machine state (Status Word) are saved on the stack to allow resumption of the interrupted program. Interrupts fall into three classes: hardware initiated, INT instructions, and instruction exceptions. Hardware initiated interrupts occur in response to an external input and are classified as non-maskable or maskable.

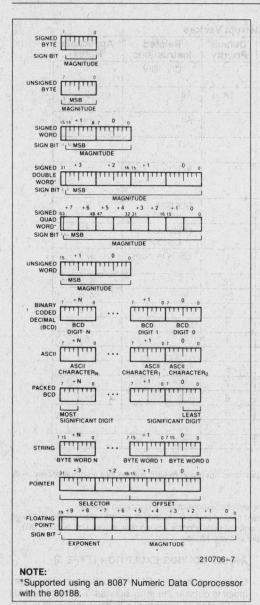

NOTE:
*Supported using an 8087 Numeric Data Coprocessor with the 80188.

Figure 7. 80188 Supported Data Types

Programs may cause an interrupt with an INT instruction. Instruction exceptions occur when an unusual condition, which prevents further instruction processing, is detected while attempting to execute an instruction. If the exception was caused by executing an ESC instruction with the ESC trap bit set in the relocation register, the return instruction will point to the ESC instruction, or to the segment override prefix immediately preceding the ESC instruction if the prefix was present. In all other cases, the return address from an exception will point at the instruction immediately following the instruction causing the exception.

A table containing up to 256 pointers defines the proper interrupt service routine for each interrupt. Interrupts 0–31, some of which are used for instruction exceptions, are reserved. Table 4 shows the 80188 predefined types and default priority levels. For each interrupt, an 8-bit vector must be supplied to the 80188 which identifies the appropriate table entry. Exceptions supply the interrupt vector internally. In addition, internal peripherals and noncascaded external interrupts will generate their own vectors through the internal interrupt controller. INT instructions contain or imply the vector and allow access to all 256 interrupts. Maskable hardware initiated interrupts supply the 8-bit vector to the CPU during an interrupt acknowledge bus sequence. Non-maskable hardware interrupts use a predefined internally supplied vector.

Interrupt Sources

The 80188 can service interrupts generated by software or hardware. The software interrupts are generated by specific instructions (INT, ESC, unused OP, etc.) or the results of conditions specified by instructions (array bounds check, INT0, DIV, IDIV, etc.). All interrupt sources are serviced by an indirect call through an element of a vector table. This vector table is indexed by using the interrupt vector type (Table 4), multiplied by four. All hardware-generated interrupts are sampled at the end of each instruction. Thus, the software interrupts will begin service first. Once the service routine is entered and interrupts are enabled, any hardware source of sufficient priority can interrupt the service routine in progress.

Those pre-defined 80188 interrupts which cannot be masked by programming are described below.

DIVIDE ERROR EXCEPTION (TYPE 0)

Generated when a DIV or IDIV instruction quotient cannot be expressed in the number of bits in the destination.

SINGLE-STEP INTERRUPT (TYPE 1)

Generated after most instructions if the TF flag is set. Interrupts will not be generated after prefix instructions (e.g., REP), instructions which modify segment registers (e.g., POP DS), or the WAIT instruction.

NON-MASKABLE INTERRUPT—NMI (TYPE 2)

An external interrupt source which cannot be masked.

Table 4. 80188 Interrupt Vectors

Interrupt Name	Vector Type	Vector Address	Default Priority	Related Instructions	Applicable Notes
Divide Error Exception	0	00H	1	DIV, IDIV	1
Single Step Interrupt	1	04H	1A	All	2
Non-Maskable Interrupt (NMI)	2	08H	1	All	
Breakpoint Interrupt	3	0CH	1	INT	1
INTO Detected Overflow Exception	4	10H	1	INTO	1
Array Bounds Exception	5	14H	1	BOUND	1
Unused Opcode Exception	6	18H	1	Undefined Opcodes	1
ESC Opcode Exception	7	1CH	1	ESC Opcodes	1, 3
Timer 0 Interrupt	8	20H	2A		4, 5
Timer 1 Interrupt	18	48H	2B		4, 5
Timer 2 Interrupt	19	4CH	2C		4, 5
Reserved	9	24H	3		
DMA 0 Interrupt	10	28H	4		5
DMA 1 Interrupt	11	2CH	5		5
INT0 Interrupt	12	30H	6		
INT1 Interrupt	13	34H	7		
INT2 Interrupt	14	38H	8		
INT3 Interrupt	15	3CH	9		
Reserved	16, 17	40H, 44H			
Reserved	20–31	50H . . . 7CH			

NOTES:
Default priorities for the interrupt sources are used only if the user does not program each source into a unique priority level.
1. Generated as a result of an instruction execution.
2. Performed in same manner as 8088.
3. An ESC opcode will cause a trap if the power bit is set in the peripheral control block relocation register.
4. All three timers constitute one source of request to the interrupt controller. As such, they share the same priority level with respect to other interrupt sources. However, the timers have a defined priority order among themselves (2A > 2B > 2C).
5. The vector type numbers for these sources are programmable in Slave Mode.

BREAKPOINT INTERRUPT (TYPE 3)

A one-byte version of the INT instruction. It uses 12 as an index into the service routine address table (because it is a type 3 interrupt).

INTO DETECTED OVERFLOW EXCEPTION (TYPE 4)

Generated during an INTO instruction if the OF bit is set.

ARRAY BOUNDS EXCEPTION (TYPE 5)

Generated during a BOUND instruction if the array index is outside the array bounds. The array bounds are located in memory at a location indicated by one of the instruction operands. The other operand indicates the value of the index to be checked.

UNUSED OPCODE EXCEPTION (TYPE 6)

Generated if execution is attempted on undefined opcodes.

ESCAPE OPCODE EXCEPTION (TYPE 7)

Generated if execution is attempted of ESC opcodes (D8H–DFH). This exception will only be generated if a bit in the relocation register is set. The return address of this exception will point to the ESC instruction causing the exception. If a segment override prefix preceded the ESC instruction, the return address will point to the segment override prefix.

Hardware-generated interrupts are divided into two groups: maskable interrupts and non-maskable interrupts. The 80188 provides maskable hardware interrupt request pins INT0–INT3. In addition, maskable interrupts may be generated by the 80188 integrated DMA controller and the integrated timer unit. The vector types for these interrupts are shown in Table 4. Software enables these inputs by setting the Interrupt Flag bit (IF) in the Status Word. The interrupt controller is discussed in the peripheral section of this data sheet.

Further maskable interrupts are disabled while servicing an interrupt because the IF bit is reset as part of the response to an interrupt or exception. The saved Status Word will reflect the enable status of the processor prior to the interrupt. The interrupt flag will remain zero unless specifically set. The interrupt return instruction restores the Status Word, thereby restoring the original status of IF bit. If the interrupt return re-enables interrupts, and another interrupt is pending, the 80188 will immediately service the highest-priority interrupt pending, i.e., no instructions of the main line program will be executed.

Non-Maskable Interrupt Request (NMI)

A non-maskable interrupt (NMI) is also provided. This interrupt is serviced regardless of the state of the IF bit. A typical use of NMI would be to activate a power failure routine. The activation of this input causes an interrupt with an internally supplied vector value of 2. No external interrupt acknowledge sequence is performed. The IF bit is cleared at the beginning of an NMI interrupt to prevent maskable interrupts from being serviced.

Single-Step Interrupt

The 80188 has an internal interrupt that allows programs to execute one instruction at a time. It is called the single-step interrupt and is controlled by the single-step flag bit (TF) in the Status Word. Once this bit is set, an internal single-step interrupt will occur after the next instruction has been executed. The interrupt clears the TF bit and uses an internally supplied vector of 1. The IRET instruction is used to set the TF bit and transfer control to the next instruction to be single-stepped.

Initialization and Processor Reset

Processor initialization is accomplished by driving the $\overline{\text{RES}}$ input pin LOW. $\overline{\text{RES}}$ must be LOW during power-up to ensure proper device initialization. $\overline{\text{RES}}$ forces the 80188 to terminate all execution and local bus activity. No instruction or bus activity will occur as long as $\overline{\text{RES}}$ is active. After $\overline{\text{RES}}$ becomes inactive and an internal processing interval elapses, the 80188 begins execution with the instruction at physical location FFFF0(H). $\overline{\text{RES}}$ also sets some registers to predefined values as shown in Table 5.

Table 5. 80188 Initial Register State after RESET

Status Word	F002(H)
Instruction Pointer	0000(H)
Code Segment	FFFF(H)
Data Segment	0000(H)
Extra Segment	0000(H)
Stack Segment	0000(H)
Relocation Register	20FF(H)
UMCS	FFFB(H)

THE 80188 COMPARED TO THE 80186

The 80188 CPU is an 8-bit processor designed around the 80186 internal structure. Most internal functions of the 80188 are identical to the equivalent 80186 functions. The 80188 handles the external bus the same way the 80186 does with the distinction of handling only 8 bits at a time. Sixteen bit operands are fetched or written in two consecutive bus cycles. Both processors will appear identical to the software engineer, with the exception of execution time. The internal register structure is identical and all instructions have the same end result. The differences between the 80188 and the 80186 are outlined below. Internally, there are three differences between the 80188 and the 80186. All changes are related to the 8-bit bus interface.

- The queue length is 4 bytes in the 80188, whereas the 80186 queue contains 6 bytes, or three words. The queue was shortened to prevent overuse of the bus by the BIU when prefetching instructions. This was required because of the additional time necessary to fetch instructions 8 bits at a time.

- To further optimize the queue, the prefetching algorithm was changed. The 80188 BIU will fetch a new instruction to load into the queue each time there is a 1-byte hole (space available) in the queue. The 80186 waits until a 2-byte space is available.

- The internal execution time of the instruction is affected by the 8-bit interface. All 16-bit fetches and writes from/to memory take an additional four clock cycles. The CPU may also be limited by the speed of instruction fetches when a series of simple operations occur. When the more sophisticated instructions of the 80188 are being used, the queue has time to fill and the execution proceeds as fast as the execution unit will allow.

The 80188 and 80186 are completely software compatible by virtue of their identical execution units. Software that is system dependent may not be completely transferable, but software that is not system dependent will operate equally well on an 80188 or an 80186.

The hardware interface of the 80188 contains the major differences between the two CPUs. The pin assignments are nearly identical, however, with the following functional changes.

- A8–A15—These pins are only address outputs on the 80188. These address lines are latched internally and remain valid throughout a bus cycle in a manner similar to the 8085 upper address lines.
- $\overline{BHE}$ has no meaning on the 80188 and has been eliminated.

80188 Clock Generator

The 80188 provides an on-chip clock generator for both internal and external clock generation. The clock generator features a crystal oscillator, a divide-by-two counter, synchronous and asynchronous ready inputs, and reset circuitry.

Oscillator

The oscillator circuit of the 80188 is designed to be used with a parallel resonant fundamental mode crystal. This is used as the time base for the 80188. The crystal frequency selected will be double the CPU clock frequency. Use of an LC or RC circuit is not recommended with this oscillator. If an external oscillator is used, it can be connected directly to input pin X1 in lieu of a crystal. The output of the oscillator is not directly available outside the 80188. The recommended crystal configuration is shown in Figure 8.

Intel recommends the following values for crystal selection parameters.

Temperature Range:	0 to 70°C
ESR (Equivalent Series Resistance):	30Ω max
C_0 (Shunt Capacitance of Crystal):	7.0 pf max
C_L (Load Capacitance):	20 pf ±2 pf
Drive Level:	1 mW max

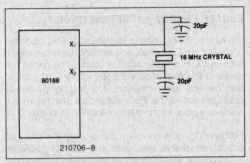

Figure 8. Recommended 8 MHz 80188 Crystal Configuration

Clock Generator

The 80188 clock generator provides the 50% duty cycle processor clock for the 80188. It does this by dividing the oscillator output by 2 forming the symmetrical clock. If an external oscillator is used, the state of the clock generator will change on the falling edge of the oscillator signal. The CLKOUT pin provides the processor clock signal for use outside the 80188. This may be used to drive other system components. All timings are referenced to the output clock.

READY Synchronization

The 80188 provides both synchronous and asynchronous ready inputs. Asynchronous ready synchronization is accomplished by circuitry which samples ARDY in the middle of T_2, T_3, and again in the middle of each T_W until ARDY is sampled HIGH. One-half CLKOUT cycle of resolution time is used for full synchronization of a rising ARDY signal. A high-to-low transition on ARDY may be used as an indication of the not ready condition but it must be performed synchronously to CLKOUT **either** in the middle of T_2, T_3, **or** T_W, or at the falling edge of T_3 or T_W.

A second ready input (SRDY) is provided to interface with externally synchronized ready signals. This input is sampled at the end of T_2, T_3, and again at the end of each T_W until it is sampled HIGH. By using this input rather than the asynchronous ready input, the half-clock cycle resolution time penalty is eliminated.

This input must satisfy set-up and hold times to guarantee proper operation of the circuit.

In addition, the 80188, as part of the integrated chip-select logic, has the capability to program WAIT states for memory and peripheral blocks. This is discussed in the Chip Select/Ready Logic description.

RESET Logic

The 80188 provides both a $\overline{\text{RES}}$ input pin and a synchronized RESET output pin for use with other system components. The $\overline{\text{RES}}$ input pin on the 80188 is provided with hysteresis in order to facilitate power-on Reset generation via an RC network. RESET output is guaranteed to remain active for at least five clocks given a $\overline{\text{RES}}$ input of at least six clocks. RESET may be delayed up to approximately two and one-half clocks behind $\overline{\text{RES}}$.

Multiple 80188 processors may be synchronized through the $\overline{\text{RES}}$ input pin, since this input resets both the processor and divide-by-two internal counter in the clock generator. In order to ensure that the divide-by-two counters all begin counting at the same time, the active going edge of $\overline{\text{RES}}$ must satisfy a 25 ns setup time before the falling edge of the 80188 clock input. In addition, in order to ensure that all CPUs begin executing in the same clock cycle, the reset must satisfy a 25 ns setup time before the rising edge of the CLKOUT signal of all the processors.

LOCAL BUS CONTROLLER

The 80188 provides a local bus controller to generate the local bus control signals. In addition, it employs a HOLD/HLDA protocol for relinquishing the local bus to other bus masters. It also provides outputs that can be used to enable external buffers and to direct the flow of data on and off the local bus.

Memory/Peripheral Control

The 80188 provides ALE, $\overline{\text{RD}}$, and $\overline{\text{WR}}$ bus control signals. The $\overline{\text{RD}}$ and $\overline{\text{WR}}$ signals are used to strobe data from memory or I/O to the 80188 or to strobe data from the 80188 to memory or I/O. The ALE line provides a strobe to latch the address when it is valid. The 80188 local bus controller does not provide a memory/$\overline{\text{I/O}}$ signal. If this is required, use the $\overline{\text{S2}}$ signal (which will require external latching), make the memory and I/O spaces nonoverlapping, or use only the integrated chip-select circuitry.

Transceiver Control

The 80188 generates two control signals for external transceiver chips. This capability allows the addition of transceivers for extra buffering without adding

external logic. These control lines, DT/$\overline{\text{R}}$ and $\overline{\text{DEN}}$, are generated to control the flow of data through the transceivers. The operation of these signals is shown in Table 6.

Table 6. Transceiver Control Signals Description

Pin Name	Function
$\overline{\text{DEN}}$ (Data Enable)	Enables the output drivers of the transceivers. It is active LOW during memory, I/O, or INTA cycles.
DT/$\overline{\text{R}}$ (Data Transmit/Receive)	Determines the direction of travel through the transceivers. A HIGH level directs data away from the processor during write operations, while a LOW level directs data toward the processor during a read operation.

Local Bus Arbitration

The 80188 uses a HOLD/HLDA system of local bus exchange. This provides an asynchronous bus exchange mechanism. This means multiple masters utilizing the same bus can operate at separate clock frequencies. The 80188 provides a single HOLD/HLDA pair through which all other bus masters may gain control of the local bus. External circuitry must arbitrate which external device will gain control of the bus when there is more than one alternate local bus master. When the 80188 relinquishes control of the local bus, it floats $\overline{\text{DEN}}$, $\overline{\text{RD}}$, $\overline{\text{WR}}$, S0–S2, $\overline{\text{LOCK}}$, AD0–AD7, A8–A19, $\overline{\text{S7}}$, and DT/$\overline{\text{R}}$ to allow another master to drive these lines directly.

The 80188 HOLD latency time, i.e., the time between HOLD request and HOLD acknowledge, is a function of the activity occurring in the processor when the HOLD request is received. A HOLD request is the highest-priority activity request which the processor may receive: higher than instruction fetching or internal DMA cycles. However, if a DMA cycle is in progress, the 80188 will complete the transfer before relinquishing the bus. This implies that if a HOLD request is received just as a DMA transfer begins, the HOLD latency time can be as great as 4 bus cycles. This will occur if a DMA word transfer operation is taking place from an odd address to an odd address. This is a total of 16 clocks or more, if WAIT states are required. In addition, if locked transfers are performed, the HOLD latency time will be increased by the length of the locked transfer.

Local Bus Controller and Reset

During RESET the local bus controller will perform the following actions:

- Drive $\overline{DEN}$, $\overline{RD}$, and $\overline{WR}$ HIGH for one clock cycle, then float.

NOTE:

$\overline{RD}$ is also provided with an internal pull-up device to prevent the processor from inadvertently entering Queue Status Mode during RESET.

- Drive $\overline{S0}-\overline{S2}$ to the inactive state (all HIGH) and then float.
- Drive $\overline{LOCK}$ HIGH and then float.
- Three-state AD0–7, A8–19, S7, DT/$\overline{R}$.
- Drive ALE LOW (ALE is never floated).
- Drive HLDA LOW.

INTERNAL PERIPHERAL INTERFACE

All the 80188 integrated peripherals are controlled by 16-bit registers contained within an internal 256-byte control block. The control block may be mapped into either memory or I/O space. Internal logic will recognize control block addresses and respond to bus cycles. During bus cycles to internal registers, the bus controller will signal the operation externally (i.e., the $\overline{RD}$, $\overline{WR}$, status, address, data, etc., lines will be driven as in a normal bus cycle), but D_{7-0}, SRDY, and ARDY will be ignored. The base address of the control block must be on an even 256-byte boundary (i.e., the lower 8 bits of the base address are all zeros). All of the defined registers within this control block may be read or written by the 80188 CPU at any time

The control block base address is programmed by a 16-bit relocation register contained within the control block at offset FEH from the base address of the control block (see Figure 9). It provides the upper 12 bits of the base address of the control block. Note that mapping the control register block into an address range corresponding to a chip-select range is not recommended (the chip select circuitry is discussed later in this data sheet. In addition, bit 12 of this register determines whether the control block will be mapped into I/O or memory space. If this bit is 1, the control block will be located in memory space. If the bit is 0, the control block will be located in I/O space. If the control register block is mapped into I/O space, the upper 4 bits of the base address must be programmed as 0 (since I/O addresses are only 16 bits wide).

Whenever mapping the 188 peripheral control block to another location, the programming of the relocation register should be done with a byte write (i.e. OUT DX,AL). Any access to the control block is done 16 bits at a time. Thus, internally, the relocation register will get written with 16 bits of the AX register while externally, the BIU will run only one 8-bit bus cycle. If a word instruction is used (i.e. OUT DX,AX), the relocation register will be written on the first bus cycle. The Bus Interface Unit (BIU) will then run a second bus cycle which is unnecessary. The address of the second bus cycle will no longer be within the control block (i.e. the control block was moved on the first cycle), and therefore, will require the generation of an external ready signal to complete the cycle. For this reason we recommend byte operations to the relocation register. Byte instructions may also be used for the other registers in the control block and will eliminate half of the bus cycles required if a word operation had been specified. Byte operations are only valid on even addresses though, and are undefined on odd addresses.

In addition to providing relocation information for the control block, the relocation register contains bits which place the interrupt controller into Slave Mode, and cause the CPU to interrupt upon encountering ESC instructions. At RESET, the relocation register is set to 20FFH which maps the control block to start at FF00H in I/O space. An offset map of the 256-byte control register block is shown in Figure 10.

CHIP-SELECT/READY GENERATION LOGIC

The 80188 contains logic which provides programmable chip-select generation for both memories and peripherals. In addition, it can be programmed to provide READY (or WAIT state) generation. It can also provide latched address bits A1 and A2. The chip-select lines are active for all memory and I/O cycles in their programmed areas, whether they be generated by the CPU or by the integrated DMA unit.

Memory Chip Selects

The 80188 provides 6 memory chip select outputs for 3 address areas: upper memory, lower memory, and midrange memory. One each is provided for upper memory and lower memory, while four are provided for midrange memory.

The range for each chip select is user-programmable and can be set to 2K, 4K, 8K, 16K, 32K, 64K, 128K (plus 1K and 256K for upper and lower chip selects). In addition, the beginning or base address

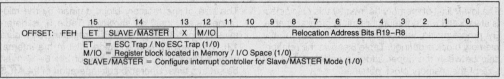

ET = ESC Trap / No ESC Trap (1/0)
M/IO = Register block located in Memory / I/O Space (1/0)
SLAVE/MASTER = Configure interrupt controller for Slave/MASTER Mode (1/0)

Figure 9. Relocation Register

	OFFSET
Relocation Register	FEH
DMA Descriptors Channel 1	DAH
	D0H
DMA Descriptors Channel 0	CAH
	C0H
Chip-Select Control Registers	A8H
	A0H
Timer 2 Control Registers	66H
	60H
Timer 1 Control Registers	5EH
	58H
Timer 0 Control Registers	56H
	50H
Interrupt Controller Registers	3EH
	20H

Figure 10. Internal Register Map

of the midrange memory chip select may also be selected. Only one chip select may be programmed to be active for any memory location at a time. All chip select sizes are in bytes.

Upper Memory $\overline{CS}$

The 80188 provides a chip select, called $\overline{UCS}$, for the top of memory. The top of memory is usually used as the system memory because after reset the 80188 begins executing at memory location FFFF0H.

The upper limit of memory defined by this chip select is always FFFFFH, while the lower limit is programmable. By programming the lower limit, the size of the select block is also defined. Table 7 shows the relationship between the base address selected and the size of the memory block obtained.

Table 7. UMCS Programming Values

Starting Address (Base Address)	Memory Block Size	UMCS Value (Assuming R0 = R1 = R2 = 0)
FFC00	1K	FFF8H
FF800	2K	FFB8H
FF000	4K	FF38H
FE000	8K	FE38H
FC000	16K	FC38H
F8000	32K	F838H
F0000	64K	F038H
E0000	128K	E038H
C0000	256K	C038H

The lower limit of this memory block is defined in the UMCS register (see Figure 11). This register is at offset A0H in the internal control block. The legal values for bits 6–13 and the resulting starting address and memory block sizes are given in Table 7. Any combination of bits 6–13 not shown in Table 7 will result in undefined operation. After reset, the UMCS register is programmed for a 1K area. It must be reprogrammed if a larger upper memory area is desired.

The internal generation of any 20-bit address whose upper 16 bits are equal to or greater than the UMCS value (with bits 0–5 as "0") asserts $\overline{UCS}$. UMCS bits R2–R0 specify the ready mode for the area of memory defined by the chip select register, as explained later.

Lower Memory $\overline{CS}$

The 80188 provides a chip select for low memory called $\overline{LCS}$. The bottom of memory contains the interrupt vector table, starting at location 00000H.

The lower limit of memory defined by this chip select is always 0H, while the upper limit is programmable. By programming the upper limit, the size of the memory block is defined. Table 8 shows the relationship between the upper address selected and the size of the memory block obtained.

Table 8. LMCS Programming Values

Upper Address	Memory Block Size	LMCS Value (Assuming R0 = R1 = R2 = 0)
003FFH	1K	0038H
007FFH	2K	0078H
00FFFH	4K	00F8H
01FFFH	8K	01F8H
03FFFH	16K	03F8H
07FFFH	32K	07F8H
0FFFFH	64K	0FF8H
1FFFFH	128K	1FF8H
3FFFFH	256K	3FF8H

The upper limit of this memory block is defined in the LMCS register (see Figure 12) at offset A2H in the internal control block. The legal values for bits 6–15 and the resulting upper address and memory block sizes are given in Table 8. Any combination of bits 6–15 not shown in Table 8 will result in undefined operation. After RESET, the LMCS register value is undefined. However, the $\overline{\text{LCS}}$ chip-select line will not become active until the LMCS register is accessed.

Any internally generated 20-bit address whose upper 16 bits are less than or equal to LMCS (with bits 0–5 "1") will assert $\overline{\text{LCS}}$. LMCS register bits R2–R0 specify the READY mode for the area of memory defined by this chip-select register.

Mid-Range Memory $\overline{\text{CS}}$

The 80188 provides four $\overline{\text{MCS}}$ lines which are active within a user-locatable memory block. This block can be located within the 80188 1M byte memory address space exclusive of the areas defined by $\overline{\text{UCS}}$ and $\overline{\text{LCS}}$. Both the base address and size of this memory block are programmable.

The size of the memory block defined by the mid-range select lines, as shown in Table 9, is determined by bits 8–14 of the MPCS register (see Figure 13). This register is at location A8H in the internal control block. One and only one of bits 8–14 must be set at a time. Unpredictable operation of the $\overline{\text{MCS}}$ lines will otherwise occur. Each of the four chip-select lines is active for one of the four equal contiguous divisions of the mid-range block. If the total block size is 32K, each chip select is active for 8K of memory with $\overline{\text{MCS0}}$ being active for the first range and $\overline{\text{MCS3}}$ being active for the last range.

The EX and MS in MPCS relate to peripheral functionality as described in a later section.

Table 9. MPCS Programming Values

Total Block Size	Individual Select Size	MPCS Bits 14–8
8K	2K	0000001B
16K	4K	0000010B
32K	8K	0000100B
64K	16K	0001000B
128K	32K	0010000B
256K	64K	0100000B
512K	128K	1000000B

The base address of the mid-range memory block is defined by bits 15–9 of the MMCS register (see Figure 14). This register is at offset A6H in the internal control block. These bits correspond to bits A19–A13 of the 20-bit memory address. Bits A12–A0 of the base address are always 0. The base address may be set at any integer multiple of the size of the total memory block selected. For example, if the mid-range block size is 32K (or the size of the block for which each $\overline{\text{MCS}}$ line is active is 8K), the block could be located at 10000H or 18000H, but not at 14000H, since the first few integer multiples of a 32K memory block are 0H, 8000H, 10000H, 18000H, etc. After RESET, the contents of both of these registers are undefined. However, none of the $\overline{\text{MCS}}$ lines will be active until both the MMCS and MPCS registers are accessed.

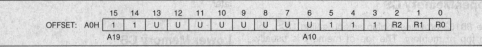

Figure 11. UMCS Register

Figure 12. LMCS Register

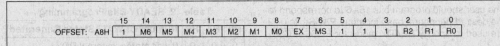

OFFSET: A8H	15	14	13	12	11	10	9	8	7	6	5	4	3	2	1	0
	1	M6	M5	M4	M3	M2	M1	M0	EX	MS	1	1	1	R2	R1	R0

Figure 13. MPCS Register

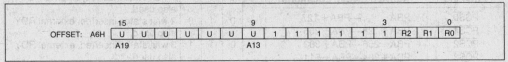

OFFSET: A6H	15						9						3			0
	U	U	U	U	U	U	1	1	1	1	1	1	R2	R1	R0
	A19						A13									

Figure 14. MMCS Register

MMCS bits R2–R0 specify READY mode of operation for all four mid-range chip selects.

The 512K block size for the mid-range memory chip selects is a special case. When using 512K, the base address would have to be at either locations 00000H or 80000H. If it were to be programmed at 00000H when the $\overline{\text{LCS}}$ line was programmed, there would be an internal conflict between the $\overline{\text{LCS}}$ ready generation logic and the $\overline{\text{MCS}}$ ready generation logic. Likewise, if the base address were programmed at 80000H, there would be a conflict with the $\overline{\text{UCS}}$ ready generation logic. Since the $\overline{\text{LCS}}$ chip-select line does not become active until programmed, while the $\overline{\text{UCS}}$ line is active at reset, the memory base can be set only at 00000H. If this base address is selected, however, the $\overline{\text{LCS}}$ range must not be programmed.

Peripheral Chip Selects

The 80188 can generate chip selects for up to seven peripheral devices. These chip selects are active for seven contiguous blocks of 128 bytes above a programmable base address. The base address may be located in either memory or I/O space.

Seven $\overline{\text{CS}}$ lines called $\overline{\text{PCS0-6}}$ are generated by the 80188. The base address is user-programmable;

however it can only be a multiple of 1K bytes, i.e., the least significant 10 bits of the starting address are always 0.

$\overline{\text{PCS5}}$ and $\overline{\text{PCS6}}$ can also be programmed to provide latched address bits A1 and A2. If so programmed, they cannot be used as peripheral selects. These outputs can be connected directly to the A0 and A1 pins used for selecting internal registers of 8-bit peripheral chips.

The starting address of the peripheral chip-select block is defined by the PACS register (see Figure 15). The register is located at offset A4H in the internal control block. Bits 15–6 of this register correspond to bits 19–10 of the 20-bit Programmable Base Address (PBA) of the peripheral chip-select block. Bits 9–0 of the PBA of the peripheral chip-select block are all zeros. If the chip-select block is located in I/O space, bits 12–15 must be programmed zero, since the I/O address is only 16 bits wide. Table 10 shows the address range of each peripheral chip select with respect to the PBA contained in PACS register.

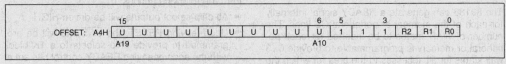

OFFSET: A4H	15								6	5		3			0
	U	U	U	U	U	U	U	U	U	U	1	1	1	R2	R1	R0
	A19									A10						

Figure 15. PACS Register

The user should program bits 15–6 to correspond to the desired peripheral base location. PACS bits 0–2 are used to specify READY mode for PCS0–PCS3.

Table 10. PCS Address Ranges

PCS Line	Active between Locations
PCS0	PBA —PBA + 127
PCS1	PBA + 128—PBA + 255
PCS2	PBA + 256—PBA + 383
PCS3	PBA + 384—PBA + 511
PCS4	PBA + 512—PBA + 639
PCS5	PBA + 640—PBA + 767
PCS6	PBA + 768—PBA + 895

The mode of operation of the peripheral chip selects is defined by the MPCS register (which is also used to set the size of the mid-range memory chip-select block, see Figure 13). The register is located at offset A8H in the internal control block. Bit 7 is used to select the function of PCS5 and PCS6, while bit 6 is used to select whether the peripheral chip selects are mapped into memory or I/O space. Table 11 describes the programming of these bits. After RESET, the contents of both the MPCS and the PACS registers are undefined, however none of the PCS lines will be active until both of the MPCS and PACS registers are accessed.

Table 11. MS, EX Programming Values

Bit	Description
MS	1 = Peripherals mapped into memory space.
	0 = Peripherals mapped into I/O space.
EX	0 = 5 PCS lines. A1, A2 provided.
	1 = 7 PCS lines. A1, A2 are not provided.

MPCS bits 0–2 specify the READY mode for PCS4–PCS6 as outlined below.

READY Generation Logic

The 80188 can generate a READY signal internally for each of the memory or peripheral CS lines. The number of WAIT states to be inserted for each peripheral or memory is programmable to provide 0–3 wait states for all accesses to the area for which the chip select is active. In addition, the 80188 may be programmed to either ignore external READY for each chip-select range individually or to factor external READY with the integrated ready generator.

READY control consists of 3 bits for each CS line or group of lines generated by the 80188. The interpretation of the READY bits is shown in Table 12.

Table 12. READY Bits Programming

R2	R1	R0	Number of WAIT States Generated
0	0	0	0 wait states, external RDY also used.
0	0	1	1 wait state inserted, external RDY also used.
0	1	0	2 wait states inserted, external RDY also used.
0	1	1	3 wait states inserted, external RDY also used.
1	0	0	0 wait states, external RDY ignored.
1	0	1	1 wait state inserted, external RDY ignored.
1	1	0	2 wait states inserted, external RDY ignored.
1	1	1	3 wait states inserted, external RDY ignored.

The internal READY generator operates in parallel with external READY, not in series if the external READY is used (R2 = 0). For example, if the internal generator is set to insert two wait states, but activity on the external READY lines will insert four wait states, the processor will only insert four wait states, not six. This is because the two wait states generated by the internal generator overlapped the first two wait states generated by the external ready signal. Note that the external ARDY and SRDY lines are always ignored during cycles accessing internal peripherals.

R2–R0 of each control word specifies the READY mode for the corresponding block, with the exception of the peripheral chip selects: R2–R0 of PACS set the PCS0–3 READY mode, R2–R0 of MPCS set the PCS4–6 READY mode.

Chip Select/Ready Logic and Reset

Upon RESET, the Chip-Select/Ready Logic will perform the following actions:

- All chip-select outputs will be driven HIGH.
- Upon leaving RESET, the UCS line will be programmed to provide chip selects to a 1K block with the accompanying READY control bits set at 011 to insert 3 wait states in conjunction with external READY (i.e., UMCS resets to FFFBH).
- No other chip select or READY control registers have any predefined values after RESET. They will not become active until the CPU accesses their control registers. Both the PACS and MPCS registers must be accessed before the PCS lines will become active.

DMA Channels

The 80188 DMA controller provides two independent DMA channels. Data transfers can occur between memory and I/O spaces (e.g., Memory to I/O) or within the same space (e.g., Memory to Memory or I/O to I/O). Each DMA channel maintains both a 20-bit source and destination pointer which can be optionally incremented or decremented after each data transfer. Each data transfer consumes 2 bus cycles (a minimum of 8 clocks), one cycle to fetch data and the other to store data. This provides a data transfer rate of one MByte/sec at 8 MHz.

DMA Operation

Each channel has six registers in the control block which define each channel's operation. The control registers consist of a 20-bit Source pointer (2 words), a 20-bit Destination pointer (2 words), a 16-bit Transfer Count Register, and a 16-bit Control Word.

The format of the DMA Control Blocks is shown in Table 13. The Transfer Count Register (TC) specifies the number of DMA transfers to be performed. Up to 64K byte transfers can be performed with automatic termination. The Control Word defines the channel's operation (see Figure 17). All registers may be modified or altered during any DMA activity. Any changes made to these registers will be reflected immediately in DMA operation.

Table 13. DMA Control Block Format

Register Name	Register Address	
	Ch. 0	Ch. 1
Control Word	CAH	DAH
Transfer Count	C8H	D8H
Destination Pointer (upper 4 bits)	C6H	D6H
Destination Pointer	C4H	D4H
Source Pointer (upper 4 bits)	C2H	D2H
Source Pointer	C0H	D0H

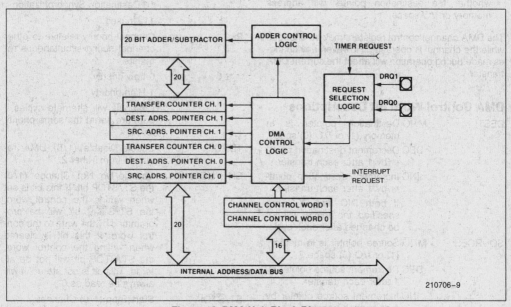

Figure 16. DMA Unit Block Diagram

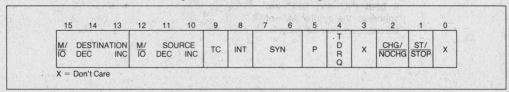

Figure 17. DMA Control Register

DMA Channel Control Word Register

Each DMA Channel Control Word determines the mode of operation for the particular 80188 DMA channel. This register specifies:

- the mode of synchronization;
- whether interrupts will be generated after the last transfer;
- whether DMA activity will cease after a programmed number of DMA cycles;
- the relative priority of the DMA channel with respect to the other DMA channel;
- whether the source pointer will be incremented, decremented, or maintained constant after each transfer;
- whether the source pointer addresses memory or I/O space;
- whether the destination pointer will be incremented, decremented, or maintained constant after each transfer; and
- whether the destination pointer will address memory or I/O space.

The DMA channel control registers may be changed while the channel is operating. However, any changes made during operation will affect the current DMA transfer.

DMA Control Word Bit Descriptions

DEST: M/$\overline{\text{IO}}$ Destination pointer is in memory (1) or I/O (0) space.

DEC Decrement destination pointer by 1 after each transfer.

INC Increment destination pointer by 1 after each transfer.

If both INC and DEC are specified, the pointer will not be changed after each cycle.

SOURCE: M/$\overline{\text{IO}}$ Source pointer is in memory (1) or I/O (0) space.

DEC Decrement source pointer by 1 after each transfer.

INC Increment source pointer by 1 after each transfer.

If both INC and DEC are specified, the pointer will not be changed after each cycle.

TC: If set, DMA will terminate when the contents of the transfer count register reach zero. The ST/$\overline{\text{STOP}}$ bit will also be reset at this point. If cleared, the DMA controller will decrement the transfer count register for each DMA cycle, but DMA transfers will not stop when the transfer count register reaches zero.

INT: Enable interrupts to CPU upon transfer count termination.

SYN: 00 No synchronization.

NOTE:

When unsynchronized transfers are specified, the TC bit will be ignored and the ST bit will be cleared upon the transfer count reaching zero, stopping the channel.

01 Source Synchronization.

10 Destination Synchronization.

11 Unused.

P: Channel priority relative to other channel during simultaneous requests.

0 Low priority.

1 High priority.

Channels will alternate cycles if both are set at the same priority level.

TDRQ: Enable/Disable (1/0) DMA requests from Timer 2.

CHG/$\overline{\text{NOCHG}}$:   Change/Do Not Change (1/0) the ST/$\overline{\text{STOP}}$ bit. If this bit is set when writing the control word, the ST/$\overline{\text{STOP}}$ bit will be programmed by the write to the control word. If this bit is cleared when writing the control word, the ST/$\overline{\text{STOP}}$ bit will not be altered. This bit is not stored; it will always be read as 0.

ST/$\overline{\text{STOP}}$:   Start/Stop (1/0) Channel.

DMA Destination and Source Pointer Registers

Each DMA channel maintains a 20-bit source and a 20-bit destination pointer. Each of these pointers takes up two full 16-bit registers in the peripheral control block. The lower four bits of the upper register contain the upper four bits of the 20-bit physical address (see Figure 18). These pointers may be individually incremented or decremented after each transfer. Each pointer may point into either memory or I/O space. Since the DMA channels can perform transfers to or from odd addresses, there is no restriction on values for the pointer registers.

DMA Transfer Count Register

Each DMA channel maintains a 16-bit transfer count register (TC). The register is decremented after every DMA cycle, regardless of the state of the TC bit in the DMA Control Register. If the TC bit in the DMA control word is set or if unsynchronized transfers are programmed, DMA activity will terminate when the transfer count register reaches zero.

DMA Requests

Data transfers may be either source or destination synchronized, that is either the source of the data or the destination of the data may request the data transfer. In addition, DMA transfers may be unsyn-

chronized; that is, the transfer will take place continually until the correct number of transfers has occurred. When source or unsynchronized transfers are performed, the DMA channel may begin another transfer immediately after the end of a previous DMA transfer. This allows a complete transfer to take place every 2 bus cycles or eight clock cycles (assuming no wait states). When destination synchronized transfers are performed, data will not be fetched from the source address until the destination device signals that it is ready to receive it. Also, the DMA controller will relinquish control of the bus after every transfer. If no other bus activity is initiated, another destination synchronized DMA cycle will begin after two processor clocks. This allows the destination device time to remove its request if another transfer is not desired. Since the DMA controller will relinquish the bus, the CPU can initiate a bus cycle. As a result, a complete bus cycle will often be inserted between destination synchronized transfers. Table 14 shows the maximum DMA transfer rates.

Table 14. Maximum DMA Transfer Rates @ CLKOUT = 8 MHz

Type of Synchronization Selected	CPU Running	CPU Halted
Unsynchronized	1.0 MBytes/sec	1.0 MBytes/sec
Source Synch	1.0 MBytes/sec	1.0 MBytes/sec
Destination Synch	0.67 MBytes/sec	0.80 MBytes/sec

HIGHER REGISTER ADDRESS	XXX	XXX	XXX	A19–A16
LOWER REGISTER ADDRESS	A15–A12	A11–A8	A7–A4	A3–A0

15   0

XXX = Don't Care

Figure 18. DMA Pointer Register Format

DMA Acknowledge

No explicit DMA acknowledge pulse is provided. Since both source and destination pointers are maintained, a read from a requesting source, or a write to a requesting destination, should be used as the DMA acknowledge signal. Since the chip-select lines can be programmed to be active for a given block of memory or I/O space, and the DMA pointers can be programmed to point to the same given block, a chip-select line could be used to indicate a DMA acknowledge.

DMA Priority

The DMA channels may be programmed to give one channel priority over the other, or they may be programmed to alternate cycles when both have DMA requests pending. DMA cycles always have priority over internal CPU cycles except between locked memory accesses or word accesses to odd memory locations; also, an external bus hold takes priority over an internal DMA cycle. Because an interrupt request cannot suspend a DMA operation and the CPU cannot access memory during a DMA cycle, interrupt latency time will suffer during sequences of continuous DMA cycles. An NMI request, however, will cause all internal DMA activity to halt. This allows the CPU to quickly respond to the NMI request.

DMA Programming

DMA cycles will occur whenever the ST/STOP bit of the Control Register is set. If synchronized transfers

are programmed, a DRQ must also be generated. Therefore, the source and destination transfer pointers, and the transfer count register (if used) must be programmed before the ST/STOP bit is set.

Each DMA register may be modified while the channel is operating. If the CHG/NOCHG bit is cleared when the control register is written, the ST/STOP bit of the control register will not be modified by the write. If multiple channel registers are modified, it is recommended that a LOCKED string transfer be used to prevent a DMA transfer from occurring between updates to the channel registers.

DMA Channels and Reset

Upon RESET, the DMA channels will perform the following actions:

- The ST/STOP bit for each channel will be reset to STOP.
- Any transfer in progress is aborted.

TIMERS

The 80188 provides three internal 16-bit programmable timers (see Figure 19). Two of these are highly flexible and are connected to four external pins (2 per timer). They can be used to count external events, time external events, generate nonrepetitive waveforms, etc. The third timer is not connected to any external pins, and is useful for real-time coding and time delay applications. In addition, the third timer can be used as a prescaler to the other two, or as a DMA request source.

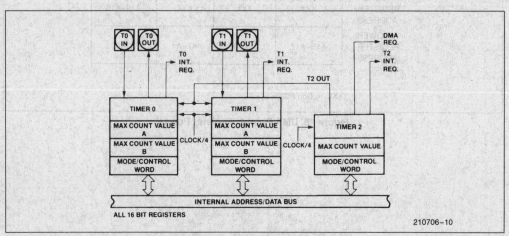

Figure 19. Timer Block Diagram

Timer Operation

The timers are controlled by 11 16-bit registers in the peripheral control block. The configuration of these registers is shown in Table 15. The count register contains the current value of the timer. It can be read or written at any time independent of whether the timer is running or not. The value of this register will be incremented for each timer event. Each of the timers is equipped with a MAX COUNT register, which defines the maximum count the timer will reach. After reaching the MAX COUNT register value, the timer count value will reset to zero during that same clock, i.e., the maximum count value is never stored in the count register itself. Timers 0 and 1 are, in addition, equipped with a second MAX COUNT register, which enables the timers to alternate their count between two different MAX COUNT values. If a single MAX COUNT register is used, the timer output pin will switch LOW for a single clock, 2 clocks after the maximum count value has been reached. In the dual MAX COUNT register mode, the output pin will indicate which MAX COUNT register is currently in use, thus allowing nearly complete freedom in selecting waveform duty cycles. For the timers with two MAX COUNT registers, the RIU bit in the control register determines which is used for the comparison.

Each timer gets serviced every fourth CPU-clock cycle, and thus can operate at speeds up to one-quarter the internal clock frequency (one-eighth the crystal rate). External clocking of the timers may be done at up to a rate of one-quarter of the internal CPU-clock rate (2 MHz for an 8 MHz CPU clock). Due to internal synchronization and pipelining of the timer circuitry, a timer output may take up to 6 clocks to respond to any individual clock or gate input.

Since the count registers and the maximum count registers are all 16 bits wide, 16 bits of resolution are provided. Any Read or Write access to the timers will add one wait state to the minimum four-clock bus cycle, however. This is needed to synchronize and coordinate the internal data flows between the internal timers and the internal bus.

The timers have several programmable options.

- All three timers can be set to halt or continue on a terminal count.

- Timers 0 and 1 can select between internal and external clocks, alternate between MAX COUNT registers and be set to retrigger on external events.

- The timers may be programmed to cause an interrupt on terminal count.

These options are selectable via the timer mode/control word.

Timer Mode/Control Register

The mode/control register (see Figure 20) allows the user to program the specific mode of operation or check the current programmed status for any of the three integrated timers.

Table 15. Timer Control Block Format

Register Name	Register Offset		
	Tmr. 0	Tmr. 1	Tmr. 2
Mode/Control Word	56H	5EH	66H
Max Count B	54H	5CH	not present
Max Count A	52H	5AH	62H
Count Register	50H	58H	60H

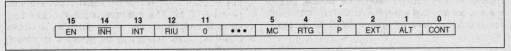

15	14	13	12	11	•••	5	4	3	2	1	0
EN	INH	INT	RIU	0		MC	RTG	P	EXT	ALT	CONT

Figure 20. Timer Mode/Control Register

EN

The enable bit provides programmer control over the timer's RUN/HALT status. When set, the timer is enabled to increment subject to the input pin constraints in the internal clock mode (discussed previously). When cleared, the timer will be inhibited from counting. All input pin transitions during the time EN is zero will be ignored. If CONT is zero, the EN bit is automatically cleared upon maximum count.

INH

The inhibit bit allows for selective updating of the enable (EN) bit. If $\overline{INH}$ is a one during the write to the mode/control word, then the state of the EN bit will be modified by the write. If $\overline{INH}$ is a zero during the write, the EN bit will be unaffected by the operation. This bit is not stored; it will always be a 0 on a read.

INT

When set, the INT bit enables interrupts from the timer, which will be generated on every terminal count. If the timer is configured in dual MAX COUNT register mode, an interrupt will be generated each time the value in MAX COUNT register A is reached, and each time the value in MAX COUNT register B is reached. If this enable bit is cleared after the interrupt request has been generated, but before a pending interrupt is serviced, the interrupt request will still be in force. (The request is latched in the Interrupt Controller.)

RIU

The Register In Use bit indicates which MAX COUNT register is currently being used for comparison to the timer count value. A zero value indicates register A. The RIU bit cannot be written, i.e., its value is not affected when the control register is written. It is always cleared when the ALT bit is zero.

MC

The Maximum Count bit is set whenever the timer reaches its final maximum count value. If the timer is configured in dual MAX COUNT register mode, this bit will be set each time the value in MAX COUNT register A is reached, and each time the value in MAX COUNT register B is reached. This bit is set regardless of the timer's interrupt-enable bit. The MC bit gives the user the ability to monitor timer status through software instead of through interrupts. Programmer intervention is required to clear this bit.

RTG

Retrigger bit is only active for internal clocking (EXT = 0). In this case it determines the control function provided by the input pin.

If RTG = 0, the input level gates the internal clock on and off. If the input pin is HIGH, the timer will count; if the input pin is LOW, the timer will hold its value. As indicated previously, the input signal may be asynchronous with respect to the 80188 clock.

When RTG = 1, the input pin detects LOW-to-HIGH transitions. The first such transition starts the timer running, clearing the timer value to zero on the first clock, and then incrementing thereafter. Further transitions on the input pin will again reset the timer to zero, from which it will start counting up again. If CONT = 0, when the timer has reached maximum count, the EN bit will be cleared, inhibiting further timer activity.

P

The prescaler bit is ignored unless internal clocking has been selected (EXT = 0). If the P bit is a zero, the timer will count at one-fourth the internal CPU clock rate. If the P bit is a one, the output of timer 2 will be used as a clock for the timer. Note that the user must initialize and start timer 2 to obtain the prescaled clock.

EXT

The external bit selects between internal and external clocking for the timer. The external signal may be asynchronous with respect to the 80188 clock. If this bit is set, the timer will count LOW-to-HIGH transitions on the input pin. If cleared, it will count an internal clock while using the input pin for control. In this mode, the function of the external pin is defined by the RTG bit. The maximum input to output transition latency time may be as much as 6 clocks. However, clock inputs may be pipelined as closely together as every 4 clocks without losing clock pulses.

ALT

The ALT bit determines which of two MAX COUNT registers is used for count comparison. If ALT = 0, register A for that timer is always used, while if ALT = 1, the comparison will alternate between register A and register B when each maximum count is reached. This alternation allows the user to change one MAX COUNT register while the other is being used, and thus provides a method of generating non-repetitive waveforms. Square waves and pulse outputs of any duty cycle are a subset of available signals obtained by not changing the final count registers. The ALT bit also determines the function of the timer output pin. If ALT is zero, the output pin will go LOW for one clock, the clock after the maximum count is reached. If ALT is one, the output pin will reflect the current MAX COUNT register being used (0/1 for B/A).

CONT

Setting the CONT bit causes the associated timer to run continuously, while resetting it causes the timer to halt upon maximum count. If CONT = 0 and ALT = 1, the timer will count to the MAX COUNT register A value, reset, count to the register B value, reset, and halt.

Not all mode bits are provided for timer 2. Certain bits are hardwired as indicated below:

ALT = 0, EXT = 0, P = 0, RTG = 0, RIU = 0

Count Registers

Each of the three timers has a 16-bit count register. The contents of this register may be read or written by the processor at any time. If the register is written while the timer is counting, the new value will take effect in the current count cycle.

Max Count Registers

Timers 0 and 1 have two MAX COUNT registers, while timer 2 has a single MAX COUNT register. These contain the number of events the timer will count. In timers 0 and 1, the MAX COUNT register used can alternate between the two max count values whenever the current maximum count is reached. A timer resets when the timer count register equals the max count value being used. If the timer count register or the max count register is changed so that the max count is less than the timer count, the timer does not immediately reset. Instead, the timer counts up to 0FFFFH, "wraps around" to zero, counts up to the max count value, and then resets.

Timers and Reset

Upon RESET, the Timers will perform the following actions:

- All EN (Enable) bits are reset preventing timer counting.
- For Timers 0 and 1, the RIU bits are reset to zero and the ALT bits are set to one. This results in the Timer Out pins going HIGH.

INTERRUPT CONTROLLER

The 80188 can receive interrupts from a number of sources, both internal and external. The internal interrupt controller serves to merge these requests on a priority basis, for individual service by the CPU.

Internal interrupt sources (Timers and DMA channels) can be disabled by their own control registers or by mask bits within the interrupt controller. The 80188 interrupt controller has its own control register that sets the mode of operation for the controller.

The interrupt controller will resolve priority among requests that are pending simultaneously. Nesting is provided so interrupt service routines for lower priority interrupts may be interrupted by higher priority interrupts. A block diagram of the interrupt controller is shown in Figure 21.

The 80188 has a special Slave Mode in which the internal interrupt controller acts as a slave to an external master. The controller is programmed into this mode by setting bit 14 in the peripheral control block relocation register. (See Slave Mode section.)

MASTER MODE OPERATION

Interrupt Controller External Interface

Five pins are provided for external interrupt sources. One of these pins is NMI, the non-maskable interrupt. NMI is generally used for unusual events such as power-fail interrupts. The other four pins may be configured in any of the following ways:

- As four interrupt input lines with internally generated interrupt vectors.
- As an interrupt line and interrupt acknowledge line pair (Cascade Mode) with externally generated interrupt vectors plus two interrupt input lines with internally generated vectors.
- As two pairs of interrupt/interrupt acknowledge lines (Cascade Mode) with externally generated interrupt vectors.

External sources in the Cascade Mode use externally generated interrupt vectors. When an interrupt is acknowledged, two INTA cycles are initiated and the vector is read into the 80188 on the second cycle. The capability to interface to external 8259A programmable interrupt controllers is provided when the inputs are configured in Cascade Mode.

Interrupt Controller Modes of Operation

The basic modes of operation of the interrupt controller in Master Mode are similar to the 8259A. The interrupt controller responds identically to internal interrupts in all three modes: the difference is only in the interpretation of function of the four external interrupt pins. The interrupt controller is set into one of these three modes by programming the correct bits in the INT0 and INT1 control registers. The modes of interrupt controller operation are as follows:

FULLY NESTED MODE

When in the fully nested mode four pins are used as direct interrupt requests as in Figure 22. The vectors for these four inputs are generated internally. An in-service bit is provided for every interrupt source. If a lower-priority device requests an interrupt while the in-service bit (IS) is set, no interrupt will be generated by the interrupt controller. In addition, if another interrupt request occurs from the same interrupt source while the in-service bit is set, no interrupt will be generated by the interrupt controller. This allows interrupt service routines to operate with interrupts enabled, yet be suspended only by interrupts of higher priority than the in-service interrupt.

When a service routine is completed, the proper IS bit must be reset by writing the proper pattern to the EOI register. This is required to allow subsequent interrupts from this interrupt source and to allow servicing of lower-priority interrupts. An EOI command is executed at the end of the service routine just before the return from interrupt instruction. If the fully nested structure has been upheld, the next highest-priority source with its IS bit set is then serviced.

CASCADE MODE

The 80188 has four interrupt pins and two of them have dual functions. In the fully nested mode the four pins are used as direct interrupt inputs and the corresponding vectors are generated internally. In the Cascade Mode, the four pins are configured into interrupt input-dedicated acknowledge signal pairs. The interconnection is shown in Figure 23. INT0 is an interrupt input interfaced to an 8259A, while INT2/INTA0 serves as the dedicated interrupt acknowledge signal to that peripheral. The same is true for INT1 and INT3/INTA1. Each pair can selectively be placed in the Cascade Mode by programming the proper value into INT0 and INT1 control registers. The use of the dedicated acknowledge signals eliminates the need for the use of external logic to generate INTA and device select signals.

The primary Cascade Mode allows the capability to serve up to 128 external interrupt sources through the use of external master and slave 8259As. Three levels of priority are created, requiring priority resolution in the 80188 interrupt controller, the master 8259As, and the slave 8259As. If an external interrupt is serviced, one IS bit is set at each of these levels. When the interrupt service routine is completed, up to three end-of-interrupt commands must be issued by the programmer.

SPECIAL FULLY NESTED MODE

This mode is entered by setting the SFNM bit in INT0 or INT1 control register. It enables complete nestability with external 8259A masters. Normally, an interrupt request from an interrupt source will not be recognized unless the in-service bit for that source is reset. If more than one interrupt source is connected to an external interrupt controller, all of the interrupts will be funneled through the same 80188 interrupt request pin. As a result, if the external interrupt controller receives a higher-priority interrupt, its interrupt will not be recognized by the 80188 controller until the 80188 in-service bit is reset. In Special Fully Nested Mode, the 80188 interrupt controller will allow interrupts from an external pin regardless of the state of the in-service bit for an interrupt source in order to allow multiple interrupts from a single pin. An in-service bit will continue to be set, however, to inhibit interrupts from other lower-priority 80188 interrupt sources.

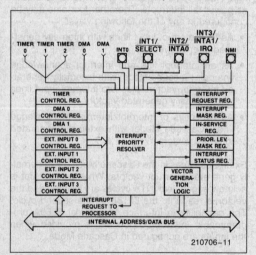

210706–11

Figure 21. Interrupt Controller Block Diagram

Special procedures should be followed when resetting IS bits at the end of interrupt service routines. Software polling of the IS register in the external master 8259A is required to determine if there is more than one bit set. If so, the IS bit in the 80188 remains active and the next interrupt service routine is entered.

Operation in a Polled Environment

The controller may be used in a polled mode if interrupts are undesirable. When polling, the processor disables interrupts and then polls the interrupt controller whenever it is convenient. Polling the interrupt controller is accomplished by reading the Poll Word (Figure 32). Bit 15 in the poll word indicates to the processor that an interrupt of high enough priority is requesting service. Bits 0–4 indicate to the processor the type vector of the highest-priority source requesting service. Reading the Poll Word causes the In-Service bit of the highest priority source to be set.

It is desirable to be able to read the Poll Word information without guaranteeing service of any pending interrupt, i.e., not set the indicated in-service bit. The 80188 provides a Poll Status Word in addition to the conventional Poll Word to allow this to be done. Poll Word information is duplicated in the Poll Status Word, but reading the Poll Status Word does not set the associated in-service bit. These words are located in two adjacent memory locations in the register file.

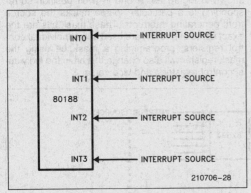

Figure 22. Fully Nested (Direct) Mode Interrupt Controller Connections

Master Mode Features

PROGRAMMABLE PRIORITY

The user can program the interrupt sources into any of eight different priority levels. The programming is done by placing a 3-bit priority level (0–7) in the control register of each interrupt source. (A source with a priority level of 4 has higher priority over all priority levels from 5 to 7. Priority registers containing values lower than 4 have greater priority). All interrupt sources have preprogrammed default priority levels (see Table 4).

If two requests with the same programmed priority level are pending at once, the priority ordering scheme shown in Table 4 is used. If the serviced interrupt routine reenables interrupts, other interrupt requests can be serviced.

END-OF-INTERRUPT COMMAND

The end-of-interrupt (EOI) command is used by the programmer to reset the In-Service (IS) bit when an interrupt service routine is completed. The EOI command is issued by writing the proper pattern to the EOI register. There are two types of EOI commands, specific and nonspecific. The nonspecific command does not specify which IS bit is reset. When issued, the interrupt controller automatically resets the IS bit of the highest priority source with an active service routine. A specific EOI command requires that the programmer send the interrupt vector type to the interrupt controller indicating which source's IS bit is to be reset. This command is used when the fully nested structure has been disturbed or the highest priority IS bit that was set does not belong to the service routine in progress.

TRIGGER MODE

The four external interrupt pins can be programmed in either edge- or level-trigger mode. The control register for each external source has a level-trigger mode (LTM) bit. All interrupt inputs are active HIGH. In the edge sense mode or the level-trigger mode, the interrupt request must remain active (HIGH) until the interrupt request is acknowledged by the 80188 CPU. In the edge-sense mode, if the level remains high after the interrupt is acknowledged, the input is disabled and no further requests will be generated. The input level must go LOW for at least one clock cycle to re-enable the input. In the level-trigger mode, no such provision is made: holding the interrupt input HIGH will cause continuous interrupt requests.

INTERRUPT VECTORING

The 80188 Interrupt Controller will generate interrupt vectors for the integrated DMA channels and the integrated Timers. In addition, the Interrupt Controller will generate interrupt vectors for the external interrupt lines if they are not configured in Cascade or Special Fully Nested Modes. The interrupt vectors generated are fixed and cannot be changed (see Table 4).

Interrupt Controller Registers

The Interrupt Controller register model is shown in Figure 24. It contains 15 registers. All registers can both be read or written unless specified otherwise.

IN-SERVICE REGISTER

This register can be read from or written into. The format is shown in Figure 25. It contains the In-Service bit for each of the interrupt sources. The In-Service bit is set to indicate that a source's service routine is in progress. When an In-Service bit is set, the interrupt controller will not generate interrupts to the CPU when it receives interrupt requests from devices with a lower programmed priority level. The TMR bit is the In-Service bit for all three timers; the D0 and D1 bits are the In-Service bits for the two DMA channels; the I0–I3 are the In-Service bits for the external interrupt pins. The IS bit is set when the processor acknowledges an interrupt request either by an interrupt acknowledge or by reading the poll register. The IS bit is reset at the end of the interrupt service routine by an end-of-interrupt command.

INTERRUPT REQUEST REGISTER

The internal interrupt sources have interrupt request bits inside the interrupt controller. The format of this register is shown in Figure 25. A read from this register yields the status of these bits. The TMR bit is the logical OR of all timer interrupt requests. D0 and D1 are the interrupt request bits for the DMA channels.

The state of the external interrupt input pins is also indicated. The state of the external interrupt pins is not a stored condition inside the interrupt controller, therefore the external interrupt bits cannot be written. The external interrupt request bits are set when an interrupt request is given to the interrupt controller, so if edge-triggered mode is selected, the bit in the register will be HIGH only after an inactive-to-active transition. For internal interrupt sources, the register bits are set when a request arrives and are reset when the processor acknowledges the requests.

Writes to to the interrupt request register will affect the D0 and D1 interrupt request bits. Setting either bit will cause the corresponding interrupt request while clearing either bit will remove the corresponding interrupt request. All other bits in the register are read-only.

MASK REGISTER

This is a 16-bit register that contains a mask bit for each interrupt source. The format for this register is shown in Figure 25. A one in a bit position corresponding to a particular source masks the source from generating interrupts. These mask bits are the exact same bits which are used in the individual control registers; programming a mask bit using the mask register will also change this bit in the individual control registers, and vice versa.

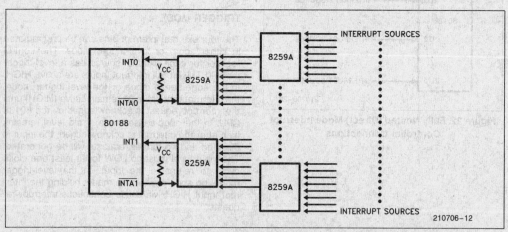

Figure 23. Cascade and Special Fully Nested Mode Interrupt Controller Connections

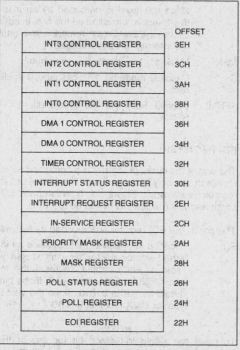

	OFFSET
INT3 CONTROL REGISTER	3EH
INT2 CONTROL REGISTER	3CH
INT1 CONTROL REGISTER	3AH
INT0 CONTROL REGISTER	38H
DMA 1 CONTROL REGISTER	36H
DMA 0 CONTROL REGISTER	34H
TIMER CONTROL REGISTER	32H
INTERRUPT STATUS REGISTER	30H
INTERRUPT REQUEST REGISTER	2EH
IN-SERVICE REGISTER	2CH
PRIORITY MASK REGISTER	2AH
MASK REGISTER	28H
POLL STATUS REGISTER	26H
POLL REGISTER	24H
EOI REGISTER	22H

Figure 24. Interrupt Controller Registers (Master Mode)

PRIORITY MASK REGISTER

This register masks all interrupts below a particular interrupt priority level. The format of this register is shown in Figure 26. The code in the lower three bits of this register inhibits interrupts of priority lower (a higher priority number) than the code specified. For example, 100 written into this register masks interrupts of level five (101), six (110), and seven (111). The register is reset to seven (111) upon RESET so no interrupts are masked due to priority number.

INTERRUPT STATUS REGISTER

This register contains general interrupt controller status information. The format of this register is shown in Figure 27. The bits in the status register have the following functions:

DHLT: DMA Halt Transfer; setting this bit halts all DMA transfers. It is automatically set whenever a non-maskable interrupt occurs, and it is reset when an IRET instruction is executed. This bit allows prompt service of all non-maskable interrupts. This bit may also be set by the programmer.

IRTx: These three bits represent the individual timer interrupt request bits. These bits differentiate between timer interrupts, since the timer IR bit in the interrupt request register is the "OR" function of all timer interrupt requests. Note that setting any one of these three bits initiates an interrupt request to the interrupt controller.

Figure 25. In-Service, Interrupt Request, and Mask Register Formats

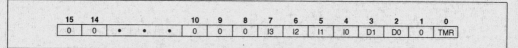

Figure 26. Priority Mask Register Format

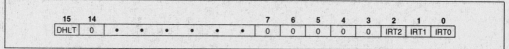

Figure 27. Interrupt Status Register Format (non-RMX Mode)

TIMER, DMA 0, 1; CONTROL REGISTERS

These registers are the control words for all the internal interrupt sources. The format for these registers is shown in Figure 28. The three bit positions PR0, PR1, and PR2 represent the programmable priority level of the interrupt source. The MSK bit inhibits interrupt requests from the interrupt source. The MSK bits in the individual control registers are the exact same bits as are in the Mask Register; modifying them in the individual control registers will also modify them in the Mask Register, and vice versa.

INT0-INT3 CONTROL REGISTERS

These registers are the control words for the four external input pins. Figure 29 shows the format of the INT0 and INT1 Control registers; Figure 30 shows the format of the INT2 and INT3 Control registers. In Cascade Mode or Special Fully Nested Mode, the control words for INT2 and INT3 are not used.

The bits in the various control registers are encoded as follows:

PR0-2: Priority programming information. Highest priority = 000, lowest priority = 111.

LTM: Level-trigger mode bit. 1 = level-triggered; 0 = edge-triggered. Interrupt Input levels are active high. In level-triggered mode, an interrupt is generated whenever the external line is high. In edge-triggered mode, an interrupt will be generated only

when this level is preceded by an inactive-to-active transition on the line. In both cases, the level must remain active until the interrupt is acknowledged.

MSK: Mask bit, 1 = mask; 0 = non-mask.

C: Cascade mode bit, 1 = cascade; 0 = direct.

SFNM: Special Fully Nested Mode bit, 1 = SFNM.

EOI REGISTER

The end of the interrupt register is a command register which can only be written into. The format of this register is shown in Figure 31. It initiates an EOI command when written to by the 80188 CPU.

The bits in the EOI register are encoded as follows:

S_x: Encoded information that specifies an interrupt source vector type as shown in Table 4. For example, to reset the In-Service bit for DMA channel 0, these bits should be set to 01010, since the vector type for DMA channel 0 is 10.

NOTE:
To reset the single In-Service bit for any of the three timers, the vector type for timer 0 (8) should be written in this register.

NSPEC/: A bit that determines the type of EOI command. Nonspecific = 1, Specific = 0.
SPEC

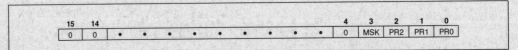

Figure 28. Timer/DMA Control Register Formats

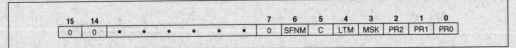

Figure 29. INT0/INT1 Control Register Formats

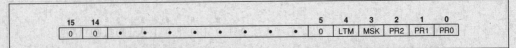

Figure 30. INT2/INT3 Control Register Formats

POLL AND POLL STATUS REGISTERS

These registers contain polling information. The format of these registers is shown in Figure 32. They can only be read. Reading the Poll register constitutes a software poll. This will set the IS bit of the highest priority pending interrupt. Reading the poll status register will not set the IS bit of the highest priority pending interrupt; only the status of pending interrupts will be provided.

Encoding of the Poll and Poll Status register bits are as follows:

S_x: Encoded information that indicates the vector type of the highest priority interrupting source. Valid only when INTREQ = 1.

INTREQ: This bit determines if an interrupt request is present. Interrupt Request = 1; no Interrupt Request = 0.

SLAVE MODE OPERATION

When Slave Mode is used, the internal 80188 interrupt controller will be used as a slave controller to an external master interrupt controller. The internal 80188 resources will be monitored by the internal interrupt controller, while the external controller functions as the system master interrupt controller. Upon reset, the 80188 will be in Master Mode. To provide for slave mode operation bit 14 of the relocation register should be set.

Because of pin limitations caused by the need to interface to an external 8259A master, the internal interrupt controller will no longer accept external inputs. There are however, enough 80188 interrupt controller inputs (internally) to dedicate one to each timer. In this mode, each timer interrupt source has its own mask bit, IS bit, and control word.

In Slave Mode each peripheral must be assigned a unique priority to ensure proper interrupt controller operation. Therefore, it is the programmer's responsibility to assign correct priorities and initialize interrupt control regisers before enable interrupts.

Slave Mode External Interface

The configuration of the 80188 with respect to an external 8259A master is shown in Figure 33. The INT0 (pin 45) input is used as the 80188 CPU interrupt input. IRQ (pin 41) functions as an output to send the 80188 slave-interrupt-request to one of the 8 master-PIC-inputs.

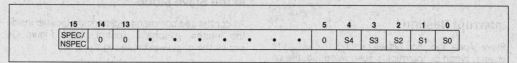

Figure 31. EOI Register Format

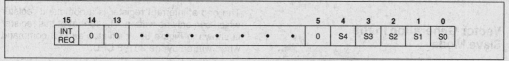

Figure 32. Poll and Poll Status Register Format

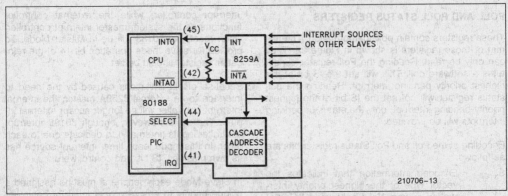

Figure 33. Slave Mode Interrupt Controller Connections

Correct master-slave interface requires decoding of the slave addresses (CAS0–2). Slave 8259As do this internally. Because of pin limitations, the 80188 slave address will have to be decoded externally. SELECT (pin 44) is used as a slave-select input. Note that the slave vector address is transferred internally, but the READY input must be supplied externally.

INTA0 (pin 42) is used as an acknowledge output, suitable to drive the INTA input of an 8259A.

Interrupt Nesting

Slave Mode operation allows nesting of interrupt requests. When an interrupt is acknowledged, the priority logic masks off all priority levels except those with equal or higher priority.

Vector Generation in the Slave Mode

Vector generation in Slave Mode is exactly like that of an 8259A or 82C59A slave. The interrupt controller generates an 8-bit vector type number which the CPU multiplies by four to use as an address into the vector table. The five most significant bits of this type number are user-programmable while the three least significant bits are defined according to Figure 34. The significant five bits of the vector are programmed by writing to the Interrupt Vector register at offset 20H.

Specific End-of-Interrupt

In Slave Mode the specific EOI command operates to reset an in-service bit of a specific priority. The user supplies a 3-bit priority-level value that points to an in-service bit to be reset. The command is executed by writing the correct value in the Specific EOI register at offset 22H.

Interrupt Controller Registers in the Slave Mode

All control and command registers are located inside the internal peripheral control block. Figure 34 shows the offsets of these registers.

END-OF-INTERRUPT REGISTER

The end-of-interrupt register is a command register which can only be written. The format of this register is shown in Figure 35. It initiates an EOI command when written by the 80188 CPU.

The bits in the EOI register are encoded as follows:

VT_x: Three least-significant vector type bits corresponding to the source for which the IS bit is to be reset. Figure 34 indicates these bits.

IN-SERVICE REGISTER

This register can be read from or written into. It contains the in-service bit for each of the internal interrupt sources. The format for this register is shown in Figure 36. Bit positions 2 and 3 correspond to the DMA channels; positions 0, 4, and 5 correspond to the integral timers. The source's IS bit is set when the processor acknowledges its interrupt request.

INTERRUPT REQUEST REGISTER

This register indicates which internal peripherals have interrupt requests pending. The format of this register is shown in Figure 36. The interrupt request bits are set when a request arrives from an internal source, and are reset when the processor acknowledges the request. As in Master Mode, D0 and D1 are read/write, all other bits are read only.

MASK REGISTER

This register contains a mask bit for each interrupt source. The format for this register is shown in Figure 36. If the bit in this register corresponding to a particular interrupt source is set, any interrupts from that source will be masked. These mask bits are exactly the same bits which are used in the individual control registers, i.e., changing the state of a mask bit in this register will also change the state of the mask bit in the individual interrupt control register corresponding to the bit.

CONTROL REGISTERS

These registers are the control words for all the internal interrupt sources. The format of these registers is shown in Figure 37. Each of the timers and both of the DMA channels have their own Control Register.

The bits of the Control Registers are encoded as follows:

pr$_x$: 3-bit encoded field indicating a priority level for the source.

msk: mask bit for the priority level indicated by pr$_x$ bits.

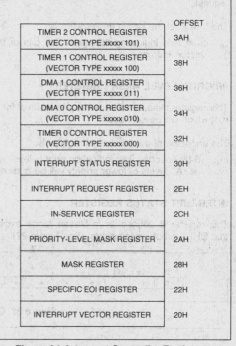

	OFFSET
TIMER 2 CONTROL REGISTER (VECTOR TYPE xxxxx 101)	3AH
TIMER 1 CONTROL REGISTER (VECTOR TYPE xxxxx 100)	38H
DMA 1 CONTROL REGISTER (VECTOR TYPE xxxxx 011)	36H
DMA 0 CONTROL REGISTER (VECTOR TYPE xxxxx 010)	34H
TIMER 0 CONTROL REGISTER (VECTOR TYPE xxxxx 000)	32H
INTERRUPT STATUS REGISTER	30H
INTERRUPT REQUEST REGISTER	2EH
IN-SERVICE REGISTER	2CH
PRIORITY-LEVEL MASK REGISTER	2AH
MASK REGISTER	28H
SPECIFIC EOI REGISTER	22H
INTERRUPT VECTOR REGISTER	20H

Figure 34. Interrupt Controller Registers (Slave Mode)

15	14	13					8	7	6	5	4	3	2	1	0
0	0	0	•	•	•	•	0	0	0	0	0	0	VT2	VT1	VT0

Figure 35. Specific EOI Register Format

15	14	13					8	7	6	5	4	3	2	1	0
0	0	0	•	•	•	•	0	0	0	TMR2	TMR1	D1	D0	0	TMR0

Figure 36. In-Service, Interrupt Request, and Mask Register Format

INTERRUPT VECTOR REGISTER

This register provides the upper five bits of the interrupt vector address. The format of this register is shown in Figure 38. The interrupt controller itself provides the lower three bits of the interrupt vector as determined by the priority level of the interrupt request.

The format of the bits in this register is:

t_x: 5-bit field indicating the upper five bits of the vector address.

PRIORITY-LEVEL MASK REGISTER

This register indicates the lowest priority-level interrupt which will be serviced.

The encoding of the bits in this register is:

m_x: 3-bit encoded field indication priority-level value. All levels of lower priority will be masked.

INTERRUPT STATUS REGISTER

This register is defined as in Master Mode except that DHLT is not implemented. (See Figure 27).

Interrupt Controller and Reset

Upon RESET, the interrupt controller will perform the following actions:

- All SFNM bits reset to 0, implying Fully Nested Mode.
- All PR bits in the various control registers set to 1. This places all sources at lowest priority (level 111).
- All LTM bits reset to 0, resulting in edge-sense mode.
- All Interrupt Service bits reset to 0.
- All Interrupt Request bits reset to 0.
- All MSK (Interrupt Mask) bits set to 1 (mask).
- All C (Cascade) bits reset to 0 (non-Cascade).
- All PRM (Priority Mask) bits set to 1, implying no levels masked.
- Initialized to Master Mode.

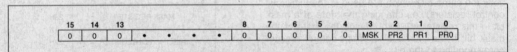

Figure 37. Control Word Format

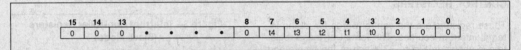

Figure 38. Interrupt Vector Register Format

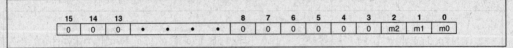

Figure 39. Priority Level Mask Register

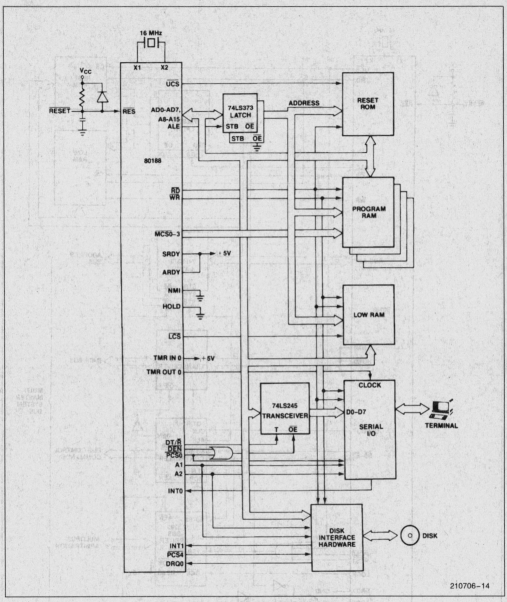

Figure 40. Typical 80188 Computer

210706–14

intel

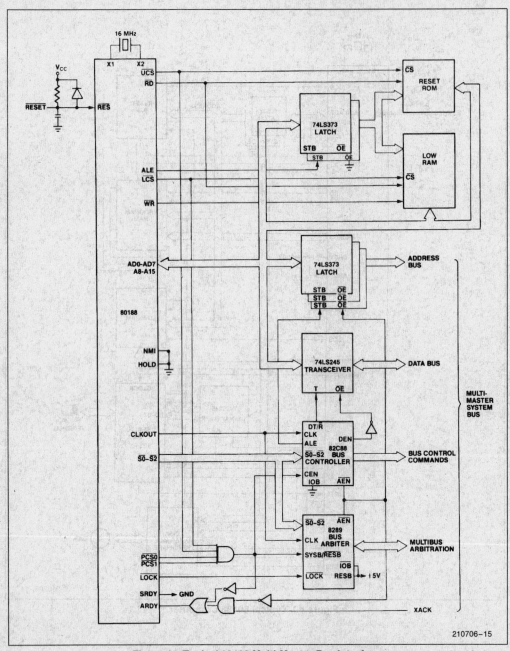

Figure 41. Typical 80188 Multi-Master Bus Interface

210706-15

ABSOLUTE MAXIMUM RATINGS*

Ambient Temperature under Bias ....0°C to +70°C

Storage Temperature .... −65°C to +150°C

Voltage on any Pin with
  Respect to Ground............. −1.0V to +7V

Power Dissipation .... 3 Watt

Notice: Stresses above those listed under "Absolute Maximum Ratings" may cause permanent damage to the device. This is a stress rating only and functional operation of the device at these or any other conditions above those indicated in the operational sections of this specification is not implied. Exposure to absolute maximum rating conditions for extended periods may affect device reliability.

D.C. CHARACTERISTICS (T_A = 0°C to +70°C, V_{CC} = 5V ±10%)
Applicable to 80188 (8 MHz)

Symbol	Parameter	Min	Max	Units	Test Conditions
V_{IL}	Input Low Voltage	−0.5	+0.8	V	
V_{IH}	Input High Voltage (All except X1 and $\overline{RES}$)	2.0	V_{CC} + 0.5	V	
V_{IH1}	Input High Voltage ($\overline{RES}$)	3.0	V_{CC} + 0.5	V	
V_{CLI}	X1 Input Low Voltage	−0.5	0.6	V	
V_{CHI}	X1 Input High Voltage	3.9	V_{CC} + 1.0	V	
V_{OL}	Output Low Voltage		0.45	V	I_a = 2.5 mA for $\overline{S0}$–$\overline{S2}$ I_a = 2.0 mA for all other outputs
V_{OH}	Output High Voltage	2.4		V	I_{oa} = −400 μA
I_{CC}	Power Supply Current		600*	mA	T_A = −40°C
			550	mA	T_A = 0°C
			415	mA	T_A = +70°C
I_{LI}	Input Leakage Current		±10	μA	0V < V_{IN} < V_{CC}
I_{LO}	Output Leakage Current		±10	μA	0.45V < V_{OUT} < V_{CC}
V_{CLO}	Clock Output Low		0.6	V	I_a = 4.0 mA
V_{CHO}	Clock Output High	4.0		V	I_{oa} = −200 μA
C_{IN}	Input Capacitance		10	pF	
C_{IO}	I/O Capacitance		20	pF	

*For extended temperature parts only.

PIN TIMINGS

A.C. CHARACTERISTICS (T_A = 0°C to + 70°C, V_{CC} = 5V ± 10%)

80188 Timing Requirements All Timings Measured At 1.5 Volts Unless Otherwise Noted

Symbol	Parameter	80188 (8 MHz) Min	80188 (8 MHz) Max	Units	Test Conditions
T_{DVCL}	Data in Setup (A/D)	20		ns	
T_{CLDX}	Data in Hold (A/D)	10		ns	
T_{ARYHCH}	Asynchronous Ready (ARDY) active setup time[1]	20		ns	
T_{ARYLCL}	ARDY inactive setup time	35		ns	
T_{CLARX}	ARDY hold time	15		ns	
T_{ARYCHL}	Asynchronous Ready inactive hold time	15		ns	
T_{SRYCL}	Synchronous Ready (SRDY) Transition Setup Time[2]	20		ns	
T_{CLSRY}	SRDY Transition Hold Time[2]	15		ns	
T_{HVCL}	HOLD Setup[1]	25		ns	
T_{INVCH}	INTR, NMI, TEST, TMR IN, Setup[1]	25		ns	
T_{INVCL}	DRQ0, DRQ1, Setup[1]	25		ns	
80188 Master Interface Timing Responses					
T_{CLAV}	Address Valid Delay	5	55	ns	
T_{CLAX}	Address Hold	10		ns	
T_{CLAZ}	Address Float Delay	T_{CLAX}	35	ns	
T_{CHCZ}	Command Lines Float Delay		45	ns	
T_{CHCV}	Command Lines Valid Delay (after float)		55	ns	
T_{LHLL}	ALE Width	$T_{CLCL}-35$		ns	
T_{CHLH}	ALE Active Delay		35	ns	C_L = 20–200 pF
T_{CHLL}	ALE Inactive Delay		35	ns	all outputs (except T_{CLTMV})
T_{LLAX}	Address Hold to ALE Inactive	$T_{CHCL}-25$		ns	@ 8 MHz
T_{CLDV}	Data Valid Delay	10	44	ns	
T_{CLDOX}	Data Hold Time	10		ns	
T_{WHDX}	Data Hold after WR	$T_{CLCL}-40$		ns	
T_{CVCTV}	Control Active Delay 1	5	50	ns	
T_{CHCTV}	Control Active Delay 2	10	55	ns	
T_{CVCTX}	Control Inactive Delay	5	55	ns	
T_{CVDEX}	DEN Inactive Delay (Non-Write Cycle)	10	70	ns	

1. To guarantee recognition at next clock.
2. To guarantee proper operation.

PIN TIMINGS (Continued)

A.C. CHARACTERISTICS

(T_A = 0°C to +70°C, V_{CC} = 5V ±10%) (Continued)

80188 Master Interface Timing Responses (Continued)

Symbol	Parameter	80188 (8 MHz) Min	80188 (8 MHz) Max	Units	Test Conditions
T_{AZRL}	Address Float to $\overline{RD}$ Active	0		ns	
T_{CLRL}	$\overline{RD}$ Active Delay	10	70	ns	
T_{CLRH}	$\overline{RD}$ Inactive Delay	10	55	ns	
T_{RHAV}	$\overline{RD}$ Inactive to Address Active	$T_{CLCL}-40$		ns	
T_{CLHAV}	HLDA Valid Delay	5	50	ns	
T_{RLRH}	$\overline{RD}$ Width	$2T_{CLCL}-50$		ns	
T_{WLWH}	$\overline{WR}$ Width	$2T_{CLCL}-40$		ns	
T_{AVLL}	Address Valid to ALE Low	$T_{CLCH}-25$		ns	
T_{CHSV}	Status Active Delay	10	55	ns	
T_{CLSH}	Status Inactive Delay	10	65	ns	
T_{CLTMV}	Timer Output Delay		60	ns	100 pF max
T_{CLRO}	Reset Delay		60	ns	
T_{CHQSV}	Queue Status Delay		35	ns	
T_{CHDX}	Status Hold Time	10		ns	
T_{AVCH}	Address Valid to Clock High	10		ns	
T_{CLLV}	$\overline{LOCK}$ Valid/Invalid Delay	5	65	ns	

80188 Chip-Select Timing Responses

Symbol	Parameter	Min	Max	Units	Test Conditions
T_{CLCSV}	Chip-Select Active Delay		66	ns	
T_{CXCSX}	Chip-Select Hold from Command Inactive	35		ns	
T_{CHCSX}	Chip-Select Inactive Delay	5	35	ns	

80188 CLKIN Requirements

Symbol	Parameter	Min	Max	Units	Test Conditions
T_{CKIN}	CLKIN Period	62.5	250	ns	
T_{CKHL}	CLKIN Fall Time		10	ns	3.5 to 1.0V
T_{CKLH}	CLKIN Rise Time		10	ns	1.0 to 3.5V
T_{CLCK}	CLKIN Low Time	25		ns	1.5V
T_{CHCK}	CLKIN High Time	25		ns	1.5V

PIN TIMINGS (Continued)

A.C. CHARACTERISTICS (Continued)

($T_A = 0°C$ to $+70°C$, $V_{CC} = 5V \pm 10\%$) (Continued)

80188 CLKOUT Timing (200 pF load)

Symbol	Parameter	80188 (8 MHz)		Units	Test Conditions
		Min	Max		
T_{CICO}	CLKIN to CLKOUT Skew		50	ns	
T_{CLCL}	CLKOUT Period	125	500	ns	
T_{CLCH}	CLKOUT Low Time	$\frac{1}{2} T_{CLCL} - 7.5$		ns	1.5V
T_{CHCL}	CLKOUT High Time	$\frac{1}{2} T_{CLCL} - 7.5$		ns	1.5V
T_{CH1CH2}	CLKOUT Rise Time		15	ns	1.0 to 3.5V
T_{CL2CL1}	CLKOUT Fall Time		15	ns	3.5 to 1.0V

Explanation of the AC Symbols

Each timing symbol has from 5 to 7 characters. The first character is always a "T" (stands for time). The other characters, depending on their positions, stand for the name of a signal or the logical status of that signal. The following is a list of all the characters and what they stand for.

A: Address

ARY: Asynchronous Ready Input

C: Clock Output

CK: Clock Input

CS: Chip Select

CT: Control (DT/$\overline{R}$, $\overline{DEN}$, . . .)

D: Data Input

DE: $\overline{DEN}$

H: Logic Level High

IN: Input (DRQ0, TIM0, . . .)

L: Logic Level Low or ALE

O: Output

QS: Queue Status (QS1, QS2)

R: $\overline{RD}$ Signal, RESET Signal

S: Status ($\overline{S0}$, $\overline{S1}$, $\overline{S2}$)

SRY: Synchronous Ready Input

V: Valid

W: WR Signal

X: No Longer a Valid Logic Level

Z: Float

Examples:

T_{CLAV}— Time from Clock Low to Address Valid

T_{CHLH}— Time from Clock High to ALE High

T_{CLCSV}— Time from Clock LOW to Chp Select Valid

WAVEFORMS

Major Cycle Timing

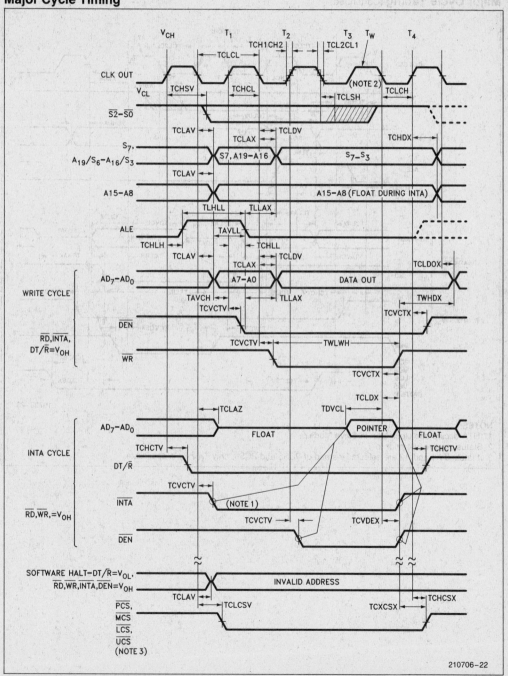

WAVEFORMS (Continued)

Major Cycle Timing (Continued)

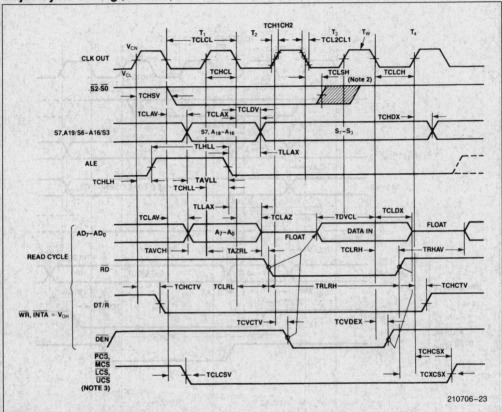

210706–23

NOTES:
1. INTA occurs one clock later in Slave Mode.
2. Status inactive just prior to T₄.
3. If latched A1 and A2 are selected instead of $\overline{PCS5}$ and $\overline{PCS6}$, only T_{CLCSV} is applicable.

WAVEFORMS (Continued)

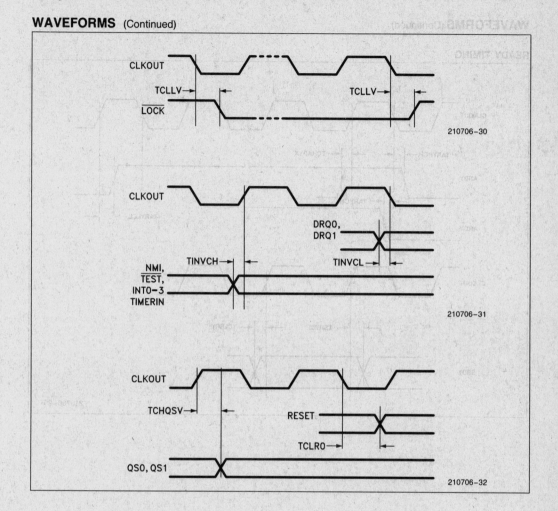

210706–30

210706–31

210706–32

WAVEFORMS (Continued)

READY TIMING

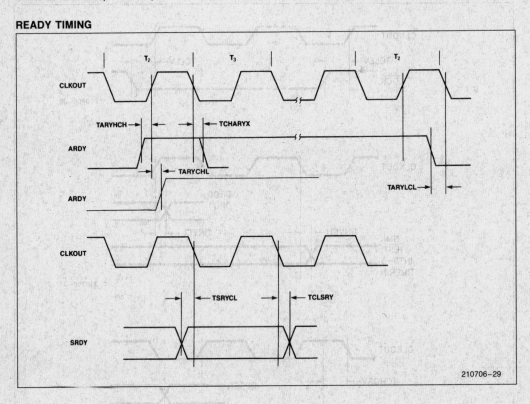

210706–29

WAVEFORMS (Continued)

HOLD/HLDA TIMING (Entering Hold)

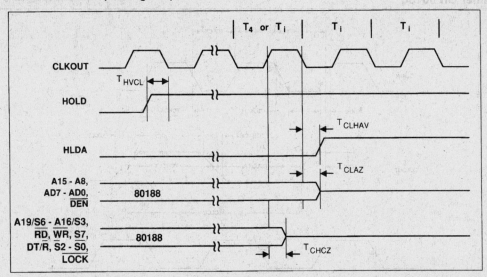

HOLD/HLDA TIMING (Leaving Hold)

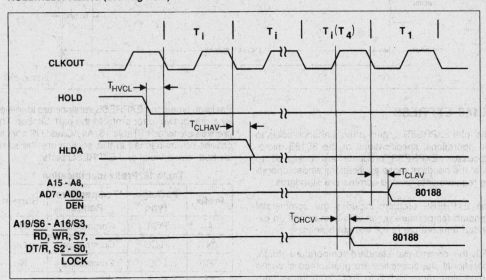

210706–33

WAVEFORMS (Continued)

Timer On 80188

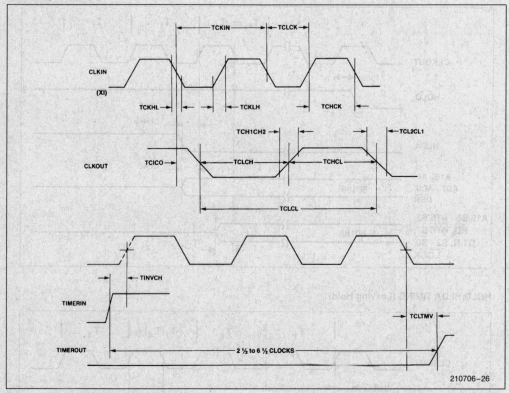

210706–26

80188 EXPRESS

The Intel EXPRESS system offers enhancements to the operational specifications of the 80188 microprocessor. EXPRESS products are designed to meet the needs of those applications whose operating requirements exceed commercial standards.

The EXPRESS program includes the commercial standard temperature range with burn-in and an extended temperature range without burn-in.

With the commercial standard temperature range, operational characteristics are guaranteed over the temperature range of 0°C to 70°C. With the extended temperature range option, operational characteristics are guaranteed over the range of −40°C to +85°C.

The optional burn-in is dynamic, for a minimum time of 160 hours at 125°C with V_{CC} = 5.5V ±0.25V, following guidelines in MIL-STD-883, Method 1015.

Package types and EXPRESS versions are identified by a one or two-letter prefix to the part number. The prefixes are listed in Table 16. All AC and DC specifications not mentioned in this section are the same for both commercial and EXPRESS parts.

Table 16. Prefix Identification

Prefix	Package Type	Temperature Range	Burn-In
A	PGA	Commercial	No
N	PLCC	Commercial	No
R	LCC	Commercial	No
TA	PGA	Extended	No
QR	LCC	Commercial	Yes

NOTE:
Not all package/temperature range combinations are available.

80188 EXECUTION TIMINGS

A determination of 80188 program execution timing must consider the bus cycles necessary to prefetch instructions as well as the number of execution unit cycles necessary to execute instructions. The following instruction timings represent the minimum execution time in clock cycles for each instruction. The timings given are based on the following assumptions:

- The opcode, along with any data or displacement required for execution of a particular instruction, has been prefetched and resides in the queue at the time it is needed.
- No wait states or bus HOLDs occur.

All instructions which involve memory accesses can also require one or two additional clocks above the minimum timings shown due to the asynchronous handshake between the Bus Interface Unit (BIU) and execution unit.

All jumps and calls include the time required to fetch the opcode of the next instruction at the destination address.

The 80188 8-bit BIU is noticeably limited in its performance relative to the execution unit. A sufficient number of prefetched bytes may not reside in the prefetch queue much of the time. Therefore, actual program execution time may be substantially greater than that derived from adding the instruction timings shown.

INSTRUCTION SET SUMMARY

Function	Format				Clock Cycles	Comments
DATA TRANSFER						
MOV = Move:						
Register to register/memory	1 0 0 0 1 0 0 w	mod reg r/m			2/12*	
Register/memory to register	1 0 0 0 1 0 1 w	mod reg r/m			2/9*	
Immediate to register/memory	1 1 0 0 0 1 1 w	mod 000 r/m	data	data if w = 1	12/13*	8/16-bit
Immediate to register	1 0 1 1 w reg	data	data if w = 1		3/4	8/16-bit
Memory to accumulator	1 0 1 0 0 0 0 w	addr-low	addr-high		8*	
Accumulator to memory	1 0 1 0 0 0 1 w	addr-low	addr-high		9*	
Register/memory to segment register	1 0 0 0 1 1 1 0	mod 0 reg r/m			2/13	
Segment register to register/memory	1 0 0 0 1 1 0 0	mod 0 reg r/m			2/15	
PUSH = Push:						
Memory	1 1 1 1 1 1 1 1	mod 1 1 0 r/m			20	
Register	0 1 0 1 0 reg				14	
Segment register	0 0 0 reg 1 1 0				13	
Immediate	0 1 1 0 1 0 s 0	data	data if s = 0		14	
PUSHA = Push All	0 1 1 0 0 0 0 0				68	
POP = Pop:						
Memory	1 0 0 0 1 1 1 1	mod 0 0 0 r/m			24	
Register	0 1 0 1 1 reg				14	
Segment register	0 0 0 reg 1 1 1	(reg ≠ 01)			12	
POPA = Pop All	0 1 1 0 0 0 0 1				83	
XCHG = Exchange:						
Register/memory with register	1 0 0 0 0 1 1 w	mod reg r/m			4/17*	
Register with accumulator	1 0 0 1 0 reg				3	
IN = Input from:						
Fixed port	1 1 1 0 0 1 0 w	port			10*	
Variable port	1 1 1 0 1 1 0 w				8*	
OUT = Output to:						
Fixed port	1 1 1 0 0 1 1 w	port			9*	
Variable port	1 1 1 0 1 1 1 w				7*	
XLAT = Translate byte to AL	1 1 0 1 0 1 1 1				15	
LEA = Load EA to register	1 0 0 0 1 1 0 1	mod reg r/m			6	
LDS = Load pointer to DS	1 1 0 0 0 1 0 1	mod reg r/m	(mod ≠ 11)		26	
LES = Load pointer to ES	1 1 0 0 0 1 0 0	mod reg r/m	(mod ≠ 11)		26	
LAHF = Load AH with flags	1 0 0 1 1 1 1 1				2	
SAHF = Store AH into flags	1 0 0 1 1 1 1 0				3	
PUSHF = Push flags	1 0 0 1 1 1 0 0				13	

Shaded areas indicate instructions not available in 8086, 8088 microsystems.
*Note: Clock cycles shown for byte transfer. For word operations, add 4 clock cycles for all memory transfers.

INSTRUCTION SET SUMMARY (Continued)

Function	Format					Clock Cycles	Comments
DATA TRANSFER (Continued)							
POPF = Pop flags	1 0 0 1 1 1 0 1					12	
SEGMENT = **Segment Override:**							
CS	0 0 1 0 1 1 1 0					2	
SS	0 0 1 1 0 1 1 0					2	
DS	0 0 1 1 1 1 1 0					2	
ES	0 0 1 0 0 1 1 0					2	
ARITHMETIC							
ADD = **Add:**							
Reg/memory with register to either	0 0 0 0 0 0 d w	mod reg r/m				3/10*	
Immediate to register/memory	1 0 0 0 0 0 s w	mod 0 0 0 r/m	data	data if s w = 01		4/16*	
Immediate to accumulator	0 0 0 0 0 1 0 w	data	data if w = 1			3/4	8/16-bit
ADC = **Add with carry:**							
Reg/memory with register to either	0 0 0 1 0 0 d w	mod reg r/m				3/10*	
Immediate to register/memory	1 0 0 0 0 0 s w	mod 0 1 0 r/m	data	data if s w = 01		4/16*	
Immediate to accumulator	0 0 0 1 0 1 0 w	data	data if w = 1			3/4	8/16-bit
INC = **Increment:**							
Register/memory	1 1 1 1 1 1 1 w	mod 0 0 0 r/m				3/15*	
Register	0 1 0 0 0 reg					3	
SUB = **Subtract:**							
Reg/memory and register to either	0 0 1 0 1 0 d w	mod reg r/m				3/10*	
Immediate from register/memory	1 0 0 0 0 0 s w	mod 1 0 1 r/m	data	data if s w = 01		4/16*	
Immediate from accumulator	0 0 1 0 1 1 0 w	data	data if w = 1			3/4	8/16-bit
SBB = **Subtract with borrow:**							
Reg/memory and register to either	0 0 0 1 1 0 d w	mod reg r/m				3/10*	
Immediate from register/memory	1 0 0 0 0 0 s w	mod 0 1 1 r/m	data	data if s w = 01		4/16*	
Immediate from accumulator	0 0 0 1 1 1 0 w	data	data if w = 1			3/4	8/16-bit
DEC = **Decrement:**							
Register/memory	1 1 1 1 1 1 1 w	mod 0 0 1 r/m				3/15*	
Register	0 1 0 0 1 reg					3	
CMP = **Compare:**							
Register/memory with register	0 0 1 1 1 0 1 w	mod reg r/m				3/10*	
Register with register/memory	0 0 1 1 1 0 0 w	mod reg r/m				3/10*	
Immediate with register/memory	1 0 0 0 0 0 s w	mod 1 1 1 r/m	data	data if s w = 01		3/10*	
Immediate with accumulator	0 0 1 1 1 1 0 w	data	data if w = 1			3/4	8/16-bit
NEG = Change sign register/memory	1 1 1 1 0 1 1 w	mod 0 1 1 r/m				3/10*	
AAA = ASCII adjust for add	0 0 1 1 0 1 1 1					8	
DAA = Decimal adjust for add	0 0 1 0 0 1 1 1					4	
AAS = ASCII adjust for subtract	0 0 1 1 1 1 1 1					7	
DAS = Decimal adjust for subtract	0 0 1 0 1 1 1 1					4	

Shaded areas indicate instructions not available in 8086, 8088 microsystems.
*Note: Clock cycles shown for byte transfer. For word operations, add 4 clock cycles for all memory transfers.

INSTRUCTION SET SUMMARY (Continued)

Function	Format				Clock Cycles	Comments
ARITHMETIC (Continued)						
MUL = Multiply (unsigned):	1 1 1 1 0 1 1 w	mod 1 0 0 r/m				
Register-Byte					26–28	
Register-Word					35–37	
Memory-Byte					32–34	
Memory-Word					41–43*	
IMUL = Integer multiply (signed):	1 1 1 1 0 1 1 w	mod 1 0 1 r/m				
Register-Byte					25–28	
Register-Word					34–37	
Memory-Byte					31–34	
Memory-Word					40–43*	
IMUL = Integer Immediate multiply (signed)	0 1 1 0 1 0 s 1	mod reg r/m	data	data if s = 0	22–25/ 29–32	
DIV = Divide (unsigned):	1 1 1 1 0 1 1 w	mod 1 1 0 r/m				
Register-Byte					29	
Register-Word					38	
Memory-Byte					35	
Memory-Word					44*	
IDIV = Integer divide (signed):	1 1 1 1 0 1 1 w	mod 1 1 1 r/m				
Register-Byte					44–52	
Register-Word					53–61	
Memory-Byte					50–58	
Memory-Word					59–67*	
AAM = ASCII adjust for multiply	1 1 0 1 0 1 0 0	0 0 0 0 1 0 1 0			19	
AAD = ASCII adjust for divide	1 1 0 1 0 1 0 1	0 0 0 0 1 0 1 0			15	
CBW = Convert byte to word	1 0 0 1 1 0 0 0				2	
CWD = Convert word to double word	1 0 0 1 1 0 0 1				4	
LOGIC **Shift/Rotate Instructions:**						
Register/Memory by 1	1 1 0 1 0 0 0 w	mod TTT r/m			2/15	
Register/Memory by CL	1 1 0 1 0 0 1 w	mod TTT r/m			5 + n/17 + n	
Register/Memory by Count	1 1 0 0 0 0 0 w	mod TTT r/m	count		5 + n/17 + n	
AND = And:						
Reg/memory and register to either	0 0 1 0 0 0 d w	mod reg r/m			3/10*	
Immediate to register/memory	1 0 0 0 0 0 0 w	mod 1 0 0 r/m	data	data if w = 1	4/16*	
Immediate to accumulator	0 0 1 0 0 1 0 w	data	data if w = 1		3/4	8/16-bit

	TTT	Instruction
	0 0 0	ROL
	0 0 1	ROR
	0 1 0	RCL
	0 1 1	RCR
	1 0 0	SHL/SAL
	1 0 1	SHR
	1 1 1	SAR

Shaded areas indicate instructions not available in 8086, 8088 microsystems.
*Note: Clock cycles shown for byte transfer. For word operations, add 4 clock cycles for all memory transfers.

INSTRUCTION SET SUMMARY (Continued)

Function	Format				Clock Cycles	Comments
LOGIC (Continued)						
TEST = And function to flags, no result:						
Register/memory and register	1 0 0 0 0 1 0 w	mod reg r/m			3/10*	
Immediate data and register/memory	1 1 1 1 0 1 1 w	mod 0 0 0 r/m	data	data if w = 1	4/10*	
Immediate data and accumulator	1 0 1 0 1 0 0 w	data	data if w = 1		3/4	8/16-bit
OR = Or:						
Reg/memory and register to either	0 0 0 0 1 0 d w	mod reg r/m			3/10*	
Immediate to register/memory	1 0 0 0 0 0 0 w	mod 0 0 1 r/m	data	data if w = 1	4/16*	
Immediate to accumulator	0 0 0 0 1 1 0 w	data	data if w = 1		3/4	8/16-bit
XOR = Exclusive or:						
Reg/memory and register to either	0 0 1 1 0 0 d w	mod reg r/m			3/10*	
Immediate to register/memory	1 0 0 0 0 0 0 w	mod 1 1 0 r/m	data	data if w = 1	4/16*	
Immediate to accumulator	0 0 1 1 0 1 0 w	data	data if w = 1		3/4	8/16-bit
NOT = Invert register/memory	1 1 1 1 0 1 1 w	mod 0 1 0 r/m			3/10*	
STRING MANIPULATION:						
MOVS = Move byte/word	1 0 1 0 0 1 0 w				14*	
CMPS = Compare byte/word	1 0 1 0 0 1 1 w				22*	
SCAS = Scan byte/word	1 0 1 0 1 1 1 w				15*	
LODS = Load byte/wd to AL/AX	1 0 1 0 1 1 0 w				12*	
STOS = Store byte/wd from AL/AX	1 0 1 0 1 0 1 w				10*	
INS = Input byte/wd from DX port	0 1 1 0 1 1 0 w				14	
OUTS = Output byte/wd to DX port	0 1 1 0 1 1 1 w				14	
Repeated by count in CX (REP/REPE/REPZ/REPNE/REPNZ)						
MOVS = Move string	1 1 1 1 0 0 1 0	1 0 1 0 0 1 0 w			8 + 8n*	
CMPS = Compare string	1 1 1 1 0 0 1 z	1 0 1 0 0 1 1 w			5 + 22n*	
SCAS = Scan string	1 1 1 1 0 0 1 z	1 0 1 0 1 1 1 w			5 + 15n*	
LODS = Load string	1 1 1 1 0 0 1 0	1 0 1 0 1 1 0 w			6 + 11n*	
STOS = Store string	1 1 1 1 0 0 1 0	1 0 1 0 1 0 1 w			6 + 9n*	
INS = Input string	1 1 1 1 0 0 1 0	0 1 1 0 1 1 0 w			8 + 8n*	
OUTS = Output string	1 1 1 1 0 0 1 0	0 1 1 0 1 1 1 w			8 + 8n*	

Shaded areas indicate instructions not available in 8086, 8088 microsystems.
*Note: Clock cycles shown for byte transfer. For word operations, add 4 clock cycles for all memory transfers.

INSTRUCTION SET SUMMARY (Continued)

Function	Format			Clock Cycles	Comments
CONTROL TRANSFER					
CALL = Call:					
Direct within segment	1 1 1 0 1 0 0 0	disp-low	disp-high	19	
Register/memory indirect within segment	1 1 1 1 1 1 1 1	mod 0 1 0 r/m		17/27	
Direct intersegment	1 0 0 1 1 0 1 0	segment offset		31	
		segment selector			
Indirect intersegment	1 1 1 1 1 1 1 1	mod 0 1 1 r/m	(mod ≠ 11)	54	
JMP = Unconditional jump:					
Short/long	1 1 1 0 1 0 1 1	disp-low		14	
Direct within segment	1 1 1 0 1 0 0 1	disp-low	disp-high	14	
Register/memory indirect within segment	1 1 1 1 1 1 1 1	mod 1 0 0 r/m		11/21	
Direct intersegment	1 1 1 0 1 0 1 0	segment offset		14	
		segment selector			
Indirect intersegment	1 1 1 1 1 1 1 1	mod 1 0 1 r/m	(mod ≠ 11)	34	
RET = Return from CALL:					
Within segment	1 1 0 0 0 0 1 1			20	
Within seg adding immed to SP	1 1 0 0 0 0 1 0	data-low	data-high	22	
Intersegment	1 1 0 0 1 0 1 1			30	
Intersegment adding immediate to SP	1 1 0 0 1 0 1 0	data-low	data-high	33	
JE/JZ = Jump on equal/zero	0 1 1 1 0 1 0 0	disp		4/13	JMP not taken/JMP taken
JL/JNGE = Jump on less/not greater or equal	0 1 1 1 1 1 0 0	disp		4/13	
JLE/JNG = Jump on less or equal/not greater	0 1 1 1 1 1 1 0	disp		4/13	
JB/JNAE = Jump on below/not above or equal	0 1 1 1 0 0 1 0	disp		4/13	
JBE/JNA = Jump on below or equal/not above	0 1 1 1 0 1 1 0	disp		4/13	
JP/JPE = Jump on parity/parity even	0 1 1 1 1 0 1 0	disp		4/13	
JO = Jump on overflow	0 1 1 1 0 0 0 0	disp		4/13	
JS = Jump on sign	0 1 1 1 1 0 0 0	disp		4/13	
JNE/JNZ = Jump on not equal/not zero	0 1 1 1 0 1 0 1	disp		4/13	
JNL/JGE = Jump on not less/greater or equal	0 1 1 1 1 1 0 1	disp		4/13	
JNLE/JG = Jump on not less or equal/greater	0 1 1 1 1 1 1 1	disp		4/13	
JNB/JAE = Jump on not below/above or equal	0 1 1 1 0 0 1 1	disp		4/13	
JNBE/JA = Jump on not below or equal/above	0 1 1 1 0 1 1 1	disp		4/13	
JNP/JPO = Jump on not par/par odd	0 1 1 1 1 0 1 1	disp		4/13	

Shaded areas indicate instructions not available in 8086, 8088 microsystems.

*Note: Clock cycles shown for byte transfer. For word operations, add 4 clock cycles for all memory transfers.

INSTRUCTION SET SUMMARY (Continued)

Function	Format				Clock Cycles	Comments
CONTROL TRANSFER (Continued)						
JNO = Jump on not overflow	01110001	disp			4/13	
JNS = Jump on not sign	01111001	disp			4/13	
JCXZ = Jump on CX zero	11100011	disp			5/15	
LOOP = Loop CX times	11100010	disp			6/16	LOOP not taken/LOOP taken
LOOPZ/LOOPE = Loop while zero/equal	11100001	disp			6/16	
LOOPNZ/LOOPNE = Loop while not zero/equal	11100000	disp			6/16	
ENTER = Enter Procedure	11001000	data-low	data-high	L		
L = 0					19	
L = 1					29	
L > 1					$26 + 20(n - 1)$	
LEAVE = Leave Procedure	11001001				8	
INT = Interrupt:						
Type specified	11001101	type			47	
Type 3	11001100				45	if INT. taken/ if INT. not taken
INTO = Interrupt on overflow	11001110				48/4	
IRET = Interrupt return	11001111				28	
BOUND = Detect value out of range	01100010	mod reg r/m			33–35	
PROCESSOR CONTROL						
CLC = Clear carry	11111000				2	
CMC = Complement carry	11110101				2	
STC = Set carry	11111001				2	
CLD = Clear direction	11111100				2	
STD = Set direction	11111101				2	
CLI = Clear interrupt	11111010				2	
STI = Set interrupt	11111011				2	
HLT = Halt	11110100				2	
WAIT = Wait	10011011				6	if $\overline{\text{TEST}}$ = 0
LOCK = Bus lock prefix	11110000				2	
ESC = Processor Extension Escape	11011TTT	mod LLL r/m			6	
	(TTT LLL are opcode to processor extension)					
NOP = No Operation	10010000				3	

Shaded areas indicate instructions not available in 8086, 8088 microsystems.
*Note: Clock cycles shown for byte transfer. For word operations, add 4 clock cycles for all memory transfers.

80188

FOOTNOTES

The Effective Address (EA) of the memory operand is computed according to the mod and r/m fields:

if mod = 11 then r/m is treated as a REG field

if mod = 00 then DISP = 0*, disp-low and disp-high are absent

if mod = 01 then DISP = disp-low sign-extended to 16-bits, disp-high is absent

if mod = 10 then DISP = disp-high: disp-low

if r/m = 000 then EA = (BX) + (SI) + DISP

if r/m = 001 then EA = (BX) + (DI) + DISP

if r/m = 010 then EA = (BP) + (SI) + DISP

if r/m = 011 then EA = (BP) + (DI) + DISP

if r/m = 100 then EA = (SI) + DISP

if r/m = 101 then EA = (DI) + DISP

if r/m = 110 then EA = (BP) + DISP*

if r/m = 111 then EA = (BX) + DISP

DISP follows 2nd byte of instruction (before data if required)

*except if mod = 00 and r/m = 110 then EA = disp-high: disp-low.

EA calculation time is 4 clock cycles for all modes, and is included in the execution times given whenever appropriate.

Segment Override Prefix

0	0	1	reg	1	1	0

reg is assigned according to the following:

reg	Segment Register
00	ES
01	CS
10	SS
11	DS

REG is assigned according to the following table:

16-Bit (w = 1)	8-Bit (w = 0)
000 AX	000 AL
001 CX	001 CL
010 DX	010 DL
011 BX	011 BL
100 SP	100 AH
101 BP	101 CH
110 SI	110 DH
111 DI	111 BH

The physical addresses of all operands addressed by the BP register are computed using the SS segment register. The physical addresses of the destination operands of the string primitive operations (those addressed by the DI register) are computed using the ES segment, which may not be overridden.

REVISION HISTORY

The sections significantly revised since version -010 are:

Pin Description Table	Added note to $\overline{\text{TEST}}$ pin requiring proper RESET at power-up to configure pin as input.
	Renamed pin 44 to INT1/$\overline{\text{SELECT}}$ and pin 41 to INT3/$\overline{\text{INTA1}}$/IRQ to better describe their functions in Slave Mode.
Initialization and Processor Reset	Added reminder to drive $\overline{\text{RES}}$ pin LOW during power-up.
Major Cycle Timing Waveform	Clarified applicability of T_{CLCSV} to latched A1 and A2 in footnote.
HOLD/HLDA Timing Waveforms	Redrawn to indicate correct relationship of HOLD inactive to HLDA inactive.
Instruction Set Summary	Corrected clock count for ENTER instruction.
Slave Mode Operation	The three low order bits associated with vector generation and performing EOI are not alterable; however, the priority levels are programmable. This information is a clarification only.

The sections significantly revised since version -009 are:

Pin Description Table	Various descriptions rewritten for clarity.
Interrupt Vector Table	Redrawn for clarity.
A.C. Characteristics	Added reminder that T_{SRYCL} and T_{CLSRY} must be met.
Explanation of the A.C. Symbols	New section.
Major Cycle Timing Waveforms	T_{CLRO} indicated.

The sections significantly revised since version -008 are:

Pin Description Table	Noted $\overline{\text{RES}}$ to be low more than 4 clocks. Connections to X1 and X2 clarified.
DMA Control Bit Descriptions	Moved and clarified note concerning TC condition for ST/$\overline{\text{STOP}}$ clearing during unsynchronized transfers.
Interrupt Controller, etc.	Renamed iRMX Mode to Slave Mode.
Interrupt Request Register	Noted that D0 and D1 are read/write, others read-only.
Execution Timings	Clarified effect of bus width.
A.C. Characteristics	10 MHz 80188 no longer offered.

The sections significantly revised since version -007 are:

A.C. Characteristics	Several timings changed in anticipation of test change (all listed in ns): T_{CLAV} (min.) at 10 MHz from 50 to 44; T_{CVCTV} (min.) at 8 MHz from 10 to 5; T_{CVCTV} (max.) from 70 to 50 at 8 MHz and 56 to 40 at 10 MHz.

80C188
CHMOS HIGH INTEGRATION 16-BIT MICROPROCESSOR

- **Operation Modes Include:**
  - Enhanced Mode Which Has
    - DRAM Refresh Control Unit
    - Power-Save Mode
  - Compatible Mode
    - NMOS 80188 Pin for Pin Replacement for Non-Numerics Applications

- **Integrated Feature Set**
  - Enhanced 80C86/C88 CPU
  - Clock Generator
  - 2 Independent DMA Channels
  - Programmable Interrupt Controller
  - 3 Programmable 16-Bit Timers
  - Dynamic RAM Refresh Control Unit
  - Programmable Memory and Peripheral Chip Select Logic
  - Programmable Wait State Generator
  - Local Bus Controller
  - Power Save Mode
  - System-Level Testing Support (High Impedance Test Mode)

- **Available in 16 MHz (80C188-16), 12.5 MHz (80C188-12) and 10 MHz (80C188) Versions**

- **Direct Addressing Capability to 1 MByte Memory and 64 KByte I/O**

- **Completely Object Code Compatible with All Existing 8086/8088 Software and Also Has 10 Additional Instructions over 8086/8088**

- **Complete System Development Support**
  - All 8088 and NMOS 80188 Software Development Tools Can Be Used for 80C186 System Development
    - ASM86 Assembler, PL/M-86, Pascal-86, Fortran-86, C-86 and System Utilities
    - In-Circuit-Emulator (ICE™-188)

- **Available in 68 Pin:**
  - Plastic Leaded Chip Carrier (PLCC)
  - Ceramic Pin Grid Array (PGA)
  - Ceramic Leadless Chip Carrier (JEDEC A Package)

  (See Packaging Outlines and Dimensions, Order Number 231369)

- **Available in EXPRESS Extended Temperature Range (−40°C to +85°C)**

The Intel 80C188 is a CHMOS high integration microprocessor. It has features which are new to the 80186 family which include a DRAM refresh control unit and power-save mode. When used in "compatible" mode, the 80C188 is 100% pin-for-pin compatible with the NMOS 80188 (except for 8087 applications). The "enhanced" mode of operation allows the full feature set of the 80C188 to be used. The 80C188 is upward compatible with 8086 and 8088 software and fully compatible with 80186 and 80188 software, except for numerics applications.

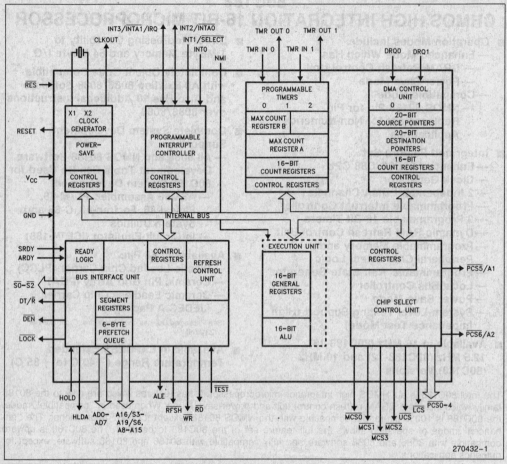

Figure 1. 80C188 Block Diagram

270432–1

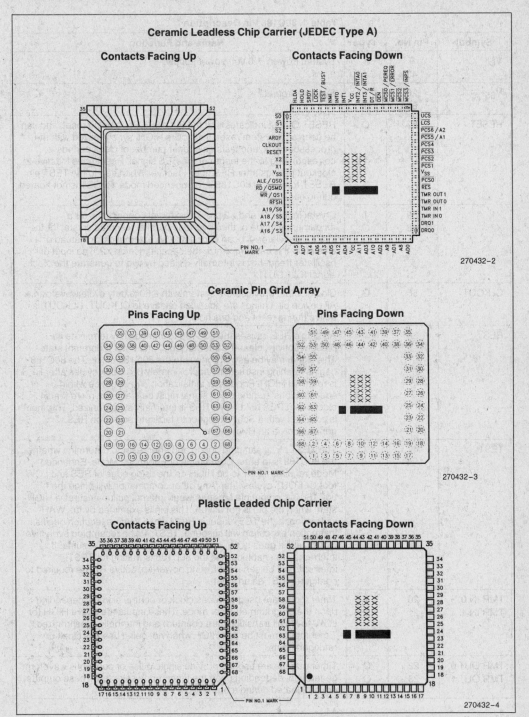

Figure 2. 80C188 Pinout Diagrams

Table 1. 80C188 Pin Description

Symbol	Pin No.	Type	Name and Function
V$_{CC}$	9 43	I I	System Power: +5 volt power supply.
V$_{SS}$	26 60	I I	System Ground.
RESET	57	O	RESET Output indicates that the 80C188 CPU is being reset, and can be used as a system reset. It is active HIGH, synchronized with the processor clock, and lasts an integer number of clock periods corresponding to the length of the $\overline{RES}$ signal. Reset goes inactive 2 clockout periods after $\overline{RES}$ goes inactive. When tied to the $\overline{TEST}$ pin, RESET forces the 80C188 into enhanced mode. RESET is not floated during bus hold.
X1 X2	59 58	I O	Crystal Inputs X1 and X2 provide external connections for a fundamental mode or third overtone parallel resonant crystal for the internal oscillator. X1 can connect to an external clock instead of a crystal. In this case, minimize the capacitance on X2. The input or oscillator frequency is internally divided by two to generate the clock signal (CLKOUT).
CLKOUT	56	O	Clock Output provides the system with a 50% duty cycle waveform. All device pin timings are specified relative to CLKOUT. CLKOUT is active during reset and bus hold.
$\overline{RES}$	24	I	An active $\overline{RES}$ causes the 80C188 to immediately terminate its present activity, clear the internal logic, and enter a dormant state. This signal may be asynchronous to the 80C188 clock. The 80C188 begins fetching instructions approximately 6½ clock cycles after $\overline{RES}$ is returned HIGH. For proper initialization, V$_{CC}$ must be within specifications and the clock signal must be stable for more than 4 clocks with $\overline{RES}$ held LOW. $\overline{RES}$ is internally synchronized. This input is provided with a Schmitt-trigger to facilitate power-on $\overline{RES}$ generation via an RC network.
$\overline{TEST}$	47	I/O	The $\overline{TEST}$ pin is sampled during and after reset to determine whether the 80C188 is to enter Compatible or Enhanced Mode. Enhanced Mode requires $\overline{TEST}$ to be HIGH on the rising edge of $\overline{RES}$ and LOW four CLKOUT cycles later. Any other combination will place the 80C188 in Compatible Mode. A weak internal pullup ensures a HIGH state when the pin is not driven. This pin is examined by the WAIT instruction. If the $\overline{TEST}$ input is HIGH when WAIT execution begins, instruction execution will suspend. $\overline{TEST}$ will be resampled every five clocks until it goes LOW, at which time execution will resume. If interrupts are enabled while the 80C188 is waiting for $\overline{TEST}$, interrupts will be serviced. During power-up, active $\overline{RES}$ is required to configure $\overline{TEST}$ as an input.
TMR IN 0 TMR IN 1	20 21	I I	Timer Inputs are used either as clock or control signals, depending upon the programmed timer mode. These inputs are active HIGH (or LOW-to-HIGH transitions are counted) and internally synchronized. Timer Inputs must be tied HIGH when not being used as clock or retrigger inputs.
TMR OUT 0 TMR OUT 1	22 23	O O	Timer outputs are used to provide single pulse or continous waveform generation, depending upon the timer mode selected. These outputs are not floated during a bus hold.

Table 1. 80C188 Pin Description (Continued)

Symbol	Pin No.	Type	Name and Function
DRQ0 DRQ1	18 19	I I	DMA Request is asserted HIGH by an external device when it is ready for DMA Channel 0 or 1 to perform a transfer. These signals are level-triggered and internally synchronized.
NMI	46	I	The Non-Maskable Interrupt input causes a Type 2 interrupt. An NMI transition from LOW to HIGH is latched and synchronized internally, and initiates the interrupt at the next instruction boundary. NMI must be asserted for at least one CLKOUT period. The Non-Maskable Interrupt cannot be avoided by programming.
INT0 INT1/$\overline{\text{SELECT}}$ INT2/$\overline{\text{INTA0}}$ INT3/$\overline{\text{INTA1}}$/IRQ	45 44 42 41	I I I/O I/O	Maskable Interrupt Requests can be requested by activating one of these pins. When configured as inputs, these pins are active HIGH. Interrupt Requests are synchronized internally. INT2 and INT3 may be configured to provide active-LOW interrupt-acknowledge output signals. All interrupt inputs may be configured to be either edge- or level-triggered. To ensure recognition, all interrupt requests must remain active until the interrupt is acknowledged. When slave mode is selected, the function of these pins changes (see Interrupt Controller section of this data sheet).
A19/S6 A18/S5 A17/S4 A16/S3	65 66 67 68	O O O O	Address Bus Outputs (16–19) and Bus Cycle Status (3–6) indicate the four most significant address bits during T_1. These signals are active HIGH. During T_2, T_3, T_W, and T_4, status information is available on these lines as encoded below: During T_2, T_3, T_W, and T_4, the S6 pin is LOW to indicate a CPU-initiated bus cycle or HIGH to indicate a DMA-initiated bus cycle. During the same T-states, S3, S4, and S5 are always LOW. These outputs are floated during a bus hold or reset.
A15 A14 A13 A12 A11 A10 A9 A8	1 3 5 7 10 12 14 16	O O O O O O O O	Address-Only Bus (15–8) contains valid addresses from T_1–T_4. The bus is active high. These outputs are floated during a bus hold or reset.
AD7 AD6 AD5 AD4 AD3 AD2 AD1 AD0	2 4 6 8 11 13 15 17	I/O I/O I/O I/O I/O I/O I/O I/O	Address/Data Bus (7–0) signals constitute the time multiplexed memory or I/O address (T_1) and data (T_2, T_3, T_W, and T_4) bus. The bus is active high. These pins are floated during a bus hold or reset.
$\overline{\text{RFSH}}$	64	O	In compatible mode, $\overline{\text{RFSH}}$ is HIGH. In enhanced mode, $\overline{\text{RFSH}}$ is asserted LOW to signify a refresh bus cycle. The $\overline{\text{RFSH}}$ output pin floats during bus hold or reset, regardless of operating mode.

Table 1. 80C186 Pin Description (Continued)

Symbol	Pin No.	Type	Name and Function
ALE/QS0	61	O	Address Latch Enable/Queue Status 0 is provided by the 80C188 to latch the address. ALE is active HIGH, with addresses guaranteed valid on the trailing edge.
WR/QS1	63	O	Write Strobe/Queue Status 1 indicates that the data on the bus is to be written into a memory or an I/O device. It is active LOW, and floats during bus hold or reset. When the 80C188 is in queue status mode, the ALE/QS0 and WR/QS1 pins provide information about processor/instruction queue interaction.

QS1	QS0	Queue Operation
0	0	No queue operation
0	1	First opcode byte fetched from the queue
1	1	Subsequent byte fetched from the queue
1	0	Empty the queue

Symbol	Pin No.	Type	Name and Function
RD/QSMD	62	O/I	Read Strobe is an active LOW signal which indicates that the 80C188 is performing a memory or I/O read cycle. It is guaranteed not to go LOW before the A/D bus is floated. An internal pull-up ensures that RD/QSMD is HIGH during RESET. Following RESET the pin is sampled to determine whether the 80C188 is to provide ALE, RD and WR, or queue status information. To enable Queue Status Mode, RD must be connected to GND. RD will float during bus HOLD.
ARDY	55	I	Asynchronous Ready informs the 80C188 that the addressed memory space or I/O device will complete a data transfer. The ARDY pin accepts a rising edge that is asynchronous to CLKOUT and is active HIGH. The falling edge of ARDY must be synchronized to the 80C188 clock. Connecting ARDY HIGH will always assert the ready condition to the CPU. If this line is unused, it should be tied LOW to yield control to the SRDY pin.
SRDY	49	I	Synchronous Ready informs the 80C188 that the addressed memory space or I/O device will complete a data transfer. The SRDY pin accepts an active-HIGH input synchronized to CLKOUT. The use of SRDY allows a relaxed system timing over ARDY. This is accomplished by elimination of the one-half clock cycle required to internally synchronize the ARDY input signal. Connecting SRDY high will always assert the ready condition to the CPU. If this line is unused, it should be tied LOW to yield control to the ARDY pin.

Table 1. 80C188 Pin Description (Continued)

Symbol	Pin No.	Type	Name and Function
$\overline{\text{LOCK}}$	48	O	$\overline{\text{LOCK}}$ output indicates that other system bus masters are not to gain control of the system bus. $\overline{\text{LOCK}}$ is active LOW. The $\overline{\text{LOCK}}$ signal is requested by the LOCK prefix instruction and is activated at the beginning of the first data cycle associated with the instruction immediately following the LOCK prefix. It remains active until the completion of that instruction. No instruction prefetching will occur while $\overline{\text{LOCK}}$ is asserted. $\overline{\text{LOCK}}$ floats during bus hold or reset.

Symbol	Pin No.	Type	Name and Function
$\overline{\text{S0}}$	52	O	Bus cycle status $\overline{\text{S0}}$–$\overline{\text{S2}}$ are encoded to provide bus-transaction
$\overline{\text{S1}}$	53	O	information:
$\overline{\text{S2}}$	54	O	

80C188 Bus Cycle Status Information

$\overline{\text{S2}}$	$\overline{\text{S1}}$	$\overline{\text{S0}}$	Bus Cycle Initiated
0	0	0	Interrupt Acknowledge
0	0	1	Read I/O
0	1	0	Write I/O
0	1	1	Halt
1	0	0	Instruction Fetch
1	0	1	Read Data from Memory
1	1	0	Write Data to Memory
1	1	1	Passive (no bus cycle)

The status pins float during HOLD.
$\overline{\text{S2}}$ may be used as a logical M/$\overline{\text{IO}}$ indicator, and $\overline{\text{S1}}$ as a DT/$\overline{\text{R}}$ indicator.

Symbol	Pin No.	Type	Name and Function
HOLD	50	I	HOLD indicates that another bus master is requesting the local bus. The HOLD input is active HIGH. The 80C188 generates HLDA (HIGH) in response to a HOLD request. Simultaneous with the issuance of HLDA, the 80C188 will float the local bus and control lines. After HOLD is detected as being LOW, the 80C188 will lower HLDA. When the 80C188 needs to run another bus cycle, it will again drive the local bus and control lines.
HLDA	51	O	
			In Enhanced Mode, HLDA will go low when a DRAM refresh cycle is pending in the 80C188 and an external bus master has control of the bus. It will be up to the external master to relinquish the bus by lowering HOLD so that the 80C188 may execute the refresh cycle.
$\overline{\text{UCS}}$	34	O/I	Upper Memory Chip Select is an active LOW output whenever a memory reference is made to the defined upper portion (1K–256K block) of memory. $\overline{\text{UCS}}$ does not float during bus hold. The address range activating $\overline{\text{UCS}}$ is software programmable.
			$\overline{\text{UCS}}$ and $\overline{\text{LCS}}$ are sampled upon the rising edge of $\overline{\text{RES}}$. If both pins are held low, the 80C188 will enter ONCE Mode. In ONCE Mode all pins assume a high impedance state and remain so until a subsequent RESET. $\overline{\text{UCS}}$ has a weak internal pullup that is active during RESET to ensure that the 80C188 does not enter the ONCE mode inadvertently.

Table 1. 80C188 Pin Description (Continued)

Symbol	Pin No.	Type	Name and Function
$\overline{\text{LCS}}$	33	O/I	Lower Memory Chip Select is active LOW whenever a memory reference is made to the defined lower portion (1K–256K) of memory. $\overline{\text{LCS}}$ does not float during bus HOLD. The address range activating $\overline{\text{LCS}}$ is software programmable. $\overline{\text{UCS}}$ and $\overline{\text{LCS}}$ are sampled upon the rising edge of $\overline{\text{RES}}$. If both pins are held low, the 80C186 will enter ONCE Mode. In ONCE Mode all pins assume a high impedance state and remain so until a subsequent RESET. $\overline{\text{LCS}}$ has a weak internal pullup that is active only during RESET to ensure that the 80C188 does not enter ONCE Mode inadvertently.
$\overline{\text{MCS0}}$ $\overline{\text{MCS1}}$ $\overline{\text{MCS2}}$ $\overline{\text{MCS3}}$	38 37 36 35	O O O O	Mid-Range Memory Chip Select signals are active LOW when a memory reference is made to the defined mid-range portion of memory (8K–512K). These lines do not float during bus HOLD. The address ranges activating $\overline{\text{MCS0}}$–3 are software programmable.
$\overline{\text{PCS0}}$ $\overline{\text{PCS1}}$ $\overline{\text{PCS2}}$ $\overline{\text{PCS3}}$ $\overline{\text{PCS4}}$	25 27 28 29 30	O O O O O	Peripheral Chip Select signals 0–4 are active LOW when a reference is made to the defined peripheral area (64K I/O space or 1 Mbyte memory space). These lines do not float during bus HOLD. The address ranges activating $\overline{\text{PCS0}}$–4 are software programmable.
$\overline{\text{PCS5}}$/A1	31	O	Peripheral Chip Select 5 or Latched A1 may be programmed to provide a sixth peripheral chip select, or to provide an internally latched A1 signal. The address range activating $\overline{\text{PCS5}}$ is software-programmable. $\overline{\text{PCS5}}$/A1 does not float during bus HOLD. When programmed to provide latched A1, this pin will retain the previously latched value during HOLD.
$\overline{\text{PCS6}}$/A2	32	O	Peripheral Chip Select 6 or Latched A2 may be programmed to provide a seventh peripheral chip select, or to provide an internally latched A2 signal. The address range activating $\overline{\text{PCS6}}$ is software-programmable. $\overline{\text{PCS6}}$/A2 does not float during bus HOLD. When programmed to provide latched A2, this pin will retain the previously latched value during HOLD.
DT/$\overline{\text{R}}$	40	O	Data Transmit/Receive controls the direction of data flow through an external data bus transceiver. When LOW, data is transferred to the 80C188. When HIGH the 80C188 places write data on the data bus. DT/$\overline{\text{R}}$ floats during a bus hold or RESET.
$\overline{\text{DEN}}$	39	O	Data Enable is provided as a data bus transceiver output enable. $\overline{\text{DEN}}$ is active LOW during each memory and I/O access. $\overline{\text{DEN}}$ is HIGH whenever DT/$\overline{\text{R}}$ changes state. During RESET, $\overline{\text{DEN}}$ is driven HIGH for one clock, then floated. $\overline{\text{DEN}}$ also floats during HOLD.

FUNCTIONAL DESCRIPTION

Introduction

The following Functional Description describes the base architecture of the 80C188. The 80C188 is a very high integration 16-bit microprocessor. It combines 15–20 of the most common microprocessor system components onto one chip. The 80C188 is object code compatible with the 8086/8088 microprocessors and adds 10 new instruction types to the 8086/8088 instruction set.

The 80C188 has two major modes of operation, Compatible and Enhanced. In Compatible Mode the 80C188 is completely compatible with NMOS 80188, with the exception of 8087 support. The Enhanced mode adds two new features to the system design. These are Power-Save control and Dynamic RAM refresh.

80C188 BASE ARCHITECTURE

The 8086, 8088, 80186, and 80188 families all contain the same basic set of registers, instructions, and addressing modes. The 80C188 processor is upward compatible with the 8086 and 8088 CPUs.

Register Set

The 80C188 base architecture has fourteen registers as shown in Figures 3a and 3b. These registers are grouped into the following categories.

General Registers

Eight 16-bit general purpose registers may be used for arithmetic and logical operands. Four of these (AX, BX, CX, and DX) can be used as 16-bit registers or split into pairs of separate 8-bit registers.

Segment Registers

Four 16-bit special purpose registers select, at any given time, the segments of memory that are immediately addressable for code, stack, and data. (For usage, refer to Memory Organization.)

Base and Index Registers

Four of the general purpose registers may also be used to determine offset addresses of operands in memory. These registers may contain base addresses or indexes to particular locations within a segment. The addressing mode selects the specific registers for operand and address calculations.

Status and Control Registers

Two 16-bit special purpose registers record or alter certain aspects of the 80C188 processor state. These are the Instruction Pointer Register, which contains the offset address of the next sequential instruction to be executed, and the Status Word Register, which contains status and control flag bits (see Figures 3a and 3b).

Status Word Description

The Status Word records specific characteristics of the result of logical and arithmetic instructions (bits 0, 2, 4, 6, 7, and 11) and controls the operation of the 80C186 within a given operating mode (bits 8, 9, and 10). The Status Word Register is 16-bits wide. The function of the Status Word bits is shown in Table 2.

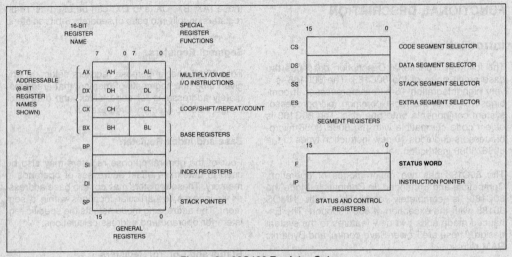

Figure 3a. 80C188 Register Set

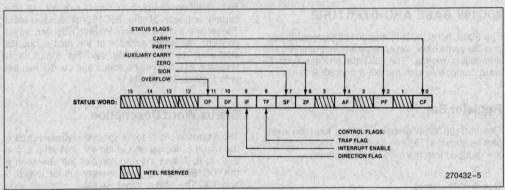

Figure 3b. Status Word Format

Table 2. Status Word Bit Functions

Bit Position	Name	Function
0	CF	Carry Flag—Set on high-order bit carry or borrow; cleared otherwise
2	PF	Parity Flag—Set if low-order 8 bits of result contain an even number of 1-bits; cleared otherwise
4	AF	Set on carry from or borrow to the low order four bits of AL; cleared otherwise
6	ZF	Zero Flag—Set if result is zero; cleared otherwise
7	SF	Sign Flag—Set equal to high-order bit of result (0 if positive, 1 if negative)
8	TF	Single Step Flag—Once set, a single step interrupt occurs after the next instruction executes. TF is cleared by the single step interrupt.
9	IF	Interrupt-enable Flag—When set, maskable interrupts will cause the CPU to transfer control to an interrupt vector specified location.
10	DF	Direction Flag—Causes string instructions to auto decrement the appropriate index register when set. Clearing DF causes auto increment.
11	OF	Overflow Flag—Set if the signed result cannot be expressed within the number of bits in the destination operand; cleared otherwise

Instruction Set

The instruction set is divided into seven categories: data transfer, arithmetic, shift/rotate/logical, string manipulation, control transfer, high-level instructions, and processor control. These categories are summarized in Figure 4.

An 80C188 instruction can reference anywhere from zero to several operands. An operand can reside in a register, in the instruction itself, or in memory. Specific operand addressing modes are discussed later in this data sheet.

Memory Organization

Memory is organized in sets of segments. Each segment is a linear contiguous sequence of up to 64K (2^{16}) 8-bit bytes. Memory is addressed using a two-component address (a pointer) that consists of a 16-bit base segment and a 16-bit offset. The 16-bit base values are contained in one of four internal segment register (code, data, stack, extra). The physical address is calculated by shifting the base value LEFT by four bits and adding the 16-bit offset value to yield a 20-bit physical address (see Figure 5). This allows for a 1 MByte physical address size.

All instructions that address operands in memory must specify the base segment and the 16-bit offset value. For speed and compact instruction encoding, the segment register used for physical address generation is implied by the addressing mode used (see Table 3). These rules follow the way programs are written (see Figure 6) as independent modules that require areas for code and data, a stack, and access to external data areas.

Special segment override instruction prefixes allow the implicit segment register selection rules to be overridden for special cases. The stack, data, and extra segments may coincide for simple programs.

GENERAL PURPOSE	
MOV	Move byte or word
PUSH	Push word onto stack
POP	Pop word off stack
PUSHA	Push all registers on stack
POPA	Pop all registers from stack
XCHG	Exchange byte or word
XLAT	Translate byte
INPUT/OUTPUT	
IN	Input byte or word
OUT	Output byte or word
ADDRESS OBJECT	
LEA	Load effective address
LDS	Load pointer using DS
LES	Load pointer using ES
FLAG TRANSFER	
LAHF	Load AH register from flags
SAHF	Store AH register in flags
PUSHF	Push flags onto stack
POPF	Pop flags off stack
ADDITION	
ADD	Add byte or word
ADC	Add byte or word with carry
INC	Increment byte or word by 1
AAA	ASCII adjust for addition
DAA	Decimal adjust for addition
SUBTRACTION	
SUB	Subtract byte or word
SBB	Subtract byte or word with borrow
DEC	Decrement byte or word by 1
NEG	Negate byte or word
CMP	Compare byte or word
AAS	ASCII adjust for subtraction
DAS	Decimal adjust for subtraction
MULTIPLICATION	
MUL	Multiply byte or word unsigned
IMUL	Integer multiply byte or word
AAM	ASCII adjust for multiply
DIVISION	
DIV	Divide byte or word unsigned
IDIV	Integer divide byte or word
AAD	ASCII adjust for division
CBW	Convert byte to word
CWD	Convert word to doubleword

MOVS	Move byte or word string
INS	Input bytes or word string
OUTS	Output bytes or word string
CMPS	Compare byte or word string
SCAS	Scan byte or word string
LODS	Load byte or word string
STOS	Store byte or word string
REP	Repeat
REPE/REPZ	Repeat while equal/zero
REPNE/REPNZ	Repeat while not equal/not zero
LOGICALS	
NOT	"Not" byte or word
AND	"And" byte or word
OR	"Inclusive or" byte or word
XOR	"Exclusive or" byte or word
TEST	"Test" byte or word
SHIFTS	
SHL/SAL	Shift logical/arithmetic left byte or word
SHR	Shift logical right byte or word
SAR	Shift arithmetic right byte or word
ROTATES	
ROL	Rotate left byte or word
ROR	Rotate right byte or word
RCL	Rotate through carry left byte or word
RCR	Rotate through carry right byte or word
FLAG OPERATIONS	
STC	Set carry flag
CLC	Clear carry flag
CMC	Complement carry flag
STD	Set direction flag
CLD	Clear direction flag
STI	Set interrupt enable flag
CLI	Clear interrupt enable flag
EXTERNAL SYNCHRONIZATION	
HLT	Halt until interrupt or reset
WAIT	Wait for TEST pin active
LOCK	Lock bus during next instruction
NO OPERATION	
NOP	No operation
HIGH LEVEL INSTRUCTIONS	
ENTER	Format stack for procedure entry
LEAVE	Restore stack for procedure exit
BOUND	Detects values outside prescribed range

Figure 4. 80C188 Instruction Set

CONDITIONAL TRANSFERS	
JA/JNBE	Jump if above/not below nor equal
JAE/JNB	Jump if above or equal/not below
JB/JNAE	Jump if below/not above nor equal
JBE/JNA	Jump if below or equal/not above
JC	Jump if carry
JE/JZ	Jump if equal/zero
JG/JNLE	Jump if greater/not less nor equal
JGE/JNL	Jump if greater or equal/not less
JL/JNGE	Jump if less/not greater nor equal
JLE/JNG	Jump if less or equal/not greater
JNC	Jump if not carry
JNE/JNZ	Jump if not equal/not zero
JNO	Jump if not overflow
JNP/JPO	Jump if not parity/parity odd
JNS	Jump if not sign

JO	Jump if overflow
JP/JPE	Jump if parity/parity even
JS	Jump if sign
UNCONDITIONAL TRANSFERS	
CALL	Call procedure
RET	Return from procedure
JMP	Jump
ITERATION CONTROLS	
LOOP	Loop
LOOPE/LOOPZ	Loop if equal/zero
LOOPNE/LOOPNZ	Loop if not equal/not zero
JCXZ	Jump if register CX = 0
INTERRUPTS	
INT	Interrupt
INTO	Interrupt if overflow
IRET	Interrupt return

Figure 4. 80C188 Instruction Set (Continued)

To access operands that do not reside in one of the four immediately available segments, a full 32-bit pointer can be used to reload both the base (segment) and offset values.

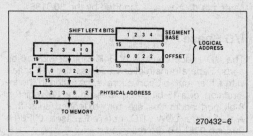

Figure 5. Two Component Address

Table 3. Segment Register Selection Rules

Memory Reference Needed	Segment Register Used	Implicit Segment Selection Rule
Instructions	Code (CS)	Instruction prefetch and immediate data.
Stack	Stack (SS)	All stack pushes and pops; any memory references which use BP Register as a base register.
External Data (Global)	Extra (ES)	All string instruction references which use the DI register as an index.
Local Data	Data (DS)	All other data references.

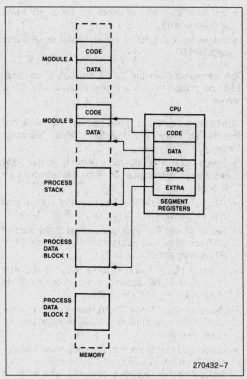

Figure 6. Segmented Memory Helps Structure Software

Addressing Modes

The 80C188 provides eight categories of addressing modes to specify operands. Two addressing modes are provided for instructions that operate on register or immediate operands:

- *Register Operand Mode:* The operand is located in one of the 8- or 16-bit general registers.
- *Immediate Operand Mode:* The operand is included in the instruction.

Six modes are provided to specify the location of an operand in a memory segment. A memory operand address consists of two 16-bit components: a segment base and an offset. The segment base is supplied by a 16-bit segment register either implicitly chosen by the addressing mode or explicitly chosen by a segment override prefix. The offset, also called the effective address, is calculated by summing any combination of the following three address elements:

- the *displacement* (an 8- or 16-bit immediate value contained in the instruction);
- the *base* (contents of either the BX or BP base registers); and
- the *index* (contents of either the SI or DI index registers).

Any carry out from the 16-bit addition is ignored. Eight-bit displacements are sign extended to 16-bit values.

Combinations of these three address elements define the six memory addressing modes, described below.

- *Direct Mode:* The operand's offset is contained in the instruction as an 8- or 16-bit displacement element.
- *Register Indirect Mode:* The operand's offset is in one of the registers SI, DI, BX, or BP.
- *Based Mode:* The operand's offset is the sum of an 8- or 16-bit displacement and the contents of a base register (BX or BP).
- *Indexed Mode:* The operand's offset is the sum of an 8- or 16-bit displacement and the contents of an index register (SI or DI).
- *Based Indexed Mode:* The operand's offset is the sum of the contents of a base register and an Index register.
- *Based indexed Mode with Displacement:* The operand's offset is the sum of a base register's contents, an index register's contents, and an 8- or 16-bit displacement.

Data Types

The 80C188 directly supports the following data types:

- *Integer:* A signed binary numeric value contained in an 8-bit byte or a 16-bit word. All operations assume a 2's complement representation.
- *Ordinal:* An unsigned binary numeric value contained in an 8-bit byte or a 16-bit word.
- *Pointer:* A 16- or 32-bit quantity, composed of a 16-bit offset component or a 16-bit segment base component in addition to a 16-bit offset component.
- *String:* A contiguous sequence of bytes or words. A string may contain from 1 to 64K bytes.
- *ASCII:* A byte representation of alphanumeric and control characters using the ASCII standard of character representation.
- *BCD:* A byte (unpacked) representation of the decimal digits 0–9.
- *Packed BCD:* A byte (packed) representation of two decimal digits (0–9). One digit is stored in each nibble (4-bits) of the byte.

In general, individual data elements must fit within defined segment limits. Figure 7 graphically represents the data types supported by the 80C188.

I/O Space

The I/O space consists of 64K 8-bit or 32K 16-bit ports. Separate instructions address the I/O space with either an 8-bit port address, specified in the instruction, or a 16-bit port address in the DX register. 8-bit port addresses are zero extended such that $A_{15}-A_8$ are LOW. I/O port addresses 00F8(H) through 00FF(H) are reserved.

Interrupts

An interrupt transfers execution to a new program location. The old program address (CS:IP) and machine state (Status Word) are saved on the stack to allow resumption of the interrupted program. Interrupts fall into three classes: hardware initiated, INT instructions, and instruction exceptions. Hardware initiated interrupts occur in response to an external input and are classified as non-maskable or maskable.

Programs may cause an interrupt with an INT instruction. Instruction exceptions occur when an unusual condition, which prevents further instruction processing, is detected while attempting to execute an instruction. If the exception was caused by attempted execution of an ESC instruction, the return instruction will point to the ESC instruction, or to the segment override prefix immediately preceding the ESC instruction if the prefix was present. In all other cases, the return address from an exception will point at the instruction immediately following the instruction causing the exception.

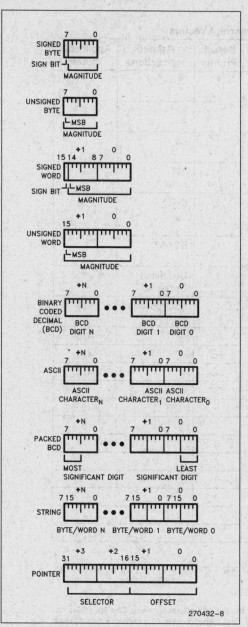

Figure 7. 80C188 Supported Data Types

A table containing up to 256 pointers defines the proper interrupt service routine for each interrupt. Interrupts 0–31, some of which are used for instruction exceptions, are reserved. Table 4 shows the 80C188 predefined types and default priority levels. For each interrupt, an 8-bit vector must be supplied to the 80C186 which identifies the appropriate table entry. Exceptions supply the interrupt vector internally. In addition, internal peripherals and noncascaded external interrupts will generate their own vectors through the internal interrupt controller. INT instructions contain or imply the vector and allow access to all 256 interrupts. Maskable hardware initiated interrupts supply the 8-bit vector to the CPU during an interrupt acknowledge bus sequence. Non-maskable hardware interrupts use a predefined internally supplied vector.

Interrupt Sources

The 80C188 can service interrupts generated by software or hardware. The software interrupts are generated by specific instructions (INT, ESC, unused OP, etc.) or the results of conditions specified by instructions (array bounds check, INT0, DIV, IDIV, etc.). All interrupt sources are serviced by an indirect call through an element of a vector table. This vector table is indexed by using the interrupt vector type (Table 4), multiplied by four. All hardware-generated interrupts are sampled at the end of each instruction. Thus, the software interrupts will begin service first. Once the service routine is entered and interrupts are enabled, any hardware source of sufficient priority can interrupt the service routine in progress.

Those pre-defined 80C188 interrupts which cannot be masked by programming are described below.

DIVIDE ERROR EXCEPTION (TYPE 0)

Generated when a DIV or IDIV instruction quotient cannot be expressed in the number of bits in the destination.

SINGLE-STEP INTERRUPT (TYPE 1)

Generated after most instructions if the TF flag in the status word is set. This interrupt allows programs to execute one instruction at a time. Interrupts will not be generated after prefix instructions (e.g., REP), instructions which modify segment registers (e.g., POP DS), or the WAIT instruction. Vectoring to the single-step interrupt service routine clears the TF bit. An IRET instruction in the interrupt service routine restores the TF bit to logic "1" and transfers control to the next instruction to be single-stepped.

NON-MASKABLE INTERRUPT—NMI (TYPE 2)

An external interrupt source which is serviced regardless of the state of the IF bit. No external acknowledge sequence is performed. The IF bit is cleared at the beginning of an NMI interrupt to prevent maskable interrupts from being serviced. A typical use of NMI would be to activate a power failure routine.

Table 4. 80C188 Interrupt Vectors

Interrupt Name	Vector Type	Vector Address	Default Priority	Related Instructions	Applicable Notes
Divide Error Exception	0	00H	1	DIV, IDIV	1
Single Step Interrupt	1	04H	1A	All	2
Non-Maskable Interrupt (NMI)	2	08H	1	All	
Breakpoint Interrupt	3	0CH	1	INT	1
INTO Detected Overflow Exception	4	10H	1	INTO	1
Array Bounds Exception	5	14H	1	BOUND	1
Unused-Opcode Exception	6	18H	1	Undefined Opcodes	1
ESC Opcode Exception	7	1CH	1	ESC Opcodes	1, 3
Timer 0 Interrupt	8	20H	2A		4, 5
Timer 1 Interrupt	18	48H	2B		4, 5
Timer 2 Interrupt	19	4CH	2C		4, 5
Reserved	9	24H	3		
DMA 0 Interrupt	10	28H	5		5
DMA 1 Interrupt	11	2CH	5		5
INT0 Interrupt	12	30H	6		
INT1 Interrupt	13	34H	7		
INT2 Interrupt	14	38H	8		
INT3 Interrupt	15	3CH	9		
Reserved	16, 17	40H, 44H			
Reserved	20–31	50H . . . 7CH			

NOTES:

Default priorities for the interrupt sources are used only if the user does not program each source to a unique priority level.

1. Generated as a result of an instruction execution.

2. Performed in same manner as 8088.

3. An ESC opcode will cause a trap regardless of the 80C188 operating mode. The 80C188 is not directly compatible with the 80188 in this respect. The instruction set of a numerics coprocessor cannot be executed.

4. All three timers constitute one source of request to the interrupt controller. As such, they share the same priority level with respect to other interrupt sources. However, the timers have a defined priority order among themselves (2A > 2B > 2C).

5. The vector type numbers for these sources are programmable in Slave Mode.

BREAKPOINT INTERRUPT (TYPE 3)

A one-byte version of the INT instruction. It uses 12 as an index into the service routine address table (because it is a type 3 interrupt).

INTO DETECTED OVERFLOW EXCEPTION (TYPE 4)

Generated during an INTO instruction if the OF bit is set.

ARRAY BOUNDS EXCEPTION (TYPE 5)

Generated during a BOUND instruction if the array index is outside the array bounds. The array bounds are located in memory at a location indicated by one of the instruction operands. The other operand indicates the value of the index to be checked.

UNUSED OPCODE EXCEPTION (TYPE 6)

Generated if execution is attempted on undefined opcodes.

ESCAPE OPCODE EXCEPTION (TYPE 7)

Generated if execution is attempted of ESC opcodes (D8H–DFH). The 80C188 does not check an escape opcode trap bit as does the 80C186. On the 80C188, ESC traps occcur in both compatible and enhanced operating modes. The return address of

this exception will point to the ESC instruction causing the exception. If a segment override prefix preceded the ESC instruction, the return address will point to the segment override prefix.

NOTE:

Unlike the 80188, all numerics coprocessor opcodes cause a trap. The 80C188 does not support the numerics interface.

Hardware-generated interrupts are divided into two groups: maskable interrupts and non-maskable interrupts. The 80C188 provides maskable hardware interrupt request pins INT0–INT3. In addition, maskable interrupts may be generated by the 80C188 integrated DMA controller and the integrated timer unit. The vector types for these interrupts is shown in Table 4. Software enables these inputs by setting the interrupt flag bit (IF) in the Status Word. The interrupt controller is discussed in the peripheral section of this data sheet.

Further maskable interrupts are disabled while servicing an interrupt because the IF bit is reset as part of the response to an interrupt or exception. The saved Status Word will reflect the enable status of the processor prior to the interrupt. The interrupt flag will remain zero unless specifically set. The interrupt return instruction restores the Status Word, thereby restoring the original status of IF bit. If the interrupt return re-enables interrupts, and another interrupt is pending, the 80C188 will immediately service the highest-priority interrupt pending, i.e., no instructions of the main line program will be executed.

Initialization and Processor Reset

Processor initialization is accomplished by driving the $\overline{RES}$ input pin LOW. $\overline{RES}$ must be LOW during power-up to ensure proper device initialization. $\overline{RES}$ forces the 80C188 to terminate all execution and local bus activity. No instruction or bus activity will occur as long as $\overline{RES}$ is active. After $\overline{RES}$ becomes inactive and an internal processing interval elapses, the 80C188 begins execution with the instruction at physical location FFFF0(H). $\overline{RES}$ also sets some registers to predefined values as shown in Table 5.

Table 5. 80C188 Initial Register State after RESET

Status Word	F002(H)
Instruction Pointer	0000(H)
Code Segment	FFFF(H)
Data Segment	0000(H)
Extra Segment	0000(H)
Stack Segment	0000(H)
Relocation Register	20FF(H)
UMCS	FFFB(H)

THE 80C188 COMPARED TO THE 80C186

The 80C188 is an 8-bit processor designed based on the 80C186 internal structure. Most internal functions of the 80C188 are identical to the equivalent 80C186 functions. The 80C188 handles the external bus the same way the 80C186 does with the distinction of handling only 8 bits at a time. Sixteen-bit operands are fetched or written in two consecutive bus cycles. The processors will look the same to the software engineer, with the exception of execution time. The internal register structure is identical and all instructions except numerics instructions have the same end result. Internally, there are four differences between the 80C188 and the 80C186. All changes are related to the 8-bit bus interface.

- The queue length is 4 bytes in the 80C188, whereas the 80C186 queue contains 6 bytes, or three words. The queue was shortened to prevent overuse of the bus by the BIU when prefetching instructions. This was required because of the additional time necessary to fetch instructions 8 bits at a time.

- To further optimize the queue, the prefetching algorithm was changed. The 80C188 BIU will fetch a new instruction to load into the queue each time there is a 1-byte hole (space available) in the queue. The 80C186 waits until a 2-byte space is available.

- The internal execution time of an instruction is affected by the 8-bit interface. All 16-bit fetches and writes from/to memory take an additional four clock cycles. The CPU may also be limited by the rate of instruction fetches when a series of simple operations occur. When the more sophisticated instructions of the 80C188 are being used, the queue has more time to fill and the execution proceeds more closely to the speed at which the execution unit will allow.

- The 80C188 does not have a numerics interface, since the 80C186 numerics interface inherently requires 16-bit communication with the numerics coprocessor.

The 80C188 and 80C186 are completely software compatible (except for numerics instructions) by virtue of their identical execution units. However, software that is system dependent may not be completely transferable.

The bus interface and associated control signals vary somewhat between the two processors. The pin assignments are nearly identical, with the following functional changes:

- A8–A15—These pins are only address outputs on the 80C188. These address lines are latched internally and remain valid throughout the bus cycle.

- $\overline{BHE}$ has no meaning on the 80C188. However, it was necessary to designate this pin the $\overline{RFSH}$ pin in order to provide an indication of DRAM refresh bus cycles.

80C188 CLOCK GENERATOR

The 80C188 provides an on-chip clock generator for both internal and external clock generation. The clock generator features a crystal oscillator, a divide-by-two counter, synchronous and asynchronous ready inputs, and reset circuitry.

Oscillator

The 80C188 oscillator circuit is designed to be used either with a parallel resonant fundamental or third-overtone mode crystal, depending upon the frequency range of the application as shown in Figure 8c. This is used as the time base for the 80C188. The crystal frequency chosen should be twice the required processor frequency. Use of an LC or RC circuit is not recommended.

The output of the oscillator is not directly available outside the 80C188. The two recommended crystal configurations are shown in Figures 8a and 8b. When used in third-overtone mode the tank circuit shown in Figure 8b is recommended for stable operation. The sum of the stray capacitances and loading capacitors should equal the values shown. It is advisable to limit stray capacitance between the X1 and X2 pins to less than 10 pF. While a fundamental-mode circuit will require approximately 1 ms for start-up, the third-overtone arrangement may require 1 ms to 3 ms to stabilize.

Alternately, the oscillator may be driven from an external source as shown in Figure 8d. The configuration shown in Figure 8e is not recommended.

Intel recommends the following values for crystal selection parameters:

Temperature Range:	0 to 70°C
ESR (Equivalent Series Resistance):	40Ω max
C_0 (Shunt Capacitance of Crystal):	7.0 pF max
C_1 (Load Capacitance):	20 pF ± 2 pF
Drive Level:	1 mW max

Clock Generator

The 80C188 clock generator provides the 50% duty cycle processor clock for the 80C188. It does this by dividing the oscillator output by 2 forming the symmetrical clock. If an external oscillator is used, the state of the clock generator will change on the falling edge of the oscillator signal. The CLKOUT pin provides the processor clock signal for use outside the 80C188. This may be used to drive other system components. All timings are referenced to the output clock.

READY Synchronization

The 80C188 provides both synchronous and asynchronous ready inputs. Asynchronous ready synchronization is accomplished by circuitry which samples ARDY in the middle of T_2, T_3 and again in the middle of each T_W until ARDY is sampled HIGH. One-half CLKOUT cycle of resolution time is used for full synchronization of a rising ARDY signal. A high-to-low transition on ARDY may be used as an indication of the not ready condition but it must be performed synchronously to CLKOUT **either** in the middle of T_2, T_3 or T_W, **or** at the falling edge of T_3 or T_W.

A second ready input (SRDY) is provided to interface with externally synchronized ready signals. This input is sampled at the end of T_2, T_3 and again at the end of each T_W until it is sampled HIGH. By using this input rather than the asynchronous ready input, the half-clock cycle resolution time penalty is eliminated. This input must satisfy set-up and hold times to guarantee proper operation of the circuit.

In addition, the 80C188, as part of the integrated chip-select logic, has the capability to program WAIT states for memory and peripheral blocks. This is discussed in the Chip Select/Ready Logic description.

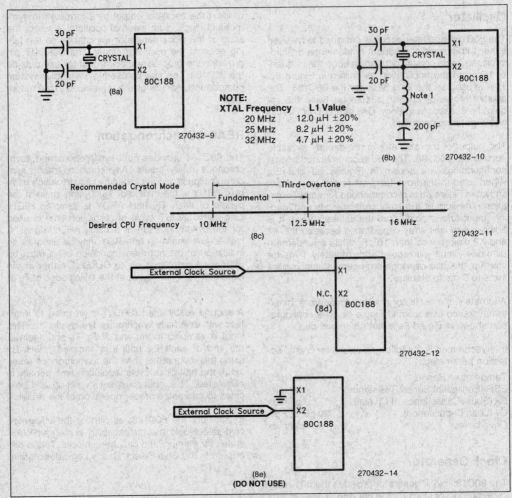

Figure 8. 80C188 Oscillator Configurations (see text)

RESET Logic

The 80C188 provides both a $\overline{RES}$ input pin and a synchronized RESET output pin for use with other system components. The $\overline{RES}$ input pin on the 80C188 is provided with hysteresis in order to facilitate power-on Reset generation via an RC network. RESET output is guaranteed to remain active for at least five clocks given a $\overline{RES}$ input of at least six clocks. RESET may be delayed up to approximately two and one-half clocks behind $\overline{RES}$.

LOCAL BUS CONTROLLER

The 80C188 provides a local bus controller to generate the local bus control signals. In addition, it employs a HOLD/HLDA protocol for relinquishing the local bus to other bus masters. It also provides outputs that can be used to enable external buffers and to direct the flow of data on and off the local bus.

Memory/Peripheral Control

The 80C188 provides ALE, $\overline{RD}$, and $\overline{WR}$ bus control signals. The $\overline{RD}$ and $\overline{WR}$ signals are used to strobe data from memory or I/O to the 80C188 or to strobe data from the 80C188 to memory or I/O. The ALE line provides a strobe to latch the address when it is valid. The 80C188 local bus controller does not provide a memory/$\overline{I/O}$ signal. If this is required, use the $\overline{S2}$ signal (which will require external latching), make the memory and I/O spaces nonoverlapping, or use only the integrated chip-select circuitry.

Transceiver Control

The 80C188 generates two control signals for external transceiver chips. This capability allows the addition of transceivers for extra buffering without adding external logic. These control lines, DT/$\overline{R}$ and $\overline{DEN}$, are generated to control the flow of data through the transceivers. The operation of these signals is shown in Table 6.

Table 6. Transceiver Control Signals Description

Pin Name	Function
$\overline{DEN}$ (Data Enable)	Enables the output drivers of the transceivers. It is active LOW during memory, I/O, or INTA cycles.
DT/$\overline{R}$ (Data Transmit/Receive)	Determines the direction of travel through the transceivers. A HIGH level directs data away from the processor during write operations, while a LOW level directs data toward the processor during a read operation.

Local Bus Arbitration

The 80C188 uses a HOLD/HLDA system of local bus exchange. This provides an asynchronous bus exchange mechanism. This means multiple masters utilizing the same bus can operate at separate clock frequencies. The 80C188 provides a single HOLD/HLDA pair through which all other bus masters may gain control of the local bus. External circuitry must arbitrate which external device will gain control of the bus when there is more than one alternate local bus master. When the 80C188 relinquishes control of the local bus, it floats $\overline{DEN}$, $\overline{RD}$, $\overline{WR}$, $\overline{S0}$–$\overline{S2}$, $\overline{LOCK}$, AD0–AD7, A8–A19, S7/$\overline{RFSH}$, and DT/$\overline{R}$ to allow another master to drive these lines directly.

The 80C188 HOLD latency time, i.e., the time between HOLD request and HOLD acknowledge, is a function of the activity occurring in the processor when the HOLD request is received. A HOLD request is second only to DRAM refresh requests in priority of activity requests the processor may receive. Any bus cycle in progress will be completed before the 80C188 relinquishes the bus. This implies that if a HOLD request is received just as a DMA transfer begins, the HOLD latency can be as great as 4 bus cycles. This will occur if a DMA word transfer operation is taking place from an odd address to an odd address. This is a total of 16 clock cycles or more if WAIT states are required. In addition, if locked transfers are performed, the HOLD latency time will be increased by the length of the locked transfer.

If the 80C188 has relinquished the bus and a refresh request is pending, HLDA is removed (driven LOW) to signal the remote processor that the 80C188 wishes to regain control of the bus. The 80C188 will wait until HOLD is removed before taking control of the bus to run the refresh cycle.

Local Bus Controller and Reset

During RESET, the local bus controller will perform the following action:

- Drive $\overline{DEN}$, $\overline{RD}$, and $\overline{WR}$ HIGH for one clock cycle, then float them.
- Drive $\overline{S0}$–$\overline{S2}$ to the inactive state (all HIGH) and then float.
- Drive $\overline{LOCK}$ HIGH and then float.
- Float AD0–AD7, A8–A19, S7/$\overline{RFSH}$, DT/$\overline{R}$.
- Drive ALE LOW.
- Drive HLDA LOW.

$\overline{RD}$/$\overline{QSMD}$, $\overline{UCS}$, $\overline{LCS}$, and $\overline{TEST}$ pins have internal pullup devices which are active while $\overline{RES}$ is applied. Excessive loading or grounding certain of these pins causes the 80C188 to enter an alternative mode of operation:

- $\overline{RD}$/$\overline{QSMD}$ LOW results in Queue Status Mode.
- $\overline{UCS}$ and $\overline{LCS}$ LOW results in ONCE Mode.
- $\overline{TEST}$ LOW (and HIGH later) results in Enhanced Mode.

INTERNAL PERIPHERAL INTERFACE

All the 80C188 integrated peripherals are controlled by 16-bit registers contained within an internal 256-byte control block. The control block may be mapped into either memory or I/O space. Internal logic will recognize control block addresses and respond to bus cycles. During bus cycles to internal registers, the bus controller will signal the operation externally (i.e., the $\overline{RD}$, $\overline{WR}$, status, address, data, etc., lines will be driven as in a normal bus cycle), but D_{15-0}, SRDY, and ARDY will be ignored. The base address of the control block must be on an even 256-byte boundary (i.e., the lower 8 bits of the base address are all zeros). All of the defined registers within this control block may be read or written by the 80C188 CPU at any time.

The control block base address is programmed by a 16-bit relocation register contained within the control block at offset FEH from the base address of the control block (see Figure 9). It provides the upper 12 bits of the base address of the control block. The control block is effectively an internal chip select range and must abide by all the rules concerning chip selects (the chip select circuitry is discussed later in this data sheet). Any access to the 256 bytes of the control block activates an internal chip select.

Other chip selects may overlap the control block only if they are programmed to zero wait states and ignore external ready. In addition, bit 12 of this register determines whether the control block will be mapped into I/O or memory space. If this bit is 1, the control block will be located in memory space. If the bit is 0, the control block will be located in I/O space. If the control register block is mapped into I/O space, the upper 4 bits of the base address must be programmed as 0 (since I/O addresses are only 16 bits wide).

In addition to providing relocation information for the control block, the relocation register contains bits which place the interrupt controller into Slave Mode. At RESET, the relocation register is set to 20FFH, which maps the control block to start at FF00H in I/O space. An offset map of the 256-byte control register block is shown in Figure 10.

CHIP-SELECT/READY GENERATION LOGIC

The 80C188 contains logic which provides programmable chip-select generation for both memories and peripherals. In addition, it can be programmed to provide READY (or WAIT state) generation. It can also provide latched address bits A1 and A2. The chip-select lines are active for all memory and I/O cycles in their programmed areas, whether they be generated by the CPU or by the integrated DMA unit.

Memory Chip Selects

The 80C188 provides 6 memory chip select outputs for 3 address areas; upper memory, lower memory, and midrange memory. One each is provided for upper memory and lower memory, while four are provided for midrange memory.

The range for each chip select is user-programmable and can be set to 2K, 4K, 8K, 16K, 32K, 64K, 128K (plus 1K and 256K for upper and lower chip selects). In addition, the beginning or base address of the midrange memory chip select may also be selected. Only one chip select may be programmed to be active for any memory location at a time. All chip select sizes are in bytes.

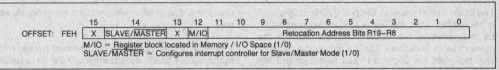

OFFSET: FEH	15	14	13	12	11	10	9	8	7	6	5	4	3	2	1	0
	X	SLAVE/$\overline{\text{MASTER}}$		X	M/$\overline{\text{IO}}$				Relocation Address Bits R19–R8							

M/$\overline{\text{IO}}$ = Register block located in Memory / I/O Space (1/0)
SLAVE/$\overline{\text{MASTER}}$ = Configures interrupt controller for Slave/Master Mode (1/0)

Figure 9. Relocation Register

	OFFSET
Relocation Register	FEH
DMA Descriptors Channel 1	DAH
	D0H
DMA Descriptors Channel 0	CAH
	C0H
Chip-Select Control Registers	A8H
	A0H
Time 2 Control Registers	66H
	60H
Time 1 Control Registers	5EH
	58H
Time 0 Control Registers	56H
	50H
Interrupt Controller Registers	3EH
	20H

Figure 10. Internal Register Map

Upper Memory $\overline{\text{CS}}$

The 80C188 provides a chip select, called $\overline{\text{UCS}}$, for the top of memory. The top of memory is usually used as the system memory because after reset the 80C188 begins executing at memory location FFFF0H.

The upper limit of memory defined by this chip select is always FFFFFH, while the lower limit is programmable. By programming the lower limit, the size of the select block is also defined. Table 7 shows the relationship between the base address selected and the size of the memory block obtained.

Table 7. UMCS Programming Values

Starting Address (Base Address)	Memory Block Size	UMCS Value (Assuming R0 = R1 = R2 = 0)
FFC00	1K	FFF8H
FF800	2K	FFB8H
FF000	4K	FF38H
FE000	8K	FE38H
FC000	16K	FC38H
F8000	32K	F838H
F0000	64K	F038H
E0000	128K	E038H
C0000	256K	C038H

The lower limit of this memory block is defined in the UMCS register (see Figure 11). This register is at offset A0H in the internal control block. The legal values for bits 6–13 and the resulting starting address and memory block sizes are given in Table 7. Any combination of bits 6–13 not shown in Table 7 will result in undefined operation. After reset, the UMCS register is programmed for a 1K area. It must be reprogrammed if a larger upper memory area is desired.

The internal generation of any 20-bit address whose upper 16 bits are equal to or greater than the UMCS value (with bits 0–5 as "0") asserts $\overline{\text{UCS}}$. UMCS bits R2–R0 specify the ready mode for the area of memory defined by the chip select register, as explained later.

Lower Memory $\overline{\text{CS}}$

The 80C188 provides a chip select for low memory called $\overline{\text{LCS}}$. The bottom of memory contains the interrupt vector table, starting at location 00000H.

The lower limit of memory defined by this chip select is always 0H, while the upper limit is programmable. By programming the upper limit, the size of the memory block is defined. Table 8 shows the relationship between the upper address selected and the size of the memory block obtained.

Table 8. LMCS Programming Values

Upper Address	Memory Block Size	LMCS Value (Assuming R0 = R1 = R2 = 0)
003FFH	1K	0038H
007FFH	2K	0078H
00FFFH	4K	00F8H
01FFFH	8K	01F8H
03FFFH	16K	03F8H
07FFFH	32K	07F8H
0FFFFH	64K	0FF8H
1FFFFH	128K	1FF8H
3FFFFH	256K	3FF8H

The upper limit of this memory block is defined in the LMCS register (see Figure 12) at offset A2H in the internal control block. The legal values for bits 6–15 and the resulting upper address and memory block sizes are given in Table 8. Any combination of bits 6–15 not shown in Table 8 will result in undefined operation. After RESET, the LMCS register value is undefined. However, the $\overline{LCS}$ chip-select line will not become active until the LMCS register is accessed.

Any internally generated 20-bit address whose upper 16 bits are less than or equal to LMCS (with bits 0–5 "1") will assert $\overline{LCS}$. LMCS register bits R2–R0 specify the READY mode for the area of memory defined by this chip-select register.

Mid-Range Memory $\overline{CS}$

The 80C188 provides four $\overline{MCS}$ lines which are active within a user-locatable memory block. This block can be located within the 80C188 1M byte memory address space exclusive of the areas defined by $\overline{UCS}$ and $\overline{LCS}$. Both the base address and size of this memory block are programmable.

The size of the memory block defined by the mid-range select lines, as shown in Table 9, is determined by bits 8–14 of the MPCS register (see Figure 13). This register is at location A8H in the internal control block. One and only one of bits 8–14 must be set at a time. Unpredictable operation of the $\overline{MCS}$ lines will otherwise occur. Each of the four chip-select lines is active for one of the four equal contiguous divisions of the mid-range block. If the total block size is 32K, each chip select is active for 8K of memory with $\overline{MCS0}$ being active for the first range and $\overline{MCS3}$ being active for the last range.

The EX and MS in MPCS relate to peripheral functionality as described in a later section.

Table 9. MPCS Programming Values

Total Block Size	Individual Select Size	MPCS Bits 14–8
8K	2K	0000001B
16K	4K	0000010B
32K	8K	0000100B
64K	16K	0001000B
128K	32K	0010000B
256K	64K	0100000B
512K	128K	1000000B

The base address of the mid-range memory block is defined by bits 15–9 of the MMCS register (see Figure 14). This register is at offset A6H in the internal control block. These bits correspond to bits A19–A13 of the 20-bit memory address. Bits A12–A0 of the base address are always 0. The base address may be set at any integer multiple of the size of the total memory block selected. For example, if the mid-range block size is 32K (or the size of the block for which each $\overline{MCS}$ line is active is 8K), the block could be located at 10000H or 18000H, but not at 14000H, since the first few integer multiples of a 32K memory block are 0H, 8000H, 10000H, 18000H, etc. After RESET, the contents of both registers are undefined. However, none of the $\overline{MCS}$ lines will be active until both the MMCS and MPCS registers are accessed.

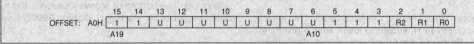

OFFSET: A0H	15	14	13	12	11	10	9	8	7	6	5	4	3	2	1	0
	1	1	U	U	U	U	U	U	U	U	U	1	1	1	R2	R1	R0

A19   A10

Figure 11. UMCS Register

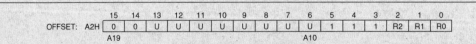

OFFSET: A2H	15	14	13	12	11	10	9	8	7	6	5	4	3	2	1	0
	0	0	U	U	U	U	U	U	U	U	1	1	1	R2	R1	R0

A19   A10

Figure 12. LMCS Register

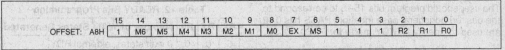

	15	14	13	12	11	10	9	8	7	6	5	4	3	2	1	0
OFFSET: A8H	1	M6	M5	M4	M3	M2	M1	M0	EX	MS	1	1	1	R2	R1	R0

Figure 13. MPCS Register

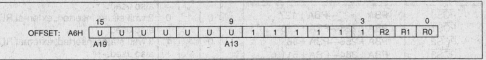

	15						9						3		0
OFFSET: A6H	U	U	U	U	U	U	U	1	1	1	1	1	1	R2	R1	R0
	A19						A13								

Figure 14. MMCS Register

MMCS bits R2–R0 specify READY mode of operation for all four mid-range chip selects.

The 512K block size for the mid-range memory chip selects is a special case. When using 512K, the base address would have to be at either locations 00000H or 80000H. If it were to be programmed at 00000H when the $\overline{\text{LCS}}$ line was programmed, there would be an internal conflict between the $\overline{\text{LCS}}$ ready generation logic and the $\overline{\text{MCS}}$ ready generation logic. Likewise, if the base address were programmed at 80000H, there would be a conflict with the $\overline{\text{UCS}}$ ready generation logic. Since the $\overline{\text{LCS}}$ chip-select line does not become active until programmed, while the $\overline{\text{UCS}}$ line is active at reset, the memory base can be set only at 00000H. If this base address is selected, however, the $\overline{\text{LCS}}$ range must not be programmed.

Peripheral Chip Selects

The 80C188 can generate chip selects for up to seven peripheral devices. These chip selects are active for seven contiguous blocks of 128 bytes above a programmable base address. The base address may be located in either memory or I/O space.

Seven $\overline{\text{CS}}$ lines called $\overline{\text{PCS0}}$–6 are generated by the 80C188. The base address is user-programmable; however it can only be a multiple of 1K bytes, i.e., the least significant 10 bits of the starting address are always 0.

$\overline{\text{PCS5}}$ and $\overline{\text{PCS6}}$ can also be programmed to provide latched address bits A1 and A2. If so programmed, they cannot be used as peripheral selects. These outputs can be connected directly to the A0 and A1 pins used for selecting internal registers of 8-bit peripheral chips.

The starting address of the peripheral chip-select block is defined by the PACS register (see Figure 15). The register is located at offset A4H in the internal control block. Bits 15–6 of this register correspond to bits 19–10 of the 20-bit Programmable Base Address (PBA) of the peripheral chip-select block. Bits 9–0 of the PBA of the peripheral chip-select block are all zeros. If the chip-select block is located in I/O space, bits 12–15 must be programmed zero, since the I/O address is only 16 bits wide. Table 10 shows the address range of each peripheral chip select with respect to the PBA contained in PACS register.

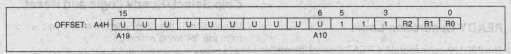

	15								6	5		3		0
OFFSET: A4H	U	U	U	U	U	U	U	U	U	U	1	1	1	R2	R1	R0
	A19								A10					

Figure 15. PACS Register

The user should program bits 15–6 to correspond to the desired peripheral base location. PACS bits 0–2 are used to specify READY mode for $\overline{PCS0}$–$\overline{PCS3}$.

Table 10. PCS Address Ranges

$\overline{PCS}$ Line	Active between Locations
$\overline{PCS0}$	PBA —PBA+127
$\overline{PCS1}$	PBA+128—PBA+255
$\overline{PCS2}$	PBA+256—PBA+383
$\overline{PCS3}$	PBA+384—PBA+511
$\overline{PCS4}$	PBA+512—PBA+639
$\overline{PCS5}$	PBA+640—PBA+767
$\overline{PCS6}$	PBA+768—PBA+895

The mode of operation of the peripheral chip selects is defined by the MPCS register (which is also used to set the size of the mid-range memory chip-select block, see Figure 13). The register is located at offset A8H in the internal control block. Bit 7 is used to select the function of $\overline{PCS5}$ and $\overline{PCS6}$, while bit 6 is used to select whether the peripheral chip selects are mapped into memory or I/O space. Table 11 describes the programming of these bits. After RESET, the contents of both the MPCS and the PACS registers are undefined, however none of the PCS lines will be active until both of the MPCS and PACS registers are accessed.

Table 11. MS, EX Programming Values

Bit	Description
MS	1 = Peripherals mapped into memory space.
	0 = Peripherals mapped into I/O space.
EX	0 = 5 $\overline{PCS}$ lines. A1, A2 provided.
	1 = 7 $\overline{PCS}$ lines. A1, A2 are not provided.

MPCS bits 0–2 specify the READY mode for $\overline{PCS4}$–$\overline{PCS6}$ as outlined below.

READY Generation Logic

The 80C188 can generate a READY signal internally for each of the memory or peripheral $\overline{CS}$ lines. The number of WAIT states to be inserted for each peripheral or memory is programmable to provide 0–3 wait states for all accesses to the area for which the chip select is active. In addition, the 80C188 may be programmed to either ignore external READY for each chip-select range individually or to factor external READY with the integrated ready generator.

READY control consists of 3 bits for each $\overline{CS}$ line or group of lines generated by the 80C188. The interpretation of the READY bits is shown in Table 12.

Table 12. READY Bits Programming

R2	R1	R0	Number of WAIT States Generated
0	0	0	0 wait states, external RDY also used.
0	0	1	1 wait state inserted, external RDY also used.
0	1	0	2 wait states inserted, external RDY also used.
0	1	1	3 wait states inserted, external RDY also used.
1	0	0	0 wait states, external RDY ignored.
1	0	1	1 wait state inserted, external RDY ignored.
1	1	0	2 wait states inserted, external RDY ignored.
1	1	1	3 wait states inserted, external RDY ignored.

The internal READY generator operates in parallel with external READY, not in series, if the external READY is used (R2 = 0). For example, if the internal generator is set to insert two wait states, but activity on the external READY lines will insert four wait states, the processor will only insert four wait states, not six. This is because the two wait states generated by the internal generator overlapped the first two wait states generated by the external ready signal. Note that the external ARDY and SRDY lines are always ignored during cycles accessing internal peripherals.

R2–R0 of each control word specifies the READY mode for the corresponding block, with the exception of the peripheral chip selects: R2–R0 of PACS set the $\overline{PCS0}$–3 READY mode, R2–R0 of MPCS set the $\overline{PCS4}$–6 READY mode.

Chip Select/Ready Logic and Reset

Upon RESET, the Chip-Select/Ready Logic will perform the following actions:

- All chip-select outputs will be driven HIGH.
- Upon leaving RESET, the $\overline{UCS}$ line will be programmed to provide chip selects to a 1K block with the accompanying READY control bits set at 011 to insert 3 wait states in conjunction with external READY (i.e., UMCS resets to FFFBH).
- No other chip select or READY control registers have any predefined values after RESET. They will not become active until the CPU accesses their control registers. Both the PACS and MPCS registers must be accessed before the $\overline{PCS}$ lines will become active.

DMA CHANNELS

The 80C188 DMA controller provides two independent DMA channels. Data transfers can occur between memory and I/O spaces (e.g., Memory to I/O) or within the same space (e.g., Memory to Memory or I/O to I/O). Each DMA channel maintains both a 20-bit source and destination pointer which can be optionally incremented or decremented after each data transfer. Each data transfer consumes 2 bus cycles (a minimum of 8 clocks), one cycle to fetch data and the other to store data.

DMA Operation

Each channel has six registers in the control block which define each channel's operation. The control registers consist of a 20-bit Source pointer (2 words), a 20-bit destination pointer (2 words), a 16-bit Transfer Count Register, and a 16-bit Control Word. The format of the DMA Control Blocks is shown in Table 13. The Transfer Count Register

(TC) specifies the number of DMA transfers to be performed. Up to 64K byte transfers can be performed with automatic termination. The Control Word defines the channel's operation (see Figure 17). All registers may be modified or altered during any DMA activity. Any changes made to these registers will be reflected immediately in DMA operation.

Table 13. DMA Control Block Format

Register Name	Register Address	
	Ch. 0	Ch. 1
Control Word	CAH	DAH
Transfer Count	C8H	D8H
Destination Pointer (upper 4 bits)	C6H	D6H
Destination Pointer	C4H	D4H
Source Pointer (upper 4 bits)	C2H	D2H
Source Pointer	C0H	D0H

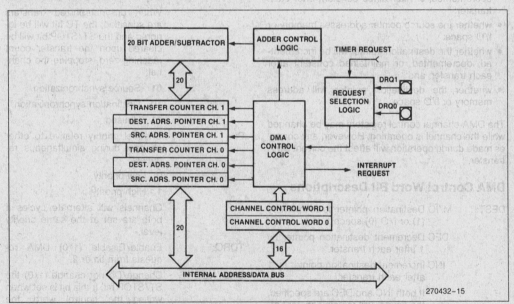

Figure 16. DMA Unit Block Diagram

270432–15

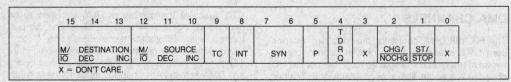

15	14	13	12	11	10	9	8	7	6	5	4	3	2	1	0
M/IO	DESTINATION DEC INC		M/IO	SOURCE DEC INC		TC	INT	SYN		P	T D R Q	X	CHG/NOCHG	ST/STOP	X

X = DON'T CARE.

Figure 17. DMA Control Register

DMA Channel Control Word Register

Each DMA Channel Control Word determines the mode of operation for the particular 80C188 DMA channel. This register specifies:

- the mode of synchronization;
- whether interrupts will be generated after the last transfer;
- whether DMA activity will cease after a programmed number of DMA cycles;
- the relative priority of the DMA channel with respect to the other DMA channel;
- whether the source pointer will be incremented, decremented, or maintained constant after each transfer;
- whether the source pointer addresses memory or I/O space;
- whether the destination pointer will be incremented, decremented, or maintained constant after each transfer; and
- whether the destination pointer will address memory or I/O space.

The DMA channel control registers may be changed while the channel is operating. However, any changes made during operation will affect the current DMA transfer.

DMA Control Word Bit Descriptions

DEST: M/IO Destination pointer is in memory (1) or I/O (0) space.

        DEC Decrement destination pointer by 1 after each transfer.

        INC Increment destination pointer by 1 after each transfer.

        If both INC and DEC are specified, the pointer will remain constant after each cycle.

SOURCE: M/IO Source pointer is in memory (1) or I/O (0) space.

        DEC Decrement source pointer by 1 after each transfer.

        INC Increment source pointer by 1 after each transfer.

        If both INC and DEC are specified, the pointer will remain constant after each cycle.

TC: If set, DMA will terminate when the contents of the transfer count register reach zero. The ST/STOP bit will also be reset at this point. If cleared, the DMA controller will decrement the transfer count register for each DMA cycle, but the DMA transfers will not stop when the transfer count register reaches zero.

INT: Enable interrupts to CPU upon transfer count termination.

SYN: 00 No synchronization.

NOTE:

When unsynchronized transfers are specified, the TC bit will be ignored and the ST/STOP bit will be cleared upon the transfer count reaching zero, stopping the channel.

        01 Source synchronization.

        10 Destination synchronization.

        11 Unused.

P: Channel priority relative to other channel during simultaneous requests.

        0 Low priority.

        1 High priority.

    Channels will alternate cycles if both are set at the same priority level.

TDRQ: Enable/Disable (1/0) DMA requests from timer 2.

CHG/NOCHG: Change/Do not change (1/0) the ST/STOP bit. If this bit is set when writing the control word, the ST/STOP bit will be programmed by the write to the control word. If this bit is cleared when writing the control word, the ST/STOP bit will not be altered. This bit is not stored; it will always be read as 0.

ST/STOP: Start/Stop (1/0) channel.

DMA Destination and Source Pointer Registers

Each DMA channel maintains a 20-bit source and a 20-bit destination pointer. Each of these pointers takes up two full 16-bit registers in the peripheral control block. For each DMA Channel to be used, all four pointer registers must be initialized. The lower four bits of the upper register contain the upper four bits of the 20-bit physical address (see Figure 18). These pointers may be individually incremented or decremented after each transfer.

Each pointer may point into either memory or I/O space. Since the upper four bits of the address are not automatically programmed to zero, the user must program them in order to address the normal 64K I/O space. There is no restriction on values for the pointer registers.

DMA Transfer Count Register

Each DMA channel maintains a 16-bit transfer count register (TC). The register is decremented after every DMA cycle, regardless of the state of the TC bit in the DMA Control Register. If the TC bit in the DMA control word is set or if unsynchronized transfers are programmed, however, DMA activity will terminate when the transfer count register reaches zero.

DMA Requests

Data transfers may be either source or destination synchronized, that is either the source of the data or the destination of the data may request the data transfer. In addition, DMA transfers may be unsynchronized; that is, the transfer will take place continually until the correct number of transfers has occurred. When source or unsynchronized transfers are performed, the DMA channel may begin another transfer immediately after the end of a previous DMA transfer. This allows a complete transfer to take place every 2 bus cycles or eight clock cycles (assuming no wait states). When destination synchronization is performed, data will not be fetched from the source address until the destination device signals that it is ready to receive it. Also, the DMA controller will relinquish control of the bus after every transfer. If no other bus activity is initiated, another destination synchronized DMA cycle will begin after two processor clocks. This allows the destination device time to remove its request if another transfer is not desired. Since the DMA controller will relinquish the bus, the CPU can initiate a bus cycle. As a result, a complete bus cycle will often be inserted between destination synchronized transfers. Table 14 shows the maximum DMA transfer rates.

Table 14. Maximum DMA Transfer Rates at CLKOUT = 16 MHz

Type of Synchronization Selected	CPU Running	CPU Halted
Unsynchronized	2.0 MBytes/sec	2.0 MBytes/sec
Source Synch	2.0 MBytes/sec	2.0 MBytes/sec
Destination Synch	1.3 MBytes/sec	1.6 MBytes/sec

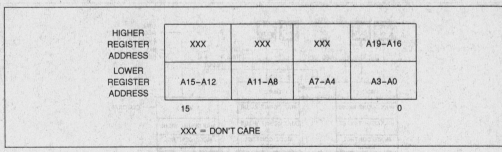

Figure 18. DMA Pointer Register Format

DMA Acknowledge

No explicit DMA acknowledge pulse is provided. Since both source and destination pointers are maintained, a read from a requesting source, or a write to a requesting destination, should be used as the DMA acknowledge signal. Since the chip-select lines can be programmed to be active for a given block of memory or I/O space, and the DMA pointers can be programmed to point to the same given block, a chip-select line could be used to indicate a DMA acknowledge.

DMA Priority

The DMA channels may be programmed to give one channel priority over the other, or they may be programmed to alternate cycles when both have DMA requests pending. DMA cycles always have priority over internal CPU cycles except between locked memory accesses; also, an external bus hold takes priority over an internal DMA cycle. Because an interrupt request cannot suspend a DMA operation and the CPU cannot access memory during a DMA cycle, interrupt latency time will suffer during sequences of continuous DMA cycles. An NMI request, however, will cause all internal DMA activity to halt. This allows the CPU to quickly respond to the NMI request.

DMA Programming

DMA cycles will occur whenever the ST/$\overline{\text{STOP}}$ bit of the Control Register is set. If synchronized transfers are programmed, a DRQ must also be generated. Therefore the source and destination transfer point-

ers, and the transfer count register (if used) must be programmed before the ST/STOP bit is set.

Each DMA register may be modified while the channel is operating. If the CHG/NOCHG bit is cleared when the control register is written, the ST/STOP bit of the control register will not be modified by the write. If multiple channel registers are modified, it is recommended that a LOCKED string transfer be used to prevent a DMA transfer from occurring between updates to the channel registers.

DMA Channels and Reset

Upon RESET, the state of the DMA channels will be as follows:

* The ST/$\overline{\text{STOP}}$ bit for each channel will be reset to $\overline{\text{STOP}}$.
* Any transfer in progress is aborted.
* The values of the transfer count registers, source pointers and destination pointers are indeterminate.

TIMERS

The 80C188 provides three internal 16-bit programmable timers (see Figure 19). Two of these are highly flexible and are connected to four external pins (2 per timer). They can be used to count external events, time external events, generate nonrepetitive waveforms, etc. The third timer is not connected to any external pins, and is useful for real-time coding and time delay applications. In addition, the third timer can be used as a prescaler to the other two, or as a DMA request source.

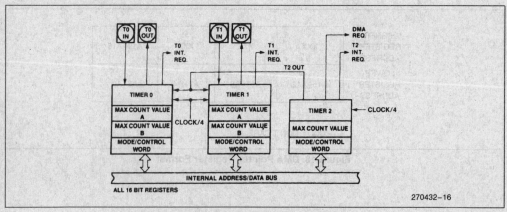

Figure 19. Timer Block Diagram

Timer Operation

The timers are controlled by 11 16-bit registers in the peripheral control block. The configuration of these registers is shown in Table 15. The count register contains the current value of the timer. It can be read or written at any time independent of whether the timer is running or not. The value of this register will be incremented for each timer event. Each of the timers is equipped with a MAX COUNT register, which defines the maximum count the timer will reach. After reaching the MAX COUNT register value, the timer count value will reset to zero during that same clock, i.e., the maximum count value is never stored in the count register itself. Timers 0 and 1 are, in addition, equipped with a second MAX COUNT register, which enables the timers to alternate their count between two different MAX COUNT values. If a single MAX COUNT register is used, the timer output pin will switch LOW for a single clock, 1 clock after the maximum count value has been reached. In the dual MAX COUNT register mode, the output pin will indicate which MAX COUNT register is currently in use, thus allowing nearly complete freedom in selecting waveform duty cycles. For the timers with two MAX COUNT registers, the RIU bit in the control register determines which is used for the comparison.

Each timer gets serviced every fourth CPU-clock cycle, and thus can operate at speeds up to one-quarter the internal clock frequency (one-eighth the crystal rate). External clocking of the timers may be done at up to a rate of one-quarter of the internal CPU-clock rate. Due to internal synchronization and pipelining of the timer circuitry, a timer output may take up to 6 clocks to respond to any individual clock or gate input.

Since the count registers and the maximum count registers are all 16 bits wide, 16 bits of resolution are provided. Any Read or Write access to the timers will add one wait state to the minimum four-clock bus cycle, however. This is needed to synchronize and coordinate the internal data flows between the internal timers and the internal bus.

The timers have several programmable options.

- All three timers can be set to halt or continue on a terminal count.

- Timers 0 and 1 can select between internal and external clocks, alternate between MAX COUNT registers and be set to retrigger on external events.

- The timers may be programmed to cause an interrupt on terminal count.

These options are selectable via the timer mode/control word.

Timer Mode/Control Register

The mode/control register (see Figure 20) allows the user to program the specific mode of operation or check the current programmed status for any of the three integrated timers.

Table 15. Timer Control Block Format

Register Name	Register Offset		
	Tmr. 0	Tmr. 1	Tmr. 2
Mode/Control Word	56H	5EH	66H
Max Count B	54H	5CH	not present
Max Count A	52H	5AH	62H
Count Register	50H	58H	60H

15	14	13	12	11		5	4	3	2	1	0
EN	INH	INT	RIU	0	...	MC	RTG	P	EXT	ALT	CONT

Figure 20. Timer Mode/Control Register

EN:

The enable bit provides programmer control over the timer's RUN/HALT status. When set, the timer is enabled to increment subject to the input pin constraints in the internal clock mode (discussed previously). When cleared, the timer will be inhibited from counting. All input pin transitions during the time EN is zero will be ignored. If CONT is zero, the EN bit is automatically cleared upon maximum count.

$\overline{INH}$:

The inhibit bit allows for selective updating of the enable (EN) bit. If $\overline{INH}$ is a one during the write to the mode/control word, then the state of the EN bit will be modified by the write. If $\overline{INH}$ is a zero during the write, the EN bit will be unaffected by the operation. This bit is not stored; it will always be a 0 on a read.

INT:

When set, the INT bit enables interrupts from the timer, which will be generated on every terminal count. If the timer is configured in dual MAX CONT register mode, an interrupt will be generated each time the value in MAX COUNT register A is reached, and each time the value in MAX COUNT register B is reached. If this enable bit is cleared after the interrupt request has been generated, but before a pending interrupt is serviced, the interrupt request will still be in force. (The request is latched in the Interrupt Controller).

RIU:

The Register In Use bit indicates which MAX COUNT register is currently being used for comparison to the timer count value. A zero value indicates register A. The RIU bit cannot be written, i.e., its value is not affected when the control register is written. It is always cleared when the ALT bit is zero.

MC:

The Maximum Count bit is set whenever the timer reaches its final maximum count value. If the timer is configured in dual MAX COUNT register mode, this bit will be set each time the value in MAX COUNT register A is reached, and each time the value in MAX COUNT register B is reached. This bit is set regardless of the timer's interrupt-enable bit. The MC bit gives the user the ability to monitor timer status through software instead of through interrupts.

Programmer intervention is required to clear this bit.

RTG:

Retrigger bit is only active for internal clocking (EXT = 0). In this case it determines the control function provided by the input pin.

If RTG = 0, the input level gates the internal clock on and off. If the input pin is HIGH, the timer will count; if the input pin is LOW, the timer will hold its value. As indicated previously, the input signal may be asynchronous with respect to the 80C188 clock.

When RTG = 1, the input pin detects LOW-to-HIGH transitions. The first such transition starts the timer running, clearing the timer value to zero on the first clock, and then incrementing thereafter. Further transitions on the input pin will again reset the timer to zero, from which it will start counting up again. If CONT = 0, when the timer has reached maximum count, the EN bit will be cleared, inhibiting further timer activity.

P:

The prescaler bit is ignored unless internal clocking has been selected (EXT = 0). If the P bit is a zero, the timer will count at one-fourth the internal CPU clock rate. If the P bit is a one, the output of timer 2 will be used as a clock for the timer. Note that the user must initialize and start timer 2 to obtain the prescaled clock.

EXT:

The external bit selects between internal and external clocking for the timer. The external signal may be asynchronous with respect to the 80C188 clock. If this bit is set, the timer will count LOW-to-HIGH transitions on the input pin. If cleared, it will count an internal clock while using the input pin for control. In this mode, the function of the external pin is defined by the RTG bit. The maximum input to output transition latency time may be as much as 6 clocks. However, clock inputs may be pipelined as closely together as every 4 clocks without losing clock pulses.

ALT:

The ALT bit determines which of two MAX COUNT registers is used for count comparison. If ALT = 0, register A for that timer is always used, while if ALT = 1, the comparison will alternate between register A and register B when each maximum count is reached. This alternation allows the user to change one MAX COUNT register while the other is being used, and thus provides a method of generating non-repetitive waveforms. Square waves and pulse outputs of any duty cycle are a subset of available signals obtained by not changing the final count registers. The ALT bit also determines the function of the timer output pin. If ALT is zero, the output pin will go LOW for one clock, the clock after the maximum count is reached. If ALT is one, the output pin will reflect the current MAX COUNT register being used (0/1 for B/A).

CONT:

Setting the CONT bit causes the associated timer to run continuously, while resetting it causes the timer to halt upon maximum count. If CONT = 0 and ALT = 1, the timer will count to the MAX COUNT register A value, reset, count to the register B value, reset, and halt.

Not all mode bits are provided for timer 2. Certain bits are hardwired as indicated below:

ALT = 0, EXT = 0, P = 0, RTG = 0, RIU = 0

Count Registers

Each of the three timers has a 16-bit count register. The contents of this register may be read or written by the processor at any time. If the register is written while the timer is counting,the new value will take effect in the current count cycle.

The count registers should be programmed before attempting to use the timers since they are not automatically initialized to zero.

Max Count Registers

Timers 0 and 1 have two MAX COUNT registers, while timer 2 has a single MAX COUNT register. These contain the number of events the timer will count. In timers 0 and 1, the MAX COUNT register used can alternate between the two max count values whenever the current maximum count is reached.

A timer resets when the timer count register equals the max count value being used. If the timer count register or the max count register is changed so that the max count is less than the timer count, the timer does not immediately reset. Instead, the timer counts up to 0FFFFH, "wraps around" to zero, counts up to the max count value, and then resets.

Timers and Reset

Upon RESET, the state of the timers will be as follows:

- All EN (Enable) bits are reset preventing timer counting.
- For Timers 0 and 1, the RIU bits are reset to zero and the ALT bits are set to one. This results in the Timer Out pins going HIGH.
- The contents of the count registers are indeterminate.

INTERRUPT CONTROLLER

The 80C188 can receive interrupts from a number of sources, both internal and external. The internal interrupt controller serves to merge these requests on a priority basis, for individual service by the CPU.

Internal interrupt sources (Timers and DMA channels) can be disabled by their own control registers or by mask bits within the interrupt controller. The 80C188 interrupt controller has its own control register that sets the mode of operation for the controller.

The interrupt controller will resolve priority among requests that are pending simultaneously. Nesting is provided so interrupt service routines for lower priority interrupts may be interrupted by higher priority interrupts. A block diagram of the interrupt controller is shown in Figure 21.

The 80C188 has a special Slave Mode in which the internal interrupt controller acts as a slave to an external master. The controller is programmed into this mode by setting bit 14 in the peripheral control block relocation register. (See Slave Mode section.)

MASTER MODE OPERATION

Interrupt Controller External Interface

Five pins are provided for external interrupt sources. One of these pins is NMI, the non-maskable interrupt. NMI is generally used for unusual events such as power-fail interrupts. The other four pins may be configured in any of the following ways:

- As four interrupt input lines with internally generated interrupt vectors.
- As an interrupt line and interrupt acknowledge line pair (cascade mode) with externally generated interrupt vectors plus two interrupt input lines with internally generated vectors.
- As two pairs of interrupt/interrupt acknowledge lines (Cascade Mode) with externally generated interrupt vectors.

External sources in the Cascade Mode use externally generated interrupt vectors. When an interrupt is acknowledged, two INTA cycles are initiated and the vector is read into the 80C188 on the second cycle. The capability to interface to external 82C59A programmable interrupt controllers is provided when the inputs are configured in Cascade Mode.

Interrupt Controller Modes of Operation

The basic modes of operation of the interrupt controller in master mode are similar to the 82C59A. The interrupt controller responds identically to internal interrupts in all three modes: the difference is only in the interpretation of function of the four external interrupt pins. The interrupt controller is set into one of these three modes by programming the correct bits in the INT0 and INT1 control registers. The modes of interrupt controller operation are as follows:

Fully Nested Mode

When in the fully nested mode four pins are used as direct interrupt requests as in Figure 22. The vectors for these four inputs are generated internally. An in-service bit is provided for every interrupt source. If a lower-priority device requests an interrupt while the in service bit (IS) is set, no interrupt will be generated by the interrupt controller. In addition, if another interrupt request occurs from the same interrupt source while the in-service bit is set, no interrupt will be generated by the interrupt controller. This allows interrupt service routines to operate with interrupts enabled, yet be suspended only by interrupts of higher priority than the in-service interrupt.

When a service routine is completed, the proper IS bit must be reset by writing the proper pattern to the EOI register. This is required to allow subsequent interrupts from this interrupt source and to allow servicing of lower-priority interrupts. An EOI command is executed at the end of the service routine just before the return from interrupt instruction. If the fully nested structure has been upheld, the next highest-priority source with its IS bit set is then serviced.

Cascade Mode

The 80C188 has four interrupt pins and two of them have dual functions. In the fully nested mode the four pins are used as direct interrupt inputs and the corresponding vectors are generated internally. In the Cascade Mode, the four pins are configured into interrupt input-dedicated acknowledge signal pairs. The interconnection is shown in Figure 23. INT0 is an interrupt input interfaced to an 82C59A, while INT2/INTA0 serves as the dedicated interrupt acknowledge signal to that peripheral. The same is true for INT1 and INT3/INTA1. Each pair can selectively be placed in the Cascade or non-Cascade Mode by programming the proper value into INT0 and INT1 control registers. The use of the dedicated acknowledge signals eliminates the need for the use of external logic to generate INTA and device select signals.

The primary Cascade Mode allows the capability to serve up to 128 external interrupt sources through the use of external master and slave 82C59As. Three levels of priority are created, requiring priority resolution in the 80C188 interrupt controller, the master 82C59As, and the slave 82C59As. If an external interrupt is serviced, one IS bit is set at each of these levels. When the interrupt service routine is completed, up to three end-of-interrupt commands must be issued by the programmer.

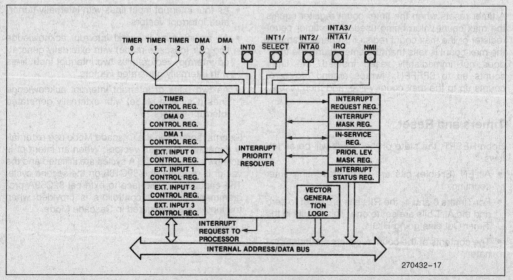

Figure 21. Interrupt Controller Block Diagram

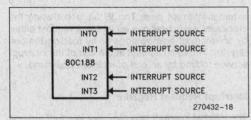

Figure 22. Fully Nested (Direct) Mode Interrupt Controller Connections

Special Fully Nested Mode

This mode is entered by setting the SFNM bit in INT0 or INT1 control register. It enables complete nestability with external 82C59A masters. Normally, an interrupt request from an interrupt source will not be recognized unless the in-service bit for that source is reset. If more than one interrupt source is connected to an external interrupt controller, all of the interrupts will be funneled through the same 80C188 interrupt request pin. As a result, if the external interrupt controller receives a higher-priority interrupt, its interrupt will not be recognized by the 80C188 controller until the 80C188 in-service bit is reset. In Special Fully Nested Mode, the 80C188 interrupt controller will allow interrupts from an external pin regardless of the state of the in-service bit for an interrupt source in order to allow multiple interrupts from a single pin. An in-service bit will continue to be set, however, to inhibit interrupts from other lower-priority 80C188 interrupt sources.

Special procedures should be followed when resetting IS bits at the end of interrupt service routines. Software polling of the IS register in the external master 82C59A is required to determine if there is more than one bit set. If so, the IS bit in the 80C188 remains active and the next interrupt service routine is entered.

Operation in a Polled Environment

The controller may be used in a polled mode if interrupts are undesirable. When polling, the processor disables interrupts and then polls the interrupt controller whenever it is convenient. Polling the interrupt controller is accomplished by reading the Poll Word (Figure 32). Bit 15 in the poll word indicates to the processor that an interrupt of high enough priority is requesting service. Bits 0–4 indicate to the processor the type vector of the highest-priority source requesting service. Reading the Poll Word causes the In-Service bit of the highest priority source to be set.

It is desirable to be able to read the Poll Word information without guaranteeing service of any pending

interrupt, i.e., not set the indicated in-service bit. The 80C188 provides a Poll Status Word in addition to the conventional Poll Word to allow this to be done. Poll Word information is duplicated in the Poll Status Word, but reading the Poll Status Word does not set the associated in-service bit. These words are located in two adjacent memory locations in the register file.

Master Mode Features

Programmable Priority

The user can program the interrupt sources into any of eight different priority levels. The programming is done by placing a 3-bit priority level (0–7) in the control register of each interrupt source. (A source with a priority level of 4 has higher priority over all priority levels from 5 to 7. Priority registers containing values lower than 4 have greater priority). All interrupt sources have preprogrammed default priority levels (see Table 4).

If two requests with the same programmed priority level are pending at once, the priority ordering scheme shown in Table 4 is used. If the serviced interrupt routine reenables interrupts, other interrupt requests can be serviced.

End-of-Interrupt Command

The end-of-interrupt (EOI) command is used by the programmer to reset the In-Service (IS) bit when an interrupt service routine is completed. The EOI command is issued by writing the proper pattern to the EOI register. There are two types of EOI commands, specific and nonspecific. The nonspecific command does not specify which IS bit is reset. When issued, the interrupt controller automatically resets the IS bit of the highest priority source with an active service routine. A specific EOI command requires that the programmer send the interrupt vector type to the interrupt controller indicating which source's IS bit is to be reset. This command is used when the fully nested structure has been disturbed or the highest priority IS bit that was set does not belong to the service routine in progress.

Trigger Mode

The four external interrupt pins can be programmed in either edge- or level-trigger mode. The control register for each external source has a level-trigger mode (LTM) bit. All interrupt inputs are active HIGH. In the edge sense mode or the level-trigger mode, the interrupt request must remain active (HIGH) until the interrupt request is acknowledged by the

80C188 CPU. In the edge-sense mode, if the level remains high after the interrupt is acknowledged, the input is disabled and no further requests will be generated. The input level must go LOW for at least one clock cycle to re-enable the input. In the level-trigger mode, no such provision is made: holding the interrupt input HIGH will cause continuous interrupt requests.

Interrupt Vectoring

The 80C186 Interrupt Controller will generate interrupt vectors for the integrated DMA channels and the integrated Timers. In addition, the Interrupt Controller will generate interrupt vectors for the external interrupt lines if they are not configured in Cascade or Special Fully Nested Mode. The interrupt vectors generated are fixed and cannot be changed (see Table 4).

Interrupt Controller Registers

The Interrupt Controller register model is shown in Figure 24. It contains 15 registers. All registers can both be read or written unless specified otherwise.

In-Service Register

This register can be read from or written into. The format is shown in Figure 25. It contains the In-Service bit for each of the interrupt sources. The In-Service bit is set to indicate that a source's service routine is in progress. When an In-Service bit is set, the interrupt controller will not generate interrupts to the CPU when it receives interrupt requests from devices with a lower programmed priority level. The TMR bit is the In-Service bit for all three timers; the D0 and D1 bits are the In-Service bits for the two DMA channels; the I0–I3 are the In-Service bits for the external interrupt pins. The IS bit is set when the processor acknowledges an interrupt request either by an interrupt acknowledge or by reading the poll register. The IS bit is reset at the end of the interrupt service routine by an end-of-interrupt command.

Interrupt Request Register

The internal interrupt sources have interrupt request bits inside the interrupt controller. The format of this register is shown in Figure 25. A read from this register yields the status of these bits. The TMR bit is the logical OR of all timer interrupt requests. D0 and D1 are the interrupt request bits for the DMA channels.

The state of the external interrupt input pins is also indicated. The state of the external interrupt pins is not a stored condition inside the interrupt controller, therefore external interrupt bits cannot be written. The external interrupt request bits are set when an interrupt request is given to the interrupt controller, so if edge-triggered mode is selected, the bit in the register will be HIGH only after an inactive-to-active transition. For internal interrupt sources, the register bits are set when a request arrives and are reset when the processor acknowledges the requests.

Writes to the interrupt request register will affect the D0 and D1 interrupt request bits. Setting either bit will cause the corresponding interrupt request while clearing either bit will remove the corresponding interrupt request. All other bits in the register are read-only.

Mask Register

This is a 16-bit register that contains a mask bit for each interrupt source. The format for this register is shown in Figure 25. A one in a bit position corre-

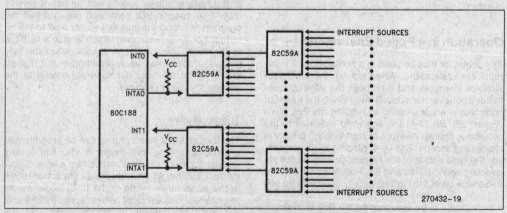

Figure 23. Cascade and Special Fully Nested Mode Interrupt Controller Connections

sponding to a particular source masks the source from generating interrupts. These mask bits are the exact same bits which are used in the individual control registers; programming a mask bit using the mask register will also change this bit in the individual control registers, and vice versa.

	OFFSET
INT3 CONTROL REGISTER	3EH
INT2 CONTROL REGISTER	3CH
INT1 CONTROL REGISTER	3AH
INT0 CONTROL REGISTER	38H
DMA 1 CONTROL REGISTER	36H
DMA 0 CONTROL REGISTER	34H
TIMER CONTROL REGISTER	32H
INTERRUPT STATUS REGISTER	30H
INTERRUPT REQUEST REGISTER	2EH
IN-SERVICE REGISTER	2CH
PRIORITY MASK REGISTER	2AH
MASK REGISTER	28H
POLL STATUS REGISTER	26H
POLL REGISTER	24H
EOI REGISTER	22H

Figure 24. Interrupt Controller Registers (Master Mode)

Priority Mask Register

This register masks all interrupts below a particular interrupt priority level. The format of this register is shown in Figure 26. The code in the lower three bits of this register inhibits interrupts of priority lower (a higher priority number) than the code specified. For example, 100 written into this register masks interrupts of level five (101), six (110), and seven (111). The register is reset to seven (111) upon RESET so no interrupts are masked due to priority number.

Interrupt Status Register

This register contains general interrupt controller status information. The format of this register is shown in Figure 27. The bits in the status register have the following functions:

DHLT: DMA Halt Transfer; setting this bit halts all DMA transfers. It is automatically set whenever a non-maskable interrupt occurs, and it is reset when an IRET instruction is executed. This bit allows prompt service of all non-maskable interrupts. This bit may also be set by the programmer.

IRTx: These three bits represent the individual timer interrupt request bits. These bits differentiate between timer interrupts, since the timer IR bit in the interrupt request register is the "OR" function of all timer interrupt request. Note that setting any one of these three bits initiates an interrupt request to the interrupt controller.

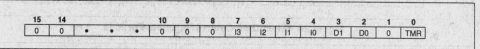

15	14				10	9	8	7	6	5	4	3	2	1	0
0	0	•	•	•	0	0	0	I3	I2	I1	I0	D1	D0	0	TMR

Figure 25. In-Service, Interrupt Request, and Mask Register Formats

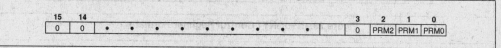

15	14											3	2	1	0
0	0	•	•	•	•	•	•	•	•	•		0	PRM2	PRM1	PRM0

Figure 26. Priority Mask Register Format

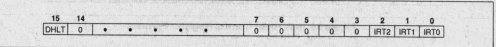

15	14						7	6	5	4	3	2	1	0
DHLT	0	•	•	•	•	•	0	0	0	0	0	IRT2	IRT1	IRT0

Figure 27. Interrupt Status Register Format (Master Mode)

Timer, DMA 0, 1; Control Register

These registers are the control words for all the internal interrupt sources. The format for these registers is shown in Figure 28. The three bit positions PR0, PR1, and PR2 represent the programmable priority level of the interrupt source. The MSK bit inhibits interrupt requests from the interrupt source. The MSK bits in the individual control registers are the exact same bits as are in the Mask Register; modifying them in the individual control registers will also modify them in the Mask Register, and vice versa.

INT0-INT3 Control Registers

These registers are the control words for the four external input pins. Figure 29 shows the format of the INT0 and INT1 Control registers; Figure 30 shows the format of the INT2 and INT3 Control registers. In Cascade Mode or Special Fully Nested Mode, the control words for INT2 and INT3 are not used.

The bits in the various control registers are encoded as follows:

PR0-2: Priority programming information. Highest Priority = 000, Lowest Priority = 111

LTM: Level-trigger mode bit. 1 = level-triggered; 0 = edge-triggered. Interrupt Input levels are active high. In level-triggered mode, an interrupt is generated whenever the external line is high. In edge-triggered mode, an interrupt will be generated only when this

level is preceded by an inactive-to-active transition on the line. In both cases, the level must remain active until the interrupt is acknowledged.

MSK: Mask bit, 1 = mask; 0 = non-mask.

C: Cascade mode bit, 1 = cascade; 0 = direct

SFNM: Special Fully Nested Mode bit, 1 = SFNM

EOI Register

The end of the interrupt register is a command register which can only be written into. The format of this register is shown in Figure 31. It initiates an EOI command when written to by the 80C188 CPU.

The bits in the EOI register are encoded as follows:

S_x: Encoded information that specifies an interrupt source vector type as shown in Table 4. For example, to reset the In-Service bit for DMA channel 0, these bits should be set to 01010, since the vector type for DMA channel 0 is 10.

NOTE:

To reset the single In-Service bit for any of the three timers, the vector type for timer 0 (8) should be written in this register.

NSPEC/: A bit that determines the type of EOI command. Nonspecific = 1, Specific = 0.
SPEC

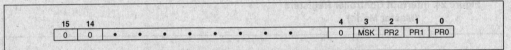

Figure 28. Timer/DMA Control Registers Formats

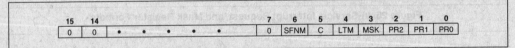

Figure 29. INT0/INT1 Control Register Formats

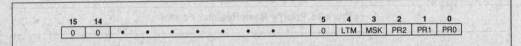

Figure 30. INT2/INT3 Control Register Formats

Poll and Poll Status Registers

These registers contain polling information. The format of these registers is shown in Figure 32. They can only be read. Reading the Poll register constitutes a software poll. This will set the IS bit of the highest priority pending interrupt. Reading the poll status register will not set the IS bit of the highest priority pending interrupt; only the status of pending interrupts will be provided.

Encoding of the Poll and Poll Status register bits are as follows:

S_x: Encoded information that indicates the vector type of the highest priority interrupting source. Valid only when INTREQ = 1.

INTREQ: This bit determines if an interrupt request is present. Interrupt Request = 1; no Interrupt Request = 0.

SLAVE MODE OPERATION

When Slave Mode is used, the internal 80C188 interrupt controller will be used as a slave controller to an external master interrupt controller. The internal 80C188 resources will be monitored by the internal interrupt controller, while the external controller functions as the system master interrupt controller.

Upon reset, the 80C188 will be in master mode. To provide for slave mode operation bit 14 of the relocation register should be set.

Because of pin limitations caused by the need to interface to an external 82C59A master, the internal interrupt controller will no longer accept external inputs. There are however, enough 80C188 interrupt controller inputs (internally) to dedicate one to each timer. In this mode, each timer interrupt source has its own mask bit, IS bit, and control word.

In Slave Mode each peripheral must be assigned a unique priority to ensure proper interrupt controller operation. Therefore, it is the programmer's responsibility to assign correct priorities and initialize interrupt control registers before enabling interrupts.

Slave Mode External Interface

The configuration of the 80C188 with respect to an external 82C59A master is shown in Figure 33. The INT0 (Pin 45) input is used as the 80C188 CPU interrupt input. IRQ (Pin 41) functions as an output to send the 80C188 slave-interrupt-request to one of the 8 master-PIC-inputs.

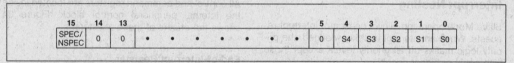

Figure 31. EOI Register Format

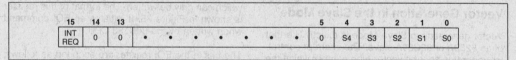

Figure 32. Poll and Poll Status Register Format

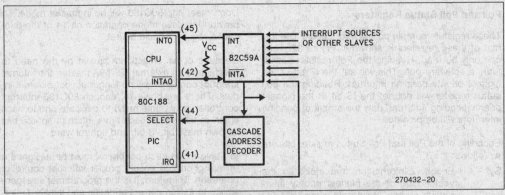

Figure 33. Slave Mode Interrupt Controller Connections

Correct master-slave interface requires decoding of the slave addresses (CAS0-2). Slave 82C59As do this internally. Because of pin limitations, the 80C188 slave address will have to be decoded externally. SELECT (Pin 44) is used as a slave-select input. Note that the slave vector address is transferred internally, but the READY input must be supplied externally.

INTA0 (Pin 42) is used as an acknowledge output, suitable to drive the INTA input of an 82C59A.

Interrupt Nesting

Slave Mode operation allows nesting of interrupt requests. When an interrupt is acknowledged, the priority logic masks off all priority levels except those with equal or higher priority.

Vector Generation in the Slave Mode

Vector generation in Slave Mode is exactly like that of an 8259A or 82C59A slave. The interrupt controller generates an 8-bit vector type number which the CPU multiplies by four to use as an address into the vector table. The five most significant bits of this type number are user-programmable while the three least significant bits are defined according to Figure 34. The significant five bits of the vector are programmed by writing to the Interrupt Vector register at offset 20H.

Specific End-of-Interrupt

In Slave Mode the specific EOI command operates to reset an in-service bit of a specific priority. The user supplies a 3-bit priority-level value that points to an in-service bit to be reset. The command is executed by writing the correct value in the Specific EOI register at offset 22H.

Interrupt Controller Registers in the Slave Mode

All control and command registers are located inside the internal peripheral control block. Figure 34 shows the offsets of these registers.

End-of-Interrupt Register

The end-of-interrupt register is a command register which can only be written. The format of this register is shown in Figure 35. It initiates an EOI command when written by the 80C188 CPU.

The bits in the EOI register are encoded as follows:

VT_x: Three least-significant vector type bits corresponding to the source for which the IS bit is to be reset. Figure 34 indicates these bits.

In-Service Register

This register can be read from or written into. It contains the in-service bit for each of the internal interrupt sources. The format for this register is shown in Figure 36. Bit positions 2 and 3 correspond to the DMA channels; positions 0, 4, and 5 correspond to the integral timers. The source's IS bit is set when the processor acknowledges its interrupt request.

Interrupt Request Register

This register indicates which internal peripherals have interrupt requests pending. The format of this register is shown in Figure 36. The interrupt request bits are set when a request arrives from an internal source, and are reset when the processor acknowledges the request. As in Master Mode, D0 and D1 are read/write; all other bits are read only.

Mask Register

This register contains a mask bit for each interrupt source. The format for this register is shown in Figure 36. If the bit in this register corresponding to a particular interrupt source is set, any interrupts from that source will be masked. These mask bits are exactly the same bits which are used in the individual control registers, i.e., changing the state of a mask bit in this register will also change the state of the mask bit in the individual interrupt control register corresponding to the bit.

Control Registers

These registers are the control words for all the internal interrupt sources. The format of these registers is shown in Figure 37. Each of the timers and both of the DMA channels have their own Control Register.

The bits of the Control Registers are encoded as follows:

pr_x: 3-bit encoded field indicating a priority level for the source.

msk: mask bit for the priority level indicated by pr_x bits.

	OFFSET
TIMER 2 CONTROL REGISTER (VECTOR TYPE xxxxx101)	3AH
TIMER 1 CONTROL REGISTER (VECTOR TYPE xxxxx100)	38H
DMA 1 CONTROL REGISTER (VECTOR TYPE xxxxx011)	36H
DMA 0 CONTROL REGISTER (VECTOR TYPE xxxxx010)	34H
TIMER 0 CONTROL REGISTER (VECTOR TYPE xxxxx000)	32H
INTERRUPT STATUS REGISTER	30H
INTERRUPT-REQUEST REGISTER	2EH
IN-SERVICE REGISTER	2CH
PRIORITY-LEVEL MASK REGISTER	2AH
MASK REGISTER	28H
SPECIFIC EOI REGISTER	22H
INTERRUPT VECTOR REGISTER	20H

Figure 34. Interrupt Controller Registers (Slave Mode)

15	14	13					8	7	6	5	4	3	2	1	0
0	0	0	•	•	•	•	0	0	0	0	0	0	VT2	VT1	VT0

Figure 35. Specific EOI Register Format

15	14	13					8	7	6	5	4	3	2	1	0
0	0	0	•	•	•	•	0	0	0	TMR2	TMR1	D1	D0	0	TMR0

Figure 36. In-Service, Interrupt Request, and Mask Register Format

Interrupt Vector Register

This register provides the upper five bits of the interrupt vector address. The format of this register is shown in Figure 38. The interrupt controller itself provides the lower three bits of the interrupt vector as determined by the priority level of the interrupt request.

The format of the bits in this register is:

t_x: 5-bit field indicating the upper five bits of the vector address.

Priority-Level Mask Register

This register indicates the lowest priority-level interrupt which will be serviced.

The encoding of the bits in this register is:

m_x: 3-bit encoded field indication priority-level value. All levels of lower priority will be masked.

Interrupt Status Register

This register is defined as in Master Mode except that DHLT is not implemented (see Figure 27).

Interrupt Controller and Reset

Upon RESET, the interrupt controller will perform the following actions:

- All SFNM bits reset to 0, implying Fully Nested Mode.
- All PR bits in the various control registers set to 1. This places all sources at lowest priority (level 111).
- All LTM bits reset to 0, resulting in edge-sense mode.
- All Interrupt Service bits reset to 0.
- All Interrupt Request bits reset to 0.
- All MSK (Interrupt Mask) bits set to 1 (mask).
- All C (Cascade) bits reset to 0 (non-Cascade).
- All PRM (Priority Mask) bits set to 1, implying no levels masked.
- Initialized to Master Mode.

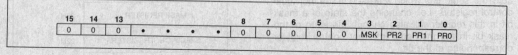

Figure 37. Control Word Format

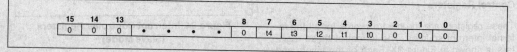

Figure 38. Interrupt Vector Register Format

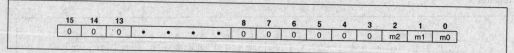

Figure 39. Priority Level Mask Register

Enhanced Mode Operation

In Compatible Mode the 80C188 operates with all the features of the NMOS 80188, with the exception of 8087 support (i.e. no numeric coprocessing is possible). Queue-Status information is still available for design purposes other than 8087 support.

All the Enhanced Mode features are completely masked when in Compatible Mode. A write to any of the Enhanced Mode registers will have no effect, while a read will not return any valid data.

In Enhanced Mode, the 80C188 will operate with Power-Save and DRAM refresh, in addition to all the Compatible Mode features.

Entering Enhanced Mode

Enhanced mode can be entered by tying the RESET output signal from the 80C188 to the TEST/BUSY input.

Queue-Status Mode

The queue-status mode is entered by strapping the $\overline{RD}$ pin low. $\overline{RD}$ is sampled at RESET and if LOW, the 80C188 will reconfigure the ALE and $\overline{WR}$ pins to be QS0 and QS1 respectively. This mode is available on the 80C188 in both Compatible and Enhanced Modes.

DRAM Refresh Control Unit Description

The Refresh Control Unit (RCU) automatically generates DRAM refresh bus cycles. The RCU operates only in Enhanced Mode. After a programmable period of time, the RCU generates a memory read request to the BIU. If the address generated during a refresh bus cycle is within the range of a properly programmed chip select, that chip select will be activated when the BIU executes the refresh bus cycle. The ready logic and wait states programmed for that region will also be in force. If no chip select is activated, then external ready is automatically required to terminate the refresh bus cycle.

If the HLDA pin is active when a DRAM refresh request is generated (indicating a bus hold condition), then the 80C188 will deactivate the HLDA pin in order to perform a refresh cycle. The circuit external to the 80C188 must remove the HOLD signal for at least one clock in order to execute the refresh cycle. The sequence of HLDA going inactive while HOLD is being held active can be used to signal a pending refresh request.

All registers controlling DRAM refresh may be read and written in Enhanced Mode. When the processor is operating in Compatible Mode, they are deselected and are therefore inaccessible. Some fields of these registers cannot be written and are always read as zeros.

DRAM Refresh Addresses

The address generated during a refresh cycle is determined by the contents of the MDRAM register (see Figure 40) and the contents of a 9-bit counter. Figure 41 illustrates the origin of each bit.

	15	14	13	12	11	10	9	8	7	6	5	4	3	2	1	0
MDRAM: Offset E0H	M6	M5	M4	M3	M2	M1	M0	0	0	0	0	0	0	0	0	0

Bits 0–8:   Reserved, read back as 0.

Bits 9–15:   M0–M6, are address bits A13–A19 of the 20-bit memory refresh address. These bits should correspond to any chip select address to be activated for the DRAM partition. These bits are cleared to 0 on RESET.

Figure 40. Memory Partition Register

A19	A18	A17	A16	A15	A14	A13	A12	A11	A10	A9	A8	A7	A6	A5	A4	A3	A2	A1	A0
M6	M5	M4	M3	M2	M1	M0	0	0	0	CA8	CA7	CA6	CA5	CA4	CA3	CA2	CA1	CA0	1

M6–M0:   Bits defined by MDRAM Register

CA8–CA0:   Bits defined by refresh address counter. These bits change according to a linear/feedback shift register; they do not directly follow a binary count.

Figure 41. Addresses Generated by RCU

	15	14	13	12	11	10	9	8	7	6	5	4	3	2	1	0
CDRAM: Offset E2H	0	0	0	0	0	0	0	C8	C7	C6	C5	C4	C3	C2	C1	C0

Bits 0–8: C0–C8, clock divisor register, holds the number of CLKOUT cycles between each refresh request.

Bits 9–15: Reserved, read back as 0.

Figure 42. Clock Pre-Scaler Register

	15	14	13	12	11	10	9	8	7	6	5	4	3	2	1	0
EDRAM: Offset E4H	E	0	0	0	0	0	0	T8	T7	T6	T5	T4	T3	T2	T1	T0

Bits 0–8: T0–T8, refresh clock counter outputs. Read only.

Bits 9–14: Reserved, read back as 0.

Bit 15: Enable RCU, set to 0 on RESET.

Figure 43. Enable RCU Register

Refresh Control Unit Programming and Operation

After programming the MDRAM and the CDRAM registers (Figures 40 and 42), the RCU is enabled by setting the "E" bit in the EDRAM register (Figure 43). The clock counter (T0–T8 of EDRAM) will be loaded from C0–C8 of CDRAM during T_3 of instruction cycle that sets the "E" bit. The clock counter is then decremented at each subsequent CLKOUT.

A refresh is requested when the value of the counter has reached 1 and the counter is reloaded from CDRAM. In order to avoid missing refresh requests, the value in the CDRAM register should always be at least 18 (12H). Clearing the "E" bit at anytime will clear the counter and stop refresh requests, but will not reset the refresh address counter.

POWER-SAVE CONTROL

Power Save Operation

The 80C188, when in Enhanced Mode, can enter a power saving state by internally dividing the processor clock frequency by a programmable factor. This divided frequency is also available at the CLKOUT

pin. The PDCON register contains the two-bit fields for selecting the clock division factor and the enable bit.

All internal logic, including the Refresh Control Unit and the timers, will have their clocks slowed down by the division factor. To maintain a real time count or a fixed DRAM refresh rate, these peripherals must be re-programmed when entering and leaving the power-save mode.

The power-save mode is exited whenever an interrupt is processed by automatically resetting the enable bit. If the power-save mode is to be re-entered after serving the interrupt, the enable bit will need to be set in software before returning from the interrupt routine.

The internal clocks of the 80C188 will begin to be divided during the T_3 state of the instruction cycle that sets the enable bit. Clearing the enable bit will restore full speed in the T_3 state of that instruction.

At no time should the internal clock frequency be allowed to fall below 0.5 MHz. This is the minimum operational frequency of the 80C188. For example, an 80C188 running with a 12 MHz crystal (6 MHz CLOCKOUT) should never have a clock divisor greater than eight.

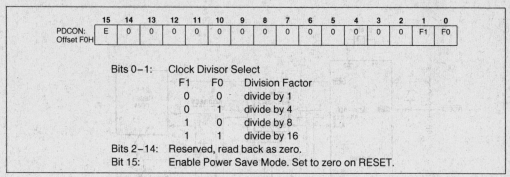

	15	14	13	12	11	10	9	8	7	6	5	4	3	2	1	0
PDCON: Offset F0H	E	0	0	0	0	0	0	0	0	0	0	0	0	0	F1	F0

Bits 0–1:   Clock Divisor Select

F1	F0	Division Factor
0	0	divide by 1
0	1	divide by 4
1	0	divide by 8
1	1	divide by 16

Bits 2–14:   Reserved, read back as zero.

Bit 15:   Enable Power Save Mode. Set to zero on RESET.

Figure 44. Power-Save Control Register

ONCE™ Test Mode

To facilitate testing and inspection of devices when fixed into a target system, the 80C188 has a test mode available which allows all pins to be placed in a high-impedance state. ONCE stands for "ON Circuit Emulation". When placed in this mode, the 80C188 will put all pins in the high-impedance state until RESET.

The ONCE mode is selected by tying the $\overline{UCS}$ and the $\overline{LCS}$ LOW during RESET. These pins are sampled on the low-to-high transition of the $\overline{RES}$ pin. The $\overline{UCS}$ and the $\overline{LCS}$ pins have weak internal pull-up resistors similar to the $\overline{RD}$ and $\overline{TEST}$ pins to guarantee normal operation.

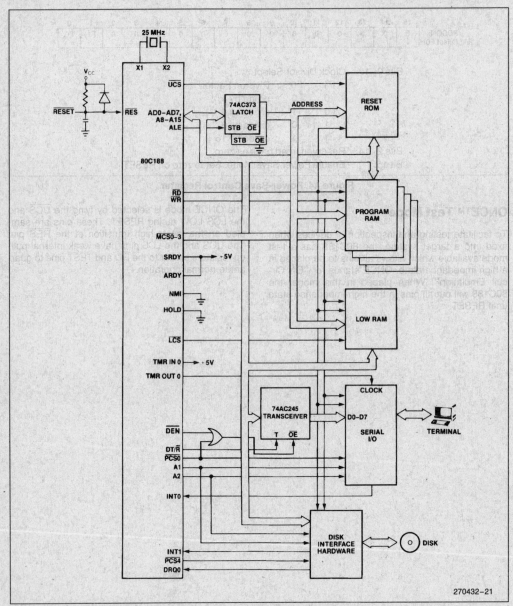

270432–21

Figure 45. Typical 80C188 Computer

ABSOLUTE MAXIMUM RATINGS*

Ambient Temperature under Bias ....0°C to +70°C

Storage Temperature .... −65°C to +150°C

Voltage on Any Pin with
   Respect to Ground .... −1.0V to +7.0V

Package Power Dissipation 1W

Not to exceed the maximum allowable die temperature based on thermal resistance of the package.

*Notice: Stresses above those listed under "Absolute Maximum Ratings" may cause permanent damage to the device. This is a stress rating only and functional operation of the device at these or any other conditions above those indicated in the operational sections of this specification is not implied. Exposure to absolute maximum rating conditions for extended periods may affect device reliability.

NOTICE: This data sheet is only valid for devices indicated in the Specification Level Markings section. Specifications contained in the following tables are subject to change.

D.C. CHARACTERISTICS

T_A = 0°C to +70°C, V_{CC} = 5V ±10% except V_{CC} = 5V ± 5% at f > 12.5 MHz

Symbol	Parameter	Min	Max	Units	Test Conditions
V_{IL}	Input Low Voltage (Except X1)	−0.5	$0.2\,V_{CC}$ − 0.3	V	
V_{IL2}	Clock Input Low Voltage (X1)	−0.5	0.6	V	
V_{IH}	Input High Voltage (All except X1, RES, ARDY and SRDY)	$0.2\,V_{CC}$ + 0.9	V_{CC} + 0.5	V	
V_{IH1}	Input High Voltage (RES)	3.0	V_{CC} + 0.5	V	
V_{IH2}	Input High Voltage (SRDY, ARDY)	$0.2\,V_{CC}$ + 1.1	V_{CC} + 0.5	V	
V_{IH3}	Clock Input High Voltage (X1)	3.9	V_{CC} + 0.5	V	
V_{OL}	Output Low Voltage		0.45	V	I_{OL} = 2.5 mA (S0, 1, 2) I_{OL} = 2.0 mA (others)
V_{OH}	Output High Voltage	2.4	V_{CC}	V	I_{OH} = −2.4 mA @ 2.4V(4)
		V_{CC} − 0.5	V_{CC}	V	I_{OH} = −200 μA @ V_{CC} −0.5
I_{CC}	Power Supply Current		150	mA	@16 MHz, 0°C V_{CC} = 5.25V(3)
			120	mA	@12.5 MHz, 0°C V_{CC} = 5.5V(3)
			100	mA	@10 MHz, 0°C V_{CC} = 5.5V(3)
I_{LI}	Input Leakage Current		±10	μA	@0.5 MHz $0.45V \le V_{IN} \le V_{CC}$
I_{LO}	Output Leakage Current		±10	μA	@0.5 MHz $0.45V \le V_{OUT} \le V_{CC}$(1)
V_{CLO}	Clock Output Low		0.45	V	I_{CLO} = 4.0 mA
V_{CHO}	Clock Output High	V_{CC} − 0.5		V	I_{CHO} = −500 μA
C_{IN}	Input Capacitance		10	pF	@ 1 MHz(2)
C_{IO}	Output or I/O Capacitance		20	pF	@ 1 MHz(2)

NOTES:
1. Pins being floated during HOLD or by invoking the ONCE Mode.
2. Characterization conditions are a) Frequency = 1 MHz; b) Unmeasured pins at GND; c) V_{IN} at +5.0V or 0.45V. This parameter is not tested.
3. Current is measured with the device in RESET with X1 and X2 driven and all other non-power pins open.
4. RD/QSMD, UCS, LCS, TEST pins have internal pullup devices. Loading some of these pins above I_{OH} = −200 μA can cause the 80C188 to go into alternative modes of operation. See the section on Local Bus Controller and Reset for details.

POWER SUPPLY CURRENT

Current is linearly proportional to clock frequency and is measured with the device in RESET with X1 and X2 driven and all other non-power pins open.

Maximum current is given by I_{CC} = 8.4 mA × freq. (MHz) + 15 mA.

Typical current is given by I_{CC} (typ.) = 6.4 mA X freq. (MHz) + 4.0 mA. "Typicals" are based on a limited number of samples taken from early manufacturing lots measured at V_{CC} = 5V and room temperature. "Typicals" are not guaranteed.

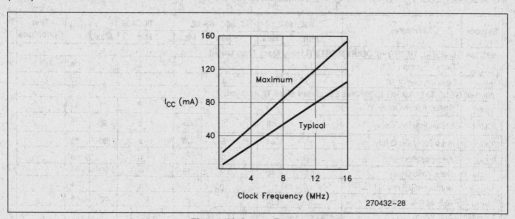

Figure 46. I_{CC} vs Frequency

A. C. CHARACTERISTICS

MAJOR CYCLE TIMINGS (READ CYCLE)

$T_A = 0°C$ to $+70°C$, $V_{CC} = 5V \pm 10\%$ except $V_{CC} = 5V \pm 5\%$ at $f > 12.5$ MHz

All timings are measured at 1.5V and 100 pF loading on CLKOUT unless otherwise noted.
All output test conditions are with $C_L = 50\text{-}200$ pF (10 MHz) and $C_L = 50\text{-}100$ pF (12.5-16 MHz).
For A.C. tests, input $V_{IL} = 0.45V$ and $V_{IH} = 2.4V$ except at X1 where $V_{IH} = V_{CC} - 0.5V$.

Symbol	Parameter	80C188 Min	80C188 Max	80C188-12 Min	80C188-12 Max	80C188-16 Min	80C188-16 Max	Unit	Test Conditions
80C188 GENERAL TIMING REQUIREMENTS (Listed More Than Once)									
T_{DVCL}	Data in Setup (A/D)	15		15		15		ns	
T_{CLDX}	Data in Hold (A/D)	3		3		3		ns	
80C188 GENERAL TIMING RESPONSES (Listed More Than Once)									
T_{CHSV}	Status Active Delay	5	45	5	35	5	31	ns	
T_{CLSH}	Status Inactive Delay	5	46	5	35	5	30	ns	
T_{CLAV}	Address Valid Delay	5	44	5	36	5	33	ns	
T_{CLAX}	Address Hold	0		0		0		ns	
T_{CLDV}	Data Valid Delay	5	40	5	36	5	33	ns	
T_{CHDX}	Status Hold Time	10		10		10		ns	
T_{CHLH}	ALE Active Delay		30		25		20	ns	
T_{LHLL}	ALE Width	$T_{CLCL} - 15$		$T_{CLCL} - 15$		$T_{CLCL} - 15$		ns	
T_{CHLL}	ALE Inactive Delay		30		25		20	ns	
T_{AVLL}	Address Valid to ALE Low	$T_{CLCH} - 18$		$T_{CLCH} - 15$		$T_{CLCH} - 15$		ns	Equal Loading
T_{LLAX}	Address Hold from ALE Inactive	$T_{CHCL} - 15$		$T_{CHCL} - 15$		$T_{CHCL} - 15$		ns	Equal Loading
T_{AVCH}	Address Valid to Clock High	0		0		0		ns	
T_{CLAZ}	Address Float Delay	T_{CLAX}	30	T_{CLAX}	25	T_{CLAX}	20	ns	
T_{CLCSV}	Chip-Select Active Delay	3	42	3	33	3	30	ns	
T_{CXCSX}	Chip-Select Hold from Command Inactive	$T_{CLCH} - 10$		$T_{CLCH} - 10$		$T_{CLCH} - 10$		ns	Equal Loading
T_{CHCSX}	Chip-Select Inactive Delay	5	35	5	30	5	25	ns	
T_{DXDL}	$\overline{DEN}$ Inactive to DT/$\overline{R}$ Low	0		0		0		ns	Equal Loading
T_{CVCTV}	Control Active Delay 1	3	44	3	37	3	31	ns	
T_{CVDEX}	$\overline{DEN}$ Inctive Delay	5	44	5	37	5	31	ns	
T_{CHCTV}	Control Active Delay 2	5	44	5	37	5	31	ns	
T_{CLLV}	$\overline{LOCK}$ Valid/Invalid Delay	3	40	3	37	3	35	ns	
80C188 TIMING RESPONSES (Read Cycle)									
T_{AZRL}	Address Float to $\overline{RD}$ Active	0		0		0		ns	
T_{CLRL}	$\overline{RD}$ Active Delay	5	44	5	37	5	31	ns	
T_{RLRH}	$\overline{RD}$ Pulse Width	$2T_{CLCL} - 30$		$2T_{CLCL} - 25$		$2T_{CLCL} - 25$		ns	
T_{CLRH}	$\overline{RD}$ Inactive Delay	5	44	5	37	5	31	ns	
T_{RHLH}	$\overline{RD}$ Inactive to ALE High	$T_{CLCH} - 14$		$T_{CLCH} - 14$		$T_{CLCH} - 14$		ns	Equal Loading
T_{RHAV}	$\overline{RD}$ Inactive to Address Active	$T_{CLCL} - 15$		$T_{CLCL} - 15$		$T_{CLCL} - 15$		ns	Equal Loading

270432–33

A.C. CHARACTERISTICS

READ CYCLE WAVEFORMS

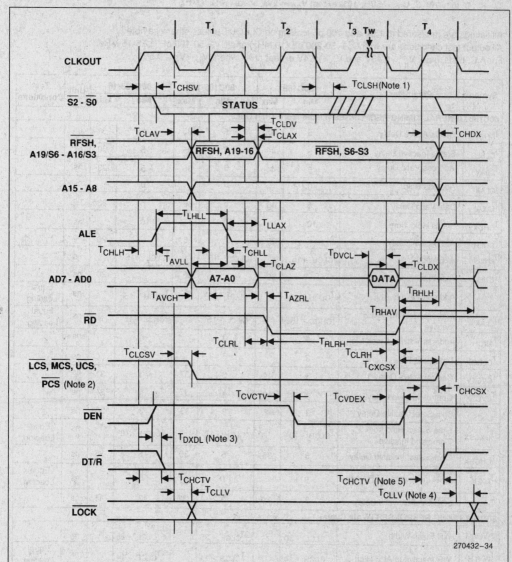

270432–34

NOTES:
1. Status inactive in state preceding T_4.
2. If latched A_1 and A_2 are selected instead of $\overline{PCS5}$ and $\overline{PCS6}$, only T_{CLCSV} is applicable.
3. For write cycle followed by read cycle.
4. T_1 of next bus cycle.
5. Changes in T-state preceding next bus cycle if followed by write.

A. C. CHARACTERISTICS
MAJOR CYCLE TIMINGS (WRITE CYCLE)

$T_A = 0\ ^{\circ}C$ to $+70\ ^{\circ}C$, $V_{CC} = 5V \pm 10\%$ except $V_{CC} = 5V \pm 5\%$ at $f > 12.5$ MHz

All timings are measured at 1.5V and 100 pF loading on CLKOUT unless otherwise noted.
All output test conditions are with $C_L = 50\text{-}200$ pF (10 MHz) and $C_L = 50\text{-}100$ pF (12.5-16 MHz).
For A.C. tests, input $V_{IL} = 0.45V$ and $V_{IH} = 2.4V$ except at X1 where $V_{IH} = V_{CC}\ 0.5V$.

Symbol	Parameter	80C188		80C188-12		80C188-16		Unit	Test Conditions
		Min	Max	Min	Max	Min	Max		
80C188 GENERAL TIMING RESPONSES (Listed More Than Once)									
T_{CHSV}	Status Active Delay	5	45	5	35	5	31	ns	
T_{CLSH}	Status Inactive Delay	5	46	5	35	5	30	ns	
T_{CLAV}	Address Valid Delay	5	44	5	36	5	33	ns	
T_{CLAX}	Address Hold	0		0		0		ns	
T_{CLDV}	Data Valid Delay	5	40	5	36	5	33	ns	
T_{CHDX}	Status Hold Time	10		10		10		ns	
T_{CHLH}	ALE Active Delay		30		25		20	ns	
T_{LHLL}	ALE Width	$T_{CLCL} - 15$		$T_{CLCL} - 15$		$T_{CLCL} - 15$		ns	
T_{CHLL}	ALE Inactive Delay		30		25		20	ns	
T_{AVLL}	Address Valid to ALE Low	$T_{CLCH} - 18$		$T_{CLCH} - 15$		$T_{CLCH} - 15$		ns	Equal Loading
T_{LLAX}	Address Hold from ALE Inactive	$T_{CHCL} - 15$		$T_{CHCL} - 15$		$T_{CHCL} - 15$		ns	Equal Loading
T_{AVCH}	Address Valid to Clock High	0		0		0		ns	
T_{CLDOX}	Data Hold Time	3		3		3		ns	
T_{CVCTV}	Control Active Delay 1	3	44	3	37	3	31	ns	
T_{CVCTX}	Control Inactive Delay	3	44	3	37	3	31	ns	
T_{CLCSV}	Chip-Select Active Delay	3	42	3	33	3	30	ns	
T_{CXCSX}	Chip-Select Hold from Command Inactive	$T_{CLCH} - 10$		$T_{CLCH} - 10$		$T_{CLCH} - 10$		ns	Equal Loading
T_{CHCSX}	Chip-Select Inactive Delay	5	35	5	30	5	25	ns	
T_{DXDL}	$\overline{DEN}$ Inactive to DT/$\overline{R}$ Low	0		0		0		ns	Equal Loading
T_{CLLV}	$\overline{LOCK}$ Valid/Invalid Delay	3	40	3	37	3	35	ns	
80C188 TIMING RESPONSES (Write Cycle)									
T_{WLWH}	$\overline{WR}$ Pulse Width	$2T_{CLCL} - 30$		$2T_{CLCL} - 25$		$2T_{CLCL} - 25$		ns	
T_{WHLH}	$\overline{WR}$ Inactive to ALE High	$T_{CLCH} - 14$		$T_{CLCH} - 14$		$T_{CLCH} - 14$		ns	Equal Loading
T_{WHDX}	Data Hold After $\overline{WR}$	$T_{CLCL} - 34$		$T_{CLCL} - 20$		$T_{CLCL} - 20$		ns	Equal Loading
T_{WHDEX}	$\overline{WR}$ Inactive to $\overline{DEN}$ Inactive	$T_{CLCH} - 10$		$T_{CLCH} - 10$		$T_{CLCH} - 10$		ns	Equal Loading

270432–35

A.C. CHARACTERISTICS

WRITE CYCLE WAVEFORMS

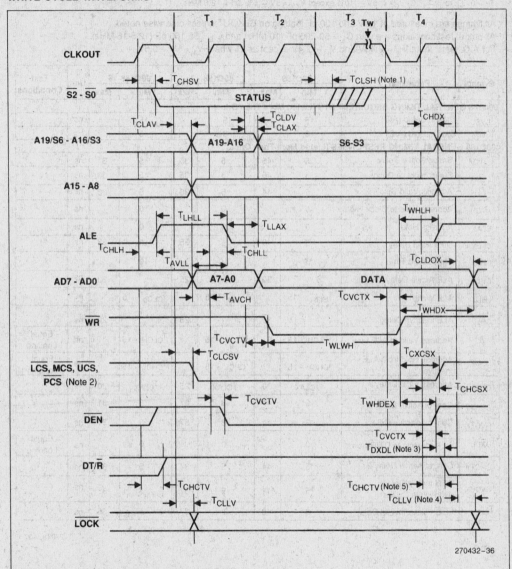

270432-36

NOTES:
1. Status inactive in state preceding T_4.
2. If latched A_1 and A_2 are selected instead of $\overline{PCS5}$ and $\overline{PCS6}$, only T_{CLCSV} is applicable.
3. For write cycle followed by read cycle.
4. T_1 of next bus cycle.
5. Changes in T-state preceding next bus cycle if followed by read, INTA, or halt.

A. C. CHARACTERISTICS

MAJOR CYCLE TIMINGS (INTERRUPT ACKNOWLEDGE CYCLE)

$T_A = 0^\circ$ C to $+ 70^\circ$ C, $V_{CC} = 5V \pm$ 10% except $V_{CC} = 5V \pm 5\%$ at f > 12.5 MHz

All timings are measured at 1.5V and 100 pF loading on CLKOUT unless otherwise noted.
All output test conditions are with C_L = 50-200 pF (10 MHz) and C_L = 50-100 pF (12.5-16 MHz).
For A.C. tests, input V_{IL} = 0.45V and V_{IH} = 2.4V except at X1 where $V_{IH} = V_{CC} - 0.5V$.

Symbol	Parameter	80C188		80C188-12		80C188-16		Unit	Test Conditions
		Min	Max	Min	Max	Min	Max		
80C188 GENERAL TIMING REQUIREMENTS (Listed More Than Once)									
T_{DVCL}	Data in Setup (A/D)	15		15		15		ns	
T_{CLDX}	Data in Hold (A/D)	3		3		3		ns	
80C188 GENERAL TIMING RESPONSES (Listed More Than Once)									
T_{CHSV}	Status Active Delay	5	45	5	35	5	31	ns	
T_{CLSH}	Status Inactive Delay	5	46	5	35	5	30	ns	
T_{CLAV}	Address Valid Delay	5	44	5	36	5	33	ns	
T_{AVCH}	Address Valid to Clock High	0		0		0		ns	
T_{CLAX}	Address Hold	0		0		0		ns	
T_{CLDV}	Data Valid Delay	5	40	5	36	5	33	ns	
T_{CHDX}	Status Hold Time	10		10		10		ns	
T_{CHLH}	ALE Active Delay		30		25		20	ns	
T_{LHLL}	ALE Width	T_{CLCL} - 15		T_{CLCL} - 15		T_{CLCL} - 15		ns	
T_{CHLL}	ALE Inactive Delay		30		25		20	ns	
T_{AVLL}	Address Valid to ALE Low	T_{CLCH} - 18		T_{CLCH} - 15		T_{CLCH} - 15		ns	Equal Loading
T_{LLAX}	Address Hold from ALE Inactive	T_{CHCL} - 15		T_{CHCL} - 15		T_{CHCL} - 15		ns	Equal Loading
T_{CLAZ}	Address Float Delay	T_{CLAX}	30	T_{CLAX}	25	T_{CLAX}	20	ns	
T_{CVCTV}	Control Active Delay 1	3	44	3	37	3	31	ns	
T_{CVCTX}	Control Inactive Delay	3	44	3	37	3	31	ns	
T_{DXDL}	$\overline{DEN}$ Inactive to DT/$\overline{R}$ Low	0		0		0		ns	Equal Loading
T_{CHCTV}	Control Active Delay 2	5	44	5	37	5	31	ns	
T_{CVDEX}	$\overline{DEN}$ Inctive Delay (Non-Write Cycles)	5	44	5	37	5	31	ns	
T_{CLLV}	$\overline{LOCK}$ Valid/Invalid Delay	3	40	3	37	3	35	ns	

270432–37

A. C. CHARACTERISTICS
INTERRUPT ACKNOWLEDGE CYCLE WAVEFORMS

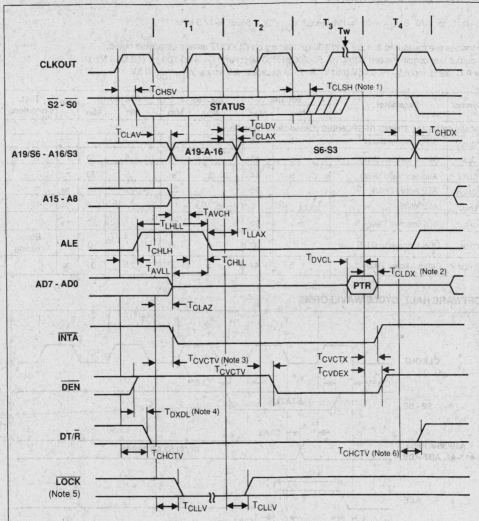

NOTES:

1. Status inactive in state preceding T_4.
2. The data hold time lasts only until $\overline{INTA}$ goes inactive, even if the $\overline{INTA}$ transition occurs prior to $T_{CLDX}(min)$.
3. $\overline{INTA}$ occurs one clock later in Slave Mode.
4. For write cycle followed by interrupt acknowledge cycle.
5. $\overline{LOCK}$ is active upon T_1 of the first interrupt acknowledge cycle and inactive upon T_2 of the second interrupt acknowledge cycle.
6. Changes in T-state preceding next bus cycle if followed by write.

270432–38

A. C. CHARACTERISTICS

SOFTWARE HALT CYCLE TIMINGS

$T_A = 0^{\circ}C$ to $+70^{\circ}C$, $V_{CC} = 5V \pm 10\%$ except $V_{CC} = 5V \pm 5\%$ at $f > 12.5$ MHz

All timings are measured at 1.5V and 100 pF loading on CLKOUT unless otherwise noted.
All output test conditions are with $C_L = 50\text{-}200$ pF (10 MHz) and $C_L = 50\text{-}100$ pF (12.5-16 MHz).
For A.C. tests, input $V_{IL} = 0.45V$ and $V_{IH} = 2.4V$ except at X1 where $V_{IH} = V_{CC} - 0.5V$.

Symbol	Parameter	80C188		80C188-12		80C188-16		Unit	Test Conditions
		Min	Max	Min	Max	Min	Max		
80C188 GENERAL TIMING RESPONSES (Listed More Than Once)									
T_{CHSV}	Status Active Delay	5	45	5	35	5	31	ns	
T_{CLSH}	Status Inactive Delay	5	46	5	35	5	30	ns	
T_{CLAV}	Address Valid Delay	5	44	5	36	5	33	ns	
T_{CHLH}	ALE Active Delay		30		25		20	ns	
T_{LHLL}	ALE Width	$T_{CLCL} - 15$		$T_{CLCL} - 15$		$T_{CLCL} - 15$		ns	
T_{CHLL}	ALE Inactive Delay		30		25		20	ns	
T_{DXDL}	$\overline{DEN}$ Inactive to DT/$\overline{R}$ Low		0		0		0	ns	Equal Loading
T_{CHCTV}	Control Active Delay 2	5	44	5	37	5	31	ns	

SOFTWARE HALT CYCLE WAVEFORMS

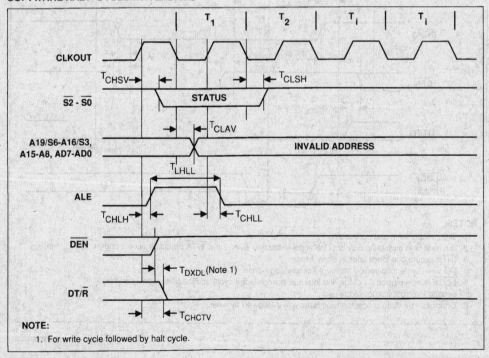

NOTE:
1. For write cycle followed by halt cycle.

A. C. CHARACTERISTICS

CLOCK TIMINGS

$T_A = 0^\circ$ C to $+70^\circ$ C, $V_{CC} = 5V \pm 10\%$ except $V_{CC} = 5V \pm 5\%$ at f > 12.5 MHz

All timings are measured at 1.5V and 100 pF loading on CLKOUT unless otherwise noted.
All output test conditions are with C_L = 50-200 pF (10 MHz) and C_L = 50-100 pF (12.5-16 MHz).
For A.C. tests, input V_{IL} = 0.45V and V_{IH} = 2.4V except at X1 where $V_{IH} = V_{CC} - 0.5V$.

Symbol	Parameter	80C188		80C188-12		80C188-16		Unit	Test Conditions
		Min	Max	Min	Max	Min	Max		
80C188 CLKIN REQUIREMENTS Measurements taken with following conditions: External clock input to X1 and X2 not connected (float)									
T_{CKIN}	CLKIN Period	50	1000	40	1000	31.25	1000	ns	
T_{CLCK}	CLKIN Low Time	20		16		13		ns	1.5 V [2]
T_{CHCK}	CLKIN High Time	20		16		13		ns	1.5 V [2]
T_{CKHL}	CLKIN Fall Time		5		5		5	ns	3.5 to 1.0V
T_{CKLH}	CLKIN Rise Time		5		5		5	ns	1.0 to 3.5V
80C188 CLKOUT TIMING									
T_{CICO}	CLKIN to CLKOUT Skew		25		21		17	ns	
T_{CLCL}	CLKOUT Period	100	2000	80	2000	62.5	2000	ns	
T_{CLCH}	CLKOUT Low Time	0.5 T_{CLCL} -8		0.5 T_{CLCL} -7		0.5 T_{CLCL} -7		ns	C_L=100pF (2)
		0.5 T_{CLCL} -6		0.5 T_{CLCL} -5		0.5 T_{CLCL} -5		ns	C_L=50pF (3)
T_{CHCL}	CLKOUT High Time	0.5 T_{CLCL} -8		0.5 T_{CLCL} -7		0.5 T_{CLCL} -7		ns	C_L=100pF (4)
		0.5 T_{CLCL} -6		0.5 T_{CLCL} -5		0.5 T_{CLCL} -5		ns	C_L=50pF (3)
T_{CH1CH2}	CLKOUT Rise Time		10		10		10	ns	1.0 to 3.5V
T_{CL2CL1}	CLKOUT Fall Time		10		10		10	ns	3.5 to 1.0V

NOTES:

1. T_{CLCK} and T_{CHCK} (CLKIN Low and High times) should not have a duration less than 40% of T_{CKIN}.
2. Tested under worst case conditions: V_{CC} = 5.5V (5.25V @ 16 MHz). $T_A = 70\,^\circ$C.
3. Not Tested.
4. Tested under worst case conditions: V_{CC} = 4.5V (4.75V @ 16 MHz). $T_A = 0\,^\circ$C.

CLOCK WAVEFORMS

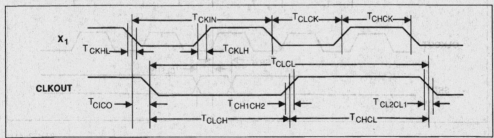

270432-40

A. C. CHARACTERISTICS

READY, PERIPHERAL, AND QUEUE STATUS TIMINGS

$T_A = 0°$ C to $+ 70°$ C, $V_{CC} = 5V \pm$ 10% except $V_{CC} = 5V \pm$ 5% at f > 12.5 MHz

All timings are measured at 1.5V and 100 pF loading on CLKOUT unless otherwise noted.
All output test conditions are with $C_L = 50$-200 pF (10 MHz) and $C_L = 50$-100 pF (12.5-16 MHz).
For A.C. tests, input $V_{IL} = 0.45V$ and $V_{IH} = 2.4V$ except at X1 where $V_{IH} = V_{CC} - 0.5V$.

Symbol	Parameter	80C188		80C188-12		80C188-16		Unit	Test Conditions
		Min	Max	Min	Max	Min	Max		
80C188 READY AND PERIPHERAL TIMING REQUIREMENTS									
T_{SRYCL}	Synchronous Ready(SRDY) Transition Setup Time [1]	15		15		15		ns	
T_{CLSRY}	SRDY Transition Hold Time [1]	15		15		15		ns	
T_{ARYCH}	ARDY Resolution Transition Setup Time [2]	15		15		15		ns	
T_{CLARX}	ARDY Active Hold Time [1]	15		15		15		ns	
T_{ARYCHL}	ARDY Inactive Holding Time	15		15		15		ns	
T_{ARYLCL}	Asynchronous Ready (ARDY) Setup Time [1]	25		25		25		ns	
T_{INVCH}	INTx, NMI, $\overline{TEST}$/BUSY, TMR IN Setup Time [2]	15		15		15		ns	
T_{INVCL}	DRQ0, DRQ1 Setup Time [2]	15		15		15		ns	
80C188 PERIPHERAL AND QUEUE STATUS TIMING RESPONSES									
T_{CLTMV}	Timer Output Delay		40		33		27	ns	
T_{CHQSV}	Queue Status Delay		37		32		30	ns	

NOTES:
1. To guarantee proper operation.
2. To guarantee recognition at clock edge.

SYNCHRONOUS READY (SRDY) WAVEFORMS

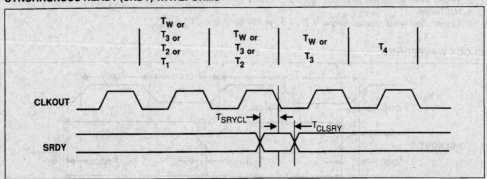

A. C. CHARACTERISTICS

ASYNCHRONOUS READY (ARDY) WAVEFORMS

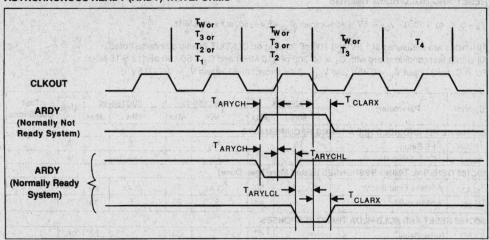

PERIPHERAL AND QUEUE STATUS WAVEFORMS

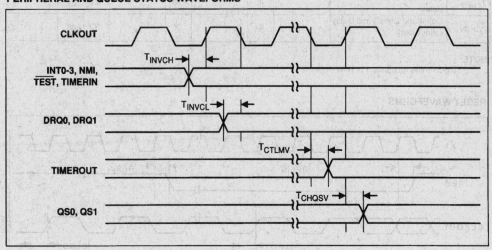

270432–42

A. C. CHARACTERISTICS

RESET AND HOLD/HLDA TIMINGS

$T_A = 0^\circ$ C to $+70^\circ$ C, $V_{CC} = 5V \pm 10\%$ except $V_{CC} = 5V \pm 5\%$ at f > 12.5 MHz

All timings are measured at 1.5V and 100 pF loading on CLKOUT unless otherwise noted.
All output test conditions are with $C_L = 50$-200 pF (10 MHz) and $C_L = 50$-100 pF (12.5-16 MHz).
For A.C. tests, input $V_{IL} = 0.45V$ and $V_{IH} = 2.4V$ except at X1 where $V_{IH} = V_{CC}$- 0.5V.

Symbol	Parameter	80C188		80C188-12		80C188-16		Unit	Test Conditions
		Min	Max	Min	Max	Min	Max		
80C188 RESET AND HOLD/HLDA TIMING REQUIREMENTS									
T_{RESIN}	RES Setup	15		15		15		ns	
T_{HVCL}	HOLD Setup (1)	15		15		15		ns	
80C188 GENERAL TIMING RESPONSES (Listed More Than Once)									
T_{CLAZ}	Address Float Delay	T_{CLAX}	30	T_{CLAX}	25	T_{CLAX}	20	ns	
T_{CLAV}	Address Valid Delay	5	44	5	36	5	33	ns	
80C188 RESET AND HOLD/HLDA TIMING RESPONSES									
T_{CLRO}	Reset Delay		40		33		27	ns	
T_{CLHAV}	HLDA Valid Delay	3	40	3	33	3	25	ns	
T_{CHCZ}	Command Lines Float Delay		40		33		28	ns	
T_{CHCV}	Command Lines Valid Delay (after Float)		44		36		32	ns	

NOTE:
1. To guarantee recognition at next clock.

RESET WAVEFORMS

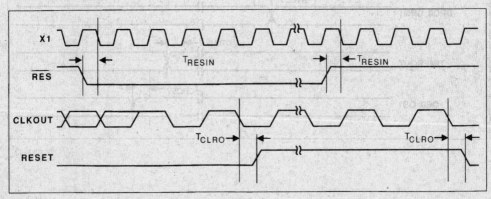

270432-43

A. C. CHARACTERISTICS

HOLD/HLDA WAVEFORMS (Entering Hold)

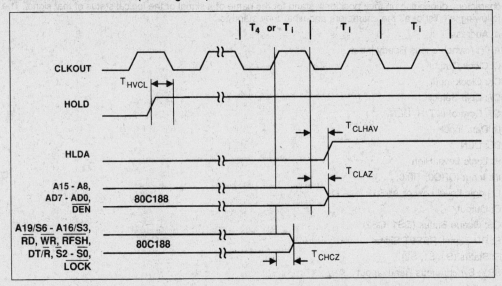

HOLD/HLDA WAVEFORMS (Leaving Hold)

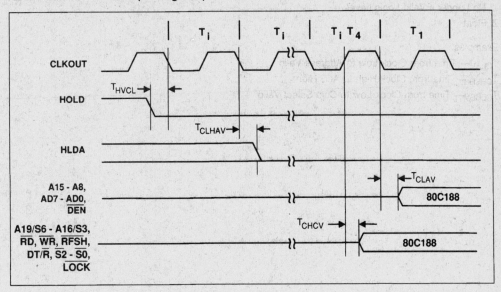

270432–44

EXPLANATION OF THE AC SYMBOLS

Each timing symbol has from 5 to 7 characters. The first character is always a "T" (stands for time). The other characters, depending on their positions, stand for the name of a signal or the logical status of that signal. The following is a list of all the characters and what they stand for.

A: Address

ARY: Asynchronous Ready Input

C: Clock Output

CK: Clock Input

CS: Chip Select

CT: Control (DT/$\overline{R}$, $\overline{DEN}$, . . .)

D: Data Input

DE: $\overline{DEN}$

H: Logic Level High

IN: Input (DRQ0, TIM0, . . .)

L: Logic Level Low or ALE

O: Output

QS: Queue Status (QS1, QS2)

R: $\overline{RD}$ Signal, RESET Signal

S: Status ($\overline{S0}$, $\overline{S1}$, $\overline{S2}$)

SRY: Synchronous Ready Input

V: Valid

W: WR Signal

X: No Longer a Valid Logic Level

Z: Float

Examples:

T$_{CLAV}$— Time from Clock Low to Address Valid

T$_{CHLH}$— Time from Clock High to ALE High

T$_{CLCSV}$— Time from Clock Low to Chip Select Valid

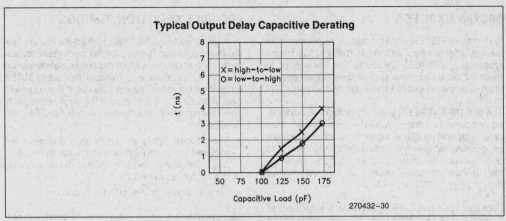

Figure 47. Capacitive Derating Curve

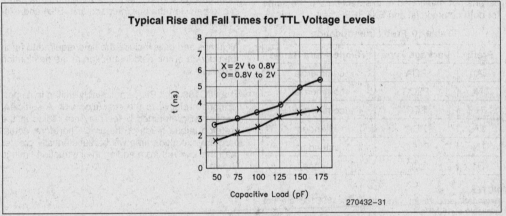

Figure 48. TTL Level Slew Rates for Output Buffers

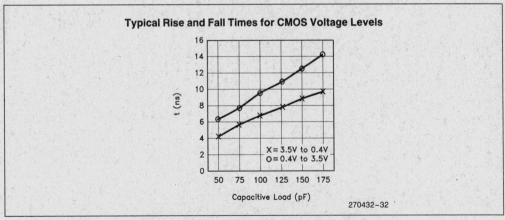

Figure 49. CMOS Level Slew Rates for Output Buffers

80C188 EXPRESS

The Intel EXPRESS system offers enhancements to the operational specifications of the 80C188 microprocessor. EXPRESS products are designed to meet the needs of those applications whose operating requirements exceed commercial standards.

The 80C188 EXPRESS program includes an extended temperature range. With the commercial standard temperature range operational characteristics are guaranteed over the temperature range of 0°C to +70°C. With the extended temperature range option, operational characteristics are guaranteed over the range of −40°C to +85°C.

Package types and EXPRESS versions are identified by a one or two-letter prefix to the part number. The prefixes are listed in Table 16. All AC and DC specifications not mentioned in this section are the same for both commercial and EXPRESS parts.

Table 16. Prefix Identification

Prefix	Package Type	Temperature Range
A	PGA	commercial
N	PLCC	commercial
R	LCC	commercial
TA	PGA	extended
TN	PLCC	extended
TR	LCC	extended

NOTE:
Extended temperature versions of the 80C188 are not available at 16 MHz.

80C188 EXECUTION TIMINGS

A determination of 80C188 program execution timing must consider the bus cycles necessary to prefetch instructions as well as the number of execution unit cycles necessary to execute instructions. The following instruction timings represent the minimum execution time in clock cycles for each instruction. The timings given are based on the following assumptions:

- The opcode, along with any data or displacement required for execution of a particular instruction, has been prefetched and resides in the queue at the time it is needed.
- No wait states or bus HOLDs occur.

All instructions which involve memory accesses can require one or two additional clocks above the minimum timings shown due to the asynchronous handshake between the bus interface unit (BIU) and execution unit.

All jumps and calls include the time required to fetch the opcode of the next instruction at the destination address.

The 80C188 8-bit BIU is noticeably limited in its performance relative to the execution unit. A sufficient number of prefetched bytes may not reside in the prefetch queue much of the time. Therefore, actual program execution time will be substantially greater than that derived from adding the instruction timings shown.

INSTRUCTION SET SUMMARY

Function	Format				Clock Cycles	Comments
DATA TRANSFER						
MOV = Move:						
Register to Register/Memory	1000100w	mod reg r/m			2/12*	
Register/memory to register	1000101w	mod reg r/m			2/9*	
Immediate to register/memory	1100011w	mod 000 r/m	data	data if w = 1	12/13	8/16-bit
Immediate to register	1011w reg	data	data if w = 1		3/4	8/16-bit
Memory to accumulator	1010000w	addr-low	addr-high		8*	
Accumulator to memory	1010001w	addr-low	addr-high		9*	
Register/memory to segment register	10001110	mod 0 reg r/m			2/13	
Segment register to register/memory	10001100	mod 0 reg r/m			2/15	
PUSH = Push:						
Memory	11111111	mod 1 1 0 r/m			20	
Register	01010 reg				14	
Segment register	000 reg 110				13	
Immediate	011010s0	data	data if s = 0		14	
PUSHA = Push All	01100000				68	
POP = Pop:						
Memory	10001111	mod 0 0 0 r/m			24	
Register	01011 reg				14	
Segment register	000 reg 111	(reg ≠ 01)			12	
POPA = Pop All	01100001				83	
XCHG = Exchange:						
Register/memory with register	1000011w	mod reg r/m			4/17*	
Register with accumulator	10010 reg				3	
IN = Input from:						
Fixed port	1110010w	port			10*	
Variable port	1110110w				8*	
OUT = Output to:						
Fixed port	1110011w	port			9*	
Variable port	1110111w				7*	
XLAT = Translate byte to AL	11010111				15	
LEA = Load EA to register	10001101	mod reg r/m			6	
LDS = Load pointer to DS	11000101	mod reg r/m	(mod ≠ 11)		26	
LES = Load pointer to ES	11000100	mod reg r/m	(mod ≠ 11)		26	
LAHF = Load AH with flags	10011111				2	
SAHF = Store AH into flags	10011110				3	
PUSHF = Push flags	10011100				13	
POPF = Pop flags	10011101				12	

Shaded areas indicate instructions not available in 8086, 8088 microsystems.

*NOTE:
Clock cycles shown for byte transfer. For word operations, add 4 clock cycles for all memory transfers.

INSTRUCTION SET SUMMARY (Continued)

Function	Format				Clock Cycles	Comments
DATA TRANSFER (Continued)						
SEGMENT = Segment Override:						
CS	`00101110`				2	
SS	`00110110`				2	
DS	`00111110`				2	
ES	`00100110`				2	
ARITHMETIC						
ADD = Add:						
Reg/memory with register to either	`000000dw`	`mod reg r/m`			3/10*	
Immediate to register/memory	`100000sw`	`mod 000 r/m`	data	data if s w = 01	4/16*	
Immediate to accumulator	`0000010w`	data	data if w = 1		3/4	8/16-bit
ADC = Add with carry:						
Reg/memory with register to either	`000100dw`	`mod reg r/m`			3/10*	
Immediate to register/memory	`100000sw`	`mod 010 r/m`	data	data if s w = 01	4/16*	
Immediate to accumulator	`0001010w`	data	data if w = 1		3/4	8/16-bit
INC = Increment:						
Register/memory	`1111111w`	`mod 000 r/m`			3/15*	
Register	`01000 reg`				3	
SUB = Subtract:						
Reg/memory and register to either	`001010dw`	`mod reg r/m`			3/10*	
Immediate from register/memory	`100000sw`	`mod 101 r/m`	data	data if s w = 01	4/16*	
Immediate from accumulator	`0010110w`	data	data if w = 1		3/4	8/16-bit
SBB = Subtract with borrow:						
Reg/memory and register to either	`000110dw`	`mod reg r/m`			3/10*	
Immediate from register/memory	`100000sw`	`mod 011 r/m`	data	data if s w = 01	4/16*	
Immediate from accumulator	`0001110w`	data	data if w = 1		3/4	8/16-bit
DEC = Decrement						
Register/memory	`1111111w`	`mod 001 r/m`			3/15*	
Register	`01001 reg`				3	
CMP = Compare:						
Register/memory with register	`0011101w`	`mod reg r/m`			3/10*	
Register with register/memory	`0011100w`	`mod reg r/m`			3/10*	
Immediate with register/memory	`100000sw`	`mod 111 r/m`	data	data if s w = 01	3/10*	
Immediate with accumulator	`0011110w`	data	data if w = 1		3/4	8/16-bit
NEG = Change sign register/memory	`1111011w`	`mod 011 r/m`			3/10*	
AAA = ASCII adjust for add	`00110111`				8	
DAA = Decimal adjust for add	`00100111`				4	
AAS = ASCII adjust for subtract	`00111111`				7	
DAS = Decimal adjust for subtract	`00101111`				4	

Shaded areas indicate instructions not available in 8086, 8088 microsystems.

*NOTE:
Clock cycles shown for byte transfer. For word operations, add 4 clock cycles for all memory transfers.

INSTRUCTION SET SUMMARY (Continued)

Function	Format				Clock Cycles	Comments
ARITHMETIC (Continued)						
MUL = Multiply (unsigned):	1 1 1 1 0 1 1 w	mod 100 r/m				
Register-Byte					26–28	
Register-Word					35–37	
Memory-Byte					32–34	
Memory-Word					41–43*	
IMUL = Integer multiply (signed):	1 1 1 1 0 1 1 w	mod 1 0 1 r/m				
Register-Byte					25–28	
Register-Word					34–37	
Memory-Byte					31–34	
Memory-Word					40–43*	
IMUL = Integer Immediate multiply (signed)	0 1 1 0 1 0 s 1	mod reg r/m	data	data if s=0	22–25/ 29–32	
DIV = Divide (unsigned):	1 1 1 1 0 1 1 w	mod 1 1 0 r/m				
Register-Byte					29	
Register-Word					38	
Memory-Byte					35	
Memory-Word					44*	
IDIV = Integer divide (signed):	1 1 1 1 0 1 1 w	mod 1 1 1 r/m				
Register-Byte					44–52	
Register-Word					53–61	
Memory-Byte					50–58	
Memory-Word					59–67*	
AAM = ASCII adjust for multiply	1 1 0 1 0 1 0 0	0 0 0 0 1 0 1 0			19	
AAD = ASCII adjust for divide	1 1 0 1 0 1 0 1	0 0 0 0 1 0 1 0			15	
CBW = Convert byte to word	1 0 0 1 1 0 0 0				2	
CWD = Convert word to double word	1 0 0 1 1 0 0 1				4	
LOGIC						
Shift/Rotate Instructions:						
Register/Memory by 1	1 1 0 1 0 0 0 w	mod TTT r/m			2/15	
Register/Memory by CL	1 1 0 1 0 0 1 w	mod TTT r/m			5+n/17+n	
Register/Memory by Count	1 1 0 0 0 0 0 w	mod TTT r/m	count		5+n/17+n	

	TTT Instruction
0 0 0	ROL
0 0 1	ROR
0 1 0	RCL
0 1 1	RCR
1 0 0	SHL/SAL
1 0 1	SHR
1 1 1	SAR

Function	Format				Clock Cycles	Comments
AND = And:						
Reg/memory and register to either	0 0 1 0 0 0 d w	mod reg r/m			3/10*	
Immediate to register/memory	1 0 0 0 0 0 0 w	mod 1 0 0 r/m	data	data if w=1	4/16*	
Immediate to accumulator	0 0 1 0 0 1 0 w	data	data if w=1		3/4	8/16-bit

Shaded areas indicate instructions not available in 8086, 8088 microsystems.

*NOTE:
Clock cycles shown for byte transfer. For word operations, add 4 clock cycles for all memory transfers.

INSTRUCTION SET SUMMARY (Continued)

Function	Format				Clock Cycles	Comments
LOGIC (Continued)						
TEST = And function to flags, no result:						
Register/memory and register	1 0 0 0 0 1 0 w	mod reg r/m			3/10*	
Immediate data and register/memory	1 1 1 1 0 1 1 w	mod 0 0 0 r/m	data	data if w = 1	4/10*	
Immediate data and accumulator	1 0 1 0 1 0 0 w	data	data if w = 1		3/4	8/16-bit
OR = Or:						
Reg/memory and register to either	0 0 0 0 1 0 d w	mod reg r/m			3/10*	
Immediate to register/memory	1 0 0 0 0 0 0 w	mod 0 0 1 r/m	data	data if w = 1	4/16*	
Immediate to accumulator	0 0 0 0 1 1 0 w	data	data if w = 1		3/4	8/16-bit
XOR = Exclusive or:						
Reg/memory and register to either	0 0 1 1 0 0 d w	mod reg r/m			3/10*	
Immediate to register/memory	1 0 0 0 0 0 0 w	mod 1 1 0 r/m	data	data if w = 1	4/16*	
Immediate to accumulator	0 0 1 1 0 1 0 w	data	data if w = 1		3/4	8/16-bit
NOT = Invert register/memory	1 1 1 1 0 1 1 w	mod 0 1 0 r/m			3/10*	
STRING MANIPULATION						
MOVS = Move byte/word	1 0 1 0 0 1 0 w				14*	
CMPS = Compare byte/word	1 0 1 0 0 1 1 w				22*	
SCAS = Scan byte/word	1 0 1 0 1 1 1 w				15*	
LODS = Load byte/wd to AL/AX	1 0 1 0 1 1 0 w				12*	
STOS = Store byte/wd from AL/AX	1 0 1 0 1 0 1 w				10*	
INS = Input byte/wd from DX port	0 1 1 0 1 1 0 w				14	
OUTS = Output byte/wd to DX port	0 1 1 0 1 1 1 w				14	
Repeated by count in CX (REP/ REPE/REPZ/REPNE/REPNZ)						
MOVS = Move string	1 1 1 1 0 0 1 0	1 0 1 0 0 1 0 w			8 + 8n*	
CMPS = Compare string	1 1 1 1 0 0 1 z	1 0 1 0 0 1 1 w			5 + 22n*	
SCAS = Scan string	1 1 1 1 0 0 1 z	1 0 1 0 1 1 1 w			5 + 15n*	
LODS = Load string	1 1 1 1 0 0 1 0	1 0 1 0 1 1 0 w			6 + 11n*	
STOS = Store string	1 1 1 1 0 0 1 0	1 0 1 0 1 0 1 w			6 + 9n*	
INS = Input string	1 1 1 1 0 0 1 0	0 1 1 0 1 1 0 w			8 + 8n*	
OUTS = Output string	1 1 1 1 0 0 1 0	0 1 1 0 1 1 1 w			8 + 8n*	
CONTROL TRANSFER						
CALL = Call:						
Direct within segment	1 1 1 0 1 0 0 0	disp-low	disp-high		19	
Register/memory indirect within segment	1 1 1 1 1 1 1 1	mod 0 1 0 r/m			17/27	
Direct intersegment	1 0 0 1 1 0 1 0	segment offset			31	
		segment selector				
Indirect intersegment	1 1 1 1 1 1 1 1	mod 0 1 1 r/m	(mod ≠ 11)		54	

Shaded areas indicate instructions not available in 8086, 8088 microsystems.

*NOTE:
Clock cycles shown for byte transfer. For word operations, add 4 clock cycles for all memory transfers.

INSTRUCTION SET SUMMARY (Continued)

Function	Format			Clock Cycles	Comments
CONTROL TRANSFER (Continued) **JMP** = Unconditional jump:					
Short/long	11101011	disp-low		14	
Direct within segment	11101001	disp-low	disp-high	14	
Register/memory indirect within segment	11111111	mod 1 0 0 r/m		11/21	
Direct intersegment	11101010	segment offset		14	
		segment selector			
Indirect intersegment	11111111	mod 1 0 1 r/m	(mod ≠ 11)	34	
RET = Return from CALL:					
Within segment	11000011			20	
Within seg adding immed to SP	11000010	data-low	data-high	22	
Intersegment	11001011			30	
Intersegment adding immediate to SP	11001010	data-low	data-high	33	
JE/JZ = Jump on equal/zero	01110100	disp		4/13	JMP not taken/JMP taken
JL/JNGE = Jump on less/not greater or equal	01111100	disp		4/13	
JLE/JNG = Jump on less or equal/not greater	01111110	disp		4/13	
JB/JNAE = Jump on below/not above or equal	01110010	disp		4/13	
JBE/JNA = Jump on below or equal/not above	01110110	disp		4/13	
JP/JPE = Jump on parity/parity even	01111010	disp		4/13	
JO = Jump on overflow	01110000	disp		4/13	
JS = Jump on sign	01111000	disp		4/13	
JNE/JNZ = Jump on not equal/not zero	01110101	disp		4/13	
JNL/JGE = Jump on not less/greater or equal	01111101	disp		4/13	
JNLE/JG = Jump on not less or equal/greater	01111111	disp		4/13	
JNB/JAE = Jump on not below/above or equal	01110011	disp		4/13	
JNBE/JA = Jump on not below or equal/above	01110111	disp		4/13	
JNP/JPO = Jump on not par/par odd	01111011	disp		4/13	
JNO = Jump on not overflow	01110001	disp		4/13	
JNS = Jump on not sign	01111001	disp		4/13	
JCXZ = Jump on CX zero	11100011	disp		5/15	
LOOP = Loop CX times	11100010	disp		6/16	LOOP not taken/LOOP taken
LOOPZ/LOOPE = Loop while zero/equal	11100001	disp		6/16	
LOOPNZ/LOOPNE = Loop while not zero/equal	11100000	disp		6/16	
ENTER = Enter Procedure	11001000	data-low	data-high	L	
L = 0				19	
L = 1				29	
L > 1				26 + 20(n − 1)	
LEAVE = Leave Procedure	11001001			8	

Shaded areas indicate instructions not available in 8086, 8088 microsystems.

INSTRUCTION SET SUMMARY (Continued)

Function	Format		Clock Cycles	Comments
CONTROL TRANSFER (Continued) **INT** = Interrupt:				
Type specified	11001101	type	47	
Type 3	11001100		45	if INT. taken/ if INT. not taken
INTO = Interrupt on overflow	11001110		48/4	
IRET = Interrupt return	11001111		28	
BOUND = Detect value out of range	01100010	mod reg r/m	33–35	
PROCESSOR CONTROL				
CLC = Clear carry	11111000		2	
CMC = Complement carry	11110101		2	
STC = Set carry	11111001		2	
CLD = Clear direction	11111100		2	
STD = Set direction	11111101		2	
CLI = Clear interrupt	11111010		2	
STI = Set interrupt	11111011		2	
HLT = Halt	11110100		2	
WAIT = Wait	10011011		6	if $\overline{TEST}$ = 0
LOCK = Bus lock prefix	11110000		2	
NOP = No Operation	10010000		3	

Shaded areas indicate instructions not available in 8086, 8088 microsystems.

FOOTNOTES

The Effective Address (EA) of the memory operand is computed according to the mod and r/m fields:

if mod	=	11 then r/m is treated as a REG field
if mod	=	00 then DISP = 0*, disp-low and disp-high are absent
if mod	=	01 then DISP = disp-low sign-extended to 16-bits, disp-high is absent
if mod	=	10 then DISP = disp-high: disp-low
if r/m	=	000 then EA = (BX) + (SI) + DISP
if r/m	=	001 then EA = (BX) + (DI) + DISP
if r/m	=	010 then EA = (BP) + (SI) + DISP
if r/m	=	011 then EA = (BP) + (DI) + DISP
if r/m	=	100 then EA = (SI) + DISP
if r/m	=	101 then EA = (DI) + DISP
if r/m	=	110 then EA = (BP) + DISP*
if r/m	=	111 then EA = (BX) + DISP

DISP follows 2nd byte of instruction (before data if required)

*except if mod = 00 and r/m = 110 then EA = disp-high: disp-low.

EA calculation time is 4 clock cycles for all modes, and is included in the execution times given whenever appropriate.

Segment Override Prefix

0	0	1	reg	1	1	0

reg is assigned according to the following:

reg	Segment Register
00	ES
01	CS
10	SS
11	DS

REG is assigned according to the following table:

16-Bit (w = 1)	8-Bit (w = 0)
000 AX	000 AL
001 CX	001 CL
010 DX	010 DL
011 BX	011 BL
100 SP	100 AH
101 BP	101 CH
110 SI	110 DH
111 DI	111 BH

The physical addresses of all operands addressed by the BP register are computed using the SS segment register. The physical addresses of the destination operands of the string primitive operations (those addressed by the DI register) are computed using the ES segment, which may not be overridden.

REVISION HISTORY

The sections significantly revised since version -003 are:

Pin Description Table
Added note to $\overline{TEST}$ pin requiring proper RESET at power-up to configure pin as input.

Renamed pin 44 to INT1/$\overline{SELECT}$ and pin 41 to INT3/$\overline{INTA1}$/IRQ to better describe their functions in Slave Mode.

Initialization and Processor Reset
Added reminder to drive $\overline{RES}$ pin LOW during power-up.

Read and Write Cycle Waveforms
Clarified applicability of T_{CLCSV} to latched A1 and A2 in footnotes.

Instruction Set Summary
Corrected clock count for ENTER instruction.

Slave Mode Operation
The three low order bits associated with vector generation and performing EOI are not alterable; however, the priority levels are programmable. This information is a clarification only.

The sections significantly revised since version -002 are:

Front Page
Deleted references to burn-in devices.

Local Bus Controller and Reset
Clarified effects of excessive loading on pins with internal pullup devices. Equivalent resistance no longer shown.

D.C. Characteristics
Renamed V_{CLI} to V_{IL1}. Renamed V_{CHI} to V_{IH3}. Changed V_{OH} (min) from 0.8 V_{CC} to V_{CC} − 0.5V. Changed I_{CC} (max) from 180 mA to 150 mA at 16 MHz, 150 mA to 120 mA at 12.5 MHz, and 120 mA to 100 mA at 10 MHz. Changed V_{CLO} (max) from 0.5V to 0.45V. Changed V_{CHO} (min) from 0.8 V_{CC} to V_{CC} − 0.5V. Clarified effect of excessive loading on pins with internal pullup devices.

Power Supply Current
Added equation and graph for maximum current.

A.C. Characteristics
Many timings changed (all listed in ns): T_{DVCL} (min) at 16 MHz from 10 to 15; T_{CLDX} (min) from 5 to 3; T_{CLAV} (max) at 10 MHz from 50 to 44; T_{CHCV} (max) from 45 to 44 at 10 MHz and from 37 to 36 at 12.5 MHz; T_{LHLL} (min) from T_{CLCL} − 30 to T_{CLCL} − 15; T_{LLAX} (min) at 10 MHz from T_{CHCL} − 20 to T_{CHCL} − 15; T_{CVCTV} (max) from 56 to 44 at 10 MHz, and from 47 to 37 at 12.5 MHz; T_{CVDEX} (max) from 56 to 44 at 10 MHz, 47 to 37 at 12.5 MHz, and from 35 to 31 at 16 MHz; T_{RHAV} (min) from T_{CLCL} − 40 at 10 MHz and T_{CLCL} − 20 at 12.5 MHz and 16 MHz to T_{CLCL} − 15 at all frequencies; T_{RLRH} (min) from 2 T_{CLCL} − 46 to 2 T_{CLCL} − 30 at 10 MHz, from 2 T_{CLCL} − 40 to 2 T_{CLCL} − 25 at 12.5 MHz, and T_{CLCL} − 30 to 2 T_{CLCL} − 25 at 16 MHz; T_{WLWH} (min) from 2 T_{CLCL} − 34 to 2 T_{CLCL} − 30 at 10 MHz, and 2 T_{CLCL} − 30 to 2 T_{CLCL} − 25 at 12.5 MHz, T_{AVLL} (min) from T_{CLCH} − 19 to T_{CLCH} − 18 at 10 MHz; T_{CLSH} (max) at 10 MHz from 50 to 46; T_{CLTMV} (max) from 48 to 40 at 10 MHz; 40 to 33 at 12.5 MHz, and 30 to 27 at 16 MHz; T_{CLRO} (max) from 48 to 40 at 10 MHz, 40 to 33 at 12.5 MHz, and 37 to 27 at 16 MHz; T_{CHQSV} (max) from 28 to 37 at 10 MHz, 28 to 32 at 12.5 MHz, and 25 to 30 at 16 MHz; T_{CHDX} (min) from 5 to 10; T_{CLLV} (max) at 10 MHz from 45 to 40 and at 12.5 MHz from 40 to 37; T_{CLCSV} (max) from 45 to 42 at 10 MHz; T_{CHCSX} (max) from 32 to 35 at 10 MHz, 28 to 30 at 12.5 MHz, and 23 to 25 at 16 MHz; and T_{CH1CH2} and T_{CL2CL1} (max) at 16 MHz from 8 to 10. Added new timings for T_{WHDEX}, T_{RHLH}, and T_{WHLH}. Established minimum timing for T_{CLCSV}.

Timing Waveforms	Section rearranged to show waveforms on same or facing page relative to corresponding tabular data. T_{CLSRY} drawn to same clock edge as T_{SRYCL}. Drawing changed to indicate one less clock between HOLD inactive and HLDA inactive.
Specification Level Markings	New section.

The sections significantly revised since version -001 are:

LCC Contact Diagram	Corrections made to upper address pins.
Pin Description Table	Various descriptions rewritten for clarity.
Interrupt Vector Table	Redrawn for clarity.
ESC Opcode Exception Description	Note added concerning ESC trap.
Oscillator Configurations	Deleted drive of X2 with inverted X1.
RESET Logic	Deleted paragraph concerning setup times for synchronization of multiple processors.
Local Bus Arbitration	Added description of HLDA when a refresh cycle is pending.
Local Bus Controller and Reset	Added description of pullup devices for appropriate pins.
DMA Controller	Added reminder to initialize transfer count registers and pointer registers.
Timers	Added reminder to initialize count registers.
DRAM Refresh Addresses	Refresh address counter described in figure.
D.C. Characteristics	V_{IH2} indicated for SRDY, ARDY. I_{CC} (max.) now indicated for all devices.
Power Supply Current	Typical I_{CC} indicated.
A.C. Characteristics	Input V_{IH} test condition at X1 added. T_{CLDOX}, T_{CVCTV}, T_{CVCTX}, T_{CLHAV} and T_{CLLV} minimums reduced from 5 ns to 3 ns. T_{CLCH} min. and T_{CHCL} min. relaxed by 2 ns. Added reminder that T_{SRYCL} and T_{CLSRY} must be met.
Explanation of the A.C. Symbols	New section.
Major Cycle Timing Waveforms	T_{DXDL} indicated in Read Cycle. T_{CLRO} indicated.
Rise/Fall Times and Capacitive Derating Curves	New Figures added.
Instruction Set Summary	ESC deleted.

SPECIFICATION LEVEL MARKINGS

Current 80C188 devices bear backside lot code information consisting of seven digits followed by letters. The second, third, and fourth digits comprise a manufacturing data code. This preliminary data sheet applies only to 80C188 devices with a date code corresponding to week 25 of 1989 (backside markings x925xxx XXX) or later.

82188
INTEGRATED BUS CONTROLLER FOR
8086, 8088, 80186, 80188 PROCESSORS

- ■ Provides Flexibility in System Configurations
  - — Supports 8087 Math Coprocessor in 8 MHz 80186 and 80188 Systems
  - — Provides a Low-cost Interface for 8086, 8088 Systems to an 82586 LAN Coprocessor or 82730 Text Coprocessor
- ■ Facilitates Interface to one or more Multimaster Busses

- ■ Supports Multiprocessor, Local Bus Systems
- ▣ Allows use of 80186/80188 High-Integration Features
- ■ 3-State, Command Output Drivers
- ■ Available in EXPRESS
  - — Standard Temperature Range
  - — Extended Temperature Range
- ■ Available in Plastic DIP or Cerdip Package

  (See Packaging Outlines and Dimensions, Order #231369)

The 82188 Integrated Bus Controller (IBC) is a 28-pin HMOS III component for use with 80186, 80188, 8086 and 8088 systems. The IBC provides command and control timing signals plus a configurable $\overline{RQ}/\overline{GT} \longleftrightarrow$ HOLD-HLDA converter. The device may be used to interface an 8087 Math Coprocessor with an 80186 or 80188 Processor. Also, an 82586 Local Area Network (LAN) Coprocessor or 82730 Text Coprocessor may be interfaced to an 8086 or 8088 with the IBC.

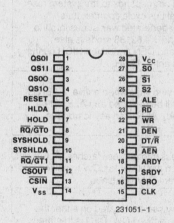

Figure 1.
82188 Pin Configuration

231051–1

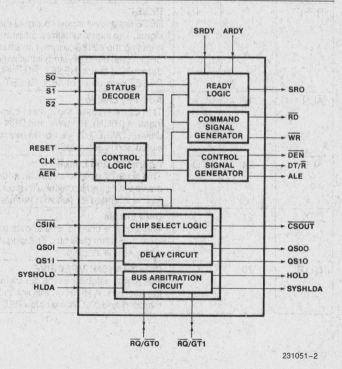

231051–2

Figure 2.
82188 Block Diagram

August 1989
Order Number: 231051-005

PIN DESCRIPTIONS

Symbol	Pin No.	Type	Name and Function
S̄0̄ S̄1̄ S̄2̄	27 26 25	I	**Status Input Pins** S̄0̄–S̄2̄ correspond to the status pins of the CPU. The 82188 uses the status lines to detect and identify the processor bus cycles. The 82188 decodes S̄0̄–S̄2̄ to generate the command and control signals. S̄0̄–S̄2̄ are also used to insert 3 wait states into the SRO line during the first 256 80186 bus cycles after RESET. A HIGH input on all three lines indicates that no bus activity is taking place. The status input lines contain weak internal pull-up devices.

S̄2̄	S̄1̄	S̄0̄	Bus Cycle Initiated
0	0	0	interrupt acknowledge
0	0	1	read I/O
0	1	0	write I/O
0	1	1	halt
1	0	0	instruction fetch
1	0	1	read data from memory
1	1	0	write data to memory
1	1	1	passive (no bus cycle)

Symbol	Pin No.	Type	Name and Function
CLK	15	I	**CLOCK** CLK is the clock signal generated by the CPU or clock generator device. CLK edges establish when signals are sampled and generated.
RESET	5	I	**RESET** RESET is a level triggered signal that corresponds to the system reset signal. The signal initializes an internal bus cycle counter, thus enabling the 82188 to insert internally generated wait states into the SRO signal during system initialization. The 82188 mode is also determined during RESET. R̄D̄, W̄R̄, and D̄EN̄ are driven HIGH during RESET regardless of ĀEN̄. RESET is active HIGH.
ĀEN̄	19	I	**Address Enable** This signal enables the system command lines when active. If ĀEN̄ is inactive (HIGH), R̄D̄, W̄R̄, and D̄EN̄ will be tri-stated and ALE will be driven LOW (DT/R̄ will not be effected). ĀEN̄ is an asynchronous signal and is active LOW.
ALE	24	O	**Address Latch Enable** This signal is used to strobe an address into address latches. ALE is active HIGH and latch should occur on the HIGH to LOW transition. ALE is intended for use with transparent D-type latches.
D̄EN̄	21	O	**Data Enable** This signal is used to enable data transceivers located on either the local or system data bus. The signal is active LOW. D̄EN̄ is tri-stated when ĀEN̄ is inactive.
DT/R̄	20	O	**Data TRANSMIT/RECEIVE** This signal establishes the direction of data flow through the data transceivers. A HIGH on this line indicates TRANSMIT (write to I/O or memory) and a LOW indicates RECEIVE (Read from I/O or memory).

PIN DESCRIPTIONS (Continued)

Symbol	Pin No.	Type	Name and Function
$\overline{RD}$	23	O	**READ** This signal instructs an I/O or memory device to drive its data onto the data bus. The $\overline{RD}$ signal is similiar to the $\overline{RD}$ signal of the 80186(80188) in Non-Queue-Status Mode. $\overline{RD}$ is active LOW and is tri-stated when $\overline{AEN}$ is inactive.
$\overline{WR}$	22	O	**WRITE** This signal instructs an I/O or memory device to record the data presented on the data bus. The $\overline{WR}$ signal is similiar to the $\overline{WR}$ signal of the 80186(80188) in Non-Queue-Status Mode. $\overline{WR}$ is active LOW and is tri-stated when $\overline{AEN}$ is inactive.
HOLD	7	O	**HOLD** The HOLD signal is used to request bus control from the 80186 or 80188. The request can come from either the 8087 ($\overline{RQ}/\overline{GTO}$) or from the third processor (SYSHOLD). The signal is active HIGH.
HLDA	6	I	**HOLD Acknowledge** 80186 MODE—This line serves to translate the HLDA output of the 80186(80188) to the appropriate signal of the device requesting the bus. HLDA going active (HIGH) indicates that the 80186 has relinquished the bus. If the requesting device is the 8087, HLDA will be translated into the grant pulse of the $\overline{RQ}/\overline{GTO}$ line. If the requesting device is the optional third processor, HLDA will be routed into the SYSHLDA line. This pin also determines the mode in which the 82188 will operate. If this line is HIGH during the falling edge of RESET, the 82188 will enter the 8086 mode. If LOW, the 82188 will enter the 80186 mode. For 8086 mode, this pin should be strapped to V_{CC}.
$\overline{RQ}/\overline{GTO}$	8	I/O	**Request/Grant O** $\overline{RQ}/\overline{GTO}$ is connected to $\overline{RQ}/\overline{GTO}$ of the 8087 Numeric Coprocessor. When initiated by the 8087, $\overline{RQ}/\overline{GTO}$ will be translated to HOLD-HLDA to acquire the bus from the 80186(80188). This line is bidirectional, and is active LOW. $\overline{RQ}/\overline{GTO}$ has a weak internal pull-up device to prevent erroneous request/grant signals.
$\overline{RQ}/\overline{GT}1$	11	I/O	**Request/Grant 1** 80186 Mode—In 80186 Mode, $\overline{RQ}/\overline{GT}1$ allows a third processor to take control of the local bus when the 8087 has bus control. For a HOLD-HLDA type third processor, the 82188's $\overline{RQ}/\overline{GT}1$ line should be connected to the $\overline{RQ}/\overline{GT}1$ line of the 8087. 8086 MODE—In 8086 Mode, $\overline{RQ}/\overline{GT}1$ is connected to either $\overline{RQ}/\overline{GTO}$ or $\overline{RQ}/\overline{GT}1$ of the 8086. $\overline{RQ}/\overline{GT}1$ will start its request/grant sequence when the SYSHOLD line goes active. In 8086 Mode, $\overline{RQ}/\overline{GT}1$ is used to gain bus control from the 8086 or 8088. $\overline{RQ}/\overline{GT}1$ is a bidirectional line and is active LOW. This line has a weak internal pull-up device to prevent erroneous request/grant signals.

PIN DESCRIPTIONS (Continued)

Symbol	Pin No.	Type	Name and Function
SYSHOLD	9	I	**System Hold** 80186 MODE–SYSHOLD serves as a hold input for an optional third processor in an 80186(80188)-8087 system. If the 80186(80188) has bus control, SYSHOLD will be routed to HOLD to gain control of the bus. If the 8087 has bus control, SYSHOLD will be translated to $\overline{RQ/GT}1$ to gain control of the bus. 8086 MODE–SYSHOLD serves as a hold input for a coprocessor in an 8086 or 8088 system. SYSHOLD is translated to $\overline{RQ/GT}1$ of the 82188 to allow the coprocessor to take control of the bus. SYSHOLD may be an asynchronous signal.
SYSHLDA	10	O	**System Hold Acknowledge** SYSHLDA serves as a hold acknowledge line to the processor or coprocessor connected to it. The device connected to the SYSHOLD-SYSHLDA lines is allowed the bus when SYSHLDA goes active (HIGH).
SRDY	17	I	**Synchronous Ready** The SRDY input serves the same function as SRDY of the 80186(80188). The 82188 combines SRDY with ARDY to form a synchronized ready output signal (SRO). SRDY must be synchronized external to the 82188 and is active HIGH. If tied to V_{CC}, SRO will remain active (HIGH) after the first 256 80186 cycles following RESET. If only ARDY is to be used, SRDY should be tied LOW.
ARDY	18	I	**Asynchronous Ready** The ARDY input serves the same function as ARDY of the 80186(80188). ARDY may be an asynchronous input, and is active HIGH. Only the rising edge of ARDY is synchronized by the 82188. The falling edge must be synchronized external to the 82188. If connected to V_{CC}, SRO will remain active (HIGH) after the first 256 80186 bus cycles following RESET. If only SRDY is to be used, ARDY should be connected LOW.
SRO	16	O	**Synchronous READY Output** SRO provides a synchronized READY signal which may be interfaced directly with the SRDY of the 80186(80188) and READY of the 8087. The SRO signal is an accumulation of the synchronized ARDY signal, the SRDY signal, and the internally generated wait state signal.
QS0I QS1I	1 2	I	**Queue-Status Inputs** QS0I, QS1I are connected to the Queue-Status lines of the 80186(80188) to allow synchronization of the queue-status signals to 8087 timing requirements.
QS0O QS1O	3 4	O	**Queue-Status Outputs** QS0O, QS1O are connected to the queue-status pins of the 8087. The signals produced meet 8087 Queue-Status input requirements.

PIN DESCRIPTIONS (Continued)

Symbol	Pin No.	Type	Name and Function
$\overline{\text{CSIN}}$	13	I	**Chip-Select Input** $\overline{\text{CSIN}}$ is connected to one of the chip-select lines of the 80186(80188). $\overline{\text{CSIN}}$ informs the 82188 that a bank select is taking place. The 82188 routes this signal to the chip-select output ($\overline{\text{CSOUT}}$). $\overline{\text{CSIN}}$ is active LOW. This line is not used when memory and I/O device addresses are decoded external to the 80186(80188).
$\overline{\text{CSOUT}}$	12	O	**Chip-Select Output** This signal is used as a chip-select line for a bank of memory devices. It is active when $\overline{\text{CSIN}}$ is active or when the 8087 has bus control. $\overline{\text{CSOUT}}$ is active LOW.

FUNCTIONAL DESCRIPTION

BUS CONTROLLER

The 82188 Integrated Bus Controller (IBC) generates system control and command signals. The signals generated are determined by the Status Decoding Logic. The bus controller logic interprets status lines $\overline{S0}$–$\overline{S2}$ to determine what type of bus cycle is taking place. The appropriate signals are then generated by the Command and Control Signal Generators.

The Address Enable ($\overline{\text{AEN}}$) line allows the command and control signals to be disabled. When $\overline{\text{AEN}}$ is inactive (HIGH), the command signals and $\overline{\text{DEN}}$ will be tri-stated, and ALE will be held low (DT/$\overline{\text{R}}$ will be uneffected). $\overline{\text{AEN}}$ inactive will allow other systems to take control of the bus. Control and command signals respond to a change in the $\overline{\text{AEN}}$ signal within 40 ns.

The command signals consist of $\overline{\text{RD}}$ and $\overline{\text{WR}}$. The 82188's $\overline{\text{RD}}$ and $\overline{\text{WR}}$ signals are similiar to $\overline{\text{RD}}$ and $\overline{\text{WR}}$ of the 80186(80188) in the non-Queue-Status Mode. These command signals do not differentiate between memory and I/O devices. $\overline{\text{RD}}$ and $\overline{\text{WR}}$ can be conditioned by $\overline{S2}$ of the 80186(80188) to obtain separate signals for I/O and memory devices. $\overline{\text{RD}}$ is asserted during INTA cycles, unlike $\overline{\text{RD}}$ on the 80186(80188).

The control commands consist of Data Enable ($\overline{\text{DEN}}$), Data Transmit/Receive (DT/$\overline{\text{R}}$), and Address Latch Enable (ALE). The control commands are similiar to those generated by the 80186(80188). $\overline{\text{DEN}}$ determines when the external bus should be enabled onto the local bus. DT/$\overline{\text{R}}$ determines the direction of the data transfer, and ALE determines when the address should be strobed into the latches (used for demultiplexing the address bus). DT/$\overline{\text{R}}$ does not go to an inactive (high) state at the end of bus cycles, unlike DT/$\overline{\text{R}}$ on the 80186(80188).

MODE SELECT

The 82188 Integrated Bus Controller (IBC) is configurable. The device has two modes: 80186 Mode and 8086 Mode. Selecting the mode of the device configures the Bus Arbitration Logic (see BUS ARBITRATION section for details). In 80186 Mode, the 82188 IBC may be used as a bus controller/interface device for an 80186(80188), 8087, and optional third processor system. In 8086 Mode, the 82188 IBC may be used as an interface device allowing a maximum mode 8086(8088) to interface with a coprocessor that uses a HOLD-HLDA bus exchange protocol.

The mode of the 82188 is determined during RESET. If the HLDA line is LOW at the falling edge of RESET (as in the case when tied to the HLDA line of the 80186 or 80188), the 82188 will enter into 80186 Mode. If the HLDA line is HIGH at the falling edge of RESET, the 82188 will enter 8086 Mode. In 8086 Mode, only the Bus Arbitration Logic is used. The eight pins used in 8086 Mode are: SYSHOLD, SYSHLDA, HLDA, CLK, RESET, $\overline{\text{RQ}}$/$\overline{\text{GT}}$1, V_{CC}, and V_{SS}. The other pins may be left unconnected.

BUS ARBITRATION

The Bus Exchange Logic interfaces up to three sets of bus exchange signals:

- HOLD-HLDA
- SYSHOLD-SYSHLDA
- $\overline{\text{RQ}}$/$\overline{\text{GT}}$0 ($\overline{\text{RQ}}$/$\overline{\text{GT}}$1)

This logic executes translating, routing, and arbitrating functions. The logic translates HOLD-HLDA signals to $\overline{\text{RQ}}$/$\overline{\text{GT}}$ signals and $\overline{\text{RQ}}$/$\overline{\text{GT}}$ signals to HOLD-HLDA signals. The logic also determines which set of bus exchange signals are to be interfaced. The mode of the 82188 and the priority of the devices requesting the bus determine the routing of the bus exchange signals.

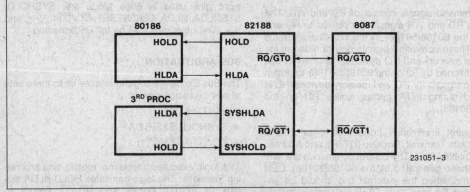

80186 MODE

In 80186 Mode, a system may have three potential bus masters: the 80186 or 80188 CPU, the 8087 Numerics Coprocessor, and a third processor (such as the 82586 LAN or 82730 Text Coprocessor). The third processor may have either a HOLD-HLDA or $\overline{RQ}/\overline{GT}$ bus exchange protocol. The possible bus exchange signal connections and paths for 80186 Mode are shown in Figures 3 & 4 and Tables 1 & 2, respectively. If no HOLD-HLDA type third processor is used, SYSHOLD should be tied LOW to prevent an erroneous SYSHOLD signal. In 80186 mode, the bus priorities are:

Highest Priority . . . . Third Processor
Second Highest Priority 8087
Default Priority 80186

— THREE-PROCESSOR SYSTEM OPERATION (HOLD-HLDA TYPE THIRD PROCESSOR)

In the configuration shown in Figure 3, the third processor requests the bus by sending SYSHOLD HIGH. The 82188 will route (and translate if necessary) the request to the current bus master. This includes routing the request to HOLD if the 80186(80188) is the current bus master or routing and translating the request to $\overline{RQ}/\overline{GT}1$ if the 8087 is in control of the bus. The third processor's request is not passed through the 8087 if the 80186 is the bus master (see Table 1).

The 8087 requests the bus using $\overline{RQ}/\overline{GT}0$. The request pulse from the 8087 will be translated and routed to HOLD if the 80186 is the bus master. If the third processor has control of the bus, the grant pulse to the 8087 will be delayed until the third processor relinquishes the bus (sending SYSHOLD LOW). In this case, HOLD will remain HIGH during the third processor-to-8087 bus control transfer. The 80186 will not be granted the bus until both coprocessors have released it.

Table 1. Bus Exchange Paths (80186 Mode) (HOLD-HLDA Type 3rd Proc)

Requesting Device	Current Bus Master		
	80186	8087	3rd Proc
80186	n/a	n/a	n/a
8087	$\overline{RQ}/\overline{GT}0 \longleftrightarrow \frac{HOLD}{HLDA}$	n/a	n/a
3rd Proc	$\frac{SYSHOLD}{SYSHLDA} \longleftrightarrow \frac{HOLD}{HLDA}$	$\frac{SYSHOLD}{SYSHLDA} \longleftrightarrow \overline{RQ}/\overline{GT}1$	n/a

**Figure 3.
Bus Exchange Signal Connections (80186 Mode) for a Three Local Processor System
(HOLD-HLDA Type 3rd Proc)**

Table 2. Bus Exchange Paths (80186 Mode) ($\overline{RQ}/\overline{GT}$ Type 3rd Proc)

Requesting Device	Current Bus Master		
	80186	8087	3rd Proc
80186	n/a	n/a	n/a
8087	$\overline{RQ}/\overline{GT}0 \longleftrightarrow \dfrac{\text{HOLD}}{\text{HLDA}}$	n/a	n/a
3rd Proc	$\overline{RQ}/\overline{GT}1 \longleftrightarrow \overline{RQ}/\overline{GT}0 \longleftrightarrow \dfrac{\text{HOLD}}{\text{HLDA}}$	$\overline{RQ}/\overline{GT}1$	n/a

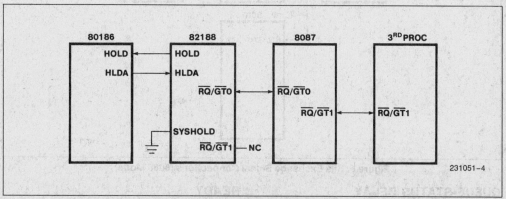

231051–4

Figure 4.
Bus Exchange Signal Connections (80186 Mode) for a Three Local Processor System
($\overline{RQ}/\overline{GT}$ Type 3rd Proc)

When the bus is requested from the 80186(80188), a bus priority decision is made. This decision is made when the HLDA line goes active. Upon receipt of the HLDA signal, the highest-priority requesting device will be acknowledged the bus. For example, if the 8087 initially requested the bus, the bus will be granted to the third processor if SYSHOLD became active before HLDA was received by the 82188. In this case, the grant pulse to the 8087 will be delayed until the third processor relinquishes the bus.

— THREE-PROCESSOR SYSTEM OPERATION ($\overline{RQ}/\overline{GT}$ TYPE THIRD PROCESSOR)

In the configuration shown in Figure 4, the third processor requests the bus by initiating a request/grant sequence with the 8087's $\overline{RQ}/\overline{GT}1$ line. The 8087 will grant the bus if it is the current bus master or will pass the request on if the 80186 is the current bus master (see Table 2). In this configuration, the 82188's Bus Arbitration Logic translates $\overline{RQ}/\overline{GT}0$ to HOLD-HLDA. The 8087 provides the bus arbitration in this configuration.

8086 MODE

The 8086 Mode allows an 8086, 8088 system to contain both $\overline{RQ}/\overline{GT}$ and HOLD-HLDA type coprocessors simultaneously. In 8086 Mode, two possible bus masters may be interfaced by the 82188; an 8086 or 8088 CPU and a coprocessor which uses a HOLD-HLDA bus exchange protocol (typically an 82586 LAN Coprocessor or an 82730 Text Coprocessor). The bus exchange signal connections for 8086 Mode are shown in Figure 5. Bus arbitration signals used in the 8086 Mode are:

- $\overline{RQ}/\overline{GT}1$
- SYSHOLD
- SYSHLDA

In 8086 Mode, no arbitration is necessary since only two devices are interfaced. The coprocessor has bus priority over the 8086(8088). SYSHOLD-SYSHLDA are routed and translated directly to $\overline{RQ}/\overline{GT}1$. $\overline{RQ}/\overline{GT}1$ of the 82188 may be tied to either $\overline{RQ}/\overline{GT}0$ or $\overline{RQ}/\overline{GT}1$ of the 8086(8088).

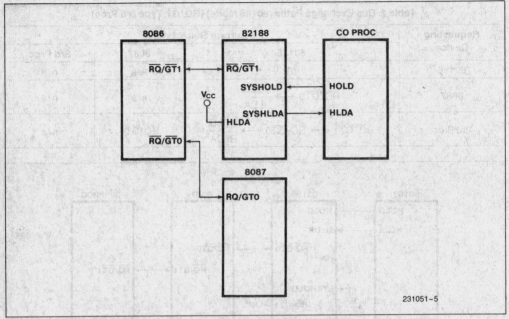

231051-5

Figure 5. Bus Exchange Signal Connections (8086 Mode)

QUEUE-STATUS DELAY

The Queue-Status Delay logic is used to delay the queue-status signals from the 80186(80188) to meet 8087 queue-status timing requirements. QS0I, QS1I correspond to the queue-status lines of the 80186(80188). The 82188 delays these signals by one clock phase. The delayed signals are interfaced to the 8087 queue-status lines by QS0O, QS1O.

CHIP-SELECT

The Chip-Select Logic allows the utilization of the chip select circuitry of the 80186(80188). Normally, this circuitry could not be used in an 80186(80188)-8087 system since the 8087 contains no chip select circuitry. The Chip-Select Logic contains two external connections: Chip-Select Input ($\overline{CSIN}$) and Chip-Select Output ($\overline{CSOUT}$). $\overline{CSOUT}$ is active when either $\overline{CSIN}$ is active or when the 8087 has control of the bus.

By using $\overline{CSOUT}$ to select memory containing data structures, no external decoding is necessary. The 80186 may gain access to this memory bank through the $\overline{CSIN}$ line while the 8087 will automatically obtain access when it becomes the bus master. Note that this configuration limits the amount of memory accessible by the 8087 to the physical memory bank selected by $\overline{CSOUT}$. Systems where the 8087 must access the full 1 Megabyte address space must use an external decoding scheme.

READY

The Ready logic allows two types of Ready signals: a Synchronous Ready Signal (SRDY) and an Asynchronous Ready Signal (ARDY). These signals are similiar to SRDY and ARDY of the 80186. Wait states will be inserted when both SRDY and ARDY are LOW. Inserting wait states allows slower memory and I/O devices to be interfaced to the 80186(80188)-8087 system.

ARDY's LOW-to-HIGH transition is synchronized to the CPU clock by the 82188. The 82188 samples ARDY at the beginning of T2, T3 and Tw until sampled HIGH. Note that ARDY of the 82188 is sampled one phase earlier than ARDY of the 80186. ARDY's falling edge must be synchronous to the CPU clock. ARDY allows an easy interface with devices that emit an asynchronous ready signal.

The SRDY signal allows direct interface to devices that emit a synchronized ready signal. SRDY must be synchronized to the CPU clock for both of its transitions. SRDY is sampled in the middle of T2, T3 and in the middle of each Tw. An 82188-80186(80188)'s SRDY setup time is 30 ns longer than the 80186(80188)'s SRDY setup time. SRDY eliminates the half-clock cycle penalty necessary for ARDY to be internally sychronized.

The sychronized ready output (SRO) is the accumulation of SRDY, ARDY, and the internal wait-state generator. SRO should be connected to SRDY of the 80186(80188) (with 80186(80188)'s ARDY tied LOW), and READY of the 8087.

SRDY	ARDY	SRO
0	0	0
1	X	1
X	1	1

The internal wait state generator allows for synchronization between the 80186(80188) and 8087 in 80186 mode. Upon RESET, the 82188 automatically inserts 3 wait-states per 80186(80188) bus cycle, overlapped with any externally produced wait-states created by ARDY and SRDY.

Since the 8087 has no provision for internal wait-state generation, only externally created wait states will be effective. The 82188, upon RESET, will inject 3 wait states for each of the first 256 80186(80188) bus cycles onto the SRO line. This will allow the 8087 to match the 80186(80188)'s timing.

The internally-generated wait states are overlapped with those produced by the SRDY and ARDY lines. Overlapping the injected wait states insures a minimum of three wait states for the first 256 80186(80188) bus cycles after RESET. Systems with a greater number of wait states will not be affected. Internal wait state generation by the 82188 will stop on the 256th 80186(80188) bus cycle after RESET. To maintain sychronization between the 80186(80188) and 8087, the following conditions are necessary:

- The 80186(80188)'s control block must be mapped in I/O space before it is written to or read from.

- All memory chip-select lines must be set to 0 WAIT STATES, EXTERNAL READY ALSO USED within the first 256 80186(80188) bus cycles after RESET.

An equivalent READY logic diagram is shown in Figure 6.

SYSTEM CONSIDERATIONS

In any 82188 configuration, clock compatibility must be considered. Depending on the device, a 50% or a 33% duty-cycle clock is needed. For example, the 80186 and 80188 (as well as the 82188, 82586, and 82730) requires a 50% duty-cycle clock. The 8086, 8088 and their 'kit' devices' (8087, 8089, 82C88, and 8289) clock requirements, on the other hand, require a 33% duty-cycle clock signal. The system designer must make sure clock requirements of all the devices in the system are met.

Figure 7 demonstrates the usage of the 82188 in 80186 Mode where it is used to interface an 8087 into an 80186 system. In this case, the clock requirements of the 8087 are met by specifying the 10 MHz (8087-1) device, but clocking the system at a maximum rate of 8 MHz.

Status bit six (S6) from the main processor (8086, 8088, 80186, or 80188) is used by the 8087 to track the instruction flow. S6 is multiplexed with address bit 19 (A19). If the third processor generates only 16 bits of address, S6 is not generated. A19/S6 must be driven high by external circuitry during the status portion of bus cycles controlled by the third processor.

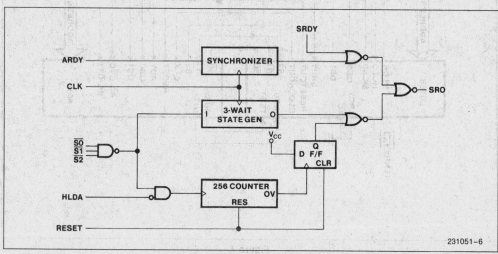

Figure 6. Equivalent 82188 READY Circuit

231051–6

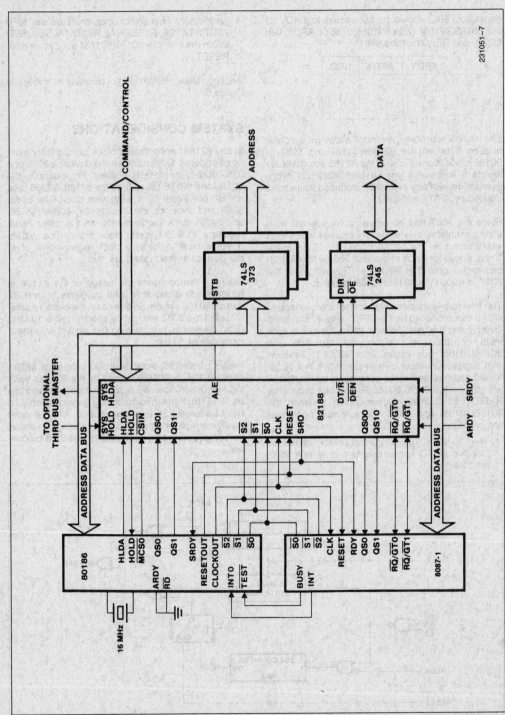

Figure 7.
80186/8087-1 System Using the 82188 in 80186 Mode

ABSOLUTE MAXIMUM RATINGS *

Temperature Under Bias . . . . 0°C to 70°C

Storage Temperature. . . . . −65°C to 150°C

Case Temperature . . . . 0°C to +85°C

Voltage on any Pin with
Respect to GND . . . . −1.0V to 7.0V

Power Dissipation . . . . 0.7 Watts

*Notice: Stresses above those listed under "Absolute Maximum Ratings" may cause permanent damage to the device. This is a stress rating only and functional operation of the device at these or any other conditions above those indicated in the operational sections of this specification is not implied. Exposure to absolute maximum rating conditions for extended periods may affect device reliability.

DC CHARACTERISTICS

(V_{CC} = 5V ± 10%, T_A = 0°C to 70°C, T_{CASE} = 0°C to +85°C)

Symbol	Parameter	Min	Max	Units	Test Cond.
V_{IL}	Input Low Voltage	−0.5	+0.8	volts	
V_{IH}	Input High Voltage	2.0	V_{CC} + 0.5	volts	
V_{OL}	Output Low Voltage		0.45	volts	I_{OL} = 2 mA
V_{OH}	Output High Voltage	2.4		volts	I_{OH} = −400 μA
I_{CC}	Power Supply Current		100	mA	T_A = 25°C
I_{LI}	Input Leakage Current		±10	μA	$0V < V_{IN} < V_{CC}$
I_{LO}	Output Leakage Current		±10	μA	$0.45 < V_{OUT} < V_{CC}$
V_{CLI}	CLK Input Low Voltage	−0.5	+0.6	volts	
V_{CHI}	CLK Input High Voltage	3.9	V_{CC} +1.0	volts	
C_{IN}	Input Capacitance		10	pF	
C_{IO}	I/O Capacitance		20	pF	

AC CHARACTERISTICS

(V_{CC} = 5V ± 10%, T_A = 0°C to 70°C, T_{CASE} = 0°C to +85°C)

TIMING REQUIREMENTS

Symbol	Parameter	Min	Max	Units	Notes
TCLCL	Clock Period	125	500	ns	
TCLCH	Clock LOW Time	½TCLCL-7.5		ns	
TCHCL	Clock HIGH Time	½TCLCL-7.5		ns	
TARYHCL	ARDY Active Setup Time	20		ns	
TCHARYL	ARDY Hold Time	15		ns	8
TARYLCH	ARDY Inactive Setup Time	35		ns	
TSRYHCL	SRDY Input Setup Time	65,50		ns	1
TSVCH	STATUS Active Setup Time	55		ns	
TSXCL	STATUS Inactive Setup Time	50		ns	
TQIVCL	QS0I, QS1I Setup Time	15		ns	
THAVGV	HLDA Setup Time	50		ns	
TSHVCL	SYSHOLD Asynchronous Setup Time	25		ns	
TGVCH	$\overline{RQ}/\overline{GT}$ Input Setup Time	0		ns	6

TIMING RESPONSES

Symbol	Parameter	Min	Max	Units	Notes
TSVLH	STATUS Valid to ALE Delay		30	ns	4
TCHLL	ALE Inactive Delay		30	ns	
TCLML	RD, WR Active Delay	10	70	ns	
TCLMH	RD, WR Inactive Delay	10	55	ns	
TSVDTV	STATUS to DT/R Delay		30	ns	3
TCLDTV	DT/R Active Delay		55	ns	3
TCHDNV	DEN Active Delay	10	55	ns	
TCHDNX	DEN Inactive Delay	10	55	ns	
TCLQOV	QS0O, QS1O Delay	5	50	ns	
TCHHV	HOLD Delay		50	ns	2,6
TCLSAV	SYSHLDA Delay		50	ns	6
TCLGV	RQ/GT Output Delay		40	ns	6
TGVHV	RQ/GT0 To HOLD Delay		50	ns	2,6
TCLLH	ALE Active Delay		30	ns	4
TAELCV	Command Enable Delay		40	ns	
TAEHCX	Command Disable Delay		40	ns	
TCHRO	SRO Output Delay	5	30	ns	5,6
TSRYHRO	SRDY To SRO Delay		30	ns	5
TCSICSO	CSIN To CSOUT Delay		30	ns	
TCLCSOV	CLK Low to CSOUT Delay	10		ns	
TCLCSOH	CLK Low to CSOUT Inactive Delay	10		ns	

NOTES (applicable to both spec listing and timing diagrams):
1. TSRYHOL = (80186's) TSRYCL + 30 ns = 65 ns for 6 MHz operation and 50 ns for 8 MHz operation.
2. Timing not tested.
3. DT/R will be asserted to the latest of TSVDTV & TCLDTV.
4. ALE will be asserted to the latest of TSVLH & TCLLH.
5. SRO will be asserted to the latest of TCHRO & TSRYHRO.
6. CL = 20–100 pF
7. Address/Data bus shown for reference only.
8. The falling edge of ARDY must be synchronized to CLK.

A.C. TESTING INPUT, OUTPUT WAVEFORM

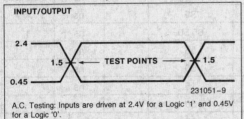

A.C. Testing: Inputs are driven at 2.4V for a Logic '1' and 0.45V for a Logic '0'.

A.C. TESTING LOAD CIRCUIT

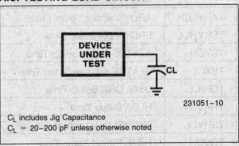

CL includes Jig Capacitance
CL = 20–200 pF unless otherwise noted

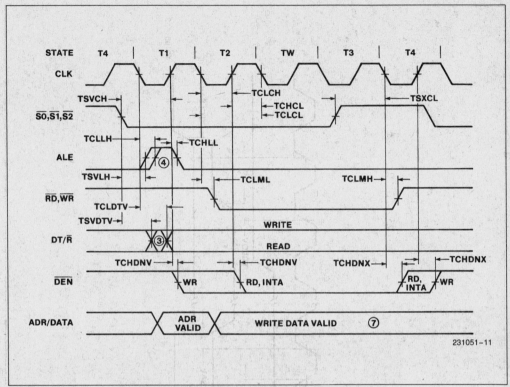

Command and Control Waveforms–80186 Mode

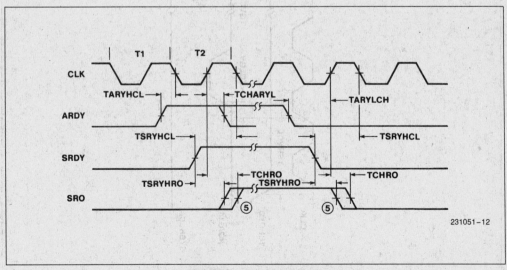

READY Timing–80186 Mode

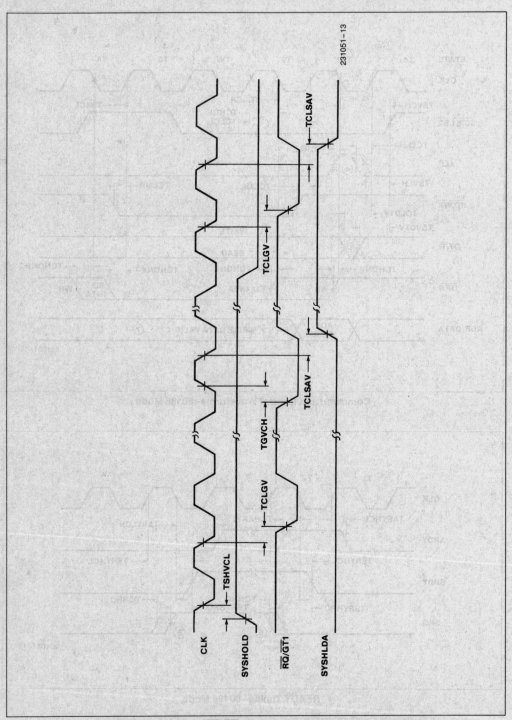

231051–13

SYSHOLD-SYSHLDA to $\overline{RQ}/\overline{GT}1$ Timing–80186 Mode and 8086 Mode

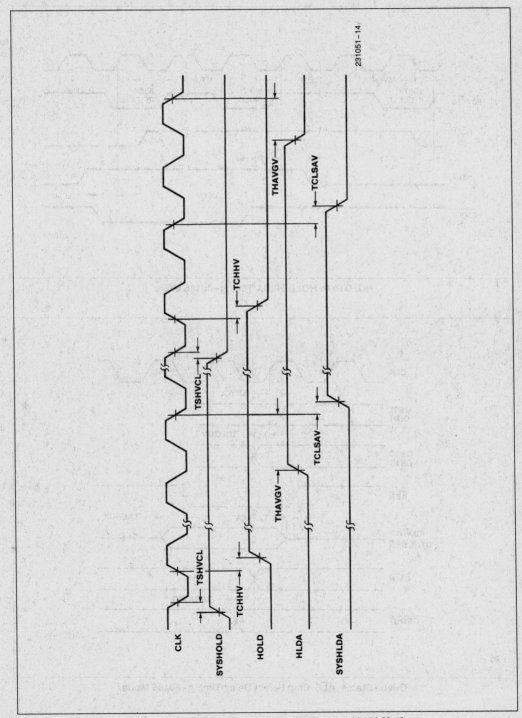

231051−14

SYSHOLD-SYSHLDA To HOLD-HLDA Timing−80186 Mode

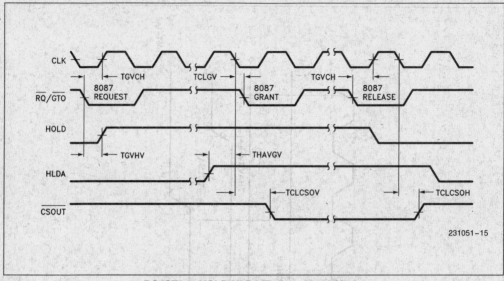

RQ/GT0 to HOLD-HLDA Timing–80186 Mode

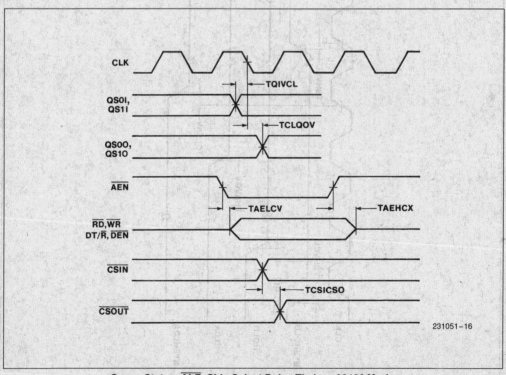

Queue Status, ALE, Chip Select Delay Timing–80186 Mode

REVISION HISTORY

The sections significantly revised since version -004 are:

Bus Controller   Added note describing $\overline{RD}$ during $\overline{INTA}$ and DT/$\overline{R}$ compared to the 80186/80188.

System Considerations   Use of 82188 with 80186 and 8087-1, all at 8 MHz, is clarified.

The sections significantly revised since version -002 are:

AC Characteristics T_{QIVCL} (min.) changed from 10 ns to 15 ns. Minimum timings for T_{CLML}, T_{CLMH}, and T_{CHDNV} changed from 0 ns to 10 ns. T_{CHDNX} (min.) changed from 5 ns to 10 ns. Minimum timings or T_{SVDTV}, T_{CLDTV}, and T_{CLLH} are no longer indicated (they were 0 ns). T_{CLCSOV} and T_{CLCSOH} added.

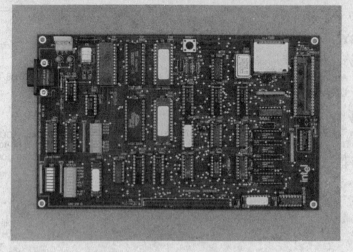

LOW COST CODE EVALUATION TOOL

Intel's EV80C186 evaluation board provides a hardware environment for code execution and software debugging at a relatively low cost. The board features the 80C186 advanced, CHMOS, 16-bit data controller, the highest performance member of the industry standard 80186 family. The board allows you to take full advantage of the power of the 80186 family. The EV80C186 provides zero wait-state, 12.5 MHz execution of your code. Plus, it can be quickly reconfigured to use an 80C188, 80186 or 80188, allowing for exact analysis of code execution speeds in a particular application.

Popular features such as single-step program execution and sixteen software breakpoints are standard on the EV80C186. Intel provides a complete code development environment using assembler (ASM-86) as well as high-level languages such as Intel's iC-86, FORTRAN-86, Pascal-86 or PL/M-86 to accelerate development schedules.

The evaluation board is hosted on an IBM PC* or BIOS-compatible clone, already a standard development solution in most of today's engineering environments. The source code for the on-board monitor (written in ASM-86) is public domain. The program is about 2K, and can be modified to be included in your target hardware. In this way, the provided PC host software can be used throughout the development phase.

EV80C186 FEATURES

- Zero Wait-State 12.5 MHz Execution Speed
- 16K Bytes of SRAM/ROMsim
- DRAM Sockets and Control Logic
- CMOS, low-power board
- Concurrent Interrogation of Memory and Registers
- Sixteen Software Breakpoints
- Two Single-Step Modes
- High-Level Language Support
- RS-232-C Communication Link

FULL SPEED EXECUTION

The EV80C186 executes your code from on-board ROMsim at 12.5 MHz with zero wait-states. By changing oscillators on the 80C186, any execution speed up to 16 MHz can be evaluated. The boards host interface baud-rate is not affected by this crystal change.

16K BYTES OF ROMSIM

The board comes with 16K bytes of SRAM to be used as ROMsim for your code and for data memory as needed. This memory is configured as sixteen bits wide. If you are using an 80188/80C188, the lower byte is actually a 32K x 8 SRAM, providing 32K bytes for your application.

DRAM SOCKETS AND CONTROL LOGIC

The EV80C186 comes with sockets ready for 512K bytes of DRAM; the necessary control logic is already there. Also, if you are using an 80C186 or 80C188, the monitor will set up the DRAM refresh controller for you.

TOTALLY CMOS BOARD

The EV80C186 board is built totally with CMOS components. Its power consumption is therefore low, requiring 5 volts at 400 mA. The board also requires +/- 12 volts at 15 mA.

CONCURRENT INTERROGATION OF MEMORY AND REGISTERS

The monitor for the EV80C186 allows you to read and modify external memory and read internal registers while your code is running in the board. You may only modify internal registers while your code is halted.

SIXTEEN SOFTWARE BREAKPOINTS

There are sixteen breakpoints available which automatically substitute an INT3 instruction for your code instruction at the breakpoint location. The substitution occurs when execution is started. If processor is halted or a breakpoint is reached, your code is restored in the ROMsim.

TWO STEP MODES

There are two single-step modes available. The first stepping mode uses the Trap Flag feature of the '86 architecture. The second mode also uses the Trap Flag except for subroutine calls which are treated as one indivisible instruction by placing an INT3 after them.

HIGH LEVEL LANGUAGE SUPPORT

The host software for the EV80C186 board is able to load absolute object code generated by ASM-86, iC-86, FORTRAN-86, Pascal-86 or PL/M-86, all of which are available from Intel.

RS-232-C COMMUNICATION LINK

The EV80C186 communicates with the host using an Intel 82510 UART provided on board.

PERSONAL COMPUTER REQUIREMENTS

The EV80C186 Evaluation Board is hosted on an IBM PC, XT, AT or BIOS-compatible clone. The PC must meet the following minimum requirements:

- **512K Bytes of Memory**
- **One 360K Byte floppy Disk Drive**
- **PC DOS 3.1 or Later**

- **A Serial Port (COM1 or COM2) at 9600 Baud**
- **ASM-86, iC-86, FORTRAN-86, Pascal-86 or PL/M-86**
- **A text editor such as AEDIT**

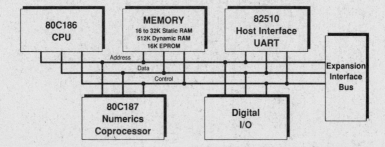

80186 Development Support Tools

2

COMPLETE SOFTWARE DEVELOPMENT SUPPORT FOR THE 8086/80186 FAMILY OF MICROPROCESSORS

Intel supports application development for the 8086/80186 family of microprocessors (8086, 8088, 80186, 80188 and real mode 80286 and 80386 designs) with a complete set of development languages and utilities. These tools include a macro assembler and compilers for C, PL/M, FORTRAN and Pascal. A linker/relocator program, library manager, numerics support libraries, and object-to-hex utility are also available. Intel software tools generate fast and efficient code. They are designed to give maximum control over the processor. Most importantly, they are designed to get your application up and running in an embedded system fast and with maximum design productivity.

FEATURES

- Macro assembler for speed-critical code
- NEW windowed, interactive source level debugger works with all Intel languages
- ANSI Compatible iC-86 package for structured C programming, with many processor specific extensions
- PL/M compiler for high-level language programs with support for many low-level hardware functions
- FORTRAN for ANSI-compatible, numeric intensive applications
- Pascal for developing modular, portable applications that are easy to maintain
- Linker program for linking modules generated by Intel compilers and assemblers

- Locator for generating programs with absolute addresses for execution from ROM based systems
- AEDIT Source Code and text editor
- Library manager for creating and maintaining object module libraries
- Complete numeric support libraries including a software emulator for the 8087
- Object-to-hex conversion utility for burning code into (E)PROMS
- Hosted on IBM PC XT/AT* or compatibles running DOS, DEC VAX* or MicroVAX* systems running VMS, and Intel Systems 86/3XX or 286/3XX running iRMX® Operating System

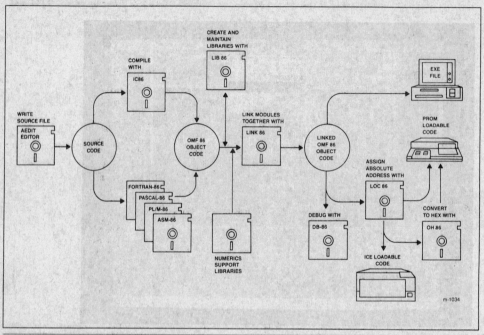

Figure 1: The Application Development Process

ASM-86 MACRO ASSEMBLER

ASM-86 is the macro assembler for the 8086/80186 family of components. It is used to translate symbolic assembly language source into relocatable object code where utmost speed, small code size and hardware control are critical. Intel's exclusive macro facility in ASM-86 saves development and maintenance time, since common code sequences need only be developed once. The assembler's simplified instruction set reduces the number of mnemonics that the programmer needs to remember. This assembler also saves development time by performing extensive checks on consistent usage of variables and labels. Inconsistencies are detected when the program is assembled, before linking or debugging is started.

NEW FOR 1989: SOURCE LEVEL DEBUGGER

DB-86 is an on-host software execution environment with source level debug capabilities for object modules produced by iC-86, ASM-86, PL/M-86, Pascal-86 and FORTRAN-86. Its powerful, source-oriented interface allows users to focus their efforts on finding bugs rather than spending time learning and manipulating the debug environment.

- **Ease of learning.** Drop-down menus make the tool easy to learn for new or casual users. A command line interface is also provided for more complex problems.
- **Extensive debug modes.** Watch windows, conditional breakpoints (breakpoints triggered by program conditions), trace points, and fixed and temporary breakpoints can be set and modified as needed.
- **See into your program.** You can browse source and call stack, observe processor registers, output screen, and watch window variables accessed by either the pull down menu or by a single keystroke using function keys.
- **Full debug symbolics for maximum productivity.** The user need not know whether a variable is an unsigned integer, a real, or a structure; the debugger utilizes the wealth of variable typing information available in Intel languages to display program variables in their respective type formats.
- **Support for overlaid programs and the numeric coprocessor.**

iC-86 SOFTWARE PACKAGE

Intel's iC-86 brings the full power of the C programming language to 8086, 8088, 80186 and 80188-based microprocessor systems. It can also be used to develop real mode programs for execution on the 80286 or 80386. iC-86 has been developed specifically for embedded microprocessor-based applications. iC-86 meets the draft proposed ANSI C standard. Key features of the iC-86 compiler include:

- **Highly Optimized.** Four levels of optimization are available. Important optimization features include a jump optimizer and improved register manipulation via register history.

- **ROMable Code and Libraries.** The iC-86 compiler produces ROMable code which can be loaded directly into embedded target systems. Libraries are also completely ROMable, retargetable and reentrant.

- **Supports Small, Medium, Compact, and Large memory segmentation models.**

- **Symbolics.** The iC-86 compiler boosts programming productivity by providing extensive debug information, including type information and symbols. The symbolics information can be used to debug using Intel ICE™ emulators and the new DB-86 Source level debugger.

- **Built-in functions.** iC-86 is loaded with built-in functions. The flags register, I/O ports, interrupts, and numerics chip can be controlled directly, without the need for assembly language coding. You spend more of your productive time programming in C and less with Assembler. Built-in functions also improve compile-time and run-time performance since the compiler generates in-line code instructions instead of function calls to assembly instructions.

- **Standard Language.** iC-86 conforms to the 1988 Draft Proposed ANSI standard for the C language. iC-86 code is fully linkable with other modules written in other Intel 8086/186 languages, allowing programmers to use the optimal language for any task.

PL/M-86 SOFTWARE PACKAGE

PL/M-86 is a high-level programming language designed to support the software requirements of advanced 16-bit microprocessors. PL/M-86 provides the productivity advantages of a high-level language while providing the low-level hardware access features of assembly language. Key features of PL/M-86 include:

- **Structured programming.** PL/M-86 supports modular and structured programming, making programs easier to understand, maintain and debug.

- **Built-in functions.** PL/M-86 includes an extensive list of functions, including TYPE CONVERSION functions, STRING manipulations, and functions for interrogating 8086/186 hardware flags.

- **Interrupt handling.** The INTERRUPT attribute allows you to define interrupt handling procedures. The compiler generates code to save and restore all registers for INTERRUPT procedures.

- **Compiler controls.** Compile-time options increase the flexibility of the PL/M-86 compiler. They include: optimization, conditional compilation, the inclusion of common PL/M source files from disk, cross-reference of symbols, and optional assembly language code in the listing file.

- **Data types.** PL/M-86 supports seven data types, allowing the compiler to perform three different kinds of arithmetic: signed, unsigned and floating point.

- **Language compatibility.** PL/M-86 object modules are compatible with all other object modules generated by Intel 8086/186 languages.

FORTRAN-86 SOFTWARE PACKAGE

FORTRAN-86 meets the ANSI FORTRAN 77 Language Subset Specification and includes almost all of the features of the full standard. This compatibility assures portability of existing FORTRAN programs and shortens the development process, since programmers are immediately productive without retraining.

FORTRAN-86 provides extensive support for numeric processing tasks and applications, with features such as:

- Support for single, double, double extended precision, complex, and double complex floating-point data types
- Support for proposed REALMATH IEEE floating point standard
- Full support for all other data types: integer, logical and character
- Optional hardware (8087 numeric data processor) or software (simulator) floating-point support at link time

PASCAL-86 SOFTWARE PACKAGE

Pascal-86 conforms to the ISO Pascal standard, facilitating application portability, training and maintenance. It has also been enhanced with microcomputer support features such as interrupt handling, direct port I/O and separate compilation.

A well-defined and documented run-time operating system interface allows the user to execute applications under user-designed operating systems as an alternate to the development system environment. Program modules compiled under Pascal-86 are compatible and linkable with modules written in other Intel 8086/186 languages, so developers can implement each module in the language most appropriate for the task at hand.

Pascal-86 object modules contain symbol and type information for program debugging using Intel ICE™ emulators and the DB-86 debugger.

LINK-86 LINKER

Intel's LINK-86 utility is used to combine multiple object modules into a single program and resolve references between independently compiled modules. The resulting linked module can be either a bound load-time-locatable module or simply a relocatable module. A .EXE option allows modules to be generated which can be executed directly on a DOS system.

LINK-86 greatly increases productivity by allowing you to use modular programming. The incremental link capability allows new modules to be easily added to existing software. Because applications can be broken into separate modules, they're easier to design, test and maintain. Standard modules can be reused in different applications, saving software development time.

LOC-86 LOCATOR

The LOC-86 utility changes relocatable 8086/186 object modules into absolute object modules. Its default address assignment algorithm will automatically assign absolute addresses to the object modules prior to loading of the code into the target system. This frees you from concern about the final arrangement of the object code in memory. You still have the power to override the control and specify absolute addresses for various Segments, Classes, and Groups in memory. You may also reserve various parts of memory.

LOC-86 is a powerful tool for embedded development because it simplifies set up of the bootstrap loader and initialization code for execution from ROM based systems. The locator will also optionally generate a print file containing diagnostic information to assist in program debugging.

NUMERICS SUPPORT LIBRARY

The Numerics Support Library greatly facilitates the use of floating-point calculations from programs written in Assembler, PL/M, and C. It adds to these languages many of the functions that are built into applications programming languages, such as Pascal and FORTRAN. A full 8087 software emulator and interface libraries are included for precision floating point calculations without the use of the 8087 component. The decimal conversion library aids the translation between decimal and binary formats. A Common Elementary Function library provides support for transcendental, rounding and other common functions, not directly handled by the numeric processor. An Error Handler Module makes it easy to write interrupt routines that recover from floating-point error conditions.

LIB-86 LIBRARIAN

The Intel LIB-86 utility creates and maintains libraries of software object modules. Standard modules can be placed in a library and linked to your application using the LINK-86 utility.

AEDIT SOURCE CODE AND TEXT EDITOR

AEDIT is a full-screen text editing system designed specifically for software engineers and technical writers. With the facilities for automatic program block indentation, HEX display and input, and full macro support, AEDIT is an essential tool for any programming environment. And with AEDIT, the output file is the pure ASCII text (or HEX code) you input—no special characters or proprietary formats.

Dual file editing means you can create source code and its supporting documents at the same time. Keep your program listing with its errors in the background for easy reference while correcting the source in the foreground. Using the split-screen windowing capability, it is easy to compare two files, or copy text from one to the other. The DOS system-escape command eliminates the need to leave the editor to compile a program, get a directory listing, or execute any other program executable at the DOS system level.

OH-86 OBJECT-TO-HEXADECIMAL CONVERTER

The OH-86 utility converts Intel 8086/186 object modules into standard hexadecimal format, allowing the code to be loaded directly into PROM using industry standard PROM programmers.

SERVICE, SUPPORT AND TRAINING

Intel augments its 8086/186 family development tools with a full array of seminars, classes and workshops. In addition, on-site consulting services, field application engineering expertise, telephone hotline support, and software and hardware maintenance contracts are available to help assure your design success.

ORDERING INFORMATION

D86ASM86NL	ASM-86	Assembler for PC XT or AT system (or compatible) running DOS 3.0 or higher
VVSASM86	ASM-86	Assembler for VAX/VMS
MVVSASM86	ASM-86	Assembler for MicroVAX/VMS
R86ASM86SU	ASM-86	Assembler for Intel 86/3XX systems running iRMX 86 operating system
R286ASM86EU	ASM-86	Assembler for Intel 286/3XX systems running iRMX II™ operating system
Note:		ASM-86 includes Macro Assembler, Link-86, Loc-86, Lib-86, Cross-Reference utility, OH-86, Numerics Support, and DB-86 Source Level Debugger. (DB-86 available in DOS version only.)
D86C86NL	iC-86	Software Package for IBM PC XT/AT running PC DOS 3.0 or higher
VVSC86	iC-86	Software Package for VAX/VMS
MVVSC86	iC-86	Software Package for MicroVAX/VMS
R86C86SU	iC-86	Software Package for Intel System 8086/3XX running iRMX 86 operating system
D86PLM86NL	PL/M-86	Software Package for IBM PC XT/AT running PC DOS 3.0 or higher
VVSPLM86	PL/M-86	Software Package for VAX/VMS
MVVSPLM86	PL/M-86	Software Package for MicroVAX/VMS
R86PLM86SU	PL/M-86	Software Package for Intel System 8086/3XX running iRMX 86 operating system
D86FOR86NL	FORTRAN-86	Software Package for PC XT/AT (or compatible) running PC-DOS 3.0 or higher
VVSFORT86	FORTRAN-86	Software Package for VAX/VMS 4.3 and later
MVVSFORT86	FORTRAN-86	Software Package for MicroVAX/VMS
R86FOR86SU	FORTRAN-86	Software Package for Intel System 86/3XX running iRMX 86 operating system
D86PAS86NL	PASCAL-86	Software Package for IBM PC XT/AT running PC DOS 3.0 or higher
VVSPAS86	PASCAL-86	Software Package for VAX/VMS
MVVPAS86	PASCAL-86	Software Package for MicroVAX/VMS
R86PAS86SU	PASCAL-86	Software Package for Intel System 86/3XX running iRMX 86
D86EDNL		AEDIT Source Code Editor for IBM PC XT/AT running PC DOS 3.0 or higher

REAL-TIME SOFTWARE ANALYSIS FOR THE 8086/88, 80186/188, 80286, AND 80386

Intel's iPAT™ Performance Analysis Tool enables OEMs developing applications based on the 8086/88, 80186/188, 80286, or 80386 microprocessors to analyze real-time software execution in their prototype systems at speeds up to 20 MHz. Through such analysis, it is possible to speed-tune applications with real-time data, optimize use of operating systems (such as Intel's iRMX® II Real-Time Multitasking Executive for the 80286 and 80386, and iRMK™ Real-Time Multitasking Kernel for the 80386), characterize response characteristics, and determine code execution coverage by real-time test suites. Analysis is performed symbolically, non-intrusively, and in real-time with 100% sampling in the microprocessor prototype environment. iPAT supports analysis of OEM-developed software built using 8086, 80286, and 80386 assemblers and compilers supplied by Intel and other vendors.

All iPAT Performance Analysis Tool products are serially linked to DOS computer systems (such as IBM* PC AT, PC XT, and PS/2* Model 80) to host iPAT control and graphic display software. Several means of access to the user's prototype microprocessor system are supported. For the 80286 (real and protected mode), a 12.5 MHz iPAT-286 probe can be used with the iPATCORE system. For the 8086/88 (MAX MODE designs only), a 10 MHz iPAT-88 probe can be used with the iPATCORE system. iPATCORE systems also can be connected to sockets provided on the ICE™-286 and ICE-186 in-circuit emulators, or interfaced to IICE in-circuit emulators with probes supporting the 8086/88, 80186/188, or 80286. The 20 MHz iPAT™-386™ probe, also supported by the common iPATCORE system, can be operated either in "piggyback" fashion connected to an Intel ICE in-circuit emulator for the Intel386™, or directly connected to a prototype system independent of an ICE. iPAT-386 supports all models of 80386 applications anywhere in the lowest 16 Megabytes of the 80386 linear address space.

iPAT FEATURES

- Up to 20 MHz real-time analysis
- Histograms and analysis tables
- Performance profiles of up to 125 partitions
- Code execution coverage over up to 252K
- Hardware or software interrupt analysis
- Simple use with function keys and graphics
- Use with or without Intel ICEs

MOST COMPLETE REAL-TIME ANALYSIS AVAILABLE TODAY

iPAT Performance Analysis Tools use in-circuit probes containing proprietary chip technology to achieve full sampling in real-time non-intrusively.

MEETS THE REAL-TIME DESIGNER'S NEEDS

The iPAT products include support for interactions between real-time software and hardware interrupts, real-time operating systems, "idle time," and full analysis of real-time process control systems.

SPEED-TUNING YOUR SOFTWARE

By examining iPAT histogram and tabular information about procedure usage (including or not including their interaction with other procedures, hardware, operating systems, or interrupt service routines) for critical functions, the software engineer can quickly pinpoint trouble spots. Armed with this information, bottlenecks can be eliminated by means such as changes to algorithms, recoding in assembler, or adjusting system interrupt priorities. Finally, iPAT can be used to prove the acceptibility of the developer's results.

EFFICIENCY AND EFFECTIVENESS IN TESTING

With iPAT code execution coverage information, product evaluation with test suites can be performed more effectively and in less time. The evaluation team can quickly pinpoint areas of code that are executed or not executed under real-time conditions. By this means, the evaluation team can substantially remove the "black box" aspect of testing and assure 100% hits on the software under test. Coverage information can be used to document testing at the module, procedure, and line level. iPAT utilities also support generation of instruction-level code coverage information.

ANALYSIS WITH OR WITHOUT SYMBOLICS

If your application is developed with "debug" symbolics generated by Intel 8086, 80286, or 80386 assemblers and compilers, iPAT can use them — automatically. Symbolic names also can be defined within the iPAT environment, or conversion tools supplied with the iPAT products can be used to create symbolic information from virtually any vendor's map files for 8086, 80286, and 80836 software tools.

REAL OR PROTECTED MODE

iPAT supports 80286 and 80386 protected mode symbolic information generated by Intel 80286 and 80386 software tools. It can work with absolute addresses, as well as base-offset or selector-offset references to partitions in the prototype system's execution address space.

FROM ROM-LOADED TO OPERATING SYSTEM LOADED APPLICATIONS

The software analysis provided by iPAT watches absolute execution addresses in-circuit in real time, but also supports use of various iPAT utilities to determine the load locations for load-time located software, such as applications running under iRMXII, DOS, Microsoft Windows*, or MS* OS/2.

USE STANDALONE OR WITH ICE

The iPAT-386, iPAT-286, and iPAT-86/88 probes, together with an iPATCORE system, provide standalone software analysis independent of an ICE (in-circuit emulator) system. The iPATCORE system and DOS-hosted software also can be used together with ICE-386, ICE-286, and I²ICE-86/88, 186/188, or 286 in-circuit emulators and DOS-hosted software. Under the latter scenario, the user can examine prototype software characteristics in real-time on one DOS host while another DOS host is used to supply input or test conditions to the protype through an ICE. It also is possible to use an iPATCORE and I²ICE system with integrated host software on a single Intel Series III or Series IV development system or on a DOS computer.

UTILITIES FOR YOUR NEEDS

Various utilities supplied with iPAT products support generation of symbolic information from map files associated with 3rd-party software tools, extended analysis of iPAT code execution coverage analysis data, and convenience in the working environment. For example, symbolics can be generated for maps produced by most software tools, instruction-level code execution information can be produced, and iRMXII-format disks can be read/written in DOS floppy drives to facilitate file transfer.

WORLDWIDE SERVICE AND SUPPORT

All iPAT Performance Analysis Tool products are supported by Intel's worldwide service and support. Total hardware and software support is available, including a hotline number when the need is there.

CONFIGURATION GUIDE

For all of the following application requirements, the iPAT system is supported with iPAT 2.0 (or greater) or iPAT/IICE 1.2 (or greater) host software, as footnoted.

Application Software	Option	iPAT Order Codes	Host System
80386 Embedded	#1	iPAT386DOS1, iPATCORE	DOS
iRMK on 80386	#1	iPAT386DOS, iPATCORE	DOS
iRMXII OS-Loaded or Embedded on 386	#1	iPAT386DOS, iPATCORE	DOS
OS/2-Loaded on 386	#1	iPAT386DOS, iPATCORE	DOS
iRMXII OS-Loaded or Embedded	#1	iPAT286DOS, iPATCORE	DOS
80286 Embedded	#1	iPAT286DOS, iPATCORE	DOS
	#2	ICEPATKIT2	DOS
	#3	IICEPATKIT3	DOS
	#4	IIIPATD, iPATCORE3	DOS4
	#5	IIIPATB, iPATCORE3	Series III4
	#6	IIIPATC, iPATCORE3	Series IV4
DOS OS-Loaded 80286	#1	iPAT286DOS, iPATCORE	DOS
OS/2 OS-Loaded 80286	#1	iPAT286DOS, iPATCORE	DOS
80186/188 Embedded	#1	ICEPATKIT2	DOS
	#2	IICEPATKIT3	DOS
	#3	IIIPATD, iPATCORE3	DOS4
	#4	IIIPATB, iPATCORE3	Series III4
	#5	IIIPATC, iPATCORE3	Series IV4
DOS OS-Loaded 8086/88	#1	iPAT88DOS, iPATCORE	DOS
8086/88 Embedded	#1	iPAT88DOS, iPATCORE	DOS
	#2	IICEPATKIT3	DOS
	#3	IIIPATD, iPATCORE3	DOS4
	#4	IIIPATB, iPATCORE3	Series III4
	#5	IIIPATC, iPATCORE3	Series IV4

Notes:

1. Operable standalone or with ICE-386 (separate product; separate host). iPAT-386 probe connects directly to prototype system socket, or to optional 4 probe-to-socket hinge cable (order code TA386A), or to ICE-386 probe socket.
2. Requires ICE-186 or ICE-286 in-circuit emulator system.
3. Requires IICE in-circuit emulator system.
4. Includes iPAT/IICE integrated software (iPAT/ICE 1.2 or greater), which only supports sequential iPAT and ICE operation on one host, rather than in parallel on two hosts (iPAT 2.0 or greater).

SPECIFICATIONS

HOST COMPUTER REQUIREMENTS

All iPAT Performance Analysis Tool products are hosted on IBM PC AT, PC XT, or PS/2 Model 80 personal computers, or 100% compatibles, and use a serial link for host-to-iPAT communications. At least a PC AT class system is recommended. The DOS host system must meet the following minimum requirements:

- 640K Bytes of Memory
- 360K Byte or 1.2M Byte floppy disk drive
- Fixed disk drive
- A serial port (COM1 or COM2) supporting 9600 baud data transfer
- DOS 3.0 or later
- IBM or 100% compatible BIOS

PHYSICAL DESCRIPTIONS

Unit	Width Inches	Width Cm.	Height Inches	Height Cm.	Length Inches	Length Cm.
iPATCORE	8.25	21.0	1.75	4.5	13.75	35.0
Power Supply	7.75	20.0	4.25	11.0	11.0	28.0
iPAT-386 probe	3.0	7.6	0.50	1.3	4.0	10.1
iPAT-286 probe	4.0	10.2	1.12	2.8	6.0	15.3
iPAT-86 probe	4.0	10.2	1.12	2.8	6.0	15.3
iPATCABLE (to ICE-186/286)	4.0	10.2	.25	.6	36.0	91.4
IIIPATB,C,D (IICE board)	12.0	30.5	12.0	30.5	.5	1.3
Serial cables PC AT/XT PS/2					144.0	370.0

ELECTRICAL CONSIDERATIONS

The iPATCORE system power supply uses an AC power source at 100V, 120V, 220V, or 240V over 47Hz to 63Hz. 2 amps (AC) at 100V or 120V; 1 amp at 220V or 240V.

iPAT-386, iPAT-286 and iPAT-86/88 probes are externally powered, impose no power demands on the user's prototype, and can thus be used to analyze software activity through power down and power up of a prototype system. For ICE-386, ICE-286, ICE-186, and IICE microprocessor probes, see the appropriate in-circuit emulator factsheets.

ENVIRONMENTAL SPECIFICATIONS

Operating Temperature: 10°C to 40°C (50°F to 104°F) ambient

Operating Humidity: Maximum of 85% relative humidity, non-condensing

I²ICE™ IN-CIRCUIT EMULATION SYSTEM

IN-CIRCUIT EMULATOR FOR THE 8086/80186/80286 FAMILY OF MICROPROCESSORS

The I²ICE™ In-Circuit Emulator is a high-performance, cost-effective debug environment for developing systems with the Intel 8086/80186/80286 family of microprocessors. With 10 MHz emulation, a window-oriented user interface, and compatibility with Intel's iPAT™ Performance Analysis Tool, the I²ICE Emulator gives you unmatched speed and control over all phases of hardware/software debug.

FEATURES

- Emulation speeds up to 10 MHz with 8086/88, 80186/188 and 80286 microprocessors
- 8087 and 80287 numeric coprocessor support
- Hosted on IBM PC AT*, AT BIOS, or compatibles
- ICEVIEW™ window-oriented user interface with pull-down menus and context-sensitive help
- Source and symbol display using all Intel languages

- 1K frame bus and execution trace buffer
- Symbolic debugging for flexible access to memory location and program variables
- Flexible breakpointing for quick problem isolation
- Memory expandable to 288K with zero wait states
- Worldwide service and support
- iPAT option for software speed tuning

intel

September, 1989
Order Number: 280800-001

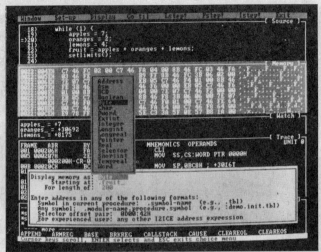

Plate 1. An example of the ICEVIEW™ user interface showing source, memory, watch, and trace.

ONE TOOL FOR THE ENTIRE DEVELOPMENT PROCESS

The I²ICE Emulator allows hardware and software design to proceed simultaneously, so you can develop software even before prototype hardware is available. With 32K of zero wait-state mappable memory (and an additional 256K with optional memory boards), you can use the I²ICE Emulator to debug at any stage of the development cycle: hardware development, software development, system integration or system test.

HIGH-SPEED, REAL-TIME EMULATION

The I²ICE Emulator delivers full-speed, real-time emulation at speeds up to 10 MHz. Based on Intel's exclusive microprocessor technology, the I²ICE Emulator matches each chip's electrical and timing characteristics without memory or interrupt intrusions, ensuring design accuracy and eliminating surprises. The performance of your prototype is the performance you can expect from your final product.

EASY-TO-USE ICEVIEW™ INTERFACE

The ICEVIEW interface makes the I²ICE Emulator easy to learn and use by providing easy access to application information and ICE functions. Pull-down menus and windows boost productivity for both new and experienced users. Multiple on-screen windows allow you to access the source display, execution trace, register, and other important information, all at the same time. You can watch the information change as you modify and step through your program. You can even customize window size and screen positions.

A command line interface is also available with syntax checking and context-sensitive prompts. ICEVIEW works with monochrome, CGA and the latest EGA color displays.

SYMBOLIC DEBUG SPEEDS DEVELOPMENT

The extensive debug symbolics generated by the Intel 8086 and 80286 assemblers and compilers can increase your development productivity. Symbolics with automatic formatting are available for all primitive types, regardless of whether the variables are globals, locals (stack-resident) or pointers. The virtual symbol table supports all symbolics, even in very large programs. Aliasing can be used to reduce keystrokes and save time.

POWERFUL BREAK AND TRACE CAPABILITY FOR FAST PROBLEM ISOLATION

The I²ICE Emulator allows up to eight simultaneous break/trace conditions to be set (four execution, four bus), a timesaver when solving hardware/software integration problems. Break and trace points can be set on specified line numbers, on procedures, or on symbolic data events, such as writing a variable to a value or range of values. You can break or trace on specific hardware events, such as a read or write to a specific address, data or I/O port, or on a combination of events.

MULTIPROCESSOR, PROTECTED MODE, AND COPROCESSOR SUPPORT

Up to four I²ICE systems can be linked and controlled simultaneously from one PC host, enabling you to debug multiprocessor systems. The I²ICE Emulator with an 80286 probe supports all 80286 protected mode capabilities. It also supports the 8087 and 80287 numeric coprocessors.

iPAT™ FOR SOFTWARE PERFORMANCE AND CODE COVERAGE ANALYSIS

The I²ICE Emulator interfaces to Intel's iPAT Performance Analysis Tool for examining software execution speeds and code coverage in real time. iPAT displays critical performance data about your code in easy-to-understand histograms and tables. Elusive bottlenecks are readily seen, allowing you to focus your attention to get the most performance out of your product.

iPAT also performs code execution coverage, letting you perform product evaluations faster and more effectively. iPAT pinpoints areas in your code either executed or not executed according to specific conditions, taking the guesswork out of software evaluations.

EASY INTERFACE TO EXTERNAL INSTRUMENTS

The I²ICE system includes external emulation clips and software support for setting breakpoints, tracepoints and arm/disarm conditions on external events, making it easy to connect external logic analyzers and signal generators. You can debug complex hardware/software interactions with a high level of productivity.

WORLDWIDE SERVICE AND SUPPORT

The I²ICE Emulator is supported by Intel's worldwide service and support organization. In addition to an extended warranty, you can choose from hotline support, on-site systems engineering assistance, and a variety of hands- on training workshops.

SPECIFICATIONS

HOST REQUIREMENTS

IBM PC/AT or 100% PC AT BIOS compatible
DOS 3.1 or later
640K bytes of memory
360K bytes or 1.2 MB floppy disk drive
Hard disk drive
Monochrome, CGA or EGA monitor (EGA recommended)

PHYSICAL DESCRIPTION

Unit	Width		Height		Length	
	cm	in	cm	in	cm	in
I²ICE chassis	43.2	17.0	21.0	8.25	61.3	24.13
Probe base	21.6	8.5	7.6	3.0	25.4	10.0

Host/chassis cable   15 ft. (4.6 m)

ELECTRICAL CHARACTERISTICS

90-132 V or 180-264 V (selectable)
47-63 Hz
12 amps (AC)

ENVIRONMENTAL SPECIFICATIONS

Operating temperature: 0-40°C (32-104°F) ambient
Operating humidity: Maximum of 85% relative humidity, non-condensing

ORDERING INFORMATION

Kit Code	Contents
pIII010KITD	I²ICE system 10 MHz 8086/8088 support kit for IBM PC host. Includes probe, chassis, and host interface module and software.
pIII111KITD	I²ICE system 10 MHz 80186 support kit for IBM PC host. Includes probe, chassis, host interface module and software. Note: For 80188 support, the III198 option below must also be ordered.
III198	10 MHz 80188 support conversion kit to convert 80186 probe to 80188 probe.
pIII212KITD	I²ICE system, 10 MHz 80286 support kit for IBM PC AT host. Includes probe, chassis, host interface module and software.
III010PATC86D	I²ICE system 10 MHz 8086/8088 support kit with iPAT Performance Analysis Tool for PC AT host. Includes I²ICE probe, chassis, host interface module, iPAT tool option, cables and software. Also includes iC-86 compiler, 86 Macro Assembler, utilities, and AEDIT text editor.
III111PATC86D	As above for 10 MHz 80186 support.
III212PATC86D	As above for 10 MHz 80286 support. Note: C-286 and RLL-286 and ASM-286 must be ordered separately.
954D	I²ICE PC AT host software. Includes ICEVIEW™ windowed human interface.

Note: I²ICE probes, chassis, software, cables and iPAT options are available separately.

PROGRAMMER SUPPORT

AEDIT is a full-screen text editing system designed specifically for software engineers and technical writers. With the facilities for automatic program block indentation, HEX display and input, and full macro support, AEDIT is an essential tool for any programming environment. And with AEDIT, the output file is the pure ASCII text (or HEX code) you input—no special characters or proprietary formats.

Dual file editing means you can create source code and its supporting documents at the same time. Keep your program listing with its errors in the background for easy reference while correcting the source in the foreground. Using the split-screen windowing capability, it is easy to compare two files, or copy text from one to the other. The DOS system-escape command eliminates the need to leave the editor to compile a program, get a directory listing, or execute any other program executable at the DOS system level.

There are no limits placed on the size of the file or the length of the lines processed with AEDIT. It even has a batch mode for those times when you need to make automatic string substitutions or insertions in a number of separate text files.

AEDIT FEATURES

- Complete range of editing support—from document processing to HEX code entry and modification
- Supports system escape for quick execution of PC-DOS System level commands
- Full macro support for complex or repetitive editing tasks
- Hosted on PC-DOS and RMX operating systems
- Dual file support with optional split-screen windowing
- No limit to file size or line length
- Quick response with an easy to use menu driven interface
- Configurable and extensible for complete control of the editing process

© Intel Corporation 1989

September, 1989
Order Number: 280804-002

FEATURES

POWERFUL TEXT EDITOR

As a text editor, AEDIT is versatile and complete. In addition to simple character insertion and cursor positioning commands, AEDIT supports a number of text block processing commands. Using these commands you can easily move, copy, or delete both small and large blocks of text. AEDIT also provides facilities for forward or reverse string searches, string replacement and query replace.

AEDIT removes the restriction of only inserting characters when adding or modifying text. When adding text with AEDIT you may choose to either insert characters at the current cursor location, or over-write the existing text as you type. This flexibility simplifies the creation and editing of tables and charts.

USER INTERFACE

The menu-driven interface AEDIT provides makes it unnecessary to memorize long lists of commands and their syntax. Instead, a complete list of the commands or options available at any point is always displayed at the bottom of the screen. This makes AEDIT both easy to learn and easy to use.

FULL FLEXIBILITY

In addition to the standard PC terminal support provided with AEDIT, you are able to configure AEDIT to work with almost any terminal. This along with user-definable macros and full adjustable tabs, margins, and case sensitivity combine to make AEDIT one of the most flexible editors available today.

MACRO SUPPORT

AEDIT will create macros by simply keeping track of the command and text that you type, "learning" the function the macro is to perform. The editor remembers your actions for later execution, or you may store them in a file to use in a later editing session.

Alternatively, you can design a macro using AEDIT's powerful macro language. Included with the editor is an extensive library of useful macros which you may use or modify to meet your individual editing needs.

TEXT PROCESSING

For your documentation needs, paragraph filling or justification simplifies the chore of document formatting. Automatic carriage return insertion means you can focus on the content of what you are typing instead of how close you are to the edge of the screen.

SERVICE, SUPPORT, AND TRAINING

Intel augments its development tools with a full array of seminars, classes, and workshops; on-site consulting services; field application engineering expertise; telephone hot-line support; and software and hardware maintenance contracts. This full line of services will ensure your design success.

SPECIFICATIONS

HOST SYSTEM

AEDIT for PC-DOS has been designed to run on the IBM* PC XT, IBM PC AT, and compatibles. It has been tested and evaluated for the PC-DOS 3.0 or greater operating system.

Versions of AEDIT are available for the iRMX™-86 and RMX II Operating System.

ORDERING INFORMATION

D86EDINL	AEDIT Source Code Editor Release 2.2 for PC-DOS with supporting documentation
122716	AEDIT-DOS Users Guide
122721	AEDIT-DOS Pocket Reference
RMX864WSU	AEDIT for iRMX-86 Operating System
R286EDI286EU	AEDIT for iRMX II Operating System

For direct information on Intel's Development Tools, or for the number of your nearest sales office or distributor, call 800-874-6835 (U.S.). For information or literature on additional Intel products, call 800-548-4725 (U.S. and Canada).

INTEL iC-86/286 COMPILER

The Intel iC-86/286 compiler is the C compiler to use for 8086/186/286 embedded microprocessor designs. In addition to outstanding execution speed, Intel's iC-86/286 compiler generates compact, efficient code which can be easily loaded into ROM-based systems. The iC-86/286 compiler is also fully supported by the Intel DB86 windowed source-level software debugger and in-circuit emulation tools.

iC-86/286 COMPILER FEATURES

- Optimized for embedded systems
- Built-in functions for automatic machine code generation
- ROMable code and libraries
- Integrated debugging with Intel ICE™ and I²ICE™
- Compliance with draft ANSI standard
- Supports Small, Medium, Compact, and Large memory models
- PL/M compatible subsystems
- Selector data type support
- Linkable with other Intel 8086/286 languages such as ASM and PL/M
- ROMable and reentrant libraries
- Ability to mix memory models with "near" and "far" pointers
- C and PL/M calling conventions for compatibility with PL/M and other C programs
- iRMX® interface libraries included

BUILT-IN FUNCTIONS

The iC-86/286 compiler features more than 35 processor-specific functions that directly generate machine code within the C language.

Built-in functions eliminate the need for in-line assembly language coding or making calls to assembly functions. This increases code performance and reduces programming time.

With built-ins you can enable or disable interrupts and directly control hardware I/O without having to exit C for assembler. This means you can write high performance software for real time applications without having to keep track of every architectural detail, as you would in assembly language. For example, to generate an INT instruction, you simply type:

```
causeinterrupt (number)
```

Or, the following iC-86 instruction will cause the processor to come to a halt with interrupts enabled:

```
halt( )
```

EMBEDDED COMPONENT SUPPORT

iC-86/286 compiler was designed specifically for embedded microprocessor applications. It produces ROMable code which can be loaded directly into target systems via Intel ICE emulators and debugged *without modification* for fast, easy, development and debugging.

HIGHLY OPTIMIZED

The iC-86/286 compiler has four levels of optimization for tailoring performance to your application. Important optimization features include a jump optimizer and improved register manipulation using register history.

RUN-TIME SUPPORT

Run-time libraries for the iC-86/286 compiler are designed for use in many environments. Both DOS and iRMX interface libraries are included so programs executing on those systems can take advantage of operating system features. The interface libraries conform to the ANSI standard. They also meet the IEEE standard POSIX interface so you can easily retarget the libraries for use in applications that do not run on DOS or iRMX.

The libraries are completely ROMable and re-entrant making it easy to adapt them for embedded, multi-tasking or real-time applications.

Both the DOS and iRMX-I operating system interface libraries are provided with iC-86 hosted on DOS. The iRMX-I hosted version of iC-86 includes the iRMX interface libraries only.

iC-286 compiler includes iRMX-II interface libraries only.

INTEGRATED DEBUG TOOLS

The iC-86/286 compiler is part of a completely integrated set of development tools from Intel (Fig. 1).

Code output from the compiler can be easily linked with modules written in assembler and high-level languages, such as PL/M, Fortran, and Pascal.

Linked modules and programs can be debugged using Intel's DB86 windowed source-level software debugger. The debugger uses an advanced interface with windows and pull-down menus for the ultimate in debug productivity. Watch windows can be opened to observe changing program variables and processor registers. You can readily switch between program modules and view the calling sequence and call stack.

Intel's DB86 Software Debugger

Naturally code generated by iC-86/286 works completely with Intel's I²ICE, ICE-186, ICE-286 and ICE-386 family of in-circuit emulators as well as the iPAT™ performance analysis tool. This complete set of tools gives you the power to quickly debug, test, integrate and optimize your application code for the target system.

ICE-186, iPAT

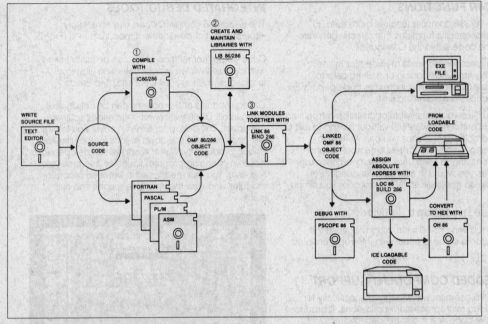

Figure 1: The Application Development Process

SERVICE AND SUPPORT

Intel's development tools are backed by our worldwide service and support organization dedicated to solving any problems encountered by our customers. Several hardware and software service programs are available

which include hotline support, consulting, training, technical newsletters, bulletin boards and other services. The iC-86/286 compiler includes 90 days of software support under warranty.

SPECIFICATIONS

ENVIRONMENT

Hardware Requirements	DOS Version:	IBM PC XT or AT (or 100% Compatible) running DOS 3.1 or greater.
	iRMX Version:	iRMX-I system for iC-86 iRMX-II system for iC-286
Memory Requirements	DOS Version:	256 KB
	iRMX Version:	374 KB
Media	DOS Version:	5¼″ DS/DD Diskettes 3½″ DS/DD Diskettes
	iRMX Version:	DS/DD iRMX Standard Format

STANDARDS

iC-86/286 conforms to the X3J11 ANSI draft proposal for the C programming language.

ORDERING INFORMATION

Order Code	Host Environment	Target Code
D86C86NL	DOS	8086/186
D86C286NL	DOS	80286
R86C86	iRMX-I	8086/186
R286C286	iRMX-II	80286

Other programming tools:

Order Code	Host Environment	Description
D86PAK86NL	DOS	8086/186 Assembler, DB86 Debugger, Utilities AEDIT text editor
D86ASM86KIT	DOS	8086/186 Assembler, DB86 Debugger, Utilities
D86ASM286NL	DOS	80286 Assembler
R86ASM86	iRMX-I	8086/186 Assembler, Utilities
R286ASM286	iRMX-II	80286 Assembler, Utilities
RMXIISFTSCP	iRMX-II	80286 Softscope Debugger

2-18

ICE™-186 IN-CIRCUIT EMULATOR

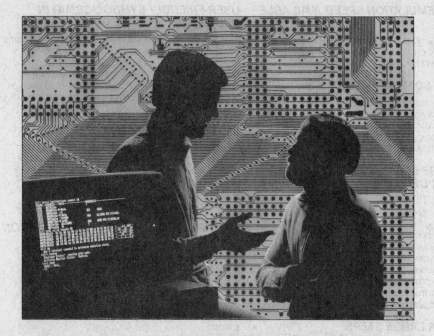

HIGH PERFORMANCE REAL-TIME EMULATION

Intel's ICE-186 emulator delivers real-time emulation for the 80C186 microprocessor at speeds up to 12.5 MHz. The in-circuit emulator is a versatile and efficient tool for developing, debugging and testing products designed with the Intel 80C186 microprocessor. The ICE-186 emulator provides real time, full speed emulation in a user's system. Popular features such as symbolic debug, 2K bytes trace memory, and single-step program execution are standard on the ICE-186 emulator. Intel provides a complete development environment using assembler (ASM86) as well as high-level languages such as Intel's iC86, PL/M86, Pascal 86 and Fortran 86 to accelerate development schedules.

The ICE-186 emulator supports a subset of the 80C186 features at 12.5 MHz and at the TTL level characteristics of the component. The emulator is hosted on IBM's Personal Computer AT, already available as a standard development solution in most of today's engineering environments. The ICE-186 emulator operates in prototype or standalone mode, allowing software development and debug before a prototype system is available. The ICE-186 emulator is ideally suited for developing real-time applications such as industrial automation, computer peripherals, communications, office automation, or other applications requiring the full power of the 12.5 MHz 80C186 microprocessor.

ICE™-186 FEATURES

- Full 12.5 MHz Emulation Speed
- 2K Frames Deep Trace Memory
- Two-Level Breakpoints with Occurrence Counters
- Single-Step Capability
- 128K Bytes Zero Wait-State Mapped Memory
- Supports DRAM Refresh
- High-Level Language Support

- Symbolic Debug
- RS-232-C and GPIB Communication Links
- Crystal Power Accessory
- Interface for Intel Performance Analysis Tool (iPAT)
- Interface for Optional General Purpose Logic Analyzer
- Tutorial Software
- Complete Intel Service and Support

October, 1989
Order Number: 280726-003

HIGHEST EMULATION SPEED AVAILABLE TODAY

The ICE-186 emulator supports development and debug of time-critical hardware and software using Intel's 12.5 MHz 80C186 microprocessor.

RETRACE SOFTWARE TRACKS

This emulator captures up to 2,048 frames of processor activity, including both execution and data bus activity. With this trace memory, large blocks of program code can be traced in real time and viewed for program flow and behavior characteristics.

HARDWARE BREAKPOINTS FOR COMPLEX DEBUG

User-defined "TIL-THEN" breakpoint statements stop emulation at specific execution addresses or bus events. During the hardware and software integration phase, breakpoint statements can be defined as execution addresses and/or bus addresses and/or bus access types such as memory and I/O reads or writes. Additionally, event counters provide another level of breakpoint control for sophisticated state machine constructs used to specify emulation breakpoints/tracepoints.

SMALL OR LARGE STEPS

A stepping command can be used to view program execution one instruction at a time or in preset instruction blocks. When used in conjunction with symbolic debug, code execution can be monitored quickly and precisely.

DEBUG CODE WITHOUT A PROTOTYPE

Even before prototype hardware is available, the ICE-186 emulator working in conjunction with the Crystal Power Accessory (CPA) creates a "virtual" application environment. 128K bytes of zero wait-state memory is available for mapped memory and I/O resource addressing in 4K increments. The CPA provides emulator diagnostics as well as the ability to use the emulator without a prototype.

DON'T LOSE MEMORY

The ICE-186 emulator continues DRAM refresh signals even when emulation has been halted, thus ensuring DRAM memory will not be lost. During interrogation mode the ICE-186 emulator will keep the timers functioning and correctly respond to interrupts in real-time.

HIGH LEVEL LANGUAGE SUPPORT OPTIMIZED FOR INTEL TOOLS

The ICE-186 supports emulation for programs written in Intel's ASM86 or any of Intel's high-level languages:

PL/M-86	Fortran-86
Pascal-86	C-86

These languages are optimized for the Intel 80186/80188 component architectures to deliver a tightly integrated, high performance development environment.

USER-FRIENDLY SYMBOLICS AID IN DEBUG

Symbolics allow access to program symbols by name rather than cumbersome physical addresses. Symbolic debug speeds the debugging process by reducing reliance on memory maps. In a dynamic development process, user variables can be used as parameters for ICE-186 commands resulting in a consistent debug environment.

SUPPORTS FAST BREAKS

"Fastbreaks" is a feature which allows the emulation processor to halt, access memory, and return to emulation as quickly as possible. A fastbreak never takes more than 5625 clock cycles (most types of fastbreaks are considerably less). This feature is particularly useful in embedded applications.

MULTIPLE HIGH-SPEED COMMUNICATION LINKS

Two communication links are available for use in conjunction with the host IBM PC AT. The ICE-186 emulator uses either serial (RS-232-C) or a parallel (GPIB) link. A user supplied National Instruments (IEEE-488) GPIB communication board provides parallel transfers at rates up to 300K bytes per second.

SOFTWARE ANALYSIS (iPAT)

Intel's Performance Analysis Tool (iPAT) is designed to increase team productivity with features like interrupt latency measurement, code coverage analysis and software module performance analysis. These features enable the user to design reliable, high performance embedded control products. The ICE-186 emulator has an external 60 pin connector for iPAT.

BUILT-IN SUPPORT FOR LOGIC ANALYSIS

General-purpose logic analyzers can be used in conjunction with the ICE-186 to provide detailed timing of specific events. The ICE-186 emulator provides an external sync signal for triggering logic analysis, making complex trigger sequence programming easy. An additional 60 pin connector is included for the logic analyzer.

WORLDWIDE SERVICE AND SUPPORT

The ICE-186 emulator is supported by Intel's worldwide service and support organization. Total hardware and software support is available including a hotline number when the need is there.

Note: This emulator does not support use of the 8087.

PERSONAL COMPUTER REQUIREMENTS

The ICE-186 emulator is hosted on an IBM PC AT. The emulator has been tested and evaluated on an IBM PC AT. The PC AT must meet the following minimum requirements:

- 640K Bytes of Memory
- Intel Above Board with at Least 1M Byte of Expansion Memory
- One 360K Bytes or One 1.2M Bytes floppy Disk Drive
- One 20M Bytes Fixed-Disk Drive
- PC DOS 3.2 or Later
- A serial Port (COM1 or COM2) Supporting Minimally at 9600 Baud Data Transfers, or a National Instruments GPIB-PC2A board.
- IBM PC AT BIOS

PHYSICAL DESCRIPTION AND CHARACTERISTICS

The ICE-186 Emulator consists of the following components:

Unit	Width Inches	Width Cm.	Height Inches	Height Cm.	Length Inches	Length Cm.
Emulator Control Unit	10.40	26.40	1.70	4.30	20.70	52.60
Power Supply	7.60	19.00	4.15	10.70	11.00	27.90
User Probe	3.70	9.40	.65	1.60	7.00	17.80
User Cable/ Plcc					22.00	55.90
Hinge Cable					3.40	8.60
Crystal Power Accessory	4.30	10.90	.60	1.50	6.70	17.00
CPA Power Cable					9.00	22.90

ELECTRICAL CONSIDERATIONS

Icc 1050mA
I_{IH} 70μA Max.
I_{IL} −1.5mA Max
I_{OH} −1.0mA Max.

TIMING CONSIDERATIONS

		COMPONENT SPEC Min.	COMPONENT SPEC Max.	ICE-186 SPEC Min.	ICE-186 SPEC Max.
Symbol	Parameter				
TD_{VCL}	Data in Setup (A/D)	15		24	
TA_{RYCH}	Async Ready (ARDY) Resolution Transition Setup Time	15		23	
TS_{RYCL}	Synchronous Ready (SRDY) Transition Setup Time	15		25	
TH_{VCL}	HOLD Setup	15		32	
TI_{NVCH}	NMI	15		32	
	/TEST	15		31	
	INTR,TIMERIN Setup Time	15		17	
TI_{NVCL}	DRQ0, DRQ1, Setup Time	15		19	
TC_{LAZ}	Address Float Delay				
	READ Cycles	TC_{LAX}	25	5	36
	INTA cycles	TC_{LAX}	25	0	25
	HLDA	TC_{LAX}	25	10	50
TL_{HLL}	ALE Width (min)	TC_{LCL}-30		TC_{LCL}-32	
TC_{HLH}	ALE Active Delay*		25		42
(N/A)	CLKOUT Low to ALE Active**	(N/A)			19
TC_{HLL}	ALE Inactive Delay		25		40
TL_{LAX}	Address Hold to ALE Inactive (min)	TC_{HCL}-15		TC_{HCL}-28	
TC_{VCTX}	Control Inactive Delay	5	37	1	40
TA_{ZRL}	Address Float to /RD Active	0		−30	
TA_{VLL}	Address VAlid to ALE Low (min)	TC_{LCH}-15		TC_{LCH}-19	
TC_{HQSV}	Que Status Delay		28		35
TD_{XDL}	/DEN Inactive to DT /R Low	0		−7	
TC_{ICO}	CLKIN to CLKOUT Skew		21		37

ICE-186 User AC Differences

Consult User Guide for Additional Specifications.

*Applies only when the ALEMODE variable is set to START.
**Applies only when the ALEMODE variable is set to END.

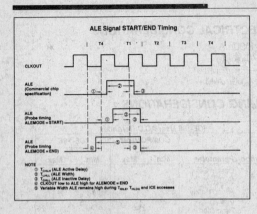

ALE Signal START/END Timing

NOTE
① T$_{CHLH}$ (ALE Active Delay)
② T$_{LHLL}$ (ALE Width)
③ T$_{CHLL}$ (ALE Inactive Delay)
④ CLKOUT low to ALE high for ALEMODE = END
⑤ Variable Width ALE remains high during T$_{DLST}$, T$_{HLDA}$ and ICE accesses

ENVIRONMENTAL SPECIFICATIONS

Operating Temperature 10°C to 40°C Ambient
Storage Temperature −40°C to 70°C

ORDERING INFORMATION

ICE186	ICE-186 System including ICE software (Requires DOS 3.XX PC AT with Above Board)
ICE 186AB	ICE 186 with Above Board included
ICE186IPAT	ICE-186 System including ICE S/W packages and the iPAT system (Requires DOS 3.XX PC AT with Above Board)
D86ASM86NL	86 macro assembler 86 builder/ binder/mapper utilities for DOS 3.XX.
D86C86NL	86 C compiler and run time libraries for DOS 3.XX.
D86PAS86NL	86 Pascal Compiler for DOS 3.XX.
D86PLM86NL	86 PL/M compiler for DOS 3.XX.
D86FOR86NL	86 Fortran compiler for DOS 3.XX.
ICEPAT KIT	iPAT Kit (Performance Analysis Tool) for ICE 186
ICEXONCE	Adapter for on-circuit emulation
ICEXLCC	Adapter for LCC component
ICEXPGA	Adapter for PGA component

ICE™-188 IN-CIRCUIT EMULATOR

HIGH PERFORMANCE REAL-TIME EMULATION

Intel's ICE-188 emulator delivers real-time emulation for the 80C188 microprocessor at speeds up to 12.5 MHz. The in-circuit emulator is a versatile and efficient tool for developing, debugging and testing products designed with the Intel 80C188 microprocessor. The ICE-188 emulator provides real time, full speed emulation in a user's system. Popular features such as symbolic debug, 2K bytes trace memory, and single-step program execution are standard on the ICE-188 emulator. Intel provides a complete development environment using assembler (ASM86) as well as high-level languages such as Intel's iC86, PL/M86, Pascal 86 and Fortran 86 to accelerate development schedules.

The ICE-188 emulator supports a subset of the 80C188 features at 12.5 MHz and at the TTL level characteristics of the component. The emulator is hosted on IBM's Personal Computer AT, already available as a standard development solution in most of today's engineering environments. The ICE-188 emulator operates in prototype or standalone mode, allowing software development and debug before a prototype system is available. The ICE-188 emulator is ideally suited for developing real-time applications such as industrial automation, computer peripherals, communications, office automation, or other applications requiring the full power of the 12.5 MHz 80C188 microprocessor.

ICE™-188 FEATURES

- Full 12.5 MHz Emulation Speed
- 2K Frames Deep Trace Memory
- Two-Level Breakpoints with Occurrence Counters
- Single-Step Capability
- 128K Bytes Zero Wait-State Mapped Memory
- Supports DRAM Refresh
- High-Level Language Support

- Symbolic Debug
- RS-232-C and GPIB Communication Links
- Crystal Power Accessory
- Interface for Intel Performance Analysis Tool (iPAT)
- Interface for Optional General Purpose Logic Analyzer
- Tutorial Software
- Complete Intel Service and Support

© Intel Corporation 1989

October, 1989
Order Number: 280816-001

HIGHEST EMULATION SPEED AVAILABLE TODAY

The ICE-188 emulator supports development and debug of time-critical hardware and software using Intel's 12.5 MHz 80C188 microprocessor.

RETRACE SOFTWARE TRACKS

This emulator captures up to 2,048 frames of processor activity, including both execution and data bus activity. With this trace memory, large blocks of program code can be traced in real time and viewed for program flow and behavior characteristics.

HARDWARE BREAKPOINTS FOR COMPLEX DEBUG

User-defined "TIL-THEN" breakpoint statements stop emulation at specific execution addresses or bus events. During the hardware and software integration phase, breakpoint statements can be defined as execution addresses and/or bus addresses and/or bus access types such as memory and I/O reads or writes. Additionally, event counters provide another level of breakpoint control for sophisticated state machine constructs used to specify emulation breakpoints/tracepoints.

SMALL OR LARGE STEPS

A stepping command can be used to view program execution one instruction at a time or in preset instruction blocks. When used in conjunction with symbolic debug, code execution can be monitored quickly and precisely.

DEBUG CODE WITHOUT A PROTOTYPE

Even before prototype hardware is available, the ICE-188 emulator working in conjunction with the Crystal Power Accessory (CPA) creates a "virtual" application environment. 128K bytes of zero wait-state memory is available for mapped memory and I/O resource addressing in 4K increments. The CPA provides emulator diagnostics as well as the ability to use the emulator without a prototype.

DON'T LOSE MEMORY

The ICE-188 emulator continues DRAM refresh signals even when emulation has been halted, thus ensuring DRAM memory will not be lost. During interrogation mode the ICE-188 emulator will keep the timers functioning and correctly respond to interrupts in real-time.

HIGH LEVEL LANGUAGE SUPPORT OPTIMIZED FOR INTEL TOOLS

The ICE-188 supports emulation for programs written in Intel's ASM86 or any of Intel's high-level languages:

PL/M-86	Fortran-86
Pascal-86	C-86

These languages are optimized for the Intel 80186/80188 component architectures to deliver a tightly integrated, high performance development environment.

USER-FRIENDLY SYMBOLICS AID IN DEBUG

Symbolics allow access to program symbols by name rather than cumbersome physical addresses. Symbolic debug speeds the debugging process by reducing reliance on memory maps. In a dynamic development process, user variables can be used as parameters for ICE-188' commands resulting in a consistent debug environment.

SUPPORTS FAST BREAKS

"Fastbreaks" is a feature which allows the emulation processor to halt, access memory, and return to emulation as quickly as possible. A fastbreak never takes more than 5625 clock cycles (most types of fastbreaks are considerably less). This feature is particularly useful in embedded applications.

MULTIPLE HIGH-SPEED COMMUNICATION LINKS

Two communication links are available for use in conjunction with the host IBM PC AT. The ICE-188 emulator uses either serial (RS-232-C) or a parallel (GPIB) link. A user supplied National Instruments (IEEE-488) GPIB communication board provides parallel transfers at rates up to 300K bytes per second.

SOFTWARE ANALYSIS (iPAT)

Intel's Performance Analysis Tool (iPAT) is designed to increase team productivity with features like interrupt latency measurement, code coverage analysis and software module performance analysis. These features enable the user to design reliable, high performance embedded control products. The ICE-188 emulator has an external 60 pin connector for iPAT.

BUILT-IN SUPPORT FOR LOGIC ANALYSIS

General-purpose logic analyzers can be used in conjunction with the ICE-188 to provide detailed timing of specific events. The ICE-188 emulator provides an external sync signal for triggering logic analysis, making complex trigger sequence programming easy. An additional 60 pin connector is included for the logic analyzer.

WORLDWIDE SERVICE AND SUPPORT

The ICE-188 emulator is supported by Intel's worldwide service and support organization. Total hardware and software support is available including a hotline number when the need is there.

Note: This emulator does not support use of the 8087.

SPECIFICATIONS

PERSONAL COMPUTER REQUIREMENTS

The ICE-188 emulator is hosted on an IBM PC AT. The emulator has been tested and evaluated on an IBM PC AT. The PC AT must meet the following minimum requirements:

- 640K Bytes of Memory
- Intel Above Board with at Least 1M Byte of Expansion Memory
- One 360K Bytes or One 1.2M Bytes floppy Disk Drive
- One 20M Bytes Fixed-Disk Drive
- PC DOS 3.2 or Later
- A serial Port (COM1 or COM2) Supporting Minimally at 9600 Baud Data Transfers, or a National Instruments GPIB-PC2A board.
- IBM PC AT BIOS

PHYSICAL DESCRIPTION AND CHARACTERISTICS

The ICE-188 Emulator consists of the following components:

Unit	Width Inches	Width Cm.	Height Inches	Height Cm.	Length Inches	Length Cm.
Emulator Control Unit	10.40	26.40	1.70	4.30	20.70	52.60
Power Supply	7.60	19.00	4.15	10.70	11.00	27.90
User Probe	3.70	9.40	.65	1.60	7.00	17.80
User Cable/ Plcc					22.00	55.90
Hinge Cable					3.40	8.60
Crystal Power Accessory	4.30	10.90	.60	1.50	6.70	17.00
CPA Power Cable					9.00	22.90

ELECTRICAL CONSIDERATIONS

Icc 1050mA
I_{IH} 70μA Max.
I_{IL} −1.5mA Max
I_{OH} −1.0mA Max.

TIMING CONSIDERATIONS

		COMPONENT SPEC		ICE-188 SPEC	
Symbol	Parameter	Min.	Max.	Min.	Max.
TD_{VCL}	Data in Setup (A/D)	15		24	
TA_{RYCH}	Async Ready (ARDY) Resolution Transition Setup Time	15		23	
TS_{RYCL}	Synchronous Ready (SRDY) Transition Setup Time	15		25	
TH_{VCL}	HOLD Setup	15		32	
TI_{NVCH}	NMI	15		32	
	/TEST	15		31	
	INTR,TIMERIN Setup Time	15		17	
TI_{NVCL}	DRQ0, DRQ1, Setup Time	15		19	
TC_{LAZ}	Address Float Delay				
	READ Cycles	TC_{LAX}	25	5	36
	INTA cycles	TC_{LAX}	25	0	25
	HLDA	TC_{LAX}	25	10	50
TL_{HLL}	ALE Width (min)	TC_{LCL}-30		TC_{LCL}-32	
TC_{HLH}	ALE Active Delay*		25		42
(N/A)	CLKOUT Low to ALE Active**	(N/A)			19
TC_{HLL}	ALE Inactive Delay		25		40
TL_{LAX}	Address Hold to ALE Inactive (min)	TC_{HCL}-15		TC_{HCL}-28	
TC_{VCTX}	Control Inactive Delay	5	37	1	40
TA_{ZRL}	Address Float to /RD Active	0		−30	
TA_{VLL}	Address VAlid to ALE Low (min)	TC_{LCH}-15		TC_{LCH}-19	
TC_{HQSV}	Que Status Delay		28		35
TD_{XDL}	/DEN Inactive to DT /R Low	0		−7	
TC_{ICO}	CLKIN to CLKOUT Skew		21		37

ICE-188 User AC Differences

Consult User Guide for Additional Specifications.

*Applies only when the ALEMODE variable is set to START.
**Applies only when the ALEMODE variable is set to END.

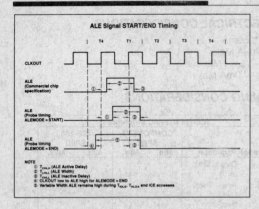

ALE Signal START/END Timing

CLKOUT

ALE
(Commercial chip
specification)

ALE
(Probe timing
ALEMODE = START)

ALE
(Probe timing
ALEMODE = END)

NOTE
① T_CHLH (ALE Active Delay)
② T_LHLL (ALE Width)
③ T_CHLL (ALE Inactive Delay)
④ CLKOUT low to ALE high for ALEMODE = END
⑤ Variable Width ALE remains high during T_IDLE, T_HLDA and ICE accesses

ENVIRONMENTAL SPECIFICATIONS

Operating Temperature 10°C to 40°C Ambient
Storage Temperature −40°C to 70°C

ORDERING INFORMATION

ICE188	ICE-188 System including ICE software (Requires DOS 3.XX PC AT with Above Board)
ICE 188AB	ICE 188 with Above Board included
D86ASM86NL	86 macro assembler 86 builder/binder/mapper utilities for DOS 3.XX.
D86C86NL	86 C compiler and run time libraries for DOS 3.XX.
D86PAS86NL	86 Pascal Compiler for DOS 3.XX.
D86PLM86NL	86 PL/M compiler for DOS 3.XX.
D86FOR86NL	86 Fortran compiler for DOS 3.XX.
ICEPAT KIT	iPAT Kit (Performance Analysis Tool) for ICE 188
ICEXONCE	Adapter for on-circuit emulation
ICEXLCC	Adapter for LCC component
ICEXPGA	Adapter for PGA component
UP188	User probe to convert ICE-186 to support 80C188 component

For direct information on Intel's Development Tools, or for the number of your nearest sales office or distributor, call 800-874-6835 (U.S.). For information or literature on additional Intel products, call 800-548-4725 (U.S. and Canada).

80960KA/KB Product Overview and Data Sheets

80960KA-KB
PRODUCT OVERVIEW

INTRODUCTION

This chapter provides an overview of the Intel 80960KB processor (which is part of the 80960K series of embedded-processor products).

All of the processors in the 80960K series of products are based on the Intel 80960 architecture. Most of the information in this overview also applies to the 80960KA processor. The only difference between the 80960KB and 80960KA processors is that the 80960KA does not provide on-chip support for floating-point operations or operations on decimal numbers.

OVERVIEW OF THE 80960KB ARCHITECTURE

The 80960KB processor introduced the 80960 architecture – a new 32-bit architecture from Intel. This architecture has been designed to meet the needs of embedded applications such as machine control, robotics, process control, avionics, and instrumentation.

The 80960 architecture can best be characterized as a high-performance computing engine. It features high-speed instruction execution and ease of programming. It is also easily extensible, allowing processors and controllers based on this architecture to be conveniently customized to meet the needs of specific processing and control applications.

The following are some of the important attributes of the 80960 architecture:

- Full 32-bit registers
- High-speed, pipelined instruction execution
- A convenient program execution environment with 32 general-purpose registers and a versatile set of special-function registers
- A highly optimized procedure call mechanism that features on-chip caching of local variables and parameters
- Extensive facilities for handling interrupts and faults
- Extensive tracing facilities to support efficient program debugging and monitoring
- Register scoreboarding and write buffering to permit efficient operation when used with lower performance memory subsystems.

OVERVIEW OF THE SINGLE PROCESSOR SYSTEM ARCHITECTURE

The central processing module, memory module, and I/O module form the natural boundaries for the hardware system architecture. The modules are connected together by the high bandwidth 32-bit multiplexed L-bus, which can transfer data at a maximum sustained rate of 53M bytes per second for an 80960 processor operating at 20 MHz.

Figure 1 shows a simplified block diagram of one possible system configuration. The heart of this system is the 80960KB processor, which fetches instructions, executes code, manipulates stored information, and interacts with I/O devices. The high bandwidth L-bus connects the 80960KB processor to memory and I/O modules. The 80960KB processor stores system data, instructions, and programs in the memory module. By accessing various peripheral devices in the I/O module, the 80960KB processor supports communication to terminals, modems, printers, disks, and other I/O devices.

80960KB Processor and the L-Bus

The 80960KB processor performs bus operations using multiplexed address and data signals, and provides all the necessary control signals. For example, standard control signals, such as Address Latch Enable ($\overline{\text{ALE}}$), Address/Data Status ($\overline{\text{ADS}}$), Write/Read Command (W/$\overline{\text{R}}$), Data Transmit/Receive (DT/$\overline{\text{R}}$), and Data Enable ($\overline{\text{DEN}}$), are provided by the 80960KB processor. The 80960 processor also generates byte enable signals that specify which bytes on the 32-bit data lines are valid for the transfer.

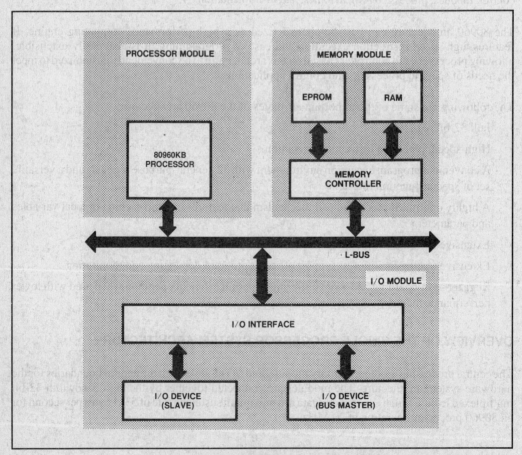

Figure 1. Basic 80960MC System Configuration

The L-bus supports burst transactions, which access up to four data words at a maximum rate of one word per clock cycle. The 80960KB processor uses the two low-order address lines to indicate how many words are to be transferred. The 80960KB processor performs burst transactions to load the on-chip 512-byte instruction cache to minimize memory accesses for instruction fetches. Burst transactions can also be used for data access.

To transfer control of the bus to an external bus master, the 80960KB provides two arbitration signals: hold request (HOLD) and hold acknowledge (HLDA). After receiving HOLD, the processor grants control of the bus to an external master by asserting HLDA.

The 80960KB processor provides a flexible interrupt structure by using an on-chip interrupt controller, an external interrupt controller, or both. The type of interrupt structure is specified by an internal interrupt vector register. For a system with multiple processors, another method is available, called inter-agent communication (IAC) where a processor can interrupt another processor by sending an IAC message.

Memory Module

A memory module can consist of a memory controller, Erasable Programmable Read Only Memory (EPROM), and static or dynamic Random Access Memory (RAM). The memory controller first conditions the L-bus signals for memory operation. It demultiplexes the address and data lines, generates the chip select signals from the address, detects the start of the cycle for burst mode operation, and latches the byte enable signals.

The memory controller generates the control signals for EPROM, SRAM, and DRAM. Specifically, it provides the control signals, multiplexed row/column address, and refresh control for dynamic RAMs. The controller can be designed to accomodate the burst transaction of the 80960KB processor by using the static column mode or nibble mode features of the dynamic RAM. In addition to supplying the operational signals, the controller generates the READY signal to indicate that data can be transferred to or from the 80960KB processor.

The 80960KB processor directly addresses up to 4G bytes of physical memory. The processor does not allow burst accesses to cross a 16-byte boundary, to ease the design of the controller. Each address specifies a four-byte data word within the block. Individual data bytes can be accessed by using the four byte-enable signals from the 80960KB processor. Chapter 5 provides design guidelines for the memory controller.

I/O Module

The I/O module consists of the I/O components and the interface circuit. I/O components can be used to allow the 80960KB processor to use most of its clock cycles for computational and system management activities. Time consuming tasks can be off-loaded to specialized slave-type components, such as the 8259A Programmable Interrupt Controller or the 82530 Serial Communication Controller. Some tasks may require a master-type component, such as the 82586 Local Area Network Control.

The interface circuit performs several functions. It demultiplexes the address and data lines, generates the chip select signals from the address, produces the I/O read or I/O write command from the processor's W/R signal, latches the byte enable signals, and generates the READY signals. Since some of these functions are identical to those of the memory controller, the same logic can be used for both interfaces. For master-type peripherals that operate on a 16-bit data bus, the interface circuit translates the 32-bit data bus to a 16-bit data bus.

The 80960KB processor uses memory-mapped addresses to access I/O devices. This allows the CPU to use may of the same instructions to exchange information for both memory and peripheral devices. Thus, the powerful memory-type instructions can be used to perform 8-, 16-, and 32-bit data transfers.

HIGH PERFORMANCE PROGRAM EXECUTION

Much of the design of the 80960 architecture has been aimed at maximizing the processor's computational and data processing speed through the use of increased parallelism. The following paragraphs describe several of the mechanisms and techniques used to accomplish this goal.

Load and Store Model

One of the more important features of the 80960 architecture is its performance of most operations on operands in registers, rather than in memory. For example, all arithmetic, logic, comparison, branching and bit operations are performed with registers and literals.

This feature provides two benefits. First, it increases program execution speed by minimizing the number of memory accesses necessary to execute a program. Second, it reduces the memory latency encountered when using slower, lower-cost memory parts.

To support this concept, the architecture provides a generous supply of general-purpose registers. For each procedure, 32 registers are available, 28 of which are available for general use. Thse registers are divided into two types: global and local. Both types of registers can be used for general storage of operands. The only difference is that global registers retain their contents across procedure boundaries, whereas the processor allocates a new set of local registers each time a new procedure is called.

The architecture also provides a set of fast, versatile load and store instructions. These instructions allow burst transfers of 1, 2, 4, 8, 12, or 16 bytes of information between memory and the registers.

On-Chip Caching of Code and Data

To further reduce memory accesses, the architecture offers two mechanisms for caching code and data on chip: an instruction cache and multiple sets of local registers. The instruction cache allows prefetching of blocks of instruction from memory. This helps ensure that the instruction execution pipeline is supplied with a steady stream of instructions. It also reduces the number of memory accesses required when performing iterative operations such as loops. The architecture allows the size of the instruction cache to vary. For the 80960KB processor, it is 512 bytes.

To optimize the architecture's procedure call mechanism, the processor provides multiple sets of local registers. This allows the processor to perform procedure calls without having to write the local registers out to the stack in memory. The number of register sets depends on the processor implementation. The 80960KB processor provides four sets of local registers.

Overlapped Instruction Execution

The 80960 architecture also enhances program execution speed by overlapping the execution of some instructions. In the 80960K series of processors, this is accomplished through register scoreboarding.

Register scoreboarding permits instruction execution to continue while data is being fetched from memory. When a load instruction is executed, the processor sets one or more scoreboard bits to indicate the target registers to be loaded. After the target registers are loaded, the scoreboard bits are cleared. While the target registers are being loaded, the processor is allowed to execute other instructions that do not use these registers.

The processor uses the scoreboard bits to ensure that the target registers are not used until the loads complete. (Scoreboard bits are checked transparently from software.) This technique allows code to be executed such that some instructions can be executed in zero clock cycles (that is, executed for free).

Single-Clock Instructions

The 80960 architecture is designed to let a processor execute commonly used instructions, such as moves, adds, subtracts, logical operations, and branches, in a minimum number of clock cycles (preferably one cycle). The architecture supports this concept in several ways. For example, the load and store model described earlier eliminates the clock cycles required to perform memory-to-memory operations, by concentrating on register-to-register operations.

In addition, all of the instructions in the 80960 architecture are 32 bits long and aligned on 32-bit boundaries. This lets instructions be decoded in one clock cycle, and eliminates the need for an instruction-alignment stage in the pipeline.

The 80960KB processor takes full advantage of these features of the architecture, resulting in more than 50 instructions that can be executed in a single clock cycle.

Efficient Interrupt Model

The 80960 architecture provides an efficient mechanism for servicing interrupts from external sources. To handle interrupts, the processor maintains an interrupt table of 248 interrupt vectors, 240 of which are available for general use. When an interrupt is signaled, the processor uses a pointer to the interrupt table to perform an implicit call to an interrupt handler procedure. In performing this call, the processor automatically saves the state of the processor prior to receiving the interrupt, performs the interrupt routine, then restores the state of the processor. A separate interrupt stack is also provided to segregate interrupt handling from application programs.

The interrupt handling facilities also allow interrupts to be evaluated by priority. The processor is then able to store interrupt vectors that are lower in priority than the current processor task in a pending interrupt section of the interrupt table. The processor checks and services the pending interrupts at defined times.

SIMPLIFIED PROGRAMMING ENVIRONMENT

Because of its streamlined execution environment, processors based on the 80960 architecture are particularly easy to program. The following paragraphs describe some of the architecture features that simplify programming.

Highly Efficient Procedure Call Mechanism

The procedure call mechanism makes procedure calls and parameter passing between procedures simple and compact. Each time a call instruction is issued, the processor automatically automatically saves the current set of local registers and allocates a new set for the called procedure. Likewise, on a return from a procedure, the current set of local registers is deallocated and the local registers for the procedure being returned to are restored. This means a program never has to explicitly save and restore those local variables that are stored in local registers.

Versatile Instruction Set and Addressing

The selection of instructions and addressing modes also simplifies programming. A full set of load, store, move, arithmetic, comparison, and branch instructions are provided, with operations on both integer and ordinal data types. Operations on bits and bit strings are simplified by a complete set of Boolean and bit-field instructions.

The addressing modes are efficient and straighforward, while at the same time providing the necessary indexing and scaling modes required to address complex arrays and record structures. The large 4-gigabyte address space provides ample room to store programs and data. The availabilty of 32 addressing lines allows some address lines to be memory-mapped to control hardware functions.

Extensive Fault Handling Capability

To aid in program development, the 80960 architecture defines a wide range of faults that the processor detects, including arithmetic faults, invalid operations, invalid operands, and machine faults. Whan a fault is detected, the processor makes an implicit call call to a fault handler routine, in a way similar to the interrupt mechanism descrbed previously. The information collected for each fault allows program developers to quickly correct faulting code, and allows automatic recovery from some faults.

Debugging and Monitoring

To support debugging systems, the 80960 architecture provides a mechanism for monitoring processor activity by means of trace events. When the processor detects a trace event, it signals a trace fault and calls a fault handler. Intel provides several tools that use this feature, including an in-circuit emulator (ICE) device.

SUPPORT FOR ARCHITECTURAL EXTENSIONS

The 80960 architecture provides several features that enable processors based on this architecture to be easily customized to meet the needs of specific embedded applications, such as signal processing, array processing, or graphics processing.

The most important of these features is the set of 32 special function registers. These registers provide a convenient interface to circuitry in the processor or pins that can be connected to external hardware. They can be used to control timers, to perform operations on special data types, or to perform I/O functions. The special function registers are similar to the global registers. They can be addressed by all of the register access instructions.

EXTENSIONS INCLUDED IN THE 80960K SERIES PROCESSORS

The 80960K series of processors provides a complete implementation of the 80960 architecture, plus several extensions to that architecture. These extensions fall into two categories: floating-point processing and interagent communication.

On-Chip Floating Point

The 80960KB processor provides a complete implementation of the IEEE standard for binary floating-point arithmetic (IEEE 754-185). This implementation includes a full set of floating point operations, including add, subtract, multiply, divide, trigonometric functions, and logarithmic functions. These operations are performed on single precision (32-bit), double precision (64-bit), and extended precision (80-bit) real numbers.

One of the benefits of this implementation is that the floating-point handling facilities are integrated into the normal instruction execution environment. Single and double precision floating-point values are stored in the same registers as non-floating point values. Four 80-bit floating-point registers are provided to hold extended-precision values.

80960KA-KB PRODUCT OVERVIEW

Interagent Communication

All of the processors in the 80960K series provide an interagent communication (IAC) mechanism, allowing agents connected to the processor's bus to communicate with one another. This mechanism operates similarly to the interrupt mechanism, except that IAC messages are passed through dedicated sections of memory. The sort of tasks handled with IAC messages are processor reinitialization, stopping the processor, purging the instruction cache, and forcing the processor to check pending interrupts.

3-8

80960KA
EMBEDDED 32-BIT PROCESSOR

- **High-Performance Embedded Architecture**
  - 25 MIPS Burst Execution at 25 MHz
  - 9.4 MIPS* Sustained Execution at 25 MHz
- **512-Byte On-Chip Instruction Cache**
  - Direct Mapped
  - Parallel Load/Decode for Uncached Instructions
- **Pin Compatible with 80960KB**
- **Multiple Register Sets**
  - Sixteen Global 32-Bit Registers
  - Sixteen Local 32-Bit Registers
  - Four Local Register Sets Stored On-Chip
  - Register Scoreboarding

- **Built-In Interrupt Controller**
  - 32 Priority Levels 256 Vectors
  - Supports 8259A
  - 3.4 μs Latency @ 25 MHz
- **Easy to Use, High Bandwidth 32-Bit Bus**
  - 66.7 MBytes/s Burst
  - Up to 16-Bytes Transferred per Burst
- **4 Gigabyte, Linear Address Space**
- **132-Lead Pin Grid Array (PGA) Package**
- **132-Lead Plastic Quad Flat Pack (PQFP)**
- **Uses 85C960 Bus Controller**
- **Supported by 27C202 and 27960KX Burst EPROMs**

The 80960KA is a member of Intel's new 32-bit processor family, the i960 series, which is designed especially for embedded applications. It is based on the family's high performance, common core architecture, and includes a 512-byte instruction cache and a built-in interrupt controller. The 80960KA has a large register set, multiple parallel execution units, and a high-bandwidth, burst bus. Using advanced RISC technology, this high performance processor is capable of execution rates in excess of 9.4 million instructions per second.* The 80960KA is well-suited for a wide range of embedded applications, including laser printers, image processing, industrial control, robotics, and telecommunications.

*Relative to Digital Equipment Corporation's VAX-11/780** at 1 MIPS

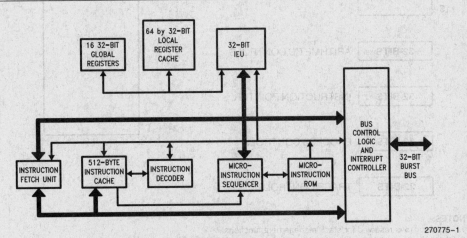

Figure 1. The 80960KA's Highly Parallel Microarchitecture

270775-1

**VAX-11™ is a trademark of Digital Equipment Corporation.

November 1989
Order Number: 270775-001

THE 960 SERIES

The 80960KA is a member of a new family of 32-bit microprocessors from Intel known as the i960 Series. This series was especially designed to serve the needs of embedded applications. The embedded market includes applications as diverse as industrial automation, avionics, image processing, graphics, robotics, telecommunications, and automobiles. These types of applications require high integration, low power consumption, quick interrupt response times, and high performance. Since time to market is critical, embedded microprocessors need to be easy to use in both hardware and software designs.

All members of the 80960 series share a common core architecture which utilizes RISC technology so that, except for special functions, the family members are object code compatible. Each new processor in the series will add its own special set of functions to the core to satisfy the needs of a specific application or range of applications in the embedded market. For example, future processors may include a DMA controller, a timer, or an A/D converter.

Software written for the 80960KA will run without modification on any other member of the 80960 family. It is also pin-compatible with the 80960KB, which includes an integrated floating-point unit, and the 80960MC, a military-grade version with support for multitasking, memory management, multiprocessing, and fault tolerance.

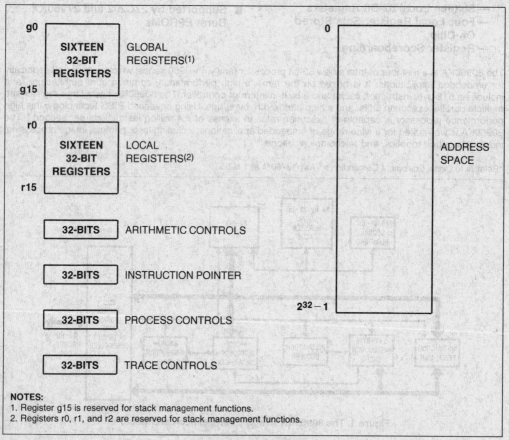

NOTES:
1. Register g15 is reserved for stack management functions.
2. Registers r0, r1, and r2 are reserved for stack management functions.

Figure 2. Register Set

KEY PERFORMANCE FEATURES

The 80960KA's architecture is based on the most recent advances in RISC technology and is grounded in Intel's long experience in designing embedded controllers. Many features contribute to the 80960KA's exceptional performance:

1. Large Register Set. Modern compilers can take advantage of a large number of registers to optimize execution speed. For maximum flexibility, the 80960KA provides 32 32-bit registers and four 80-bit floating-point registers. (See Figure 2.)

2. Fast Instruction Execution. Simple functions make up the bulk of instructions in most programs, so that execution speed can be greatly improved by ensuring that these core instructions execute in as short a time as possible. The most-frequently executed instructions such as register-register moves, add/subtract, logical operations, and shifts execute in one to two cycles (Table 1 contains a list of instructions.)

3. Load/Store Architecture. One way to improve execution speed is to reduce the number of times that the processor must access memory to perform an operation. Like other processors based on RISC technology, the 80960KA has a Load/Store architecture, only the LOAD and STORE instructions reference memory; all other instructions operate on registers.

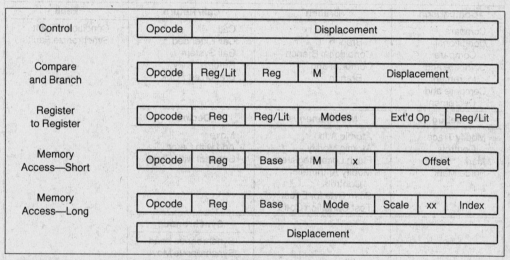

Figure 3. Instruction Formats

Table 1. 80960KA Instruction Set

Data Movement	Arithmetic	Logical	Bit and Bit Field
Load Store Move Load Address	Add Subtract Multiply Divide Remainder Modulo Shift	And Not And And Not Or Exclusive Or Not Or Or Not Nor Exclusive Nor Not Nand Rotate	Set Bit Clear Bit Not Bit Check Bit Alter Bit Scan for Bit Scan over Bit Extract Modify
Comparison	**Branch**	**Call/Return**	**Fault**

Compare
Conditional
  Compare
Compare and
  Increment
Compare and
  Decrement
	Unconditional
	  Branch
	Conditional Branch
	Compare and
	  Branch
		Call
		Call Extended
		Call System
		Return
		Branch and Link
			Conditional Fault
			Synchronize Faults

Debug	**Miscellaneous**	**Decimal**	

Modify Trace
  Controls
Mark
Force Mark
	Atomic Add
	Atomic Modify
	Flush Local Registers
	Modify Arithmetic
	  Controls
	Scan Byte for Equal
	Test Condition Code
		Move
		Add with Carry
		Subtract with Carry	

		Synchronous	
		Synchronous Load Synchronous Move	

4. Simple Instruction Formats. All instructions in the 80960KA are 32-bits long and must be aligned on word boundaries. This alignment makes it possible to eliminate the instruction-alignment stage in the pipeline. To simplify the instruction decoder further, there are only five instruction formats and each instruction uses only one format. (See Figure 3.)

5. Overlapped Instruction Execution. A load operation allows execution of subsequent instructions to continue before the data has been returned from memory, so that these instructions can overlap the load. The 80960KA manages this process transparently to software through the use of a register scoreboard. Conditional instructions also make use of a scoreboard so that subsequent unrelated instructions can be executed while the conditional instruction is pending.

6. Integer Execution Optimization. When the result of an operation is used as an operand in a subsequent calculation, the value is sent immediately to its destination register. Yet at the same time, the value is put back on a bypass path to the ALU, thereby saving the time that otherwise would be required to retrieve the value for the next operation.

7. Bandwidth Optimizations. The 80960KA gets optimal use of its memory bus bandwidth because the bus is tuned for use with the cache: the line size of the instruction cache matches the maximum burst size for instruction fetches. The 80960KA automatically fetches four words in a burst and stores them directly in the cache. Due to the size of the cache and the fact that it is continually filled in anticipation of needed instructions in the program flow, the 80960KA is exceptionally insensitive to memory wait states. In fact, each wait state causes only a 7% degradation in system perfomance. The benefit is that the 80960KA will deliver outstanding performance even with a low cost memory system.

8. Cache Bypass. If there is a cache miss, the processor fetches the needed instruction, then sends it on to the instruction decoder at the same time it updates the cache. Thus, no extra time is taken to load and read the cache.

Memory Space and Addressing Modes

The 80960KA offers a linear programming environment so that all programs running on the processor are contained in a single address space. The maximum size of the address space is 4 Gigabytes (2^{32} bytes).

For ease of use, the 80960KA has a small number of addressing modes, but includes all those necessary

to ensure efficient compiler implementations of high-level languages such as C, Fortran and Ada. Table 2 lists the memory addressing modes.

Data Types

The 80960KA recognizes the following data types:

Numeric:
- 8-, 16-, 32- and 64-bit ordinals
- 8-, 16, 32- and 64-bit integers

Non-Numeric:
- Bit
- Bit Field
- Triple-Word (96 bits)
- Quad-Word (128 bits)

Large Register Set

The programming environment of the 80960KA includes a large number of registers. In fact, 32 registers are available at any time. The availability of this many registers greatly reduces the number of memory accesses required to execute most programs, which leads to greater instruction processing speed.

There are two types of general-purpose registers: local and global. The global registers consist of sixteen 32-bit registers (G0 through G15) These registers perform the same function as the general-purpose registers provided in other popular microprocessors. The term global refers to the fact that these registers retain their contents across procedure calls.

The local registers, on the other hand, are procedure specific. For each procedure call, the 80960KA allocates 16 local registers (R0 through R15). Each local register is 32 bits wide.

Multiple Register Sets

To further increase the efficiency of the register set, multiple sets of local registers are stored on-chip. This cache holds up to four local register frames, which means that up to three procedure calls can be made without having to access the procedure stack resident in memory.

Although programs may have procedure calls nested many calls deep, a program typically oscillates back and forth between only two or three levels. As

Table 2. Memory Addressing Modes

- 12-Bit Offset
- 32-Bit Offset
- Register-Indirect
- Register + 12-Bit Offset
- Register + 32-Bit Offset
- Register + (Index-Register × Scale-Factor)
- Register × Scale Factor + 32-Bit Displacement
- Register + (Index-Register × Scale-Factor) + 32-Bit Displacement

Scale-Factor is 1, 2, 4, 8 or 16

a result, with four stack frames in the cache, the probability of there being a free frame on the cache when a call is made is very high. In fact, runs of representative C-language programs show that 80% of the calls are handled without needing to access memory.

If there are four or more active procedures and a new procedure is called, the processor moves the oldest set of local registers in the register cache to a

procedure stack in memory to make room for a new set of registers. Global register G15 is used by the processor as the frame pointer (FP) for the procedure stack.

Note that the global registers are not exchanged on a procedure call, but retain their contents, making them available to all procedures for fast parameter passing. An illustration of the register cache is shown in Figure 4.

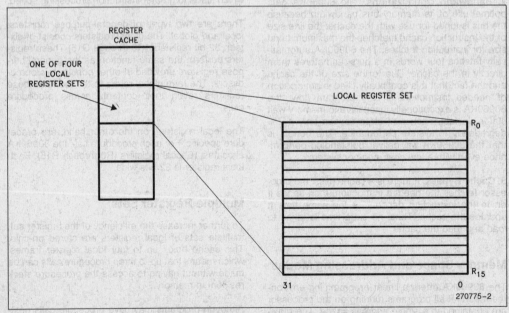

Figure 4. Multiple Register Sets Are Stored On-Chip

Instruction Cache

To further reduce memory accesses, the 80960KA includes a 512-byte on-chip instruction cache. The instruction cache is based on the concept of locality of reference; that is, most programs are not usually executed in a steady stream but consist of many branches and loops that lead to jumping back and forth within the same small section of code. Thus, by maintaining a block of instructions in a cache, the number of memory references required to read instructions into the processor can be greatly reduced.

To load the instruction cache, instructions are fetched in 16-byte blocks, so that up to four instructions can be fetched at one time. An efficient prefetch algorithm increases the probability that an instruction will already be in the cache when it is needed.

Code for small loops will often fit entirely within the cache, leading to a great increase in processing speed since further memory references might not be necessary until the program exits the loop. Similarly, when calling short procedures, the code for the calling procedure is likely to remain in the cache, so it will be there on the procedure's return.

Register Scoreboarding

The instruction decoder has been optimized in several ways. One of these optimizations is the ability to do instruction overlapping by means of register scoreboarding.

Register scoreboarding occurs when a LOAD instruction is executed to move a variable from memory into a register. When the instruction is initiated, a scoreboard bit on the target register is set. When the register is actually loaded, the bit is reset. In between, any reference to the register contents is accompanied by a test of the scoreboard bit to insure that the load has completed before processing continues. Since the processor does not have to wait for the LOAD to be completed, it can go on to execute additional instructions placed in between the LOAD instruction and the instruction that uses the register contents, as shown in the following example:

```
LOAD R4, address 1
LOAD R5, address 2
Unrelated instruction
Unrelated instruction
ADD R4, R5, R6
```

In essence, the two unrelated instructions between the LOAD and ADD instructions are executed for free (i.e., take no apparent time to execute) because they are executed while the register is being loaded. Up to three instructions can be pending at one time with three corresponding scoreboard bits set. By exploiting this feature, system programmers and compilers have a useful tool for optimizing execution speed.

High Bandwidth Local Bus

An 80960KA CPU resides on a high-bandwidth address/data bus known as the local bus (L-Bus). The L-Bus provides a direct communication path between the processor and the memory and I/O subsystem interfaces. The processor uses the local bus to fetch instructions, manipulate memory, and respond to interrupts. Its features include:

- 32-bit multiplexed address/data path
- Four-word burst capability, which allows transfers from 1 to 16 bytes at a time
- High bandwidth reads and writes at 66.7 MBytes per second
- Special signal to indicate whether a memory transaction can be cached

Figure 5 identifies the groups of signals which constitute the L-Bus. Table 4 lists the function of the L-Bus and other processor-support signals, such as the interrupt lines.

Interrupt Handling

The 80960KA can be interrupted in one of two ways: by the activation of one of four interrupt pins or by sending a message on the processor's data bus.

The 80960KA is unusual in that it automatically handles interrupts on a priority basis and tracks pending interrupts through its on-chip interrupt controller. Two of the interrupt pins can be configured to provide 8259A handshaking for expansion beyond four interrupt lines.

Debug Features

The 80960KA has built-in debug capabilities. There are two types of breakpoints and six different trace modes. The debug features are controlled by two internal 32-bit registers, the Process-Controls Word and the Trace-Controls Word. By setting bits in these control words, a software debug monitor can closely control how the processor responds during program execution.

The 80960KA has both hardware and software breakpoints. It provides two hardware breakpoint registers on-chip which can be set by a special command to any value. When the instruction pointer matches the value in one of the breakpoint registers, the breakpoint will fire, and a breakpoint handling routine is called automatically.

The 80960KA also provides software breakpoints through the use of two instructions, MARK and FMARK. These instructions can be placed at any point in a program and will cause the processor to halt execution at that point and call the breakpoint handling routine. The breakpoint mechanism is easy to use and provides a powerful debugging tool.

Tracing is available for instructions (single-step execution), calls and returns, and branching. Each different type of trace may be enabled separately by a special debug instruction. In each case, the 80960KA executes the instruction first and then calls a trace handling routine (usually part of a software debug monitor). Further program execution is halted until the trace routine is completed. When the trace event handling routine is completed, instruction execution resumes at the next instruction. The

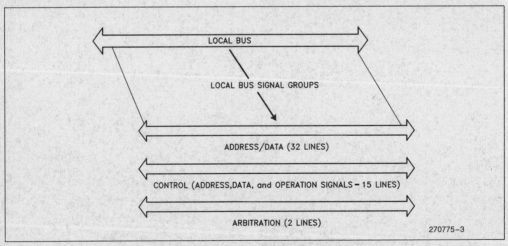

Figure 5. Local Bus Signal Groups

80960KA's tracing mechanisms, which are implemented completely in hardware, greatly simplify the task of testing and debugging software.

FAULT DETECTION

The 80960KA has an automatic mechanism to handle faults. There are ten fault types including trace, arithmetic, and floating-point faults. When the processor detects a fault, it automatically calls the appropriate fault handling routine and saves the current instruction pointer and necessary state information to make efficient recovery possible. The processor posts diagnostic information on the type of fault to a Fault Record. Like interrupt handling routines, fault handling routines are usually written to meet the needs of a specific application and are often included as part of the operating system or kernel.

For each of the ten fault types, there are numerous subtypes that provide specific information about a fault. For example, a floating-point fault may have its subtype set to an Overflow or Zero-Divide fault. The fault handler can use this specific information to respond correctly to the fault.

BUILT-IN TESTABILITY

Upon reset, the 80960KA automatically conducts an extensive internal test (self-test) of its major blocks of logic. Then, before executing its first instruction, it does a zero check sum on the first eight words in memory to ensure that the system has been loaded correctly. If a problem is discovered at any point during the self-test, the 80960KA will assert its FAILURE pin and will not begin program execution. The self-test takes approximately 47,000 cycles to complete.

System manufacturers can use the 80960KA's self-test feature during incoming parts inspection. No special diagnostic programs need to be written, and the test is both thorough and fast. The self-test capability helps ensure that defective parts will be discovered before systems are shipped, and once in the field, the self-test makes it easier to distinguish between problems caused by processor failure and problems resulting from other causes.

CHMOS

The 80960KA is fabricated using Intel's CHMOS IV (Complementary High Speed Metal Oxide Semiconductor) process. This advanced technology eliminates the frequency and reliability limitations of older CMOS processes and opens a new era in microprocessor performance. It combines the high performance capabilities of Intel's industry-leading HMOS technology with the high density and low power characteristics of CMOS. The 80960KA is available at 16, 20 and 25 MHz.

Table 4a. 80960KA Pin Description: L-Bus Signals

Symbol	Type	Name and Function
CLK2	I	**SYSTEM CLOCK** provides the fundamental timing for 80960KA systems. It is divided by two inside the 80960KA to generate the internal processor clock.
LAD_{31} $-LAD_0$	I/O T.S.	**LOCAL ADDRESS/DATA BUS** carries 32-bit physical addresses and data to and from memory. During an address (T_a) cycle, bits 2–31 contain a physical word address (bits 0–1 indicate SIZE; see below). During a data (T_d) cycle, bits 0–31 contain read or write data. The LAD lines are active HIGH and float to a high impedance state when not active. **SIZE,** which is comprised of bits 0–1 of the LAD lines during a T_a cycle, specifies the size of a burst transfer in words. LAD_1 LAD_0 0 0 1 Word 0 1 2 Words 1 0 3 Words 1 1 4 Words
$\overline{ALE}$	O T.S.	**ADDRESS-LATCH ENABLE** indicates the transfer of a physical address. ALE is asserted during a T_a cycle and deasserted before the beginning of the T_d state. It is active LOW and floats to a high impedance state during a hold cycle (T_h or T_{hr}).

I/O = Input/Output, O = Output, I = Input, O.D. = Open-Drain, T.S. = tri-state

Table 4a. 80960KA Pin Description: L-Bus Signals (Continued)

Symbol	Type	Name and Function
$\overline{ADS}$	O, O.D.	**ADDRESS/DATA STATUS** indicates an address state. ADS is asserted every T_a state and deasserted during the following T_d state. For a burst transaction, $\overline{ADS}$ is asserted again every T_d state where $\overline{READY}$ was asserted in the previous cycle.
W/$\overline{R}$	O, O.D.	**WRITE/READ** specifies, during a T_a cycle, whether the operation is a write or read. It is latched on-chip and remains valid during T_d cycles.
DT/$\overline{R}$	O, O.D.	**DATA TRANSMIT/RECEIVE** indicates the direction of data transfer to and from the L-Bus. It is low during T_a and T_d cycles for a read or interrupt acknowledgement; it is high during T_a and T_d cycles for a write. DT/$\overline{R}$ never changes state when $\overline{DEN}$ is asserted (see Timing Diagrams).
$\overline{DEN}$	O, O.D.	**DATA ENABLE** is asserted during T_d cycles and indicates transfer of data on the LAD bus lines.
$\overline{READY}$	I	**READY** indicates that data on LAD lines can be sampled or removed. If $\overline{READY}$ is not asserted during a T_d cycle, the T_d cycle is extended to the next cycle by inserting a wait state (T_W), and $\overline{ADS}$ is not asserted in the next cycle.
$\overline{LOCK}$	I/O, O.D.	**BUS LOCK** prevents other bus masters from gaining control of the L-Bus following the current cycle (if they would assert $\overline{LOCK}$ to do so). $\overline{LOCK}$ is used by the processor or any bus agent when it performs indivisible Read/Modify/Write (RMW) operations. Do not leave $\overline{LOCK}$ unconnected. It must be pulled high for the processor to function properly. For a read that is designated as a RMW-read, $\overline{LOCK}$ is examined. if asserted, the processor waits until it is not asserted; if not asserted, the processor asserts $\overline{LOCK}$ during the T_a cycle and leaves it asserted. A write that is designated as an RMW-write deasserts $\overline{LOCK}$ in the T_a cycle. During the time $\overline{LOCK}$ is asserted, a bus agent can perform a normal read or write but no RMW operations. $\overline{LOCK}$ is also held asserted during an interrupt-acknowledge transaction.
$\overline{BE_3}$–$\overline{BE_0}$	O, O.D.	**BYTE ENABLE LINES** specify which data bytes (up to four) on the bus take part in the current bus cycle. $\overline{BE_3}$ corresponds to LAD_{31}–LAD_{24} and $\overline{BE_0}$ corresponds to LAD_7–LAD_0. The byte enables are provided in advance of data. The byte enables asserted during T_a specify the bytes of the first data word. The byte enables asserted during T_d specify the bytes of the next data word (if any), that is, the word to be transmitted following the next assertion of $\overline{READY}$. The byte enables during the T_d cycles preceding the last assertion of $\overline{READY}$ are undefined. The byte enables are latched on-chip and remain constant from one T_d cycle to the next when $\overline{READY}$ is not asserted. For reads, the byte enables specify the byte(s) that the processor will actually use. L-Bus agents are required to assert only adjacent byte enables (e.g., asserting just $\overline{BE_0}$ and $\overline{BE_2}$ is not permitted), and are required to assert at least one byte enable. To produce address bits A_0 and A_1 externally, they can be decoded from the byte enables.

I/O = Input/Output, O = Output, I = Input, O.D. = Open-Drain, T.S. = tri-state

Table 4a. 80960KA Pin Description: L-Bus Signals (Continued)

Symbol	Type	Name and Function
HOLD/ HLDAR	I	**HOLD:** If the processor is the primary bus master (PBM), the input is interpreted as HOLD, a request from a secondary bus master to acquire the bus. When the processor receives HOLD and grants another master control of the bus, it floats its tri-state bus lines and then asserts HLDA and enters the T_h state. When HOLD is deasserted, the processor will deassert HLDA and go to either the T_i or T_a state. **HOLD ACKNOWLEDGE RECEIVED:** If the processor is a secondary bus master (SBM), the input is HLDAR, which indicates, when HOLDR output is high, that the processor has acquired the bus. Processors and other agents can be told at reset if they are the primary bus master (PBM).
HLDA/ HOLDR	O T.S.	**HOLD ACKNOWLEDGE:** If the processor is a primary bus master, the output is HLDA, which relinquishes control of the bus to another bus master. **HOLD REQUEST:** For secondary bus masters (SBM), the output is HOLDR, which is a request to acquire the bus. The bus is said to be acquired if the agent is a primary bus master and does not have its HLDA output asserted, or if the agent is a secondary bus master and has its HOLD input and HLDA output asserted.
CACHE	O T.S.	**CACHE** indicates if an access is cacheable during a T_a cycle. It is not asserted during any synchronous access, such as a synchronous load or move instruction used for sending an IAC message. The CACHE signal floats to a high impedance state when the processor is idle.

Table 4b. 80960KA Pin Description: Module Support Signals

Symbol	Type	Name and Function
BADAC	I	**BAD ACCESS,** if asserted in the cycle following the one in which the last READY of a transaction is asserted, indicates that an unrecoverable error has occurred on the current bus transaction, or that a synchronous load/store instruction has not been acknowledged. **STARTUP:** During system reset, the BADAC signal is interpreted differently. If the signal is high, it indicates that this processor will perform system initialization. If it is low, another processor in the system will perform system initialization instead.
RESET	I	**RESET** clears the internal logic of the processor and causes it to re-initialize. During RESET assertion, the input pins are ignored (except for BADAC and IAC/INT₀), the tri-state output pins are placed in a high impedance state, and other output pins are placed in their non-asserted state. RESET must be asserted for at least 41 CLK2 cycles for a predictable RESET. The HIGH to LOW transition of RESET should occur after the rising edge of both CLK2 and the external bus CLK, and before the next rising edge of CLK2.
FAILURE	O O.D.	**INITIALIZATION FAILURE** indicates that the processor has failed to initialize correctly. After RESET is deasserted and before the first bus transaction begins, FAILURE is asserted while the processor performs a self-test. If the self-test completes successfully, then FAILURE is deasserted. Next, the processor performs a zero checksum on the first eight words of memory. If it fails, FAILURE is asserted for a second time and remains asserted; if it passes, system initialization continues and FAILURE remains deasserted.
N.C.	N/A	**NOT CONNECTED** indicates pins should not be connected. Never connect any pin marked N.C.

I/O = Input/Output, O = Output, I = Input, O.D. = Open-Drain, T.S. = tri-state

Table 4b. 80960KA Pin Description: Module Support Signals (Continued)

Symbol	Type	Name and Function
$\overline{\text{IAC}}$ $\overline{\text{INT0}}$	I	**INTERAGENT COMMUNICATION REQUEST/INTERRUPT 0** indicates either that there is a pending IAC message for the processor or an interrupt. The bus interrupt control register determines in which way the signal should be interpreted. To signal an interrupt or IAC request in a synchronous system, this pin (as well as the other interrupt pins) must be enabled by being deasserted for at least one bus cycle and then asserted for at least one additional bus cycle; in an asynchronous system, the pin must remain deasserted for at least two bus cycles and then be asserted for at least two more bus cycles. **LOCAL PROCESSOR NUMBER:** This signal is interpreted differently during system reset. If the signal is at a high voltage level, it indicates that this processor is a primary bus master (Local Processor Number = 0); if it is at a low voltage level, it indicates that this processor is a secondary bus master (Local Processor Number = 1).
INT1	I	**INTERRUPT 1,** like $\overline{\text{INT0}}$, provides direct interrupt signaling.
INT2/ INTR	I	**INTERRUPT 2/INTERRUPT REQUEST:** The bus control registers determines how this pin is interpreted. If INT2, it has the same interpretation as the $\overline{\text{INT0}}$ and INT1 pins. If INTR, it is used to receive an interrupt request from an external interrupt controller.
$\overline{\text{INT3}}$/ $\overline{\text{INTA}}$	I/O O.D.	**INTERRUPT 3/INTERRUPT ACKNOWLEDGE:** The bus interrupt control register determines how this pin is interpreted. If $\overline{\text{INT3}}$, it has the same interpretation as the $\overline{\text{INT0}}$, INT1, and INT2 pins. If $\overline{\text{INTA}}$, it is used as an output to control interrupt-acknowledge bus transactions. The $\overline{\text{INTA}}$ output is latched on-chip and remains valid during T_d cycles; as an output, it is open-drain.

I/O = Input/Output, O = Output, I = Input, O.D. = Open-Drain, T.S. = tri-state

ELECTRICAL SPECIFICATIONS

Power and Grounding

The 80960KA is implemented in CHMOS IV technology and has modest power requirements. Its high clock frequency and numerous output buffers (address/data, control, error, and arbitration signals) can cause power surges as multiple output buffers drive new signal levels simultaneously. For clean on-chip power distribution at high frequency, 12 V_{CC} and 13 V_{SS} pins separately feed functional units of the 80960KA in the PGA.

Power and ground connections must be made to all power and ground pins of the 80960KA. On the circuit board, all V_{CC} pins must be strapped closely together, preferably on a power plane. Likewise, all V_{SS} pins should be strapped together, preferably on a ground plane. These pins may not be connected together within the chip.

Power Decoupling Recommendations

Liberal decoupling capacitance should be placed near the 80960KA. The processor can cause transient power surges when driving the L-Bus, particularly when it is connected to a large capacitive load.

Low inductance capacitors and interconnects are recommended for best high frequency electrical performance. Inductance can be reduced by shortening the board traces between the processor and decoupling capacitors as much as possible. Capacitors specifically designed for PGA packages are also commercially available and offer the lowest possible inductance.

Connection Recommendations

For reliable operation, always connect unused inputs to an appropriate signal level. In particular, if one or more interrupt lines are not used, they should be pulled up. No inputs should ever be left floating.

All open-drain outputs require a pullup device. While in some cases a simple pullup resistor will be adequate, we recommend a network of pullup and pulldown resistors biased to a valid V_{IH} ($\geq 3.4V$) and terminated in the characteristic impedance of the circuit board. Figure 6 shows our recommendations for the resistor values for both a low and high current drive network, which assumes that the circuit board has a characteristic impedance of 100Ω. The advantage of terminating the output signals in this fashion is that it limits signal swing and reduces AC power consumption.

Characteristic Curves

Figure 7 shows the typical supply current requirements over the operating temperature range of the processor at supply voltage (V_{CC}) of 5V. Figure 8 shows the typical power supply current (I_{CC}) required by the 80960KA at various operating frequencies when measured at three input voltage (V_{CC}) levels.

For a given output current (I_{OL}), the curve in Figure 9 shows the worst case output low voltage (V_{OL}).

Figure 10 shows the typical capacitive derating curve for the 80960KA measured from 1.5V on the system clock (CLK) to 0.8V on the falling edge and 2.0V on the rising edge of the L-Bus address/data (LAD) signals.

Test Load Circuit

Figure 13 illustrates the load circuit used to test the 80960KA's tristate pins, and Figure 14 shows the load circuit used to test the open drain outputs. The open drain test uses an active load circuit in the form of a matched diode bridge. Since the open-drain outputs sink current, only the I_{OL} legs of the bridge are necessary and the I_{OH} legs are not used. When the 80960KA driver under test is turned off, the output pin is pulled up to V_{REF} (i.e., V_{OH}). Diode D_1 is turned off and the I_{OL} current source flows through diode D_2.

When the 80960KA open-drain driver under test is on, diode D_1 is also on, and the voltage on the pin being tested drops to V_{OL}. Diode D_2 turns off and I_{OL} flows through diode D_1.

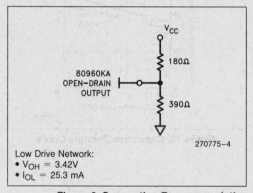

Low Drive Network:
• $V_{OH} = 3.42V$
• $I_{OL} = 25.3$ mA

270775–4

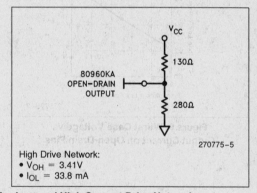

High Drive Network:
• $V_{OH} = 3.41V$
• $I_{OL} = 33.8$ mA

270775–5

Figure 6. Connection Recommendations for Low and High Current Drive Networks

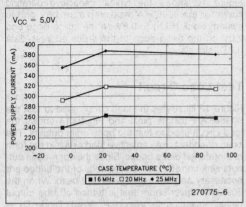

Figure 7. Typical Supply Current (I_{CC})

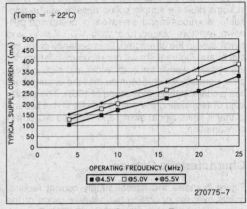

Figure 8. Typical Current vs Frequency

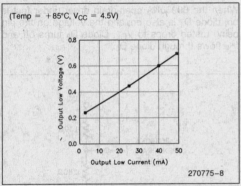

Figure 9. Worst Case Voltage vs
Output Current on Open-Drain Pins

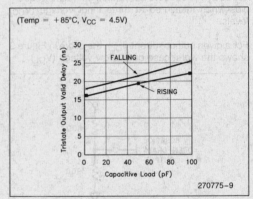

Figure 10. Capacitive Derating Curve

ABSOLUTE MAXIMUM RATINGS*

Operating Temperature . . . . 0°C to +85°C Case

Storage Temperature . . . . −65°C to +150°C

Voltage on Any Pin . . . . −0.5V to V_{CC} + 0.5V

Power Dissipation . . . . 2.5W (25 MHz)

Notice: Stresses above those listed under "Absolute Maximum Ratings" may cause permanent damage to the device. This is a stress rating only and functional operation of the device at these or any other conditions above those indicated in the operational sections of this specification is not implied. Exposure to absolute maximum rating conditions for extended periods may affect device reliability.

D.C. CHARACTERISTICS

80960KA (16 MHz): T_{CASE} = 0°C to +85°C, V_{CC} = 5V ± 10%

80960KA (20 and 25 MHz): T_{CASE} = 0°C to +85°C, V_{CC} = 5V ± 5%

Symbol	Parameter	Min	Max	Units	Test Conditions
V_{IL}	Input Low Voltage	−0.3	+0.8	V	
V_{IH}	Input High Voltage	2.0	V_{CC} + 0.3	V	
V_{CL}	CLK2 Input Low Voltage	−0.3	+1.0	V	
V_{CH}	CLK2 Input High Voltage	0.55 V_{CC}	V_{CC} + 0.3	V	
V_{OL}	Output Low Voltage		0.45 0.60	V	(1, 5) (6)
V_{OH}	Output High Voltage	2.4		V	(2, 4)
I_{CC}	Power Supply Current: 16 MHz 20 MHz 25 MHz		 375 420 480	 mA mA mA	 T_A = 0°C T_A = 0°C T_A = 0°C
I_{LI}	Input Leakage Current		±15	µA	0 ≤ V_O ≤ V_{CC}
I_{LO}	Output Leakage Current		±15	µA	0.45 ≤ V_O ≤ V_{CC}
C_{IN}	Input Capacitance		10	pF	f_C = 1 MHz(3)
C_O	I/O or Output Capacitance		12	pF	f_C = 1 MHz(3)
C_{CLK}	Clock Capacitance		10	pF	f_C = 1 MHz(3)

NOTES:
1. For tri-state outputs, this parameter is measured at:
   Address/Data . . . . 4.0 mA
   Controls . . . . 5.0 mA
2. This parameter is measured at:
   Address/Data . . . . −1.0 mA
   Controls . . . . −0.9 mA
   ALE . . . . −5.0 mA
3. Input, output, and clock capacitance are not tested.
4. Not measured on open-drain outputs.
5. For open-drain outputs . . . . 25 mA
6. For open-drain outputs . . . . 40 mA

A.C. SPECIFICATIONS

This section describes the AC specifications for the 80960KA pins. All input and output timings are specified relative to the 1.5V level of the rising edge of CLK2, and refer to the time at which the signal reaches (for output delay and input setup) or leaves (for hold time) the TTL levels of LOW (0.8V) or HIGH (2.0V). All AC testing should be done with input voltages of 0.4V and 2.4V, except for the clock (CLK2), which should be tested with input voltages of 0.45V and 0.55 V_{CC}.

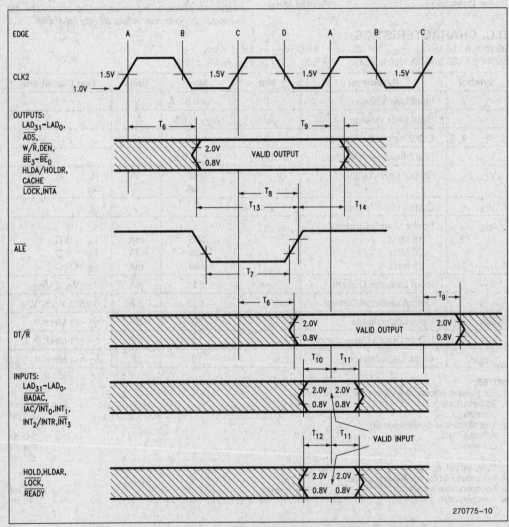

Figure 11. Drive Levels and Timing Relationships for 80960KA Signals
(See Figure 17 for Timing of HOLD/HOLDA)

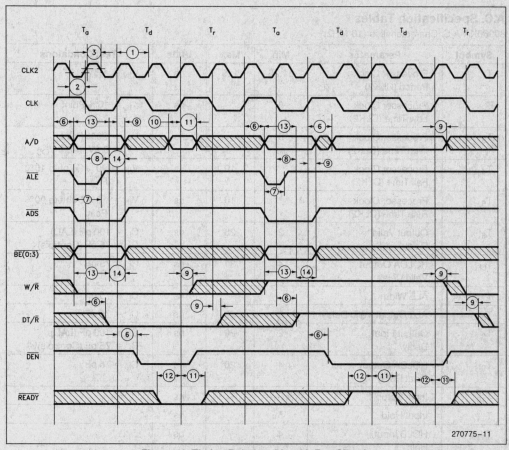

Figure 12. Timing Relationship of L-Bus Signals

270775–11

A.C. Specification Tables

80960KA A.C. Characteristics (16 MHz)

Symbol	Parameter	Min	Max	Units	Test Conditions
T_1	Processor Clock Period (CLK2)	31.25	125	ns	V_{IN} = 1.5V
T_2	Processor Clock Low Time (CLK2)	8		ns	V_{IL} = 10% Point = 1.2V
T_3	Processor Clock High Time (CLK2)	8		ns	V_{IH} = 90% Point = 0.1V + 0.5 V_{CC}
T_4	Processor Clock Fall Time (CLK2)		10	ns	V_{IN} = 90% Point to 10% Point
T_5	Processor Clock Rise Time (CLK2)		10	ns	V_{IN} = 10% Point to 90% Point
T_6	Output Valid Delay	2	25	ns	C_L = 100 pF (LAD) C_L = 75 pF (Controls)
T_{6H}	HOLDA Output Valid Delay	4	31	ns	C_L = 75 pF
T_7	$\overline{ALE}$ Width	15		ns	C_L = 75 pF
T_8	$\overline{ALE}$ Output Valid Delay	0	20	ns	C_L = 75 pF[2]
T_9	Output Float Delay	2	20	ns	C_L = 100 pF (LAD) C_L = 75 pF (Controls)[2]
T_{9H}	HOLDA Output Float Delay	4	20	ns	C_L = 75 pF
T_{10}	Input Setup 1	3		ns	
T_{11}	Input Hold	5		ns	
T_{11H}	HOLD Input Hold	4		ns	
T_{12}	Input Setup 2	8		ns	
T_{13}	Setup to $\overline{ALE}$ Inactive	10		ns	C_L = 100 pF (LAD) C_L = 75 pF (Controls)
T_{14}	Hold after $\overline{ALE}$ Inactive	8		ns	C_L = 100 pF (LAD) C_L = 75 pF (Controls)
T_{15}	Reset Hold	3		ns	
T_{16}	Reset Setup	5		ns	
T_{17}	Reset Width	1281		ns	41 CLK2 Periods Minimum

NOTES:
1. $\overline{IAC}/\overline{INT}_0$, INT_1, $INT_2/INTR$, $\overline{INT}_3$ can be asynchronous.
2. A float condition occurs when the maximum output current becomes less than I_{LO}. Float delay is not tested, but should be no longer than the valid delay.

80960KA A.C. Characteristics (20 MHz)

Symbol	Parameter	Min	Max	Units	Test Conditions
T_1	Processor Clock Period (CLK2)	25	125	ns	$V_{IN} = 1.5V$
T_2	Processor Clock Low Time (CLK2)	6		ns	$V_{IL} = 10\%$ Point $= 1.2V$
T_3	Processor Clock High Time (CLK2)	6		ns	$V_{IH} = 90\%$ Point $= 0.1V + 0.5 V_{CC}$
T_4	Processor Clock Fall Time (CLK2)		10	ns	$V_{IN} = 90\%$ Point to 10% Point
T_5	Processor Clock Rise Time (CLK2)		10	ns	$V_{IN} = 10\%$ Point to 90% Point
T_6	Output Valid Delay	2	20	ns	$C_L = 60$ pF (LAD) $C_L = 50$ pF (Controls)
T_{6H}	HOLDA Output Valid Delay	4	26	ns	$C_L = 50$ pF
T_7	$\overline{ALE}$ Width	12		ns	$C_L = 50$ pF
T_8	$\overline{ALE}$ Output Valid Delay	0	20	ns	$C_L = 50$ pF[2]
T_9	Output Float Delay	2	20	ns	$C_L = 60$ pF (LAD) $C_L = 50$ pF (Controls)[2]
T_{9H}	HOLDA Output Float Delay	4	20	ns	$C_L = 50$ pF
T_{10}	Input Setup 1	3		ns	
T_{11}	Input Hold	5		ns	
T_{11H}	HOLD Input Hold	4		ns	
T_{12}	Input Setup 2	7		ns	
T_{13}	Setup to $\overline{ALE}$ Inactive	10		ns	$C_L = 60$ pF (LAD) $C_L = 50$ pF (Controls)
T_{14}	Hold after $\overline{ALE}$ Inactive	8		ns	$C_L = 60$ pF (LAD) $C_L = 50$ pF (Controls)
T_{15}	Reset Hold	3		ns	
T_{16}	Reset Setup	5		ns	
T_{17}	Reset Width	1025		ns	41 CLK2 Periods Minimum

NOTES:
1. $\overline{IAC}/\overline{INT}_0$, INT_1, $INT_2/INTR$, $\overline{INT}_3$ can be asynchronous.
2. A float condition occurs when the maximum output current becomes less than I_{LO}. Float delay is not tested, but should be no longer than the valid delay.

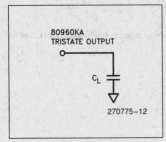

Figure 13. Test Load Circuit for TRI-STATE Output Pins

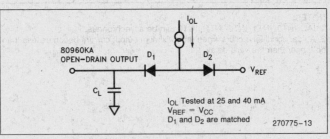

Figure 14. Test Load Circuit for Open-Drain Output Pins

80960KA A.C. Characteristics (25 MHz)

Symbol	Parameter	Min	Max	Units	Test Conditions
T_1	Processor Clock Period (CLK2)	20	125	ns	$V_{IN} = 1.5V$
T_2	Processor Clock Low Time (CLK2)	5		ns	$V_{IL} = 10\%$ Point $= 1.2V$
T_3	Processor Clock High Time	5		ns	$V_{IH} = 90\%$ Point $= 0.1V + 0.5\ V_{CC}$
T_4	Processor Clock Fall Time (CLK2)		10	ns	$V_{IN} = 90\%$ Point to 10% Point
T_5	Processor Clock Rise Time (CLK2)		10	ns	$V_{IN} = 10\%$ Point to 90% Point
T_6	Output Valid Delay	2	18	ns	$C_L = 60$ pF (LAD) $C_L = 50$ pF (Controls)
T_{6H}	HOLDA Output Valid Delay	4	24	ns	$C_L = 50$ pF
T_7	ALE Width	12		ns	$C_L = 50$ pF
T_8	ALE Output Valid Delay	0	20	ns	$C_L = 50$ pF[2]
T_9	Output Float Delay	2	18	ns	$C_L = 60$ pF (LAD) $C_L = 50$ pF (Controls)
T_{9H}	HOLDA Output Float Delay	4	20	ns	$C_L = 50$ pF
T_{10}	Input Setup 1	3		ns	
T_{11}	Input Hold	5		ns	
T_{11H}	HOLD Input Hold	4		ns	
T_{12}	Input Setup 2	7		ns	
T_{13}	Setup to ALE Inactive	10		ns	$C_L = 60$ pF (LAD) $C_L = 50$ pF (Controls)
T_{14}	Hold after ALE Inactive	8		ns	$C_L = 60$ pF (LAD) $C_L = 50$ pF (Controls)
T_{15}	Reset Hold	3		ns	
T_{16}	Reset Setup	7		ns	
T_{17}	Reset Width	820		ns	41 CLK2 Periods Minimum

NOTES:
1. IAC/INT0, INT1, INT2/INTR, INT3 can be asynchronous.
2. A float condition occurs when the maximum output current becomes less than I_{LO}. Float delay is not tested, but should be no longer than the valid delay.

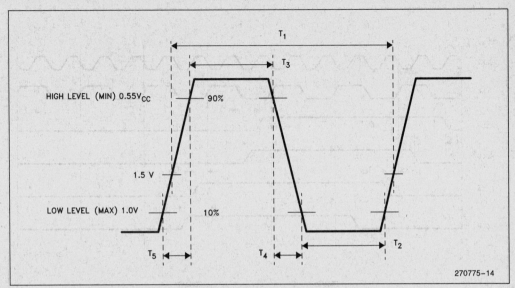

Figure 15. Processor Clock Pulse (CLK2)

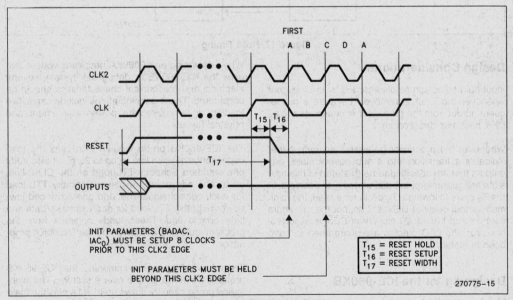

T_{15} = RESET HOLD
T_{16} = RESET SETUP
T_{17} = RESET WIDTH

INIT PARAMETERS (BADAC, IAC$_0$) MUST BE SETUP 8 CLOCKS PRIOR TO THIS CLK2 EDGE

INIT PARAMETERS MUST BE HELD BEYOND THIS CLK2 EDGE

Figure 16. RESET Signal Timing

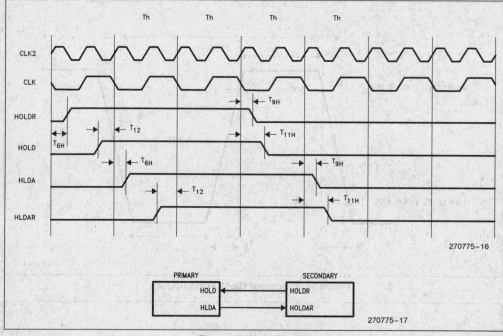

Figure 17. Hold Timing

Design Considerations

Input hold times can be disregarded by the designer whenever the input is removed because a subsequent output from the processor is deasserted (e.g., DEN becomes deasserted).

Whenever the processor generates an output that indicates a transition into a subsequent state, any outputs that are specified to be tri-stated in this new state are guaranteed to be tri-stated. For example, in the T_d cycle following a T_a cycle for a read, the minimum output delay of DEN is 2 ns, but the maximum float time of LAD is 20 ns. When DEN is asserted, however, the LAD outputs are guaranteed to have been tri-stated.

Designing for the ICE-960KB

The 80960KB In-Circuit Emulator assists in debugging both 80960KA and 80960KB hardware and software designs. The product consists of a probe module, cable, and control unit. Because of the high operating frequency of 80960KA systems, the probe module connects directly to the 80960KA socket.

When designing an 80960KA hardware system that uses the ICE-960KB to debug the system, several electrical and mechanical characteristics should be considered. These considerations include capacitive loading, drive requirement, power requirement, and physical layout.

The ICE-960KB probe module increases the load capacitance of each line by up to 25 pF. It also adds one standard Schottky TTL load on the CLK2 line, up to one advanced low-power Schottky TTL load for each control signal line, and one advanced low-power Schottky TTL load for each address/data and byte enable line. These loads originate from the probe module and are driven by the 80960KA processor.

To achieve high noise immunity, the ICE-960KB probe is powered by the user's system. The high-speed probe circuitry draws up to 1.1A plus the maximum current (I_{CC}) of the 80960KA processor.

The mechanical considerations are shown in Figure 18, which illustrates the lateral clearance requirements for the ICE-960KB probe as viewed from above the socket of the 80960KA processor.

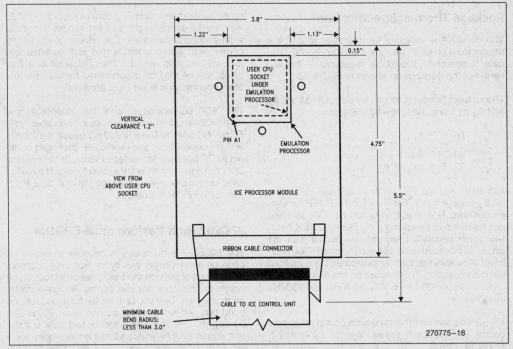

VERTICAL
CLEARANCE 1.2"

USER CPU
SOCKET
UNDER
EMULATION
PROCESSOR

PIN A1

EMULATION
PROCESSOR

VIEW FROM
ABOVE USER CPU
SOCKET

ICE PROCESSOR MODULE

RIBBON CABLE CONNECTOR

CABLE TO ICE CONTROL UNIT

MINIMUM CABLE
BEND RADIUS:
LESS THAN 3.0"

3.8"
1.22"
1.13"
0.15"
4.75"
5.5"

270775–18

Figure 18. ICE-960KB Lateral Clearance Requirements

MECHANICAL DATA

Package Dimensions and Mounting

The 80960KA is available in two different packages: a 132-lead ceramic pin-grid array (PGA) and a 132-lead plastic quad flat pack (PQFP). Pins in the ceramic package are arranged 0.100 inch (2.54 mm) center-to-center, in a 14 by 14 matrix, three rows around. (See Figure 19.) The plastic package uses fine-pitch gull wing leads arranged in a single row along the perimeter of the package with 0.025 inch (0.64 mm) spacing. (See Figure 20.) Dimensions are given in Figure 21 and Table 7.

There are a wide variety of sockets available for the ceramic PGA package including low-insertion or zero-insertion force mountings, and a choice of terminals such as soldertail, surface mount, or wire wrap. Several applicable sockets are shown in Figure 22.

The PQFP is normally surface mounted to take best advantage of the plastic package's small footprint and low cost. In some applications, however, designers may prefer to use a socket, either to improve heat dissipation or reduce repair costs. Figures 23a and 23b show two of the many sockets available.

Pin Assignment

The PGA and PQFP have different pin assignments. Figure 24 shows the view from the bottom of the PGA (pins facing up) and Figure 25 shows a view from the top of the PGA (pins facing down). Figure 20 shows the top view of the PQFP; notice that the pins are numbered in order from 1 to 132 around the package's perimeter. Tables 5 and 6 list the function of each pin in the PGA, and Tables 8 and 9 list the function of each pin in the PQFP.

V_{CC} and GND connections must be made to multiple V_{CC} and GND pins. Each V_{CC} and GND pin must be connected to the appropriate voltage or ground and externally strapped close to the package. We recommend that you include separate power and ground planes in your circuit board for power distribution.

NOTE:

Pins identified as N.C., "No Connect," should never be connected. The 80960KA PGA and PQFP packages both contain 53 N.C. pins

Package Thermal Specification

The 80960KA is specified for operation when case temperature is within the range 0°C to +85°C. The case temperature should be measured at the top center of the package as shown in Figure 26.

The ambient temperature can be calculated from θ_{jc} and θ_{ja} by using the following equations:

$$T_J = T_C + P*\theta_{jc}$$
$$T_A = T_J - P*\theta_{ja}$$
$$T_C = T_A + P*[\theta_{ja} - \theta_{jc}]$$

Values for θ_{ja} and θ_{jc} are given in Table 10 for the PGA package and in Table 11 for the PQFP for various airflows. Note that the θ_{ja} for the PGA package can be reduced by adding a heatsink, while a heatsink is not generally used with the plastic package since it is intended to be surface mounted. The maximum allowable ambient temperature (T_A) permitted without exceeding T_C is shown by the charts in Figures 27 through 29 for 16 MHz, 20 MHz, and 25 MHz respectively.

The curves assume the maximum permitted supply current (I_{CC}) at each speed, V_{CC} of 5.0V, and a T_{CASE} of +85°C.

If you will be using the 80960KA in a harsh environment where the ambient temperature may exceed the limits for the normal commercial part, you should consider using an extended temperature part. These parts are designed by the prefix "TA" and are available at 16 and 20 MHz in the ceramic PGA package. Figure 30 shows the maximum allowable ambient temperature for the 20 MHz extended temperature TA80960KA at various airflows. The curve assumes an I_{CC} of 420 mA, V_{CC} of 5.0V, and a T_{CASE} of +125°C.

WAVEFORMS

Figures 31 through 36 show the waveforms for various transactions on the 80960KA's local bus.

SUPPORT COMPONENTS

85C960 Burst Bus Controller

The Intel 85C960 performs burst logic, ready generation, and address decode for the 80960KA and 80960KB. The burst logic supports both standard and burst mode memories and peripherals. The ready generation and timing control supports 0 to 15 wait states across eight address ranges for read/write and burst accesses. The address decoder decodes eight address inputs into four external and four internal chip selects. The wait state and chip select values may be programmed by the user; the timing control and burst logic are fixed.

The 85C960 operates with the 80960KA and 80960KB at all frequencies and consumes only 50 mA at 25 MHz. The 85C960 is housed in a 28-pin, 300-mil ceramic DIP and plastic DIP packages or 28-pin PLCC package for surface mount. In the ceramic DIP package the part is UV-erasable, which makes it easy to revise designs. Order the 85C960 data sheet (No. 290192) for full details.

27C202 High-Performance EPROM

The 80960KA's burst bus is capable of accepting code on almost every bus cycle. For every address the processor puts on the bus, it can read four 32-bit words on the next four bus cycles. A high-performance memory system can make best use of the burst bus. Along with fast access time (70 ns and 90 ns), the 27C202 also offers a fast data tristate, fast output enable time, and X16 configuration for a two-bank interleave design. As a result the 27C202 can achieve 1-0-0-0 performance (one wait state on the first access and zero wait-states on the remaining three) or 16 MHz and 20 MHz designs. For further information order the 27C202 data sheet (No. 290136).

27960KX Burst Mode EPROM

Intel 27960KX one-megabit EPROM is designed specifically to support the 80960KA and 80960KB. It uses a burst interface to offer near zero wait-state performance without the high cost of alternative memory technologies. The 27960KX removes the need for "dumping" code and data stored in slow EPROMs or ROMs into expensive high-speed "shadow" RAM.

Internally, the 27960KX is organized in blocks of four bytes that are accessed sequentially. The address of the four-byte block is latched and incremented internally. After a set number of wait-states (1 or 2), data is output one word at a time each subsequent clock cycle. High-performance outputs provide zero wait-state data-to-data burst accesses. Extra power and ground pins dedicated to the output reduce the effect of fast output switching on the device. The 27960KX offers 1-0-0-0 performance at 20 MHz and 2-0-0-0 performance at 25 MHz. Full details can be found in the 27960KX data sheet (No. 290237)

Table 5. 80960KA PGA Pinout—In Pin Order

Pin	Signal	Pin	Signal	Pin	Signal	Pin	Signal
A1	V_{CC}	C6	LAD_{20}	H1	$W/\overline{R}$	M10	V_{SS}
A2	V_{SS}	C7	LAD_{13}	H2	$\overline{BE}_0$	M11	V_{CC}
A3	LAD_{19}	C8	LAD_8	H3	$\overline{LOCK}$	M12	N.C.
A4	LAD_{17}	C9	LAD_3	H12	N.C.	M13	N.C.
A5	LAD_{16}	C10	V_{CC}	H13	N.C.	M14	N.C.
A6	LAD_{14}	C11	V_{SS}	H14	N.C.	N1	V_{SS}
A7	LAD_{11}	C12	$\overline{INT}_3/\overline{INTA}$	J1	$DT/\overline{R}$	N2	N.C.
A8	LAD_9	C13	INT_1	J2	$\overline{BE}_2$	N3	N.C.
A9	LAD_7	C14	$\overline{IAC}/\overline{INT}_0$	J3	V_{SS}	N4	N.C.
A10	LAD_5	D1	$\overline{ALE}$	J12	N.C.	N5	N.C.
A11	LAD_4	D2	$\overline{ADS}$	J13	N.C.	N6	N.C.
A12	LAD_1	D3	HLDA/HLDR	J14	N.C.	N7	N.C.
A13	$INT_2/INTR$	D12	V_{CC}	K1	$\overline{BE}_3$	N8	N.C.
A14	V_{CC}	D13	N.C.	K2	$\overline{FAILURE}$	N9	N.C.
B1	LAD_{23}	D14	N.C.	K3	V_{SS}	N10	N.C.
B2	LAD_{24}	E1	LAD_{28}	K12	V_{CC}	N11	N.C.
B3	LAD_{22}	E2	LAD_{26}	K13	N.C.	N12	N.C.
B4	LAD_{21}	E3	LAD_{27}	K14	N.C.	N13	N.C.
B5	LAD_{18}	E12	N.C.	L1	$\overline{DEN}$	N14	N.C.
B6	LAD_{15}	E13	V_{SS}	L2	N.C.	P1	V_{CC}
B7	LAD_{12}	E14	N.C.	L3	V_{CC}	P2	N.C.
B8	LAD_{10}	F1	LAD_{29}	L12	V_{SS}	P3	N.C.
B9	LAD_6	F2	LAD_{31}	L13	N.C.	P4	N.C.
B10	LAD_2	F3	CACHE	L14	N.C.	P5	N.C.
B11	CLK2	F12	N.C.	M1	N.C.	P6	N.C.
B12	LAD_0	F13	N.C.	M2	V_{CC}	P7	N.C.
B13	RESET	F14	N.C.	M3	V_{SS}	P8	N.C.
B14	V_{SS}	G1	LAD_{30}	M4	V_{SS}	P9	N.C.
C1	HOLD/HLDAR	G2	$\overline{READY}$	M5	V_{CC}	P10	N.C.
C2	LAD_{25}	G3	$\overline{BE}_1$	M6	N.C.	P11	N.C.
C3	$\overline{BADAC}$	G12	N.C.	M7	N.C.	P12	N.C.
C4	V_{CC}	G13	N.C.	M8	N.C.	P13	V_{SS}
C5	V_{SS}	G14	N.C.	M9	N.C.	P14	V_{CC}

Table 6. 80960KA PGA Pinout—In Signal Order

Signal	Pin	Signal	Pin	Signal	Pin	Signal	Pin
$\overline{ADS}$	D2	LAD_{15}	B6	N.C.	J14	N.C.	P9
$\overline{ALE}$	D1	LAD_{16}	A5	N.C.	K13	N.C.	P10
$\overline{BADAC}$	C3	LAD_{17}	A4	N.C.	K14	N.C.	P11
$\overline{BE_0}$	H2	LAD_{18}	B5	N.C.	L13	N.C.	P12
$\overline{BE_1}$	G3	LAD_{19}	A3	N.C.	L14	N.C.	L2
$\overline{BE_2}$	J2	LAD_{20}	C6	N.C.	M1	$\overline{READY}$	G2
$\overline{BE_3}$	K1	LAD_{21}	B4	N.C.	M6	RESET	B13
CACHE	F3	LAD_{22}	B3	N.C.	M7	V_{CC}	A1
CLK2	B11	LAD_{23}	B1	N.C.	M8	V_{CC}	A14
$\overline{DEN}$	L1	LAD_{24}	B2	N.C.	M9	V_{CC}	C4
DT/$\overline{R}$	J1	LAD_{25}	C2	N.C.	M12	V_{CC}	C10
$\overline{FAILURE}$	K2	LAD_{26}	E2	N.C.	M13	V_{CC}	D12
HLDA/HOLDR	D3	LAD_{27}	E3	N.C.	M14	V_{CC}	K12
HOLD/HLDAR	C1	LAD_{28}	E1	N.C.	N2	V_{CC}	L3
$\overline{IAC}/\overline{INT}_0$	C14	LAD_{29}	F1	N.C.	N3	V_{CC}	M2
INT_1	C13	LAD_{30}	G1	N.C.	N4	V_{CC}	M5
INT_2/INTR	A13	LAD_{31}	F2	N.C.	N5	V_{CC}	M11
$\overline{INT}_3/\overline{INTA}$	C12	$\overline{LOCK}$	H3	N.C.	N6	V_{CC}	P1
LAD_0	B12	N.C.	D13	N.C.	N7	V_{CC}	P14
LAD_1	A12	N.C.	D14	N.C.	N8	V_{SS}	A2
LAD_2	B10	N.C.	E12	N.C.	N9	V_{SS}	B14
LAD_3	C9	N.C.	E14	N.C.	N10	V_{SS}	C5
LAD_4	A11	N.C.	F12	N.C.	N11	V_{SS}	C11
LAD_5	A10	N.C.	F13	N.C.	N12	V_{SS}	E13
LAD_6	B9	N.C.	F14	N.C.	N13	V_{SS}	J3
LAD_7	A9	N.C.	G12	N.C.	N14	V_{SS}	K3
LAD_8	C8	N.C.	G13	N.C.	P2	V_{SS}	L12
LAD_9	A8	N.C.	G14	N.C.	P3	V_{SS}	M3
LAD_{10}	B8	N.C.	H12	N.C.	P4	V_{SS}	M4
LAD_{11}	A7	N.C.	H13	N.C.	P5	V_{SS}	M10
LAD_{12}	B7	N.C.	H14	N.C.	P6	V_{SS}	N1
LAD_{13}	C7	N.C.	J12	N.C.	P7	V_{SS}	P13
LAD_{14}	A6	N.C.	J13	N.C.	P8	W/$\overline{R}$	H1

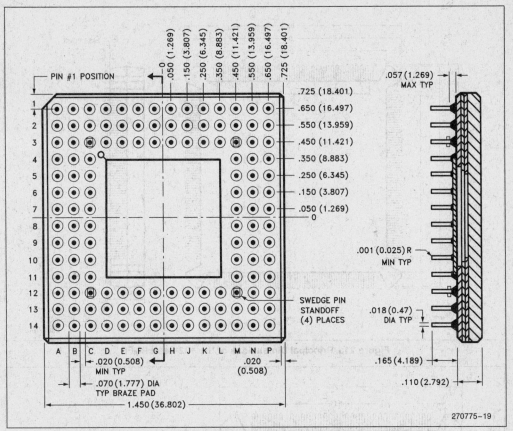

Figure 19. A 132-Lead Pin-Grid Array (PGA) Used to Package the 80960KA

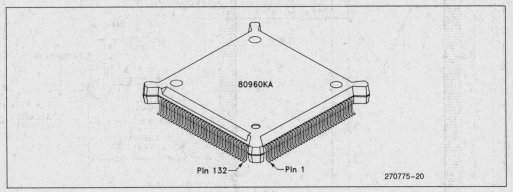

Figure 20. The 132-Lead Plastic Quad Flat Pack (PQFP) used to Package the 80960KA

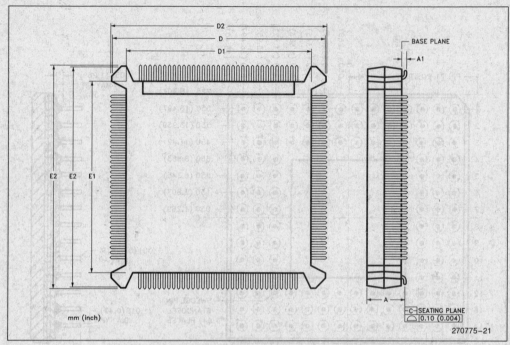

Figure 21a. Principal Dimensions of the 132-Lead PQFP

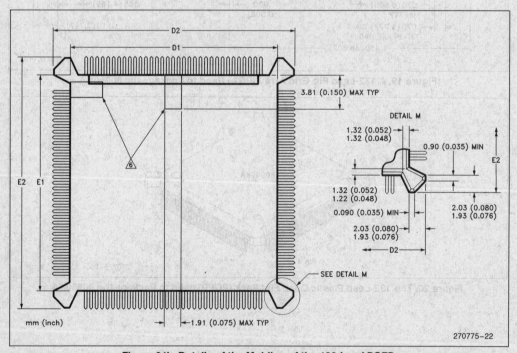

Figure 21b. Details of the Molding of the 132-Lead PQFP

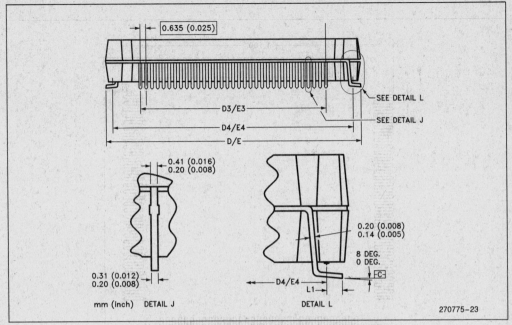

Figure 21c. Terminal Details for the 132-Lead PQFP

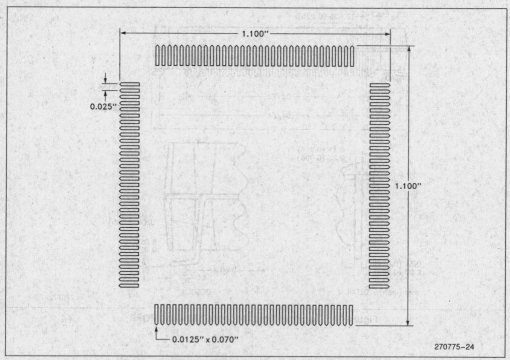

Figure 21d. Board Footprint Area for the 132-Lead PQFP

Table 7. Package Dimension: 80960KA PQFP

Symbol	Description	Inches		MM	
		Min	Max	Min	Max
N	Leadcount	132 Leads		132 Leads	
A	Package Height	0.160	0.170	4.060	4.320
A1	Standoff	0.020	0.030	0.510	0.760
D,E	Terminal Dimension	1.075	1.085	27.310	27.560
D1,E1	Package Body	0.947	0.953	24.050	24.210
D2,E2	Bumper Distance Without Flash With Flash	1.097 1.097	1.103 1.110	27.860 27.860	28.010 28.190
D3,E3	Lead Dimension	0.800 REF		20.32 REF	
D4,E4	Foot Radius Location	1.023	1.037	25.890	26.330
L1	Foot Length	0.020	0.030	0.510	0.760

- Low insertion force (LIF) soldertail 55274-1
- Amp tests indicate 50% reduction in insertion force compared to machined sockets

Other socket options
- Zero insertion force (ZIF) soldertail 55583-1
- Zero insertion force (ZIF) Burn-in version 55573-2

Amp Incorporated
(Harrisburg, PA 17105 U.S.A.
Phone 717-564-0100)

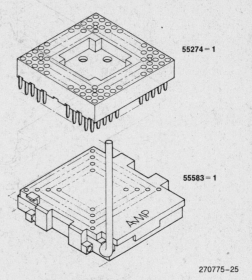

270775-25

Cam handle locks in low profile position when 80960KA is installed (handle UP for open and DOWN for closed positions).

Courtesy Amp Incorporated

Peel-A-Way* Mylar and Kapton Socket Terminal Carriers
- Low insertion force surface mount CS132-37TG
- Low insertion force soldertail CS132-01TG
- Low insertion force wire-wrap CS132-02TG (two-level)
  CS132-03TG (thee-level)
- Low insertion force press-fit CS132-05TG

Advanced Interconnections
(5 Division Street)
Warwick, RI 02818 U.S.A.
Phone 401-885-0485)

Peel-A-Way Carrier No. 132:
   Kapton Carrier is KS132
   Mylar Carrier is MS132

Molded Plastic Body KS132 is shown below:

270775-26

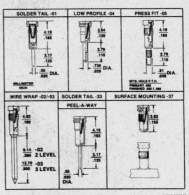

270775-27

Courtesy Advanced Interconnections
(Peel-A-Way Terminal Carriers
U.S. Patent No. 4442938)

*Peel-A-Way is a trademark of Advanced Interconnections.

Figure 22. Several Socket Options for Mounting the 80960KA

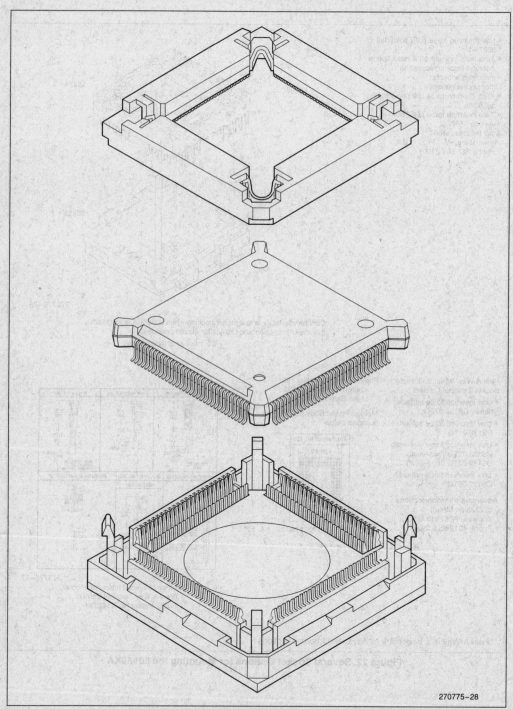

**Figure 23a. AMP Micropitch Socket for the 132-Lead Plastic
Quad Flat Pack, 0.025″ Lead Spacing, Gull Wing Leads**

270775–28

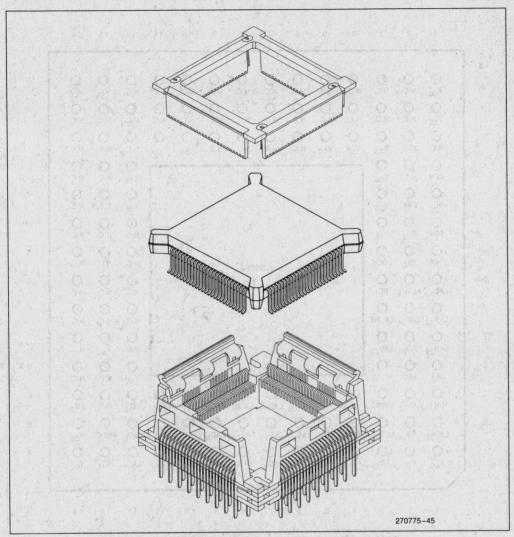

270775–45

Figure 23b. 3M Plastic Bumper and Flat Package and Lid

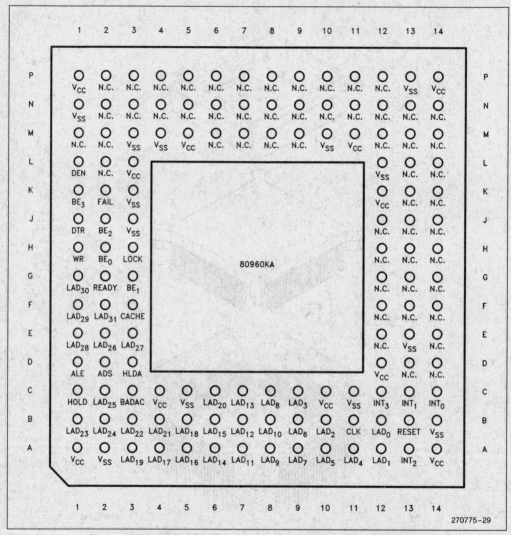

Figure 24. 80960KA PGA Pinout—View from Bottom (Pins Facing Up)

270775–29

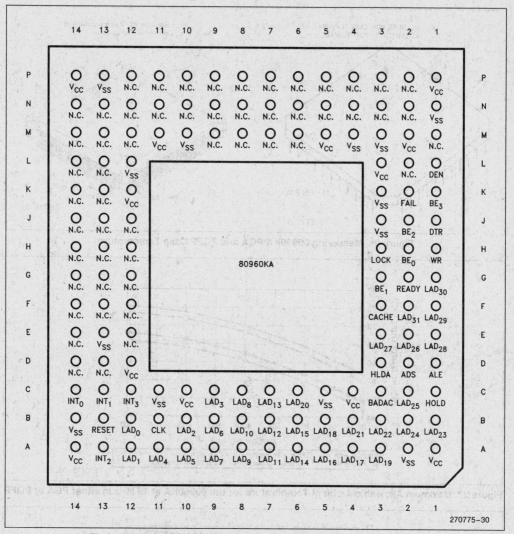

Figure 25. 80960KA PGA Pinout—View from Top (Pins Facing Down)

270775–30

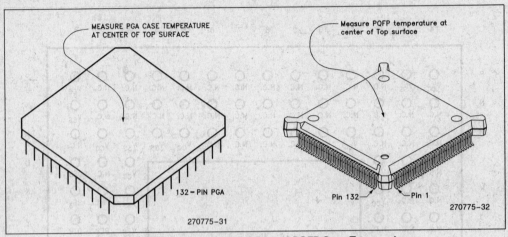

Figure 26. Measuring 80960KA PGA and PQFP Case Temperature

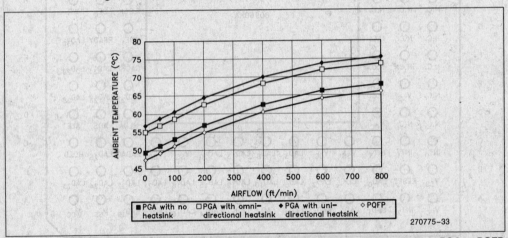

Figure 27. Maximum Allowable Ambient Temperature for the 80960KA at 16 MHz in either PGA or PQFP

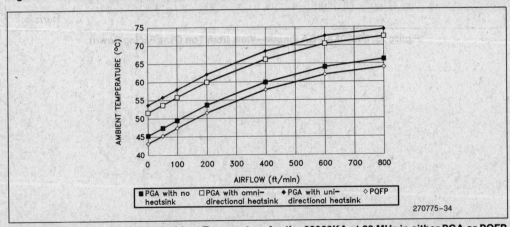

Figure 28. Maximum Allowable Ambient Temperature for the 80960KA at 20 MHz in either PGA or PQFP

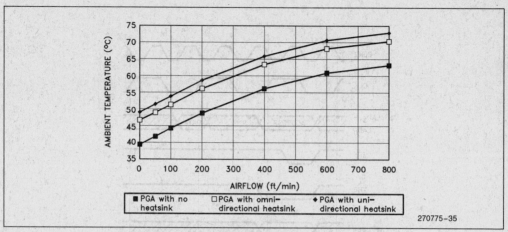

270775-35

**Figure 29. Maximum Allowable Ambient Temperature for
the 80960KA at 25 MHz (available in PGA only)**

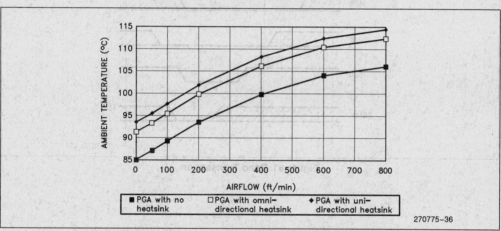

270775-36

**Figure 30. Maximum Allowable Ambient Temperature for the Extended
Temperature TA-80960KA at 20 MHz (available in PGA only)**

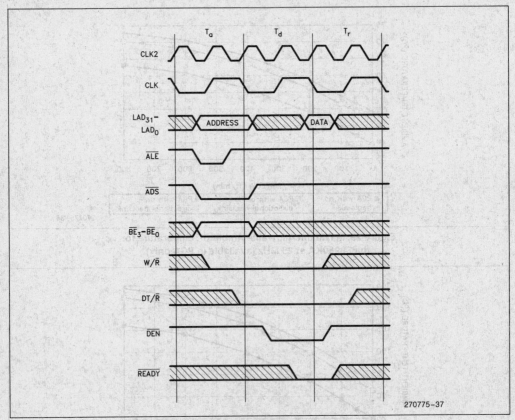

270775–37

Figure 31. Read Transaction

Table 8. 80960KA Plastic Package Pinout - In Pin Order

Pin	Signal	Pin	Signal	Pin	Signal	Pin	Signal
1	HLDA/HOLR	34	N.C.	67	V_{ss}	100	LAD0
2	$\overline{ALE}$	35	V_{cc}	68	V_{ss}	101	LAD1
3	LAD26	36	V_{cc}	69	N.C.	102	LAD2
4	LAD27	37	N.C.	70	V_{cc}	103	V_{ss}
5	LAD28	38	N.C.	71	V_{cc}	104	LAD3
6	LAD29	39	N.C.	72	N.C.	105	LAD4
7	LAD30	40	N.C.	73	N.C.	106	LAD5
8	LAD31	41	N.C.	74	N.C.	107	LAD6
9	V_{ss}	42	N.C.	75	N.C.	108	LAD7
10	CACHE	43	N.C.	76	N.C.	109	LAD8
11	$W/\overline{R}$	44	N.C.	77	N.C.	110	LAD9
12	$\overline{READY}$	45	N.C.	78	N.C.	111	LAD10
13	$DT/\overline{R}$	46	N.C.	79	V_{ss}	112	LAD11
14	$\overline{BE0}$	47	N.C.	80	V_{ss}	113	LAD112
15	$\overline{BE1}$	48	N.C.	81	N.C.	114	V_{ss}
16	$\overline{BE2}$	49	N.C.	82	V_{cc}	115	LAD13
17	$\overline{BE3}$	50	N.C.	83	V_{cc}	116	LAD14
18	$\overline{FAILURE}$	51	N.C.	84	N.C.	117	LAD15
19	V_{ss}	52	V_{ss}	85	$\overline{IAC/INT0}$	118	LAD16
20	$\overline{LOCK}$	53	V_{ss}	86	INT1	119	LAD17
21	$\overline{DEN}$	54	N.C.	87	INT2/INTR	120	LAD18
22	DEBUG	55	V_{cc}	88	$\overline{INT3/INTA}$	121	LAD19
23	N.C.	56	V_{cc}	89	N.C.	122	LAD20
24	N.C.	57	N.C.	90	V_{ss}	123	LAD21
25	N.C.	58	N.C.	91	CLK2	124	LAD22
26	V_{ss}	59	N.C.	92	V_{cc}	125	V_{ss}
27	V_{ss}	60	N.C.	93	RESET	126	LAD23
28	N.C.	61	N.C.	94	N.C.	127	LAD24
29	V_{cc}	62	N.C.	95	N.C.	128	LAD25
30	V_{cc}	63	N.C.	96	N.C.	129	$\overline{BADAC}$
31	N.C.	64	N.C.	97	N.C.	130	HOLD/HLDAR
32	V_{ss}	65	N.C.	98	N.C.	131	N.C.
33	V_{ss}	66	N.C.	99	N.C.	132	$\overline{ADS}$

Table 9. 80960KA Plastic Package Pinout - In Signal Order

Signal	Pin	Signal	Pin	Signal	Pin	Signal	Pin
$\overline{\text{ADS}}$	132	LAD21	123	N.C.	45	N.C.	98
$\overline{\text{ALE}}$	2	LAD22	124	N.C.	46	N.C.	99
$\overline{\text{BADAC}}$	129	LAD23	126	N.C.	47	N.C.	131
$\overline{\text{BE0}}$	14	LAD24	127	N.C.	48	$\overline{\text{READY}}$	12
$\overline{\text{BE1}}$	15	LAD25	128	N.C.	49	RESET	93
$\overline{\text{BE2}}$	16	LAD26	3	N.C.	50	V_{CC}	29
$\overline{\text{BE3}}$	17	LAD27	4	N.C.	51	V_{CC}	30
CACHE	10	LAD28	5	N.C.	54	V_{CC}	35
CLK2	91	LAD29	6	N.C.	57	V_{CC}	36
DEBUG	22	LAD3	104	N.C.	58	V_{CC}	55
$\overline{\text{DEN}}$	21	LAD30	7	N.C.	59	V_{CC}	56
DT/$\overline{\text{R}}$	13	LAD31	8	N.C.	60	V_{CC}	70
$\overline{\text{FAILURE}}$	18	LAD4	105	N.C.	61	V_{CC}	71
HLDA/HOLR	1	LAD5	106	N.C.	62	V_{CC}	82
HOLD/HLDAR	130	LAD6	107	N.C.	63	V_{CC}	83
$\overline{\text{IAC}}$/INT0	85	LAD7	108	N.C.	64	V_{CC}	92
INT1	86	LAD8	109	N.C.	65	V_{SS}	9
INT2/INTR	87	LAD9	110	N.C.	66	V_{SS}	19
INT3/$\overline{\text{INTA}}$	88	$\overline{\text{LOCK}}$	20	N.C.	69	V_{SS}	26
LAD0	100	N.C.	23	N.C.	72	V_{SS}	27
LAD1	101	N.C.	24	N.C.	73	V_{SS}	32
LAD10	112	N.C.	25	N.C.	74	V_{SS}	33
LAD11	111	N.C.	28	N.C.	75	V_{SS}	52
LAD12	113	N.C.	31	N.C.	76	V_{SS}	53
LAD13	115	N.C.	34	N.C.	77	V_{SS}	67
LAD14	116	N.C.	37	N.C.	78	V_{SS}	68
LAD15	117	N.C.	38	N.C.	81	V_{SS}	79
LAD16	118	N.C.	39	N.C.	84	V_{SS}	80
LAD17	119	N.C.	40	N.C.	89	V_{SS}	90
LAD18	120	N.C.	41	N.C.	94	V_{SS}	103
LAD19	121	N.C.	42	N.C.	95	V_{SS}	114
LAD2	102	N.C.	43	N.C.	96	V_{SS}	125
LAD20	122	N.C.	44	N.C.	97	W/$\overline{\text{R}}$	11

Table 10. 80960KA PGA Package Thermal Characteristics

Parameter	Thermal Resistance—°C/Watt						
	Airflow—ft./min (m/sec)						
	0 (0)	50 (0.25)	100 (0.50)	200 (1.01)	400 (2.03)	600 (3.04)	800 (4.06)
θ Junction-to-Case (Case Measured as shown in Figure 26)	2	2	2	2	2	2	2
θ Case-to-Ambient (No Heatsink)	19	18	17	15	12	10	9
θ Case-to-Ambient (with Omnidirectional Heatsink)	16	15	14	12	9	7	6
θ Case-to-Ambient (with Unidirectional) Heatsink)	15	14	13	11	8	6	5

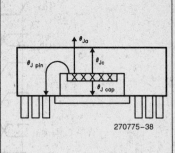

270775–38

NOTES:
1. This table applies to 80960KA PGA plugged into socket or soldered directly into board.
2. $\theta_{JA} = \theta_{JC} + \theta_{CA}$.
3. $\theta_{J\text{-}CAP} = 4°C/w$ (approx.)
$\theta_{J\text{-}PIN} = 4°C/w$ (inner pins) (approx.)
$\theta_{J\text{-}PIN} = 8°C/w$ (outer pins) (approx.)

Table 11. 80960KA PQFP Package Thermal Characteristics

Parameter	PQFP Thermal Resistance—°C/Watt						
	Airflow—ft./min (m/sec)						
	0 (0)	50 (0.25)	100 (0.50)	200 (1.01)	400 (2.03)	600 (3.04)	800 (4.06)
θ Junction-to-Case (Case Measured as shown in Figure 26)	6	6	6	6	6	6	6
θ Case-to-Ambient (No Heatsink)	20	19	18	16	13	11	10

NOTES:
1. This table applies to 80960KA PQFP soldered directly into board.
2. $\theta_{JA} = \theta_{JC} + \theta_{CA}$.
3. $\theta_{JL} = 18°C/Watt$
$\theta_{JB} = 18°C/Watt$

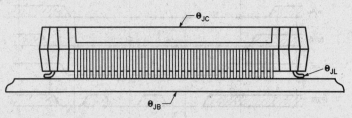

270775–39

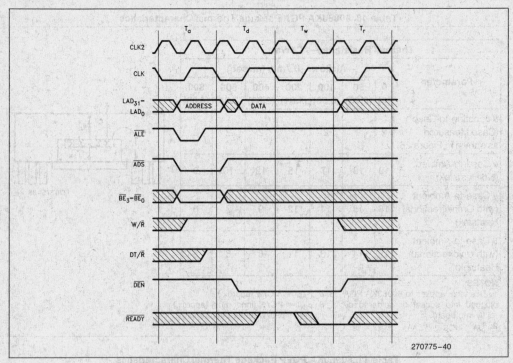

270775-40

Figure 32. Write Transaction with One Wait State

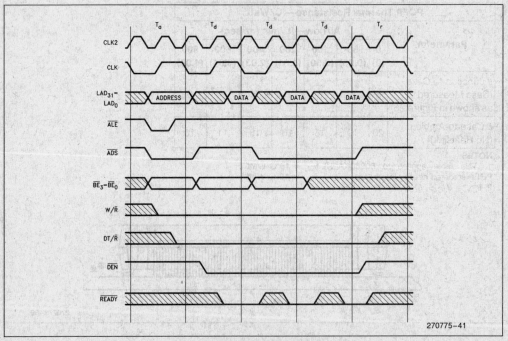

270775-41

Figure 33. Burst Read Transaction

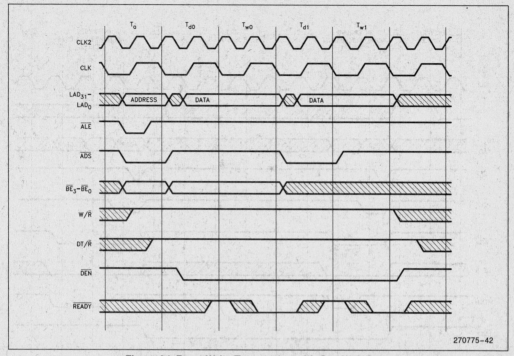

Figure 34. Burst Write Transaction with One Wait State

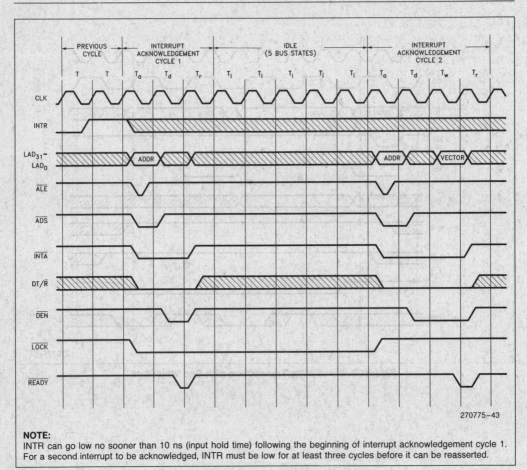

270775–43

NOTE:
INTR can go low no sooner than 10 ns (input hold time) following the beginning of interrupt acknowledgement cycle 1. For a second interrupt to be acknowledged, INTR must be low for at least three cycles before it can be reasserted.

Figure 35. Interrupt Acknowledge Transaction

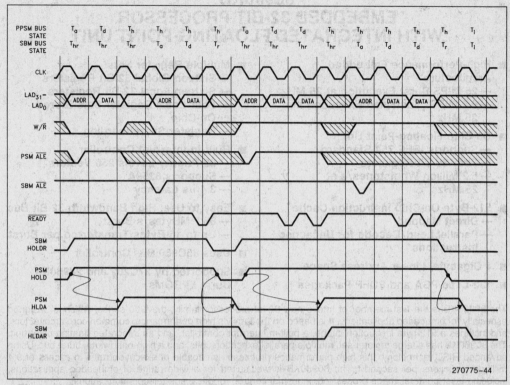

Figure 36. Bus Exchange Transaction (PBM = Primary Bus Master, SBM = Secondary Bus Master)

270775–44

80960KB
EMBEDDED 32-BIT PROCESSOR
WITH INTEGRATED FLOATING-POINT UNIT

- **High-Performance Embedded Architecture**
  - 25 MIPS Burst Execution at 25 MHz
  - 9.4 MIPS* Sustained Execution at 25 MHz
- **On-Chip Floating-Point Unit**
  - Supports IEEE 754 Standard
  - Four 80-Bit Registers
  - 5.2 Million Whetstones/s at 25 MHz
- **512-Byte On-Chip Instruction Cache**
  - Direct Mapped
  - Parallel Load/Decode for Uncached Instructions
- **4 Gigabyte, Linear Address Space**
- **132-Lead PGA and PQFP Packages**

- **Multiple Register Sets**
  - Sixteen Global 32-Bit Registers
  - Sixteen Local 32-Bit Registers
  - Four Local Register Sets Stored On-Chip
  - Register Scoreboarding
- **Built-In Interrupt Controller**
  - 32 Priority Levels 256 Vectors
  - Supports 8259A
  - 3.4 μs Latency
- **Easy to Use, High Bandwidth 32-Bit Bus**
  - 66.7 MBytes/s Burst
  - Up to 16-Bytes Transferred per Burst
- **Uses 85C960 Bus Controller**
- **Supported by 27C202 and 27960KX Burst EPROMs**

The 80960KB is the first member of Intel's new 32-bit processor family, the i960 series, which is designed especially for embedded applications. It is based on the family's high performance, common core architecture, and includes a 512-byte instruction cache, a built-in interrupt controller, and an integrated floating-point unit. The 80960KB has a large register set, multiple parallel execution units, and a high-bandwidth, burst bus. Using advanced RISC technology, this high performance processor is capable of execution rates in excess of 9.4 million instructions per second.* The 80960KB is well-suited for a wide range of embedded applications, including laser printers, image processing, industrial control, robotics, and telecommunications.

*Relative to Digital Equipment Corporation's VAX-11/780** at 1 MIPS

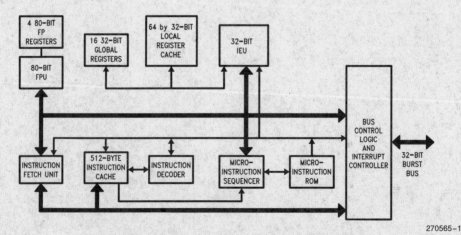

Figure 1. The 80960KB's Highly Parallel Microarchitecture

270565-1

**VAX-11™ is a trademark of Digital Equipment Corporation.

November 1989
Order Number: 270565-003

THE 960 SERIES

The 80960KB is the first member of a new family of 32-bit microprocessors from Intel known as the 960 Series. This series was especially designed to serve the needs of embedded applications. The embedded market includes applications as diverse as industrial automation, avionics, image processing, graphics, robotics, telecommunications, and automobiles. These types of applications require high integration, low power consumption, quick interrupt response times, and high performance. Since time to market is critical, embedded microprocessors need to be easy to use in both hardware and software designs.

All members of the 80960 series share a common core architecture which utilizes RISC technology so that, except for special functions, the family members are object code compatible. Each new processor in the series will add its own special set of functions to the core to satisfy the needs of a specific application or range of applications in the embedded market. For example, future processors may include a DMA controller, a timer, or an A/D converter.

The 80960KB includes an integrated floating-point unit. Intel also offers a pin-compatible version, called the 80960KA, without an FPU, and a military-grade version, the 80960MC, with support for memory management, mutitasking, multiprocessing, and fault tolerance.

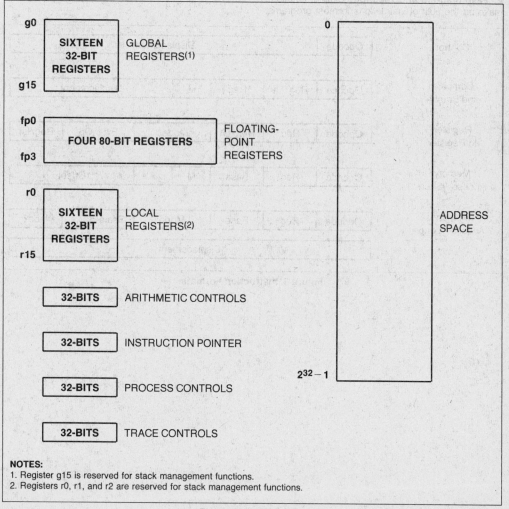

NOTES:
1. Register g15 is reserved for stack management functions.
2. Registers r0, r1, and r2 are reserved for stack management functions.

Figure 2. Register Set

KEY PERFORMANCE FEATURES

The 80960KB's architecture is based on the most recent advances in RISC technology and is grounded in Intel's long experience in designing embedded controllers. Many features contribute to the 80960KB's exceptional performance:

1. Large Register Set. Having a large number of registers reduces the number of times that a processor needs to access memory. Modern compilers can take advantage of this feature to optimize execution speed. For maximum flexibility, the 80960KB provides 32 32-bit registers and four 80-bit floating-point registers. (See Figure 2.)

2. Fast Instruction Execution. Simple functions make up the bulk of instructions in most programs,

so that execution speed can be greatly improved by ensuring that these core instructions execute in as short a time as possible. The most-frequently executed instructions such as register-register moves, add/subtract, logical operations, and shifts execute in one to two cycles (Table 1 contains a list of instructions.)

3. Load/Store Architecture. Like other processors based on RISC technology, the 80960KB has a Load/Store architecture, only the LOAD and STORE instructions reference memory; all other instructions operate on registers. This type of architecture simplifies instruction decoding and is used in combination with other techniques to increase parallelism.

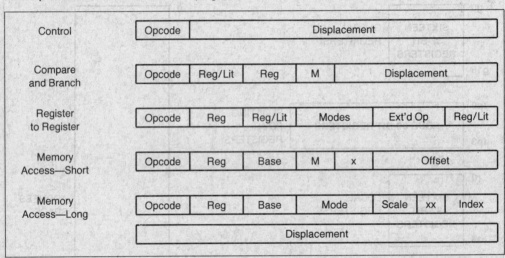

Figure 3. Instruction Formats

Table 1. 80960KB Instruction Set

Data Movement	Arithmetic	Logical	Bit and Bit Field
Load	Add	And	Set Bit
Store	Subtract	Not And	Clear Bit
Move	Multiply	And Not	Not Bit
Load Address	Divide	Or	Check Bit
	Remainder	Exclusive Or	Alter Bit
	Modulo	Not Or	Scan for Bit
	Shift	Or Not	Scan over Bit
	Extended Multiply	Nor	Extract
	Extended Divide	Exclusive Nor	Modify
		Not	
		Nand	
		Rotate	

Comparison	Branch	Call/Return	Fault
Compare	Unconditional	Call	Conditional Fault
Conditional	Branch	Call Extended	Synchronize Faults
Compare	Conditional Branch	Call System	
Compare and	Compare and	Return	
Increment	Branch	Branch and Link	
Compare and			
Decrement			

Debug	Miscellaneous	Decimal	
Modify Trace	Atomic Add	Move	
Controls	Atomic Modify	Add with Carry	
Mark	Flush Local Registers	Subtract with Carry	
Force Mark	Modify Arithmetic		
	Controls		
	Scan Byte for Equal		
	Test Condition Code		

Conversion	Floating-Point	Synchronous	
Convert Real to Integer	Move Real	Synchronous Load	
Convert Integer to Real	Add	Synchronous Move	
	Subtract		
	Multiply		
	Divide		
	Remainder		
	Scale		
	Round		
	Square Root		
	Sine		
	Cosine		
	Tangent		
	Arctangent		
	Log		
	Log Binary		
	Log Natural		
	Exponent		
	Classify		
	Copy Real Extended		
	Compare		

4. Simple Instruction Formats. All instructions in the 80960KB are 32-bits long and must be aligned on word boundaries. This alignment makes it possible to eliminate the instruction-alignment stage in the pipeline. To simplify the instruction decoder further, there are only five instruction formats and each instruction uses only one format. (See Figure 3.)

5. Overlapped Instruction Execution. A load operation allows execution of subsequent instructions to continue before the data has been returned from memory, so that these instructions can overlap the load. The 80960KB manages this process transparently to software through the use of a register scoreboard. Conditional instructions also make use of a scoreboard so that subsequent unrelated instructions can be executed while the conditional instruction is pending.

6. Integer Execution Optimization. When the result of an operation is used as an operand in a subsequent calculation, the value is sent immediately to its destination register. Yet at the same time, the value is put back on a bypass path to the ALU, thereby saving the time that otherwise would be required to retrieve the value for the next operation.

7. Bandwidth Optimizations. The 80960KB gets optimal use of its memory bus bandwidth because the bus is tuned for use with the cache: the line size of the instruction cache matches the maximum burst size for instruction fetches. The 80960KB automatically fetches four words in a burst and stores them directly in the cache. Due to the size of the cache and the fact that it is continually filled in anticipation of needed instructions in the program flow, the 80960KB is exceptionally insensitive to memory wait states. In fact, each wait state causes only a 7% degradation in system perfomance. The benefit is that the 80960KB will deliver outstanding performance even with a low cost memory system.

8. Cache Bypass. If there is a cache miss, the processor fetches the needed instruction, then sends it on to the instruction decoder at the same time it updates the cache. Thus, no extra time is taken to load and read the cache.

Memory Space and Addressing Modes

The 80960KB offers a linear programming environment so that all programs running on the processor are contained in a single address space. The maximum size of the address space is 4 Gigabytes (2^{32} bytes).

For ease of use, the 80960KB has a small number of addressing modes, but includes all those necessary

to ensure efficient compiler implementations of high-level languages such as C, Fortran and Ada. Table 2 lists the memory addressing modes.

Data Types

The 80960KB recognizes the following data types:

Numeric:
- 8-, 16-, 32- and 64-bit ordinals
- 8-, 16, 32- and 64-bit integers
- 32-, 64- and 80-bit real numbers

Non-Numeric:
- Bit
- Bit Field
- Triple-Word (96 bits)
- Quad-Word (128 bits)

Large Register Set

The programming environment of the 80960KB includes a large number of registers. In fact, 36 registers are available at any time. The availability of this many registers greatly reduces the number of memory accesses required to execute most programs, which leads to greater instruction processing speed.

There are two types of general-purpose registers: local and global. The 20 global registers consist of sixteen 32-bit registers (G0 through G15) and four 80-bit registers (FP0 through FP3). These registers perform the same function as the general-purpose registers provided in other popular microprocessors. The term global refers to the fact that these registers retain their contents across procedure calls.

The local registers, on the other hand, are procedure specific. For each procedure call, the 80960KB allocates 16 local registers (R0 through R15). Each local register is 32 bits wide. Any register can also be used for single or double-precision floating-point operations; the 80-bit floating-point registers are provided for extended precision.

Multiple Register Sets

To further increase the efficiency of the register set, multiple sets of local registers are stored on-chip. This cache holds up to four local register frames, which means that up to three procedure calls can be made without having to access the procedure stack resident in memory.

Although programs may have procedure calls nested many calls deep, a program typically oscillates back and forth between only two or three levels. As

Table 2. Memory Addressing Modes

- 12-Bit Offset
- 32-Bit Offset
- Register-Indirect
- Register + 12-Bit Offset
- Register + 32-Bit Offset
- Register + (Index-Register × Scale-Factor)
- Register × Scale Factor + 32-Bit Displacement
- Register + (Index-Register × Scale-Factor) + 32-Bit Displacement

Scale-Factor is 1, 2, 4, 8 or 16

a result, with four stack frames in the cache, the probability of there being a free frame on the cache when a call is made is very high. In fact, runs of representative C-language programs show that 80% of the calls are handled without needing to access memory.

If there are four or more active procedures and a new procedure is called, the processor moves the oldest set of local registers in the register cache to a procedure stack in memory to make room for a new set of registers. Global register G15 is used by the processor as the frame pointer (FP) for the procedure stack.

Note that the global and floating-point registers are not exchanged on a procedure call, but retain their contents, making them available to all procedures for fast parameter passing. An illustration of the register cache is shown in Figure 4.

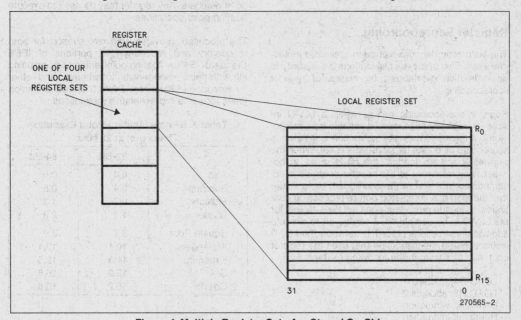

Figure 4. Multiple Register Sets Are Stored On-Chip

Instruction Cache

To further reduce memory accesses, the 80960KB includes a 512-byte on-chip instruction cache. The instruction cache is based on the concept of locality of reference; that is, most programs are not usually executed in a steady stream but consist of many branches and loops that lead to jumping back and forth within the same small section of code. Thus, by maintaining a block of instructions in a cache, the number of memory references required to read instructions into the processor can be greatly reduced.

To load the instruction cache, instructions are fetched in 16-byte blocks, so that up to four instructions can be fetched at one time. An efficient prefetch algorithm increases the probability that an instruction will already be in the cache when it is needed.

Code for small loops will often fit entirely within the cache, leading to a great increase in processing speed since further memory references might not be necessary until the program exits the loop. Similarly, when calling short procedures, the code for the calling procedure is likely to remain in the cache, so it will be there on the procedure's return.

Register Scoreboarding

The instruction decoder has been optimized in several ways. One of these optimizations is the ability to do instruction overlapping by means of register scoreboarding.

Register scoreboarding occurs when a LOAD instruction is executed to move a variable from memory into a register. When the instruction is initiated, a scoreboard bit on the target register is set. When the register is actually loaded, the bit is reset. In between, any reference to the register contents is accompanied by a test of the scoreboard bit to insure that the load has completed before processing continues. Since the processor does not have to wait for the LOAD to be completed, it can go on to execute additional instructions placed in between the LOAD instruction and the instruction that uses the register contents, as shown in the following example:

```
LOAD R4, address 1
LOAD R5, address 2
Unrelated instruction
Unrelated instruction
ADD R4, R5, R6
```

In essence, the two unrelated instructions between the LOAD and ADD instructions are executed for free (i.e., take no apparent time to execute) because they are executed while the register is being loaded. Up to three LOAD instructions can be pending at one time with three corresponding scoreboard bits set. By exploiting this feature, system programmers and compilers have a useful tool for optimizing execution speed.

Floating-Point Arithmetic

In the 80960KB, floating-point arithmetic has been made an integral part of the architecture. Having the floating-point unit integrated on-chip provides two advantages. First, it improves the performance of the chip for floating-point applications, since no additional bus overhead is associated with floating-point calculations, thereby leaving more time for other bus operations such as I/O. Second, the cost of using floating-point operations is reduced because a separate coprocessor chip is not required.

The 80960KB floating-point (real number) data types include single-precision (32-bit), double-precision (64-bit), and extended precision (80-bit) floating-point numbers. Any register may be used to execute floating-point operations.

The processor provides hardware support for both mandatory and recommended portions of IEEE Standard 754 for floating-point arithmetic, including all arithmetic, exponential, logarithmic, and other transcendental functions. Table 3 shows execution times for some representative instructions.

Table 3. Sample Floating-Point Execution Times (μs) at 25 MHz

	32-Bit	64-Bit
Add	0.4	0.5
Subtract	0.4	0.5
Multiply	0.7	1.3
Divide	1.3	2.9
Square Root	3.7	3.9
Arctangent	10.1	13.1
Exponent	11.3	12.5
Sine	15.2	16.6
Cosine	15.2	16.6

High Bandwidth Local Bus

An 80960KB CPU resides on a high-bandwidth address/data bus known as the local bus (L-Bus). The L-Bus provides a direct communication path between the processor and the memory and I/O subsystem interfaces. The processor uses the local bus to fetch instructions, manipulate memory, and respond to interrupts. Its features include:

- 32-bit multiplexed address/data path
- Four-word burst capability, which allows transfers from 1 to 16 bytes at a time
- High bandwidth reads and writes at 66.7 MBytes per second
- Special signal to indicate whether a memory transaction can be cached

Figure 5 identifies the groups of signals which constitute the L-Bus. Table 4 lists the function of the L-Bus and other processor-support signals, such as the interrupt lines.

Interrupt Handling

The 80960KB can be interrupted in one of two ways: by the activation of one of four interrupt pins or by sending a message on the processor's data bus.

The 80960KB is unusual in that it automatically handles interrupts on a priority basis and tracks pending interrupts through its on-chip interrupt controller. Two of the interrupt pins can be configured to provide 8259A handshaking for expansion beyond four interrupt lines.

Debug Features

The 80960KB has built-in debug capabilities. There are two types of breakpoints and six different trace modes. The debug features are controlled by two internal 32-bit registers, the Process-Controls Word and the Trace-Controls Word. By setting bits in these control words, a software debug monitor can closely control how the processor responds during program execution.

The 80960KB has both hardware and software breakpoints. It provides two hardware breakpoint registers on-chip which can be set by a special command to any value. When the instruction pointer matches the value in one of the breakpoint registers, the breakpoint will fire, and a breakpoint handling routine is called automatically.

The 80960KB also provides software breakpoints through the use of two instructions, MARK and FMARK. These instructions can be placed at any point in a program and will cause the processor to halt execution at that point and call the breakpoint handling routine. The breakpoint mechanism is easy to use and provides a powerful debugging tool.

Tracing is available for instructions (single-step execution), calls and returns, and branching. Each different type of trace may be enabled separately by a special debug instruction. In each case, the 80960KB executes the instruction first and then calls a trace handling routine (usually part of a software debug monitor). Further program execution is halted until the trace routine is completed. When the trace event handling routine is completed, instruction execution resumes at the next instruction. The

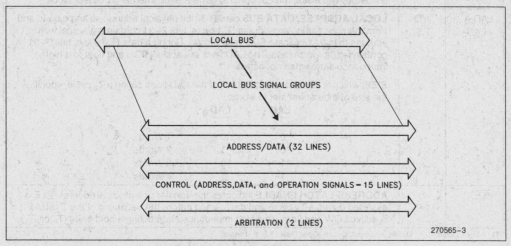

Figure 5. Local Bus Signal Groups

80960KB's tracing mechanisms, which are implemented completely in hardware, greatly simplify the task of testing and debugging software.

FAULT DETECTION

The 80960KB has an automatic mechanism to handle faults. There are ten fault types including trace, arithmetic, and floating-point faults. When the processor detects a fault, it automatically calls the appropriate fault handling routine and saves the current instruction pointer and necessary state information to make efficient recovery possible. The processor posts diagnostic information on the type of fault to a Fault Record. Like interrupt handling routines, fault handling routines are usually written to meet the needs of a specific application and are often included as part of the operating system or kernel.

For each of the ten fault types, there are numerous subtypes that provide specific information about a fault. For example, a floating-point fault may have its subtype set to an Overflow or Zero-Divide fault. The fault handler can use this specific information to respond correctly to the fault.

BUILT-IN TESTABILITY

Upon reset, the 80960KB automatically conducts an extensive internal test (self-test) of its major blocks of logic. Then, before executing its first instruction, it does a zero check sum on the first eight words in memory to ensure that the system has been loaded correctly. If a problem is discovered at any point during the self-test, the 80960KB will assert its FAILURE pin and will not begin program execution. The self-test takes approximately 47,000 cycles to complete.

System manufacturers can use the 80960KB's self-test feature during incoming parts inspection. No special diagnostic programs need to be written, and the test is both thorough and fast. The self-test capability helps ensure that defective parts will be discovered before systems are shipped, and once in the field, the self-test makes it easier to distinguish between problems caused by processor failure and problems resulting from other causes.

CHMOS

The 80960KB is fabricated using Intel's CHMOS IV (Complementary High Speed Metal Oxide Semiconductor) process. This advanced technology eliminates the frequency and reliability limitations of older CMOS processes and opens a new era in microprocessor performance. It combines the high performance capabilities of Intel's industry-leading HMOS technology with the high density and low power characteristics of CMOS. The 80960KB is available at 16, 20 and 25 MHz.

Table 4a. 80960KB Pin Description: L-Bus Signals

Symbol	Type	Name and Function
CLK2	I	**SYSTEM CLOCK** provides the fundamental timing for 80960KB systems. It is divided by two inside the 80960KB to generate the internal processor clock.
LAD_{31} $-LAD_0$	I/O T.S.	**LOCAL ADDRESS/DATA BUS** carries 32-bit physical addresses and data to and from memory. During an address (T_a) cycle, bits 2–31 contain a physical word address (bits 0–1 indicate SIZE; see below). During a data (T_d) cycle, bits 0–31 contain read or write data. The LAD lines are active HIGH and float to a high impedance state when not active.
		SIZE, which is comprised of bits 0–1 of the LAD lines during a T_a cycle, specifies the size of a burst transfer in words.
		<table><tr><td>$\underline{LAD_1}$</td><td>$\underline{LAD_0}$</td><td></td></tr><tr><td>0</td><td>0</td><td>1 Word</td></tr><tr><td>0</td><td>1</td><td>2 Words</td></tr><tr><td>1</td><td>0</td><td>3 Words</td></tr><tr><td>1</td><td>1</td><td>4 Words</td></tr></table>
ALE	O T.S.	**ADDRESS-LATCH ENABLE** indicates the transfer of a physical address. ALE is asserted during a T_a cycle and deasserted before the beginning of the T_d state. It is active LOW and floats to a high impedance state during a hold cycle (T_h or T_{hr}).

I/O = Input/Output, O = Output, I = Input, O.D. = Open-Drain, T.S. = tri-state

Table 4a. 80960KB Pin Description: L-Bus Signals (Continued)

Symbol	Type	Name and Function
$\overline{ADS}$	O O.D.	**ADDRESS/DATA STATUS** indicates an address state. ADS is asserted every T_a state and deasserted during the the following T_d state. For a burst transaction, $\overline{ADS}$ is asserted again every T_d state where $\overline{READY}$ was asserted in the previous cycle.
$W/\overline{R}$	O O.D.	**WRITE/READ** specifies, during a T_a cycle, whether the operation is a write or read. It is latched on-chip and remains valid during T_d cycles.
$DT/\overline{R}$	O O.D.	**DATA TRANSMIT/RECEIVE** indicates the direction of data transfer to and from the L-Bus. It is low during T_a and T_d cycles for a read or interrupt acknowledgement; it is high during T_a and T_d cycles for a write. $\overline{DT/R}$ never changes state when $\overline{DEN}$ is asserted (see Timing Diagrams).
$\overline{DEN}$	O O.D.	**DATA ENABLE** is asserted during T_d cycles and indicates transfer of data on the LAD bus lines.
$\overline{READY}$	I	**READY** indicates that data on LAD lines can be sampled or removed. If $\overline{READY}$ is not asserted during a T_d cycle, the T_d cycle is extended to the next cycle by inserting a wait state (T_W), and $\overline{ADS}$ is not asserted in the next cycle.
$\overline{LOCK}$	I/O O.D.	**BUS LOCK** prevents other bus masters from gaining control of the L-Bus following the current cycle (if they would assert $\overline{LOCK}$ to do so). $\overline{LOCK}$ is used by the processor or any bus agent when it performs indivisible Read/Modify/Write (RMW) operations. Do not leave $\overline{LOCK}$ unconnected. It must be pulled high for the processor to function properly. For a read that is designated as a RMW-read, $\overline{LOCK}$ is examined. if asserted, the processor waits until it is not asserted; if not asserted, the processor asserts $\overline{LOCK}$ during the T_a cycle and leaves it asserted. A write that is designated as an RMW-write deasserts $\overline{LOCK}$ in the T_a cycle. During the time $\overline{LOCK}$ is asserted, a bus agent can perform a normal read or write but no RMW operations. $\overline{LOCK}$ is also held asserted during an interrupt-acknowledge transaction.
$\overline{BE_3}-\overline{BE_0}$	O O.D.	**BYTE ENABLE LINES** specify which data bytes (up to four) on the bus take part in the current bus cycle. $\overline{BE_3}$ corresponds to $LAD_{31}-LAD_{24}$ and $\overline{BE_0}$ corresponds to LAD_7-LAD_0. The byte enables are provided in advance of data. The byte enables asserted during T_a specify the bytes of the first data word. The byte enables asserted during T_d specify the bytes of the next data word (if any), that is, the word to be transmitted following the next assertion of $\overline{READY}$. The byte enables during the T_d cycles preceding the last assertion of $\overline{READY}$ are undefined. The byte enables are latched on-chip and remain constant from one T_d cycle to the next when $\overline{READY}$ is not asserted. For reads, the byte enables specify the byte(s) that the processor will actually use. L-Bus agents are required to assert only adjacent byte enables (e.g., asserting just $\overline{BE_0}$ and $\overline{BE_2}$ is not permitted), and are required to assert at least one byte enable. To produce address bits A_0 and A_1 externally, they can be decoded from the byte enables.

I/O = Input/Output, O = Output, I = Input, O.D. = Open-Drain, T.S. = tri-state

Table 4a. 80960KB Pin Description: L-Bus Signals (Continued)

Symbol	Type	Name and Function
HOLD/ HLDAR	I	**HOLD:** If the processor is the primary bus master (PBM), the input is interpreted as HOLD, a request from a secondary bus master to acquire the bus. When the processor receives HOLD and grants another master control of the bus, it floats its tri-state bus lines and then asserts HLDA and enters the T_h state. When HOLD is deasserted, the processor will deassert HLDA and go to either the T_i or T_a state. **HOLD ACKNOWLEDGE RECEIVED:** If the processor is a secondary bus master (SBM), the input is HLDAR, which indicates, when HOLDR output is high, that the processor has acquired the bus. Processors and other agents can be told at reset if they are the primary bus master (PBM).
HLDA/ HOLDR	O T.S.	**HOLD ACKNOWLEDGE:** If the processor is a primary bus master, the output is HLDA, which relinquishes control of the bus to another bus master. **HOLD REQUEST:** For secondary bus masters (SBM), the output is HOLDR, which is a request to acquire the bus. The bus is said to be acquired if the agent is a primary bus master and does not have its HLDA output asserted, or if the agent is a secondary bus master and has its HOLD input and HLDA output asserted.
CACHE	O T.S.	**CACHE** indicates if an access is cacheable during a T_a cycle. It is not asserted during any synchronous access, such as a synchronous load or move instruction used for sending an IAC message. The CACHE signal floats to a high impedance state when the processor is idle.

Table 4b. 80960KB Pin Description: Module Support Signals

Symbol	Type	Name and Function
$\overline{\text{BADAC}}$	I	**BAD ACCESS,** if asserted in the cycle following the one in which the last $\overline{\text{READY}}$ of a transaction is asserted, indicates that an unrecoverable error has occurred on the current bus transaction, or that a synchronous load/store instruction has not been acknowledged. **STARTUP:** During system reset, the $\overline{\text{BADAC}}$ signal is interpreted differently. If the signal is high, it indicates that this processor will perform system initialization. If it is low, another processor in the system will perform system initialization instead.
RESET	I	**RESET** clears the internal logic of the processor and causes it to re-initialize. During RESET assertion, the input pins are ignored (except for $\overline{\text{BADAC}}$ and $\overline{\text{IAC}}/\overline{\text{INT}}_0$), the tri-state output pins are placed in a high impedance state, and other output pins are placed in their non-asserted state. RESET must be asserted for at least 41 CLK2 cycles for a predictable RESET. The HIGH to LOW transition of RESET should occur after the rising edge of both CLK2 and the external bus CLK, and before the next rising edge of CLK2.
$\overline{\text{FAILURE}}$	O O.D.	**INITIALIZATION FAILURE** indicates that the processor has failed to initialize correctly. After RESET is deasserted and before the first bus transaction begins, $\overline{\text{FAILURE}}$ is asserted while the processor performs a self-test. If the self-test completes successfully, then $\overline{\text{FAILURE}}$ is deasserted. Next, the processor performs a zero checksum on the first eight words of memory. If it fails, $\overline{\text{FAILURE}}$ is asserted for a second time and remains asserted; if it passes, system initialization continues and $\overline{\text{FAILURE}}$ remains deasserted.
N.C.	N/A	**NOT CONNECTED** indicates pins should not be connected. Never connect any pin marked N.C.

I/O = Input/Output, O = Output, I = Input, O.D. = Open-Drain, T.S. = tri-state

Table 4b. 80960KB Pin Description: Module Support Signals (Continued)

Symbol	Type	Name and Function
$\overline{\text{IAC}}$ $\overline{\text{INT0}}$	I	**INTERAGENT COMMUNICATION REQUEST/INTERRUPT 0** indicates either that there is a pending IAC message for the processor or an interrupt. The bus interrupt control register determines in which way the signal should be interpreted. To signal an interrupt or IAC request in a synchronous system, this pin (as well as the other interrupt pins) must be enabled by being deasserted for at least one bus cycle and then asserted for at least one additional bus cycle; in an asynchronous system, the pin must remain deasserted for at least two bus cycles and then be asserted for at least two more bus cycles. **LOCAL PROCESSOR NUMBER:** This signal is interpreted differently during system reset. If the signal is at a high voltage level, it indicates that this processor is a primary bus master (Local Processor Number = 0); if it is at a low voltage level, it indicates that this processor is a secondary bus master (Local Processor Number = 1).
INT1	I	**INTERRUPT 1,** like $\overline{\text{INT0}}$, provides direct interrupt signaling.
INT2/ INTR	I	**INTERRUPT 2/INTERRUPT REQUEST:** The bus control registers determines how this pin is interpreted. If INT2, it has the same interpretation as the $\overline{\text{INT0}}$ and INT1 pins. If INTR, it is used to receive an interrupt request from an external interrupt controller.
$\overline{\text{INT3}}$/ $\overline{\text{INTA}}$	I/O O.D.	**INTERRUPT 3/INTERRUPT ACKNOWLEDGE:** The bus interrupt control register determines how this pin is interpreted. If $\overline{\text{INT3}}$, it has the same interpretation as the $\overline{\text{INT0}}$, INT1, and INT2 pins. If $\overline{\text{INTA}}$, it is used as an output to control interrupt-acknowledge bus transactions. The $\overline{\text{INTA}}$ output is latched on-chip and remains valid during T_d cycles; as an output, it is open-drain.

I/O = Input/Output, O = Output, I = Input, O.D. = Open-Drain, T.S. = tri-state

ELECTRICAL SPECIFICATIONS

Power and Grounding

The 80960KB is implemented in CHMOS IV technology and has modest power requirements. Its high clock frequency and numerous output buffers (address/data, control, error, and arbitration signals) can cause power surges as multiple output buffers drive new signal levels simultaneously. For clean on-chip power distribution at high frequency, 12 V_{CC} and 13 V_{SS} pins separately feed functional units of the 80960KB in the PGA.

Power and ground connections must be made to all power and ground pins of the 80960KB. On the circuit board, all V_{CC} pins must be strapped closely together, preferably on a power plane. Likewise, all V_{SS} pins should be strapped together, preferably on a ground plane. These pins may not be connected together within the chip.

Power Decoupling Recommendations

Liberal decoupling capacitance should be placed near the 80960KB. The processor can cause transient power surges when driving the L-Bus, particularly when it is connected to a large capacitive load.

Low inductance capacitors and interconnects are recommended for best high frequency electrical performance. Inductance can be reduced by shortening the board traces between the processor and decoupling capacitors as much as possible. Capacitors specifically designed for PGA packages are also commercially available and offer the lowest possible inductance.

Connection Recommendations

For reliable operation, always connect unused inputs to an appropriate signal level. In particular, if one or more interrupt lines are not used, they should be pulled up. No inputs should ever be left floating.

All open-drain outputs require a pullup device. While in some cases a simple pullup resistor will be adequate, we recommend a network of pullup and pull-down resistors biased to a valid V_{IH} ($\geq 3.4V$) and terminated in the characteristic impedance of the circuit board. Figure 6 shows our recommendations for the resistor values for both a low and high current drive network, which assumes that the circuit board has a characteristic impedance of 100Ω. The advantage of terminating the output signals in this fashion is that it limits signal swing and reduces AC power consumption.

Characteristic Curves

Figure 7 shows the typical supply current requirements over the operating temperature range of the processor at supply voltage (V_{CC}) of 5V. Figure 8 shows the typical power supply current (I_{CC}) required by the 80960KB at various operating frequencies when measured at three input voltage (V_{CC}) levels.

For a given output current (I_{OL}), the curve in Figure 9 shows the worst case output low voltage (V_{OL}).

Figure 10 shows the typical capacitive derating curve for the 80960KB measured from 1.5V on the system clock (CLK) to 0.8V on the falling edge and 2.0V on the rising edge of the L-Bus address/data (LAD) signals.

Test Load Circuit

Figure 13 illustrates the load circuit used to test the 80960KB's tristate pins, and Figure 14 shows the load circuit used to test the open drain outputs. The open drain test uses an active load circuit in the form of a matched diode bridge. Since the open-drain outputs sink current, only the I_{OL} legs of the bridge are necessary and the I_{OH} legs are not used. When the 80960KB driver under test is turned off, the output pin is pulled up to V_{REF} (i.e., V_{OH}). Diode D_1 is turned off and the I_{OL} current source flows through diode D_2.

When the 80960KB open-drain driver under test is on, diode D_1 is also on, and the voltage on the pin being tested drops to V_{OL}. Diode D_2 turns off and I_{OL} flows through diode D_1.

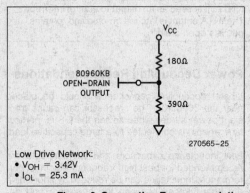

Low Drive Network:
- V_{OH} = 3.42V
- I_{OL} = 25.3 mA

270565–25

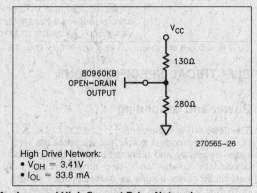

High Drive Network:
- V_{OH} = 3.41V
- I_{OL} = 33.8 mA

270565–26

Figure 6. Connection Recommendations for Low and High Current Drive Networks

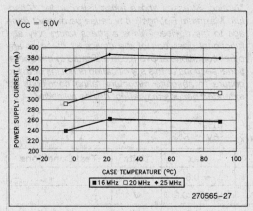

Figure 7. Typical Supply Current (I_CC)

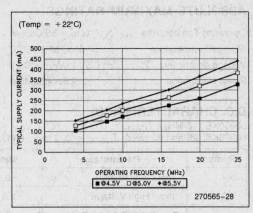

Figure 8. Typical Current vs Frequency

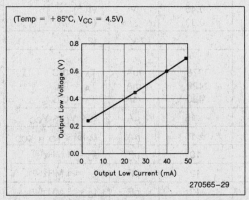

**Figure 9. Worst Case Voltage vs Output Current
on Open-Drain Pins**

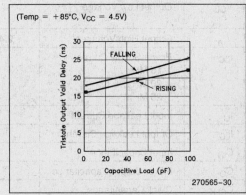

Figure 10. Capacitive Derating Curve

ABSOLUTE MAXIMUM RATINGS*

Operating Temperature . . . . 0°C to +85°C Case

Storage Temperature . . . . −65°C to +150°C

Voltage on Any Pin . . . . −0.5V to V_{CC} + 0.5V

Power Dissipation . . . . 2.5W (25 MHz)

Notice: Stresses above those listed under "Absolute Maximum Ratings" may cause permanent damage to the device. This is a stress rating only and functional operation of the device at these or any other conditions above those indicated in the operational sections of this specification is not implied. Exposure to absolute maximum rating conditions for extended periods may affect device reliability.

D.C. CHARACTERISTICS

80960KB (16 MHz): T_{CASE} = 0°C to +85°C, V_{CC} = 5V ± 10%

80960KB (20 and 25 MHz): T_{CASE} = 0°C to +85°C, V_{CC} = 5V ± 5%

Symbol	Parameter	Min	Max	Units	Test Conditions
V_{IL}	Input Low Voltage	−0.3	+0.8	V	
V_{IH}	Input High Voltage	2.0	V_{CC} + 0.3	V	
V_{CL}	CLK2 Input Low Voltage	−0.3	+1.0	V	
V_{CH}	CLK2 Input High Voltage	0.55 V_{CC}	V_{CC} + 0.3	V	
V_{OL}	Output Low Voltage		0.45 0.60	V	(1, 5) (6)
V_{OH}	Output High Voltage	2.4		V	(2, 4)
I_{CC}	Power Supply Current: 16 MHz 20 MHz 25 MHz		 375 420 480	 mA mA mA	 T_A = 0°C T_A = 0°C T_A = 0°C
I_{LI}	Input Leakage Current		±15	μA	$0 \leq V_O \leq V_{CC}$
I_{LO}	Output Leakage Current		±15	μA	$0.45 \leq V_O \leq V_{CC}$
C_{IN}	Input Capacitance		10	pF	f_C = 1 MHz(3)
C_O	I/O or Output Capacitance		12	pF	f_C = 1 MHz(3)
C_{CLK}	Clock Capacitance		10	pF	f_C = 1 MHz(3)

NOTES:
1. For tri-state outputs, this parameter is measured at:
   Address/Data . . . . 4.0 mA
   Controls . . . . 5.0 mA
2. This parameter is measured at:
   Address/Data . . . . −1.0 mA
   Controls . . . . −0.9 mA
   ALE . . . . −5.0 mA
3. Input, output, and clock capacitance are not tested.
4. Not measured on open-drain outputs.
5. For open-drain outputs . . . . 25 mA
6. For open-drain outputs . . . . 40 mA

AC SPECIFICATIONS

This section describes the AC specifications for the 80960KB pins. All input and output timings are specified relative to the 1.5V level of the rising edge of CLK2, and refer to the time at which the signal reaches (for output delay and input setup) or leaves (for hold time) the TTL levels of LOW (0.8V) or HIGH (2.0V). All AC testing should be done with input voltages of 0.4V and 2.4V, except for the clock (CLK2), which should be tested with input voltages of 0.45V and 0.55 V_{CC}.

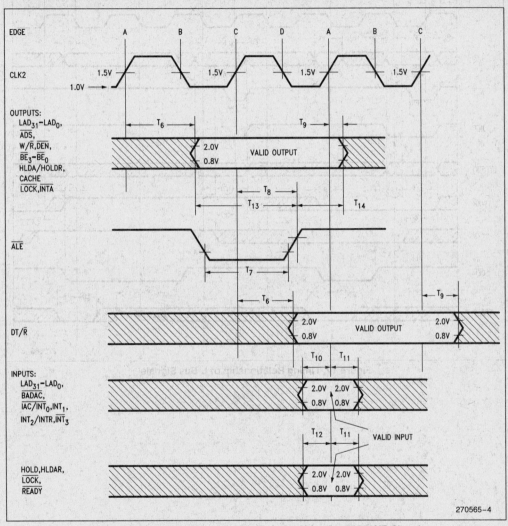

Figure 11. Drive Levels and Timing Relationships for 80960KB Signals

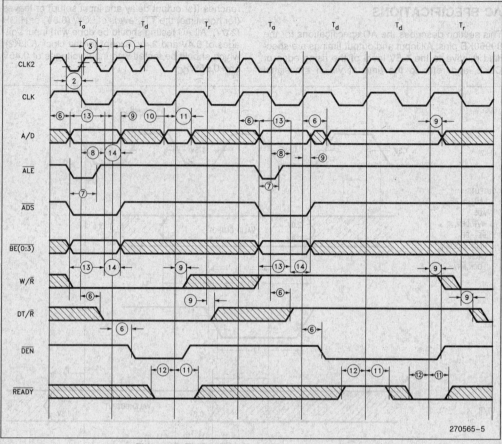

Figure 12. Timing Relationship of L-Bus Signals

270565-5

A.C. Specification Tables

80960KB A.C. Characteristics (16 MHz)

Symbol	Parameter	Min	Max	Units	Test Conditions
T_1	Processor Clock Period (CLK2)	31.25	125	ns	$V_{IN} = 1.5V$
T_2	Processor Clock Low Time (CLK2)	8		ns	$V_{IL} = 10\%$ Point $= 1.2V$
T_3	Processor Clock High Time (CLK2)	8		ns	$V_{IH} = 90\%$ Point $= 0.1V + 0.5\ V_{CC}$
T_4	Processor Clock Fall Time (CLK2)		10	ns	$V_{IN} = 90\%$ Point to 10% Point
T_5	Processor Clock Rise Time (CLK2)		10	ns	$V_{IN} = 10\%$ Point to 90% Point
T_6	Output Valid Delay	2	25	ns	$C_L = 100$ pF (LAD) $C_L = 75$ pF (Controls)
T_{6H}	HOLDA Output Valid Delay	4	31	ns	$C_L = 75$ pF
T_7	$\overline{ALE}$ Width	15		ns	$C_L = 75$ pF
T_8	$\overline{ALE}$ Output Valid Delay	5	20	ns	$C_L = 75$ pF[2]
T_9	Output Float Delay	2	20	ns	$C_L = 100$ pF (LAD) $C_L = 75$ pF (Controls)[2]
T_{9H}	HOLDA Output Float Delay	4	20	ns	$C_L = 75$ pF
T_{10}	Input Setup 1	3		ns	
T_{11}	Input Hold	5		ns	
T_{11H}	HOLD Input Hold	4		ns	
T_{12}	Input Setup 2	8		ns	
T_{13}	Setup to $\overline{ALE}$ Inactive	10		ns	$C_L = 100$ pF (LAD) $C_L = 75$ pF (Controls)
T_{14}	Hold after $\overline{ALE}$ Inactive	8		ns	$C_L = 100$ pF (LAD) $C_L = 75$ pF (Controls)
T_{15}	Reset Hold	3		ns	
T_{16}	Reset Setup	5		ns	
T_{17}	Reset Width	1281		ns	41 CLK2 Periods Minimum

NOTES:
1. $\overline{IAC}/\overline{INT}_0$, INT_1, $INT_2/INTR$, $\overline{INT}_3$ can be asynchronous.
2. A float condition occurs when the maximum output current becomes less than I_{LO}. Float delay is not tested, but should be no longer than the valid delay.

80960KB AC Characteristics (20 MHz)

Symbol	Parameter	Min	Max	Units	Test Conditions
T_1	Processor Clock Period (CLK2)	25	125	ns	$V_{IN} = 1.5V$
T_2	Processor Clock Low Time (CLK2)	6		ns	$V_{IL} = 10\%$ Point $= 1.2V$
T_3	Processor Clock High Time (CLK2)	6		ns	$V_{IH} = 90\%$ Point $= 0.1V + 0.5 V_{CC}$
T_4	Processor Clock Fall Time (CLK2)		10	ns	$V_{IN} = 90\%$ Point to 10% Point
T_5	Processor Clock Rise Time (CLK2)		10	ns	$V_{IN} = 10\%$ Point to 90% Point
T_6	Output Valid Delay	20	20	ns	$C_L = 60$ pF (LAD) $C_L = 50$ pF (Controls)
T_{6H}	HOLDA Output Valid Delay	4	21	ns	$C_L = 50$ pF
T_7	$\overline{ALE}$ Width	12		ns	$C_L = 50$ pF
T_8	$\overline{ALE}$ Output Valid Delay	5	20	ns	$C_L = 50$ pF[2]
T_9	Output Float Delay	2	20	ns	$C_L = 60$ pF (LAD) $C_L = 50$ pF (Controls)[2]
T_{9H}	HOLDA Output Float Delay	4	20	ns	$C_L = 50$ pF
T_{10}	Input Setup 1	3		ns	
T_{11}	Input Hold	5		ns	
T_{11H}	HOLD	4		ns	
T_{12}	Input Setup 2	7		ns	
T_{13}	Setup to $\overline{ALE}$ Inactive	10		ns	$C_L = 60$ pF (LAD) $C_L = 50$ pF (Controls)
T_{14}	Hold after $\overline{ALE}$ Inactive	8		ns	$C_L = 60$ pF (LAD) $C_L = 50$ pF (Controls)
T_{15}	Reset Hold	3		ns	
T_{16}	Reset Setup	5		ns	
T_{17}	Reset Width	1025		ns	41 CLK2 Periods Minimum

NOTES:
1. $\overline{IAC}/\overline{INT}_0$, INT_1, $INT_2/INTR$, $\overline{INT}_3$ can be asynchronous.
2. A float condition occurs when the maximum output current becomes less than I_{LO}. Float delay is not tested, but should be no longer than the valid delay.

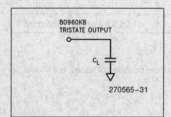

Figure 13. Test Load Circuit for TRI-STATE Output Pins

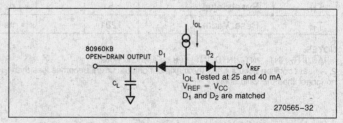

Figure 14. Test Load Circuit for Open-Drain Output Pins

80960KB AC Characteristics (25 MHz)

Symbol	Parameter	Min	Max	Units	Test Conditions
T_1	Processor Clock Period (CLK2)	20	125	ns	$V_{IN} = 1.5V$
T_2	Processor Clock Low Time (CLK2)	5		ns	$V_{IL} = 10\%$ Point $= 1.2V$
T_3	Processor Clock High Time	5		ns	$V_{IH} = 90\%$ Point $= 0.1V + 0.5 V_{CC}$
T_4	Processor Clock Fall Time (CLK2)		10	ns	$V_{IN} = 90\%$ Point to 10% Point
T_5	Processor Clock Rise Time (CLK2)		10	ns	$V_{IN} = 10\%$ Point to 90% Point
T_6	Output Valid Delay	2	18	ns	$C_L = 60$ pF (LAD) $C_L = 50$ pF (Controls)
T_{6H}	HOLDA Output Valid Delay	4	24	ns	$C_L = 50$ pF
T_7	$\overline{ALE}$ Width	12		ns	$C_L = 50$ pF
T_8	$\overline{ALE}$ Output Valid Delay	5	20	ns	$C_L = 50$ pF (2)
T_9	Output Float Delay	2	18	ns	$C_L = 60$ pF (LAD) $C_L = 50$ pF (Controls)
T_{9H}	HOLDA Output Float Delay	4	20	ns	$C_L = 50$ pF
T_{10}	Input Setup 1	3		ns	
T_{11}	Input Hold	5		ns	
T_{11H}	HOLD Input Hold	4		ns	
T_{12}	Input Setup 2	7		ns	
T_{13}	Setup to $\overline{ALE}$ Inactive	10		ns	$C_L = 60$ pF (LAD) $C_L = 50$ pF (Controls)
T_{14}	Hold after $\overline{ALE}$ Inactive	8		ns	$C_L = 60$ pF (LAD) $C_L = 50$ pF (Controls)
T_{15}	Reset Hold	3		ns	
T_{16}	Reset Setup	5		ns	
T_{17}	Reset Width	820		ns	41 CLK2 Periods Minimum

NOTES:
1. $\overline{IAC}/\overline{INT0}$, INT1, INT2/INTR, $\overline{INT3}$ can be asynchronous.
2. A float condition occurs when the maximum output current becomes less than I_{LO}. Float delay is not tested, but should be no longer than the valid delay.

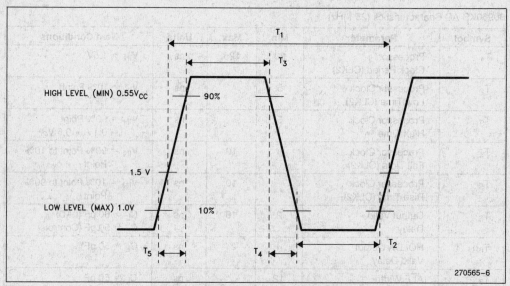

Figure 15. Processor Clock Pulse (CLK2)

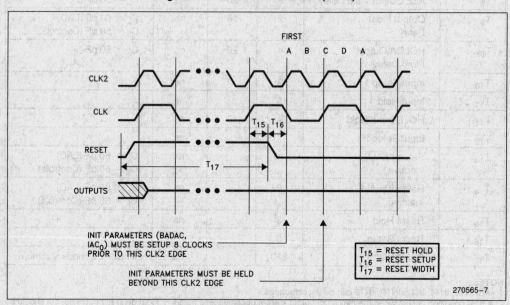

FIRST

A B C D A

CLK2

CLK

RESET

OUTPUTS

T_{15} T_{16}

T_{17}

INIT PARAMETERS (BADAC,
IAC$_0$) MUST BE SETUP 8 CLOCKS
PRIOR TO THIS CLK2 EDGE

INIT PARAMETERS MUST BE HELD
BEYOND THIS CLK2 EDGE

T_{15} = RESET HOLD
T_{16} = RESET SETUP
T_{17} = RESET WIDTH

270565–7

Figure 16. RESET Signal Timing

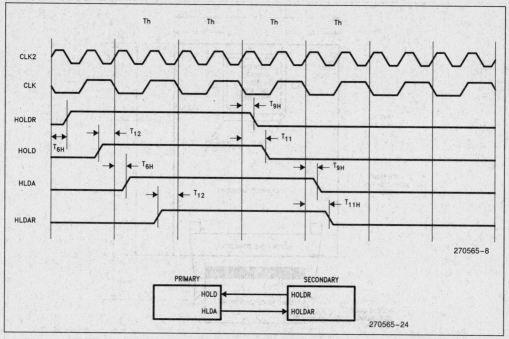

Figure 17. Hold Timing

Design Considerations

Input hold times can be disregarded by the designer whenever the input is removed because a subsequent output from the processor is deasserted (e.g., DEN becomes deasserted).

Whenever the processor generates an output that indicates a transition into a subsequent state, any outputs that are specified to be tri-stated in this new state are guaranteed to be tri-stated. For example, in the T_d cycle following a T_a cycle for a read, the minimum output delay of DEN is 2 ns, but the maximum float time of LAD is 20 ns. When DEN is asserted, however, the LAD outputs are guaranteed to have been tri-stated.

Designing for the ICE-960KB

The 80960KB In-Circuit Emulator assists in debugging both 80960KA and 80960KB hardware and software designs. The product consists of a probe module, cable, and control unit. Because of the high operating frequency of 80960KB systems, the probe module connects directly to the 80960KB socket.

When designing an 80960KB hardware system that uses the ICE-960KB to debug the system, several electrical and mechanical characteristics should be considered. These considerations include capacitive loading, drive requirement, power requirement, and physical layout.

The ICE-960KB probe module increases the load capacitance of each line by up to 25 pF. It also adds one standard Schottky TTL load on the CLK2 line, up to one advanced low-power Schottky TTL load for each control signal line, and one advanced low-power Schottky TTL load for each address/data and byte enable line. These loads originate from the probe module and are driven by the 80960KB processor.

To achieve high noise immunity, the ICE-960KB probe is powered by the user's system. The high-speed probe circuitry draws up to 1.1A plus the maximum current (I_{CC}) of the 80960KB processor.

The mechanical considerations are shown in Figure 18, which illustrates the lateral clearance requirements for the ICE-960KB probe as viewed from above the socket of the 80960KB processor.

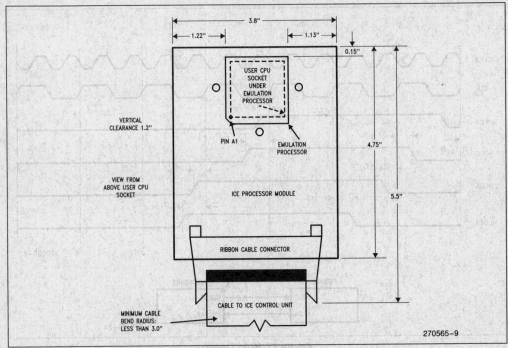

Figure 18. ICE-960KB Lateral Clearance Requirements

MECHANICAL DATA

Package Dimensions and Mounting

The 80960KB is available in two different packages: a 132-lead ceramic pin-grid array (PGA) and a 132-lead plastic quad flat pack (PQFP). Pins in the ceramic package are arranged 0.100 inch (2.54 mm) center-to-center, in a 14 by 14 matrix, three rows around. (See Figure 19.) The plastic package uses fine-pitch gull wing leads arranged in a single row along the perimeter of the package with 0.025 inch (0.64 mm) spacing. (See Figure 20.) Dimensions are given in Figure 21 and Table 7.

There are a wide variety of sockets available for the ceramic PGA package including low-insertion or zero-insertion force mountings, and a choice of terminals such as soldertail, surface mount, or wire wrap. Several applicable sockets are shown in Figure 22.

The PQFP is normally surface mounted to take best advantage of the plastic package's small footprint and low cost. In some applications, however, designers may prefer to use a socket, either to improve heat dissipation or reduce repair costs. Figures 22, 23b and 23c show two of the many sockets available.

Pin Assignment

The PGA and PQFP have different pin assignments. Figure 24 shows the view from the bottom of the PGA (pins facing up) and Figure 25 shows a view from the top of the PGA (pins facing down). Figure 20 shows the top view of the PQFP; notice that the pins are numbered in order from 1 to 132 around the package's perimeter. Tables 5 and 6 list the function of each pin in the PGA, and Tables 8 and 9 list the function of each pin in the PQFP.

V_{CC} and GND connections must be made to multiple V_{CC} and GND pins. Each V_{CC} and GND pin must be connected to the appropriate voltage or ground and externally strapped close to the package. We recommend that you include separate power and ground planes in your circuit board for power distribution.

NOTE:
Pins identified as N.C., "No Connect," should never be connected. The 80960KB PGA and PQFP packages both contain 53 N.C. pins.

Package Thermal Specification

The 80960KB is specified for operation when case temperature is within the range 0°C to +85°C. The case temperature should be measured at the top center of the package as shown in Figure 26.

The ambient temperature can be calculated from θ_{jc} and θ_{ja} by using the following equations:

$$T_J = T_C + P^*\theta_{jc}$$
$$T_A = T_J - P^*\theta_{ja}$$
$$T_C = T_A + P^*[\theta_{ja} - \theta_{jc}]$$

Values for θ_{ja} and θ_{jc} are given in Table 10 for the PGA package and in Table 11 for the PQFP for various airflows. Note that the θ_{ja} for the PGA package can be reduced by adding a heatsink, while a heatsink is not generally used with the plastic package since it is intended to be surface mounted. The maximum allowable ambient temperature (T_A) permitted without exceeding T_C is shown by the charts in Figures 27 through 29 for 16 MHz, 20 MHz, and 25 MHz respectively.

The curves assume the maximum permitted supply current (I_{CC}) at each speed, V_{CC} of 5.0V, and a T_{CASE} of +85°C.

If you will be using the 80960KB in a harsh environment where the ambient temperature may exceed the limits for the normal commercial part, you should consider using an extended temperature part. These parts are designed by the prefix "TA" and are available at 16 and 20 MHz in the ceramic PGA package. Figure 30 shows the maximum allowable ambient temperature for the 20 MHz extended temperature TA80960KB at various airflows. The curve assumes an I_{CC} of 420 mA, V_{CC} of 5.0V, and a T_{CASE} of +125°C.

WAVEFORMS

Figures 31 through 36 show the waveforms for various transactions on the 80960KB's local bus.

SUPPORT COMPONENTS

85C960 Burst Bus Controller

The Intel 85C960 performs burst logic, ready generation, and address decode for the 80960KA and 80960KB. The burst logic supports both standard and burst mode memories and peripherals. The ready generation and timing control supports 0 to 15 wait states across eight address ranges for read/write and burst accesses. The address decoder decodes eight address inputs into four external and four internal chip selects. The wait state and chip select values may be programmed by the user; the timing control and burst logic are fixed.

The 85C960 operates with the 80960KA and 80960KB at all frequencies and consumes only 50 mA at 25 MHz. The 85C960 is housed in a 28-pin, 300-mil ceramic DIP and plastic DIP packages or 28-pin PLCC package for surface mount. In the ceramic DIP package the part is UV-erasable, which makes it easy to revise designs. Order the 85C960 data sheet (No. 290192) for full details.

27C202 High-Performance EPROM

The 80960KB's burst bus is capable of accepting code on almost every bus cycle. For every address the processor puts on the bus, it can read four 32-bit words on the next four bus cycles. A high-performance memory system can make best use of the burst bus. Along with fast access time (70 and 90 ns), the 27C202 also offers a fast data tristate, fast output enable time, and X16 configuration for a two-bank interleave design. As a result the 27C202 can achieve 1-0-0-0 performance (one wait state on the first access and zero wait-states on the remaining three) for 16 and 20 MHz designs. For further information order the 27C202 data sheet (No. 290136).

27960KX Burst Mode EPROM

Intel 27960KX one-megabit EPROM is designed specifically to support the 80960KA and 80960KB. It uses a burst interface to offer near zero wait-state performance without the high cost of alternative memory technologies. The 27960KX removes the need for "dumping" code and data stored in slow EPROMs or ROMs into expensive high-speed "shadow" RAM.

Internally, the 27960KX is organized in blocks of four bytes that are accessed sequentially. The address of the four-byte block is latched and incremented internally. After a set number of wait-states (1 or 2), data is output one word at a time each subsequent clock cycle. High-performance outputs provide zero wait-state data-to-data burst accesses. Extra power and ground pins dedicated to the output reduce the effect of fast output switching on the device. The 27960KX offers 1-0-0-0 performance at 20 MHz and 2-0-0-0 performance at 25 MHz. Full details can be found in the 27960KX data sheet (No. 290337).

Table 5. 80960KB PGA Pinout—In Pin Order

Pin	Signal	Pin	Signal	Pin	Signal	Pin	Signal
A1	V_{CC}	C6	LAD_{20}	H1	$W/\overline{R}$	M10	V_{SS}
A2	V_{SS}	C7	LAD_{13}	H2	$\overline{BE}_0$	M11	V_{CC}
A3	LAD_{19}	C8	LAD_8	H3	$\overline{LOCK}$	M12	N.C.
A4	LAD_{17}	C9	LAD_3	H12	N.C	M13	N.C.
A5	LAD_{16}	C10	V_{CC}	H13	N.C.	M14	N.C.
A6	LAD_{14}	C11	V_{SS}	H14	N.C.	N1	V_{SS}
A7	LAD_{11}	C12	$\overline{INT}_3/\overline{INTA}$	J1	$DT/\overline{R}$	N2	N.C.
A8	LAD_9	C13	INT_1	J2	$\overline{BE}_2$	N3	N.C.
A9	LAD_7	C14	$\overline{IAC}/\overline{INT}_0$	J3	V_{SS}	N4	N.C.
A10	LAD_5	D1	$\overline{ALE}$	J12	N.C	N5	N.C.
A11	LAD_4	D2	$\overline{ADS}$	J13	N.C.	N6	N.C.
A12	LAD_1	D3	HLDA/HLDR	J14	N.C.	N7	N.C.
A13	$INT_2/INTR$	D12	V_{CC}	K1	$\overline{BE}_3$	N8	N.C.
A14	V_{CC}	D13	N.C.	K2	$\overline{FAILURE}$	N9	N.C.
B1	LAD_{23}	D14	N.C.	K3	V_{SS}	N10	N.C.
B2	LAD_{24}	E1	LAD_{28}	K12	V_{CC}	N11	N.C.
B3	LAD_{22}	E2	LAD_{26}	K13	N.C.	N12	N.C.
B4	LAD_{21}	E3	LAD_{27}	K14	N.C.	N13	N.C.
B5	LAD_{18}	E12	N.C.	L1	$\overline{DEN}$	N14	N.C.
B6	LAD_{15}	E13	V_{SS}	L2	N.C.	P1	V_{CC}
B7	LAD_{12}	E14	N.C.	L3	V_{CC}	P2	N.C.
B8	LAD_{10}	F1	LAD_{29}	L12	V_{SS}	P3	N.C.
B9	LAD_6	F2	LAD_{31}	L13	N.C.	P4	N.C.
B10	LAD_2	F3	CACHE	L14	N.C.	P5	N.C.
B11	CLK2	F12	N.C.	M1	N.C.	P6	N.C.
B12	LAD_0	F13	N.C.	M2	V_{CC}	P7	N.C.
B13	RESET	F14	N.C.	M3	V_{SS}	P8	N.C.
B14	V_{SS}	G1	LAD_{30}	M4	V_{SS}	P9	N.C.
C1	HOLD/HLDAR	G2	$\overline{READY}$	M5	V_{CC}	P10	N.C.
C2	LAD_{25}	G3	$\overline{BE}_1$	M6	N.C.	P11	N.C.
C3	$\overline{BADAC}$	G12	N.C.	M7	N.C.	P12	N.C.
C4	V_{CC}	G13	N.C.	M8	N.C.	P13	V_{SS}
C5	V_{SS}	G14	N.C.	M9	N.C.	P14	V_{CC}

Table 6. 80960KB PGA Pinout—In Signal Order

Signal	Pin	Signal	Pin	Signal	Pin	Signal	Pin
$\overline{ADS}$	D2	LAD_{15}	B6	N.C.	J14	N.C.	P9
$\overline{ALE}$	D1	LAD_{16}	A5	N.C.	K13	N.C.	P10
$\overline{BADAC}$	C3	LAD_{17}	A4	N.C.	K14	N.C.	P11
$\overline{BE_0}$	H2	LAD_{18}	B5	N.C.	L13	N.C.	P12
$\overline{BE_1}$	G3	LAD_{19}	A3	N.C.	L14	N.C.	L2
$\overline{BE_2}$	J2	LAD_{20}	C6	N.C.	M1	$\overline{READY}$	G2
$\overline{BE_3}$	K1	LAD_{21}	B4	N.C.	M6	RESET	B13
CACHE	F3	LAD_{22}	B3	N.C.	M7	V_{CC}	A1
CLK2	B11	LAD_{23}	B1	N.C.	M8	V_{CC}	A14
$\overline{DEN}$	L1	LAD_{24}	B2	N.C.	M9	V_{CC}	C4
DT/$\overline{R}$	J1	LAD_{25}	C2	N.C.	M12	V_{CC}	C10
$\overline{FAILURE}$	K2	LAD_{26}	E2	N.C.	M13	V_{CC}	D12
HLDA/HOLDR	D3	LAD_{27}	E3	N.C.	M14	V_{CC}	K12
HOLD/HLDAR	C1	LAD_{28}	E1	N.C.	N2	V_{CC}	L3
$\overline{IAC}/\overline{INT}_0$	C14	LAD_{29}	F1	N.C.	N3	V_{CC}	M2
INT_1	C13	LAD_{30}	G1	N.C.	N4	V_{CC}	M5
INT_2/INTR	A13	LAD_{31}	F2	N.C.	N5	V_{CC}	M11
$\overline{INT}_3/\overline{INTA}$	C12	$\overline{LOCK}$	H3	N.C.	N6	V_{CC}	P1
LAD_0	B12	N.C.	D13	N.C.	N7	V_{CC}	P14
LAD_1	A12	N.C.	D14	N.C.	N8	V_{SS}	A2
LAD_2	B10	N.C.	E12	N.C.	N9	V_{SS}	B14
LAD_3	C9	N.C.	E14	N.C.	N10	V_{SS}	C5
LAD_4	A11	N.C.	F12	N.C.	N11	V_{SS}	C11
LAD_5	A10	N.C.	F13	N.C.	N12	V_{SS}	E13
LAD_6	B9	N.C.	F14	N.C.	N13	V_{SS}	J3
LAD_7	A9	N.C.	G12	N.C.	N14	V_{SS}	K3
LAD_8	C8	N.C.	G13	N.C.	P2	V_{SS}	L12
LAD_9	A8	N.C.	G14	N.C.	P3	V_{SS}	M3
LAD_{10}	B8	N.C.	H12	N.C.	P4	V_{SS}	M4
LAD_{11}	A7	N.C.	H13	N.C.	P5	V_{SS}	M10
LAD_{12}	B7	N.C.	H14	N.C.	P6	V_{SS}	N1
LAD_{13}	C7	N.C.	J12	N.C.	P7	V_{SS}	P13
LAD_{14}	A6	N.C.	J13	N.C.	P8	W/$\overline{R}$	H1

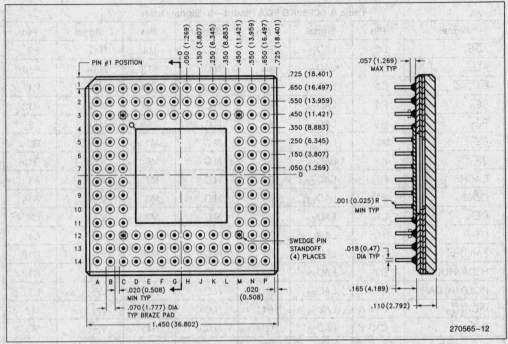

Figure 19. A 132-Lead Pin-Grid Array (PGA) Used to Package the 80960KB

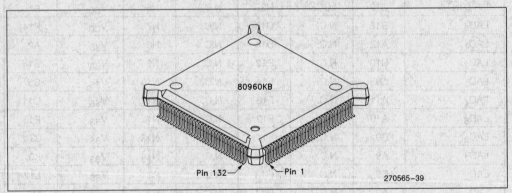

Figure 20. The 132-Lead Plastic Quad Flat Pack (PQFP) used to Package the 80960KB

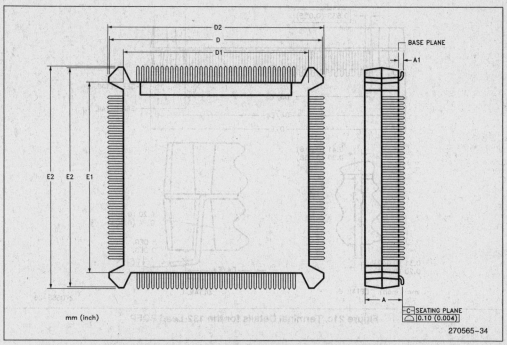

Figure 21a. Principal Dimensions of the 132-Lead PQFP

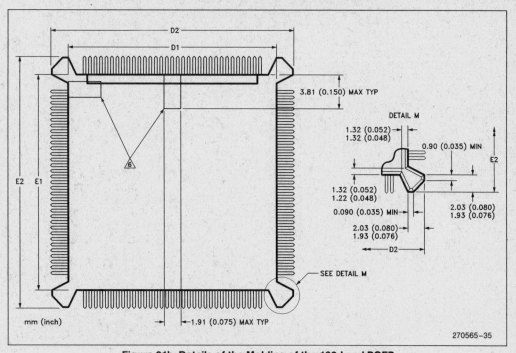

Figure 21b. Details of the Molding of the 132-Lead PQFP

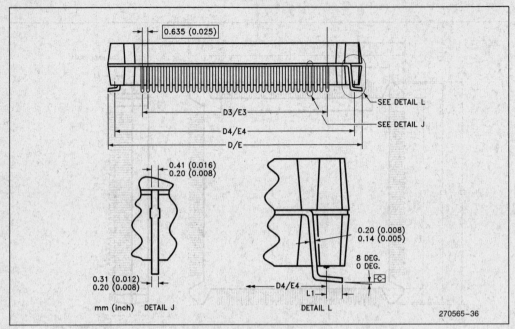

Figure 21c. Terminal Details for the 132-Lead PQFP

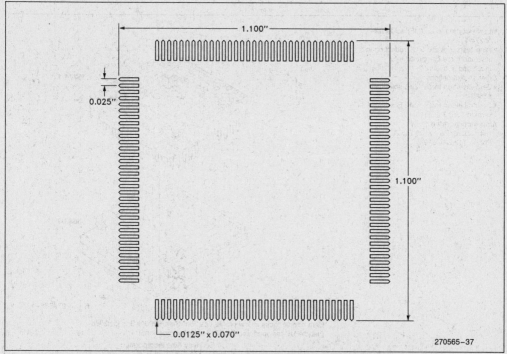

Figure 21d. Board Footprint Area for the 132-Lead PQFP

Table 7. Package Dimension: 80960KB PQFP

Symbol	Description	Inches		MM	
		Min	Max	Min	Max
N	Leadcount	132 Leads		132 Leads	
A	Package Height	0.160	0.170	4.060	4.320
A1	Standoff	0.020	0.030	0.510	0.760
D,E	Terminal Dimension	1.075	1.085	27.310	27.560
D1,E1	Package Body	0.947	0.953	24.050	24.210

D2,E2	Bumper Distance
	  Without Flash
	  With Flash
		
		1.097
		1.097
			
			1.103
			1.110
				
				27.860
				27.860
					
					28.010
					28.190

D3,E3	Lead Dimension	0.800 REF		20.32 REF	
D4,E4	Foot Radius Location	1.023	1.037	25.890	26.330
L1	Foot Length	0.020	0.030	0.510	0.760

- Low insertion force (LIF) soldertail 55274-1
- Amp tests indicate 50% reduction in insertion force compared to machined sockets

Other socket options
- Zero insertion force (ZIF) soldertail 55583-1
- Zero insertion force (ZIF) Burn-in version 55573-2

Amp Incorporated
(Harrisburg, PA 17105 U.S.A
Phone 717-564-0100)

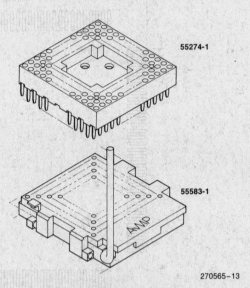

55274-1

55583-1

270565–13

Cam handle locks in low profile position when 80960KB is installed
(handle UP for open and DOWN for closed positions).

Courtesy Amp Incorporated

Peel-A-Way* Mylar and Kapton Socket Terminal Carriers
- Low insertion force surface mount CS132-37TG
- Low insertion force soldertail CS132-01TG
- Low insertion force wire-wrap CS132-02TG (two-level) CS132-03TG (thee-level)
- Low insertion force press-fit CS132-05TG

Advanced Interconnections
(5 Division Street)
Warwick, RI 02818 U.S.A.
Phone 401-885-0485)

Peel-A-Way Carrier No. 132:
Kapton Carrier is KS132
Mylar Carrier is MS132

Molded Plastic Body KS132 is shown below:

FOOT PRINT NO. 132

1.400 SQ.

.100 TYP

14 x 14 x 3 ROWS

270565–14

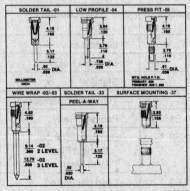

270565–15

Courtesy Advanced Interconnections
(Peel-A-Way Terminal Carriers
U.S. Patent No. 4442938)

*Peel-A-Way is a trademark of Advanced Interconnections.

Figure 22. Several Socket Options for Mounting the 80960KB

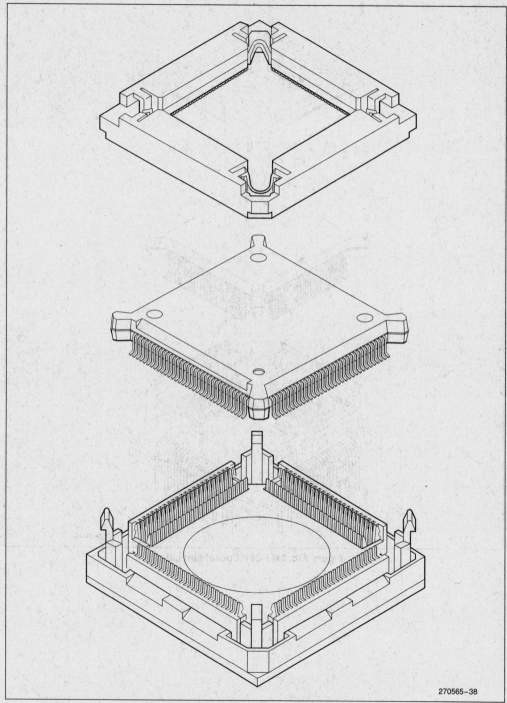

**Figure 23a. AMP Micropitch Socket for the 132-Lead Plastic
Quad Flat Pack, 0.025″ Lead Spacing, Gull Wing Leads**

270565–38

270565–46

Figure 23b. 3M PQFP Socket and Lid

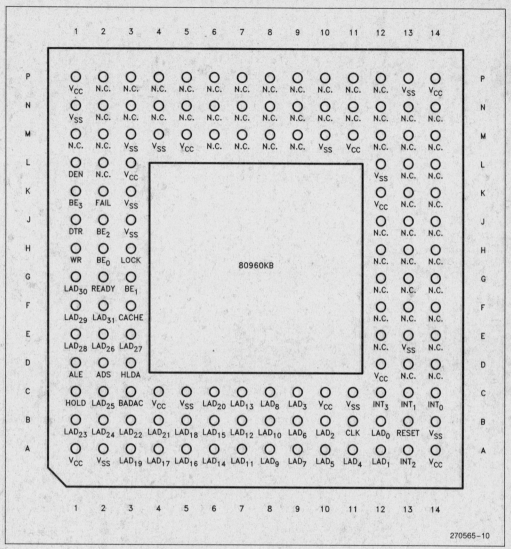

Figure 24. 80960KB PGA Pinout—View from Bottom (Pins Facing Up)

270565–10

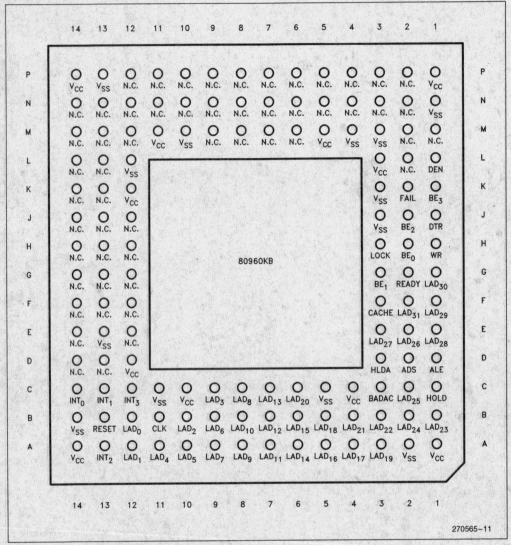

Figure 25. 80960KB PGA Pinout—View from Top (Pins Facing Down)

270565–11

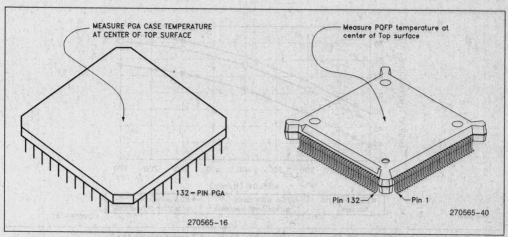

Figure 26. Measuring 80960KB PGA and PQFP Case Temperature

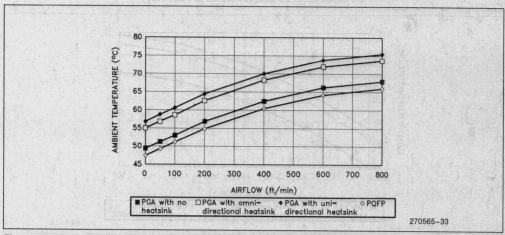

Figure 27. Maximum Allowable Ambient Temperature for the 80960KB at 16 MHz in either PGA or PQFP

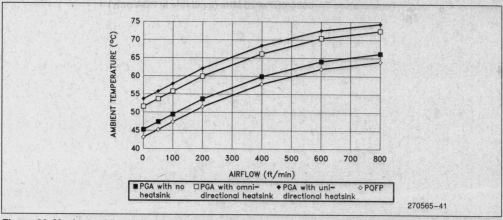

Figure 28. Maximum Allowable Ambient Temperature for the 80960KB at 20 MHz in either PGA or PQFP

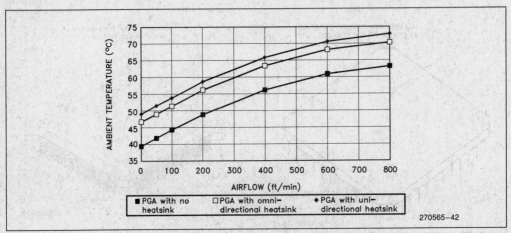

**Figure 29. Maximum Allowable Ambient Temperature for
the 80960KB at 25 MHz (available in PGA only)**

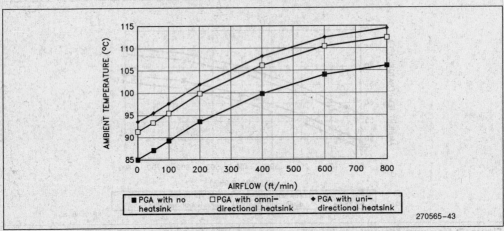

**Figure 30. Maximum Allowable Ambient Temperature for the Extended
Temperature TA-80960KB at 20 MHz (available in PGA only)**

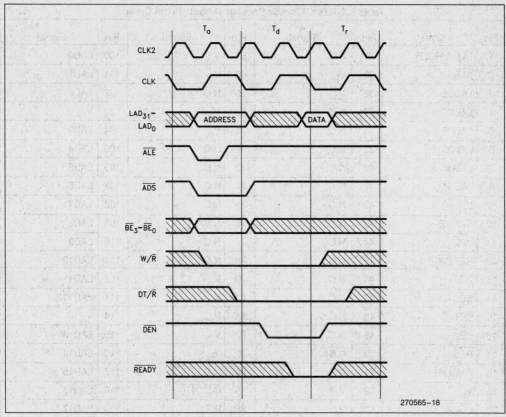

Figure 31. Read Transaction

270565–18

Table 8. 80960KB Plastic Package Pinout - In Pin Order

Pin	Signal	Pin	Signal	Pin	Signal	Pin	Signal
1	HLDA/HOLR	34	N.C	67	V_{SS}	100	LAD0
2	$\overline{ALE}$	35	V_{CC}	68	V_{SS}	101	LAD1
3	LAD26	36	V_{CC}	69	N.C.	102	LAD2
4	LAD27	37	N.C.	70	V_{CC}	103	V_{SS}
5	LAD28	38	N.C.	71	V_{CC}	104	LAD3
6	LAD29	39	N.C.	72	N.C.	105	LAD4
7	LAD30	40	N.C.	73	N.C.	106	LAD5
8	LAD31	41	N.C.	74	N.C.	107	LAD6
9	V_{SS}	42	N.C.	75	N.C.	108	LAD7
10	CACHE	43	N.C.	76	N.C.	109	LAD8
11	$W/\overline{R}$	44	N.C.	77	N.C.	110	LAD9
12	$\overline{READY}$	45	N.C.	78	N.C.	111	LAD10
13	$DT/\overline{R}$	46	N.C.	79	V_{SS}	112	LAD11
14	$\overline{BE0}$	47	N.C.	80	V_{SS}	113	LAD112
15	$\overline{BE1}$	48	N.C.	81	N.C.	114	V_{SS}
16	$\overline{BE2}$	49	N.C.	82	V_{CC}	115	LAD13
17	$\overline{BE3}$	50	N.C.	83	V_{CC}	116	LAD14
18	$\overline{FAILURE}$	51	N.C.	84	N.C.	117	LAD15
19	V_{SS}	52	V_{SS}	85	$\overline{IAC/INT0}$	118	LAD16
20	$\overline{LOCK}$	53	V_{SS}	86	INT1	119	LAD17
21	$\overline{DEN}$	54	N.C.	87	INT2/INTR	120	LAD18
22	DEBUG	55	V_{CC}	88	$\overline{INT3/INTA}$	121	LAD19
23	N.C.	56	V_{CC}	89	N.C.	122	LAD20
24	N.C.	57	N.C.	90	V_{SS}	123	LAD21
25	N.C.	58	N.C.	91	CLK2	124	LAD22
26	V_{SS}	59	N.C.	92	V_{CC}	125	V_{SS}
27	V_{SS}	60	N.C.	93	RESET	126	LAD23
28	N.C.	61	N.C.	94	N.C.	127	LAD24
29	V_{CC}	62	N.C.	95	N.C.	128	LAD25
30	V_{CC}	63	N.C.	96	N.C.	129	$\overline{BADAC}$
31	N.C.	64	N.C.	97	N.C.	130	HOLD/HLDAR
32	V_{SS}	65	N.C.	98	N.C.	131	N.C.
33	V_{SS}	66	N.C.	99	N.C.	132	$\overline{ADS}$

Table 9. 80960KB Plastic Package Pinout - In Signal Order

Signal	Pin	Signal	Pin	Signal	Pin	Signal	Pin
ADS	132	LAD21	123	N.C.	45	N.C.	98
ALE	2	LAD22	124	N.C.	46	N.C.	99
BADAC	129	LAD23	126	N.C.	47	N.C.	131
BE0	14	LAD24	127	N.C.	48	READY	12
BE1	15	LAD25	128	N.C.	49	RESET	93
BE2	16	LAD26	3	N.C.	50	V_{CC}	29
BE3	17	LAD27	4	N.C.	51	V_{CC}	30
CACHE	10	LAD28	5	N.C.	54	V_{CC}	35
CLK2	91	LAD29	6	N.C.	57	V_{CC}	36
DEBUG	22	LAD3	104	N.C.	58	V_{CC}	55
DEN	21	LAD30	7	N.C.	59	V_{CC}	56
DT/R	13	LAD31	8	N.C.	60	V_{CC}	70
FAILURE	18	LAD4	105	N.C.	61	V_{CC}	71
HLDA/HOLR	1	LAD5	106	N.C.	62	V_{CC}	82
HOLD/HLDAR	130	LAD6	107	N.C.	63	V_{CC}	83
IAC/INT0	85	LAD7	108	N.C.	64	V_{CC}	92
INT1	86	LAD8	109	N.C.	65	V_{SS}	9
INT2/INTR	87	LAD9	110	N.C.	66	V_{SS}	19
INT3/INTA	88	LOCK	20	N.C.	69	V_{SS}	26
LAD0	100	N.C.	23	N.C.	72	V_{SS}	27
LAD1	101	N.C.	24	N.C.	73	V_{SS}	32
LAD10	112	N.C.	25	N.C.	74	V_{SS}	33
LAD11	111	N.C.	28	N.C.	75	V_{SS}	52
LAD12	113	N.C.	31	N.C.	76	V_{SS}	53
LAD13	115	N.C.	34	N.C.	77	V_{SS}	67
LAD14	116	N.C.	37	N.C.	78	V_{SS}	68
LAD15	117	N.C.	38	N.C.	81	V_{SS}	79
LAD16	118	N.C.	39	N.C.	84	V_{SS}	80
LAD17	119	N.C.	40	N.C.	89	V_{SS}	90
LAD18	120	N.C.	41	N.C.	94	V_{SS}	103
LAD19	121	N.C.	42	N.C.	95	V_{SS}	114
LAD2	102	N.C.	43	N.C.	96	V_{SS}	125
LAD20	122	N.C.	44	N.C.	97	W/R	11

Table 10. 80960KB PGA Package Thermal Characteristics

Thermal Resistance—°C/Watt							
Parameter	**Airflow—ft./min (m/sec)**						
	0 **(0)**	**50** **(0.25)**	**100** **(0.50)**	**200** **(1.01)**	**400** **(2.03)**	**600** **(3.04)**	**800** **(4.06)**
θ Junction-to-Case (Case Measured as shown in Figure 26)	2	2	2	2	2	2	2
θ Case-to-Ambient (No Heatsink)	19	18	17	15	12	10	9
θ Case-to-Ambient (with Omnidirectional Heatsink)	16	15	14	12	9	7	6
θ Case-to-Ambient (with Unidirectional) Heatsink)	15	14	13	11	8	6	5

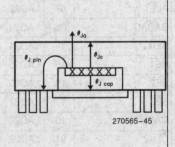

270565–45

NOTES:
1. This table applies to 80960KB PGA plugged into socket or soldered directly into board.
2. $\theta_{JA} = \theta_{JC} + \theta_{CA}$.
3. $\theta_{J\text{-}CAP}$ = 4°C/w (approx.)
$\theta_{J\text{-}PIN}$ = 4°C/w (inner pins) (approx.)
$\theta_{J\text{-}PIN}$ = 8°C/w (outer pins) (approx.)

Table 11. 80960KB PQFP Package Thermal Characteristics

PQFP Thermal Resistance—°C/Watt							
Parameter	**Airflow—ft./min (m/sec)**						
	0 **(0)**	**50** **(0.25)**	**100** **(0.50)**	**200** **(1.01)**	**400** **(2.03)**	**600** **(3.04)**	**800** **(4.06)**
θ Junction-to-Case (Case Measured as shown in Figure 26)	6	6	6	6	6	6	6
θ Case-to-Ambient (No Heatsink)	20	19	18	16	13	11	10

NOTES:
1. This table applies to 80960KB PQFP soldered directly into board.
2. $\theta_{JA} = \theta_{JC} + \theta_{CA}$.
3. θ_{JL} = 18°C/Watt
θ_{JB} = 18°C/Watt

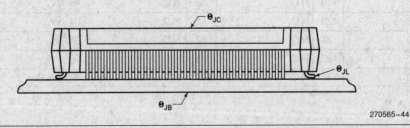

270565–44

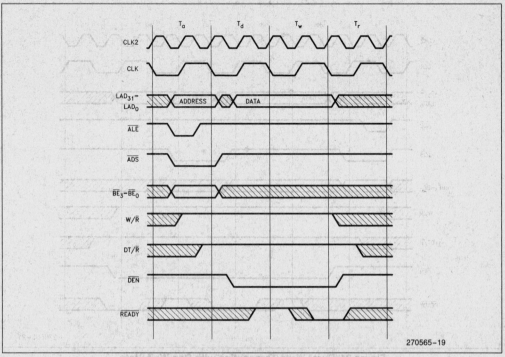

Figure 32. Write Transaction with One Wait State

270565-19

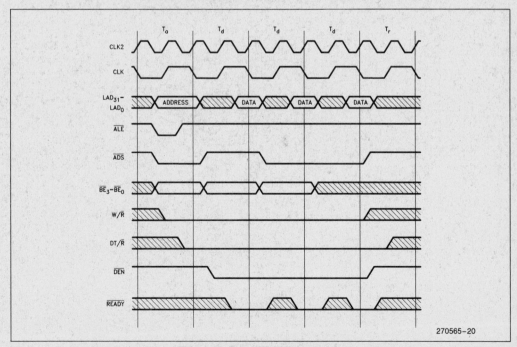

Figure 33. Burst Read Transaction

270565-20

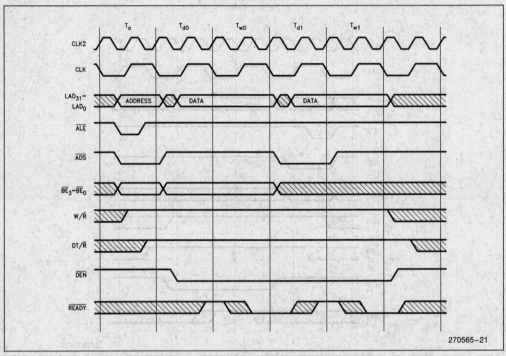

Figure 34. Burst Write Transaction with One Wait State

270565–21

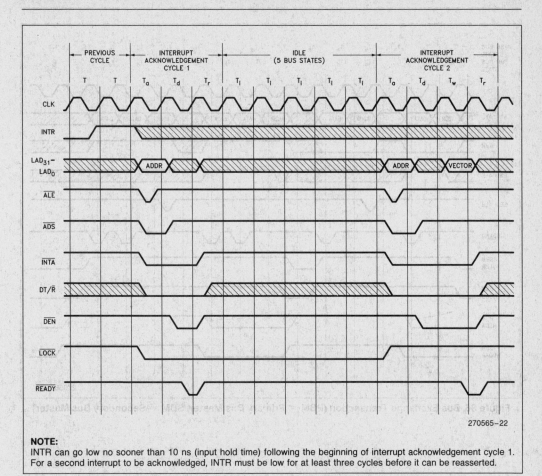

NOTE:
INTR can go low no sooner than 10 ns (input hold time) following the beginning of interrupt acknowledgement cycle 1.
For a second interrupt to be acknowledged, INTR must be low for at least three cycles before it can be reasserted.

270565–22

Figure 35. Interrupt Acknowledge Transaction

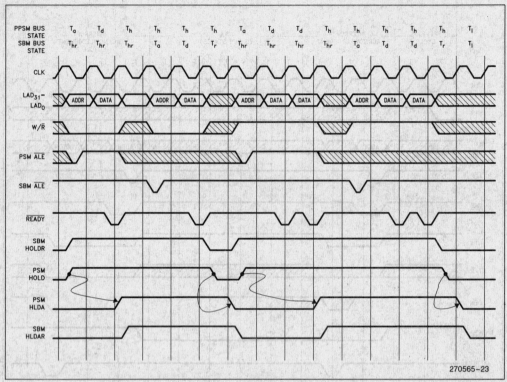

Figure 36. Bus Exchange Transaction (PBM = Primary Bus Master, SBM = Secondary Bus Master)

80960CA Product Overview and Data Sheets

80960CA PRODUCT OVERVIEW

1.0 PURPOSE

The *80960CA Product Overview* is a summary of the features and operation of Intel's 80960CA Embedded Processor. The Product Overview is intended for those who are not familiar with the 80960 architecture or the 80960CA, a product built around this architecture. The 80960CA Product Overview provides a programmer or a system designer with a quick, global view of software and hardware design considerations for the 80960CA. For further information, refer to the following reference documents:

— The *80960CA User's Manual* contains detailed technical information and examples for designing embedded systems using the 80960CA.

— The *80960CA Data Sheet* provides electrical specifications for the device, such as the DC and AC parameters, operating conditions, and packaging specifications.

2.0 80960CA 32-BIT EMBEDDED PROCESSOR

The 80960CA (Figure 2-1) is optimized for embedded processing applications. This product features the high-performance C-Series core plus built-in system peripherals, effectively integrating a high-speed CPU and system components onto a single silicon die. The 80960CA is a member of Intel's 80960 embedded processor family. Each member of the 80960 family is based on a common architectural definition referred to as the *core architecture*.

An 80960 family member, such as the 80960CA, is made up of an implementation of the core architecture plus application-specific extensions. These extensions may consist of integrated peripherals, instruction-set extensions, or additional registers and caches beyond those defined by the architecture. The common core architecture provides a basis for code compatibility for all 80960 family products, while application-specific extensions optimize a particular product for a class of applications.

The 80960 architectural target is the execution of multiple instructions per clock (i.e., fractional clocks per instruction). By defining an architecture which supports parallel instruction execution and out-of-order instruction execution, performance advances are not constrained by the system clock.

The 80960CA is capable of launching and executing instructions in parallel. This is accomplished by the use of advanced silicon technology as well as innovative "microarchitectural" constructs. The term microarchitecture refers to the implementation of the instruction set and programming resources. For example, different microarchitectures may have different pipeline construction, internal bus widths, register set porting, degrees of parallelism, and cache parameterization (two-way, four-way, etc.).

A principal objective of the 80960 architecture is to provide the framework to allow microarchitectural advances to translate directly into increased performance without architectural limitations.

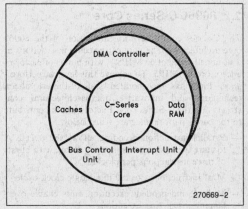

Figure 2-1. 80960CA

2.1 80960 Architecture

Embedded applications are cost sensitive, require a different mix of instructions than reprogrammable applications, have demanding interrupt response requirements, and often use real-time executives rather than full-blown operating systems. The 80960 architecture was developed with these factors in mind. Several key optimizations which are provided by the architecture are explained below.

Instruction Set: Powerful Boolean operations are provided. Frequently executed functions are available as single instructions for greater code density and performance. Call, Return, Compare-and-Branch, Conditional-Compare, Compare-and-Increment or Decrement, and Bit-Field-Extract are each single instructions.

Interrupts: A priority interrupt structure simplifies the management of real-time events. With 31 discrete levels of priority and 248 possible interrupt-handling procedures, this structure provides the low latency and high throughput interrupt handling required in embedded processor applications.

Faults: A generalized fault-handling mechanism simplifies the task of detecting errant arithmetic calculations or other conditions that typically require a significant amount of in-line user code.

Application-Specific Extensions: The core architecture is designed to accept application-specific extensions such as instruction set extensions (e.g., string functions, floating point), special purpose registers, larger caches, on-chip program and data memory, a memory management and protection unit, fault-tolerance support, multiprocessing support, and real-time peripherals (DMA, serial ports, etc.).

2.2 80960 C-Series Core

The C-series core is an implementation of the 80960 core architecture. The core can execute instructions at a sustained speed of 66 MIPS$_{(1)}$ with bursts of performance up to 99 MIPS. To achieve this level of performance, Intel has incorporated state-of-the-art silicon technology and innovative microarchitectural constructs into the C-Series core. Factors which contribute to the core's performance are listed below.

— Parallel instruction decoding allows the 80960CA to start two instructions in every clock, with bursts of three instructions per clock.

— Most instructions execute in a single clock cycle.

— Multiple independent execution units enable overlapping instruction execution.

— Advanced silicon technology allows operation with a 33 MHz internal clock.

— Efficient instruction pipeline is designed to minimize pipeline break losses.

— Register and resource scoreboarding transparently manage parallel execution.

— Branch look-ahead feature enables branches to execute in parallel with other instructions.

— Local register cache is integrated on-chip.

— 1 Kbyte two-way set associative instruction cache is integrated on-chip.

— 1 Kbyte Static Data RAM is integrated on-chip.

These factors combine to make the 80960CA an ultra-high performance computing engine.

NOTE:
1. Single clock instructions at 33 MHz.

2.3 80960CA System Peripherals

The 80960CA features several extensions to the core architecture in the form of integrated peripherals. These peripherals are intended to reduce the external system requirements needed for embedded applications. These peripherals are described below.

Bus Controller Unit: A 32-bit high-performance bus controller interfaces the 80960CA to external memory and peripherals. The bus controller transfers instructions or data at a maximum rate of 132 Mbytes per second.$_{(2)}$ Internally programmable wait states and 16 separately configurable memory regions allow the bus controller to interface with a variety of memory subsystems with minimum system complexity and maximum performance.

DMA Controller: A four channel DMA controller performs high speed data transfers between peripherals and memory. The DMA controller provides advanced features such as data chaining, byte assembly and disassembly, and a fly-by mode capable of transfer speeds of up to 66 Mbytes per second. The DMA controller features a performance and flexibility which is only possible by integrating the DMA controller and the 80960CA core.

Interrupt Controller: A priority interrupt controller manages 8 external interrupt inputs, 4 internal interrupt sources from the DMA controller, and a single non-maskable interrupt input (NMI). A total of 248 external interrupt sources are supported by the interrupt controller by configuring the 8 external interrupt pins as an 8-bit input port. The interrupt controller provides the mechanism for the low latency and high throughput interrupt service featured by the 80960CA. The interrupt latency for the 80960CA is typically less than 1 μs.

3.0 EXECUTION ENVIRONMENT

The *Execution Environment* (Figure 3-1) refers to the resources which are available for executing code on the 80960CA. The following sections describe the elements of the execution environment.

3.1 Registers and Literals

The 80960CA provides four types of working data registers: *Global Registers, Local Registers, Special Function Registers* (SFRs), and *Control Registers.*

Global and local registers are general purpose 32-bit data registers. The SFRs and the control registers provide a programmer's interface to the on-chip peripherals (i.e., the DMA controller, interrupt controller, and bus controller).

NOTE:
2. 33 MHz internal clock, load or instruction fetch on 0 wait state, pipelined burst bus.

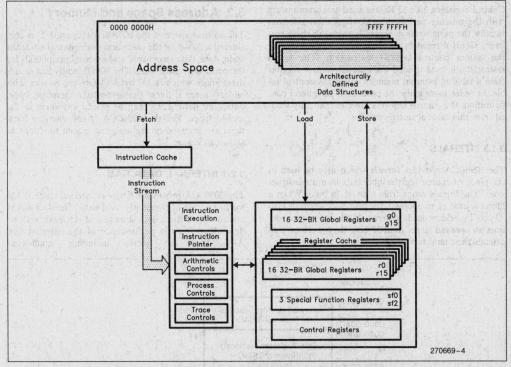

Figure 3-1. Execution Environment

The 80960 architecture is a register-oriented architecture. That is, operands and results of instructions are placed in working data registers rather than in memory. Since the architecture is register oriented, an ample supply of registers is provided. The architecture's working register set consists of 16, 32-bit global registers and 16, 32-bit local registers.

3.1.1 GLOBAL AND LOCAL REGISTERS

The procedure call and return mechanism, which is part of the 80960 architecture, inspires the names given to the local and global registers. When a procedure call or return is executed, the contents of global registers are preserved across procedure boundaries. In other words, the same set of global registers is used for each procedure. A new set of local registers, however, is allocated for each procedure. The 80960's call and return mechanism is explained in Section 3.8.

The 80960CA supplies 16, 32-bit global registers designated **g0** through **g15**. Registers **g0** through **g14** are general purpose global registers. Register **g15** is reserved for the current Frame Pointer. This register is available in assembly language as the **fp** register. The **fp** contains the address of the first byte in the current stack frame. The **fp** register and the stack frame are described in Section 3.8.

The 80960CA supplies 16, 32-bit **Local Registers** designated **r0** through **r15**. Registers **r3** through **r15** are general purpose local registers. Registers **r0**, **r1**, and **r2** are reserved for special functions as follows: **r0** contains the Previous Frame Pointer, **r1** contains the Stack Pointer, and **r2** is reserved for the Return Instruction Pointer. These registers are available in assembly language as, respectively, the **pfp**, **sp**, and **rip** registers. The **pfp**, **sp**, and **rip** registers manage stack frame linkage for the 80960's procedure call and return mechanism. The function of these registers is decribed in Section 3.8.

3.1.2 SPECIAL FUNCTION REGISTERS AND CONTROL REGISTERS

The 80960CA uses 3 Special Function Registers (SFRs) for communicating with on-chip peripherals. These SFR's are an architectural extension specific to the 80960CA. The SFRs on the 80960CA are designated as **sf0**, **sf1**, and **sf2**. SFRs are accessed as source operands by most of the 80960CA's instructions. The registers serve as part of the programmer's interface to the DMA and interrupt controller.

Control registers, like SFRs are used to communicate with the on-chip peripherals. Configuration information for the peripherals is generally stored in these registers. Control registers can only be accessed by using the system control (**sysctl**) instruction. The **sysctl** instruction is used to load the internal control register from a table in external memory called the control table. In order to simplify the process of peripheral configuration, the control registers are automatically loaded from this table at initialization.

3.1.3 LITERALS

The 80960CA provides *literals* which may be used in the place of source register operands in most instructions. The literals range from 0 to 31 (5 bits). When a literal is used as an operand, the processor expands it to 32 bits by adding leading zeros. If the instruction defines an operand larger than 32 bits, the processor zero extends the literal to the operand size.

3.2 Address Space and Memory

The address space of the 80960CA (Figure 3-2) is considered a subset of the execution environment since the code, data, data structures, and external peripherals for the processor reside here. The 80960 family has an address space which is 2^{32} bytes (4 Gbytes) in size. This address space is linear (unsegmented); therefore, code, data, and peripherals may be placed anywhere in the usable space. For the 80960CA, some memory locations are reserved or are assigned special functions as shown in Figure 3-2.

3.2.1 INTERNAL DATA RAM

The 80960CA provides 1 Kbyte of internal static RAM for fast access of frequently used data. The data RAM allows time critical data storage and retrieval, with no dependence on the performance of the external bus. Any load or store, including quad-word

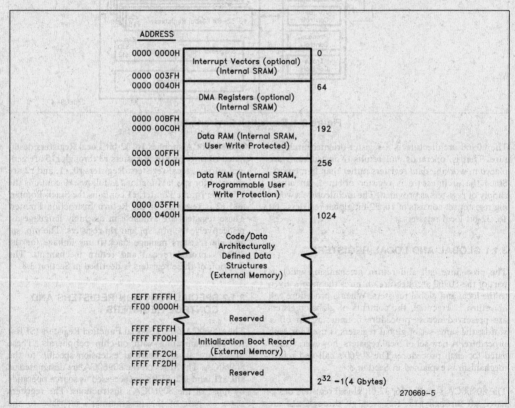

Figure 3-2. Address Space

operations, execute in a single clock cycle when directed to internal data RAM. The data RAM is located at address 00H in the processor's address space. When the DMA controller is in use, 32 bytes of data RAM are reserved for each active DMA channel. Additionally, 64 bytes of data RAM are reserved for 16 interrupt vectors which may be cached internally to reduce interrupt latency. The data RAM reserved for the DMA controller and the interrupt controller can be used for additional data storage when these peripherals are not used.

Two execution modes are possible on the 80960CA, *user mode* or *supervisor mode*. These modes are used to implement a protection model in which system data structures are isolated from user code. As shown in Figure 3-2, the first 256 bytes of data RAM are always write protected when a program is executing in user mode but may always be written when executing in supervisor mode. The remainder of the data RAM can be programmed for this protection feature. The user and supervisor modes are described further in Section 3.7.

3.2.2 RESERVED ADDRESS SPACE

The upper 16 Mbytes of memory (FF000000H–FFFFFFFFH) are reserved for specific functions and extensions to the 80960 architecture. The 12 words in reserved space (FFFFFF00H–FFFFFF2CH) are used to start up the processor when it comes out of reset. These 12 words are called the *initialization boot record*.

3.2.3 ARCHITECTURALLY DEFINED DATA STRUCTURES

To execute a program on the 80960CA, data structures specific to the 80960 architecture must reside in the processor's address space. Architecture-defined data structures include stacks, initialization structures, and various procedure entry tables. These data structures may generally be located anywhere in the address space. Pointers to each data structure are specified when the 80960CA is initialized. The architecture-defined data structures include:

— Interrupt Table — User Stack

— System-Procedure — Interrupt Stack
  Table — Supervisor Stack

— Fault Table

In addition to the data structure defined by the architecture, the 80960CA requires several implementation-specific data structures which are used for configuring peripherals and initialization. These data structures include:

— Control Table

— Process Control Block

— Initialization Boot Record

Each data structure will be explained in more detail later in this product overview.

3.3 Memory Addressing Modes

The 80960CA offers a variety of modes for memory addressing. The addressing modes available are summarized in Table 3-1.

Absolute addressing is used to reference an address as an offset from address 0 of the processor's address space. At the machine level, absolute addressing may be implemented in one of two ways depending on the size of the absolute offset from address 0. Two instruction formats, MEMA and MEMB, are used to provide absolute addressing modes. For the MEMA format, the offset is an ordinal number ranging from 0 to 2048. For the MEMB format, the offset is an integer (called a displacement) ranging from $-2^{31}-1$ to 2^{31}. An assembler will choose the MEMA or MEMB format based on the size of the offset.

Register-indirect addressing modes use a 32-bit ordinal value in a register as the base for the address calculation. Offsets and indexes are added to this address base depending on the particular addressing mode. The *register-indirect-with-index* addressing mode adds a scaled index to the address base. The index is specified as a value in a register. The scale value may be selected as 1, 2, 4, 8, or 16.

The *index-with-displacement* addressing mode uses a scaled index plus an integer displacement. No address base is used in this address calculation.

The *IP-with-displacement* addressing mode is used with load and store instructions to make them IP relative. In this mode, an integer displacement plus a constant of 8 is added to the IP of the instruction to calculate the next address.

Table 3-1. Memory Addressing Modes

Mode	Description
Absolute Offset	Offset
Absolute Displacement	Displacement
Register Indirect	Abase
Register Indirect with Offset	Abase + Offset
Register Indirect with Index	Abase + (Index*Scale)
Register Indirect with Index and Displacement	Abase + (Index*Scale) + Displacement
Index with Displacement	(Index*Scale) + Displacement
Register Indirect with Displacement	Abase + Displacement
IP with Displacement	IP + Displacement + 8

3.4 Data Types

The 80960CA operates on the following data types (Figure 3-3):

— Integer (8, 16, 32, and 64 bits)
— Ordinal (8, 16, 32, and 64 bits)
— Bit
— Bit Field
— Triple Word (96 bits)
— Quad Word (128 bits)

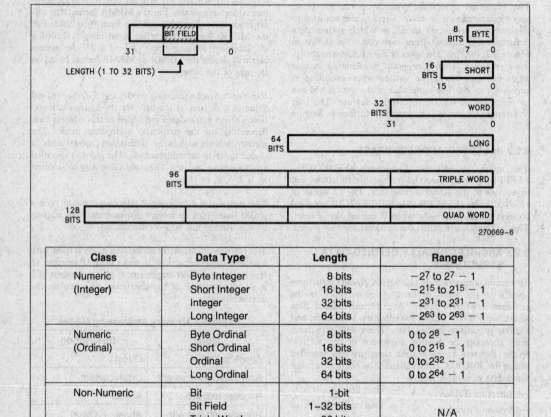

Class	Data Type	Length	Range
Numeric (Integer)	Byte Integer	8 bits	-2^7 to $2^7 - 1$
	Short Integer	16 bits	-2^{15} to $2^{15} - 1$
	Integer	32 bits	-2^{31} to $2^{31} - 1$
	Long Integer	64 bits	-2^{63} to $2^{63} - 1$
Numeric (Ordinal)	Byte Ordinal	8 bits	0 to $2^8 - 1$
	Short Ordinal	16 bits	0 to $2^{16} - 1$
	Ordinal	32 bits	0 to $2^{32} - 1$
	Long Ordinal	64 bits	0 to $2^{64} - 1$
Non-Numeric	Bit	1-bit	N/A
	Bit Field	1–32 bits	
	Triple Word	96 bits	
	Quad Word	128 bits	

Figure 3-3. Data Types

The following sections describe the data types supported by the 80960CA.

3.4.1 NUMERIC DATA TYPES

Integers and ordinals are considered numeric data types since the processor performs arithmetic operations with this data. The integer data type is a signed binary value in standard 2's complement representation. The ordinal data type is an unsigned binary value.

3.4.2 NON-NUMERIC DATA TYPES

The remaining data types (bit field, triple word, and quad word) represent groupings of bits or bytes that the processor can operate on as a whole, regardless of the nature of the data contained in the group. These data types facilitate the moving of blocks of bits or bytes.

3.5 Instruction Set

The 80960CA features a comprehensive instruction set (Table 3-2). Much of the instruction set is that of a RISC architecture. Unlike pure RISC machines, however, the 80960CA provides an extension to the RISC instruction set with instructions that perform complex functions such as procedure calls and returns, high-speed multiplies, and other complex control, arithmetic, and logical operations. The instruction set allows functionally complex yet highly compact code to be written for embedded control applications where memory is a valuable commodity.

3.5.1 INSTRUCTION GROUPS

The 80960CA instruction set is most easily described if grouped by the functions listed below:

— Data Movement
— Address Computation
— Logical and Arithmetic
— Bit and Bit Field
— Comparison
— Branch
— Call and Return
— Fault
— Debug
— Processor Management

The instructions which make up each of these groups are described in the following sections.

3.5.1.1 Data Movement Instructions

The data movement instructions move data from memory to registers, from registers to memory, and between registers. The load instructions copy bytes, words, or multiple words from memory to a selected register or group of registers. Conversely, the store instructions copy bytes, words, or groups of words from a selected register or group of registers to memory. The move instructions copy data between registers.

Load Instructions

- **ld**   load word
- **ldob**   load ordinal byte
- **ldos**   load ordinal short
- **ldib**   load integer byte
- **ldis**   load integer short
- **ldl**   load long
- **ldt**   load triple
- **ldq**   load quad

Store Instructions

- **st**   store word
- **stob**   store ordinal byte
- **stos**   store ordinal short
- **stib**   store integer byte
- **stis**   store integer short
- **stl**   store long
- **stt**   store triple
- **stq**   store quad

Move Instructions

- **mov**   move word
- **movl**   move long
- **movt**   move triple
- **movq**   move quad

3.5.1.2 Address Computation Instructions

The load address (**lda**) instruction causes a 32-bit address to be computed and placed in a destination register. The address is computed based on the addressing mode selected. The load and store instructions perform a function identical to that of the **lda** instruction when calculating a source or destination address. The **lda** instruction is useful for loading a 32-bit constant into a register.

3.5.1.3 Logical and Arithmetic Instructions

Logical instructions perform bitwise Boolean operations on operands in registers. Since this group of instructions performs only bitwise manipulations of data, separate logical instructions for integer and ordinal data types do not exist. In the table below, src1 and src2 represent processor registers or literals which are the operands for these instructions.

Table 3-2. Instruction Set Summary

Data Movement	Arithmetic	Logical	Bit and Bit Field
Load	Add	And	Set Bit
Store	Subtract	Not And	Clear Bit
Move	Multiply	And Not	Not Bit
	Divide	Or	Check Bit
	Remainder	Exclusive Or	Alter Bit
	Modulo	Not Or	Scan for Bit
			Scan for Byte
	Shift	Or Not	Span over Bit
	Extended	Nor	Extract
	Shift	Exclusive Nor	Modify
	Extended	Not	
	Multiply	Nand	
	Extended	Rotate	
	Divide		
	Add with		
	Carry		
	Subtract with		
	Carry		

Comparison	Branch	Call and Return	Fault
Compare	Unconditional	Call	Conditional
Condition	Branch	Call Extended	Fault
Compare	Conditional	Call System	Synchronize
Compare and	Branch	Return	Faults
Increment	Branch and		
Compare and	Link		
Decrement	Condition		
Condition Test	Compare		
	and Conditional		
	Branch		

Debug	Processor Management	Address Computation	Atomic
Modify Trace	Modify	Load Address	Atomic Add
Controls	Process		Atomic Modify
Mark	Controls		
Force Mark	Modify		
	Arithmetic		
	Controls		
	System Control		
	Update DMA		
	Setup DMA		
	Flush Local		
	Registers		

Logical Instructions

- **and**   src1 and src2
- **notand**   src1 and (not src2)
- **andnot**   (not src1) and src2
- **or**   src1 or src2
- **notor**   src1 or (not src2)
- **ornot**   (not src1) or src2
- **xor**   src1 xor src2
- **xnor**   src1 xnor src2
- **nor**   not (src1 or src2)
- **nand**   not (src1 and src2)
- **not**   not (src1)

Arithmetic instructions perform add, subtract, multiply, divide, and shift operations on integer or ordinal operands in registers.

Arithmetic Instructions

- **addi**   add integer
- **addo**   add ordinal
- **subi**   subtract integer
- **subo**   subtract ordinal
- **muli**   multiply integer
- **mulo**   multiply ordinal
- **divi**   divide integer
- **divo**   divide ordinal
- **remi**   remainder integer
- **remo**   remainder ordinal
- **modi**   modulo integer
- **rotate** rotate bit left
- **shli**   shift left integer
- **shlo**   shift left ordinal
- **shri**   shift right integer
- **shro**   shift right ordinal
- **shrdi**   shift right dividing integer

Extended arithmetic instructions facilitate computation on ordinals and integers which are longer than 32 bits. In add with carry and subtract with carry instructions, the carry out from the previous arithmetic instruction is used in the computation. The extended multiply instruction multiplies two ordinal source operands producing a long ordinal result (64 bits). The extended divide instruction divides a long ordinal dividend by an ordinal divisor and produces a 64-bit result. The extended shift right instruction shifts a 64-bit source value and produces the lower order 32 bits of the shifted value.

Extended Arithmetic Instructions

- **addc**   add ordinal with carry
- **subc**   subtract ordinal with carry
- **emul**   extended multiply
- **ediv**   extended divide
- **eshro**   shift right extended ordinal

The atomic instructions perform read-modify-write operations on operands in memory. They allow a system to insure that when an atomic operation is performed on a specified memory location, the operation will be completed before another agent is allowed to perform an operation on the same memory. These instructions are required to enable synchronization between interrupt handlers and background tasks in any system. They are also particularly useful in systems where several agents (processors, coprocessors, or external logic) have access to the same system memory for communication.

Atomic Instructions

- **atadd**   atomic add
- **atmod**   atomic modify

3.5.1.4 Bit and Bit Field Instructions

The bit instructions operate on a specified bit in a register.

Bit Instructions

- **setbit**   set bit
- **clrbit**   clear bit
- **notbit**   not bit
- **alterbit** alter bit
- **scanbit** scan for bit
- **spanbit** span over bit

Bit field instructions operate on a specified contiguous group of bits in a register. This group of bits can be from 0 to 32 bits in length.

Bit Field Instructions

- **extract**   extract field
- **modify**   modify field
- **scanbyte** scan for byte

3.5.1.5 Branch Instructions

The branch instructions allow the direction of program flow to be changed by explicitly modifying the *Instruction Pointer (IP)*. The target IP in a branch instruction is generally specified as a displacement to be added to the current IP. The extended branch instructions allow IP calculation using any addressing mode.

The unconditional branch instructions always alter program flow when executed.

Unconditional Branch Instructions

- **b**   branch
- **bx**   branch extended

The RISC branch-and-link instructions automatically save a Return Instruction Pointer (RIP) before the jump is taken. The RIP is the address of the instruction following the branch and link.

Branch and Link Instructions

- **bal**　branch and link
- **balx**　branch and link extended

Conditional branch instructions alter program flow only if the *condition code flags* in the arithmetic control register match a value specified in the instruction. The condition code flags indicate conditions of equality or inequality between two operands in a previously executed instruction. The arithmetic control register and condition code flags are described in Section 3.6.

Based on a *branch prediction flag* located in the machine level instruction, the 80960CA will assume that an instruction usually takes or does not take a conditional branch. By executing along the predicted path of program flow, delays due to breaks in the instruction stream are often avoided. This feature of the 80960CA is referred to as *branch prediction*. The 80960CA incorporates the branch prediction feature because code using a conditional branch instruction usually favors a single direction of program flow.

The branch prediction flag is specified at the assembly level by appending a *.t* or *.f* to a conditional branch instruction meaning, respectively, "assume branch taken" or "assume branch not taken". For example, the assembler mnemonic **be.t** means that the processor will assume that this branch-if-equal instruction usually branches when encountered. In the following table .p represents the branch prediction flag.

Conditional Branch Instructions

- **be.p**　branch if equal
- **bne.p**　branch if not equal
- **bl.p**　branch if less
- **ble.p**　branch if less or equal
- **bg.p**　branch if greater
- **bge.p**　branch if greater or equal
- **bo.p**　branch if ordered
- **bno.p**　branch if unordered

Compare and conditional branch instructions compare two operands, then branch according to the immediate results.

Conditional Compare and Conditions Branch Instructions

- **cmpibe.p**　compare integer and branch if equal
- **cmpibne.p**　compare integer and branch if not equal
- **cmpibl.p**　compare integer and branch if less
- **cmpible.p**　compare integer and branch if less or equal
- **cmpibg.p**　compare integer and branch if greater
- **cmpibge.p**　compare integer and branch if greater or equal
- **cmpibo.p**　compare integer and branch if ordered
- **cmpibno.p**　compare integer and branch if unordered
- **cmpobe.p**　compare ordinal and branch if equal
- **cmpobne.p**　compare ordinal and branch if not equal
- **cmpobl.p**　compare ordinal and branch if less
- **cmpoble.p**　compare ordinal and branch if less or equal
- **cmpobg.p**　compare ordinal and branch if greater
- **cmpobge.p**　compare ordinal and branch if greater or equal
- **bbs.p**　check bit and branch if set
- **bbc.p**　check bit and branch if clear

3.5.1.6 Compare and Condition Test Instructions

The 80960CA provides several types of instructions that are used to compare two operands. The condition code flags in the arithmetic control register are set to indicate whether one operand is less than, equal to, or greater than the other operand.

Compare Instructions

- **cmpi**　compare integer
- **cmpo**　compare ordinal
- **chkbit**　check bit

Conditional compare instructions test the existing status of the condition code flags before a compare is performed. These conditional compare instructions are provided to optimize two-sided range comparisons (i.e. to test if a value is less than one number but greater than another).

Conditional Compare Instructions

- **concmpi**   conditional compare integer
- **concmpo**   conditional compare ordinal

The compare and increment and compare and decrement instructions set the condition code flags based on a comparison of two register sources, decrements or increments one of the sources, and finally stores this result in a destination register.

- **cmpinci**   compare and increment integer
- **cmpinco**   compare and increment ordinal
- **cmpdeci**   compare and decrement integer
- **cmpdeco**   compare and decrement ordinal

The condition test instructions allow the state of the condition code flags to be tested. Based on the outcome of the comparison, a true or false code is stored in a destination register. The branch prediction flag is used in this instruction to reduce the execution time of the instruction when the test outcome is predicted correctly. For example **teste.t** (test if equal) will execute in a shorter time if the condition code flags test true for the equal condition. Analogous to the function of the branch prediction flag in the conditional compare and branch instructions, the prediction flag in this case eliminates breaks in the micro-instruction sequence which is used to implement the condition test instructions.

Condition Test Instructions

- **teste.p**   test if equal
- **testne.p**   test if not equal
- **testl.p**   test if less
- **testle.p**   test if less or equal
- **testg.p**   test if greater
- **testge.p**   test if greater or equal
- **testo.p**   test if ordered
- **testno.p**   test if not ordered

3.5.1.7 Call and Return Instructions

The 80960CA features an on-chip call and return mechanism for making procedure calls to local and system procedures. The call instructions and the call and return mechanism is described in Section 3.8.

Call and Return Instructions

- **call**   call
- **callx**   call extended
- **calls**   call system
- **ret**   return

3.5.1.8 Fault Instructions

The 80960CA will fault automatically as the result of certain errant operations which may occur when executing code. Fault procedures are then invoked automatically to handle the various types of faults. In addition, the fault instructions permit a fault to be generated explicitly based on the value of the condition code flags. The branch prediction flag in these instructions is used to reduce the execution time of these instructions when the state of the condition code flags are guessed correctly.

Conditional Fault Instructions

- **faulte.p**   fault if equal
- **faultne.p** fault if not equal
- **faultl.p**   fault if less
- **faultle.p** fault if less or equal
- **faultg.p**   fault if greater
- **faultge.p** fault if greater or equal
- **faulto.p**   fault if ordered
- **faultno.p** fault if unordered

The **syncf** instruction causes the processor to wait for all faults to be generated which are associated with any prior uncompleted instructions.

- **syncf**   synchronize faults

3.5.1.9 Debug Instructions

The processor supports debugging and monitoring of program activity through the use of trace events. The debug instructions support debugging and monitoring software.

Debug Instructions

- **modtc**   modify trace controls
- **mark**   mark
- **fmark**   force mark

3.5.1.10 Processor Management Instructions

The 80960CA provides several instructions for direct control of processor functions and for configuring the 80960CA's peripherals. A brief description of the processor management instructions is given below.

Processor Management Instructions

- **modpc**   modify process controls
- **modac**   modify arithmetic controls
- **sysctl**   system control instruction
- **udma**   update DMA SRAM
- **sdma**   setup DMA
- **flushreg**   flush local registers

3.6 Arithmetic Controls

The *Arithmetic Control (AC) Register* is a 32-bit on-chip register (Figure 3-4). The AC register is used primarily to monitor and control the execution of 80960CA arithmetic instructions. The processor reads and modifies bits in the AC register when performing many arithmetic operations. The AC register is also used to control the faulting conditions for some instructions. The **modac** instruction allows the user to directly read or modify the AC register.

The processor sets the condition code flags (bits 0–2) to indicate equality or inequality as the result of certain instructions (such as the compare instructions). Other instructions, such as the conditional branch instructions, take action based on the value of the condition code flags. Table 3-3 shows the functional assignment for each condition code flag.

Table 3-3. Arithmetic Condition Codes

Condition Code	Condition
001	Greater Than
010	Equal
100	Less Than

The integer overflow flag (bit 8) and the integer overflow mask (bit 12) are used in conjunction with the arithmetic integer overflow fault. The mask bit masks the integer overflow fault. When the fault is masked, and an integer overflow occurs, the integer overflow flag is set but no fault handling action is taken. If the fault is not masked, and an integer overflow occurs, the integer overflow fault is taken and the integer overflow flag is not set.

The no imprecise faults flag (bit 15) determines if imprecise faults are allowed to occur. Fault handling and precise and imprecise faults in the 80960CA are discussed in Section 3.10.

3.7 Process Management

Process management refers to the monitoring and control of certain properties of an executing process. The following sections describe the mechanisms available on the 80960CA to perform this function.

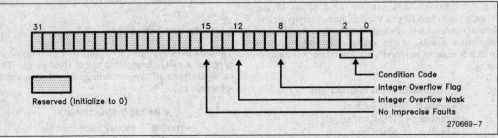

Figure 3-4. Arithmetic Control Register

3.7.1 PROCESS CONTROL REGISTER

The *Process Control (PC) Register* (Figure 3-5) provides access to process state information. The function for the PC register is described below.

Execution Mode Flag—This flag indicates that the processor is executing in user mode (0) or supervisor mode (1).

Priority Field—This 5-bit field indicates the current executing priority of the processor. Priority values range from 0 to 31, with 0 as the lowest and 31 as the highest priority.

State Flag—This flag determines the executing state of the processor. The processor state is either executing state (0) or interrupted state (1).

Trace Enable Bit and Trace Fault Pending Flags— These fields control and monitor trace activity in the processor. The Trace Enable Bit enables fault generation for trace events. The Trace Fault Pending Flag indicates that a trace event has been detected.

The process controls can be modified by software with the modify process controls (**modpc**) instruction. The **modpc** instruction may only write the PC register when the processor is in supervisor mode.

3.7.2 PRIORITIES

The 80960 architecture defines a means to assign priorities to executing programs and interrupts. The current priority of the processor is stored in the priority field of the PC register. This priority is used to determine if an interrupt will be serviced and in which order multiple pending interrupts will be serviced. Setting the priority of an executing program above that of interrupts allows critical code to be prioritized and executed without interruption.

The priority field of the PC register can be modified directly using the **modpc** instruction. The priority field is also modified to reflect the priority of serviced interrupts. On a return from an interrupt routine, the priori-

ty of the processor is restored to its priority before the interrupt occurred.

3.7.3 PROCESSOR STATES AND MODES

The 80960CA may execute programs in *user mode* or *supervisor mode.* The user-supervisor protection mechanism allows a system to be designed in which kernel code and data reside in the same address space as user code and data, but access to the kernel procedures and data is only allowed through a tightly controlled interface. This interface is the system call table and the interrupt mechanism. The 80960CA provides a supervisor pin (SUP) to implement memory systems which protect code and data from possible corruption by programs executing in user mode. Some instructions and functions of the 80960CA are also insulated from code executing in user mode.

The processor has two operating states: executing and interrupted. In executing state, the processor can execute in user or supervisor mode. In the interrupted state, the processor always executes in supervisor mode.

3.8 Call and Return Mechanism

The 80960 architecture features a built-in call and return mechanism. This mechanism is designed to make procedure calls simple and fast, and to provide a flexible method for storing and handling variables that are local to a procedure. A call automatically allocates a new set of local registers and a new stack frame. All linkage information is maintained by the processor, making procedure calls and returns virtually transparent to the user. A system call instruction is provided as a method for calling privileged procedures such as a kernel service. The call and return model supports efficient translation of structured high level code (such as C, or ADA) to 80960 machine language.

The procedure call and return mechanism provides a number of significant benefits which contribute to the performance and ease of use of the 80960CA.

1) The call and return instructions are implemented entirely on-chip, resulting in an extremely high performance implementation of these commonly used functions.

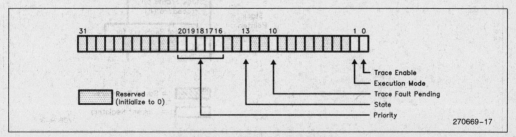

Figure 3-5. Process Control Register

2) A single instruction to implement each call or return operation results in code density improvements compared to processors which require multiple instructions to encode these functions.

3) By implementing the call and return functions as single instructions, the 80960 architecture is open for further optimization of these instructions, while maintaining assembly-level compatibility.

4) A program does not have to explicitly save or restore the variables stored in the local registers when a call or return is executed. The processor does this implicitly on procedure calls and on returns.

5) The call and return mechanism provides a structure for storing a virtually unlimited number of local variables for each procedure: the on-chip local registers provide quick access to often used variables and the stack provides space for additional variables.

3.8.1 LOCAL REGISTERS AND THE STACK FRAME

At any point in a program, the 80960 has access to a local register set and a section of the procedure stack referred to as a stack frame. When a call is executed, a new stack frame is allocated for the called procedure. Additionally, the current local register set is saved by the processor, freeing these registers for use by the newly called procedure. In this way, every procedure has a unique stack and unique set of local registers. When a

return is executed, the current local register set and current stack frame are deallocated. The previous local register set and previous stack frame are restored. This call and return mechanism is illustrated in Figure 3-6 where n is procedure depth for the currently executing procedure.

The procedure stack structure is defined by the 80960 architecture. The procedure stack always grows upward (i.e. towards higher addresses) and the stack pointer (SP) always points to the next available byte of the stack frame. The 80960CA requires that each stack frame begins on a 16-byte boundary. Due to this alignment requirement, a padding space of 0 to 15 bytes may exist between adjacent stack frames in memory. When a stack frame is allocated, the first 16 words are always assigned as storage for the local registers; therefore, the SP initially points to the 17th word in the stack frame. It should be noted that although each stack frame is assigned storage space for the local registers, these locations in the stack are not guaranteed to contain the values of the saved local registers. This is because several sets of local registers are cached on-chip rather than written to the stack in external memory. This caching mechanism is described in detail later in this section.

3.8.2 PROCEDURE LINKING

The 80960 architecture automatically manages procedure linkage. One global register and three local registers are reserved for procedure linkage information.

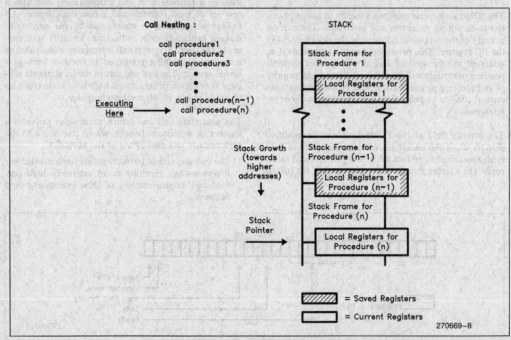

Figure 3-6. Call and Return Mechanism

Figure 3-7 describes the pointer structure used to link frames and to provide a unique SP for each frame. Register **g15** is the *Frame Pointer (FP)*. The FP is the address of the first byte of the current (topmost) stack frame. The FP is always updated to point to the current frame when calls and returns are executed. Register **r0** is the *Previous Frame Pointer (PFP)*. The PFP is the address of the first byte of the stack frame which was created prior to the frame containing this PFP. Register **r1** is the *Stack Pointer (SP)*. The SP points to the next available byte of the stack frame. Register **r2** is reserved for the *Return Instruction Pointer (RIP)*. The RIP is the address of the instruction which follows a call instruction, this is also the target address for the return from that procedure. The RIP is automatically stored in register **r2** of the calling procedure when a call is executed.

3.8.3 PARAMETER PASSING

Parameters may be passed by value or passed by reference between procedures. The global registers, the stack, or predefined data structures in memory may be used to pass these parameters.

The global registers provide the fastest method for passing parameters. The values to be passed into a procedure reside in the global registers of the calling procedure. When a procedure is called, the values in the global registers are preserved. If more parameters are to be passed than will fit in the global registers, additional parameters may be passed in the stack of the calling procedure, or in a data structure which is referenced by a pointer passed in the global registers.

3.8.4 LOCAL REGISTER CACHE

The 80960CA provides an on-chip cache for saving and restoring the local registers on calls and returns. This cache greatly enhances performance of the call and return mechanism on the 80960CA. Movement of data between the local registers and the register cache is typically accomplished in only 4 processor clocks with no external bus traffic. When this cache is filled, the registers associated with the oldest stack frame are moved to the area reserved for those registers on the physical stack (Figure 3-7).

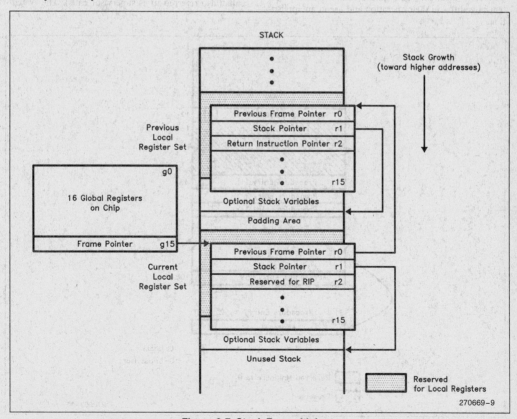

Figure 3-7. Stack Frame Linkage

The local register cache is a physical extension of the internal data RAM. The part of the data RAM used for this cache is not visible to the user and is large enough to hold up to 5 sets of local registers. The register cache may be extended to hold up to 15 sets of local registers. When extended, each new register set consumes 16 words of the user's data RAM, beginning at the highest address and growing downward. The size of the local register cache is selected when the processor is initialized.

In some cases, the contents of the cached local register sets may require examination or modification (e.g. for fault handling). Since the local registers are cached, the **flushreg** instruction is provided to flush the local register cache to the locations reserved for the registers on the stack. This insures that the values in external memory are consistent with the values held in the local register cache.

3.8.5 LOCAL AND SYSTEM CALLS

The 80960CA provides two methods for making procedure calls: local calls and system calls. Local and system calls differ in their operation and use in an application.

The local call instructions initiate a procedure call using the call and return mechanism described earlier. The stack frames for these procedure calls are allocated on the *local procedure stack*. A local call is made using either of two local call instructions: **call** or **callx**. The **call** instruction specifies the address of the called procedure using an IP plus displacement addressing mode with a range of -2^{23} to $2^{23}-4$ bytes from the current IP. The **callx** (call extended) instruction specifies the address of the calling procedure using any of the 80960's addressing modes.

A system call is made using the **calls** instruction. This call is similar to a local call except that the processor gets the IP for the called procedure from a data structure called the *system procedure table*. The **calls** instruction requires a procedure number operand. This procedure number serves as an index into the system procedure table, which contains IP's for specific procedures. The system procedure table is shown in Figure 3-8.

The system call mechanism supports two types of procedure calls: system-local calls and system-supervisor calls (also referred to as supervisor calls). The system-

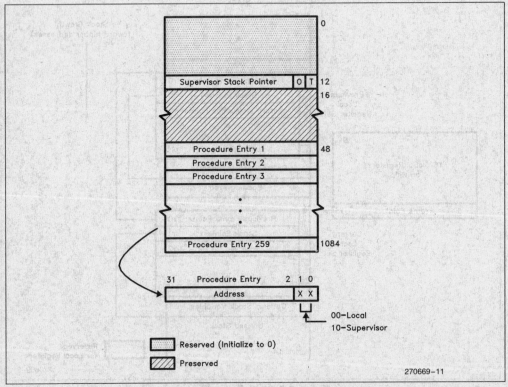

Figure 3-8. System Procedure Table

local call performs the same action as the local call instructions with one exception: the IP target for a system-local call is fetched from the system-procedure table. The supervisor call differs from the local call as follows:

1) A supervisor call causes the processor to switch to another stack (called the supervisor stack).

2) A supervisor call causes the processor to switch to the supervisor execution mode and asserts the 80960CA's supervisor (SUP) pin for all bus accesses.

The system call mechanism offers several benefits. The system call promotes the portability of application software. System calls are commonly used for kernel services. By calling these services with a procedure number rather than a specific IP, application software does not have to be changed each time the implementation of the kernel service is modified. Additionally, the ability to switch to a different execution mode and stack allows kernel procedures and data to be insulated from application code.

3.8.6 IMPLICIT PROCEDURE CALLS

The call and return mechanism described for procedure calls applies to several classes of call instructions as well as to the context switching initiated by interrupts and faults. When an interrupt or fault condition occurs, an implicit call is performed that saves the current state of the processor before branching to the interrupt or fault handling procedure. When this context switch occurs, the local registers are saved and a new stack frame is allocated. Additionally, the values of the AC register and PC register are saved when the implicit call occurs. These values are restored on the return from the interrupt or fault handler.

3.9 Interrupts

An interrupt is a temporary break in the control stream of a program so that the processor can handle another task. Interrupts may be triggered by the instruction stream or by hardware sources internal and external to the 80960CA. An interrupt request is associated with a vector (i.e. an address) of an interrupt handling procedure. The processor will branch to the handling procedure when an interrupt is serviced. When the handling action is completed, the processor is restored to its state prior to the interrupt.

3.9.1 INTERRUPT VECTORS AND PRIORITY

Interrupt vectors are simply instruction pointers (addresses) to interrupt handling procedures. The 80960 architecture defines 248 interrupt vectors. This means

that 248 unique interrupt handling procedures may be used. An 8-bit interrupt vector number is associated with each interrupt vector. This number ranges from 8 to 255. Each interrupt vector has a priority from 1 to 31, which is determined by the 5 most significant bits of the interrupt vector number. Priority 1 is the lowest priority and 31 is the highest. Priority 0 interrupts are not defined.

The 80960CA executes with a unique priority ranging from 0 to 31. When an interrupt is serviced, the processor's priority switches to the priority corresponding to that of the interrupt request. When a return from an interrupt procedure is executed, the process priority is restored to its value prior to servicing the interrupt. This priority switching is handled automatically by the 80960CA.

The 80960CA compares its current priority and the priority of an interrupt request to determine whether to service an interrupt immediately or to delay service. If a requested interrupt priority is greater than the processor's current priority or equal to 31, the processor services the interrupt immediately; otherwise, the processor saves (posts) the interrupt request as a pending interrupt so that it can be serviced later. When the processor's priority falls below the priority of a pending interrupt, the pending interrupt is serviced. With the mechanism described, interrupts with a priority of 0 will never be serviced. For this reason, vectors numbered 0 to 7 are not defined.

3.9.2 INTERRUPT TABLE

The interrupt table (Figure 3-9) is an architecturally defined data structure which holds the interrupt vectors and information on pending interrupts. The first 36 bytes of the table are used to post interrupts. The 31 most significant bits in the 32-bit pending priorities field represent a possible priority (1 to 31) of a pending interrupt. When the processor posts an interrupt in the interrupt table, the bit corresponding to the interrupt's priority is set. For example, if an interrupt with a priority of 10 is posted in the interrupt table, bit 10 is set in the pending priorities field.

The pending interrupts field contains a 256-bit string in which each bit represents an interrupt vector. When the processor posts an interrupt in the interrupt table, the bit corresponding to the vector number of that interrupt is set.

Portions of the interrupt table are cached on-chip in a non-transparent fashion. This caching is implemented to minimized interrupt latency by reducing the number of accesses to the table in external memory when an interrupt is serviced.

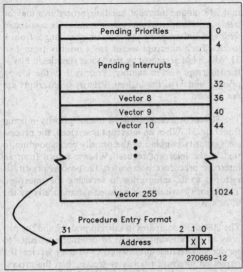

Figure 3-9. Interrupt Table

3.9.3 INTERRUPT STACK

Stack frames for interrupt handling procedures are allocated on a separate *interrupt stack*. The interrupt stack can be located anywhere in the processor's address space. The beginning address of the interrupt stack is specified when the processor is initialized.

3.9.4 INTERRUPT HANDLING ACTION

When an interrupt is serviced, the processor saves the processor state and calls the interrupt procedure. The processor state is restored upon return from the interrupt procedure.

This interrupt service mechanism is handled by an implicit call operation. When the interrupt is serviced, the current local registers are saved. A new local register set and stack frame are allocated on the interrupt stack for the interrupt handler procedure and the processor switches to supervisor execution mode. In addition to the local registers, the current value of the AC and PC registers are saved as an interrupt record on the interrupt stack.

3.9.5 PENDING INTERRUPTS

Any of the 248 interrupts can be requested by software. The system control instruction (**sysctl**) is provided to support this feature. When the system control instruction requests an interrupt, one of two actions may occur depending on the priority of the requested interrupt

and the current process priority. 1) The interrupt is serviced immediately, or 2) the interrupt is posted (the pending priorities field and the pending interrupts field are modified to reflect a pending interrupt).

Interrupts may also be requested by hardware sources internal and external to the 80960CA. Managing the hardware sources and posting these interrupts is handled by the interrupt controller. Interrupts requested by hardware are posted in an internal register, not in the interrupt table. A mask register enables or disables interrupts from each hardware source. Requesting and posting hardware interrupts is described in Section 4.4 Interrupt Controller.

3.9.6 INTERRUPT LATENCY

The time required to perform an interrupt task switch is referred to as the *interrupt latency*. The latency is the time measured between the activation of an interrupt source and the execution of the first instruction for the interrupt-handling procedure for the source.

Interrupt latency for the 80960CA varies depending on conditions such as:

— Complex instructions are executing when the interrupt occurs (e.g. **sysctl**, **call**, **ret**, etc.).

— Outstanding loads to a local register are pending, delaying the interrupt context switch.

— Division, multiplication, or other multi-cycle instructions with a local register as destination are executing.

The 80960CA has been designed to optimize latency and throughput for interrupts. Two processor features are designed for this purpose:

First, in the interrupt table, all interrupt vectors with an index whose least significant four bits are 0010_2 can be cached in internal data RAM. The processor will automatically read these vectors from data RAM when the interrupt is serviced. This feature reduces the added latency due to an external access of the interrupt table for that vector. The NMI vector is always cached in data RAM.

Second, an instruction cache locking mechanism allows interrupt procedures or segments of interrupt procedures to be stored in the instruction cache. These routines are always executed from the internal cache, eliminating external code fetches and reducing latency and increasing throughput for the interrupt.

3.10 Fault Handling and Instruction Tracing

The 80960CA is able to detect various conditions in code or in its internal state that could cause the processor to deliver incorrect or inappropriate results or that could cause it to head down an undesirable control path. These conditions are referred to as faults. The 80960 architecture provides fault handling mechanisms to detect and, in most cases, fully recover from a fault.

The 80960CA provides on-chip debug support by triggering trace events and servicing the trace fault. A trace event is activated when a particular instruction or type of instruction is encountered in an instruction stream. The trace event optionally signals a fault. A fault handling procedure for the trace fault can act as a debug monitor and analyze the state of the processor when the trace event occurred.

3.10.1 FAULT TYPES AND SUBTYPES

All of the faults that the processor detects are predefined. These faults are divided into types and subtypes, each of which is given a number. Table 3-4 lists the faults that the processor detects arranged by type and subtype.

Table 3-4. Fault Types and Subtypes

Fault Type	Fault Subtype	Fault Record
Parallel		XX00 00XX
Trace	Instruction Type	XX01 0002
	Branch Trace	XX01 0004
	Call Trace	XX01 0008
	Return Trace	XX01 0010
	Prereturn Trace	XX01 0020
	Supervisor Trace	XX01 0040
	Breakpoint Trace	XX01 0080
Operation	Invalid Opcode	XX02 0001
	Unimplemented	X002 0002
	Invalid Operand	XX02 0004
Arithmetic	Integer Overflow	XX03 0001
	Arithmetic Zero-Divide	XX03 0002
Constraint	Range	XX05 0001
	Privileged	XX05 0002
Protection	Length	XX07 0001
Type	Mismatch	XX0A 0001

NOTE: X refers to preserved locations in the fault record.

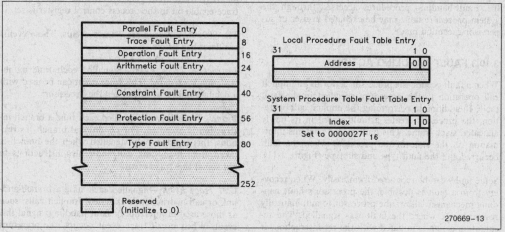

Figure 3-10. Fault Table

270669–13

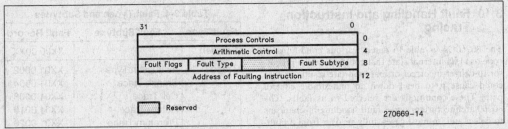

Figure 3-11. Fault Record

3.10.2 FAULT TABLE

The fault table (Figure 3-10) provides the processor with a pathway to fault handling procedures. The fault table is an architecture-defined data structure, which may be located anywhere in the processor's address space. The location of the fault table is specified at initialization. When a fault occurs, an entry in the table is selected based on the type of fault that occurs. The entry in the fault table contains a pointer to a specific fault handler.

The fault table can contain two types of entries (Figure 3-10). The first type of entry is simply a pointer to the address of the fault-handling procedure. The second type of entry is an index into the system-procedure table. Fault-handling procedures accessed through the system-procedure table may be executed in user or supervisor execution mode.

3.10.3 FAULT HANDLING ACTION

When a fault occurs, the processor performs an implicit call operation to the procedure specified in the fault table. In addition to performing the implicit call operation, the processor creates a fault record in its newly allocated stack frame. This fault record contains information on the state of the processor when the fault occurred and the fault type and subtype (Figure 3-11).

Some faults can be recovered from easily. When recovery from a fault is possible, the processor's fault handling mechanism allows the processor to automatically resume work where the fault was signalled. The resumption action is initiated with the **ret** instruction. If simple recovery from a fault is not possible, then the fault handling procedure may call a debug monitor, initiate a reset, or take other actions to recover from the fault.

3.10.4 TRACING AND DEBUG

The 80960CA provides a facility for monitoring the activity of the processor by tracing the instruction stream. A trace event occurs at points in a program where certain types of instructions are encountered or a certain IP or data address is encountered. When a trace event occurs, a trace fault can be generated and a trace-fault handler called which displays or analyzes the state of the processor.

3.10.4.1 Trace Events

The *Trace Control (TC) Register* (Figure 3-12) is used to specify the types of instructions which cause trace events. When a mode bit in the TC register is set, specific instructions will generate trace events. For example, if the branch trace mode bit is enabled and a branch instruction is executed, a branch trace event will be signalled. An event flag is used to record trace events. A single event flag is provided for each mode bit. Any trace event generates a trace fault when the trace enable bit in the process control register is set.

The 80960CA recognizes 7 trace events. These events are described below.

Instruction Trace Event—Signalled each time an instruction is executed. This trace event can be used with a debug monitor to single step the processor.

Branch Trace Event—Signalled each time a branch instruction is executed. For conditional branch instructions, this event is only signalled when the branch is taken. Branch-and-link, call, and return instructions do not signal this trace event.

Call Trace Event—Signalled each time a branch-and-link or call instruction is executed. Implicit calls, such as those used in interrupt or fault handling, signal this event. When a call trace event occurs, the prereturn trace flag (bit 3 in local register **r0**) is set by the processor to indicate a prereturn trace pending.

Pre-Return Trace Event—Signalled just prior to any **ret** instruction. This event is only signalled if the pre-return trace flag in register **r0** is set. Since the pre-return trace flag is set when a call trace event occurs, the call trace mode must be enabled before a pre-return trace event can be signalled.

Return Trace Event—Signalled each time a **ret** instruction is executed.

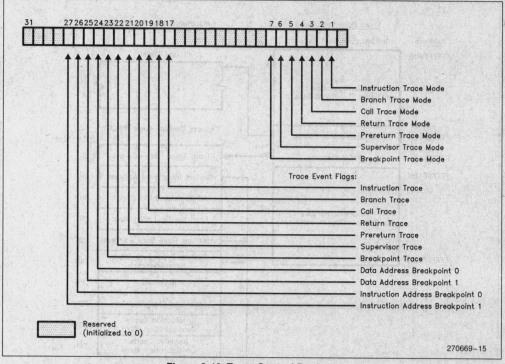

Figure 3-12. Trace Control Register

Supervisor Trace Event—Signalled each time a **calls** instruction is executed where the selected entry type is supervisor, or when a **ret** from supervisor mode is executed.

Breakpoint Trace Events—Signalled each time a **mark** instruction, **fmark** instruction, or specified address is encountered in the instruction stream. The **mark** instruction signals an event when the breakpoint trace mode is enabled, the **fmark** (force mark) instruction will generate a breakpoint trace event regardless of the value of the breakpoint trace mode bit.

Two IP breakpoint registers and two internal data address breakpoint registers are provided on the 80960CA. These breakpoints are loaded with an instruction or data address using the system control (**sysctl**) instruction. When the address is encountered and the breakpoint trace mode bit is set, a breakpoint trace event occurs. A corresponding instruction or data address event flag is set in the TC register when the address is encountered.

3.10.5 PROCESSOR INITIALIZATION

The Initial Memory Image (IMI) are the data structures needed to initialize the 80960CA (Figure 3-13). The initialization boot record, in reserved memory beginning at FFFFFF00H, contains a pointer to the Processor Control Block (PRCB). The PRCB in turn holds pointers to the data structures which are necessary to execute code on the 80960CA. The PRCB also holds several fields which contain information to initially configure the 80960CA.

Processor initialization begins by asserting the $\overline{\text{RESET}}$ pin. At initialization the processor optionally performs an internal self-test. A bus confidence test is also performed by calculating a checksum of 8 words read from external memory. If either of these self-tests fails, the $\overline{\text{FAIL}}$ pin indicates the failure and the processor aborts initialization. If the self-test passes, the 80960CA continues with initialization and branches to the first address of the user's code.

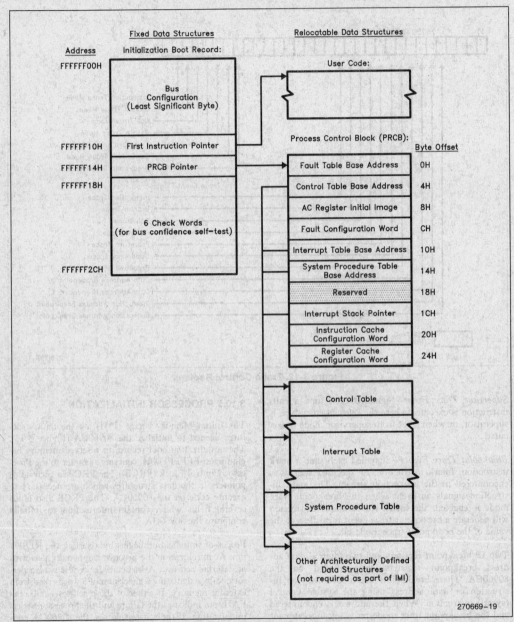

Figure 3-13. Initial Memory Image

4.0 80960CA SYSTEM IMPLEMENTATION

This section is an overview of the peripherals integrated with the 80960CA core. The features and operation of the Bus Controller, DMA Controller, Interrupt Controller, and the interfaces between these peripherals and the core are described.

4.1 Peripheral Interface

A program communicates with the on-chip peripherals by reading or modifying the special function registers (SFRs) or by loading control registers. The SFRs generally serve to transfer status information and data between a peripheral and the core, and the control registers serve to configure the peripherals. SFRs are accessed directly as instruction operands. The control registers are loaded by using the system control (**sysctl**) instruction.

4.2 Bus Controller Unit

The Bus Controller Unit (BCU) manages the data and instruction path between the 80960CA and external memory. Data operations and instruction fetches share a 32-bit data bus. Memory addresses are output on a separate 32-bit address bus. The BCU incorporates several advanced features to simplify the bus interface to external memory. A programmable *memory region configuration table* allows the characteristics of the external bus to be programmed differently for 16 separate regions in memory. The attributes of the external bus which are programmable include wait states and external ready control, data bus width (8, 16, or 32 bits), burst mode, address pipelining, and byte ordering. The region programmable bus options are described in this section.

4.2.1 BUS TRANSFERS, ACCESSES, AND REQUESTS

The distinction between *transfer, bus access,* and *bus request,* as these terms apply to the 80960CA, must be presented before beginning a discussion of the BCU.

Transfer—A *bus transfer* is defined simply as a movement of code or data between a memory system and the 80960CA. A write transfer occurs when the memory system is the destination of a data movement. A read transfer occurs when the 80960CA is the destination for a data or a code fetch from memory.

Bus Access—A *bus access* is defined as an address cycle and one or more transfers. In burst mode, an access can consist of a single address cycle and 1 to 4 transfers.

Bus Request—A *bus request* is issued by the core and directed to the Bus Controller. A bus request is sent to the BCU when a load, store, or an atomic instruction is executed, or when an instruction fetch is needed. Bus requests are also issued by the core to perform DMA transfers. A bus request can consist of one or more bus accesses. For example, an aligned word (32-bit) request to an 8-bit memory region will result in four byte-length accesses.

4.2.2 BUS CONTROL COPROCESSOR

The 80960CA's peripherals are often referred to as coprocessors, since their operation is decoupled from the execution of the instruction stream. As an integrated coprocessor, the BCU receives bus requests and independently carries out the action of moving data or code between the processor and external memory. The BCU uses a three deep queue to store pending bus requests. The queue decouples the core from the BCU, since a series of adjacent requests may be issued faster than the BCU can service each request. Two of the three queue entries store requests from a user's program (loads, stores, fetches, etc.). The third queue entry is used by requests originating from a DMA operation. This queue entry takes user requests when the DMA is turned off. The 80960CA alternates service of requests issued by the user program and requests issued by a DMA operation.

4.2.3 SIGNAL DESCRIPTIONS

The external bus signals consist of 30 address signals, 4 byte enables, 32 data lines, and various control signals.

D31–D0   32-bit Data Bus (bi-directional)—32-, 16-, and 8-bit values are transmitted and received on these lines. The 8- and 16-bit quantities are transferred on the low order data lines when a memory region is configured respectively for an 8- or 16-bit bus.

A31–A2   30-bit Address (outputs)—The 30-bit address bus identifies all external addresses to word (4-byte) boundaries. The byte enable lines indicate the selected byte in each word.

$\overline{BE3}$–$\overline{BE0}$ Byte Enables (outputs)—The byte enables select which of 4 addressed bytes are active in a memory access. When a memory region is configured for an 8-bit bus width, $\overline{BE1}$ and $\overline{BE0}$ act as the lower two bits of the address. For a 16-bit memory region, $\overline{BE1}$, $\overline{BE3}$, and $\overline{BE0}$ are encoded to provide A1, $\overline{BHE}$, and $\overline{BLE}$ respectively.

W/$\overline{R}$ Write or Read (output)—This signal is low for read accesses and high for write accesses.

$\overline{ADS}$ Address Strobe (output)—Indicates valid address and the start of a new bus access.

DT/R̄ Data Transmit or Receive (output)—Direction control for data transceivers; similar to W/R̄.

DEN Data Enable (output)—Low during a bus request after the first address cycle. This signal is used to control data transceivers and to indicate the end of a bus request.

WAIT Wait (output)—Indicates that wait states are being inserted by the internal wait state generator.

READY Ready (input)—Signals that data is valid for a read transfer or ends data hold for a write transfer. This function can be disabled for a memory region.

BTERM Burst Terminate (input)—Terminates a burst access. Another address is generated to complete the request when the signal is deasserted. This function can be disabled for a memory region.

D/C Data or Code (output)—Indicates a data transfer or a code fetch.

DMA DMA Access (output)—Indicates that a bus request was initiated by either the user program or the DMA.

SUP Supervisor Access (output)—Indicates that a bus access originated from a bus request issued in supervisor mode. This signal can be used to protect system data structures, or peripherals from errant modification by the user code.

LOCK Lock (output)—Indicates that an atomic memory operation is in progress. This signal can be used to inhibit external agents from modifying memory which is atomically accessed.

BLAST Burst Last (output)—Indicates the last transfer in a burst access.

HOLD Hold (input)—HOLD can be used by a bus requester to request access to the bus. The processor asserts HLDA after the current bus request or locked requests have completed.

HOLDA Hold Acknowledge (output)—Indicates to a bus requester that the processor has relinquished control of the bus.

BREQ Bus Request (output)—Indicates that requests are queued in the bus controller and are waiting to be serviced. BREQ can be used for external bus arbitration logic in conjunction with HOLD and HLDA to regain bus mastership.

Figure 4-1 shows the timing for a simple, non-burst, non-pipelined read and write access. The timing relations for the key control signals are shown in this figure.

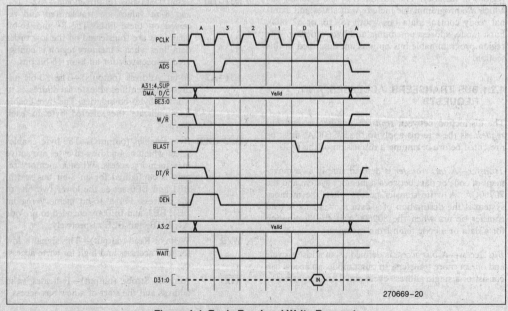

Figure 4-1. Basic Read and Write Request
4-24

4.2.4 MEMORY REGION CONFIGURATION TABLE

The BCU can be configured differently for 16 separate sections (referred to as regions) of the address space. The four most significant bits of a memory address define the location of each region in memory. The bus characteristics in a region are specified in the *memory region configuration table*. When a bus request is serviced, the BCU accesses the configuration table entry for the region addressed and services the request based on the bus characteristics programmed for that region. The characteristics programmed for each region are listed below:

- Burst Mode (on/off)
- Wait States (5 parameters)
- Bus Width (8-, 16-, or 32-bit)
- Ready Inputs (on/off)
- Address Pipelining (on/off)
- Byte Ordering (Big/Little Endian)

The flexibility of region programming simplifies the bus interface in applications where a memory system is made up of a variety of sub-systems, such as SRAM, DRAM, ROM, and memory mapped peripherals. Each memory sub-system can be mapped into a different region in memory, and that region can be configured specifically for the requirements of the particular memory sub-system.

The configuration table is made up of 16 on-chip control registers (Figure 4-2). Each register is programmed with the configuration information for a single region. Since the region table is located on-chip, access to region information does not affect the performance of the bus.

4.2.4.1 Burst Accesses

The 80960CA BCU is capable of burst accesses to memory systems which are designed to support this feature. Burst mode is intended to get the most performance from low cost memory systems. A burst access is a single address cycle followed by successive data or instruction transfers. The transfers reference data or instructions at sequential addresses starting at the address which began the burst access (Figure 4-3). In a burst memory system, the upper 28 bits of an address remain fixed while the lower two bits A2 and A3 increment to access subsequent locations.

Wait state timing for the first access of a burst request is controlled independently from the timing for subsequent accesses. A memory sub-system using static column mode or page mode DRAMs, for example, can take advantage of the short column access times for these devices by using burst mode. Interleaved ROM or EPROM systems can also be constructed which simultaneously access several words and then use burst mode to multiplex the multi-word array onto the data bus.

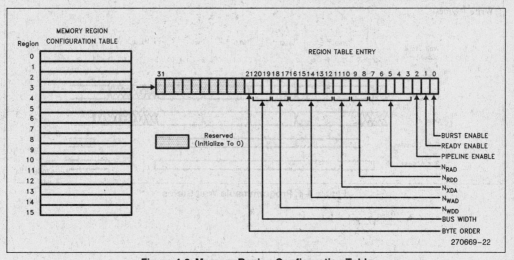

Figure 4-2. Memory Region Configuration Table

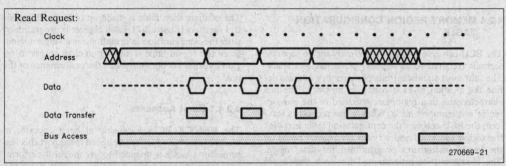

Figure 4-3. Burst Memory Request

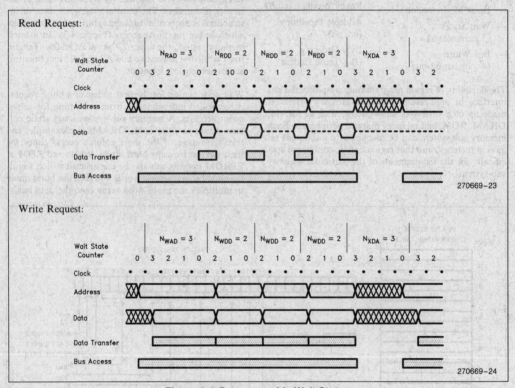

Figure 4-4. Programmable Wait States

4.2.4.2 Programmable Wait State Generation

The 80960CA may be interfaced with a variety of memory sub-systems and peripherals with a minimum system cost and complexity. To achieve this interface flexibility, the 80960CA implements an internal programmable wait state generator. Internally generated wait states eliminate the potential system delays which come from generating wait states with external logic.

Wait states are programmed for each region in the memory region configuration table. The number of wait states is programmable over a range which allows efficient control of memory devices ranging from ultra-fast SRAMs to slow peripherals. An external ready signal is also provided for external wait state control.

The wait states which can be generated by the 80960CA are shown in Figure 4-4. In this table N is the number of wait states inserted. The wait states for read accesses and for write accesses are described by three parameters each. For read accesses, N_{RAD} is the number of states between the address cycle and the first data cycle and N_{RDD} is the number of states between consecutive data cycles in a burst access. For writes, N_{WAD} is the number of states that data is held after an address cycle, and N_{WDD} is the number of states that data is held for consecutive data cycles in a burst write. For both reads and writes, N_{XDA} is the number of dead cycles after the last data cycle and before the next address.

4.2.4.3 READY Control

The memory region configuration table allows the ready input (READY) to be enabled or disabled for each region. If the ready input is disabled, the external input has no effect on the wait states generated for a memory access; all wait states are generated internally. If the ready input is enabled, it works in conjunction with the programmable wait state generator. In this case, the ready input has no effect until the number of programmed wait states has expired. When the wait state counter reaches 0, the ready input is sampled, and wait states continue or are terminated based on the value of the ready input. In order to gain complete external control over wait states, all wait state parameters for a region can be set to 0.

4.2.4.4 Pipelined Reads

The 80960CA BCU provides an address pipelining mode (Figure 4-5) to optimize the performance of instruction and data fetches from external memory. When the pipelined read mode is enabled, an address cycle overlaps with the last data cycle in each access, effectively reducing the total time needed for each access. Pipelining mode is selected in each region by programming the memory region configuration table.

4.2.4.5 Byte Ordering

One of two configurations for byte ordering, often referred to as little endian or big endian, is selected for each region by programming the memory region configuration table. The byte ordering options make the 80960CA capable of sharing memory with a processor which uses either byte ordering scheme. Byte ordering refers to the way that the 80960CA relates internal data to the way that data is stored or fetched from memory. The little endian configuration orders the bytes in a short-word or word so that the least significant byte of the quantity is positioned at the lowest address and the most significant byte at the highest address in memory. Conversely, for the big endian configuration, the least significant byte is positioned at the highest address, and the most significant byte at the lowest address. For example, for little endian ordering, byte 0 for word data would be found in memory at an address of the form XXXX XXX0H and, for big endian, at address XXXX XXX3H.

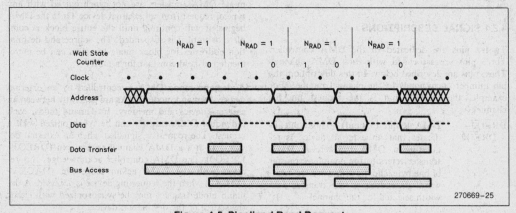

Figure 4-5. Pipelined Read Request

4.2.4.6 Data Alignment

The 80960CA can service any aligned or non-aligned bus request. Aligned requests are directed to their natural boundary in memory. In other words, the addresses for aligned requests are even multiples of the length of the data transferred. Non-aligned requests are not serviced directly by the BCU but are assisted by microcode. Microcode automatically breaks non-aligned requests into multiple aligned requests which are then reissued to the BCU. Depending on the degree of non-alignment and the length of the original request, the resulting requests by microcode will consist of a combination of byte, short-word, and double-word requests. The BCU is able to generate an operation-unaligned fault when a non-aligned bus request is first received. This fault can be selectively masked at initialization.

4.3 DMA Controller

The DMA controller is a high-performance, full-functioned integrated peripheral. The DMA controller can manage 4 channels of DMA transfer concurrent with program execution. Separate external control for each channel is provided. Each channel supports high-performance memory to memory transfers where the source and destination can be any combination of internal data RAM or external memory. The DMA Controller supports various types of transfers such as high-speed fly-by transfers and data chaining with the use of linked descriptor lists in memory.

The 80960CA's DMA controller is implemented using dedicated hardware and microcode. Because of the efficiency of the core, it is possible for the microcode to execute DMA transfers at high speeds. DMA transfers are performed by the core concurrently with execution of the user's program. Internal DMA logic is used for sampling requests, synchronizing transfers with external devices, and handling the service of multiple active channels.

4.3.1 SIGNAL DESCRIPTIONS

Twelve pins are dedicated to the DMA controller. Three pins are associated with each DMA channel. These pins are described below. In this description, the pin number corresponds to the channel number. For example, the DREQ0 pin is the request pin for channel 0.

$\overline{\text{DREQ3}}-$
$\overline{\text{DREQ0}}$ — DMA Request (input)—This input indicates that an external device is requesting a DMA transfer. A DMA transfer refers to the complete transfer of one byte, short-word, word, or quad-word, depending on the transfer data width selected for the channel.

$\overline{\text{DACK3}}-$
$\overline{\text{DACK0}}$ — DMA Acknowledge (output)—This output becomes active when the requesting device is accessed.

$\overline{\text{EOP3}}/\text{TC3}-$
$\overline{\text{EOP0}}/\text{TC0}$ — End of Process (input) or Terminal Count (output)—This pin functions either as an input ($\overline{\text{EOPx}}$) or as an output (TCx). When programmed as an output, the pin is driven active for one clock after byte count reaches zero and a DMA terminates. When programmed as an input, an external device can cause the DMA operation to terminate.

4.3.2 DMA TRANSFERS

The 80960CA DMA controller supports a variety of transfer modes and variations of these modes, allowing the DMA to adapt to a number of hardware systems and the performance requirements of these systems.

4.3.2.1 Standard Block and Demand Mode Transfers

A standard DMA transfer is made up of multiple bus requests. Loads from a source address are followed by stores to a destination address. The DMA controller issues the proper combination of these bus requests to execute the DMA transfer. For example, a typical DMA transfer between memory and an 8-bit peripheral could appear as a single byte load request directed to the source memory, followed by a single byte store request directed to the 8-bit peripheral.

The DMA controller has two basic transfer modes: block mode (unsynchronized) and demand mode (synchronized). Any DMA transfer will be serviced by one of these basic transfer modes.

A block mode DMA is initiated by software. Block mode DMAs are generally between memory. Block mode DMA transfers are not synchronized with any type of request from an external device. Once the DMA begins, it will continue until the entire block is complete or until it is suspended. The source and destination addresses for block mode transfers can be incremented or held constant for a DMA.

A demand mode DMA is controlled by an external device. Demand mode DMAs are generally between an external device and memory. In demand mode, each individual DMA transfer can be synchronized with a request. The request is signalled when an external device activates a DMA channel request pin ($\overline{\text{DREQ3}}-$ $\overline{\text{DREQ0}}$). The DMA controller acknowledges this request with the DMA acknowledge pin ($\overline{\text{DACK3}}-$ $\overline{\text{DACK0}}$) when the requesting device is accessed. A demand mode transfer may be synchronized with either the source or the destination device.

4.3.2.2 Fly-by Transfers

A fly-by transfer mode is provided for the most performance-critical DMA applications. Fly-by mode also makes very efficient use of the external bus during a DMA. Standard DMA transfers involve multiple bus requests: load requests directed to the source and a store request directed to the destination. Fly-by transfers only require a single bus request. For a fly-by transfer, memory sees a load or a store on the bus while the requesting device is selected by the DMA acknowledge pin. The data is never actually read from or written to the 80960CA. For memory to device transfers, the processor issues a load, and, while reading the memory, accesses the external device with the DMA acknowledge pin. The data is then written directly to the destination device with a single bus request. For a device to memory transfer, the reverse operation is performed. The DMA issues a store, and, while writing the memory, accesses the source device with the DMA acknowledge pin. In this case, the processor floats the data bus and the device's data is written directly into memory.

4.3.2.3 Data Chaining

Each DMA channel can be programmed in a data chaining mode. In this mode, all transfer information is taken from a linked-list descriptor in memory (Figure 4-6). Data chaining is started by specifying a pointer to a descriptor in memory. The transfer continues until

the number of bytes in the byte count field in the descriptor is transferred. At this time, another linked-list descriptor may be executed. The next descriptor is specified by the next-pointer field in the current description. Data chaining continues until a null pointer is encountered in the next-pointer field. Data chaining can be designated as source chaining, destination chaining, or both.

In data chaining mode, an option exists which allows chaining descriptors to be updated while the DMA is running. When this option is enabled, the DMA sets a bit in the DMA's special function register after loading a descriptor and then checks this bit before loading the next descriptor. If the bit has been cleared by the user, the DMA continues; otherwise, the DMA waits for the next descriptor to be set up and for the user to clear the bit. An interrupt can be generated when each buffer is complete or when the DMA is terminated with a null pointer or the EOP pin.

4.3.3 TRANSFER CHARACTERISTICS

The DMA controller provides the programmer with a number of options for configuring the characteristics of a DMA transfer. Intelligent selection of transfer characteristics works to balance DMA performance and functionality with performance of the user program when the DMA is in progress.

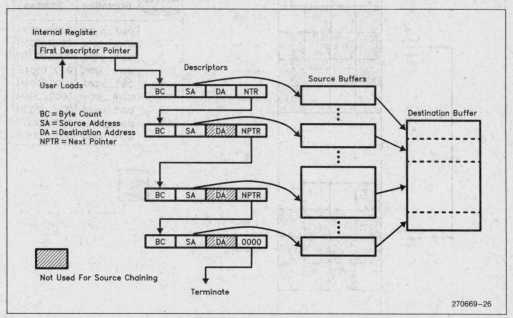

Figure 4-6. Source Data Chaining

The DMA controller provides features to optimize transfers by moving a maximum amount of data for each bus request issued. This is controlled by specifying the width of the source and destination directed bus requests for a DMA transfer, and by on-chip assembly or disassembly of the transfer when source and destination are not of equal widths.

Data alignment is performed automatically by the DMA controller when the source and destination of a transfer are not aligned. The alignment algorithm is optimized for many transfers, providing a performance comparable to the aligned transfer cases.

4.3.3.1 Transfer Data Length

The transfer data length specifies the length of bus requests directed to the source and destination in a standard DMA transfer. Byte, short, word, or quad-word loads and stores are selected for either source or destination when a DMA channel is set up. Assembly and disassembly of data is automatically performed when the source and destination widths are different. This feature provides the most efficient use of the bus when DMA transfers occur between a source and a destination with different external bus widths.

The DMA controller provides the option of using quad word transfers to enhance DMA performance. When quad transfers are specified, the DMA will request a four-word load request and four-word store request for each DMA transfer. The trade-off for the added DMA performance is latency on the external bus, preventing requests by the core, or by another DMA channel from being immediately serviced.

4.3.3.2 Data Alignment

The DMA controller supports transfer of source and destination data aligned to different byte boundaries in memory. The DMA implements microcode algorithms to transfer some non-aligned data with a performance level approaching that for aligned transfers. The DMA accomplishes this by attempting to issue the maximum number of aligned bus requests during a DMA (Figure 4-7). As shown, most of the overhead due to non-aligned DMAs is incurred at the beginning and end of the DMA. DMAs with low byte counts, therefore, do not benefit as much from the data alignment features of the DMA. The alignment feature is optimized for 8-bit to 8-bit, 32-bit to 32-bit and for 8-bit and 32-bit combinations of source and destination lengths.

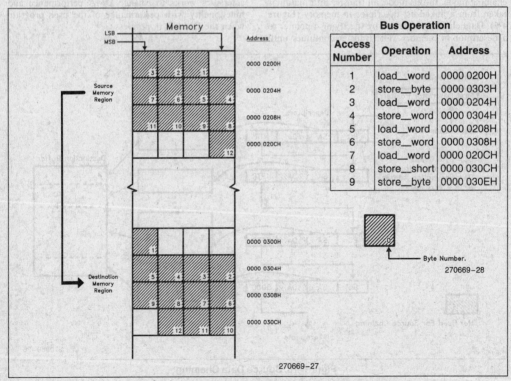

Figure 4-7. DMA Data Alignment

4.3.3.3 Channel Priority

The DMA controller arbitrates the priority of the 4 DMA channels. If multiple DMA channels are enabled, the DMA controller will determine in which order each channel is serviced.

The DMA controller can be configured in one of two priority modes, fixed mode or rotating mode. The fixed mode assumes a fixed priority for each channel with channel 0 having the highest priority, followed by channels 1, 2, and 3, with channel 3 having the lowest priority. The rotating mode updates a channel's priority to the lowest priority after that channel's DMA is made. This insures that a single channel is never locked out by other active channels. The priority sequence is always in the same order, with priority rotating from the low channel numbers to the high channel numbers.

4.3.3.4 Performance and Latency Considerations

DMA operations and the user program share the resources of the core and of the external bus. DMA performance and the performance of the user program are coupled directly to the balance of load sharing between these two processes. The core resources necessary to perform a DMA transfer vary depending on the way a channel has been configured. For example, byte assembly and disassembly requires more processor overhead per byte of transfer than does a transfer in which the source and destination transfer lengths are equal. The performance of a DMA is also tightly coupled to the user program's use of the external bus. If the user program does not make frequent bus requests, the requests by the DMA controller will be serviced with little or no delay.

The user can enhance performance of the DMA with trade-offs in system complexity and flexibility. Aligned transfers eliminate the microcode overhead needed to perform the internal alignments. DMAs between regions of equal transfer widths eliminate overhead for

assembly and disassembly. Source or destination memory configured as burst memory will provide the most efficient use of the DMA controller when the quad-transfer feature is enabled. Using the fly-by mode reduces the number of bus requests needed for a DMA since fly-by mode uses only a single load or a single store request for each transfer.

4.3.4 DMA CONTROL AND CONFIGURATION

The DMA Controller uses an SFR register, the DMA command (DMAC) register, and the setup DMA (**sdma**) instruction for configuration and control of a DMA. The **sdma** instruction is used to configure each DMA channel. Transfer widths, byte count, source and destination addresses for a DMA are specified in this instruction.

The DMAC register (Figure 4-8) is described below.

The *channel enable field* enables a DMA once the channel is set up. Clearing these bits will also cause a DMA transfer to be suspended.

The *terminal count field* signals that byte count has reached zero and a DMA has ended.

The *channel active field* indicates that a channel is idle or active. If set, this bit indicates that the channel is active. This implies that the channel is servicing a transfer or has a request pending. The active bits are status information only.

The *channel done field* indicates that a DMA operation is complete. The done bits are status information only.

The *channel wait field* is used for handshaking with a user program in data chaining mode. The DMA sets these bits when a new linked-list descriptor is read. The DMA will not read the next descriptor until this bit is cleared by the user. The user can set up the next descriptor and then clear the channel wait bits to dynamically change descriptors.

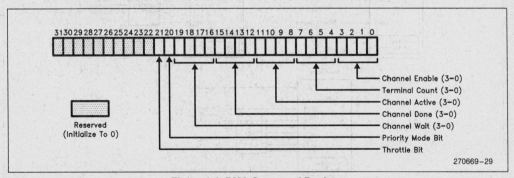

Figure 4-8. DMA Command Register

A *priority mode bit* selects rotating or fixed priority mode.

The *throttle bit* selects the maximum amount of core resources that the DMA microcode will receive in relation to the execution of the user program.

4.3.5 DMA INTERRUPTS

The DMA controller is the source of 4 hardware interrupts in the 80960CA. The DMA Controller can be programmed to request an interrupt when a DMA is complete, or when a buffer transfer is completed in chaining mode. Each channel requests a different interrupt.

4.4 Interrupt Controller

The 80960CA *Interrupt Controller* manages interrupts which are requested by external agents or by the DMA Controller. The interrupt controller manages 4 internal DMA interrupt sources, a single NMI (Non-Maskable Interrupt) pin, and 8 external interrupt pins. Up to 248 external interrupt sources can be supported by the interrupt controller. The interrupt controller handles the prioritization of software interrupts, hardware interrupts, and the process priority, and signals the core when interrupts are to be serviced. The interrupt controller provides the low-latency interrupt service featured on the 80960CA.

4.4.1 EXTERNAL INTERRUPTS

The 80960CA provides 8 interrupt pins and one NMI pin for detecting external requests. The interrupt controller allows the 8 interrupt pins to be configured as dedicated inputs capable of requesting 8 interrupts, or as a vectored input capable of requesting up to 248 interrupts. The NMI pin is always a dedicated input. The interrupt controller pins are described below.

$\overline{\text{XINT7}}-$
$\overline{\text{XINT0}}$ External Interrupts (inputs)—These pins can be used as dedicated inputs, or acting together as an 8-bit number, request any interrupt. The inputs are edge or level detected, and are optionally debounced internally.

$\overline{\text{NMI}}$ Non-Maskable Interrupt (input)—NMI requests the highest priority interrupt. NMI is always taken and is not maskable (as the name implies), and not interruptable.

4.4.2 INTERRUPT MODES

The 8 external interrupt pins can be configured in one of three modes: dedicated mode, expanded mode, or mixed mode (Figure 4-9).

4.4.2.1 Dedicated Mode Interrupts

In dedicated mode, each of the 8 interrupt pins acts as a dedicated input. When an external event is detected on an interrupt pin, a unique interrupt is requested for that pin. It is possible to map each dedicated pin to one of a number of possible interrupt vectors. This is accomplished by programming the interrupt map (IMAP) control registers with an interrupt vector number for each pin. (Recall that interrupt vector numbers are 8-bit values which reference the 248 vectors in the interrupt table.)

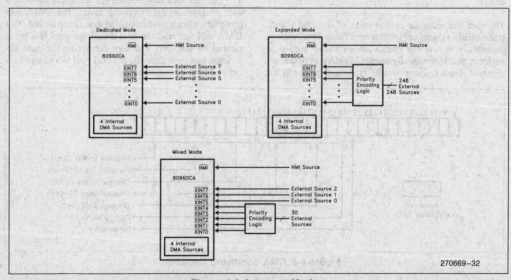

Figure 4-9. Interrupt Modes

Only the upper four bits of the vector number can be programmed for a dedicated mode interrupt. The lower four bits are fixed at the value 0010_2. With four programmable bits, one of 15 interrupt vectors is available for each dedicated pin. These interrupt vectors span the even priority levels from priority 2 to 30. The vector at priority 0 is not defined.

The 15 interrupt vectors available to dedicated sources can be cached in internal data RAM. If this interrupt vector caching feature is selected, the processor will automatically fetch the vector from data RAM, eliminating the latency caused by a bus request for a vector in external memory.

The DMA Controller can request four interrupts to signal the end of a DMA for each of four channels. The four interrupt signals from the DMA are handled by the interrupt controller in the same way as an interrupt pin configured as a dedicated input. Each of the four DMA sources may request one of 15 interrupts by programming the IMAP for that source.

4.4.2.2 Expanded Mode Interrupts

In expanded mode, external hardware considers the interrupt pins ($\overline{\text{XINT0}}-\overline{\text{XINT7}}$) as an 8-bit binary number. This number is used directly as the interrupt vector number. Each of the 248 possible interrupt vectors can be referenced in this way, allowing a separate external source for each vector. External hardware is responsible for recognizing individual hardware sources and then driving the interrupt vector number corresponding to that source onto the interrupt pins.

4.4.2.3 Mixed Mode Interrupts

In mixed mode, the 8 interrupt pins are divided into two functional sets. One set functions in dedicated mode, the other in expanded mode. In mixed mode, three pins are dedicated interrupt pins ($\overline{\text{XINT7}}-\overline{\text{XINT5}}$). A programmable vector number is associated with each of these pins. The remaining five interrupt pins ($\overline{\text{XINT4}}-\overline{\text{XINT0}}$) are treated as the most significant five bits of the expanded mode vector number. The lower order bits are internally forced to 010_2 to form the full 8-bit value for the vector number.

4.4.3 INTERRUPT CONTROLLER SETUP

The interrupt controller uses two special function registers to manage interrupt requests by hardware sources. The hardware interrupt pending register (IPND) and the hardware interrupt mask register (IMSK) are addressed as sf0 and sf1 respectively. A single bit in each register corresponds to each of the 8 possible external sources and 4 DMA sources for hardware interrupts. The IMSK register performs the function of masking hardware interrupts and the IPND register implements posting of interrupts requested by hardware. When configured for expanded or mixed mode interrupts, bit 0 of the IMSK register globally masks the expanded mode interrupts.

4.4.4. NON-MASKABLE INTERRUPT

In addition to the maskable hardware interrupts, a single *Non-Maskable Interrupt (NMI)* is provided. A dedicated NMI pin is used to request this interrupt. NMI is defined as a higher priority than any hardware interrupt, software interrupt, or process priority. The NMI procedure, therefore, can never be interrupted and must execute the return instruction before other procedures can execute. The NMI procedure is entered through vector 248. This vector is cached in internal data RAM at initialization to reduce latency for the NMI.

APPENDIX A
80960CA CORE IMPLEMENTATION

The 80960CA Core is a high-performance implementation of the 80960 Core Architecture. This section briefly describes the microarchitecture of the 80960CA core and the key constructs used to achieve parallel instruction execution.

The 80960CA core can be divided into the 6 main subunits listed below.

— Instruction Sequencer

— Register File

— Execution Unit

— Multiply and Divide Unit

— Address Generation Unit

— Static Data RAM and Local Register Cache

Figure A-1 is a simple block diagram of the 80960CA. The nucleus of the processor is the Instruction Sequencer and Register File. The other subunits of the core, referred to as coprocessors, radiate from these units, connecting to either the register (REG) side or the memory (MEM) side of the processor. The Instruction Sequencer issues directives, via the REG and MEM interfaces, which target a specific coprocessor. That coprocessor then executes an express function virtually decoupled from the IS and the other coproces-

sors. The REG and MEM data busses shown in Figure A-1 are used to transfer data between the common Register File and the coprocessors.

A.1 Instruction Sequencer

The *Instruction Sequencer (IS)* decodes the instruction stream and drives the decoded instruction stream onto the coprocessor interfaces. In a single clock, the IS decodes up to 4 instruction and issues up to three of these instructions to the on-chip coprocessors or to the IS itself. One register (REG) format, one memory (MEM) format, and one control or control and branch (CTRL or COBR) format instruction can be issued at one time. These instructions are directed respectively to the REG coprocessors, the MEM coprocessors, or to the IS. The ability to issue multiple instructions in parallel can result in the simultaneous execution of many instructions at once. An optimizing compiler or hand optimization of assembly code can easily produce an instruction stream which takes full advantage of the parallel execution of the core.

A technique known as *resource scoreboarding* is used to manage the parallel execution of instructions and the common resources of the processor. A coprocessor, for example, can scoreboard itself, indicating that it cannot

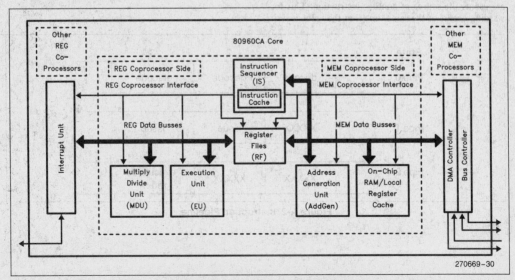

Figure A-1. 80960CA Block Diagram

act on another instruction until an instruction currently executing on that coprocessor is completed. A specific form of resource scoreboarding is referred to as *register scoreboarding*. When the computation stage of an instruction takes more than one clock, the destination register or registers for the result are scoreboarded as busy. A subsequent operation needing that particular register will be delayed until the multi-clock operation is completed. Instructions which do not use the scoreboarded registers can be executed in parallel.

The IS manages a three stage parallel instruction pipeline (Figure A-2). In the first stage of the pipeline (pipe 0), the address of the next instruction is calculated. This address may be the next sequential instruction, the target of a branch, or a location in microcode. In the second stage of the pipeline (pipe 1), the instructions are issued to the rest of the machine. In the third stage (pipe 2), the instruction computation is started, and for single cycle instructions, a result is returned.

Several microarchitectural features of the core are designed to minimize performance loss due to pipeline breaks.

Branch Prediction—To minimize pipeline breaks due to branching, the user can specify the direction that a conditional branch instruction will usually follow. The processor will execute along the specified instruction path with no pipeline break. If the branch direction specified was the direction actually selected by execution of the conditional branch, no pipeline break occurs. The direction of the branch guess is determined by a bit value in the CTRL format instructions.

Register Bypassing—Register bypassing is a feature which forwards the result of an instruction for immediate use as the source of another instruction. This forwarding occurs at the same time that the value is written to its destination register. Bypassing the register file saves the one clock cycle break which would otherwise occur while waiting for the value to be written to the register file and the register scoreboard to be cleared.

On-chip Cache—The on-chip instruction cache and local register cache eliminate many pipeline breaks which will occur if the IS is forced to wait for code or data to be moved between the 80960CA and external memory.

Register File Access—The Register File allows multiple instructions to gain access to the register set simultaneously. This eliminates pipeline breaks which would be caused by a loss of access to the register set by any coprocessor.

A.1.1 INSTRUCTION CACHE

The IS includes a 1 Kbyte two-way set associative instruction cache capable of delivering up to four instructions each clock to the Instruction Sequencer. The cache allows inner loops of code to execute with no external instruction fetches.

A.1.2 MICROCODE ROM

The 80960CA uses *microcode ROM* to implement complex instructions and functions. This includes calls, returns, DMA transfers, and initialization sequences. Microcode provides an inexpensive and simple method for implementing complex instructions in the mostly RISC environment of the 80960CA. When the IS encounters a microcoded instruction, it automatically branches to the microcode routine. The 80960CA performs this microcode branch in 0 clocks.

State	1	2	3
Pipe 0	decode	decode	decode
Pipe 1	XXXXX	issue	issue
Pipe 2	XXXXX	XXXXX	execute & return

Figure A-2. Instruction Pipeline

A.2 Register File

The *Register File (RF)* contains the 16 local and 16 global registers. The register file has six ports (Figure A-3), allowing parallel access of the register set by several 80960CA coprocessors. This parallel access results in an ability to execute one simple logic or arithmetic instruction, one memory operation (load/store), and one address calculation per clock.

MEM coprocessors interface to the RF with a 128-bit wide load bus and a 128-bit wide store bus. These busses enable movement of up to 4 words per clock to and from the RF. These busses also allow LOAD data from a previous read access and STORE data from a current write access to be processed in the register file simultaneously. An additional 32-bit port allows an address or address reduction operand to be simultaneously fetched by the Address Generation Unit.

REG coprocessors interface to the RF with two 64-bit source busses and a single 64-bit destination bus. With this bus structure, two source operands are simultaneously issued to a REG coprocessor when an instruction is issued. A 64-bit destination bus allows the result from the previous operation to be written to the RF at the same time that the current operation's source operands are issued.

A.3 Execution Unit

The Execution Unit is the 32-bit Arithmetic and Logic Unit of the 80960CA Core. The EU can be viewed as a self-contained REG coprocessor with its own instruction set. As such, the EU is responsible for executing or supporting the execution of all the integer and ordinal arithmetic instructions, the logic and shift instructions, the move instructions, the bit and bit field instructions, and the compare operations. The EU performs any arithmetic or logical instructions in a single clock.

A.4 Multiply Divide Unit

The *Multiply and Divide Unit (MDU)* is a REG coprocessor which performs integer and ordinal multiply, divide, remainder, and modulo operations. The MDU detects integer overflow and divide by zero errors. The MDU is optimized for multiplication, performing 32-bit multiplies in 4 clocks. The MDU performs multiplies and divides in parallel with the main execution unit.

A.5 Address Generation Unit

The *Address Generation Unit (AGU)* is a MEM coprocessor which computes the effective addresses for memory operations. It directly executes the load address instruction (**lda**) and calculates addresses for loads and stores based on the addressing mode specified in these instructions. The address calculations are performed in parallel with the main execution unit (EU).

A.6 Data RAM and Local Register Cache

The *Data RAM and Local Register Cache* is part of a 1.5 Kbyte block of on-chip Static RAM (SRAM). 1 Kbyte of this SRAM is mapped into the 80960CA's address space from location 00000000H to 000003FFH. A portion of the remaining 512 bytes is dedicated to the Local Register Cache. This part of internal SRAM is not directly visible to the user. Loads and Stores, including quad-word accesses, to the internal SRAM are typically performed in only one clock. The complete local register set, therefore, can be moved to the local register cache in only four clocks.

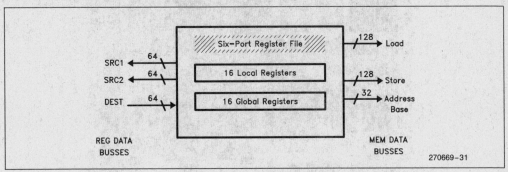

Figure A-3. Six-Port Register File

80960CA-33, -25, -16
32-BIT HIGH PERFORMANCE EMBEDDED PROCESSOR

- Two Instructions/clock sustained execution
- Four 59 Mbytes/s DMA Channels with Data Chaining
- Demultiplexed 32-Bit Burst Bus with Pipelining

■ 32-bit Parallel Architecture
— Two Instructions/clock Execution
— Load/Store Architecture
— 16, 32-bit Global Registers
— 16, 32-bit Local Registers
— Load/Store 128-bits per Clock
— Operate on 1, 8, 16, 32, 64-bit Data
— Manipulate 64-Bit Bit Fields
— 11 Addressing Modes
— Full Parallel Fault Model
— Supervisor Protection Model

■ Fast Procedure Call/Return Model
— Full Procedure Call in 4 clocks
— RISC Call in 2 clocks (BAL)

■ On-Chip Register Cache
— Caches Registers on Call/Ret
— Minimum of 6 Frames provided
— Number of Frames Programmable, up to 15

■ On-Chip Instruction Cache
— 1 Kbyte Two-Way Set Associative
— 128-bit Path to Instruction Sequencer
— Cache-Lock Modes
— Cache-Off Mode

■ High Bandwidth On-Chip Data Ram
— 1 Kbytes On-chip RAM for Data
— Sustain 128-bits per clock access
— Supervisor Protection Provided

■ Four On-Chip DMA Channels
— 59 Mbytes/s Fly-by Transfers
— 32 Mbytes/s Two-Cycle Transfers
— Data Chaining
— Data Packing/Unpacking
— Programmable Priority Method

■ 32-Bit Demultiplexed Burst Bus
— 128-bit Paths to *and* from Registers
— Burst Bus for DRAM Interfacing
— Address Pipelining
— Fully Programmable Wait States
— Supports 8, 16 or 32-bit Bus Widths
— Supports Unaligned Accesses
— Supervisor Protection Pin
— "Big-Endian" Mode Provided

■ High-Speed Interrupt Controller
— Up to 248 External Interrupts
— 32 Fully Programmable Priorities
— Multi-mode 8-bit Interrupt Port
— Four Internal DMA Interrupts
— Separate, Non-maskable Interrupt Pin
— Context Switch in 750 ns Typical

270727–1

Figure 1. 80960CA Die Photo

1.0 PURPOSE

This document provides a preview of the electrical characteristics expected of the 33, 25 and 16 MHz versions of the 80960CA. For a detailed description of any 80960CA functional topic, other than parametric performance, consult the latest 80960CA Product Overview (Order No. 270669), or the 80960CA User's Manual (Order No. 270710).

2.0 80960CA OVERVIEW

The 80960CA is the second-generation member of the 80960 Family of embedded processors. The 80960CA is object code compatible with the 32-bit 80960 Core Architecture while including Special Function Register extensions to control on-chip peripherals, and instruction set extensions to shift 64-bit operands and configure on-chip hardware. Multiple 128-bit internal busses, on-chip instruction caching and a sophisticated instruction scheduler allow the processor to sustain execution of two instructions every clock, and peak at execution of 3 instructions per clock.

A 32-bit demultiplexed and pipelined burst bus provides a 132 Mbyte/s bandwidth to a system's high-speed external memory sub-system. In addition, the 80960CA's on-chip caching of instructions, procedure context and critical program data substantially decouples system performance from the wait states associated with accesses to the system's slower, cost sensitive, main memory sub-system.

The 80960CA bus controller also integrates full wait state and bus width control for highest system performance with minimal system design complexity. Unaligned access and Big Endien byte order support reduces the cost of porting existing applications to the 80960CA.

The processor also integrates four compete data-chaining DMA channels and a high-speed interrupt controller on-chip. The DMA channels perform: single-cycle or two-cycle transfers, data packing and unpacking, and data chaining. Block transfers, in addition to source or destination synchronized transfers are provided.

The interrupt controller provides full programmability of 248 interrupt sources into 32 priority levels with a typical interrupt task switch ("latency") time of 750 ns.

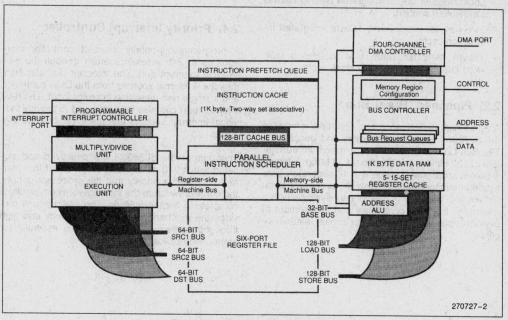

Figure 2. 80960CA Block Diagram

2.1. The C-Series Core

The C-Series core is a very high performance micro-architectural implementation of the 80960 Core Architecture. The C-Series core can sustain execution of two instructions per clock (66 MIPs at 33 MHz). To achieve this level of performance, Intel has incorporated state-of-the-art silicon technology and innovative microarchitectural constructs into the implementation of the C-Series core. Factors which contribute to the core's performance follow.

— Advanced silicon technology allows operation with a 33 MHz internal clock.

— Parallel instruction decoding allows issue of up to three instructions per clock.

— Most instructions execute in a single clock.

— Parallel instruction decode allows sustained, simultaneous execution of two single-clock instructions every clock cycle.

— Efficient instruction pipeline is designed to minimize pipeline break losses.

— Register and resource scoreboarding allow simultaneous multi-clock instruction execution.

— Branch look-ahead and prediction allows many branches to execute with no pipeline break.

— Local Register Cache integrated on-chip caches Call/Return context.

— Two-way set associative, 1Kbyte integrated instruction cache

— 1Kbyte integrated Data RAM sustains a four-word (128-bit) access every clock cycle.

2.2. Pipelined, Burst Bus

A 32-bit high performance bus controller interfaces the 80960CA to external memory and peripherals. The Bus Control Unit features a maximum transfer rate of 132 Mbytes per second (at 33 MHz). Internally programmable wait states and 16 separately configurable memory regions allow the processor to interface with a variety of memory subsystems with a minimum of system complexity and a maximum of performance. The Bus Controller's main features include:

— Demultiplexed, Burst Bus to exploit most efficient DRAM access modes

— Address Pipelining to reduce memory cost while maintaining performance

— 32-, 16- and 8-bit modes for I/O interfacing ease.

— Full internal wait state generation to reduce system cost

— Little and Big Endien support to ease application development

— Unaligned access support for code portability

— Three-deep request queue to decouple the bus from the core

— Direct interface to 27C960 Burst EPROM

2.3. Flexible DMA Controller

A four channel DMA controller provides high speed DMA control for data transfers involving peripherals and memory. The DMA provides advanced features such as data chaining, byte assembly and disassembly, and a high performance fly-by mode capable of transfer speed of up to 59 MBytes per second at 33 MHz. The DMA controller features a performance and flexibility which is only possible by integrating the DMA controller and the 80960CA core.

2.4. Priority Interrupt Controller

A programmable-priority interrupt controller manages up to 248 external sources through the 8-bit external interrupt port. The Interrupt Unit also handles the 4 internal sources from the DMA controller, and a single non-maskable interrupt input. The 8-bit interrupt port can also be configured to provide individual interrupt sources that are level, or edge triggered.

Interrupts in the 80960CA are prioritized and signaled within 270 ns of the request, and if the interrupt is of higher priority that the processor priority, the context switch to the interrupt routine typically is complete in another 480 ns. The interrupt unit provides the mechanism for the low latency and high throughput interrupt service which is essential for embedded applications.

2.5. Instruction Set Summary

The following table summarizes the 80960CA instruction set by logical groupings. See the 80960CA User's Manual for a complete description of the instruction set.

Data Movement	Arithmetic	Logical	Bit, Bit Field and Byte
Load	Add	And	Set Bit
Store	Subtract	Not And	Clear Bit
Move	Multiply	And Not	Not Bit
Load Address	Divide	Or	Alter Bit
	Remainder	Exclusive Or	Scan for Bit
	Modulo	Not Or	Span over Bit
	Shift	Or Not	Extract
	*Extended	Nor	Modify
	Shift	Exclusive Nor	Scan Byte for Equal
	Extended	Not	
	Multiply	Nand	
	Extended		
	Divide		
	Add with		
	Carry		
	Subtract with		
	Carry		
	Rotate		
Comparison	**Branch**	**Call and Return**	**Fault**
Compare	Unconditional	Call	Conditional
Conditional	Branch	Call Extended	Fault
Compare	Conditional	Call System	Synchronize
Compare and	Branch	Return	Faults
Increment		Branch and Link	
Compare and			
Decrement	Compare and		
Condition Test	Branch		
Check Bit			
Debug	**Processor Management**	**Atomic**	
Modify Trace	Modify	Atomic Add	
Controls	Process	Atomic Modify	
Mark	Controls		
Force Mark	Modify		
	Arithmetic		
	Controls		
	*System Control		
	*DMA Control		
	Flush Local		
	Registers		

NOTE:
Instructions marked by (*) are 80960CA extensions to the 80960 instruction set.

3.0 PACKAGE INFORMATION

3.1. Package Introduction

This section describes the pins, pinouts and thermal characteristics for the 80960CA in the 168-pin Ceramic Pin Grid Array (PGA) package. For complete package specifications and information, see the Intel Packaging Specification (Order # 231369).

3.2. Pin Descriptions

The 80960CA pins are described in this section. Table 1 presents the legend for interpreting the pin descriptions in the following tables.

The pins associated with the 32-bit demultiplexed processor bus are described in Table 2. The pins associated with basic processor configuration and control are described in Table 3. The pins associated with the 80960CA DMA Controller and Interrupt Unit are described in Table 4.

Figure 3 provides an example pin description table entry. The "I/O" signifies that the data pins are input-output. The "S" indicates the pins are synchronous to PCLK2:1. The "H(Z)" indicates that these pins float while the processor bus is in a Hold Acknowledge state. The "R(Z)" notation indicates that the pins also float while $\overline{RESET}$ is low.

All pins float while the processor is in the ONCE™ mode.

Table 1. Pin Description Nomenclature

Symbol	Description
I	Input only pin
O	Output only pin
I/O	Pin can be either an input or output
-	Pins "must be" connected as described
S(. . .)	Synchronous. Inputs must meet setup and hold times relative to PCLK2:1 for proper operation of the processor. All outputs are synchronous to PCLK2:1. S(E) Edge sensitive input S(L) Level sensitive input
A(. . .)	Asynchronous. Inputs may be asynchronous to PCLK2:1. A(E) Edge sensitive input A(L) Level sensitive input
H(. . .)	While the processor's bus is in the Hold Acknowledge state, the pin: H(1)　is driven to V_{CC} H(0)　is driven to V_{SS} H(Z)　floats H(Q)　continues to be a valid output
R(. . .)	While the processor's $\overline{RESET}$ # pin is low, the pin R(1)　is driven to V_{CC} R(0)　is driven to V_{SS} R(Z)　floats R(Q)　continues to be a valid output

Name	Type	Description
D31:0	I/O S(L) H(Z) R(Z)	**DATA BUS** carries 32, 16, or 8-bit data quantities depending on bus width configuration. The least significant bit of the data is carried on D0 and the most significant on D31. When the bus is configured for 8 bit data, the lower 8 data lines, D7:0 are used. For 16 bit data widths, D15:0 are used. For 32 bit data the full data bus is used.

Figure 3. Example Pin Description Entry

Table 2. 80960CA Pin Description—External Bus Signals

Name	Type	Description
A31:2	O S H(Z) R(Z)	**ADDRESS BUS** carries the upper 30 bits of the physical address. A31 is the most significant address bit and A2 is the least significant. During a bus access, A31:2 identify all external addresses to word (4-byte) boundaries. The byte enable signals indicate the selected byte in each word. During burst accesses, A3 and A2 increment to indicate successive data cycles.
D31:0	I / O S(L) H(Z) R(Z)	**DATA BUS** carries 32, 16, or 8-bit data quantities depending on bus width configuration. The least significant bit of the data is carried on D0 and the most significant on D31. When the bus is configured for 8 bit data, the lower 8 data lines, D7:0 are used. For 16 bit bus widths, D15:0 are used. For 32 bit bus widths the full data bus is used.
$\overline{BE3}$ $\overline{BE2}$ $\overline{BE1}$ $\overline{BE0}$	O S H(Z) R(Z)	**BYTE ENABLES** select which of the four bytes addressed by A31:2 are active during an access to a memory region configured for a 32-bit data-bus width. $\overline{BE3}$ applies to D31:24; $\overline{BE2}$ applies to D23:16; $\overline{BE1}$ applies to D15:8; and $\overline{BE0}$ applies to D7:0. 32-bit bus: $\overline{BE3}$ –Byte Enable 3 –enable D31:24 $\overline{BE2}$ –Byte Enable 2 –enable D23:16 $\overline{BE1}$ –Byte Enable 1 –enable D15:8 $\overline{BE0}$ –Byte Enable 0 –enable D7:0 For accesses to a memory region configured for a 16-bit data-bus width, the processor directly encodes $\overline{BE3}$, $\overline{BE1}$ and $\overline{BE0}$ to provided $\overline{BHE}$, A1 and $\overline{BLE}$ respectively. 16-bit bus: $\overline{BE3}$ –Byte High Enable ($\overline{BHE}$) –enable D15:8 $\overline{BE2}$ –Not used (is driven high or low) $\overline{BE1}$ –Address Bit 1 (A1) $\overline{BE0}$ –Byte Low Enable ($\overline{BLE}$) –enable D7:0 For accesses to a memory region configured for an 8-bit data bus width, the processor directly encodes $\overline{BE1}$ and $\overline{BE0}$ to provide A1 and A0 respectively. 8-bit bus: $\overline{BE3}$ –Not used (is driven high or low) $\overline{BE2}$ –Not used (is driven high or low) $\overline{BE1}$ –Address Bit 1 (A1) $\overline{BE0}$ –Address Bit 0 (A0)
W/$\overline{R}$	O S H(Z) R(Z)	**WRITE/READ** is low (0) for read accesses and high (1) for write accesses. The W/$\overline{R}$ signal changes in the same clock cycle as $\overline{ADS}$. It remains valid for the entire access in non-pipelined regions. In pipelined regions, W/$\overline{R}$ may not be valid in the last cycle of a read accesses.
$\overline{ADS}$	O S H(Z) R(1)	**ADDRESS STROBE** indicates valid address and the start of a new bus access. $\overline{ADS}$ is asserted for the first clock of a bus access.

Table 2. 80960CA Pin Description—External Bus Signals (Continued)

Name	Type	Description
READY	I S(L) H(Z) R(Z)	READY is an input which signals the termination of a data transfer. READY is used to indicate that read data on the bus is valid, or that a write-data transfer has completed. The READY signal works in conjunction with the internally programmed wait-state generator. If READY is enabled in a region, the pin is sampled after the programmed number of wait-states has expired. If the READY pin is deasserted high, wait states will continue to be inserted until READY becomes asserted low. This is true for the N_{RAD}, N_{RDD}, N_{WAD}, and N_{WDD} wait states. The N_{XDA} wait states cannot be extended.
BTERM	I S(L) H(Z) R(Z)	BURST TERMINATE is an input which signals the termination of an access. The assertion of BTERM causes another address cycle to occur. The BTERM signal works in conjunction with the internally programmed wait-state generator. If READY and BTERM are enabled in a region, the BTERM pin is sampled after the programmed number of wait states has expired. When BTERM is asserted (low), READY is ignored.
WAIT	O S H(Z) R(1)	WAIT indicates the status of the internal wait state generator. WAIT is active when wait states are being caused by the internal wait state generator and not by the READY or BTERM inputs. WAIT can be used to derive a write-data strobe. WAIT can also be thought of as a READY output that the processor provides when it is inserting wait states.
BLAST	O S H(Z) R(0)	BURST LAST indicates the last transfer in a bus access. BLAST is asserted in the last data transfer of burst and non-burst accesses after the wait state counter reaches zero. BLAST remains active until the clock following the last cycle of the last data transfer of a bus access. If the READY or BTERM input is used to extend wait states, the BLAST signal remains active until READY or BTERM terminates the access.
DT/R̄	O S H(Z) R(1)	DATA TRANSMIT/RECEIVE indicates direction for data transceivers. DT/R̄ is used in conjunction with DEN to provide control for data transceivers attached to the external bus. When DT/R̄ is low (0), the signal indicates that the processor will receive data. Conversely, when high (1) the signal indicates that the processor will send data. DT/R̄ will change only while DEN is high.
DEN	O S H(Z) H(Z)	DATA ENABLE indicates data cycles in a bus access. DEN is asserted (low) at the start of the first data cycle of a bus access and is deasserted (high) at the end of the last data cycle. DEN is used in conjunction with DT/R̄ to provide control for data transceivers attached to the external bus. DEN will remain asserted for sequential reads from pipelined memory regions. DEN will be high when DT/R̄ changes.
LOCK	O S H(Z) R(1)	BUS LOCK indicates that an atomic read-modify-write operation is in progress. LOCK may be used to prevent external agents from accessing memory which is currently involved in an atomic operation. LOCK is asserted (0) in the first clock of an atomic operation, and deasserted in the clock cycle following the last bus access for the atomic operation. To allow the most flexibility for a memory system enforcement of locked accesses, the processor will acknowledge a bus hold request when LOCK is asserted. The processor will perform DMA transfers while LOCK is active.
HOLD	I S(L) H(Z) R(Z)	HOLD REQUEST signals that an external agent requests access to the external bus. The processor asserts HOLDA after completing the current bus request. HOLD, HOLDA, and BREQ are used together to arbitrate access to the processor's external bus by external bus agents.

Table 2. 80960CA Pin Description—External Bus Signals (Continued)

Name	Type	Description
HOLDA	O S H(1) R(Q)	**HOLD ACKNOWLEDGE** indicates to a bus requestor that the processor has relinquished control of the external bus. When HOLDA is asserted, the external address bus, data bus, and bus control signals are floated. HOLD, HOLDA, and BREQ are used together to arbitrate access to the processor's external bus by external bus agents. Since the processor will grant HOLD requests and enter the Hold Acknowledge state even while $\overline{RESET}$ is active, the state of the HOLDA pin will be independent of the $\overline{RESET}$ pin.
BREQ	O S H(Q) R(0)	**BUS REQUEST** indicates that the processor wishes to perform a bus request. BREQ can be used by external bus arbitration logic in conjunction with HOLD and HOLDA to determine when to return mastership of the external bus to the processor.
D/$\overline{C}$	O S H(Z) R(0)	**DATA OR CODE** indicates that a bus access is a data access (1) or a instruction access (0). D/$\overline{C}$ has the same timing as W/$\overline{R}$
$\overline{DMA}$	O S H(Z) R(1)	**DMA ACCESS** indicates whether the bus access was initiated by the DMA controller. $\overline{DMA}$ will be asserted (low) for any DMA access. $\overline{DMA}$ will be deasserted (high) for all other accesses.
$\overline{SUP}$	O S H(Z) R(0)	**SUPERVISOR ACCESS** indicates whether the bus access originates from a request issued while in supervisor mode. $\overline{SUP}$ will be asserted (low) when the access has supervisor privileges, and will be deasserted (high) otherwise. $\overline{SUP}$ can be used to isolate supervisor code and data structures from non-supervisor access.

Table 3. 80960CA Pin Description—Processor Control Signals

Name	Type	Description
$\overline{RESET}$	I A(L) H(Z) R(Z) N(Z)	**RESET** causes the chip to reset. When $\overline{RESET}$ is asserted (low), all external signals return to the reset state. When $\overline{RESET}$ is deasserted, initialization begins. When the two-x clock mode is selected, $\overline{RESET}$ must remain asserted for 16 PCLK2:1 cycles before being deasserted in order to guarantee correct initialization of the processor. When the one-x clock mode is selected, $\overline{RESET}$ must remain asserted for 10,000 PCLK2:1 cycles before being deasserted in order to guarantee correct initialization of the processor. The CLKMODE pin selects one-x or two-x input clock division of the CLKIN pin. The processor's Hold Acknowledge bus state functions while the chip is reset. If the processor's bus is in the Hold Acknowledge state when $\overline{RESET}$ is activated, the processor will internally reset, but will maintain the Hold Acknowledge state on external pins until the Hold request is removed. If a hold request is made while the processor is in the reset state, the processor bus will grant HOLDA and enter the Hold Acknowledge state.
$\overline{FAIL}$	O S H(Q) R(0)	**FAIL** indicates failure of the processor's self-test performed at initialization. When $\overline{RESET}$ is deasserted and the processor begins initialization, the $\overline{FAIL}$ pin is asserted (0). An internal self-test is performed as part of the initialization process. If this self-test passes, the $\overline{FAIL}$ pin is deasserted (1) otherwise it remains asserted. The $\overline{FAIL}$ pin is reasserted while the processor performs and external bus self-confidence test. If this self-test passes, the processor deasserts the $\overline{FAIL}$ pin and branches to the users initialization routine, otherwise the $\overline{FAIL}$ pin remains asserted. Internal self-test and the use of the $\overline{FAIL}$ pin can be disabled with the STEST pin.

Table 3. 80960CA Pin Description—Processor Control Signals (Continued)

Name	Type	Description
STEST	I S(L) H(Z) R(Z)	**SELF TEST** causes the processor's internal self-test feature to be enabled or disabled at initialization. STEST is read on the rising edge of $\overline{\text{RESET}}$. When asserted (high) the processor's internal self-test and external bus confidence tests are performed during processor initialization. When deasserted (low), no self-tests are performed during initialization.
$\overline{\text{ONCE}}$™	I A(L) H(Z) R(Z)	**ON CIRCUIT EMULATION** causes all outputs to be floated when asserted (low). $\overline{\text{ONCE}}$ is continuously sampled while $\overline{\text{RESET}}$ is low, and is latched on the rising edge of $\overline{\text{RESET}}$. To place the processor in the ONCE state: (1) assert $\overline{\text{RESET}}$ and $\overline{\text{ONCE}}$ (order does not matter) (2) wait for at least 16 clocks in one-x mode, or 10,000 clocks in two-x mode, after V_{CC} and CLKIN are within operating specifications (3) deassert $\overline{\text{RESET}}$ (4) wait at least 16 clocks (The processor will now be latched in the ONCE state as long as $\overline{\text{RESET}}$ is high.) To exit the ONCE state, bring V_{CC} and CLKIN to operating conditions, then assert $\overline{\text{RESET}}$ and bring $\overline{\text{ONCE}}$ high prior to deasserting $\overline{\text{RESET}}$. CLKIN must operate within the specified operating conditions of the processor until step 4 above has been completed. The CLKIN may then be changed to D.C. to achieve the lowest possible ONCE mode leakage current. $\overline{\text{ONCE}}$ can be used by emulator products or for board testers to effectively make an installed processor transparent in the board.
CLKIN	I A(E) H(Z) R(Z)	**CLOCK INPUT** is an input for the external clock needed to run the processor. The external clock is internally divided as prescribed by the CLKMODE pin to produce PCLK2:1.
CLKMODE	I A(L) H(Z) R(Z)	**CLOCK MODE** selects the division factor applied to the external clock input (CLKIN). When CLKMODE is high (1), CLKIN is divided by one to create PCLK2:1 and the processor's internal clock. When CLKMODE is low (0), CLKIN is divided by two to create PCLK2:1 and the processor's internal clock. CLKMODE should be tied high, or low in a system, as the clock mode is not latched by the processor. If left unconnected, the processor will internally pull the CLKMODE pin low (0), enabling the two-x clock mode.
PCLK2 PCLK1	O S H(Q) R(Q)	**PROCESSOR OUTPUT CLOCKS** provide a timing reference for all inputs and outputs of the processor. All inputs and output timings are specified in relation to PCLK2 and PCLK1. PCLK2 and PCLK1 are identical signals. Two output pins are provided to allow flexibility in the system's allocation of capacitive loading on the clock. PCLK2:1 may also be connected at the processor to form a single clock signal.
V_{SS}	–	**GROUND** connections consist of 24 pins which must be shorted externally to a V_{SS} board plane.
V_{CC}	–	**POWER** connections consist of 24 pins which must be shorted externally to a V_{CC} board plane.
N/C	–	**NO CONNECT** pins must not be connected in a system.

Table 4. 80960CA Pin Description—DMA and Interrupt Unit Control Signals

Name	Type	Description
DREQ3 DREQ2 DREQ1 DREQ0	I A(L) H(Z) R(Z)	**DMA REQUEST** causes a DMA transfer to be requested. Each of the four signals requests a transfer on a single channel. DREQ0 requests channel 0, DREQ1 requests channel 1, etc. When two or more channels are requested simultaneously, the channel with the highest priority is serviced first. The channel priority mode is programmable.
DACK3 DACK2 DACK1 DACK0	O S H(Z) R(1)	**DMA ACKNOWLEDGE** indicates that a DMA transfer is being executed. Each of the four signals acknowledges a transfer for a single channel. DACK0 acknowledges channel 0, DACK1 acknowledges channel 1, etc. DACK3:0 are active (0) when the requesting device of a DMA is accessed.
EOP3/TC3 EOP2/TC2 EOP1/TC1 EOP0/TC0	I / O A(L) H(Z) R(Z)	**END OF PROCESS/TERMINAL COUNT** can be programmed as either an input (EOP3:0) or as an output (TC3:0), but not both. Each pin is individually programmable. When programmed as an input, EOPx causes the termination of a current DMA transfer for the channel corresponding to the EOPx pin. EOP0 corresponds to channel 0, EOP1 corresponds to channel 1, etc. When a channel is configured for source *and* destination chaining, the EOP pin for that channel causes termination of only the current buffer transferred and causes the next buffer to be transferred. EOP3:0 are asynchronous inputs. When programmed as an output, the channel's TCx pin indicates that the channel byte count has reached 0 and a DMA has terminated. TCx is driven active (0) for a single clock cycle after the last DMA transfer is completed on the external bus. TC3:0 are synchronous outputs.
XINT7 XINT6 XINT5 XINT4 XINT3 XINT2 XINT1 XINT0	I A(E/L) H(Z) R(Z)	**EXTERNAL INTERRUPT PINS** cause interrupts to be requested. These pins can be configured in three modes. In the Dedicated Mode, each pin is a dedicated external interrupt source. Dedicated inputs can be individually programmed to be level (low) or edge (falling) activated. In the Expanded Mode, the 8 pins act together as an 8-bit vectored interrupt source. The interrupt pins in this mode are level activated. Since the interrupt pins are active low, the vector number requested is the one's complement of the positive logic value place on the port. This eliminates glue logic to interface to combinational priority encoders which output negative logic. In the Mixed Mode, XINT7:5 are dedicated sources and XINT4:0 act as the 5 most significant bits of an expanded mode vector. The least significant bits are set to 010 internally.
NMI	I A(E) H(Z) R(Z)	**NON-MASKABLE INTERRUPT** causes a non-maskable interrupt event to occur. NMI is the highest priority interrupt recognized. NMI is an edge (falling) activated source.

3.3. 80960CA Pinout

Tables 5 and 6 list the 80960CA pin names with package location. Figure 4-a depicts the complete 80960CA pinout as viewed from the top side of the

component (i.e., pins facing down). Figure 4-b shows the complete 80960CA pinout as viewed from the pin-side of the package (i.e., pins facing up). See **Section 4.0, Electrical Specifications** for specifications and recommended connections.

Table 5. Pin Name with Package Location

Address Bus	Data Bus	Bus Control	Processor Control	I/O
Name . . Location	*Name . . Location*	*Name . . Location*	*Name . . . . Location*	*Name . . Location*
A31 . . . . S15	D31 . . . . R03	$\overline{BE3}$ S05	RESET A16	$\overline{DREQ3}$ A07
A30 . . . . Q13	D30 . . . . Q05	$\overline{BE2}$ S06		$\overline{DREQ2}$ B06
A29 . . . . R14	D29 . . . . S02	$\overline{BE1}$ S07	FAIL A02	$\overline{DREQ1}$ A06
A28 . . . . Q14	D28 . . . . Q04	$\overline{BE0}$ R09		$\overline{DREQ0}$ B05
A27 . . . . S16	D27 . . . . R02		STEST B02	
A26 . . . . R15	D26 . . . . Q03	W/$\overline{R}$ S10		$\overline{DACK3}$ A10
A25 . . . . S17	D25 . . . . S01		$\overline{ONCE}$	$\overline{DACK2}$ A09
A24 . . . . Q15	D24 . . . . R01	$\overline{ADS}$ R06		$\overline{DACK1}$ A08
A23 . . . . R16	D23 . . . . Q02		CKLIN C13	$\overline{DACK0}$ B08
A22 . . . . R17	D22 . . . . P03	READY S03	CLKMODE C14	
A21 . . . . Q16	D21 . . . . Q01	$\overline{BTERM}$ R04	PCLK1 . . . . B14	EOP/$\overline{TC3}$ . . . A11
A20 . . . . P15	D20 . . . . P02		PCLK2 . . . . B13	EOP/$\overline{TC2}$ . . . A12
A19 . . . . P16	D19 . . . . P01	$\overline{WAIT}$ S12		EOP/$\overline{TC1}$ . . . A13
A18 . . . . Q17	D18 . . . . N02	$\overline{BLAST}$ S08	$\mathbf{V_{SS}}$	EOP/$\overline{TC0}$ . . . A14
A17 . . . . P17	D17 . . . . N01		*Location*	
A16 . . . . N16	D16 . . . . M01	DT/$\overline{R}$ S11	C07, C08, C09,	$\overline{XINT7}$ C17
A15 . . . . N17	D15 . . . . L01	$\overline{DEN}$ S09	C10, C11, C12, F15, G03, G15,	$\overline{XINT6}$ C16
A14 . . . . M17	D14 . . . . L02		H03, H15, J03,	$\overline{XINT5}$ B17
A13 . . . . L16	D13 . . . . K01	$\overline{LOCK}$ S14	J15, K03, K15, L03, L15, M03,	$\overline{XINT4}$ C15
A12 . . . . L17	D12 . . . . J01		M15, Q07, Q08,	$\overline{XINT3}$ B16
A11 . . . . K17	D11 . . . . H01	HOLD R05	Q09, Q10, Q11	$\overline{XINT2}$ A17
A10 . . . . J17	D10 . . . . H02	HOLDA S04	$\mathbf{V_{CC}}$	$\overline{XINT1}$ A15
A9 . . . . S17	D9 . . . . G01	BREQ R13	*Location*	$\overline{XINT0}$ B15
A8 . . . . G17	D8 . . . . F01		B07, B09, B10,	
A7 . . . . G16	D7 . . . . E01	D/$\overline{C}$ S13	B11, B12, C06, E15, F03, F16,	$\overline{NMI}$ D15
A6 . . . . F17	D6 . . . . F02	$\overline{DMA}$ R12	G02, H16, J02,	
A5 . . . . E17	D5 . . . . D01	$\overline{SUP}$ Q12	J16, K02, K16, M02,	
A4 . . . . E16	D4 . . . . E02		M16, N03, N15, Q06, R07, R08, R10, R11	
A3 . . . . D17	D3 . . . . C01		**No Connect**	
A2 . . . . D16	D2 . . . . D02		*Location*	
	D1 . . . . C02		A01, A03, A04, A05, B01, B03, B04, C03, C04, C05, D03	
	D0 . . . . E03			

Table 6. Pin Name with Package Location

Address Bus		Data Bus		Bus Control		Processor Control		I/O	
Location	*Name*	*Location*	*Name*	*Location*	*Name*	*Location*	*Name*	*Location*	*Name*
A01	NC	C01	D3	G01	D9	M01	D16	R01	D24
A02	$\overline{\text{FAIL}}$	C02	D1	G02	V_{CC}	M02	V_{CC}	R02	D27
A03	NC	C03	NC	G03	V_{SS}	M03	V_{SS}	R03	D31
A04	NC	C04	NC	G15	V_{SS}	M15	V_{SS}	R04	$\overline{\text{BTERM}}$
A05	NC	C05	NC	G16	A7	M16	V_{CC}	R05	HOLD
A06	$\overline{\text{DREQ1}}$	C06	V_{CC}	G17	A8	M17	A14	R06	$\overline{\text{ADS}}$
A07	$\overline{\text{DREQ3}}$	C07	V_{SS}					R07	V_{CC}
A08	$\overline{\text{DACK1}}$	C08	V_{SS}	H01	D11	N01	D17	R08	V_{CC}
A09	$\overline{\text{DACK2}}$	C09	V_{SS}	H02	D10	N02	D18	R09	$\overline{\text{BE0}}$
A10	$\overline{\text{DACK3}}$	C10	V_{SS}	H03	V_{SS}	N03	V_{CC}	R10	V_{CC}
A11	$\overline{\text{EOP}}$/TC0	C11	V_{SS}	H15	V_{SS}	N15	V_{CC}	R11	V_{CC}
A12	$\overline{\text{EOP}}$/TC1	C12	V_{SS}	H16	V_{CC}	N16	A16	R12	$\overline{\text{DMA}}$
A13	$\overline{\text{EOP}}$/TC2	C13	CLKIN	H17	A9	N17	A15	R13	BREQ
A14	$\overline{\text{EOP}}$/TC3	C14	CLKMODE					R14	A29
A15	$\overline{\text{XINT1}}$	C15	$\overline{\text{XINT4}}$	J01	D12	P01	D19	R15	A26
A16	$\overline{\text{RESET}}$	C16	$\overline{\text{XINT6}}$	J02	V_{CC}	P02	D20	R16	A23
A17	$\overline{\text{XINT2}}$	C17	$\overline{\text{XINT7}}$	J03	V_{SS}	P03	D22	R17	A22
				J15	V_{SS}	P15	A20		
B01	NC	D01	D5	J16	V_{CC}	P16	A19	S01	D25
B02	STEST	D02	D2	J17	A10	P17	A17	S02	D29
B03	NC	D03	NC					S03	$\overline{\text{READY}}$
B04	NC	D15	$\overline{\text{NMI}}$	K01	D13	Q01	D21	S04	HOLDA
B05	$\overline{\text{DREQ0}}$	D16	A2	K02	V_{CC}	Q02	D23	S05	$\overline{\text{BE3}}$
B06	$\overline{\text{DREQ2}}$	D17	A3	K03	V_{SS}	Q03	D26	S06	$\overline{\text{BE2}}$
B07	V_{CC}			K15	V_{SS}	Q04	D28	S07	$\overline{\text{BE1}}$
B08	$\overline{\text{DACK0}}$	E01	D7	K16	V_{CC}	Q05	D30	S08	$\overline{\text{BLAST}}$
B09	V_{CC}	E02	D4	K17	A11	Q06	V_{CC}	S09	$\overline{\text{DEN}}$
B10	V_{CC}	E03	D0			Q07	V_{SS}	S10	W/$\overline{\text{R}}$
B11	V_{CC}	E15	V_{CC}	L01	D15	Q08	V_{SS}	S11	DT/$\overline{\text{R}}$
B12	V_{CC}	E16	A4	L02	D14	Q09	V_{SS}	S12	$\overline{\text{WAIT}}$
B13	PCLK2	E17	A5	L03	V_{SS}	Q10	V_{SS}	S13	D/$\overline{\text{C}}$
B14	PCLK1			L15	V_{SS}	Q11	V_{SS}	S14	$\overline{\text{LOCK}}$
B15	$\overline{\text{XINT0}}$	F01	D8	L16	A13	Q12	$\overline{\text{SUP}}$	S15	A31
B16	$\overline{\text{XINT3}}$	F02	D6	L17	A12	Q13	A30	S16	A27
B17	$\overline{\text{XINT5}}$	F03	V_{CC}			Q14	A28	S17	A25
		F15	V_{SS}			Q15	A24		
		F16	V_{CC}			Q16	A21		
		F17	A6			Q17	A18		

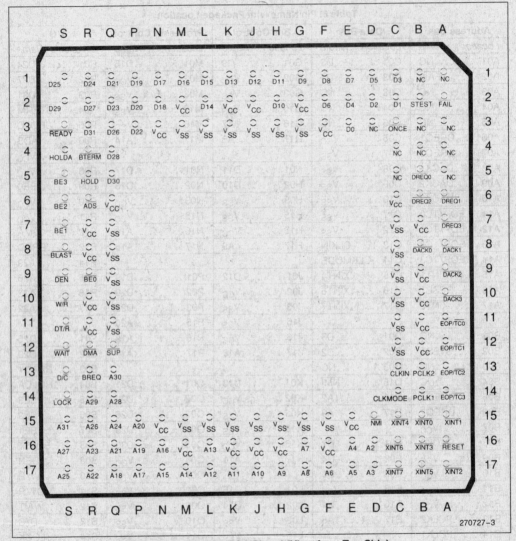

Figure 4a. 80960CA PGA Pinout (View from Top Side)

270727-3

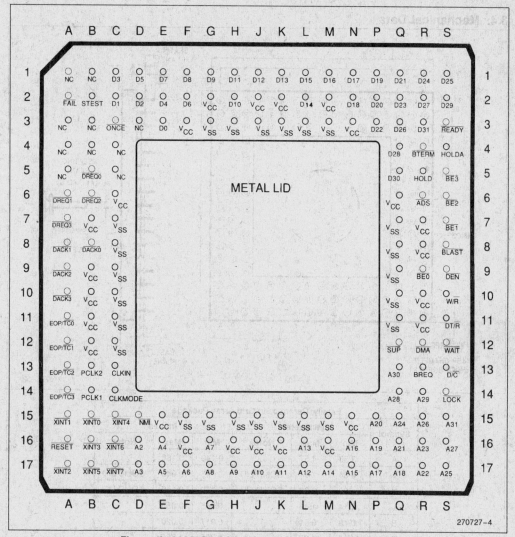

Figure 4b. 80960CA PGA Pinout (View from Bottom Side)

270727–4

3.4. Mechanical Data

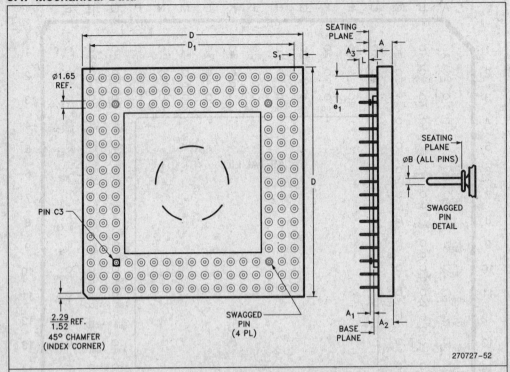

Family: Ceramic Pin Grid Array Package						
Symbol	**Millimeters**			**Inches**		
	Min	**Max**	**Notes**	**Min**	**Max**	**Notes**
A	3.56	4.57		0.140	0.180	
A₁	0.64	1.14	SOLID LID	0.025	0.045	SOLID LID
A₂	23	0.30	SOLID LID	0.110	0.140	SOLID LID
A₃	1.14	1.40		0.045	0.055	
B	0.43	0.51		0.017	0.020	
D	44.07	44.83		1.735	1.765	
D₁	40.51	40.77		1.595	1.605	
e₁	2.29	2.79		0.090	0.110	
L	2.54	3.30		0.100	0.130	
N	168			168		
S₁	1.52	2.54		0.060	0.100	
ISSUE	IWS REV X 7/15/88					

Figure 5. 168 Lead Ceramic PGA Package Dimensions

Table 7. Ceramic PGA Package Dimension Symbols

Letter or Symbol	Description of Dimensions
A	Distance from seating plane to highest point of body
A_1	Distance between seating plane and base plane (lid)
A_2	Distance from base plane to highest point of body
A_3	Distance from seating plane to bottom of body
B	Diameter of terminal lead pin
D	Largest overall package dimension of length
D_1	A body length dimension, outer lead center to outer lead center
e_1	Linear spacing between true lead position centerlines
L	Distance from seating plane to end of lead
S_1	Other body dimension, outer lead center to edge of body

NOTES:
1. Controlling dimension: millimeter.
2. Dimension "e_1" ("e") is non-cumulative.
3. Seating plane (standoff) is defined by P.C. board hole size: 0.0415–0.0430 inch.
4. Dimensions "B", "B_1" and "C" are nominal.
5. Details of Pin 1 identifier are optional.

3.5. Package Thermal Specifications

The 80960CA is specified for operation when T_C (the case temperature) is within the range of 0°C–100°C. T_C may be measured in any environment to determine whether the 80960CA is within specified operating range. The case temperature should be measured at the center of the top surface, opposite the pins.

T_A (the ambient temperature) can be calculated from θ_{CA} (thermal resistance from case to ambient) with the following equation:

$$T_A = T_C - P^*\theta_{CA}$$

Typical values for θ_{CA} at various airflows are given in Table 8 for the 1.75 sq. in., 168 pin, ceramic PGA.

Table 9 shows the maximum T_A allowable (without exceeding T_C) at various airflows and operating frequencies (f_{PCLK}).

Note that T_A is greatly improved by attaching fins or a heat sink to the package. P (the maximum power consumption) is calculated by using the maximum I_{CC} (I_{CC} HOT) as tabulated in Section 4.4, **DC Characteristics**, and V_{CC} of 5V.

Table 8. Thermal Resistance (θ_{CA}) at Various Airflows In °C/Watt

	Airflow-ft/min (m/sec)					
	0	200	400	600	800	1000
	(0)	(1.01)	(2.03)	(3.04)	(4.06)	(5.07)
θ_{CA} with Heat Sink*	13	9	5.5	5.0	3.9	3.4
θ_{CA} without Heat Sink	17	14	11	9	7.1	6.6

* 0.285″ high unidirectional heat sink (Al alloy 6061, 50 mil fin width, 150 mil center-to-center fin spacing).

Table 9. Maximum T_A at Various Airflows In °C

	f_{PCLK}	Airflow-ft/min (m/sec)					
	(MHz)	0	200	400	600	800	1000
		(0)	(1.01)	(2.03)	(3.04)	(4.06)	(5.07)
T_A with Heat Sink*	33	64	75	84	86	89	90
	25	70	79	87	88	91	92
	16	80	86	91	92	94	95
T_A without Heat Sink	33	53	61	69	75	80	81
	25	61	68	75	79	84	85
	16	74	79	83	86	89	90

* 0.285″ high unidirectional heat sink (Al alloy 6061, 50 mil fin width, 150 mil center-to-center fin spacing).

4.0 ELECTRICAL SPECIFICATIONS

4.1. Absolute Maximum Ratings

Parameter	Maximum Rating
Storage Temperature	−65 °C to +150 °C
Case Temperature Under Bias	−65 °C to +110 °C
Supply Voltage wrt. V_{SS}	−0.5V to +6.5V
Voltage on Other pins wrt V_{SS}	−0.5V to V_{CC} +0.5V

Notice: Stresses above those listed under "Absolute Maximum Ratings" may cause permanent damage to the device. This is a stress rating only and functional operation of the device at these or any other conditions above those indicated in the operational sections of this specification is not implied. Exposure to absolute maximum rating conditions for extended periods may affect device reliability.

NOTICE: Specifications contained within the following tables are subject to change.

4.2. Operating Conditions

Operating Conditions (A80960CA-33, -25, -16)

Symbol	Parameter		Min	Max	Units	Notes
V_{CC}	Supply Voltage		4.5	5.5	V	
f_{CLK2x}	Input Clock Frequency (2-x Mode)	A80960CA-33	0	66	MHz	
		A80960CA-25	0	50	MHz	
		A80960CA-16	0	32	MHz	
f_{CLK1x}	Input Clock Frequency (1-x Mode)	A80960CA-33	8	33	MHz	
		A80960CA-25	8	25	MHz	(1)
		A80960CA-16	8	16	MHz	
T_C	Case Temperature Under Bias	A80960CA-33, -25, -16	0	100	°C	

NOTE:
(1) When in the 1-x input clock mode, CLKIN is an input to an internal phase-locked loop and must maintain a minimum frequency of 8 MHz for proper processor operation. However, in the 1-x Mode, CLKIN may still be stopped when the processor is in reset. If CLKIN is stopped, the specified RESET low time must be provided once CLKIN restarts and has stabilized.

4.3. Recommended Connections

Power and ground connections must be made to multiple V_{CC} and V_{SS} (GND) pins. Every 80960CA-based circuit board should include power (V_{CC}) and ground (V_{SS}) planes for power distribution. Every V_{CC} pin must be connected to the power plane, and every V_{SS} pin must be connected to the ground plane. Pins identified as "N.C." **must not** be connected in the system.

Liberal decoupling capacitance should be placed near the 80960CA. The processor can cause transient power surges when its numerous output buffers transition, particularly when connected to large capacitive loads.

Low inductance capacitors and interconnects are recommended for best high frequency electrical performance. Inductance can be reduced by shortening the board traces between the processor and decoupling capacitors as much as possible. Capacitors specifically designed for PGA packages will offer the lowest possible inductance.

For reliable operation, always connect unused inputs to an appropriate signal level. In particular, any unused interrupt (XINT, NMI) or DMA (DREQ) input should be connected to V_{CC} through a pull-up resistor, as should BTERM if not used. Pull-up resistors should be in the range of 20 KΩ for each pin tied high. If READY or HOLD are not used, the unused input should be connected to ground. **N.C. pins must always remain unconnected.**

NOTICE: *The information in this datasheet is a PREVIEW of expected device performance. This datasheet should not be used as the basis for a final design. Once parametric information corresponding to a production device is available, an updated datasheet will be published to supercede this document.*

4.4. D.C. Specifications

D.C. Characteristics

(A80960CA-33, -25, -16 under the conditions described in **Section 4.2, Operating Conditions**.)

Symbol	Parameter	Min	Max	Units	Notes
V_{IL}	Input Low Voltage for all pins except $\overline{RESET}$	−0.3	0.8	V	
V_{IH}	Input High Voltage for all pins except $\overline{RESET}$	2.0	V_{CC} + 0.3	V	
V_{OL}	Output Low Voltage		0.45	V	I_{OL} = 5 mA
V_{OH}	Output High Voltage $\quad I_{OH} = -1mA$	2.4		V	
	$I_{OH} = -200\mu A$	V_{CC} − 0.5		V	
V_{ILR}	Input Low Voltage for $\overline{RESET}$	− 0.3	2.0	V	
V_{IHR}	Input High Voltage for $\overline{RESET}$	3.0	V_{CC} + 0.3	V	
V_{RH}	Input Hysterisis on $\overline{RESET}$	0.35	0.65	V	
I_{LI1}	Input Leakage Current for each pin *except*: BTERM, ONCE, STEST, DREQ3:0, EOP3:0/TC3:0, NMI, XINT7:0, READY, HOLD		±15	μA	$0V \le V_{IN} \le V_{CC}$ (1)
I_{LI2}	Input Leakage Current for: BTERM, ONCE, STEST, DREQ3:0, EOP3:0/TC3:0, NMI, XINT7:0	0	250	μA	V_{IN} = 0.45V (2)
I_{LI3}	Input Leakage Current for: READY, HOLD	0	500	μA	V_{IN} = 2.4V (3)
I_{LO}	Output Leakage Current		±15	μA	$0.45V \le V_{OUT} \le V_{CC}$
I_{CC}	Supply Current (A80960CA-33) I_{CC} (I_{CC1}) $\quad I_{CC}$ HOT (I_{CC2})		700 550	mA mA	(4) (5)
I_{CC}	Supply Current (A80960CA-25) I_{CC} (I_{CC1}) $\quad I_{CC}$ HOT (I_{CC2})		550 450	mA mA	(4) (5)
I_{CC}	Supply Current (A80960CA-16) I_{CC} (I_{CC1}) $\quad I_{CC}$ HOT (I_{CC2})		375 300	mA mA	(4) (5)
I_{ONCE}	ONCE-mode Supply Current $I_{ONCE1} \quad$ A80960CA-33 $I_{ONCE2} \quad$ A80960CA-25 $I_{ONCE3} \quad$ A80960CA-16 $I_{ONCE4} \quad$ A80960CA-33, -25, -16		10 7.5 5 5	mA mA mA mA	(7) (7) (8) (8)
C_{IN}	Input Capacitance for: CLKIN, RESET, ONCE, READY, HOLD, DREQ3:0 XINT7:0, NMI, BTERM, CLKMODE	0	15	pF	FC = 1 MHz
C_{OUT}	Output Capacitance of each output pin		15	pF	F_C = 1 MHz, (6)

NOTES:
(1) No Pull-up or pull-down.
(2) These pins have internal pullup resistors.
(3) These pins have internal pulldown resistors.
(4) Measured at worst case frequency, V_{CC} and temperature, with device operating and outputs loaded to the test conditions described in **Section 4.5.2, A.C. Test Conditions.**
(5) At maximum operation temperature, with all other conditions as noted in (4).
(6) Output Capacitance is the capacitive load of a floating output pin.
(7) With CLKIN operating.
(8) With CLKIN at D.C.

4.5. A.C. Specifications

4.5.1. A.C. SPECIFICATION TABLES

A.C. Characteristics — A80960CA-33

(A80960CA-33 only, under the conditions described in **Section 4.2, Operating Conditions** and **Section 4.5.2, A.C. Test Conditions**.)

Symbol	Parameter		Min	Max	Units	Notes
	INPUT CLOCK[9]					
T_F	CLKIN Frequency		0	66	MHz	(1)
T_C	CLKIN Period	In One-X Mode (f_{CLK1x})	30.3	125	ns	(1,12)
		In Two-X Mode (f_{CLK2x})	15.15	∞	ns	(1)
T_{CS}	CLKIN Period Stability	In One-X Mode (f_{CLK1x})		±0.1%	Δ	(1,13)
T_{CH}	CLKIN High Time	In One-X Mode (f_{CLK1x})	6	62.5	ns	(1,12)
		In Two-X Mode (f_{CLK2x})	6	∞	ns	(1)
T_{CL}	CLKIN Low Time	In One-X Mode (f_{CLK1x})	6	62.5	ns	(1,12)
		In Two-X Mode (f_{CLK2x})	6	∞	ns	(1)
T_{CR}	CLKIN Rise Time		0	6	ns	(1)
T_{CF}	CLKIN Fall Time		0	6	ns	(1)
	OUTPUT CLOCKS[8]					
T_{CP}	CLKIN to PCLK2:1 Delay	In One-X Mode (f_{CLK1x})	−2	2	ns	(1,3,13)
		In Two-X Mode (f_{CLK2x})	2	25	ns	(1,3)
T	PCLK2:1 Period	In One-X Mode (f_{CLK1x})		T_C	ns	(1,13)
		In Two-X Mode (f_{CLK2x})		$2T_C$	ns	(1,3)
T_{PH}	PCLK2:1 High Time		(T/2) − 2	T/2	ns	(1,13)
T_{PL}	PCLK2:1 Low Time		(T/2) − 2	T/2	ns	(1,13)
T_{PR}	PCLK2:1 Rise Time		1	4	ns	(1,3)
T_{PF}	PCLK2:1 Fall Time		1	4	ns	(1,3)
	SYNCHRONOUS OUTPUTS[8]					
T_{OV}	Output Valid Delay, Output Hold					(6)
T_{OH}	T_{OV1}, T_{OH1}	A31:28	3	16	ns	
	T_{OV2}, T_{OH2}	A27:4	3	18	ns	
	T_{OV3}, T_{OH3}	A3:2	3	16	ns	
	T_{OV4}, T_{OH4}	$\overline{BE3:0}$	3	18	ns	
	T_{OV5}, T_{OH5}	$\overline{ADS}$	3	18	ns	
	T_{OV6}, T_{OH6}	W/$\overline{R}$	3	18	ns	
	T_{OV7}, T_{OH7}	D/$\overline{C}$,SUP,$\overline{DMA}$	4	18	ns	
	T_{OV8}, T_{OH8}	$\overline{BLAST}$, $\overline{WAIT}$	3	18	ns	
	T_{OV9}, T_{OH9}	$\overline{DEN}$	3	18	ns	
	T_{OV10}, T_{OH10}	$\overline{HOLDA}$, $\overline{BREQ}$	4	18	ns	
	T_{OV11}, T_{OH11}	$\overline{LOCK}$	4	20	ns	
	T_{OV12}, T_{OH12}	$\overline{DACK3:0}$, $\overline{EOP3:0}$/$\overline{TC3:0}$	4	18	ns	
	T_{OV13}, T_{OH13}	D31:0	3	18	ns	
	T_{OV14}, T_{OH14}	DT/$\overline{R}$	T/2 + 3	T/2 + 18	ns	
T_{OF}	Output Float for all outputs		3	22	ns	(6)
	SYNCHRONOUS INPUTS[9]					
T_{IS}	Input Setup					
	T_{IH1}	D31:0	3		ns	(1,11)
	T_{IH2}	$\overline{READY}$, $\overline{BTERM}$	10		ns	(1,11)
	T_{IH3}	$\overline{HOLD}$	15		ns	(1,11)
T_{IH}	Input Hold					
	T_{IH1}	D31:0	3		ns	(1,11)
	T_{IH2}	$\overline{READY}$,$\overline{BTERM}$	5		ns	(1,11)
	T_{IH3}	$\overline{HOLD}$	3		ns	(1,11)

A.C. Characteristics — A80960CA-33

A80960CA-33 only, under the conditions described in **Section 4.2, Operating Conditions** and **Section 4.5.2, A.C. Test Conditions.**) (Continued)

Symbol	Parameter	Min	Max	Units	Notes
RELATIVE OUTPUT TIMINGS(8,6)					
T_{AVSH1}	A31:2 Valid to $\overline{ADS}$ Rising	T − 4	T + 4	ns	
T_{AVSH2}	$\overline{BE3:0}$, W/$\overline{R}$, $\overline{SUP}$, D/$\overline{C}$, $\overline{DMA}$, $\overline{DACK3:0}$ Valid to $\overline{ADS}$ Rising	T − 4	T + 4	ns	
T_{AVEL1}	A31:2 Valid to $\overline{DEN}$ Falling	T − 4	T + 4	ns	
T_{AVEL2}	$\overline{BE3:0}$, W/$\overline{R}$, $\overline{SUP}$, $\overline{INST}$, $\overline{DMA}$, $\overline{DACK3:0}$ Valid to $\overline{DEN}$ Falling	T − 4	T + 4	ns	
T_{NLQV}	$\overline{WAIT}$ Falling to Output Data Valid	±4		ns	
T_{DVNH}	Output Data Valid to $\overline{WAIT}$ Rising	N*T − 4	2N*T + 4	ns	(4)
T_{NLNH}	$\overline{WAIT}$ Falling to $\overline{WAIT}$ Rising	N*T ± 4		ns	(4)
T_{NHQX}	Output Data Hold after $\overline{WAIT}$ Rising	N*T − 4	N*T + 4	ns	(4)
T_{EHQX}	Output Data Hold after $\overline{DEN}$ Rising	− 4	∞	ns	(5)
T_{EHTV}	DT/$\overline{R}$ Hold after $\overline{DEN}$ High	T/2 − 4	∞	ns	(5)
T_{TVEL}	DT/$\overline{R}$ Valid to $\overline{DEN}$ Falling	T/2 − 4	T/2 + 4	ns	(6)
RELATIVE INPUT TIMINGS(6)					
T_{XDX}	Input Data Hold after A31:2, $\overline{BE3:0}$, W/$\overline{R}$, D/$\overline{C}$, $\overline{SUP}$, $\overline{DMA}$, $\overline{LOCK}$, $\overline{DEN}$, $\overline{DACK3:0}$ invalid	0		ns	(9)
T_{IS4}	$\overline{RESET}$ Input Setup	10		ns	(7)
T_{IH4}	$\overline{RESET}$ Input hold	5		ns	(7)
T_{IS5}	$\overline{DREQ3:0}$ Input Setup	10		ns	(7)
T_{IH5}	$\overline{DREQ3:0}$ Input hold	5		ns	(7)

NOTES:
(1) See **Section 4.5.3, A.C. Timing Waveforms** for waveforms and definitions.
(2) See Figure 19 for capacitive derating information for output delays and hold times.
(3) See Figure 20 for capacitive derating information for rise and fall times.
(4) Where N is the number of wait states that are inserted by the combination of Bus Controller Region Table entries and the $\overline{READY}$ input conditions. When there are no wait states in an access, $\overline{WAIT}$ never goes active.
(5) Output Data and/or DT/$\overline{R}$ may be driven indefinitely following a cycle if there is no subsequent bus activity.
(6) See Notes 1, 2, and 3.
(7) Since asynchronous inputs are synchronized internally by the 80960CA they have no required setup or hold times in order to be recognized and for proper operation. However, in order to guarantee recognition of the input at a particular rising edge of PCLK2:1 the setup times shown must be met. Asynchronous inputs must be active for at least two consecutive PCLK2:1 rising edges to be seen by the processor.
(8) These specifications are guaranteed by the processor.
(9) These specifications must be met by the system for proper operation of the processor.
(10) This timing is independent of loading on PCLK2:1. The derating curves do not apply.
(11) This timing is dependent upon the loading of PCLK2:1. Use the derating curves of **Section 4.5.3** to adjust the timing for PCLK2:1 loading.
(12) In the One-x input clock mode the maximum input clock period is limited to 125 ns while the processor is operating. When the processor is in reset, the input clock may stop even in One-x mode.
(13) When in the One-x input clock mode, these specifications assume a stable input clock with a period variation of less than ±0.1% between adjacent cycles.

A.C. Characteristics — A80960CA-25

(A80960CA-25 only, under the conditions described in **Section 4.2, Operating Conditions** and **Section 4.5.2, A.C. Test Conditions**.)

Symbol	Parameter		Min	Max	Units	Notes
INPUT CLOCK[9]						
T_F	CLKIN Frequency		0	50	MHz	(1)
T_C	CLKIN Period	In One-X Mode (f_{CLK1x})	40	125	ns	(1,12)
		In Two-X Mode (f_{CLK2x})	20	∞	ns	(1)
T_{CS}	CLKIN Period Stability	In One-X Mode (f_{CLK1x})		$\pm 0.1\%$	Δ	(1,13)
T_{CH}	CLKIN High Time	In One-X Mode (f_{CLK1x})	8	62.5	ns	(1,12)
		In Two-X Mode (f_{CLK2x})	8	∞	ns	(1)
T_{CL}	CLKIN Low Time	In One-X Mode (f_{CLK1x})	8	62.5	ns	(1,12)
		In Two-X Mode (f_{CLK2x})	8	∞	ns	(1)
T_{CR}	CLKIN Rise Time		0	6	ns	(1)
T_{CF}	CLKIN Fall Time		0	6	ns	(1)
OUTPUT CLOCKS[8]						
T_{CP}	CLKIN to PCLK2:1 Delay	In One-X Mode (f_{CLK1x})	-2	4	ns	(1,3,13)
		In Two-X Mode (f_{CLK2x})	2	25	ns	(1,3)
T	PCLK2:1 Period	In One-X Mode (f_{CLK1x})		T_C	ns	(1,13)
		In Two-X Mode (f_{CLK2x})		$2T_C$	ns	(1,3)
T_{PH}	PCLK2:1 High Time		$(T/2) - 3$	$T/2$	ns	(1,13)
T_{PL}	PCLK2:1 Low Time		$(T/2) - 3$	$T/2$	ns	(1,13)
T_{PR}	PCLK2:1 Rise Time		1	4	ns	(1,3)
T_{PF}	PCLK2:1 Fall Time		1	4	ns	(1,3)
SYNCHRONOUS OUTPUTS[8]						
T_{OV} T_{OH}	Output Valid Delay, Output Hold					(6)
	T_{OV1}, T_{OH1}	A31:28	3	20	ns	
	T_{OV2}, T_{OH2}	A27:4	3	20	ns	
	T_{OV3}, T_{OH3}	A3:2	3	20	ns	
	T_{OV4}, T_{OH4}	$\overline{BE3:0}$	3	20	ns	
	T_{OV5}, T_{OH5}	$\overline{ADS}$	3	20	ns	
	T_{OV6}, T_{OH6}	$W/\overline{R}$	3	20	ns	
	T_{OV7}, T_{OH7}	$D/\overline{C}, SUP, \overline{DMA}$	4	20	ns	
	T_{OV8}, T_{OH8}	$\overline{BLAST}, \overline{WAIT}$	3	20	ns	
	T_{OV9}, T_{OH9}	$\overline{DEN}$	3	20	ns	
	T_{OV10}, T_{OH10}	$\overline{HOLDA}, \overline{BREQ}$	4	20	ns	
	T_{OV11}, T_{OH11}	$\overline{LOCK}$	4	22	ns	
	T_{OV12}, T_{OH12}	$\overline{DACK3:0}, \overline{EOP3:0/TC3:0}$	4	20	ns	
	T_{OV13}, T_{OH13}	D31:0	3	20	ns	
	T_{OV14}, T_{OH14}	$DT/\overline{R}$	$T/2 + 3$	$T/2 + 20$	ns	
T_{OF}	Output Float for all outputs		3	22	ns	(6)
SYNCHRONOUS INPUTS[9]						
T_{IS}	Input Setup					
	T_{IH1}	D31:0	5		ns	(1,11)
	T_{IH2}	$\overline{READY}, \overline{BTERM}$	15		ns	(1,11)
	T_{IH3}	$\overline{HOLD}$	15		ns	(1,11)
T_{IH}	Input Hold					
	T_{IH1}	D31:0	5		ns	(1,11)
	T_{IH2}	$\overline{READY}, \overline{BTERM}$	5		ns	(1,11)
	T_{IH3}	$\overline{HOLD}$	3		ns	(1,11)

A.C. Characteristics — A80960CA-25

(A80960CA-25 only, under the conditions described in **Section 4.2, Operating Conditions** and **Section 4.5.2, A.C. Test Conditions.**) (Continued)

Symbol	Parameter	Min	Max	Units	Notes
RELATIVE OUTPUT TIMINGS(8,6)					
T_{AVSH1}	A31:2 Valid to $\overline{ADS}$ Rising	T − 4	T + 4	ns	
T_{AVSH2}	$\overline{BE3:0}$, W/$\overline{R}$, $\overline{SUP}$, D/$\overline{C}$, $\overline{DMA}$, $\overline{DACK3:0}$ Valid to $\overline{ADS}$ Rising	T − 4	T + 4	ns	
T_{AVEL1}	A31:2 Valid to $\overline{DEN}$ Falling	T − 4	T + 4	ns	
T_{AVEL2}	$\overline{BE3:0}$, W/$\overline{R}$, $\overline{SUP}$, $\overline{INST}$, $\overline{DMA}$, $\overline{DACK3:0}$ Valid to $\overline{DEN}$ Falling	T − 4	T + 4	ns	
T_{NLQV}	$\overline{WAIT}$ Falling to Output Data Valid	±4		ns	
T_{DVNH}	Output Data Valid to $\overline{WAIT}$ Rising	N*T − 4	N*T + 4	ns	(4)
T_{NLNH}	$\overline{WAIT}$ Falling to $\overline{WAIT}$ Rising	N*T ± 4		ns	(4)
T_{NHQX}	Output Data Hold after $\overline{WAIT}$ Rising	N*T − 4	N*T + 4	ns	(4)
T_{EHQX}	Output Data Hold after $\overline{DEN}$ Rising	− 4	∞	ns	(5)
T_{EHTV}	DT/$\overline{R}$ Hold after $\overline{DEN}$ High	T/2 − 4	∞	ns	(5)
T_{TVEL}	DT/$\overline{R}$ Valid to $\overline{DEN}$ Falling	T/2 − 4	T/2 + 4	ns	(6)
RELATIVE INPUT TIMINGS(6)					
T_{XDX}	Input Data Hold after A31:2, $\overline{BE3:0}$, W/$\overline{R}$, D/$\overline{C}$, $\overline{SUP}$, $\overline{DMA}$, $\overline{LOCK}$, $\overline{DEN}$, $\overline{DACK3:0}$ invalid	0		ns	(9)
T_{IS4}	$\overline{RESET}$ Input Setup	10		ns	(7)
T_{IH4}	$\overline{RESET}$ Input hold	5		ns	(7)
T_{IS5}	$\overline{DREQ3:0}$ Input Setup	10		ns	(7)
T_{IH5}	$\overline{DREQ3:0}$ Input hold	5		ns	(7)

NOTES:
(1) See **Section 4.5.3, A.C. Timing Waveforms** for waveforms and definitions.
(2) See Figure 19 for capacitive derating information for output delays and hold times.
(3) See Figure 20 for capacitive derating information for rise and fall times.
(4) Where N is the number of wait states that are inserted by the combination of Bus Controller Region Table entries and the $\overline{READY}$ input conditions. When there are no wait states in an access, $\overline{WAIT}$ never goes active.
(5) Output Data and/or DT/$\overline{R}$ may be driven indefinitely following a cycle if there is no subsequent bus activity.
(6) See Notes 1, 2, and 3.
(7) Since asynchronous inputs are synchronized internally by the 80960CA they have no required setup or hold times in order to be recognized and for proper operation. However, in order to guarantee recognition of the input at a particular rising edge of PCLK2:1 the setup times shown must be met. Asynchronous inputs must be active for at least two consecutive PCLK2:1 rising edges to be seen by the processor.
(8) These specifications are guaranteed by the processor.
(9) These specifications must be met by the system for proper operation of the processor.
(10) This timing is independent of loading on PCLK2:1. The derating curves do not apply.
(11) This timing is dependent upon the loading of PCLK2:1. Use the derating curves of **Section 4.5.4** to adjust the timing for PCLK2:1 loading.
(12) In the One-x input clock mode the maximum input clock period is limited to 125 ns while the processor is operating. When the processor is in reset, the input clock may stop even in One-x mode.
(13) When in the One-x input clock mode, these specifications assume a stable input clock with a period variation of less than ±0.1% between adjacent cycles.

A.C. Characteristics — A80960CA-16

(A80960CA-16 only, under the conditions described in **Section 4.2, Operating Conditions** and **Section 4.5.2, A.C. Test Conditions**.) (Continued)

Symbol	Parameter		Min	Max	Units	Notes
INPUT CLOCK[9]						
T_F	CLKIN Frequency		0	50	MHz	(1)
T_C	CLKIN Period	In One-X Mode (f_{CLK1x})	62.5	125	ns	(1,12)
		In Two-X Mode (f_{CLK2x})	31.25	∞	ns	(1)
T_{CS}	CLKIN Period Stability	In One-X Mode (f_{CLK1x})		$\pm 0.1\%$	Δ	(1,13)
T_{CH}	CLKIN High Time	In One-X Mode (f_{CLK1x})	10	62.5	ns	(1,12)
		In Two-X Mode (f_{CLK2x})	10	∞	ns	(1)
T_{CL}	CLKIN Low Time	In One-X Mode (f_{CLK1x})	10	62.5	ns	(1,12)
		In Two-X Mode (f_{CLK2x})	10	∞	ns	(1)
T_{CR}	CLKIN Rise Time		0	6	ns	(1)
T_{CF}	CLKIN Fall Time		0	6	ns	(1)
OUTPUT CLOCKS[8]						
T_{CP}	CLKIN to PCLK2:1 Delay	In One-X Mode (f_{CLK1x})	-2	5	ns	(1,3,13)
		In Two-X Mode (f_{CLK2x})	2	25	ns	(1,3)
T	PCLK2:1 Period	In One-X Mode (f_{CLK1x})	T_C		ns	(1,13)
		In Two-X Mode (f_{CLK2x})	$2T_C$		ns	(1,3)
T_{PH}	PCLK2:1 High Time		$(T/2) - 4$	$T/2$	ns	(1,13)
T_{PL}	PCLK2:1 Low Time		$(T/2) - 4$	$T/2$	ns	(1,13)
T_{PR}	PCLK2:1 Rise Time		1	4	ns	(1,3)
T_{PF}	PCLK2:1 Fall Time		1	4	ns	(1,3)
SYNCHRONOUS OUTPUTS[8]						
T_{OV}	Output Valid Delay, Output Hold					(6)
T_{OH}	T_{OV1}, T_{OH1}	A31:28	3	22	ns	
	T_{OV2}, T_{OH2}	A27:4	3	22	ns	
	T_{OV3}, T_{OH3}	A3:2	3	22	ns	
	T_{OV4}, T_{OH4}	$\overline{BE3:0}$	3	22	ns	
	T_{OV5}, T_{OH5}	$\overline{ADS}$	3	22	ns	
	T_{OV6}, T_{OH6}	$W/\overline{R}$	3	22	ns	
	T_{OV7}, T_{OH7}	$D/\overline{C}, \overline{SUP}, \overline{DMA}$	4	22	ns	
	T_{OV8}, T_{OH8}	$\overline{BLAST}, \overline{WAIT}$	3	22	ns	
	T_{OV9}, T_{OH9}	$\overline{DEN}$	3	22	ns	
	T_{OV10}, T_{OH10}	$\overline{HOLDA}, \overline{BREQ}$	4	22	ns	
	T_{OV11}, T_{OH11}	$\overline{LOCK}$	4	22	ns	
	T_{OV12}, T_{OH12}	$\overline{DACK3:0}, \overline{EOP3:0/TC3:0}$	4	22	ns	
	T_{OV13}, T_{OH13}	D31:0	3	22	ns	
	T_{OV14}, T_{OH14}	$DT/\overline{R}$	$T/2 + 3$	$T/2 + 22$	ns	
T_{OF}	Output Float for all outputs		3	22	ns	(6)
SYNCHRONOUS INPUTS[9]						
T_{IS}	Input Setup					
	T_{IH1}	D31:0	5		ns	(1,11)
	T_{IH2}	$\overline{READY}, \overline{BTERM}$	18		ns	(1,11)
	T_{IH3}	$\overline{HOLD}$	15		ns	(1,11)
T_{IH}	Input Hold					
	T_{IH1}	D31:0	5		ns	(1,11)
	T_{IH2}	$\overline{READY}, \overline{BTERM}$	5		ns	(1,11)
	T_{IH3}	$\overline{HOLD}$	5		ns	(1,11)

A.C. Characteristics — A80960CA-16

(A80960CA-16 only, under the conditions described in **Section 4.2, Operating Conditions** and **Section 4.5.2, A.C. Test Conditions**.) (Continued)

Symbol	Parameter	Min	Max	Units	Notes
RELATIVE OUTPUT TIMINGS(8,6)					
T_{AVSH1}	A31:2 Valid to $\overline{ADS}$ Rising	T − 4	T + 4	ns	
T_{AVSH2}	$\overline{BE3:0}$, W/$\overline{R}$, $\overline{SUP}$, D/$\overline{C}$, $\overline{DMA}$, $\overline{DACK3:0}$ Valid to $\overline{ADS}$ Rising	T − 4	T + 4	ns	
T_{AVEL1}	A31:2 Valid to $\overline{DEN}$ Falling	T − 4	T + 4	ns	
T_{AVEL2}	$\overline{BE3:0}$, W/$\overline{R}$, $\overline{SUP}$, $\overline{INST}$, $\overline{DMA}$, $\overline{DACK3:0}$ Valid to $\overline{DEN}$ Falling	T − 4	T + 4	ns	
T_{NLQV}	$\overline{WAIT}$ Falling to Output Data Valid	±4		ns	
T_{DVNH}	Output Data Valid to $\overline{WAIT}$ Rising	N*T − 4	N*T + 4	ns	(4)
T_{NLNH}	$\overline{WAIT}$ Falling to $\overline{WAIT}$ Rising	N*T ± 4		ns	(4)
T_{NHQX}	Output Data Hold after $\overline{WAIT}$ Rising	N*T − 4	N*T + 4	ns	(4)
T_{EHQX}	Output Data Hold after $\overline{DEN}$ Rising	− 4	∞	ns	(5)
T_{EHTV}	DT/$\overline{R}$ Hold after $\overline{DEN}$ High	T/2 − 4	∞	ns	(5)
T_{TVEL}	DT/$\overline{R}$ Valid to $\overline{DEN}$ Falling	T/2 − 4	T/2 + 4	ns	(6)
RELATIVE INPUT TIMINGS(6)					
T_{XDX}	Input Data Hold after A31:2, $\overline{BE3:0}$, W/$\overline{R}$, D/$\overline{C}$, $\overline{SUP}$, $\overline{DMA}$, $\overline{LOCK}$, $\overline{DEN}$, $\overline{DACK3:0}$ invalid	0		ns	(9)
T_{IS4}	$\overline{RESET}$ Input Setup	10		ns	(7)
T_{IH4}	$\overline{RESET}$ Input hold	5		ns	(7)
T_{IS5}	$\overline{DREQ3:0}$ Input Setup	10		ns	(7)
T_{IH5}	$\overline{DREQ3:0}$ Input hold	5		ns	(7)

NOTES:
(1) See **Section 4.5.3, A.C. Timing Waveforms** for waveforms and definitions.
(2) See Figure 19 for capacitive derating information for output delays and hold times.
(3) See Figure 20 for capacitive derating information for rise and fall times.
(4) Where N is the number of wait states that are inserted by the combination of Bus Controller Region Table entries and the $\overline{READY}$ input conditions. When there are no wait states in an access, $\overline{WAIT}$ never goes active.
(5) Output Data and/or DT/$\overline{R}$ may be driven indefinitely following a cycle if there is no subsequent bus activity.
(6) See Notes 1, 2, and 3.
(7) Since asynchronous inputs are synchronized internally by the 80960CA they have no required setup or hold times in order to be recognized and for proper operation. However, in order to guarantee recognition of the input at a particular rising edge of PCLK2:1 the setup times shown must be met. Asynchronous inputs must be active for at least two consecutive PCLK2:1 rising edges to be seen by the processor.
(8) These specifications are guaranteed by the processor.
(9) These specifications must be met by the system for proper operation of the processor.
(10) This timing is independent of loading on PCLK2:1. The derating curves do not apply.
(11) This timing is dependent upon the loading of PCLK2:1. Use the derating curves of **Section 4.5.4** to adjust the timing for PCLK2:1 loading.
(12) In the One-x input clock mode the maximum input clock period is limited to 125 ns while the processor is operating. When the processor is in reset, the input clock may stop even in One-x mode.
(13) When in the One-x input clock mode, these specifications assume a stable input clock with a period variation of less than ±0.1% between adjacent cycles.

4.5.2. A.C. TEST CONDITIONS

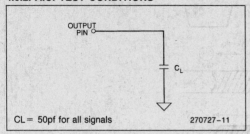

CL = 50pf for all signals   270727–11

Figure 6. A.C. Test Load

The A.C Specifications in Section 4.5 are tested with the 50 pf load shown in Figure 6. See **Section 4.5.4, Derating Curves**, to see how timings vary with load capacitance.

Specifications are measured at the 1.5V crossing point, unless otherwise indicated. Input waveforms are assumed to have a rise-and-fall time of ≤ 2 ns from 0.8V to 2.0V. See **Section 4.5.3, A.C. Timing Waveforms**, for A.C. spec definitions, test points, and illustrations.

4.5.3. A.C. TIMING WAVEFORMS

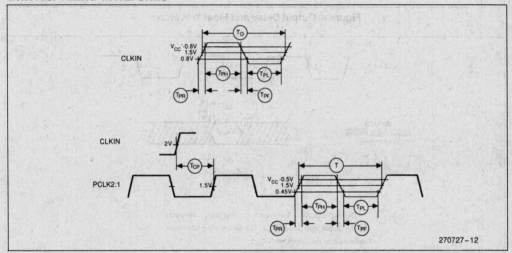

Figure 7. Input and Output Clocks Waveform

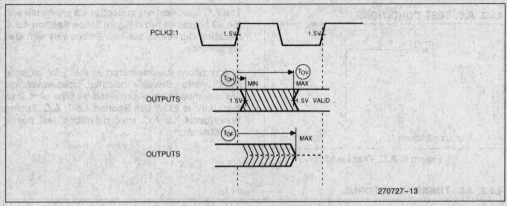

Figure 8. Output Delay and Float Waveform

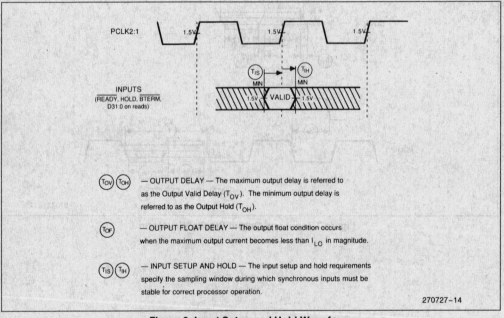

Figure 9. Input Setup and Hold Waveform

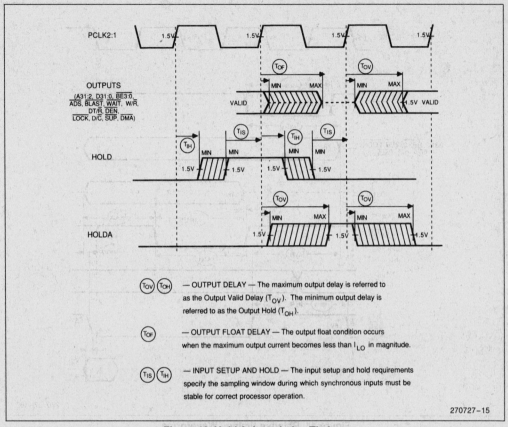

Figure 10. Hold Acknowledge Timings

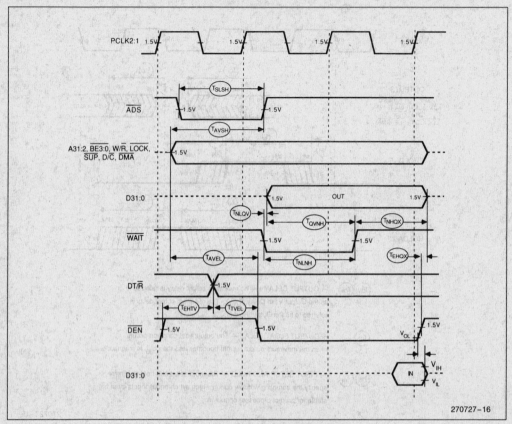

Figure 11. Relative-timings Waveforms.

270727–16

DERATING CURVES

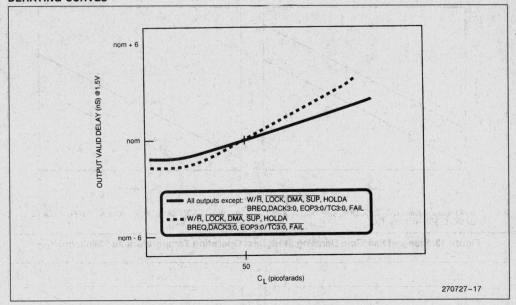

Figure 12. Output Delay or Hold vs. Load Capacitance

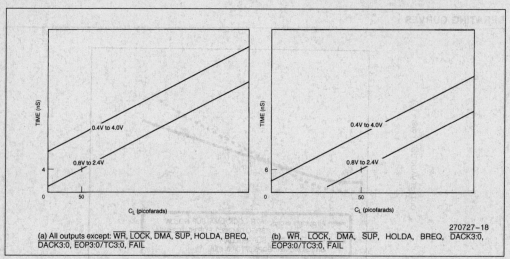

(a) All outputs except: WR, LOCK, DMA, SUP, HOLDA, BREQ, DACK3:0, EOP3:0/TC3:0, FAIL

(b) WR, LOCK, DMA, SUP, HOLDA, BREQ, DACK3:0, EOP3:0/TC3:0, FAIL

270727–18

Figure 13. Rise and Fall Time Derating at Highest Operating Temperature and Minimum V$_{CC}$

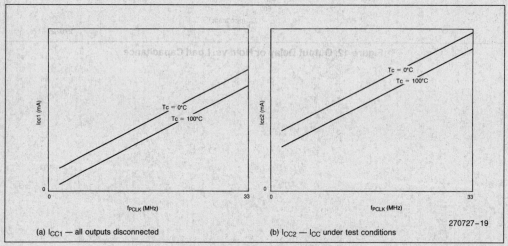

(a) I$_{CC1}$ — all outputs disconnected

(b) I$_{CC2}$ — I$_{CC}$ under test conditions

270727–19

Figure 14. I$_{CC}$ vs Frequency and Temperature

5.0 RESET AND HOLD ACKNOWLEDGE

The following table lists the condition of each processor output pin while $\overline{RESET}$ is asserted (low).

Table 10. Reset Conditions

Pins	State During Reset (HOLDA inactive)[1]
A31:A2	Floating
D31:D0	Floating
$\overline{BE3:0}$	Floating
W/$\overline{R}$	Driven low (Read)
$\overline{ADS}$	Driven high (Inactive)
$\overline{WAIT}$	Driven high (Inactive)
$\overline{BLAST}$	Driven low (Active)
DT/$\overline{R}$	Driven low (Receive)
$\overline{DEN}$	Driven high (Inactive)
$\overline{LOCK}$	Driven high (Inactive)
BREQ	Driven low (Inactive)
D/$\overline{C}$	Floating
$\overline{DMA}$	Floating
$\overline{SUP}$	Floating
$\overline{FAIL}$	Driven low (Active)
$\overline{DACK3}$	Driven high (Inactive)
$\overline{DACK2}$	Driven high (Inactive)
$\overline{DACK1}$	Driven high (Inactive)
$\overline{DACK0}$	Driven high (Inactive)
$\overline{EOP/TC3}$	Floating (set to input mode)
$\overline{EOP/TC2}$	Floating (set to input mode)
$\overline{EOP/TC1}$	Floating (set to input mode)
$\overline{EOP/TC0}$	Floating (set to input mode)

The following table lists the condition of each processor output pin while HOLDA is asserted (low).

Table 11. Hold Acknowledge Conditions

Pins	State During HOLDA
A31:A2	Floating
D31:D0	Floating
$\overline{BE3:0}$	Floating
W/$\overline{R}$	Floating
$\overline{ADS}$	Floating
$\overline{WAIT}$	Floating
$\overline{BLAST}$	Floating
DT/$\overline{R}$	Floating
$\overline{DEN}$	Floating
$\overline{LOCK}$	Floating
BREQ	Driven (high or low)
D/$\overline{C}$	Floating
$\overline{DMA}$	Floating
$\overline{SUP}$	Floating
$\overline{FAIL}$	Driven high (Inactive)
$\overline{DACK3}$	Driven high (Inactive)
$\overline{DACK2}$	Driven high (Inactive)
$\overline{DACK1}$	Driven high (Inactive)
$\overline{DACK0}$	Driven high (Inactive)
$\overline{EOP/TC3}$	Driven if output
$\overline{EOP/TC2}$	Driven if output
$\overline{EOP/TC1}$	Driven if output
$\overline{EOP/TC0}$	Driven if output

NOTE:
(1) With regard to bus output pin state only, the Hold Acknowledge state takes precedence over the reset state. Although asserting the $\overline{RESET}$ pin will internally reset the processor, the processor's bus output pins will not enter the reset state if it has granted Hold Acknowledge to a previous HOLD request (HOLDA is active). Furthermore, the processor will grant new HOLD requests and enter the Hold Acknowledge state even while in reset.

For example, if HOLDA is not active and the processor is in the reset state, then HOLD is asserted, the processor's bus pins will enter the Hold Acknowledge state and HOLDA will be granted. The processor will not be able to perform memory accesses until the HOLD request is removed, even if the $\overline{RESET}$ pin is brought high. This operation is provided to simplify boot-up synchronization among multiple processors sharing the same bus.

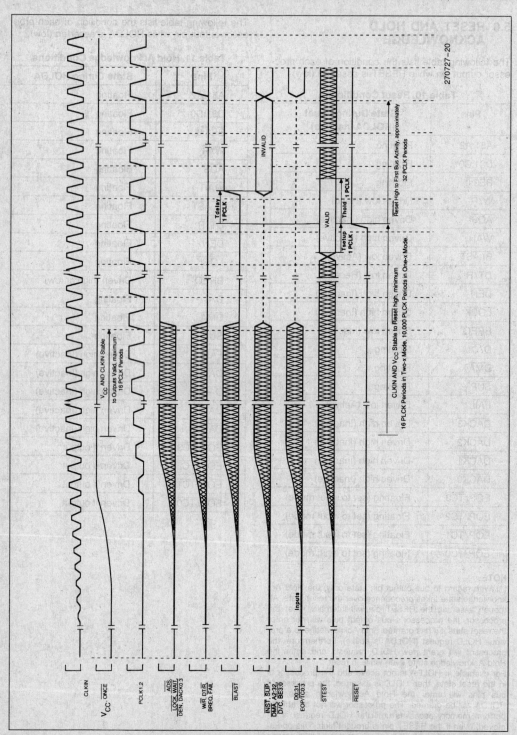

Figure 15. Cold Reset Waveform

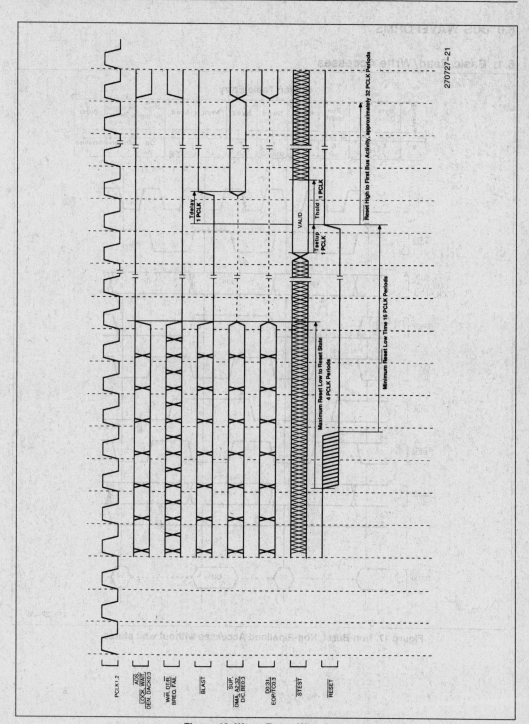

270727–21

Figure 16. Warm Reset Waveform

6.0 BUS WAVEFORMS

6.1. Basic Read/Write Accesses

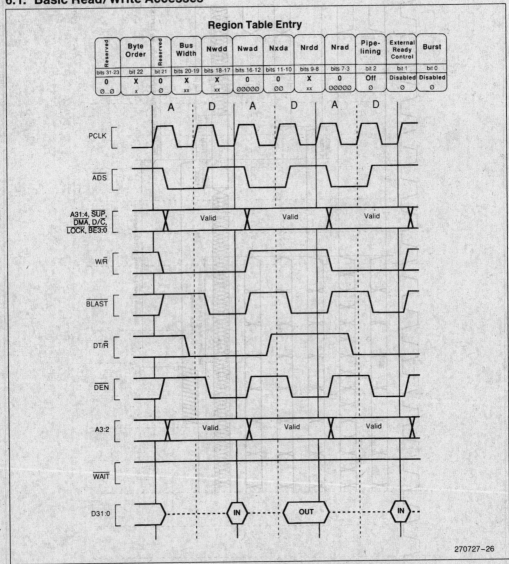

Figure 17. Non-Burst, Non-Pipelined Accesses without wait states.

270727-26

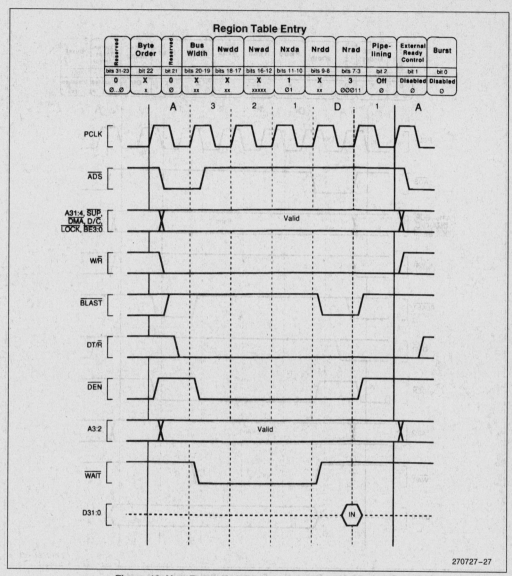

Figure 18. Non-Burst, Non-Pipelined Read with wait states.

270727–27

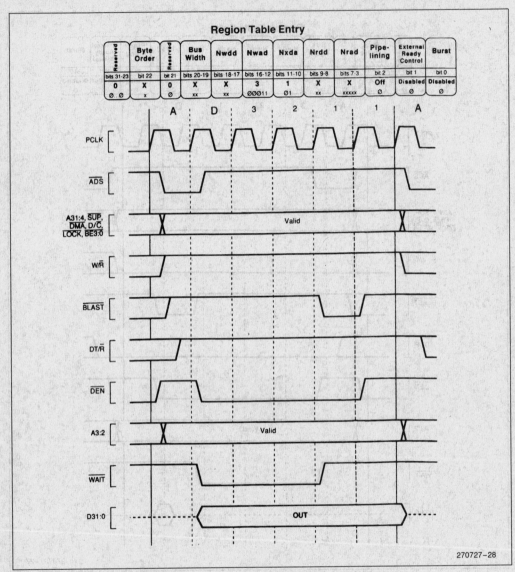

Figure 19. Non-Burst, Non-Pipelined Write with wait states.

270727–28

6.2. Burst Accesses

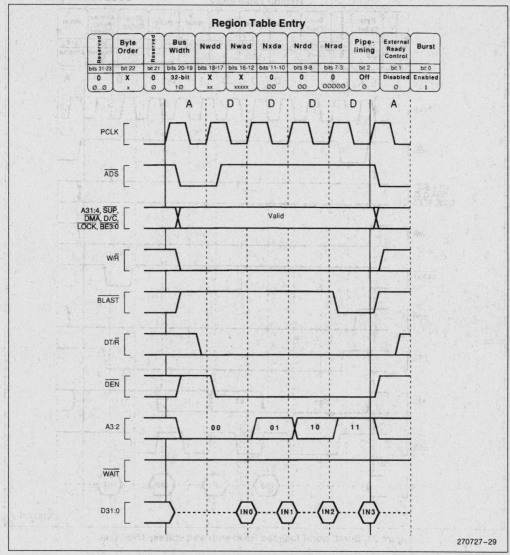

Figure 20. Burst, Non-Pipelined Read without wait states, 32-bit bus.

270727–29

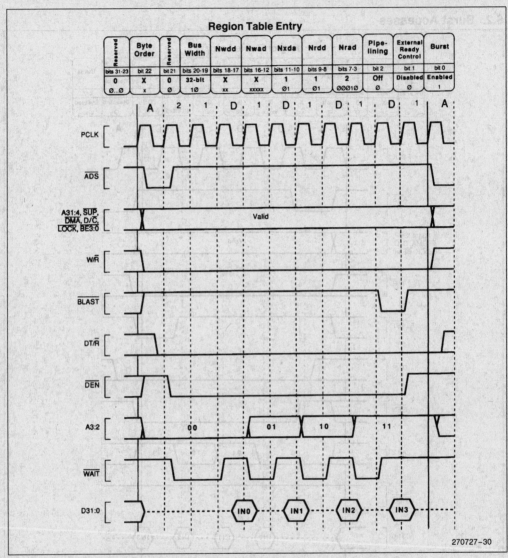

Figure 21. Burst, Non-Pipelined Read with wait states, 32-bit bus.

270727–30

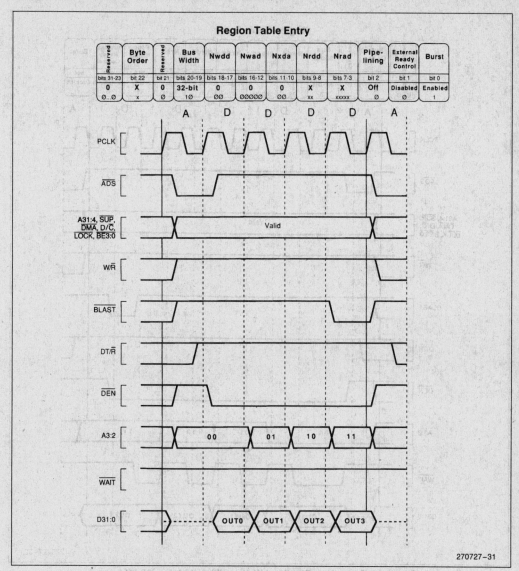

Figure 22. Burst, Non-Pipelined Write without wait states, 32-bit bus.

270727–31

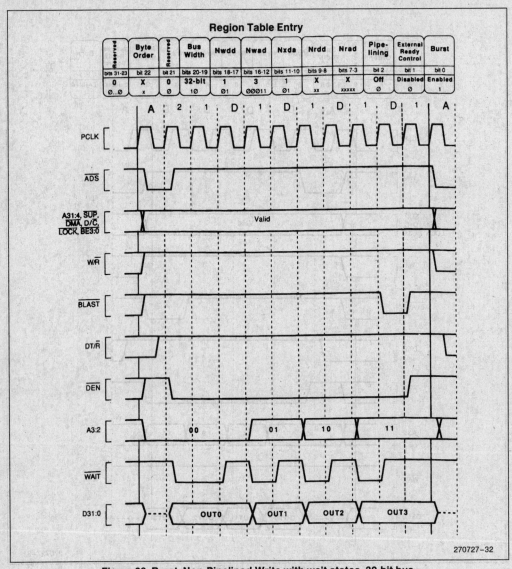

Region Table Entry

Reserved	Byte Order	Reserved	Bus Width	Nwdd	Nwad	Nxda	Nrdd	Nrad	Pipe-lining	External Ready Control	Burst
bits 31-23	bit 22	bit 21	bits 20-19	bits 18-17	bits 16-12	bits 11-10	bits 9-8	bits 7-3	bit 2	bit 1	bit 0
0	X	0	32-bit	1	3	1	X	X	Off	Disabled	Enabled
Ø...Ø	x	Ø	1Ø	Ø1	ØØØ11	Ø1	xx	xxxxx	Ø	Ø	1

Figure 23. Burst, Non-Pipelined Write with wait states, 32-bit bus.

270727–32

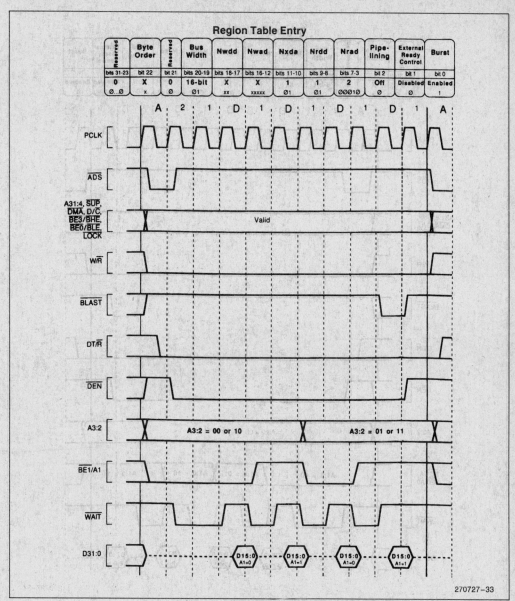

Region Table Entry

Reserved	Byte Order	Reserved	Bus Width	Nwdd	Nwad	Nxda	Nrdd	Nrad	Pipe-lining	External Ready Control	Burst
bits 31-23	bit 22	bit 21	bits 20-19	bits 18-17	bits 16-12	bits 11-10	bits 9-8	bits 7-3	bit 2	bit 1	bit 0
0	X	0	16-bit	X	X	1	1	2	Off	Disabled	Enabled
Ø...Ø	x	Ø	Ø1	xx	xxxxx	Ø1	Ø1	ØØØ1Ø	Ø	Ø	1

Figure 24. Burst, Non-Pipelined Read with wait states, 16-bit bus.

270727–33

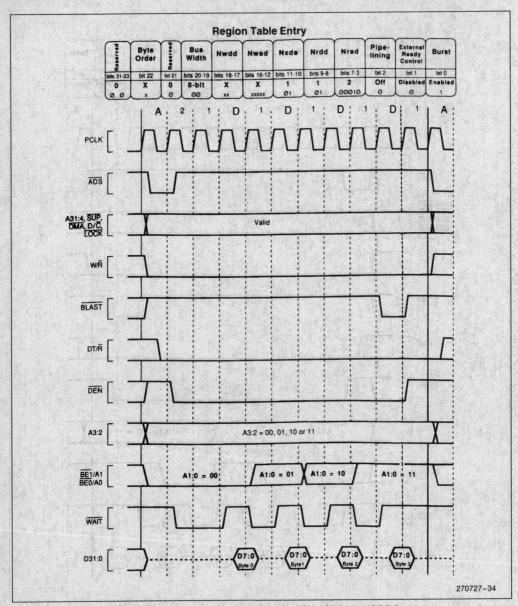

Region Table Entry

Reserved	Byte Order	Reserved	Bus Width	Nwdd	Nwad	Nxda	Nrdd	Nrad	Pipe-lining	External Ready Control	Burst
bits 31-23	bit 22	bit 21	bits 20-19	bits 18-17	bits 16-12	bits 11-10	bits 9-8	bits 7-3	bit 2	bit 1	bit 0
0	X	0	8-bit	X	X	1	1	2	Off	Disabled	Enabled
Ø..Ø	x	Ø	ØØ	xx	xxxxx	Ø1	Ø1	ØØØ1Ø	Ø	Ø	1

Figure 25. Burst, Non-Pipelined Read with wait states, 8-bit bus.

270727-34

6.3. Pipelined Accesses

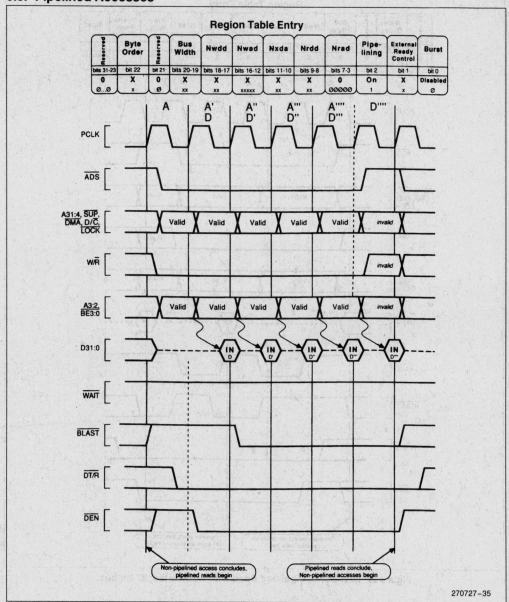

Region Table Entry

Reserved	Byte Order	Reserved	Bus Width	Nwdd	Nwad	Nxda	Nrdd	Nrad	Pipe-lining	External Ready Control	Burst
bits 31-23	bit 22	bit 21	bits 20-19	bits 18-17	bits 16-12	bits 11-10	bits 9-8	bits 7-3	bit 2	bit 1	bit 0
0	X	0	X	X	X	X	X	0	On	X	Disabled
Ø...Ø	x	Ø	xx	xx	xxxxx	xx	xx	ØØØØØ	1	x	Ø

Figure 26. Non-Burst, Pipelined Read without wait states, 32-bit bus.

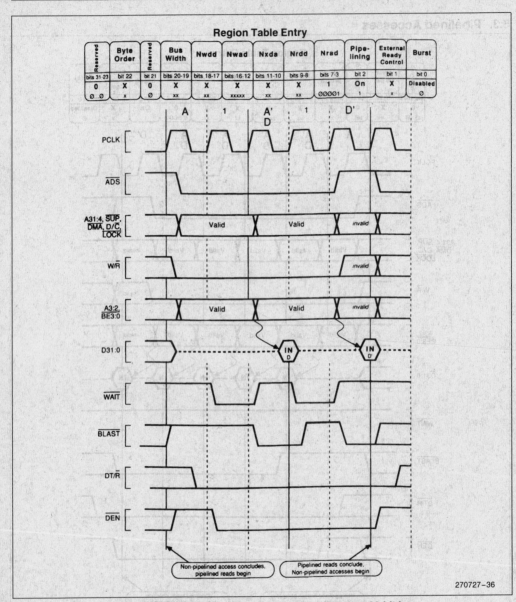

Region Table Entry

Reserved	Byte Order	Reserved	Bus Width	Nwdd	Nwad	Nxda	Nrdd	Nrad	Pipe-lining	External Ready Control	Burst
bits 31-23	bit 22	bit 21	bits 20-19	bits 18-17	bits 16-12	bits 11-10	bits 9-8	bits 7-3	bit 2	bit 1	bit 0
0	X	0	X	X	X	X	X	1	On	X	Disabled
0...0	x	0	xx	xx	xxxxx	xx	xx	00001	1	x	0

Figure 27. Non-Burst, Pipelined Read with wait states, 32-bit bus.

270727-36

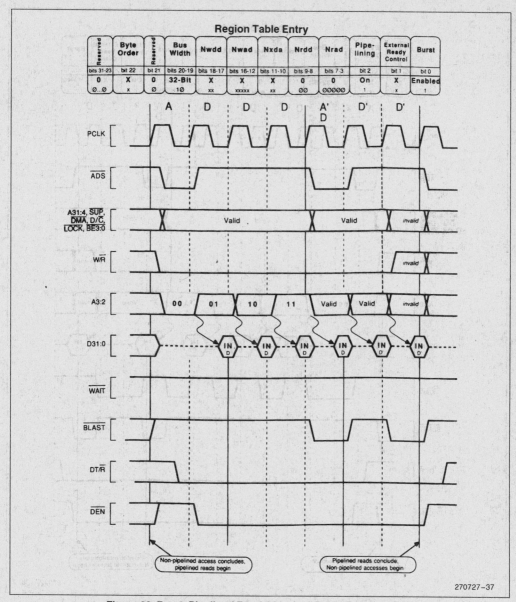

Figure 28. Burst, Pipelined Read without wait states, 32-bit bus.

270727-37

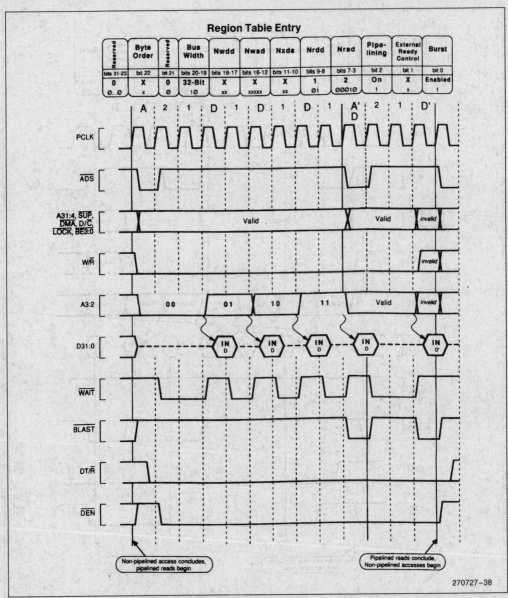

Figure 29. Burst, Pipelined Read with wait states, 32-bit bus.

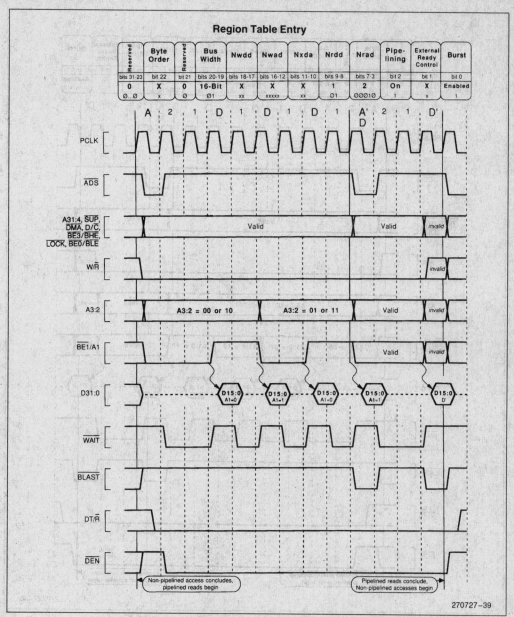

Figure 30. Burst, Pipelined Read with wait states, 16-bit bus.

270727-39

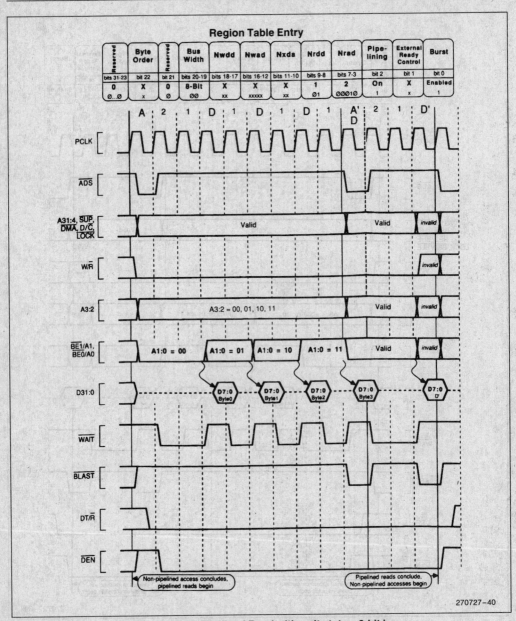

Figure 31. Burst, Pipelined Read with wait states, 8-bit bus.

270727–40

6.4. Using READY

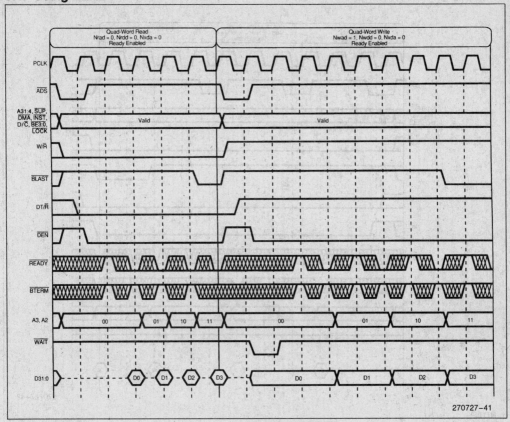

Figure 32. Using External READY

6.5. Using $\overline{\text{BTERM}}$

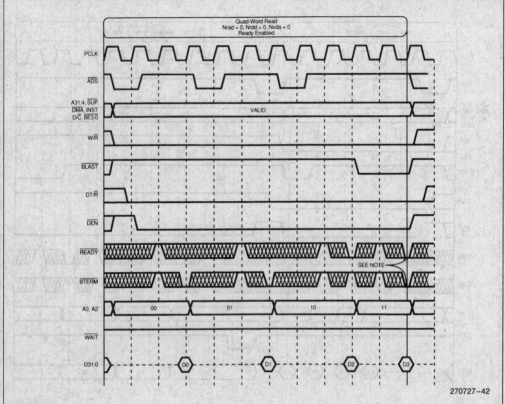

270727-42

NOTE:
$\overline{\text{READY}}$ adds memory access time to data transfers, whether or not the bus access is a burst access. $\overline{\text{BTERM}}$ interrupts a bus access, whether or not the bus access has more data transfers pending. Either the $\overline{\text{READY}}$ signal or the $\overline{\text{BTERM}}$ signal will terminate a bus access if the signal is asserted during the last (or only) data transfer of the bus access.

Figure 33. Terminating a Burst with $\overline{\text{BTERM}}$

6.6. Unaligned Requests

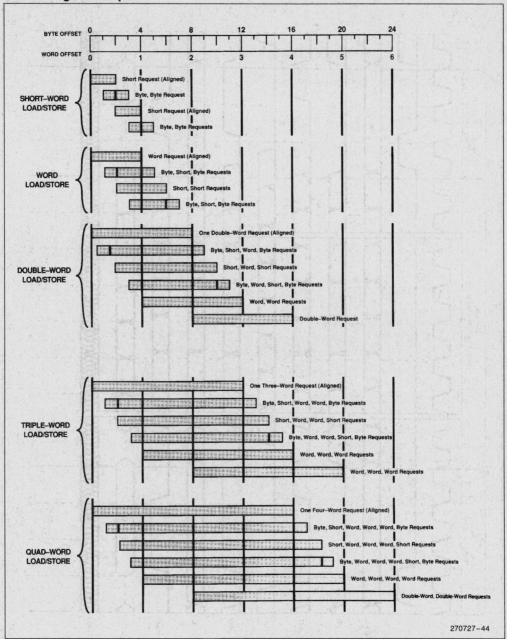

Figure 34.

270727-44

6.7. Idle Bus

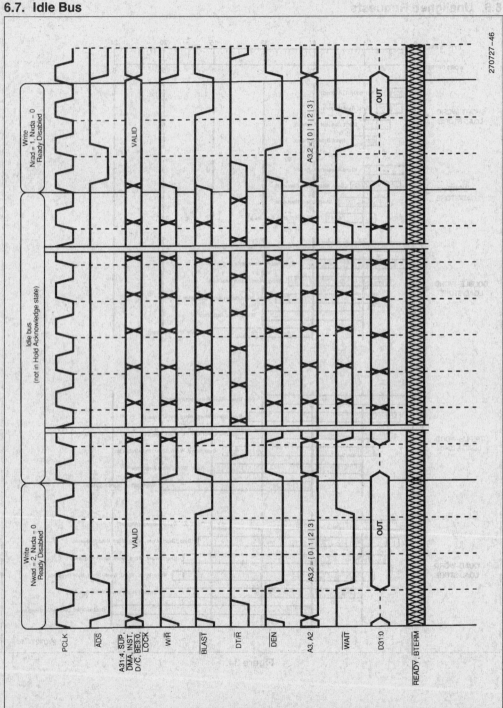

Figure 35. Idle Bus Operation

7.0 ON-CIRCUIT EMULATION™ (ONCE)

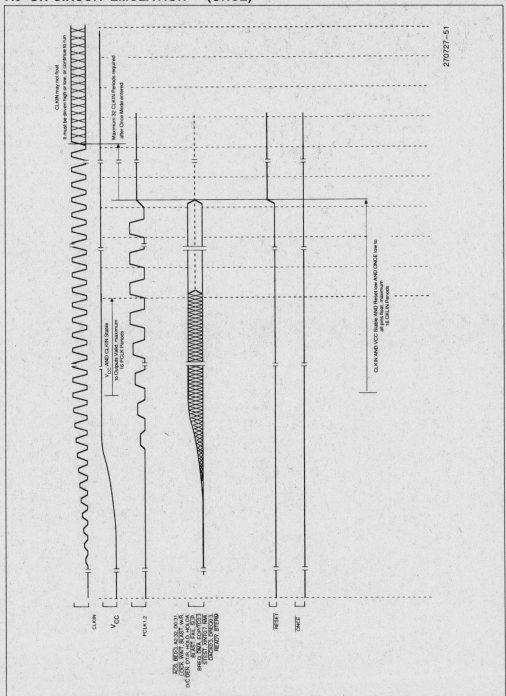

Figure 36. Entering the ONCE™ State

80960MC Product Overview and Data Sheets

5

80960MC
PRODUCT OVERVIEW

This chapter provides an overview of the architecture of the 80960MC processor.

The 80960MC processor is the military-grade member of a new family of processors from Intel. This processor family is based on a new 32-bit architecture called the 80960 architecture. The 80960 architecture has been designed specifically to meet the needs of embedded applications such as avionics, aerospace, weapons systems, robotics, and instrumentation, where high reliability is critical. It represents a renewed commitment from Intel to provide reliable, high-performance processors and controllers for the embedded processor marketplace.

The 80960 architecture can best be characterized as a high-performance computing engine. It features high-speed instruction execution and ease of programming. It is also easily extensible, allowing processors and controllers based on this architecture to be conveniently customized to meet the needs of specific processing and control applications.

Some of the important attributes of the 80960 architecture include:

- full 32-bit registers

- high-speed, pipelined instruction execution

- a convenient program execution environment with 32 general-purpose registers and a versatile set of special-function registers

- a highly optimized procedure call mechanism that features on-chip caching of local variables and parameters

- extensive facilities for handling interrupts and faults

- extensive tracing facilities to support efficient program debugging and monitoring

- register scoreboarding and write buffering to permit efficient operation with lower performance memory subsystems

The 80960MC processor implements the 80960 architecture, plus it offers several extensions to the architecture. Some of these extensions, such as on-chip support for floating-point arithmetic, virtual memory management, and multitasking, are designed to enhance overall system performance. Several other extensions are designed to enhance system reliability and robustness. These extensions include facilities for hardware enforced protection of software modules and for creating fault tolerant systems through the use of redundant processors.

The following sections describe those features of the 80960 architecture that are provided to streamline code execution and simplify programming. The extensions to this architecture provided in the 80960MC processor are described at the end of the chapter.

HIGH PERFORMANCE PROGRAM EXECUTION

Much of the design of the 80960 architecture has been aimed at maximizing the processor's computational and data processing speed through increased parallelism. The following paragraphs describe several of the mechanisms and techniques used to accomplish this goal, including:

- an efficient load and store memory-access model
- caching of code and procedural data
- overlapped execution of instructions
- many one or two clock-cycle instructions

Load and Store Model

One of the more important features of the 80960 architecture is that most of its operations are performed on operands in registers, rather than in memory. For example, all the arithmetic, logical, comparison, branching, and bit operations are performed with registers and literals.

This feature provides two benefits. First, it increases program execution speed by minimizing the number of memory accesses required to execute a program. Second, it reduces memory latency encountered when using slower, lower-cost memory parts.

To support this concept, the architecture provides a generous supply of general-purpose registers. For each procedure, 32 registers are available (28 of which are available for general use). These registers are divided into two types: global and local. Both these types of registers can be used for general storage of operands. The only difference is that global registers retain their contents across procedure boundaries, whereas the processor allocates a new set of local registers each time a new procedure is called.

The architecture also provides a set of fast, versatile load and store instructions. These instructions allow burst transfers of 1, 2, 4, 8, 12, or 16 bytes of information between memory and the registers.

On-Chip Caching of Code and Data

To further reduce memory accesses, the architecture offers two mechanisms for caching code and data on chip: an instruction cache and multiple sets of local registers. The instruction cache allows prefetching of blocks of instruction from memory, which helps insure that the instruction execution pipeline is supplied with a steady stream of instructions. It also reduces the number of memory accesses required when performing iterative operations such as loops. (The size of the instruction cache can vary. With the 80960MC processor, it is 512 bytes.)

To optimize the architecture's procedure call mechanism, the processor provides multiple sets of local registers. This allows the processor to perform most procedure calls without having to write the local registers out to the stack in memory.

(The number of local-register sets provided depends on the processor implementation. The 80960MC processor provides four sets of local registers.)

Overlapped Instruction Execution

Another technique that the 80960 architecture employs to enhance program execution speed is overlapping the execution of some instructions. This is accomplished through two mechanisms: register scoreboarding and branch prediction.

Register scoreboarding permits instruction execution to continue while data is being fetched from memory. When a load instruction is executed, the processor sets one or more scoreboard bits to indicate the target registers to be loaded. After the target registers are loaded, the scoreboard bits are cleared. While the target registers are being loaded, the processor is allowed to execute other instructions that do not use these registers. The processor uses the scoreboard bits to insure that target registers are not used until the loads are complete. (The checking of scoreboard bits is transparent to software.) The net result of using this technique is that code can often be optimized in such a way as to allow some instructions to be executed parallel.

Single-Clock Instructions

It is the intent of the 80960 architecture that a processor be able to execute commonly used instructions such as move, add, subtract, logical operations, compare and branch in a minimum number of clock cycles (preferable one clock cycle). The architecture supports this concept in several ways. For example, the load and store model described earlier in this chapter (with its concentration on register-to-register operations) allows simple operations to be performed without the overhead of memory-to-memory operations.

Also, all the instructions in the 80960 architecture are 32 bits or 64 bits long and aligned on 32-bit boundaries. This feature allows instructions to be decoded in one clock cycle. It also eliminates the need for an instruction-alignment stage in the pipeline.

The design of the 80960MC processor takes full advantage of these features of the architecture, resulting in more than 50 instructions that can be executed in a single clock-cycle.

Efficient Interrupt Model

The 80960 architecture provides an efficient mechanism for servicing interrupts from external sources. To handle interrupts, the processor maintains an interrupt table of 248 interrupt vectors (240 of which are available for general use). When an interrupt is signaled, the processor uses a pointer from the interrupt table to perform an implicit call to an interrupt handler procedure. In performing this call, the processor automatically saves the state of the processor prior to receiving the interrupt; performs the interrupt routine; and then restores the state of the processor. A separate interrupt stack is also provided to segregate interrupt handling from application programs.

The interrupt handling facilities also feature a method of prioritizing interrupts. Using this technique, the processor is able to store interrupts that are lower in priority than the task the processor is currently working on in a pending interrupt section of the interrupt table. At certain defined times, the processor checks the pending interrupts and services them.

SIMPLIFIED PROGRAMMING ENVIRONMENT

Partly as a side benefit of its streamlined execution environment and partly by design, processors based on the 80960 architecture are particularly easy to program. For example, the large number of general-purpose registers allows relatively complex algorithms to be executed with a minimum number of memory accesses. The following paragraphs describe some of the other features that simplify programming.

Highly Efficient Procedure Call Mechanism

The procedure call mechanism makes procedure calls and parameter passing between procedures simple and compact. Each time a call instruction is issued, the processor automatically saves the current set of local registers and allocates a new set of local registers for the called procedure. Likewise, on a return from a procedure, the current set of local registers is deallocated and the local registers for the procedure being returned to are restored. On a procedure call, the program thus never has to explicitly save and restore those local variables and parameters that are stored in local registers.

Versatile Instruction Set and Addressing

The selection of instructions and addressing modes also simplifies programming. The architecture offers a full set of load, store, move, arithmetic, comparison, and branch instructions, with operations on both integer and ordinal data types. It also provides a complete set of Boolean and bit-field instructions, to simplify operations on bits and bit strings.

The addressing modes are efficient and straightforward, while at the same time providing the necessary indexing and scaling modes required to address complex arrays and record structures.

The large 4-gigabyte address space provides ample room to store programs and data. The availability of 32 addressing lines allows some address lines to be memory-mapped to control hardware functions.

Extensive Fault Handling Capability

To aid in program development, the 80960 architecture defines a wide selection of faults that the processor detects, including arithmetic faults, invalid operands, invalid operations, and machine faults. When a fault is detected, the processor makes an implicit call to a fault handler routine, using a mechanism similar to that described above for interrupts. The information collected for each fault allows program developers to quickly correct faulting code. It also allows automatic recovery from some faults.

Debugging and Monitoring

To support debugging systems, the 80960 architecture provides a mechanism for monitoring processor activity by means of trace events. The processor can be configured to detect as many as seven different trace events, including branches, calls, supervisor calls, returns, prereturns, breakpoints, and the execution of any instruction. When the processor detects a trace event, it signals a trace fault and calls a fault handler. Intel provides several tools that use this feature, including an in-circuit emulator (ICE) device.

SUPPORT FOR ARCHITECTURAL EXTENSIONS

The 80960 architecture described earlier in this chapter provides a high-performance computing engine for use as the computational and data-processing core of embedded processors or controllers. The architecture also provides several features that enable processors based on this architecture to be easily customized to meet the needs of specific embedded applications, such as signal processing, array processing, or graphics processing.

The most important of these features is a set of 32 special-function registers. These registers provide a convenient interface to circuitry in the processor or to pins that can be connected to external hardware. They can be used to control timers, to perform operations on special data types, or to perform I/O functions.

The special-function registers are similar to the global registers. They can be addressed by all the register-access instructions.

EXTENSIONS INCLUDED IN THE 80960MC PROCESSOR

The extensions to the 80960 architecture included in the 80960MC processor are built on top of the processor's core computing engine. These extensions are aimed at improving the efficiency and reliability of embedded systems.

On-Chip Floating Point

The 80960MC processor provides a complete implementation of the IEEE standard for binary floating-point arithmetic (IEEE 754-185). This implementation includes a full set of floating-point operations, including add, subtract, multiply, divide, trigonometric functions, and logarithmic functions. These operations are performed on single precision (32-bit), double precision (64-bit), and extended precision (80-bit) real numbers.

One of the benefits of this implementation is that the floating-point handling facilities are completely integrated into the normal instruction execution environment. Single- and double-precision floating-point values are stored in the same registers as non-floating point values. Also, four 80-bit floating-point registers are provided to hold extended-precision values.

String and Decimal Operations

The 80960MC processor provides several instructions for moving, filling, and comparing byte strings in memory. These instructions speed up string operations and reduce the amount of code required to handle strings.

The decimal instructions perform move, add with carry, and subtract with carry operations on binary-coded decimal (BCD) strings.

Virtual-Memory Support

Another of the 80960MC processor's important features is support for virtual-memory management. When using the processor in virtual-memory mode, the processor provides each process (or task) with an address space of up to 2^{32} bytes. This address space is paged into physical memory in 4K-byte pages. On-chip memory-management facilities handle virtual-to-physical address translation. A translation look-aside buffer (TLB) speeds address translation by storing virtual-to-physical address translations for frequently accessed parts of memory, such as the location of the page tables and the location of often used system data structures.

Protection

The 80960MC processor offers two mechanisms for protecting critical data structures or software modules. The first is the ability to use page rights bits to restrict access to individual pages. Page rights allow various levels of access to be assigned to a page, ranging from no access to read only to read-write.

The second protection mechanism is a user/supervisor protection model. This two-level protection model provides hardware enforced protection of kernel procedures and data structures. When using this protection mechanism, privileged procedures and data are placed in protected pages of memory. These pages can then be accessed only through a procedure table, which provides a tightly controlled interface to kernel functions.

Multitasking

The 80960MC processor offers a variety of process management facilities to support concurrent execution of multiple tasks. These facilities can be divided into two groups: process scheduling and interprocess communications.

The process scheduling facilities consist of a set of general-purpose data structures and instructions, which are designed to support several different multitasking schemes. For example, the processor provides a set of instructions that allow the kernel to explicitly dispatch a task (bind it to the processor) and to suspend a task (save the current state of a task so that another task can be bound to the processor). These instructions can be used within kernel procedures to schedule, dispatch, and preempt multiple tasks.

The processor also provides a unique feature called *self dispatching*. Here, the kernel schedules tasks by queuing them to a dispatch port. Thereafter, the processor handles the dispatching, preempting, and rescheduling of the tasks automatically, independent of the kernel. When using this mechanism, tasks can be scheduled by priority, with up to 32 priority levels to choose from.

The processor's interprocess communication facilities include support for semaphores and communication ports. These facilities allow synchronization of interdependent tasks and asynchronous communication between tasks.

Multiprocessing

The 80960MC processor provides several mechanisms designed to simplify the design of multiple-processor systems, allowing several processors to run in parallel, using shared memory resources. One of these mechanisms is the self-dispatching capability described above. Here, two or more processors can schedule and dispatch processes from a single dispatch port, with each processor equally sharing the processing load.

The processor also provides an interagent communication (IAC) mechanism that allows processors to exchange messages among themselves on the bus. This mechanism operates similarly to the interrupt mechanism, except that IAC messages are passed through dedicated sections of memory. The IAC mechanism can be used to preempt processes running on another processor, to manage interrupt handling, or to initialize and synchronize several processors.

A set of atomic instructions are also provided to synchronize memory accesses. Multiple processors can then access shared memory without inserting inaccuracies and ambiguities into shared data structures.

Fault Tolerance

The 80960 family of components supports fault-tolerant system design through the use of the M82965 Bus Extension Unit component. The M82965 allows two processors to be operated in tandem to form a self-checking module. The two M82965s check the outputs of two processors (a master and a checker) cycle-by-cycle. If the checking M82965 detects a difference between outputs, it signals an error. A software recovery procedure can then be initiated.

This fault detection mechanism supports several fault detection and recovery techniques, including self healing, and continuous-operation (non-stop) systems.

LOOK FOR MORE IN THE FUTURE

The 80960 architecture offers exceptional performance, plus a wealth of useful features to help in the design of efficient and reliable embedded systems. But equally important, it offers lots of room to grow. The 80960MC processor provides average instruction processing rates of 7.5 million instructions per second (7.5 MIPS) at 20 MHz clock rate and 10 MIPS at a 25 MHz clock rate[1].

---

[1] 1 MIP is equivalent to the performance of a Digital Equipment Corp. VAX 11/780.

However, the 80960MC is only the beginning. With improvements in VLSI technology, future implementations of the 80960 architecture will offer even greater performance. They will also offer a variety of useful extensions to solve specific control and monitoring needs in the field of embedded applications.

80960MC
EMBEDDED 32-BIT MICROPROCESSOR
WITH INTEGRATED FLOATING-POINT UNIT
AND MEMORY MANAGEMENT UNIT

Military

- **High-Performance Embedded Architecture**
  - 20 MIPS Burst Execution at 20 MHz
  - 7.5 MIPS* Sustained Execution at 20 MHz

- **On-Chip Floating-Point Unit**
  - Supports IEEE 754 Floating-Point Standard
  - Full Transcendental Support
  - Four 80-Bit Registers
  - 4 Million Whetstones/Second at 20 MHz

- **512-Byte On-Chip Instruction Cache**
  - Direct Mapped
  - Parallel Load/Decode for Uncached Instructions

- **Multiple Register Sets**
  - Sixteen Global 32-Bit Registers
  - Sixteen Local 32-Bit Registers
  - Four Local Register Sets Stored On-Chip (Sixteen 32-Bit Registers per Set)
  - Register Scoreboarding

- **On-Chip Memory Management Unit**
  - 4 Gigabyte Virtual Address Space per Task
  - 4 Kbyte Pages with Supervisor/User Protection

- **Built-In Interrupt Controller**
  - 32 Priority Levels
  - 248 Vectors
  - Supports M8259A

- **Easy to Use, High Bandwidth 32-Bit Bus**
  - 43 MBytes/s Burst
  - Up to 16-Bytes Transferred per Burst

- **Multitasking and Multiprocessor Support**
  - Automatic Task Dispatching
  - Prioritized Task Queues

- **Advanced Package Technology**
  - 132 Lead Ceramic Pin Grid Array
  - 164 Lead Ceramic Quad Flatpack

- **Military Temperature Range**
  - $-55°C$ to $+125°C$ (T_C)

The 80960MC is the enhanced military member of Intel's new 32-bit microprocessor family, the 960 series, which is designed especially for embedded applications. It is based on the family's high performance, common core architecture, and includes a 512-byte instruction cache, a built-in interrupt controller, an integrated floating-point unit and a memory management unit. The 80960MC has a large register set, multiple parallel execution units, and a high-bandwidth, burst bus. Using advanced RISC technology, this high performance processor can respond to interrupts in under 5 μs and is capable of execution rates in excess of 7.5 million instructions per second.* The 80960MC is well-suited for a wide range of military and other high reliability applications, including avionics, airborne radar, navigation, and instrumentation.

*Relative to Digital Equipment Corporation's VAX-11/780** at 1 MIPS

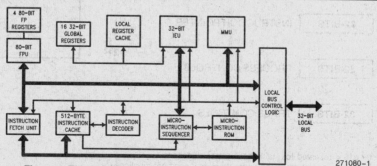

Figure 1. The 80960MC's Highly Parallel Microarchitecture

271080–1

**VAX-11™ is a trademark of Digital Equipment Corporation.

THE 960 SERIES

The 80960MC is the enhanced military member of a new family of 32-bit microprocessors from Intel known as the 960 Series. This series was especially designed to serve the needs of embedded applications. The embedded market includes applications as diverse as industrial automation, avionics, image processing, graphics, robotics, telecommunications, and automobiles. These types of applications require high integration, low power consumption, quick interrupt response times, and high performance. Since time to market is critical, embedded microprocessors need to be easy to use in both hardware and software designs.

All members of the 80960 series share a common core architecture which utilizes RISC technology so that, except for special functions, the family members are object code compatible. Each new processor in the series will add its own special set of functions to the core to satisfy the needs of a specific application or range of applications in the embedded market. For example, future processors may include a DMA controller, a timer, or an A/D converter.

The 80960MC includes an integrated Floating Point Unit (FPU), a Memory Management Unit (MMU), multitasking support, and multiprocessor support. There are also two commercial members of the family: the 80960KB processor with integrated FPU and the 80960KA without floating-point.

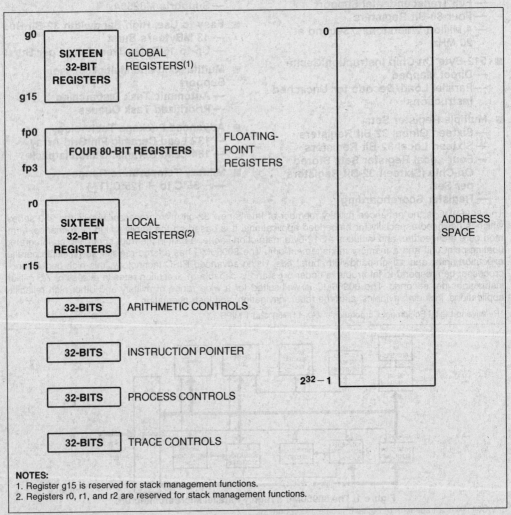

Figure 2. Register Set

NOTES:
1. Register g15 is reserved for stack management functions.
2. Registers r0, r1, and r2 are reserved for stack management functions.

KEY PERFORMANCE FEATURES

The 80960MC's architecture is based on the most recent advances in RISC technology and is grounded in Intel's long experience in designing embedded controllers. Many features contribute to the 80960MC's exceptional performance:

1. Large Register Set. Having a large number of registers reduces the number of times that a processor needs to access memory. Modern compilers can take advantage of this feature to optimize execution speed. For maximum flexibility, the 80960MC provides thirty-two 32-bit registers (sixteen local and sixteen global) and four 80-bit floating-point global registers. (See Figure 2.)

2. Fast Instruction Execution. Simple functions make up the bulk of instructions in most programs, so that execution speed can be greatly improved by ensuring that these core instructions execute in as short a time as possible. The most-frequently executed instructions such as register-register moves, add/subtract, logical operations, and shifts execute in one to two cycles (Table 1 contains a list of instructions.)

3. Load/Store Architecture. Like other processors based on RISC technology, the 80960MC has a Load/Store architecture, only the LOAD and STORE instructions reference memory; all other instructions operate on registers. This type of architecture simplifies instruction decoding and is used in combination with other techniques to increase parallelism.

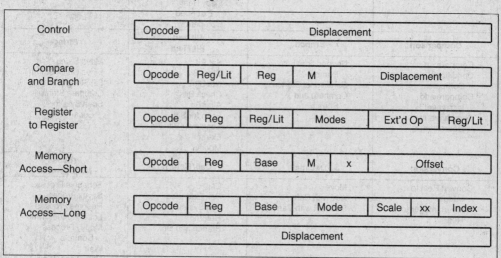

Figure 3. Instruction Formats

Table 1. 80960MC Instruction Set

Data Movement	Arithmetic	Floating Point	Logical
Load	Add	Add	And
Store	Subtract	Subtract	Not And
Move	Multiply	Multiply	And Not
Load Address	Divide	Divide	Or
Load Physical	Remainder	Remainder	Exclusive Or
Address	Modulo	Scale	Not Or
	Shift	Round	Or Not
		Square Root	Nor
		Sine	Exclusive Nor
		Cosine	Not
		Tangent	Nand
		Arctangent	Rotate
		Log	
		Log Binary	
		Log Natural	
		Exponent	
		Classify	
		Copy Real	
		Extended	
		Compare	

Comparison	Branch	Bit and Bit Field	String
Compare	Unconditional	Set Bit	Move String
Conditional	Branch	Clear Bit	Move Quick String
Compare	Conditional Branch	Not Bit	Fill String
Compare and	Compare and	Check Bit	Compare String
Increment	Branch	Alter Bit	Scan Byte for
Compare and		Scan for Bit	Equal
Decrement		Scan over Bit	
		Extract	
		Modify	

Conversion	Decimal	Call/Return	Process Management
Convert Real to	Move	Call	Schedule Process
Integer	Add with Carry	Call Extended	Saves Process
Convert Integer to	Subtract with Carry	Call System	Resume Process
Real		Return	Load Process Time
		Branch and Link	Modify Process
			Controls
			Wait
			Conditional Wait
			Signal
			Receive
			Conditional
			Receive
			Send
			Send Service
			Atomic Add
			Atomic Modify

Fault	Debug	Miscellaneous	
Conditional Fault	Modify Trace	Flush Local	
Synchronize Faults	Controls	Registers	
	Mark	Inspect Access	
	Force Mark	Modify Arithmetic	
		Controls	
		Test Condition	
		Code	

4. Simple Instruction Formats. All instructions in the 80960MC are 32-bits long and must be aligned on word boundaries. This alignment makes it possible to eliminate the instruction-alignment stage in the pipeline. To simplify the instruction decoder further, there are only five instruction formats and each instruction uses only one format. (See Figure 3.)

5. Overlapped Instruction Execution. A load operation allows execution of subsequent instructions to continue before the data has been returned from memory, so that these instructions can overlap the load. The 80960MC manages this process transparently to software through the use of a register scoreboard. Conditional instructions also make use of a scoreboard so that subsequent unrelated instructions can be executed while the conditional instruction is pending.

6. Integer Execution Optimization. When the result of an operation is used as an operand in a subsequent calculation, the value is sent immediately to its destination register. Yet at the same time, the value is put back on a bypass path to the ALU, thereby saving the time that otherwise would be required to retrieve the value for the next operation.

7. Bandwidth Optimizations. The 80960MC gets optimal use of its memory bus bandwidth because the bus is tuned for use with the cache: the line size of the instruction cache matches the maximum burst size for instruction fetches. The 80960MC automatically fetches four words in a burst and stores them directly in the cache. Due to the size of the cache and the fact that it is continually filled in anticipation of needed instructions in the program flow, the 80960MC is exceptionally insensitive to memory wait states. In fact, each wait state causes only a 7% degradation in system perfomance. The benefit is that the 80960MC will deliver outstanding performance even with a low cost memory system.

8. Cache Bypass. If there is a cache miss, the processor fetches the needed instruction, then sends it on to the instruction decoder at the same time it updates the cache. Thus, no extra time is taken to load and read the cache.

Memory Space and Addressing Modes

The 80960MC allows each task (process) to address a logical memory space of up to 4 Gbytes. In turn, each task's address space is divided into four 1-Gbyte regions and each region can be mapped to physical addresses by one or two levels of page tables. The region with the highest addresses (Region 3) is common to all tasks.

In keeping with RISC design principles, the number of addressing modes has been kept to a minimum but includes all those necessary to ensure efficient execution of high-level languages such as Ada, C, and Fortran. Table 2 lists the memory addressing modes.

Data Types

The 80960MC recognizes the following data types:

Numeric:
- 8-, 16-, 32- and 64-bit ordinals
- 8-, 16, 32- and 64-bit integers
- 32-, 64- and 80-bit real numbers

Non-Numeric:
- Bit
- Bit Field
- Triple-Word (96 bits)
- Quad-Word (128 bits)

Large Register Set

The programming environment of the 80960MC includes a large number of registers. In fact, 36 registers are available at any time. The availability of this many registers greatly reduces the number of memory accesses required to execute most programs, which leads to greater instruction processing speed.

There are two types of general-purpose registers: local and global. The 20 global registers consist of sixteen 32-bit registers (G0 through G15) and four 80-bit registers (FP0 through FP3). These registers perform the same function as the general-purpose registers provided in other popular microprocessors. The term global refers to the fact that these registers retain their contents across procedure calls.

The local registers, on the other hand, are procedure specific. For each procedure call, the 80960MC allocates 16 local registers (R0 through R15). Each local register is 32 bits wide. Any register can also be used for floating-point operations; the 80-bit floating-point registers are provided for extended precision.

Multiple Register Sets

To further increase the efficiency of the register set, multiple sets of local registers are stored on-chip. This cache holds up to four local register frames, which means that up to three procedure calls can be made without having to access the procedure stack resident in memory.

Table 2. Memory Addressing Modes

- 12-Bit Offset
- 32-Bit Offset
- Register-Indirect
- Register + 12-Bit Offset
- Register + 32-Bit Offset
- Register + (Index-Register × Scale-Factor)
- Register × Scale Factor + 32-Bit Displacement
- Register + (Index-Register × Scale-Factor) + 32-Bit Displacement

Scale-Factor is 1, 2, 4, 8 or 16

Although programs may have procedure calls nested many calls deep, a program typically oscillates back and forth between only two or three levels. As a result, with four stack frames in the cache, the probability of there being a free frame on the cache when a call is made is very high. In fact, runs of representative C-language programs show that 80% of the calls are handled without needing to access memory.

If there are four or more active procedures and a new procedure is called, the processor moves the oldest set of local registers in the register cache to a procedure stack in memory to make room for a new set of registers. Global register G15 is used by the processor as the frame pointer (FP) for the procedure stack.

Note that the global and floating-point registers are not exchanged on a procedure call, but retain their contents, making them available to all procedures for fast parameter passing. An illustration of the register cache is shown in Figure 4.

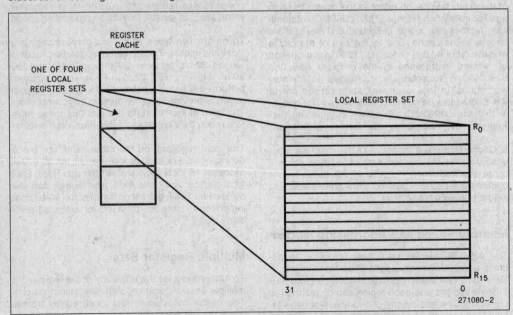

Figure 4. Multiple Register Sets Are Stored On-Chip

Instruction Cache

To further reduce memory accesses, the 80960MC includes a 512-byte on-chip instruction cache. The instruction cache is based on the concept of locality of reference; that is, most programs are not usually executed in a steady stream but consist of many branches and loops that lead to jumping back and forth within the same small section of code. Thus, by maintaining a block of instructions in a cache, the number of memory references required to read instructions into the processor can be greatly reduced.

To load the instruction cache, instructions are fetched in 16-byte blocks, so that up to four instructions can be fetched at one time. An efficient prefetch algorithm increases the probability that an instruction will already be in the cache when it is needed.

Code for small loops will often fit entirely within the cache, leading to a great increase in processing speed since further memory references might not be necessary until the program exits the loop. Similarly, when calling short procedures, the code for the calling procedure is likely to remain in the cache, so it will be there on the procedure's return.

Register Scoreboarding

The instruction decoder has been optimized in several ways. One of these optimizations is the ability to do instruction overlapping by means of register scoreboarding.

Register scoreboarding occurs when a LOAD instruction is executed to move a variable from memory into a register. When the instruction is initiated, a scoreboard bit on the target register is set. When the register is actually loaded, the bit is reset. In between, any reference to the register contents is accompanied by a test of the scoreboard bit to insure that the load has completed before processing continues. Since the processor does not have to wait for the LOAD to be completed, it can go on to execute additional instructions placed in between the LOAD instruction and the instruction that uses the register contents, as shown in the following example:

```
LOAD R4, address 1
LOAD R5, address 2
Unrelated instruction
Unrelated instruction
ADD R4, R5, R6
```

In essence, the two unrelated instructions between the LOAD and ADD instructions are executed for free (i.e., take no apparent time to execute) because they are executed while the register is being loaded. Up to three LOAD instructions can be pending at one time with three corresponding scoreboard bits set. By exploiting this feature, system programmers and compilers have a useful tool for optimizing execution speed.

Memory Management and Protection

The 80960MC will be especially useful for multitasking applications that require software protection and a very large address space. To ensure the highest level of performance possible, the memory management unit and translation look-aside buffer (TLB) are contained on-chip.

The 80960MC supports a conventional form of demand-paged virtual memory in which the address space is divided into 4 Kbyte pages. Studies have shown that a 4 Kbyte page is the optimum size for a broad range of applications.

Each page table entry includes a 2-bit page rights field that specifies whether the page is a no-access, read-only, or read-write page. This field is interpreted differently depending on whether the current task (process) is executing in user or supervisor mode, as shown below:

Rights	User	Supervisor
00	No Access	Read-Only
01	No Access	Read-Write
10	Read-Only	Read-Write
11	Read-Write	Read-Write

Floating-Point Arithmetic

In the 80960MC, floating-point arithmetic has been made an integral part of the architecture. Having the floating-point unit integrated on-chip provides two advantages. First, it improves the performance of the chip for floating-point applications, since no additional bus overhead is associated with floating-point calculations, thereby leaving more time for other bus operations such as I/O. Second, the cost of using floating-point operations is reduced because a separate coprocessor chip is not required.

The 80960MC floating-point (real number) data types include single-precision (32-bit), double-precision (64-bit), and extended precision (80-bit) floating-point numbers. Any register may be used to execute floating-point operations.

The processor provides hardware support for both mandatory and recommended portions of IEEE Standard 754 for floating-point arithmetic, including all arithmetic, exponential, logarithmic, and other transcendental functions. Table 3 shows execution times for some representative instructions.

Table 3. Sample Floating-Point Execution Times (µs) at 20 MHz

	32-Bit	64-Bit
Add	0.5	0.7
Subtract	0.5	0.7
Multiply	1.0	1.8
Divide	1.8	3.8
Square Root	5.0	5.2
Arctangent	13.4	17.5
Exponent	15.0	16.7
Sine	20.3	22.1
Cosine	20.3	22.1

Multitasking Support

Multitasking programs commonly involve the monitoring and control of an external operation, such as the activities of a process controller or the movements of a machine tool. These programs generally consist of a number of processes that run independently of one another, but share a common database or pass data among themselves.

The 80960MC offers several hardware functions designed to support multitasking systems. One unique feature, called self-dispatching, allows a processor to switch itself automatically among scheduled tasks. When self-dispatching is used, all the operating system is required to do is place the task in the scheduling queue.

When the processor becomes available, it dispatches the task from the beginning of the queue and then executes it until it becomes blocked, interrupted, or until its time-slice expires. It then returns the task to the end of the queue (i.e., automatically reschedules it) and dispatches the next ready task.

During these operations, no communication between the processor and the operating system is necessary until the running task is complete or an interrupt is issued.

Synchronization and Communication

The 80960MC also offers instructions to set up and test semaphores to ensure that concurrent tasks remain synchronized and no data inconsistency results. Special data structures, known as communication ports, provide the means for exchanging parameters and data structures. Transmission of information by means of communication ports is asynchronous and automatically buffered by the processor.

Communication between tasks by means of ports can be carried out independently of the operating system. Once the ports have been set up by the programmer, the processor handles the message passing automatically.

High Bandwidth Local Bus

An 80960MC CPU resides on a high-bandwidth address/data bus known as the local bus (L-Bus). The L-Bus provides a direct communication path between the processor and the memory and I/O subsystem interfaces. The processor uses the local bus to fetch instructions, manipulate memory, and respond to interrupts. Its features include:

- 32-bit multiplexed address/data path
- Four-word burst capability, which allows transfers from 1 to 16 bytes at a time
- High bandwidth reads and writes at 43 MBytes per second
- Special signal to indicate whether a memory transaction can be cached

Figure 5 identifies the groups of signals which constitute the L-Bus. Table 4 lists the function of the L-Bus and other processor-support signals, such as the interrupt lines.

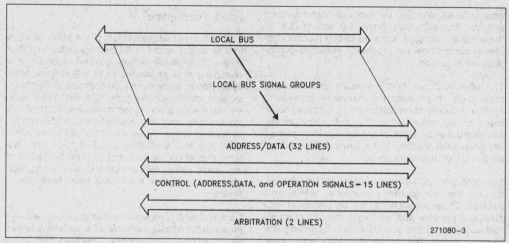

Figure 5. Local Bus Signal Groups

Multiple Processor Support

One means of increasing the processing power of a system is to run two or more processors in parallel. Since microprocessors are not generally designed to run in tandem with other processors, designing such a system is usually difficult and costly.

The 80960MC solves this problem by offering a number of functions to coordinate the actions of multiple processors. First, messages can be passed between processors to initiate actions such as flushing a cache, stopping or starting another processor, or preempting a task. The messages are passed on the bus and allow multiple processors to run together smoothly, with rare need to lock the bus or memory.

Second, a set of synchronization instructions help maintain the coherency of memory. These instructions permit several processors to modify memory at the same time without inserting inaccuracies or ambiguities into shared data structures.

The self-dispatching mechanism, in addition to being used in single-processor systems, provides the means to increase the performance of a system merely by adding processors. Each processor can either work on the same pool of tasks (sharing the same queue with other processors) or can be restricted to its own queue.

When processors perform system operations, they synchronize themselves by using atomic operations and sending special messages between each other. And changing the number of processors in a system never requires a software change. Software will execute correctly regardless of the number of processors in the system; systems with more processors simply execute faster.

Interrupt Handling

The 80960MC can be interrupted in one of two ways: by the activation of one of four interrupt pins or by sending a message on the processor's data bus.

The 80960MC is unusual in that it automatically handles interrupts on a priority basis and tracks pending interrupts through its on-chip interrupt controller. Two of the interrupt pins can be configured to provide M8259A handshaking for expansion beyond four interrupt lines.

An interrupt message is made up of a vector number and an interrupt priority. If the interrupt priority is greater than that of the currently running task, the processor accepts the interrupt and uses the vector as an index into the interrupt table. If the priority of the interrupt message is below that of the current task, the processor saves the information in a section of the interrupt table reserved for pending interrupts.

Debug Features

The 80960MC has built-in debug capabilities. There are two types of breakpoints and six different trace modes. The debug features are controlled by two internal 32-bit registers, the Process-Controls Word and the Trace-Controls Word. By setting bits in these control words, a software debug monitor can closely control how the processor responds during program execution.

The 80960MC has both hardware and software breakpoints. It provides two hardware breakpoint registers on-chip which can be set by a special command to any value. When the instruction pointer matches the value in one of the breakpoint registers, the breakpoint will fire, and a breakpoint handling routine is called automatically.

The 80960MC also provides software breakpoints through the use of two instructions, MARK and FMARK. These instructions can be placed at any point in a program and will cause the processor to halt execution at that point and call the breakpoint handling routine. The breakpoint mechanism is easy to use and provides a powerful debugging tool.

Tracing is available for instructions (single-step execution), calls and returns, and branching. Each different type of trace may be enabled separately by a special debug instruction. In each case, the 80960MC executes the instruction first and then calls a trace handling routine (usually part of a software debug monitor). Further program execution is halted until the trace routine is completed. When the trace event handling routine is completed, instruction execution resumes at the next instruction. The 80960MC's tracing mechanisms, which are implemented completely in hardware, greatly simplify the task of testing and debugging software.

FAULT DETECTION

The 80960MC has an automatic mechanism to handle faults. There are ten fault types including trace, arithmetic, and floating-point faults. When the processor detects a fault, it automatically calls the appropriate fault handling routine and saves the current instruction pointer and necessary state information to make efficient recovery possible. The processor posts diagnostic information on the type of fault to a Fault Record. Like interrupt handling routines, fault handling routines are usually written to meet the needs of a specific application and are often included as part of the operating system or kernel.

For each of the ten fault types, there are numerous subtypes that provide specific information about a fault. For example, a floating-point fault may have its subtype set to an Overflow or Zero-Divide fault. The fault handler can use this specific information to respond correctly to the fault.

Fault Tolerance

The term fault tolerance refers to the ability of a system to detect errors in its own operation and then take self-corrective action to prevent errors from corrupting data or leading to wrong actions. Many fault-tolerant systems rely on software to do checking and provide recovery; the 80960MC's fault-tolerant mechanisms are based exclusively on hardware mechanisms and the replication of VLSI components and buses. When the 80960MC processor is used with Intel's M82965 Bus Extension Unit, systems can easily be built to tolerate the failure of any single component or bus and continue to operate correctly. Figure 6 shows a small fault-tolerant system.

Each 80960MC processor is able to detect hardware errors automatically because of a capability known as Functional Redundancy Checking (FRC), so called because a second or redundant processor checks the operations of the first or master processor. FRC provides the low-level hardware support upon which hardware fault-tolerant modules are constructed.

While FRC can be used alone to provide automatic error detection, a completely fault-tolerant system must also be able to reconfigure itself, replacing the set of failed components with another pair that is still working.

In order to do so, the M82965 Bus Extension Unit enables two pairs of master/checker components to be combined to form primary and shadow processors in a configuration known as Quad Modular Redundancy (QMR).

Each procesor module in a QMR system is paired with another self-checking module which operates in lock step. The mechanism is known as module shadowing because a shadow is ready to fill in if the primary fails (or vice versa). Fault detection and recovery occur automatically without the intervention of either application or operating system software. When a fault is detected, the faulty pair is automatically disabled and the remaining pair takes over. Only then is the operating system notified that a failure has occurred.

Interagent Communications (IAC)

In order to coordinate their actions, processors in a multiple processor system need a means for communicating with each other. The 80960MC does this through a mechanism known as Interagent Communication messages or IACs.

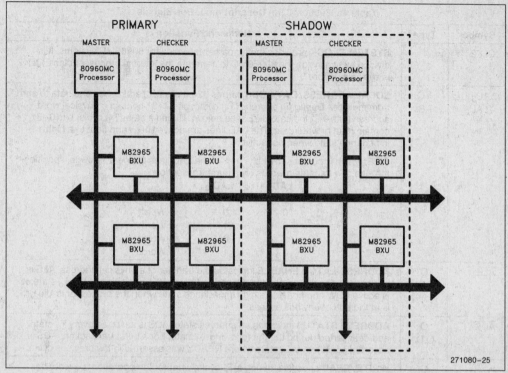

Figure 6. A Small Fault-Tolerant System Using Quad Modular Redundancy

IAC messages cause a variety of actions including starting and stopping processors, flushing instruction caches and TLBs, and sending interrupts to other processors in the system. The upper 16 Mbytes of the processor's physical memory space is reserved for sending and receiving IAC messages. The M82965 provides internal registers for storing and forwarding IAC messages, but it isn't necessary to use BXUs in order to use IAC messages.

BUILT-IN TESTABILITY

Upon reset, the 80960MC automatically conducts an exhaustive internal test of its major blocks of logic.

Then, before executing its first instruction, it does a zero check sum on the first eight words in memory to ensure that the system has been loaded correctly. If a problem is discovered at any point during the self-test, the 80960MC will assert its FAILURE pin and will not begin program execution. The self-test takes approximately 47,000 cycles to complete.

System manufacturers can use the 80960MC's self-test feature during incoming parts inspection. No special diagnostic programs need to be written, and the test is both thorough and fast. The self-test ca-

pability helps ensure that defective parts will be discovered before systems are shipped, and once in the field, the self-test makes it easier to distinguish between problems caused by processor failure and problems resulting from other causes.

COMPATIBILITY WITH 80960K-SERIES

Application programs written for the 80960K-Series microprocessors can be run on the 80960MC without modification. The 80960K-Series instruction set forms the core of the 80960MC's instructions, so binary compatibility is assured.

CHMOS

The 80960MC is fabricated using Intel's CHMOS III (Complementary High Speed Metal Oxide Semiconductor) process. This advanced technology eliminates the frequency and reliability limitations of older CMOS processes and opens a new era in microprocessor performance. It combines the high performance capabilities of Intel's industry-leading HMOS III technology with the high density and low power characteristics of CMOS. The 80960MC is available in a 16 MHz version.

Table 4a. 80960MC Pin Description: L-Bus Signals

Symbol	Type	Name and Function
CLK2	I	**SYSTEM CLOCK** provides the fundamental timing for 80960MC systems. It is divided by two inside the 80960MC to generate the internal processor clock. CLK2 is shown in Figure 9.
LAD_{31} $-LAD_0$	I/O T.S.	**LOCAL ADDRESS/DATA BUS** carries 32-bit physical addresses and data to and from memory. During an address (T_a) cycle, bits 2–31 contain a physical word address (bits 0–1 indicate SIZE; see below). During a data (T_d) cycle, bits 0–31 contain read or write data. The LAD lines are active HIGH and float to a high impedance state when not active. **SIZE,** which is comprised of bits 0–1 of the LAD lines during a T_a cycle, specifies the size of a transfer in words for a burst transaction. LAD_1 LAD_0 0 0 1 Word 0 1 2 Words 1 0 3 Words 1 1 4 Words
$\overline{ALE}$	O T.S.	**ADDRESS-LATCH ENABLE** indicates the transfer of a physical address. ALE is asserted during a T_a cycle and deasserted before the beginning of the T_d state. It is active LOW and floats to a high impedance state when the processor is idle or is at the end of any bus access.
$\overline{ADS}$	O O.D.	**ADDRESS STATUS** indicates an address state. ADS is asserted every T_a state and deasserted during the the following T_d state. For a burst transaction, $\overline{ADS}$ is asserted again every T_d state where $\overline{READY}$ was asserted in the previous cycle.
W/$\overline{R}$	O O.D.	**WRITE/READ** specifies, during a T_a cycle, whether the operation is a write or read. It is latched on-chip and remains valid during T_d and T_w states.
DT/$\overline{R}$	O O.D.	**DATA TRANSMIT/RECEIVE** indicates the direction of data transfer to and from the L-Bus. It is low during T_a, T_w and T_d cycles for a read or interrupt acknowledgement; it is high during T_a, T_w and T_d cycles for a write. DT/$\overline{R}$ never changes state when $\overline{DEN}$ is asserted (see Timing Diagrams).
$\overline{DEN}$	O O.D.	**DATA ENABLE** is asserted during T_d and T_w cycles and indicates transfer of data on the LAD bus lines.
$\overline{READY}$	I	**READY** indicates that data on LAD lines can be sampled or removed. If $\overline{READY}$ is not asserted during a T_d cycle, the T_d cycle is extended to the next cycle by inserting wait states (T_w), and $\overline{ADS}$ is not asserted in the next cycle.
$\overline{LOCK}$	I/O O.D.	**BUS LOCK** prevents other bus masters from gaining control of the L-Bus following the current cycle (if they would assert $\overline{LOCK}$ to do so). $\overline{LOCK}$ is used by the processor or any bus agent when it performs indivisible Read/Modify/Write (RMW) operations. For a read that is designated as a RMW-read, $\overline{LOCK}$ is examined. if asserted, the processor waits until it is not asserted; if not asserted, the processor asserts $\overline{LOCK}$ during the T_a cycle and leaves it asserted. A write that is designated as an RMW-write deasserts $\overline{LOCK}$ in the T_a cycle.

I/O = Input/Output, O = Output, I = Input, O.D. = Open-Drain, T.S. = three state
$T_a = T_{Address}$, $T_d = T_{Data}$, $T_w = T_{Wait}$, $T_r = T_{Recovery}$, $T_i = T_{Idle}$, $T_h = T_{Hold}$

Table 4a. 80960MC Pin Description: L-Bus Signals (Continued)

Symbol	Type	Name and Function
$\overline{BE_3}$–$\overline{BE_0}$	O O.D.	**BYTE ENABLE LINES** specify which data bytes (up to four) on the bus take part in the current bus cycle. $\overline{BE_3}$ corresponds to LAD_{31}–LAD_{24} and $\overline{BE_0}$ corresponds to LAD_7–LAD_0. The byte enables are provided in advance of data. The byte enables asserted during T_a specify the bytes of the first data word. The byte enables asserted during T_d specify the bytes of the next data word (if any), that is, the word to be transmitted following the next assertion of $\overline{READY}$. The byte enables during the T_d cycles preceding the last assertion of $\overline{READY}$ are undefined. The byte enables are latched on-chip and remain constant from one T_d cycle to the next when $\overline{READY}$ is not asserted. For reads, the byte enables specify the byte(s) that the processor will actually use. 80960MC's will assert only adjacent byte enables (e.g., asserting just $\overline{BE_0}$ and $\overline{BE_2}$ is not permitted), and are required to assert at least one byte enable. Accesses must also be naturally aligned (e.g., asserting $\overline{BE_1}$ and $\overline{BE_2}$ is not allowed even though they are adjacent). To produce address bits A_0 and A_1 externally, they can be decoded from the byte enables.
HOLD (HLDAR)	I	**HOLD** indicates a request from a secondary bus master to acquire the bus. If the processor is initialized as the primary bus master this input will be interpreted as HOLD. When the processor receives HOLD and grants another master control of the bus, it floats its three-state bus lines, asserts HOLD ACKNOWLEDGE, and enters the T_h state. When HOLD is deasserted, the processor will deassert HOLD ACKNOWLEDGE and go to either the T_i or T_a state. **HOLD ACKNOWLEDGE RECEIVED** indicates that the processor has acquired the bus. If the processor is initialized as the secondary bus master this input is interpreted as HLDAR. HOLD timing is shown in Figure 11.
HLDA (HOLDR)	O T.S.	**HOLD ACKNOWLEDGE** relinquishes control of the bus to another bus master. If the processor is initialized as the primary bus master this output will be interpreted as HLDA. When HOLD is deasserted, the processor will deassert HLDA and go to either the T_i or T_a state. **HOLD REQUEST** indicates a request to acquire the bus. If the processor is initialized as the secondary bus master this output will be interpreted as HOLDR. HOLD timing is shown in Figure 11.
CACHE	O T.S.	**CACHE** indicates if an access is cacheable during a T_a cycle. The CACHE signal floats to a high impedance state when the processor is idle.

I/O = Input/Output, O = Output, I = Input, O.D. = Open-Drain, T.S. = three state
T_a = $T_{Address}$, T_d = T_{Data}, T_W = T_{Wait}, T_r = $T_{Recovery}$, T_i = T_{Idle}, T_h = T_{Hold}

Table 4b. 80960MC Pin Description: Module Support Signals

Symbol	Type	Name and Function
$\overline{\text{BADAC}}$	I	**BAD ACCESS,** if asserted in the cycle following the one in which the last $\overline{\text{READY}}$ of a transaction is asserted, indicates that an unrecoverable error has occurred on the current bus transaction, or that a synchronous load/store instruction has not been acknowledged. **STARTUP:** During system reset, the $\overline{\text{BADAC}}$ signal is interpreted differently. If the signal is high, it indicates that this processor will perform system initialization. If it is low, another processor in the system will perform system initialization instead.
RESET	I	**RESET** clears the internal logic of the processor and causes it to re-initialize. During RESET assertion, the input pins are ignored (except for $\overline{\text{BADAC}}$ and $\overline{\text{IAC}}/\overline{\text{INT}_0}$), the tri-state output pins are placed in a high impedance state, and other output pins are placed in their non-asserted state. RESET must be asserted for at least 41 CLK2 cycles for a predictable RESET. The HIGH to LOW transition of RESET should occur after the rising edge of both CLK2 and the external bus CLK, and before the next rising edge of CLK2. RESET timing is shown in Figure 10.
$\overline{\text{FAILURE}}$	O O.D.	**INITIALIZATION FAILURE** indicates that the processor has failed to initialize correctly. After RESET is deasserted and before the first bus transaction begins, $\overline{\text{FAILURE}}$ is asserted while the processor performs a self-test. If the self-test completes successfully, then $\overline{\text{FAILURE}}$ is deasserted. Next, the processor performs a zero checksum on the first eight words of memory. If it fails, $\overline{\text{FAILURE}}$ is asserted for a second time and remains asserted; if it passes, system initialization continues and $\overline{\text{FAILURE}}$ remains deasserted.
N.C.	N/A	**NOT CONNECTED** indicates pins should not be connected. Never connect any pin marked N.C.
$\overline{\text{IAC}}$ $(\overline{\text{INT}_0})$	I	**INTERAGENT COMMUNICATION REQUEST/INTERRUPT 0** indicates either that there is a pending IAC message for the processor or an interrupt. The bus interrupt control register determines in which way the signal should be interpreted. To signal an interrupt or IAC request in a synchronous system, this pin (as well as the other interrupt pins) must be enabled by being deasserted for at least one bus cycle and then asserted for at least one additional bus cycle; in an asynchronous system, the pin must remain deasserted for at least two bus cycles and then be asserted for at least two more bus cycles. **LOCAL PROCESSOR NUMBER:** This signal is interpreted differently during system reset. If the signal is at a high voltage level, it indicates that this processor is a primary bus master (Local Processor Number = 0); if it is at a low voltage level, it indicates that this processor is a secondary bus master (Local Processor Number = 1).
INT$_1$	I	**INTERRUPT 1,** like $\overline{\text{INT}_0}$, provides direct interrupt signaling.
INT$_2$ (INTR)	I	**INTERRUPT 2/INTERRUPT REQUEST:** The bus control registers determines how this pin is interpreted. If INT$_2$, it has the same interpretation as the $\overline{\text{INT}_0}$ and INT1 pins. If INTR, it is used to receive an interrupt request from an external interrupt controller.
$\overline{\text{INT}_3}$ $(\overline{\text{INTA}})$	I/O O.D.	**INTERRUPT 3/INTERRUPT ACKNOWLEDGE:** The bus interrupt control register determines how this pin is interpreted. If $\overline{\text{INT}_3}$, it has the same interpretation as the $\overline{\text{INT}_0}$, INT$_1$, and INT$_2$ pins. If $\overline{\text{INTA}}$, it is used as an output to control interrupt-acknowledge bus transactions. The $\overline{\text{INTA}}$ output is latched on-chip and remains valid during T$_d$ cycles; as an output, it is open-drain.

I/O = Input/Output, O = Output, I = Input, O.D. = Open-Drain, T.S. = three state
$T_a = T_{Address}$, $T_d = T_{Data}$, $T_w = T_{Wait}$, $T_r = T_{Recovery}$, $T_i = T_{Idle}$, $T_h = T_{Hold}$

ELECTRICAL SPECIFICATIONS

Power and Grounding

The 80960MC is implemented in CHMOS III technology and has modest power requirements. Its high clock frequency and numerous output buffers (address/data, control, error, and arbitration signals) can cause power surges as multiple output buffers drive new signal levels simultaneously. For clean on-chip power distribution at high frequency, 11 V_{CC} and 13 V_{SS} pins separately feed functional units of the 80960MC.

Power and ground connections must be made to all power and ground pins of the 80960MC. On the circuit board, all V_{CC} pins must be strapped closely together, preferably on a power plane. Likewise, all V_{SS} pins should be strapped together, preferably on a ground plane.

Power Decoupling Recommendations

Liberal decoupling capacitance should be placed near the 80960MC. The processor can cause transient power surges when driving the L-Bus, particularly when it is connected to a large capacitive load.

Low inductance capacitors and interconnects are recommended for best high frequency electrical performance. Inductance can be reduced by shortening the board traces between the processor and decoupling capacitors as much as possible.

Connection Recommendations

For reliable operation, always connect unused inputs to an appropriate signal level. In particular, if one or more interrupt lines are not used, they should be pulled up or down to their respective deasserted states. No inputs should ever be left floating.

All open-drain outputs require a pullup device. While in most cases a simple pullup resistor will be adequate, a network of pullup and pulldown resistors biased to a valid V_{IH} ($\geq$ 3.4V) will limit noise and AC power consumption.

ABSOLUTE MAXIMUM RATINGS*

Case Temperature
  under Bias[5] . . . . −55°C to +125°C
Storage Temperature . . . . −65°C to +150°C
Voltage on Any Pin . . . . −0.5V to V_{CC} + 0.5V
Power Dissipation . . . . 2.8W (20 MHz)

Notice: Stresses above those listed under "Absolute Maximum Ratings" may cause permanent damage to the device. This is a stress rating only and functional operation of the device at these or any other conditions above those indicated in the operational sections of this specification is not implied. Exposure to absolute maximum rating conditions for extended periods may affect device reliability.

NOTICE: Specifications contained within the following tables are subject to change.

D.C. CHARACTERISTICS

80960MC: T_{CASE}[5] = −55°C to +125°C, V_{CC} = 5V ± 5%

Symbol	Parameter	Min	Max	Units	Test Conditions
V_{IL}	Input Low Voltage	−0.3	+0.8	V	
V_{IH}	Input High Voltage	2.0	V_{CC} + 0.3	V	
V_{CL}	CLK2 Input Low Voltage	−0.3	+1.0	V	
V_{CH}	CLK2 Input High Voltage	0.55 V_{CC}	V_{CC} + 0.3	V	
V_{OL1}	Output Low Voltage (Three-State Outputs)		0.45	V	(1)
V_{OL2}	Output Low Voltage (Open-Drain Outputs)		0.45 0.60	V V	I_{OL} = 25 mA I_{OL} = 40 mA
V_{OH}	Output High Voltage	2.4		V	(2, 4)
I_{CC}	Power Supply Current		500	mA	
I_{LI}	Input Leakage Current		±15	μA	0 ≤ V_O ≤ V_{CC}
I_{LO}	Output Leakage Current		±15	μA	0.45 ≤ V_O ≤ V_{CC}
C_{IN}	Input Capacitance		10	pF	f_C = 1 MHz(3)
C_O	I/O or Output Capacitance		12	pF	f_C = 1 MHz(3)
C_{CLK}	Clock Capacitance		10	pF	f_C = 1 MHz(3)

θ_{JA}	Thermal Resistance (Junction-to-Ambient)
	  Pin Grid Array
	  Ceramic Quad Flatpack
			
			21
			29
				
				°C/W
				°C/W	

θ_{JC}	Thermal Resistance (Junction-to-Case)
	  Pin Grid Array
	  Ceramic Quad Flatpack
			
			4
			8
				
				°C/W
				°C/W	

NOTES:
1. This parameter is measured at:
  Address/Data . . . . 4.0 mA
  Controls . . . . 5.0 mA
2. This parameter is measured at:
  Address/Data . . . . −1.0 mA
  Controls . . . . −0.9 mA
  ALE . . . . −5.0 mA
3. Input, output, and clock capacitance are not tested.
4. Not measured on open-drain outputs.
5. Case temperatures are "instant on".

AC SPECIFICATIONS

This section describes the AC specifications for the 80960MC pins. All input and output timings are specified relative to the 1.5V level of the rising edge of CLK2, and refer to the time at which the signal reaches (for output delay and input setup) or leaves (for hold time) the TTL levels of LOW (0.8V) or HIGH (2.0V). All AC testing should be done with input voltages of 0.4V and 2.4V, except for the clock (CLK2), which should be tested with input voltages of 0.45V and 0.55 V_{CC}.

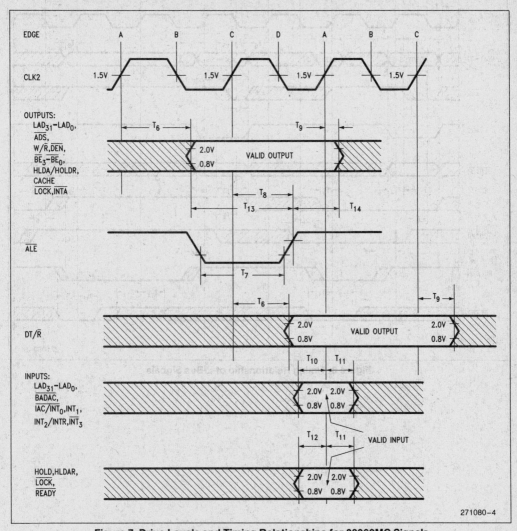

Figure 7. Drive Levels and Timing Relationships for 80960MC Signals

271080–4

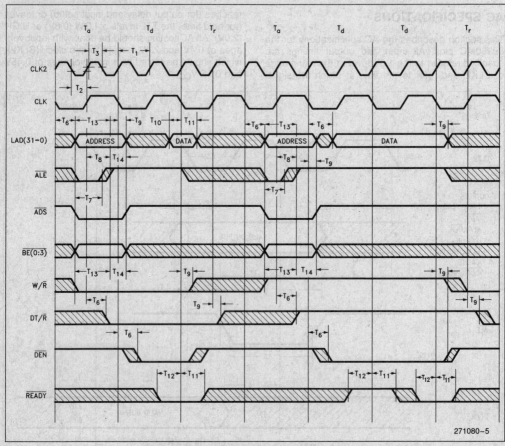

Figure 8. Timing Relationship of L-Bus Signals

271080–5

A.C. Specification Tables

80960MC A.C. Characteristics (16 MHz)

T_{case}[3] $= -55°C$ to $+125°C$, $V_{CC} = 5V \pm 5\%$

Symbol	Parameter	Min	Max	Units	Test Conditions
T_1	Processor Clock Period	31.25	125	ns	$V_{IN} = 1.5V$
T_2	Processor Clock Low Time	11		ns	$V_{IN} = 10\%$ Point $= 1.2V$
T_3	Processor Clock High Time	11		ns	$V_{IN} = 90\%$ Point $= 0.1V + 0.5 V_{CC}$
T_4	Processor Clock Fall Time		10	ns	$V_{IN} = 90\%$ Point to 10% Point
T_5	Processor Clock Rise Time		10	ns	$V_{IN} = 10\%$ Point to 90% Point
T_6	Output Valid Delay	5	35	ns	$C_L = 100$ pF (LAD) $C_L = 75$ pF (Controls)
T_7	$\overline{ALE}$ Width	15		ns	$C_L = 75$ pF
T_8	$\overline{ALE}$ Invalid Delay	5	20	ns	$C_L = 75$ pF[2]
T_9	Output Float Delay	5	20	ns	$C_L = 100$ pF (LAD) $C_L = 75$ pF (Controls)[2]
T_{10}	Input Setup 1	3		ns	
T_{11}	Input Hold	5		ns	
T_{12}	Input Setup 2	8		ns	
T_{13}	Setup to $\overline{ALE}$ Inactive	10		ns	$C_L = 100$ pF (LAD) $C_L = 75$ pF (Controls)
T_{14}	Hold after $\overline{ALE}$ Inactive	8		ns	$C_L = 100$ pF (LAD) $C_L = 75$ pF (Controls)
T_{15}	Reset Hold	5		ns	
T_{16}	Reset Setup	8		ns	
T_{17}	Reset Width	1282		ns	41 CLK2 Periods Minimum

NOTES:
1. $\overline{IAC}/\overline{INT}_0$, INT_1, $INT_2/INTR$, $\overline{INT}_3/\overline{INTA}$ can be asynchronous.
2. A float condition occurs when the maximum output current becomes less than I_{LO}. Float delay is not tested, but should be no longer than the valid delay.
3. Case temperatures are "instant on".

A.C. Specification Tables (Continued)

80960MC A.C. Characteristics (20 MHz)

T_{case}[3] $= -55°C$ to $+125°C$, $V_{CC} = 5V \pm 5\%$

Symbol	Parameter	Min	Max	Units	Test Conditions
T_1	Processor Clock Period	25	125	ns	$V_{IN} = 1.5V$
T_2	Processor Clock Low Time	8		ns	$V_{IN} = 10\%$ Point $= 1.2V$
T_3	Processor Clock High Time	8		ns	$V_{IN} = 90\%$ Point $= 0.1V + 0.5 V_{CC}$
T_4	Processor Clock Fall Time		10	ns	$V_{IN} = 90\%$ Point to 10% Point
T_5	Processor Clock Rise Time		10	ns	$V_{IN} = 10\%$ Point to 90% Point
T_6	Output Valid Delay	2	25	ns	$C_L = 100$ pF (LAD) $C_L = 75$ pF (Controls)
T_7	$\overline{ALE}$ Width	12		ns	$C_L = 75$ pF
T_8	$\overline{ALE}$ Invalid Delay	5	20	ns	$C_L = 75$ pF[2]
T_9	Output Float Delay	2	20	ns	$C_L = 100$ pF (LAD) $C_L = 75$ pF (Controls)[2]
T_{10}	Input Setup 1	3		ns	
T_{11}	Input Hold	5		ns	
T_{12}	Input Setup 2	7		ns	
T_{13}	Setup to $\overline{ALE}$ Inactive	10		ns	$C_L = 100$ pF (LAD) $C_L = 75$ pF (Controls)
T_{14}	Hold after $\overline{ALE}$ Inactive	8		ns	$C_L = 100$ pF (LAD) $C_L = 75$ pF (Controls)
T_{15}	Reset Hold	3		ns	
T_{16}	Reset Setup	5		ns	
T_{17}	Reset Width	1025		ns	41 CLK2 Periods Minimum

NOTES:
1. $\overline{IAC}/\overline{INT}_0$, INT_1, $INT_2/INTR$, $\overline{INT}_3/\overline{INTA}$ can be asynchronous.
2. A float condition occurs when the maximum output current becomes less than I_{LO}. Float delay is not tested, but should be no longer than the valid delay.
3. Case temperatures are "instant on".

A.C. Specification Tables (Continued)

80960MC A.C. Characteristics (25 MHz)

T_{case}[3] = −55°C to +125°C, V_{CC} = 5V ±5%

Symbol	Parameter	Min	Max	Units	Test Conditions
T_1	Processor Clock Period (CLK2)	20	125	ns	V_{IN} = 1.5V
T_2	Processor Clock Low Time (CLK2)	6		ns	V_{IN} = 10% Point 1.2V
T_3	Processor Clock High Time	6		ns	V_{IN} = 90% Point 0.1V + 0.5 V_{CC}
T_4	Processor Clock Fall Time (CLK2)		10	ns	V_{IN} = 90% Point to 10% Point
T_5	Processor Clock Rise Time (CLK2)		10	ns	V_{IN} = 10% Point to 90% Point
T_6	Output Valid Delay	2	18	ns	C_L = 60 pF (LAD) C_L = 50 pF (Controls)
T_7	ALE Width	12		ns	C_L = 50 pF
T_8	ALE Output Valid Delay	5	20	ns	C_L = 50 pF[2]
T_9	Output Float Delay	2	20	ns	C_L = 60 pF (LAD) C_L = 50 pF (Controls)
T_{10}	Input Setup 1	3		ns	
T_{11}	Input Hold	5		ns	
T_{12}	Input Setup 2	7		ns	
T_{13}	Setup to ALE Inactive	10		ns	C_L = 60 pF (LAD) C_L = 50 pF (Controls)
T_{14}	Hold after ALE Inactive	8		ns	C_L = 60 pF (LAD) C_L = 50 pF (Controls)
T_{15}	Reset Hold	3		ns	
T_{16}	Reset Setup	5		ns	
T_{17}	Reset Width	820		ns	41 CLK2 Periods Minimum

NOTES:
1. $\overline{IAC}/\overline{INT}_0$, INT_1, $INT_2/INTR$, $\overline{INT}_3/\overline{INTA}$ can be asynchronous.
2. A float condition occurs when the maximum output current becomes less than I_{LO}. Float delay is not tested, but should be no longer than the valid delay.
3. Case temperatures are "instant on".

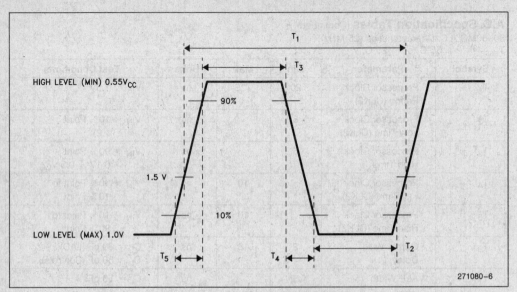

Figure 9. Processor Clock Pulse (CLK2)

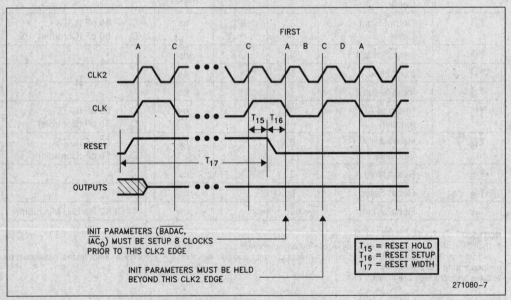

Figure 10. RESET Signal Timing

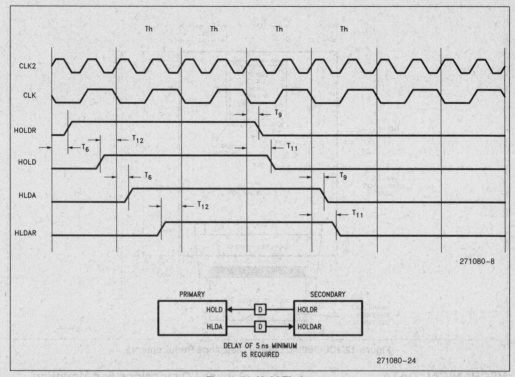

271080-8

271080-24

Figure 11. Hold Timing

Design Considerations

Input hold times can be disregarded by the designer whenever the input is removed because a subsequent output from the processor is deasserted (e.g., $\overline{DEN}$ becomes deasserted).

In other words, whenever the processor generates an output that indicates a transition into a subsequent state, the processor must have sampled any inputs for the previous state.

Similarly, whenever the processor generates an output that indicates a transition into a subsequent state, any outputs that are specified to be three stated in this new state are guaranteed to be three stated.

Designing for the ICE-960MC

The 80960MC In-Circuit Emulator assists in debugging 80960MC hardware and software designs. The product consists of a probe module, cable, and control unit. Because of the high operating frequency of 80960MC systems, the probe module connects directly to the 80960MC socket.

When designing an 80960MC hardware system that uses the ICE-960MC to debug the system, several electrical and mechanical characteristics should be considered. These considerations include capacitive loading, drive requirement, power requirement, and physical layout.

The ICE-960MC probe module increases the load capacitance of each line by up to 25 pF. It also adds one standard Schottky TTL load on the CLK2 line, up to one advanced low-power Schottky TTL load for each control signal line, and one advanced low-power Schottky TTL load for each address/data and byte enable line. These loads originate from the probe module and are driven by the 80960MC processor.

To achieve high noise immunity, the ICE-960MC probe is powered by the user's system. The high-speed probe circuitry draws up to 1.1A plus the maximum current (I_{CC}) of the 80960MC processor.

The mechanical considerations are shown in Figure 12, which illustrates the lateral clearance requirements for the ICE-960MC probe as viewed from above the socket of the 80960MC processor.

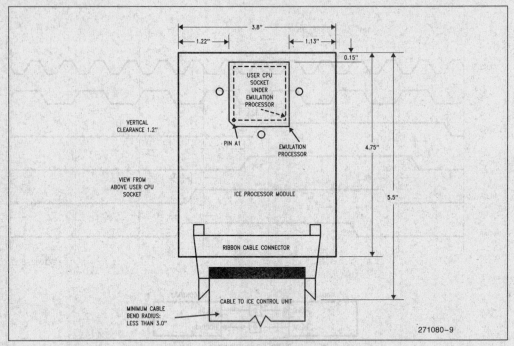

Figure 12. ICE-960MC Lateral Clearance Requirements

MECHANICAL DATA

Pin Assignment

The 80960MC is packaged in a 132-lead ceramic pin grid array and a 164-lead ceramic quad flatpack. The 80960MC pin grid array pinout as viewed from the substrate side of the component is shown in Figure 13 and from the pin side in Figure 14. The 80960MC ceramic quad flatpack pinout as viewed from the top of the package is shown in Figure 15.

V_{CC} and GND connections must be made to multiple V_{CC} and GND pins. Each V_{CC} and GND pin must be connected to the appropriate voltage or ground and externally strapped close to the package. Preferably, the circuit board should include power and ground planes for power distribution. Tables 5, 6, 7 and 8 list the function of each pin.

NOTE:
Pins identified as N.C., "No Connect," should never be connected under any circumstances.

Package Dimensions and Mounting

Pins in the pin grid array package are arranged 0.100 inch (2.54mm) center-to-center, in a 14 by 14 matrix, three rows around. (See Figure 16.)

A wide variety of available sockets allow low-insertion or zero-insertion force mountings, and a choice of terminals such as soldertail, surface mount, or wire wrap. Several applicable sockets are shown in Figure 17.

Package Thermal Specification

The 80960MC is specified for operation when its case temperature is within the range of $-55°C$ to $+125°C$. The PGA case temperature should be measured at the center of the top surface opposite the pins as shown in Figure 18. The ceramic quad flatpack case temperature should be measured at the center of the lid on the top surface of the package.

WAVEFORMS

Figures 19 through 25 show the waveforms for various transactions on the 80960MC's local bus.

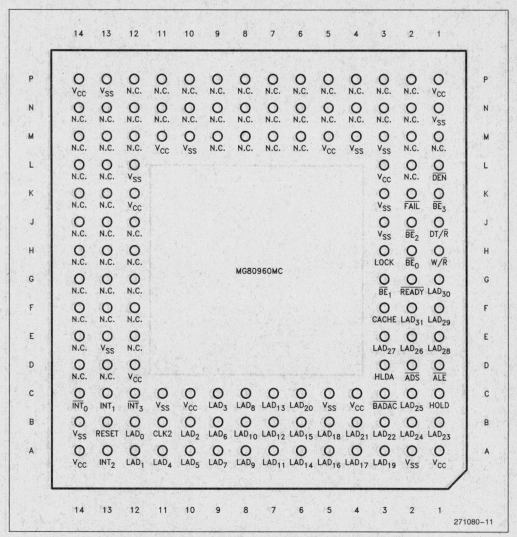

Figure 13. MG80960MC Pinout—View from Top (Pins Facing Down)

271080–11

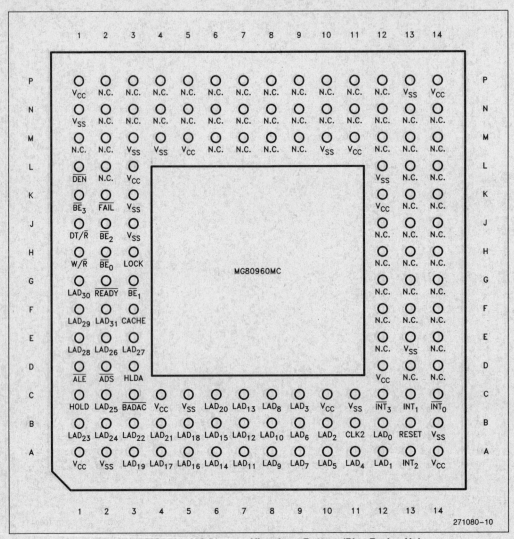

Figure 14. MG80960MC Pinout—View from Bottom (Pins Facing Up)

271080–10

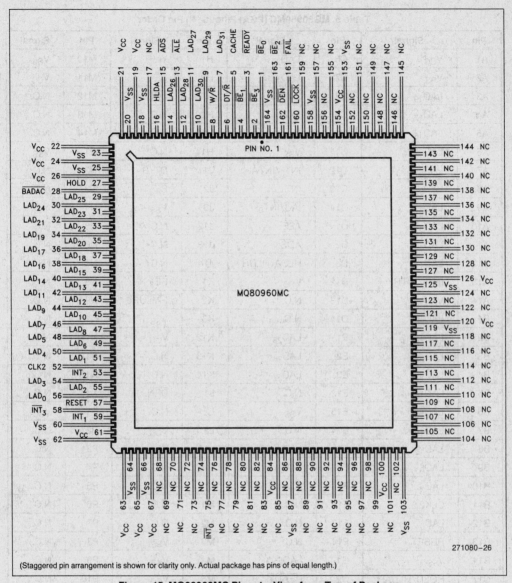

(Staggered pin arrangement is shown for clarity only. Actual package has pins of equal length.)

Figure 15. MQ80960MC Pinout—View from Top of Package

271080–26

Table 5. MG80960MC (PGA) Pinout—In Pin Order

Pin	Signal	Pin	Signal	Pin	Signal	Pin	Signal
A1	V_{CC}	C6	LAD_{20}	H1	$W/\overline{R}$	M10	V_{SS}
A2	V_{SS}	C7	LAD_{13}	H2	$\overline{BE}_0$	M11	V_{CC}
A3	LAD_{19}	C8	LAD_8	H3	$\overline{LOCK}$	M12	N.C.
A4	LAD_{17}	C9	LAD_3	H12	N.C	M13	N.C.
A5	LAD_{16}	C10	V_{CC}	H13	N.C.	M14	N.C.
A6	LAD_{14}	C11	V_{SS}	H14	N.C.	N1	V_{SS}
A7	LAD_{11}	C12	$\overline{INT}_3/\overline{INTA}$	J1	$DT/\overline{R}$	N2	N.C.
A8	LAD_9	C13	INT_1	J2	$\overline{BE}_2$	N3	N.C.
A9	LAD_7	C14	$\overline{IAC}/\overline{INT}_0$	J3	V_{SS}	N4	N.C.
A10	LAD_5	D1	$\overline{ALE}$	J12	N.C	N5	N.C.
A11	LAD_4	D2	$\overline{ADS}$	J13	N.C.	N6	N.C.
A12	LAD_1	D3	HLDA/HLDR	J14	N.C.	N7	N.C.
A13	$INT_2/INTR$	D12	V_{CC}	K1	$\overline{BE}_3$	N8	N.C.
A14	V_{CC}	D13	N.C.	K2	$\overline{FAILURE}$	N9	N.C.
B1	LAD_{23}	D14	N.C.	K3	V_{SS}	N10	N.C.
B2	LAD_{24}	E1	LAD_{28}	K12	V_{CC}	N11	N.C.
B3	LAD_{22}	E2	LAD_{26}	K13	N.C.	N12	N.C.
B4	LAD_{21}	E3	LAD_{27}	K14	N.C.	N13	N.C.
B5	LAD_{18}	E12	N.C.	L1	$\overline{DEN}$	N14	N.C.
B6	LAD_{15}	E13	V_{SS}	L2	N.C.	P1	V_{CC}
B7	LAD_{12}	E14	N.C.	L3	V_{CC}	P2	N.C.
B8	LAD_{10}	F1	LAD_{29}	L12	V_{SS}	P3	N.C.
B9	LAD_6	F2	LAD_{31}	L13	N.C.	P4	N.C.
B10	LAD_2	F3	CACHE	L14	N.C.	P5	N.C.
B11	CLK2	F12	N.C.	M1	N.C.	P6	N.C.
B12	LAD_0	F13	N.C.	M2	N.C.	P7	N.C.
B13	RESET	F14	N.C.	M3	V_{SS}	P8	N.C.
B14	V_{SS}	G1	LAD_{30}	M4	V_{SS}	P9	N.C.
C1	HOLD/HLDAR	G2	$\overline{READY}$	M5	V_{CC}	P10	N.C.
C2	LAD_{25}	G3	$\overline{BE}_1$	M6	N.C.	P11	N.C.
C3	$\overline{BADAC}$	G12	N.C.	M7	N.C.	P12	N.C.
C4	V_{CC}	G13	N.C.	M8	N.C.	P13	V_{SS}
C5	V_{SS}	G14	N.C.	M9	N.C.	P14	V_{CC}

NOTE:
Pins identified as N.C. ("No Connect") should never be connected under any circumstances.

Table 6. MG80960MC (PGA) Pinout—In Signal Order

Signal	Pin	Signal	Pin	Signal	Pin	Signal	Pin
$\overline{\text{ADS}}$	D2	LAD_{15}	B6	N.C.	J14	N.C.	P8
$\overline{\text{ALE}}$	D1	LAD_{16}	A5	N.C.	K13	N.C.	P9
$\overline{\text{BADAC}}$	C3	LAD_{17}	A4	N.C.	K14	N.C.	P10
$\overline{\text{BE}}_0$	H2	LAD_{18}	B5	N.C.	L13	N.C.	P11
$\overline{\text{BE}}_1$	G3	LAD_{19}	A3	N.C.	L14	N.C.	P12
$\overline{\text{BE}}_2$	J2	LAD_{20}	C6	N.C.	M1	N.C.	L2
$\overline{\text{BE}}_3$	K1	LAD_{21}	B4	N.C.	M2	$\overline{\text{READY}}$	G2
CACHE	F3	LAD_{22}	B3	N.C.	M6	RESET	B13
CLK2	B11	LAD_{23}	B1	N.C.	M7	V_{CC}	A1
$\overline{\text{DEN}}$	L1	LAD_{24}	B2	N.C.	M8	V_{CC}	A14
$\text{DT}/\overline{\text{R}}$	J1	LAD_{25}	C2	N.C.	M9	V_{CC}	C4
$\overline{\text{FAILURE}}$	K2	LAD_{26}	E2	N.C.	M12	V_{CC}	C10
HLDA/HOLDR	D3	LAD_{27}	E3	N.C.	M13	V_{CC}	D12
HOLD/HLDAR	C1	LAD_{28}	E1	N.C.	M14	V_{CC}	K12
$\overline{\text{IAC}}/\overline{\text{INT}}_0$	C14	LAD_{29}	F1	N.C.	N2	V_{CC}	L3
INT_1	C13	LAD_{30}	G1	N.C.	N3	V_{CC}	M5
INT_2/INTR	A13	LAD_{31}	F2	N.C.	N4	V_{CC}	M11
$\overline{\text{INT}}_3/\overline{\text{INTA}}$	C12	$\overline{\text{LOCK}}$	H3	N.C.	N5	V_{CC}	P1
LAD_0	B12	N.C.	D13	N.C.	N6	V_{CC}	P14
LAD_1	A12	N.C.	D14	N.C.	N7	V_{SS}	A2
LAD_2	B10	N.C.	E12	N.C.	N8	V_{SS}	B14
LAD_3	C9	N.C.	E14	N.C.	N9	V_{SS}	C5
LAD_4	A11	N.C.	F12	N.C.	N10	V_{SS}	C11
LAD_5	A10	N.C.	F13	N.C.	N11	V_{SS}	E13
LAD_6	B9	N.C.	F14	N.C.	N12	V_{SS}	J3
LAD_7	A9	N.C.	G12	N.C.	N13	V_{SS}	K3
LAD_8	C8	N.C.	G13	N.C.	N14	V_{SS}	L12
LAD_9	A8	N.C.	G14	N.C.	P2	V_{SS}	M3
LAD_{10}	B8	N.C.	H12	N.C.	P3	V_{SS}	M4
LAD_{11}	A7	N.C.	H13	N.C.	P4	V_{SS}	M10
LAD_{12}	B7	N.C.	H14	N.C.	P5	V_{SS}	N1
LAD_{13}	C7	N.C.	J12	N.C.	P6	V_{SS}	P13
LAD_{14}	A6	N.C.	J13	N.C.	P7	$\text{W}/\overline{\text{R}}$	H1

NOTE:
Pins identified as N.C. ("No Connect") should never be connected under any circumstances.

Table 7. MQ80960MC (CQP) Pinout—In Pin Order

Pin	Signal	Pin	Signal	Pin	Signal	Pin	Signal
1	$\overline{BE}_0$	42	LAD_{11}	83	N.C.	124	N.C.
2	$\overline{BE}_3$	43	LAD_{12}	84	V_{CC}	125	V_{SS}
3	$\overline{READY}$	44	LAD_9	85	N.C.	126	V_{CC}
4	$\overline{BE}_1$	45	LAD_{10}	86	N.C.	127	N.C.
5	CACHE	46	LAD_7	87	V_{SS}	128	N.C.
6	$DT/\overline{R}$	47	LAD_8	88	N.C.	129	N.C.
7	LAD_{31}	48	LAD_5	89	N.C.	130	N.C.
8	$W/\overline{R}$	49	LAD_6	90	N.C.	131	N.C.
9	LAD_{29}	50	LAD_4	91	N.C.	132	N.C.
10	LAD_{30}	51	LAD_1	92	N.C.	133	N.C.
11	LAD_{27}	52	CLK_2	93	N.C.	134	N.C.
12	LAD_{28}	53	INT_2	94	N.C.	135	N.C.
13	$\overline{ALE}$	54	LAD_3	95	N.C.	136	N.C.
14	LAD_{26}	55	LAD_2	96	N.C.	137	N.C.
15	$\overline{ADS}$	56	LAD_0	97	N.C.	138	N.C.
16	HLDA	57	RESET	98	N.C.	139	N.C.
17	N.C.	58	$\overline{INT}_3$	99	N.C.	140	N.C.
18	V_{SS}	59	INT_1	100	V_{CC}	141	N.C.
19	V_{CC}	60	V_{SS}	101	N.C.	142	N.C.
20	V_{SS}	61	V_{CC}	102	N.C.	143	N.C.
21	V_{CC}	62	V_{SS}	103	V_{SS}	144	N.C.
22	V_{CC}	63	V_{CC}	104	N.C.	145	N.C.
23	V_{SS}	64	V_{SS}	105	N.C.	146	N.C.
24	V_{CC}	65	V_{CC}	106	N.C.	147	N.C.
25	V_{SS}	66	V_{SS}	107	N.C.	148	N.C.
26	V_{CC}	67	V_{CC}	108	N.C.	149	N.C.
27	HOLD	68	N.C.	109	N.C.	150	N.C.
28	$\overline{BADAC}$	69	N.C.	110	N.C.	151	N.C.
29	LAD_{25}	70	N.C.	111	N.C.	152	N.C.
30	LAD_{24}	71	N.C.	112	N.C.	153	V_{SS}
31	LAD_{23}	72	N.C.	113	N.C.	154	V_{CC}
32	LAD_{21}	73	N.C.	114	N.C.	155	N.C.
33	LAD_{22}	74	N.C.	115	N.C.	156	N.C.
34	LAD_{19}	75	$\overline{INT}_0$	116	N.C.	157	N.C.
35	LAD_{20}	76	N.C.	117	N.C.	158	V_{SS}
36	LAD_{17}	77	N.C.	118	N.C.	159	N.C.
37	LAD_{18}	78	N.C.	119	V_{SS}	160	$\overline{LOCK}$
38	LAD_{16}	79	N.C.	120	V_{CC}	161	$\overline{FAIL}$
39	LAD_{15}	80	N.C.	121	N.C.	162	$\overline{DEN}$
40	LAD_{14}	81	N.C.	122	N.C.	163	$\overline{BE}_2$
41	LAD_{13}	82	N.C.	123	N.C.	164	V_{SS}

NOTE:
Pins identified as N.C. ("No Connect") should never be connected under any circumstances.

Table 8. MQ80960MC (CQP) Pinout—In Signal Order

Signal	Pin	Signal	Pin	Signal	Pin	Signal	Pin
$\overline{ADS}$	15	LAD_{23}	31	N.C.	102	N.C.	148
$\overline{ALE}$	13	LAD_{24}	30	N.C.	104	N.C.	149
$\overline{BADAC}$	28	LAD_{25}	29	N.C.	105	N.C.	150
$\overline{BE_0}$	1	LAD_{26}	14	N.C.	106	N.C.	151
$\overline{BE_1}$	4	LAD_{27}	11	N.C.	107	N.C.	152
$\overline{BE_2}$	163	LAD_{28}	12	N.C.	108	N.C.	155
$\overline{BE_3}$	2	LAD_{29}	9	N.C.	109	N.C.	156
CACHE	5	LAD_{30}	10	N.C.	110	N.C.	157
CLK2	52	LAD_{31}	7	N.C.	111	N.C.	159
$\overline{DEN}$	162	$\overline{LOCK}$	160	N.C.	112	$\overline{READY}$	3
DT/$\overline{R}$	6	N.C.	17	N.C.	113	RESET	57
$\overline{FAILURE}$	161	N.C.	68	N.C.	114	V_{CC}	19
HLDA/HOLDR	16	N.C.	69	N.C.	115	V_{CC}	21
HOLD/HLDAR	27	N.C.	70	N.C.	116	V_{CC}	22
$\overline{IAC}/\overline{INT_0}$	75	N.C.	71	N.C.	117	V_{CC}	24
INT_1	59	N.C.	72	N.C.	118	V_{CC}	26
INT_2/INTR	53	N.C.	73	N.C.	121	V_{CC}	61
$\overline{INT_3}/\overline{INTA}$	58	N.C.	74	N.C.	122	V_{CC}	63
LAD_0	56	N.C.	76	N.C.	123	V_{CC}	65
LAD_1	51	N.C.	77	N.C.	124	V_{CC}	67
LAD_2	55	N.C.	78	N.C.	127	V_{CC}	84
LAD_3	54	N.C.	79	N.C.	128	V_{CC}	100
LAD_4	50	N.C.	80	N.C.	129	V_{CC}	120
LAD_5	48	N.C.	81	N.C.	130	V_{CC}	126
LAD_6	49	N.C.	82	N.C.	131	V_{CC}	154
LAD_7	46	N.C.	83	N.C.	132	V_{SS}	18
LAD_8	47	N.C.	85	N.C.	133	V_{SS}	20
LAD_9	44	N.C.	86	N.C.	134	V_{SS}	23
LAD_{10}	45	N.C.	88	N.C.	135	V_{SS}	25
LAD_{11}	42	N.C.	89	N.C.	136	V_{SS}	60
LAD_{12}	43	N.C.	90	N.C.	137	V_{SS}	62
LAD_{13}	41	N.C.	91	N.C.	138	V_{SS}	64
LAD_{14}	40	N.C.	92	N.C.	139	V_{SS}	66
LAD_{15}	39	N.C.	93	N.C.	140	V_{SS}	87
LAD_{16}	38	N.C.	94	N.C.	141	V_{SS}	103
LAD_{17}	36	N.C.	95	N.C.	142	V_{SS}	119
LAD_{18}	37	N.C.	96	N.C.	143	V_{SS}	125
LAD_{19}	34	N.C.	97	N.C.	144	V_{SS}	153
LAD_{20}	35	N.C.	98	N.C.	145	V_{SS}	158
LAD_{21}	32	N.C.	99	N.C.	146	V_{SS}	164
LAD_{22}	33	N.C.	101	N.C.	147	W/$\overline{R}$	8

NOTE:
Pins identified as N.C. ("No Connect") should never be connected under any circumstances.

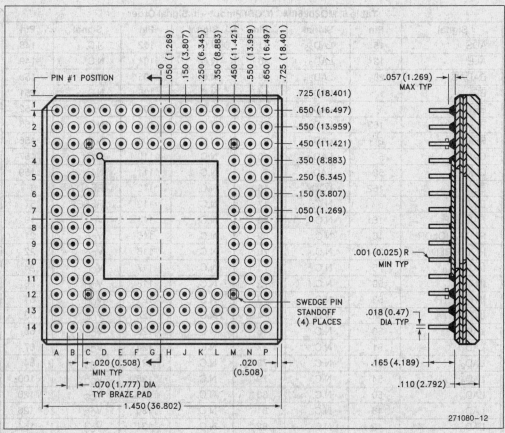

271080-12

Figure 16. A 132-Lead Pin-Grid Array (PGA) Used to Package the MG80960MC

- Low insertion force (LIF) soldertail 55274-1
- Amp tests indicate 50% reduction in insertion force compared to machined sockets

Other socket options

- Zero insertion force (ZIF) soldertail 55583-1
- Zero insertion force (ZIF) Burn-in version 55573-2

Amp Incorporated
(Harrisburg, PA 17105 U.S.A
Phone 717-564-0100)

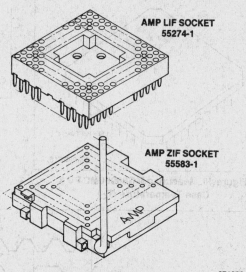

AMP LIF SOCKET 55274-1

AMP ZIF SOCKET 55583-1

271080–13

Cam handle locks in low profile position when MG80960MC is installed (handle UP for open and DOWN for closed positions).

Courtesy Amp Incorporated

Peel-A-Way* Mylar and Kapton Socket Terminal Carriers

- Low insertion force surface mount CS132-37TG
- Low insertion force soldertail CS132-01TG
- Low insertion force wire-wrap CS132-02TG (two-level) CS132-03TG (thee-level)
- Low insertion force press-fit CS132-05TG

Advanced Interconnections
(5 Division Street)
Warwick, RI 02818 U.S.A.
Phone 401-885-0485)

Peel-A-Way Carrier No. 132:
Kapton Carrier is KS132
Mylar Carrier is MS132

Molded Plastic Body KS132 is shown below:

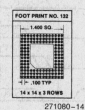

FOOT PRINT NO. 132

1.400 SQ.

.100 TYP

14 x 14 x 3 ROWS

271080–14

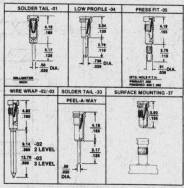

271080–15

Courtesy Advanced Interconnections
(Peel-A-Way Terminal Carriers
U.S. Patent No. 4442938)

*Peel-A-Way is a trademark of Advanced Interconnections.

Figure 17. Several Socket Options for Mounting the MG80960MC

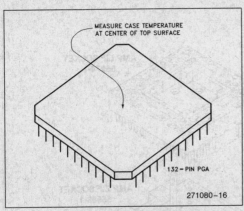

Figure 18. Measuring MG80960MC PGA
Case Temperature (T_C)

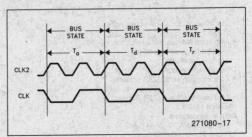

Figure 19. System and Processor
Clock Relationship

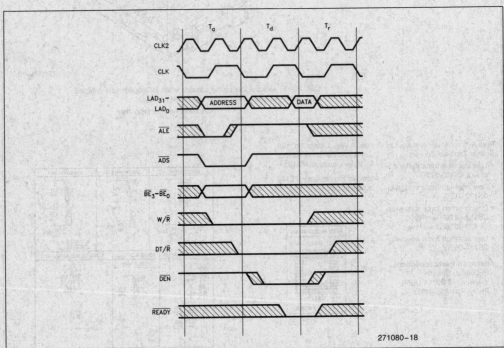

Figure 20. Read Transaction

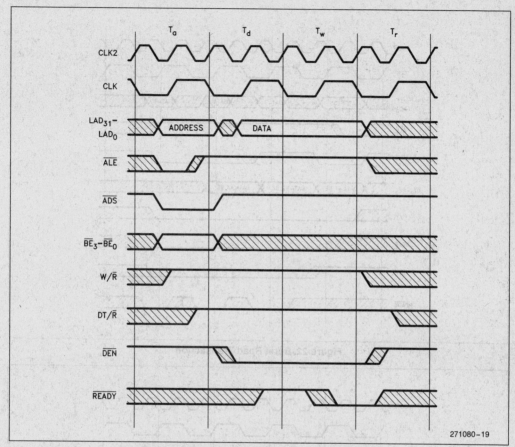

Figure 21. Write Transaction with One Wait State

271080-19

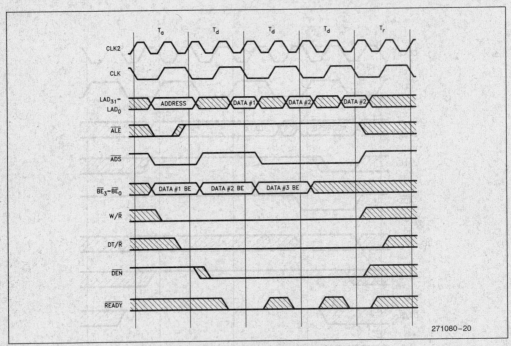

271080–20

Figure 22. Burst Read Transaction

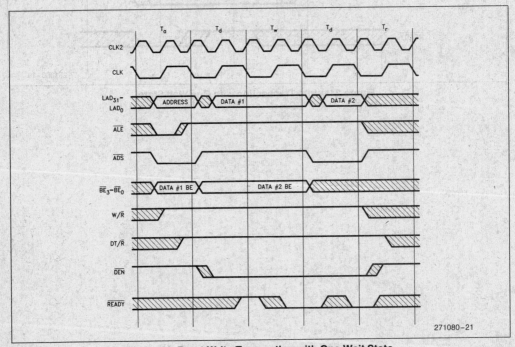

271080–21

Figure 23. Burst Write Transaction with One Wait State

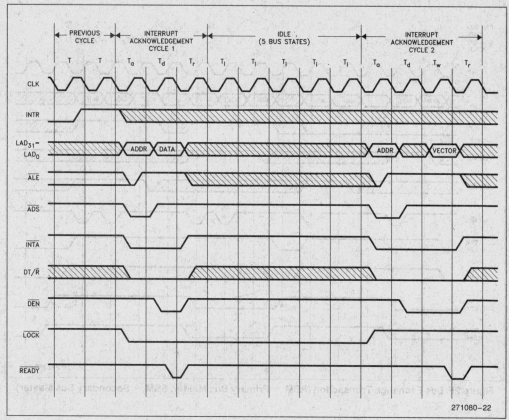

Figure 24. Interrupt Acknowledge Transaction

271080-22

5-45

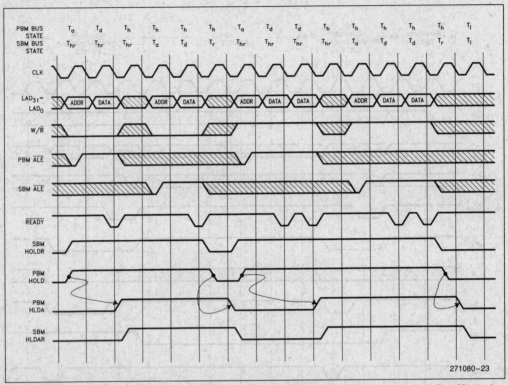

Figure 25. Bus Exchange Transaction (PBM = Primary Bus Master, SBM = Secondary Bus Master)

Revision History

1. 20 MHz timing specifications were added.
2. Pin 158, ceramic quad pack, (see Figure 15) changed from NC (No Connect) to V_{SS}.

M82965
FAULT TOLERANT BUS EXTENSION UNIT
Military

- **Multiprocessor Support**
  - **Connect up to 32 Processor and Memory Modules in a Single System**

- **Multiple Bus Support with No External Logic**
  - **Connect up to Four 32-Bit Buses for High-Bandwidth Access to Interleaved Memory**

- **Software-Transparent Fault Tolerance**
  - **Recover from a Single-Point Failure in a Module or Bus without Affecting Program Execution**

- **Cache Control Support**
  - **Provides Directory, Coherency Logic, and Control Signals for a Two-Way Set-Associative Cache**
  - **Single BXU Supports 64 Kbytes**
  - **Combine up to Four BXUs to Support 256 Kbytes**

- **Message Passing**
  - **Supports Interagent Communication**
  - **Redundant Error Reporting Network**

- **Two I/O Prefetch Channels**
  - **Provides High-Bandwidth, Low Latency Access to Memory or I/O for Sequential Transfers**

- **Memory Module Support**
  - **Interfaces Discrete Memory Controller and DRAM Array to AP-Bus**

- **Advanced CHMOS III Technology**

- **Advanced Package Technology**
  - **132 Lead Ceramic Pin Grid Array**
  - **164 Lead Ceramic Quad Flatpack**

- **Military Temperature Range:**
  $-55°C$ to $+125°C$ (T_C)

The M82965 Bus Extension Unit (BXU) is the key to building multiprocessor and fault-tolerant systems with the 80960MC 32-bit microprocessor. BXUs connect to each other in an expandable matrix that can support up to 32 processor and memory modules in a single, high-performance system. No external interface logic is required. The BXU increases overall system performance by providing hardware support for local caches, I/O prefetch, message passing, and multiprocessor arbitration. Through redundant modules, fault-tolerant systems based on the BXU can sustain a single-point failure and then reconfigure themselves automatically, while application programs continue undisrupted. Truly a VLSI building block, the M82965 BXU supports a wide range of fault tolerance and performance options to meet a diverse set of cost, performance, and reliability needs.

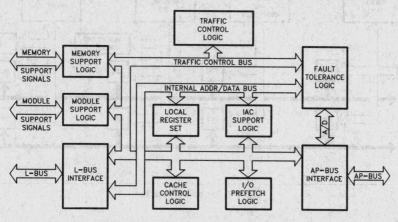

Figure 1. M82965 Block Diagram

271082-1

October 1989
Order Number: 271082-003

FUNCTIONAL OVERVIEW

The M82965 Bus Extension Unit (BXU) is the key component in building multiprocessor and fault-tolerant system designs with the 80960MC 32-bit microprocessor. Its primary function is to connect the Local bus (L-Bus) of a system module to a system-wide bus called the Advanced Processor Bus (AP-Bus), allowing the system to expand incrementally as each new module or AP-Bus is added.

Several important features are provided within the BXU which streamline 80960MC multiprocessor system operation. To increase the available system bus bandwidth, multiple BXUs can be employed within each system module to support up to four AP-Buses. To reduce AP-Bus traffic, BXU components can directly support a two-way set-associative cache. I/O prefetch channels are incorporated within each BXU to reduce the time necessary to transfer large blocks of data from shared system memory or I/O. BXUs support processor-to-processor communication by recognizing, storing, and exchanging Interagent Communication (IAC) messages with other BXUs along the AP-Bus. Requests for access to the AP-Bus are resolved through BXU arbitration logic which ensures that no system modules will suffer from resource starvation.

BXUs support fault tolerant system operation through several mechanisms used to detect, isolate and recover from hardware errors. Paired BXUs monitor each other's operation on a cycle-by-cycle basis through a method called Functional Redundancy Checking (FRC). Errors on the AP-Bus are detected through interlaced parity bits on the address/data and control lines, signal duplication on the transaction control lines, and a bus timer used to monitor the bus for non-response to a request. Recovery mechanisms include the capability to marry FRC modules in a primary-shadow pair (Quad Modular Redundancy), so that if either fails, the surviving spouse can take over operations immediately. Transient errors on the AP-Bus are automatically retried, and in the case of permanent errors, the failed bus is disabled and all memory accesses switched to a backup bus.

MULTIPROCESSOR SUPPORT

A multiprocessor 80960MC system is composed of a set of modules connected to an AP-Bus. Figure 2 shows the three possible types of modules: active, passive, and the combination of both an active and passive module. Active modules contain up to two 80960MC processors, cache or private memory, and a BXU. Passive modules contain a memory array and controller and a BXU. Active/Passive modules contain either processors and global memory, or master and slave I/O devices.

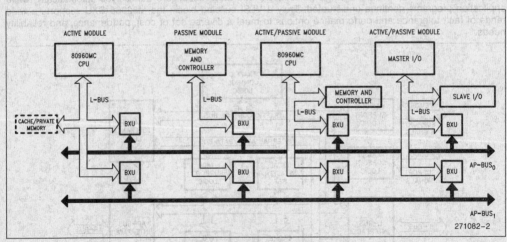

Figure 2. Types of Modules

Local Bus

In a multiprocessor system each module has its own Local Bus (L-Bus), which is typically confined to a single board. The L-Bus is provided to interconnect components within a module. It is a 32-bit multiplexed, synchronous bus with a maximum bandwidth of 43 Mbytes per second at 16 MHz. It has been designed to interface with standard support components using minimal glue logic. The L-Bus uses HOLD/HOLDA for arbitration with bus slaves and LOCK for signaling indivisible operations. A READY signal can be used to lengthen bus transactions.

Local Bus protocol permits both primary and secondary bus masters to coexist on the bus (often a processor and a DMA, or occasionally two processors). A secondary bus master must obtain use of the L-Bus from the bus master through the use of HOLDR/HOLDAR. A BXU is always used as a master in a memory module and is generally used as a slave in a processor module. Fifty BXU pins are dedicated to L-Bus and module support operations (including cache control). The L-Bus control registers are shown in Table 1.

Table 1. L-Bus Control Registers

Register	Description
Physical-ID (Local)	This register contains a unique identifier for a specific BXU on the L-Bus. It corresponds to the AP-Bus Physical-ID register.
Logical-ID (Local)	This register holds the Logical-ID of the BXU. It corresponds to the AP-Bus Logical-ID register.
LBI Control	This is the major control register for BXU functions on the L-Bus. It is used to set the interleaving factor for the cache, determines if the BXU should act as a master on the L-Bus, and indicates whether the BXU is in memory or processor mode.
System Bus ID	This register uniquely identifies the BXU as attached to one of four AP-Buses.
Local-Bus Test	This register allows system diagnostics to check on the type of recognition that was done on the previous L-Bus request.
Match 0	The contents of this register determine which bits in the L-Bus address should be recognized by the BXU. This register provides a base address for a partition of memory recognized by the BXU.
Mask 0	The contents of this register determine if certain bits in the Match 0 register should be ignored (i.e., marked "don't care") during address recognition.
Match 1	Same function as Match Register 0.
Mask 1	Same function as Mask Register 0.
Match 2	Same function as Match Register 0.
Mask 2	Same function as Mask Register 0.
Private Memory Match	Private memory address recognizer.
Private Memory Mask	Private memory mask register.

Advanced Processor Bus

A highly optimized multiprocessing bus called the Advanced Processor Bus (AP-Bus) interconnects 80960MC system modules. The AP-Bus is synchronous, in that all components in the system, including processors and BXUs, are driven by the same clock edge. It is a 32-bit multiplexed bus with a maximum bandwidth of 43 Mbytes per second at 16 MHz.

Transactions over the AP-Bus are encoded into pairs of request and reply packets. A request packet defines the operation, amount of data, and the location (or address) where the transaction will occur. In the case of a write request, the packet will also include data. The reply packet indicates whether or not the action completed successfully, and in the case of read replies, will also include the requested data. Table 2 lists the various types of AP-Bus operations.

The AP-Bus supports a pipelining feature that allows up to three requests to be pending at any time. Reply packets are returned in the order requested unless deferred, but requests and replies may be intermixed. For example, two requests may be made, followed by a single reply packet, then another request packet, before being completed by two reply packets.

The AP-Bus consists of 47 bi-directional signals, a clock signal, a RESET signal, and five module support signals which are used to interface system modules to the AP-Bus (see Figure 3). The BXU is the only component that attaches to the AP-Bus.

BXUs connect to each other in the form of a matrix to allow orderly growth in the system by the addition of buses or modules. An 80960MC multiprocessing system allows up to 32 modules and four AP-Buses. In practice, the number of modules in a system will be somewhat less in order to meet the AP-Bus's timing and electrical specifications; a practical limit may be 20 to 25 connections to an AP-Bus. Table 3 contains a summary of the functions of the AP-Bus Interface Registers.

Table 2. Types of AP-Bus Operations

Packet Type	Base Action	Specific Operation
Request	Write	Write Word(s)
		RMW Write Word(s)
	Read	Read Word(s)
		RMW Read Word(s)
Reply	Accepted	Read Reply Word(s)
		Acknowledge (Write Reply)
	Refused	Reissue
		Not Acknowledged (NACK)
		Bad Access

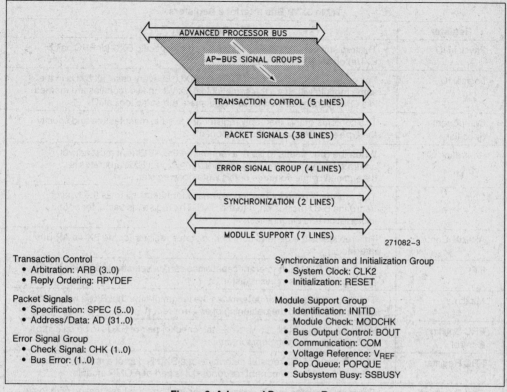

271082-3

Transaction Control
- Arbitration: ARB (3..0)
- Reply Ordering: RPYDEF

Packet Signals
- Specification: SPEC (5..0)
- Address/Data: AD (31..0)

Error Signal Group
- Check Signal: CHK (1..0)
- Bus Error: (1..0)

Synchronization and Initialization Group
- System Clock: CLK2
- Initialization: RESET

Module Support Group
- Identification: INITID
- Module Check: MODCHK
- Bus Output Control: BOUT
- Communication: COM
- Voltage Reference: V_{REF}
- Pop Queue: POPQUE
- Subsystem Busy: SSBUSY

Figure 3. Advanced Processor Bus

M82965

ADVANCE INFORMATION

Table 3. AP-Bus Interface Registers

Register	Description
Physical ID	This register contains a unique identifier for a specific BXU (or FRC pair of BXUs) on an AP-Bus.
Logical ID	This register holds the logical ID for the BXU. In every case, all BXUs in the same module will share the same logical ID. When two modules are married in a QMR configuration, they will also share the same logical ID.
Component Specifier	The contents of this read-only register are fixed at manufacture and specify the type and stepping of the component.
Arbitration ID	When the BXU needs to issue a request on the AP-Bus, it must actively arbitrate for the bus. The time and order in which a BXU arbitrates is determined by the contents of this write-only register.
Com	This register is used for loading external information, such as the type of board the BXU resides on, into the BXU. The register is useful for both initialization and diagnostics.
AP-Bus Control	This register is the general control and status register for the BXU's AP-Bus interface.
FT1	Most of the BXU fault-tolerant capabilities can be selectively enabled by altering control bits in this register.
Maxtime	The value in this register determines the length of time that BXUs will remain quiescent following the beginning of an error report.
FRC Splitting Control	Writing to this register allows a master/checker pair of BXUs to be split into separately functioning components.
FRC Register	The contents of this register determine of a BXU is part of a master/checker pair and how the component responds if it is part of a QMR module.
Test Detection	Bits in this register enable parity logic and other internal self testing diagnostic features.
AP Match	Bits in this register are compared against the corresponding bits in the AP-Bus address cycle and determine which partition of the address space is recognized by this BXU.
AP Mask	If a bit in this register is cleared, it will cause the corresponding bit position in the Address Match register to be ignored during comparisons.

Memory addressing over the AP-Bus is divided into 16-byte blocks. The location of a bus transaction is defined by a 32-bit address. Each address points to a single byte that is part of a larger 16-byte block. All transactions are performed on a single block or portion of a block, and do not overlap multiple blocks.

Modes of Operation

The BXU operates in either Processor or Memory mode. Processor mode provides support for Active or Active/Passive modules, while Memory mode supports Passive modules. The functions of several BXU signals are dependent on the operating mode of the BXU.

In Processor mode, the BXU supports cache, I/O prefetch and IAC message functions. The BXU can act as either a master or slave on the L-Bus and requests can flow in either direction between the AP-Bus and the L-Bus. The assumption is, however, that most traffic will flow from the L-Bus out onto the AP-Bus. In a processor-only module, there is no need for the BXU to participate in arbitration for the L-Bus, since it will operate only as a slave.

In Memory mode, the BXU always operates as a master on the L-Bus and no requests are ever accepted from the L-Bus. All requests flow from the AP-Bus into the module. In this mode, the BXU supports memory functions and signaling, but does not provide caching or I/O prefetch.

Read-Modify-Write Transactions

Read-Modify-Write (RMW) operations are provided to give BXUs the ability to read and modify a location as a single indivisible action. A RMW-Read operation initiates the indivisible action by asserting the LOCK signal on the L-bus. A RMW-Write operation is used to terminate the action.

When an RMW-Read transaction occurs, the block of memory addressed is marked by the BXU controlling that portion of memory as locked (the lock covers a fixed address space based on address bits 4 and 6). Once locked, any other RMW-Reads to this block will be rejected, but the block remains available for other types of memory operations.

When an RMW-Read is issued, the BXU controlling the affected memory will either respond with data in a normal Read Reply (and set the appropriate lock), or it will respond with a Reissue Reply indicating that the requested block is already locked. If refused, the requesting BXU will wait a short interval and then put the RMW-Read request back into the arbitration process and try again.

RMW-Writes are equivalent to Write Word(s) except that it resets the lock for that memory location. The only valid reply packet is the Ack (Write Reply).

Interagent Communications (IAC) Support

Bus Extension Units and 80960MC processors communicate by sending Interagent Communication (IAC) messages, which are a set of memory-mapped addresses recognized by all BXUs. These messages are used for such system functions as initialization, cache flushing, access to error logs and interrupts. The upper 16 Mbytes of the 80960MC's 4 Gigabyte address range are reserved for IAC communications.

IAC requests fall into two major groups: messages and register requests. Messages are sent between processors to cause a processor to perform a specific action (e.g., start, stop, flush cache, etc.) and are held in the IAC message support registers; Table 4 summarizes the function of these four registers. Register requests are used by software to read and write to BXU registers in order to control the system operation or configuration.

An IAC message always originates on an L-Bus and usually from a processor. From the originator, the request flows to the BXU where it may be handled internally or propagated on to the AP-Bus. If the IAC is sent on to the AP-Bus, the final destination of the IAC (another BXU) must reside on that bus. The IAC will not be propagated onto another L-Bus or AP-Bus. IAC messages can be one to four words long.

Although each L-Bus (processor or memory module) may be connected to as many as four AP-Buses, at any point in time only one bus will be designated as the message bus. All IAC messages will flow over that bus. The BXUs on the message bus are responsible for handling the IAC message traffic on behalf of the processors residing on their L-Bus (an L-Bus may support one or two processors).

AP-Bus 0 normally serves as the message bus. If AP-Bus 0 is not functional, then AP-Bus 1 serves as the message bus, completely transparent to the software. Processors are unaware of which bus is actually acting as the message bus.

I/O Prefetch Support

The BXU offers two I/O prefetch channels to provide high bandwidth, low latency access to memory for sequential transfers. Each channel buffers 32 bytes of data in two 16-byte blocks. As data is requested from the buffers, the BXU automatically prefetches the next data block. The BXU can take

Table 4. IAC Support Registers

Register	Description
Processor 0 Priority	This register holds the priority of the task (process) which Processor 0 on the BXU's L-Bus is currently executing.
Processor 0 Message	This register buffers four words of data from an IAC message for Processor 0.
Processor 1 Priority	This register holds the priority of the task (process) which Processor 1 on the BXU's L-Bus is currently executing.
Processor 1 Message	This register buffers four words of data from an IAC message for Processor 1.

advantage of the three-deep AP-Bus pipeline to quickly fill the buffers if it ever gets behind because of momentary surges in AP-Bus traffic. In this way, the prefetch logic acts to provide stable, bounded response times, even in large multiprocessor configurations.

Because the normal operation of the BXU hides the latency of write requests by replying immediately on the L-Bus, the prefetch unit operates only for read requests. On a read request from the L-Bus, the prefetch logic returns the amount of data requested. Any processor or intelligent device used with the BXU must guarantee that it will split all memory requests that cross 16-byte boundaries into two requests.

Cache Support

The main function of a cache is to provide local high speed storage for frequently accessed memory locations. Storing the information locally, the cache intercepts memory references and handles them directly without transferring the request to the AP-Bus. This action results in lower traffic on the AP-Bus and decreased latency on the L-Bus, leading to improved performance for a processor on the L-Bus. It also increases potential system performance in a multiprocessor system by reducing each processor's demand for AP-Bus bandwidth, thereby allowing more processors in a system.

The BXU provides cache directory, coherency logic, and control signals, while external SRAM is used for data storage. A CACHE signal output from the 80960MC processor indicates to the BXU whether a request is cacheable. The operation of the BXU cache is not dependent on the size of the data transfer and therefore can support partial writes. Both data and instructions can be contained within the local cache.

The BXU supports a two-way, set associative cache with 256 sets. The (read address) tag field is 20 bits long and consists of LAD lines 31–12. There are eight bits that indicate if a line is valid (a line is 16 bytes). The control bits in the cache control registers can be used to mask some of these bits to change cache configurations. All entries in the directory can be invalidated by sending an INVALIDATE CACHE Command to each BXU in the module. Figure 4 shows one example of a BXU cache directory and its relation to L-Bus addresses.

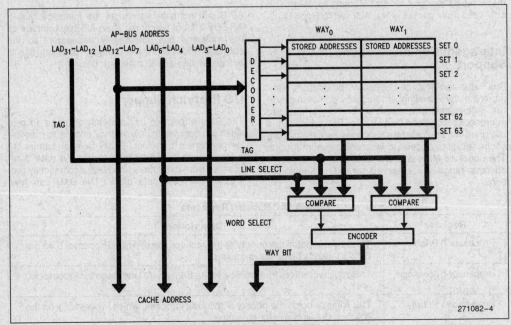

Figure 4. Example of a Cache Directory Array

A single BXU supports 64 Kbytes of cache. When a processor module uses multiple BXUs (and therefore multiple buses), the BXUs cooperate to provide a larger directory and addressing for a larger cache. The best way to view this larger directory is to think of it as having an increased number of sets. Thus a cache managed by two BXUs will have a directory consisting of 512 sets instead of 256. The maximum size cache is 256 Kbytes (four BXUs supporting four AP-Buses per processor module).

The cache is managed using a write-through policy that guarantees that the shared system memory will always have the most recent copy of all data; BXU caches never contain the only copy of revised data. Any time a processor updates a cache entry, it always causes a write request on the AP-Bus, so that there are never any hidden updates. In addition, all BXUs monitor AP-Bus traffic to detect if an update is being made to a location which they are storing in their own cache. If so, that line in the cache directory is marked invalid. This procedure guarantees that a BXU cache will always return correct data even when a system uses multiple caches, when multiple processors treat a single data item differently (some caching, some not), or when two processors are used on a single L-Bus.

An example of an SRAM control design using a single BXU is shown in Figure 5. The BXU supplies six memory control signals to interface the directory and control logic with an external cache composed of static RAM: Cache Read ($\overline{CR}$), Cache Write ($\overline{CW}$), Way0 ($\overline{WY0}$), Way1 ($\overline{WY1}$), Word0 ($\overline{WD0}$), and Word1 ($\overline{WD1}$). SRAM control also requires use of the L-Bus byte enable ($\overline{BE3}-\overline{BE0}$) signals and certain address lines. To simplify latching the byte enable signals, the BXU asserts $\overline{READY}$ on all address and recovery cycles as well as when it is transferring data.

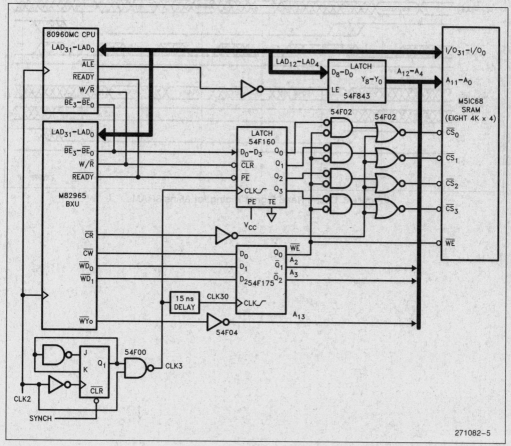

Figure 5. Sample Cache SRAM Control Design Using a BXU

271082–5

M82965

The tight timing specifications of SRAMs require a small amount of external logic to interface a static RAM cache to a BXU. Since all BXU cache signals have a relatively wide clock to data valid specification (T_{cd}), external flip-flops are used to achieve tighter resolution of the Cache Write and Word edges. The address bits are latched using ALE from the processor. Way0 selects between the two "ways" in the cache directory, and Way1 selects between the cache and private memory (if present on the L-Bus).

In order to ensure that the cache is filled properly, the byte enable latch is cleared on read requests. If the processor made a read request for two bytes that missed the cache, the BXU would first write the entire 16-byte block, then return the requested information to the processor. If the byte enable latches weren't set, then the write into the cache wouldn't work correctly because not all byte enables would be asserted. Byte enable information does not need to be held on reads because data is always returned in full words and the processor selects the portion of the word that it needs internally. Signal timings are shown in Figures 6–10.

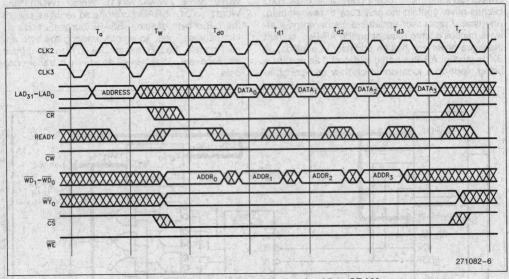

Figure 6. Cache Read Signal Timing for 35 ns SRAMs

271082–6

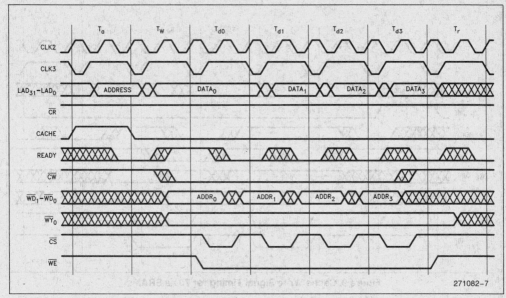

Figure 7. Cache Write Signal Timing for 35 ns SRAMs

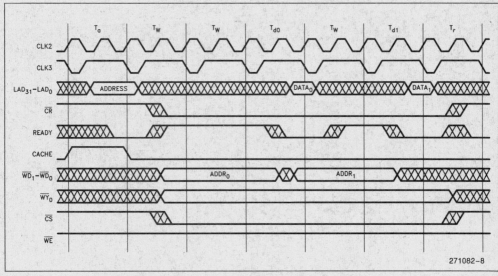

Figure 8. Cache Read Signal Timing for 70 ns SRAMs

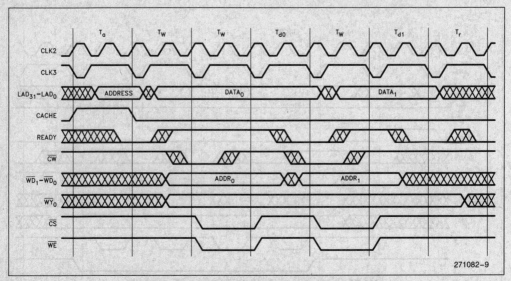

Figure 9. Cache Write Signal Timing for 70 ns SRAMs

271082-9

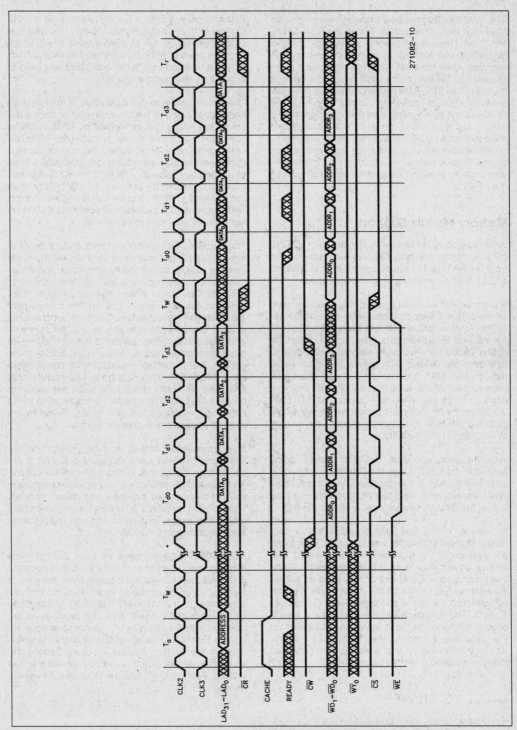

Figure 10. Cache Signal Timing for a 4-Word Read with a Cache Fill for 35 ns SRAMs

The BXU has four memory address recognizers for the L-Bus plus an additional recognizer for initialization RAM. Three of the memory address recognizers (Mask2–0 and Match2–0) map to shared system memory, while the fourth address recognizer maps requests to SRAM on the local bus, called private memory. The INIT-RAM recognizer serves two functions: it enables bootstrap software to use the SRAM cache as a scratch pad during system initialization, and it provides the means for executing a memory test on the SRAM cache. The private memory recognizer allows SRAM to be used on the local bus as normal memory in addition to a cache. Private memory is not accessable by other modules on the AP-Bus.

Memory Module Support

When operating in Memory mode, the BXU is a Local Bus master and only handles requests inbound from the AP-Bus. The cache control logic is disabled since it is unnecessary in a memory module.

A read request received by an idle BXU will be seen on the L-Bus 1.5 clock cycles after it was received on the AP-Bus. BXUs offer two reply speed options for inbound Read requests. The high-performance option, called the "fast reply" mode, allows data to flow onto the AP-Bus with only a half-cycle delay through the BXU. This option requires the L-Bus memory controller to be able to supply data on every clock cycle. In the "slow reply" mode, the BXU buffers the entire AP-Bus reply packet before sending it onto the AP-Bus. This option permits the use of slower, less costly memory.

Write requests are fully buffered before being passed to the L-Bus. Once the BXU has received an error-free packet, it initiates the L-Bus transaction. When the last data word has been accepted on the L-Bus, the BXU generates a reply on the AP-Bus.

In memory mode, the BXU provides two or four Ready-Modify-Write locks with timeouts. Four locks are available if the module is not interleaved with other modules, two locks if it is interleaved. When interleaving occurs, address bit 4 is used as part of the address recognition for the module, which thereby restricts a module to use either locks 0 and 2, or 1 and 3. This approach ensures that if a bus switch occurs, the locks that may have been allocated on the failed bus will not overlap with locks that are currently allocated on the surviving bus (since all traffic is rerouted to the surviving bus).

FAULT TOLERANCE

Three basic tenets form the basis for the implementation of 80960MC fault tolerant systems. First, fault tolerant functions are achieved through the replication of VLSI components. Second, the system is partitioned into a set of confinement areas which form the basis of error detection and recovery. Third, only bus-oriented communication paths are used to provide system communication.

The BXU is unique in that it provides all the functions necessary to detect, isolate, and recover from a failure in any single system module or AP-Bus. Unlike many other fault tolerant system designs, 80960MC systems do not rely on voter components for fault detection, thereby eliminating one potential source of single-point failures. Although the BXU registers must be initialized by software, all the fault tolerant mechanisms are built into the hardware, and correct fault recovery of a system built using the BXU does not depend on software intervention.

The purpose of a confinement area is to inhibit damage from error propagation and to isolate the faulty area for subsequent recovery and repair. A confinement area is defined as a unit (system module or AP-Bus) that has a limited number of tightly controlled interfaces. Figure 11 shows the confinement areas within a small system. Detection mechanisms exist at every interface to ensure that no inconsistent data can leave the confinement area and corrupt other confinement areas. When a fault occurs in the system, it is immediately isolated to a confinement area. The fault is known to be in that confinement area, and all other confinement areas are known to be fault-free. All intermodule communication in an 80960MC system occurs over buses. There are no point-to-point or daisy-chained signals.

This arrangement makes modular growth and on-line repair possible since no signal definition is dependent on the number of resources in the system. The presence or absence of any module cannot prevent communication between any other modules. The AP-Bus provides a uniform communications matrix that allows multiprocessor and fault-tolerant systems to expand modularly.

In 80960MC systems, there are three distinct steps in responding to an error. First, the error is detected and isolated to a confinement area. Next, the error is reported to all the modules in the system. This action prevents the incorrect data from propagating into another confinement area and provides all the modules with the information required to perform recovery. Finally, the faulty confinement area is isolated from the system. Recovery occurs through the application of redundant resources available in the system. Table 5 describes the fault-tolerant control registers.

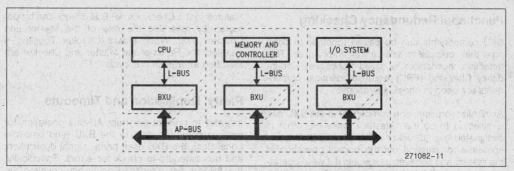

271082–11

Figure 11. Fault Confinement Areas in an 80960MC System

Table 5. Fault Tolerance Support Registers and Commands

Register	Description
Test Type	The Test Report command instructs the BXU to test the error reporting network. The type of error report generated is determined by the content of this register.
Spouse ID	In a QMR module, this register holds the module ID of the FRC module to which this module is married.
QMR	The contents of this register determine if a module is part of a QMR pair, and if it should function as the primary or shadow in the pair.
Module Error ID	Identifies the BXU as part of a specific module confinement area.
Bus Error ID	Determines the Bus ID contents in an error report.
Error Log	Records the type of the most recent error report received and the number of errors that have occurred since the last Terminate Permanant Error Window command.
Error Record	Holds the contents of the previous error report.
FT2	Holds additional fault-tolerant control parameters.
Test Report Command	The Test Report command instructs the BXU to test the error reporting network. The type of error report generated is determined by the contents of the Test Type Register.
Primary Catastrophe Command	A write to this register causes a Primary Catastrophe error report, usually indicating a primary module power failure.
Shadow Catastrophe Command	A write to this register causes a Shadow Catastrophe error report, usually indicating a shadow module power failure.
Terminate Permanent Error Window Command	A write to this register closes the permanent error window, so that a reoccurance of a previous error is not recorded as permanent.
Attach Bus Command	A write to this register causes the identified bus to be attached to the system and become active.
Detach Bus Command	A write to this register causes the identified bus to be detached from the system and become inactive.
Sync Refresh Command	A write to this register causes BXUs in memory mode to assert their ForceRef pin and enables AP-Bus address matching.

Functional Redundancy Checking

BXU components can be paired together to compare their outputs to ensure that they agree. This detection mechanism is called Functional Redundancy Checking (FRC) because identical components are used to check operations.

At initialization time, one component in the BXU pair is selected to be the "Master", while the other is designated the "Checker". The Master BXU is responsible for carrying out the normal operation of the system and behaves as it would if it were operating in a non-fault tolerant system. The Checker BXU, in contrast, disables its AP-Bus outputs and instead monitors the AP-Bus pins of the Master (see Figure 12). The Checker BXU is responsible for duplicating the operation of the Master and using its internal comparison circuitry to detect any inconsistency between its result and the output of the Master.

The Master and Checker BXUs run in lock step, comparing operations cycle-by-cycle. If at any point the Master or Checker disagree, an FRC error will be signaled and an error reporting cycle will begin.

When using the FRC mechanism, the BXU pins comprising the electrical connection to the AP-Bus must be connected together. A BXU provides FRC coverage on the AD, SPEC, BOUT and MODCHK pins.

Failures in the Checker's AP-Bus drivers can be detected by reversing the role of the Master and Checker BXU. When Master/Checker Toggling is enabled, the Roles of the Master and Checker are switched after each bus cycle.

Parity, Duplication and Timeouts

In order to prevent incorrect AP-Bus operation for passing corrupted data to the BXU (and onto the Local Bus), the BXU uses parity, signal duplication, and bus timeouts to check for errors. Specifically, the AP-Bus has interlaced parity bits covering the AD and SPEC signals, signal duplication is used on both arbitration and RPYDEF, and a bus timer is set to monitor the bus for non-response to a request.

The BXU calculates two separate parity bits across alternate AD and SPEC signals, which are indicated by the CHK0 and CHK1 pins. CHK0 is even parity across the even AD and SPEC pins, and CHK1 is even parity across the odd pins. Since the arbitration and RPYDEF lines are driven independently by multiple bus agents (BXUs), parity cannot be used for error detection, rather the detection of errors is done by duplicating each set of lines, one set for Masters, the other set for Checkers. Consequently, each BXU connects to only one arbitration network. If there is a disagreement between the two sets of signals on

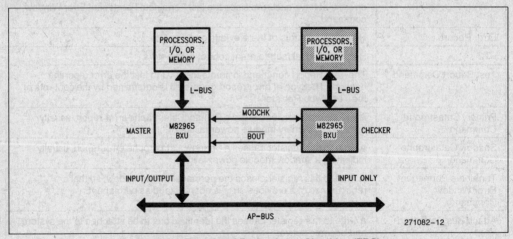

Figure 12. Functional Redundancy Checking (FRC)

the AP-Bus, it will be detected through an FRC disagreement. The BXU uses a timer to determine if no response has been received and too long a period has elapsed since the bus request was made. During normal operation the timer is active whenever the bus pipeline is not empty. The timer is reset on every bus reply or deferral. If the BXU was the source of the requests and a timeout occurs, it signals a Bad Access Reply on the AP-Bus. The timer is nominally 256 clocks.

Error Reporting

The error reporting network is the backbone of fault isolation and recovery. When an error is detected, the BXU detecting the error reports its type and location to all other nodes in the system. The error reporting network is designed so that, independent of an error in the system, each node not only receives an error report, but is guaranteed to receive the same error report. Each BXU in the system uniformly logs each error report, and is able to use this information to proceed independently with the appropriate recovery procedure.

The BXU has two serial Error Reporting Lines associated with each bus interface (BERLs for the AP-Bus and LERLs for the Local Bus). An indentical serial error report is sent over each pair of lines associated with each bus.

An AP-Bus error reporting cycle consists of five phases: Reporting, Partner Communications, Transient Waiting Period, Retry, and the Permanent Error Window (see Figure 13). The reporting phase lasts 256 cycles from the beginning of the first report received on the BXU's error reporting lines. The BXU becomes quiescent as soon as it detects the start bit of an error report and remains quiescent through the Transient Waiting Period.

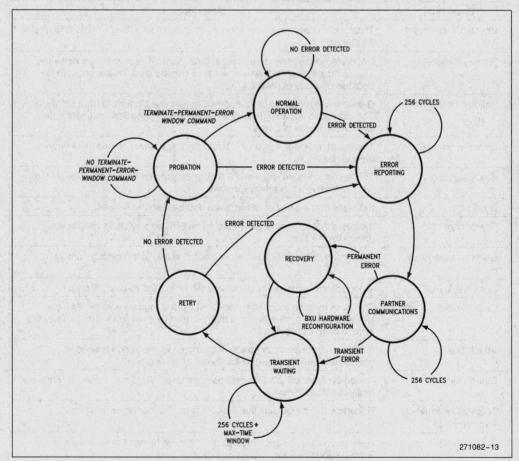

271082–13

Figure 13. Error Reporting Cycle

During partner communications, BXUs communicate with each other via their POPQUE lines to determine whether to retry accesses in the case that one of the AP-Buses is removed from the system. Partner ordering lasts 256 cycles.

Transient waiting enables the system to sustain disturbances from mechanical vibrations and brief electrical transients without needing to permanently reconfigure the system. The BXUs simply wait a predetermined time for the transient to subside. The duration of the Transient Waiting Period is adjustable and can be set by software (16 μs to 500 ms at 16 MHz). During this period, the BXU completes its internal recovery mechanisms (if the error is permanent). Since the transient waiting mechanism on the buses depends on all buses moving to the retry state at the same time, all BXUs must have identical values for the Transient Waiting Period.

During the RETRY phase, all accesses that were pending at the time that the error report was received will be retried. At the same time as RETRY begins, the BXU enters the Permanent Error Window. During this interval, the BXU watches for the error to reoccur.

Each BXU has two registers that are used for logging error reports. The ERROR LOG register contains the current error report and the ERROR RECORD register contains the previous error report. When a error report is received, the contents of the ERROR LOG register are copied into the ERROR RECORD register. Both registers are accessible by software and are the primary means by which the software routines responsible for system management communicate with the hardware fault handling mechanisms. Table 6 lists the types of errors that can be reported.

Table 6. Error Types Reported

Error Type	Description
Unsafe Confinement Area	This type of report is issued when an error is detected that would make a retry dangerous.
Primary Catastophe	Generated in response to a Primary Catastrophe Command from software. The command is usually issued when all primary modules are about to fail because of a loss of power.
Shadow Catastophe	Generated in response to a Shadow Catastrophe Command from software. The command is usually issued when all shadow modules are about to fail because of a loss of power.
Error Reporting Error	The report indicates that a BXU has detected a failure on one of its error reporting lines.
Bus Arbitration	This report is issued when an FRC error is detected on the $\overline{\text{BOUT}}$ pin of the BXU indicating a bus arbitration error.
Bus Parity	Indicates that a parity error has been detected on the AP-Bus.
Component	Indicates that a checker has detected an FRC error while its master was driving the AP-Bus.
Uncorrectable Array Error	An uncorrectable error has been detected in one of the memory arrays.
Correctable ECC	A correctable error has been detected in one of the memory arrays.
COM Altered	This error report occurs when the COM input is toggled (two cycles high, followed by two cycles low) and may be used by external circuits to notify the system of an external fault.
Attach Bus	Issued in response to an Attach Bus command, this report is used to reactivate a bus that was previously out of service.
Detach Bus	Issued in response to a Detach Bus command, this report is used to remove a faulty bus from the system.
Terminate Permanent Error Window	Receiving this report signifies the end of the Permanent Error Window.
Sync Refresh	Used to synchronize memory modules that are being married to form a Primary/Shadow Pair.

The BXU's hardware compares the contents of the two error reporting registers to determine if a bus retry has resulted in a repeat of the previous error (which therefore must be considered a permanent error). Software can clear the two registers by sending a Terminate Permanent Error Window command. The registers allow software to monitor the health of the system and to respond appropriately in case of hardware problems. The availability of this information simplifies diagnostic routines.

The ERROR LOG register is handled independently by hardware and software; hardware always responds immediately to an error report so that it is never lost by failure of software to respond. During normal system operation, software should never write to this register, since it is both read and written by hardware. The ERROR LOG register is cleared on a cold start, but its contents are retained across a warm start.

RECOVERY MECHANISMS

Module Shadowing

Automatic recovery from permanent single-point failures in a module is accomplished through module shadowing, or what is more formally called Quad Modular Redundancy (QMR). Using this technique, two FRC pairs (master/checker) of the same type are logically linked to form a primary/shadow pair (see Figure 14). The marriage of the two modules is performed by software which sets the logical ID of the two modules equal and restarts them in lock step (or synchronous operation). There is no direct electrical connection between a primary/shadow pair. They are usually on separate boards so that either can be removed in the case of a failure in that module.

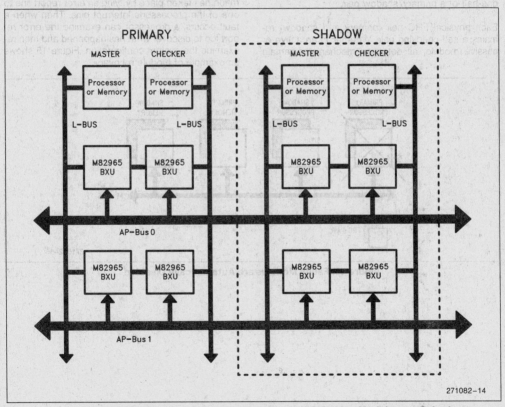

Figure 14. In Quad Modular Redundancy (QMR), Self-Checking Modules are Paired

The primary/shadow pair operate in lock step so that there is always a complete and current backup for an FRC pair. At any point in time, one FRC pair will be active (i.e., sending its output to the AP-Bus) while the other will be passive (i.e., its outputs will be disabled). Initially, the primary FRC pair is active and is responsible for issuing requests or replies to the AP-Bus. Data leaves only by means of the active FRC pair.

As an option, the roles of active and passive modules are switched after every second bus cycle. (In contrast, master/checker pairs are toggled every cycle). This ping-pong action exercises all of the logic in both primary and shadow modules. Any latent failure that exists in the AP-Bus drivers will be detected immediately. All of the logic to perform this lock step operation is contained in the BXU and neither the processors nor any discrete logic contained in a module is aware that the module is participating as one-half of a primary/shadow pair.

Each physical FRC pair (primary and shadow) remains a self-checking pair. Whether in an active or passive module, all detection mechanisms remain enabled and continuously check the operation of that module. Neither the primary nor the shadow check the operation of the other; FRC is used for fault detection, while module shadowing (Quad Modular Redundancy) is used to ensure immediate recovery.

Automatic Module Recovery

If a permanent error is detected in either a primary or a shadow FRC pair, the faulty pair will immediately be disabled as all BXUs in the pair shutdown. The surviving spouse then separates itself from the faulty FRC pair and operates as an active pair on every bus cycle. At that point, recovery is complete.

Hardware recovery is autonomous and requires no software intervention to complete. The operating system can be informed that a hardware reconfiguration has taken place by tying an error report line to one of the processor's interrupt pins. Then when a fault occurs, a processor can examine the error report log to discover what has happened and then re-examine the system configuration. Figure 15 shows an example of module recovery.

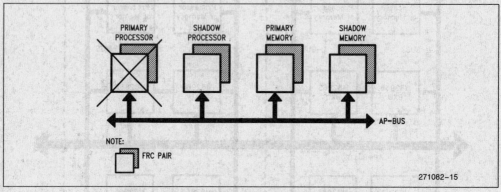

Figure 15. Faulty Modules are Automatically Disabled

Bus Switching

All AP-Buses in an 80960MC system are physically identical, but when a system is operational each bus handles a unique address range. The BXU has been designed so that it is possible to pair together two AP-Busses and have them act as redundant or alternate resources for each other. AP-Bus 0 is paired with AP-Bus 1 and AP-Bus 2 is paired with AP-Bus 3. In order for an FRC pair to have an additional bus, it must also have another pair of Master/Checker BXUs. Normally the memory addresses will be interleaved between the two (or four) buses, but this isn't necessary for bus switching.

Since the AP-Bus does not hold state information (as do processors and memory), all buses in the sys-

tem may be used during normal operation. There is no degradation of throughput to achieve bus redundancy. Each bus is fully operational.

When a permanent error has been detected on an AP-Bus, all BXUs on the faulty bus disable themselves. L-Bus requests for the failed bus will be ignored by the disabled BXUs and picked up instead by the BXUs attached to the backup bus. If a BXU has a cache, the BXU invalidates its cache directory since the directory must be reorganized to match the new (and larger) address space, including a new interleaving factor. Figure 16 shows an example of bus switching.

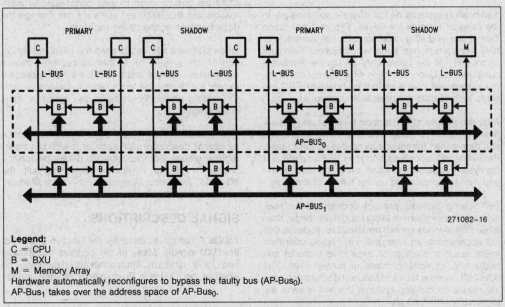

Legend:
C = CPU
B = BXU
M = Memory Array
Hardware automatically reconfigures to bypass the faulty bus (AP-Bus₀).
AP-Bus₁ takes over the address space of AP-Bus₀.

271082–16

Figure 16. If a Bus Fails, Its Backup Bus Takes Over Immediately

Self-Healing Systems

In some applications it is important to guarantee the integrity of the data, but momentary interruptions in processing can occur without seriously affecting operations or jeopardizing human lives. For these applications, a cost effective approach may be to use self-healing systems.

Self-healing systems use Functional Redundancy Checking to ensure that all errors are detected and that faults are confined within a module. Fault recovery is not automatic; recovery and reconfiguration is done by software following error detection. Self-healing systems are less costly than fully fault-tolerant systems because fewer components are necessary.

Self-healing systems do not operate continuously in the case of a hardware failure. Program execution cannot proceed after detection of a permanent error until the system has been reconfigured. Transient errors will still be taken care of by the hardware components. Upon detection of a permanent error, the system will cease operation, however FRC ensures that no data will have been corrupted.

After the system stops, it must be reset and a diagnostic program run which reads the BXU errors logs and determines the most appropriate action to take. Recovery and reconfiguration may be complete and the system back on-line within a few seconds to several minutes, depending on the nature of the fault.

Self-healing systems are not appropriate for real-time applications where program delays longer than a few milliseconds cannot be tolerated. In these critical applications, an interruption in system operation might result in damage to expensive material and equipment, or endangerment of human lives. The 80960MC system fault tolerant architecture provides the means for building systems that will recover automatically within 48 μs.

BXU Registers

Initialization and control of the BXU is done by reading and writing the BXU's internal registers. The registers are mapped to the upper 16 Mbytes of the 80960MC processor's physical address space.

Initialization of a system using BXUs occurs in three stages. In the first stage which immediately follows RESET, all registers (except for the registers containing error report information) are loaded with 0 or with values sampled off a set of pins.

During this stage the BXU's System Bus ID and mode of operation are established. In the second stage, software assigns logical, physical, and arbitration IDs to each BXU. Then in the third stage, the COM pin can be used to load board-specific information into the BXU and software can change the default values of any of the registers.

Once software has established the initial configuration of the system, no further interaction between the system software and the BXU may be necessary except for testing the error reporting functions and for making on-line changes to the system's initial configuration.

This Advance Information Data Sheet contains a functional description for each of the BXU's major register groups. For more specific details on controlling each of the registers, please consult the *80960MC Hardware Designer's Reference Manual.*

SIGNAL DESCRIPTIONS

Tables 7 through 11 describe the function of each of the BXU signals. Many of the pins are multiplexed and have different interpretations depending on whether the BXU is in Processor or Memory mode.

Table 7. M82965 BXU L-Bus Signals

Symbol	Type	Name and Function
LAD_{31} –LAD_0	I/O T.S.	**LOCAL ADDRESS/DATA BUS:** Carries 32-bit physical addresses and data to and from a processor or memory. During an address (T_a) cycle, bits 2–31 contain a physical word addres (bits 0–1 indicate SIZE; see below). During a data (T_d) cycle, bits 0–31 contain read or write data. The LAD lines are active HIGH and float to a three-state OFF when the bus is not acquired. **SIZE:** Which is comprised of bits 0–1 of the LAD bus during a T_a cycle, specifies the size of a transfer in words. LAD_1 LAD_0 0 0 1 Word 0 1 2 Words 1 0 3 Words 1 1 4 Words
$\overline{ALE}$	O T.S.	**ADDRESS-LATCH ENABLE:** Indicates the transfer of a physical address. $\overline{ALE}$ is asserted during a T_a cycle, and deasserted during T_d cycles and the second half of T_a cycles. It is active LOW and floats to a three-state OFF when the L-Bus is not acquired.
$\overline{ADS}$	I/O O.D.	**ADDRESS STATUS:** Is used to detect address cycles and additional data cycles.
CACHE	I	**CACHEABLE:** During a T_a cycle, specifies whether data is cacheable. **When operating in the MEMORY mode this pin should be tied to ground through a 10 kΩ resistor.**
W/$\overline{R}$	I/O O.D.	**WRITE/READ:** specifies, during a T_a cycle, whether the operation is a write or read. It is latched on-chip and remains valid during T_d cycles.
$\overline{CW}/\overline{DEN}$	O O.D.	**CACHE WRITE:** (Defined only when the BXU is in PROCESSOR mode). This signal indicates that the cache SRAM should be written with data from the L-Bus and is used to generate the chip select, and write enable signals required by the SRAM. The signal is open drain so it can be shared among multiple BXUs controlling a single set of SRAMs. **DATA ENABLE:** (Defined only when the BXU is in MEMORY mode). Is asserted during T_D cycles and indicates transfer of data on the local AD bus lines.
$\overline{CR}/$ DT/$\overline{R}$	O O.D.	**CACHE READ:** (Defined only when the BXU is in PROCESSOR mode). This signal indicates that the cache SRAM should drive data onto the L-Bus in response to a read request and is used to generate the chip select and output enable signals required by the SRAM. This signal is open drain so it can be shared among multiple BXUs controlling a single cache. **DATA TRANSMIT/RECEIVE:** (Defined only when the BXU is in MEMORY mode). Indicates the direction of data transfer. It is low during T_a and T_d cycles for a read or interrupt acknowledgement; it is high during T_a and T_d cycles for a write. DT/$\overline{R}$ never changes state when $\overline{DEN}$ is asserted.
$\overline{LOCK}$	I	**BUS LOCK:** Is used by the BXU to distinguish between normal reads and RMW-reads, normal writes and RMW-writes. An 80960MC processor asserts $\overline{LOCK}$ at the beginning of an RMW cycle, and the BXU recognizes it as an RMW-read. If the read operation is accepted by the module serving memory, the processor drops $\overline{LOCK}$, and executes an RMW-write. $\overline{LOCK}$ is also held asserted during an interrupt-acknowledge transaction.
$\overline{READY}$	I/O O.D	**READY:** Indicates that data on LAD lines can be sampled or removed. If $\overline{READY}$ is not asserted during a T_d cycle, the T_d cycle is extended to the next cycle, and $\overline{ADS}$ is not asserted in the next cycle. $\overline{READY}$ is driven on T_a, T_r and T_i cycles.

NOTES:
I/O = Input/Output, I = Input, O = Output, O.D. = Open Drain, T.S. = three-state

Table 7. M82965 BXU L-Bus Signals (Continued)

Symbol	Type	Name and Function
$\overline{BE_3}-$ $\overline{BE_0}$	I/O O.D.	**BYTE ENABLES:** Specify which data bytes on the local bus will take part in the next bus cycle. $\overline{BE_3}$ corresponds to $LAD_{24}-LAD_{31}$ and $\overline{BE_0}$ corresponds to LAD_0-LAD_7.
HOLD/ HOLDAR	I	**HOLD:** Indicates that a master I/O peripheral requests control of the bus. When the BXU receives HOLD and grants the peripheral control of the bus, it floats the bus lines and then asserts HLDA and enters the T_h state. When HOLD is deasserted, the BXU will deassert HLDA and go to either the T_i or T_a state. **HOLD ACKNOWLEDGE REQUEST:** Is an input to the secondary bus master that the primary bus master has relinquished control of the bus.
HLDA/ HOLDR	O	**HOLD ACKNOWLEDGE:** Relinquishes control of the bus to a master I/O peripheral. **HOLD REQUST:** Is used by a Secondary Bus Master to request use of the bus from the Primary Bus Master.

Table 8. M82965 BXU L-Bus Module Support Signals

Symbol	Type	Name and Function
$\overline{BADAC}$	O O.D.	**BAD ACCESS:** If asserted in the cycle following the one in which the last $\overline{READY}$ of a transaction is asserted as a result of a bad access, it indicates that the transaction has exceeded the AP-Bus time-out period.
$\overline{IAC_0}/\overline{ERR}$	I/O O.D.	**INTERAGENT COMMUNICATION: PROCESSOR 0:** (Defined only when the BXU is in PROCESSOR mode). Is an open-drain output that indicates that there is a pending IAC message for Processor 0 on the BXU's local bus. **EXTERNAL ERROR:** (Defined only when the BXU is in MEMORY mode). Is an input that indicates that an error has been detected in external logic (e.g., a failure in a discrete memory controller).
$\overline{IAC_1}/\overline{FRF}$	O O.D.	**INTERAGENT COMMUNICATION: PROCESSOR 1:** (Defined only when the BXU is in PROCESSOR mode). Is an open-drain output that indicates that there is a pending IAC message for Processor 1 on the BXU's local bus. **FORCE REFRESH:** (Defined only when the BXU is in memory mode). Is an open-drain output that tells the external memory controller to immediately execute a refresh operation.
$\overline{PFETCH}$	I	**PREFETCH:** Is used in conjunction with the Cache and Write/Read ($W/\overline{R}$) signals to define the type of request being issued (0 = LO, 1 = HI):

$\overline{PFETCH}$	CACHE	$W/\overline{R}$	
0	0	0	Read using Prefetch Channel 0
0	0	1	Start for Prefetch Channel 0
0	1	0	Read using Prefetch Channel 1
0	1	1	Start for Prefetch Channel 1
1	0	0	Noncacheable Read
1	0	1	Noncacheable Write
1	1	0	Cacheable Read
1	1	1	Cacheable Write

NOTES:
I/O = Input/Output, I = Input, O = Output, O.D. = Open Drain

Table 9. M82965 BXU AP-Bus Signals

Symbol	Type	Name and Function
$\overline{AD}_{31}-\overline{AD}_0$	I/O O.D.	**SYSTEM ADDRESS/DATA LINES:** Carry 32-bit addresses and data between modules (BXUs) on an AP-Bus. The content of the AD lines is defined by the SPEC encoding during the same bus cycle.
$\overline{SPEC}_5-\overline{SPEC}_0$	I/O O.D.	**PACKET SPECIFICATION:** Signals define the packet type and the parameters required for the transaction: $SPEC_5$: **REQUEST:** Is asserted if the packet is a request packet. $SPEC_4$: **MULTICYCLE:** Is asserted if the packet consists of more than one bus cycle. $SPEC_3-SPEC_2$: **CYCLE COUNT:** These two bits are used in conjunction with Request and Multicycle signals to specify the length of the packet (in bus cycles) and the data length (in words). $SPEC_1-SPEC_0$: **OPERATION/STATUS TYPE:** These two bits identify the specific operation or status conveyed by the packet.
$\overline{CHK}_1-\overline{CHK}_0$	I/O O.D.	**CHECK SIGNALS:** Provide interlaced parity for the $\overline{SPEC}$ and $\overline{AD}$ lines.
$\overline{ARB}_3-\overline{ARB}_0$	I/O O.D.	**ARBITRATION:** Signals are used by the bus agents (BXUs) to determine which agent has access to the bus next. These signals have a timing that is one-half cycle out of phase with the $\overline{AD}$ lines.
$\overline{RPYDEF}$	I/O O.D.	**REPLY DEFER:** Signal allows an agent to give up its "slot" on the bus temporarily if its access is going to take a long time. This action reorders the pipeline, moving the deferred request to the bottom of the queue, resets the bus time-out counter and permits another agent to use the bus.
$\overline{BERL}_1-\overline{BERL}_0$	I/O O.D.	**BUS ERROR REPORT LINES:** Is used to signal errors from bus transactions or from within modules connected to the bus.

NOTES:
I/O = Input/Output, I = Input, O = Output, O.D. = Open Drain

Table 10. M82965 BXU AP-Bus (Local Agent) Support Signals

Symbol	Type	Name and Function
CLK2	I	**SYSTEM CLOCK:** Provides the base timing and synchronization for all agents (BXUs) in the system. It is sourced to all agents from a central clock and is twice the frequency of the bus cycle. **NOTE:** The clock skew over the AP-Bus for a typical system should be no greater than 6 ns for correct system operation.
BOUT	I/O O.D.	**BUS OUTPUT CONTROL:** Is asserted whenever a component is driving the AP-Bus. Functional Redundancy Checks on BOUT can be used to detect arbitration failures.
MODCHK	I/O O.D.	**MODULE CHECK:** Is connected between Master/Checker pairs, allowing a Functional Redundancy Check to be performed on internal states.
INITID	I	**INITIALIZE ID:** Is connected to one of the 32 AD lines and is used in conjunction with the IDENTIFY DEVICE IAC to provide a unique address for each BXU at initialization time.
V_{REF}	I	**VOLTAGE REFERENCE:** Provides a stable voltage reference for the input buffers of components connected to the AP-Bus. External hardware must provide a V_{REF}/W voltage (see Table 14) on the V_{REF} pin during normal operation of the component. The V_{REF} pin is also used to distinguish between a warm start (system memory and the Error Record register retain their state) and a cold start (system memory and BXU registers are cleared).
RESET	I	**RESET:** Forces all agents on the bus to reset and synchronize. The bus cycle begins the first CLK2 period after RESET is deasserted. The RESET signal is the way a BXU is synchronized to the rest of the system.
COM	I/O O.D.	**COMMUNICATION:** Can be used to load information into a component as part of the initialization sequence or to inform external logic that the component has failed. The BXU will asserted COM if it has shut itself off due to a failure in its module. The COM signal is not involved in any aspect of AP-Bus operation, but can be used to load board-dependent information into the BXU or to signal the rest of the system that an external error has occurred.

NOTES:
I/O = Input/Output, I = Input, O = Output, O.D. = Open Drain

Table 11. M82965 BXU Module Support Signals

Symbol	Type	Name and Function
$\overline{WY_0}/\overline{COR}$	O O.D.	**WAY$_0$:** (When the BXU is in processor mode). Indicates which one of the two "ways" in a directory set had a cache hit. The line is intended to drive the SRAM address pins and will remain stable throughout the length of a cache access. **CORRECT:** (When the BXU is in memory mode). Is used by the BXU to tell an external ECC controller to correct the memory data as it flows onto the local bus. If this signal is not asserted, then the memory data may flow directly onto the local bus with only error checking, but no correction.
$\overline{WY_1}/\overline{MEM}$	O O.D.	**WAY$_1$:** (Defined only when the BXU is in PROCESSOR mode). Indicates if the access is for the cache or private memory half of the SRAM. The line is intended to drive the SRAM address lines directly and will remain stable throughout the length of a cache access. **MEMORY/REGISTER REQUEST:** (Defined only when the BXU is in MEMORY mode). This signal allows mapping some of the BXU's register space out to the registers in an external controller. If the signal is high, the associated L-Bus request is a memory request; otherwise, the L-Bus request is to an external register on the board.
$\overline{WD_0}/\overline{UNC}$	I/O O.D.	**WORD$_0$:** (Only defined when the BXU is in PROCESSOR mode). Provides the low order bit of the word address for the SRAM. Together with WORD$_1$, the two bits indicate which of the four words within an address line should be addressed. Because SRAM timing is critical, an external latch could be required. The signals change for each word of data transferred. **UNCORRECTABLE ECC:** (Only defined when the BXU is in MEMORY mode). Is an input used by the external ECC logic to signal to the BXU that it has detected an uncorrectable memory error.
$\overline{WD_1}/\overline{ECC}$	I/O O.D.	**WORD$_1$:** (Defined only when the BXU is in PROCESSOR mode). Provides the high order bit of the word address for the SRAM. Together with WORD$_0$, the two bits indicate which of the four words within an address line should be addressed. Because SRAM timing is critical, an external latch will be required. The signals change for each word of data transferred. **ECC ERROR:** (Defined only when the BXU is in MEMORY mode). Is an input used by the external ECC logic to signal to the BXU that it has detected a memory error. The signal will be asserted even though external logic may be correcting the error and providing correct data on the L-Bus. If the BXU is asserting its CORRECT signal, the ECC ERROR signal will be ignored. Only the $\overline{UNC}$ pin will be checked for an error indication under these conditions.
$\overline{SSBUSY}$	I/O O.D.	**SUBSYSTEM BUSY:** Connects together all BXUs in a module that are in the same subsystem. When the signal is pulled low (BUSY), the BXUs will accept a request address, but will not continue with the data cycles. This signal is used to ensure that the BXUs always handle RMW-writes, Interagent Communication messages, and retries correctly. An external signal is needed because BXUs can generate AP-Bus requests internally because of the prefetcher, or their internal logic can be tied up handling an IAC request from the AP-Bus.

Table 11. M82965 BXU Module Support Signals (Continued)

Symbol	Type	Name and Function
$\overline{POPQUE}$	I/O O.D.	**POP QUEUE:** Is used by the two BXUs acting as bus backups for each other to communicate status on the completion of outstanding L-Bus requests. Usually, this signal is asserted when the oldest write in the queue has completed. During the partner ordering period, a different protocol is used to convey the status of all write requests outstanding.
$\overline{LERL_1} - \overline{LERL_0}$	I/O O.D.	**LOCAL ERROR REPORTING LINES:** Are identical to the BERL signals defined for the AP-Bus, but are used on the module side to connect all BXUs on a single L-Bus.

NOTES:
I/O = Input/Output, I = Input, O = Output, O.D. = Open Drain

MECHANICAL DATA

Pin Assignment

The MG82965 BXU (PGA package) pinout as viewed from the top side of the component (pins down) is shown in Figure 17 and from the bottom side (pins up) in Figure 18.

V_{CC} and GND connections must be made to multiple V_{CC} and GND pins. Each V_{CC} and GND pin must be connected to the appropriate voltage or ground and externally strapped close to the package. Preferably, the circuit board should include power and ground planes for power distribution. Table 12 lists the function of each pin.

Many of the signals are multiplexed and several signals have different interpretations depending on whether the BXU is used in Processor or Memory mode.

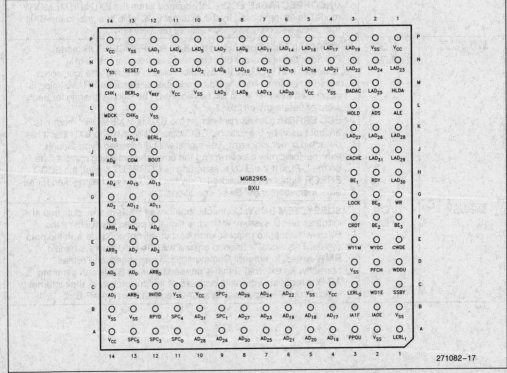

Figure 17. MG82965 BXU Pinout—View from Top Side (Pins Down)

271082–17

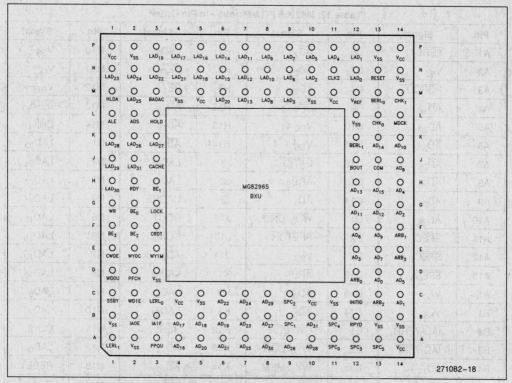

Figure 18. MG82965 BXU Pinout—View from Bottom Side (Pins Up)

271082–18

Table 12. M82965 PGA Pinout—In Pin Order

Pin	Signal	Pin	Signal	Pin	Signal	Pin	Signal
A1	$\overline{LERL}_1$	C6	$\overline{AD}_{22}$	H1	LAD_{30}	M10	V_{SS}
A2	V_{SS}	C7	$\overline{AD}_{24}$	H2	$\overline{READY}$	M11	V_{CC}
A3	$\overline{POPQUE}$	C8	$\overline{AD}_{29}$	H3	$\overline{BE}_1$	M12	V_{REF}
A4	$\overline{AD}_{16}$	C9	$\overline{SPEC}_2$	H12	$\overline{AD}_{13}$	M13	$\overline{BERL}_0$
A5	$\overline{AD}_{20}$	C10	V_{CC}	H13	$\overline{AD}_{15}$	M14	$\overline{CHK}_1$
A6	$\overline{AD}_{21}$	C11	V_{SS}	H14	$\overline{AD}_4$	N1	LAD_{23}
A7	$\overline{AD}_{25}$	C12	$\overline{INITID}$	J1	LAD_{29}	N2	LAD_{24}
A8	$\overline{AD}_{30}$	C13	$\overline{ARB}_2$	J2	LAD_{31}	N3	LAD_{22}
A9	$\overline{AD}_{26}$	C14	$\overline{AD}_1$	J3	$CACHE$	N4	LAD_{21}
A10	$\overline{AD}_{28}$	D1	$\overline{WD}_0/\overline{UNC}$	J12	$\overline{BOUT}$	N5	LAD_{18}
A11	$\overline{SPEC}_0$	D2	$\overline{PFETCH}$	J13	$\overline{COM}$	N6	LAD_{15}
A12	$\overline{SPEC}_3$	D3	V_{SS}	J14	$\overline{AD}_8$	N7	LAD_{12}
A13	$\overline{SPEC}_5$	D12	$\overline{ARB}_0$	K1	LAD_{28}	N8	LAD_{10}
A14	V_{CC}	D13	$\overline{AD}_0$	K2	LAD_{26}	N9	LAD_6
B1	V_{SS}	D14	$\overline{AD}_5$	K3	LAD_{27}	N10	LAD_2
B2	$\overline{IAC}_0/\overline{ERR}$	E1	$\overline{CW}/\overline{DEN}$	K12	$\overline{BERL}_1$	N11	$CLK2$
B3	$\overline{IAC}_1/\overline{FRF}$	E2	$\overline{WY}_0/\overline{COR}$	K13	$\overline{AD}_{14}$	N12	LAD_0
B4	$\overline{AD}_{17}$	E3	$\overline{WY}_1/\overline{MEM}$	K14	$\overline{AD}_{10}$	N13	$RESET$
B5	$\overline{AD}_{18}$	E12	$\overline{AD}_3$	L1	$\overline{ALE}$	N14	V_{SS}
B6	$\overline{AD}_{19}$	E13	$\overline{AD}_7$	L2	$\overline{ADS}$	P1	V_{CC}
B7	$\overline{AD}_{23}$	E14	$\overline{ARB}_3$	L3	$HOLD$	P2	V_{SS}
B8	$\overline{AD}_{27}$	F1	$\overline{BE}_3$	L12	V_{SS}	P3	LAD_{19}
B9	$\overline{SPEC}_1$	F2	$\overline{BE}_2$	L13	$\overline{CHK}_0$	P4	LAD_{17}
B10	$\overline{AD}_{31}$	F3	$\overline{CR}/DT/\overline{R}$	L14	$\overline{MODCHK}$	P5	LAD_{16}
B11	$\overline{SPEC}_4$	F12	$\overline{AD}_6$	M1	$HLDA$	P6	LAD_{14}
B12	$\overline{RPYDEF}$	F13	$\overline{AD}_9$	M2	LAD_{25}	P7	LAD_{11}
B13	V_{SS}	F14	$\overline{ARB}_1$	M3	$\overline{BADAC}$	P8	LAD_9
B14	V_{SS}	G1	$W/\overline{R}$	M4	V_{SS}	P9	LAD_7
C1	$\overline{SSBUSY}$	G2	$\overline{BE}_0$	M5	V_{CC}	P10	LAD_5
C2	$\overline{WD}_1/\overline{ECC}$	G3	$\overline{LOCK}$	M6	LAD_{20}	P11	LAD_4
C3	$\overline{LERL}_0$	G12	$\overline{AD}_{11}$	M7	LAD_{13}	P12	LAD_1
C4	V_{CC}	G13	$\overline{AD}_{12}$	M8	LAD_8	P13	V_{SS}
C5	V_{SS}	G14	$\overline{AD}_2$	M9	LAD_3	P14	V_{CC}

Table 13. M82965 Pinout—In Signal Order

Signal	PGA Pin	Signal	PGA Pin	Signal	PGA Pin	Signal	PGA Pin
$\overline{AD}_0$	D13	$\overline{ALE}$	L1	LAD_8	M8	$\overline{SPEC}_0$	A11
$\overline{AD}_1$	C14	$\overline{ARB}_0$	D12	LAD_9	P8	$\overline{SPEC}_1$	B9
$\overline{AD}_2$	G14	$\overline{ARB}_1$	F14	LAD_{10}	N8	$\overline{SPEC}_2$	C9
$\overline{AD}_3$	E12	$\overline{ARB}_2$	C13	LAD_{11}	P7	$\overline{SPEC}_3$	A12
$\overline{AD}_4$	H14	$\overline{ARB}_3$	E14	LAD_{12}	N7	$\overline{SPEC}_4$	B11
$\overline{AD}_5$	D14	$\overline{BADAC}$	M3	LAD_{13}	M7	$\overline{SPEC}_5$	A13
$\overline{AD}_6$	F12	$\overline{BE}_0$	G2	LAD_{14}	P6	$\overline{SSBUSY}$	C1
$\overline{AD}_7$	E13	$\overline{BE}_1$	H3	LAD_{15}	N6	V_{CC}	A14
$\overline{AD}_8$	J14	$\overline{BE}_2$	F2	LAD_{16}	P5	V_{CC}	C4
$\overline{AD}_9$	F13	$\overline{BE}_3$	F1	LAD_{17}	P4	V_{CC}	C10
$\overline{AD}_{10}$	K14	$\overline{BERL}_0$	M13	LAD_{18}	N5	V_{CC}	M5
$\overline{AD}_{11}$	G12	$\overline{BERL}_1$	K12	LAD_{19}	P3	V_{CC}	M11
$\overline{AD}_{12}$	G13	$\overline{BOUT}$	J12	LAD_{20}	M6	V_{CC}	P1
$\overline{AD}_{13}$	H12	CACHE	J3	LAD_{21}	N4	V_{CC}	P14
$\overline{AD}_{14}$	K13	$\overline{CHK}_0$	L13	LAD_{22}	N3	V_{REF}	M12
$\overline{AD}_{15}$	H13	$\overline{CHK}_1$	M14	LAD_{23}	N1	V_{SS}	A2
$\overline{AD}_{16}$	A4	CLK2	N11	LAD_{24}	N2	V_{SS}	B1
$\overline{AD}_{17}$	B4	$\overline{COM}$	J13	LAD_{25}	M2	V_{SS}	B13
$\overline{AD}_{18}$	B5	$\overline{CR}/DT/\overline{R}$	F3	LAD_{26}	K2	V_{SS}	B14
$\overline{AD}_{19}$	B6	$CW/\overline{DEN}$	E1	LAD_{27}	K3	V_{SS}	C5
$\overline{AD}_{20}$	A5	HLDA	M1	LAD_{28}	K1	V_{SS}	C11
$\overline{AD}_{21}$	A6	HOLD	L3	LAD_{29}	J1	V_{SS}	D3
$\overline{AD}_{22}$	C6	$\overline{IAC}_0/\overline{ERR}$	B2	LAD_{30}	H1	V_{SS}	L12
$\overline{AD}_{23}$	B7	$\overline{IAC}_1/\overline{FRF}$	B3	LAD_{31}	J2	V_{SS}	M4
$\overline{AD}_{24}$	C7	$\overline{INITID}$	C12	$\overline{LERL}_0$	C3	V_{SS}	M10
$\overline{AD}_{25}$	A7	LAD_0	N12	$\overline{LERL}_1$	A1	V_{SS}	N14
$\overline{AD}_{26}$	A9	LAD_1	P12	$\overline{LOCK}$	G3	V_{SS}	P2
$\overline{AD}_{27}$	B8	LAD_2	N10	$\overline{MODCHK}$	L14	V_{SS}	P13
$\overline{AD}_{28}$	A10	LAD_3	M9	$\overline{PFETCH}$	D2	$\overline{WD}_0/\overline{UNC}$	D1
$\overline{AD}_{29}$	C8	LAD_4	P11	$\overline{POPQUE}$	A3	$\overline{WD}_1/\overline{ECC}$	C2
$\overline{AD}_{30}$	A8	LAD_5	P10	$\overline{READY}$	H2	$W/\overline{R}$	G1
$\overline{AD}_{31}$	B10	LAD_6	N9	RESET	N13	$\overline{WY}_0/\overline{COR}$	E2
$\overline{ADS}$	L2	LAD_7	P9	$\overline{RPYDEF}$	B12	$\overline{WY}_1/\overline{MEM}$	E3

Package Dimensions and Mounting

The MG82965 BXU is packaged in either a 132-lead ceramic pin-grid array (PGA) or a 164-pin CQP package. (Contact factory for details on CQP availability.) Pins in the PGA package are arranged 0.100 inch (2.54 mm) center-to-center, in a 14 by 14 matrix, three rows around. See Figure 19.

A wide variety of available sockets allows low-insertion or zero-insertion force mountings, and a choice of terminals such as soldertail, surface mount, or wire-wrap. Figure 20 shows several applicable sockets.

Package Thermal Specification

The M82965 BXU is specified for operation when its case temperature is within the range of −55°C to +125°C. The PGA case temperature should be measured at the center of the top surface opposite the pins as shown in Figure 21.

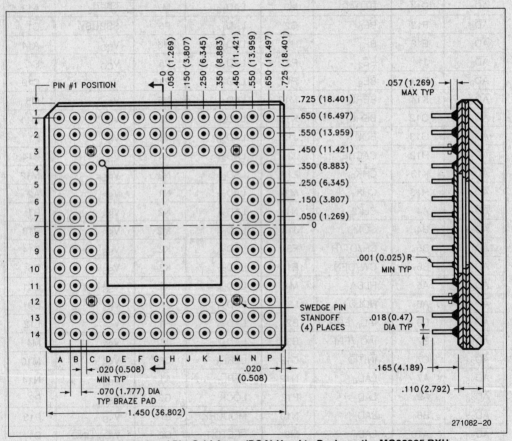

271082−20

Figure 19. A 132-Lead Pin-Grid Array (PGA) Used to Package the MG82965 BXU

- Low insertion force (LIF) soldertail 55274-1
- Amp tests indicate 50% reduction in insertion force compared to machined sockets

Other socket options

- Zero insertion force (ZIF) soldertail 55583-1
- Zero insertion force (ZIF) Burn-in version 55573-2

Amp Incorporated
(Harrisburg, PA 17105 U.S.A
Phone 717-564-0100)

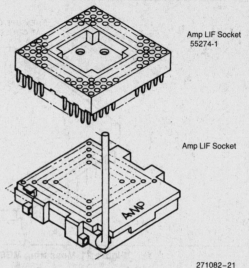

Amp LIF Socket
55274-1

Amp LIF Socket

271082–21

Cam handle locks in low profile position when MG82965 is installed (handle UP for open and DOWN for closed positions).

Courtesy Amp Incorporated

Peel-A-Way* and Kapton Socket Terminal Carriers

- Low insertion force surface mount CS132-37TG
- Low insertion force soldertail CS132-01TG
- Low insertion force wire-wrap CS132-02TG (two-level) CS132-03TG (three-level)
- Low insertion force press-fit CS132-05TG

Advanced Interconnections
(5 Division Street)
Warwick, RI 02818 U.S.A.
Phone 401-885-0485)

Peel-A-Way Carrier No. 132:
Kapton Carrier is KS132
Mylar Carrier is MS132

Molded Plastic Body KS132 is shown below:

FOOT PRINT NO. 132
├─ 1.400 SQ. ─┤
─┤├─ .100 TYP
14 x 14 x 3 ROWS

271082–22

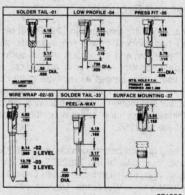

271082–23

Courtesy Advanced Interconnections
(Peel-A-Way Terminal Carriers
U.S. Patent No. 4442938)

*Peel-A-Way is a trademark of Advanced Interconnections.

Figure 20. Several Socket Options for Mounting the M82965 BXU

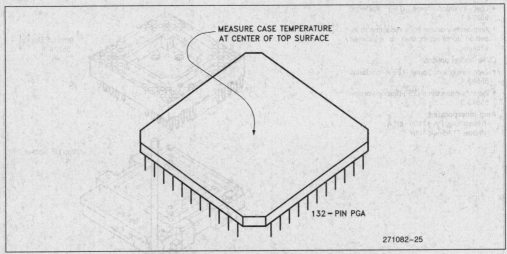

MEASURE CASE TEMPERATURE
AT CENTER OF TOP SURFACE

132 – PIN PGA

271082–25

Figure 21. Measuring MG82965 Case Temperature

ELECTRICAL SPECIFICATIONS

Power and Grounding

The M82965 is implemented in CHMOS III technology and has modest power requirements. Its high clock frequency and numerous output buffers (address/data, control, error, and arbitration signals) can cause power surges as multiple output buffers drive new signal levels simultaneously. For clean on-chip power distribution at high frequency, seven V_{CC} and thirteen V_{SS} pins separately feed functional units of the M82965.

Power and ground connections must be made to all V_{CC} and V_{SS} pins of the M82965. On the circuit board, all V_{CC} pins must be strapped closely together, preferably on a V_{CC} plane. Likewise, all V_{SS} pins should be strapped together, preferably on a ground plane.

Power Decoupling Recommendations

Liberal decoupling capacitance should be placed near the M82965. The BXU when driving its two 32-bit address/data buses (AP-Bus and L-Bus) can cause transient power surges, particularly when driving large capacitive loads.

Low inductance capacitors and interconnects are recommended for best high frequency electrical performance. Inductance can be reduced by shortening the board traces between the BXU and decoupling capacitors as much as possible.

Connection Recommendations

For reliable operation, always connect unused inputs to an appropriate signal level. In particular, if PFETCH or $\overline{LERL}_{0-1}$ are not used, they should be pulled up and if the CACHE input is not used (i.e., BXU operating in the Memory mode) it should be tied low through a 10 kΩ resistor. No inputs should ever be left floating.

All open-drain outputs require a pullup device. While in most cases a simple pullup resistor will be adequate, a network of pullup and pulldown resistors biased to a valid V_{IH} (e.g., 3.5V) will limit noise and AC power consumption, especially on the AP-Bus.

ABSOLUTE MAXIMUM RATINGS*

Case Temperature
under Bias[1]........... $-55°C$ to $+125°C$ Case
Storage Temperature .... $-65°C$ to $+150°C$
Voltage on Any Pin.......... $-0.5V$ to $V_{CC} + 0.5V$
Power Dissipation......................2.5W

*Notice: Stresses above those listed under "Absolute Maximum Ratings" may cause permanent damage to the device. This is a stress rating only and functional operation of the device at these or any other conditions above those indicated in the operational sections of this specification is not implied. Exposure to absolute maximum rating conditions for extended periods may affect device reliability.

NOTICE: Specifications contained within the following tables are subject to change.

Table 14. D.C. Characteristics (T_{CASE}[1] = $-55°C$ to $+125°C$, V_{CC} = 5V $\pm5\%$)

Symbol	Parameter	Min	Max	Units	Test Conditions
V_{IL}	Input Low Voltage	-0.3	$+0.8$	V	
V_{ILA}	Input Low Voltage: AP-Bus	-0.5	$+1.0$	V	
V_{IH}	Input High Voltage	2.0	$V_{CC} + 0.3$	V	
V_{IHA}	Input High Voltage: AP-Bus	2.0	V_{CC}	V	
$V_{REF/C}$	V_{REF} Trip Point Cold Start	$V_{CC} - 0.7$		V	
$V_{REF/W}$	V_{REF} Trip Point Warm Start	1.7	1.8	V	
V_{CL}	CLK2 Input Low Voltage	-0.3	$+1.0$	V	
V_{CH}	CLK2 Input High Voltage	0.55 V_{CC}	V_{CC}	V	
V_{OL}	Output Low Voltage: I_{OL} = 4 mA: LAD Lines I_{OL} = 5 mA: Controls[4] I_{OL} = 25 mA: L-Bus Open-Drain Outputs I_{OL} = 80 mA: AP-Bus[2] Open-Drain Outputs		0.45 0.45 0.45 0.70	V V V V	
V_{OH}	Output High Voltage: I_{OH} = 1 mA: LAD Lines I_{OH} = 0.9 mA: Controls[4] I_{OH} = 5.0 mA: ALE	 2.4 2.4 2.4		 V V V	
I_{CC}	Power Supply Current		450	mA	
I_{LI}	Input Leakage Current		±15	μA	$0V \le V_O \le V_{CC}$
I_{LO}	Output Leakage Current		±15	μA	$0.45V \le V_O \le V_{CC}$
C_{IN}	Input Capacitance		10	pF	Notes 2, 3
C_O	I/O or Output Capacitance		12	pF	Notes 2, 3
C_{CLK}	Clock Capacitance		12	pF	Notes 2, 3

NOTES:
1. Case temperatures are "instant on."
2. Not 100% tested.
3. Test frequency = 1 MHz, T_C = 25°C, unmeasured pins at GND.
4. "Controls" include all L-Bus I/O pins not otherwise specified.

A.C. SPECIFICATIONS

This section describes the A.C. specifications for the M82965 pins. All input and output timings are specified relative to the 1.5V level of the rising edge of CLK2, and refer to the time at which the signal reaches (for output delay and input setup) or leaves (for hold time) the TTL levels of LOW (0.8V) or HIGH (2.0V).

All A.C. testing should be done with input voltages of 0.45V and 2.4V.

Maximum output hold times are the same as minimum output delays. Tri-state signals have no resistive load or termination.

The Output Delay specified for open-drain signals includes both the low to high and high to low transitions. The float delay is the amount of time that the pulldown transistor may remain active. This specification is provided to help system designers calculate propagation delay for terminations other than the one used for testing.

Table 15. M82965 A.C. Timing Specifications (T_C[1] = −55°C to +125°C, V_{CC} = 5V ±5%)

Symbol	Parameter	Min	Max	Units	Test Conditions
T_1	Clock Period	31.25	125	ns	V_{IN} = 1.5V
T_2	Clock Low Time	11		ns	V_{IN} = 10% Point = 1.2V
T_3	Clock High Time	11		ns	V_{IN} = 90% Point = 0.1V + 0.5 V_{CC}
T_4	Clock Fall Time		10	ns	V_{IN} = 90% Point to 10% Point[2]
T_5	Clock Rise Time		10	ns	V_{IN} = 10% Point to 90% Point[2]
T_6	Output Valid Delay:				
	LAD	4	35	ns	C_L = 100 pF
	$\overline{WY}$	4	35	ns	C_L = 125 pF
	$\overline{CW}$, $\overline{WD}$, SS Busy	4	30	ns	C_L = 75 pF
	$\overline{CR}$	4	45	ns	C_L = 75 pF
	Controls[3]	2	35	ns	C_L = 75 pF
T_7	$\overline{ALE}$ Width	15		ns	C_L = 75 pF
T_8	$\overline{ALE}$ Invalid Delay		20	ns	C_L = 75 pF
T_9	Output Float Delay:				
	LAD	5	20	ns	C_L = 100 pF
	$\overline{WY}$	5	22	ns	C_L = 125 pF
	Controls[3]	5	22	ns	C_L = 75 pF
T_{10}	Input Setup Time:				
	$\overline{LOCK}$, HOLD, HOLDAR, $\overline{READY}$	8		ns	10% Point
	$\overline{ECC}$, $\overline{UNC}$	15		ns	10% Point
	Controls[3]	3		ns	10% Point
T_{11}	Input Data Hold	10		ns	90% Point
T_{12}	Setup to $\overline{ALE}$ Inactive	10		ns	C_L = 100 pF (LAD) C_L = 75 pF (Controls)
T_{13}	Hold after $\overline{ALE}$ Inactive	8		ns	C_L = 100 pF (LAD) C_L = 75 pF (Controls)
T_{14}	RESET Hold	5		ns	
T_{15}	RESET Setup	8		ns	
T_{16}	RESET Width	1250		ns	40 CLK2 Periods Minimum
T_{17}	Clock to Data Valid (AP-Bus)		17	ns	C_L = 50 pF I_{OL} = 50 mA
T_{18}	Clock to High[2] Impedance (AP-Bus)		14	ns	
T_{19}	Output Hold (AP-Bus)	5		ns	C_L = 50 pF I_{OL} = 50 mA
T_{20}	Input Setup (AP-Bus)	7		ns	
T_{21}	Input Hold (AP-Bus)	10		ns	

NOTES:
1. Case temperatures are "Instant On".
2. Not 100% tested.
3. "Controls" include all L-Bus I/O pins not otherwise specified.

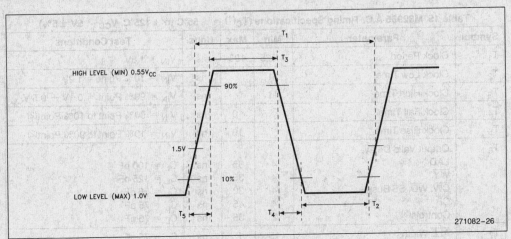

Figure 22. CLK2 Timing

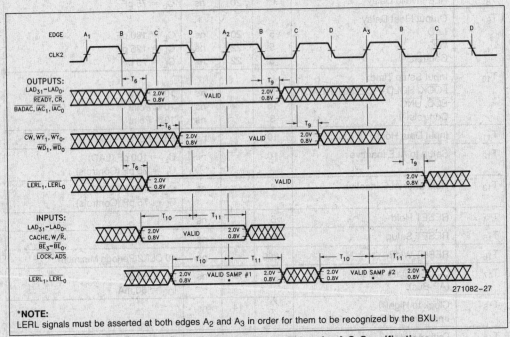

*NOTE:
LERL signals must be asserted at both edges A_2 and A_3 in order for them to be recognized by the BXU.

Figure 23. Drive Levels and Measurement Points for A.C. Specifications.
L-Bus Timings for the BXU as a Bus Slave

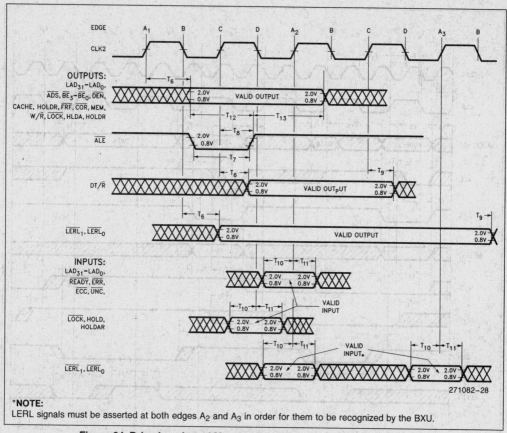

*NOTE:
LERL signals must be asserted at both edges A_2 and A_3 in order for them to be recognized by the BXU.

**Figure 24. Drive Levels and Measurement Points for A.C. Specifications.
L-Bus Timings for the BXU as a Bus Master**

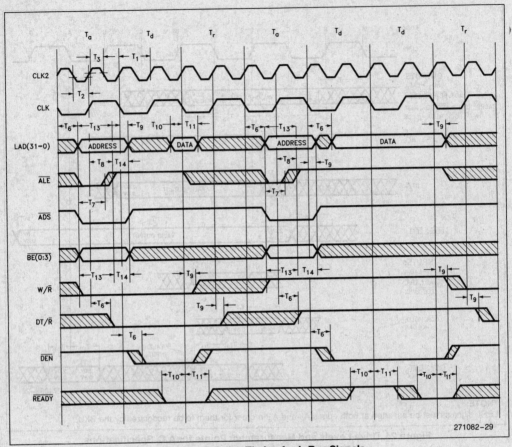

Figure 25. Relative Timing for L-Bus Signals

271082–29

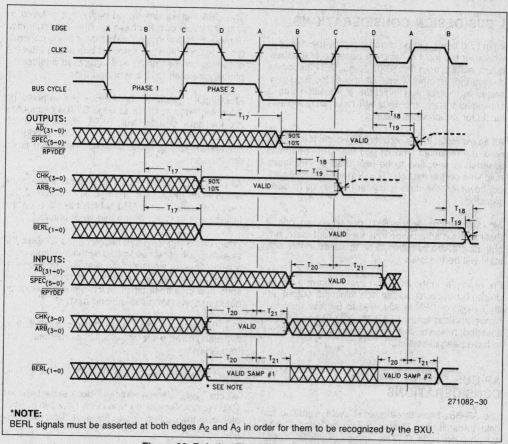

*NOTE:
BERL signals must be asserted at both edges A_2 and A_3 in order for them to be recognized by the BXU.

Figure 26. Relative Timing for AP-Bus Signals

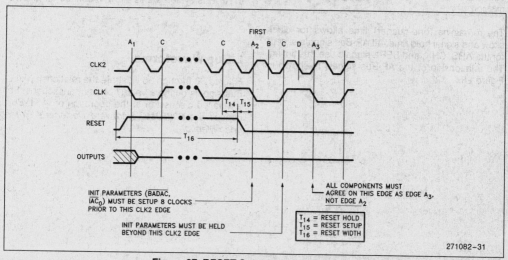

Figure 27. RESET Setup and HOLD Timing

L-BUS DESIGN CONSIDERATIONS

Input hold times can be disregarded by the designer whenever the input is removed because of a subsequent output from the BXU (e.g., $\overline{\text{DEN}}$ becomes deasserted). In other words, whenever the BXU generates an output that indicates a transition into a subsequent state, the BXU will have sampled any inputs for the previous state.

As an example, in the recovery (T_r) cycle following a read, the minimum time ($t_{6\ Min}$) that $\overline{\text{DEN}}$ becomes asserted is specified to be less than the minimum hold time on the data ($t_{11\ Min}$). When $\overline{\text{DEN}}$ is asserted, however, the data is guaranteed to have been sampled.

Similarly, whenever the BXU generates an output that indicates a transition to a subsequent state, any outputs that are specified to be tri-stated in this new state will be tri-stated.

For example, in the data (T_d) cycle following an address (T_a) cycle for a read, the minimum output delay ($t_{6\ Min}$) of $\overline{\text{DEN}}$ is specified to be less than the maximum float time of LAD ($t_{9\ Max}$). When $\overline{\text{DEN}}$ is asserted, however, the LAD outputs are guaranteed to have been tri-stated.

AP-BUS SIGNAL TIMING CONSIDERATIONS

The AP-Bus uses three-quarter cycle signaling for data transmission. Data is driven on edge D and sampled on edge C. This approach allows three-quarters of the bus cycle to be used for data transmission.

The remaining (one-quarter) time allows for clock skew and signal hold time. All AP-Bus signals except for the ARB, CHK, and BERL signals use this timing. The relationship of the AP-Bus signals is shown in Figure 28.

The CHK signals (interlaced parity) are delayed by one-half cycle or one phase to allow for generation of parity from the internal data that is being transmitted. The CHK lines are sampled one phase after the data has been sampled and compared against the parity generated for the received data.

Most input signals on the AP-Bus are sampled on the rising edge of CLK2 at edge C. The exceptions are the error signals CHK, BERL and ARB, which are sampled on the rising edge of CLK2 at edge A. Regardless of the edge, the setup and hold times are the same.

All outputs on the AP-Bus are driven relative to the falling edge of CLK2 at the middle of phase 2, except CHK, BERL and ARB, which transition on the falling edge of CLK2 at the middle of phase 1.

When designing a system based on the AP-Bus, the system topology will be limited by the available propagation time for signals in the system. The propagation time must allow for settling of ringing, ground shift, and crosstalk, all of which are dependent on board and system materials and design.

The following equation gives the propagation time available, given a specific clock implementation and frequency:

$$T_{PROP} = 2T_1 - (T_3 + T_4 + T_5 + (T_{18}\ \text{or}\ T_{19}) + T_{10a} + T_{skew})$$

Where T_{skew} is the worst case clock skew between BXUs (clock skew is the time delay between any two clocks in the system due to physical distribution limits).

In AP-Bus systems, this skew is defined as follows:

$$T_{skew} \le T_3 + T_{20} - T_{11}$$

L-Bus Waveforms

Figures 30 through 36 illustrate the relationship of L-Bus signals during a variety of bus transactions. For a detailed discussion of the operation of the L-Bus, consult the *80960MC Hardware Designer's Reference Manual*.

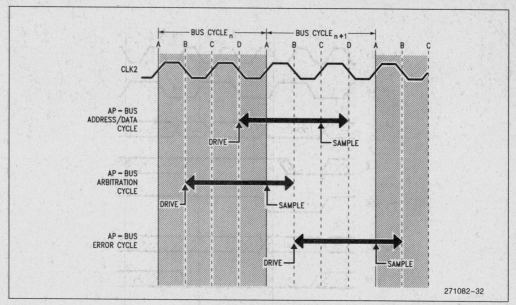

271082–32

Figure 28. AP-Bus Signal Timing

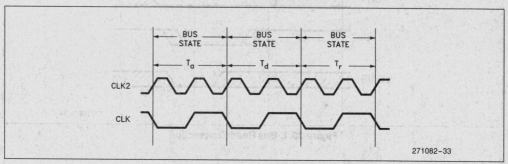

271082–33

Figure 29. System and Processor Clock Relationship

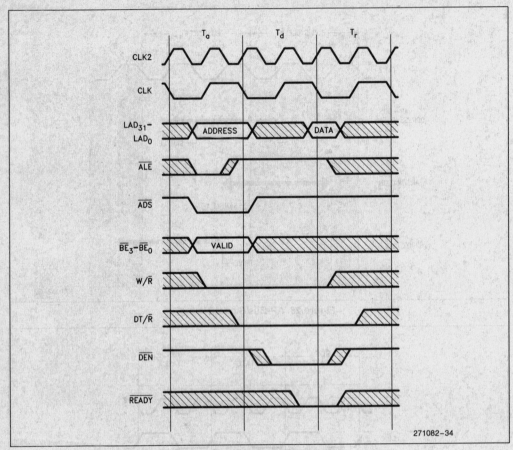

271082–34

Figure 30. L-Bus Read Transaction

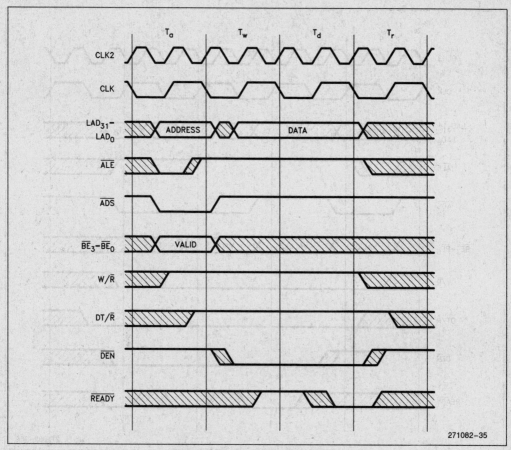

271082–35

Figure 31. L-Bus Write Transaction

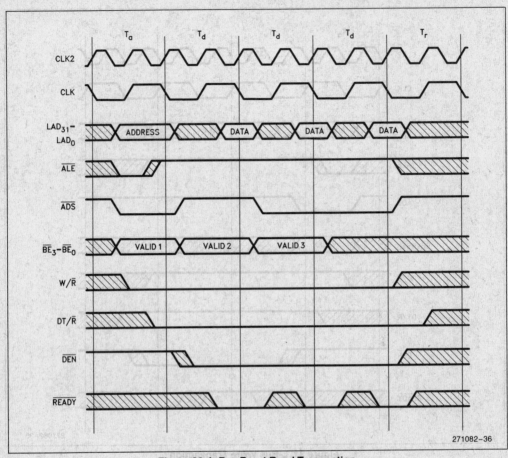

271082-36

Figure 32. L-Bus Burst Read Transaction

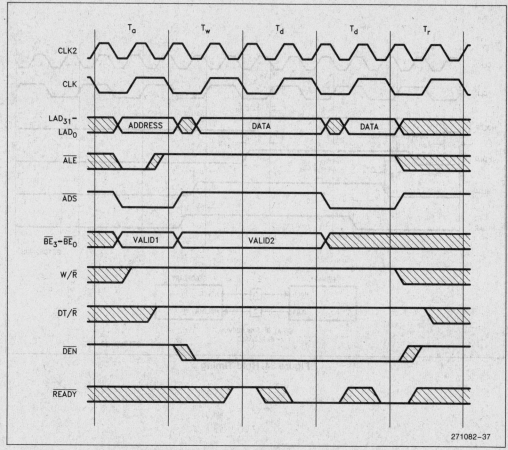

Figure 33. L-Bus Burst Write Transaction with One Wait State

271082-37

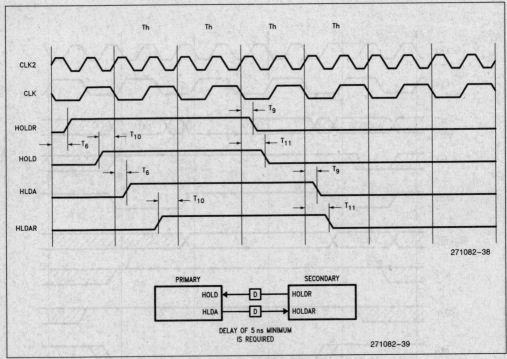

271082–38

271082–39

Figure 34. Hold Timing

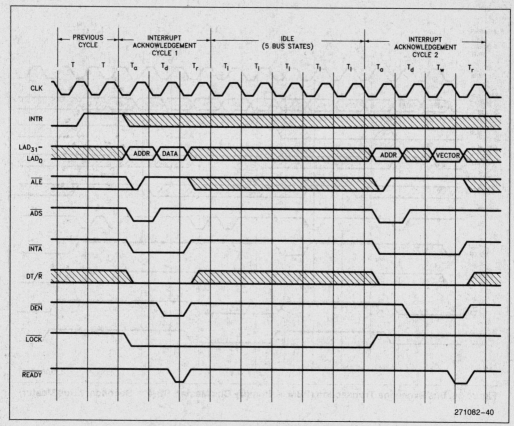

271082–40

Figure 35. Interrupt Acknowledge Transaction

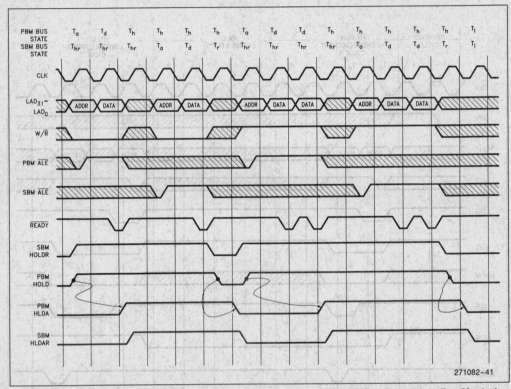

Figure 36. Bus Exchange Transaction (PBM = Primary Bus Master, SBM = Secondary Bus Master)

Memories & Peripherals
Data Sheets

85C960
1-MICRON CHMOS
80960 K-SERIES BUS CONTROL µPLD

- Burst Logic, Ready Control, and Address Decode Support for 80960 KA/KB Embedded Controllers in Single Chip

- Burst Logic Supports Both Standard and New Generation "Burst Mode" Memories and Peripherals

- Ready/Timing Control Supports 0–15 Wait States across 8 Address Ranges, Read/Write Accesses, Burst Transactions

- 8 Dedicated Inputs Decoded into 8 Latched Chip Selects (4 External/Internal; 4 Internal Only)

- Operates with 80960KA/KB at 16 MHz, 20 MHz, and 25 MHz

- UV Erasable (CerDIP) or OTP™

- 100% Generically Testable Logic Array

- Based on Low Power CHMOS IIIE Technology

- Available in 28-Pin 300-mil CerDIP and PDIP Packages and in 28-Pin PLCC Package
  (See Packaging Spec., Order Number #231369)

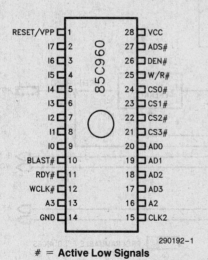

290192–1

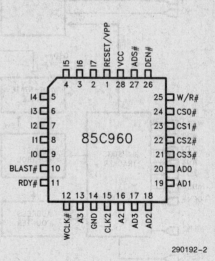

290192–2

\# = Active Low Signals

Figure 1. Pinout Diagam

October 1989
Order Number: 290192-001

GENERAL DESCRIPTION

The Intel 85C960 is a single-chip burst/ready/decode µPLD (Microcomputer Programmable Logic Device) designed to interface 80960 KA/KB embedded controllers to system memory and I/O. The 85C960 provides programmable chip selects, a programmable read/write access wait state/ready generator, and burst address (A2, A3) cycling. Burst transaction cycling of A2, A3, and WCLK# (Write Clock) is also supported for intelligent peripherals on the bus.

For its programmable functions, the 85C960 uses advanced EPROM cells as logic array and wait-state table memory elements. Coupled with Intel's proprietary CHMOS IIIE technology, the result is a programmable device able to support Intel's 32-bit 80960 KA/KB embedded controllers at speeds up to 25 MHz.

ARCHITECTURE DESCRIPTION

The 85C960 µPLD integrates burst control, ready generation, and chip select decoding into a single device. Figure 2 shows the architecture of the 85C960. Table 1 lists and describes each signal on the device. The 85C960 replaces 6–10 separate PLD/discrete logic devices in small- and medium-sized 80960 systems. For medium- to large-sized systems, the 85C960 can be supplemented with an additional decoder, such as the 85C508, and a second 85C960. Figure 3 shows a single 85C960 in a typical application.

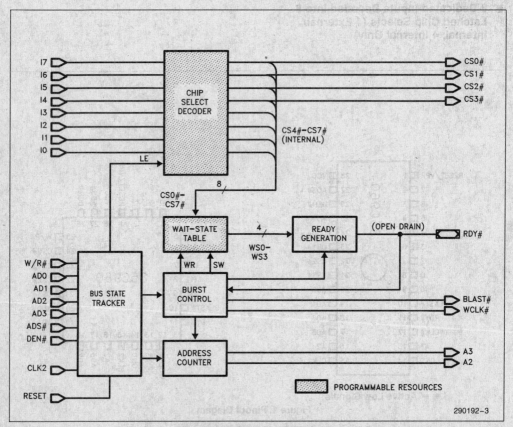

Figure 2. 85C960 Block Diagram

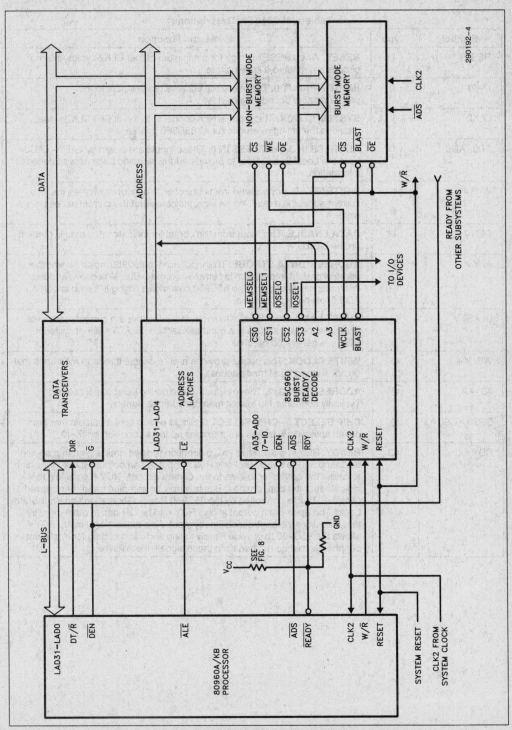

290192-4

Figure 3. 85C960 in an 80960 System

Table 1. 85C960 Pin Descriptions

Symbol	Type	Name and Function
RESET	I	**RESET.** When RESET is high for a minimum of four CLK2 cycles, internal circuits are reset to a known state.
I7–I0	I	**INPUT 7–INPUT 0.** These are the address range inputs to the programmable decode logic array.
CLK2	I	**SYSTEM CLOCK.** This input, which connects to the 80960 CLK2 signal, provides the timing reference for all 85C960 operations.
AD3–AD0	I	**ADDRESS IN 3–ADDRESS IN 0.** These inputs are driven by LAD0–LAD3 from the Local Bus (L-Bus) to provide addressing and burst access decode information.
W/R#	I	**WRITE/READ.** Write/Read from controller. When low, indicates that the current access is a read. When high, indicates that the current access is a write.
DEN#	I	**DATA ENABLE.** This input from the controller indicates that data is present on the L-Bus.
ADS#	I	**ADDRESS/DATA STROBE.** This input from the 80960 indicates whether address or data information is currently on the L-Bus. When low, address information is changing. The 85C960 chip select timing is based in part on ADS# low during Ta states.
BLAST#	O	**BURST LAST.** This signal, when low, indicates that the current read/write access is the last access in a burst transaction. BLAST# is not cycled if RDY# is generated off-chip.
WCLK#	O	**WRITE CLOCK.** This output provides a write enable strobe to memories that do not support burst mode access.
A3, A2	O	**ADDRESS OUT 3, 2.** These outputs cycle during burst transactions. Typically connected to lowest memory address signals.
CS3#–CS0#	O	**CHIP SELECT 3–CHIP SELECT 0.** Single p-term select outputs that are driven active (low) for the programmed address condition on I7–I0.
RDY#	I/O	**READY.** RDY# is an active low, bidirectional, open-drain signal that should be connected to the controller's Ready input. As an output, RDY# goes high to cause the controller to extend the current access. RDY# goes low to indicate that the data on the L-Bus bus may be sampled (read) or removed (write). RDY# is controlled by the 85C960 Ready Generation and Wait-State Logic. The open-drain output allows RDY# to be OR-tied to other circuitry that may drive the controller's Ready input. As a bidirectional input, RDY# allows the 85C960 to provide Ready timing and burst cycling for intelligent peripherals that do not generate these signals themselves.

80960 L-Bus (Local Bus) cycles are monitored by the **Bus State Tracker** to synchronize the functional blocks in the 85C960 to the L-Bus. CLK2 provides the timing reference for all 85C960 operations.

Four external chip selects (CS0#–CS3#) are generated by the programmable **Chip Select Decoder.** These four signals provide decoded selects to memory and I/O devices and are routed to the programmable **Wait-State Table** so that the 85C960 can generate RDY# at the appropriate time. Four additional selects are decoded (internal only) and routed to the Wait-State Table so that the 85C960 can generate RDY# for up to four additional address ranges.

The **Ready Generation** block generates RDY# to the controller under control of the **Wait-State Table.** Depending on the contents programmed into this table and the current type of access, from 0–15 wait states can be introduced into each bus cycle. An independent wait state value can be chosen for each select and each access type. Four access types are possible: read first, read subsequent, write first, and write subsequent.

The **Burst Control** and **Address Counter** blocks control burst transaction timing to memory and I/O. Note that the RDY# pin is sampled by the Burst Control block to allow the 85C960 to generate burst transaction timing for other bus peripherals. WCLK# provides a write enable strobe for memory and I/O that do not support burst mode. BLAST# informs burst-mode devices that the current access is the last one in a burst transaction. A2 and A3 are cycled to select the address location for each access.

FUNCTIONAL DESCRIPTION

The following paragraphs provide a detailed description of each functional block in the 85C960 μPLD.

Chip Select Decoder

The Chip Select Decoder, shown in Figure 4, is a high speed, single p-term (product-term) latched decoder circuit with eight inputs (I0–I7) and eight latched outputs. Each output goes low when its associated product term is true. Four of these outputs (CS0#–CS3#) are available externally to be used as device selects. The remaining four outputs (CS4#–CS7#) are available internally so that the 85C960 can provide ready and burst timing for four more device selects. (The actual selects for these four additional devices/resources must be generated by external logic.)

The input to each latch is a single NAND p-term that can be connected to the dedicated inputs. The true

and complements of all inputs (I7–I0) are available to all eight NAND p-terms.

Each intersecting point in the logic array is connected or not connected based on the value programmed in the EPROM array. Initially (EPROM erased state), no connections exist between any p-term and any input. Connections can be made by programming the appropriate EPROM cells. Since p-terms are implemented as NANDs, a true condition on a p-term drives the output low. Current consumption is higher when both true and complement p-terms for the same input are programmed.

Selects are latched on the falling edge of an internal Latch Enable (LE), which is generated from ADS#, DEN#, and CLK2. The proper combination of these signals occurs during an 80960 address state (Ta). Figure 5 shows the relationship of the internal LE and external chip selects to the three signals at the end of a Ta state. All selects are cleared to an inactive high state at the start of a recovery state. (Tr). All eight selects (four external and four internal) are routed to the Wait-State Table.

Wait State Table

Chip selects, WR (Write/Read), and SW (Subsequent Word) feed the Wait-State Table. Each chip select points to a set of four wait state values while WR and SW determine which of the four values to route to the Ready Generation block (see Figure 6). The four values are grouped into read and write groups with each group having a value for the first access and subsequent access (second through fourth). The four-bit wait-state value is sent to the Ready Generation block (via WS0#–WS3#) to be used as an initial count value. If two selects are active, the resulting count value is the logical bit AND of the two individual values. If more than two selects are active and the individual count values are not the same, the resulting count value is indeterminate. If no select is active, no count value is loaded (and the Ready Generation circuit is disabled).

Ready Generation

RDY# is high at the start of each burst transaction. The RDY Generator begins to count down from the wait state value, decrementing the counter at the start of each wait state. When the internal counter reaches 0000, RDY# is pulled low (CLK2c during the data state). On the next CLK2c edge (for a wait state), RDY# is released, allowing an external resistor to pull RDY# high. Figure 7 shows the timing for a four-word burst write transaction with 1 wait state for the first access and 0 wait states for the remaining three accesses (Burst Write 1-0-0-0).

RDY# is an open-drain I/O pin, which must be connected to pullup and pulldown resistors as shown in Figure 8. During a wait-state access, RDY# is pulled high to cause the controller to extend the current access so that the memory or peripheral chip has time to present data to the bus (read), or sample data on the bus (write). RDY# is released on the

CLK2a edge of a Tr state. If a Read or Write access occurs without a chip select having been decoded on-chip, the RDY# output buffer is disabled and RDY# is sampled as an input. This allows the 85C960 to cycle A2, A3, and WCLK# to provide burst transaction timing for other bus controllers. RDY# may be OR-tied with other bus controllers so they can access the processor Ready signal.

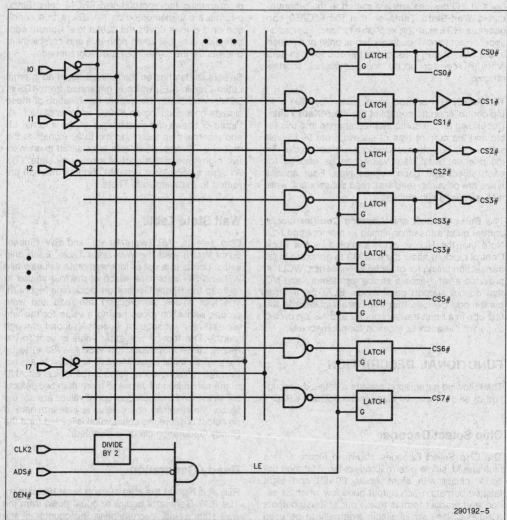

Figure 4. 85C960 Chip Select Decoder Block

290192–5

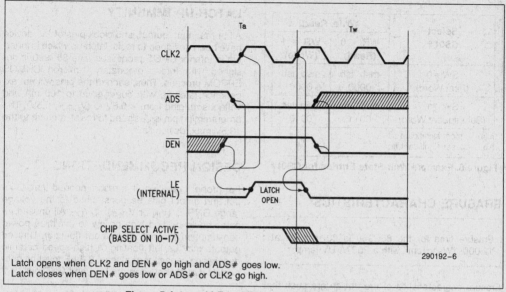

Latch opens when CLK2 and DEN# go high and ADS# goes low.
Latch closes when DEN# goes low or ADS# or CLK2 go high.

290192-6

Figure 5. Internal LE and External Chip Select Timing

Burst Transactions

AD3, AD2 are latched to indicate the starting address of a burst transaction. The 85C960 places these two signals out on A3 and A2, respectively, then cycles the two addresses upward until the last access of the burst. The 85C960 assumes that the processor handles splitting of the burst transaction when a 16-byte boundary is crossed.

AD0 and AD1 specify the size of the burst transfer in double-words as shown in Table 2.

Table 2. AD0–AD1 vs Burst Size

AD1	AD0	No. of Words Transferred
0	0	1
0	1	2
1	0	3
1	1	4

WCLK#, BLAST# Generation

WCLK# is the write enable signal for writing to non-burst mode memories. When low, address outputs A2 and A3 are valid. Its trailing edge (low-to-high transition) can be used to latch data into non-burst mode memories. WCLK# is only provided during writes; during reads, WCLK# remains high.

BLAST# indicates that the current access is the last access in a burst transaction. BLAST# is used by burst-mode memories to reset internal address counters. BLAST# is not cycled when RDY# is generated off-chip.

POWER-ON CHARACTERISTICS

85C960 inputs and outputs begin responding 1 μs (max.) after V_{CC} power-up (V_{CC} = 4.75V) or after a power-loss/power-up sequence. RESET must be synchronous to CLK2 and must be held high for a minimum of 4 clock cycles after V_{CC} reaches 4.75 V. After 4 clock cycles, A2 and A3 are high, CS0#–CS3# (and CS4#–CS7#), BLAST#, WCLK# are high, and the open drain RDY# signal is inactive.

Select CS0f #	Write/Read	
	WR = 0 (Read)	WR = 1 (Write)
SW = 0 (First Word)	msb lsb 0000	msb lsb 0000
SW = 1 (Subsequent Word)	msb lsb 0011	msb lsb 0010

msb = most significant bit
lsb = least significant bit

Figure 6. Example Wait-State Entries for CS0f #

ERASURE CHARACTERISTICS

Erasure time for the 85C960 is 20 minutes at 12,000 μWsec/cm^2 with a 2537Å UV lamp.

Erasure characteristics of the device are such that erasure begins to occur upon exposure to light with wavelengths shorter than approximately 4000Å. It should be noted that sunlight and certain types of fluorescent lamps have wavelengths in the 3000Å–4000Å range. Data shows that constant exposure to room level fluorescent lighting could erase the typical 85C960 in approximately two years, while it would take approximately two weeks to erase the device when exposed to direct sunlight. If the device is to be exposed to these lighting conditions for extended periods of time, conductive opaque labels should be placed over the device window to prevent unintentional erasure.

The recommended erasure procedure for the 85C960 is exposure to shortwave ultraviolet light with a wavelength of 2537Å. The integrated dose (i.e., UV intensity × exposure time) for erasure should be a minimum of fifteen (15) Wsec/cm^2. The erasure time with this dosage is approximately 20 minutes using an ultraviolet lamp with a 12,000 μW/cm^2 power rating. The device should be placed within 1 inch of the lamp tubes during exposure. The maximum integrated dose the 85C960 can be exposed to without damage is 7258 Wsec/cm^2 (1 week at 12,000 μW/cm^2). Exposure to high intensity UV light for longer periods may cause permanent damage to the device.

LATCH-UP IMMUNITY

All of the input, output, and clock pins of the device have been designed to resist latch-up which is inherent in inferior CMOS processes. The 85C960 is designed with Intel's proprietary 1-micron CHMOS EPROM process. Thus, each of the pins will not experience latch-up with currents up to 100 mA and voltages ranging from −0.5V to (V$_{CC}$ + 0.5V). The programming pin is designed to resist latch-up to the 13.5V max. device limit.

DESIGN RECOMMENDATIONS

For proper operation, it is recommended that all input and output pins be constrained to the voltage range GND ≤ (V$_{IN}$ or V$_{OUT}$) ≤ V$_{CC}$. All unused inputs should be tied high or low to minimize power consumption (do not leave them floating). Unused outputs may be left floating. A high-speed ceramic decoupling capacitor of at least 0.2 μF must be connected directly between the V$_{CC}$ and GND pin.

As with all CMOS devices, ESD handling procedures should be used with the 85C960 to prevent damage to the device during programming, assembly, and test.

FUNCTIONAL TESTING

Since the programmable sections of the 85C960 are controlled by EPROM elements, the device is completely testable during the manufacturing process. Each programmable EPROM bit controlling the internal logic is tested using application independent test patterns. EPROM cells in the device are 100% tested for programming and erasure. After testing, the devices are erased before shipments to the customers. No post-programming tests of the EPROM array are required.

The testability and reliability of EPROM-based programmable logic devices is an important feature over similar devices based on fuse technology. Fuse-based programmable logic devices require a user to perform post-programming tests to insure device functionality. During the manufacturing process, tests on fuse-based parts can only be performed in very restricted ways in order to avoid pre-programming the array.

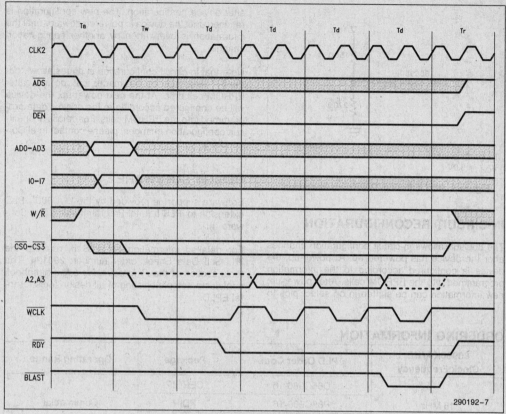

Figure 7. Burst Write Transaction (1-0-0-0)

290192–7

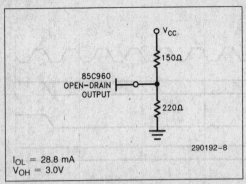

$I_{OL} = 28.8$ mA
$V_{OH} = 3.0$V

Figure 8. RDY # Pullup/Pulldown Resistors

IN-CIRCUIT RECONFIGURATION

The 85C960 allows in-circuit configuration changes after the device has powered up. At power-up, the device is configured according to the information programmed into the EPROM cells. After power-up, new information can be shifted in on select pins to alter device configuration. The new configuration is retained until the device is powered down or until the information is overwritten by another configuration change.

Note that in-circuit configuration changes allow "on-the-fly" changes to be made, but do not alter EPROM cell data. At the next power-up, the device will be configured according to the original data programmed into the EPROM cells. For details on in-circuit configuration changes, please contact Intel Corporation.

DESIGN SOFTWARE

Software support is provided by the LOC960 μPLD extension to iPLS II (Intel Programmable Logic Software II).

For detailed information on iPLS II, refer to the iPLDS II Data Sheet, order number: 290134. The tools section of the *Programmable Logic* handbook contains a complete listing of all design tools for Intel EPLDs.

ORDERING INFORMATION

80960KA/KB Clock Frequency	μPLD Order Code	Package	Operating Range
16 MHz	D85C960-16	CERDIP	Commercial
	P85C960-16	PDIP	
	N85C960-16	PLCC	
20 MHz	D85C960-20	CERDIP	Commercial
	P85C960-20	PDIP	
	N85C960-20	PLCC	
25 MHz	D85C960-25	CERDIP	Commercial
	P85C960-25	PDIP	
	N85C960-25	PLCC	

ABSOLUTE MAXIMUM RATINGS*

Supply Voltage (V_{CC})[1] . . . . $-2.0V$ to $+7.0V$

Programming Supply
 Voltage (V_{PP})[1] . . . . $-2.0V$ to $+13.5V$

D.C. Input Voltage (V_I)[1, 2] . . . $-0.5V$ to $V_{CC} + 0.5V$

Storage Temperature (T_{stg}) . . . . . $-65°C$ to $+150°C$

Ambient Temperature (T_A)[3] . . . . . $-10°C$ to $+85°C$

NOTES:
1. Voltages with respect to GND.
2. Minimum D.C. input is $-0.5V$. During transitions, the inputs may undershoot to $-2.0V$ or overshoot to $+7.0V$ for periods of less than 20 ns under no load conditions.
3. Under bias. Extended Temperature versions are also available.

*Notice: Stresses above those listed under "Absolute Maximum Ratings" may cause permanent damage to the device. This is a stress rating only and functional operation of the device at these or any other conditions above those indicated in the operational sections of this specification is not implied. Exposure to absolute maximum rating conditions for extended periods may affect device reliability.

NOTICE: Specifications contained within the following tables are subject to change.

RECOMMENDED OPERATING CONDITIONS

Symbol	Parameter	Min	Max	Units
V_{CC}	Supply Voltage	4.75	5.25	V
V_{IN}	Input Voltage	0	V_{CC}	V
V_O	Output Voltage	0	V_{CC}	V
T_A	Operating Temperature	0	$+70$	°C

85C960

PRELIMINARY

D.C. CHARACTERISTICS ($T_A = 0°C$ to $+70°C$, $V_{CC} = 5.0V \pm 5\%$)

Symbol	Parameter	Min	Typ	Max	Unit	Test Conditions
V_{IH}[4]	High Level Input Voltage	2.0		$V_{CC} + 0.3$	V	
V_{IL}[4]	Low Level Input Voltage	-0.3		0.8	V	
V_{OH}	High Level Output Voltage	2.4			V	$I_{OH} = -4.0$ mA D.C., V_{CC} = Min.
V_{OL1}	Low Level Output Voltage			0.4	V	$I_{OL} = 4.0$ mA D.C., V_{CC} = Min., $C_L = 30$ pF
V_{OL2}	Low Level Output Voltage for A2, A3			0.45	V	$I_{OL} = 24$ mA D.C., V_{CC} = Min., $C_L = 60$ pF
V_{OL3}	Low Level Output Voltage for Open Drain (RDY#)			0.5	V	$I_{OL} = 30$ mA D.C., V_{CC} = Min., $C_L = 30$ pF
I_I	Input Leakage Current			± 10	μA	V_{CC} = Max., GND $\leq V_{IN} \leq V_{CC}$
I_{OZ}	Output Leakage Current			± 10	μA	V_{CC} = Max., GND $\leq V_{OUT} \leq V_{CC}$
I_{SC}[5]	Output Short Circuit Current	-30		-90	mA	V_{CC} = Max., $V_{OUT} = 0.5V$
I_{CC}	Power Supply Current		10	50	mA	V_{CC} = Max., $V_{IN} = V_{CC}$ or GND, No Load, CLK2 = 50 MHz

NOTES:
4. Absolute values with respect to device GND; all over and undershoots due to system or tester noise are included.
5. Not more than 1 output should be tested at a time. Duration of that test should not exceed 1 second.

A.C. TESTING LOAD CIRCUIT (RDY#)

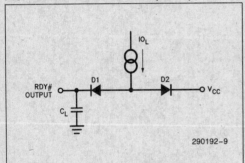

290192-9

See D.C. Characteristics Table for Current and Capacitance Specifications.
D1 and D2 are matched.

A.C. TESTING LOAD CIRCUIT (ALL OUTPUTS EXCEPT RDY#)

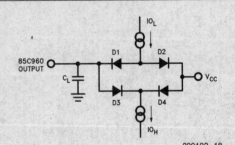

290192-18

See D.C. Characteristics Table for Current and Capacitance Specifications.
D1 and D2 are matched
D3 and D4 are matched

A.C. TESTING WAVEFORM—SYNCHRONOUS INPUTS AND OUTPUTS

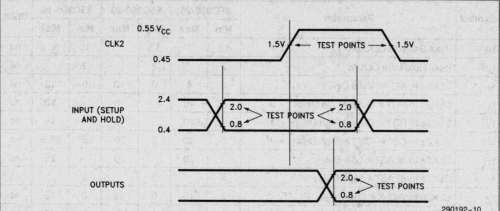

A.C. Testing: Inputs are driven at 2.4V for a Logic "1" and 0.4V for a Logic "0". CLK2 is driven at 0.55 V_{CC} for a Logic "1" and 0.45V for a Logic "0". Timing Measurements made relative to CLK2 are made from 1.5V on CLK2. Inputs and outputs are measured at 2.0V for a high and 0.8V for a low. Device input rise and fall times are less than 3 ns.

A.C. TESTING WAVEFORM—ASYNCHRONOUS INPUTS AND OUTPUTS

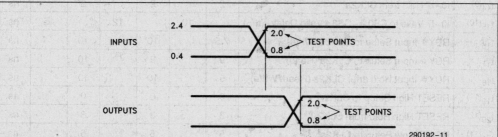

A.C. Testing: Inputs are driven at 2.4V for a Logic "1" and 0.4V for a Logic "0". Input timing is measured at 1.5V for high-to-low and low-to-high transitions. Outputs are measured at 2.0V for a high and 0.8V for a low. Device input rise and fall times are less than 3 ns.

A.C. CHARACTERISTICS (T_A = 0°C to +70°C, V_{CC} = 5.0V ±5%)

Symbol	Parameter	85C960-25		85C960-20		85C960-16		Units
		Min	Max	Min	Max	Min	Max	
t_1[6]	Input Setup to CLK2a	12		15		15		ns
t_2[6]	Input Hold from CLK2a	2		2		2		ns
t_3	CLK2a to A2, A3 Valid Delay	0	8	0	10	0	12	ns
t_4	CLK2c to RDY# Output Low Delay		10		15		18	ns
t_5[7]	CLK2c to RDY# Output High Delay		10		15		18	ns
t_6	CLK2a to CS0#–CS3# High Delay	5	40	5	50	5	62.5	ns
t_7	CLK2a to BLAST# Low Delay		20		20		25	ns
t_8	CLK2a to BLAST# High Delay	5		5		5		ns
t_9	CLK2b to WCLK# Low Delay	0	10	0	12	0	15	ns
t_{10}	CLK2d to WCLK# High Delay	2	10	2	12	2	15	ns
t_{11}[8]	ADS# Low to CS0#–CS3# Low Delay		10		12		15	ns
t_{12}[8]	CLK2c to CS0#–CS3# Low Delay		12		15		18	ns
t_{13}[9]	I0–I7 Setup to CLK2a	5		7		10		ns
t_{14}[9]	I0–I7 Hold from CLK2a	2		2		2		ns
t_{15}[10]	I0–I7 Valid to CS0#–CS3# Valid Delay–(t_{PD})		10		12		15	ns
t_{16}	RDY# Input Setup to CLK2d (Write)	7.5		10		10		ns
t_{17}	RDY# Input Setup to CLK2a (Read)	9		9		10		ns
t_{18}	RDY# Input Hold after CLK2a (Read/Write)	5		10		10		ns
t_{19}[11]	RESET High Setup to CLK2 ↑	0		0		0		ns
t_{20}[12]	RESET High Hold from CLK2 ↑	3		3		3		ns
t_{21}[11]	RESET Low Setup to CLK2a	5		5		5		ns

NOTES:
6. Applies to ADS#, DEN#, W/R#, and AD0–AD3. DEN# is high during the entire Ta state in 80960 KA/KB systems.
7. RDY# is an open-drain output. Specified time includes RDY# output float delay and pull-up/pull-down resistors (Figure 8). RDY# remains low for a minimum of 10 ns at the start of a Tr state and goes high by CLK2a of the next Tx state.
8. Chip Select Decoder latches are transparent flow-through types. Latches open when ADS# is low, DEN# is high, and CLK2 goes high during the middle of a Tx state (CLK2c). Since DEN# is high during the entire Ta state in 80960 KA/KB systems, only CLK2c and ADS# are specified.
9. Chip Select Decoder latches are transparent flow-through types. Latches close when ADS# is high or DEN# is low, or when CLK2 goes high at the start of a Tx state (CLK2a) after the latches have opened. Since ADS# is low and DEN# is high at the end of a Ta in 80960 KA/KB systems, setup and hold times are specified with reference to CLK2a only.
10. Propagation delay while latches are open (transparent); one output switching (high-to-low).
11. RESET must be held high for a minimum of 4 CLK2 cycles (80960 specifies 41 CLK2 cycles minimum).
12. RESET must hold after the low-to-high transition immediately prior to CLK2a. CLK2a is defined as the first low-to-high transition after RESET goes low.

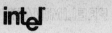
CLK2 EDGES

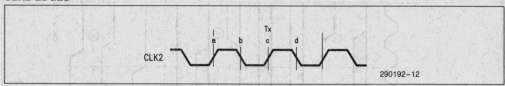

290192–12

CAPACITANCE ($T_A = 0°C$ to $+70°C$; $V_{CC} = 5.0V \pm 5\%$)

Symbol	Parameter	Min	Typ	Max	Unit	Conditions
C_{IN}	Input Capacitance		6	10	pF	$V_{IN} = 0V$, f = 1.0 MHz
C_{OUT}	Output Capacitance		6	10	pF	$V_{OUT} = 0V$, f = 1.0 MHz
C_{CLK}	CLK2 Capacitance		6	10	pF	$V_{IN} = 0V$, f = 1.0 MHz
C_{VPP}	V_{PP} Pin Capacitance		10	25	pF	V_{PP} on Pin 1 (RESET)
C_{RDY}	RDY # Capacitance		6	10	pF	$V_{OUT} = 0V$, f = 1.0 MHZ

85C960

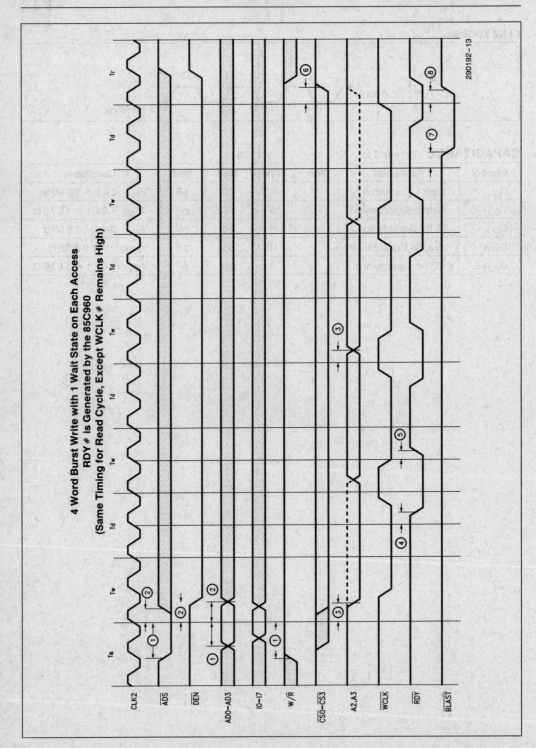

WCLK# TIMING

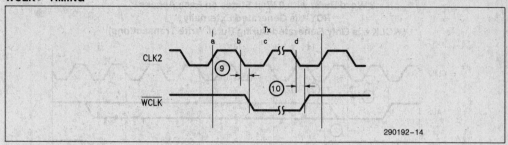

290192–14

I0–I7 AND CS0#–CS3# TIMING

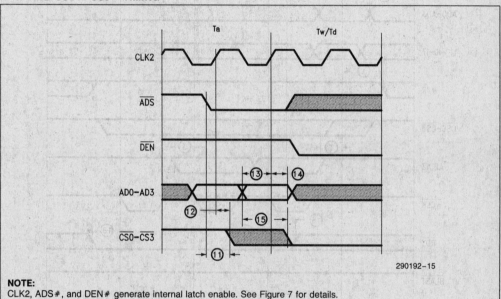

290192–15

NOTE:
CLK2, ADS#, and DEN# generate internal latch enable. See Figure 7 for details.

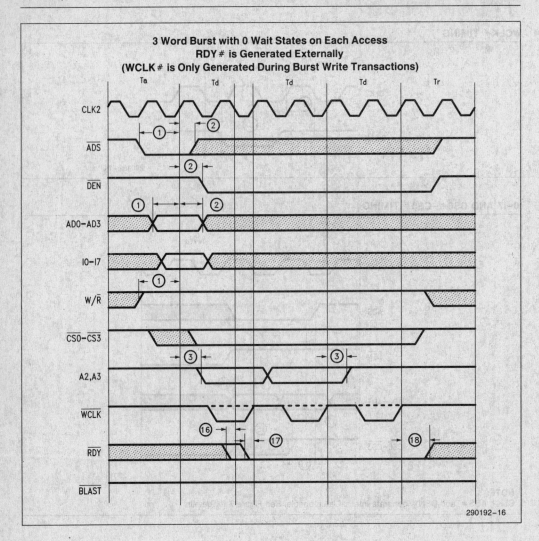

3 Word Burst with 0 Wait States on Each Access
RDY# is Generated Externally
(WCLK# is Only Generated During Burst Write Transactions)

290192-16

RESET INPUT TIMING

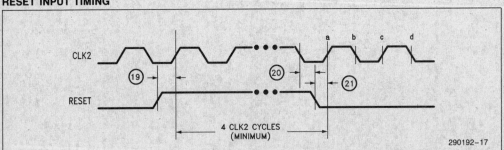

4 CLK2 CYCLES
(MINIMUM)

290192-17

27C202
Fast Word-Wide 256K (16K x 16) EPROM

- **High Speed**
  - 70 ns Access Time Maximizes CPU Performance
- **Low-Power CHMOS***
  - 100 mA Active, 15 mA Standby
- **High Drive Capability**
  - 4 mA Source/16 mA Sink Handles Large Arrays
- **High-Density Upgrade Pinout**
  - Matches 27210 1M EPROM

- **Rapid Programming**
  - 4 Second Throughput for Automated Manufacturing
- **Simple Interfacing**
  - TTL and CMOS Compatible
  - 2-Line Output Control
- **Versatile Package Options**
  - Standard 40-Pin DIP
  - Compact Surface-Mount 44-Lead PLCC**
  - 44-Lead Cerquad

(See Packaging Spec., Order No. 231369)

The Intel 27C202 is a high-performance, 262,144-bit, electrically programmable read only memory organized as 16 K-words of 16 bits each. Its high-density, word-wide configuration provides high integration for today's speed-critical applications.

The 27C202 meets no-wait-state performance requirements for many advanced 32-bit microprocessors. The large 256 K-bit capacity is well suited for high-end embedded control applications. The 27C202's organization provides an optimal single-chip firmware solution for code needs of monolithic 16-bit digital signal processors. System interfacing is simple, given two-line output control common to all standard Intel EPROMs. In addition, both TTL and CMOS logic can be used with the 27C202.

Three different packages are available for the 27C202. The standard 40-pin Dual-In-Line Package (DIP) provides for conventional device handling and socketing. Also, a 44-lead, One-Time-Programmable (OTP™) Plastic Leaded Chip Carrier (PLCC) allows lowest-cost, automated, surface-mount manufacturing. The 44-lead windowed Cerquad package allows reprogramming with the same compact dimensions as the PLCC package.

The Quick-Pulse Programming™ algorithm, with throughput times as fast as 4 seconds per device, improves manufacturing efficiency.

The 27C202 is manufactured on Intel's advanced CHMOS* III-E process, which is optimized for high-performance products.

The 27C202 will be replaced by the 27C202C mid-1990. The 27C202C will be functionally identical to the 27C202 in the read mode. The 27C202C's memory array will use a 1-transistor cell, versus the 27C202's 2-transistor cell, and will program with a standard one-pass algorithm.

*CHMOS is a patented process of Intel Corporation.   **PLCC package availability TBD

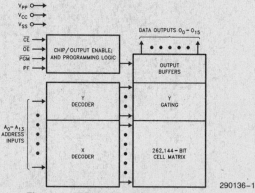

Figure 1. 27C202 Block Diagram

October 1989
Order Number: 290136-006

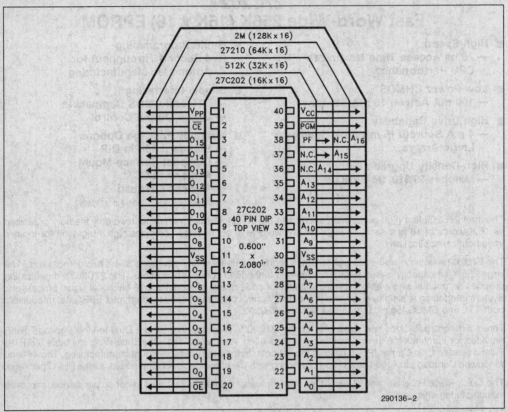

Figure 2. DIP Pin Configurations

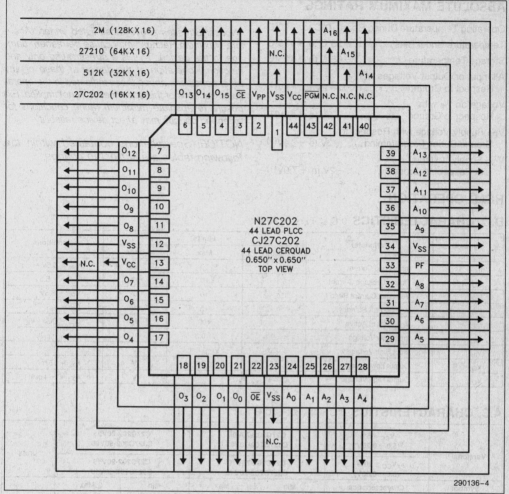

Figure 3. Cerquad**/PLCC Lead Configurations

290136–4

Pin Names

$A_0 - A_{15}$	Addresses
$\overline{CE}$	Chip Enable
$\overline{OE}$	Output Enable
$O_0 - O_{15}$	Outputs
$\overline{PGM}$	Program Enable
PF	Program Function
N.C.	No Connect

*CHMOS is a patented process of Intel Corporation.

NOTES:
1. Upgrade paths to higher densities are shown next to 27C202 pinouts.
2. Each 27C202 V_{CC} and V_{SS} pin specified must be tied individually to their respective power supplies. See System Design Considerations.

**Cerquad is available in a socket only version until the third quarter of 1990.

ABSOLUTE MAXIMUM RATINGS*

Operating Temperature During Read . 0°C to +70°C
Temperature Under Bias . . . . −55°C to +125°C
Storage Temperature . . . . −65°C to +125°C
All Input or Output Voltages with
   Respect to Ground . . . . −2V to +7V[1]
Voltage on A_9 with
   Respect to Ground . . . . −2V to +14V[1]
V_{PP} Supply Voltage with Respect to
   Ground During Programming . . . . −2V to +14V[1]
V_{CC} Supply Voltage
   with Respect to Ground . . . . −2V to +7.0V[1]

*Notice: Stresses above those listed under "Absolute Maximum Ratings" may cause permanent damage to the device. This is a stress rating only and functional operation of the device at these or any other conditions above those indicated in the operational sections of this specification is not implied. Exposure to absolute maximum rating conditions for extended periods may affect device reliability.

NOTICE: Specifications contained within the following tables are subject to change.

READ OPERATION

D.C. CHARACTERISTICS $0°C \leq T_A \leq +70°C$

Symbol	Parameter	Limits			Conditions
		Min	Max	Units	
I_{LI}	Input Load Current		10	µA	$V_{IN} = 5.5V$
I_{LO}	Output Leakage Current		10	µA	$V_{OUT} = 5.5V$
I_{PP1}	V_{PP} Load Current Read		10	µA	$V_{PP} = 5.5V$
I_{SB}	V_{CC} Current Standby		15	mA	$\overline{CE} = V_{IH}$
I_{CC}[2]	V_{CC} Current Active		100	mA	$\overline{CE} = OE = V_{IL}$
V_{IL}	Input Low Voltage	−0.1	+0.8	V	
V_{IH}	Input High Voltage	2.0	$V_{CC} + 1$	V	
V_{OL}	Output Low Voltage		0.45	V	$I_{OL} = 16$ mA
V_{OH}	Output High Voltage	2.4		V	$I_{OH} = -4$ mA

A.C. CHARACTERISTICS $0°C \leq T_A \leq +70°C$

Versions[3]		$V_{CC} \pm 5\%$ (5.0 ±0.25V)	C27C202-70V05 CJ27C202-70V05		C27C202-90V05 CJ27C202-90V05		Units
		$V_{CC} \pm 10\%$ (5.0 ±0.50V)	C27C202-70V10 CJ27C202-70V10		C27C202-90V10 CJ27C202-90V10		
Symbol	Characteristics		Min	Max	Min	Max	
t_{ACC}[5]	Address to Output Delay			70		90	ns
t_{CE}[5]	$\overline{CE}$ to Output Delay			70		90	ns
t_{OE}[5]	$\overline{OE}$ to Output Delay			30		35	ns
t_{DF}[4]	$\overline{OE}$ High to Output Float		0	15	0	20	ns
t_{OH}[4]	Output Hold from Address, $\overline{CE}$ or $\overline{OE}$ Whichever Occurred First		0		0		ns

NOTES:
1. Specified D.C. input voltage ranges are shown in the D.C. Read and D.C. Program Characteristics tables. Absolute maximum input voltages apply to overshoot durations of 20 ns or less; otherwise device damage may occur.
2. V_{CC} current assumes no output loading, i.e., $I_{OH} = I_{OL} = 0$ mA.
3. Packaging Options: C = Ceramic Side-Brazed DIP, CJ = Cerquad.
4. This parameter is only sampled and is not 100% tested. Output Float is defined as the point where data is no longer driven.
5. A derating factor of 6 ns/100 pF should be used with output loading greater than 30 pF. This derating factor is only sampled and not 100% tested.

CAPACITANCE[1] $T_A = 25°C, f = 1$ MHz

Symbol	Parameter	Typ	Max	Unit	Conditions
C_{IN}	Input Capacitance	12	15	pF	$V_{IN} = 0V$
C_{OUT}	Output Capacitance	12	15	pF	$V_{OUT} = 0V$
C_{VPP}	V_{PP} Input Capacitance		75	pF	$V_{PP} = 0V$

A.C. TESTING INPUT/OUTPUT WAVEFORM

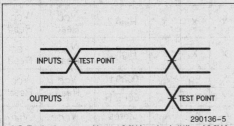

290136–5

A.C. Testing inputs are driven at 3.0V for a Logic "1" and 0.0V for a Logic "0". Timing measurements are made at 1.5V for both Logic "1" and Logic "0" output levels. Rise and fall times are 5 ns.

A.C. TESTING LOAD CIRCUIT

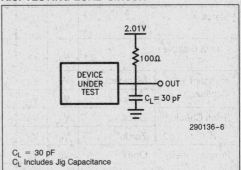

290136–6

$C_L = 30$ pF
C_L Includes Jig Capacitance

A.C. WAVEFORMS

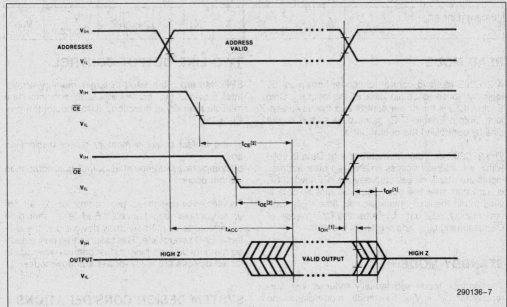

290136–7

NOTES:
1. These parameters are only sampled and are not 100% tested.
2. $\overline{OE}$ may be delayed up to $t_{CE}-t_{OE}$ after the falling edge of $\overline{CE}$ without impact on t_{CE}.

DEVICE OPERATION

Table 1 shows 27C202 operating modes. All inputs are TTL levels indicated in DC Characteristics unless otherwise specified.

Table 1. Mode Selection

Mode	Pins	$\overline{CE}$	$\overline{OE}$	$\overline{PGM}$	PF	A_9	A_0	Outputs	V_{CC}	V_{PP}
Read		V_{IL}	V_{IL}	X	X	A_9	A_0	D_{OUT}	V_{CC} Read	V_{CC} Read
Standby		V_{IH}	X	X	X	X	X	High Z	V_{CC} Read	V_{CC} Read
Output Disable		V_{IL}	V_{IH}	X	X	X	X	High Z	V_{CC} Read	V_{CC} Read
int$_e$ligent Identifier	Manufacturer	V_{IL}	V_{IL}	X	X	V_H	V_{IL}	0089 H	V_{CC} Read	V_{CC} Read
	Device	V_{IL}	V_{IL}	X	X	V_H	V_{IH}	66FE H		
Blank Checks	Ones	V_{IL}	V_{IL}	V_{IH}	V_{IH}	A_9	A_0	Zeros	V_{CC} Program	V_{PP}
	Zeros	V_{IL}	V_{IL}	V_{IH}	V_{IL}	A_9	A_0	Ones		
Program Verify	Ones	V_{IL}	V_{IL}	V_{IH}	V_{IH}	A_9	A_0	Ones	V_{CC} Program	V_{PP}
	Zeros	V_{IL}	V_{IL}	V_{IH}	V_{IL}	A_9	A_0	Zeros		
Program	Ones	V_{IL}	V_{IH}	V_{IL}	V_{IH}	A_9	A_0	D_{IN}	V_{CC} Program	V_{PP}
	Zeros	V_{IL}	V_{IH}	V_{IL}	V_{IL}	A_9	A_0			
Program Inhibit		V_{IH}	X	X	X	X	X	High Z	V_{CC} Program	V_{PP}

READ MODE

A 27C202 has two control functions; both must be logically active to obtain data at the outputs. Chip Enable ($\overline{CE}$) is the power control and the device-select. Output Enable ($\overline{OE}$) gates data to the output pins by controlling the output buffer.

The 27C202 operates asynchronously. Data is valid within the address access time (t_{ACC}) after address inputs are stable on selected devices ($\overline{CE}$ low). If $\overline{CE}$ is activated after the addresses are stable, data is valid within the chip enable access time (t_{CE}). Outputs display valid data t_{OE} after the falling edge of $\overline{OE}$, assuming t_{ACC} and t_{CE} times are met.

STANDBY MODE

The standby mode substantially reduces V_{CC} current. When $\overline{CE}$ = V_{IH}, the standby mode places the outputs in a high impedance state, independent of the $\overline{OE}$ input.

TWO LINE OUTPUT CONTROL

EPROMs are often used in larger memory arrays. Intel provides two control inputs to accommodate multiple memory connections. Two line control provides for:

a) the lowest possible memory power dissipation, and
b) complete assurance that output bus contention will not occur.

To efficiently use these two control inputs, an address decoder should enable $\overline{CE}$ while $\overline{OE}$ should be connected to all memory-array devices and the system READ control line. This assures that only selected memory devices have active outputs while deselected devices are in low-power standby mode.

SYSTEM DESIGN CONSIDERATIONS

The 27C202 is a high performance memory with exceptionally strong output drive capability for fast output response. Input levels are sensitive to power supply stability. Special considerations must be given to the large supply current swings associated with switching 16 powerful output drivers. Minimizing power supply inductance is critical. Wide, short traces with low inductance must be connected from the circuit board's ground and V_{CC} plane to each device. V_{CC} transients must be suppressed with high-frequency 0.1 μF capacitors. Where the solid ground plane of a multilayer board is not available, bulk electrolytic capacitors (typically 4.7 μF) should decouple the V_{CC} and the ground supplies for each group of four 27C202 devices.

The 30 pF load capacitance specified in the A.C. Test Conditions is not a system design limitation. The 27C202 has the output drive capability to handle the capacitive loading of large memory arrays. However, access times must be appropriately derated for loading in excess of 30 pF. T_{ACC}, T_{OE} and T_{CE} should be derated 6 ns/100 pF with output loading greater than 30 pF.

PROGRAMMING MODE

Caution: Exceeding 14V on V_{PP} will permanently damage the device.

To minimize data access time delays, the 27C202 utilizes a 2-transistor cell with differential sensing. The 2-transistor cells are partitioned into "ONES" and "ZEROS" arrays. Programming is done in two passes; once in the "ONES" half of the memory array and once in the "ZEROS" half. The same data word must be presented to the device in both passes. A program function (PF) pin is provided to control this partitioning (see Figure 5).

The programming mode is entered when V_{PP} and V_{CC} are raised to their programming voltages (see Table 2), $\overline{CE}$ and $\overline{PGM}$ are at TTL-low and $\overline{OE}$ = V_{IH}. The data to be programmed is applied 16 bits in parallel to the data output pins. TTL levels are required for the address and data inputs.

PROGRAM INHIBIT

Programming of multiple EPROMs in parallel with different data is easily accomplished by using the Program Inhibit mode. A high-level $\overline{PGM}$ or $\overline{CE}$ prevents devices from being programmed.

Except for $\overline{CE}$, all like inputs of the parallel EPROMs may be common. A TTL low-level pulse applied to the $\overline{PGM}$ input, with V_{PP} at programming voltage, $\overline{CE}$ at a TTL-low level, and $\overline{OE}$ at V_{IH} will program the selected device.

PROGRAM VERIFY/BLANK CHECK

The program verify/blank check mode is activated when the $\overline{OE}$ is at a TTL-low level, V_{PP} and V_{CC} are at their programming levels, and the program control line ($\overline{PGM}$) is at a TTL-high level. Blank Check individually confirms unprogrammed status of both arrays **(a blank check cannot be done with a normal read operation with the 2-transistor cell).** Program verify is used to check programmed status. The elevated V_{CC} voltage used during Program Verify ensures high programming margins and long-term data retention with maximum noise immunity.

The program/verify cycle begins with the "ONES" array; the Program Function pin (PF) is held at a TTL-high level. The "ONES" programming is completed when the desired "ONES" bits are verified changed from their unprogrammed state ("ZEROS").

Programming is not complete, however, until the "ZEROS" array program/verify cycle is also finished. The "ZEROS" cycle begins when PF is brought to a TTL-low level. The "ZEROS" programming is completed when the desired "ZEROS" bits are verified changed from their unprogrammed state ("ONES").

Quick-Pulse Programming™ OPERATIONS

The Quick-Pulse Programming™ algorithm is used to program Intel's 27C202. Developed to reduce substantially production programming throughput time, this algorithm can program a 27C202 in under four seconds. Actual programming time depends on the PROM programmer used.

The Quick-Pulse Programming algorithm uses a 100 microsecond initial-pulse followed by a word verification to determine when the addressed word is correctly programmed. The algorithm terminates if 25 100 μs pulses fail to program a word. This is repeated for both the "ONES" and "ZEROS" programming. Figure 5 shows the 27C202 Quick-Pulse Programming algorithm flowchart.

The entire program-pulse/word-verify sequence is performed with V_{CC} = 6.25V and V_{PP} = 12.75V. When programming is complete, all words should be compared to the original data in a standard read mode with V_{CC} = 5.0V.

int_eligent Identifier™ MODE

The int_eligent Identifier™ Mode will determine an EPROM's manufacturer and device type. Programming equipment can automatically match a device with its proper programming algorithm.

The Identifier mode is activated when A9 is at high voltage (V_H). A0 determines the information being accessed. The first address (A0 = V_{IL}) accesses the manufacturer code and the second (A0 = V_{IH}) accesses the device code.

ERASURE CHARACTERISTICS (FOR UV-WINDOW PACKAGES)

Light with wavelengths shorter than 4000 Angstroms (Å) causes EPROM erasure. Sunlight and some fluo-rescent lamps have wavelengths in the 3000–4000 Å range. Constant exposure to room-level fluores-cent light can erase an EPROM in about 3 years while direct sunlight erasure occurs within approxi-mately 1 week. Covering windowed EPROMs with opaque labels prevents such unintended erasure.

The recommended erasure procedure is to expose the EPROM to a 2537 Å ultraviolet (UV) source for a minimum integrated dose (intensity × exposure time) of 15 W-sec/cm^2. The EPROM should be placed within 1 inch of the light source and will erase in 15 to 20 minutes with a typical 12000 μW/cm^2 lamp.

Overexposure to high-intensity UV light can cause permanent device damage. The maximum integrat-ed dose allowed is 7258 W-sec/cm^2 (approximately 1 week at 12000 μW/cm^2).

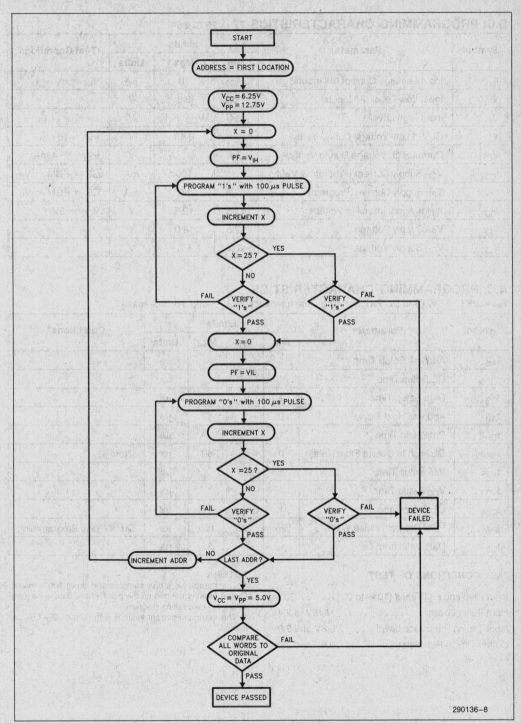

Figure 4. 27C202 Programming Algorithm

D.C. PROGRAMMING CHARACTERISTICS $T_A = 25°C \pm 5°C$

Symbol	Parameter	Limits			Test Conditions
		Min	Max	Units	
I_{LI}	Input Leakage Current (All Inputs)		10	μA	$V_{IN} = 6V$
V_{IL}	Input Low Level (All Inputs)	-0.1	0.8	V	
V_{IH}	Input High Level	2.4	$V_{CC} + 1$	V	
V_{OL}	Output Low Voltage During Verify		0.45	V	$I_{OL} = 16\ mA$
V_{OH}	Output High Voltage During Verify	2.4		V	$I_{OH} = -4\ mA$
$I_{CC2}^{(2)}$	V_{CC} Supply Current (Program & Verify)		100	mA	$\overline{CE} = \overline{PGM} = V_{IL}$
I_{PP2}	V_{PP} Supply Current (Program)		50	mA	$\overline{CE} = \overline{PGM} = V_{IL}$
V_{ID}	A_9 int$_e$ligent Identifier Voltage	11.5	12.5	V	$V_{CC} = 5V$
V_{PP}	V_{PP} Supply Voltage	12.5	13.0	V	
V_{CC}	V_{CC} Supply Voltage	6.0	6.5	V	

A.C. PROGRAMMING CHARACTERISTICS

$T_A = 25°C \pm 5\%$ (See DC Programming Characteristics for V_{CC} and V_{PP} voltages.)

Symbol	Parameter	Limits				Conditions*
		Min	Typ	Max	Units	
t_{AS}	Address Setup Time	1			μs	
t_{OES}	$\overline{OE}$ Setup Time	1			μs	
t_{DS}	Data Setup Time	1			μs	
t_{AH}	Address Hold Time	0			μs	
t_{DH}	Data Hold Time	1			μs	
t_{DFP}	$\overline{OE}$ High to Output Float Delay	0		50	ns	(Note 1)
t_{VPS}	V_{PP} Setup Time	1			μs	
t_{VCS}	V_{CC} Setup Time	1			μs	
t_{CES}	$\overline{CE}$ Setup Time	1			μs	
t_{PW}	$\overline{PGM}$ Program Pulse Width	95	100	105	μs	Quick-Pulse Programming
t_{OE}	Data Valid from $\overline{OE}$			35	ns	

*A.C. CONDITIONS OF TEST

Input Rise and Fall Times (10% to 90%) . . . . . . 20 ns

Input Pulse Levels . . . . 0.45V to 2.4V

Input Timing Reference Level . . . . 0.8V and 2.0V

Output Timing Reference Level . . . . . . 0.8V and 2.0V

NOTES:
1. This parameter is only sampled and is not 100% tested. Output Float is defined as the point where data is no longer driven—see timing diagram.
2. The maximum current value is with outputs O_0–O_{15} unloaded.

PROGRAMMING WAVEFORMS

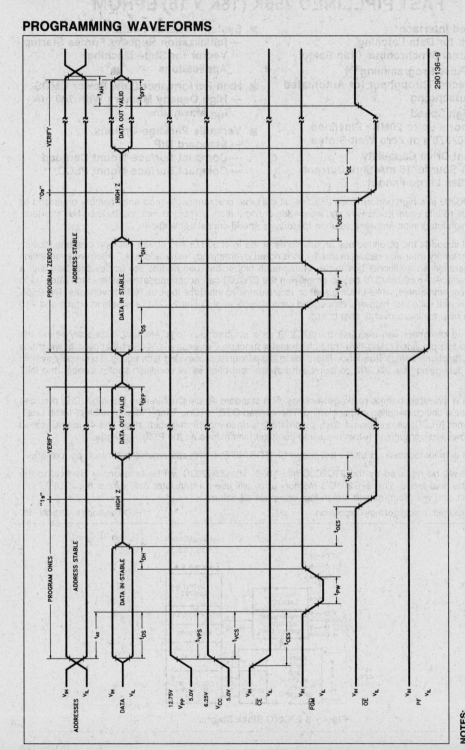

290136-9

NOTES:
1. The Input Timing Reference Level is 0.8V for V_{IL} and 2V for a V_{IH}.
2. t_{OE} and t_{DFP} are characteristics of the device but must be accommodated by the programmer.
3. When programming, a 0.1 μF capacitor is required across V_{PP} and ground to suppress spurious voltage transients which can damage the device.

27C203
FAST PIPELINED 256K (16K x 16) EPROM

- **Pipelined Interface**
  - **Clock for Data Latching**
  - **Optional Synchronous Chip Select**
- **Quick-Pulse Programming™**
  - **4 Second Throughput for Automated Manufacturing**
- **Very High Speed**
  - **Supports up to 20MHz Pipelined 80386/376's at Zero Wait-States**
- **Excellent Drive Capability**
  - **4 mA Source/16 mA Sink Current Handles Large Fanout**

- **System Initialize Feature**
  - **Initialization Register Forces Startup Vector for State Machine Applications**
- **High-Performance/Low Power CMOS**
  - **High Density Memory With 100 mA I_{CC} Maximum**
- **Versatile Package Options**
  - **Standard DIP**
  - **Compact Surface-Mount Cerquad**
  - **Compact Surface-Mount PLCC****

The Intel 27C203 is a high performance 262,144-bit erasable programmable read-only memory organized as 16K words of 16 bits each. Its density and word-wide configuration, combined with its pipelined bus interface, provides a high integration firmware solution for today's speed-critical applications.

The 27C203 supports the pipelined bus architectures of the Intel 80376 and 80386 microprocessors. Pipelining relaxes memory interface requirements by utilizing an overlapping "early address," effectively stretching the read operation an additional bus cycle. Thus, much higher bus bandwidths are achievable than with a standard interface. An 80386/376 design employing the 27C203 can accommodate system clock rates up to 20 MHz at zero wait-states, while utilizing slower, less expensive interface logic in 16 MHz versions. The 256K bit capacity is well suited for high-end embedded control applications. The 27C203's simple interface and X16 organization help minimize overall chip count.

State machine designers can also use the 27C203 as a synchronous logic element, especially where the designer needs a pipelined "data-flow-through" transfer function. For example, it can be applied to weighting or summing functions in high frequency filters using digital signal processing techniques. To simplify system design and debugging, the 27C203 contains a hardware-controlled initial condition vector through the INIT function pin.

The 27C203 is available in three package versions. The standard 40-pin Dual-In-Line Package (DIP) provides for conventional device handling and socketing. The 44-lead OTP™ (One-Time-Programmable) Plastic Leaded Chip Carrier (PLCC) allows lowest cost, automated, surface-mount manufacturing. The 44-lead Cerquad Package allows reprogramming within the same compact dimensions as the PLCC package.

The 27C203 is manufactured on Intel's advanced CHMOS* III-E, a process optimized for high performance.

The 27C203 will be replaced by the 27C203C mid 1990. The 27C203C will be functionally identical to the 27C203 in the read mode. The 27C203C's memory array will use a I-transistor cell, versus the 27C203's 2-transistor cell, and will program with a standard one-pass algorithm.

*CHMOS is a patented process of Intel Corporation.   **PLCC package availability TBD

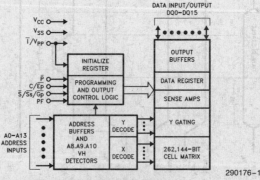

Figure 1. 27C203 Block Diagram

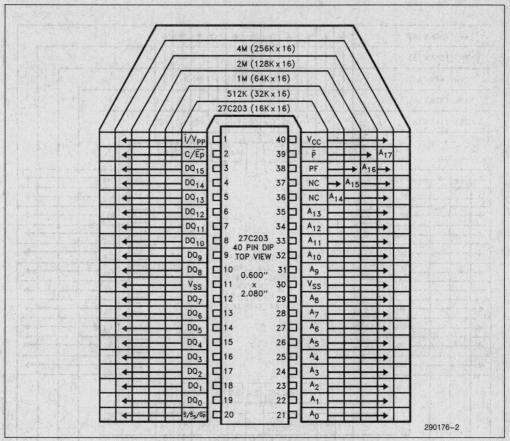

Figure 2a. DIP Pin Configuration

27C203 Pin Names

A0–A13	Address
DQ0–DQ15	Data Inputs/Outputs
C/$\overline{Ep}$	Clock/Program Chip Enable
$\overline{S}$/$\overline{Ss}$/$\overline{Gp}$	Chip Select/Program Output Enable
$\overline{P}$	Programming Enable
PF	Program Function
$\overline{I}$/V_{PP}	Initialize Register Enable/V_{PP}
NC	No Connect

NOTE:
1. Each 27C203 V_{CC} and V_{SS} pin specified must be tied individually to their respective power supplies. See System Design Considerations.

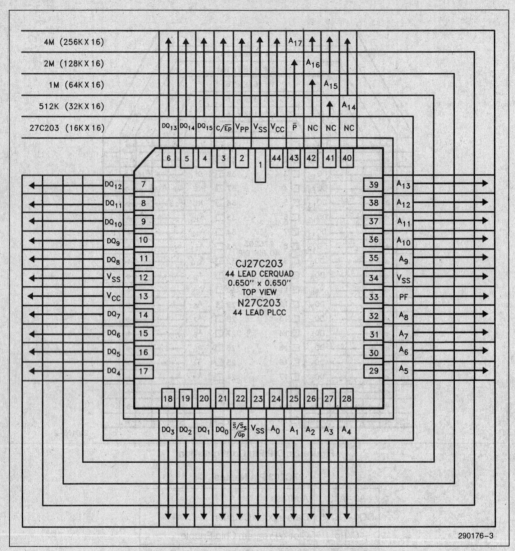

Figure 2b. Cerquad/PLCC Lead Configuration

290176–3

ABSOLUTE MAXIMUM RATINGS*

Operating temperature during read ...0°C to +70°C

Temperature under bias .... −55°C to +125°C

Storage temperature .... −65°C to +125°C

All input or output voltages
with respect to ground .... −2V to +7V[1]

Voltage on A9 with
with respect to ground .... −2V to +14V[1]

V_PP supply voltage with respect
to ground during programming .. −2V to +14V[1]

V_CC supply voltage with
respect to ground .... −2V to +7V[1]

*Notice: Stresses above those listed under "Absolute Maximum Ratings" may cause permanent damage to the device. This is a stress rating only and functional operation of the device at these or any other conditions above those indicated in the operational sections of this specification is not implied. Exposure to absolute maximum rating conditions for extended periods may affect device reliability.

NOTICE: Specifications contained within the following tables are subject to change.

EXTENDED TEMPERATURE (EXPRESS) EPROMS

The Intel EXPRESS EPROM family receives additional processing to enhance product characteristics. EXPRESS EPROMs are available with 168 +/ − 8 hour, 125°C dynamic burn-in using Intel's standard bias configuration. This process meets or exceeds most industry burn-in specifications. The standard EXPRESS EPROM operating temperature range is 0°C to +70°C. Extended operating temperature range (−40°C to +85°C) EXPRESS products are also available. Like all Intel EPROMs, the EXPRESS EPROM family is inspected to 0.1% electrical AQL. This allows reduction or elimination of incoming testing.

EXPRESS OPTIONS

Versions

Speed	Packaging Options	
Versions	DIP	Cerquad
−45V05	Q, T, L	Q, T, L
−45V10	Q, T, L	Q, T, L
−55V05	Q, T, L	Q, T, L
−55V10	Q, T, L	Q, T, L

EXPRESS EPROM PRODUCT FAMILY

Product Definitions

Type	Operating Temperature	Burn-in 125°C (hr)
Q	0°C to +70°C	168 ± 8
T	−40°C to +85°C	NONE
L	−40°C to +85°C	168 ± 8

NOTE:
1. Minimum D.C. input voltage is −0.5V. During transitions the inputs may undershoot to −2.0V for periods less than 20 ns. Maximum D.C. voltage on output pins is V_CC + 0.5V which may overshoot to V_CC +2V for periods less than 20 ns.

D.C. CHARACTERISTICS

Symbol	Parameter	Min	Typ	Max	Units	Conditions
		Limits				
I_{LI}	Input Load Current			10	μA	$V_{IN} = 5.5V$
I_{LO}	Output Leakage Current			10	μA	$V_{OUT} = 5.5V$
I_{PP1}	V_{PP} Load Current Read			10	μA	$V_{PP} = 5.5V$
I_{CC}[1]	V_{CC} Current Active		60	100	mA	
V_{IL}	Input Low Voltage	−0.1		+0.8	V	
V_{IH}	Input High Voltage	2.0		$V_{CC} + 1$	V	
V_{OL}	Output Low Voltage			.45	V	$I_{OL} = 16\,mA$
V_{OH}	Output High Voltage	2.4			V	$I_{OH} = -4mA$

A.C. CHARACTERISTICS

Versions (2)		C27C203-45V05 CJ27C203-45V05		C27C203-55V05 CJ27C203-55V05		
	$V_{CC} \pm 5\%\ (5.0 \pm 0.25V)$					
	$V_{CC} \pm 10\%\ (5.0 \pm 0.50V)$	C27C203-45V10 CJ27C203-45V10		C27C203-55V10 CJ27C203-55V10		Units
Symbol	Characteristics	Min.	Max.	Min.	Max.	
t_{AVCH}	Address Valid to Clock	45		55		ns
t_{CHAX}	Address Hold from Clock	0		0		ns
t_{CHQV}[3]	Clock to Valid Output		40		50	ns
t_{CHQZ}[4]	Clock to Output Tri-state for Synchronous Chip Deselect, S_S		15		15	ns
t_{CHCL}, t_{CLCH}	Clock Pulse Width	25		25		ns
t_{SVCH}	Setup Time to Clock for Synchronous Chip Select, $\overline{S}_S$.	10		10		ns
t_{CHSX}	Hold Time for Sync. Select	10		10		ns
t_{CHQX}[4]	Data Hold Time From Clock	0		0		ns
t_{SHQX}[4]	Data Hold Time From Select	0		0		ns
t_{SLQV}[3]	Valid Output Delay from Asynchronous Chip Select, $\overline{S}$.		35		40	ns
t_{SHQZ}[4]	Output Tri-state from Asynchronous Chip Deselect, $\overline{S}$.		10		10	ns
t_{ILQV}[3]	Initialize Register Valid Output Delay		35		40	ns
t_{ILIH}	Initialize Pulse Width	20		25		ns
t_{IHCH}	Recovery Time from Initialize to Clock	5		5		ns

NOTES:
1. V_{CC} current assumes no output loading, i.e., $I_{OH} = I_{OL}$ 0mA
2. Packaging options: C = Ceramic Side-Brazed, CJ = Cerquad.
3. A derating factor of 6 ns/100 pF should be used with output loading greater than 30 pF. This derating factor is only sampled and not 100% tested.
4. These parameters are only sampled and not 100% tested.

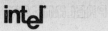
A.C. WAVEFORMS—PIPELINED BUS APPLICATION (80376/80386)

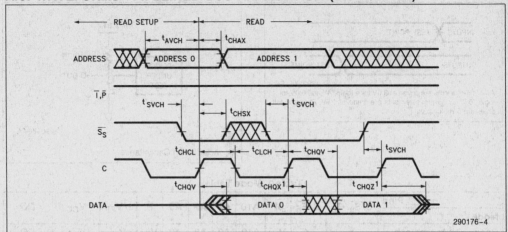

290176–4

A.C. WAVEFORMS—STATE MACHINE APPLICATION (ASYNCHRONOUS CHIP SELECT)

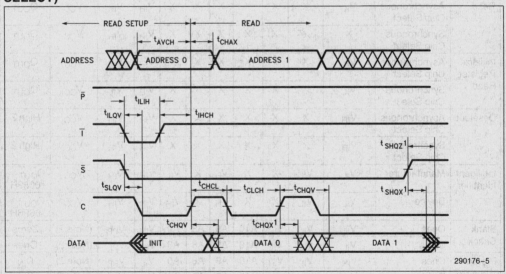

290176–5

NOTE:
1. These parameters are only sampled and not 100% tested.

CAPACITANCE[1] $T_A = 25°C, f = 1$ MHz

Symbol	Parameter	Typ	Max	Unit	Conditions
C_{IN}	Input Capacitance	12	15	pF	$V_{IN} = 0V$
C_{OUT}	Output Capacitance	12	15	pF	$V_{OUT} = 0V$
C_{VPP}	V_{PP} Input Capacitance		75	pF	$V_{PP} = 0V$

A.C. TESTING INPUT/OUTPUT WAVEFORM

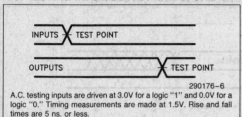

290176-6

A.C. testing inputs are driven at 3.0V for a logic "1" and 0.0V for a logic "0." Timing measurements are made at 1.5V. Rise and fall times are 5 ns. or less.

A.C. TESTING LOAD CURRENT

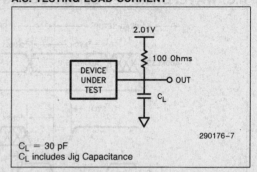

290176-7

C_L = 30 pF
C_L includes Jig Capacitance

Table 1. Mode Table

Mode	Pins	$\overline{S}/\overline{S_s}/\overline{G_p}$	$C/\overline{E_p}$	pF	A10	A9	A8	A0	$\overline{P}$	$\overline{I}/V_{PP}$	V_{CC}	DQ
Read Setup	Asynchronous Chip Select	X	⟋	V_{IH}	A10	A9	A8	A0	V_{IH}	V_{IH}	V_{CC}	DQ Prior
	Synchronous Chip Select	V_{IL}	⟋	V_{IH}	A10	A9	A8	A0	V_{IH}	V_{IH}	V_{CC}	DQ Prior
Read	Asynchronous Chip Select	V_{IL}	X	X	X	X	X	X	V_{IH}	V_{IH}	V_{CC}	Q_{OUT}
	Synchronous Chip Select	X	⟋	X	X	X	X	X	V_{IH}	V_{IH}	V_{CC}	Q_{OUT}
Initialize Register Read	Asynchronous Chip Select	V_{IL}	X	X	X	X	X	X	V_{IH}	V_{IL}	V_{CC}	Q_{OUT}
	Synchronous Chip Select	V_{IL}	⟋	X	X	X	X	X	V_{IH}	V_{IL}	V_{CC}	Q_{OUT}
Deselect	Asynchronous Chip Select	V_{IH}	X	X	X	X	X	X	V_{IH}	V_{IH}	V_{CC}	High Z
	Synchronous Chip Select	V_{IH}	⟋	X	X	X	X	X	V_{IH}	V_{IH}	V_{CC}	High Z
Int$_e$ligent Identifier	Manufacturer	V_{IL}	V_{IL}	X	X	V_H	X	V_{IL}	V_{IH}	V_{IH}	V_{CC}	Q_{OUT} = 0089H
	Device	V_{IL}	V_{IL}	X	X	V_H	X	V_{IH}	V_{IH}	V_{IH}	V_{CC}	Q_{OUT} = 66F6H
Blank Check	Ones	V_{IL}	V_{IL}	V_{IH}	A10	A9	A8	A0	V_{IH}	V_{PP}	(Note 2)	Zeros
	Zeros	V_{IL}	V_{IL}	V_{IL}	A10	A9	A8	A0	V_{IH}	V_{PP}	(Note 2)	Ones
Program	Ones	V_{IH}	V_{IL}	V_{IH}	A10	A9	A8	A0	V_{IL}	V_{PP}	(Note 2)	D_{IN}
	Zeros	V_{IH}	V_{IL}	V_{IL}	A10	A9	A8	A0	V_{IL}	V_{PP}	(Note 2)	D_{IN}

Table 1. Mode Table (Continued)

Mode		$\overline{S}/\overline{S}_s/\overline{G}_p$	$C/\overline{E}_p$	pF	A10	A9	A8	A0	$\overline{P}$	$\overline{I}/V_{PP}$	V_{CC}	DQ
Program Verify	Ones	V_{IL}	V_{IL}	V_{IH}	A10	A9	A8	A0	V_{IH}	V_{PP}	(Note 2)	Ones
	Zeros	V_{IL}	V_{IL}	V_{IL}	A10	A9	A8	A0	V_{IH}	V_{PP}	(Note 2)	Zeros
Synchronous Chip Select Program		V_{IH}	V_{IL}	X	X	X	V_H	X	V_{IL}	V_{PP}	(Note 2)	High Z
Initialize Register Program		V_{IH}	V_{IL}	X	V_H	X	X	X	V_{IL}	V_{PP}	(Note 2)	D_{IN}
Initialize Register Read		V_{IL}	V_{IL}	X	X	X	X	X	V_{IH}	V_{IL}	(Note 2)	Q_{OUT}
Program Inhibit		X	V_{IH}	X	X	X	X	X	X	V_{PP}	(Note 2)	High Z

NOTES:
1. Refer to A.C. Test Points for V_{IH} and V_{IL} levels. A V_{IH} to V_{IL} transition is represented by ⌐, and a V_{IL} to V_{IH} transition is represented by ⌐. X represents either V_{IH} or V_{IL}. See D.C. programming characteristics for V_H and V_{PP}.
2. $V_{CC} = 6.25V \pm 0.25V$ during programming.

READ MODE

The 27C203 read operation is synchronous. Data registers on the output buffers (Figure 3) allow high-bandwidth, pipelined read operations without the additional components that would normally be required. By using these data registers along with a programmable initial word feature, state machine designs can be implemented without the use of external latches.

The chip select (output enable) can be programmed to be synchronous ($\overline{S}s$) or left in the default asynchronous state ($\overline{S}$) (Figure 3). The chip select is programmed to be synchronous in pipelined bus applications so the data output triggers off the rising edge of the clock (C) signal. In state machine applications, the chip select can be programmed or left unprogrammed, depending on the needs of the design. Pipelined and state machine applications are detailed below.

PIPELINED BUS APPLICATION (80376 OR 80386)

The 27C203 pipelined EPROM interfaces with the 80376/80386 pipelined bus when programmed in the synchronous chip select mode. Figure 4 shows a 376™ embedded processor with the 27C203 in a simple embedded system.

Valid address information must be stable for the minimum address setup time (t_{AVCH}) before the data can be shifted to the outputs. The data is loaded in the data registers on the rising edge of the 27C203's C. The same C edge latches the synchronous chip select state into the chip select register. To activate the next output, the $\overline{S}s$ input must be low before the C rising edge. Following the rising edge of the C, the outputs become valid (t_{CHQV}).

To deselect the device in the next output state, the $\overline{S}s$ must be high for at least the synchronous select setup time (t_{SVCH}) before the C rising edge. Follow-

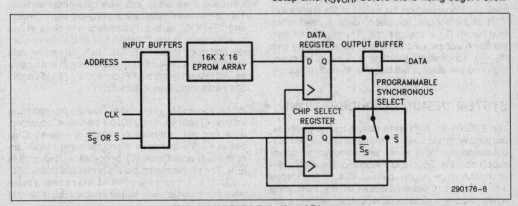

Figure 3. 27C203 Functional Diagram

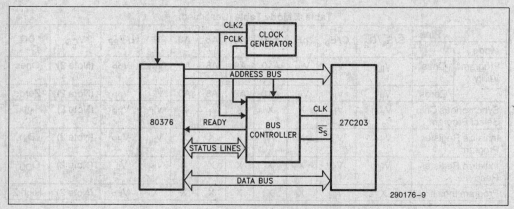

Figure 4. 27C203 in Simple 80376 Embedded System

ing the rising edge of the C, the outputs become tri-stated (t_{CHQZ}).

Buffering may be needed to avoid bus contention when different types of pipelined memories are bussed together. For common 27C203's with synchronous chip selects, the chip deselect times are sufficiently fast to minimize active output overlap. The synchronization of one device's selection with another's deselection is accomplished through common clock inputs (C must be common with multiple synchronously selected devices).

STATE MACHINE APPLICATION

A programmable initial word feature, combined with the data registers, optimize the 27C203 for state machine designs. The 16-bit initial word is active (t_{ILQV}) when the Initialize Register Enable pin ($\overline{I}$) is brought low for a minimum pulse width (t_{ILIH}). A recovery time (t_{IHCH}) is required before the next C rising edge.

The chip select can be programmed to be either synchronous ($\overline{Ss}$) or left in the default asynchronous state ($\overline{S}$), depending on the needs of the application. With asynchronous operation, data is read when chip select ($\overline{S}$) is brought low. The registered data will then become valid in the chip select access time (t_{SLQV}). To deselect the device, $\overline{S}$ must be raised high and the outputs will become tri-stated (t_{SHQZ}).

SYSTEM DESIGN CONSIDERATIONS

The 27C203 is a high performance memory with exceptionally strong output drive capability for fast output response. Input levels are sensitive to power supply stability. Special considerations must be given to the large supply current swings associated with switching 16 powerful output drivers. Minimizing power supply inductance is critical. Wide, short

traces with low inductance must be connected from the circuit board's ground and V_{CC} plane to each device. V_{CC} transients must be suppressed with high-frequency 0.1 μF capacitors. Where the solid ground plane of a multilayer board is not available, bulk electrolytic capacitors (typically 4.7μF) should decouple the V_{CC} and the ground supplies for each group of four 27C203 devices.

The 30pF load capacitance specified in the A.C. Test Conditions is not a system design limitation. The 27C203 has the output drive capability to handle the capacitive loading of large memory arrays. However, access times must be appropriately derated for loading in excess of 30pF. t_{CHQV}, t_{SLQV} and t_{ILQV} should be derated 6ns/100pF with output loading greater than 30pF.

PROGRAMMING MODE

Caution: Exceeding 14V on V_{PP} will permanently damage the device.

To minimize data access time delays, the 27C203 utilizes a 2-transistor cell with differential sensing. The 2-transistor cells are partitioned into "ONES" and "ZEROS" arrays. Programming is done in two passes; once in the "ONES" half of the memory array and once in the "ZEROS" half. The same data word must be presented to the device in both passes. A program function (PF) pin is provided to control this partitioning (see Figure 5).

When V_{PP} and V_{CC} are raised to their programming voltage (Table 2), the 27C203 becomes asynchronous and the programming mode is entered. Chip Select ($\overline{S}/\overline{Ss}$) becomes a programming output enable ($\overline{Gp}$), and Clock (C) becomes a chip enable ($\overline{Ep}$). The programming pin ($\overline{P}$) is brought to the TTL-low level to activate the EPROM programming pulse while the programming output enable ($\overline{Gp}$) is held at a TTL-high level.

Outputs are active whenever $\overline{Gp}$ and $\overline{Ep}$ are low. $\overline{Ep}$ does not need to be toggled as it does while serving the read mode Clock function. This facilitates gang programming by allowing $\overline{Gp}$ to be a common verify control line while $\overline{Ep}$ controls individual device selection, eliminating bus contention.

PROGRAM INHIBIT

Programming of multiple EPROMs in parallel with different data is easily accomplished by using the Program Inhibit mode. A high-level $\overline{P}$ or $\overline{Ep}$ prevents devices from being programmed.

Except for $\overline{Ep}$, all like inputs of the parallel EPROMs may be common. A TTL low-level pulse applied to the $\overline{P}$ input, with V_{PP} at programming voltage, $\overline{Ep}$ at a TTL-low level and $\overline{G}_p$ at V_{IH} will program the selected device.

PROGRAM VERIFY/BLANK CHECK

The program verify mode is activated when the programming output enable pin ($\overline{Gp}$) is at a TTL-low level, V_{PP} and V_{CC} are at their programming levels, and the program control line ($\overline{P}$) is at a TTL-high level. Blank Check individually confirms unprogrammed status of both arrays **(a blank check cannot be done with a normal read operation with the 2-transistor cell)**. Program verify is used to check programmed status. The elevated V_{CC} voltage used during Program Verify ensures high programming margins and long-term data retention with maximum noise immunity.

The program/verify cycle begins with the "ONES" array; the Program Function pin (PF) is held at a TTL-high level. The "ONES" programming is completed when the desired "ONES" bits are verified changed from their unprogrammed state ("ZEROS")

Programming is not complete, however, until the "ZEROS" array program/verify cycle is also finished. The "ZEROS" cycle begins when PF is brought to a TTL-low level. The "ZEROS" programming is completed when the desired "ZEROS" bits are verified changed from their unprogrammed state ("ONES").

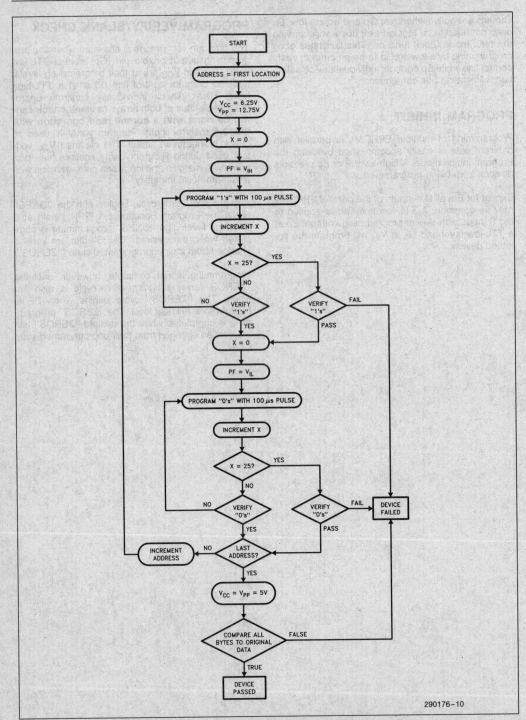

Figure 5. 27C203 Quick-Pulse Programming™ Algorithm

Quick-Pulse Programming™ Operations

The Quick-Pulse Programming algorithm is used to program Intel's 27C203. Developed to substantially reduce production programming throughput time, this algorithm can program a 27C203 in under four seconds. Actual programming time depends on the PROM programmer used.

The Quick-Pulse Programming algorithm uses a 100 microsecond initial-pulse followed by a word verification to determine when the addressed word is correctly programmed. The algorithm terminates if 25 100 μs pulses fail to program a word. This is repeated for both the "ONES" and "ZEROS" programming. Figure 5 shows the 27C203 Quick-Pulse Programming algorithm flowchart.

The entire program-pulse/word-verify sequence is performed with V_{CC} = 6.25V and V_{PP} = 12.75V. When programming is complete, all words should be compared to the original data in a standard read mode with V_{CC} = 5.0V.

int_eligent Identifier™ Mode

The int_eligent Identifier Mode will determine an EPROM's manufacturer and device type. Programming equipment can automatically match a device with its proper programming algorithm.

The Identifier mode is activated when A9 is at high voltage (V_H). A0 determines the information being accessed. The first address (A0 = V_{IL}) accesses the manufacturer code and the second (A0 = V_{IH}) accesses the device code.

SPECIAL FEATURE PROGRAMMING

The Chip Select synchronous state ($\overline{Ss}$) and the initialize register contents are both UV-erasable and user-programmable. Programming operations for these special 27C203 features are described below and waveforms are shown in Figure 7.

SYNCHRONOUS CHIP SELECT PROGRAMMING

The chip select pin's default (erased) state is asynchronous ($\overline{S}$). The synchronous state ($\overline{Ss}$) is programmed by raising A8 to V_H (Figure 7) for twenty five 100 microsecond program pulses. Program verify is accomplished with a functionality check; when $\overline{Ss}$ is programmed, the state of the outputs, valid or tri-state, can only be changed with a clock (C) rising edge.

INITIALIZE REGISTER CONTENTS PROGRAMMING

When the initialize register enable pin is brought low, the initialize register contents override the output generated by normal read oprations. The contents are all "ZEROS" in the erased state. To program the register, A10 is raised to V_H (Figure 7). The remaining setup and programming parameters are the same as the program "ONES" mode, with the data inputs set to the desired initial-condition-vector data. The initialize register read mode or the initialize register verify mode allow programming verification.

Erasure Characteristics (for UV-Window Packages)

Light with wavelengths shorter than 4000 Angstroms (Å) causes EPROM erasure. Sunlight and some florescent lamps have wavelengths in the 3000Å– 4000Å range. Constant exposure to room-level florescent light can erase an EPROM in about three years while direct sunlight erasure can occur within one week. Covering windowed EPROMs with opaque labels prevents such unintended erasure.

The recommended erasure procedure is to expose the EPROM to a 2537Å ultraviolet (UV) source for a minimum integrated dose (intensity x exposure time) of 15 W-sec/cm^2. The EPROM should be placed within one inch of the light source and will erase in 15-20 minutes with a typical 12000 μW/cm^2 lamp.

Overexposure to high-intensity UV light can cause permanent device damage. The maximum integrated dose allowed is 7258 W-sec/cm^2 (approximately 1 week at 12000 μW/cm).

D.C. Programming Characteristics $T_A = 25°C \pm 5°C$

Table 2

Symbol	Parameter	Limits			Conditions
		Min	Max	Units	
I_{IL}	Input Low Load Current		10	μA	$V_{IN} = 0V$
I_{IH}	Input High Load Current		10	μA	$V_{IN} = 6V$
I_{OZL}	Tri-state Low Leakage		10	μA	$V_{OUT} = 0V$
I_{OZH}	Tri-state High Leakage		15	μA	$V_{OUT} = 6V$
I_{CC}[1]	V_{CC} Current Active		100	mA	$\overline{Ep} = \overline{P} = V_{IL}$
V_{IL}	Input Low Voltage	-0.1	$+0.8$	V	
V_{IH}	Input High Voltage	2.0	$V_{CC} + 1$	V	
V_{OL}	Verify Output Low Volt.		0.45	V	$I_{OL} = 16$ mA
V_{OH}	Verify Output High Volt.	2.4		V	$I_{OH} = -4$ mA
I_{PP}	V_{PP} Supply Current		50	mA	$\overline{Ep} = \overline{P} = V_{IL}$
V_H	Input High Voltage	11.5	12.5	V	$V_{CC} = 5V$
V_{PP}	V_{PP} Supply Voltage	12.5	13.0	V	
V_{CC}	V_{CC} Supply Voltage	6.0	6.5	V	

A.C. Programming Characteristics $T_A = 25°C \pm 5°C$

Symbol	Parameter	Limits			Conditions
		Min	Max	Units	
t_{AVPL}	Address Setup Time	1		μs	
t_{DZGL}	$\overline{Gp}$ Setup Time	1		μs	
t_{DVPL}	Data Setup Time			μs	
t_{FVPL}	PF Setup Time	1		μs	
t_{GHAX}	Address Hold Time	0		μs	
*t_{PHDX}	Data Hold Time	1		μs	
t_{GHQX}	Output Deselect Time	0	50	ns	(Note 2)
t_{VPS}	V_{PP} Setup time	1		μs	
t_{VCS}	V_{CC} Setup Time	1		μs	
t_{ELPL}	$\overline{Ep}$ Setup Time	1		μs	
t_{AHPL}	Special Functions Address Setup Time	1		μs	A8 or A10 = V_H
t_{PLPH}	Program ($\overline{P}$) Pulse Width	95	105	μs	Quick-Pulse™ Programming
t_{GLQV}	Data Valid from $\overline{OE}$		50	μs	
t_{AVQV}	Intelligent Identifier Valid from Address Valid		100	ns	A9 = V_H Other A's = V_{IL}
t_{ILQV}	Initialize Register Verify from $\overline{I}$ Low		100	ns	$A_{10} = V_H$
t_{PLPH2}	Synchronous Chip Select Program Pulse Width	95	105	μs	$A_8 = V_H$

NOTES:

1. The maximum current value is with outpus DQ0–DQ15 unloaded.
2. This parameter is only sampled and is not 100% tested. Output float is defined as the point where data is no longer driven. See timing diagram.
3. V_{CC} must be applied simultaneously or before V_{PP} and removed simultaneously or after V_{PP}.

AC Conditions of Test

Input Rise and Fall Times (10% to 90%)............20 ns
Input Pulse Levels ....0.45V to 2.4V
Input Timing Reference Level ....0.8V to 2.0V
Output Timing Reference Level..............0.8V to 2.0V

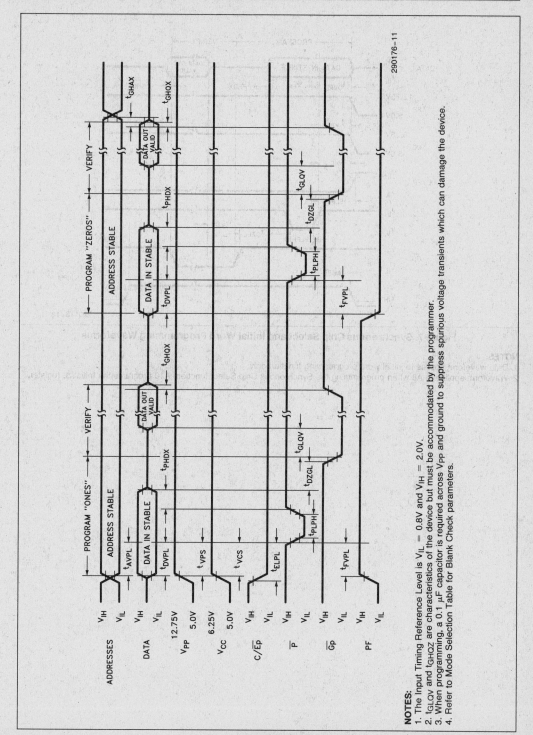

290176-11

NOTES:
1. The Input Timing Reference Level is $V_{IL} = 0.8V$ and $V_{IH} = 2.0V$.
2. t_{GLQV} and t_{GHQZ} are characteristics of the device but must be accommodated by the programmer.
3. When programming, a 0.1 μF capacitor is required across V_{PP} and ground to suppress spurious voltage transients which can damage the device.
4. Refer to Mode Selection Table for Blank Check parameters.

Figure 6. Programming Waveforms

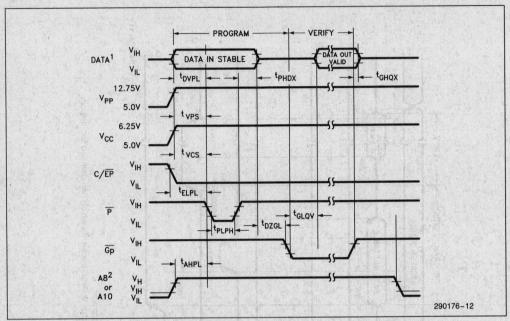

Figure 7. Synchronous Chip Select and Initial Word Programming Waveforms

NOTES:
1. Data waveform applies to initial word programming function only.
2. Waveform applies to A8 when programming the Synchronous Chip Select function. A10 programs the Initialize register.

27960CX
PIPELINED BURST ACCESS 1M (128K x 8) EPROM

- **Synchronous 4 Byte Data Burst Access**
- **No Glue Interface to 80960CA**
- **High Performance Clock to Data Out Time**
  - **Zero Wait State Data to Data Burst**
  - **Up to 33 MHz 80960CA Performance**
- **Asynch Microcontroller Reset Function**
  - **Returns to Known State with Hi-Z Outputs**

- **Pipelined Addressing for Optimal Bus Bandwidth on 80960CA**
  - **Next Addressing Overlaps Last Data Byte**
- **CHMOS-IIIE for High Performance and Low Power**
  - **125 mA Active, 30 mA Standby**
  - **TTL Compatible Inputs**
- **1 Mbit Density Configures as 128K x 8**
  - **Pin Out Upgrade Path to 512K x 8**

The 27960CX is a member of a new family of a high performance CMOS EPROMs with synchronous burst access. The 27960CX has a 1 Mbit capacity, configured as 128K x 8, and is packaged in either 44-lead Cerquad or 44-lead PLCC. The pinout has two No Connect (N/C) pins for a density upgrade path to 4 Mbit (512K x 8).

The synchronous 4 byte burst access provides a no glue interface to the 80960CA bus. Internally the 27960CX is organized in blocks of 4 bytes which are accessed sequentially. A burst access begins on the first clock pulse after $\overline{ADS}$ and $\overline{CS}$ are asserted. The address of a four byte block is latched in the first clock cycle. After a number of wait states (1 or 2), data is output one byte at a time on each subsequent clock cycle. A burst access is terminated at the rising edge of CLK when $\overline{BLAST}$ is asserted.

High performance outputs provide zero wait state data-to-data burst accesses at clock frequencies up to 33 MHz. Extra power and ground pins dedicated to the outputs reduce the effect of fast output switching on device performance. The pipelining capability of the 27960CX allows the address to overlap the previous data, further optimizing bus bandwidth in 80960CA applications.

The internal state machine of the 27960CX is factory figured to generate either 1 or 2 wait states between the address and the first byte of data. An asynchronous microcontroller reset feature puts the outputs in a high impedance state and resets the internal state machine to a known state where a new burst access can begin.

The 27960CX is manufactured on Intel's 1 micron CHMOS-IIIE technology.

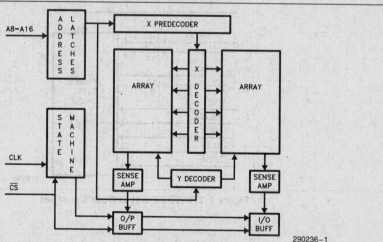

290236–1

Figure 1. 27960CX Burst EPROM Block Diagram

October 1989
Order Number: 290236-002

27960CX BURST EPROM

EPROMs are established as the preferred code storage device in embedded applications. The non-volatile, flexible, reliable, cost effective EPROM makes a product easier to design, manufacture and service. Until recently, however, EPROMs could not match the performance needs of high-end systems. The 27960CX was designed to support the 80960CA embedded controller. It utilizes the burst interface to offer near zero-wait state performance without the high cost normally associated with this performance.

In embedded designs, board space and cost must be kept at a minimum without impacting performance and reliability. The 27960CX removes the need for expensive high-speed shadow RAM backed up by slow EPROM or ROM for non-volatile code storage. Code optimization concerns are reduced with "off-chip" code fetches no longer crippling to system performance. FONTs can be run directly out of these EPROMs at the same performance as high-speed DRAMs. With the 27960CX, the EPROM is the ideal code or FONT storage device for your 80960CA system.

Architecture

The 27960CX is a 128K x 8, high-performance CMOS EPROM with a synchronous burst access. It is available in surface mount 44-lead PLCC and 44-lead CERQUAD* (reprogrammable) packages.

*CERQUAD is available in a socket only version until the third quarter of 1990.

The 27960CX provides a no-glue, synchronous burst interface to the 80960CA's bus. It operates in pipelined or non-pipelined modes. Internally, the 27960CX is organized in blocks of 4 bytes which are accessed sequentially. A burst access begins on the first clock pulse after $\overline{ADS}$ is asserted. The address of the four byte block is latched in the clock cycle following $\overline{ADS}$. After a set number of wait states (1 or 2), data is output one byte at a time on each subsequent clock cycle. A burst access is terminated at the rising edge of CLK when $\overline{BLAST}$ is asserted. High performance outputs provide zero wait state data-to-data burst access at clock frequencies up to 33 MHz. Extra power and ground pins dedicated to the outputs reduce the effect of fast output switching on device performance.

The pipelining capability of the 27960CX allows the address to overlap the last data byte of the burst, further optimizing bus band-width in 80960CA applications. In the pipelined mode, with a non-buffered interface, the 27960CX gives 4 bytes of data in 6 clock cycles at 33 MHz. In a 32-bit configuration, this translates into a read band-width of 88 Mbytes/sec. Performance capability of the 27960CX in different 80960CA systems is given in Table I.

Systems can be designed with the 27960CX in 8-, 16- or 32-bit data widths and can also boot-up from the EPROM.

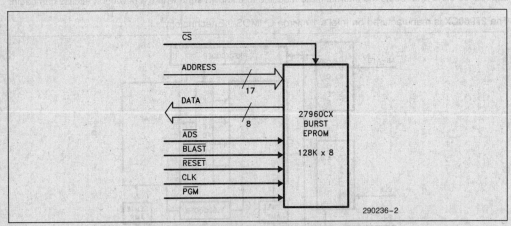

Figure 2. 27960CX Burst EPROM Signal Set

Table 1. Performance Capability

33 MHz   2 WS   Non-Buffered: 4 Words/6 Clock Cycles → 88 Mbytes/Sec

ADDR	A00	WS	WS	—	—	—	A01	WS	WS	—	—	—	A02	WS
DATA	—	—	—	D00	D01	D02	D03	—	—	D10	D11	D12	D13	—
PCLK	C1	C2	C3	C4	C5	C6	C7	C1	C2	C3	C4	C5	C6	C1

25 MHz   2 WS   Buffered: 4 Words/6 Clock Cycles → 66 Mbytes/Sec

ADDR	A00	WS	WS	—	—	—	A01	WS	WS	—	—	—	A02	WS
DATA	—	—	—	D00	D01	D02	D03	—	—	D10	D11	D12	D13	—
PCLK	C1	C2	C3	C4	C5	C6	C7	C1	C2	C3	C4	C5	C6	C1

20 MHz   1 WS   Buffered: 4 Words/5 Clock Cycles → 64 Mbytes/Sec

ADDR	A00	WS	—	—	—	A01	WS	—	—	—	A02	WS
DATA	—	—	D00	D01	D02	D03	—	D10	D11	D12	D13	—
PCLK	C1	C2	C3	C4	C5	C6	C1	C2	C3	C4	C5	C1

16 MHz   1 WS   Buffered: 4 Words/5 Clock Cycles → 51 Mbytes/Sec

ADDR	A00	WS	—	—	—	A01	WS	—	—	—	A02	WS
DATA	—	—	D00	D01	D02	D03	—	D10	D11	D12	D13	—
PCLK	C1	C2	C3	C4	C5	C6	C1	C2	C3	C4	C5	C1

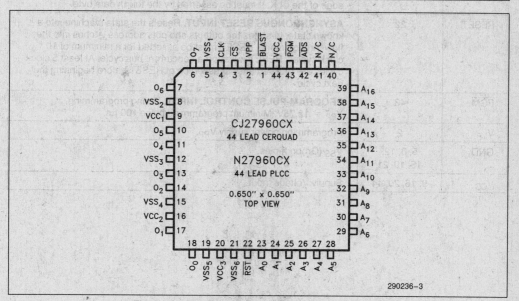

Figure 3. 27960CX 44 Lead PLCC/CERQUAD Pinout

PIN DESCRIPTIONS

Symbol	Pin	Function
A0–A16	23–39	**ADDRESS INPUTS.** During a burst operation, A2–A16 provides the base address pointing to a block of four consective bytes. A0, A1 selects the first byte of the burst access. An internal address generator increments addresses for subsequent bytes of the burst.
D0–D7	6, 7, 10, 11, 13, 14, 17, 18	Data Inputs/Outputs.
$\overline{ADS}$	42	**ADDRESS STROBE.** Indicates the start of a new bus access. It is active low in the first clock cycle of a bus access.
$\overline{CS}$	3	**CHIP SELECT.** Master device enable. When asserted (active low) data can be written to and read from the device. In read mode, $\overline{CS}$ enables the state machine and the I/O circuitry. A memory access begins on the first rising edge of CLK after $\overline{ADS}$ and $\overline{CS}$ are asserted. **NOTE:** 1. The address decode path is independent of $\overline{CS}$, i.e., X and Y decoding is always powered up. 2. For programming, $\overline{CS}$ should remain low for the entire cycle. Program and verify functions are done one byte at a time. 3. $\overline{CS}$ going high does not terminate a concurrent burst cycle.
$\overline{BLAST}$	1	**BURST LAST.** Terminates a concurrent burst data cycle at the rising edge of the CLK. It must be asserted by the fourth data byte.
$\overline{RESET}$	22	**ASYNCHRONOUS RESET INPUT.** Resets the state machine into a known state, tri-states the outputs and puts address latches into the flow through mode. $\overline{RESET}$ must be asserted for a minimum of 10 clock cycles. $\overline{RESET}$ will abort a concurrent bus cycle. At least 5 clock cycles are required after deassertion of $\overline{RESET}$ before beginning the next cycle.
$\overline{PGM}$	43	**PROGRAM-PULSE CONTROL INPUT.** During programming, V_{PP} = 12.75V. Minimum programming pulse 100 μs.
V_{PP}	2	Programming power supply V_{PP}.
GND	5, 8, 12, 15, 19, 21	V_{SS} (Ground) pins.
V_{CC}	9, 16, 20, 44	Supply Voltage Input.

INTERFACE EXAMPLE

1.0 Overview

This example illustrates 8-, 16- and 32-bit wide burst access EPROM interfaces to the 80960CA. The designs offer a simple "no-glue" interface to the 80960CA's bus.

A non-buffered 27960CX burst EPROM system organized as 128K x 32 is shown (Figure 4A). Since the 27960CX is capable of driving a 60 pF load, large, non-buffered systems can be implemented by stacking up 2 banks of 4 EPROMs, giving a memory size of 256K x 32. The input capacitance load seen on the address lines (due to the EPROM only) is 24 pF for a 128K x 32 system and 48 pF for a 256K x 32 system. The EPROM is specified at 6 pF for input capacitance and 15 pF max, 12 pF typical for output capacitance. Larger systems can be implemented with buffers (Figure 4B).

Chip Select Logic

Higher order address lines are decoded to provide $\overline{CS}$. Qualification with other signals is not required. The chip select logic can be implemented with standard asynchronous decoders, PAL's or PLD's (like Intel's 85C508).

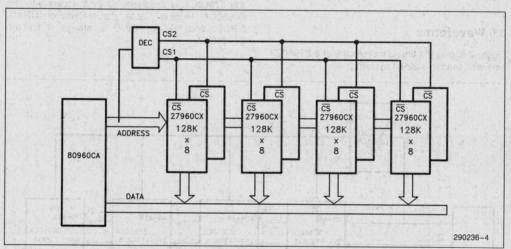

Figure 4A. 256K x 32 Non-Buffered EPROM Memory System

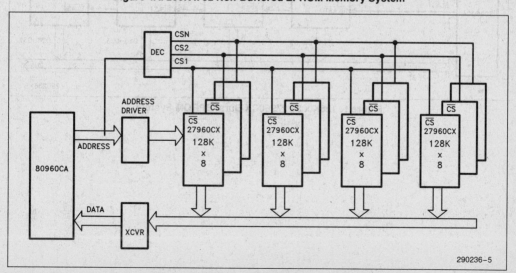

Figure 4B. Buffered EPROM Memory System

2.0 Schematics

Figure 5 shows a non-buffered, 128K x 32 27960CX EPROM system.

Chip select logic is the only external logic that is required for this interface, and can be derived from the global system chip select circuitry.

In a non-buffered, 16-bit system (Figure 6A). $\overline{BE1}$, and A2 connect to the lower order address bits of the 27960CX. $\overline{BE1}$ connects to A0 of both EPROMs while A2 connects to both A1's.

In a non-buffered, 8-bit system (Figure 6B). $\overline{BE0}$ and $\overline{BE1}$ connect to A0 and A1 respectively.

3.0 Waveforms

Figure 7 shows the timing waveforms of a 27960CX pipelined read in a 32-bit system.

a) $\overline{CS}$ Setup Time

$\overline{CS}$ setup time is defined as the time between $\overline{CS}$ being asserted and the first rising edge of CLK (during address state). Since a memory access begins on the first rising edge of CLK after $\overline{ADS}$ and $\overline{CS}$ are asserted, a minimum $\overline{CS}$ setup time of 5 ns at 33 MHz operation and 6 ns at 20 MHz operation is required. With the 80960CA's maximum valid address delay of 18 ns at 33 MHz, 7 ns remains for $\overline{CS}$ decoding logic.

b) Bootup

The wait-state configuration (1 or 2 wait-states) of the 27960CX is programmed by the user into the 80960CA Region Table parameters of NRAD, NRDD, and NXDA. NRDD is always 0 for the 27960CX.

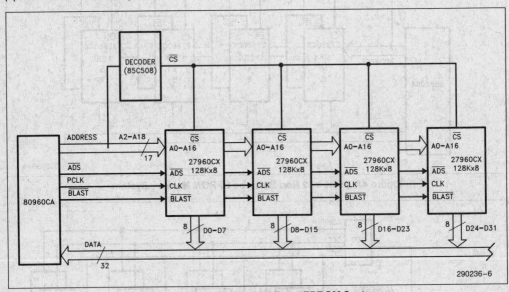

Figure 5. 128K x 32 27960CX Burst EPROM System

290236-6

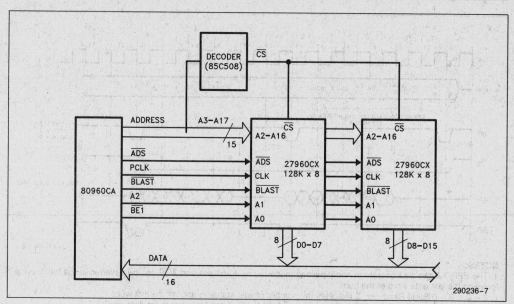

Figure 6A. 27960CX Burst EPROM in a 16-Bit System

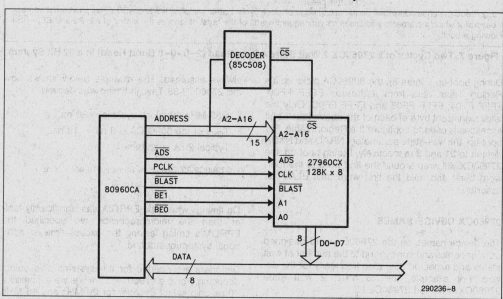

Figure 6B. 27960CX Burst EPROM in a 8-Bit System

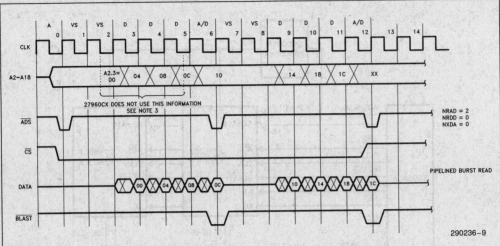

NOTES:
1. The EPROM can also operate in non pipelined mode i.e, next address and $\overline{ADS}$ can be asserted in the clock cycle following the last data word of the burst.
2. 2 – 0 – 0 – 0 Burst Read → 2 indicates the number of wait states to access the first word
 0's indicate the number of wait states for subsequent data words:
 0 in this case!
3. 27960CX latches addresses on the falling edge of clock cycle 1 after sampling $\overline{CS}$ and $\overline{ADS}$ it has an internal address generator which increments addresses for subsequent words of the burst. It ignores the states of A2, A3 and $\overline{BE0}$–$\overline{BE3}$ during a burst.

Figure 7. Two Cycles of a 27960CX 2 Wait State 4 Byte Read (2–0–0–0 Burst Read) in a 32 Bit System

During boot-up (Figure 8), the 80960CA picks up it's Region Table data from addresses FFFF FF00; FFFF FF04; FFFF FF08 and FFFF FF0C. Only the least significant byte of each of the above four 32-bit accesses is used to configure the Region Table. For boot-up, the wait-state parameters NRAD and NXDA default to 31 and 3 respectively. During boot-up, the 27960CX will wrap around the first word of the four-word burst and hold the first word until $\overline{BLAST}$ is asserted.

27960CX DEVICE NAMES

The device names on the 27960CX were designed as memnonics and correspond to the number of wait states and expected operation frequency for the device. For example, the 25 MHz, 2 wait state 27960CX is named 27960C2-25.

AC TIMINGS DERIVATION

The AC timings for the 27960CX were generated specifically to meet the requirements of the 80960CA microprocessor. In each timing case the applicable 80960CA clock frequency and AC timing were taken together with an address buffer delay (if needed) and a typical 2 ns guardband to generate the 27960CX AC timing. Worst case timings were always assumed. The example below shows how the 27960C2-33 Tavc₀h timing was derived.

@33 MHz the clock cycle is ~ 30 ns.

T_{OV2} of the 80960CA is 3 ns – 18 ns.

Typical 2 ns guardband.

27960C2-33 Tavc₀h = 30 ns – 18 ns – 2 ns
 = 10 ns

On timings where the EPROM was significantly faster than the microprocessor, we specified the EPROM's timing leaving the excess time as additional system guardband.

Decoders are needed for the systems chip select decoding. For the 27960CX's timings we assumed a 10 ns chip select decoder for 20 MHz and 16 MHz frequencies and a 5 ns – 7 ns decoder for 25 MHz and 33 MHz systems. The example below shows how the 27960C3-33 Tsvch timing was derived.

@33 MHz the clock cycle is ~ 30 ns.

T_{OV2} of the 80960CA is 3 ns – 18 ns.

Decoder = 7 ns

27960C3-33 Tsvch = 30 ns – 18 ns – 7 ns
 = 5 ns

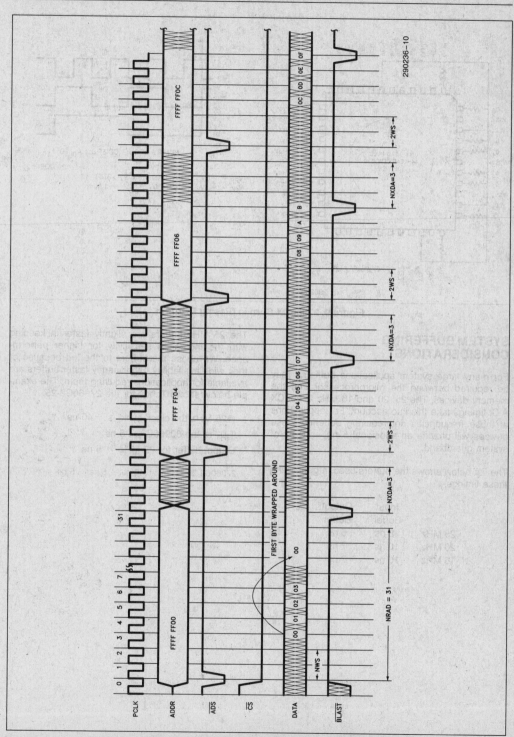

Figure 8. 27960CX/80960CA Bootup Timing

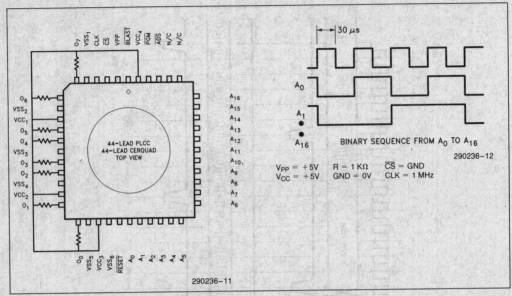

Figure 9. 27960CX Burn in Biasing Diagram

SYSTEM BUFFERING CONSIDERATIONS

For many large system applications buffering may be required between the microprocessor and the memory devices. The 25, 20 and 16 MHz 27960CX A.C. timings take this into account. For applications at those frequencies not requiring buffering these devices will provide an additional 5 ns – 10 ns of system guardband.

The list below shows the buffers used in generating these timings.

	Input Buffer	Output Buffer
25 MHz	8 ns	5 ns
20 MHz	10 ns	7 ns
16 MHz	10 ns	7 ns

The 25 MHz buffers are slightly faster in keeping with the increased sensitivity for higher performance. We chose the buffers to the left because of their wide availability. Significantly faster buffers are available for applications requiring them. The example below shows Tchqv for the 27960C2-25.

@25 MHz the clock cycle is ~40 ns.

T_{IH1} of the 80960CA is 5 ns.

Output buffer for 25 MHz = 5 ns

27960C2-25 Tchqv = 40 ns – 5 ns – 5 ns
= 30 ns

ABSOLUTE MAXIMUM RATINGS*

Read Operating Temperature . . . . . . 0°C to +70°C[8]

Case Temperature Under Bias . . −10°C to +80°C[8]

Storage Temperature . . . . −65°C to +125°C

All Input or Output Voltages
with Respect to Ground . . . . . . −0.6V to +6.5V[4]

Voltage on Pin A9
with Respect to Ground . . . . . −0.6V to +13.0V[4]

V_{PP} Supply Voltage
with Respect to Ground . . . . . −0.6V to +14.0V[4]

V_{CC} Supply Voltage
with Respect to Ground . . . . . . −0.6V to +7.0V[4]

Notice: Stresses above those listed under "Absolute Maximum Ratings" may cause permanent damage to the device. This is a stress rating only and functional operation of the device at these or any other conditions above those indicated in the operational sections of this specification is not implied. Exposure to absolute maximum rating conditions for extended periods may affect device reliability.

NOTICE: Specifications contained within the following tables are subject to change.

READ OPERATION

D.C. CHARACTERISTICS 0°C < T_A +70°C, V_{CC}: 10%, TTL Inputs

Symbol	Parameter		Notes	Min	Max	Units	Test Conditions
I_{LI}	Input Load Current				1	μA	V_{IN} = 5.5V
I_{LO}	Output Leakage Current				10	μA	V_{OUT} = 5.5V
I_{PP}	V_{PP} Load Current Read				10	μA	V_{PP} = 0 to V_{CC}, $\overline{PGM}$ = V_{IH}
I_{SB}	V_{CC} Standby	Switching	2		45	mA	$\overline{CS}$ = V_{IH}, f = 33 MHz
		Stable	2		30	mA	$\overline{CS}$ = V_{IH}
I_{CC}	V_{CC} Active Current		1, 3, 7		125	mA	$\overline{CS}$ = V_{IL}, f = 33 MHz, I_{OUT} = 0 mA
V_{IL}	Input Low Voltage		4	−0.5	0.8	V	
V_{IH}	Input High Voltage			2.0	V_{CC} + 1	V	
V_{OL}	Output Low Voltage				0.45	V	I_{OL} = 2.1 mA
V_{OH1}	Output High Voltage		5	V_{CC} − 0.8		V	I_{OH} = −100 μA
V_{OH2}	Output High Voltage		5	2.4		V	I_{OH} = −400 μA
I_{OS}	Output Short Circuit		6		100	mA	

NOTES:
1. Maximum value is with outputs unloaded.
2. I_{CC} standby current assumes no output loading i.e., I_{OH} = I_{OL} = 0 mA.
3. I_{CC} is the sum of current through V_{CC3} + V_{CC4} and does not include the current through V_{CC1} and V_{CC2}. (V_{CC1} and V_{CC2} supply power to the output drivers. V_{CC3} and V_{CC4} supply power to the reset of the device.)
4. Minimum D.C. input voltage is −0.5V during transitions. Inputs may undershoot to −2.0V for periods less than 20 ns.
5. Maximum D.C. output voltage is V_{CC} + 0.5V; overshoot may be V_{CC} + 2.0V for periods less than 20 ns.
6. One output shorted for no more than one second. I_{OS} is sampled but not 100% tested.
7. I_{CC} max measured with a 0.11 μF capacitor between V_{CC} and V_{SS}.
8. This specification defines commercial product operating temperatures.

EXPLANATION OF A.C. SYMBOLS

The nomenclature used for timing parameters are as per IEEE STD 662-1980 IEEE Standard Terminology for Semiconductor Memory.

Each timing symbol has five characters. The first is always a "t" (for time). The second character represents a signal name. e.g., (CLK, $\overline{ADS}$, etc.). The third character represents the signal's level (high or low) for the signal indicated by the second character. The fourth character represents a signal name at which a transition occurs marking the end of the time interval being specified.

The fifth character represents the signal level indicated by the fourth character. The list below shows character representations.

A:	Address	R:	$\overline{Reset}$
B:	$\overline{BLAST}$	Q:	Data
C:	Clock	S:	$\overline{Chip\ Select}$
H:	Logic High Level	t:	Time
L:	$\overline{ADS}$/Logic Low Level	V:	Valid
P:	V_{PP} Programming Voltage	Z:	Tristate Level
X:	No longer a valid "driven" logic level		

A.C. CHARACTERISTICS Read $0°C < T_A < +70°C$, 10% V_{CC}

		Product Name		27960C2-33		27960C2-25		27960C1-20		27960C1-16		
		Read Timing		33 MHz 2 Wait State		25 MHz 2 Wait State		20 MHz 1 Wait State		16 MHz 1 Wait State		Units
No.	Symbol	Characteristic	Notes	Min	Max	Min	Max	Min	Max	Min	Max	
1	t_{AVC0H}	Address Valid to CLK High	CLK0	10		10		14		22		ns
2	t_{CNHAX}	CLK High to Address Invalid	(2)	0		0		0		0		ns
3	t_{LLCH}	$\overline{ADS}$ low to CLK High		8		8		14		22		ns
4	t_{CHLH}	CLK high to $\overline{ADS}$ High	(5)	3	22	3	32	3	36	3	40	ns
5	t_{SVCH}	Chip Select Valid to CLK High	(1)	5		5		6		14		ns
6	t_{CNHSX}	CLK High to Chip Select Invalid	(2)	0		0		0		0		ns
7	t_{CHQV}	CLK High to Data Valid			27		30		36		40	ns
8	t_{CHQX}	CLK High to Data Invalid		5		5		5		5		ns
9	t_{CHQZ}	CLK High to Data Hi-Z	(6)		20		25		25		30	ns
10	t_{BVCH}	$\overline{BLAST}$ Valid to CLK High		8		8		14		22		ns
11	t_{CHBX}	CLK High to $\overline{BLAST}$ Invalid	(3)	3	22	3	32	3	36	3	40	ns

NOTES:
1. Valid signal level is meant to be either a logic high or logic low.
2. TC_NHSX—The subscript N represents the number of wait states for this parameter. $\overline{CS}$ can be de-asserted (high) after the number of wait states (N) has expired. The EPROM will continue to burst out data for the current cycle.
3. BLAST # must be returned high before the next rising clock edge.
4. The sum of TCHQV + TAVCH + NCLK will not equal actual TAVQV if independent test conditions are used to obtain TAVCH and TCHQV (N = number of wait states).
5. $\overline{ADS}$ must be returned high before the next rising clock edge.
6. Sampled but not 100% tested. The transition is measured ±500 mV from steady state voltage.
7. For capacitive loads above 60 pF, T_{CHQV} can be derated by 1 ns/10 pF.

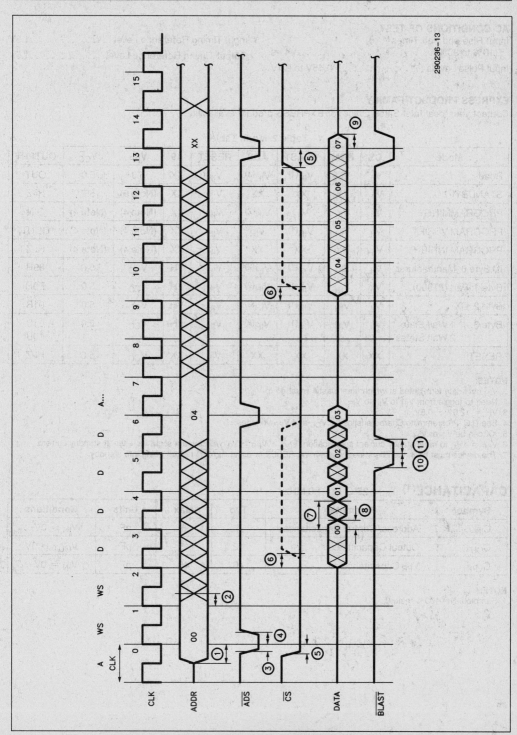

Figure 10. 27960CX   2 Wait State AC Waveforms

AC CONDITIONS OF TEST

Input Rise and Fall Times
(10% to 90%). . . . . 4 ns

Input Pulse Levels . . . . 0.45V to 2.4V

Input Timing Reference Level 1.5V

Output Timing Reference Level 1.5V

EXPRESS PRODUCT FAMILY

Contact your local Intel Sales Office for EXPRESS product availability.

Table 2. Mode Table

Mode	$\overline{CS}$	$\overline{PGM}$	BLAST	ADS	RESET	A9	V_{PP}	V_{CC}	OUTPUT
Read	V_{IL}	V_{IH}	V_{IH}(1)	V_{IH}(2)	V_{IH}	XX	5.0	5.0	OUT
STANDBY(7)	V_{IH}	XX	XX	XX	V_{IH}	XX	(Note 6)	5.0	Hi-Z
PROGRAMMING	V_{IL}	V_{IL}	V_{IH}	V_{IH}(2)	V_{IH}	XX	(Note 4)	(Note 4)	DIN
PROGRAM VERIFY	V_{IL}	V_{IH}	V_{IH}(1)	V_{IH}	V_{IH}	XX	(Note 4)	(Note 4)	DOUT
PROGRAM INHIBIT	V_{IH}	XX	XX	XX	V_{IH}	XX	(Note 4)	(Note 4)	Hi-Z
ID Byte 0: Manufacturer	V_{IL}	V_{IH}	V_{IH}(1)	V_{IH}(2)	V_{IH}	VH	V_{CC}	5.0	89H
Byte 1: Part (27960)	V_{IL}	V_{IH}	V_{IH}(1)	V_{IH}(2)	V_{IH}	VH	V_{CC}	5.0	E0H
Byte 2: CX	V_{IL}	V_{IH}	V_{IH}(1)	V_{IH}(2)	V_{IH}	VH	V_{CC}	5.0	01B
Byte 3: 1 Wait State 2 Wait States	V_{IL}	V_{IH}	V_{IH}(1)	V_{IH}(2)	V_{IH}	VH	V_{CC}	5.0	01B 10B
RESET	XX	XX	XX	XX	V_{IL}	XX	V_{CC}	5.0	Hi-Z

NOTES:
1. V_{IH} until data terminated at which time Blast# must go to V_{IL}.
2. Need to toggle from V_{IH} to V_{IL} to V_{IH}.
3. VH = 12.0V ± 0.5V.
4. See D.C. Programming Characteristics for V_{CC} and V_{PP} voltages.
5. XX can be V_{IL} or V_{IH}.
6. V_{PP} = V_{CC} to meet standy current specification. V_{CC} > V_{PP} > V_{IL} will cause a slight increase in standby current.
7. The device must be in the idle state (by asserting $\overline{RESET}$ or using $\overline{BLAST}$) before going into standby.

CAPACITANCE(1) T_A = 25°C, f = 1.0 MHz

Symbol	Parameter	Typ	Max	Units	Conditions
C_{IN}	Address/Control Capacitance	4	6	pF	V_{IN} = 0V
C_{OUT}	Output Capacitance	12	15	pF	V_{OUT} = 0V
C_{VPP}	V_{PP} Capacitance	40	45	pF	V_{IN} = 0V

NOTE:
1. Sampled. Not 100% tested.

A.C. INPUT/OUTPUT REFERENCE WAVEFORMS

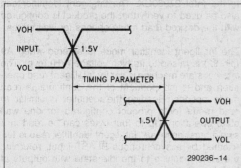

290236–14

Input and output timings are measured from 1.5V. Timing values are specified assuming maximum input and output rise and fall time = 4 ns.

A.C. TESTING LOAD CIRCUIT

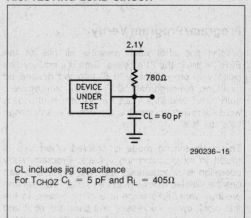

290236–15

CL includes jig capacitance
For T_{CHQZ} C_L = 5 pF and R_L = 405Ω

CLOCK CHARACTERISTICS

Versions		33 MHz		25 MHz		20 MHz		16 MHz		Units
Symbol	Parameter	Min	Max	Min	Max	Min	Max	Min	Max	
CLK	Period	30.3		40		50		62.5		ns
T_{PR}	Rise Time	1	4	1	4	1	4	1	4	ns
T_{PF}	Fall Time	1	4	1	4	1	4	1	4	ns
T_{PL}	Low Time	(T/2) − 2	T/2	(T/2) − 3	T/2	(T/2) − 4	T/2	(T/2) − 4	T/2	ns
T_{PH}	High Time	(T/2) − 2	T/2	(T/2) − 3	T/2	(T/2) − 4	T/2	(T/2) − 4	T/2	ns
Max Rise Time for Programming CLK = 100 ns										

CLOCK WAVEFORM

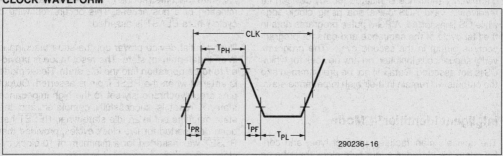

290236–16

PROGRAMMING MODES

Program/Program Verify

Initially, and after each erasure, all bits of the EPROM are in the "1's" state. Data is introduced by selectively programming "0's" into the desired bit locations. Although only "0's" can be programmed, both "1's" and "0's" can be present in the data word. Ultraviolet erasure is the only way to change "0's" to "1's".

The programming mode is entered when V_{PP} is raised to its programming voltage. Program/verify operation is synchronous with the clock and can only be initiated following an idle state. Program and program verify take place in 3 clock cycles. In the first clock cycle, addresses and data are input and programming occurs. Program verify follows in the second clock cycle and the third clock cycle terminates synchronous program/verify operation, returning the state machine to the idle state with outputs at high impedance.

As in the read mode, A2–A16 point to a four byte block in the memory array. During programming, A0 and A1 point to an individual byte within the four byte block that is to be accessed. Only one byte is accessed in each 3 cycle program/verify sequence.

Program Inhibit

The Program Inhibit mode allows parallel programming and verification of multiple devices with different data. With V_{PP} at its program voltage, a program/verify sequence is initiated for any device that receives a valid $\overline{ADS}$ pulse and rising clock edge while $\overline{CS}$ is asserted. A $\overline{PGM}$ pulse programs data in the first cycle of the sequence and data for program verify is output in the second cycle. The program/verify sequence is inhibited on any devices for which $\overline{CS}$ is not asserted. Data will not be programmed and the outputs will remain in their high impedance state.

int$_e$ligent Identifier™ Mode

The device's manufacturer, product type, and configuration are stored in a four byte block that can be accessed by using the int$_e$ligent Identifier mode.

The programmer can verify the device identifier and choose the programming algorithm that corresponds to the Intel 27960CX. The int$_e$ligent identifier can also be used to verify that the product is configured with the desired read mode options for wait states.

The int$_e$ligent identifier mode is entered when A9 (pin 32) is raised to its high voltage (VH) level. The internal state machine is set for int$_e$ligent read operation and is independent of the configurable read mode options. Reading the identifier is similar to read mode for a product configured for one wait state operation. Up to four bytes can be read in a single burst access. int$_e$ligent identifier read is terminated by a synchronous $\overline{BLAST}$ input, returning the state machine to the idle state with outputs at high impedance.

The four byte block code for the int$_e$ligent identifier code is located at address 0000H through 0003H and is encoded as follows:

MEANING	(A1, A0)	DATA
Intel ID	Byte 00	89h
27960	Byte 01	E0h
CX	Byte 10	01b
1 Wait State	Byte 11	01b
2 Wait States	Byte 11	10b

RESET MODE

Due to the synchronous nature of the 27960CX, the various operating modes must be initiated from a known idle state. During normal operation, the internal state machine returns to an idle state at the termination of a bus access. This occurs following a cycle where $\overline{BLAST}$ is asserted.

During initial device power up, the state machine is in an indeterminant state. The reset mode is provided to force operation into the idle state. Reset mode is entered when the $\overline{RESET}$ pin is asserted. Output pins are asynchronously set to the high impedance state. A reset is successfully completed and the state machine set in an idle state when $\overline{RESET}$ has been deasserted for five clock cycles, provided that $\overline{RESET}$ was asserted for a minimum of 10 clock cycles.

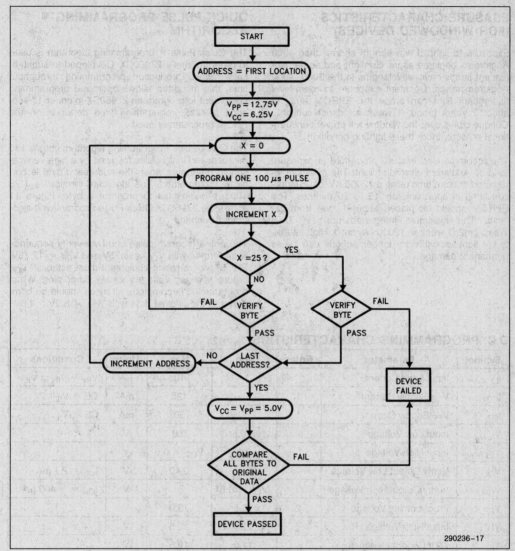

Figure 11. Quick-Pulse Programming™ Algorithm

290236–17

ERASURE CHARACTERISTICS (FOR WINDOWED DEVICES)

Exposure to light of wavelength shorter than 4000 Angstroms begins erasure. Sunlight and some fluorescent lamps have wavelengths in the 3000–4000 Angstrom range. Constant exposure to room-level fluorescent light can erase the EPROM array in about 3 years (about 1 week for direct sunlight). Opaque labels over the window will prevent unintentional erasure under these lighting conditions.

The recommended erasure procedure is exposure to 2537 Angstrom ultraviolet light. The minimum integrated erasure time using a 12000 fW/cm2 ultraviolet lamp is approximately 15 to 20 minutes. The EPROM should be placed about 1 inch from the lamp. The maximum integrated dose is 7258 Wsec/cm2 (1 week @ 12000 fW/cm2). High intensity UV light exposure for longer periods can cause permanent damage.

QUICK-PULSE PROGRAMMING™ ALGORITHM

The Quick-Pulse™ programming algorithm is used to program Intel's 27960CX. Developed to substantially reduce production programming throughput time, this algorithm allows optimized programming equipment to program an 27960CX in under 17 seconds. Actual programming time depends on the PROM programmer used.

The Quick-Pulse Programming algorithm uses a 100 microsecond initial pulse followed by a byte verification to determine when the addressed byte is correctly programmed. The algorithm terminates if 25 100 μs pulses fail to program a byte. Figure 11 shows the 27960CX Quick-Pulse Programming algorithm flowchart.

The entire program-pulse and byte-verify sequence is performed with V_{CC} = 6.25V and V_{PP} = 12.75V. PROM programming equipment must establish V_{CC} before applying voltages to any other pins. When programming is complete, all bytes should be compared to the original data with V_{CC} = 5.0V.

D.C. PROGRAMMING CHARACTERISTICS T_A = 25° ±5°C

Symbol	Parameter	Notes	Min	Max	Units	Conditions
I_{LI}	Input Load Current			10	μA	$V_{IN} = V_{IH}$ or V_{IL}
I_{CC2}	V_{CC} Supply Current	1		125	mA	$CE = V_{IL}$
I_{PP}	V_{PP} Supply Current	1		50	mA	$CE = V_{IL}$
V_{IL}	Input Low Voltage		−0.5	0.8	V	
V_{IH}	Input High Voltage		2.0	V_{CC} + 0.5	V	
V_{OL}	Verify Output Low Voltage			0.40	V	I_{OL} = 2.1 mA
V_{OH}	Verify Output High Voltage		V_{CC} − 0.8		V	I_{OH} = −400 μA
V_{PP}	Programming Voltage	2	12.5	13.0	V	
VH	Input High Voltage		11.5	12.5	V	
V_{ID}	A9 int$_e$ligent Identifier		11.5	12.5	V	
V_{CC}	Quick-Pulse		6.0	6.5	V	
V_{PP}	Quick-Pulse		12.5	13.0	V	$\overline{CS} = \overline{PGM} = V_{IL}$

NOTES:
1. The maximium current value is with outputs unloaded.
2. V_{CC} must be applied simultaneously or before V_{PP} and remove simultaneously or after V_{PP}.
3. During programming clock levels are V_{IH} and V_{IL}.

A.C. PROGRAMMING, RESET AND ID CHARACTERISTICS $0°C < T_A < +70°C$

No.	Symbol	Characteristic	Min	Max	Units	Conditions
1	t_{AVPL}	Address Valid to $\overline{PGM}$ Low	2		μs	
2	t_{CHAX}	CLK(1) High to Address Invalid	50		ns	
3	t_{LLCH}	$\overline{ADS}$ Low to CLK High	50		ns	(Note 1)
4	t_{CHLH}	CLK High to $\overline{ADS}$ High	50		ns	(Note 2)
5	t_{SVCH}	$\overline{CS}$ Valid to CLK High	50		ns	
6	t_{CHSX}	CLK High to $\overline{CS}$ Invalid			ns	(Note 3)
7	t_{CHQV}	CLK(1) High to DATA (Out) Valid		100	ns	
8	t_{CHQX}	CLK High to DATA (Out) Invalid	0		ns	
9	t_{BVCH}	$\overline{BLAST}$ Valid to CLK High	50		ns	
10	t_{CHBX}	CLK High to $\overline{BLAST}$ Invalid	50		ns	(Note 4)
11	t_{QVPL}	DATA Valid to $\overline{PGM}$ Low	2		μs	
12	t_{PLPH}	Program Pulse Width	95	105	μs	
13	t_{PHQX}	$\overline{PGM}$ High to DATA Invalid	2		μs	
14	t_{CLPL}	CLK Low to $\overline{PGM}$ Low	50		ns	
15	t_{QZCH}	DATA in Tri-State to CLK High	2		μs	
16	t_{VCS}	V_{CC} High Voltage to CLK High	2		μs	
17	t_{VPS}	V_{PP} High Voltage to CLK High	2		μs	
18	t_{A9HCH}	A9 High Voltage to CLK High	2		μs	
19	t_{CHA9X}	CLK High to A9 Not High Voltage	2		μs	
20	t_{RVCH}	$\overline{RESET}$ Valid to CLK High	50		ns	(Note 6)
21	t_{CHCL}	CLK High to CLK Low	100		ns	(Note 5)
22	t_{CLCH}	CLK Low to CLK High	100		ns	(Note 5)

NOTES:
1. If $\overline{CS}$ is low, $\overline{ADS}$ can go low no sooner than the falling edge of the previous CLK.
2. $\overline{ADS}$ must return high prior to the next rising edge of clock.
3. $\overline{CS}$ must remain low until after the rising edge of CLK1.
4. $\overline{BLAST}$ must return high prior to the next rising edge of CLK.
5. Max CLK rise time is 100 ns.
6. Reset must be low for 10 clock cycles and high for 5 clock cycles.

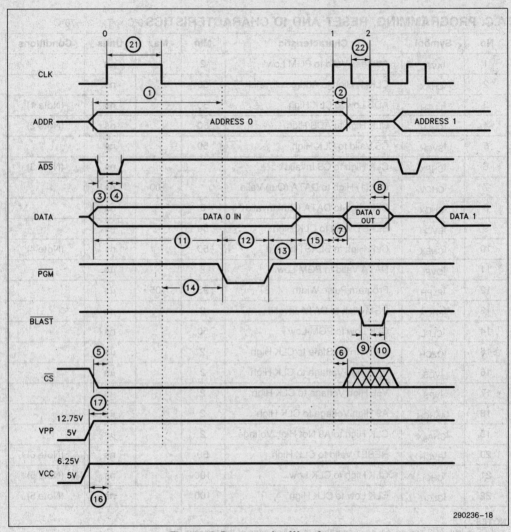

Figure 12. Programming Waveforms

290236–18

RESET and int_eligent Identifier Waveforms

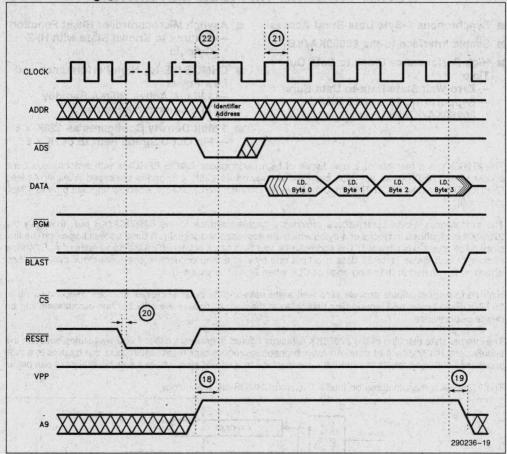

Figure 13. Reset and ID Waveforms

27960KX
BURST ACCESS 1M (128K x 8) EPROM

- **Synchronous 4-Byte Data Burst Access**
- **Simple Interface to the 80960KA/KB**
- **High Performance Clock to Data Out Time**
  - **Zero Wait State Data to Data Burst**
  - **Supports 16, 20 and 25 MHz 80960KA/KB Devices**

- **Asynch Microcontroller Reset Function**
  - **Returns to Known State with Hi-Z Outputs**
- **CHMOS-IIIE for High Performance and Low Power**
  - **125 mA Active, 30 mA Standby**
  - **TTL Compatible Inputs**
- **1 Mbit Density Configures as 128K x 8**
  - **Pin Out Upgrade Path to 512K x 8**

The 27960KX is a member of a new family of high performance CMOS EPROMs with synchronous burst access. The 27960KX has a 1 Mbit capacity, configured as 128K x 8, and is packaged in either 44-lead CERQUAD or 44-lead PLCC. The pinout has two No Connect (N/C) pins for a density upgrade path to 4 Mbit (512K x 8).

The synchronous 4-byte burst access provides a simple interface to the 80960KA/KB bus. Internally the 27960KX is organized in blocks of 4 bytes which are accessed sequentially. A burst access begins on the first clock pulse after $\overline{CS}$ is asserted. The address of a four byte block is latched on the rising edge of $\overline{ALE}$. After a number of wait states (1 or 2), data is output one byte at a time on each subsequent clock cycle. A burst access is terminated at the rising edge of CLK when $\overline{BLAST}$ is asserted.

High performance outputs provide zero wait state data-to-data burst accesses at clock frequencies up to 25 MHz. Extra power and ground pins dedicated to the outputs reduce the effect of fast output switching on device performance.

The internal state machine of the 27960KX is factory figured to generate either 1 or 2 wait states between the address and the first byte of data. An asynchronous microcontroller reset feature puts the outputs in a high impedance state and resets the internal state machine to a known state where a new burst access can begin.

The 27960KX is manufactured on Intel's 1 micron CHMOS-IIIE technology.

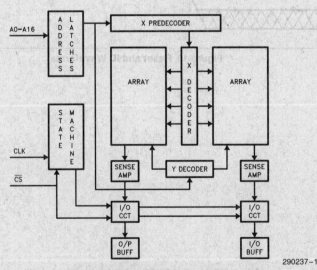

290237-1

Figure 1. 27960KX Burst EPROM Block Diagram

October 1989
Order Number: 290237-002

27960KX BURST EPROM

EPROMs are established as the preferred code storage device in embedded applications. The non-volatile, flexible, reliable, cost effective EPROM makes a product easier to design, manufacture and service. Until recently, however, EPROMs could not match the performance needs of high-end systems. The 27960KX was designed to support the 80960KA/KB embedded controllers. It utilizes the burst interface to offer near zero-wait state performance without the high cost normally associated with this performance.

In embedded designs, board space and cost must be kept at a minimum without impacting performance and reliability. The 27960KX removes the need for expensive high-speed shadow RAM backed up by slow EPROM or ROM for non-volatile code storage. Code optimization concerns are reduced with "off-chip" code fetches no longer crippling to system performance. FONTs can be run directly out of these EPROMs at the same performance as high-speed DRAMs. With the 27960KX, the EPROM is the ideal code or FONT storage device for your 80960KA/KB system.

Architecture

The 27960KX is a 128K x 8, high-performance CMOS EPROM with a synchronous burst access. It is available in surface mount 44-lead PLCC and 44-lead CERQUAD* (reprogrammable) packages.

The 27960KX provides a simple, synchronous burst interface to the 80960KA/KB's bus. Internally, the 27960KX is organized in blocks of 4 bytes which are accessed sequentially. A burst access begins on the first clock pulse after $\overline{CS}$ is asserted. The address of the four byte block is latched by the rising edge of $\overline{ALE}$. After a set number of wait states (1 or 2), data is output one byte at a time on each subsequent clock cycle. A burst access is terminated at the rising edge of CLK if $\overline{BLAST}$ is asserted. High performance outputs provide zero wait state data-to-data burst access at clock frequencies up to 25 MHz. Extra power and ground pins dedicated to the outputs reduce the effect of fast output switching on device performance.

The 27960KX gives 4 bytes of data in 8 clock cycles at 25 MHz and 4 bytes of data in 7 clock cycles at 20 MHz. In a 32-bit configuration, this translates into a read bandwidth of 50 Mbytes/sec and 45 Mbytes/sec respectively. Performance capability of the 27960KX in different 80960KA/KB systems is given in Table 1.

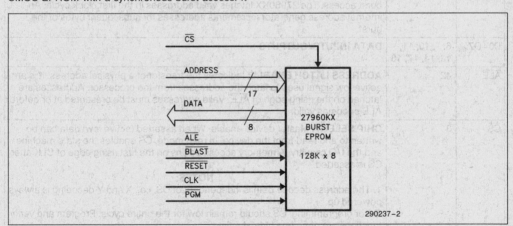

290237-2

Figure 2. 27960KX Burst EPROM Signal Set

*CERQUAD is available in a socket only version until the third quarter of 1990.

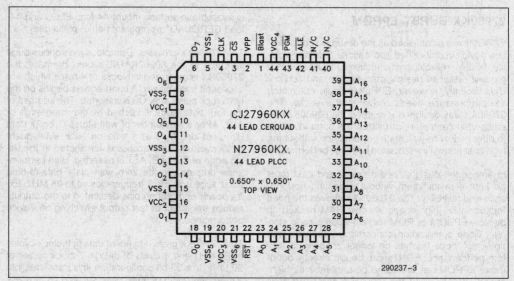

Figure 3. 27960KX 44-Lead PLCC/CERQUAD Pinout

PIN DESCRIPTIONS

Symbol	Pin	Function
A0–A16:	23–39	**ADDRESS INPUTS:** During a burst operation, A2–A16 provide the base address pointing to a block of four consecutive bytes. A0, A1 select the first byte of the burst access. The 27960KX latches valid addresses in the first clock cycle. An internal address generator increments addresses for subsequent bytes of the burst.
D0–D7:	6, 7, 10, 11, 13, 14, 17, 18	**DATA INPUTS/OUTPUTS**
$\overline{ALE}$	42	**ADDRESS LATCH ENABLE:** Indicates the transfer of a physical address. It is an active low signal used to latch the addresses from the processor. Addresses are latched on the rising edge of $\overline{ALE}$. Valid addresses must be presented at or before $\overline{ALE}$ becomes valid.
$\overline{CS}$	3	**CHIP SELECT:** Master device enable. When asserted (active low) data can be written to and read from the device. In read mode, $\overline{CS}$ enables the state machine and the I/O circuitry. A memory access begins on the first rising edge of CLK after $\overline{CS}$ is asserted. **NOTES:** 1. The address decode path is independent of $\overline{CS}$, i.e., X and Y decoding is always powered up. 2. For programming, $\overline{CS}$ should remain low for the entire cycle. Program and verify functions are done one byte at a time. 3. $\overline{CS}$ going high does not terminate a concurrent burst cycle. 4. $\overline{CS}$ must be deasserted between bursts.
$\overline{BLAST}$	1	**BURST LAST:** Terminates a concurrent burst data cycle at the rising edge of the CLK. It must be asserted by the fourth data byte.
$\overline{RESET}$	22	**ASYNCHRONOUS RESET INPUT:** Resets the state machine into a known state, tri-states the outputs and puts address latches into the flow through mode. The duration of RESET should be 10 CLK cycles minimum. Reset will abort a concurrent bus cycle. At least 5 clock cycles are required after deassertion of RESET before beginning the next cycle.

PIN DESCRIPTIONS (Continued)

Symbol	Pin	Function
$\overline{PGM}$	43	**PROGRAM-PULSE CONTROL INPUT:** During programming, $V_{PP} = 12.75V$. Minimum programming pulse $= 100\ \mu s$.
V_{PP}	2	**PROGRAMMING POWER SUPPLY V_{PP}**
GND	5, 8, 12, 15, 19, 21	V_{SS} **(GROUND) PINS**
V_{CC}	9, 16, 20, 44	**SUPPLY VOLTAGE INPUT**

Table 1. Performance Capability

```
25 MHz. 2 WS. NON-BUFFERED : 4 WORDS/8 CLOCK CYCLES  →  50 MBYTES/SEC

ADDR|A00|WS |WS |   |   |   |   |   |RS |A01|WS |WS |   |   |   |   |RS |A03|WS
    |   |   |   | - | - | - |   |   |   |   |   |   | - | - | - | - |   |   |
DATA| - | - | - |D00|   |D02|D03| - | - | - | - |D10|D11|D12|D13|   |   |
    |   |   |   |   |DO1|   |   |   |   |   |   |   |   |   |   |   |   |
CLK |C1 |C2 |C3 |C4 |C5 |C6 |C7 |C8 |C1 |C2 |C3 |C4 |C5 |C6 |C7 |C8 |

20 MHz. 1 WS. NON-BUFFERED : 4 WORDS/7 CLOCK CYCLES  →  45 MBYTES/SEC

ADDR|A00|WS |   |   |   |   |RS |A01|WS |   |   |   |   |RS |A03|WS
    |   |   | - | - | - | - |   |   |   | - | - | - | - |   |   |
DATA| - | - |D00|D01|D02|D03| - | - | - |D10|D11|D12|D13|
CLK |C1 |C2 |C3 |C4 |C5 |C6 |C7 |C1 |C2 |C3 |C4 |C5 |C6 |C7 |

16 MHz. 1 WS. BUFFERED : 4 WORDS/7 CLOCK CYCLES  →  36 MBYTES/SEC

ADDR|A00|WS |   |   |   |   |RS |A01|WS |   |   |   |   |RS |A03|WS
    |   |   | - | - | - | - |   |   |   | - | - | - | - |   |   |
DATA| - | - |D00|D01|D02|D03| - | - | - |D10|D11|D12|D13|
CLK |C1 |C2 |C3 |C4 |C5 |C6 |C7 |C1 |C2 |C3 |C4 |C5 |C6 |C7 |
```

INTERFACE EXAMPLE

1. Overview

The following design offers a simple interface to the 80960KA/KB's bus.

A non-buffered 27960KX burst EPROM system is shown (Figure 4). Since the 27960KX is capable of driving a 60 pF load, large, non-buffered systems can be implemented by stacking up 2 banks of 4 EPROMs, giving a memory size of 256K x 32. The input capacitance load seen on the address lines (due to the EPROM only) is 24 pF for a 128K x 32 system and 48 pF for a 256K x 32 system. The EPROM is specified at 6 pF for input capacitance and 15 pF max, 12 pF typical for output capacitance. Larger systems can be implemented with buffers.

Chip Select Logic

Higher order address lines are decoded to provide $\overline{CS}$. Qualification with other signals is not required. The chip select logic can be implemented with standard asynchronous decoders, PAL's or PLD's (like Intel's 85C960).

2. Waveforms

Figure 5 shows the timing waveforms of 27960KX pipelined reads in a 32-bit system.

a. $\overline{CS}$ setup time

$\overline{CS}$ setup time is defined as the time between $\overline{CS}$ being asserted and the first rising edge of CLK (during address state). Since a memory access begins on the first rising edge of CLK after $\overline{CS}$ is asserted, a minimum $\overline{CS}$ setup time of 5 ns at 25 MHz operation and 6 ns at 20 MHz operation is required. With the 80960KA/KB's maximum valid address delay of 24 ns at 25 MHz, 9 ns remains for $\overline{CS}$ decoding logic.

b. $\overline{CS}$ Deassert between bursts

$\overline{CS}$ must be deasserted after every Burst Read.

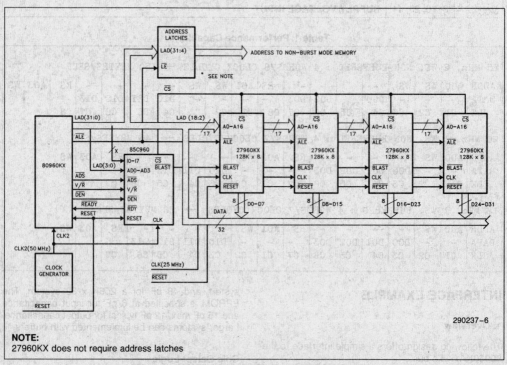

NOTE:
27960KX does not require address latches

290237-6

Figure 4. 128K x 32 27960KX Burst EPROM System

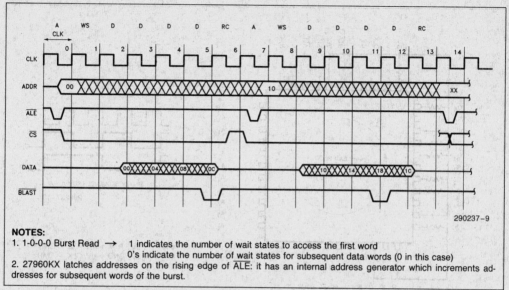

NOTES:
1. 1-0-0-0 Burst Read ⟶ 1 indicates the number of wait states to access the first word
   0's indicate the number of wait states for subsequent data words (0 in this case)
2. 27960KX latches addresses on the rising edge of ALE: it has an internal address generator which increments addresses for subsequent words of the burst.

Figure 5. Two Cycles of a 27960KX 1 Wait State, 4-Byte Read (1-0-0-0 Burst Read) in a 32-Bit System

27960KX DEVICE NAMES

The device names on the 27960KX were derived as mnemonics and correspond to the number of wait states and expected operation frequency for the device. For example, the 25 MHz, 2 wait state 27960KX is named 27960K2-25.

AC TIMINGS

The A.C. timings for the 27960KX were generated specifically to meet the requirements of the 80960KA/KB microprocessor. In each timing case the applicable 80960KA/KB clock frequency and A.C. timing were taken together with an address buffer delay (if needed) and a 2 ns clock skew

guardband to generate the 27960KX AC timing. Worst case timings were always assumed. The example below shows how the 27960K1-20 Tavc$_0$h timing was derived.

@20 MHz the clock cycle is ~ 50 ns.
t$_6$ of the 80960KA/KB is 5–30 ns.
2 ns clock skew guardband.

27960K1-20 Tavc$_0$h = 50 ns − 30 ns − 2 ns
$$= 18 ns$$

On timings where the EPROM was significantly faster than the microprocessor, we specified the EPROM's timing leaving the excess time as additional system guardband.

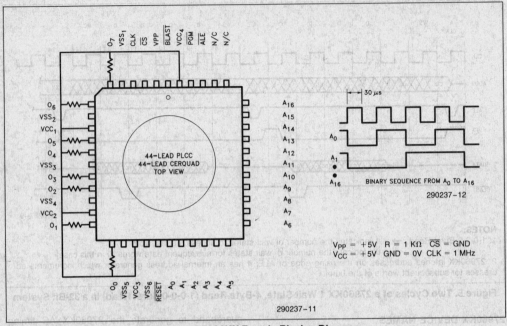

290237–11

Figure 6. 27960KX Burn in Biasing Diagram

Decoders are needed for the systems chip select decoding. For the 27960KX's timings we assumed a 5–10 ns chip select decoder for 16 MHz and 20 MHz frequencies and a 5–9 ns decoder for 25 MHz systems. The example below shows how the 27960K2-25 Tsvch timing was derived.

@25 MHz the clock cycle is ~40 ns.
t_6 of the 80960KA/KB is 5–24 ns.
Decoder = 9 ns
2 ns clock skew guardband

27960K2-25 Tsvch = 40 ns − 24 ns − 9 ns − 2 ns
              = 5 ns

SYSTEM BUFFERING CONSIDERATIONS

For many large system applications buffering may be required between the microprocessor and the memory devices. The 20 MHz − 2 WS and 16 MHz 27960KX A.C. timings take this into account. For applications at these frequencies not requiring buffering these devices will provide an additional 5–10 ns of system guardband.

The list below shows the buffers used in generating these timings.

	Input Buffer	Output Buffer
20 MHz	8–10 ns	7 ns
16 MHz	10 ns	7 ns

The 20 MHz buffers are slightly faster in keeping with the increased sensitivity for higher performance. We chose the above buffers because of their wide availability. Significantly faster buffers are available for applications requiring them. The example below shows Tchqv for the 27960K1-20.

@20 MHz the clock cycle is ~50 ns.
t_{10} of the 80960KA/KB is 3 ns.
Output buffer for 20 MHz = 7 ns.
2 ns clock skew guardband

27960K1-20 Tchqv = 50 ns − 7 ns − 3 ns − 2 ns
              = 38 ns

ABSOLUTE MAXIMUM RATINGS*

Read Operating Temperature ...... 0°C to +70°C[8]

Case Temperature under Bias .. −10°C to +80°C[8]

Storage Temperature .... −65°C to +150°C

All Input or Output Voltages ..... −0.6V to +6.5V[4]
    with Respect to Ground

Voltage on Pin A9 .... −0.6V to +13.0V[4]
    with Respect to Ground

V_{PP} Supply Voltage .... −0.6V to +14.0V[4]
    with Respect to Ground

V_{CC} Supply Voltage .... −0.6V to +7.0V[4]
    with Respect to Ground

Notice: Stresses above those listed under "Absolute Maximum Ratings" may cause permanent damage to the device. This is a stress rating only and functional operation of the device at these or any other conditions above those indicated in the operational sections of this specification is not implied. Exposure to absolute maximum rating conditions for extended periods may affect device reliability.

NOTICE: Specifications contained within the following tables are subject to change.

READ OPERATION

D.C. CHARACTERISTICS 0°C < T_A < +70°C, V_{CC}: 10%, TTL Inputs

Symbol	Parameter	Notes	Min	Max	Units	Test Conditions
I_{LI}	Input Load Current			1	μA	V_{IN} = 5.5V
I_{LO}	Output Leakage Current			10	μA	V_{OUT} = 5.5V
I_{PP}	V_{PP} Load Current Read			10	μA	V_{PP} = 0 to V_{CC}, $\overline{PGM}$ = V_{IH}
I_{SB}	V_{CC} Standby Switching	2		45	mA	$\overline{CS}$ = V_{IH}, f = 33 MHz
	Stable	2		30	mA	$\overline{CS}$ = V_{IH}
I_{CC}	V_{CC} Active Current	1, 3, 7		125	mA	$\overline{CS}$ = V_{IL}, f = 33 MHz, I_{OUT} = 0 mA
V_{IL}	Input Low Voltage	4	−0.5	0.8	V	
V_{IH}	Input High Voltage		2.0	V_{CC}+1	V	
V_{OL}	Output Low Voltage			0.45	V	IOL = 2.1 mA
V_{OH1}	Output High Voltage	5	V_{CC}−0.8		V	IOH = 100 μA
V_{OH2}	Output High Voltage	5	2.4		V	IOH = 400 μA
I_{OS}	Output Short Circuit	6		100	mA	

NOTES:
1. Maximum value is with outputs unloaded.
2. I_{CC} standby current assumes no output loading, i.e., I_{OH} = I_{OL} = 0 mA.
3. I_{CC} is the sum of current through V_{CC3} + V_{CC4} and does not include the current through V_{CC1} and V_{CC2}. (V_{CC1} and V_{CC2} supply power to the output drivers. V_{CC3} and V_{CC4} supply power to the rest of the device.)
4. Minimum DC input voltage is −0.5V during transitions. Inputs may undershoot to −2.0V for periods less than 20 ns.
5. Maximum DC output voltage is V_{CC} + 0.5V; overshoot may be V_{CC} + 2.0V for periods less than 20 ns.
6. One output shorted for no more than one second. I_{OS} is sampled but not 100% tested.
7. I_{CC} max measured with a 0.11 μF capacitor between V_{CC} and V_{SS}.
8. This specification defines commercial product operating temperatures.

EXPLANATION OF A.C. SYMBOLS

The nomenclature used for timing parameters are as per IEEE STD 662-1980 IEEE Standard Terminology for Semiconductor Memory.

Each timing symbol has five characters. The first is always a "t" (for time). The second character represents a signal name, e.g., (CLK, ALE, etc.). The third character represents the signal's level (high or low) for the signal indicated by the second character. The fourth character represents a signal name at which a transition occurs marking the end of the time interval being specified.

The fifth character represents the signal level indicated by the fourth character. The list below shows character representations.

A:	Address	R:	$\overline{Reset}$
B:	$\overline{BLAST}$	Q:	Data
C:	Clock	S:	$\overline{Chip\ Select}$
H:	Logic High Level	t:	Time
L:	$\overline{ALE}$/Logic Low Level	V:	Valid
P:	V_{PP} Programming Voltage	Z:	Tristate level
X:	No longer a valid "driven" logic level		

A.C. CHARACTERISTICS: READ $0\,°C < T_A < +70\,°C$, 10% V_{CC}

Product Name				27960K2-25		27960K1-20		27960K2-20		27960K1-16		
READ TIMING			Notes	25 MHz 2 Wait States		20 MHz 1 Wait State		20 MHz 2 Wait States		16 MHz 1 Wait State		Units
No	Symbol	Characteristic		Min	Max	Min	Max	Min	Max	Min	Max	
1	t_{AVC_0H}	Address Valid to CLK High	CLK 0	12		18		10		15		ns
2	t_{LLAV}	$\overline{ALE}$ Low to Address Valid	CLK 1	0		0		0		0		ns
3	t_{LLLH}	$\overline{ALE}$ Low to $\overline{ALE}$ High		12		12		12		12		ns
4	t_{LHAX}	$\overline{ALE}$ High to Address Invalid		8		8		8		8		ns
5	t_{SVCH}	Chip Select Valid to CLK High	(1, 5)	5		8		6		8		ns
6	t_{C_NHSX}	CLK High to Chip Select Invalid	(2)	0		0		0		0		ns
7	t_{CHQV}	CLK High to Data Valid			45		45		38		45	ns
8	t_{CHQX}	CLK High to Data Invalid		6		7		7		7		ns
9	t_{CHQZ}	CLK High to Data Hi-Z	(6)		25		30		30		35	ns
10	t_{BVCH}	$\overline{BLAST}$ Valid to CLK High		15		15		15		15		ns
11	t_{CHBX}	CLK High to $\overline{BLAST}$ Invalid	(3)	5	35	5	45	5	45	5	45	ns

NOTES:
1. Valid signal level is meant to be either a logic high or logic low.
2. t_{C_NHSX}—The subscript N represents the number of wait states for this parameter. $\overline{CS}$ can be de-asserted (high) after the number of wait states (N) has expired. The EPROM will continue to burst out data for the current cycle.
3. $\overline{BLAST}$ must be returned high before the next rising clock edge.
4. The sum of $t_{CHQV} + t_{AVCH} + NCLK$ will not equal actual t_{AVQV} if independent test conditions are used to obtain t_{AVCH} and t_{CHQV} (N = number of wait states).
5. $\overline{CS}$ must be deasserted after every burst read (see Figure 7).
6. Sampled but not 100% tested. The transition is measured ±500 mV from steady state voltage.
7. For capacitive loads above 60 pF, T_{CHQV} can be derated by 1 ns/10 pF.

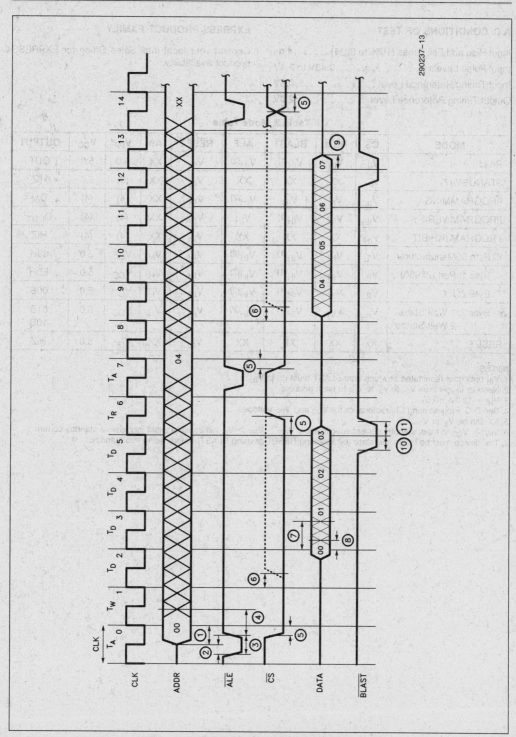

Figure 7. 27960KX 1 WS A.C. Read Waveforms

A.C. CONDITIONS OF TEST

Input Rise and Fall Times (10% to 90%) . . . . 4 ns
Input Pulse Levels . . . . 0.45V to 2.4V
Input Timing Reference Level 0.8V
Output Timing Reference Level 2.0V

EXPRESS PRODUCT FAMILY

Contact your local Intel Sales Office for EXPRESS product availability.

Table 2. Mode Table

MODE	$\overline{CS}$	$\overline{PGM}$	BLAST	$\overline{ALE}$	RESET	A9	V_{PP}	V_{CC}	OUTPUT
Read	V_{IL}	V_{IH}	$V_{IH}^{(1)}$	$V_{IH}^{(2)}$	V_{IH}	XX	5.0	5.0	OUT
STANDBY (7)	V_{IH}	XX	XX	XX	V_{IH}	XX	(6)	5.0	HiZ
PROGRAMMING	V_{IL}	V_{IL}	V_{IH}	$V_{IH}^{(2)}$	V_{IH}	XX	(4)	(4)	D_{IN}
PROGRAM VERIFY	V_{IL}	V_{IH}	$V_{IH}^{(1)}$	V_{IH}	V_{IH}	XX	(4)	(4)	D_{OUT}
PROGRAM INHIBIT	V_{IH}	XX	XX	XX	V_{IH}	XX	(4)	(4)	HiZ
ID Byte 0: Manufacturer	V_{IL}	V_{IH}	$V_{IH}^{(1)}$	$V_{IH}^{(2)}$	V_{IH}	V_H	V_{CC}	5.0	89H
Byte 1: Part (27960)	V_{IL}	V_{IH}	$V_{IH}^{(1)}$	$V_{IH}^{(2)}$	V_{IH}	V_H	V_{CC}	5.0	E0H
Byte 2: KX	V_{IL}	V_{IH}	$V_{IH}^{(1)}$	$V_{IH}^{(2)}$	V_{IH}	V_H	V_{CC}	5.0	00B
Byte 3: 1 Wait State 2 Wait States	V_{IL}	V_{IH}	$V_{IH}^{(1)}$	$V_{IH}^{(2)}$	V_{IH}	V_H	V_{CC}	5.0	01B 10B
RESET	XX	XX	XX	XX	V_{IL}	XX	V_{CC}	5.0	HiZ

NOTES:
1. V_{IH} until data terminated at which time $\overline{BLAST}$ must go to V_{IL}.
2. Need to toggle from V_{IH} to V_{IL} to V_{IH} to latch address.
3. V_H = 12.0V ±0.5V.
4. See D.C. Programming Characteristics for V_{CC} and V_{PP} voltages.
5. XX can be V_{IL} or V_{IH}.
6. V_{PP} = V_{CC} to meet standby current specification. $\underline{V_{CC} > V_{PP} > V_{IL}}$ will cause a slight increase in standby current.
7. The device must be in the idle state (by asserting $\overline{RESET}$ or using $\overline{BLAST}$) before going into standby.

CAPACITANCE(1) $T_A = 25°C. f = 1.0$ MHz

Symbol	Parameter	Typ	Max	Units	Conditions
C_{IN}	Address/Control Capacitance	4	6	pF	$V_{IN} = 0V$
C_{OUT}	Output Capacitance	12	15	pF	$V_{OUT} = 0V$
C_{VPP}	V_{PP} Capacitance	40	45	pF	$V_{IN} = 0V$

NOTE:
1. Sampled, not 100% tested

A.C. INPUT/OUTPUT REFERENCE WAVEFORMS

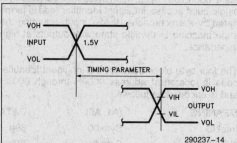

290237-14

A.C. test inputs are driven at 2.4V (V_{OH}) for a logic '1'
and 0.45V (V_{OL}) for a logic '0'.
Input timing begins at 1.5V.
Output timing ends at V_{IH} (2.0V) and V_{IL} (0.8V)
Input Rise and fall times (10% to 90%) < 4.0 ns

A.C. TESTING LOAD CIRCUIT

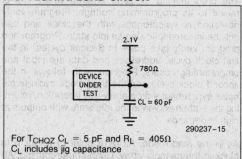

290237-15

For T_{CHQZ} C_L = 5 pF and R_L = 405Ω
C_L includes jig capacitance

CLOCK CHARACTERISTICS

Versions		25 MHz		20 MHz		16 MHz		Units
Symbol	Parameter	Min	Max	Min	Max	Min	Max	
CLK	Period	40		50		62.5		ns
T_5	Rise Time		10		10		10	ns
T_4	Fall Time		10		10		10	ns
T_2	Low Time	7		8		11		ns
T_3	High Time	7		8		11		ns

Max Rise Time for Programming CLK = 100 ns

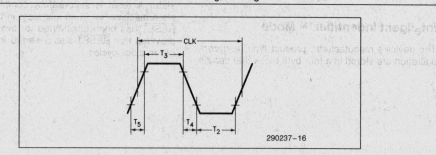

290237-16

PROGRAMMING MODES

Program/Program Verify

Initially, and after each erasure, all bits of the EPROM are in the "1's" state. Data is introduced by selectively programming "0's" into the desired bit locations. Although only "0's" can be programmed, both "1's" and "0's" can be present in the data word. Ultraviolet erasure is the only way to change "0's" to "1's".

The programming mode is entered when Vpp is raised to its programming voltage. Program/verify operation is synchronous with the clock and can only be initiated following an idle state. Program and program verify take place in 3 clock cycles. In the first clock cycle, addresses and data are input and programming occurs. Program verify follows in the second clock cycle and the third clock cycle terminates synchronous program/verify operation, returning the state machine to the idle state with outputs at high impedance.

As in the read mode, A2–A16 point to a four byte block in the memory array. During programming, A0 and A1 point to an individual byte within the four byte block that is to be accessed. Only one byte is accessed in each 3 cycle program/verify sequence.

Program Inhibit

The Program Inhibit mode allows parallel programming and verification of multiple devices with different data. With Vpp at its program voltage, a program/verify sequence is initiated for any device that receives a valid $\overline{ALE}$ pulse and rising clock edge while $\overline{CS}$ is asserted. A $\overline{PGM}$ pulse programs data in the first cycle of the sequence and data for program verify is output in the second cycle. The program/verify sequence is inhibited on any devices for which $\overline{CS}$ is not asserted during the first ($\overline{ALE}$) cycle. Data will not be programmed and the outputs will remain in their high impedance state.

int$_e$ligent Indentifier™ Mode

The device's manufacturer, product type, and configuration are stored in a four byte block that can be accessed by using the int$_e$ligent Identifier mode. The programmer can verify the device identifier and choose the programming algorithm that corresponds to the Intel 27960KX. The int$_e$ligent Identifier can also be used to verify that the product is configured with the desired read mode options for wait states.

The int$_e$ligent Identifier mode is entered when A9 (pin 32) is raised to its high voltage (V_H) level. The internal state machine is set for int$_e$ligent read operation and is independent of the configurable read mode options. Reading the Identifier is similar to read mode for a product configured for one wait state operation. Up to four bytes can be read in a single burst access. int$_e$ligent Identifier read is terminated by a synchronous $\overline{BLAST}$ input, returning the state machine to the idle state with outputs at high impedance.

The four byte block code for the int$_e$ligent Identifier code is located at address 0000H through 0003H and is encoded as follows:

MEANING	(A1, A0)	DATA
Intel ID	Byte 00	89h
27960	Byte 01	E0h
KX	Byte 10	00b
1 wait state	Byte 11	01b
2 wait states	Byte 11	10b

RESET MODE

Due to the synchronous nature of the 27960KX, the various operating modes must be initiated from a known idle state. During normal operation, the internal state machine returns to an idle state at the termination of a bus access. This occurs following a cycle where $\overline{BLAST}$ is asserted. It stays there until another bus access is initiated.

During initial device power up, the state machine is in an indeterminant state. The reset mode is provided to force operation in to the idle state. Reset mode is entered when the $\overline{RESET}$ pin is asserted. Output pins are asynchronously set to the high impedance state. A reset is successfully completed and the state machine set in an idle state in the cycle after $\overline{RESET}$ has been deasserted for five clock cycles, provided that $\overline{RESET}$ was asserted for a minumum of ten clock cycles.

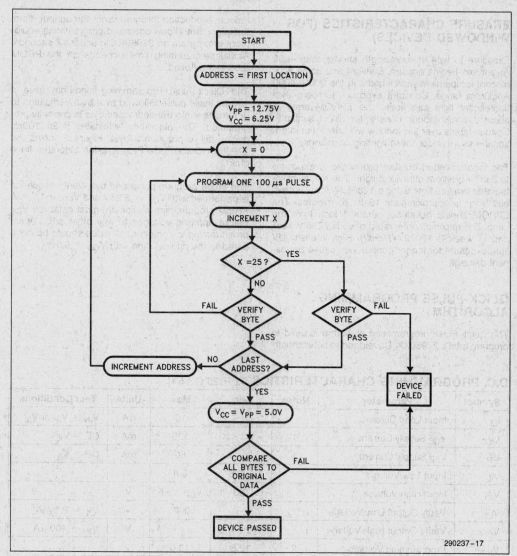

Figure 8. Quick-Pulse Programming™ Algorithm

290237–17

ERASURE CHARACTERISTICS (FOR WINDOWED DEVICES)

Exposure to light of wavelength shorter than 4000 Angstroms begins erasure. Sunlight and some fluorescent lamps have wavelengths in the 3000–4000 Angstrom range. Constant exposure to room-level fluorescent light can erase the EPROM array in about 3 years (about 1 week for direct sunlight). Opaque labels over the window will prevent unintentional erasure under these lighting conditions.

The recommended erasure procedure is exposure to 2537 Angstrom ultraviolet light. The minimum integrated erasure time using a 12000 fW/cm2 ultraviolet lamp is approximately 15 to 20 minutes. The EPROM should be placed about 1 inch from the lamp. The maximum integrated dose is 7258 Wsec/cm2 (1 week @ 12000 fW/cm2). High intensity UV light exposure for longer periods can cause permanent damage.

QUICK-PULSE PROGRAMMING ALGORITHM

The Quick-Pulse programming algorithm is used to program Intel's 27960KX. Developed to substantially reduce production programming throughput time, this algorithm allows optimized programming equipment to program an 27960KX in under 17 seconds. Actual programming time depends on the PROM programmer used.

The Quick-Pulse Programming algorithm uses a 100 μs initial pulse followed by a byte verfication to determine when the addressed byte is correctly programmed. The algorithm terminates if 25 100μs pulses fail to program a byte. Figure 8 shows the 27960KX Quick-Pulse Programming algorithm flowchart.

The entire program-pulse and byte-verify sequence is performed with V_{CC} = 6.25V and V_{PP} = 12.75V. PROM programming equipment must establish V_{CC} before applying voltages to any other pins. When programming is complete, all bytes should be compared to the original data with V_{CC} = 5.0V.

D.C. PROGRAMMING CHARACTERISTICS T_A = 25°C ±5°C

Symbol	Parameter	Notes	Min	Max	Units	Test Conditions
I_{LI}	Input Load Current			10	μA	$V_{IN} = V_{IH}$ or V_{IL}
I_{CC2}	V_{CC} Supply Current	1		125	mA	CE = V_{IL}
I_{PP}	V_{PP} Supply Current	1		50	mA	CE = V_{IL}
V_{IL}	Input Low Voltage		−0.5	0.8	V	
V_{IH}	Input High Voltage		2.0	V_{CC} + 0.5	V	
V_{OL}	Verify Output Low Voltage			0.40	V	I_{OL} = 2.1 mA
V_{OH}	Verify Output High Voltage		V_{CC} − 0.8		V	I_{OH} = 400 μA
V_{PP}	Programming Voltage	2	12.5	13.0	V	
V_H	Input High Voltage		11.5	12.5	V	
V_{ID}	A9 inteligent Identifier		11.5	12.5	V	
V_{CC}	Quick-Pulse		6.0	6.5	V	
V_{PP}	Quick-Pulse		12.5	13.0	V	$\overline{CS} = \overline{PGM} = V_{IL}$

NOTES:
1. The maximum current value is with outputs unloaded.
2. V_{CC} must be applied simultaneously or before V_{PP} and remove simultaneously or after V_{PP}.
3. During programming clock levels are V_{IH} and V_{IL}.

A.C. PROGRAMMING, RESET AND ID CHARACTERISTICS $0°C < T_A < +70°C$

No	Symbol	Characteristic	Min	Max	Units	Conditions
1	t_{AVPL}	Address Valid to $\overline{PGM}$ Low	2		μs	
2	t_{CHAX}	CLK(1) High to Address Invalid	50		ns	
3	t_{LLCH}	$\overline{ALE}$ Low to CLK High	50		ns	Note 1
4	t_{CHLH}	CLK High to $\overline{ALE}$ High	50		ns	Note 2
5	t_{SVCH}	$\overline{CS}$ Valid to CLK High	50		ns	
6	t_{CHSX}	CLK High to $\overline{CS}$ Invalid			ns	Note 3
7	t_{CHQV}	CLK(1) High to DATA (Out) Valid		100	ns	
8	t_{CHQX}	CLK High to DATA (Out) Invalid	0		ns	
9	t_{BVCH}	$\overline{BLAST}$ Valid to CLK High	50		ns	
10	t_{CHBX}	CLK High to $\overline{BLAST}$ Invalid	50		ns	Note 4
11	t_{QVPL}	DATA Valid to $\overline{PGM}$ Low	2		μs	
12	t_{PLPH}	Program Pulse Width	95	105	μs	
13	t_{PHQX}	$\overline{PGM}$ High to DATA Invalid	2		μs	
14	t_{CLPL}	CLK Low to $\overline{PGM}$ Low	50		ns	
15	t_{QZCH}	DATA in Tri-State to CLK High	2		μs	
16	t_{VCS}	V_{CC} High Voltage to CLK High	2		μs	
17	t_{VPS}	V_{PP} High Voltage to CLK High	2		μs	
18	t_{A9HCH}	A9 High Voltage to CLK High	2		μs	
19	t_{CHA9X}	CLK High to A9 not High Voltage	2		μs	
20	t_{RVCH}	$\overline{RESET}$ Valid to CLK High	50		ns	Note 6
21	t_{CHCL}	CLK High to CLK Low	100		ns	Note 5
22	t_{CLCH}	CLK Low to CLK High	100		ns	Note 5

NOTES:
1. If $\overline{CS}$ is low, $\overline{ALE}$ can go low no sooner than the falling edge of the previous CLK.
2. $\overline{ALE}$ must return high prior to the next rising edge of clock.
3. $\overline{CS}$ must remain low until after the rising edge CLK 1.
4. $\overline{BLAST}$ must return high prior to the next rising edge of CLK.
5. Max CLK rise time is 100 ns.
6. Reset must be held low for 10 cycles and high for 5 cycles before performing a read.

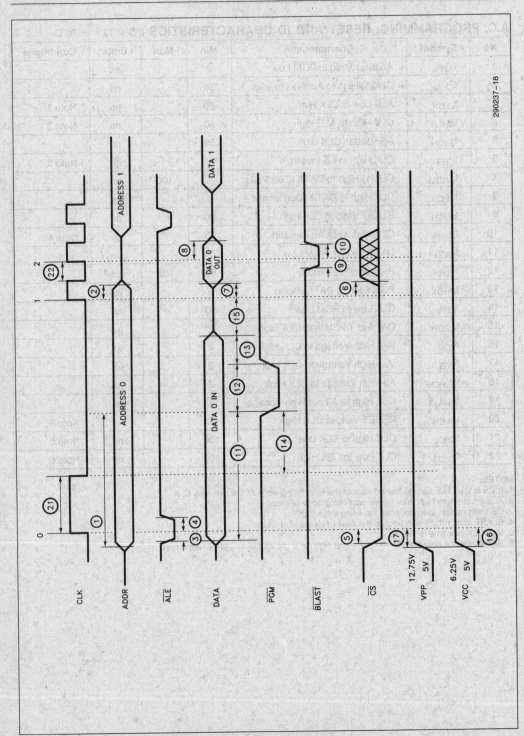

290237–18

Figure 9. Programming Waveforms

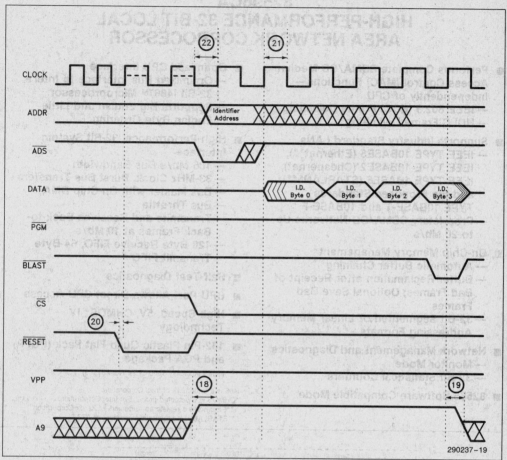

Figure 10. Reset and ID Waveforms

290237–19

82596CA
HIGH-PERFORMANCE 32-BIT LOCAL AREA NETWORK COPROCESSOR

- **Performs Complete CSMA/CD Medium Access Control (MAC) Functions— Independently of CPU**
  - **IEEE 802.3 (EOC) Frame Delimiting**
  - **HDLC Frame Delimiting**

- **Supports Industry Standard LANs**
  - **IEEE TYPE 10BASE5 (Ethernet**), IEEE TYPE 10BASE2 (Cheapernet), IEEE TYPE 1BASE5 (STARLAN***), and the Proposed Standards TYPE 10BASE-T and 10BASE-F**
  - **Proprietary CSMA/CD Networks Up to 20 Mb/s**

- **On-Chip Memory Management**
  - **Automatic Buffer Chaining**
  - **Buffer Reclamation after Receipt of Bad Frames; Optional Save Bad Frames**
  - **32-Bit Segmented or Linear Memory Addressing Formats**

- **Network Management and Diagnostics**
  - **Monitor Mode**
  - **32-Bit Statistical Counters**

- **82586 Software Compatible Mode**

- **Optimized CPU Interface**
  - **Optimized Bus Interface to Intel's 32-Bit i486™ Microprocessor**
  - **Supports Big Endian and Little Endian Byte Ordering**

- **High-Performance, 32-Bit System Interface**
  - **106 Mb/s Bus Bandwidth**
  - **33-MHz Clock, Burst Bus Transfers**
  - **Bus Master with On-Chip DMA**
  - **Bus Throttle**
  - **Transmits and Receives Back-to-Back Frames at 10 Mb/s**
  - **128-Byte Receive FIFO, 64-Byte Transmit FIFO**

- **Self-Test Diagnostics**

- **CPU Port Allows Direct CPU Access**

- **High-Speed, 5V, CHMOS* IV Technology**

- **132-Pin Plastic Quad Flat Pack (PQFP) and PGA Package**

  (See Packaging Spec Order No. 231369)

i486 is a trademark of Intel Corporation.
*CHMOS is a patented process of Intel Corporation.
**Ethernet is a registered trademark of Xerox Corporation.
***STARLAN is a registered trademark of AT&T.

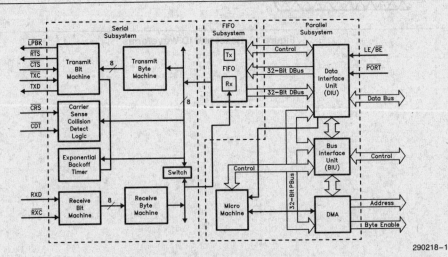

Figure 1. 82596CA Block Diagram

290218–1

October 1989
Order Number: 290218-002

The 82596CA is an intelligent, high-performance 32-bit Local Area Network coprocessor. The 82596CA implements the CSMA/CD access method and can be configured to support all existing IEEE 802.3 standards—TYPEs 10BASE5, 10BASE2, 1BASE5, and 10BROAD36. It can also be used to implement the proposed standards TYPE 10BASE-T and 10BASE-F. The 82596CA performs high-level commands, command chaining, and interprocessor communications via shared memory, thus relieving the host CPU of many tasks associated with network control. All time-critical functions are performed independently of the CPU, this increases network performance and efficiency. The 82596CA bus interfaces is optimized for Intel's i486™ 32-bit microprocessor.

The 82596CA implements all IEEE 802.3 Medium Access Control and channel interface functions, these include framing, preamble generation and stripping, source address generation, destination address checking, short-frame detection, and automatic length-field handling. Data rates up to 20 Mb/s are supported.

The 82596CA provides a powerful host system interface. It manages memory structures automatically, with command chaining and bidirectional data chaining. An on-chip DMA controller manages four channels, this allows autonomous transfer of data blocks (buffers and frames) and relieves the CPU of byte transfer overhead. Buffers containing errored or collided frames can be automatically recovered without CPU intervention. The 82596CA provides an upgrade path for existing 82586 software drivers by providing an 82586-software-compatible mode that supports the current 82586 memory structure. The 82586CA also has a Flexible memory structure and a Simplified memory structure. The 82596CA can address up to 4 gigabytes of memory. The 82596CA supports Little Endian and Big Endian byte ordering.

The 82596CA bus interface is optimized to Intel's i486 microprocessor, providing a bus transfer rate of up to 106 MB/s at 33 MHz. The bus interface employs bus throttle timers to regulate 82596CA bus

use. Two large, independent FIFOs—128 bytes for Receive and 64 bytes for Transmit—tolerate long bus latencies and provide programmable thresholds that allow the user to optimize bus overhead for any worst-case bus latency. The high-performance bus is capable of back-to-back transmission and reception during the IEEE 802.3 9.6-μs Interframe Spacing (IFS) period.

The 82596CA provides a wide range of diagnostics and network management functions, these include internal and external loopback, exception condition tallies, channel activity indicators, optional capture of all frames regardless of destination address (promiscuous mode), optional capture of errored or collided frames, and time domain reflectometry for locating fault points on the network cable. The statistical counters, in 32-bit segmented and linear modes, are 32-bits each and include CRC errors, alignment errors, overrun errors, resource errors, short frames, and received collisions. The 82596CA also features a monitor mode for network analysis. In this mode the 82596CA can capture status bytes, and update statistical counters, of frames monitored on the link without transferring the contents of the frames to memory. This can be done concurrently while transmitting and receiving frames destined for that station.

The 82596CA can be used in both baseband and broadband networks. It can be configured for maximum network efficiency (minimum contention overhead) with networks of any length. Its highly flexible CSMA/CD unit supports address field lengths of zero through six bytes—configurable to either IEEE 802.3/Ethernet or HDLC frame delimitation. It also supports 16- or 32-bit cyclic redundancy checks. The CRC can be transferred directly to memory for receive operations, or dynamically inserted for transmit operations. The CSMA/CD unit can also be configured for full duplex operation or CSMA/DCR (Collision Sense Multiple Access with Deterministic Collision Resolution).

The 82596CA is fabricated with Intel's reliable, 5-V, CHMOS IV technology. It is available in a 132-pin PQFP or PGA package.

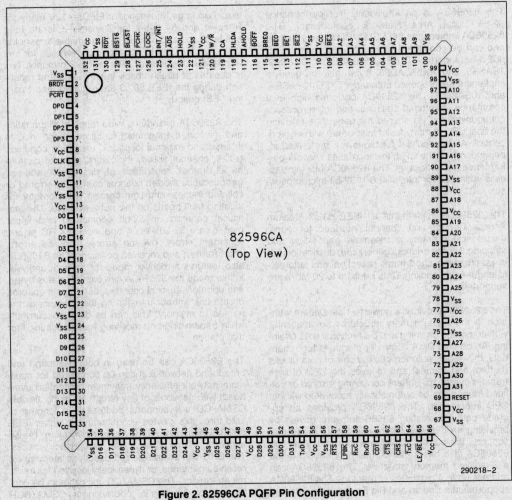

Figure 2. 82596CA PQFP Pin Configuration

290218-2

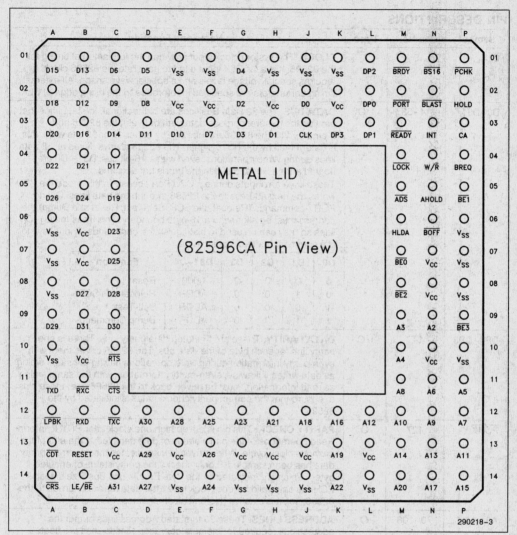

Figure 3. 82596CA PGA Pinout

290218-3

PIN DESCRIPTIONS

Symbol	Pin No.	Type	Name and Function
CLK	9	I	**CLOCK.** The system clock input provides the fundamental timing for the 82596. It is a 1X CLK input used to generate the 82596 clock. It requires special voltage levels and a special wave shape. All external timing parameters are specified in reference to the rising edge of CLK.
D0–D31	14–53	I/O	**DATA BUS.** The 32 Data Bus lines are bidirectional, tri-state lines that provide the general purpose data path between the 82596 and memory. With the 82596 the bus can be either 16 or 32 bits wide; this is determined by the $\overline{BS16}$ signal. The 82596 always drives all 32 data lines during Write operations, even with a 16-bit bus. D31– D0 are floated after a Reset or when the bus is not acquired. These lines are inputs during a CPU Port access; in this mode the CPU writes the next address to the 82596 through the data lines. During $\overline{PORT}$ commands (Relocatable SCP, Self-Test, Reset and Dump) the address must be aligned to a 16-byte boundary. This frees the D_3–D_0 lines so they can be used to distinguish the commands. The following is a summary of the decoding data.
DP0–DP3	4–7	I/O	**DATA PARITY.** These are tri-stated data parity pins. There is one parity line for each byte of the data bus. The 82596 drives them with even-parity information during write operations having the same timing as data writes. Likewise, even-parity information, with the same timing as read information, must be driven back to the 82596 over these pins to ensure that the correct parity check status is indicated by the 82596.
PCHK	127	O	**PARITY CHECK.** This pin is driven high one clock after $\overline{RDY}$ to inform Read operations of the parity status of data sampled at the end of the previous clock cycle. When driven low it indicates that incorrect parity data has been sampled. It only checks the parity status of enabled bytes, which are indicated by the Byte Enable and Bus Size signals. $\overline{PCHK}$ is only valid for one clock time after data read is returned to the 82596; i.e., it is inactive (high) at all other times.
A31-A2	70–108	O	**ADDRESS LINES.** These 30 tri-stated Address lines output the address bits required for memory operation. These lines are floated after a Reset or when the bus is not acquired.
$\overline{BE3}$–$\overline{BE0}$	109–114	O	**BYTE ENABLE.** These tri-stated signals are used to indicate which bytes are involved with the current memory access. The number of Byte Enable signals asserted indicates the physical size of the data being transferred (1, 2, 3, or 4 bytes). • $\overline{BE0}$ indicates D7–D0 • $\overline{BE1}$ indicates D15–D8 • $\overline{BE2}$ indicates D23–D16 • $\overline{BE3}$ indicates D31–D24 These lines are floated after a Reset or when the bus is not acquired.

D0	D1	D2	D3	D31–D4	Function
0	0	0	0	0000	Reset
0	1	0	0	ADDR	Relocatable SCP
1	0	0	0	ADDR	Self-Test
1	1	0	0	ADDR	Dump Command

PIN DESCRIPTIONS (Continued)

Symbol	Pin No.	Type	Name and Function
W/R̄	120	O	**WRITE/READ.** This dual function pin is used to distinguish Write and Read cycles. This line is floated after a Reset or when the bus is not acquired.
ADS̄	124	O	**ADDRESS STATUS.** The 82596 uses this tri-state pin to indicate to indicate that a valid bus cycle has begun and that A31–A2, BE3̄–BE0̄, and W/R̄ are being driven. It is asserted during t1 bus states. This line is floated after a Reset or when the bus is not acquired.
RDȲ	130	I	**READY.** Active low. This signal is the acknowledgment from addressed memory that the transfer cycle can be completed. When high, it causes wait states to be inserted. It is ignored at the end of the first clock of the bus cycle's data cycle. This active-low signal does not have an internal pull-up resistor. This signal must meet the setup and hold times to operate correctly.
BRDȲ	2	I	**BURST READY.** Active low. Burst Ready, like RDȲ, indicates that the external system has presented valid data on the data pins in response to a Read, or that the external system has accepted the 82596 data in response to a Write request. Also, like RDȲ, this signal is ignored at the end of the first clock in a bus cycle. If the 82596 can still receive data from the previous cycle, ADS̄ will not be asserted in the next clock cycle; however, Address and Byte Enable will change to reflect the next data item expected by the 82596. BRDȲ will be sampled during each succeeding clock and if active, the data on the pins will be strobed to the 82596 or to external memory (read/write). BRDȲ operates exactly like READY during the last data cycle of a burst sequence and during nonburstable cycles.
BLAST̄	128	O	**BURST LAST.** A signal (active low) on this tri-state pin indicates that the burst cycle is finished and when BRDȲ is next returned it will be treated as a normal ready; i.e., another set of addresses will be driven with ADS̄ or the bus will go idle. BLAST̄ is not asserted if the bus is not acquired.
AHOLD	117	I	**ADDRESS HOLD.** This hold signal is active high, it allows another bus master to access the 82596 address bus. In a system where an 82596 and a i486 processor share the local bus, AHOLD allows the cache controller to make a cache invalidation cycle while the 82596 holds the address lines. In response to a signal on this pin, the 82596 immediately (i.e. during the next clock) stops driving the entire address bus (A31–A2); the rest of the bus can remain active. For example, data can be returned for a previously specified bus cycle during Address Hold. The 82596 will not begin another bus cycle while AHOLD is active.
BOFF̄	116	I	**BACKOFF.** This signal is active low, it informs the 82596 that another bus master requires access to the bus before the 82596 bus cycle completes. The 82596 immediately (i.e. during the next clock) floats its bus. Any data returned to the 82596 while BOFF̄ is asserted is ignored. BOFF̄ has higher priority than RDȲ or BRDȲ; if two such signals are returned in the same clock period, BOFF̄ is given preference. The 82596 remains in Hold until BOFF̄ goes high, then the 82596 resumes its bus cycle by driving out the address and status, and asserting ADS̄. If Backoff is asserted when the 82596 is not on the bus, the 82596 will not request the bus (HOLD) when BOFF̄ goes active.

PIN DESCRIPTIONS (Continued)

Symbol	Pin No.	Type	Name and Function
LOCK	126	O	**LOCK.** This tri-state pin is used to distinguish locked and unlocked bus cycles. LOCK generates a semaphore handshake to the CPU. LOCK can be active for several memory cycles, it goes active during the first locked memory cycle (t1) and goes inactive at the last locked cycle (t2). This line is floated after a Reset or when the bus is not acquired. LOCK can be disabled via the sysbus byte.
BS16	129	I	**BUS SIZE.** This signal allows the 82596CA to work with either 16- or 32-bit bytes. Inserting BS16 low causes the 82596 to perform two 16-bit memory accesses when transferring 32-bit data. In little endian mode the D15–D0 lines are driven when BS16 is inserted, in Big Endian mode the D31–D16 lines are driven.
HOLD	123	O	**HOLD.** The HOLD signal is active high, the 82596 uses it to request local bus mastership at the end of the current CPU bus transfer cycle or at the end of the current DMA burst transfer cycle. In normal operation HOLD goes inactive before HLDA. The 82596 can be forced off the bus by deasserting HLDA or if the bus throttle timers expire.
HLDA	118	I	**HOLD ACKNOWLEDGE.** The HLDA signal is active high, it indicates that the CPU has received the Hold request and that bus control has been given to the 82596. HLDA is internally synchronized; after HOLD is detected low, the CPU drives HLDA low. **NOTE** *Do not connect HLDA to V_{CC}—it will cause a deadlock.* A user wanting to give the 82596 permanent access to the bus should connect HLDA to HOLD. If HLDA goes inactive before HOLD, the 82596 will release the bus (by deasserting HOLD) within a maximum of within a specified number of bus cycles.
BREQ	115	I	**BUS REQUEST.** This signal, when configured to an externally activated mode, is used to trigger the bus throttle timers.
PORT	3	I	**PORT.** When this signal is received, the 82596 latches the data on the data bus into an internal 32-bit register. When the CPU is asserting this signal it can write into the 82596 (via the data bus). This signal is internally polled only when the 82596 does not hold the bus. On a 16-bit bus this pin must be activated twice during all CPU Port access commands.
RESET	69	I	**RESET.** This active high, internally synchronized signal causes the 82596 to terminate current activity. The signal must be high for at least five system clock cycles. After five system clock cycles and four serial clock cycles the 82596 will execute a Reset when it receives a high RESET signal. When RESET returns to low the 82596 waits for the first CA signal and then begins the initialization sequence.
LE/BE	65	I	**LITTLE ENDIAN/BIG ENDIAN.** This dual-function pin is used to select byte ordering. When LE/BE is high, little endian byte ordering is used; when low, big endian byte ordering is used for data in frames (bytes) and for control (SCB, RFD, CBL, etc).

PIN DESCRIPTIONS (Continued)

Symbol	Pin No.	Type	Name and Function
CA	119	I	**CHANNEL ATTENTION.** The CPU uses this pin to force the 82596 to begin executing memory resident Command blocks. The CA signal is internally synchronized. The signal must be high for at least one system clock. It is latched internally on the high to low edge and then detected by the 82596. The first CA after a Reset forces the 82596 into the initialization sequence beginning at location 00FFFFF6h or an SCP address written to the 82596 using CPU Port access. All subsequent CA signals cause the 82596 to begin executing new command sequences from the SCB.
INT/$\overline{\text{INT}}$	125	O	**INTERRUPT.** A high signal on this pin notifies the CPU that the 82596 is requesting an interrupt. This signal is an edge triggered interrupt signal, and can be configured to be active high or low.
V$_{CC}$	18 Pins		**POWER.** +5 V ±10%.
V$_{SS}$	18 Pins		**GROUND.** 0 V.
TxD	54	O	**TRANSMIT DATA.** This pin transmits data to the serial link. It is high when not transmitting.
$\overline{\text{TxC}}$	64	O	**TRANSMIT CLOCK.** This signal provides the fundamental timing for the serial subsystem. The clock is also used to transmit data synchronously on the TxD pin. For NRZ encoding, data is transferred to the TxD pin on the high to low clock transition. For Manchester encoding, the transmitted bit center is aligned with the low to high transition.
$\overline{\text{LPBK}}$	58	1	**LOOPBACK.** This TTL-level control signal enables the loopback mode. In this mode serial data on the TxD input is routed through the 82C501 internal circuits and back to the RxD output without driving the transceiver cable. To enable this signal, both internal and external loopback need to be set with the Configure command.
RxD	60	I	**RECEIVE DATA.** This pin receives NRZ serial data only. It must be high when not receiving.
$\overline{\text{RxC}}$	59	I	**RECEIVE CLOCK.** This signal provides timing information to the internal shifting logic. For NRZ data the state of the RxD pin is sampled on the high to low transition of the clock.
$\overline{\text{RTS}}$	57	O	**REQUEST TO SEND.** When this signal is low the 82596 informs the external interface that it has data to transmit. It is forced high after a Reset or when transmission is stopped.
$\overline{\text{CTS}}$	62	I	**CLEAR TO SEND.** An active-low signal that enables the 82596 to send data. It is normally used as an interface handshake to $\overline{\text{RTS}}$. Asserting $\overline{\text{CTS}}$ high stops transmission. $\overline{\text{CTS}}$ is internally synchronized. If $\overline{\text{CTS}}$ goes inactive, meeting the setup time to the $\overline{\text{TxC}}$ negative edge, the transmission will stop and $\overline{\text{RTS}}$ will go inactive within, at most, two $\overline{\text{TxC}}$ cycles.

PIN DESCRIPTIONS (Continued)

Symbol	Pin No.	Type	Name and Function
$\overline{CRS}$	63	I	**CARRIER SENSE.** This signal is active low, it is used to notify the 82596 that traffic is on the serial link. It is only used if the 82596 is configured for external Carrier Sense. In this configuration external circuitry is required for detecting traffic on the serial link. $\overline{CRS}$ is internally synchronized. To be accepted, the signal must remain active for at least two serial clock cycles (for CRSF = 0).
$\overline{CDT}$	61	I	**COLLISION DETECT.** This active-low signal informs the 82596 that a collision has occurred. It is only used if the 82596 is configured for external Collision Detect. External circuitry is required for collision detection. $\overline{CDT}$ is internally synchronized. To be accepted, the signal must remain active for at least two serial clock cycles (for CDTF = 0).

82596 AND HOST CPU INTERACTION

The 82596CA and the host CPU communicate through shared memory. Because of its on-chip DMA capability, the 82596 can make data block transfers (buffers and frames) independently of the CPU; this greatly reduces the CPU byte transfer overhead. The 82596CA bus interface is optimized for Intel's 32-bit 486 microprocessor.

The 82596 is a multitasking coprocessor that comprises two independent logical units—the Command Unit (CU) and the Receive Unit (RU). The CU executes commands from shared memory. The RU handles all activities related to frame reception. The independence of the CU and RU enables the 82596 to engage in both activities simultaneously—the CU can fetch and execute commands from memory while the RU is storing received frames in memory. The CPU is only involved with this process after the CU has executed a sequence of commands or the RU has finished storing a sequence of frames.

The CPU and the 82596 use the hardware signals Interrupt (INT) and Channel Attention (CA) to initiate communication with the System Control Block (SCB), see Figure 4. The 82596 uses INT to alert the CPU of a change in the contents of the SCB, the CPU uses CA to alert the 82596.

The 82596 has a CPU Port Access state that allows the CPU to execute certain functions. The 82596 $\overline{PORT}$ pin and data bus pins are used to enable this feature. The CPU can perform four operations when the 82596 is in this state.

- Write an alternative System Configuration Pointer (SCP). This can be used when the 82596 cannot use the default SCP address space.

- Write a different Dump Command Pointer and execute Dump. This can be used for troubleshooting No Response problems.

- Perform a software reset. The CPU can reset the 82596 without disturbing the rest of the system.

- Perform a self-test. This can be used for board testing; the 82596 will execute a self-test and write the results to memory.

82596 BUS INTERFACE

The 82596CA has bus interface timings and pin definitions that are compatible with Intel's 32-bit i486 microprocessor. This eliminates the need for additional bus interface logic. Operating at 33 MHz, the 82596's bus bandwidth can be as high as 106 MB/s. Since Ethernet only requires 1.25 MB/s, this leaves a considerable amount of bandwidth for the CPU. The 82596 also has a bus throttle to regulate its use of the bus. Two timers can be programmed through the SCB: one controls the maximum time the 82596 can remain on the bus, the other controls the time the 82596 must stay off the bus (see Figure 5). The bus throttle can be programmed to trigger internally with HLDA or externally with BREQ. These timers can restrict the 82596 HOLD activation time and improve bus utilization.

82596 MEMORY ADDRESSING

The 82596 has a 32-bit memory address range, which allows addressing up to four gigabytes of memory. The 82596 has three memory addressing modes (see Table 1).

- **82586 Mode.** The 82596 has a 24-bit memory address range. The System Control Block, Command List, Receive Descriptor List, and Buffer Descriptors must reside in one 64-KB memory segment.

- **32-Bit Segmented Mode.** The 82596 has a 32-bit memory address range. The System Control Block, Command List, Receive Descriptor List, and Buffer Descriptors must reside in one 64-KB memory segment.

- **Linear Mode.** The 82596 has a 32-bit memory address range. Any memory structure can reside anywhere within the 32-bit memory address range.

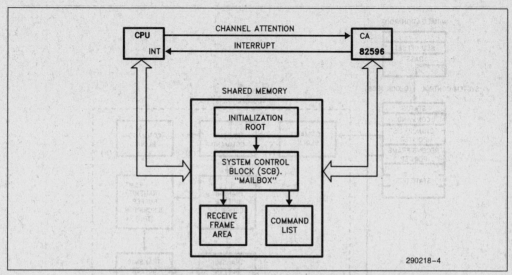

Figure 4. 82596 and Host CPU Intervention

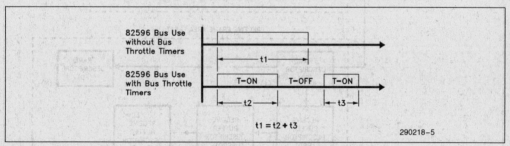

Figure 5. Bus Throttle Timers

Table 1. 82596 Memory Addressing Formats

Entity	Operation Mode		
	82586	**32-Bit Segmented**	**Linear**
ISCP Address	24-Bit Linear	32-Bit Linear	32-Bit Linear
SCB Address	Base (24) + Offset (16)	Base (32) + Offset (16)	32-Bit Linear
Command Block Pointers	Base (24) + Offset (16)	Base (32) + Offset (16)	32-Bit Linear
Rx Frame Descriptors	Base (24) + Offset (16)	Base (32) + Offset (16)	32-Bit Linear
Tx Frame Descriptors	Base (24) + Offset (16)	Base (32) + Offset (16)	32-Bit Linear
Rx Buffer Descriptors	Base (24) + Offset (16)	Base (32) + Offset (16)	32-Bit Linear
Tx Buffer Descriptors	Base (24) + Offset (16)	Base (32) + Offset (16)	32-Bit Linear
Rx Buffers	24-Bit Linear	32-Bit Linear	32-Bit Linear
Tx Buffers	24-Bit Linear	32-Bit Linear	32-Bit Linear

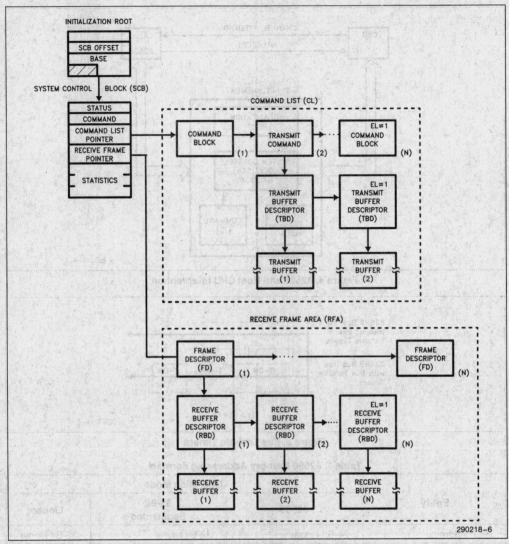

Figure 6. 82596 Shared Memory Structure

82596 SYSTEM MEMORY STRUCTURE

The Shared Memory structure consists of four parts: the Initialization Root, the System Control Block, the Command List, and the Receive Frame Area (see Figure 6).

The Initialization Root is in an established location known to the host CPU and the 82596 (00FFFFF6h). However, the CPU can establish the Initialization Root in another location by using the CPU Port access. This root is accessed during initialization, and points to the System Control Block.

The System Control Block serves as a bidirectional mail drop for the host CPU and the 82596 CU and RU. It is the central point through which the CPU and the 82596 exchange control and status information. The SCB has two areas. The first contains instructions from the CPU to the 82596. These include: control of the CU and RU (Start, Abort, Suspend, and Resume), a pointer to the list of CU commands, a pointer to the Receive Frame Area, a set of Interrupt Acknowledge bits, and the T-ON and T-OFF timers for the bus throttle. The second area contains status information the 82596 is sending to the CPU. Such as, the CU and RU states (Idle, Active

Ready, Suspended, No Receive Resources, etc.), interrupt bits (Command Completed, Frame Received, CU Not Ready, and RU Not Ready), and statistical counters.

The Command List functions as a program for the CU; individual commands are placed in memory units called Command Blocks (CBs). These CBs contain the parameters and status of specific high-level commands called Action Commands; e.g., Transmit or Configure.

Transmit causes the 82596 to transmit a frame. The Transmit CB contains the destination address, the length field, and a pointer to a list of linked buffers holding the frame that is to be constructed from several buffers scattered throughout memory. The Command Unit operates without CPU intervention; the DMA for each buffer, and the prefetching of references to new buffers, is performed in parallel. The CPU is notified only after a transmission is complete.

The Receive Frame Area is a list of Free Frame Descriptors (descriptors not yet used) and a list of user-prepared buffers. Frames arrive at the 82596 unsolicited; the 82596 must always be ready to receive and store them in the Free Frame Area. The Receive Unit fills the buffers when it receives frames, and reformats the Free Buffer List into received-frame structures. The frame structure is, for all practical purposes, identical to the format of the frame to be transmitted. The first Frame descriptor is referenced by the SCB. Unless the 82596 is configured to Save Bad Frames, the frame descriptor, and the associated buffer descriptor, which is wasted when a bad frame is received, are automatically reclaimed and returned to the Free Buffer List.

Receive buffer chaining (storing incoming frames in a linked buffer list) significantly improves memory utilization. Without buffer chaining, the user must allocate consecutive blocks of memory, each capable of containing a maximum frame (for Ethernet, 1518 bytes). Since an average frame is about 200 bytes, this is very inefficient. With buffer chaining, the user can allocate small buffers and the 82596 will only use those that are needed.

Figure 7 A–D illustrates how the 82596 uses the Receive Frame Area. Figure 7A shows an unused Receive Frame Area composed of Free Frame Descriptors and Free Receive Buffers prepared by the user. The SCB points to the first Frame Descriptor of the Frame Descriptor List. Figure 7B shows the same Receive Frame Area after receiving one frame. This first frame occupies two Receive Buffers and one Frame Descriptor—a valid received frame

will only occupy one Frame Descriptor. After receiving this frame the 82596 sets the next Free Frame Descriptor RBD pointer to the next Free RBD. Figure 7C shows the RFA after receiving a second frame. In this example the second frame occupies only one Receive Buffer and one RFD. The 82596 again sets the RBD pointer. This process is repeated again in Figure 7D, showing the reception of another frame using one Receive Buffer; in this example there is an extra Frame Descriptor.

TRANSMIT AND RECEIVE MEMORY STRUCTURES

There are three memory structures for reception and transmission. The 82586 memory structure, the Flexible memory structure, and the Simplified memory structure. The 82586 mode is selected by configuring the 82596 during initialization. In this mode all the 82596 memory structures are compatible with the 82586 memory structures.

When the 82596 is not configured to the 82586 mode, the other two memory structures, Simplified and Flexible, are available for transmitting and receiving. These structures can be selected on a frame-by-frame basis by setting the S/F bit in the Transmit Command and the Receive Frame Descriptor (see Figures 29, 30, 41, and 42). The Simplified memory structure offers a simple structure for ease of programming (see Figure 8). All information about a frame is contained in one structure; for example, during reception the RFD and data field are contained in one structure.

The Flexible memory structure (see Figure 9) has a variable control field that allows the programmer to specify the amount of receive data the RFD will contain for receive operations and the amount of transmit data the Transmit Command Block will contain for transmit operations. For example, when the variable control field in the RFD is set to 20 bytes during a reception, the first 20 bytes of the data field are stored in the RFD, and the remainder of the data field is stored in the Receive Data Buffers. This is useful for capturing frame headers when header information is contained in the data field. The header information can then be automatically stored in the RFD partitioned from the Receive Data Buffer.

The variable control field can also be used for the Transmit Command when the Flexible memory structure is used. The quantity of data field bytes to be transmitted from the Transmit Command Block is specified by the variable control field.

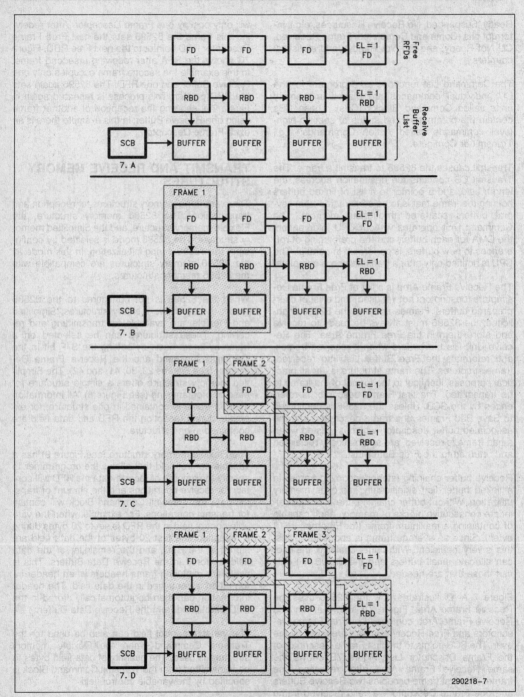

Figure 7. Frame Reception in the RFA

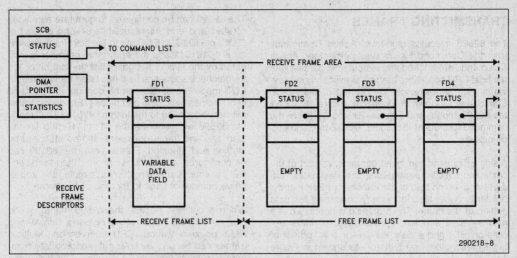

Figure 8. Simplified Memory Structure

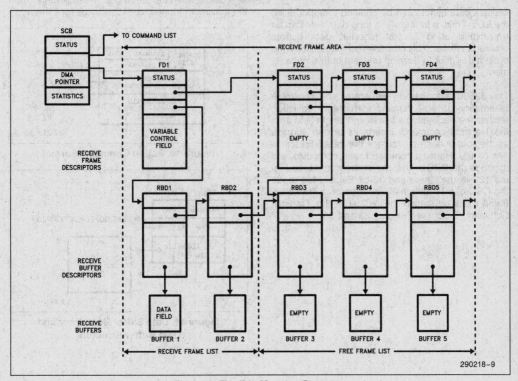

Figure 9. Flexible Memory Structure

TRANSMITTING FRAMES

The 82596 executes high-level Action Commands from the Command List in system memory. Action Commands are fetched and executed in parallel with the host CPU operation, thereby significantly improving system performance. The format of the Action Commands is shown in Figure 10. Figure 28 shows the 82586 mode, and Figures 29 and 30 show the command formats of the Linear and 32-bit Segmented modes.

A single Transmit command contains, as part of the command-specific parameters, the destination address and length field of the transmitted frame and a pointer to buffer area in memory containing the data portion of the frame. The data field is contained in a memory data structure consisting of a buffer descriptor (BD) and a data buffer—or a linked list of buffer descriptors and buffers—as shown in Figure 11.

Multiple data buffers can be chained together using the BDs. Thus, a frame with a long data field can be transmitted using several (shorter) data buffers chained together. This chaining technique allows the system designer to develop efficient buffer management.

The 82596 automatically generates the preamble (alternating 1s and 0s) and start frame delimiter, fetches the destination address and length field from the Transmit command, inserts its unique address as the source address, fetches the data field specified by the Transmit command, and computes and appends the CRC to the end of the frame (see Figure 12). In the Linear and 32-bit Segmented mode the CRC can be optionally inserted on a frame-by-frame basis by setting the NC bit in the Transmit Command Block (see Figures 29 and 30).

The 82596 can be configured to generate two types of start and end frame delimiters—End of Carrier (EOC) or HDLC. In EOC mode the start frame delimiter is 10101011 and the end frame delimiter is indicated by the lack of a signal after the last bit of the frame check sequence field has been transmitted. In EOC mode the 82596 can be configured to extend short frames by adding pad bytes (7Eh) during transmission, according to the length field. In HDLC mode the 82596 will generate the 01111110 flag for the start and end frame delimiters, and do standard bit stuffing and stripping. Furthermore, the 82596 can be configured to pad frames shorter than the specified minimum frame length by appending the appropriate number of flags to the end of the frame.

When a collision occurs, the 82596 manages the jam, random wait, and retry processes, reinitializing DMA pointers without CPU intervention. Multiple frames can be sent by linking the appropriate number of Transmit commands together. This is particularly useful when transmitting a message larger than the maximum frame size (1518 bytes for Ethernet).

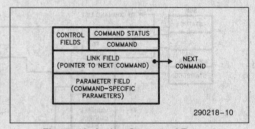

Figure 10. Action Command Format

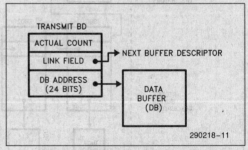

Figure 11. Data Buffer Descriptor and Data Buffer Structure

PREAMBLE	START FRAME DELIMITER	DESTINATION ADDRESS	SOURCE ADDRESS	LENGTH FIELD	DATA FIELD	FRAME CHECK SEQUENCE	END FRAME DELIMITER

Figure 12. Frame Format

RECEIVING FRAMES

To reduce CPU overhead, the 82596 is designed to receive frames without CPU supervision. The host CPU first sets aside an adequate receive buffer space and then enables the 82596 Receive Unit. Once enabled, the RU watches for arriving frames and automatically stores them in the Receive Frame Area (RFA). The RFA contains Receive Frame Descriptors, Receive Buffer Descriptors, and Data Buffers (see Figure 13). The individual Receive Frame Descriptors make up a Receive Descriptor List (RDL) used by the 82596 to store the destination and source addresses, the length field, and the status of each frame received (see Figure 14).

Once enabled, the 82596 checks each passing frame for an address match. The 82596 will recognize its own unique address, one or more multicast addresses, or the broadcast address. If a match is found the 82596 stores the destination and source addresses and the length field in the next available RFD. It then begins filling the next available Data Buffer on the FBL, which is pointed to by the current RFD, with the data portion of the incoming frame. As one Data Buffer is filled, the 82596 automatically fetches the next DB on the FBL until the entire frame is received. This buffer chaining technique is particularly memory efficient because it allows the system designer to set aside buffers to fit frames much shorter than the maximum allowable frame length.

Once the entire frame is received without error, the 82596 does the following housekeeping tasks.

- The actual count field of the last Buffer Descriptor used to hold the frame just received is updated with the number of bytes stored in the associated Data Buffer.
- The next available Receive Frame Descriptor is fetched.
- The address of the next available Buffer Descriptor is written to the next available Receive Frame Descriptor.
- A frame received interrupt status bit is posted in the SCB.
- An interrupt is sent to the CPU.

If a frame error occurs, for example a CRC error, the 82596 automatically reinitializes its DMA pointers and reclaims any data buffers containing the bad frame. The 82596 will continue to receive frames without CPU help as long as Receive Frame Descriptors and Data Buffers are available.

82596 NETWORK MANAGEMENT AND DIAGNOSTICS

The behavior of data communication networks is normally very complex because of their distributed and asynchronous nature. It is particularly difficult to pinpoint a failure when it occurs. The 82596 has extensive diagnostic and network management functions that help improve reliability and testability. The 82596 reports on the following events after each frame is transmitted.

- Transmission successful.
- Transmission unsuccessful. Lost Carrier Sense.
- Transmission unsuccessful. Lost Clear to Send.
- Transmission unsuccessful. A DMA underrun occurred because the system bus did not keep up with the transmission.
- Transmission unsuccessful. The number of collisions exceeded the maximum allowed.
- Number of Collisions. The number of collisions experienced during the frame.
- Heartbeat Indicator. This indicates the presence of a heartbeat during the last Interframe Spacing (IFS) after transmission.

When configured to Save Bad Frames the 82596 checks each incoming frame and reports the following errors.

- CRC error. Incorrect CRC in a properly aligned frame.
- Alignment error. Incorrect CRC in a misaligned frame.
- Frame too short. The frame is shorter than the value configured for minimum frame length.
- Overrun. Part of the frame was not placed in memory because the system bus did not keep up with incoming data.
- Out of buffer. Part of the frame was discarded because of insufficient memory storage space.
- Receive collision. A collision was detected during reception.
- Length error. A frame not matching the frame length parameter was detected.

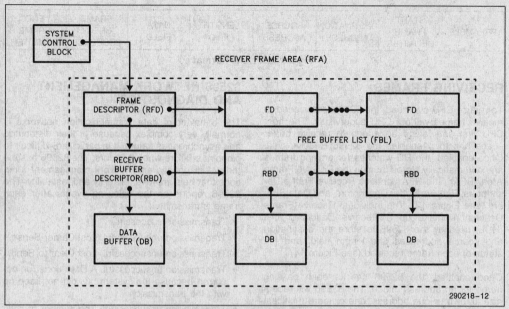

Figure 13. Receive Frame Area Diagram

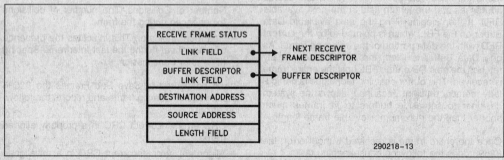

Figure 14. Receive Frame Descriptor

NETWORK PLANNING AND MAINTENANCE

To properly plan, operate, and maintain a communication network, the network management entity must accumulate information on network behavior. The 82596 provides a rich set of network-wide diagnostics that can serve as the basis for a network management entity.

Information on network activity is provided in the status of each frame transmitted. The 82596 reports the following activity indicators after each frame.

- Number of collisions. The number of collisions the 82596 experienced while attempting to transmit the frame.
- Deferred transmission. During the first transmission attempt the 82596 had to defer to traffic on the link.

The 82596 updates its 32-bit statistical counters after each received frame that both passes address filtering and is longer than the Minimum Frame Length configuration parameter. The 82596 reports the following statistics.

- CRC errors. The number of well-aligned frames that experienced a CRC error.
- Alignment errors. The number of misaligned frames that experienced a CRC error.
- No resources. The number of frames that were discarded because of insufficient resources for reception.
- Overrun errors. The number of frames that were not completely stored in memory because the system bus did not keep up with incoming data.
- Receive Collision counter. The number of collisions detected during receive.
- Short Frame counter. The number of frames that were discarded because they were shorter than the configured minimum frame length.

The 82596 can be configured to Promiscuous mode. In this mode it captures all frames transmitted on the network without checking the Destination Address. This is useful when implementing a monitoring station to capture all frames for analysis.

A useful method of capturing frame headers is to use the Simplified memory mode, configure the 82596 to Save Bad Frames, and configure the 82596 to Promiscuous mode with space in the RFD allocated for specific number of receive data bytes.

The 82596 will receive all frames and put them in the RFD. Frames that exceed the available space in the RFD will be truncated, the status will be updated, and the 82596 will retrieve the next RFD. This allows the user to capture the initial data bytes of each frame (for instance, the header) and discard the remainder of the frame.

The 82596 also has a monitor mode for network analysis. During normal operation the receive function enables the 82596 to receive frames that pass address filtering. These frames must have the Start of Frame Delimiter (SFD) field and must be longer than the absolute minimum frame length of 5 bytes (6 bytes in case of Multicast address filtering). Contents and status of the received frames are transferred to memory. The monitor function enables the 82596 to simply evaluate the incoming frames. The 82596 can monitor the frames that pass or do not pass the address filtering. It can also monitor frames which do not have the SFD fields. The 82596 can be configured to only keep statistical information about monitor franes. Three options are available in the Monitor mode. These options are selected by the two monitor mode configuration bits available in the configuration command.

When the first option is selected, the 82596 receives good frames and passes them to memory while monitoring frames that do not pass address filtering or are shorter than the minimum frame size (these frames are not transferred to memory). When this option is used the 82596 updates six counters: CRC errors, alignment errors, no resource errors, overrun errors, short frames and total good frames received.

When the second option is selected, the receive function is completely disabled. The 82596 monitors only those frames that pass address filterings and meet the minimum frame length requirement. When this option is used the 82596 updates six counters: CRC errors, alignment errors, total frames (good and bad), short frames, collisions detected and total good frames.

When the third option is selected, the receive function is completely disabled. The 82596 monitors all frames, including frames that do not have a Start Frame Delimiter. When this option is used the 82596 updates six counters: CRC errors, alignment errors, total frames (good and bad), short frames, collisions detected and total good frames.

STATION DIAGNOSTICS AND SELF-TEST

The 82596 provides a large set of diagnostic and network management functions. These include internal and external loopback and time domain reflectometry for locating fault points in the network cable. The 82596 ensures software reliability by dumping the contents of the 82596 internal registers into system memory. The 82596 has a self-test mode that enables it to run an internal self-test and place the results in system memory.

82586 SOFTWARE COMPATIBILITY

The 82596 has a software-compatible state in which all its memory structures are compatible with the 82586 memory structure. This includes all the Action Commands, the Receive Frame Area (including the RFD, Buffer Descriptors, and Data Buffers), the System Control Block, and the initialization procedures. There are two minor differences between the 82596 in the 82586-Compatible memory structure and the 82586.

- When the internal and external loopback bits in the Configure command are set to 11 the 82596 is in external loopback and the $\overline{\text{LPBK}}$ pin is activated; in the 82586 this situation would produce internal loopback.
- During a Dump command both the 82596 and 82586 dump the same number of bytes; however, the data format is different.

INITIALIZING THE 82596

A Reset command is issued to the 82596 to prepare it for normal operation. The 82596 is initialized through two data structures that are addressed by two pointers, the System Configuration Pointer (SCP) and the Intermediate System Configuration Pointer (ISCP). The initialization procedure begins when a Channel Attention signal is asserted after RESET. The 82596 uses the address of the double word that contains the SCP as a default— 00FFFFF4h. Before the CA signal is asserted this default address can be changed to any other available address by asserting the $\overline{\text{PORT}}$ pin and providing the desired address over the D_{31}–D_4 pins of the address bus. Pins D_3–D_0 must be 0010; i.e., any alternative address must be aligned to 16-byte boundaries. All addresses sent to the 82596 must be word aligned, which means that all pointers and memory structures must start on an even address (A_0 = zero).

SYSTEM CONFIGURATION POINTER (SCP)

The SCP contains the sysbus byte and the location of the next structure of the initialization process, the ISCP. The following parameters are selected in the SYSBUS.

- The 82596 operation mode.
- The Bus Throttle timer triggering method.
- Lock enabled.
- Interrupt polarity.

Byte ordering is determined by the LE/$\overline{\text{BE}}$ pin. LE/$\overline{\text{BE}}$ = 1 selects Little Endian byte ordering and LE/$\overline{\text{BE}}$ = 0 selects Big Endian byte ordering.

NOTE:
In the following X indicates a bit not checked 82596 mode. This bit must be set to 0 in all other modes.

The following diagram illustrates the format of the SCP.

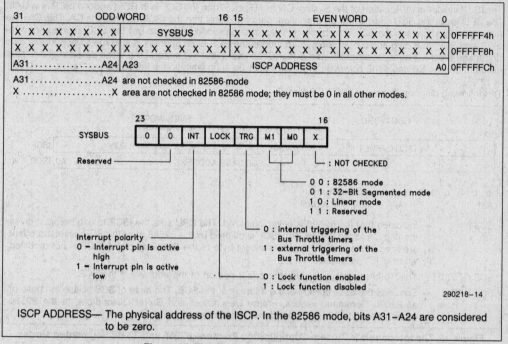

Figure 15. The System Configuration Pointer

Writing the Sysbus

When writing the sysbus byte it is important to pay attention to the byte order.

- When a Little Endian processor is used, the sysbus byte is located at byte address 00FFFFF6h (or address $n+2$ if an alternative SCP address n was programmed).
- When a processor using Big Endian byte ordering is used, the sysbus, alternative SCP, and ISCP addresses will be different.
  - The sysbus byte is located at 00FFFFF5h.
  - If an alternative SCP address is programmed, the sysbus byte should be at byte address $n+1$.

INTERMEDIATE SYSTEM CONFIGURATION POINTER (ISCP)

The ISCP indicates the location of the System Control Block. Often the SCP is in ROM and the ISCP is in RAM. The CPU loads the SCB address (or an equivalent data structure) into the ISCP and asserts CA. This Channel Attention signal causes the 82596 to begin its initialization procedure and to get the SCB address from the ISCP and SCP. In 82586 and 32-bit Segmented modes the SCP base address is also the base address of all Command Blocks, Frame Descriptors, and Buffer Descriptors (but not buffers). All these data structures must reside in one 64-KB segment; however, in Linear mode no such limitation is imposed.

The following diagram illustrates the ISCP format.

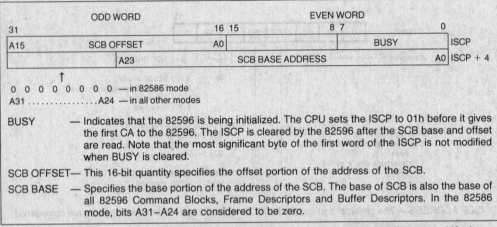

BUSY — Indicates that the 82596 is being initialized. The CPU sets the ISCP to 01h before it gives the first CA to the 82596. The ISCP is cleared by the 82596 after the SCB base and offset are read. Note that the most significant byte of the first word of the ISCP is not modified when BUSY is cleared.

SCB OFFSET— This 16-bit quantity specifies the offset portion of the address of the SCB.

SCB BASE — Specifies the base portion of the address of the SCB. The base of SCB is also the base of all 82596 Command Blocks, Frame Descriptors and Buffer Descriptors. In the 82586 mode, bits A31–A24 are considered to be zero.

Figure 16. The Intermediate System Configuration Pointer—82586 and 32-Bit Segmented Modes

```
            ODD WORD                                 EVEN WORD
31                            16  15                 8  7              0
0  0  0  ..................................  0  0  0 │  BUSY         │ ISCP
A31              SCB ABSOLUTE ADDRESS                           A0  │ ISCP + 4
```

BUSY — Indicates that the 82596 is being initialized. The ISCP is set to 01h by the CPU before its first CA to the 82596. It is cleared by the 82596 after the SCB address is read.

SCB ADDRESS— This 32-bit quantity specifies the physical address of the SCB.

Figure 17. The Intermediate System Configuration Pointer—Linear Mode.

Table 2. CPU Port Interface

Function	D31 .... D4	D3	D2	D1	D0
RESET	0 .... A4	0	0	0	0
SELF TEST	A31 Self Test Results Address A4	0	0	0	1
SCP	A31 Alternate SCP Address A4	0	0	1	0
DUMP	A31 Dump Area Pointer A4	0	0	1	1

INITIALIZATION PROCESS

The CPU sets up the SCP, ISCP, and the SCB structures, and, if desired, an alternative SCP address. It also sets BUSY to 01h. The 82596 is initialized when a Channel Attention signal follows a Reset signal, causing the 82596 to access the System Configuration Pointer. The sysbus byte, the operational mode, the bus throttle timer triggering method, the interrupt polarity, and the state of LOCK are read. After reset the Bus Throttle timers are set to T-ON or T-OFF; the timers are essentially disabled—the T-ON value is infinite, the T-OFF value is zero. After the SCP is read, the 82596 reads the ISCP and saves the SCB address. In 82586 and 32-bit Segmented modes this address is represented as a base address plus the offset (this base address is also the base address of all the control blocks). In Linear mode the base address is also an absolute address. The 82596 clears BUSY, sets CX and CNR to equal 1 in the SCB, clears the SCB command word, sends an interrupt to the CPU, and awaits another Channel Attention signal. RESET configures the 82596 to its default state before CA is asserted.

CONTROLLING THE 82596CA

The host CPU controls the 82596 with the commands, data structures, and methods described in this section. The CPU and the 82596 communicate through shared memory structures. The 82596 contains two independent units: the Command Unit and the Receive Unit. The Command Unit executes commands from the CPU, and the Receive Unit handles frame reception. These two units are controlled and monitored by the CPU through a shared memory structure called the System Control Block (SCB). The CPU and the 82596 use the CA and INT signals to communicate with the SCB.

82596 CPU ACCESS INTERFACE

The 82596 has a CPU access interface that allows the host CPU to do four things.
- Write an alternative System Configuration Pointer address.
- Write an alternative Dump area pointer and perform Dump.
- Execute a software reset.
- Execute a self-test.

The following events initiate the CPU access state.
- Presence of an address on the $D_{31}-D_4$ data bus pins.
- The D_3-D_0 pins are used to select one of the four functions.
- The $\overline{PORT}$ input pin is asserted, as in a regular write cycle.

NOTE.
The SCP Dump and Self-Test addresses must be 16-byte aligned.

To carry out 16-bit operations, the 82596 waits until it receives two write cycles. The first write holds the internal machines and the second activates the $\overline{PORT}$ command.

The $\overline{PORT}$ Reset is useful when only the 82596 needs to be reset. The CPU must wait for 10-system and 5-serial clocks before issuing another CA to the 82596; this new CA begins a new initialization process.

The Dump function is useful for troubleshooting No Response problems. If the chip is in a No Response state, the $\overline{PORT}$ Dump operation can be executed and a $\overline{PORT}$ Reset can be used to reinitialize the 82596 without disturbing the rest of the system.

The Self-Test function can be used for board testing; the 82596 will execute a self-test and write the results to memory.

MEMORY ADDRESSING FORMATS

The 82596 accesses memory by 32-bit addresses. There are two types of 32-bit addresses: linear and segmented. The type of address used depends on the 82596 operating mode and the type of memory structure it is addressing. The 82596 has three operating modes.

- 82586 Mode
  - A Linear address is a single 24-bit entity. Address pins $A_{31}-A_{24}$ are always zero.
  - A Segmented address uses a 24-bit base and a 16-bit offset.
- 32-bit Segmented Mode
  - A Linear address is a single 32-bit entity.
  - A Segmented address uses a 32-bit base and a 16-bit offset.

NOTE

In the previous two memory addressing modes, each command header (CB, TBD, RFD, RBD, and SCB) must wholly reside within one segment. If the 82596 encounters a memory structure that does not follow this restriction, the 82596 will fetch the next contiguous location in memory (beyond the segment).

- Linear Mode
  - A Linear address is a single 32-bit entity.
  - There are no Segmented addresses.

Linear addresses are primarily used to address transmit and receive data buffers. In the 82586 and 32-bit Segmented modes, segmented addresses (base plus offset) are used for all Command Blocks, Buffer Descriptors, Frame Descriptors, and System Control Blocks. When using Segmented addresses, only the offset portion of the entity being addressed is specified in the block. The base for all offsets is the same—that of the SCB. The following table summarizes the different address formats.

Entity	Operation Mode		
	82586	**32-Bit Segmented**	**Linear**
ISCP Address	24-Bit Linear	32-Bit Linear	32-Bit Linear
SCB Address	Base (24) + Offset (16)	Base (32) + Offset (16)	32-Bit Linear
Command Block Pointers	Base (24) + Offset (16)	Base (32) + Offset (16)	32-Bit Linear
Rx Frame Descriptors	Base (24) + Offset (16)	Base (32) + Offset (16)	32-Bit Linear
Tx Frame Descriptors	Base (24) + Offset (16)	Base (32) + Offset (16)	32-Bit Linear
Rx Buffer Descriptors	Base (24) + Offset (16)	Base (32) + Offset (16)	32-Bit Linear
Tx Buffer Descriptors	Base (24) + Offset (16)	Base (32) + Offset (16)	32-Bit Linear
Rx Buffers	24-Bit Linear	32-Bit Linear	32-Bit Linear
Tx Buffers	24-Bit Linear	32-Bit Linear	32-Bit Linear

All addresses presented to the 82596 must be word aligned; i.e., all pointers and memory structures must start on even addresses (A_0 = zero).

LITTLE ENDIAN AND BIG ENDIAN BYTE ORDERING

The 82596 supports both Little Endian and Big Endian byte ordering for its memory structures.

The 82596 supports Big Endian byte ordering for word and byte entities. Dword entities are not supported with Big Endian byte ordering. This results in slightly different 82596 memory structures for Big Endian operation. These structures will be defined in the *82596 Technical Reference Manual*.

NOTE
All 82596 memory entities must be word or dword aligned.

An example of a dword entity is a frame header, whereas the raw data of the frame are byte entities. Both 32- and 16-bit buses are supported. When a 16-bit bus is used with Big Endian memory organization, data lines $D_{15}-D_0$ are used. The 82596 has an internal crossover that handles these swap operations.

COMMAND UNIT (CU)

The Command Unit is the logical unit that executes Action Commands from a list of commands very similar to a CPU program. A Command Block is associated with each Action Command. The CU is modeled as a logical machine that takes, at any given time, one of the following states.

- **Idle.** The CU is not executing a command and is not associated with a CB on the list. This is the initial state.
- **Suspended.** The CU is not executing a command; however, it is associated with a CB on the list.
- **Active.** The CU is executing an Action Command and pointing to its CB.

The CPU can affect CU operation in two ways: by issuing a CU Control Command or by setting bits in the Command word of the Action Command.

RECEIVE UNIT (RU)

The Receive Unit is the logical unit that receives frames and stores them in memory. The RU is modeled as a logical machine that takes, at any given time, one of the following states.

- **Idle.** The RU has no memory resources and is discarding incoming frames. This is the initial state.
- **No Resources.** The RU has no memory resources and is discarding incoming frames. This state differs from Idle in that the RU accumulates statistics on the number of discarded frames.
- **Suspended.** The RU has memory available for storing frames, but is discarding them.
- **Ready.** The RU has memory available and is storing incoming frames.

The CPU can affect RU operation in three ways: by issuing an RU Control Command, by setting bits in the Frame Descriptor Command word of the frame being received, or by setting the EL bit of the current buffer's Buffer Descriptor.

SYSTEM CONTROL BLOCK (SCB)

The SCB is a memory block that plays a major role in communications between the CPU and the 82596. Such communications include the following.

- Commands issued by the CPU
- Status reported by the 82596

Control commands are sent to the 82596 by writing them into the SCB and then asserting CA. The 82596 examines the command, performs the required action, and then clears the SCB command word. Control commands perform the following types of tasks.

- Operation of the Command Unit (CU). The SCB controls the CU by specifying the address of the Command Block List (CBL) and by starting, suspending, resuming, or aborting execution of CBL commands.

- Operation of the Bus Throttle. The SCB controls the Bus Throttle timers by providing them with new values and sending the Load and Start timer commands. The timers can be operated in both the 32-bit Segmented and Linear modes.
- Reception of frames by the Receive Unit (RU). The SCB controls the RU by specifying the address of the Receive Frame Area and by starting, suspending, resuming, or aborting frame reception.
- Acknowledgment of events that cause interrupts.
- Resetting the chip.

The 82596 sends status reports to the CPU via the System Control Block. The SCB contains four types of status reports.

- The cause of the current interrupts. These interrupts are caused by one or more of the following 82596 events.
  - The Command Unit completes an Action Command that has its I bit set.
  - The Receive Unit receives a frame.
  - The Command Unit becomes inactive.
  - The Receive Unit becomes not ready.
- The status of the Command Unit.
- The status of the Receive Unit.
- Status reports from the 82596 regarding reception of corrupted frames.

Events can be cleared only by CPU acknowledgment. If some events are not acknowledged by the ACK field the Interrupt signal (INT) will be reissued after Channel Attention (CA) is processed. Furthermore, if a new event occurs while an interrupt is set, the interrupt is temporarily cleared to trigger edge-triggered interrupt controllers.

The CPU uses the Channel Attention line to cause the 82596 to examine the SCB. This signal is trailing-edge triggered—the 82596 latches CA on the trailing edge. The latch is cleared by the 82596 before the SCB control command is read.

31	ODD WORD				16	15		EVEN WORD				0	
ACK	X	CUC	R	RUC	X X X X	STAT	0	CUS	0	RUS	0 0 0 0		SCB
RFA OFFSET						CBL OFFSET							SCB + 4
ALIGNMENT ERRORS						CRC ERRORS							SCB + 8
OVERRUN ERRORS						RESOURCE ERRORS							SCB + 12

Figure 18. SCB—82586 Mode

31	ODD WORD				16	15		EVEN WORD			0	
ACK	0	CUC	R	RUC	0 0 0 0	STAT	0	CUS	RUS	T 0 0 0		SCB
RFA OFFSET						CBL OFFSET						SCB + 4
CRC ERRORS												SCB + 8
ALIGNMENT ERRORS												SCB + 12
RESOURCE ERRORS (*)												SCB + 16
OVERRUN ERRORS (*)												SCB + 20
RCVCDT ERRORS (*)												SCB + 24
SHORT FRAME ERRORS												SCB + 28
T-ON		TIMER		T-OFF				TIMER				SCB + 32

*In monitor mode these counters change function

Figure 19. SCB—32-Bit Segmented Mode

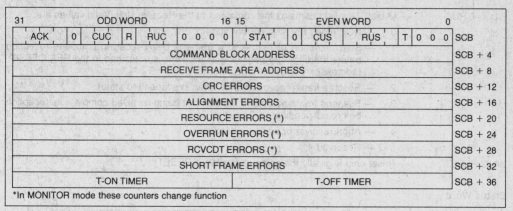

31		ODD WORD					16	15		EVEN WORD			0	
ACK	0	CUC	R	RUC	0 0 0 0		STAT	0	CUS		RUS	T	0 0 0	SCB
COMMAND BLOCK ADDRESS														SCB + 4
RECEIVE FRAME AREA ADDRESS														SCB + 8
CRC ERRORS														SCB + 12
ALIGNMENT ERRORS														SCB + 16
RESOURCE ERRORS (*)														SCB + 20
OVERRUN ERRORS (*)														SCB + 24
RCVCDT ERRORS (*)														SCB + 28
SHORT FRAME ERRORS														SCB + 32
T-ON TIMER							T-OFF TIMER							SCB + 36

*In MONITOR mode these counters change function

Figure 20. SCB—Linear Mode

Command Word

31								16	
ACK	< >	CUC	RE	RUC	0	0	0	0	SCB + 2

These bits specify the action to be performed as a result of a CA. This word is set by the CPU and cleared by the 82596. Defined bits are:

Bit 31 ACK-CX — Acknowledges that the CU completed an Action Command.

Bit 30 ACK-FR — Acknowledges that the RU received a frame.

Bit 29 ACK-CNA — Acknowledges that the Command Unit became not active.

Bit 28 ACK-RNR — Acknowledges that the Receive Unit became not ready.

Bits 24–26 CUC — (3 bits) This field contains the command to the Command Unit. Valid values are:

    0 — NOP (does not affect current state of the unit).

    1 — Start execution of the first command on the CBL. If a command is executing, complete it before starting the new CBL. The beginning of the CBL is in CBL OFFSET (address).

    2 — Resume the operation of the Command Unit by executing the next command. This operation assumes that the Command Unit has been previously suspended.

    3 — Suspend execution of commands on CBL after current command is complete.

    4 — Abort current command immediately.

    5 — Loads the Bus Throttle timers so they will be initialized with their new values after the active timer (T-ON or T-OFF) reaches Terminal Count. If no timer is active new values will be loaded immediately. This command is not valid in 82586 mode.

    6 — Loads and immediately restarts the Bus Throttle timers with their new values. This command is not valid in 82586 mode.

    7 — Reserved.

Bits 4–6 RUC — (3 bits) This field contains the command to the Receive Unit. Valid values are:

0 — NOP (does not alter current state of unit).

1 — Start reception of frames. If a frame is being received complete reception before starting. The beginning of the RFA is contained in the RFA OFFSET (address).

2 — Resume frame reception (only when in suspended state).

3 — Suspend frame reception. If a frame is being received complete its reception before suspending.

4 — Abort receiver operation immediately.

5–7 — Reserved.

Bit 23 RESET — Reset chip (logically the same as hardware RESET).

Status Word

15										0	
STAT		0	CUS	0	RUS	0	0	0	0	SCB

8356 mode

15									0	
STAT		0	CUS	RUS	T	0	0	0	SCB

32-Bit Segmented and Linear mode.

Indicates the status of the 82596. This word is modified only by the 82596. Defined bits are:

Bit 15 CX — The CU finished executing a command with its / (interrupt) bit set.

Bit 14 FR — The RU finished receiving a frame.

Bit 13 CNA — The Command Unit left the Active state.

Bit 12 RNR — The Receive Unit left the Ready state.

Bits 8–10 CUS — (3 bits) This field contains the status of the command unit. Valid values are:

0 — Idle

1 — Suspended

2 — Active

3–7 — Not used

Bit 3 T — Bus Throttle timers loaded (not in 82586 mode).

Bits 4–7 RUS — This field contains the status of the receive unit. Valid values are:

0h (0000) — Idle

1h (0001) — Suspended

2h (0010) — No Resources. This bit indicates both no resources due to lack of RFDs in the RDL and no resources due to lack of RBDs in the FBL.

4h (0100) — Ready

8h (1000) — No more RBDs (not in the 82586 mode)

Ah (1010) — No resources due to no more RBDs

No other combinations are allowed

SCB OFFSET ADDRESSES

CBL Offset (Address)

In 82586 and 32-bit Segmented modes this 16-bit quantity indicates the offset portion of the address for the first Command Block on the CBL. In Linear mode it is a 32-bit linear address for the first Command Block on the CBL. It is accessed only if CUC equals Start.

RFA Offset (Address)

In 82586 and 32-bit Segmented modes this 16-bit quantity indicates the offset portion of the address for the Receive Frame Area. In Linear mode it is a 32-bit linear address for the Receive Frame Area. It is accessed only if RUC equals Start.

SCB STATISTICAL COUNTERS

CRCERRS

This 32-bit quantity contains the number of aligned frames discarded because of a CRC error. This counter is updated, if needed, regardless of the RU state.

ALNERRS

This 32-bit quantity contains the number of frames that both are misaligned (i.e., where $\overline{CRS}$ deasserts on a nonoctet boundary) and contain a CRC error. The counter is updated, if needed, regardless of the RU state.

RSCERRS

This 32-bit quantity contains the number of good frames discarded because there were no resources to contain them. Frames intended for a host whose RU is in the No Receive Resources state, fall into this category. This counter is updated only if the RU is in the No Resources state. When in Monitor mode (configuration bits = 0x) this counter counts the total number of frames—bad and good. If $x=0$ the counter counts all frames, including frames that do not have the SFD. If $x=1$ the counter counts all frames longer than the minimum frame size and passing address filtering.

OVRNERRS

This 32-bit quantity contains the number of frames known to be lost because the local system bus was not available. If the traffic problem lasts longer than the duration of one frame, the frames that follow the first are lost without an indicator, and they are not counted. This counter is updated, if needed, regardless of the RU state.

RCVCDT

This 32-bit quantity contains the number of collisions detected during frame reception. In Monitor mode this counter counts the number of collisions detected during frame reception and all received frames shorter than the minimum frame length.

SHRTFRM

This 32-bit quantity contains the number of received frames shorter than the minimum frame length. In Monitor mode this counter counts the total number of frames received, including frames that do not have the SFD.

Statistical Counter Operation

- The CPU is responsible for clearing all error counters before initializing the 82596. The 82596 updates these counters by reading them, adding 1, and then writing them back to the SCB.
- The counters are wraparound counters. After reaching FFFFFFFFh the counters wrap around to zero.
- The 82596 updates the required counters for each frame. It is possible for more than one counter to be updated; multiple errors will result in all affected counters being updated.
- The 82596 executes the read-counter/increment/write-counter operation without relinquishing the bus (locked operation). This is to ensure that no logical contention exists between the 82596 and the CPU due to both attempting to write to the counters simultaneously. In the dual-port memory configuration the CPU should not execute any write operation to a counter if LOCK is asserted.
- The counters are 32-bits wide and their behavior is fully compatible with the IEEE 802.1 standard. The 82596 supports all relevant statistics (mandatory, optional, and desired) through the status of the transmit and receive header and directly through SCB statistics.

ACTION COMMANDS AND OPERATING MODES

This section lists all the Action Commands of the Command Unit Command Block List (CBL). Each command contains the Command field, the Status and Control fields, the link to the next Action Command, and any command-specific parameters. There are three basic types of action commands: 82596 Configuration and Setup, Transmission, and Diagnostics. The following is a list of the actual commands.

- NOP
- Individual Address Setup
- Configure
- MC Setup

- Transmit
- TDR
- Dump
- Diagnose

The 82596 has three addressing modes. In the 82586 mode all the Action Commands look exactly like those of the 82586.

- **82586 Mode.** The 82596 software and memory structure is compatible with the 82586.
- **32-Bit Segmented Mode.** The 82596 can access the entire system memory and use the two new memory structures—Simplified and Flexible—while still using the segmented approach. This does not require any significant changes to existing software.
- **Linear Mode.** The 82596 operates in a flat, linear, 4 gigabyte memory space without segmentation. It can also use the two new memory structures.

In the 32-bit Segmented mode there are some differences between the 82596 and 82586 action commands, mainly in programming and activating new 82596 features. Those bits marked "don't care" in the compatible mode are not checked; however, we strongly recommend that those bits all be zeroes; this will allow future enhancements and extensions.

In the Linear mode all of the address offsets become 32-bit address pointers. All new 82596 features are accessible in this mode, and all bits previously marked "don't care" must be zeroes.

The Action Commands, and all other 82596 memory structures, must begin on even byte boundaries, i.e., they must be word aligned.

NOP

This command results in no action by the 82596 except for those performed in the normal command processing. It is used to manipulate the CBL manipulation. The format of the NOP command is shown in Figure 21.

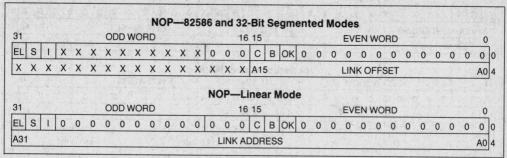

Figure 21

where:

LINK POINTER	— In the 82586 or 32-bit Segmented modes this is a 16-bit offset to the next Command Block. In the Linear mode this is the 32-bit address of the next Command Block.
EL	— If set, this bit indicates that this command block is the last on the CBL.
S	— If set to one, suspend the CU upon completion of this CB.
I	— If set to one, the 82596 will generate an interrupt after execution of the command is complete. If I is not set to one, the CX bit will not be set.
CMD (bits 16–18)	— The NOP command. Value: 0h.
Bits 19–28	— Reserved (zero in the 32-bit Segmented and Linear modes).
C	— This bit indicates the execution status of the command. The CPU initially resets it to zero when the Command Block is placed on the CBL. Following a command Completion, the 82596 will set it to one.
B	— This bit indicates that the 82596 is currently executing the NOP command. It is initially reset to zero by the CPU. The 82596 sets it to one when execution begins and to zero when execution is completed. This bit is also set when the 82596 prefetches the command.

NOTE:

The C and B bits are modified in one operation.

OK	— Indicates that the command was executed without error. If set to one no error occurred (command executed OK). If zero an error occured.

INDIVIDUAL ADDRESS SETUP

This command is used to load the 82596 with the Individual Address. This address is used by the 82596 for inserting the Source Address during transmission and recognizing the Destination Address during reception. After RESET, and prior to Individual Address Setup Command execution, the 82596 assumes the Broadcast Address is the Individual Address in all aspects, i.e.:

- This will be the Individual Address Match reference.
- This will be the Source Address of a transmitted frame (for AL-LOC=0 mode only).

The format of the Individual Address Setup command is shown in Figure 22.

IA Setup—82586 and 32-Bit Segmented Modes

31	ODD WORD	16	15	EVEN WORD	0	
EL	S	I	X X X X X X X X X X X	0 0 1	C B OK A	0 0 0 0 0 0 0 0 0 0 0 0 0 0 0	0
INDIVIDUAL ADDRESS		1st byte	A15	LINK OFFSET	A0	4
Nth byte	5th byte		4th byte	3rd byte		8

IA Setup—Linear Mode

31	ODD WORD	16	15	EVEN WORD	0	
EL	S	I	0 0 0 0 0 0 0 0 0 0 0 0	0 0 1	C B OK A	0 0 0 0 0 0 0 0 0 0 0 0 0 0 0	0
A31	LINK ADDRESS				A0	4
4th byte	5th byte		INDIVIDUAL ADDRESS	1st byte		8
			Nth byte	5th byte		C

Figure 22

where:

LINK ADDRESS, EL, B, C, I, S — As per standard Command Block (see the NOP command for details)

A — Indicates that the command was abnormally terminated due to CU Abort control command. If one, then the command was aborted, and if necessary it should be repeated. If this bit is zero, the command was not aborted.

Bits 19–28 — Reserved (zero in the 32-bit Segmented and Linear modes).

CMD (bits 16–18) — The Address Setup command. Value: 1h.

INDIVIDUAL ADDRESS — The individual address of the node, 0 to 16 bytes long.

The least significant bit of the Individual Address must be zero for Ethernet (see the Command Structure). However, no enforcement of 0 is provided by the 82596. Thus, an Individual Address with 1 as its least significant bit is a valid Individual Address in all aspects.

The default address length is 6 bytes long, as in 802.3. If a different length is used the IA Setup command should be executed after the Configure command.

CONFIGURE

The Configure command loads the 82596 with its operating parameters. It allows changing some of the parameters by specifying a byte count less than the maximum number of configuration bytes (12 in the 82586 mode, 16 in the 32-Bit Segmented and Linear modes). The 82596 configuration depends on its mode of operation.

- In the 82586 mode the maximum number of configuration bytes is 12. Any number larger than 12 will be reduced to 12 and any number less than 4 will be increased to 4.
- The additional features of the serial side are disabled in the 82586 mode.
- In both the 32-Bit Segmented and Linear modes there are four additional configuration bytes, which hold parameters for additional 82596 features. If these parameters are not accessed, the 82596 will follow their default values.

The format of the Configure command is shown in Figure 23, 24 and 25.

31	ODD WORD		16	15	EVEN WORD		0	
EL	S	I	X X X X X X X X X X	0 1 0	C	B	OK	A 0 0 0 0 0 0 0 0 0 0 0 0 0	0
Byte 7		Byte 6		A15		LINK OFFSET	A0	4
Byte 11		Byte 10		Byte 9			Byte 8	8
Byte 15		Byte 14		Byte 13			Byte 12	1
X X X X X X X X X X X X X X X X X X X X X X X X					Byte 16			1

Figure 23. CONFIGURE—82586 Mode

31	ODD WORD		16	15	EVEN WORD		0	
EL	S	I	0 0 0 0 0 0 0 0 0 0 0	0 1 0	C	B	OK	A 0 0 0 0 0 0 0 0 0 0 0 0 0	0
Byte 7		Byte 6		A15		LINK OFFSET	A0	4
Byte 11		Byte 10		Byte 9			Byte 8	8
Byte 15		Byte 14		Byte 13			Byte 12	12
Byte 19		Byte 18		Byte 17			Byte 16	16

Figure 24. CONFIGURE—32-Bit Segmented Mode

31	ODD WORD		16	15	EVEN WORD		0	
EL	S	I	0 0 0 0 0 0 0 0 0 0 0	0 1 0	C	B	OK	A 0 0 0 0 0 0 0 0 0 0 0 0 0	0
A31			LINK ADDRESS				A0	4
Byte 11		Byte 10		Byte 9			Byte 8	8
Byte 15		Byte 14		Byte 13			Byte 12	12
Byte 19		Byte 18		Byte 17			Byte 16	16
X X X X X X X X X X X X X X X X					Byte 21		Byte 20	20

Figure 25. CONFIGURE—Linear Mode

LINK ADDRESS, — As per standard Command Block (see the NOP command for details)
EL, B, C, I, S

A   — Indicates that the command was abnormally terminated due to a CU Abort control command. If 1, then the command was aborted and if necessary it should be repeated. If this bit is 0, the command was not aborted.

Bits 19–28   — Reserved (zero in the 32-Bit Segmented and Linear Modes)

CMD (bits 16–18) — The CONFIGURE command. Value: 2h.

The interpretation of the fields follows:

7	6	5	4	3	2	1	0
P	X	X	X		BYTE COUNT		

BYTE 6—82586 and 32-Bit Segmented Mode
BYTE 8—Linear Mode

BYTE CNT (Bits 0–3)   Byte Count. Number of bytes, including this one, that hold parameters to be configured.

PREFETCHED (Bit 7)   Enable the 82596 to write the prefetched bit in all prefetch RBDs.

NOTE:
The P bit is valid only in the new memory structure modes. In 82586 mode this bit is disabled (i.e., no prefetched mark).

7							0
MONITOR		X	X	FIFO LIMIT			

BYTE 7—82586 and 32-Bit Segmented Mode
BYTE 9—Linear Mode

FIFO Limit (Bits 0–3)	FIFO limit.
MONITOR # (Bits 6–7)	Receive monitor options. If the Byte Count of the configure command is less than 12 bytes then these Monitor bits are ignored.

DEFAULT: C8h

7							0
SAV BF	1	0	0	0	0	0	0

BYTE 8—82586 and 32-Bit Segmented Mode
BYTE 10—Linear Mode

SAV BF (Bit 7)	0—Received bad frames are not saved in the memory.
	1—Received bad frames are saved in the memory.

DEFAULT: 40h

7				0
LOOP BACK MODE	PREAMBLE LENGTH	NO SRC ADD INS	ADDRESS LENGTH	

BYTE 9—82586 and 32-Bit Segmented Mode
BYTE 11—Linear Mode

ADR LEN (Bits 0–2)	Address length (any kind).
NO SCR ADD INS (Bit 3)	No Source Address Insertion. In the 82586 this bit is called AL LOC.
PREAM LEN (Bits 4–5)	Preamble length.
LP BCK MODE (Bits 6–7)	Loopback mode.

DEFAULT: 26h

7				0
BOF METD	EXPONENTIAL PRIORITY	0	LINEAR PRIORITY	

BYTE 10—82586 and 32-Bit Segmented Mode
BYTE 12—Linear Mode

LIN PRIO (Bits 0–2)	Linear Priority.
EXP PRIO (Bits 4–6)	Exponential Priority.
BOF METD (Bit 7)	Exponential Backoff method.

DEFAULT: 00h

7			0
	INTER FRAME SPACING		

BYTE 11—82586 and 32-Bit Segmented Mode
BYTE 13—Linear Mode

INTERFRAME SPACING	Interframe spacing.

DEFAULT: 60h

7							0
			SLOT TIME - LOW				

BYTE 12—82586 and 32-Bit Segmented Mode
BYTE 14—Linear Mode

SLOT TIME (L)　　　　　　Slot time, low byte.
DEFAULT: 00h

7			0
MAXIMUM RETRY NUMBER	0	SLOT TIME - HIGH	

BYTE 13—82586 and 32-Bit Segmented Mode
BYTE 15—Linear Mode

SLOT TIME (H)　　　　　　Slot time, high part.
(Bits 0–2)

RETRY NUM (Bits 4–7)　　Number of transmission retries on collision.
DEFAULT: F2h

7							0
PAD	BIT STUFF	CRC16/ CRC32	NO CRC INSER	Tx ON NO CRS	MAN/ NRZ	BC DIS	PRM MODE

BYTE 14—82586 and 32-Bit Segmented Mode
BYTE 16—Linear Mode

PRM (Bit 0)　　　　　　Promiscuous mode.
BC DIS (Bit 1)　　　　　Broadcast disable.
MANCH/NRZ (Bit 2)　　Manchester or NRZ encoding. See specific timing requirements for TXC in Manchester mode.
TONO CRS (Bit 3)　　　Transmit on no CRS.
NOCRC INS (Bit 4)　　No CRC insertion.
CRC-16/CRC-32 (Bit 5)　CRC type.
BIT STF (Bit 6)　　　　Bit stuffing.
PAD (Bit 7)　　　　　　Padding.
DEFAULT: 00h

7				0
CDT SRC	COLLISION DETECT FILTER	CRS SRC	CARRIER SENSE FILTER	

BYTE 15—82586 and 32-Bit Segmented Mode
BYTE 17—Linear Mode

CRSF (Bits 0–2)　　Carrier Sense filter (length).
CRS SRC (Bit 3)　　Carrier Sense source.
CDTF (Bits 4–6)　　Collision Detect filter (length).
CDT SRC (Bit 7)　　Collision Detect source.
DEFAULT: 00h

```
7                                                                    0
|_____MINIMUM FRAME LENGTH_____|
```

BYTE 16—82586 and 32-Bit Segmented Mode
BYTE 18—Linear Mode

MIN FRAME LEN   Minimum frame length.

DEFAULT: 40h

```
7                                                                    0
| MONITOR | MC_ALL | CDBSAC | AUTOTX | CRCINM | LNGFLD | PRECRS |
```

BYTE 17—32-Bit Segmented Mode
BYTE 19—Linear Mode

PRECRS (Bit 0)   Preamble until Carrier Sense

LNGFLD (Bit 1)   Length field. Enables padding at the End-of-Carrier framing (802.3).

CRCINM (Bit 2)   Rx CRC appended to the frame in memory.

AUTOTX (Bit 3)   Auto retransmit.

CDBSAC (Bit 4)   Collision Detect by source address recognition.

MC_ALL (Bit 5)   Enable to receive all MC frames.

MONITOR (Bits 6–7)   Receive monitor options.

DEFAULT: FFH

```
7                                                                    0
| DCR | FDX |              DCR SLOT ADDRESS                        |
```

BYTE 18—32-Bit Segmented Mode
BYTE 20—Linear Mode

DCR SLOT ADDRESS   Station index in DCR mode.
   (Bits 0–5)

FDX (Bit 6)   Enables Full Duplex operation.

DCR (Bit 7)   Enables Deterministic collision resolution.

DEFAULT: 00h

```
7                                                                    0
| DIS_BOF | MULT_IA |        DCR NUMBER OF STATIONS               |
```

BYTE 19—32-Bit Segmented Mode
BYTE 21—Linear Mode

DCR NUMBER OF   Number of stations in DCR mode.
   STATIONS (Bits 0–5)

MULT_IA (Bit 6)   Multiple individual address.

DIS_BOF (Bit 7)   Disable the backoff algorithm.

DEFAULT: 3Fh

A reset (hardware or software) configures the 82596 according to the following defaults.

Table 4. Configuration Defaults

	Parameter	Default Value	Units/Meaning
	ADDRESS LENGTH	**6	Bytes
	A/L FIELD LOCATION	0	Located in FD
*	AUTO RETRANSMIT	1	Auto Retransmit Enable
	BITSTUFFING/EOC	0	EOC
	BROADCAST DISABLE	0	Broadcast Reception Enabled
*	CDBSAC	1	Disabled
	CDT FILTER	0	Bit Times
	CDT SRC	0	External Collision Detection
*	CRC IN MEMORY	1	CRC Not Transferred to Memory
	CRC-16/CRC-32	**0	CRC-32
	CRS FILTER	0	0 Bit Times
	CRS SRC	0	External CRS
*	DCR	0	Disable DCR Protocol
*	DCR Slot Number	0	DCR Disabled
*	DCR Number of Stations	63	Stations
*	DISBOF	0	Backoff Enabled
	EXT LOOPBACK	0	Disabled
	EXPONENTIAL PRIORITY	**0	802.3 Algorithm
	EXPONENTIAL BACKOFF METHOD	**0	802.3 Algorithm
*	FULL DUPLEX (FDX)	0	CSMA/CD Protocol (No FDX)
	FIFO THRESHOLD	8	TX: 32 Bytes, RX: 64 Bytes
	INT LOOPBACK	0	Disabled
	INTERFRAME SPACING	**96	Bit Times
	LINEAR PRIORITY	**0	802.3 Algorithm
*	LENGTH FIELD	1	Padding Disabled
	MIN FRAME LENGTH	**64	Bytes
*	MC ALL	1	Disabled
*	MONITOR	11	Disabled
	MANCHESTER/NRZ	0	NRZ
*	MULIA	0	Disabled
	NUMBER OF RETRIES	**15	Maximum Number of Retries
	NO CRC INSERTION	0	CRC Appended to Frame
	PREFETCH BIT IN RBD	0	Disabled (Valid Only in New Modes)
	PREAMBLE LENGTH	**7	Bytes
*	Preamble Until CRS	1	Disabled
	PROMISCUOUS MODE	0	Address Filter On
	PADDING	0	No Padding
	SLOT TIME	**512	Bit Times
	SAVE BAD FRAME	0	Discards Bad Frames
	TRANSMIT ON NO CRS	0	Disabled

NOTES
1. This configuration setup is compatible with the IEEE 802.3 specification.
2. The Asterisk "*" signifies a new configuration parameter not available in the 82586.
3. The default value of the Auto retransmit configuration parameter is enabled[1].
4. Double Asterisk "**" signifies IEEE 802.3 requirements.

MULTICAST-SETUP

This command is used to load the 82596 with the Multicast-IDs that should be accepted. As noted previously, the filtering done on the Multicast-IDs is not perfect and some unwanted frames may be accepted. This command resets the current filter and reloads it with the specified Multicast-IDs. The format of the Multicast-addresses setup command is:

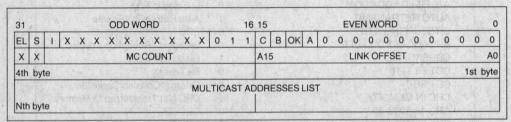

Figure 26. MC Setup—Compatible and 32-Bit Segmented Modes

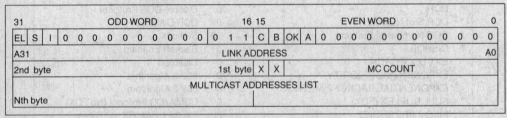

Figure 27. MC Setup—Linear Mode

where:

LINK ADDRESS, EL, B, C, I, S	— As per standard Command Block (see the NOP command for details)
A	— Indicates that the command was abnormally terminated due to a CU Abort control command. If one, then the command was aborted and if necessary it should be repeated. If this bit is zero, the command was not aborted.
Bits 19–28	— Reserved (0 in both the 32-Bit Segmented and Linear Modes).
CMD (bits 16–18)	— The MC SETUP command value: 3h.
MC-CNT	— This 14-bit field indicates the number of bytes in the MC LIST field. The MC CNT must be a multiple of the ADDR LEN; otherwise, the 82596 reduces the MC CNT to the nearest ADDR LEN multiple. MC CNT = 0 implies resetting the Hash table which is equivalent to disabling the Multicast filtering mechanism.
MC LIST	— A list of Multicast Addresses to be accepted by the 82596. The least significant bit of each MC address must be 1.

NOTE:

The list is sequential; i.e., the most significant byte of an address is immediately followed by the least significant byte of the next address.

    — When the 82596 is configured to recognize multiple Individual Address (Multi-IA), the MC-Setup command is also used to set up the Hash table for the individual address.

The least significant bit in the first byte of each IA address must be 0.

TRANSMIT

This command is used to transmit a frame of user data onto the serial link. The format of a Transmit command is as follows.

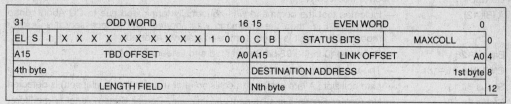

Figure 28. TRANSMIT—82586 Mode

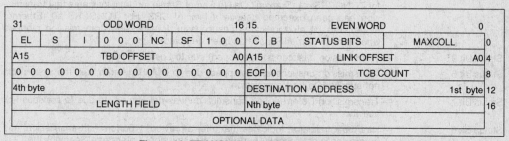

Figure 29. TRANSMIT—32-Bit Segmented Mode

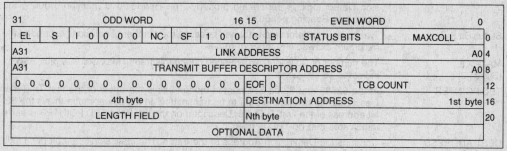

Figure 30. TRANSMIT—Linear Mode

31	COMMAND WORD		16	
EL	S	I 0 0 0 0 0 0 0 0 0 NC SF 1 0 0	2	

↑   ↑

0: No CRC Insertion disable, Configured command forces the action.

1: No CRC Insertion enable, this mode will overwrite the configuration command value.

0: Simplified Mode, all the Tx data is in the Transmit Command Block. The Transmit Buffer Descriptor Address field is all 1s.

1: Flexible Mode. Data is in the TCB and in a linked list of TBDs.

where:

LINK ADDRESS, EL, B, C, I, S	— As per standard Command Block (see the NOP command for details).
OK (Bit 13)	— Error free completion.
A (Bit 12)	— Indicates that the command was abnormally terminated due to CU Abort control command. If 1, then the command was aborted, and if necessary it should be repeated. If this bit is 0, the command was not aborted.
Bits 19–28	— Reserved (0 in the 32-bit Segmented and Linear modes).
CMD (Bits 16–18)	— The transmit command: 4h.
Status Bit 11	— Late collision. A late collision (a collision after the slot time is elapsed) is detected.
Status Bit 10	— No Carrier Sense signal during transmission. Carrier Sense signal is monitored from the end of Preamble transmission until the end of the Frame Check Sequence for TONOCRS = 1 (Transmit On No Carrier Sense mode) it indicates that transmission has been executed despite a lack of CRS. For TONOCRS = 0 (Ethernet mode), this bit also indicates unsuccessful transmission (transmission stopped when lack of Carrier Sense has been detected).
Status Bit 9	— Transmission unsuccessful (stopped) due to Loss of $\overline{\text{CTS}}$.
Status Bit 8	— Transmission unsuccessful (stopped) due to DMA Underrun; i.e., the system did not supply data for transmission.
Status Bit 7	— Transmission Deferred, i.e., transmission was not immediate due to previous link activity.
Status Bit 6	— Heartbeat Indicator, Indicates that after a previously performed transmission, and before the most recently performed transmission, (Interframe Spacing) the CDT signal was monitored as active. This indicates that the Ethernet Transceiver Collision Detect logic is performing properly. The Heartbeat is monitored during the Interframe Spacing period.
Status Bit 5	— Transmission attempt was stopped because the number of collisions exceeded the maximum allowable number of retries.
MAX-COL (Bits 3–0)	— The number of Collisions experienced during this frame. Max Col = 0 plus S5 = 1 indicates 16 collisions.
TBD POINTER	— In the 82586 and 32-bit Segmented modes this is the offset of the first Tx Buffer Descriptor containing the data to be transmitted. In the Linear mode this is the 32-bit address of the first Tx Buffer Descriptor on the list. If the TBD POINTER is all 1s it indicates that no TBD is used.
DEST ADDRESS	— Contains the Destination Address of the frame. The least significant bit (MC) indicates the address type.
	MC = 0: Individual Address.
	MC = 1: Multicast or Broadcast Address.
	If the Destination Address bits are all 1s this is a Broadcast Address.
LENGTH FIELD	— The contents of this 2-byte field are user defined. In 802.3 it contains the length of the data field. It is placed in memory in the same order it is transmitted; i.e., most significant byte first, least significant byte second.
TCB COUNT	— This 14-bit counter indicates the number of bytes that will be transmitted from the Transmit Command Block, starting from the third byte after the TCB COUNT field (address $n + 12$ in the 32-bit Segmented mode, $N + 16$ in the Linear mode). The TCB COUNT field can be any number of bytes (including an odd byte), this allows the user to transmit a frame with a header having an odd number of bytes. The TCB COUNT field is not used in the 82586 mode.
EOF Bit	— Indicates that the whole frame is kept in the Transmit Command Block. In the Simplified memory model it must be always asserted.

The interpretation of what is transmitted depends on the No Source Address insertion configuration bit and the memory model being used.

NOTES

1. The Destination Address and the Length Field are sequential. The Length Field immediately follows the most significant byte of the Destination Address.

2. In case the 82596 is configured with No Source Address insertion bit equal to 0, the 82596 inserts its configured Source Address in the transmitted frame.

- In the 82586 mode, or when the Simplified memory model is used, the Destination and Length fields of the transmitted frame are taken from the Transmit Command Block.

- If the FLEXIBLE memory model is used, the Destination and Length fields of the transmitted frame can be found either in the TCB or TBD, depending on the TCB COUNT.

3. If the 82596 is configured with the Address/Length Field Location equal to 1, the 82596 does not insert its configured Source Address in the transmitted frame. The first (2 × Address Length) + 2 bytes of the transmitted frame are interpreted as Destination Address, Source Address, and Length fields respectively. The location of the first transmitted byte depends on the operational mode of the 82596:

- In the 82586 mode, it is always the first byte of the first Tx Buffer.

- In both the 32-bit Segmented and Linear modes it depends on the SF bit and TCB COUNT:

 — In the Simplified memory mode the first transmitted byte is always the third byte after the TCB COUNT field.

 — In the Flexible mode, if the TCB COUNT is greater than 0 then it is the third byte after the TCB COUNT field. If TCB COUNT equals 0 then it is first byte of the first Tx Buffer.

- Transmit frames shorter than six bytes are invalid. The transmission will be aborted (only in 82586 mode) because of a DMA Underrun.

4. Frames which are aborted during transmission are jammed. Such an interruption of transmission can be caused by any reason indicated by any of the status bits 8, 9, 10 and 12.

JAMMING RULES

1. Jamming will not start before completion of preamble transmission.

2. Collisions detected during transmission of the last 11 bits will not result in jamming.

The format of a Transmit Buffer Descriptor is:

82586 Mode

31 ODD WORD	16	15	13	EVEN WORD	0
NEXT TBD OFFSET		EOF	X	SIZE (ACT COUNT)	0
X X X X X X X X		TRANSMIT BUFFER ADDRESS			4

32-Bit Segmented Mode

31 ODD WORD	16	15	13	EVEN WORD	0
NEXT TBD OFFSET		EOF	0	SIZE (ACT COUNT)	0
TRANSMIT BUFFER ADDRESS					4

Linear Mode

31 ODD WORD	16	15	13	EVEN WORD	0
0 0 0 0 0 0 0 0	0 0 0 0 0 0 0 0	EOF	0	SIZE (ACT COUNT)	0
NEXT TBD ADDRESS					4
TRANSMIT BUFFER ADDRESS					8

Figure 31

where:

EOF	— This bit indicates that this TBD is the last one associated with the frame being transmitted. It is set by the CPU before transmit.
SIZE (ACT COUNT)	— This 14-bit quantity specifies the number of bytes that hold information for the current buffer. It is set by the CPU before transmission.
NEXT TBD ADDRESS	— In the 82586 and 32-bit Segmented modes, it is the offset of the next TBD on the list. In the Linear mode this is the 32-bit address of the next TBD on the list. It is meaningless if EOF = 1.
BUFFER ADDRESS	— The starting address of the memory area that contains the data to be sent. In the 82586 mode, this is a 24-bit address (A31–A24 are considered to be zero). In the 32-bit Segmented and Linear modes this is a 32-bit address.

TDR

This operation activates Time Domain Reflectomet, which is a mechanism to detect open or short circuits on the link and their distance from the diagnosing station. The TDR command has no parameters. The TDR transmit sequence was changed, compared to the 82586, to form a regular transmission. The TDR bit stream is as follows.

— Preamble
— Source address
— Another Source address (the TDR frame is transmitted back to the sending station, so DEST ADR = SRC ADR).
— Data field containing 7Eh patterns.
— Jam Pattern, which is the inverse CRC of the transmitted frame.

Maximum length of the TDR frame is 2048 bits. If the 82596 senses collision while transmitting the TDR frame it transmits the jam pattern and stops the transmission. The 82596 then triggers an internal timer (STC); the timer is reset at the beginning of transmission and reset if CRS is returned. The timer measures the time elapsed from the start of transmission until an echo is returned. The echo is indicated by Collision Detect going active or a drop in the Carrier Sense signal. The following table lists the possible cases that the 82596 is able to analyze.

Conditions of TDR as Interpreted by the 82596

Condition	Transceiver Type Ethernet	Non Ethernet
Carrier Sense was inactive for 2048-bit-time periods	Short or Open on the Transceiver Cable	NA
Carrier Sense signal dropped	Short on the Ethernet cable	NA
Collision Detect went active	Open on the Ethernet cable	Open on the Serial Link
The Carrier Sense Signal did not drop or the Collision Detect did not go active within 2048-bit time period	No Problem	No Problem

An Ethernet transceiver is defined as one that returns transmitted data on the receive pair and activates the Carrier Sense Signal while transmitting. A Non-Ethernet Transceiver is defined as one that does not do so.

The format of the Time Domain Reflectometer command is:

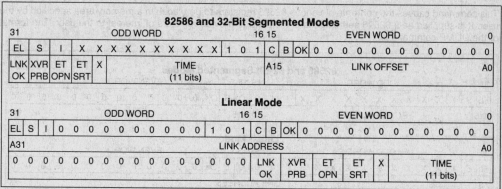

Figure 32. TDR

where:

LINK ADDRESS, EL, B, C, I, S	— As per standard Command Block (see the NOP command for details).
A	— Indicates that the command was abnormally terminated due to CU Abort control command. If one, then the command was aborted, and if necessary it should be repeated. If this bit is zero, the command was not aborted.
Bits 19–28	— Reserved (0 in the 32-bit Segmented and Linear Modes).
CMD (Bits 16–18)	— The TDR command. Value: 5h.
TIME	— An 11-bit field that specifies the number of TxC cycles that elapsed before an echo was observed. No echo is indicated by a reception consisting of "1s" only. Because the network contains various elements such as transceiver links, transceivers, Ethernet, repeaters etc., the TIME is not exactly proportional to the problems distance.
LNK OK (Bit 15)	— No link problem identified. TIME = 7FFh.
XCVR PRB (Bit 14)	— Indicates a Transceiver problem. Carrier Sense was inactive for 2048-bit time period. LNK OK = 0. TIME = 7FFh.
ET OPN (Bit 13)	— The transmission line is not properly terminated. Collision Detect went active and LNK OK = 0.
ET SRT (Bit 12)	— There is a short circuit on the transmission line. Carrier Sense Signal dropped and LNK OK = 0.

DUMP

This command causes the contents of various 82596 registers to be placed in a memory area specified by the user. It is supplied as a 82596 self-diagnostic tool, and to provide registers of interest to the user. The format of the DUMP command is:

82586 and 32-Bit Segmented Modes

31	ODD WORD	16 15	EVEN WORD	0
EL	S	I	X	X	X	X	X	X	X	X	X	X	1	1	0	C	B	OK	0 0 0 0 0 0 0 0 0 0 0 0 0 0 0
A15	BUFFER OFFSET	A0 A15	LINK OFFSET	A0

Linear Mode

31	ODD WORD	16 15	EVEN WORD	0
EL	S	I	X	X	X	X	X	X	X	X	X	X	1	1	0	C	B	OK	0 0 0 0 0 0 0 0 0 0 0 0 0 0 0
A31	LINK ADDRESS	A0
A31	BUFFER ADDRESS	A0

Figure 33. Dump

where:

LINK ADDRESS, EL, B, C, I, S	— As per standard Command Block (see the NOP command for details).
OK	— Indicates error free completion.
Bits 19–28	— Reserved (0 in the 32-bit Segmented and Linear Modes).
CMD (Bits 16–18)	— The Dump Status command. Value: 6h.
BUFFER POINTER	— In the 82586 and 32-bit Segmented modes this is the 16-bit-offset portion of the dump area address. In the Linear mode this is the 32-bit linear address of the dump area.

Dump Area Information Format

- In a Dump executed by a port command, the data of the Dump will be written to the buffer, and no status (O.K. etc. . . .) will be written into memory.
- The 82596 is not Dump compatible with the 82596 because of the 32-bit internal architecture. In 82586 mode the 82596 will dump the same number of bytes as the 82586. The compatible data will be marked with an asterisk.
- The size of the dump area when in the 82586 mode is 170 bytes.
- The DUMP area format of the 32-bit Segmented and Linear modes is described in Figure 35.
- The size of the dump area of the 32-bit Segmented and Linear modes is 304 bytes.
- When the Dump is executed by the Port command an extra word will be appended to the Dump Area. The extra word is a copy of the Dump Area status word (containing the C, B, and OK Bits). The C and OK Bits are set when the 82596 has completed the Port Dump command.

15 14 13 12 11 10 9 8 7 6 5 4 3 2 1 0	
DMA CONTROL REGISTER*	00
CONFIGURE BYTES* 7, 6	02
CONFIGURE BYTES* 9,8	04
CONFIGURE BYTES* 11, 10	06
CONFIGURE BYTES* 13, 12	08
CONFIGURE BYTES* 15, 14	0A
I.A. BYTES 1, 0*	0C
I.A. BYTES 3, 2*	0E
I.A. BYTES 5, 4*	10
LAST T.X. STATUS*	12
T.X. CRC BYTES 1, 0*	14
T.X. CRC BYTES 3, 2*	16
R.X. CRC BYTES 1, 0*	18
R.X. CRC BYTES 3, 2*	1A
R.X. TEMP MEMORY 1, 0*	1C
R.X. TEMP MEMORY 3, 2*	1E
R.X. TEMP MEMORY 5, 4*	20
LAST RECEIVED STATUS*	22
HASH REGISTER BYTES 1, 0*	24
HASH REGISTER BYTES 3, 2*	26
HASH REGISTER BYTES 5, 4*	28
HASH REGISTER BYTES 7, 6*	2A
SLOT TIME COUNTER*	2C
WAIT TIME COUNTER*	2E
MICRO MACHINE	30
	.
REGISTER FILE	.
	.
60 BYTES	6A
MICRO MACHINE LFSR	6C
MICRO MACHINE	6E
	.
FLAG ARRAY	.
	.
14 BYTES	7A
QUEUE MEMORY	7C
	.
CU PORT	.
8 BYTES	82
MICRO MACHINE ALU	84
RESERVED	86
M.M. TEMP A ROTATE R	88
M.M. TEMP A	8A
T.X. DMA BYTE COUNT	8C
M.M. INPUT PORT ADDRESS	8E
T.X. DMA ADDRESS	90
M.M. OUTPUT PORT	92
R.X. DMA BYTE COUNT	94
R.U. DMA ADDRESS	96
M.M. OUTPUT PORT ADDRESS REGISTER	98
RESERVED	9A
BUS THROTTLE TIMERS	9C
DIU CONTROL REGISTER	9E
RESERVED	A0
DMA CONTROL REGISTER	A2
BIU CONTROL REGISTER	A4
M.M. DISPATCHER REG.	A6
M.M. STATUS REGISTER	A8

Figure 34. Dump Area Format—82586 Mode

31		0	
CONFIGURE BYTES 9, 8, 7, 6			00
CONFIGURE BYTES 13, 12, 11, 10			04
CONFIGURE BYTES 17, 16, 15, 14			08
I.A. BYTES 1, 0		CONFIGURE BYTES 19, 18	0C
I.A. BYTES 5, 2			10
TX CRC BYTES 0, 1		LAST T.X. STATUS	14
RX CRC BYTES 0, 1		TX CRC BYTES 3, 2	18
RX TEMP MEMORY 1, 0		RX CRC BYTES 3, 2	1C
R.X. TEMP MEMORY 5, 2			20
HASH REGISTERS 1, 0		LAST R.X. STATUS	24
HASH REGISTER BYTES 5, 2			28
SLOT TIME COUNTER		HASH REGISTERS 7, 6	2C
RECEIVE FRAME LENGTH		WAIT-TIME COUNTER	30
MICRO MACHINE			34
			.
REGISTER FILE			.
			.
128 BYTES			B0
MICRO MACHINE LFSR			B4
MICRO MACHINE			B8
			.
FLAG ARRAY			.
			.
28 BYTES			D0
M.M. INPUT PORT			D4
16 BYTES			.
			E0
MICRO MACHINE ALU			E4
RESERVED			E8
M.M. TEMP A ROTATE R.			EC
M.M. TEMP A			F0
T.X. DMA BYTE COUNT			F4
M.M. INPUT PORT ADDRESS REGISTER			F8
T.X. DMA ADDRESS			FC
M.M. OUTPUT PORT REGISTER			100
R.X. DMA BYTE COUNT			104
M.M. OUTPUT PORT ADDRESS REGISTER			108
R.X. DMA ADDRESS REGISTER			10C
RESERVED			110
BUS THROTTLE TIMERS			114
DIU CONTROL REGISTER			118
RESERVED			11C
DMA CONTROL REGISTER			120
BIU CONTROL REGISTER			124
M.M. DISPATCHER REG.			128
M.M. STATUS REGISTER			12C

**Figure 35. Dump Area Format—Linear and
32-Bit Segmented Mode**

DIAGNOSE

The Diagnose Command triggers an internal self-test procedure that checks internal 82596 hardware, which includes:

- Exponential Backoff Random Number Generator (Linear Feedback Shift Register).
- Exponential Backoff Timeout Counter.
- Slot Time Period Counter.
- Collision Number Counter.
- Exponential Backoff Shift Register.
- Exponential Backoff Mask Logic.
- Timer Trigger Logic.

This procedure checks the operation of the Backoff block, which resides in the serial side and is not easily controlled. The Diagnose command is performed in two phases.

The format of the 82596 Diagnose command is:

82586 and 32-Bit Segmented Modes																															

82586 and 32-Bit Segmented Modes

31			ODD WORD												16	15				EVEN WORD											0
EL	S	I	X	X	X	X	X	X	X	X	X	X	1	1	1	C	B	OK	0	F	0	0	0	0	0	0	0	0	0	0	0
X	X	X	X	X	X	X	X	X	X	X	X	X	X	X	X	A15				LINK OFFSET											A0

Linear Mode

31			ODD WORD												16	15				EVEN WORD											0
EL	S	I	0	0	0	0	0	0	0	0	0	0	1	1	1	C	B	OK	0	F	0	0	0	0	0	0	0	0	0	0	0
A31							LINK ADDRESS																								A0

Figure 36. Diagnose

where:

LINK ADDRESS, EL, B, C, I, S	— As per standard Command Block (see the NOP command for details).
Bits 19–28	— Reserved (0 in the 32-bit Segmented and Linear Modes).
CMD (bits 16–18)	— The Diagnose command. Value: 7h.
OK (bit 13)	— Indicates error free completion.
F (fail)	— Indicates that the self-test procedure has failed.

RECEIVE FRAME DESCRIPTOR

Each received frame is described by one Receive Frame Descriptor (see Figure 37). Two new memory structures are available for the received frames. The structures are available only in the Linear and 32-bit Segmented modes.

Simplified Memory Structure

The first is the Simplified memory structure, the data section of the received frame is part of the RFD and is located immediately after the Length Field. Receive Buffer Descriptors are not used with the Simplified structure, it is primarily used to make programming easier. If the length of the data area described in the Size Field is smaller than the incoming frame, the following happens.

1. The received frame is truncated.

2. The No Resource error counter is updated.

3. If the 82596 is configured to Save Bad Frames the RFD is not reused; otherwise, the same RFD is used to hold the next received frame, and the only action taken regarding the truncated frame is to update the counter.

4. The 82596 continues to receive the next frame in the next RFD.

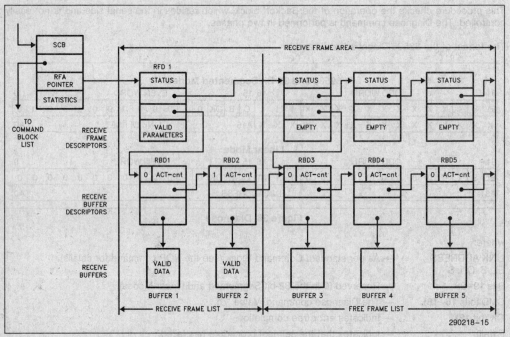

Figure 37. The Receive Frame Area

Note that this sequence is very useful for monitoring. If the 82596 is configured to Save Bad Frames, to receive in Promiscuous mode, and to use the Simplified memory structure, any programmed length of received data can be saved in memory.

The Simplified memory structure is shown in Figure 38.

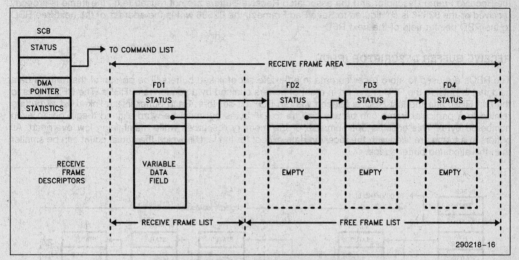

Figure 38. RFA Simplified Memory Structure

Flexible Memory Structure

The second structure is the Flexible memory structure, the data structure of the received frame is stored in both the RFD and in a linked list of Receive Buffers—Receive Buffer Descriptors. The received frame is placed in the RFD as configured in the Size field. Any remaining data is placed in a linked list of RBDs.

The Flexible memory structure is shown in Figure 39.

Buffers on the receive side can be different lengths. The 82596 will not place more bytes into a buffer than indicated in the associated RBD. The 82596 will fetch the next RBD before it is needed. The 82596 will attempt to receive frames as long as the FBL is not exhausted. If there are no more buffers, the 82596 Receive Unit will enter the No Resources state. Before starting the RU, the CPU must place the FBL pointer in the RBD pointer field of the first RFD. All remaining RBD pointer fields for subsequent RFDs should be "1s." If the Receive Frame Descriptor and the associated Receive Buffers are not reused (e.g., the frame is properly received or the 82596 is configured to Save Bad Frames), the 82596 writes the address of the next free RBD to the RBD pointer field of the next RFD.

RECEIVE BUFFER DESCRIPTOR (RBD)

The RBDs are used to store received data in a flexible set of linked buffers. The portion of the frame's data field that is outside the RFD is placed in a set of buffers chained by a sequence of RBDs. The RFD points to the first RBD, and the last RBD is flagged with an EOF bit set to 1. Each buffer in the linked list of buffers related to a particular frame can be any size up to 2^{14} bytes but must be word aligned (begin on an even numbered byte). This ensures optimum use of the memory resources while maintaining low overhead. All buffers in a frame are filled with the received data except for the last, in which the actual count can be smaller than the allocated buffer space.

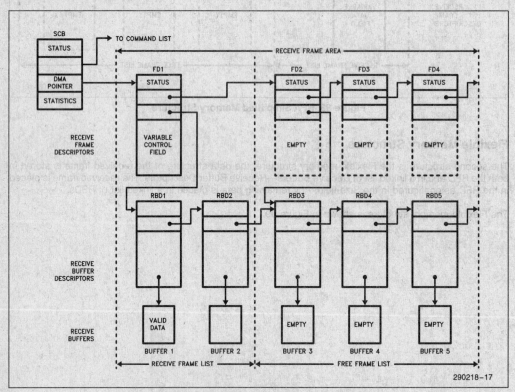

Figure 39. RFA Flexible Memory Structure

31 ODD WORD 16	15 EVEN WORD 0	
EL S X X X X X X X X X X X X X X	C B OK 0 STATUS BITS 0 0 0 0 0 0	0
A15 RBD OFFSET A0	A15 LINK OFFSET A0	4
4th byte	DESTINATION ADDRESS 1st byte	8
SOURCE ADDRESS 1st byte	Nth byte	12
Nth byte	4th byte	16
X X X X X X X X X X X X X X X X	LENGTH FIELD	20

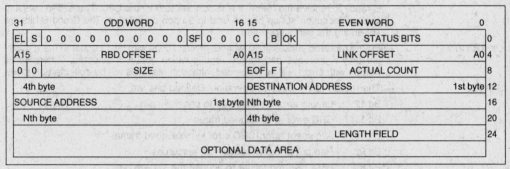

Figure 40. Receive Frame Descriptor—82586 Mode

31 ODD WORD 16	15 EVEN WORD 0	
EL S 0 0 0 0 0 0 0 0 0 0 SF 0 0 0	C B OK STATUS BITS	0
A15 RBD OFFSET A0	A15 LINK OFFSET A0	4
0 0 SIZE	EOF F ACTUAL COUNT	8
4th byte	DESTINATION ADDRESS 1st byte	12
SOURCE ADDRESS 1st byte	Nth byte	16
Nth byte	4th byte	20
	LENGTH FIELD	24
OPTIONAL DATA AREA		

Figure 41. Receive Frame Descriptor—32-Bit Segmented Mode

31 ODD WORD 16	15 EVEN WORD 0	
EL S 0 0 0 0 0 0 0 0 0 0 SF 0 0 0	C B OK STATUS BITS	0
A31 LINK ADDRESS A0		4
A31 RECEIVE BUFFER DESCRIPTOR ADDRESS A0		8
0 0 SIZE	EOF F ACTUAL COUNT	12
4th byte	DESTINATION ADDRESS 1st byte	16
SOURCE ADDRESS 1st byte	Nth byte	20
Nth byte	4th byte	24
	LENGTH FIELD	28
OPTIONAL DATA AREA		

Figure 42. Receive Frame Descriptor—Linear Mode

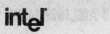

where:

EL	— When set, this bit indicates that this RFD is the last one on the RDL.
S	— When set, this bit suspends the RU after receiving the frame.
SF	— This bit selects between the Simplified or the Flexible mode.

0 — Simplified mode, all the RX data is in the RFD. RBD ADDRESS field is all "1s."

1 — Flexible mode. Data is in the RFD and in a linked list of Receive Buffer Descriptors.

C	— This bit indicates the completion of frame reception. It is set by the 82596.
B	— This bit indicates that the 82596 is currently receiving this frame, or that the 82596 is ready to receive the frame. It is initially set to 0 by the CPU. The 82596 sets it to 1 when reception set up begins, and to 0 upon completion. The C and B bits are set during the same operation.
OK (bit 13)	— Frame received successfully, without errors. RFDs with bit 13 equal to 0 are possible only if the save bad frames, configuration option is selected. Otherwise all frames with errors will be discarded, although statistics will be collected on them.
STATUS	— The results of the Receive operation. Defined bits are,

Bit 12: Length error if configured to check length

Bit 11: CRC error in an aligned frame

Bit 10: Alignment error (CRC error in misaligned frame)

Bit 9: Ran out of buffer space—no resources

Bit 8: DMA Overrun failure to acquire the system bus.

Bit 7: IA Match Bit. The destination address of the received frame matched the IA adress.

Bit 6: No EOP flag (for Bit stuffing only)

Bits 1–5: Zeros

Bit 0: Receive collision, a collision is detected during reception.

LINK ADDRESS	— A 16-bit offset (32-bit address in the Linear mode) to the next Receive Frame Descriptor. The Link Address of the last frame can be used to form a cyclical list.
RBD POINTER	— The offset (address in the Linear mode) of the first RBD containing the received frame data. An RBD pointer of all ones indicates no RBD.
EOF F SIZE ACT COUNT	— These fields are for the Simplified and Flexible memory models. They are exactly the same as the respective fields in the Receive Buffer Descriptor. See the next section for detailed explanation of their functions.
MC	— Multicast bit.
DESTINATION ADDRESS	— The contents of the destination address of the receive frame. The field is 0 to 6 bytes long.
SOURCE ADDRESS	— The contents of the Source Address field of the received frame. It is 0 to 6 bytes long.

LENGTH FIELD — The contents of this 2-byte field are user defined. In 802.3 it contains the length of the data field. It is placed in memory in the same order it is received, i.e., most significant byte first, least significant byte second.

NOTES

1. The Destination address, Source address and Length fields are packed, i.e., one field immediately follows the next.

2. The affect of Address/Length Location (No Source Address Insertion) configuration parameter while receiving is as follows:

— 82586 Mode: The Destination address, Source address and Length field are not used, they are placed in the RX data buffers.

— 32-Bit Segmented and Linear Modes: when the Simplified memory model is used, the Destination address, Source address and Length fields reside in their respective fields in the RFD. When the Flexible memory strucrture is used the Destination address, Source address, and Length field locations depend on the SIZE field of the RFD. They can be placed in the RFD, in the RX data buffers, or partially in the RFD and the rest in the RX data buffers, depending on the SIZE field value.

82586 Mode

31	ODD WORD	16	15		EVEN WORD	0	
A15	NEXT RBD OFFSET	A0	EOF	F	ACTUAL COUNT	0	0
X X X X X X X X	A23		RECEIVE BUFFER ADDRESS			A0	4
X X X X X X X X X X X X X X X X		EL	X		SIZE		8

32-Bit Segmented Mode

31	ODD WORD	16	15		EVEN WORD	0	
A15	NEXT RBD OFFSET	A0	EOF	F	ACTUAL COUNT	0	0
A31		RECEIVE BUFFER ADDRESS				A0	4
0 0 0 0 0 0 0 0 0 0 0 0 0 0 0 0 0		EL	P		SIZE		8

Linear Mode

31	ODD WORD	16	15		EVEN WORD	0	
0 0 0 0 0 0 0 0 0 0 0 0 0 0 0 0 0		EOF	F		ACTUAL COUNT	0	0
A31	NEXT RBD ADDRESS					A0	4
A31	RECEIVE BUFFER ADDRESS					A0	8
0 0 0 0 0 0 0 0 0 0 0 0 0 0 0 0		EL	P		SIZE		

Figure 43. Receive Buffer Descriptor

where:

EOF — Indicates that this is the last buffer related to the frame. It is cleared by the CPU before starting the RU, and is written by the 82596 at the end of reception of the frame.

F — Indicates that this buffer has already been used. The Actual Count has no meaning unless the F bit equals one. This bit is cleared by the CPU before starting the RU, and is set by the 82596 after the associated buffer has been. This bit has the same meaning as the Complete bit in the RFD and CB.

ACT COUNT — This 14-bit quantity indicates the number of meaningful bytes in the buffer. It is cleared by the CPU before starting the RU, and is written by the 82596 after the associated buffer has already been used. In general, after the buffer is full, the Actual Count value equals the size field of the same buffer. For the last buffer of the frame, Actual Count can be less than the buffer size.

NEXT BD ADDRESS — The offset (absolute address in the Linear mode) of the next RBD on the list. It is meaningless if EL = 1.

BUFFER ADDRESS — The starting address of the memory area that contains the received data. In the 82586 mode, this is a 24-bit address (with pins A24–A31 = 0). In the 32-bit Segmented and Linear modes this is a 32-bit address.

EL — Indicates that the buffer associated with this RBD is last in the FBL.

P — This bit indicates that the 82596 has already prefetched the RBDs and any change in the RBD data will be ignored. This bit is valid only in the new 82596 memory modes, and if this feature has been enabled during configure command. The 82596 Prefetches the RBDs in locked cycles; after prefetching the RBD the 82596 performs a write cycle where the P bit is set to one and the rest of the data remains unchanged. The CPU is responsible for resetting it in all RBDs. The 82596 will not check this bit before setting it.

SIZE — This 14-bit quantity indicates the size, in bytes, of the associated buffer. This quantity must be an even number.

ELECTRICAL AND TIMING CHARACTERISTICS

D.C. CHARACTERISTICS

$T_C = 0°C–85°C$, $V_{CC} = 5V \pm 10\%$ LE/$\overline{BE}$ have MOS levels (see V_{MIL}, V_{MIH}).
All other signals have TTL levels (see V_{IL}, V_{IH}, V_{OL}, V_{OH}).

Symbol	Parameter	Min	Max	Units	Test Conditions
V_{IL}	Input Low Voltage (TTL)	-0.3	$+0.8$	V	
V_{IH}	Input High Voltage (TTL)	2.0	$V_{CC} + 0.3$	V	
V_{MIL}	Input Low Voltage (MOS)	-0.3	$+0.8$	V	
V_{MIH}	Input High Voltage (MOS)	3.7	$V_{CC} + 0.3$	V	
V_{OL}	Output Low Voltage (TTL)		0.45	V	$I_{OL} = 4.0$ mA[1]
V_{CIL}	$\overline{RXC}$, $\overline{TXC}$ Input Low Voltage	-0.5	0.6	V	
V_{CIH}	$\overline{RXC}$, $\overline{TXC}$ Input High Voltage	3.3	$V_{CC} + 0.5$	V	
V_{OH}	Output High Voltage (TTL)	2.4		V	$I_{OH} = 0.9mA–1$ mA[1]
I_{LI}	Input Leakage Current		± 15	μA	$0 \leq V_{IN} \leq V_{CC}$
I_{LO}	Output Leakage Current		± 15	μA	$0.45 < V_{OUT} < V_{CC}$
C_{IN}	Capacitance of Input Buffer		10	pF	FC = 1 MHz
C_{OUT}	Capacitance of Input/Output Buffer		12	pF	FC = 1 MHz
C_{CLK}	CLK Capacitance		20	pF	FC = 1 MHz
I_{CC}	Power Supply		200	mA	At 25 MHz
I_{CC}	Power Supply		300	mA	At 33 MHz

NOTE:
1. The value here will be reviewed when a typical system will be introduced.

A.C. CHARACTERISTICS

82596CA INPUT/OUTPUT SYSTEM TIMINGS

C_L on all outputs is 20 pF to 50 pF unless otherwise specified.
All timing requirements are given in nanoseconds.

Symbol	Parameter	25 MHz		Test Conditions
		Min	Max	
	Operating Frequency	12.5 MHz	25 MHz	1X CLK Input
T1	CLK2 Period	20	40	
T1a	CLK Period Stability		0.1%	Adjacent CLK Δ
T2	CLK High	14		2.0V
T3	CLK Low	14	11	0.8V
T4	CLK Rise Time		4	0.8V to 2.0V
T5	CLK Fall Time		4	2.0V to 0.8V
T6	BEn, LOCK, and A2–A31 Valid Delay	3	22	
T6a	BLAST, PCHK Valid Delay	3	27	
T7	BEn, LOCK, BLAST, A2–A31 Float Delay	0		Before CLK Edge
T8	W/R and ADS Valid Delay	3	22	
T9	W/R and ADS Float Delay	0		Before CLK Edge
T10	D0–D31, DPn Write Data Valid Delay	3	22	From T2
T11	D0–D31, DPn Write Data Float Delay	0	15	2
T12	HOLD Valid Delay	3	22	Same as BREQ of i486
T13	CA and BREQ Setup Time	7		1, 4
T14	CA and BREQ Hold Time	3		1, 4
T15	BS16 Setup Time	8		4
T16	BS16 Hold Time	3		4
T17	BRDY, RDY Setup Time	8		4
T18	BRDY, RDY Hold Time	3		4
T19	D0–D31, DPn READ Setup Time	5		4
T20	D0–D31, DPn READ Hold Time	3		4
T21	AHOLD and HLDA Setup Time	10		1, 4
T22	AHOLD Hold Time	3		1, 4
T22a	HLDA Hold Time	3		1, 4
T23	RESET Setup Time	10		1, 4
T24	RESET Hold Time	3		1, 4
T25	INT/INT Valid Delay	1	26	
T26	CA and BREQ Pulse Width	1 T1	1 T1	
T27	D0–D31 CPU PORT Access Setup Time	5		4
T28	D0–D31 CPU PORT Access Hold Time	3		4
T29	PORT Setup Time	7		4
T30	PORT Hold Time	3		4
T31	BOFF Setup Time	10		4
T32	BOFF Hold Time	3		4

A.C. CHARACTERISTICS

82596CA INPUT/OUTPUT SYSTEM TIMINGS

C_L on all outputs is 20 pF to 50 pF unless otherwise specified.
All timing requirements are given in nanoseconds.

Symbol	Parameter	33 MHz		Test Conditions
		Min	Max	
	Operating Frequency	12.5 MHz	33 MHz	1X CLK Input
T1	CLK Period	30	80	
T1a	CLK Period Stability		0.1%	Adjacent CLK Δ
T2	CLK High	11		2.0V
T3	CLK Low	11		0.8V
T4	CLK Rise Time		3	0.8V to 2.0V
T5	CLK Fall Time		3	2.0V to 0.8V
T6	BEn, LOCK, and A2–A31 Valid Delay	3	19	
T6a	BLAST, PCHK Valid Delay	3	22	
T7	BEn, LOCK, BLAST, A2–A31 Float Delay	0		Before CLK Edge
T8	W/R and ADS Valid Delay	3	19	
T9	W/R and ADS Float Delay	0		Before CLK Edge
T10	D0–D31, DPn Write Data Valid Delay	3	19	From T2
T11	D0–D31, DPn Write Data Float Delay	0		2
T12	HOLD Valid Delay	3	19	Same as BREQ of i486
T13	CA and BREQ Setup Time	7		1, 4
T14	CA and BREQ Hold Time	3		1, 4
T15	BS16 Setup Time	6		4
T16	BS16 Hold Time	3		4
T17	BRDY, RDY Setup Time	6		4
T18	BRDY, RDY Hold Time	3		4
T19	D0–D31, DPn READ Setup Time	5		4
T20	D0–D31, DPn READ Hold Time	3		4
T21	AHOLD and HLDA Setup Time	8		1, 4
T22	AHOLD Hold Time	3		1, 4

A.C. CHARACTERISTICS

82596CA INPUT/OUTPUT SYSTEM TIMINGS

C_L on all outputs is 20 pF to 50 pF unless otherwise specified.
All timing requirements are given in nanoseconds.

Symbol	Parameter	33 MHz Min	33 MHz Max	Test Conditions
T22a	HLDA Hold Time	3		1, 4
T23	RESET Setup Time	8		1, 4
T24	RESET Hold Time	3		1, 4
T25	INT/$\overline{INT}$ Valid Delay	1	20	
T26	CA and BREQ Pulse Width	1	1T1	
T27	D0–D31 CPU $\overline{PORT}$ Access Setup Time	5		4
T28	D0–D31 CPU $\overline{PORT}$ Access Hold Time	3		4
T29	$\overline{PORT}$ Setup Time	7		4
T30	$\overline{PORT}$ Hold Time	3		4
T31	$\overline{BOFF}$ Setup Time	8		4
T32	$\overline{BOFF}$ Hold Time	3		4

NOTES
1. To guarantee recognition at next clock
2. Before next clock edge after $\overline{RDY}$ is returned
3. C_L 20–50 pF
4. All set-up, hold and delay timings are at maximum frequency specification F__max, and must be derated according to the following equation for operation at lower frequencies:
Tderated = (Fmax/Fopr) × T
where:
Tderate = Specifies the value to derate the specification.
Fmax = Maximum operating frequency.
Fopr = Actual operating frequency.
T = Specification at maximum frequency.

TRANSMIT/RECEIVE CLOCK PARAMETERS

Symbol	Parameter	20 MHz Min	20 MHz Max	Test Conditions
T36	$\overline{TXC}$ Cycle	50		1, 3
T38	$\overline{TXC}$ Rise Time		5	1
T39	$\overline{TXC}$ Fall Time		5	1
T40	$\overline{TXC}$ High Time	19		1, 3
T41	$\overline{TXC}$ Low Time	18		1, 3
T42	TXD Rise Time		10	4
T43	TXD Fall Time		10	4
T44	TXD Transition	20		2, 4
T45	$\overline{TXC}$ Low to TXD Valid		25	4, 6
T46	$\overline{TXC}$ Low to TXD Transition		25	2, 4
T47	$\overline{TXC}$ High to TXD Transition		25	2, 4
T48	$\overline{TXC}$ Low to TXD High (At End of Transition)		25	4
$\overline{RTS}$ AND $\overline{CTS}$ PARAMETERS				
T49	$\overline{TXC}$ Low to $\overline{RTS}$ Low, Time to Activate $\overline{RTS}$		25	5
T50	$\overline{CTS}$ Low to $\overline{TXC}$ Low, $\overline{CTS}$ Setup Time		20	
T51	$\overline{TXC}$ Low to $\overline{CTS}$ Invalid, $\overline{CTS}$ Hold Time	10		7
T52	$\overline{TXC}$ Low to $\overline{RTS}$ High		25	5

TRANSMIT/RECEIVE CLOCK PARAMETERS (Continued)

Symbol	Parameter	20 MHz		Test Conditions
		Min	Max	
RECEIVE CLOCK PARAMETERS				
T53	RXC Cycle	50		1, 3
T54	RXC Rise Time		5	1
T55	RXC Fall Time		5	1
T56	RXC High Time	19		1
T57	RXC Low Time	18		1
RECEIVED DATA PARAMETERS				
T58	RXD Setup Time	20		6
T59	RXD Hold Time	10		6
T60	RXD Rise Time		10	
T61	RXD Fall Time		10	
CRS AND CDT PARAMETERS				
T62	CDT Low to TXC HIGH External Collision Detect Setup Time	20		
T63	TXC High to CDT Inactive, CDT Hold Time	10		
T64	CDT Low to Jam Start		10	
T65	CRS Low to TXC High, Carrier Sense Setup Time	20		
T66	TXC High to CRS Inactive, CRS Hold Time	10		
T67	CRS High to Jamming Start, (Internal Collision Detect)			12
T68	Jamming Period			11
T69	CRS High to RXC High, CRS Inactive Setup Time	30		
T70	RXC High to CRS High, CRS Inactive Hold Time	10		
INTERFRAME SPACING PARAMETERS				
T71	Interframe Delay			9
EXTERNAL LOOPBACK-PIN PARAMETERS				
T72	TXC Low to LPBK Low		T36	4
T73	TXC Low to LPBK High		T36	4

NOTES:

1. Special MOS levels. $V_{CIL} = 0.9V$ and $V_{CIH} = 3.0V$.
2. Manchester only.
3. Manchester. Needs 50% duty cycle.
4. 1 TTL load + 50 pF.
5. 1 TTL load + 100 pF.
6. NRZ only.
7. Abnormal end of transmission—CTS expires before RTS.
8. Normal end to transmission.
9. Programmable value:
   $T71 = N_{IFS} \cdot T36$
   where: N_{IFS} = the IFS configuration value
   (if N_{IFS} is less than 12 then N_{IFS} is forced to 12).

10. Programmable value:
    $T64 = (N_{CDF} \cdot T36) + x \cdot T36$
    (If the collision occurs after the preamble)
    where:
    N_{CDF} = the collision detect filter configuration value, and
    x = 12, 13, 14, or 15
11. $T68 = 32 \cdot T36$
12. Programmable value:
    $T67 = (N_{CSF} \cdot T36) + x \cdot T36$
    where: N_{CSF} = the Carrier Sense Filter configuration value, and
    x = 12, 13, 14, or 15
13. To guarantee recognition on the next clock.

SYSTEM INTERFACE A.C. TIMING CHARACTERISTICS

The measurements should be done at:

- T_C = 0°C–85°C, V_{CC} = 5V ±10%, C = 50 pF unless otherwise specified.
- A.C. testing inputs are driven at 2.4V for a logic "1" and 0.45V for a logic "0".
- Timing measurements are made at 1.5V for both logic "1" and "0".
- Rise and Fall time of inputs and outputs signals are measured between 0.8V and 2.0V respectively unless otherwise specified.
- All timings are relative to CLK crossing the 1.5V level.
- All A.C. parameters are valid only after 100 μs from power up.

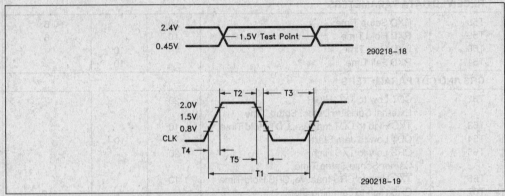

Figure 44. CLK Timings

Two types of timing specifications are presented below:

1. Input Timing—minimum setup and hold times.
2. Output Timings—output delays and float times from CLK rising edge.

Figure 45 defines how the measurements should be done:

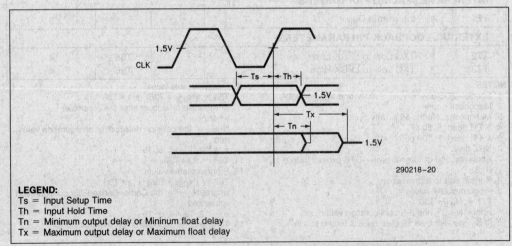

LEGEND:
Ts = Input Setup Time
Th = Input Hold Time
Tn = Minimum output delay or Minimum float delay
Tx = Maximum output delay or Maximum float delay

Figure 45. Drive Levels and Measurements Points for A.C. Specifications

INPUT WAVEFORMS

Ts = T13, T15, T17, T19, T21,   T23, T27, T29, T31
Th = T14, T16, T18, T20, T22, T22a, T24, T28, T30, T32

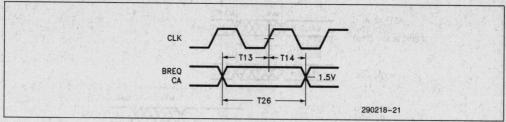

Figure 46. CA and BREQ Input Timing

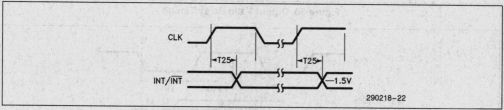

Figure 47. INT/INT Output Timing

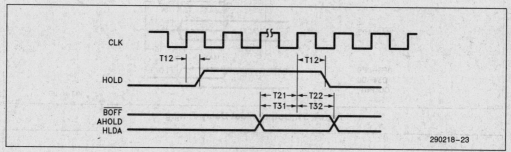

Figure 48. HOLD/HLDA Timings

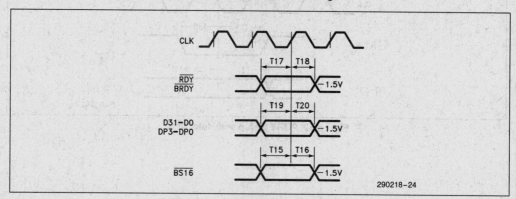

Figure 49. Input Setup and Hold Time

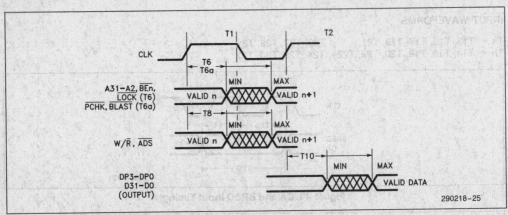

Figure 50. Output Valid Delay Timing

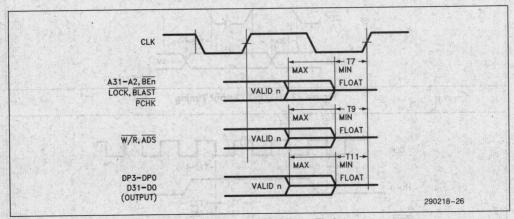

Figure 51. Output Float Delay Timing

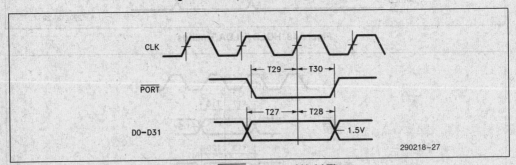

Figure 52. PORT Setup and Hold Time

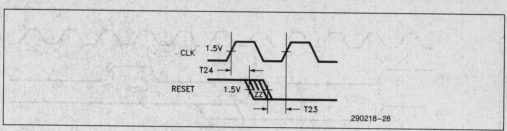

Figure 53. RESET Input Timing

SERIAL A.C. TIMING CHARACTERISTICS

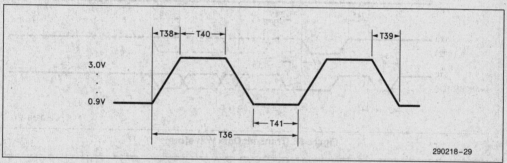

Figure 54. Serial Input Clock Timing

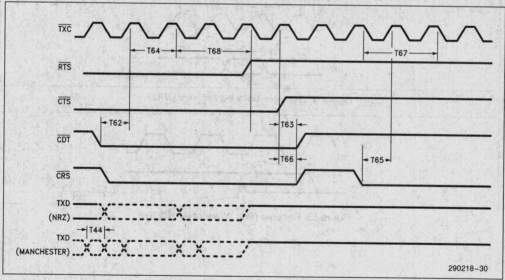

Figure 55. Transmit Data Waveforms

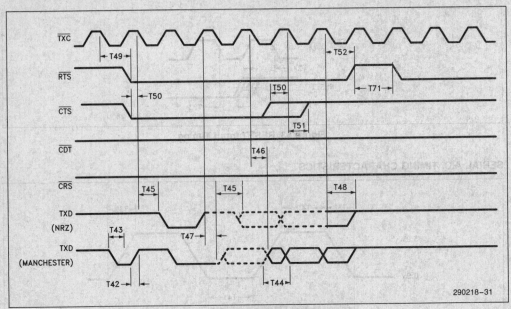

Figure 56. Transmit Data Waveforms

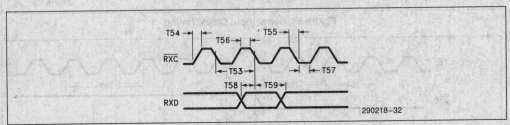

Figure 57. Receive Data Waveforms (NRZ)

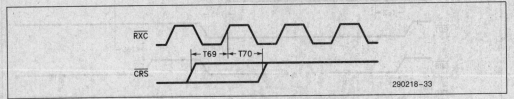

Figure 58. Receive Data Waveforms (CRS)

132 LEAD CERAMIC PIN GRID ARRAY PACKAGE INTEL TYPE A

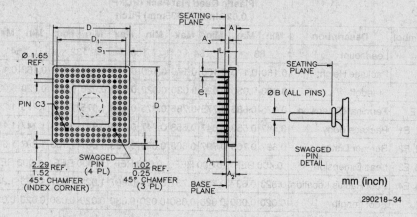

290218-34

Family: Ceramic Pin Grid Array Package						
Symbol	Millimeters			Inches		
	Min	Max	Notes	Min	Max	Notes
A	3.56	4.57		0.140	0.180	
A_1	0.76	1.27	Solid Lid	0.030	0.050	Solid Lid
A_2	2.67	3.43	Solid Lid	0.105	0.135	Solid Lid
A_3	1.14	1.40		0.045	0.055	
B	0.43	0.51		0.017	0.020	
D	36.45	37.21		1.435	1.465	
D_1	32.89	33.15		1.295	1.305	
e_1	2.29	2.79		0.090	0.110	
L	2.54	3.30		0.100	0.130	
N		132			132	
S_1	1.27	2.54		0.050	0.100	
ISSUE	IWS 10/12/88					

Intel Case Outline Drawings
Plastic Quad Flat Pack (PQFP)
0.025 Inch (0.635mm) Pitch

Symbol	Description	Min	Max	Min	Max	Min	Max	Min	Max	Min	Max	Min	Max
N	Leadcount	68		84		100		132		164		196	
A	Package Height	0.160	0.170	0.160	0.170	0.160	0.170	0.160	0.170	0.160	0.170	0.160	0.170
A1	Standoff	0.020	0.030	0.020	0.030	0.020	0.030	0.020	0.030	0.020	0.030	0.020	0.030
D, E	Terminal Dimension	0.675	0.685	0.775	0.785	0.875	0.885	1.075	1.085	1.275	1.285	1.475	1.485
D1, E1	Package Body	0.547	0.553	0.647	0.653	0.747	0.753	0.947	0.953	1.147	1.153	1.347	1.353
D2, E2	Bumper Distance	0.697	0.703	0.797	0.803	0.897	0.903	1.097	1.103	1.297	1.303	1.497	1.503
D3, E3	Lead Dimension	0.400 REF		0.500 REF		0.600 REF		0.800 REF		1.000 REF		1.200 REF	
D4, E4	Foot Radius Location	0.623	0.637	0.723	0.737	0.823	0.837	1.023	1.037	1.223	1.237	1.423	1.437
L1	Foot Length	0.020	0.030	0.020	0.030	0.020	0.030	0.020	0.030	0.020	0.030	0.020	0.030
Issue	IWS Preliminary 12/12/88												INCH

Symbol	Description	Min	Max	Min	Max	Min	Max	Min	Max	Min	Max	Min	Max
N	Leadcount	68		84		100		132		164		196	
A	Package Height	4.06	4.32	4.06	4.32	4.06	4.32	4.06	4.32	4.06	4.32	4.06	4.32
A1	Standoff	0.51	0.76	0.51	0.76	0.51	0.76	0.51	0.76	0.51	0.76	0.51	0.76
D, E	Terminal Dimension	17.15	17.40	19.69	19.94	22.23	22.48	27.31	27.56	32.39	32.64	37.47	37.72
D1, E1	Package Body	13.89	14.05	16.43	16.59	18.97	19.13	24.05	24.21	29.13	29.29	34.21	34.37
D2, E2	Bumper Distance	17.70	17.85	20.24	20.39	22.78	22.93	27.86	28.01	32.94	33.09	38.02	38.18
D3, E3	Lead Dimension	10.16 REF		12.70 REF		15.24 REF		20.32 REF		25.40 REF		30.48 REF	
D4, E4	Foot Radius Location	15.82	16.17	18.36	18.71	21.25	21.25	25.89	26.33	31.06	31.41	36.14	36.49
L1	Foot Length	0.51	0.76	0.51	0.76	0.51	0.76	0.51	0.76	0.51	0.76	0.51	0.76
Issue	IWS Preliminary 12/12/88												mm

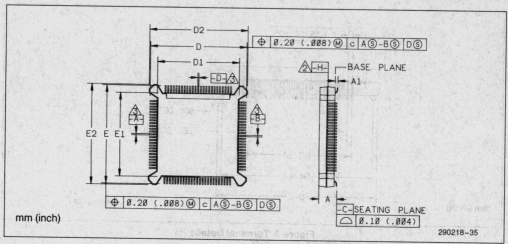

Figure 1. Principal Dimensions and Datums

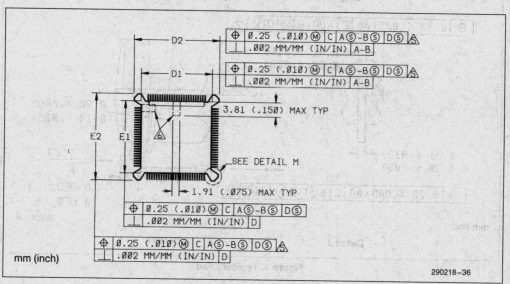

Figure 2. Molded Details

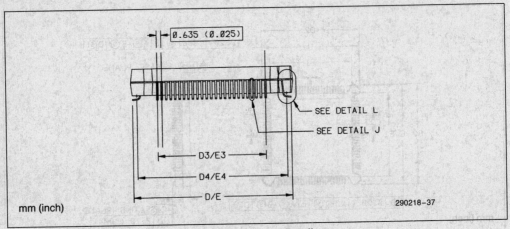

mm (inch)   290218-37

Figure 3. Terminal Details

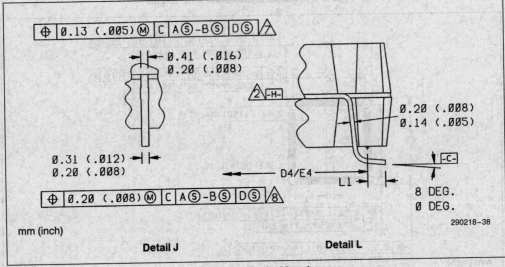

mm (inch)   290218-38

Detail J   Detail L

Figure 4. Typical Lead

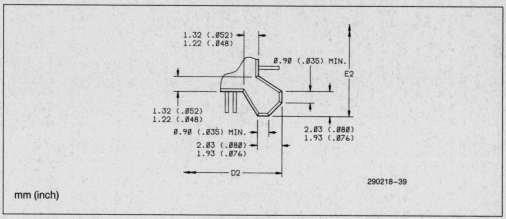

1.32 (.052)
1.22 (.048)

0.90 (.035) MIN.

E2

1.32 (.052)
1.22 (.048)

0.90 (.035) MIN.

2.03 (.080)
1.93 (.076)

2.03 (.080)
1.93 (.076)

D2

290218–39

mm (inch)

Figure 5. Detail M

REVISION HISTORY

The 82596 LAN Coprocessor data sheet version –002 contains updates and improvements to previous versions.

1. All pinout diagrams have been corrected.

2. Other TBD numbers have been supplied.

3. A more accurate description of the monitor has been supplied.

4. A.C. and D.C. parametric specifications and timings have been updated.

80960 Development Support Tools

7

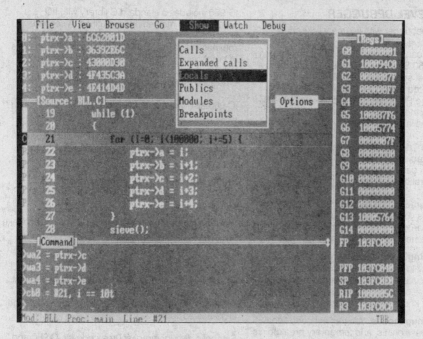

COMPREHENSIVE SOFTWARE DEVELOPMENT SUPPORT FOR 80960 EMBEDDED APPLICATIONS

The most comprehensive development support for Intel's powerful 80960 microprocessor comes, naturally, from Intel. We have every tool you need, from debugger to performance simulator, to help you get started immediately on your 80960 design. All the tools described here were designed specifically for members of the 80960 family, allowing you to take full advantage of their RISC-based design. And all are supported on a variety of hosts, including PCs, VAX* minicomputers and Sun* workstations, so you can work in a familiar environment. You can even buy 80960 software tools in handy starter kits that make development more economical.

SOFTWARE TOOLS AVAILABLE:

- Windowed, interactive, source-level DB-960 debugger
- iC-960 highly optimizing C language compiler for high-level language software development
- ASM-960 macro assembler for developing and tuning speed-critical code
- EVA-960KB plug-in execution board for benchmarking performance, evaluating architecture, and developing and debugging application code on a PC AT*.

- GEN-960 system generator for initializing your design to take advantage of 80960 on-chip features
- SIM-960 performance simulator for benchmarking/evaluating 80960CA performance
- Starter kits for supporting a wide range of development needs

intel

September, 1989
Order Number: 280796-005

SOURCE-LEVEL DEBUGGER

The DB-960 Debugger with source-level debug capabilities is available for PC ATs equipped with DOS. DB-960 can debug 80960 code executing on an Intel EVA-960 Software Execution Vehicle or on a hardware target system via a serial interface. The EVA-960 targeted debugger uses I/O resources provided by the PC, while 80960 code executes at high speed on the EVA-960. Two serial versions of DB-960 are available. DB-960CADIC plugs directly into the 80960CA socket on your prototype, offering a "plug-in and go" debug environment. DB-960D is a serial, retargetable version of DB-960 whose system debug monitor can be customized for 80960KX or 80960CA operation.

DB-960's powerful, windowed, source-oriented interface allows you to focus your efforts on finding bugs rather than on learning and manipulating the debug environment.

Ease of learning. Drop-down menus make the debugger easy to learn for new or casual users. A command line interface allows direct command entry for solving more complex problems, improving productivity of knowledgeable users.

Extensive debug modes. You can set conditional breakpoints, pass points, and temporary breakpoints as needed.

See into your program. Using pull-down menus or function keys, you can browse source and Call stacks, monitor processor registers, view screen output, and watch the values of variables change.

Full debug symbolics for maximum productivity. You need not know whether a variable is an unsigned integer, a real, or a structure: the debugger displays program variables in their respective type formats.

iC-960 COMPILER

iC-960 is a highly optimizing C language compiler for the 80960 family of microprocessors. iC-960 supports the full C language as described in the Kernighan and Ritchie book, The C Programming Language (Prentice-Hall, 1978). iC-960 includes standard ANSI extensions to the C language and is used in conjunction with ASM-960 for creating object code files.

The iC-960 compiler supports a number of processor dependent optimizations including global register allocation, constant propagation, arithmetic identity folding, redundant load/store elimination, strength reduction and register allocation/scheduling of arguments. Processor independent optimizations include common sub-expression elimination, folding of constant expressions, elimination of superfluous branches, removing unreachable code, tail recursion and procedure incorporation.

iC-960 includes a standard C library with I/O functions and mathematical routines. A second library provides low level, environment-dependent routines emulating UNIX* system calls and supplies I/O routines for the EVA-960 Software Execution Vehicle. A third library provides floating point emulation for use with the 80960KA and 80960CA.

iC-960 also includes the following enhancements for embedded application development:

Programs may be easily placed in ROM.

Memory-mapped I/O allows high-level language access to application-specific input and output.

In-line assembly simplifies the integration of C language and assembly code for speed-critical functions.

Floating point support produces in-line code to take full advantage of the floating point capability of the 80960KB and 80960MC.

The DOS-hosted version requires a 2MB AboveBoard.™ The EVA960-hosted version requires the 4MB board (EVA960KB4MB) and provides a significant compile-time speed improvement over the DOS-hosted version.

Symbolic debugging of source code for iC-960 and ASM-960 is provided by the DB-960 Source Level Debugger.

ASM-960 MACRO ASSEMBLER

The ASM-960 macro assembler is used to fine-tune sections of code for peak program execution speed on the 80960KA, 80960KB, 80960MC, and 80960CA. ASM-960 does this by giving you absolute control over program instructions. In addition to the assembler and macro preprocessor, ASM-960 includes several utilities for application program maintenance and debug:

- LINKER provides incremental program linking/locating and link-time optimization.
- ARCHIVER allows you to build reusable function libraries for applications.
- DISASSEMBLER produces assembly language from object files.
- SYMBOL DUMPER provides symbolic information from a program file for facilitating low-level debug.
- ROM IMAGE BUILDER produces a hex file suitable for PROM programmers.
- MACRO PREPROCESSOR provides code generation flexibility and improves code readability, reducing maintenance costs.

ASM-960 also supports the additional instructions supplied by the 80960CA, including branch prediction. A Floating Point Arithmetic Library (FPAL) is included for the 80960KA and 80960CA and eliminates the need to develop your own floating point code.

EVA-960KB4MB SOFTWARE EXECUTION VEHICLE

The EVA-960KB4MB is a software execution vehicle for the 80960KA/KB microprocessor. It is a single PC AT plug-in board which provides easy and convenient architecture evaluation and benchmarking, as well as software development. Used in conjunction with the C-960E Compiler, the EVA-960KB4MB execution vehicle can compile C code 3-5 times faster than the PC-AT. The EVA-960KB4B contains the following:

- 4MB of one wait-state program memory (DRAM)
- 64K bytes of zero wait-state program memory (SRAM)
- Three-channel programmable interval timer
- Hosted debug monitor which supports two hardware and 64 software breakpoints, single-step program execution, register and memory access, program download and upload.
- DOS access libraries that allow: screen display, keyboard input, read and write disk files, and the ability to spawn a DOS process that could communicate with serial or parallel I/O.
- 20 MHz operation, allowing software to operate at full speed of 80960KB

EVA-960KB4MB also operates with the DB-960 Source Level Debugger for code development/debug prior to target system availability.

GEN-960 SYSTEM GENERATOR

The 80960 System Generator (GEN-960) helps you set up data structures for standalone, embedded applications that use the on-chip features of the 80960 architecture. GEN-960 is used with other 80960 tools to generate and refine ROM or RAM code. GEN-960 supplies a set of command and template files containing assembly code and linker control commands to set up processor control blocks, inter-agent communication mechanisms, system procedure tables, and other requirements for initialization. The result is a batch file containing all the commands needed to compile, assemble and link the final target system.

- Improves engineering productivity by automating the compilation, assembly and linking process
- Supplies sample initialization code, reducing programming time
- Saves engineering time by simplifying the task of initializing each processor for on-chip capabilities

SIM-960CA PERFORMANCE SIMULATOR

The SIM-960CA Performance Simulator emulates the instruction set of the 80960CA microprocessor. You can specify wait-states and clock speed assuring accurate simulation of code execution on your target system. Using SIM-960CA's trace capability, you can trace instruction execution and read/write activity at a particular location. Timing profiles of 80960CA operations are accurate to within plus or minus 5%. Accurate estimates of actual 80960CA code performance can thus be made without an 80960CA-based target.

SOFTWARE DEVELOPMENT TOOLS

ASM960	Assembler package containing the assembler, linker/loader, macro preprocessor, archiver, ROM image builder, other object file utilities, and the 80960KA/CA floating point arithmetic library.
C960	Optimizing C Compiler, with ANSI extensions for embedded control applications; contains standard STDIO libraries and in-line assembly capability. DOS version requires 2M byte Above™Board.
GEN960	80960 System Generation software automates the compilation, assembly and linking process. Simplifies usage of 80960 sophisticated features.
SIM960CA	Performance Simulator software emulates the 80960CA instruction set allowing performance benchmarking and "fine tuning" prior to hardware prototype availability.
DB960KBDEVA	Source Level Debugger software for the 80960KB/KA with powerful debug capabilities including conditional breakpoints, source and Call stack browsing, memory/register display and modification, and ability to watch variables change value. Requires EVA-960KB4MB Software Execution Vehicle. For PC-AT hosted systems only.
DB960D	Source Level Debugger software for 80960KA/KB or CA processors resident on serially-interfaced hardware prototype systems. Includes customizable system debug monitor and serial interface protocol specifications. For PC-AT hosted systems only.
DB960CADIC	In-Circuit Source Level Debugger for 80960CA only. Includes small card with 80960CA processor, system debug monitor and serial interface. Plugs into 80960CA socket on hardware prototype system. "Ready to use" equivalent of DB960D. For PC-AT hosted systems only.
EVA960KB4MB	Software Execution Vehicle for 80960KA/KB. Includes 4M byte of on-board memory, system debug monitor and code download software. Can be used with C960E Compiler to accelerate compilation 3-5X over PC-AT alone. Required by DB960KBDEVA.

ARCHITECTURE EVALUATION STARTER KITS

960SKit3   Contains ASM960D Assembler and iC960D Compiler.

960SKit3AB   Same as 960SKit3 plus Intel Above™Board with 2M byte memory.

960SKit4   Contains ASM960M Assembler and C960M Compiler, hosted on MicroVAX/VMS.

960SKit5   Contains ASM960V Assembler and C960V C Compiler, hosted on VAX/VMS.

960SKit6   Fast development kit contains EVA960KB4MB Software Execution Vehicle and C960E Software Execution Vehicle hosted C Compiler.

960SKit7   Same as 960SKit6 plus ASM960D Assembler.

960SKit8   Contains ASM960U Assembler and C960U C Compiler, hosted on Sun 3.

DB960KIT1   Kit contains DB-960KBDEVA (KB version of DB-960 used with EVA-960) and EVA960KB4MB Software Execution Vehicle. Requires ASM960D and C960D or C960E and a PC-AT with 640K memory.

DB960KIT2   Kit contains DB-960KBDEVA (KB version of DB-960 used with EVA-960), EVA960KB4MB Software Execution Vehicle, ASM960D and C960E. Requires PC-AT with 640K memory.

DB960KIT3   Kit contains DB-960D (serial version of DB-960 supporting 80960KX and 80960CA, operating on PC-AT/DOS), ASM960D and C960D. Requires PC-AT with 640K memory.

DB960KIT7   Kit contains DB-960CADIC (in-circuit version of DB-960 supporting 80960CA, operating on PC-AT/DOS), ASM960D and C960D. Requires PC-AT with 640K memory.

For more information or the number of your nearest Intel sales office, call 800-548-4725 (good in the U.S. and Canada).

Product Code to order, by Host					
Product Category	PC-AT/DOS	EVA-960KB	VAX/VMS	mVAX/VMS	Sun 3/UNIX
Assembler	ASM960D	—	ASM960V	ASM960M	ASM960U
C Compiler	C960D	C960E	C960V	C960M	C960U
System Gen KX	GEN960D	—	GEN960V	GEN960M	GEN960U
Debugger	DB960KBDEVA	—	—	—	—
	DB960D	—	—	—	—
CA Debugger	DB960CADIC	—	—	—	—
	DB960D	—	—	—	—

*PC AT is a registered trademark of International Business Machines Corporation.
VAX/VMS and MicroVAX/VMS are trademarks of Digital Equipment Corporation.
Sun 3 is a trademark of Sun Microsystems.
AboveBoard is a trademark of Intel Corporation.

A COMPLETE ADA SOLUTION FOR REAL-TIME EMBEDDED APPLICATIONS

Ada-960 from Intel is a complete Ada development environment for 80960MC based real-time, embedded applications.

The 80960MC is a high performance, 32-bit military embedded processor especially designed to support Ada in fault-tolerant, shared-memory multiprocessor applications.

Ada-960 is hosted on VAX/VMS.* The cross-development environment inlcudes a highly optimizing Ada cross-compiler, a linker, a librarian, a source-level symbolic debugger, a target monitor, predefined packages and subprograms, the Ada run-time system, a user guide, and a detailed run-time system implementor's guide. The run-time system makes optimal use of the Ada support built into the 80960MC processor and is carefully designed for real-time embedded applications.

FEATURES

- Complete VAX/VMS* hosted Ada cross development environment
- Makes optimal use of the Ada support offered by the 80960 MC
- Run-time system is small, fast and predictable for real-time applications

- Designed for embedded applications with a highly optimizing compiler, selective linking, highly modular reconfigurable run-time, and source level symbolic debugger interfacing to a target monitor, or an emulator

THE 80960MC AND ADA: A GOOD MATCH

The Intel 80960MC embedded processor is designed to support applications written in Ada. Ada-960 from Intel is implemented to make optimal use of the Ada support built into the 80960MC.

- Ada-960 maps Ada tasks directly to 80960MC processes.
- Ada-960 uses the 80960MC embedded processor hardware to dispatch and manage Ada tasks.
- Ada-960 maps Ada task priorities directly to 80960MC process priorities.
- Ada-960 uses the 80960MC memory managment unit to provide inter-task protection.
- Ada-960 uses 80960MC semaphores to implement run-time system critical sections.
- Ada-960 uses the 80960MC on-chip floating point unit to perform floating point operations.

The unique architecture of the 80960MC allows Ada-960 to use the processor hardware to provide functionality normally implemented in software on other architectures. This includes automatic dispatching and pre-emptive priority scheduling of Ada tasks.

Ada-960's use of the 80960MC makes the run-time easily extensible to support fault-tolerant shared-memory multiprocessor configurations supported by the 80960MC embedded processor.

ADA-960 FOR REAL-TIME APPLICATIONS

Ada-960 is carefully designed for use in the development of real-time applications. Some of the real-time features of Ada-960 include:

Minimum "interrupts off" Time

The Ada-960 run-time system disables interrupts for a minimal amount of time. The "interrupts off" time does not vary with the size of the application.

Pre-emptive Priority Scheduling

Ada-960 provides a fully pre-emptive, priority-driven tasking run-time. The 80960MC hardware is used to ensure that the highest priority task is always the one that is running. The run-time system uses the 80960MC hardware to switch to a higher priority task (than the one currently executing) whenever such a task becomes ready to run.

Predictable Performance

Ada-960 provides predictable performance that is insensitive to target system load. System response time remains constant and fully deterministic as the number of tasks etc. grows.

- Ada-960 ensures that scheduling latency is independent of system load.
- Ada-960 guarantees response-time to interrupts.
- Ada-960 provides predictable memory allocation times. Memory allocation is implemented through efficient algorithms that ensure a constant upper bound on the time taken to allocate memory.

Run-time Extension

Ada-960 provides a run-time system extension package that gives applications dynamic control over tasking, scheduling, critical sections and other run-time functions.

ADA-960 FOR EMBEDDED APPLICATIONS

Ada-960 is designed for embedded applications and provides:

Small, Fast run-time System

Ada-960 provides a compact, high performance run-time system. The run-time system is very modular to support selective linking by the Ada-960 linker. The modularity of the run-time and the selective linking features of the linker ensure that all unused Ada language features are automatically omitted from the application's final executable image.

Retargetable Run-time System

Ada-960 provides an easily retargetable run-time system. The run-time system is designed to be easily retargeted to custom 80960MC boards and comes with all the necessary source files and documentation for on-site customization to specific interrupt and I/O requirments.

VAX/VMS Hosted Remote Debug

Ada-960 provides a VAX/VMS-hosted source-level, symbolic Ada debugger. The debugger allows users to debug applications on a remote 80960MC target via its interface to either the standard Intel 80960MC monitor or the standard Intel 80960MC in-circuit-emulator.

Retargetable Target Monitor

Ada-960 provides an easily retargetable target monitor. The target monitor resides on the target board. The monitor communicates with and supports the Ada debugger hosted on VAX/VMS. The target monitor is easily retargetable to custom boards. This allows the Ada debugger to be used in debugging applications on non-standard 80960MC hardware configurations.

ROMable Code and 86HEX

The Ada-960 compiler produces ROMable code. The Ada linker can produce an application's executable image in 86Hex so that the application may be easily burnt into PROM's.

Combining Ada and non-Ada Code

Ada-960 provides implementation-defined pragma FOREIGN-BODY and pragma LINKAGE-NAME to support the combination of Ada and non-Ada code.

Chapter 13 Support

Ada-960 provides chapter 13 support including representation specifications, machine-code insertion, interrupt entries, and so on.

CROSS-DEVELOPMENT ENVIRONMENT

The Ada-960 cross development environment includes tools for compiling, linking, and debugging, along with libraries and a complete set of documentation. The Ada-960 cross development environment from Intel makes the following support, documentation, tools, and software available:

Compiler

A fast, highly optimizing Ada-960 compiler that generates efficient, compact 80960MC code.

The compiler performs virtually all optimizations that are "traditional", as well as several that are Ada-specific. Each optimization is carefully tuned to the 80960MC architecture.

Optimizations performed include transformations that affect value and variable handling, code motion and elimination, tail recursion elimination, and loop strength reduction. Ada-specific data packing and code transformations such as constraint check elimination, overflow check elimination, and parameter binding are also performed. The Ada-960 code generator schedules generated machine instructions to make optimal use of parallel execution opportunities available on the 80960MC embedded processor.

Librarian

An Ada-960 librarian to manage the Ada program library. The librarian controls the interaction of compilation units and the linking of executable images. The Ada-960 librarian supports the Ada separate compilation and dependency control requirement.

Linker

An advanced Ada-960 linker to support enhanced selective linking at the subprogram level. Subprograms that are not used in an Ada application are not linked unless specifically requested. Full control over memory layout and mapping is supported with a rich command language.

Debugger

A very powerful Ada-960 source-level, symbolic Ada debugger that supports the debugging of both pure Ada and combined Ada code. The Ada-960 debugger is hosted on VAX/VMS and interfaces with target 80960MC boards through either the standard Intel 80960MC target monitor or the standard 80960MC in-circuit-emulator.

The Ada-960 debugger allows users to examine and modify their applications using the same names that appear in the source program. Users can evaluate Ada expressions, set breakpoints and tracepoints, and debug multi-tasking Ada programs.

Program breakpoints can be made conditional on arbitrary conditions, and debugger commands can be executed automatically at breakpoints.

The Ada-960 debugger can call functions and procedures in an Ada application. This feature can be used to extend the set of debugger facilities or to test parts of the application interactively.

The Ada-960 debugger allows users to display Ada variables in formats appropriate to each of their types. Users can also specify formats appropriate to the current application. Special browsing features within the debugger eliminate the need for paper listings during debugging sessions.

The Ada-960 debugger provides a flexible display of the state of Ada tasks and can display the current callstack within any task. The debugger can list tasks on various run-time queues and can suspend or change the priority of tasks.

The source level features of the Ada-960 debugger are complemented by a complete set of machine-level commands.

Script files containing debugger commands may be created in and executed by the debugger. The Ada-960 debugger can record a log of all debugging actions for later analysis or replay.

For better programmer productivity, the debugger has a multiwindow interface with separate windows for debugger commands, Ada source and program output. The Ada-960 debugger provides "scoreboard windows" for real-time display of user-selected program information.

The debugger is usable from all types of terminals and has special features to support bit-mapped displays.

Use of the debugger is possible at all optimization levels without recompilation of the Ada program.

Target Monitor

A standard Intel 80960MC target monitor that is easily retargetable to custom 80960MC boards. The target monitor comes with all the necessary source files and documentation for on-site customization to specific interrupt and I/O requirements.

ICE™

A standard Intel 80960MC in-circuit-emulator. The in-circuit-emulator delivers real-time emulation at processor speed, and allows non-intrusive debugging of applications under development.

Predefined Packages and Subprograms

An Ada-960 library containing precompiled predefined Ada packages and subprograms.

Run-time System

An Ada-960 library containing the Ada run-time system. The run-time system is small, fast, and predictable. The Ada-960 run-time is re-targetable to different 80960MC boards and is especially designed for real-time embedded applications. The run-time system is carefully designed to make optimal use of the Ada support provided by the 80960MC embedded processor.

FEATURES

The run-time system comes with all the necessary source files and documentation for on-site customization to specific interrupt and I/O conventions. Most of the run-time system is written in Intel Ada-960 with a small portion written in Intel ASM-960 assembler.

Run-time System Extension

A run-time system extension package to allow Ada applciations dynamic control over the tasking, scheduling, critical sections, and other run-time functions.

Source Code

Source code for both the run-time system and the run-time system extension.

Documentation

High quality documentation including a User Guide and a detailed Run-time System Implementor's Guide. The Run-time System Implementor's Guide provides full documentation of the interface between the Ada-960 compiler and the run-time system. It also documents the design of, and provides guidance to, modifying the run-time system.

WORLDWIDE SERVICE AND SUPPORT

Intel augments its 80960 architecture family development tools with a full array of seminars, classes, and workshops; on-site consulting services; field application engineering expertise; telephone hot-line support; and software and hardware maintenance contracts. This full line of services will ensure your design success.

ORDERING INFORMATION

For more information or the number of your nearest sales office call 800-548-4725 (good in the U.S. and Canada).

This is preliminary information. Changes to the product can be made at any time.
*VAX/VMS is a trademark of Digital Equipment Corp.

7-8

80960MC-BASED TARGET SYSTEM SUPPORTING EARLY SOFTWARE DEVELOPMENT AND BENCHMARKING

The EXV-960MC is a software execution vehicle designed to support 80960MC-based designs. Users can use the EXV-960MC board to execute and debug their application software before a functional hardware prototype is available. The EXV-960MC is also designed with programmable waitstate SRAM to support benchmarking activites. The EXV-960MC is supported by the complete set of Intel C, assembler and Ada code generation tools. Both of the VAX/VMS*-hosted 80960MC software debuggers, the SDM-960MC system debug monitor and the Ada-960MC source-level debugger, can be used for debugging software running on the EXV-960MC.

The EXV-960MC includes a MULTIBUS® I form factor board and a set of SDM-960MC target monitor EPROMS. The SDM-960MC and the Ada-960MC debugger are preconfigured to support the EXV-960MC execution environment. Designers can select the software debugger best suited to their development needs. The Ada-960MC debugger is a source-level symbolic debugger which provides a productive debugging environment for Ada applications. The SDM-960MC debug monitor offers a complete debugging facility for applications written in C, assembler or Ada.

SOFTWARE DEBUGGING SUPPORT

The SDM-960MC is a VAX/VMS*-hosted system debug monitor that provides a complete, flexible environment to execute and debug 80960MC-based applications. Users can tailor the execution environment as software development evolves. Initially, the application may require the full support of the system debug monitor to establish a run-time environment. As the application evolves, the SDM-960MC allows the application to take more of the responsibility for system functions.

The default execution environment of the SDM-960MC is the EXV-960MC execution vehicle. The VAX-hosted portion of the SDM-960MC debug monitor provides complete on-target debugging support through its interface with the target-resident portion of the SDM-960MC. To facilitate debugging on a user's custom target system, the SDM-960MC includes source and object files necessary to reconfigure the target monitor. SDM-960MC and other 80960MC development tools allow the developers to take full advantage of the 80960MC processor.

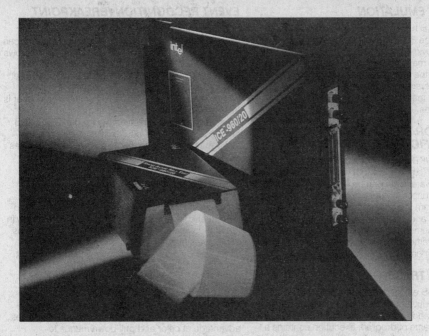

IN-CIRCUIT EMULATOR FOR THE 80960KA AND 80960KB MICROPROCESSORS

The ICE™-960KB In-Circuit Emulator delivers real-time hardware and software debugging capabilities for 80960KA/KB-based designs. The capabilities include emulation of the 80960KA/KB microprocessor, hardware and software breakpoint specification, fastbreaks, two types of trace capability, large trace buffering and sophisticated human interface. The ICE-960KB In-Circuit Emulator gives you unmatched control over all phases of hardware/software debug, including developing, integrating and testing, which improves the developers productivity and speeds time to market.

FEATURES

- Real-Time Emulation of the 80960KA/ KB microprocessors up to 20MHz
- 256K bytes of memory in Standalone Self Test Unit
- Zero wait-state operation from user system memory
- Examine and modify memory and the 80960 Registers
- 2 hardware and 32 software Breakpoints settable on any Instruction Address, and break on Trace Buffer Full
- Hosted on IBM PC-AT* running DOS (version 3.3)
- Assembly and Disassembly of code in 80960 instruction mnemonics
- Dynamically monitor or update program variables or memory with Fastbreaks

- Real-time Bus Trace with Time-Tags for tracking code execution times
- Execution Trace for tracking instruction execution inside on-chip Instruction Cache
- Stores 1024 frames of program execution history or bus cycles or both
- Versatile software featuring Color, Pulldown Menus, Forms, Command Line with Syntax Guidance and Editing, Control Constructs, Debug Procedures and DOS Command Input (shell)

REAL-TIME EMULATION

The ICE-960KB In-Circuit Emulator provides emulation of the 80960KA/KB at speeds up to 20 MHz, thus providing early detection of subtle timing problems that may arise at full speed. Intel's intimate knowledge of the component makes possible the tightest conceivable conformance between timing parameters of the emulator and the target microprocessor.

PROCESSOR/MEMORY EXAMINATION AND MODIFICATION

The 80960KA/KB registers can be accessed mnemonically (e.g. gl2, r5, fp3) with the ICE-960KB emulator software. Data can be displayed or modified in one of four bases (hexadecimal, decimal, octal, or binary). Program memory contents can be disassembled and displayed as 80960 assembly instruction mnemonics. Additionally, 80960 assembly instruction mnemonics can be assembled and stored into program memory.

PROGRAM TRACING

The ICE-960KB emulator can store 1024 frames of program execution history or 5120 cycles of the 80960KA/KB address/data bus activity in the trace buffer. Each frame of program execution contains a discontinuity address (branch, call, return, etc.), and a time-tag. This information can be used to reconstruct a history of the program execution. With the execution trace option enabled, the ICE-960KB will run at less than full speed; typically 70-90% of full-speed. Each trace frame of bus cycles contains one complete bus burst access, the address cycle followed by the four data cycles, and a time-tag. While using bus trace, the ICE-960KB runs at the full-speed of the 80960KA/KB microprocessor.

EVENT RECOGNITION (BREAKPOINT CONTROL) AND EMULATION CONTROL

Two hardware and thirty-two software breakpoints can be active at any time. The ICE-960KB emulator allows any number of breakpoints to be defined and then activated when needed. The breakpoints can be set on any instruction address. Additionally, emulation can be automatically stopped when the trace buffer is full. Besides the ability to execute program code at full speed between specified points, the ICE-960KB emulator provides the capability to single-step through program code. Fastbreaks are short pauses in program execution to examine or modify memory or 80960 registers.

STANDALONE OPERATION

Product software can be developed and debugged prior to and independent of hardware availability with the Standalone Self Test unit (SAST), which contains 256K bytes of two wait-state program memory. The SAST also provides diagnostic testing to assure full functionality of the ICE-960KB emulator.

VERSATILE AND POWERFUL HOST SOFTWARE

The easy to use ICE-960KB emulator software takes advantage of color and pull-down menus to complement its already powerful command set. The software includes: an on-line help facility, a dynamic command entry and syntax guide, screen oriented editor, assembler and disassembler, input/output redirection, command piping, DOS command entry, and the ability to customize the command set via debug procedures and literal definitions.

DEBUG PROCEDURES AND LITERALS

Debug procedures (PROCs) are user-defined groups of ICE-960KB emulator commands. They can be stored on disk and recalled during later debugging sessions. PROCs can be used to simplify the process of debugging by grouping repetitive or a required ordering of emulator commands, which can then be accessed by typing the name of the PROC. Literals are user-defined abbreviations for whole or partial ICE-960KB emulator commands. Literals are a shorthand method of customizing the emulator commands to fit your needs and preferences.

SPECIFICATIONS

HOST REQUIREMENTS

IBM PC-AT* (minimum requirements) with 640KB of
   conventional memory
1MB of RAM (Lotus, Intel, Microsoft expanded
   memory specification)
(Intel's Above™board with 1.0MB RAM is required)
20 MB Fixed Disk
At least one 5¼" Floppy Disk drive
A serial interface
80287 Numerics Coprocessor
DOS Operating System (version 3.3)

REQUIRED SYSTEM RESOURCES

The ICE-960KB emulator requires the following: a) exclusive use of the 80960KA/KB's on-chip debug registers and b) 304 bytes of target system RAM in the register save area of the stack, 256 bytes for flushing the 80960 local registers, and 48 bytes for saving the processor control block (PRCB).

SPECIFICATIONS

MECHANICAL SPECIFICATIONS

TABLE 1. ICE-960KB Emulator Physical Characteristics

Unit	Width Inches	Width cm	Height Inches	Height cm	Length Inches	Length cm	Weight lbs	Weight kg
Control unit	10.5	26.7	1.5	3.8	16.0	40.6	6.0	2.72
Processor module*	3.8	9.6	1.5	3.8	5.0	12.7		
SAST	6.0	15.2	2.0	5.1	8.0	20.3	3.5	1.59
OIB	3.8	9.6	.9	2.3	5.1	13.0		
Power supply	2.8	7.1	4.2	10.7	11.0	27.9	4.7	2.14
User cable					22.0	55.9		
Serial cable					12.0'	3.66m		

*measurement includes target adaptor

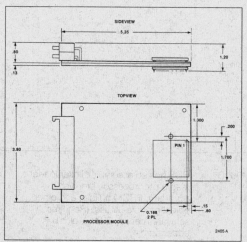

Figure 1: Processor Module

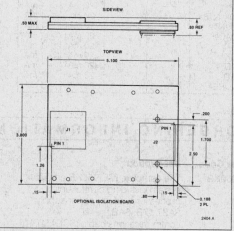

Figure 2: Optional Isolation

ELECTRICAL SPECIFICATIONS

SYNC Line Specification

The SYNCIN line must be valid for at least one instruction cycle because it is only sampled on instruction boundaries. The SYNCIN line is a standard TTL input. The SYNCOUT line is driven by a TTL open collector with a 4.75K-ohm pull-up resistor.

AD/DC Specifications

The following tables describe the DC specification differences between the ICE-960KB emulator and the 80960KA/KB microprocessor, for more details refer to the User Guide.

TABLE 2. AC Specifications With The OIB Installed

Symbol*	Parameter	Minimum	Maximum
t2	clock low time	t2 + 1nS	
t3	clock high time	t3 + 1ns	
t6	output valid delay		
	A/D 0:31	t6 + 8nS	t6 + 16Ns
	DT/R#,DEN#,BE0-3#,		
	ADS#,W/R#	t6 + 7nS	t6 + 14ns
	HLDA,CACHE,LOCK#,INTA#	t6 + 6nS	t6 + 8nS
	ALE#	t6 + 10nS	t6 + 20nS
t7	ALE# width	t7-6.5nS	
t8	ALE# disable delay	t8 + 8nS	t8 + 14nS
t9	output float delay		
	A/D 0:31	t9 + 5nS	t9 + 22nS
	DT/R#,DEN#,BEO-3#,		
	ADS#,W/R#	t9 + 7nS	t9 + 15ns
	HLDA,CACHE,LOCK#,INTA#	t9 + 6nS	t9 + 8nS
t10	input setup 1		
	A/D 0:31	t10 + 2nS	
	BADAC#,INT0-3# deassertion	t10 + 14nS	
t11	input hold		
	A/D 0:31, HOLD	t11 + 6nS	
	BADAC#,INT0-3#,READY#	t11 + 7nS	
t16	reset setup time	t16 + 6	

*symbol refers to 80960KB specification

TABLE 3. ICE-960KB Emulator DC Specifications

Symbol	Parameter	Maximum
PM-I_{CC}	Supply current with 80960KB-20	1400mA
OIB-I_{CC}	Supply current	PM-I_{CC} +1100mA

TABLE 4. Additional DC Loading

	(without OIB installed)		(with OIB installed)	
Signal	Iih Maximum	Iil Maximum	Iih Maximum	Iil Maximum
AD(0:31)	100 mA	0.6 mA	20 mA	– 1 mA
DEN#	40 mA	1.0 mA	20 mA	– 1 mA
W/R#	140 mA	1.6 mA	20 mA	– 1 mA
ADS#	140 mA	1.6 mA	20 mA	– 1 mA
CLK2	80 mA	2.2 mA	50 mA	– 2 mA
RESET			50 mA	– 2 mA
BE(0:3)#			20 mA	– 1 mA
DT/R#			20 mA	– 1 mA
INT0#,INT3#			20 mA	– 1 mA
INT1,INT2			20 mA	– 1 mA
BADAC#			20 mA	– 1 mA
ALE#			20 mA	– 1 mA
LOCK#			20 mA	– 1 mA
READY#			20 mA	– 1 mA
HOLD			20 mA	– 1 mA
FAILURE#			20 mA	– 1 mA

Power Supply

100-120V or 220-240V (Selectable)
50-60 Hz
2 amps (AC Max) @ 120V
1 amp (AC Max) @ 240V

Environmental Characteristics

Operating Temperature 10 C to 40 C (50 F to 104 F)
Operating Humidity Maximum 85% Relative
Humidity, non-condensing

ORDERING INFORMATION

Order Code	Description
ICE960KB	The complete ICE-960KB emulator system including control unit, processor module, power supply, SAST, OIB, SAB, serial communications cable (SCOM4), IEDIT, software version 1.x, and upgrade certificate for version 2.0 software. (Requires software license, Class I)
ICE960KBAB	The complete ICE-690KB emulator system including control unit, processor module, power supply, SAST, OIB, serial communications cable (SCOM4), IEDIT, software version 1.x, upgrade certificate for version 2.0 software, and 2MB Aboveboard. (Requires software license, Class I)
ICE960KB01	The complete ICE-960KB emulator system including control unit, processor module, power supply, SAST, OIB, serial communications cable (SCOM4), IEDIT, software version 1.x (version 2.0 software is not included). (Requires software license, Class I)

ASM960D DOS hosted assembler, linker/loader, macro preprocessor, archiver (librarian), PROM builder, and other object module utilities. (Requires software license, Class I, plus addendum 1)

C960D DOS hosted optimizing C compiler, with ANSI extensions for embedded applications, contains standard STDIO libraries and has inline assembly capability. Requires a 2M byte Above™board. (Requires software license, Class I)

For direct information on Intel's Development Tools, or for the number of your nearest sales office or distributor, call 800-874-6835 (U.S.). For information or literature on additional Intel products, call 800-548-4725 (U.S. and Canada).

*IBM PC/AT is a trademark of IBM

LOW COST EVALUATION TOOL

The QT960 products give you a 32-bit starter kit to begin software evaluation and hardware design at a low cost. The boards feature the 20 MHz 80960KB 32-bit embedded processor. The 80960KB has integrated floating point, instruction and register caches, and an on-chip interrupt controller. The 80960K-series are the first in a new architectural family of embedded processors from Intel built using Intel's CHMOS IV† process. These boards provide you with full access to the features of the 80960KB processor. A wire wrap prototyping area offers you easy access to board features to test your designs. Interleaved EPROM means fast execution of your code taking advantage of the 80960KB's burst bus. A programmable wait state generator simulates different memory environments useful in evaluating the performance of your code. These features make the QT960 boards useful low cost tools for the 32-bit embedded designer.

Once written, you can debug your program with NINDY, an EPROM resident debug monitor. NINDY enables you to download code, set seven different trace modes, display and modify memory or registers, and disassemble problem code sequences.

Available separately from Intel are the ASM-960 (assembly language) and iC-960 (high-level language) products which provide you with the code development environment for the QT960 boards.

The starter kit comes in two versions: the QT960F version has fast SRAM, high speed EPROM and Flash EPROM; the QT960E version has lower cost SRAM, no EPROM and Flash EPROM. Each version has NINDY in either EPROM (QT960F) or Flash EPROM (QT960E), power supply cable, and the QT960 User Manual. Both versions also include the parts list, source code of the debug monitor, and the board data base (schematics) all on diskette. Armed with this starter kit you now have a system to evaluate and prototype your product ideas quickly and at low cost.

QT 960 FEATURES

- 20 MHz Execution Speed
- 128K Bytes of Zero Wait State EPROM††
- 128K Bytes of Flash EPROM††
- 128K Bytes of Zero Wait State SRAM
- Programmable Wait State Generator
- Prototyping Wire Wrap Area
- Five Instruction Traces
- Two Hardware Breakpoints

- Display/Modify Memory and Registers
- Code Disassembly
- High Level Language Support
- RS-232 Communications Link
- The QT960E Version has 128K Bytes of Two Wait State SRAM and 128K Bytes Two Wait State EPROM

Product Order Codes: EVQT960F20 and EVQT960E20

†CHMOS IV is a patented Intel process.
††QT960F Version only.

FAST AND EASY CODE UPDATES

128K Bytes of Intel's 28F256 Flash EPROM provides an easy and quick method of changing your code in nonvolatile memory. Flash EPROM may be conveniently reprogrammed without removing it from the board while software is under development.

FAST EPROM

Interleaved fast EPROM (Intel's 27C202) on the QT960F version yields one-zero-zero-zero wait state code access. It efficiently utilizes the four word burst capabilities of the 80960KB bus maximizing program performance.

PROTOTYPING SUPPORT

A prototyping wire wrap area is provided on board with access to the system's signals and buses. This area gives you access to the board's features and allows you to easily test design ideas. A system bus connector is also provided for off board prototyping.

PROGRAMMABLE WAIT STATE GENERATOR

A software programmable wait state generator enables you to quickly model various memory speeds. Under software control you can set over 16 different wait state combinations and evaluate the performance of your target system.

DMA

The board offers you eight DMA channels accessed through a NINDY library function using Intel's 82380. In addition, off board connectors provide DMA I/O capabilities.

FIVE INSTRUCTION TRACES AND TWO HARDWARE BREAKPOINTS

NINDY utilizes the built-in trace capabilities of the 80960KB to provide you with single step, supervisor, call, return, and branch instruction tracing offering you extensive debug capabilities for software examination and modification. Two hardware breakpoints enable you to break on and examine EPROM resident code.

HIGH LEVEL LANGUAGE SUPPORT

NINDY is capable of downloading absolute object code generated by ASM-960 or iC-960. ASM-960 and iC-960 may be purchased separately from Intel.

COMMUNICATION AND SOFTWARE REQUIREMENTS

The QT960 boards communicate with the host through the RS-232 link using an Intel 82510 UART provided on board. The boards support five baud rates: 1200, 2400, 9600, 19200, and 38400. The default is 9600 baud. To communicate with the QT960 boards you must meet the following minimum software requirements:

■ Terminal Emulator   ■ XMODEM Download Capabilities

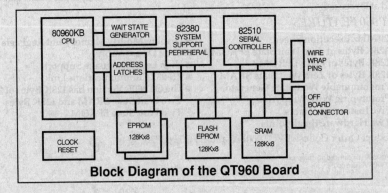

Block Diagram of the QT960 Board

```
                  PERFORMANCE STATISTICS
Number of instructions executed: 12022
Number of cycles: 6068
Total simulated time: 183.88 (micro seconds)
Speed: 65.38 MIPS (0.50 cycles per instruction)
Number of stack frames cached on chip: 8
Stack cache overflows: 0
Number of alignment errors: 0 (timing may be incorrect if > 0)  Warn: Yes
Cycles per second: 33000000
Bus utilization: 66 %
Waits: NRADWT=0 NRDDWT=0 NXDAWT=0 NWADWT=0 NWDDWT=0


                     Hits    Misses  Efficiency
Branch prediction:   1000       1    99.90 %


                          From Cache    From memory    Efficiency
Instruction words fetched:    15013            36       99.76 %


Instruction usage     Number  Percentage
Loads:                  1001     8.33
Stores:                 1001     8.33
Calls:                     1     0.01
Branches:               1002     8.33
```

SOFTWARE DEVELOPMENT TOOL FOR BENCHMARKING AND DEBUGGING 80960CA MICROPROCESSOR-BASED CODE

SIM960CA is a software simulator that emulates the instruction set of the 80960CA microprocessor. Designers can use SIM960CA to benchmark application performance and to develop and debug early 80960CA designs before 80960CA samples are available. Existing language tools such as iC960 and ASM960 can be used to develop 80960CA applications, minimizing time to market.

FEATURES

- Simulates 80960CA microprocessor
- Summarizes performance statistics, such as
  - execution speed (rated in MIPS)
  - number of cycles per instruction
  - Profile of instructions executed
    - leads, stores, calls and branches
  - bus utilization
  - 80960CA execution time between any two locations
  - branch prediction efficiency
- Display/Modification of memory and register contents

- Instruction disassembly
- Trace/break on instruction execution, address reads and writes
- Timing accuracy to + or − 5% ensuring accurate performance benchmarks
- Accepts iC960 or ASM960 COFF executable files and binary files as input
- Provides execution control − breakpoints and single stepping
- User-selectable clock, number of wait states

80960CA ARCHITECTURE SIMULATION

The SIM960CA Performance Simulator emulates the instruction set of the 80960CA microprocessor, allowing the user to specify wait states and clock speed for their target system. 80960CA applications can be developed and debugged before 80960CA component samples are available. Source code can be compiled using the 80960KX series C Compiler (iC960), Assembler (ASM960) and the resulting COFF executable file loaded into the 80960CA Performance Simulator for subsequent execution.

Using SIM960CA's trace capability, instruction execution, read and write activity at a particular location can be traced. Timing profiles of 80960CA operations are accurate to within plus or minus 5%. Estimates of actual 80960CA code performance can thus be made without an 80960CA-based target.

SIM960CA supports 80960-based C code such as standard procedures in LIBC, including STDIO routines such as PRINTF, MALLOC and MEMCPY.

PERFORMANCE STATISTICS

The SIM960CA Performance Simulator is used primarily to benchmark 80960CA performance gathering a wealth of statistics during 80960CA code execution. Some statistics that are gathered include:

- speed in MIPS (millions of instructions/sec.)
- number of cycles per instruction
- profile of instructions executed
- instructions fetched from memory
- number of instructions executed
- branch prediction efficiency
- total simulated 80960CA execution time (millionths of seconds)
- stack cache overflows
- instructions received from cache
- number of 80960CA clock cycles used
- bus utilization
- current clock speed (cycles/sec)
- wait state information

Performance statistics being gathered can be reset at any point, allowing performance analysis between any two locations. For example, execution time for a particular procedure can be measured. All timings, of course, are a function of the specified clock speed and number of wait states, selected by the user.

COMPLETE EXECUTION CONTROL

SIM960CA allows complete simulation control including control over where to begin or end the execution, number of instructions or clock cycles to execute, single stepping and the capability to execute an operating system command.

Above is a trademark of Intel Corporation. PC, XT and AT is a registered trademark of International Business Machines Corporation.

MULTIPLE DEBUG OPERATIONS

A variety of debug operations are available with SIM960CA. Users can trace instruction execution flow in a verbose or brief format. The brief format prints the address and instruction for each operation. Verbose format also prints out the cache, bus and instruction pipeline activity. 93 break or trace points can be set and deleted on instruction execution and memory read/writes. Instructions can be disassembled. Memory can be modifed or displayed in 32 bit hexadecimal, ASCII, octal or control character format. The user can flush the contents of the register cache for examination or fill memory with a specified value.

Users can also write a section of memory to a file and later read the contents of that binary file into memory.

HOST REQUIREMENTS

- IBM PC, XT or AT with 512KB of conventional memory
  (Intel Aboveboard with 2MB RAM is required for iC960 C Compiler)
- At least one 5¼″ Floppy Disk drive (360KB capacity)
- DOS Operating System (version 3.3)

ORDERING INFORMATION

Order Code	Description
SIM960CAD	80960CA Performance Simulator software, version 1.0, hosted on MS-DOS, 5.25″ flexible diskette media. Includes SIM960CA Performance Simulator User's Manual.
SIM960CAV	80960CA Performance Simulator software, version 1.0, hosted on VAX/VMS, 4-track, 1600 BPI magnetic tape. Includes SIM960CA Performance Simulator User's Manual.
SIM960CAM	80960CA Performance Simulator software, version 1.0, hosted on MicroVAX/VMS, TK-50 cartridge tape. Includes SIM960CA Performance Simulator User's Manual.

For direct information on Intel's Development Tools, or for the number of your nearest sales office or distributor, call 800-874-6835 (U.S.). For information or literature on additional Intel products, call 800-548-4725 (U.S. and Canada).

intel®

iRMK™ 960 REAL-TIME KERNEL

- 32-bit real-time multi-tasking kernel for the i960™ microprocessor family
- Flexible, modular design to ease system integration
- Fast execution with predictable response time for time-critical applications
- Compact code size (14Kbytes-including all optional modules)

- Requires only an i960 KA, KB, or MC embedded processor
- Bus independent
- Easy customization and add-on enhancements
- Easily EPROMmable
- Comprehensive development tool support

THE 32-BIT REAL-TIME KERNEL OF CHOICE
FOR THE i960™ MICROPROCESSOR

The iRMK™ 960 Real-Time Kernel is the 32-bit real-time executive developed and supported by Intel, the i960™ architecture experts. The kernel is a small, fast and highly modular package of system control software. It contains the basic software building blocks that act as the foundation in using the key features of the i960 microprocessor. The iRMK 960 software is fully supported by an array of tools that work in the most popular development environments (i.e. DOS, VAX/VMS*, SUN**).

The iRMK 960 Real-Time Kernel is available off-the-shelf. The kernel reduces the cost and risk of designing and maintaining software for numerous real-time applications such as, embedded control systems and dedicated real-time subsystems in multiprocessor environment. Use of the kernel can save man years that might otherwise be spent developing or porting another real-time kernel. This means reduced time to market for the user.

June 1989

Order Number: 281006-001

ARCHITECTURAL OVERVIEW

At the heart of the architecture are the kernel core modules consisting of a scheduler, task manager, interrupt manager, and time manager (See Figure 1). As additional building blocks, the kernel provides optional modules consisting of a mailbox manager, semaphore manager, memory manager, on-processor interrupt controller manager, and fault handler manager. The optional device managers for the 82380 Integrated System Peripheral (ISP) and 8254 Programmable Interval Timer (PIT) complete the architecture.

FUNCTIONAL FEATURES

A Full Set Of Real-Time Building Blocks

The kernel provides a full set of services for real-time applications including task management, time management, sychronization of and communications between tasks, and memory pool management.

Task Management:

The iRMK 960 kernel uses system calls to create, manage, and schedule tasks in a multi-tasking environment. It provides pre-emptive priority scheduling combined with optional time-slice (round-robin) scheduling.

The scheduling algorithm used by the kernel enables tasks to be rescheduled in a fixed amount of time regardless of the number of tasks. Applications may contain any number of tasks.

An application can integrate optional task handlers to customize task management. These handlers can execute on task creation, task switch, task deletion, and task priority change. Task handlers can be used for a wide range of functions, including saving and restoring the state of coprocessor registers on task switch, masking interrupts based on task priority, or implementing statistical and diagnostic monitors.

Interrupt Management:

iRMK 960 interrupts are managed by immediately switching control to user-written interrupt handlers when an interrupt occurs.

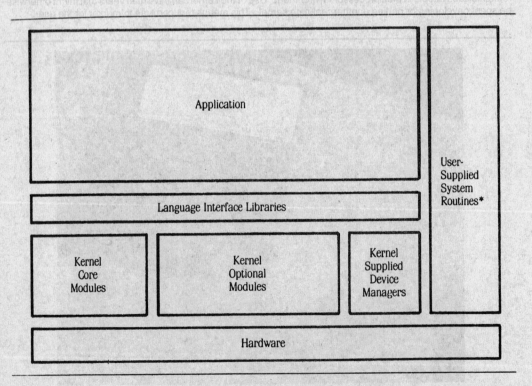

Figure 1: iRMK™ 960. Real-Time Kernel Architecture

Response to interrupts is both fast and predictable. Most of the kernel's system calls can be executed directly from interrupt handlers.

Time Management:

The time management features included in the kernel provide single-shot alarms, repetitive alarms, and a real-time clock. In addition, alarms can be reset.

These time management facilities can solve a wide range of real-time programming problems. Single-shot alarms, for example, can be used to handle timeouts. If the timeout occurs, the alarm invokes a user-written handler; if the event occurs before the timeout, the application simply deletes the alarm. Other uses for the kernel's time management facilities include polling devices with repetitive alarms, putting tasks to sleep for specifiec periods of time, or implementing a time-of-day clock.

Intertask Synchronization And Communication:

Semaphores, regions, and mailboxes are the key mechanisms the kernel uses for synchronizing tasks and communicating between tasks.

Semaphores are objects used for intertask signaling and synchronization. Tasks exchange abstract "units" with semaphores as a means of becoming synchronized. A task requests a unit from a semaphore to gain access to a resource. If the resource is available, the semaphore will have a unit to give to the task, enabling the task to proceed. A task sends a unit to a semaphore to indicate that it has released a previously obtained resource.

A special binary type of semaphore is called a Region. Regions are used to ensure mutual exclusion, thus preventing deadlock when tasks contend for control of system resources. A task holding a region's unit runs at the priority of the highest priority task waiting in queue for the region's unit.

Mailboxes are queues that can hold any number of messages and are used to exchange data between tasks. Either data or pointers can be sent using mailboxes. The kernel allows mailbox messages to be of any length. High priority messages can be placed (jammed) at the front of the message queue to ensure that they are received and processed before other messages queued at the mailbox.

To ensure that high priority tasks are not blocked by lower priority tasks, the kernel allows tasks to queue at semaphores and mailboxes in priority order. The kernel also supports first-in, first-out task queueing.

Memory Pool Management:

The iRMK 960 kernel uses the concept of memory pools to efficiently divide and manage blocks of memory. The memory pool manager provides for both fixed and variable block allocation.

Memory can be divided into any number of pools. Multiple memory pools might be created for different speed memories, or for allocating different size blocks. The times to allocate and de-allocate fixed-size areas from within a pool have a fixed upper bound.

The kernel-supplied memory manager works with flat memory architecture. Users can also write their own memory manager to provide different memory management policies or support virtual memory.

Hardware Requirements And Support

The kernel requires only an i960 microprocessor and sufficient memory for itself and its application. The kernel's design, however, recognizes that many systems use additional programmable peripheral devices and coprocessors. The kernel provides optional device managers for:

- The 82380 Intergrated System Peripheral (ISP) chip
- The 8254 Programmable Interval Timer (PIT) chip

An application can supply managers for other devices and coprocessors in addition to or in replacement of the devices listed above.

The openness of the iRMK 960 kernel is a major benefit to the OEM. The kernel is designed to be programmed into PROM or EPROM, making it easy to use in embedded designs. In addition, it can be used with any system bus, including those of MULTIBUS I and MULTIBUS II bus architectures.

A Modular Architecture For Easy Customization

The kernel is designed for maximum flexibility. It can be customized for any application. Each major function, mailboxes for example, is implemented as a separate module. The kernel's modules have not been linked together and are supplied individually. (See Table 1 for the list of kernel modules, and their approximate sizes.)

The user links only the modules needed for his application. Any module not used does not need to be linked in, and does not increase the size of the kernel in your application. The user can also replace any optional kernel module with one that implements specific features required by the application. For example, the user might want to replace the kernel's memory manager with one that supports virtual memory.

Table 1: iRMK™ 960 Kernel Modules And Approximate Sizes

Core Modules	Bytes
Task Manager	2600
Interrupt Manager	150
Time Manager	3000
Scheduler	1700
Initialization	50

Optional Modules	
Mailbox Manager	1250
Semaphore Manager	2900
Memory Manager	1260
Fault Handler Manager	50
Miscellaneous	300

Optional Device Managers	
82380 Integrated System Peripheral	4200
8254 Programmable Interval Timer	1200

Total size of the (entire) kernel (minus device managers) is about 13.5KBytes.

Developing With The iRMK™ 960 Real-Time Kernel

Kernel applications can be written using any language or compiler that produces code that executes on the i960 microprocessor. This independence is achieved by using an interface library. This library works with the idiosyncracies of a particular language — for example, the ordering of parameters. The interface library translates the calls provided by the language into a standard format expected by the kernel. Intel provides an interface library for our iC 960 compiler. The source code for this library is included, so that the user can modify it to support other compilers.

Because the kernel is supplied as unlinked object modules, applications can be developed on any system that hosts the development tools needed.

Comprehensive Development Tool Support

Intel provides a complete line of 80960 development tools for writing and debugging iRMK 960 applications. These tools include:

Software:	ASM 960 assembler
	iC 960 compiler

Note:	These tools are available for DOS, VAX/VMS*, MicroVAX*, SUN*, and EVA960KB4MB environment
Debuggers:	ICE™ 960 In-Circuit Emulator for the i960 microprocessor
	SDM™ 960 System Debug Monitor for the i960 microprocessor
Evaluation Vehicles	EVA960KB AT Bus-Compatible Board
	A960KB4MB AT Bus-Compatible Board with 4 MBytes of Memory
	QT960 Standalone Evaluation Vehicle

Intel Support, Consulting, And Training

With iRMK 960 kernel software, the developer has available the total Intel960™ architecture and real-time expertise of Intel's support engineers. Intel provides telephone support, on or off-site consulting, troubleshooting guides, and updates. The kernel includes 90 days of Intel's Technical Information Phone Service (TIPS). Extended support and consulting are also available.

Contents Of The iRMK™ 960 Kernel Development Package

The iRMK 960 Kernel comes in a comprehensive package Including:
- Kernel object modules
- Source for the kernel supplied 82380 Integrated System Peripheral and 8254 PIT device managers
- Source for the iC 960 interface library
- Source for sample applications showing the following:
  - Structure of kernel applications
  - Use of the kernel with an application written in iC 960 language
  - Compile, bind, and build sequences
  - Sample initialization code for the i960 microprocessor
  - Applications written to execute in a flat memory space
- User reference guide
- 90 days of customer support

LICENSING

iRMK 960 software requires prior execution of the standard Intel Software License Agreement (SLA). A single development copy requires a Class I license and allows iRMK 960 software to be loaded and run on one single-processor system.

SPECIFICATIONS

System Calls

The following items are system calls arranged by type:

iRMK 960 KERNEL SYSTEM CALLS LISTING

KERNEL INITIALIZATION

KN_initialize	Initialize kernel

OBJECT MANAGEMENT

KN_token_to_ptr	Returns a pointer to the area holding object
KN_current_task	Returns a pointer for the current task

TASK MANAGEMENT

KN_create_task	Creates a task
KN_delete_task	Deletes a task
KN_suspend_task	Suspends a task
KN_resume_task	Resumes a task
KN_set_priority	Change priority of a task
KN_get_priority	Return priority of a task

INTERRUPT MANAGEMENT

KN_set_interrupt	Specify interrupt handler
KN_stop_scheduling	Suspend task switching
KN_start_scheduling	Resume task switching

TIME MANAGEMENT

KN_sleep	Put calling task to sleep
KN_create_alarm	Create and start virtual alarm clock
KN_reset_alarm	Reset an existing alarm
KN_delete_alarm	Delete alarm
KN_get_time	Get time
KN_set_time	Set time
KN_tick	Notify kernel that clock tick has occurred

INTERTASK COMMUNICATION AND SYNCHRONIZATION

KN_create_semaphore	Create a semaphore
KN_delete_semaphore	Delete a semaphore
KN_send_unit	Add a unit to a semaphore
KN_receive_unit	Receive a unit from a semaphore
KN_create_mailbox	Create a mailbox
KN_delete_mailbox	Delete a mailbox
KN_send_data	Send data to a mailbox
KN_send_priority_data	Place (jam) priority message at head of message queue
KN_receive_data	Request a message from a mailbox

MEMORY MANAGEMENT

KN_create_pool	Create a memory pool
KN_delete_pool	Delete a memory pool
KN_create_area	Create a memory area from a pool
KN_delete_area	Return a memory area to a memory pool
KN_get_pool_attributes	Get a memory pool's attributes

PROGRAMMABLE INTERRUPT CONTROLLER MANAGEMENT

KN_initialize_PICs	Initialize the PIC's
KN_mask_slot	Mask out interrupts on a specified slot
KN_unmask_slot	Unmask interrupts on a specified slot
KN_send_EOI	Signal the PIC that the interrupt on a specified slot has been serviced
KN_new_masks	Change interrupt masks
KN_get_slot	Return the most important active interrupt slot
KN_get_interrupt	Get address of specified interrupt handler

PROGRAMMABLE INTERVAL CONTROLLER MANAGEMENT

KN_initialize_PIT	Initialize the PIT
KN_start_PIT	Start PIT counting
KN_get_PIT_interval	Return PIT interval

PROCESSOR RECOGNIZED FAULT HANDLING

KN_get_fault_handler	Get address of fault handler currently associated with specified fault type
KN_set_fault_handler	Establish address of fault handler for the specified fault type

PROCESSOR INTERRUPT CONTROLLER SUPPORT

KN_get_processor_ _priority	Returns value of the processor
KN_set_processor_ _priority	Change the value of the processor priority

Performance

The figures listed below were derived from a test suite running on a EVA-960 evaluation vehicle using an 80960KB running at 20 MHz. The EVA-960 has what is known as 2-1-1-1 wait-state memory; what this means is that the first instruction of a four instruction fetch takes two wait states, and each of the three successive instructions takes one wait state. The figures are the worst case values obtained from several sets of test runs. The code was generated using the iC 960 DOS hosted compiler, Version 1.1

ACTION	TIME (in usec)
Create Pool	18
Get Pool Attributes	36
Delete Pool	1
Create Area	35
Delete Area	32
Create Semaphore	6
Delete Semaphore	14
FIFO Semaphore Send Unit	7
FIFO Semaphore Receive Unit	7
Region Semaphore Send Unit	18
Region Semaphore Receive Unit	14
Create Mailbox	19
Delete Mailbox	23
Send Data	21
Receive Data	21
Create Alarm	29
Delete Alarm	30
FIFO Semaphore Send/Receive Unit w/Task Switch	75
Suspend Task w Task Switch	70
Basic Task Switch	50
Create Task	62
Suspend Task	26
Resume Task	50
Delete Task	50
Get Priority	5
Set Priority	27
Set Interrupt	3
Get Interrupt	3

MANUALS

iRMK 960 User's Manual (Intel Order # 463863-001).

TRAINING INFORMATION

Intel Customer Service Training

"80960 KA/KB Embedded Processor Training Course"

ORDERING INFORMATION

Order Code	Product Description
RMK960	iRMK 960 Real-Time Kernel

376™ Embedded Processor & Peripherals Data Sheets

8

376™ HIGH PERFORMANCE
32-BIT EMBEDDED PROCESSOR

- **Full 32-Bit Internal Architecture**
  - 8-, 16-, 32-Bit Data Types
  - 8 General Purpose 32-Bit Registers
  - Extensive 32-Bit Instruction Set
- **High Performance 16-Bit Data Bus**
  - 16 MHz CPU Clock
  - Two-Clock Bus Cycles
  - 16 Mbytes/Sec Bus Bandwidth
- **16 Mbyte Physical Memory Size**
- **High Speed Numerics Support with the 80387SX**
- **Low System Cost with the 82370 Integrated System Peripheral**
- **On-Chip Debugging Support Including Break Point Registers**

- **Complete Intel Development Support**
  - C, PL/M, Assembler
  - ICE™-376, In-Circuit Emulator
  - iRMK™ Real Time Kernel
  - iSDM™ Debug Monitor
  - DOS Based Debug
- **Extensive Third-Party Support:**
  - Languages: C, Pascal, FORTRAN, BASIC and ADA*
  - Hosts: VMS*, UNIX*, MS-DOS*, and Others
  - Real-Time Kernels
- **High Speed CHMOS Technology**
- **Available in 100 Pin Plastic Quad Flat-Pack Package and 88-Pin Pin Grid Array**
  (See Packaging Outlines and Dimensions #231369)

INTRODUCTION

The 376 32-bit embedded processor is designed for high performance embedded systems. It provides the performance benefits of a highly pipelined 32-bit internal architecture with the low system cost associated with 16-bit hardware systems. The 80376 is based on the 80386 and offers a high degree of compatibility with the 80386. All 80386 32-bit programs not dependent on paging can be executed on the 80376 and all 80376 programs can be executed on the 80386. All 32-bit 80386 language translators can be used for software development. With proper support software, any 80386-based computer can be used to develop and test 80376 programs. In addition, any 80386-based PC-AT* compatible computer can be used for hardware proto-typing for designs based on the 80376 and its companion product the 82370.

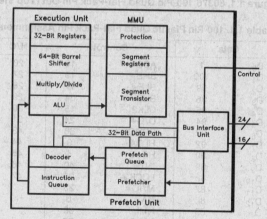

80376 Microarchitecture

240182–48

October 1989
Order Number: 240182-003

1.0 PIN DESCRIPTION

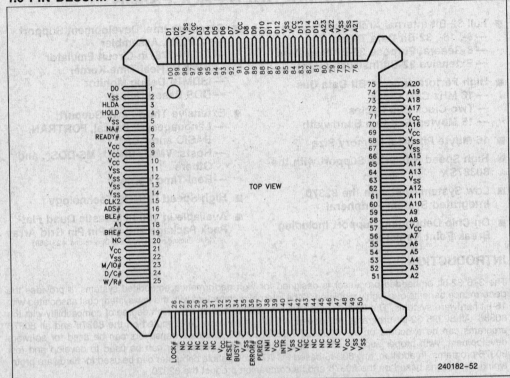

Figure 1.1. 80376 100-Pin Quad Flat-Pack Pin Out (Top View)

Table 1.1. 100-Pin Plastic Quad Flat-Pack Pin Assignments

Address		Data		Control		N/C	V_CC	V_SS
A_1	18	D_0	1	ADS#	16	20	8	2
A_2	51	D_1	100	BHE#	19	27	9	5
A_3	52	D_2	99	BLE#	17	28	10	11
A_4	53	D_3	96	BUSY#	34	29	21	12
A_5	54	D_4	95	CLK2	15	30	32	13
A_6	55	D_5	94	D/C#	24	31	39	14
A_7	56	D_6	93	ERROR#	36	43	42	22
A_8	58	D_7	92	HLDA	3	44	48	35
A_9	59	D_8	90	HOLD	4	45	57	41
A_{10}	60	D_9	89	INTR	40	46	69	49
A_{11}	61	D_{10}	88	LOCK#	26	47	71	50
A_{12}	62	D_{11}	87	M/IO#	23		84	63
A_{13}	64	D_{12}	86	NA#	6		91	67
A_{14}	65	D_{13}	83	NMI	38		97	68
A_{15}	66	D_{14}	82	PEREQ	37			77
A_{16}	70	D_{15}	81	READY#	7			78
A_{17}	72			RESET	33			85
A_{18}	73			W/R#	25			98
A_{19}	74							
A_{20}	75							
A_{21}	76							
A_{22}	79							
A_{23}	80							

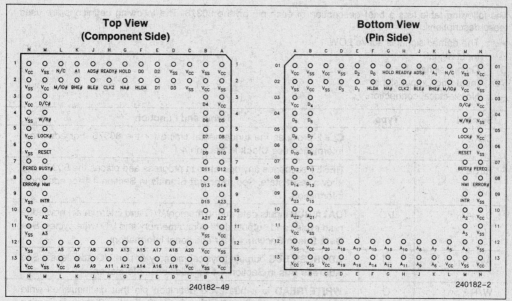

Figure 1.2. 80376 88-Pin Grid Array Pin Out

Table 1.2. 88-Pin Grid Array Pin Assignments

Pin	Label	Pin	Label	Pin	Label	Pin	Label
2H	CLK2	12D	A_{18}	2L	M/IO#	11A	V_{CC}
9B	D_{15}	12E	A_{17}	5M	LOCK#	13A	V_{CC}
8A	D_{14}	13E	A_{16}	1J	ADS#	13C	V_{CC}
8B	D_{13}	12F	A_{15}	1H	READY#	13L	V_{CC}
7A	D_{12}	13F	A_{14}	2G	NA#	1N	V_{CC}
7B	D_{11}	12G	A_{13}	1G	HOLD	13N	V_{CC}
6A	D_{10}	13G	A_{12}	2F	HLDA	11B	V_{SS}
6B	D_9	13H	A_{11}	7N	PEREQ	2C	V_{SS}
5A	D_8	12H	A_{10}	7M	BUSY#	1D	V_{SS}
5B	D_7	13J	A_9	8N	ERROR#	1M	V_{SS}
4B	D_6	12J	A_8	9M	INTR	4N	V_{SS}
4A	D_5	12K	A_7	8M	NMI	9N	V_{SS}
3B	D_4	13K	A_6	6M	RESET	11N	V_{SS}
2D	D_3	12L	A_5	2B	V_{CC}	2A	V_{SS}
1E	D_2	12M	A_4	12B	V_{CC}	12A	V_{SS}
2E	D_1	11M	A_3	1C	V_{CC}	1B	V_{SS}
1F	D_0	10M	A_2	2M	V_{CC}	13B	V_{SS}
9A	A_{23}	1K	A_1	3N	V_{CC}	13M	V_{SS}
10A	A_{22}	2J	BLE#	5N	V_{CC}	2N	V_{SS}
10B	A_{21}	2K	BHE#	10N	V_{CC}	6N	V_{SS}
12C	A_{20}	4M	W/R#	1A	V_{CC}	12N	V_{SS}
13D	A_{19}	3M	D/C#	3A	V_{CC}	1L	N/C

The following table lists a brief description of each pin on the 80376. The following definitions are used in these descriptions:

\#   The named signal is active LOW.
I   Input signal.
O   Output signal.
I/O   Input and Output signal.
—   No electrical connection.

Symbol	Type	Name and Function
CLK2	I	**CLK2** provides the fundamental timing for the 80376. For additional information see **Clock** in Section 4.1.
RESET	I	**RESET** suspends any operation in progress and places the 80376 in a known reset state. See **Interrupt Signals** in Section 4.1 for additional information.
$D_{15}-D_0$	I/O	**DATA BUS** inputs data during memory, I/O and interrupt acknowledge read cycles and outputs data during memory and I/O write cycles. See **Data Bus** in Section 4.1 for additional information.
$A_{23}-A_1$	O	**ADDRESS BUS** outputs physical memory or port I/O addresses. See **Address Bus** in Section 4.1 for additional information.
W/R\#	O	**WRITE/READ** is a bus cycle definition pin that distinguishes write cycles from read cycles. See **Bus Cycle Definition Signals** in Section 4.1 for additional information.
D/C\#	O	**DATA/CONTROL** is a bus cycle definition pin that distinguishes data cycles, either memory or I/O, from control cycles which are: interrupt acknowledge, halt, and instruction fetching. See **Bus Cycle Definition Signals** in Section 4.1 for additional information.
M/IO\#	O	**MEMORY I/O** is a bus cycle definition pin that distinguishes memory cycles from input/output cycles. See **Bus Cycle Definition Signals** in Section 4.1 for additional information.
LOCK\#	O	**BUS LOCK** is a bus cycle definition pin that indicates that other system bus masters are denied access to the system bus while it is active. See **Bus Cycle Definition Signals** in Section 4.1 for additional information.
ADS\#	O	**ADDRESS STATUS** indicates that a valid bus cycle definition and address (W/R\#, D/C\#, M/IO\#, BHE\#, BLE\# and $A_{23}-A_1$) are being driven at the 80376 pins. See **Bus Control Signals** in Section 4.1 for additional information.
NA\#	I	**NEXT ADDRESS** is used to request address pipelining. See **Bus Control Signals** in Section 4.1 for additional information.
READY\#	I	**BUS READY** terminates the bus cycle. See **Bus Control Signals** in Section 4.1 for additional information.
BHE\#, BLE\#	O	**BYTE ENABLES** indicate which data bytes of the data bus take part in a bus cycle. See **Address Bus** in Section 4.1 for additional information.
HOLD	I	**BUS HOLD REQUEST** input allows another bus master to request control of the local bus. See **Bus Arbitration Signals** in Section 4.1 for additional information.

Symbol	Type	Name and Function
HLDA	O	**BUS HOLD ACKNOWLEDGE** output indicates that the 80376 has surrendered control of its local bus to another bus master. See **Bus Arbitration Signals** in Section 4.1 for additional information.
INTR	I	**INTERRUPT REQUEST** is a maskable input that signals the 80376 to suspend execution of the current program and execute an interrupt acknowledge function. See **Interrupt Signals** in Section 4.1 for additional information.
NMI	I	**NON-MASKABLE INTERRUPT REQUEST** is a non-maskable input that signals the 80376 to suspend execution of the current program and execute an interrupt acknowledge function. See **Interrupt Signals** in Section 4.1 for additional information.
BUSY#	I	**BUSY** signals a busy condition from a processor extension. See **Coprocessor Interface Signals** in Section 4.1 for additional information.
ERROR#	I	**ERROR** signals an error condition from a processor extension. See **Coprocessor Interface Signals** in Section 4.1 for additional information.
PEREQ	I	**PROCESSOR EXTENSION REQUEST** indicates that the processor extension has data to be transferred by the 80376. See **Coprocessor Interface Signals** in Section 4.1 for additional information.
N/C	—	**NO CONNECT** should always remain unconnected. Connection of a N/C pin may cause the processor to malfunction or be incompatible with future steppings of the 80376.
V_{CC}	I	**SYSTEM POWER** provides the +5V nominal D.C. supply input.
V_{SS}	I	**SYSTEM GROUND** provides 0V connection from which all inputs and outputs are measured.

2.0 ARCHITECTURE OVERVIEW

The 80376 supports the protection mechanisms needed by sophisticated multitasking embedded systems and real-time operating systems. The use of these protection mechanisms is completely optional. For embedded applications not needing protection, the 80376 can easily be configured to provide a 16 Mbyte physical address space.

Instruction pipelining, high bus bandwidth, and a very high performance ALU ensure short average instruction execution times and high system throughput. The 80376 is capable of execution at sustained rates of 2.5–3.0 million instructions per second.

The 80376 offers on-chip testability and debugging features. Four break point registers allow conditional or unconditional break point traps on code execution or data accesses for powerful debugging of even ROM based systems. Other testability features include self-test and tri-stating of output buffers during RESET.

The Intel 80376 embedded processor consists of a central processing unit, a memory management unit and a bus interface. The central processing unit con-

sists of the execution unit and instruction unit. The execution unit contains the eight 32-bit general registers which are used for both address calculation and data operations and a 64-bit barrel shifter used to speed shift, rotate, multiply, and divide operations. The instruction unit decodes the instruction opcodes and stores them in the decoded instruction queue for immediate use by the execution unit.

The Memory Management Unit (MMU) consists of a segmentation and protection unit. Segmentation allows the managing of the logical address space by providing an extra addressing component, one that allows easy code and data relocatability, and efficient sharing.

The protection unit provides four levels of protection for isolating and protecting applications and the operating system from each other. The hardware enforced protection allows the design of systems with a high degree of integrity and simplifies debugging.

Finally, to facilitate high performance system hardware designs, the 80376 bus interface offers address pipelining and direct Byte Enable signals for each byte of the data bus.

2.1 Register Set

The 80376 has twenty-nine registers as shown in Figure 2.1. These registers are grouped into the following six categories:

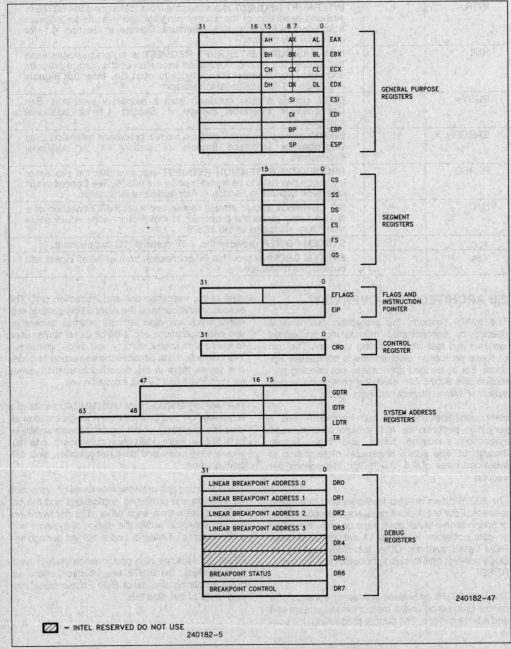

Figure 2.1. 80376 Base Architecture Registers

General Registers: The eight 32-bit general purpose registers are used to contain arithmetic and logical operands. Four of these (EAX, EBX, ECX and EDX) can be used either in their entirety as 32-bit registers, as 16-bit registers, or split into pairs of separate 8-bit registers.

Segment Registers: Six 16-bit special purpose registers select, at any given time, the segments of memory that are immediately addressable for code, stack, and data.

Flags and Instruction Pointer Registers: These two 32-bit special purpose registers in Figure 2.1 record or control certain aspects of the 80376 processor state. The EFLAGS register includes status and control bits that are used to reflect the outcome of many instructions and modify the semantics of some instructions. The Instruction Pointer, called EIP, is 32 bits wide. The Instruction Pointer controls instruction fetching and the processor automatically increments it after executing an instruction.

Control Register: The 32-bit control register, CR0, is used to control Coprocessor Emulation.

System Address Registers: These four special registers reference the tables or segments supported by the 80376/80386 protection model. These tables or segments are:

GDTR (Global Descriptor Table Register),
IDTR (Interrupt Descriptor Table Register),
LDTR (Local Descriptor Table Register),
TR (Task State Segment Register).

Debug Registers: The six programmer accessible debug registers provide on-chip support for debugging. The use of the debug registers is described in Section 2.11 **Debugging Support**.

EFLAGS REGISTER

The flag Register is a 32-bit register named EFLAGS. The defined bits and bit fields within EFLAGS, shown in Figure 2.2, control certain operations and indicate the status of the 80376 processor. The function of the flag bits is given in Table 2.1.

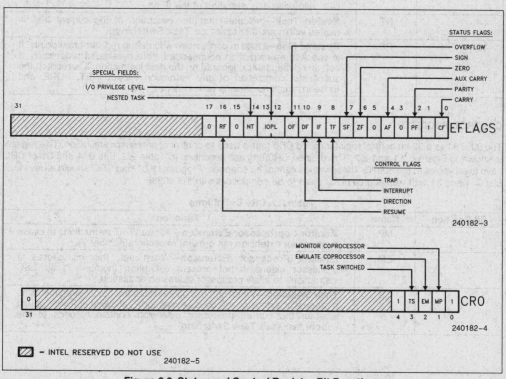

Figure 2.2. Status and Control Register Bit Functions

Table 2.1. Flag Definitions

Bit Position	Name	Function
0	CF	**Carry Flag**—Set on high-order bit carry or borrow; cleared otherwise.
2	PF	**Parity Flag**—Set if low-order 8 bits of result contain an even number of 1-bits; cleared otherwise.
4	AF	**Auxiliary Carry Flag**—Set on carry from or borrow to the low order four bits of AL; cleared otherwise.
6	ZF	**Zero Flag**—Set if result is zero; cleared otherwise.
7	SF	**Sign Flag**—Set equal to high-order bit of result (0 if positive, 1 if negative).
8	TF	**Single Step Flag**—Once set, a single step interrupt occurs after the next instruction executes. TF is cleared by the single step interrupt.
9	IF	**Interrupt-Enable Flag**—When set, external interrupts signaled on the INTR pin will cause the CPU to transfer control to an interrupt vector specified location.
10	DF	**Direction Flag**—Causes string instructions to auto-increment (default) the appropriate index registers when cleared. Setting DF causes auto-decrement.
11	OF	**Overflow Flag**—Set if the operation resulted in a carry/borrow into the sign bit (high-order bit) of the result but did not result in a carry/borrow out of the high-order bit or vice-versa.
12, 13	IOPL	**I/O Privilege Level**—Indicates the maximum CPL permitted to execute I/O instructions without generating an exception 13 fault or consulting the I/O permission bit map. It also indicates the maximum CPL value allowing alteration of the IF bit.
14	NT	**Nested Task**—Indicates that the execution of the current task is nested within another task (see **Task Switching**).
16	RF	**Resume Flag**—Used in conjunction with debug register breakpoints. It is checked at instruction boundaries before breakpoint processing. If set, any debug fault is ignored on the next instruction. It is reset at the successful completion of any instruction except IRET, POPF, and those instructions causing task switches.

CONTROL REGISTER

The 80376 has a 32-bit control register called CR0 that is used to control coprocessor emulation. This register is shown in Figures, 2.1 and 2.2. The defined CR0 bits are described in Table 2.2. Bits 0, 4 and 31 of CR0 have fixed values in the 80376. These values cannot be changed. Programs that load CR0 should always load bits 0, 4 and 31 with values previously there to be compatible with the 80386.

Table 2.2. CR0 Definitions

Bit Position	Name	Function
1	MP	**Monitor Coprocessor Extension**—Allows WAIT instructions to cause a processor extension not present exception (number 7).
2	EM	**Emulate Processor Extension**—When set, this bit causes a processor extension not present exception (number 7) on ESC instructions to allow processor extension emulation.
3	TS	**Task Switched**—When set, this bit indicates the next instruction using a processor extension will cause exception 7, allowing software to test whether the current processor extension context belongs to the current task (see **Task Switching**).

2.2 Instruction Set

The instruction set is divided into nine categories of operations:

    Data Transfer
    Arithmetic
    Shift/Rotate
    String Manipulation
    Bit Manipulation
    Control Transfer
    High Level Language Support
    Operating System Support
    Processor Control

These 80376 processor instructions are listed in Table 8.1 **80376 Instruction Set and Clock Count Summary**.

All 80376 processor instructions operate on either 0, 1, 2 or 3 operands; an operand resides in a register, in the instruction itself, or in memory. Most zero operand instructions (e.g. CLI, STI) take only one byte. One operand instructions generally are two bytes long. The average instruction is 3.2 bytes long. Since the 80376 has a 16-byte prefetch instruction queue an average of 5 instructions can be prefetched. The use of two operands permits the following types of common instructions:

    Register to Register
    Memory to Register
    Immediate to Register
    Memory to Memory
    Register to Memory
    Immediate to Memory

The operands are either 8-, 16- or 32-bit long.

2.3 Memory Organization

Memory on the 80376 is divided into 8-bit quantities (bytes), 16-bit quantities (words), and 32-bit quantities (dwords). Words are stored in two consecutive bytes in memory with the low-order byte at the lowest address. Dwords are stored in four consecutive bytes in memory with the low-order byte at the lowest address. The address of a word or Dword is the byte address of the low-order byte. For maximum performance word and dword values should be at even physical addresses.

In addition to these basic data types the 80376 processor supports segments. Memory can be divided up into one or more variable length segments, which can be shared between programs.

ADDRESS SPACES

The 80376 has three types of address spaces: **logical, linear,** and **physical.** A **logical** address (also known as a **virtual** address) consists of a selector and an offset. A selector is the contents of a segment register. An offset is formed by summing all of the addressing components (BASE, INDEX, and DISPLACEMENT), discussed in Section 2.4 **Addressing Modes,** into an effective address.

Every selector has a **logical base** address associated with it that can be up to 32 bits in length. This 32-bit **logical base** address is added to either a 32-bit offset address or a 16-bit offset address (by using the *address length prefix*)to form a final 32-bit **linear** address. This final **linear** address is then truncated so that only the lower 24 bits of this address are used to address the 16 Mbytes physical memory address space. The **logical base** address is stored in one of two operating system tables (i.e. the Local Descriptor Table or Global Descriptor Table).

Figure 2.3 shows the relationship between the various address spaces.

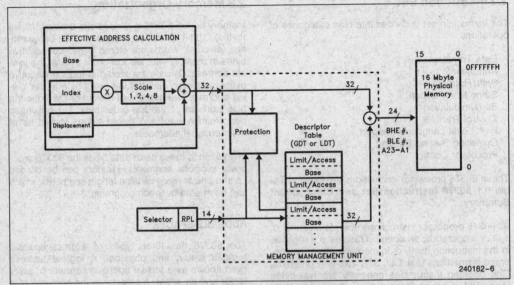

Figure 2.3. Address Translation

SEGMENT REGISTER USAGE

The main data structure used to organize memory is the segment. On the 80376, segments are variable sized blocks of linear addresses which have certain attributes associated with them. There are two main types of segments, code and data. The simplest use of segments is to have one code and data segment. Each segment is 16 Mbytes in size overlapping each other. This allows code and data to be directly addressed by the same offset.

In order to provide compact instruction encoding and increase processor performance, instructions do not need to explicitly specify which segment reg-

ister is used. The segment register is automatically chosen according to the rules of Table 2.3 (Segment Register Selection Rules). In general, data references use the selector contained in the DS register, stack references use the SS register and instruction fetches use the CS register. The contents of the Instruction Pointer provide the offset. Special segment override prefixes allow the explicit use of a given segment register, and override the implicit rules listed in Table 2.3. The override prefixes also allow the use of the ES, FS and GS segment registers.

There are no restrictions regarding the overlapping of the base addresses of any segments. Thus, all 6 segments could have the base address set to zero. Further details of segmentation are discussed in Section 3.0 Architecture.

Table 2.3. Segment Register Selection Rules

Type of Memory Reference	Implied (Default) Segment Use	Segment Override Prefixes Possible
Code Fetch	CS	None
Destination of PUSH, PUSHF, INT, CALL, PUSHA Instructions	SS	None
Source of POP, POPA, POPF, IRET, RET Instructions	SS	None
Destination of STOS, MOVS, REP STOS, REP MOVS Instructions (DI is Base Register)	ES	None
Other Data References, with Effective Address Using Base Register of:		
[EAX]	DS	CS, SS, ES, FS, GS
[EBX]	DS	CS, SS, ES, FS, GS
[ECX]	DS	CS, SS, ES, FS, GS
[EDX]	DS	CS, SS, ES, FS, GS
[ESI]	DS	CS, SS, ES, FS, GS
[EDI]	DS	CS, SS, ES, FS, GS
[EBP]	SS	CS, SS, ES, FS, GS
[ESP]	SS	CS, SS, ES, FS, GS

2.4 Addressing Modes

The 80376 provides a total of 8 addressing modes for instructions to specify operands. The addressing modes are optimized to allow the efficient execution of high level languages such as C and FORTRAN, and they cover the vast majority of data references needed by high-level languages.

Two of the addressing modes provide for instructions that operate on register or immediate operands:

Register Operand Mode: The operand is located in one of the 8-, 16- or 32-bit general registers.

Immediate Operand Mode: The operand is included in the instruction as part of the opcode.

The remaining 6 modes provide a mechanism for specifying the effective address of an operand. The linear address consists of two components: the seg-ment base address and an effective address. The effective address is calculated by summing any combination of the following three address elements (see Figure 2.3):

DISPLACEMENT: an 8-, 16- or 32-bit immediate value following the instruction.

BASE: The contents of any general purpose register. The base registers are generally used by compilers to point to the start of the local variable area. Note that if the **Address Length Prefix** is used, only BX and BP can be used as a BASE register.

INDEX: The contents of any general purpose register except for ESP. The index registers are used to access the elements of an array, or a string of characters. The index register's value can be multiplied by a scale factor, either 1, 2, 4 or 8. The scaled index is especially useful for accessing arrays or structures. Note that if the **Address Length Prefix** is used, no Scaling is available and only the registers SI and DI can be used to INDEX.

Combinations of these 3 components make up the 6 additional addressing modes. There is no performance penalty for using any of these addressing combinations, since the effective address calculation is pipelined with the execution of other instructions. The one exception is the simultaneous use of BASE and INDEX components which requires one additional clock.

As shown in Figure 2.4, the effective address (EA) of an operand is calculated according to the following formula:

$$EA = BASE_{Register} + (INDEX_{Register} \times scaling) + DISPLACEMENT$$

1. **Direct Mode:** The operand's offset is contained as part of the instruction as an 8-, 16- or 32-bit DISPLACEMENT.

2. **Register Indirect Mode:** A BASE register contains the address of the operand.

3. **Based Mode:** A BASE register's contents is added to a DISPLACEMENT to form the operand's offset.

4. **Scaled Index Mode:** An INDEX register's contents is multiplied by a SCALING factor which is added to a DISPLACEMENT to form the operand's offset.

5. **Based Scaled Index Mode:** The contents of an INDEX register is multiplied by a SCALING factor and the result is added to the contents of a BASE register to obtain the operand's offset.

6. **Based Scaled Index Mode with Displacement:** The contents of an INDEX register are multiplied by a SCALING factor, and the result is added to the contents of a BASE register and a DISPLACEMENT to form the operand's offset.

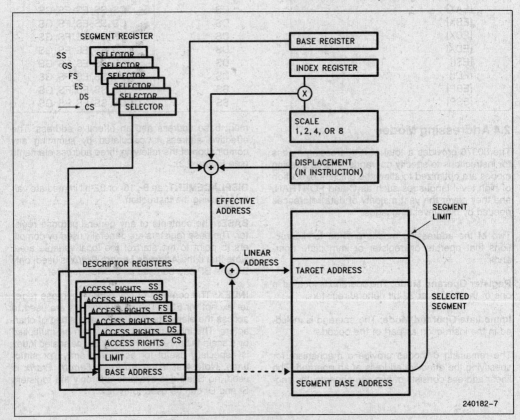

Figure 2.4. Addressing Mode Calculations

240182-7

GENERATING 16-BIT ADDRESSES

The 80376 executes code with a default length for operands and addresses of 32 bits. The 80376 is also able to execute operands and addresses of 16 bits. This is specified through the use of override prefixes. Two prefixes, the **Operand Length Prefix** and the **Address Length Prefix,** override the default 32-bit length on an individual instruction basis. These prefixes are automatically added by assem-blers. The Operand Length and Address Length Pre-fixes can be applied separately or in combination to any instruction.

The 80376 normally executes 32-bit code and uses either 8- or 32-bit displacements, and any register can be used as based or index registers. When exe-cuting 16-bit code (by prefix overrides), the displace-ments are either 8 or 16 bits, and the base and index register conform to the 16-bit model. Table 2.4 illus-trates the differences.

Table 2.4. BASE and INDEX Registers for 16- and 32-Bit Addresses

	16-Bit Addressing	32-Bit Addressing
BASE REGISTER	BX, BP	Any 32-Bit GP Register
INDEX REGISTER	SI, DI	Any 32-Bit GP Register except ESP
SCALE FACTOR	None	1, 2, 4, 8
DISPLACMENT	0, 8, 16 Bits	0, 8, 32 Bits

2.5 Data Types

The 80376 supports all of the data types commonly used in high level languages:

Bit:	A single bit quantity.
Bit Field:	A group of up to 32 contiguous bits, which spans a maximum of four bytes.
Bit String:	A set of contiguous bits, on the 80376 bit strings can be up to 16 Mbits long.
Byte:	A signed 8-bit quantity.
Unsigned Byte:	An unsigned 8-bit quantity.
Integer (Word):	A signed 16-bit quantity.
Long Integer (Double Word):	A signed 32-bit quantity. All operations assume a 2's complement representation.
Unsigned Integer (Word):	An unsigned 16-bit quantity.
Unsigned Long Integer (Double Word):	An unsigned 32-bit quantity.
Signed Quad Word:	A signed 64-bit quantity.
Unsigned Quad Word:	An unsigned 64-bit quantity.
Pointer:	A 16- or 32-bit offset only quantity which indirectly references another memory location.
Long Pointer:	A full pointer which consists of a 16-bit segment selector and either a 16- or 32-bit offset.
Char:	A byte representation of an ASCII Alphanumeric or control character.
String:	A contiguous sequence of bytes, words or dwords. A string may contain between 1 byte and 16 Mbytes.
BCD:	A byte (unpacked) representation of decimal digits 0–9.
Packed BCD:	A byte (packed) representation of two decimal digits 0–9 storing one digit in each nibble.

When the 80376 is coupled with a numerics Coprocessor such as the 80387SX then the following common Floating Point types are supported.

Floating Point: A signed 32-, 64- or 80-bit real number representation. Floating point numbers are supported by the 80387SX numerics coprocessor.

Figure 2.5 illustrates the data types supported by the 80376 processor and the 80387SX coprocessor.

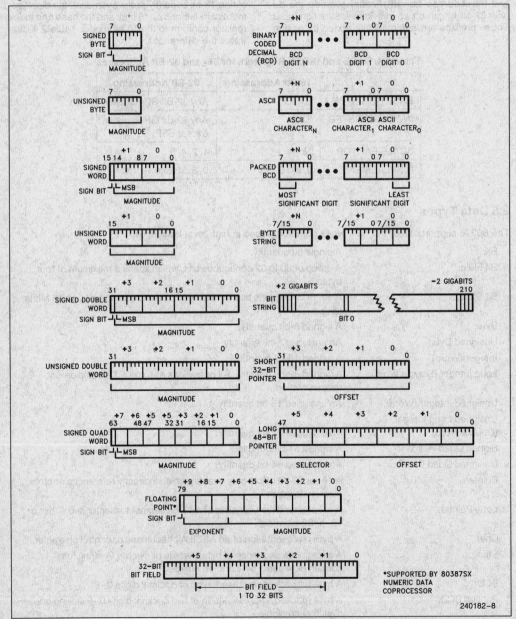

Figure 2.5. 80376 Supported Data Types

2.6 I/O Space

The 80376 has two distinct physical address spaces: physical memory and I/O. Generally, peripherals are placed in I/O space although the 80376 also supports memory-mapped peripherals. The I/O space consists of 64 Kbytes which can be divided into 64K 8-bit ports, 32K 16-bit ports, or any combination of ports which add to no more than 64 Kbytes. The M/IO# pin acts as an additional address line, thus allowing the system designer to easily determine which address space the processor is accessing. Note that the I/O address refers to a physical address.

The I/O ports are accessed by the IN and OUT instructions, with the port address supplied as an immediate 8-bit constant in the instruction or in the DX register. All 8-bit and 16-bit port addresses are zero extended on the upper address lines. The I/O instructions cause the M/IO# pin to be driven LOW. I/O port addresses 00F8H through 00FFH are reserved for use by Intel.

2.7 Interrupts and Exceptions

Interrupts and exceptions alter the normal program flow in order to handle external events, report errors or exceptional conditons. The difference between interrupts and exceptions is that interrupts are used to handle asynchronous external events while exceptions handle instruction faults. Although a program can generate a software interrupt via an INT N instruction, the processor treats software interrupts as exceptions.

Hardware interrupts occur as the result of an external event and are classified into two types: maskable or non-maskable. Interrupts are serviced after the execution of the current instruction. After the interrupt handler is finished servicing the interrupt, execution proceeds with the instruction immediately **after** the interrupted instruction.

Exceptions are classified as faults, traps, or aborts depending on the way they are reported, and whether or not restart of the instruction causing the exception is suported. **Faults** are exceptions that are detected and serviced **before** the execution of the faulting instruction. **Traps** are exceptions that are reported immediately **after** the execution of the instruction which caused the problem. **Aborts** are exceptions which do not permit the precise location of the instruction causing the exception to be determined. Thus, when an interrupt service routine has been completed, execution proceeds from the instruction immediately following the interrupted instruction. On the other hand the return address from an exception/fault routine will always point at the instruction causing the exception and include any leading instruction prefixes. Table 2.5 summarizes the possible interrupts for the 80376 and shows where the return address points to.

The 80376 has the ability to handle up to 256 different interrupts/exceptions. In order to service the interrupts, a table with up to 256 interrupt vectors must be defined. The interrupt vectors are simply pointers to the appropriate interrupt service routine. The interrupt vectors are 8-byte quantities, which are put in an Interrupt Descriptor Table. Of the 256 possible interrupts, 32 are reserved for use by Intel and the remaining 224 are free to be used by the system designer.

INTERRUPT PROCESSING

When an interrupt occurs the following actions happen. First, the current program address and the Flags are saved on the stack to allow resumption of the interrupted program. Next, an 8-bit vector is supplied to the 80376 which identifies the appropriate entry in the interrupt table. The table contains either an Interrupt Gate, a Trap Gate or a Task Gate that will point to an interrupt procedure or task. The user supplied interrupt service routine is executed. Finally, when an IRET instruction is executed the old processor state is restored and program execution resumes at the appropriate instruction.

The 8-bit interrupt vector is supplied to the 80376 in several different ways: exceptions supply the interrupt vector internally; software INT instructions contain or imply the vector; maskable hardware interrupts supply the 8-bit vector via the interrupt acknowledge bus sequence. Non-Maskable hardware interrupts are assigned to interrupt vector 2.

Maskable Interrupt

Maskable interrupts are the most common way to respond to asynchronous external hardware events. A hardware interrupt occurs when the INTR is pulled HIGH and the Interrupt Flag bit (IF) is enabled. The processor only responds to interrupts between instructions (string instructions have an "interrupt window" between memory moves which allows interrupts during long string moves). When an interrupt occurs the processor reads an 8-bit vector supplied by the hardware which identifies the source of the interrupt (one of 224 user defined interrupts).

Table 2.5. Interrupt Vector Assignments

Function	Interrupt Number	Instruction Which Can Cause Exception	Return Address Points to Faulting Instruction	Type
Divide Error	0	DIV, IDIV	Yes	FAULT
Debug Exception	1	Any Instruction	Yes	TRAP*
NMI Interrupt	2	INT 2 or NMI	No	NMI
One-Byte Interrupt	3	INT	No	TRAP
Interrupt on Overflow	4	INTO	No	TRAP
Array Bounds Check	5	BOUND	Yes	FAULT
Invalid OP-Code	6	Any Illegal Instruction	Yes	FAULT
Device Not Available	7	ESC, WAIT	Yes	FAULT
Double Fault	8	Any Instruction That Can Generate an Exception		ABORT
Coprocessor Segment Overrun	9	ESC	No	ABORT
Invalid TSS	10	JMP, CALL, IRET, INT	Yes	FAULT
Segment Not Present	11	Segment Register Instructions	Yes	FAULT
Stack Fault	12	Stack References	Yes	FAULT
General Protection Fault	13	Any Memory Reference	Yes	FAULT
Intel Reserved	14–15	—	—	—
Coprocessor Error	16	ESC, WAIT	Yes	FAULT
Intel Reserved	17–32			
Two-Byte Interrupt	0–255	INT n	No	TRAP

*Some debug exceptions may report both traps on the previous instruction, and faults on the next instruction.

Interrupts through Interrupt Gates automatically reset IF, disabling INTR requests. Interrupts through Trap Gates leave the state of the IF bit unchanged. Interrupts through a Task Gate change the IF bit according to the image of the EFLAGs register in the task's Task State Segment (TSS). When an IRET instruction is executed, the original state of the IF bit is restored.

Non-Maskable Interrupt

Non-maskable interrupts provide a method of servicing very high priority interrupts. When the NMI input is pulled HIGH it causes an interrupt with an internally supplied vector value of 2. Unlike a normal hardware interrupt no interrupt acknowledgement sequence is performed for an NMI.

While executing the NMI servicing procedure, the 80376 will not service any further NMI request, or INT requests, until an interrupt return (IRET) instruc-

tion is executed or the processor is reset. If NMI occurs while currently servicing an NMI, its presence will be saved for servicing after executing the first IRET instruction. The disabling of INTR requests depends on the gate in IDT location 2.

Software Interrupts

A third type of interrupt/exception for the 80376 is the software interrupt. An INT n instruction causes the processor to execute the interrupt service routine pointed to by the nth vector in the interrupt table.

A special case of the two byte software interrupt INT n is the one byte INT 3, or breakpoint interrupt. By inserting this one byte instruction in a program, the user can set breakpoints in his program as a debugging tool.

A final type of software interrupt, is the single step interrupt. It is discussed in **Single-Step Trap** (page 22).

INTERRUPT AND EXCEPTION PRIORITIES

Interrupts are externally-generated events. Maskable Interrupts (on the INTR input) and Non-Maskable Interrupts (on the NMI input) are recognized at instruction boundaries. When NMI and maskable INTR are **both** recognized at the **same** instruction boundary, the 80376 invokes the NMI service routine first. If, after the NMI service routine has been invoked, maskable interrupts are still enabled, then the 80376 will invoke the appropriate interrupt service routine.

As the 80376 executes instructions, it follows a consistent cycle in checking for exceptions, as shown in Table 2.6. This cycle is repeated as each instruction is executed, and occurs in parallel with instruction decoding and execution.

INSTRUCTION RESTART

The 80376 fully supports restarting all instructions after faults. If an exception is detected in the instruction to be executed (exception categories 4 through 9 in Table 2.6), the 80376 device invokes the appropriate exception service routine. The 80376 is in a state that permits restart of the instruction.

DOUBLE FAULT

A Double fault (exception 8) results when the processor attempts to invoke an exception service routine for the segment exceptions (10, 11, 12 or 13), but in the process of doing so, detects an exception.

2.8 Reset and Initialization

When the processor is Reset the registers have the values shown in Table 2.7. The 80376 will then start executing instructions near the top of physical memory, at location 0FFFFF0H. A short JMP should be executed within the segment defined for power-up (see Table 2.7). The GDT should then be initialized for a start-up data and code segment followed by a far JMP that will load the segment descriptor cache with the new descriptor values. The IDT table, after reset, is located at physical address 0H, with a limit of 256 entries.

RESET forces the 80376 to terminate all execution and local bus activity. No instruction execution or bus activity will occur as long as Reset is active. Between 350 and 450 CLK2 periods after Reset becomes inactive, the 80376 will start executing instructions at the top of physical memory.

Table 2.6. Sequence of Exception Checking

Consider the case of the 80376 having just completed an instruction. It then performs the following checks before reaching the point where the next instruction is completed:

1. Check for Exception 1 Traps from the instruction just completed (single-step via Trap Flag, or Data Breakpoints set in the Debug Registers).

2. Check for external NMI and INTR.

3. Check for Exception 1 Faults in the next instruction (Instruction Execution Breakpoint set in the Debug Registers for the next instruction).

4. Check for Segmentation Faults that prevented fetching the entire next instruction (exceptions 11 or 13).

5. Check for Faults decoding the next instruction (exception 6 if illegal opcode; or exception 13 if instruction is longer than 15 bytes, or privilege violation (i.e. not at IOPL or at CPL = 0).

6. If WAIT opcode, check if TS = 1 and MP = 1 (exception 7 if both are 1).

7. If ESCape opcode for numeric coprocessor, check if EM = 1 or TS = 1 (exception 7 if either are 1).

8. If WAIT opcode or ESCape opcode for numeric coprocessor, check ERROR# input signal (exception 16 if ERROR# input is asserted).

9. Check for Segmentation Faults that prevent transferring the entire memory quantity (exceptions 11, 12, 13).

Table 2.7. Register Values after Reset

Flag Word (EFLAGS)	uuuu0002H	(Note 1)
Machine Status Word (CR0)	uuuuuuu1H	(Note 2)
Instruction Pointer (EIP)	0000FFF0H	
Code Segment (CS)	F000H	(Note 3)
Data Segment (DS)	0000H	(Note 4)
Stack Segment (SS)	0000H	
Extra Segment (ES)	0000H	(Note 4)
Extra Segment (FS)	0000H	
Extra Segment (GS)	0000H	
EAX Register	0000H	(Note 5)
EDX Register	Component and Stepping ID	(Note 6)
All Other Registers	Undefined	(Note 7)

NOTES:
1. EFLAG Register. The upper 14 bits of the EFLAGS register are undefined, all defined flag bits are zero.
2. CR0: The defined 4 bits in the CR0 is equal to 1H.
3. The Code Segment Register (CS) will have its Base Address set to 0FFFF0000H and Limit set to 0FFFFH.
4. The Data and Extra Segment Registers (DS and ES) will have their Base Address set to 000000000H and Limit set to 0FFFFH.
5. If self-test is selected, the EAX should contain a 0 value. If a value of 0 is not found the self-test has detected a flaw in the part.
6. EDX register always holds component and stepping identifier.
7. All unidentified bits are Intel Reserved and should not be used.

2.9 Initialization

Because the 80376 processor starts executing in protected mode, certain precautions need be taken during initialization. Before any far jumps can take place the GDT and/or LDT tables need to be setup and their respective registers loaded. Before interrupts can be initialized the IDT table must be setup and the IDTR must be loaded. The example code is shown below:

```
; *******************************************************************
;
; This is an example of startup code to put either an 80376,
; 80386SX or 80386 into flat mode. All of memory is treated as
; simple linear RAM. There are no interrupt routines. The
; Builder creates the GDT-alias and IDT-alias and places them,
; by default, in GDT[1] and GDT[2]. Other entries in the GDT
; are specified in the Build file.  After initialization it jumps
; to a C startup routine. To use this template, change this jmp
; address to that of your code, or make the label of your code
; "c_startup".
;
; This code was assembled and built using version 1.2 of the
; Intel RLL utilities and Intel 386ASM assembler.
;
;        ***    This code was tested    ***
;
; *******************************************************************
```

```
NAME FLAT                    ; name of the object module

EXTRN      c_startup:near ; this is the label jmped to after init

pe_flag         equ 1
data_selc       equ 20h   ; assume code is GDT[3], data GDT[4]

INIT_CODE    SEGMENT ER PUBLIC USE32    ; Segment base at 0ffffff80h

PUBLIC GDT_DESC

gdt_desc    dq ?

PUBLIC    START

start:
    cld                      ; clear direction flag
    smsw bx                  ; check for processor (80376) at reset
    test bl,1                ; use SMSW rather than MOV for speed
    jnz pestart
realstart                    ; is an 80386 and in real mode
    db 66h                   ; force the next operand into 32-bit mode.
    mov eax,offset gdt_desc  ; move address of the GDT descriptor into eax
    xor ebx,ebx              ; clear ebx
    mov bh,ah                ; load 8 bits of address into bh
    move bl,al               ; load 8 bits of address into bl
    db 67h
    db 66h                   ; use the 32-bit form of LGDT to load
    lgdt cs:[ebx]            ; the 32-bits of address into the GDTR
    smsw ax                  ; go into protected mode (set PE bit)
    or al,pe_flag
    lmsw ax
    jmp next                 ; flush prefetch queue
pestart:
    mov ebx,offset gdt_desc
    xor eax,eax
    mov ax,bx                ; lower portion of address only
    lgdt cs:[eax]
    xor ebx,ebx              ; initialize data selectors
    mov bl,data_selc         ; GDT[3]
    mov ds,bx
    mov ss,bx
    mov es,bx
    mov fs,bx
    mov gs,bx
    jmp pejump
next:
    xor ebx,ebx              ; initialize data selectors
    mov bl,data_selc         ; GDT[3]
    mov ds,bx
    mov ss,bx
    mov es,bx
    mov fs,bx
    mov gs,bx
    db 66h                   ; for the 80386, need to make a 32-bit jump
pejump:
    jmp far ptr c_startup    ; but the 80376 is already 32-bit.

    org 70h                  ; only if segment base is at 0ffffff80h
    jmp short start
INIT_CODE ENDS
END
```

This code should be linked into your application for boot loadable code. The following build file illustrates how this is accomplished.

```
FLAT; -- build program id

SEGMENT
    *segments (dpl=0),          -- Give all user segments a DPL of 0.
    _phantom_code_ (dpl=0),     -- These two segments are created by
    _phantom_data_ (dpl=0),     -- the builder when the FLAT control is used.
    init_code  (base=0ffffff80h); -- Put startup code at the reset vector area.

GATE
    g13 (entry=13, dpl=0, trap),      -- trap gate disables interrupts
    i32 (entry=32, dpl=0, interrupt), -- interrupt gates doesn't

TABLE
    -- create GDT

    GDT (LOCATION = GDT_DESC,    -- In a buffer starting at GDT_DESC,
                                 -- BLD386 places the GDT base and
                                 -- GDT limit values. Buffer must be
                                 -- 6 bytes long. The base and limit
                                 -- values are places in this buffer
                                 -- as two bytes of limit plus
                                 -- four bytes of base in the format
                                 -- required for use by the LGDT
                                 -- instruction.
         ENTRY = (3:_phantom_code_,   -- Explicitly place segment
                  4:_phantom_data_,   -- entries into the GDT.
                  5:code32,
                  6:data,
                  7:init_code)
        );
TASK

    MAIN_TASK
        (
        DPL  = 0,              -- Task privilege level is 0.
        DATA = DATA,           -- Points to a segment that
                               -- indicates initial DS value.
        CODE = main,           -- Entry point is main, which
                               -- must be a public id.

        STACKS = (DATA),       -- Segment id points to stack
                               -- segment. Sets the initial SS:ESP.
        NO INTENABLED,         -- Disable interrupts.
        PRESENT                -- Present bit in TSS set to 1.
        );

    MEMORY
        (RANGE = (EPROM = ROM(0ffff8000h..0ffffffffh),
                  DRAM = RAM(0..0ffffh)),
         ALLOCATE = (EPROM = (MAIN_TASK)));

END

asm386 flatsim.a38 debug
asm386 application.a38 debug
bnd386 application.obj,flatsim.obj nolo debug oj (application.bnd)
bld386 application.bnd bf (flatsim.bld) bl flat
```

Commands to assemble and build a boot-loadable application named "application.a38". The initialization code is called "flatsim.a38", and build file is called "application.bld".

2.10 Self-Test

The 80376, like the 80386, has the capability to perform a self-test. The self-test checks the function of all of the Control ROM and most of the non-random logic of the part. Approximately one-half of the 80376 can be tested during self-test.

Self-Test is initiated on the 80376 when the RESET pin transitions from HIGH to LOW, and the BUSY# pin is LOW. The self-test takes about 2^{20} clocks, or approximately 33 ms with a 16 MHz 80376 processor. At the completion of self-test the processor performs reset and begins normal operation. The part has successfully passed self-test if the contents of the EAX register is zero. If the EAX register is not zero then the self-test has detected a flaw in the part. If self-test is not selected after reset, EAX may be non-zero after reset.

2.11 Debugging Support

The 80376 provides several features which simplify the debugging process. The three categories of on-chip debugging aids are:

1. The code execution breakpoint opcode (0CCH).
2. The single-step capability provided by the TF bit in the flag register, and
3. The code and data breakpoint capability provided by the Debug Registers DR0–3, DR6, and DR7.

BREAKPOINT INSTRUCTION

A single-byte software interrupt (Int 3) breakpoint instruction is available for use by software debuggers. The breakpoint opcode is 0CCh, and generates an exception 3 trap when executed.

DEBUG REGISTERS

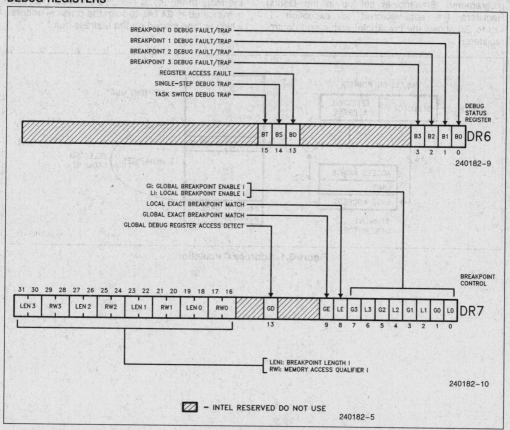

Figure 2.6. Debug Registers

SINGLE-STEP TRAP

If the single-step flag (TF, bit 8) in the EFLAG register is found to be set at the end of an instruction, a single-step exception occurs. The single-step exception is auto vectored to exception number 1.

The Debug Registers are an advanced debugging feature of the 80376. They allow data access breakpoints as well as code execution breakpoints. Since the breakpoints are indicated by on-chip registers, an instruction execution breakpoint can be placed in ROM code or in code shared by several tasks, neither of which can be supported by the INT 3 breakpoint opcode.

The 80376 contains six Debug Registers, consisting of four breakpoint address registers and two breakpoint control registers. Initially after reset, breakpoints are in the disabled state; therefore, no breakpoints will occur unless the debug registers are programmed. Breakpoints set up in the Debug Registers are auto-vectored to exception 1. Figure 2.6 shows the breakpoint status and control registers.

3.0 ARCHITECTURE

The Intel 80376 Embedded Processor has a physical address space of 16 Mbytes (2^{24} bytes) and allows the running of virtual memory programs of almost unlimited size (16 Kbytes $\times$ 16 Mbytes or 256 Gbytes (2^{38} bytes)). In addition the 80376 provides a sophisticated memory management and a hardware-assisted protection mechanism.

3.1 Addressing Mechanism

The 80376 uses two components to form the logical address, a 16-bit selector which determines the linear base address of a segment, and a 32-bit effective address. The selector is used to specify an index into an operating system defined table (see Figure 3.1). The table contains the 32-bit base address of a given segment. The linear address is formed by adding the base address obtained from the table to the 32-bit effective address. This value is truncated to 24 bits to form the physical address, which is then placed on the address bus.

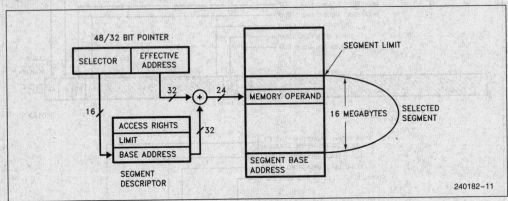

Figure 3.1. Address Calculation

3.2 Segmentation

Segmentation is one method of memory management and provides the basis for protection in the 80376. Segments are used to encapsulate regions of memory which have common attributes. For example, all of the code of a given program could be contained in a segment, or an operating system table may reside in a segment. All information about each segment, is stored in an 8-byte data structure called a descriptor. All of the descriptors in a system are contained in tables recognized by hardware.

TERMINOLOGY

The following terms are used throughout the discussion of descriptors, privilege levels and protection:

PL: **Privilege Level**—One of the four hierarchical privilege levels. Level 0 is the most privileged level and level 3 is the least privileged.

RPL: **Requestor Privilege Level**—The privilege level of the original supplier of the selector. RPL is determined by the least two significant bits of a selector.

DPL: **Descriptor Privilege Level**—This is the least privileged level at which a task may access that descriptor (and the segment associated with that descriptor). Descriptor Privilege Level is determined by bits 6:5 in the Access Right Byte of a descriptor.

CPL: **Current Privilege Level**—The privilege level at which a task is currently executing, which equals the privilege level of the code segment being executed. CPL can also be determined by examining the lowest 2 bits of the CS register, except for conforming code segments.

EPL: **Effective Privilege Level**—The effective privilege level is the least privileged of the RPL and the DPL. EPL is the numerical maximum of RPL and DPL.

Task: One instance of the execution of a program. Tasks are also referred to as processes.

DESCRIPTOR TABLES

The descriptor tables define all of the segments which are used in an 80376 system. There are three types of tables on the 80376 which hold descriptors: the Global Descriptor Table, Local Descriptor Table, and the Interrupt Decriptor Table. All of the tables are variable length memory arrays, they can range in size between 8 bytes and 64 Kbytes. Each table can hold up to 8192 8-byte descriptors. The upper 13 bits of a selector are used as an index into the descriptor table. The tables have registers associated with them which hold the 32-bit linear base address, and the 16-bit limit of each table.

Each of the tables have a register associated with it: GDTR, LDTR and IDTR; see Figure 3.2. The LGDT, LLDT and LIDT instructions load the base and limit of the Global, Local and Interrupt Descriptor Tables into the appropriate register. The SGDT, SLDT and SIDT store these base and limit values. These are privileged instructions.

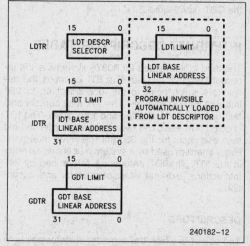

Figure 3.2. Descriptor Table Registers

Global Descriptor Table

The Global Descriptor Table (GDT) contains descriptors which are possibly available to all of the tasks in a system. The GDT can contain any type of segment descriptor except for interrupt and trap descriptors. Every 80376 system contains a GDT. A simple 80376 system contains only 2 entries in the GDT; a code and a data descriptor. For maximum performance, descriptor tables should begin on even addresses.

The first slot of the Global Descriptor Table corresponds to the null selector and is not used. The null selector defines a null pointer value.

Local Descriptor Table

LDTs contain descriptors which are associated with a given task. Generally, operating systems are designed so that each task has a separate LDT. The LDT may contain only code, data, stack, task gate, and call gate descriptors. LDTs provide a mechanism for isolating a given task's code and data segments from the rest of the operating system, while the GDT contains descriptors for segments which are common to all tasks. A segment cannot be accessed by a task if its segment descriptor does not exist in either the current LDT or the GDT. This provides both isolation and protection for a task's segments, while still allowing global data to be shared among tasks.

Unlike the 6-byte GDT or IDT registers which contain a base address and limit, the visible portion of the LDT register contains only a 16-bit selector. This selector refers to a Local Descriptor Table descriptor in the GDT (see Figure 2.1).

INTERRUPT DESCRIPTOR TABLE

The third table needed for 80376 systems is the Interrupt Descriptor Table. The IDT contains the descriptors which point to the location of up to 256 interrupt service routines. The IDT may contain only task gates, interrupt gates and trap gates. The IDT should be at least 256 bytes in size in order to hold the descriptors for the 32 Intel Reserved Interrupts. Every interrupt used by a system must have an entry in the IDT. The IDT entries are referenced by INT instructions, external interrupt vectors, and exceptions.

DESCRIPTORS

The object to which the segment selector points to is called a descriptor. Descriptors are eight-byte quantities which contain attributes about a given region of linear address space. These attributes include the 32-bit logical base address of the seg-

ment, the 20-bit length and granularity of the segment, the protection level, read, write or execute privileges, and the type of segment. All of the attribute information about a segment is contained in 12 bits in the segment descriptor. Figure 3.3 shows the general format of a descriptor. All segments on the the 80376 have three attribute fields in common: the Present bit (P), the Descriptor Privilege Level bits (DPL) and the Segment bit (S). P = 1 if the segment is loaded in physical memory, if P = 0 then any attempt to access the segment causes a not present exception (exception 11). The DPL is a two-bit field which specifies the protection level, 0–3, associated with a segment.

The 80376 has two main categories of segments: system segments, and non-system segments (for code and data). The segment bit, S, determines if a given segment is a system segment, a code segment or a data segment. If the S bit is 1 then the segment is either a code or data segment, if it is 0 then the segment is a system segment.

Note that although the 80376 is limited to a 16-Mbyte Physical address space (2^{24}), its base address allows a segment to be placed anywhere in a 4-Gbyte linear address space. When writing code for the 80376, users should keep code portability to an 80386 processor (or other processors with a larger physical address space) in mind. A segment base address can be placed anywhere in this 4-Gbyte linear address space, but a physical address will be

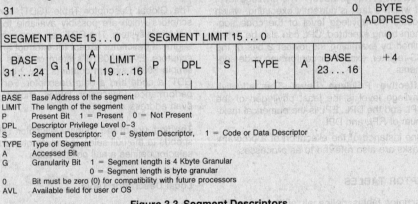

Figure 3.3. Segment Descriptors

Figure 3.4. Code and Data Descriptors

Table 3.1. Access Rights Byte Definition for Code and Data Descriptors

Bit Position	Name	Function	
7	Present (P)	P = 1	Segment is mapped into physical memory.
		P = 0	No mapping to physical memory exits
6–5	Descriptor Privilege Level (DPL)		Segment privilege attribute used in privilege tests.
4	Segment Descriptor (S)	S = 1	Code or Data (includes stacks) segment descriptor
		S = 0	System Segment Descriptor or Gate Descriptor
3	Executable (E)	E = 0	Descriptor type is data segment: ⎫ If
2	Expansion Direction (ED)	ED = 0	Expand up segment, offsets must be ≤ limit. Data
		ED = 1	Expand down segment, offsets must be > limit. Segment
1	Writable (W)	W = 0	Data segment may not be written into. (S = 1,
		W = 1	Data segment may be written into. E = 0) ⎭
3	Executable (E)	E = 1	Descriptor type is code segment: ⎫ If
2	Conforming (C)	C = 1	Code segment may only be executed when CPL ≥ DPL and CPL remains unchanged. Code Segment
1	Readable (R)	R = 0	Code segment may not be read. (S = 1,
		R = 1	Code segment may be read. E = 1) ⎭
0	Accessed (A)	A = 0	Segment has not been accessed.
		A = 1	Segment selector has been loaded into segment register or used by selector test instructions.

generated that is a truncated version of this linear address. Truncation will be to the maximum number of address bits. It is recommended to place EPROM at the highest physical address and DRAM at the lowest physical addresses.

Code and Data Descriptors (S = 1)

Figure 3.4 shows the general format of a code and data descriptor and Table 3.1 illustrates how the bits in the Access Right Byte are interpreted.

Code and data segments have several descriptor fields in common. The accessed bit, A, is set whenever the processor accesses a descriptor. The granularity bit, G, specifies if a segment length is 1-byte-granular or 4-Kbyte-granular. Base address bits 31–24, which are normally found in 80386 descriptors, are not made externally available on the 80376. They do not affect the operation of the 80376. The $A_{31}-A_{24}$ field should be set to allow an 80386 to correctly execute with EPROM at the upper 4096 Mbytes of physical memory.

System Descriptor Formats (S = 0)

System segments describe information about operating system tables, tasks, and gates. Figure 3.5 shows the general format of system segment descriptors, and the various types of system segments.

80376 system descriptors (which are the same as 80386 descriptor types 2, 5, 9, B, C, E and F) contain a 32-bit logical base address and a 20-bit segment limit.

Selector Fields

A selector has three fields: Local or Global Descriptor Table Indicator (TI), Descriptor Entry Index (Index), and Requestor (the selector's) Privilege Level (RPL) as shown in Figure 3.6. The TI bit selects either the Global Descriptor Table or the Local Descriptor Table. The Index selects one of 8K descriptors in the appropriate descriptor table. The RPL bits allow high speed testing of the selector's privilege attributes.

Segment Descriptor Cache

In addition to the selector value, every segment register has a segment descriptor cache register associated with it. Whenever a segment register's contents are changed, the 8-byte descriptor associated with that selector is automatically loaded (cached) on the chip. Once loaded, all references to that segment use the cached descriptor information instead of reaccessing the descriptor. The contents of the descriptor cache are not visible to the programmer. Since descriptor caches only change when a segment register is changed, programs which modify the descriptor tables must reload the appropriate segment registers after changing a descriptor's value.

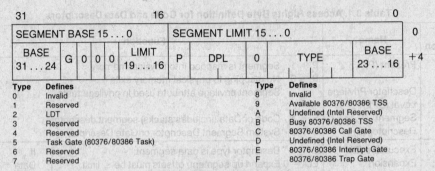

Type	Defines	Type	Defines
0	Invalid	8	Invalid
1	Reserved	9	Available 80376/80386 TSS
2	LDT	A	Undefined (Intel Reserved)
3	Reserved	B	Busy 80376/80386 TSS
4	Reserved	C	80376/80386 Call Gate
5	Task Gate (80376/80386 Task)	D	Undefined (Intel Reserved)
6	Reserved	E	80376/80386 Interrupt Gate
7	Reserved	F	80376/80386 Trap Gate

Figure 3.5. System Descriptors

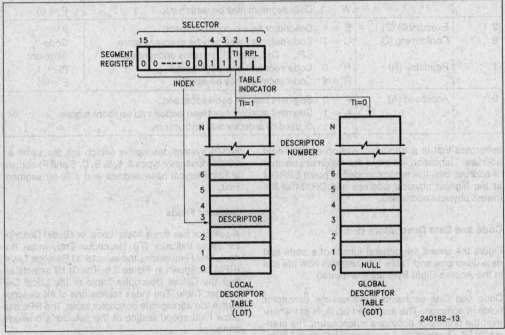

Figure 3.6. Example Descriptor Selection

3.3 Protection

The 80376 offers extensive protection features. These protection features are particularly useful in sophisticated embedded applications which use multitasking real-time operating systems. For simpler embedded applications these protection capabilities can be easily bypassed by making all applications run at privilege level (PL) 0.

RULES OF PRIVILEGE

The 80376 controls access to both data and procedures between levels of a task, according to the following rules.

—Data stored in a segment with privilege level **p** can be accessed only by code executing at a privilege level at least as privileged as **p**.

—A code segment/procedure with privilege level **p** can only be called by a task executing at the same or a lesser privilege level than **p**.

PRIVILEGE LEVELS

At any point in time, a task on the 80376 always executes at one of the four privilege levels. The Current Privilege Level (CPL) specifies what the task's privilege level is. A task's CPL may only be changed by control transfers through gate descriptors to a code segment with a different privilege level. Thus, an application program running at PL=3 may call an operating system routine at PL=1 (via a gate) which would cause the task's CPL to be set to 1 until the operating system routine was finished.

Selector Privilege (RPL)

The privilege level of a selector is specified by the RPL field. The selector's RPL is only used to establish a less trusted privilege level than the current privilege level of the task for the use of a segment. This level is called the task's effective privilege level (EPL). The EPL is defined as being the least privileged (numerically larger) level of a task's CPL and a selector's RPL. The RPL is most commonly used to verify that pointers passed to an operating system procedure do not access data that is of higher privilege than the procedure that originated the pointer. Since the originator of a selector can specify any RPL value, the Adjust RPL (ARPL) instruction is provided to force the RPL bits to the originator's CPL.

I/O Privilege

The I/O privilege level (IOPL) lets the operating system code executing at CPL=0 define the least privileged level at which I/O instructions can be used. An exception 13 (General Protection Violation) is generated if an I/O instruction is attempted when the CPL of the task is less privileged than the IOPL. The IOPL is stored in bits 13 and 14 of the EFLAGS register. The following instructions cause an exception 13 if the CPL is greater than IOPL: IN, INS, OUT, OUTS, STI, CLI and LOCK prefix.

Descriptor Access

There are basically two types of segment accesssess: those involving code segments such as control transfers, and those involving data accesses. Determining the ability of a task to access a segment involves the type of segment to be accessed, the instruction used, the type of descriptor used and CPL, RPL, and DPL as described above.

Any time an instruction loads a data segment register (DS, ES, FS, GS) the 80376 makes protection validation checks. Selectors loaded in the DS, ES, FS, GS registers must refer only to data segment or readable code segments.

Finally the privilege validation checks are performed. The CPL is compared to the EPL and if the EPL is more privileged than the CPL, an exception 13 (general protection fault) is generated.

The rules regarding the stack segment are slightly different than those involving data segments. Instructions that load selectors into SS must refer to data segment descriptors for writeable data segments. The DPL and RPL must equal the CPL of all other descriptor types or a privilege level violation will cause an exception 13. A stack not present fault causes an exception 12.

PRIVILEGE LEVEL TRANSFERS

Inter-segment control transfers occur when a selector is loaded in the CS register. For a typical system most of these transfers are simply the result of a call or a jump to another routine. There are five types of control transfers which are summarized in Table 3.2. Many of these transfers result in a privilege level transfer. Changing privilege levels is done only by control transfers, using gates, task switches, and interrupt or trap gates.

Control transfers can only occur if the operation which loaded the selector references the correct descriptor type. Any violation of these descriptor usage rules will cause an exception 13.

CALL GATES

Gates provide protected indirect CALLs. One of the major uses of gates is to provide a secure method of privilege transfers within a task. Since the operating system defines all of the gates in a system, it can ensure that all gates only allow entry into a few trusted procedures.

Table 3.2. Descriptor Types Used for Control Transfer

Control Transfer Types	Operation Types	Descriptor Referenced	Descriptor Table
Intersegment within the same privilege level	JMP, CALL, RET, IRET*	Code Segment	GDT/LDT
Intersegment to the same or higher privilege level Interrupt within task may change CPL	CALL	Call Gate	GDT/LDT
	Interrupt Instruction, Exception, External Interrupt	Trap or Interrupt Gate	IDT
Intersegment to a lower privilege level (changes task CPL)	RET, IRET*	Code Segment	GDT/LDT
	CALL, JMP	Task State Segment	GDT
Task Switch	CALL, JMP	Task Gate	GDT/LDT
	IRET** Interrupt Instruction, Exception, External Interrupt	Task Gate	IDT

*NT (Nested Task bit of flag register) = 0
**NT (Nested Task bit of flag register) = 1

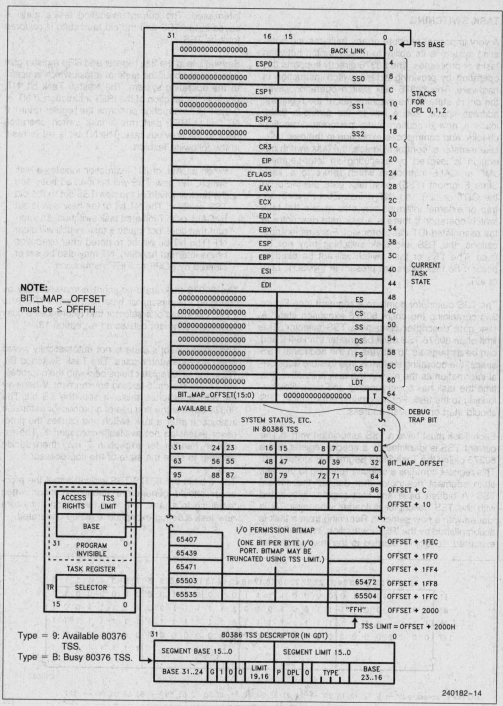

NOTE:
BIT_MAP_OFFSET
must be ≤ DFFFH

Type = 9: Available 80376
         TSS.
Type = B: Busy 80376 TSS.

Figure 3.7. 80376 TSS And TSS Registers

TASK SWITCHING

A very important attribute of any multi-tasking operating system is its ability to rapidly switch between tasks or processes. The 80376 directly supports this operation by providing a task switch instruction in hardware. The 80376 task switch operation saves the entire state of the machine (all of the registers, address space, and a link to the previous task), loads a new execution state, performs protection checks, and commences execution in the new task. Like transfer of control by gates, the task switch operation is invoked by executing an inter-segment JMP or CALL instruction which refers to a Task State Segment (TSS), or a task gate descriptor in the GDT or LDT. An INT n instruction, exception, trap or external interrupt may also invoke the task switch operation if there is a task gate descriptor in the associated IDT descriptor slot. For simple applications, the TSS and task switching may not be used. The TSS or task switch will not be used or occur if no task gates are present in the GDT, LDT or IDT.

The TSS descriptor points to a segment (see Figure 3.7) containing the entire 80376 execution state. A task gate descriptor contains a TSS selector. The limit of an 80376 TSS must be greater than 64H, and can be as large as 16 Mbytes. In the additional TSS space, the operating system is free to store additional information as the reason the task is inactive, the time the task has spent running, and open files belonging to the task. For maximum performance, TSS should start on an even address.

Each Task must have a TSS associated with it. The current TSS is identified by a special register in the 80376 called the Task State Segment Register (TR). This register contains a selector referring to the task state segment descriptor that defines the current TSS. A hidden base and limit register associated with the TSS descriptor is loaded whenever TR is loaded with a new selector. Returning from a task is accomplished by the IRET instruction. When IRET is executed, control is returned to the task which was interrupted. The current executing task's state is saved in the TSS and the old task state is restored from its TSS.

Several bits in the flag register and CR0 register give information about the state of a task which is useful to the operating system. The Nested Task bit, NT, controls the function of the IRET instruction. If NT = 0 the IRET instruction performs the regular return. If NT = 1, IRET performs a task switch operation back to the previous task. The NT bit is set or reset in the following fashion:

When a CALL or INT instruction initiates a task switch, the new TSS will be marked busy and the back link field of the new TSS set to the old TSS selector. The NT bit of the new task is set by CALL or INT initiated task switches. An interrupt that does not cause a task switch will clear NT (The NT bit will be restored after execution of the interrupt handler). NT may also be set or cleared by POPF or IRET instructions.

The 80376 task state segment is marked busy by changing the descriptor type field from TYPE 9 to TYPE 0BH. Use of a selector that references a busy task state segment causes an exception 13.

The coprocessor's state is not automatically saved when a task switch occurs. The Task Switched Bit, TS, in the CR0 register helps deal with the coprocessor's state in a multi-tasking environment. Whenever the 80376 switches tasks, it sets the TS bit. The 80376 detects the first use of a processor extension instruction after a task switch and causes the processor extension not available exception 7. The exception handler for exception 7 may then decide whether to save the state of the coprocessor.

The T bit in the 80376 TSS indicates that the processor should generate a debug exception when switching to a task. If T = 1 then upon entry to a new task a debug exception 1 will be generated.

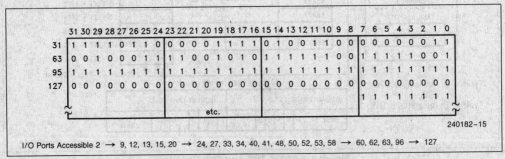

	31 30 29 28 27 26 25 24	23 22 21 20 19 18 17 16	15 14 13 12 11 10 9 8	7 6 5 4 3 2 1 0
31	1 1 1 1 0 1 1 0	0 0 0 0 1 1 1 1	0 1 0 0 1 1 0 0	0 0 0 0 0 0 1 1
63	0 0 1 0 0 0 1 1	1 1 0 0 1 0 1 0	1 1 1 1 1 1 0 0	1 1 1 1 1 0 0 1
95	1 1 1 1 1 1 1 1	1 1 1 1 1 1 1 1	1 1 1 1 1 1 1 1	1 1 1 1 1 1 1 1
127	0 0 0 0 0 0 0 0	0 0 0 0 0 0 0 0	0 0 0 0 0 0 0 0	0 0 0 0 0 0 0 0
				1 1 1 1 1 1 1 1

etc.

240182–15

I/O Ports Accessible 2 → 9, 12, 13, 15, 20 → 24, 27, 33, 34, 40, 41, 48, 50, 52, 53, 58 → 60, 62, 63, 96 → 127

Figure 3.8. Sample I/O Permission Bit Map

PROTECTION AND I/O PERMISSION BIT MAP

The I/O instructions that directly refer to addresses in the processor's I/O space are IN, INS, OUT and OUTS. The 80376 has the ability to selectively trap references to specific I/O addresses. The structure that enables selective trapping is the *I/O Permission Bit Map* in the TSS segment (see Figures 3.7 and 3.8). The I/O permission map is a bit vector. The size of the map and its location in the TSS segment are variable. The processor locates the I/O permission map by means of the **I/O map base** field in the fixed portion of the TSS. The **I/O map base** field is 16 bits wide and contains the offset of the beginning of the I/O permission map.

If an I/O instruction (IN, INS, OUT or OUTS) is encountered, the processor first checks whether CPL ≤ IOPL. If this condition is true, the I/O operation may proceed. If not true, the processor checks the I/O permission map.

Each bit in the map corresponds to an I/O port byte address; for example, the bit for port 41 is found at **I/O map base** +5 linearly, (5 × 8 = 40), bit offset 1. The processor tests all the bits that correspond to the I/O addresses spanned by an I/O operation; for example, a double word operation tests four bits corresponding to four adjacent byte addresses. If any tested bit is set, the processor signals a general protection exception. If all the tested bits are zero, the I/O operations may proceed.

It is not necessary for the I/O permission map to represent all the I/O addresses. I/O addresses not spanned by the map are treated as if they had one-bits in the map. The **I/O map base** should be at least one byte less than the TSS limit and the last byte beyond the I/O mapping information must contain all 1's.

Because the I/O permission map is in the TSS segment, different tasks can have different maps. Thus, the operating system can allocate ports to a task by changing the I/O permission map in the task's TSS.

IMPORTANT IMPLEMENTATION NOTE:
Beyond the last byte of I/O mapping information in the I/O permission bit map **must** be a byte containing all 1's. The byte of all 1's must be within the limit of the 80376's TSS segment (see Figure 3.7).

4.0 FUNCTIONAL DATA

The Intel 80376 embedded processor features a straightforward functional interface to the external hardware. The 80376 has separate parallel buses for data and address. The data bus is 16 bits in width, and bidirectional. The address bus outputs 24-bit address values using 23 address lines and two-byte enable signals.

The 80376 has two selectable address bus cycles: pipelined and non-pipelined. The pipelining option allows as much time as possible for data access by

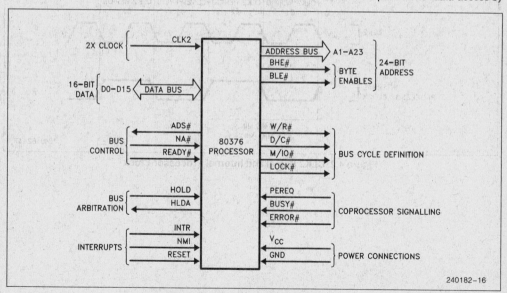

240182–16

Figure 4.1. Functional Signal Groups

starting the pending bus cycle before the present bus cycle is finished. A non-pipelined bus cycle gives the highest bus performance by executing every bus cycle in two processor clock cycles. For maximum design flexibility, the address pipelining option is selectable on a cycle-by-cycle basis.

The processor's bus cycle is the basic mechanism for information transfer, either from system to processor, or from processor to system. 80376 bus cycles perform data transfer in a minimum of only two clock periods. On a 16-bit data bus, the maximum 80376 transfer bandwidth at 16 MHz is therefore 16 Mbytes/sec. However, any bus cycle will be extended for more than two clock periods if external hardware withholds acknowledgement of the cycle.

The 80376 can relinquish control of its local buses to allow mastership by other devices, such as direct memory access (DMA) channels. When relinquished, HLDA is the only output pin driven by the 80376, providing near-complete isolation of the processor from its system (all other output pins are in a float condition).

4.1 Signal Description Overview

Ahead is a brief description of the 80376 input and output signals arranged by functional groups. Note the # symbol at the end of a signal name indicates the active, or asserted, state occurs when the signal is at a LOW voltage. When no # is present after the signal name, the signal is asserted when at the HIGH voltage level.

Example signal: M/IO#—HIGH voltage indicates Memory selected

—LOW voltage indicates I/O selected

The signal descriptions sometimes refer to A.C. timing parameters, such as "t_{25} Reset Setup Time" and "t_{26} Reset Hold Time." The values of these parameters can be found in Table 6.4.

CLOCK (CLK2)

CLK2 provides the fundamental timing for the 80376. It is divided by two internally to generate the internal processor clock used for instruction execution. The internal clock is comprised of two

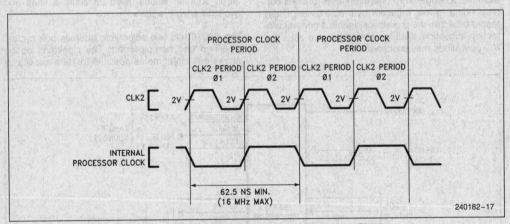

Figure 4.2. CLK2 Signal and Internal Processor Clock

phases, "phase one" and "phase two". Each CLK2 period is a phase of the internal clock. Figure 4.2 illustrates the relationship. If desired, the phase of the internal processor clock can be synchronized to a known phase by ensuring the falling edge of the RESET signal meets the applicable setup and hold times t_{25} and t_{26}.

DATA BUS ($D_{15}-D_0$)

These three-state bidirectional signals provide the general purpose data path between the 80376 and other devices. The data bus outputs are active HIGH and will float during bus hold acknowledge. Data bus reads require that read-data setup and hold times t_{21} and t_{22} be met relative to CLK2 for correct operation.

ADDRESS BUS (BHE#, BLE#, $A_{23}-A_1$)

These three-state outputs provide physical memory addresses or I/O port addresses. $A_{23}-A_{16}$ are LOW during I/O transfers except for I/O transfers automatically generated by coprocessor instructions.

During coprocessor I/O transfers, $A_{22}-A_{16}$ are driven LOW, and A_{23} is driven HIGH so that this address line can be used by external logic to generate the coprocessor select signal. Thus, the I/O address driven by the 80376 for coprocessor commands is 8000F8H, and the I/O address driven by the 80376 processor for coprocessor data is 8000FCH or 8000FEH.

The address bus is capable of addressing 16 Mbytes of physical memory space (000000H through 0FFFFFFH), and 64 Kbytes of I/O address space (000000H through 00FFFFH) for programmed I/O. The address bus is active HIGH and will float during bus hold acknowledge.

The Byte Enable outputs BHE# and BLE# directly indicate which bytes of the 16-bit data bus are involved with the current transfer. BHE# applies to $D_{15}-D_8$ and BLE# applies to D_7-D_0. If both BHE# and BLE# are asserted, then 16 bits of data are being transferred. See Table 4.1 for a complete decoding of these signals. The byte enables are active LOW and will float during bus hold acknowledge.

Table 4.1. Byte Enable Definitions

BHE#	BLE#	Function
0	0	Word Transfer
0	1	Byte Transfer on Upper Byte of the Data Bus, $D_{15}-D_8$
1	0	Byte Transfer on Lower Byte of the Data Bus, D_7-D_0
1	1	Never Occurs

BUS CYCLE DEFINITION SIGNALS (W/R#, D/C#, M/IO#, LOCK#)

These three-state outputs define the type of bus cycle being performed: W/R# distinguishes between write and read cycles, D/C# distinguishes between data and control cycles, M/IO# distinguishes between memory and I/O cycles, and LOCK# distinguishes between locked and unlocked bus cycles. All of these signals are active LOW and will float during bus acknowledge.

The primary bus cycle definition signals are W/R#, D/C# and M/IO#, since these are the signals driven valid as ADS# (Address Status output) becomes active. The LOCK# signal is driven valid at the same time the bus cycle begins, which due to address pipelining, could be after ADS# becomes active. Exact bus cycle definitions, as a function of W/R#, D/C# and M/IO# are given in Table 4.2.

LOCK# indicates that other system bus masters are not to gain control of the system bus while it is active. LOCK# is activated on the CLK2 edge that begins the first locked bus cycle (i.e., it is not active at the same time as the other bus cycle definition pins) and is deactivated when ready is returned to the end of the last bus cycle which is to be locked. The beginning of a bus cycle is determined when READY# is returned in a previous bus cycle and another is pending (ADS# is active) or the clock in which ADS# is driven active if the bus was idle. This means that it follows more closely with the write data rules when it is valid, but may cause the bus to be locked longer than desired. The LOCK# signal may be explicitly activated by the LOCK prefix on certain instructions. LOCK# is always asserted when executing the XCHG instruction, during descriptor updates, and during the interrupt acknowledge sequence.

BUS CONTROL SIGNALS (ADS#, READY#, NA#)

The following signals allow the processor to indicate when a bus cycle has begun, and allow other system hardware to control address pipelining and bus cycle termination.

Address Status (ADS#)

This three-state output indicates that a valid bus cycle definition and address (W/R#, D/C#, M/IO#, BHE#, BLE# and $A_{23}-A_1$) are being driven at the 80376 pins. ADS# is an active LOW output. Once ADS# is driven active, valid address, byte enables, and definition signals will not change. In addition, ADS# will remain active until its associated bus cycle begins (when READY# is returned for the previous bus cycle when running pipelined bus cycles). ADS# will float during bus hold acknowledge. See sections **Non-Pipelined Bus Cycles** (page 43) and **Pipelined Bus Cycles** (page 45) for additional information on how ADS# is asserted for different bus states.

Transfer Acknowledge (READY#)

This input indicates the current bus cycle is complete, and the active bytes indicated by BHE# and BLE# are accepted or provided. When READY# is sampled active during a read cycle or interrupt acknowledge cycle, the 80376 latches the input data and terminates the cycle. When READY# is sampled active during a write cycle, the processor terminates the bus cycle.

Table 4.2. Bus Cycle Definition

M/IO#	D/C#	W/R#	Bus Cycle Type	Locked?
0	0	0	INTERRUPT ACKNOWLEDGE	Yes
0	0	1	Does Not Occur	—
0	1	0	I/O DATA READ	No
0	1	1	I/O DATA WRITE	No
1	0	0	MEMORY CODE READ	No
1	0	1	HALT: Address = 2 BHE# = 1 BLE# = 0 SHUTDOWN: Address = 0 BHE# = 1 BLE# = 0	No
1	1	0	MEMORY DATA READ	Some Cycles
1	1	1	MEMORY DATA WRITE	Some Cycles

READY# is ignored on the first bus state of all bus cycles, and sampled each bus state thereafter until asserted. READY# must eventually be asserted to acknowledge every bus cycle, including Halt Indication and Shutdown Indication bus cycles. When being sampled, READY# must always meet setup and hold times t_{19} and t_{20} for correct operation.

Next Address Request (NA#)

This is used to request pipelining. This input indicates the system is prepared to accept new values of BHE#, BLE#, A_{23}–A_1, W/R#, D/C# and M/IO# from the 80376 even if the end of the current cycle is not being acknowledged on READY#. If this input is active when sampled, the next bus cycle's address and status signals are driven onto the bus, provided the next bus request is already pending internally. NA# is ignored in clock cycles in which ADS# or READY# is activated. This signal is active LOW and must satisfy setup and hold times t_{15} and t_{16} for correct operation. See **Pipelined Bus Cycles** (page 45) and **Read and Write Cycles** (page 42) for additional information.

BUS ARBITRATION SIGNALS (HOLD, HLDA)

This section describes the mechanism by which the processor relinquishes control of its local buses when requested by another bus master device. See **Entering and Exiting Hold Acknowledge** (page 52) for additional information.

Bus Hold Request (HOLD)

This input indicates some device other than the 80376 requires bus mastership. When control is granted, the 80376 floats A_{23}–A_1, BHE#, BLE#, D_{15}–D_0, LOCK#, M/IO#, D/C#, W/R# and ADS#, and then activates HLDA, thus entering the bus hold acknowledge state. The local bus will remain granted to the requesting master until HOLD becomes inactive. When HOLD becomes inactive, the 80376 will deactivate HLDA and drive the local bus (at the same time), thus terminating the hold acknowledge condition.

HOLD must remain asserted as long as any other device is a local bus master. External pull-up resistors may be required when in the hold acknowledge state since none of the 80376 floated outputs have internal pull-up resistors. See **Resistor Recommendations** (page 59) for additional information. HOLD is not recognized while RESET is active but is recognized during the time between the high-to-low transition of RESET and the first instruction fetch. If RESET is asserted while HOLD is asserted, RESET has priority and places the bus into an idle state, rather than the hold acknowledge (high-impedance) state.

HOLD is a level-sensitive, active HIGH, synchronous input. HOLD signals must always meet setup and hold times t_{23} and t_{24} for correct operation.

Bus Hold Acknowledge (HLDA)

When active (HIGH), this output indicates the 80376 has relinquished control of its local bus in response to an asserted HOLD signal, and is in the bus Hold Acknowledge state.

The Bus Hold Acknowledge state offers near-complete signal isolation. In the Hold Acknowledge state, HLDA is the only signal being driven by the 80376. The other output signals or bidirectional signals (D_{15}–D_0, BHE#, BLE#, A_{23}–A_1, W/R#, D/C#, M/IO#, LOCK# and ADS#) are in a high-impedance state so the requesting bus master may control them. These pins remain OFF throughout the time that HLDA remains active (see Table 4.3). Pull-up resistors may be desired on several signals to avoid spurious activity when no bus master is driving them. See **Resistor Recommendations** (page 59) for additional information.

When the HOLD signal is made inactive, the 80376 will deactivate HLDA and drive the bus. One rising edge on the NMI input is remembered for processing after the HOLD input is negated.

Table 4.3. Output Pin State during HOLD

Pin Value	Pin Names
1	HLDA
Float	LOCK#, M/IO#, D/C#, W/R#, ADS#, A_{23}–A_1, BHE#, BLE#, D_{15}–D_0

In addition to the normal usage of Hold Acknowledge with DMA controllers or master peripherals, the near-complete isolation has particular attractiveness during system test when test equipment drives the system, and in hardware-fault-tolerant applications.

Hold Latencies

The maximum possible HOLD latency depends on the software being executed. The actual HOLD latency at any time depends on the current bus activity, the state of the LOCK# signal (internal to the CPU) activated by the LOCK# prefix, and interrupts. The 80376 will not honor a HOLD request until the current bus operation is complete. Table 4.4 shows the types of bus operations that can affect HOLD latency, and indicates the types of delays that these operations may introduce. When considering maximum HOLD latencies, designers must select which of these bus operations are possible, and then select the maximum latency form among them.

The 80376 breaks 32-bit data or I/O accesses into 2 internally locked 16-bit bus cycles; the LOCK# signal is not asserted. The 80376 breaks unaligned 16-bit or 32-bit data or I/O accesses into 2 or 3 internally locked 16-bit bus cycles. Again the LOCK# signal is not asserted but a HOLD request will not be recognized until the end of the entire transfer.

Wait states affect HOLD latency. The 80376 will not honor a HOLD request until the end of the current bus operation, no matter how many wait states are required. Systems with DMA where data transfer is critical must insure that READY# returns sufficiently soon.

COPROCESSOR INTERFACE SIGNALS (PEREQ, BUSY#, ERROR#)

In the following sections are descriptions of signals dedicated to the numeric coprocessor interface. In addition to the data bus, address bus, and bus cycle definition signals, these following signals control communication between the 80376 and the 80387SX processor extension.

Coprocessor Request (PEREQ)

When asserted (HIGH), this input signal indicates a coprocessor request for a data operand to be transferred to/from memory by the 80376. In response, the 80376 transfers information between the coprocessor and memory. Because the 80376 has internally stored the coprocessor opcode being executed, it performs the requested data transfer with the correct direction and memory address.

PEREQ is a level-sensitive active HIGH asynchronous signal. Setup and hold times, t_{29} and t_{30}, relative to the CLK2 signal must be met to guarantee recognition at a particular clock edge. This signal is provided with a weak internal pull-down resistor of around 20 KΩ to ground so that it will not float active when left unconnected.

Coprocessor Busy (BUSY#)

When asserted (LOW), this input indicates the coprocessor is still executing an instruction, and is not yet able to accept another. When the 80376 encounters any coprocessor instruction which operates on the numerics stack (e.g. load, pop, or arithmetic operation), or the WAIT instruction, this input is first automatically sampled until it is seen to be inactive. This sampling of the BUSY# input prevents overrunning the execution of a previous coprocessor instruction.

The F(N)INIT, F(N)CLEX coprocessor instructions are allowed to execute even if BUSY# is active, since these instructions are used for coprocessor initialization and exception-clearing.

BUSY# is an active LOW, level-sensitive asynchronous signal. Setup and hold times, t_{29} and t_{30}, relative to the CLK2 signal must be met to guarantee recognition at a particular clock edge. This pin is provided with a weak internal pull-up resistor of around 20 KΩ to V$_{CC}$ so that it will not float active when left unconnected.

BUSY# serves an additional function. If BUSY# is sampled LOW at the falling edge of RESET, the 80376 processor performs an internal self-test (see **Bus Activity During and Following Reset** on page 54). If BUSY# is sampled HIGH, no self-test is performed.

Coprocessor Error (ERROR#)

When asserted (LOW), this input signal indicates that the previous coprocessor instruction generated a coprocessor error of a type not masked by the coprocessor's control register. This input is automatically sampled by the 80376 when a coprocessor instruction is encountered, and if active, the 80376 generates exception 16 to access the error-handling software.

Several coprocessor instructions, generally those which clear the numeric error flags in the coprocessor or save coprocessor state, do execute without the 80376 generating exception 16 even if ERROR# is active. These instructions are FNINIT, FNCLEX, FNSTSW, FNSTSWAX, FNSTCW, FNSTENV and FNSAVE.

ERROR# is an active LOW, level-sensitive asynchronous signal. Setup and hold times t_{29} and t_{30}, relative to the CLK2 signal must be met to guarantee recognition at a particular clock edge. This pin is provided with a weak internal pull-up resistor of around 20 KΩ to V_{CC} so that it will not float active when left unconnected.

INTERRUPT SIGNALS (INTR, NMI, RESET)

The following descriptions cover inputs that can interrupt or suspend execution of the processor's current instruction stream.

Maskable Interrupt Request (INTR)

When asserted, this input indicates a request for interrupt service, which can be masked by the 80376 Flag Register IF bit. When the 80376 responds to the INTR input, it performs two interrupt acknowledge bus cycles and, at the end of the second, latches an 8-bit interrupt vector on D_7-D_0 to identify the source of the interrupt.

INTR is an active HIGH, level-sensitive asynchronous signal. Setup and hold times, t_{27} and t_{28}, relative to the CLK2 signal must be met to guarantee recognition at a particular clock edge. To assure recognition of an INTR request, INTR should remain active until the first interrupt acknowledge bus cycle begins. INTR is sampled at the beginning of every instruction. In order to be recognized at a particular instruction boundary, INTR must be active at least eight CLK2 clock periods before the beginning of the execution of the instruction. If recognized, the 80376 will begin execution of the interrupt.

Non-Maskable Interrupt Request (NMI)

This input indicates a request for interrupt service which cannot be masked by software. The non-maskable interrupt request is always processed according to the pointer or gate in slot 2 of the interrupt table. Because of the fixed NMI slot assignment, no interrupt acknowledge cycles are performed when processing NMI.

NMI is an active HIGH, rising edge-sensitive asynchronous signal. Setup and hold times, t_{27} and t_{28}, relative to the CLK2 signal must be met to guarantee recognition at a particular clock edge. To assure recognition of NMI, it must be inactive for at least eight CLK2 periods, and then be active for at least eight CLK2 periods before the beginning of the execution of an instruction.

Once NMI processing has begun, no additional NMI's are processed until after the next IRET instruction, which is typically the end of the NMI service routine. If NMI is re-asserted prior to that time, however, one rising edge on NMI will be remembered for processing after executing the next IRET instruction.

Interrupt Latency

The time that elapses before an interrupt request is serviced (interrupt latency) varies according to several factors. This delay must be taken into account by the interrupt source. Any of the following factors can affect interrupt latency:

1. If interrupts are masked, and INTR request will not be recognized until interrupts are reenabled.

2. If an NMI is currently being serviced, an incoming NMI request will not be recognized until the 80376 encounters the IRET instruction.

3. An interrupt request is recognized only on an instruction boundary of the 80376 *Execution Unit* except for the following cases:

   — Repeat string instructions can be interrupted after each iteration.

   — If the instruction loads the Stack Segment register, an interrupt is not processed until after the following instruction, which should be an ESP load. This allows the entire stack pointer to be loaded without interruption.

   — If an instruction sets the interrupt flag (enabling interrupts), an interrupt is not processed until after the next instruction.

   The longest latency occurs when the interrupt request arrives while the 80376 processor is executing a long instruction such as multiplication, division or a task-switch.

4. Saving the Flags register and CS:EIP registers.

5. If interrupt service routine requires a task switch, time must be allowed for the task switch.

6. If the interrupt service routine saves registers that are not automatically saved by the 80376.

RESET

This input signal suspends any operation in progress and places the 80376 in a known reset state. The 80376 is reset by asserting RESET for 15 or more CLK2 periods (80 or more CLK2 periods before requesting self-test). When RESET is active, all other input pins are ignored, and all other bus pins are driven to an idle bus state as shown in Table 4.5. If RESET and HOLD are both active at a point in time, RESET takes priority even if the 80376 was in a Hold Acknowledge state prior to RESET active.

RESET is an active HIGH, level-sensitive synchronous signal. Setup and hold times, t_{25} and t_{26}, must be met in order to assure proper operation of the 80376.

Table 4.5. Pin State (Bus Idle) during RESET

Pin Name	Signal Level during RESET
ADS#	1
$D_{15}-D_0$	Float
BHE#, BLE#	0
$A_{23}-A_1$	1
W/R#	0
D/C#	1
M/IO#	0
LOCK#	1
HLDA	0

4.2 Bus Transfer Mechanism

All data transfers occur as a result of one or more bus cycles. Logical data operands of byte and word lengths may be transferred without restrictions on physical address alignment. Any byte boundary may be used, although two physical bus cycles are performed as required for unaligned operand transfers.

The 80376 processor address signals are designed to simplify external system hardware. BHE# and BLE# provide linear selects for the two bytes of the 16-bit data bus.

Byte Enable outputs BHE# and BLE# are asserted when their associated data bus bytes are involved with the present bus cycle, as listed in Table 4.6.

Table 4.6. Byte Enables and Associated Data and Operand Bytes

Byte Enable	Associated Data Bus Signals
BHE# BLE#	$D_{15}-D_8$ (Byte 1—Most Significant) D_7-D_0 (Byte 0—Least Significant)

Each bus cycle is composed of at least two bus states. Each bus state requires one processor clock period. Additional bus states added to a single bus cycle are called wait states. See **Bus Functional Description** (page 39) for additional information.

4.3 Memory and I/O Spaces

Bus cycles may access physical memory space or I/O space. Peripheral devices in the system may either be memory-mapped, or I/O-mapped, or both. As shown in Figure 4.3, physical memory addresses range from 000000H to 0FFFFFFH (16 Mbytes) and I/O addresses from 000000H to 00FFFFH (64 Kbytes). Note the I/O addresses used by the automatic I/O cycles for coprocessor communication are 8000F8H to 8000FFH, beyond the address range of programmed I/O, to allow easy generation of a coprocessor chip select signal using the A_{23} and M/IO# signals.

OPERAND ALIGNMENT

With the flexibility of memory addressing on the 80376, it is possible to transfer a logical operand that spans more than one physical Dword or word of memory or I/O. Examples are 32-bit Dword or 16-bit word operands beginning at addresses not evenly divisible by 2.

Operand alignment and size dictate when multiple bus cycles are required. Table 4.6a describes the transfer cycles generated for all combinations of logical operand lengths and alignment.

Table 4.6a. Transfer Bus Cycles for Bytes, Words and Dwords

	Byte-Length of Logical Operand								
	1	2				4			
Physical Byte Address in Memory (Low-Order Bits)	xx	00	01	10	11	00	01	10	11
Transfer Cycles	b	w	lb, hb	w	hb, l,b	lw, hw	hb, lb, mw	hw, lw	mw, hb, lb

Key:
b = byte transfer
w = word transfer
l = low-order portion
m = mid-order portion
x = don't care
h = high-order portion

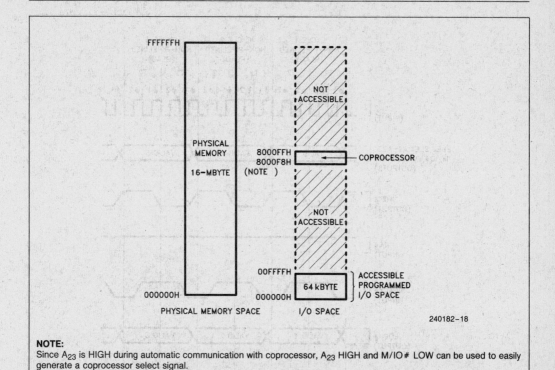

240182–18

NOTE:
Since A_{23} is HIGH during automatic communication with coprocessor, A_{23} HIGH and M/IO# LOW can be used to easily generate a coprocessor select signal.

Figure 4.3. Physical Memory and I/O Spaces

4.4 Bus Functional Description

The 80376 has separate, parallel buses for data and address. The data bus is 16 bits in width, and bidirectional. The address bus provides a 24-bit value using 23 signals for the 23 upper-order address bits and 2 Byte Enable signals to directly indicate the active bytes. These buses are interpreted and controlled by several definition signals.

The definition of each bus cycle is given by three signals: M/IO#, W/R# and D/C#. At the same time, a valid address is present on the byte enable signals, BHE# and BLE#, and the other address signals $A_{23}-A_1$. A status signal, ADS#, indicates when the 80376 issues a new bus cycle definition and address.

Collectively, the address bus, data bus and all associated control signals are referred to simply as "the bus". When active, the bus performs one of the bus cycles below:

1. Read from memory space
2. Locked read from memory space
3. Write to memory space
4. Locked write to memory space
5. Read from I/O space (or coprocessor)
6. Write to I/O space (or coprocessor)
7. Interrupt acknowledge (always locked)
8. Indicate halt, or indicate shutdown

Table 4.2 shows the encoding of the bus cycle definition signals for each bus cycle. See **Bus Cycle Definition Signals** (page 35) for additonal information.

When the 80376 bus is not performing one of the activities listed above, it is either Idle or in the Hold Acknowledge state, which may be detected by external circuitry. The idle state can be identified by the 80376 giving no further assertions on its address strobe output (ADS#) since the beginning of its most recent bus cycle, and the most recent bus cycle having been terminated. The hold acknowledge state is identified by the 80376 asserting its hold acknowledge (HLDA) output.

The shortest time unit of bus activity is a bus state. A bus state is one processor clock period (two CLK2 periods) in duration. A complete data transfer occurs during a bus cycle, composed of two or more bus states.

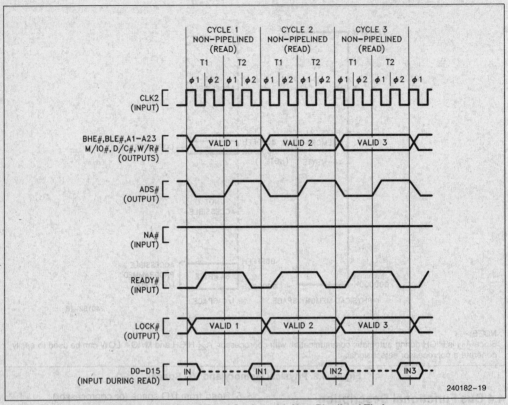

Figure 4.4. Fastest Read Cycles with Non-Pipelined Timing

The fastest 80376 bus cycle requires only two bus states. For example, three consecutive bus read cycles, each consisting of two bus states, are shown by Figure 4.4. The bus states in each cycle are named T1 and T2. Any memory or I/O address may be accessed by such a two-state bus cycle, if the external hardware is fast enough.

Every bus cycle continues until it is acknowledged by the external system hardware, using the 80376 READY# input. Acknowledging the bus cycle at the end of the first T2 results in the shortest bus cycle, requiring only T1 and T2. If READY# is not immediately asserted however, T2 states are repeated indefinitely until the READY# input is sampled active.

The pipelining option provides a choice of bus cycle timings. Pipelined or non-pipelined cycles are

selectable on a cycle-by-cycle basis with the Next Address (NA#) input.

When pipelining is selected the address (BHE#, BLE# and $A_{23}-A_1$) and definition (W/R#, D/C#, M/IO# and LOCK#) of the next cycle are available before the end of the current cycle. To signal their availability, the 80376 address status output (ADS#) is asserted. Figure 4.5 illustrates the fastest read cycles with pipelined timing.

Note from Figure 4.5 the fastest bus cycles using pipelining require only two bus states, named **T1P** and **T2P**. Therefore pipelined cycles allow the same data bandwidth as non-pipelined cycles, but address-to-data access time is increased by one T-state time compared to that of a non-pipelined cycle.

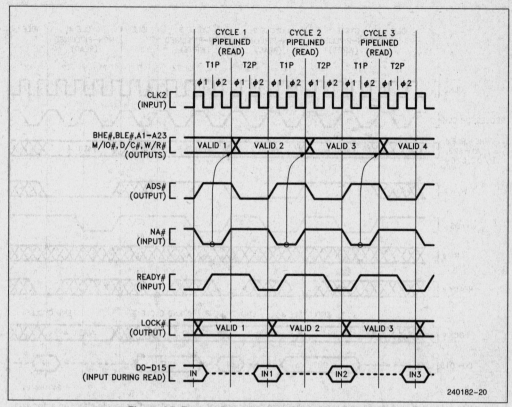

Figure 4.5. Fastest Read Cycles with Pipelined Timing

READ AND WRITE CYCLES

Data transfers occur as a result of bus cycles, classified as read or write cycles. During read cycles, data is transferred from an external device to the processor. During write cycles, data is transferred from the processor to an external device.

Two choices of bus cycle timing are dynamically selectable: non-pipelined or pipelined. After an idle bus state, the processor always uses non-pipelined timing. However the NA# (Next Address) input may be asserted to select pipelined timing for the next bus cycle. When pipelining is selected and the 80376 has a bus request pending internally, the address and definition of the next cycle is made available even before the current bus cycle is acknowledged by READY#.

Terminating a read or write cycle, like any bus cycle, requires acknowledging the cycle by asserting the READY# input. Until acknowledged, the processor inserts wait states into the bus cycle, to allow adjust-

ment for the speed of any external device. External hardware, which has decoded the address and bus cycle type, asserts the READY# input at the appropriate time.

At the end of the second bus state within the bus cycle, READY# is sampled. At that time, if external hardware acknowledges the bus cycle by asserting READY#, the bus cycle terminates as shown in Figure 4.6. If READY# is negated as in Figure 4.7, the 80376 executes another bus state (a wait state) and READY# is sampled again at the end of that state. This continues indefinitely until the cycle is acknowledged by READY# asserted.

When the current cycle is acknowledged, the 80376 terminates it. When a read cycle is acknowledged, the 80376 latches the information present at its data pins. When a write cycle is acknowledged, the write data of the 80376 remains valid throughout phase one of the next bus state, to provide write data hold time.

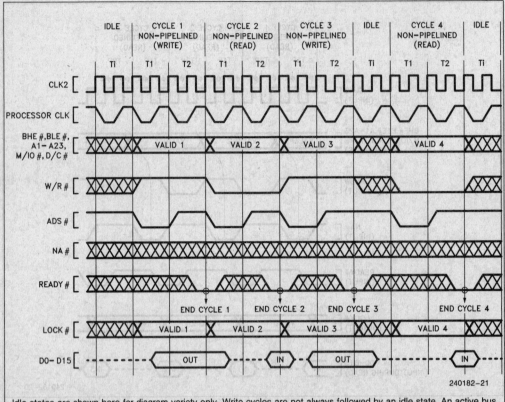

Figure 4.6. Various Non-Pipelined Bus Cycles (Zero Wait States)

Idle states are shown here for diagram variety only. Write cycles are not always followed by an idle state. An active bus cycle can immediately follow the write cycle.

Non-Pipelined Bus Cycles

Any bus cycle may be performed with non-pipelined timing. For example, Figure 4.6 shows a mixture of non-pipelined read and write cycles. Figure 4.6 shows that the fastest possible non-pipelined cycles have two bus states per bus cycle. The states are named T1 and T2. In phase one of T1, the address signals and bus cycle definition signals are driven valid and, to signal their availability, address strobe (ADS#) is simultaneously asserted.

During read or write cycles, the data bus behaves as follows. If the cycle is a read, the 80376 floats its data signals to allow driving by the external device being addressed. **The 80376 requires that all data bus pins be at a valid logic state (HIGH or LOW) at the end of each read cycle, when READY# is asserted. The system MUST be designed to meet this requirement.** If the cycle is a write, data signals are driven by the 80376 beginning in phase two of T1 until phase one of the bus state following cycle acknowledgement.

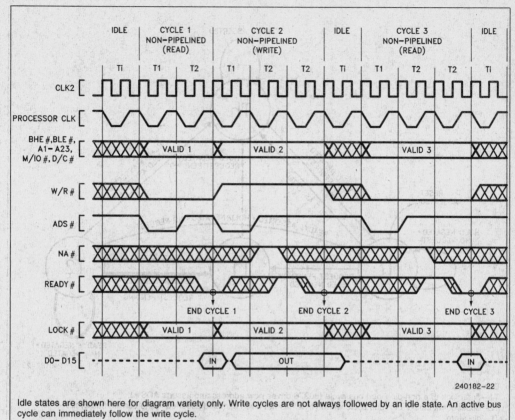

Figure 4.7. Various Non-Pipelined Bus Cycles (Various Number of Wait States)

Figure 4.7 illustrates non-pipelined bus cycles with one wait state added to Cycles 2 and 3. READY# is sampled inactive at the end of the first T2 in Cycles 2 and 3. Therefore Cycles 2 and 3 have T2 repeated again. At the end of the second T2, READY# is sampled active.

When address pipelining is not used, the address and bus cycle definition remain valid during all wait states. When wait states are added and it is desirable to maintain non-pipelined timing, it is necessary to negate NA# during each T2 state except the

last one, as shown in Figure 4.7, Cycles 2 and 3. If NA# is sampled active during a T2 other than the last one, the next state would be T2I or T2P instead of another T2.

When address pipelining is not used, the bus states and transitions are completely illustrated by Figure 4.8. The bus transitions between four possible states, T1, T2, T_i, and T_h. Bus cycles consist of T1 and T2, with T2 being repeated for wait states. Otherwise the bus may be idle, T_i, or in the hold acknowledge state T_h.

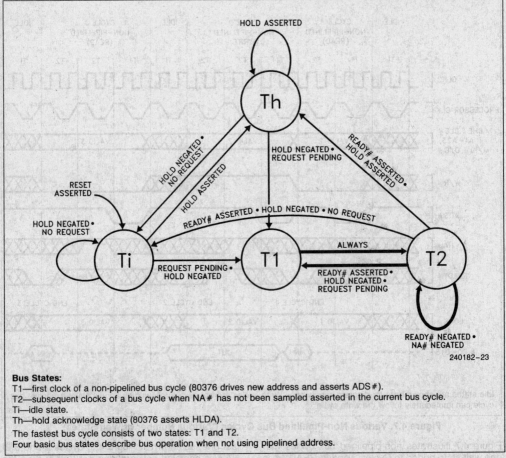

Bus States:
T1—first clock of a non-pipelined bus cycle (80376 drives new address and asserts ADS#).
T2—subsequent clocks of a bus cycle when NA# has not been sampled asserted in the current bus cycle.
Ti—idle state.
Th—hold acknowledge state (80376 asserts HLDA).

The fastest bus cycle consists of two states: T1 and T2.
Four basic bus states describe bus operation when not using pipelined address.

Figure 4.8. 80376 Bus States (Not Using Pipelined Address)

Bus cycles always begin with T1. T1 always leads to T2. If a bus cycle is not acknowledged during T2 and NA# is inactive, T2 is repeated. When a cycle is acknowledged during T2, the following state will be T1 of the next bus cycle if a bus request is pending internally, or T_i if there is no bus request pending, or T_h if the HOLD input is being asserted.

Use of pipelining allows the 80376 to enter three additional bus states not shown in Figure 4.8. Figure 4.12 on page 49 is the complete bus state diagram, including pipelined cycles.

Pipelined Bus Cycles

Pipelining is the option of requesting the address and the bus cycle definition of the next inter-

nally pending bus cycle before the current bus cycle is acknowledged with READY# asserted. ADS# is asserted by the 80376 when the next address is issued. The pipelining option is controlled on a cycle-by-cycle basis with the NA# input signal.

Once a bus cycle is in progress and the current address has been valid for at least one entire bus state, the NA# input is sampled at the end of every phase one until the bus cycle is acknowledged. During non-pipelined bus cycles NA# is sampled at the end of phase one in every T2. An example is Cycle 2 in Figure 4.9, during which NA# is sampled at the end of phase one of every T2 (it was asserted once during the first T2 and has no further effect during that bus cycle).

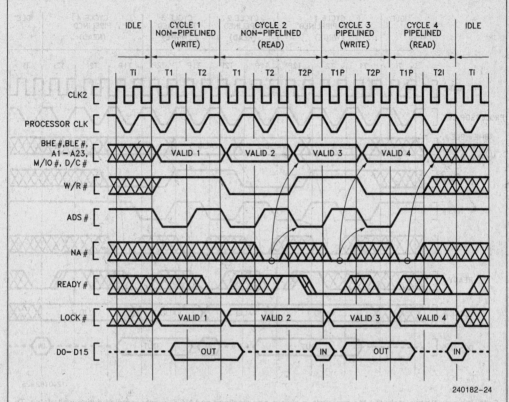

240182–24

Following any idle bus state (Ti), bus cycles are non-pipelined. Within non-pipelined bus cycles, NA# is only sampled during wait states. Therefore, to begin pipelining during a group of non-pipelined bus cycles requires a non-pipelined cycle with at least one wait state (Cylcle 2 above).

Figure 4.9. Transitioning to Pipelining during Burst of Bus Cycles

If NA# is sampled active, the 80376 is free to drive the address and bus cycle definition of the next bus cycle, and assert ADS#, as soon as it has a bus request internally pending. It may drive the next address as early as the next bus state, whether the current bus cycle is acknowledged at that time or not.

Regarding the details of pipelining, the 80376 has the following characteristics:

1. The next address and status may appear as early as the bus state after NA# was sampled active (see Figures 4.9 or 4.10). In that case, state T2P is entered immediately. However, when there is not an internal bus request already pending, the next address and status will not be available immediately after NA# is asserted and T2I is entered instead of T2P (see Figure 4.11 Cycle 3). Provided the current bus cycle isn't yet acknow-

ledged by READY# asserted, T2P will be entered as soon as the 80376 does drive the next address and status. External hardware should therefore observe the ADS# output as confirmation the next address and status are actually being driven on the bus.

2. Any address and status which are validated by a pulse on the 80376 ADS# output will remain stable on the address pins for at least two processor clock periods. The 80376 cannot produce a new address and status more frequently than every two processor clock periods (see Figures 4.9, 4.10 and 4.11).

3. Only the address and bus cycle definition of the very next bus cycle is available. The pipelining capability cannot look further than one bus cycle ahead (see Figure 4.11, Cycle 1).

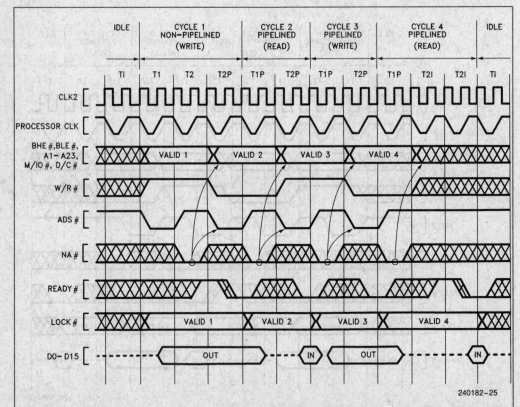

Following any idle bus state (Ti) the bus cycle is always non-pipelined and NA# is only sampled during wait states. To start, address pipelining after an idle state requires a non-pipelined cycle with at least one wait state (cycle 1 above). The pipelined cycles (2, 3, 4 above) are shown with various numbers of wait states.

Figure 4.10. Fastest Transition to Pipelined Bus Cycle Following Idle Bus State

The complete bus state transition diagram, including pipelining is given by Figure 4.12. Note it is a superset of the diagram for non-pipelined only, and the three additional bus states for pipelining are drawn in bold.

The fastest bus cycle with pipelining consists of just two bus states, T1P and T2P (recall for non-pipelined it is T1 and T2). T1P is the first bus state of a pipelined cycle.

Initiating and Maintaining Pipelined Bus Cycles

Using the state diagram Figure 4.12, observe the transitions from an idle state, T_i, to the beginning of

a pipelined bus cycle T1P. From an idle state, T_i, the first bus cycle must begin with T1, and is therefore a non-pipelined bus cycle. The next bus cycle will be pipelined, however, provided NA# is asserted and the first bus cycle ends in a T2P state (the address and status for the next bus cycle is driven during T2P). The fastest path from an idle state to a pipelined bus cycle is shown in bold below:

$T_i, T_i,$	T1–T2–T2P,	T1P–T2P,
idle states	non-pipelined cycle	pipelined cycle

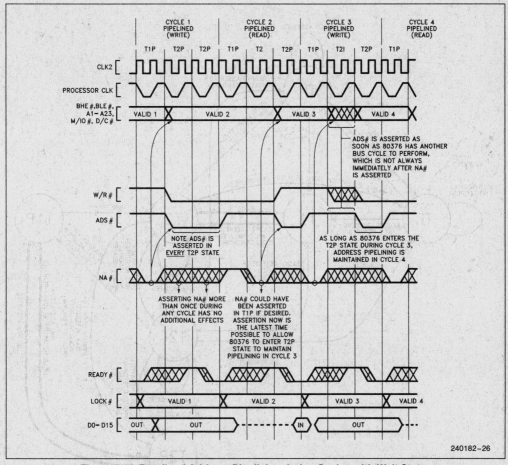

Figure 4.11. Details of Address Pipelining during Cycles with Wait States

T1–T2–T2P are the states of the bus cycle that establishes address pipelining for the next bus cycle, which begins with T1P. The same is true after a bus hold state, shown below:

T_h, T_h, T_h,   T1–T2–T2P,   T1P–T2P,

hold aknowledge   non-pipelined   pipelined
states   cycle   cycle

The transition to pipelined address is shown functionally by Figure 4.10, Cycle 1. Note that Cycle 1 is used to transition into pipelined address timing for the subsequent Cycles 2, 3 and 4, which are pipelined. The NA# input is asserted at the appropriate time to select address pipelining for Cycles 2, 3 and 4.

Once a bus cycle is in progress and the current address and status has been valid for one entire bus state, the NA# input is sampled at the end of every phase one until the bus cycle is acknowledged.

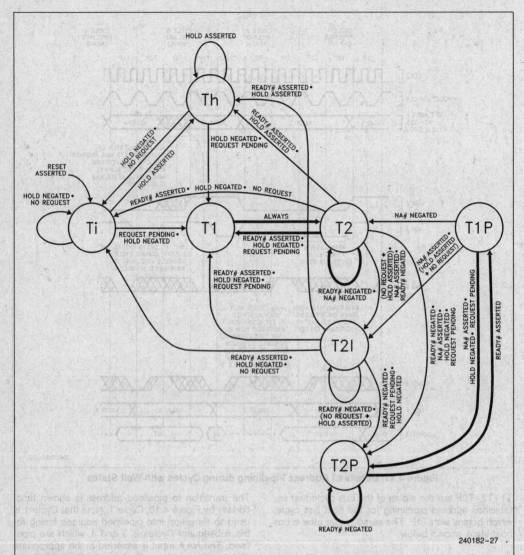

240182-27

Bus States:

T1—first clock of a non-pipelined bus cycle (80376 drives new address, status and asserts ADS#).

T2—subsequent clocks of a bus cycle when NA# has not been sampled asserted in the current bus cycle.

T2I—subsequent clocks of a bus cycle when NA# has been sampled asserted in the current bus cycle but there is not yet an internal bus request pending (80376 will not drive new address, status or assert ADS#).

T2P—subsequent clocks of a bus cycle when NA# has been sampled asserted in the current bus cycle and there is an internal bus request pending (80376 drives new address, status and asserts ADS#).

T1P—first clock of a pipelined bus cycle.

Ti—idle state.

Th—hold acknowledge state (80376 asserts HLDA).

Asserting NA# for pipelined bus cycles gives access to three more bus states: T2I, T2P and T1P.

Using pipelining the fastest bus cycle consists of T1P and T2P.

Figure 4.12. 80376 Processor Complete Bus States (Including Pipelining)

Sampling begins in T2 during Cycle 1 in Figure 4.10. Once NA# is sampled active during the current cycle, the 80376 is free to drive a new address and bus cycle definition on the bus as early as the next bus state. In Figure 4.10, Cycle 1 for example, the next address and status is driven during state T2P. Thus Cycle 1 makes the transition to pipelined timing, since it begins with T1 but ends with T2P. Because the address for Cycle 2 is available before Cycle 2 begins, Cycle 2 is called a pipelined bus cycle, and it begins with T1P. Cycle 2 begins as soon as READY# asserted terminates Cycle 1.

Examples of transition bus cycles are Figure 4.10, Cycle 1 and Figure 4.9, Cycle 2. Figure 4.10 shows transition during the very first cycle after an idle bus state, which is the fastest possible transition into address pipelining. Figure 4.9, Cycle 2 shows a transition cycle occurring during a burst of bus cycles. In any case, a transition cycle is the same whenever it occurs: it consists at least of T1, T2 (NA# is asserted at that time), and T2P (provided the 80376 has an internal bus request already pending, which it almost always has). T2P states are repeated if wait states are added to the cycle.

Note that only three states (T1, T2 and T2P) are required in a bus cycle performing a **transition** from non-pipelined into pipelined timing, for example Figure 4.10, Cycle 1. Figure 4.10, Cycles 2, 3 and 4 show that pipelining can be maintained with two-state bus cycles consisting only of T1P and T2P.

Once a pipelined bus cycle is in progress, pipelined timing is maintained for the next cycle by asserting NA# and detecting that the 80376 enters T2P during the current bus cycle. The current bus cycle must end in state T2P for pipelining to be maintained in the next cycle. T2P is identified by the assertion of ADS#. Figures 4.9 and 4.10 however, each show

pipelining ending after Cycle 4 because Cycle 4 ends in T2I. This indicates the 80376 didn't have an internal bus request prior to the acknowledgement of Cycle 4. If a cycle ends with a T2 or T2I, the next cycle will not be pipelined.

Realistically, pipelining is almost always maintained as long as NA# is sampled asserted. This is so because in the absence of any other request, a code prefetch request is always internally pending until the instruction decoder and code prefetch queue are completely full. Therefore pipelining is maintained for long bursts of bus cycles, if the bus is available (i.e., HOLD inactive) and NA# is sampled active in each of the bus cycles.

INTERRUPT ACKNOWLEDGE (INTA) CYCLES

In repsonse to an interrupt request on the INTR input when interrupts are enabled, the 80376 performs two interrupt acknowledge cycles. These bus cycles are similar to read cycles in that bus definition signals define the type of bus activity taking place, and each cycle continues until acknowledged by READY# sampled active.

The state of A_2 distinguishes the first and second interrupt acknowledge cycles. The byte address driven during the first interrupt acknowledge cycle is 4 (A_{23}–A_3, A_1, BLE# LOW, A_2 and BHE# HIGH). The byte address driven during the second interrupt acknowledge cycle is 0 (A_{23}–A_1, BLE# LOW and BHE# HIGH).

The LOCK# output is asserted from the beginning of the first interrupt acknowledge cycle until the end of the second interrupt acknowledge cycle. Four idle bus states, T_i, are inserted by the 80376 between the two interrupt acknowledge cycles for compatibility with the interrupt specification T_{RHRL} of the 8259A Interrupt Controller and the 82370 Integrated Peripheral.

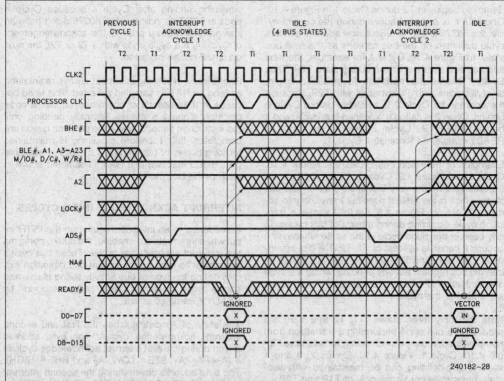

Interrupt Vector (0–255) is read on D0–D7 at end of second Interrupt Acknowledge bus cycle.
Because each Interrupt Acknowledge bus cycle is followed by idle bus states, asserting NA# has no practical effect.
Choose the approach which is simplest for your system hardware design.

Figure 4.13. Interrupt Acknowledge Cycles

During both interrupt acknowledge cycles, D_{15}–D_0 float. No data is read at the end of the first interrupt acknowledge cycle. At the end of the second interrupt acknowledge cycle, the 80376 will read an external interrupt vector from D_7–D_0 of the data bus. The vector indicates the specific interrupt number (from 0–255) requiring service.

HALT INDICATION CYCLE

The 80376 execution unit halts as a result of executing a HLT instruction. Signaling its entrance into the halt state, a halt indication cycle is performed. The halt indication cycle is identified by the state of the bus definition signals shown on page 34, **Bus Cycle Definition Signals,** and a byte address of 2. The halt indication cycle must be acknowledged by READY# asserted. A halted 80376 resumes execution when INTR (if interrupts are enabled), NMI or RESET is asserted.

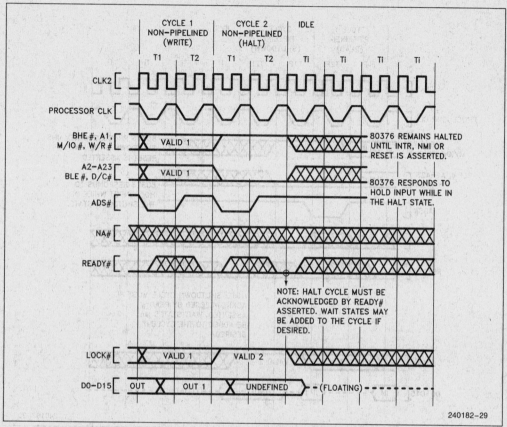

Figure 4.14. Example Halt Indication Cycle from Non-Pipelined Cycle

SHUTDOWN INDICATION CYCLE

The 80376 shuts down as a result of a protection fault while attempting to process a double fault. Signaling its entrance into the shutdown state, a shutdown indication cycle is performed. The shutdown indication cycle is identified by the state of the bus definition signals shown on page 34 **Bus Cycle Definition Signals** and a byte address of 0. The shutdown indication cycle must be acknowledged by READY# asserted. A shutdown 80376 resumes execution when NMI or RESET is asserted.

ENTERING AND EXITING HOLD ACKNOWLEDGE

The bus hold acknowledge state, T_h, is entered in response to the HOLD input being asserted. In the bus hold acknowledge state, the 80376 floats all outputs or bidirectional signals, except for HLDA. HLDA is asserted as long as the 80376 remains in the bus hold acknowledge state. In the bus hold acknowledge state, all inputs except HOLD and RESET are ignored.

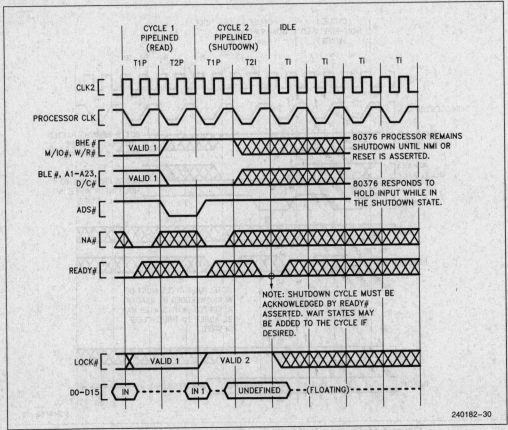

Figure 4.15. Example Shutdown Indication Cycle from Non-Pipelined Cycle

T_h may be entered from a bus idle state as in Figure 4.16 or after the acknowledgement of the current physical bus cycle if the LOCK# signal is not asserted, as in Figures 4.17 and 4.18.

T_h is exited in response to the HOLD input being negated. The following state will be T_i as in Figure 4.16 if no bus request is pending. The following bus state will be T1 if a bus request is internally pending, as in Figures 4.17 and 4.18. T_h is exited in response to RESET being asserted.

If a rising edge occurs on the edge-triggered NMI input while in T_h, the event is remembered as a non-maskable interrupt 2 and is serviced when T_h is exited unless the 80376 is reset before T_h is exited.

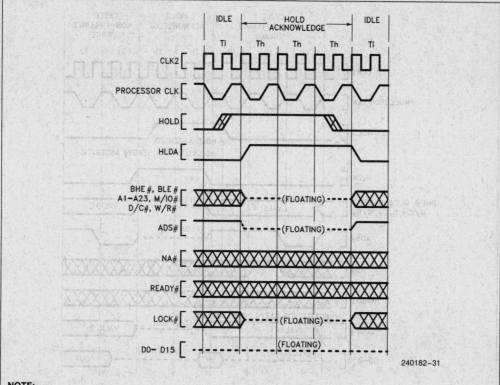

NOTE:
For maximum design flexibility the 80376 has no internal pull-up resistors on its outputs. Your design may require an external pullup on ADS# and other 80376 outputs to keep them negated during float periods.

Figure 4.16. Requesting Hold from Idle Bus

RESET DURING HOLD ACKNOWLEDGE

RESET being asserted takes priority over HOLD being asserted. If RESET is asserted while HOLD remains asserted, the 80376 drives its pins to defined states during reset, as in **Table 4.5, Pin State During Reset,** and performs internal reset activity as usual.

If HOLD remains asserted when RESET is inactive, the 80376 enters the hold acknowledge state before performing its first bus cycle, provided HOLD is still asserted when the 80376 processor would otherwise perform its first bus cycle. If HOLD remains asserted when RESET is inactive, the BUSY# input is still sampled as usual to determine whether a self test is being requested.

BUS ACTIVITY DURING AND FOLLOWING RESET

RESET is the highest priority input signal, capable of interrupting any processor activity when it is asserted. A bus cycle in progress can be aborted at any stage, or idle states or bus hold acknowledge states discontinued so that the reset state is established.

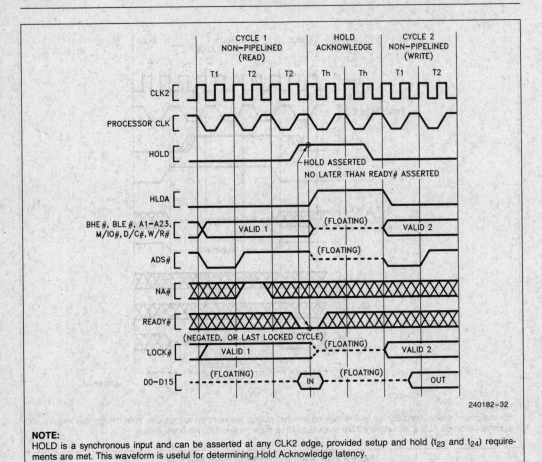

NOTE:
HOLD is a synchronous input and can be asserted at any CLK2 edge, provided setup and hold (t_{23} and t_{24}) requirements are met. This waveform is useful for determining Hold Acknowledge latency.

Figure 4.17. Requesting Hold from Active Bus (NA# Inactive)

RESET should remain asserted for at least 15 CLK2 periods to ensure it is recognized throughout the 80376, and at least 80 CLK2 periods if a 80376 self-test is going to be requested at the falling edge. RESET asserted pulses less than 15 CLK2 periods may not be recognized. RESET pulses less than 80 CLK2 periods followed by a self-test may cause the self-test to report a failure when no true failure exists.

Provided the RESET falling edge meets setup and hold times t_{25} and t_{26}, the internal processor clock phase is defined at that time as illustrated by Figure 4.19 and Figure 6.7.

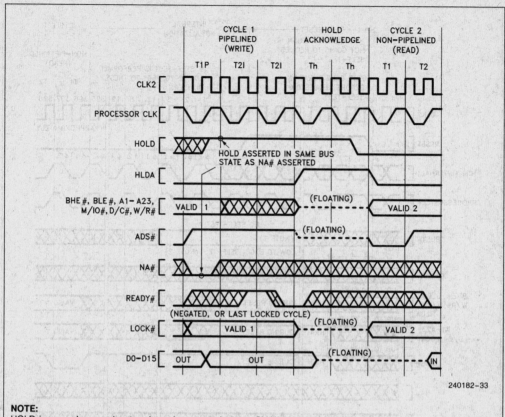

240182–33

NOTE:
HOLD is a synchronous input and can be asserted at any CLK2 edge, provided setup and hold (t_{23} and t_{24}) requirements are met. This waveform is useful for determining Hold Acknowledge latency.

Figure 4.18. Requesting Hold from Idle Bus (NA# Active)

An 80376 self-test may be requested at the time RESET goes inactive by having the BUSY# input at a LOW level as shown in Figure 4.19. The self-test requires (2^{20} + approximately 60) CLK2 periods to complete. The self-test duration is not affected by the test results. Even if the self-test indicates a problem, the 80376 attempts to proceed with the reset sequence afterwards.

After the RESET falling edge (and after the self-test if it was requested) the 80376 performs an internal initialization sequence for approximately 350 to 450 CLK2 periods.

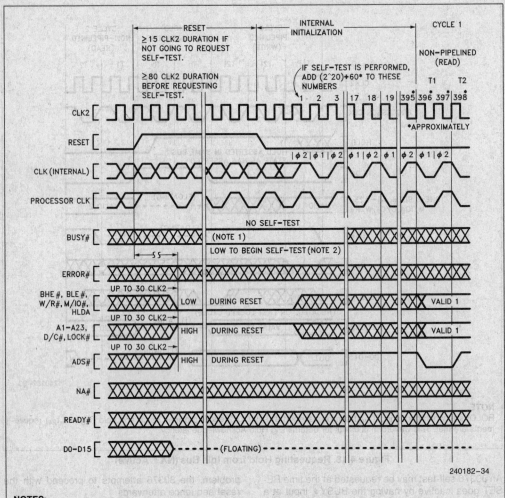

Figure 4.19. Bus Activity from Reset until First Code Fetch

NOTES:
1. BUSY# should be held stable for 8 CLK2 periods before and after the CLK2 period in which RESET falling edge occurs.
2. If self-test is requested, the 80376 outputs remain in their reset state as shown here.

4.5 Self-Test Signature

Upon completion of self-test (if self-test was requested by driving BUSY# LOW at the falling edge of RESET) the EAX register will contain a signature of 00000000H indicating the 80376 passed its self-test of microcode and major PLA contents with no problems detected. The passing signature in EAX, 00000000H, applies to all 80376 revision levels. Any non-zero signature indicates the 80376 unit is faulty.

4.6 Component and Revision Identifiers

To assist 80376 users, the 80376 after reset holds a component identifier and revision identifier in its DX register. The upper 8 bits of DX hold 33H as identification of the 80376 component. (The lower nibble, 03H, refers to the Intel386™ architecture. The upper nibble, 30H, refers to the third member of the Intel386 family). The lower 8 bits of DX hold an 8-bit unsigned binary number related to the component revision level. The revision identifier will, in general, chronologically track those component steppings which are intended to have certain improvements or distinction from previous steppings. The 80376 revision identifier will track that of the 80386 where possible.

The revision identifier is intended to assist 80376 users to a practical extent. However, the revision identifier value is not guaranteed to change with every stepping revision, or to follow a completely uniform numerical sequence, depending on the type or intention of revision, or manufacturing materials required to be changed. Intel has sole discretion over these characteristics of the component.

Table 4.7. Component and Revision Identifier History

80376 Stepping Name	Revision Identifier
A0	05H

4.7 Coprocessor Interfacing

The 80376 provides an automatic interface for the Intel 80387SX numeric floating-point coprocessor. The 80387SX coprocessor uses an I/O mapped interface driven automatically by the 80376 and assisted by three dedicated signals: BUSY#, ERROR# and PEREQ.

As the 80376 begins supporting a coprocessor instruction, it tests the BUSY# and ERROR# signals to determine if the coprocessor can accept its next instruction. Thus, the BUSY# and ERROR# inputs eliminate the need for any "preamble" bus cycles for communication between processor and coprocessor. The 80387SX can be given its command opcode immediately. The dedicated signals provide instruction synchronization, and eliminate the need of using the 80376 WAIT opcode (9BH) for 80387SX instruction synchronization (the WAIT opcode was required when the 8086 or 8088 was used with the 8087 coprocessor).

Custom coprocessors can be included in 80376 based systems by memory-mapped or I/O-mapped interfaces. Such coprocessor interfaces allow a completely custom protocol, and are not limited to a set of coprocessor protocol "primitives". Instead, memory-mapped or I/O-mapped interfaces may use all applicable 80376 instructions for high-speed coprocessor communication. The BUSY# and

ERROR# inputs of the 80376 may also be used for the custom coprocessor interface, if such hardware assist is desired. These signals can be tested by the 80376 WAIT opcode (9BH). The WAIT instruction will wait until the BUSY# input is inactive (interruptable by an NMI or enabled INTR input), but generates an exception 16 fault if the ERROR# pin is active when the BUSY# goes (or is) inactive. If the custom coprocessor interface is memory-mapped, protection of the addresses used for the interface can be provided with the segmentation mechanism of the 80376. If the custom interface is I/O-mapped, protection of the interface can be provided with the 80376 IOPL (I/O Privilege Level) mechanism.

The 80387SX numeric coprocessor interface is I/O mapped as shown in Table 4.8. Note that the 80387SX coprocessor interface addresses are beyond the 0H-0FFFFH range for programmed I/O. When the 80376 supports the 80387SX coprocessor, the 80376 automatically generates bus cycles to the coprocessor interface addresses.

Table 4.8 Numeric Coprocessor Port Addresses

Address in 80376 I/O Space	80387SX Coprocessor Register
8000F8H	Opcode Register
8000FCH	Operand Register
8000FEH	Operand Register

SOFTWARE TESTING FOR COPROCESSOR PRESENCE

When software is used to test coprocessor (80387SX) presence, it should use only the following coprocessor opcodes: FNINIT, FNSTCW and FNSTSW. To use other coprocessor opcodes when a coprocessor is known to be not present, first set EM = 1 in the 80376 CR0 register.

5.0 PACKAGE THERMAL SPECIFICATIONS

The Intel 80376 embedded processor is specified for operation when case temperature is within the range of 0°C–115°C for the ceramic 88-pin PGA package, and 0°C–110°C for the 100-pin plastic package. The case temperature may be measured in any environment, to determine whether the 80376 is within specified operating range. The case temperature should be measured at the center of the top surface.

The ambient temperature is guaranteed as long as T_C is not violated. The ambient temperature can be calculated from the θ_{jc} and θ_{ja} from the following equations:

$$T_J = T_C + P^*\theta_{jc}$$

$$T_A = T_j - P^*\theta_{ja}$$

$$T_C = T_a + P^*[\theta_{ja} - \theta_{jc}]$$

Values for θ_{ja} and θ_{jc} are given in Table 5.1 for the 100-lead fine pitch. θ_{ja} is given at various airflows. Table 5.2 shows the maximum T_a allowable (without exceeding T_c) at various airflows. Note that T_a can be improved further by attaching "fins" or a "heat sink" to the package. P is calculated using the maximum *hot* I_{CC}.

Table 5.1. 80376 Package Thermal Characteristics Thermal Resistances (°C/Watt) θ_{jc} and θ_{ja}

Package	θ_{jc}	θ_{ja} Versus Airflow-ft/min (m/sec)					
		0 (0)	200 (1.01)	400 (2.03)	600 (3.04)	800 (4.06)	1000 (5.07)
100-Lead Fine Pitch	7	33	27	24	21	18	17
88-Pin PGA	2	25	20	17	14	12	11

Assuming I_{CC} hot of 360 mA, V_{CC} of 5.0V, and a T_{CASE} of 110°C for plastic and 115°C for the 88-Pin PGA Package:

Table 5.2. 80376 Maximum Allowable Ambient Temperature at Various Airflows

Package	θ_{jc}	T_A(°C) vs Airflow-ft/min (m/sec)					
		0 (0)	200 (1.01)	400 (2.03)	600 (3.04)	800 (4.06)	1000 (5.07)
100-Lead Fine Pitch	7	63	74	79	85	91	92
88-Pin PGA	2	74	83	88	93	97	99

6.0 ELECTRICAL SPECIFICATIONS

The following sections describe recommended electrical connections for the 80376, and its electrical specifications.

6.1 Power and Grounding

The 80376 is implemented in CHMOS III technology and has modest power requirements. However, its high clock frequency and 47 output buffers (address, data, control, and HLDA) can cause power surges as multiple output buffers drive new signal levels simultaneously. For clean on-chip power distribution at high frequency, 14 V_{CC} and 18 V_{SS} pins separately feed functional units of the 80376.

Power and ground connections must be made to all external V_{CC} and GND pins of the 80376. On the circuit board, all V_{CC} pins should be connected on a V_{CC} plane and all V_{SS} pins should be connected on a GND plane.

POWER DECOUPLING RECOMMENDATIONS

Liberal decoupling capacitors should be placed near the 80376. The 80376 driving its 24-bit address bus and 16-bit data bus at high frequencies can cause transient power surges, particularly when driving large capacitive loads. Low inductance capacitors and interconnects are recommended for best high frequency electrical performance. Inductance can be reduced by shortening circuit board traces between the 80376 and decoupling capacitors as much as possible.

RESISTOR RECOMMENDATIONS

The ERROR# and BUSY# inputs have internal pull-up resistors of approximately 20 KΩ and the PEREQ input has an internal pull-down resistor of approximately 20 KΩ built into the 80376 to keep these signals inactive when the 80387SX is not present in the system (or temporarily removed from its socket).

In typical designs, the external pull-up resistors shown in Table 6.1 are recommended. However, a particular design may have reason to adjust the resistor values recommended here, or alter the use of pull-up resistors in other ways.

**Table 6.1. Recommended
Resistor Pull-Ups to V_CC**

Pin	Signal	Pull-Up Value	Purpose
16	ADS#	20 KΩ ± 10%	Lightly Pull ADS# Inactive during 80376 Hold Acknowledge States
26	LOCK#	20 KΩ ± 10%	Lightly Pull LOCK# Inactive during 80376 Hold Acknowledge States

OTHER CONNECTION RECOMMENDATIONS

For reliable operation, always connect unused inputs to an appropriate signal level. N/C pins should always remain **unconnected. Connection of N/C pins to V_CC or V_SS will result in incompatibility with future steppings of the 80376.**

Particularly when not using interrupts or bus hold (as when first prototyping), prevent any chance of spurious activity by connecting these associated inputs to GND:

—INTR
—NMI
—HOLD

If not using address pipelining connect the NA# pin to a pull-up resistor in the range of 20 KΩ to V_CC.

6.2 Absolute Maximum Ratings

Table 6.2. Maximum Ratings

Parameter	Maximum Rating
Storage Temperature	−65°C to +150°C
Case Temperature under Bias	−65°C to +120°C
Supply Voltage with Respect to V_SS	−0.5V to +6.5V
Voltage on Other Pins	−0.5V to (V_CC + 0.5)V

Table 6.2 gives a stress ratings only, and functional operation at the maximums is not guaranteed. Functional operating conditions are given in **Section 6.3, D.C. Specifications,** and **Section 6.4, A.C. Specifications.**

Extended exposure to the Maximum Ratings may affect device reliability. Furthermore, although the 80376 contains protective circuitry to resist damage from static electric discharge, always take precautions to avoid high static voltages or electric fields.

6.3 D.C. Specifications

ADVANCE INFORMATION SUBJECT TO CHANGE

Table 6.3: 80376 D.C. Characteristics

Functional Operating Range: $V_{CC} = 5V \pm 10\%$; $T_{CASE} = 0°C$ to $115°C$ 88-pin PGA, $T_{CASE} = 0°C$ to $110°C$ 100-pin plastic

Symbol	Parameter	Min	Max	Unit
V_{IL}	Input LOW Voltage	-0.3	$+0.8$	V[1]
V_{IH}	Input HIGH Voltage	2.0	$V_{CC} + 0.3$	V[1]
V_{ILC}	CLK2 Input LOW Voltage	-0.3	$+0.8$	V[1]
V_{IHC}	CLK2 Input HIGH Voltage	$V_{CC} - 0.8$	$V_{CC} + 0.3$	V[1]
V_{OL}	Output LOW Voltage			
$I_{OL} = 4$ mA:	$A_{23} - A_1$, $D_{15} - D_0$		0.45	V[1]
$I_{OL} = 5$ mA:	BHE#, BLE#, W/R#, D/C#, M/IO#, LOCK#, ADS#, HLDA		0.45	V[1]
V_{OH}	Output High Voltage			
$I_{OH} = -1$ mA:	$A_{23} - A_1$, $D_{15} - D_0$	2.4		V[1]
$I_{OH} = -0.2$ mA:	$A_{23} - A_1$, $D_{15} - D_0$	$V_{CC} - 0.5$		V[1]
$I_{OH} = -0.9$ mA:	BHE#, BLE#, W/R#, D/C#, M/IO#, LOCK#, ADS#, HLDA	2.4		V[1]
$I_{OH} = -0.18$ mA:	BHE#, BLE#, W/R#, D/C#, M/IO#, LOCK#, ADS#, HLDA	$V_{CC} - 0.5$		V[1]
I_{LI}	Input Leakage Current (For All Pins except PEREQ, BUSY# and ERROR#)		± 15	μA, $0V \leq V_{IN} \leq V_{CC}$[1]
I_{IH}	Input Leakage Current (PEREQ Pin)		200	μA, $V_{IH} = 2.4V$[1,2]
I_{IL}	Input Leakage Current (Busy# and ERROR# Pins)		-400	μA, $V_{IL} = 0.45V$[3]
I_{LO}	Output Leakage Current		± 15	μA, $0.45V \leq V_{OUT} \leq V_{CC}$[1]
I_{CC}	Supply Current at HOT		400 360	mA[4] mA[6]
C_{IN}	Input Capacitance		10	pF, $F_C = 1$ MHz[5]
C_{OUT}	Output or I/O Capacitance		12	pF, $F_C = 1$ MHz[5]
C_{CLK}	CLK2 Capacitance		20	pF, $F_C = 1$ MHz[5]

NOTES:
1. Tested at the minimum operating frequency of the part.
2. PEREQ input has an internal pull-down resistor.
3. BUSY# and ERROR# inputs each have an internal pull-up resistor.
4. I_{CC} max measurement at worse case frequency, V_{CC} and temperature (0°C).
5. Not 100% tested.
6. I_{CC} HOT max measurement at worse case frequency, V_{CC} and max temperature.

The A.C. specifications given in Table 6.4 consist of output delays, input setup requirements and input hold requirements. All A.C. specifications are relative to the CLK2 rising edge crossing the 2.0V level.

A.C. specification measurement is defined by Figure 6.1. Inputs must be driven to the voltage levels indicated by Figure 6.1 when A.C. specifications are measured. 80376 output delays are specified with minimum and maximum limits measured as shown. The minimum 80376 delay times are hold times provided to external circuitry. 80376 input setup and hold times are specified as minimums, defining the smallest acceptable sampling window. Within the sampling window, a synchronous input signal must be stable for correct 80376 processor operation.

Outputs NA#, W/R#, D/C#, M/IO#, LOCK#, BHE#, BLE#, $A_{23}-A_1$ and HLDA only change at the beginning of phase one. $D_{15}-D_0$ (write cycles) only change at the beginning of phase two. The READY#, HOLD, BUSY#, ERROR#, PEREQ and $D_{15}-D_0$ (read cycles) inputs are sampled at the beginning of phase one. The NA#, INTR and NMI inputs are sampled at the beginning of phase two.

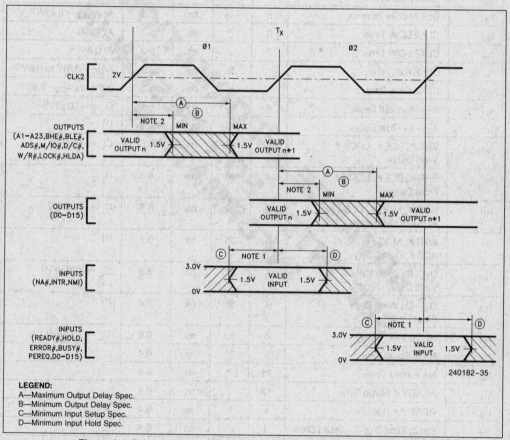

LEGEND:
A—Maximum Output Delay Spec.
B—Minimum Output Delay Spec.
C—Minimum Input Setup Spec.
D—Minimum Input Hold Spec.

240182–35

Figure 6.1. Drive Levels and Measurement Points for A.C. Specifications

6.4 A.C. Specifications

ADVANCE INFORMATION SUBJECT TO CHANGE

Table 6.4. 80376 A.C. Characteristics at 16 MHz

Functional Operating Range: V_{CC} = 5V ±10%; T_{CASE} = 0°C to 115°C for 88-pin PGA, 0°C to 110°C for 100-pin plastic

Symbol	Parameter	Min	Max	Unit	Figure	Notes
	Operating Frequency	4	16	MHz		Half CLK2 Freq
t_1	CLK2 Period	31	125	ns	6.3	
t_{2a}	CLK2 HIGH Time	9		ns	6.3	At 2[3]
t_{2b}	CLK2 HIGH Time	5		ns	6.3	At $(V_{CC} - 0.8)$V[3]
t_{3a}	CLK2 LOW Time	9		ns	6.3	At 2V[3]
t_{3b}	CLK2 LOW Time	7		ns	6.3	At 0.8V[3]
t_4	CLK2 Fall Time		8	ns	6.3	$(V_{CC} - 0.8)$V to 0.8V[3]
t_5	CLK2 Rise Time		8	ns	6.3	0.8V to $(V_{CC} - 0.8)$V[3]
t_6	$A_{23} - A_1$ Valid Delay	4	36	ns	6.5	C_L = 120 pF[4]
t_7	$A_{23} - A_1$ Float Delay	4	40	ns	6.6	[1]
t_8	BHE#, BLE#, LOCK# Valid Delay	4	36	ns	6.5	C_L = 75 pF[4]
t_9	BHE#, BLE#, LOCK# Float Delay	4	40	ns	6.6	[1]
t_{10}	W/R#, M/IO#, D/C#, ADS# Valid Delay	6	33	ns	6.5	C_L = 75 pF[4]
t_{11}	W/R#, M/IO#, D/C#, ADS# Float Delay	6	35	ns	6.6	[1]
t_{12}	$D_{15} - D_0$ Write Data Valid Delay	4	40	ns	6.5	C_L = 120 pF[4]
t_{13}	$D_{15} - D_0$ Write Data Float Delay	4	35	ns	6.6	[1]
t_{14}	HLDA Valid Delay	6	33	ns	6.6	C_L = 75 pF[4]
t_{15}	NA# Setup Time	5		ns	6.4	
t_{16}	NA# Hold Time	21		ns	6.6	
t_{19}	READY# Setup Time	19		ns	6.4	
t_{20}	READY# Hold Time	4		ns	6.4	
t_{21}	Setup Time $D_{15} - D_0$ Read Data	9		ns	6.4	
t_{22}	Hold Time $D_{15} - D_0$ Read Data	6		ns	6.4	
t_{23}	HOLD Setup Time	26		ns	6.4	
t_{24}	HOLD Hold Time	5		ns	6.4	
t_{25}	RESET Setup Time	13		ns	6.7	
t_{26}	RESET Hold Time	4		ns	6.7	

NOTE:
The 80376 does not have t_{17} or t_{18} timing specifications.

Table 6.4. 80376 A.C. Characteristics at 16 MHz

Functional Operating Range: $V_{CC} = 5V \pm 10\%$; $T_{CASE} = 0°C$ to $115°C$ for 80-pin PGA, $0°C$ to $110°C$ for 100-pin plastic (Continued)

Symbol	Parameter	Min	Max	Unit	Figure	Notes
t_{27}	NMI, INTR Setup Time	16		ns	6.4	(2)
t_{28}	NMI, INTR Hold Time	16		ns	6.4	(2)
t_{29}	PEREQ, ERROR#, BUSY# Setup Time	16		ns	6.4	(2)
t_{30}	PEREQ, ERROR#, BUSY# Hold Time	5		ns	6.4	(2)

NOTES:
1. Float condition occurs when maximum output current becomes less than I_{LO} in magnitude. Float delay is not 100% tested.
2. These inputs are allowed to be asynchronous to CLK2. The setup and hold specifications are given for testing purposes, to assure recognition within a specific CLK2 period.
3. These are not tested. They are guaranteed by design characterization.
4. Tested with C_L set to 50 pF and derated to support the indicated distributed capacitive load. See Figure 6.8 for the capacitive derating curve.

A.C. TEST LOADS

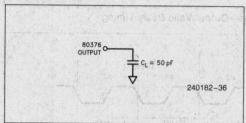

Figure 6.2. A.C. Test Loads

A.C. TIMING WAVEFORMS

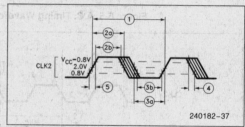

Figure 6.3. CLK2 Waveform

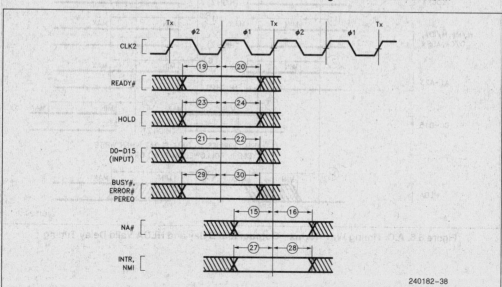

Figure 6.4. A.C. Timing Waveforms—Input Setup and Hold Timing

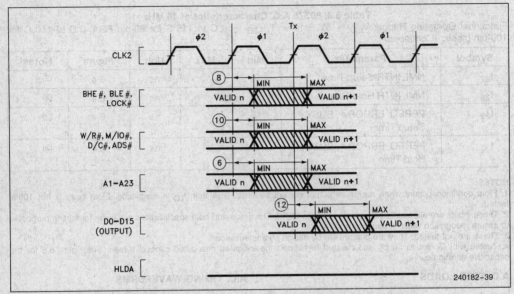

Figure 6.5. A.C. Timing Waveforms—Output Valid Delay Timing

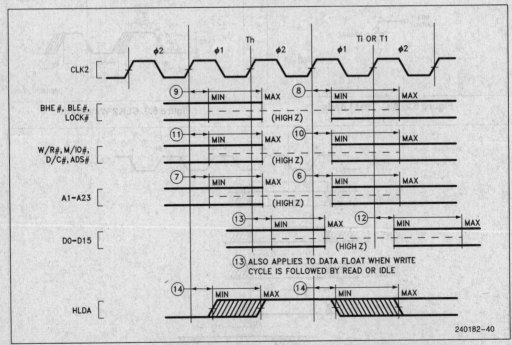

(13) ALSO APPLIES TO DATA FLOAT WHEN WRITE CYCLE IS FOLLOWED BY READ OR IDLE

Figure 6.6. A.C. Timing Waveforms—Output Float Delay and HLDA Valid Delay Timing

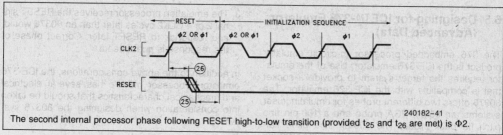

The second internal processor phase following RESET high-to-low transition (provided t_{25} and t_{26} are met) is $\Phi2$.

Figure 6.7. A.C. Timing Waveforms—RESET Setup and Hold Timing, and Internal Phase

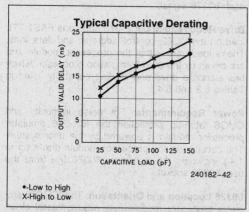

240182–42

•-Low to High
X-High to Low

Figure 6.8. Capacitive Derating Curve

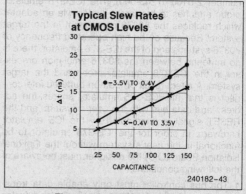

240182–43

Figure 6.9. CMOS Level Slew Rates for Output Buffers

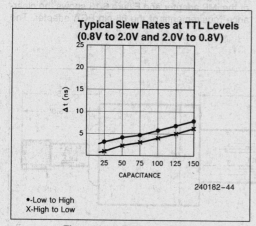

240182–44

•-Low to High
X-High to Low

Figure 6.10. TTL Level Slew Rates for Output Buffers

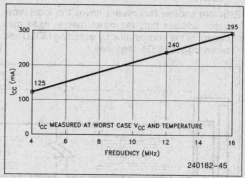

240182–45

Figure 6.11. Typical I_{CC} vs Frequency

6.5 Designing for ICE™-376 Emulator (Advanced Data)

The 376 embedded processor in-circuit emulator product is the ICE-376 emulator. Use of the emulator requires the target system to provide a socket that is compatible with the ICE-376 emulator. The 80376 offers two different probes for emulating user systems: an 88-pin PGA probe and a 100-pin fine pitch flat-pack probe. The 100-pin fine pitch flat-pack probe requires a socket, called the 100-pin PQFP, which is available from 3-M text-tool (part number 2-0100-07243-000). The ICE-376 emulator probe attaches to the target system via an adapter which replaces the 80376 component in the target system. Because of the high operating frequency of 80376 systems and of the ICE-376 emulator, there is no buffering between the 80376 emulation processor in the ICE-376 emulator probe and the target system. A direct result of the non-buffered interconnect is that the ICE-376 emulator shares the address and data bus with the user's system, and the RESET signal is intercepted by the ICE emulator hardware. In order for the ICE-376 emulator to be functional in the user's system without the Optional Isolation Board (OIB) the designer must be aware of the following conditions:

1. The bus controller must only enable data transceivers onto the data bus during valid read cycles of the 80376, other local devices or other bus masters.

2. Before another bus master drives the local processor address bus, the other master must gain control of the address bus by asserting HOLD and receiving the HLDA response.

3. The emulation processor receives the RESET signal 2 or 4 CLK2 cycles later than an 80376 would, and responds to RESET later. Correct phase of the response is guaranteed.

In addition to the above considerations, the ICE-376 emulator processor module has several electrical and mechanical characteristics that should be taken into consideration when designing the 80376 system.

Capacitive Loading: ICE-376 adds up to 27 pF to each 80376 signal.

Drive Requirements: ICE-376 adds one FAST TTL load on the CLK2, control, address, and data lines. These loads are within the processor module and are driven by the 80376 emulation processor, which has standard drive and loading capability listed in Tables 6.3 and 6.4.

Power Requirements: For noise immunity and CMOS latch-up protection the ICE-376 emulator processor module is powered by the user system. The circuitry on the processor module draws up to 1.4A including the maximum 80376 I_{CC} from the user 80376 socket.

80376 Location and Orientation: The ICE-376 emulator processor module may require lateral clearance. Figure 6.12 shows the clearance requirements of the iMP adapter and Figure 6.13 shows the clearance requirements of the 88-pin PGA adapter. The

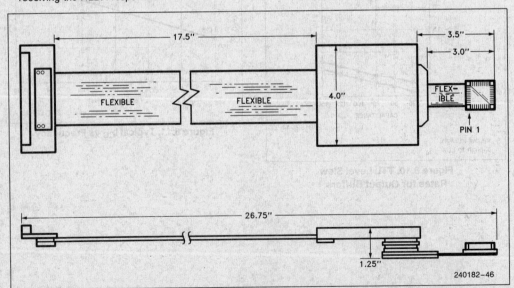

Figure 6.12. Preliminary ICE™-376 Emulator User Cable with PQFP Adapter

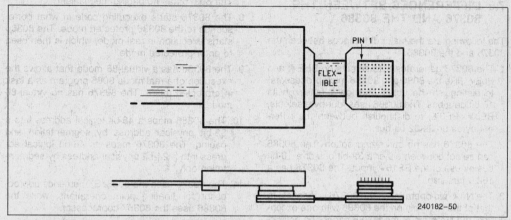

240182-50

Figure 6.13. Preliminary ICE™-376 Emulator User Cable with 88-Pin PGA Adapter

optional isolation board (OIB), which provides extra electrical buffering and has the same lateral clearance requirements as Figures 6.12 and 6.13, adds an additional 0.5 inches to the vertical clearance requirement. This is illustrated in Figure 6.14.

Optional Isolation Board (OIB) and the CLK2 speed reduction: Due to the unbuffered probe design, the ICE-376 emulator is susceptible to errors

on the user's bus. The OIB allows the ICE-376 emulator to function in user systems with faults (shorted signals, etc.). After electrical verification the OIB may be removed. When the OIB is installed, the user system must have a maximum CLK2 frequency of 20 MHz.

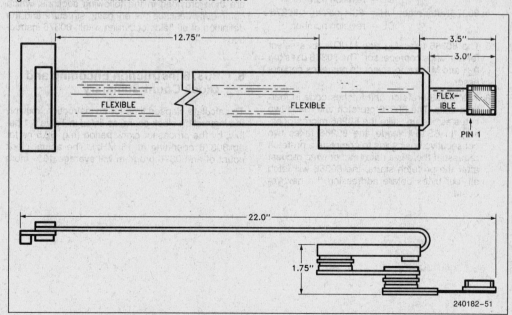

240182-51

Figure 6.14. Preliminary ICE™-376 Emulator User Cable with OIB and PQFP Adapter

7.0 DIFFERENCES BETWEEN THE 80376 AND THE 80386

The following are the major differences between the 80376 and the 80386.

1. The 80376 generates byte selects on BHE# and BLE# (like the 8086 and 80286 microprocessors) to distinguish the upper and lower bytes on its 16-bit data bus. The 80386 uses four-byte selects, BE0#–BE3#, to distinguish between the different bytes on its 32-bit bus.

2. The 80376 has no bus sizing option. The 80386 can select between either a 32-bit bus or a 16-bit bus by use of the BS16# input. The 80376 has a 16-bit bus size.

3. The NA# pin operation in the 80376 is identical to that of the NA# pin on the 80386 with one exception: the NA# pin of the 80386 cannot be activated on 16-bit bus cycles (where BS16# is LOW in the 80386 case), whereas NA# can be activated on any 80376 bus cycle.

4. The contents of all 80376 registers at reset are identical to the contents of the 80386 registers at reset, except the DX register. The DX register contains a component-stepping identifier at reset, i.e.

in 80386, after reset DH = 3 indicates 80386
DL = revision number;
in 80376, after reset DH = 33H indicates 80376
DL = revision number.

5. The 80386 uses A_{31} and M/IO# as a select for numerics coprocessor. The 80376 uses the A_{23} and M/IO# to select its numerics coprocessor.

6. The 80386 prefetch unit fetches code in four-byte units. The 80376 prefetch unit reads two bytes as one unit (like the 80286 microprocessor). In BS16# mode, the 80386 takes two consecutive bus cycles to complete a prefetch request. If there is a data read or write request after the prefetch starts, the 80386 will fetch all four bytes before addressing the new request.

7. The 80376 has no paging mechanism.

8. The 80376 starts executing code in what corresponds to the 80386 protected mode. The 80386 starts execution in real mode, which is then used to enter protected mode.

9. The 80386 has a virtual-86 mode that allows the execution of a real mode 8086 program as a task in protected mode. The 80376 has no virtual-86 mode.

10. The 80386 maps a 48-bit logical address into a 32-bit physical address by segmentation and paging. The 80376 maps its 48-bit logical address into a 24-bit physical address by segmentation only.

11. The 80376 uses the 80387SX numerics coprocessor for floating point operations, while the 80386 uses the 80387 coprocessor.

12. The 80386 can execute from 16-bit code segments. The 80376 can **only** execute from 32-bit code Segments.

8.0 INSTRUCTION SET

This section describes the 376 embedded processor instruction set. Table 8.1 lists all instructions along with instruction encoding diagrams and clock counts. Further details of the instruction encoding are then provided in the following sections, which completely describe the encoding structure and the definition of all fields occurring within 80376 instructions.

8.1 80376 Instruction Encoding and Clock Count Summary

To calculate elapsed time for an instruction, multiply the instruction clock count, as listed in Table 8.1 below, by the processor clock period (e.g. 62.5 ns for an 80376 operating at 16 MHz). The actual clock count of an 80376 program will average 10% more than the calculated clock count due to instruction sequences which execute faster than they can be fetched from memory.

Instruction Clock Count Assumptions:

1. The instruction has been prefetched, decoded, and is ready for execution.

2. Bus cycles do not require wait states.

3. There are no local bus HOLD requests delaying processor acess to the bus.

4. No exceptions are detected during instruction execution.

5. If an effective address is calculated, it does not use two general register components. One register, scaling and displacement can be used within the clock counts showns. However, if the effective address calculation uses two general register components, add 1 clock to the clock count shown.

6. Memory reference instruction accesses byte or aligned 16-bit operands.

Instruction Clock Count Notation

— If two clock counts are given, the smaller refers to a register operand and the larger refers to a memory operand.

—n = number of times repeated.

—m = number of components in the next instruction executed, where the entire displacement (if any) counts as one component, the entire immediate data (if any) counts as one component, and all other bytes of the instruction and prefix(es) each count as one component.

Misaligned or 32-Bit Operand Accesses:

— If instructions accesses a misaligned 16-bit operand or 32-bit operand on even address add:

2*   clocks for read or write.

4** clocks for read and write.

— If instructions accesses a 32-bit operand on odd address add:

4*   clocks for read or write.

8** clocks for read and write.

Wait States:

Wait states add 1 clock per wait state to instruction execution for each data access.

Table 8.1. 80376 Instruction Set Clock Count Summary

Instruction	Format			Clock Counts	Number of Data Cycles	Notes
GENERAL DATA TRANSFER						
MOV = Move:						
Register to Register/Memory	1 0 0 0 1 0 0 w	mod reg r/m		2/2*	0/1*	a
Register/Memory to Register	1 0 0 0 1 0 1 w	mod reg r/m		2/4*	0/1*	a
Immediate to Register/Memory	1 1 0 0 0 1 1 w	mod 0 0 0 r/m	immediate data	2/2*	0/1*	a
Immediate to Register (Short Form)	1 0 1 1 w reg	immediate data		2	2	
Memory to Accumulator (Short Form)	1 0 1 0 0 0 0 w	full displacement		4*	1*	a
Accumulator to Memory (Short Form)	1 0 1 0 0 0 1 w	full displacement		2¹	1*	a
Register/Memory to Segment Register	1 0 0 0 1 1 1 0	mod sreg3 r/m		22/23	0/6*	a,b,c
Segment Register to Register/Memory	1 0 0 0 1 1 0 0	mod sreg3 r/m		2/2*	0/1*	a
MOVSX = Move with Sign Extension						
Register from Register/Memory	0 0 0 0 1 1 1 1	1 0 1 1 1 1 1 w	mod reg r/m	3/6*	0/1*	a
MOVZX = Move with Zero Extension						
Register from Register/Memory	0 0 0 0 1 1 1 1	1 0 1 1 0 1 1 w	mod reg r/m	3/6*	0/1*	a
PUSH = Push:						
Register/Memory	1 1 1 1 1 1 1 1	mod 1 1 0 r/m		7/9*	2/4*	a
Register (Short Form)	0 1 0 1 0 reg			4	2	a
Segment Register (ES, CS, SS or DS)	0 0 0 sreg2 1 1 0			4	2	a
Segment Register (FS or GS)	0 0 0 0 1 1 1 1	1 0 sreg3 0 0 0		4	2	a
Immediate	0 1 1 0 1 0 s 0	immediate data		4	2	a
PUSHA = Push All	0 1 1 0 0 0 0 0			34	16	a
POP = Pop						
Register/Memory	1 0 0 0 1 1 1 1	mod 0 0 0 r/m		7/9*	2/4*	a
Register (Short Form)	0 1 0 1 1 reg			6	2	a
Segment Register (ES, SS or DS)	0 0 0 sreg2 1 1 1			25	6	a, b, c
Segment Register (FS or GS)	0 0 0 0 1 1 1 1	1 0 sreg3 0 0 1		25	6	a, b, c
POPA = Pop All	0 1 1 0 0 0 0 1			40	16	a
XCHG = Exchange						
Register/Memory with Register	1 0 0 0 0 1 1 w	mod reg r/m		3/5**	0/2**	a, m
Register with Accumulator (Short Form)	1 0 0 1 0 reg			3	0	
IN = Input from:						
Fixed Port	1 1 1 0 0 1 0 w	port number		6*	1*	f,k
				26*	1*	f,l
Variable Port	1 1 1 0 1 1 0 w			7*	1*	f,k
				27*	1*	f,l
OUT = Output to:						
Fixed Port	1 1 1 0 0 1 1 w	port number		4*	1*	f,k
				24*	1*	f,l
Variable Port	1 1 1 0 1 1 1 w			5*	1*	f,k
				26*	1*	f,l
LEA = Load EA to Register	1 0 0 0 1 1 0 1	mod reg r/m		2		

Table 8.1. 80376 Instruction Set Clock Count Summary (Continued)

Instruction	Format	Clock Counts	Number of Data Cycles	Notes
SEGMENT CONTROL				
LDS = Load Pointer to DS	`11000101` `mod reg` `r/m`	26*	6*	a, b, c
LES = Load Pointer to ES	`11000100` `mod reg` `r/m`	26*	6*	a, b, c
LFS = Load Pointer to FS	`00001111` `10110100` `mod reg` `r/m`	29*	6*	a, b, c
LGS =, Load Pointer to GS	`00001111` `10110101` `mod reg` `r/m`	29*	6*	a, b, c
LSS = Load Pointer to SS	`00001111` `10110010` `mod reg` `r/m`	26*	6*	a, b, c
FLAG CONTROL				
CLC = Clear Carry Flag	`11111000`	2		
CLD = Clear Direction Flag	`11111100`	2		
CLI = Clear Interrupt Enable Flag	`11111010`	8		f
CLTS = Clear Task Switched Flag	`00001111` `00000110`	5		e
CMC = Complement Carry Flag	`11110101`	2		
LAHF = Load AH into Flag	`10011111`	2		
POPF = Pop Flags	`10011101`	7		a, g
PUSHF = Push Flags	`10011100`	4		a
SAHF = Store AH into Flags	`10011110`	3		
STC = Set Carry Flag	`11111001`	2		
STD = Set Direction Flag	`11111101`	2		
STI = Set Interrupt Enable Flag	`11111011`	8		f
ARITHMETIC **ADD = Add**				
Register to Register	`000000dw` `mod reg` `r/m`	2		
Register to Memory	`0000000w` `mod reg` `r/m`	7**	2**	a
Memory to Register	`0000001w` `mod reg` `r/m`	6*	1*	a
Immediate to Register/Memory	`100000sw` `mod 000` `r/m` `immediate data`	2/7**	0/2**	a
Immediate to Accumulator (Short Form)	`0000010w` `immediate data`	2		
ADC = Add with Carry				
Register to Register	`000100dw` `mod reg` `r/m`	2		
Register to Memory	`0001000w` `mod reg` `r/m`	7**	2**	a
Memory to Register	`0001001w` `mod reg` `r/m`	6*	1*	a
Immediate to Register/Memory	`100000sw` `mod 010` `r/m` `immediate data`	2/7**	0/2**	a
Immediate to Accumulator (Short Form)	`0001010w` `immediate data`	2		
INC = Increment				
Register/Memory	`1111111w` `mod 000` `r/m`	2/6**	0/2**	a
Register (Short Form)	`01000` `reg`	2		
SUB = Subtract				
Register from Register	`001010dw` `mod reg` `r/m`	2		

Table 8.1. 80376 Instruction Set Clock Count Summary (Continued)

Instruction	Format	Clock Counts	Number Of Data Cycles	Notes
ARITHMETIC (Continued)				
Register from Memory	`0010100w` `mod reg` `r/m`	7**	2**	a
Memory from Register	`0010101w` `mod reg` `r/m`	6*	1	a
Immediate from Register/Memory	`100000sw` `mod 101` `r/m` immediate data	2/7**	0/1**	a
Immediate from Accumulator (Short Form)	`0010110w` immediate data	2		
SBB = Subtract with Borrow				
Register from Register	`000110dw` `mod reg` `r/m`	2		
Register from Memory	`0001100w` `mod reg` `r/m`	7**	2**	a
Memory from Register	`0001101w` `mod reg` `r/m`	6*	1*	a
Immediate from Register/Memory	`100000sw` `mod 011` `r/m` immediate data	2/7**	0/2**	a
Immediate from Accumulator (Short Form)	`0001110w` immediate data	2		
DEC = Decrement				
Register/Memory	`1111111w` `reg 001` `r/m`	2/6**	0/2**	a
Register (Short Form)	`01001` `reg`	2		
CMP = Compare				
Register with Register	`001110dw` `mod reg` `r/m`	2		
Memory with Register	`0011100w` `mod reg` `r/m`	5*	1*	a
Register with Memory	`0011101w` `mod reg` `r/m`	6**	2**	a
Immediate with Register/Memory	`100000sw` `mod 111` `r/m` immediate data	2/5*	0/1*	a
Immediate with Accumulator (Short Form)	`0011110w` immediate data	2		
NEG = Change Sign	`1111011w` `mod 011` `r/m`	2/6*	0/2*	a
AAA = ASCII Adjust for Add	`00110111`	4		
AAS = ASCII Adjust for Subtract	`00111111`	4		
DAA = Decimal Adjust for Add	`00100111`	4		
DAS = Decimal Adjust for Subtract	`00101111`	4		
MUL = Multiply (Unsigned)				
Accumulator with Register/Memory	`1111011w` `mod 100` `r/m`			
Multiplier—Byte		12–17/15–20	0/1	a,n
—Word		12–25/15–28*	0/1*	a,n
—Doubleword		12–41/17–46*	0/2*	a,n
IMUL = Integer Multiply (Signed)				
Accumulator with Register/Memory	`1111011w` `mod 101` `r/m`			
Multiplier—Byte		12–17/15–20	0/1	a,n
—Word		12–25/15–28*	0/1*	a,n
—Doubleword		12–41/17–46*	0/2*	a,n
Register with Register/Memory	`00001111` `10101111` `mod reg` `r/m`			
Multiplier—Byte		12–17/15–20	0/1	a,n
—Word		12–25/15–28*	0/1*	a,n
—Doubleword		12–41/17–46*	0/2*	a,n
Register/Memory with Immediate to Register	`011010s1` `mod reg` `r/m` immediate data			
—Word		13–26/14–27*	0/1*	a,n
—Doubleword		13–42/16–45*	0/2*	a,n

80376 PRELIMINARY

Table 8.1. 80376 Instruction Set Clock Count Summary (Continued)

Instruction	Format	Clock Counts	Number Of Data Cycles	Notes
ARITHMETIC (Continued)				
DIV = Divide (Unsigned)				
Accumulator by Register/Memory	`1111011w` `mod 110 r/m`			
Divisor—Byte		14/17	0/1	a, o
—Word		22/25*	0/1*	a, o
—Doubleword		38/43*	0/2*	a, o
IDIV = Integer Divide (Signed)				
Accumulator by Register/Memory	`1111011w` `mod 111 r/m`			
Divisor—Byte		19/22	0/1	a, o
—Word		27/30*	0/1	a, o
—Doubleword		43/48*	0/2*	a, o
AAD = ASCII Adjust for Divide	`11010101` `00001010`	19		
AAM = ASCII Adjust for Multiply	`11010100` `00001010`	17		
CBW = Convert Byte to Word	`10011000`	3		
CWD = Convert Word to Double Word	`10011001`	2		
LOGIC				
Shift Rotate Instructions				
Not Through Carry **(ROL, ROR, SAL, SAR, SHL, and SHR)**				
Register/Memory by 1	`1101000w` `mod TTT r/m`	3/7**	0/2**	a
Register/Memory by CL	`1101001w` `mod TTT r/m`	3/7**	0/2**	a
Register/Memory by Immediate Count	`1100000w` `mod TTT r/m` `immed 8-bit data`	3/7**	0/2**	a
Through Carry **(RCL and RCR)**				
Register/Memory by 1	`1101000w` `mod TTT r/m`	9/10**	0/2**	a
Register/Memory by CL	`1101001w` `mod TTT r/m`	9/10**	10/2**	a
Register/Memory by Immediate Count	`1100000w` `mod TTT r/m` `immed 8-bit data`	9/10**	0/2**	a

TTT	Instruction
000	ROL
001	ROR
010	RCL
011	RCR
100	SHL/SAL
101	SHR
111	SAR

Instruction	Format	Clock Counts	Number Of Data Cycles	Notes
SHLD = Shift Left Double				
Register/Memory by Immediate	`00001111` `10100100` `mod reg r/m` `immed 8-bit data`	3/7**	0/2**	
Register/Memory by CL	`00001111` `10100101` `mod reg r/m`	3/7**	0/2**	
SHRD = Shift Right Double				
Register/Memory by Immediate	`00001111` `10101100` `mod reg r/m` `immed 8-bit data`	3/7**	0/2**	
Register/Memory by CL	`00001111` `10101101` `mod reg r/m`	3/7**	0/2**	
AND = And				
Register to Register	`001000dw` `mod reg r/m`	2		

Table 8.1. 80376 Instruction Set Clock Count Summary (Continued)

Instruction	Format	Clock Counts	Number of Data Cycles	Notes
LOGIC (Continued)				
Register to Memory	`0010000w` `mod reg` `r/m`	7	2**	a
Memory to Register	`0010001w` `mod reg` `r/m`	6*	1*	a
Immediate to Register/Memory	`1000000w` `mod 1 0 0` `r/m` immediate data	2/7**	0/2**	a
Immediate to Accumulator (Short Form)	`0010010w` immediate data	2		
TEST = And Function to Flags, No Result				
Register/Memory and Register	`1000010w` `mod reg` `r/m`	2/5*	0/1*	a
Immediate Data and Register/Memory	`1111011w` `mod 0 0 0` `r/m` immediate data	2/5*	0/1*	a
Immediate Data and Accumulator (Short Form)	`1010100w` immediate data	2		
OR = Or				
Register to Register	`000010dw` `mod reg` `r/m`	2		
Register to Memory	`0000100w` `mod reg` `r/m`	7**	2**	a
Memory to Register	`0000101w` `mod reg` `r/m`	6*	1*	a
Immediate to Register/Memory	`1000000w` `mod 0 0 1` `r/m` immediate data	2/7**	0/2**	a
Immediate to Accumulator (Short Form)	`0000110w` immediate data	2		
XOR = Exclusive Or				
Register to Register	`001100dw` `mod reg` `r/m`	2		
Register to Memory	`0011000w` `mod reg` `r/m`	7**	2**	a
Memory to Register	`0011001w` `mod reg` `r/m`	6*	1*	a
Immediate to Register/Memory	`1000000w` `mod 1 1 0` `r/m` immediate data	2/7**	0/2**	a
Immediate to Accumulator (Short Form)	`0011010w` immediate data	2		
NOT = Invert Register/Memory	`1111011w` `mod 0 1 0` `r/m`	2/6**	0/2**	a
STRING MANIPULATION				
CMPS = Compare Byte Word	`1010011w`	10*	2*	a
INS = Input Byte/Word from DX Port	`0110110w`	9**	1**	a,f,k
		29**	1**	a,f,l
LODS = Load Byte/Word to AL/AX/EAX	`1010110w`	5*	1*	a
MOVS = Move Byte Word	`1010010w`	7**	2**	a
OUTS = Output Byte/Word to DX Port	`0110111w`	8**	1**	a,f,k
		28**	1**	a,f,l
SCAS = Scan Byte Word	`1010111w`	7*	1*	a
STOS = Store Byte/Word from AL/AX/EX	`1010101w`	4*	1*	a
XLAT = Translate String	`11010111`	5*	1*	a
REPEATED STRING MANIPULATION Repeated by Count in CX or ECX				
REPE CMPS = Compare String (Find Non-Match)	`11110011` `1010011w`	5 + 9n**	2n**	a

Table 8.1. 80376 Instruction Set Clock Count Summary (Continued)

Instruction	Format				Clock Counts	Number of Data Cycles	Notes
REPEATED STRING MANIPULATION (Continued)							
REPNE CMPS = Compare String							
(Find Match)	11110010	1010011w			5 + 9n**	2n**	a
REP INS = Input String	11110011	0110110w			7 + 6n* 27 + 6n*	1n* 1n*	a,f,k a,f,l
REP LODS = Load String	11110011	1010110w			5 + 6n*	1n*	a
REP MOVS = Move String	11110011	1010010w			7 + 4n**	2n**	a
REP OUTS = Output String	11110011	0110111w			6 + 5n* 26 + 5n*	1n* 1n*	a,f,k a,f,l
REPE SCAS = Scan String							
(Find Non-AL/AX/EAX)	11110011	1010111w			5 + 8n*	1n*	a
REPNE SCAS = Scan String							
(Find AL/AX/EAX)	11110010	1010111w			5 + 8n*	1n*	a
REP STOS = Store String	11110011	1010101w			5 + 5n*	1n*	a
BIT MANIPULATION							
BSF = Scan Bit Forward	00001111	10111100	mod reg	r/m	10 + 3n**	2n**	a
BSR = Scan Bit Reverse	00001111	10111101	mod reg	r/m	10 + 3n**	2n**	a
BT = Test Bit							
Register/Memory, Immediate	00001111	10111010	mod 100 r/m	immed 8-bit data	3/6*	0/1*	a
Register/Memory, Register	00001111	10100011	mod reg	r/m	3/12*	0/1*	a
BTC = Test Bit and Complement							
Register/Memory, Immediate	00001111	10111010	mod 111 r/m	immed 8-bit data	6/8*	0/2*	a
Register/Memory, Register	00001111	10111011	mod reg	r/m	6/13*	0/2*	a
BTR = Test Bit and Reset							
Register/Memory, Immediate	00001111	10111010	mod 110 r/m	immed 8-bit data	6/8*	0/2*	a
Register/Memory, Register	00001111	10110011	mod reg	r/m	6/13*	0/2*	a
BTS = Test Bit and Set							
Register/Memory, Immediate	00001111	10111010	mod 101 r/m	immed 8-bit data	6/8*	0/2*	a
Register/Memory, Register	00001111	10101011	mod reg	r/m	6/13*	0/2*	a
CONTROL TRANSFER							
CALL = Call							
Direct within Segment	11101000	full displacement			9 + m*	2	j
Register/Memory							
Indirect within Segment	11111111	mod 010 r/m			9 + m/12 + m	2/3	a, j
Direct Intersegment	10011010	unsigned full offset, selector			42 + m	9	c, d, j

Table 8.1. 80376 Instruction Set Clock Count Summary (Continued)

Instruction	Format	Clock Counts	Number of Data Cycles	Notes
CONTROL TRANSFER (Continued)				
(Direct Intersegment)				
Via Call Gate to Same Privilege Level		64 + m	13	a,c,d,j
Via Call Gate to Different Privilege Level, (No Parameters)		98 + m	13	a,c,d,j
Via Call Gate to Different Privilege Level, (x Parameters)		106 + 8x + m	13 + 4x	a,c,d,j
From 386 Task to 386 TSS		382	124	a,c,d,j
Indirect Intersegment	11111111 mod 0 1 1 r/m	46 + m	10	a,c,d,j
Via Call Gate to Same Privilege Level		68 + m	14	a,c,d,j
Via Call Gate to Different Privilege Level, (No Parameters)		102 + m	14	a,c,d,j
Via Call Gate to Different Privilege Level, (x Parameters)		110 + 8x + m	14 + 4x	a,c,d,j
From 386 Task to 386 TSS		399	130	a,c,d,j
JMP = Unconditional Jump				
Short	11101011 8-bit displacement	7 + m		j
Direct within Segment	11101001 full displacement	7 + m		j
Register/Memory Indirect within Segment	11111111 mod 1 0 0 r/m	9 + m/14 + m	2/4	a,j
Direct Intersegment	11101010 unsigned full offset, selector	37 + m	5	c,d,j
Via Call Gate to Same Privilege Level		53 + m	9	a,c,d,j
From 386 Task to 386 TSS		395	124	a,c,d,j
Indirect Intersegment	11111111 mod 1 0 1 r/m	37 + m	9	a,c,d,j
Via Call Gate to Same Privilege Level		59 + m	13	a,c,d,j
From 386 Task to 386 TSS		401	124	a,c,d,j

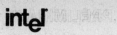
Table 8.1. 80376 Instruction Set Clock Count Summary (Continued)

Instruction	Format			Clock Counts	Number of Data Cycles	Notes
CONTROL TRANSFER (Continued)						
RET = Return from CALL:						
Within Segment	11000011			12 + m	2	a,j,p
Within Segment Adding Immediate to SP	11000010	16-bit displ		12 + m	2	a,j,p
Intersegment	11001011			36 + m	4	a,c,d,j,p
Intersegment Adding Immediate to SP	11001010	16-bit displ		36 + m	4	a,c,d,j,p
to Different Privilege Level						
Intersegment				80	4	c,d,j,p
Intersegment Adding Immediate to SP				80	4	c,d,j,p
CONDITIONAL JUMPS						
NOTE: Times Are Jump "Taken or Not Taken"						
JO = Jump on Overflow						
8-Bit Displacement	01110000	8-bit displ		7 + m or 3		j
Full Displacement	00001111	10000000	full displacement	7 + m or 3		j
JNO = Jump on Not Overflow						
8-Bit Displacement	01110001	8-bit displ		7 + m or 3		j
Full Displacement	00001111	10000001	full displacement	7 + m or 3		j
JB/JNAE = Jump on Below/Not Above or Equal						
8-Bit Displacement	01110010	8-bit displ		7 + m or 3		j
Full Displacement	00001111	10000010	full displacement	7 + m or 3		j
JNB/JAE = Jump on Not Below/Above or Equal						
8-Bit Displacement	01110011	8-bit displ		7 + m or 3		j
Full Displacement	00001111	10000011	full displacement	7 + m or 3		j
JE/JZ = Jump on Equal/Zero						
8-Bit Displacement	01110100	8-bit displ		7 + m or 3		j
Full Displacement	00001111	10000100	full displacement	7 + m or 3		j
JNE/JNZ = Jump on Not Equal/Not Zero						
8-Bit Displacement	01110101	8-bit displ		7 + m or 3		j
Full Displacement	00001111	10000101	full displacement	7 + m or 3		j
JBE/JNA = Jump on Below or Equal/Not Above						
8-Bit Displacement	01110110	8-bit displ		7 + m or 3		j
Full Displacement	00001111	10000110	full displacement	7 + m or 3		j
JNBE/JA = Jump on Not Below or Equal/Above						
8-Bit Displacement	01110111	8-bit displ		7 + m or 3		j
Full Displacement	00001111	10000111	full displacement	7 + m or 3		j
JS = Jump on Sign						
8-Bit Displacement	01111000	8-bit displ		7 + m or 3		j
Full Displacement	00001111	10001000	full displacement	7 + m or 3		j

Table 8.1. 80376 Instruction Set Clock Count Summary (Continued)

Instruction	Format			Clock Counts	Number of Data Cycles	Notes
CONDITIONAL JUMPS (Continued)						
JNS = Jump on Not Sign						
8-Bit Displacement	01111001	8-bit displ		7 + m or 3		j
Full Displacement	00001111	10001001	full displacement	7 + m or 3		j
JP/JPE = Jump on Parity/Parity Even						
8-Bit Displacement	01111010	8-bit displ		7 + m or 3		j
Full Displacement	00001111	10001010	full displacement	7 + m or 3		j
JNP/JPO = Jump on Not Parity/Parity Odd						
8-Bit Displacement	01111011	8-bit displ		7 + m or 3		j
Full Displacement	00001111	10001011	full displacement	7 + m or 3		j
JL/JNGE = Jump on Less/Not Greater or Equal						
8-Bit Displacement	01111100	8-bit displ		7 + m or 3		j
Full Displacement	00001111	10001100	full displacement	7 + m or 3		j
JNL/JGE = Jump on Not Less/Greater or Equal						
8-Bit Displacement	01111101	8-bit displ		7 + m or 3		j
Full Displacement	00001111	10001101	full displacement	7 + m or 3		j
JLE/JNG = Jump on Less or Equal/Not Greater						
8-Bit Displacement	01111110	8-bit displ		7 + m or 3		j
Full Displacement	00001111	10001110	full displacement	7 + m or 3		j
JNLE/JG = Jump on Not Less or Equal/Greater						
8-Bit Displacement	01111111	8-bit displ		7 + m or 3		j
Full Displacement	00001111	10001111	full displacement	7 + m or 3		j
JECXZ = Jump on ECX Zero	11100011	8-bit displ		9 + m or 5		j
(Address Size Prefix Differentiates JCXZ from JECXZ)						
LOOP = Loop ECX Times	11100010	8-bit displ		11 + m		j
LOOPZ/LOOPE = Loop with Zero/Equal	11100001	8-bit displ		11 + m		j
LOOPNZ/LOOPNE = Loop While Not Zero	11100000	8-bit displ		11 + m		j
CONDITIONAL BYTE SET						
NOTE: Times Are Register/Memory						
SETO = Set Byte on Overflow						
To Register/Memory	00001111	10010000	mod 000 r/m	4/5*	0/1*	a
SETNO = Set Byte on Not Overflow						
To Register/Memory	00001111	10010001	mod 000 r/m	4/5*	0/1*	a
SETB/SETNAE = Set Byte on Below/Not Above or Equal						
To Register/Memory	00001111	10010010	mod 000 r/m	4/5*	0/1*	a

Table 8.1. 80376 Instruction Set Clock Count Summary (Continued)

Instruction	Format			Clock Counts	Number of Data Cycles	Notes
CONDITIONAL BYTE SET (Continued)						
SETNB = Set Byte on Not Below/Above or Equal						
To Register/Memory	00001111	10010011	mod 000 r/m	4/5*	0/1*	a
SETE/SETZ = Set Byte on Equal/Zero						
To Register/Memory	00001111	10010100	mod 000 r/m	4/5*	0/1*	a
SETNE/SETNZ = Set Byte on Not Equal/Not Zero						
To Register/Memory	00001111	10010101	mod 000 r/m	4/5*	0/1*	a
SETBE/SETNA = Set Byte on Below or Equal/Not Above						
To Register/Memory	00001111	10010110	mod 000 r/m	4/5*	0/1*	a
SETNBE/SETA = Set Byte on Not Below or Equal/Above						
To Register/Memory	00001111	10010111	mod 000 r/m	4/5*	0/1*	a
SETS = Set Byte on Sign						
To Register/Memory	00001111	10011000	mod 000 r/m	4/5*	0/1*	a
SETNS = Set Byte on Not Sign						
To Register/Memory	00001111	10011001	mod 000 r/m	4/5*	0/1*	a
SETP/SETPE = Set Byte on Parity/Parity Even						
To Register/Memory	00001111	10011010	mod 000 r/m	4/5*	0/1*	a
SETNP/SETPO = Set Byte on Not Parity/Parity Odd						
To Register/Memory	00001111	10011011	mod 000 r/m	4/5*	0/1*	a
SETL/SETNGE = Set Byte on Less/Not Greater or Equal						
To Register/Memory	00001111	10011100	mod 000 r/m	4/5*	0/1*	a
SETNL/SETGE = Set Byte on Not Less/Greater or Equal						
To Register/Memory	00001111	01111101	mod 000 r/m	4/5*	0/1*	a
SETLE/SETNG = Set Byte on Less or Equal/Not Greater						
To Register/Memory	00001111	10011110	mod 000 r/m	4/5*	0/1*	a
SETNLE/SETG = Set Byte on Not Less or Equal/Greater						
To Register/Memory	00001111	10011111	mod 000 r/m	4/5*	0/1*	a
ENTER = Enter Procedure	11001000	16-bit displacement, 8-bit level				
L = 0				10		a
L = 1				14	1	a
L > 1				$17 + 8(n-1)$	$4(n-1)$	a
LEAVE = Leave Procedure	11001001			6		a

Table 8.1. 80376 Instruction Set Clock Count Summary (Continued)

Instruction	Format		Clock Counts ✳	Number of Data Cycles	Notes
INTERRUPT INSTRUCTIONS					
INT = Interrupt:					
Type Specified	`11001101`	`type`			
Via Interrupt or Trap Gate to Same Privilege Level			71	14	c,d,j,p
Via Interrupt or Trap Gate to Different Privilege Level			111	14	c,d,j,p
From 386 Task to 386 TSS via Task Gate			467	140	c,d,j,p
Type 3	`11001100`				
Via Interrupt or Trap Gate to Same Privilege Level			71	14	c,d,j,p
Via Interrupt or Trap Gate to Different Privilege Level			111	14	c,d,j,p
From 386 Task to 386 TSS via Task Gate			308	138	c,d,j,p
INTO = Interrupt 4 if Overflow Flag Set	`11001110`				
If OF = 1:			3		
If OF = 0					
Via Interrupt or Trap Gate to Same Privilege Level			71	14	c,d,j,p
Via Interrupt or Trap Gate to Different Privilege Level			111	14	c,d,j,p
From 386 Task to 386 TSS via Task Gate			413	138	c,d,j,p

Table 8.1. 80376 Instruction Set Clock Count Summary (Continued)

Instruction	Format	Clock Counts	Number Of Data Cycles	Notes
INTERRUPT INSTRUCTIONS (Continued)				
Bound = Out of Range	`01100010` `mod reg r/m`	✳		
Interrupt 5 if Detect Value				
if in Range		10	0	a,c,d,j,o,p
if Out of Range:				
Via Interrupt or Trap Gate				
to Same Privilege Level		71	14	c,d,j,p
Via Interrupt or Trap Gate				
to Different Privilege Level		111	14	c,d,j,p
From 386 Task to 386 TSS via Task Gate		398	138	c,d,j,p
INTERRUPT RETURN				
IRET = Interrupt Return	`11001111`			
To the Same Privilege Level (within Task)		42	5	a,c,d,j,p
To Different Privilege Level (within Task)		86	5	a,c,d,j,p
From 386 Task to 386 TSS		328	138	c,d,j,p
PROCESSOR CONTROL				
HLT = HALT	`11110100`	5		b
MOV = Move to and from Control/Debug/Test Registers				
CR0 from register	`00001111` `00100010` `11 eee reg`	10		b
Register from CR0	`00001111` `00100000` `11 eee reg`	6		b
DR0–3 from Register	`00001111` `00100011` `11 eee reg`	22		b
DR6–7 from Register	`00001111` `00100011` `11 eee reg`	16		b
Register from DR6–7	`00001111` `00100001` `11 eee reg`	14		b
Register from DR0–3	`00001111` `00100001` `11 eee reg`	22		b
NOP = No Operation	`10010000`	3		
WAIT = Wait until BUSY# Pin is Negated	`10011011`	6		

Table 8.1. 80376 Instruction Set Clock Count Summary (Continued)

Instruction	Format	Clock Counts	Number of Data Cycles	Notes
PROCESSOR EXTENSION INSTRUCTIONS				
Processor Extension Escape	`1 1 0 1 1 T T T` `mod L L L` `r/m`	See 80387SX Data Sheet		a
	TTT and LLL bits are opcode information for coprocessor.			
PREFIX BYTES				
Address Size Prefix	`0 1 1 0 0 1 1 1`	0		
LOCK = Bus Lock Prefix	`1 1 1 1 0 0 0 0`	0		f
Operand Size Prefix	`0 1 1 0 0 1 1 0`	0		
Segment Override Prefix				
CS:	`0 0 1 0 1 1 1 0`	0		
DS:	`0 0 1 1 1 1 1 0`	0		
ES:	`0 0 1 0 0 1 1 0`	0		
FS:	`0 1 1 0 0 1 0 0`	0		
GS:	`0 1 1 0 0 1 0 1`	0		
SS:	`0 0 1 1 0 1 1 0`	0		
PROTECTION CONTROL				
ARPL = Adjust Requested Privilege Level				
From Register/Memory	`0 1 1 0 0 0 1 1` `mod reg` `r/m`	20/21**	2**	a
LAR = Load Access Rights				
From Register/Memory	`0 0 0 0 1 1 1 1` `0 0 0 0 0 0 1 0` `mod reg` `r/m`	17/18*	1*	a,c,i,p
LGDT = Load Global Descriptor				
Table Register	`0 0 0 0 1 1 1 1` `0 0 0 0 0 0 0 1` `mod 0 1 0` `r/m`	13**	3*	a,e
LIDT = Load Interrupt Descriptor				
Table Register	`0 0 0 0 1 1 1 1` `0 0 0 0 0 0 0 1` `mod 0 1 1` `r/m`	13**	3*	a,e
LLDT = Load Local Descriptor				
Table Register to Register/Memory	`0 0 0 0 1 1 1 1` `0 0 0 0 0 0 0 0` `mod 0 1 0` `r/m`	24/28*	5*	a,c,e,p
LMSW = Load Machine Status Word				
From Register/Memory	`0 0 0 0 1 1 1 1` `0 0 0 0 0 0 0 1` `mod 1 1 0` `r/m`	10/13*	1*	a,e
LSL = Load Segment Limit				
From Register/Memory	`0 0 0 0 1 1 1 1` `0 0 0 0 0 0 1 1` `mod reg` `r/m`			
Byte-Granular Limit		24/27*	2*	a,c,i,p
Page-Granular Limit		29/32*	2*	a,c,i,p
LTR = Load Task Register				
From Register/Memory	`0 0 0 0 1 1 1 1` `0 0 0 0 0 0 0 0` `mod 0 0 1` `r/m`	27/31*	4*	a,c,e,p
SGDT = Store Global Descriptor				
Table Register	`0 0 0 0 1 1 1 1` `0 0 0 0 0 0 0 1` `mod 0 0 0` `r/m`	11*	3*	a
SIDT = Store Interrupt Descriptor				
Table Register	`0 0 0 0 1 1 1 1` `0 0 0 0 0 0 0 1` `mod 0 0 1` `r/m`	11*	3*	a
SLDT = Store Local Descriptor Table Register				
To Register/Memory	`0 0 0 0 1 1 1 1` `0 0 0 0 0 0 0 0` `mod 0 0 0` `r/m`	2/2*	4*	a

Table 8.1. 80376 Instruction Set Clock Count Summary (Continued)

Instruction	Format			Clock Counts	Number of Data Cycles	Notes
PROTECTION CONTROL (Continued)						
SMSW = Store Machine Status Word	00001111	00000001	mod 1 0 0 r/m	2/2*	1*	a, c
STR = Store Task Register						
To Register/Memory	00001111	00000000	mod 0 0 1 r/m	2/2*	1*	a
VERR = Verify Read Accesss						
Register/Memory	00001111	00000000	mod 1 0 0 r/m	10/11**	2**	a,c,i,p
VERW = Verify Write Accesss	00001111	00000000	mod 1 0 1 r/m	15/16**	2**	a,c,i,p

NOTES:

a. Exception 13 fault (general violation) will occur if the memory operand in CS, DS, ES, FS or GS cannot be used due to either a segment limit violation or access rights violation. If a stack limit is violated, and exception 12 (stack segment limit violation or not present) occurs.

b. For segment load operations, the CPL, RPL and DPL must agree with the privilege rules to avoid an exception 13 fault (general protection violation). The segments's descriptor must indicate "present" or exception 11 (CS, DS, ES, FS, GS not present). If the SS register is loaded and a stack segment not present is detected, an exception 12 (stack segment limit violation or not present occurs).

c. All segment descriptor accesses in the GDT or LDT made by this instruction will automatically assert LOCK# to maintain descriptor integrity in multiprocessor systems.

d. JMP, CALL, INT, RET and IRET instructions referring to another code segment will cause an exception 13 (general protection violation) if an applicable privilege rule is volated.

e. An exception 13 fault occurs if CPL is greater than 0.

f. An exception 13 fault occurs if CPL is greater than IOPL.

g. The IF bit of the flag register is not updated if CPL is greater than IOPL. The IOPL field of the flag register is updated only if CPL = 0.

h. Any violation of privelege rules as applied to the selector operand does not cause a protection exception; rather, the zero flag is cleared.

i. If the coprocessor's memory operand violates a segment limit or segment access rights, an exception 13 fault (general protection exception) will occur before the ESC instruction is executed. An exception 12 fault (stack segment limit violation or no present) will occur if the stack limit is violated by the operand's starting address.

j. The destination of a JMP, CALL, INT, RET or IRET must be in the defined limit of a code segment or an exception 13 fault (general protection violation) will occur.

k. If CPL ≤ IOPL

l. If CPL > IOPL

m. LOCK# is automatically asserted, regardless of the presence or absence of the LOCK# prefix.

n. The 80376 uses an early-out multiply algorithm. The actual number of clocks depends on the position of the most significant bit in the operand (multiplier). Clock counts given are minimum to maximum. To calculate actual clocks use the following formula:

$$\text{Actual Clock} = \text{if } m <> 0 \text{ then max } ([\log_2 |m|], 3) + 9 \text{ clocks:}$$
$$\text{if } m = 0 \text{ then 12 clocks (where m is the multiplier)}$$

o. An exception may occur, depending on the value of the operand.

p. LOCK# is asserted during descriptor table accesses.

8.2 INSTRUCTION ENCODING

Overview

All instruction encodings are subsets of the general instruction format shown in Figure 8.1. Instructions consist of one or two primary opcode bytes, possibly an address specifier consisting of the "mod r/m" byte and "scaled index" byte, a displacement if required, and an immediate data field if required.

Within the primary opcode or opcodes, smaller encoding fields may be defined. These fields vary according to the class of operation. The fields define such information as direction of the operation, size of the displacements, register encoding, or sign extension.

Almost all instructions referring to an operand in memory have an addressing mode byte following the primary opcode byte(s). This byte, the mod r/m byte, specifies the address mode to be used. Certain encodings of the mod r/m byte indicate a second addressing byte, the scale-index-base byte, follows the mod r/m byte to fully specify the addressing mode.

Addressing modes can include a displacement immediately following the mod r/m byte, or scaled index byte. If a displacement is present, the possible sizes are 8, 16 or 32 bits.

If the instruction specifies an immediate operand, the immediate operand follows any displacement bytes. The immediate operand, if specified, is always the last field of the instruction.

Figure 8.1 illustrates several of the fields that can appear in an instruction, such as the mod field and the r/m field, but the Figure does not show all fields. Several smaller fields also appear in certain instructions, sometimes within the opcode bytes themselves. Table 8.2 is a complete list of all fields appearing in the 80376 instruction set. Further ahead, following Table 8.2, are detailed tables for each field.

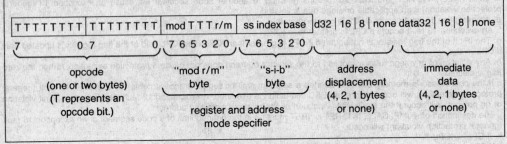

Figure 8.1. General Instruction Format

Table 8.2. Fields within 80376 Instructions

Field Name	Description	Number of Bits
w	Specifies if Data is Byte or Full Size (Full Size is either 16 or 32 Bits	1
d	Specifies Direction of Data Operation	1
s	Specifies if an Immediate Data Field Must be Sign-Extended	1
reg	General Register Specifier	3
mod r/m	Address Mode Specifier (Effective Address can be a General Register)	2 for mod; 3 for r/m
ss	Scale Factor for Scaled Index Address Mode	2
index	General Register to be used as Index Register	3
base	General Register to be used as Base Register	3
sreg2	Segment Register Specifier for CS, SS, DS, ES	2
sreg3	Segment Register Specifier for CS, SS, DS, ES, FS, GS	3
tttn	For Conditional Instructions, Specifies a Condition Asserted or a Condition Negated	4

Note: Table 8.1 shows encoding of individual instructions.

16-Bit Extensions of the Instruction Set

Two prefixes, the operand size prefix (66H) and the effective address size prefix (67H), allow overriding individually the default selection of operand size and effective address size. These prefixes may precede any opcode bytes and affect only the instruction they precede. If necessary, one or both of the prefixes may be placed before the opcode bytes. The presence of the operand size prefix (66H) and the effective address prefix will allow 16-bit data operation and 16-bit effective address calculations.

For instructions with more than one prefix, the order of prefixes is unimportant.

Unless specified otherwise, instructions with 8-bit and 16-bit operands do not affect the contents of the high-order bits of the extended registers.

Encoding of Instruction Fields

Within the instruction are several fields indicating register selection, addressing mode and so on.

ENCODING OF OPERAND LENGTH (w) FIELD

For any given instruction performing a data operation, the instruction will execute as a 32-bit operation. Within the constraints of the operation size, the w field encodes the operand size as either one byte or the full operation size, as shown in the table below.

w Field	Operand Size with 66H Prefix	Normal Operand Size
0	8 Bits	8 Bits
1	16 Bits	32 Bits

ENCODING OF THE GENERAL REGISTER (reg) FIELD

The general register is specified by the reg field, which may appear in the primary opcode bytes, or as the reg field of the "mod r/m" byte, or as the r/m field of the "mod r/m" byte.

Encoding of reg Field When w Field is not Present in Instruction

reg Field	Register Selected with 66H Prefix	Register Selected During 32-Bit Data Operations
000	AX	EAX
001	CX	ECX
010	DX	EDX
011	BX	EBX
100	SP	ESP
101	BP	EBP
110	SI	ESI
111	DI	EDI

Encoding of reg Field When w Field is Present in Instruction

reg	Register Specified by reg Field with 66H Prefix	
	Function of w Field	
	(when w = 0)	(when w = 1)
000	AL	AX
001	CL	CX
010	DL	DX
011	BL	BX
100	AH	SP
101	CH	BP
110	DH	SI
111	BH	DI

reg	Register Specified by reg Field without 66H Prefix	
	Function of w Field	
	(when w = 0)	(when w = 1)
000	AL	EAX
001	CL	ECX
010	DL	EDX
011	BL	EBX
100	AH	ESP
101	CH	EBP
110	DH	ESI
111	BH	EDI

ENCODING OF THE SEGMENT REGISTER (sreg) FIELD

The sreg field in certain instructions is a 2-bit field allowing one of the CS, DS, ES or SS segment registers to be specified. The sreg field in other instructions is a 3-bit field, allowing the FS and GS segment registers to be specified also.

2-Bit sreg2 Field

2-Bit sreg2 Field	Segment Register Selected
00	ES
01	CS
10	SS
11	DS

3-Bit sreg3 Field

3-Bit sreg3 Field	Segment Register Selected
000	ES
001	CS
010	SS
011	DS
100	FS
101	GS
110	do not use
111	do not use

ENCODING OF ADDRESS MODE

Except for special instructions, such as PUSH or POP, where the addressing mode is pre-determined, the addressing mode for the current instruction is specified by addressing bytes following the primary opcode. The primary addressing byte is the "mod r/m" byte, and a second byte of addressing information, the "s-i-b" (scale-index-base) byte, can be specified.

The s-i-b byte (scale-index-base byte) is specified when using 32-bit addressing mode and the "mod r/m" byte has r/m = 100 and mod = 00, 01 or 10. When the sib byte is present, the 32-bit addressing mode is a function of the mod, ss, index, and base fields.

The primary addressing byte, the "mod r/m" byte, also contains three bits (shown as TTT in Figure 8.1) sometimes used as an extension of the primary opcode. The three bits, however, may also be used as a register field (reg).

When calculating an effective address, either 16-bit addressing or 32-bit addressing is used. 16-bit addressing uses 16-bit address components to calculate the effective address while 32-bit addressing uses 32-bit address components to calculate the effective address. When 16-bit addressing is used, the "mod r/m" byte is interpreted as a 16-bit addressing mode specifier. When 32-bit addressing is used, the "mod r/m" byte is interpreted as a 32-bit addressing mode specifier.

Tables on the following three pages define all encodings of all 16-bit addressing modes and 32-bit addressing modes.

Encoding of Normal Address Mode with "mod r/m" byte (no "s-i-b" byte present):

mod r/m	Effective Address
00 000	DS:[EAX]
00 001	DS:[ECX]
00 010	DS:[EDX]
00 011	DS:[EBX]
00 100	s-i-b is present
00 101	DS:d32
00 110	DS:[ESI]
00 111	DS:[EDI]
01 000	DS:[EAX + d8]
01 001	DS:[ECX + d8]
01 010	DS:[EDX + d8]
01 011	DS:[EBX + d8]
01 100	s-i-b is present
01 101	SS:[EBP + d8]
01 110	DS:[ESI + d8]
01 111	DS:[EDI + d8]

mod r/m	Effective Address
10 000	DS:[EAX + d32]
10 001	DS:[ECX + d32]
10 010	DS:[EDX + d32]
10 011	DS:[EBX + d32]
10 100	s-i-b is present
10 101	SS:[EBP + d32]
10 110	DS:[ESI + d32]
10 111	DS:[EDI + d32]
11 000	register—see below
11 001	register—see below
11 010	register—see below
11 011	register—see below
11 100	register—see below
11 101	register—see below
11 110	register—see below
11 111	register—see below

Register Specified by reg or r/m during Normal Data Operations:

mod r/m	function of w field	
	(when w = 0)	(when w = 1)
11 000	AL	EAX
11 001	CL	ECX
11 010	DL	EDX
11 011	BL	EBX
11 100	AH	ESP
11 101	CH	EBP
11 110	DH	ESI
11 111	BH	EDI

Register Specified by reg or r/m during 16-Bit Data Operations: (66H Prefix)

mod r/m	function of w field	
	(when w = 0)	(when w = 1)
11 000	AL	AX
11 001	CL	CX
11 010	DL	DX
11 011	BL	BX
11 100	AH	SP
11 101	CH	BP
11 110	DH	SI
11 111	BH	DI

Encoding of 16-bit Address Mode with "mod r/m" Byte Using 67H Prefix

mod r/m	Effective Address		mod r/m	Effective Address
00 000	DS:[BX + SI]		10 000	DS:[BX + SI + d16]
00 001	DS:[BX + DI]		10 001	DS:[BX + DI + d16]
00 010	SS:[BP + SI]		10 010	SS:[BP + SI + d16]
00 011	SS:[BP + DI]		10 011	SS:[BP + DI + d16]
00 100	DS:[SI]		10 100	DS:[SI + d16]
00 101	DS:[DI]		10 101	DS:[DI + d16]
00 110	DS:d16		10 110	SS:[BP + d16]
00 111	DS:[BX]		10 111	DS:[BX + d16]
01 000	DS:[BX + SI + d8]		11 000	register—see below
01 001	DS:[BX + DI + d8]		11 001	register—see below
01 010	SS:[BP + SI + d8]		11 010	register—see below
01 011	SS:[BP + DI + d8]		11 011	register—see below
01 100	DS:[SI + d8]		11 100	register—see below
01 101	DS:[DI + d8]		11 101	register—see below
01 110	SS:[BP + d8]		11 110	register—see below
01 111	DS:[BX + d8]		11 111	register—see below

Encoding of 32-bit Address Mode ("mod r/m" byte and "s-i-b" byte present):

mod base	Effective Address
00 000	DS:[EAX + (scaled index)]
00 001	DS:[ECX + (scaled index)]
00 010	DS:[EDX + (scaled index)]
00 011	DS:[EBX + (scaled index)]
00 100	SS:[ESP + (scaled index)]
00 101	DS:[d32 + (scaled index)]
00 110	DS:[ESI + (scaled index)]
00 111	DS:[EDI + (scaled index)]
01 000	DS:[EAX + (scaled index) + d8]
01 001	DS:[ECX + (scaled index) + d8]
01 010	DS:[EDX + (scaled index) + d8]
01 011	DS:[EBX + (scaled index) + d8]
01 100	SS:[ESP + (scaled index) + d8]
01 101	SS:[EBP + (scaled index) + d8]
01 110	DS:[ESI + (scaled index) + d8]
01 111	DS:[EDI + (scaled index) + d8]
10 000	DS:[EAX + (scaled index) + d32]
10 001	DS:[ECX + (scaled index) + d32]
10 010	DS:[EDX + (scaled index) + d32]
10 011	DS:[EBX + (scaled index) + d32]
10 100	SS:[ESP + (scaled index) + d32]
10 101	SS:[EBP + (scaled index) + d32]
10 110	DS:[ESI + (scaled index) + d32]
10 111	DS:[EDI + (scaled index) + d32]

ss	Scale Factor
00	x1
01	x2
10	x4
11	x8

index	Index Register
000	EAX
001	ECX
010	EDX
011	EBX
100	no index reg**
101	EBP
110	ESI
111	EDI

**IMPORTANT NOTE:
When index field is 100, indicating "no index register," then ss field MUST equal 00. If index is 100 and ss does not equal 00, the effective address is undefined.

NOTE:
Mod field in "mod r/m" byte; ss, index, base fields in "s-i-b" byte.

ENCODING OF OPERATION DIRECTION (d) FIELD

In many two-operand instructions the d field is present to indicate which operand is considered the source and which is the destination.

d	Direction of Operation
0	Register/Memory <- - Register "reg" Field Indicates Source Operand; "mod r/m" or "mod ss index base" Indicates Destination Operand
1	Register <- - Register/Memory "reg" Field Indicates Destination Operand; "mod r/m" or "mod ss index base" Indicates Source Operand

ENCODING OF SIGN-EXTEND (s) FIELD

The s field occurs primarily to instructions with immediate data fields. The s field has an effect only if the size of the immediate data is 8 bits and is being placed in a 16-bit or 32-bit destination.

s	Effect on Immediate Data8	Effect on Immediate Data 16|32
0	None	None
1	Sign-Extend Data8 to Fill 16-Bit or 32-Bit Destination	None

ENCODING OF CONDITIONAL TEST (tttn) FIELD

For the conditional instructions (conditional jumps and set on condition), tttn is encoded with n indicating to use the condition (n = 0) or its negation (n = 1), and ttt giving the condition to test.

Mnemonic	Condition	tttn
O	Overflow	0000
NO	No Overflow	0001
B/NAE	Below/Not Above or Equal	0010
NB/AE	Not Below/Above or Equal	0011
E/Z	Equal/Zero	0100
NE/NZ	Not Equal/Not Zero	0101
BE/NA	Below or Equal/Not Above	0110
NBE/A	Not Below or Equal/Above	0111
S	Sign	1000
NS	Not Sign	1001
P/PE	Parity/Parity Even	1010
NP/PO	Not Parity/Parity Odd	1011
L/NGE	Less Than/Not Greater or Equal	1100
NL/GE	Not Less Than/Greater or Equal	1101
LE/NG	Less Than or Equal/Greater Than	1110
NLE/G	Not Less or Equal/Greater Than	1111

ENCODING OF CONTROL OR DEBUG REGISTER (eee) FIELD

For the loading and storing of the Control and Debug registers.

When Interpreted as Control Register Field

eee Code	Reg Name
000	CR0
010	Reserved
011	Reserved
Do not use any other encoding	

When Interpreted as Debug Register Field

eee Code	Reg Name
000	DR0
001	DR1
010	DR2
011	DR3
110	DR6
111	DR7
Do not use any other encoding	

9.0 REVISION HISTORY

This 80376 data sheet, version -002, contains updates and improvements to previous versions. A revision summary is listed here for your convenience.

The sections significantly revised since version -001 are:

Front Page	The 80376 Microarchitecture diagram was added.
Section 1.0	Figure 1.2 was updated to show both top and bottom views of the 88-pin PGA package.
Section 2.0	Figure 2.0 was updated to show the 16-bit registers SI, DI, BP and SP.
Section 2.1	Figure 2.2 was updated to show the correct bit polarity for bit 4 in the CR0 register.
Section 2.1	Tables 2.1 and 2.2 were updated to include additional information on the EFLAGs and CR0 registers.
Section 2.3	Figure 2.3 was updated to more accurately reflect the addressing mechanism of the 80376.
Section 2.6	In the subsection **Maskable Interrupt** a paragraph was added to describe the effect of interrupt gates on the IF EFLAGs bit.
Section 2.8	Table 2.7 was updated to reflect the correct power up condition of the CR0 register.
Section 2.10	Figure 2.6 was updated to show the correct bit positions of the BT, BS and BD bits in the DR6 register.
Section 3.0	Figure 3.1 was updated to clearly show the address calculation process.
Section 3.2	The subsection **DESCRIPTORS** was elaborated upon to clearly define the relationship between the linear address space and physical address space of the 80376.
Section 3.2	Figures 3.3 and 3.4 were updated to show the AVL bit field.
Section 3.3	The last sentence in the first paragraph of subsection **PROTECTION AND I/O PERMISSION BIT MAP** was deleted. This was an incorrect statement.
Section 4.1	In the Subsection **ADDRESS BUS (BHE#, BLE#, $A_{23}-A_1$** last sentence in the first paragraph was updated to reflect the numerics operand addresses as 8000FCH and 8000FEH. Because the 80376 sometimes does a double word I/O access a second access to 8000FEH can be seen.
Section 4.1	The Subsection **Hold Lantencies** was updated to describe how 32-bit and unaligned accesses are internally locked but do not assert the LOCK# signal.
Section 4.2	Table 4.6 was updated to show the correct active data bits during a BLE# assertion.
Section 4.4	This section was updated to correctly reflect the pipelining of the address and status of the 80376 as opposed to "Address Pipelining" which occurs on processors such as the 80286.
Section 4.6	Table 4.7 was updated to show the correct Revision number, 05H.
Section 4.7	Table 4.8 was updated to show the numerics operand register 8000FEH. This address is seen when the 80376 does a DWORD operation to the port address 8000FCH.
Section 5.0	In the first paragraph the case temperatures were updated to correctly reflect the 0°C–115°C for the ceramic package and 0°C–110°C for the plastic package.
Section 6.2	Table 6.2 was updated to correctly reflect the Case Temperature under Bias specification of −65°C–120°C.
Section 6.4	Figure 6.8 vertical axis was updated to reflect "Output Valid Delay (ns)".
Section 6.4	Figure 6.11 was updated to show typical I_{CC} vs Frequency for the 80376.
Section 6.5	This entire section was updated to reflect the new ICE-376 emulator.
Section 8.1	The clock counts and opcodes for various instructions were updated to their correct value.
Section 8.2	The section **INSTRUCTION ENCODING** was appended to the data sheet.

The sections significantly revised since version -002 are:

Section 1.0	Modified table 1.1. to list pins in alphabetical order.

82370
INTEGRATED SYSTEM PERIPHERAL

- **High Performance 32-Bit DMA Controller for 16-Bit Bus**
  - 16 MBytes/Sec Maximum Data Transfer Rate at 16 MHz
  - 8 Independently Programmable Channels
- **20-Source Interrupt Controller**
  - Individually Programmable Interrupt Vectors
  - 15 External, 5 Internal Interrupts
  - 82C59A Superset
- **Four 16-Bit Programmable Interval Timers**
  - 82C54 Compatible
- **Software Compatible to 82380**

- **Programmable Wait State Generator**
  - 0 to 15 Wait States Pipelined
  - 1 to 16 Wait States Non-Pipelined
- **DRAM Refresh Controller**
- **80376 Shutdown Detect and Reset Control**
  - Software/Hardware Reset
- **High Speed CHMOS III Technology**
- **100-Pin Plastic Quad Flat-Pack Package and 132-Pin Pin Grid Array Package**
  (See Packaging Handbook Order #231369)
- **Optimized for Use with the 80376 Microprocessor**
  - Resides on Local Bus for Maximum Bus Bandwidth

The 82370 is a multi-function support peripheral that integrates system functions necessary in an 80376 environment. It has eight channels of high performance 32-bit DMA (32-bit internal, 16-bit external) with the most efficient transfer rates possible on the 80376 bus. System support peripherals integrated into the 82370 provide Interrupt Control, Timers, Wait State generation, DRAM Refresh Control, and System Reset logic.

The 82370's DMA Controller can transfer data between devices of different data path widths using a single channel. Each DMA channel operates independently in any of several modes. Each channel has a temporary data storage register for handling non-aligned data without the need for external alignment logic.

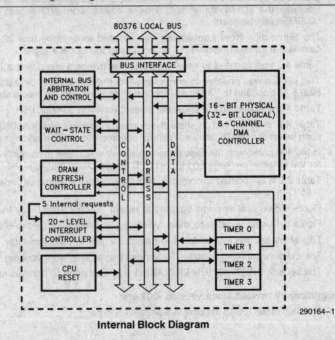

Internal Block Diagram

290164-1

October 1989
Order Number: 290164-003

Pin Descriptions

The 82370 provides all of the signals necessary to interface an 80376 host processor. It has a separate 24-bit address and 16-bit data bus. It also has a set of control signals to support operation as a bus master or a bus slave. Several special function signals exist on the 82370 for interfacing the system support peripherals to their respective system counterparts. Following are the definitions of the individual pins of the 82370. These brief descriptions are provided as a reference. Each signal is further defined within the sections which describe the associated 82370 function.

Symbol	Type	Name and Function
A_1-A_{23}	I/O	**ADDRESS BUS:** Outputs physical memory or port I/O addresses. See **Address Bus** (2.2.3) for additional information.
BHE# BLE#	I/O	**BYTE ENABLES:** Indicate which data bytes of the data bus take part in a bus cycle. See **Byte Enable** (2.2.4) for additional information.
D_0-D_{15}	I/O	**DATA BUS:** This is the 16-bit data bus. These pins are active outputs during interrupt acknowledges, during Slave accesses, and when the 82370 is in the Master Mode.
CLK2	I	**PROCESSOR CLOCK:** This pin must be connected to the processor's clock, CLK2. The 82370 monitors the phase of this clock in order to remain synchronized with the CPU. This clock drives all of the internal synchronous circuitry.
D/C#	I/O	**DATA/CONTROL:** D/C# is used to distinguish between CPU control cycles and DMA or CPU data access cycles. It is active as an output only in the Master Mode.
W/R#	I/O	**WRITE/READ:** W/R# is used to distinguish between write and read cycles. It is active as an output only in the Master Mode.
M/IO#	I/O	**MEMORY/IO:** M/IO# is used to distinguish between memory and IO accesses. It is active as an output only in the Master Mode.
ADS#	I/O	**ADDRESS STATUS:** This signal indicates presence of a valid address on the address bus. It is active as output only in the Master Mode. ADS# is active during the first T-state where addresses and control signals are valid.
NA#	I	**NEXT ADDRESS:** Asserted by a peripheral or memory to begin a pipelined address cycle. This pin is monitored only while the 82370 is in the Master Mode. In the Slave Mode, pipelining is determined by the current and past status of the ADS# and READY# signals.
HOLD	O	**HOLD REQUEST:** This is an active-high signal to the Bus Master to request control of the system bus. When control is granted, the Bus Master activates the hold acknowledge signal (HLDA).
HLDA	I	**HOLD ACKNOWLEDGE:** This input signal tells the DMA controller that the Bus Master has relinquished control of the system bus to the DMA controller.

Pin Descriptions (Continued)

Symbol	Type	Name and Function
DREQ (0–3, 5–7)	I	**DMA REQUEST:** The DMA Request inputs monitor requests from peripherals requiring DMA service. Each of the eight DMA channels has one DREQ input. These active-high inputs are internally synchronized and prioritized. Upon request, channel 0 has the highest priority and channel 7 the lowest.
DREQ4/IRQ9#	I	**DMA/INTERRUPT REQUEST:** This is the DMA request input for channel 4. It is also connected to the interrupt controller via interrupt request 9. This internal connection is available for DMA channel 4 only. The interrupt input is active low and can be programmed as either edge or level triggered. Either function can be masked by the appropriate mask register. Priorities of the DMA channel and the interrupt request are not related but follow the rules of the individual controllers. Note that this pin has a weak internal pull-up. This causes the interrupt request to be inactive, but the DMA request will be active if there is no external connection made. Most applications will require that either one or the other of these functions be used, but not both. For this reason, it is advised that DMA channel 4 be used for transfers where a software request is more appropriate (such as memory-to-memory transfers). In such an application, DREQ4 can be masked by software, freeing IRQ9# for other purposes.
EOP#	I/O	**END OF PROCESS:** As an output, this signal indicates that the current Requester access is the last access of the currently operating DMA channel. It is activated when Terminal Count is reached. As an input, it signals the DMA channel to terminate the current buffer and proceed to the next buffer, if one is available. This signal may be programmed as an asynchronous or synchronous input. EOP# must be connected to a pull-up resistor. This will prevent erroneous external requests for termination of a DMA process.
EDACK (0–2)	O	**ENCODED DMA ACKNOWLEDGE:** These signals contain the encoded acknowledgment of a request for DMA service by a peripheral. The binary code formed by the three signals indicates which channel is active. Channel 4 does not have a DMA acknowledge. The inactive state is indicated by the code 100. During a Requester access, EDACK presents the code for the active DMA channel. During a Target access, EDACK presents the inactive code 100.
IRQ (11–23)#	I	**INTERRUPT REQUEST:** These are active low interrupt request inputs. The inputs can be programmed to be edge or level sensitive. Interrupt priorities are programmable as either fixed or rotating. These inputs have weak internal pull-up resistors. Unused interrupt request inputs should be tied inactive externally.
INT	O	**INTERRUPT OUT:** INT signals that an interrupt request is pending.
CLKIN	I	**TIMER CLOCK INPUT:** This is the clock input signal to all of the 82370's programmable timers. It is independent of the system clock input (CLK2).
TOUT1/REF#	O	**TIMER 1 OUTPUT/REFRESH:** This pin is software programmable as either the direct output of Timer 1, or as the indicator of a refresh cycle in progress. As REF#, this signal is active during the memory read cycle which occurs during refresh.

Pin Descriptions (Continued)

Symbol	Type	Name and Function
TOUT2#/IRQ3#	I/O	**TIMER 2 OUTPUT/INTERRUPT REQUEST:** This is the inverted output of Timer 2. It is also connected directly to interrupt request 3. External hardware can use IRQ3# if Timer 2 is programmed as OUT = 0 (TOUT2# = 1).
TOUT3#	O	**TIMER 3 OUTPUT:** This is the inverted output of Timer 3.
READY#	I	**READY INPUT:** This active-low input indicates to the 82370 that the current bus cycle is complete. READY is sampled by the 82370 both while it is in the Master Mode, and while it is in the Slave Mode.
WSC (0–1)	I	**WAIT STATE CONTROL:** WSC0 and WSC1 are inputs used by the Wait-State Generator to determine the number of wait states required by the currently accessed memory or I/O. The binary code on these pins, combined with the M/IO# signal, selects an internal register in which a wait-state count is stored. The combination WSC = 11 disables the wait-state generator.
READYO#	O	**READY OUTPUT:** This is the synchronized output of the wait-state generator. It is also valid during CPU accesses to the 82370 in the Slave Mode when the 82370 requires wait states. READYO# should feed directly the processor's READY# input.
RESET	I	**RESET:** This synchronous input serves to initialize the state of the 82370 and provides basis for the CPURST output. RESET must be held active for at least 15 CLK2 cycles in order to guarantee the state of the 82370. After Reset, the 82370 is in the Slave Mode with all outputs except timers and interrupts in their inactive states. The state of the timers and interrupt controller must be initialized through software. This input must be active for the entire time required by the host processor to guarantee proper reset.
CHPSEL#	O	**CHIP SELECT:** This pin is driven active whenever the 82370 is addressed in a slave bus read or write cycle. It is also active during interrupt acknowledge cycles when the 82370 is driving the Data Bus. It can be used to control the local bus transceivers to prevent contention with the system bus.
CPURST	O	**CPU RESET:** CPURST provides a synchronized reset signal for the CPU. It is activated in the event of a software reset command, a processor shut-down detect, or a hardware reset via the RESET pin. The 82370 holds CPURST active for 62 clocks in response to either a software reset command or a shut-down detection. Otherwise CPURST reflects the RESET input.
V_CC		**POWER:** +5V input power.
V_SS		Ground Reference.

Table 1. Wait-State Select Inputs

Port Address	Wait-State Registers				Select Inputs	
	D7	D4	D3	D0	WSC1	WSC0
72H	MEMORY 0		I/O 0		0	0
73H	MEMORY 1		I/O 1		0	1
74H	MEMORY 2		I/O 2		1	0
	DISABLED				1	1
M/IO#	1		0			

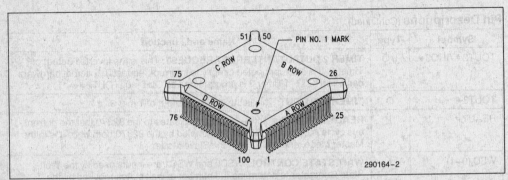

100 Pin Quad Flat-Pack Pin Out (Top View)

A Row		B Row		C Row		D Row	
Pin	Label	Pin	Label	Pin	Label	Pin	Label
1	CPURST	26	V_{CC}	51	A_{11}	76	DREQ5
2	INT	27	D_{11}	52	A_{10}	77	DREQ4/IRQ9#
3	V_{CC}	28	D_4	53	A_9	78	DREQ3
4	V_{SS}	29	D_{12}	54	A_8	79	DREQ2
5	TOUT2#/IRQ3#	30	D_5	55	A_7	80	DREQ1
6	TOUT3#	31	D_{13}	56	A_6	81	DREQ0
7	D/C#	32	D_6	57	A_5	82	IRQ23#
8	V_{CC}	33	V_{SS}	58	V_{CC}	83	IRQ22#
9	W/R#	34	D_{14}	59	A_4	84	IRQ21#
10	M/IO#	35	D_7	60	A_3	85	IRQ20#
11	HOLD	36	D_{15}	61	A_2	86	IRQ19#
12	TOUT1/REF#	37	A_{23}	62	A_1	87	IRQ18#
13	CLK2	38	A_{22}	63	V_{SS}	88	IRQ17#
14	V_{SS}	39	A_{21}	64	BLE#	89	IRQ16#
15	READYO#	40	A_{20}	65	BHE#	90	IRQ15#
16	EOP#	41	A_{19}	66	V_{SS}	91	IRQ14#
17	CHPSEL#	42	A_{18}	67	ADS#	92	IRQ13#
18	V_{CC}	43	V_{CC}	68	V_{CC}	93	IRQ12#
19	D_0	44	A_{17}	69	EDACK2	94	IRQ11#
20	D_8	45	A_{16}	70	EDACK1	95	CLKIN
21	D_1	46	A_{15}	71	EDACK0	96	WSC0
22	D_9	47	A_{14}	72	HLDA	97	WSC1
23	D_2	48	V_{SS}	73	DREQ7	98	RESET
24	D_{10}	49	A_{13}	74	DREQ6	99	READY#
25	D_3	50	A_{12}	75	NA#	100	V_{SS}

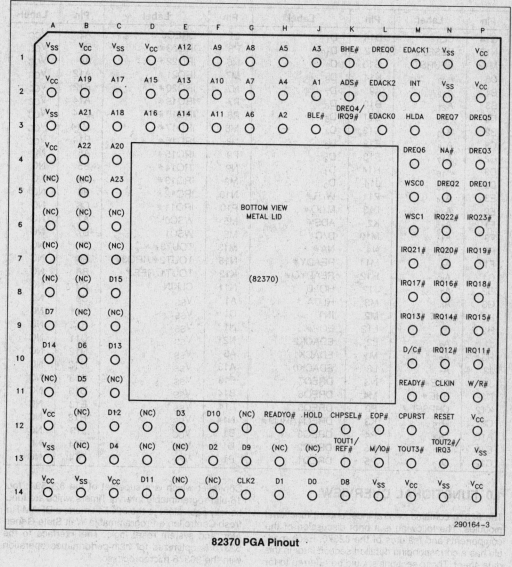

82370 PGA Pinout

290164-3

Pin	Label	Pin	Label	Pin	Label	Pin	Label
G14	CLK2	D14	D_{11}	L1	DREQ0	A2	V_{CC}
N12	RESET	F12	D_{10}	P6	IRQ23#	P2	V_{CC}
M12	CPURST	G13	D_9	N6	IRQ22#	A4	V_{CC}
C5	A_{23}	K14	D_8	M7	IRQ21#	A12	V_{CC}
B4	A_{22}	A9	D_7	N7	IRQ20#	P12	V_{CC}
B3	A_{21}	B10	D_6	P7	IRQ19#	A14	V_{CC}
C4	A_{20}	B11	D_5	P8	IRQ18#	C14	V_{CC}
B2	A_{19}	C13	D_4	M8	IRQ17#	M14	V_{CC}
C3	A_{18}	E12	D_3	N8	IRQ16#	P14	V_{CC}
C2	A_{17}	F13	D_2	P9	IRQ15#	A5	NC
D3	A_{16}	H14	D_1	N9	IRQ14#	B5	NC
D2	A_{15}	J14	D_0	M9	IRQ13#	A6	NC
E3	A_{14}	P11	W/R#	N10	IRQ12#	B6	NC
E2	A_{13}	L13	M/IO#	P10	IRQ11#	C6	NC
E1	A_{12}	K2	ADS#	M5	WSC0	A7	NC
F3	A_{11}	M10	D/C#	M6	WSC1	B7	NC
F2	A_{10}	N4	NA#	M13	TOUT3#	C7	NC
F1	A_9	M11	READY#	N13	TOUT2#/IRQ3#	A8	NC
G1	A_8	H12	READYO#	K13	TOUT1/REF#	B8	NC
G2	A_7	J12	HOLD	N11	CLKIN	B9	NC
G3	A_6	M3	HLDA	A1	V_{SS}	C9	NC
H1	A_5	M2	INT	C1	V_{SS}	A11	NC
H2	A_4	L12	EOP#	N1	V_{SS}	B12	NC
J1	A_3	L2	EDACK2	N2	V_{SS}	C11	NC
H3	A_2	M1	EDACK1	A3	V_{SS}	D12	NC
J2	A_1	L3	EDACK0	A13	V_{SS}	G12	NC
J3	BLE#	N3	DREQ7	P13	V_{SS}	B13	NC
K1	BHE#	M4	DREQ6	B14	V_{SS}	D13	NC
K12	CHPSEL#	P3	DREQ5	L14	V_{SS}	E13	NC
C8	D_{15}	K3	DREQ4/IRQ9#	N14	V_{SS}	H13	NC
A10	D_{14}	P4	DREQ3	B1	V_{CC}	J13	NC
C10	D_{13}	N5	DREQ2	D1	V_{CC}	E14	NC
C12	D_{12}	P5	DREQ1	P1	V_{CC}	F14	NC

1.0 FUNCTIONAL OVERVIEW

The 82370 contains several independent functional modules. The following is a brief discussion of the components and features of the 82370. Each module has a corresponding detailed section later in this data sheet. Those sections should be referred to for design and programming information.

1.1 82370 Architecture

The 82370 is comprised of several computer system functions that are normally found in separate LSI and VLSI components. These include: a high-performance, eight-channel, 32-bit Direct Memory Access Controller; a 20-level Programmable Interrupt Controller which is a superset of the 82C59A; four 16-bit Programmable Interval Timers which are functionally equivalent to the 82C54 timers; a DRAM Refresh Controller; a Programmable Wait State Generator; and system reset logic. The interface to the 82370 is optimized for high-performance operation with the 80376 microprocessor.

The 82370 operates directly on the 80376 bus. In the Slave Mode, it monitors the state of the processor at all times and acts or idles according to the commands of the host. It monitors the address pipeline status and generates the programmed number of wait states for the device being accessed. The 82370 also has logic to the reset of the 80376 via hardware or software reset requests and processor shutdown status.

After a system reset, the 82370 is in the Slave Mode. It appears to the system as an I/O device. It becomes a bus master when it is performing DMA transfers.

To maintain compatibility with existing software, the registers within the 82370 are accessed as bytes. If the internal logic of the 82370 requires a delay before another access by the processor, wait states are automatically inserted into the access cycle. This allows the programmer to write initialization routines, etc. without regard to hardware recovery times.

Figure 1-1 shows the basic architectural components of the 82370. The following sections briefly discuss the architecture and function of each of the distinct sections of the 82370.

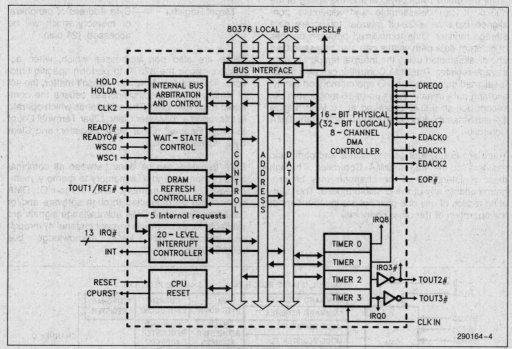

Figure 1-1. Architecture of the 82370

1.1.1 DMA CONTROLLER

The 82370 contains a high-performance, 8-channel DMA Controller. It provides a 32-bit internal data path. Through its 16-bit external physical data bus, it is capable of transferring data in any combination of bytes, words and double-words. The addresses of both source and destination can be independently incremented, decremented or held constant, and cover the entire 16-bit physical address space of the 80376. It can disassemble and assemble non-aligned data via a 32-bit internal temporary data storage register. Data transferred between devices of different data path widths can also be assembled and disassembled using the internal temporary data storage register. The DMA Controller can also transfer aligned data between I/O and memory on the fly, allowing data transfer rates up to 16 megabytes per second for an 82370 operating at 16 MHz. Figure 1-2 illustrates the functional components of the DMA Controller.

There are twenty-four general status and command registers in the 82370 DMA Controller. Through these registers any of the channels may be programmed into any of the possible modes. The operating modes of any one channel are independent of the operation of the other channels.

Each channel has three programmable registers which determine the location and amount of data to be transferred:

Byte Count Register—Number of bytes to transfer. (24-bits)

Requester Register — Byte Address of memory or peripheral which is requesting DMA service. (24-bits)

Target Register — Byte Address of peripheral or memory which will be accessed. (24-bits)

There are also port addresses which, when accessed, cause the 82370 to perform specific functions. The actual data written doesn't matter, the act of writing to the specific address causes the command to be executed. The commands which operate in this mode are: Master Clear, Clear Terminal Count Interrupt Request, Clear Mask Register, and Clear Byte Pointer Flip-Flop.

DMA transfers can be done between all combinations of memory and I/O; memory-to-memory, memory-to-I/O, I/O-to-memory, and I/O-to-I/O. DMA service can be requested through software and/or hardware. Hardware DMA acknowledge signals are available for all channels (except channel 4) through an encoded 3-bit DMA acknowledge bus (EDACK0–2).

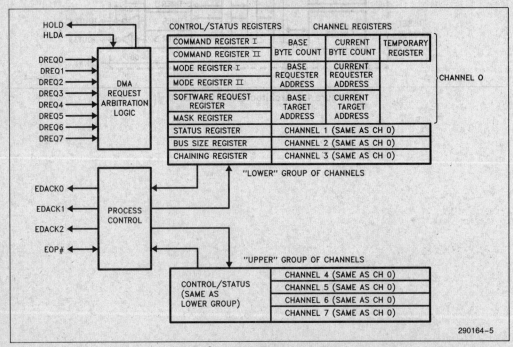

Figure 1-2. 82370 DMA Controller

The 82370 DMA Controller transfers blocks of data (buffers) in three modes: Single Buffer, Buffer Auto-Initialize, and Buffer Chaining. In the Single Buffer Process, the 82370 DMA Controller is programmed to transfer one particular block of data. Successive transfers then require reprogramming of the DMA channel. Single Buffer transfers are useful in systems where it is known at the time the transfer begins what quantity of data is to be transferred, and there is a contiguous block of data area available.

The Buffer Auto-Initialize Process allows the same data area to be used for successive DMA transfers without having to reprogram the channel.

The Buffer Chaining Process allows a program to specify a list of buffer transfers to be executed. The 82370 DMA Controller, through interrupt routines, is reprogrammed from the list. The channel is reprogrammed for a new buffer before the current buffer transfer is complete. This pipelining of the channel programming process allows the system to allocate non-contiguous blocks of data storage space, and transfer all of the data with one DMA process. The buffers that make up the chain do not have to be in contiguous locations.

Channel priority can be fixed or rotating. Fixed priority allows the programmer to define the priority of DMA channels based on hardware or other fixed pa-

rameters. Rotating priority is used to provide peripherals access to the bus on a shared basis.

With fixed priority, the programmer can set any channel to have the current lowest priority. This allows the user to reset or manually rotate the priority schedule without reprogramming the command registers.

1.1.2 PROGRAMMABLE INTERVAL TIMERS

Four 16-bit programmable interval timers reside within the 82370. These timers are identical in function to the timers in the 82C54 Programmable Interval Timer. All four of the timers share a common clock input which can be independent of the system clock. The timers are capable of operating in six different modes. In all of the modes, the current count can be latched and read by the 80376 at any time, making these very versatile event timers. Figure 1-3 shows the functional components of the Programmable Interval Timers.

The outputs of the timers are directed to key system functions, making system design simpler. Timer 0 is routed directly to an interrupt input and is not available externally. This timer would typically be used to generate time-keeping interrupts.

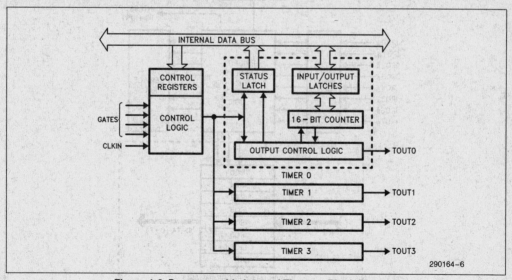

Figure 1-3. Programmable Interval Timers—Block Diagram

82370

Timers 1 and 2 have outputs which are available for general timer/counter purposes as well as special functions. Timer 1 is routed to the refresh control logic to provide refresh timing. Timer 2 is connected to an interrupt request input to provide other timer functions. Timer 3 is a general purpose timer/counter whose output is available to external hardware. It is also connected internally to the interrupt request which defaults to the highest priority (IRQ0).

1.1.3 INTERRUPT CONTROLLER

The 82370 has the equivalent of three enhanced 82C59A Programmable Interrupt Controllers. These controllers can all be operated in the Master Mode, but the priority is always as if they were cascaded. There are 15 interrupt request inputs provided for the user, all of which can be inputs from external slave interrupt controllers. Cascading 82C59As to these request inputs allows a possible total of 120 external interrupt requests. Figure 1-4 is a block diagram of the 82370 Interrupt Controller.

Each of the interrupt request inputs can be individually programmed with its own interrupt vector, allowing more flexibility in interrupt vector mapping than

was available with the 82C59A. An interrupt is provided to alert the system that an attempt is being made to program the vectors in the method of the 82C59A. This provides compatibility of existing software that used the 82C59A or 8259A with new designs using the 82370.

In the event of an unrequested or otherwise erroneous interrupt acknowledge cycle, the 82370 Interrupt Controller issues a default vector. This vector, programmed by the system software, will alert the system of unsolicited interrupts of the 80376.

The functions of the 82370 Interrupt Controller are identical to the 82C59A, except in regards to programming the interrupt vectors as mentioned above. Interrupt request inputs are programmable as either edge or level triggered and are software maskable. Priority can be either fixed or rotating and interrupt requests can be nested.

Enhancements are added to the 82370 for cascading external interrupt controllers. Master to Slave handshaking takes place on the data bus, instead of dedicated cascade lines.

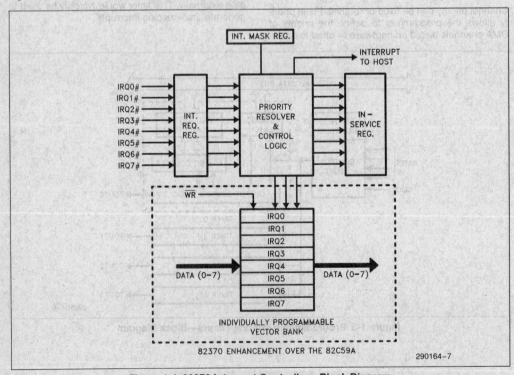

Figure 1-4. 82370 Interrupt Controller—Block Diagram

82370

1.1.4 WAIT STATE GENERATOR

The Wait State Generator is a programmable READY generation circuit for the 80376 bus. A peripheral requiring wait states can request the Wait State Generator to hold the processor's READY input inactive for a predetermined number of bus states. Six different wait state counts can be programmed into the Wait State Generator by software; three for memory accesses and three for I/O accesses. A block diagram of the 82370 Wait State Generator is shown in Figure 1-5.

The peripheral being accessed selects the required wait state count by placing a code on a 2-bit wait state select bus. This code along with the M/IO# signal from the bus master is used to select one of six internal 4-bit wait state registers which has been programmed with the desired number of wait states. From zero to fifteen wait states can be programmed into the wait state registers. The Wait State generator tracks the state of the processor or current bus master at all times, regardless of which device is the current bus master and regardless of whether or not the wait state generator is currently active.

The 82370 Wait State Generator is disabled by making the select inputs both high. This allows hardware which is intelligent enough to generate its own ready signal to be accessed without penalty. As previously mentioned, deselecting the Wait State Generator does not disable its ability to determine the proper number of wait states due to pipeline status in subsequent bus cycles.

The number of wait states inserted into a pipelined bus cycle is the value in the selected wait state register. If the bus master is operating in the non-pipelined mode, the Wait State Generator will increase the number of wait states inserted into the bus cycle by one.

On reset, the Wait State Generator's registers are loaded with the value FFH, giving the maximum number of wait states for any access in which the wait state select inputs are active.

1.1.5 DRAM REFRESH CONTROLLER

The 82370 DRAM Refresh Controller consists of a 24-bit refresh address counter and bus arbitration logic. The output of Timer 1 is used to periodically request a refresh cycle. When the controller receives the request, it requests access to the system bus through the HOLD signal. When bus control is acknowledged by the processor or current bus master, the refresh controller executes a memory read operation at the address currently in the Refresh Address Register. At the same time, it activates a refresh signal (REF#) that the memory uses to force a refresh instead of a normal read. Control of the bus is transferred to the processor at the completion of this cycle. Typically a refresh cycle will take six clock cycles to execute on an 80376 bus.

The 82370 DRAM Refresh Controller has the highest priority when requesting bus access and will interrupt any active DMA process. This allows large blocks of data to be moved by the DMA controller without affecting the refresh function. Also the DMA controller is not required to completely relinquish the bus, the refresh controller simply steals a bus cycle between DMA accesses.

The amount by which the refresh address is incremented is programmable to allow for different bus widths and memory bank arrangements.

1.1.6 CPU RESET FUNCTION

The 82370 contains a special reset function which can respond to hardware reset signals as well as a

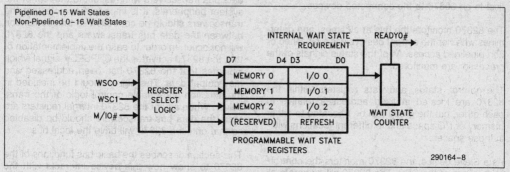

Figure 1-5. 82370 Wait State Generator—Block Diagram

8-103

software reset command. The circuit will hold the 80376's RESET line active while an external hardware reset signal is present at its RESET input. It can also reset the 80376 processor as the result of a software command. The software reset command causes the 82370 to hold the processor's RESET line active for a minimum of 62 clock cycles. The 80376 requires that its RESET line be held active for a minimum of 80 clock cycles to re-initialize. For a more detailed explanation and solution, see Appendix D (System Notes).

The 82370 can be programmed to sense the shutdown detect code on the status lines from the 80376. If the Shutdown Detect function is enabled, the 82370 will automatically reset the processor. A diagnostic register is available which can be used to determine the cause of reset.

1.1.7 REGISTER MAP RELOCATION

After a hardware reset, the internal registers of the 82370 are located in I/O space beginning at port address 0000H. The map of the 82370's registers is relocatable via a software command. The default mapping places the 82370 between I/O addresses 0000H and 00DBH. The relocation register allows this map to be moved to any even 256-byte boundary in the processor's 16-bit I/O address space or any even 64 kbyte boundary in the 24-bit memory address space.

1.2 Host Interface

The 82370 is designed to operate efficiently on the local bus of an 80376 microprocessor. The control signals of the 82370 are identical in function to those of the 80376. As a slave, the 82370 operates with all of the features available on the 80376 bus. When the 82370 is in the Master Mode, it looks identical to an 80376 to the connected devices.

The 82370 monitors the bus at all times, and determines whether the current bus cycle is a pipelined or non-pipelined access. All of the status signals of the processor are monitored.

The control, status, and data registers within the 82370 are located at fixed addresses relative to each other, but the group can be relocated to either memory or I/O space and to different locations within those spaces.

As a Slave device, the 82370 monitors the control/status lines of the CPU. The 82370 will generate all of the wait states it needs whenever it is accessed. This allows the programmer the freedom of access-

ing 82370 registers without having to insert NOPs in the program to wait for slower 82370 internal registers.

The 82370 can determine if a current bus cycle is a pipelined or a non-pipelined cycle. It does this by monitoring the ADS#, NA# and READY# signals and thereby keeping track of the current state of the 80376.

As a bus master, the 82370 looks like an 80376 to the rest of the system. This enables the designer greater flexibility in systems which include the 82370. The designer does not have to alter the interfaces of any peripherals designed to operate with the 80376 to accommodate the 82370. The 82370 will access any peripherals on the bus in the same manner as the 80376, including recognizing pipelined bus cycles.

The 82370 is accessed as an 8-bit peripheral. The 80376 places the data of all 8-bit accesses either on D(0–7) or D(8–15). The 82370 will only accept data on these lines when in the Slave Mode. When in the Master Mode, the 82370 is a full 16-bit machine, sending and receiving data in the same manner as the 80376.

2.0 80376 HOST INTERFACE

The 82370 contains a set of interface signals to operate efficiently with the 80376 host processor. These signals were designed so that minimal hardware is needed to connect the 82370 to the 80376. Figure 2-1 depicts a typical system configuration with the 80376 processor. As shown in the diagram, the 82370 is designed to interface directly with the 80376 bus.

Since the 82370 resides on the opposite side of the data bus transceivers with respect to the rest of the system peripherals, it is important to note that the transceivers should be controlled so that contention between the data bus transceivers and the 82370 will not occur. In order to ease the implementation of this, the 82370 activates the CHPSEL# signal which indicates that the 82370 has been addressed and may output data. This signal should be included in the direction and enable control logic of the transceiver. When any of the 82370 internal registers are read, the data bus transceivers should be disabled so that only the 82370 will drive the local bus.

This section describes the basic bus functions of the 82370 to show how this device interacts with the 80376 processor. Other signals which are not directly related to the host interface will be discussed in their associated functional block description.

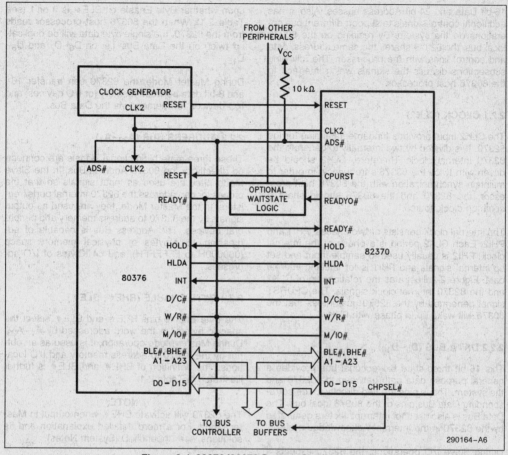

Figure 2-1. 80376/82370 System Configuration

2.1 Master and Slave Modes

At any time, the 82370 acts as either a Slave device or a Master device in the system. Upon reset, the 82370 will be in the Slave Mode. In this mode, the 80376 processor can read/write into the 82370 internal registers. Initialization information may be programmed into the 82370 during Slave Mode.

When DMA service (including DRAM Refresh Cycles generated by the 82370) is requested, the 82370 will request and subsequently get control of the 80376 local bus. This is done through the HOLD and HLDA (Hold Acknowledge) signals. When the 80376 proc-

essor responds by asserting the HLDA signal, the 82370 will switch into Master Mode and perform DMA transfers. In this mode, the 82370 is the bus master of the system. It can read/write data from/to memory and peripheral devices. The 82370 will return to the Slave Mode upon completion of DMA transfers, or when HLDA is negated.

2.2 80376 Interface Signals

As mentioned in the Architecture section, the Bus Interface module of the 82370 (see Figure 1-1) contains signals that are directly connected to the 80376 host processor. This module has separate

16-bit Data and 24-bit Address busses. Also, it has additional control signals to support different bus operations on the system. By residing on the 80376 local bus, the 82370 shares the same address, data and control lines with the processor. The following subsections discuss the signals which interface to the 80376 host processor.

2.2.1 CLOCK (CLK2)

The CLK2 input provides fundamental timing for the 82370. It is divided by two internally to generate the 82370 internal clock. Therefore, CLK2 should be driven with twice the 80376's frequency. In order to maintain synchronization with the 80376 host processor, the 82370 and the 80376 should share a common clock source.

The internal clock consists of two phases: PHI1 and PHI2. Each CLK2 period is a phase of the internal clock. PHI2 is usually used to sample input and set up internal signals and PHI1 is for latching internal data. Figure 2-2 illustrates the relationship of CLK2 and the 82370 internal clock signals. The CPURST signal generated by the 82370 guarantees that the 80376 will wake up in phase with PHI1.

2.2.2 DATA BUS ($D_0 - D_{15}$)

This 16-bit three-state bidirectional bus provides a general purpose data path between the 82370 and the system. These pins are tied directly to the corresponding Data Bus pins of the 80376 local bus. The Data Bus is also used for interrupt vectors generated by the 82370 in the Interrupt Acknowledge cycle.

During Slave I/O operations, the 82370 expects a single byte to be written or read. When the 80376 host processor writes into the 82370, either $D_0 - D_7$ or $D_8 - D_{15}$ will be latched into the 82370, depending upon whether Byte Enable bit BLE# is 0 or 1 (see Table 2-1). When the 80376 host processor reads from the 82370, the single byte data will be duplicated twice on the Data Bus; i.e. on $D_0 - D_7$ and $D_8 - D_{15}$.

During Master Mode, the 82370 can transfer 16-, and 8-bit data between memory (or I/O devices) and I/O devices (or memory) via the Data Bus.

2.2.3 ADDRESS BUS ($A_{23} - A_1$)

These three-state bidirectional signals are connected directly to the 80376 Address Bus. In the Slave Mode, they are used as input signals so that the processor can address the 82370 internal ports/registers. In the Master Mode, they are used as output signals by the 82370 to address memory and peripheral devices. The Address Bus is capable of addressing 16 Mbytes of physical memory space (000000H to FFFFFFH), and 64 Kbytes of I/O addresses.

2.2.4 BYTE ENABLE (BHE#, BLE#)

The Byte Enable pins BHE# and BLE# select the specific byte(s) in the word addressed by $A_1 - A_{23}$. During Master Mode operation, it is used as an output by the 82370 to address memory and I/O locations. The definition of BHE# and BLE# is further illustrated in Table 2-1.

NOTE:
The 82370 will activate BHE# when output in Master Mode. For a more detailed explanation and its solutions, see Appendix D (System Notes).

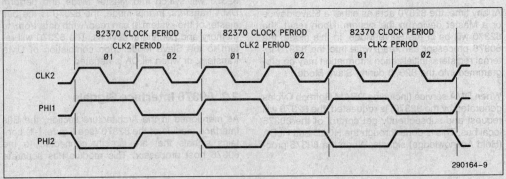

Figure 2-2. CLK2 and 82370 Internal Clock

As an output (Master Mode):

Table 2-1. Byte Enable Signals

BHE#	BLE#	Byte to be Accessed Relative to $A_{23}-A_1$	Logical Byte Presented on Data Bus During WRITE Only*	
			$D_{15}-D_8$	D_7-D_0
0	0	0, 1	B	A
0	1	1	A	A
1	0	0	U	A
1	1	(Not Used)		

U = Undefined
A = Logical D_0-D_7
B = Logical D_8-D_{15}

*NOTE:
Actual number of bytes accessed depends upon the programmed data path width.

Table 2-2. Bus Cycle Definition

M/IO#	D/C#	W/R#	As INPUTS	As OUTPUTS
0	0	0	Interrupt Acknowledge	NOT GENERATED
0	0	1	UNDEFINED	NOT GENERATED
0	1	0	I/O Read	I/O Read
0	1	1	I/O Write	I/O Write
1	0	0	UNDEFINED	NOT GENERATED
1	0	1	HALT if $A_1 = 1$ SHUTDOWN if $A_1 = 0$	NOT GENERATED
1	1	0	Memory Read	Memory Read
1	1	1	Memory Write	Memory Write

2.2.5 BUS CYCLE DEFINITION SIGNALS (D/C#, W/R#, M/IO#)

These three-state bidirectional signals define the type of bus cycle being performed. W/R# distinguishes between write and read cycles. D/C# distinguishes between processor data and control cycles. M/IO# distinguishes between memory and I/O cycles.

During Slave Mode, these signals are driven by the 80376 host processor; during Master Mode, they are driven by the 82370. In either mode, these signals will be valid when the Address Status (ADS#) is driven LOW. Exact bus cycle definitions are given in Table 2-2. Note that some combinations are recognized as inputs, but not generated as outputs. In the Master Mode, D/C# is always HIGH.

2.2.6 ADDRESS STATUS (ADS#)

This signal indicates that a valid address (A_1-A_{23}, BHE#, BLE#) and bus cycle definition (W/R#, D/C#, M/IO#) is being driven on the bus. In the Master Mode, it is driven by the 82370 as an output. In the Slave Mode, this signal is monitored as

an input by the 82370. By the current and past status of ADS# and the READY# input, the 82370 is able to determine, during Slave Mode, if the next bus cycle is a pipelined address cycle. ADS# is asserted during T1 and T2P bus states (see Bus State Definition).

NOTE:
ADS# must be qualified with the rising edge of CLK2.

2.2.7 TRANSFER ACKNOWLEDGE (READY#)

This input indicates that the current bus cycle is complete. In the Master Mode, assertion of this signal indicates the end of a DMA bus cycle. In the Slave Mode, the 82370 monitors this input and ADS# to detect a pipelined address cycle. This signal should be tied directly to the READY# input of the 80376 host processor.

2.2.8 NEXT ADDRESS REQUEST (NA#)

This input is used to indicate to the 82370 in the Master Mode that the system is requesting address pipelining. When driven LOW by either memory or peripheral devices during Master Mode, it indicates that the system is prepared to accept a new address and bus cycle definition signals from the 82370 before the end of the current bus cycle. If this input is active when sampled by the 82370, the next address is driven onto the bus, provided a bus request is already pending internally.

This input pin is monitored only in the Master Mode. In the Slave Mode, the 82370 uses the ADS# and READY# signals to determine address pipelining cycles, and NA# will be ignored.

2.2.9 RESET (RESET, CPURST)

RESET

This synchronous input suspends any operation in progress and places the 82370 in a known initial state. Upon reset, the 82370 will be in the Slave Mode waiting to be initialized by the 80376 host processor. The 82370 is reset by asserting RESET for 15 or more CLK2 periods. When RESET is asserted, all other input pins are ignored, and all other bus pins are driven to an idle bus state as shown in Table 2-3. The 82370 will determine the phase of its internal clock following RESET going inactive.

RESET is level-sensitive and must be synchronous to the CLK2 signal. The RESET setup and hold time requirements are shown in Figure 2-3.

Table 2-3. Output Signals Following RESET

Signal	Level
A_1–A_{23}, D_0–D_{15}, BHE#, BLE#	Float
D/C#, W/R#, M/IO#, ADS#	Float
READYO#	'1'
EOP#	'1' (Weak Pull-UP)
EDACK2–EDACK0	'100'
HOLD	'0'
INT	UNDEFINED*
TOUT1/REF#, TOUT2#/IRQ3#, TOUT3#	UNDEFINED*
CPURST	'0'
CHPSEL#	'1'

*NOTE:
The Interrupt Controller and Programmable Interval Timer are initialized by software commands.

CPURST

This output signal is used to reset the 80376 host processor. It will go active (HIGH) whenever one of the following events occurs: a) 82370's RESET input is active; b) a software RESET command is issued to the 82370; or c) when the 82370 detects a processor Shutdown cycle and when this detection feature is enabled (see CPU Reset and Shutdown Detect). When activated, CPURST will be held active for 62 clocks. The timing of CPURST is such that the 80376 processor will be in synchronization with the 82370. This timing is shown in Figure 2-4.

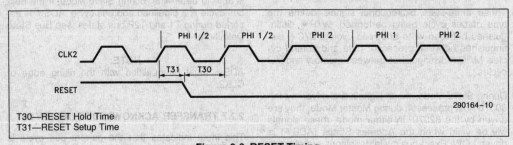

Figure 2-3. RESET Timing

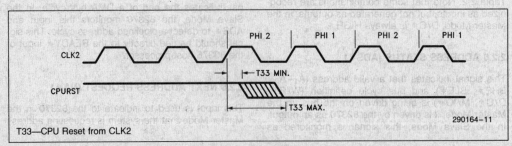

Figure 2-4. CPURST Timing

2.2.10 INTERRUPT OUT (INT)

This output pin is used to signal the 80376 host processor that one or more interrupt requests (either internal or external) are pending. The processor is expected to respond with an Interrupt Acknowledge cycle. This signal should be connected directly to the Maskable Interrupt Request (INTR) input of the 80376 host processor.

2.3 82370 Bus Timing

The 82370 internally divides the CLK2 signal by two to generate its internal clock. Figure 2-2 showed the relationship of CLK2 and the internal clock which consists of two phases: PHI1 and PHI2. Each CLK2 period is a phase of the internal clock.

In the 82370, whether it is in the Master or Slave Mode, the shortest time unit of bus activity is a bus state. A bus state, which is also referred as a 'T-state', is defined as one 82370 PHI2 clock period (i.e. two CLK2 periods). Recall in Table 2-2 various types of bus cycles in the 82370 are defined by the M/IO#, D/C# and W/R# signals. Each of these bus cycles is composed of two or more bus states. The length of a bus cycle depends on when the READY# input is asserted (i.e. driven LOW).

2.3.1 ADDRESS PIPELINING

The 82370 supports Address Pipelining as an option in both the Master and Slave Mode. This feature typically allows a memory or peripheral device to operate with one less wait state than would otherwise be required. This is possible because during a pipelined cycle, the address and bus cycle definition of the next cycle will be generated by the bus master while waiting for the end of the current cycle to be acknowledged. The pipelined bus is especially well suited for an interleaved memory environment. For 16 MHz interleaved memory designs with 100 ns access time DRAMs, zero wait state memory accesses can be achieved when pipelined addressing is selected.

In the Master Mode, the 82370 is capable of initiating, on a cycle-by-cycle basis, either a pipelined or non-pipelined access depending upon the state of the NA# input. If a pipelined cycle is requested (indicated by NA# being driven LOW), the 82370 will drive the address and bus cycle definition of the next cycle as soon as there is an internal bus request pending.

In the Slave Mode, the 82370 is constantly monitoring the ADS# and READY# signals on the processor local bus to determine if the current bus cycle is a pipelined cycle. If a pipelined cycle is detected, the 82370 will request one less wait state from the processor if the Wait State Generator feature is selected. On the other hand, during an 82370 internal register access in a pipelined cycle, it will make use of the advance address and bus cycle information. In all cases, Address Pipelining will result in a savings of one wait state.

2.3.2 MASTER MODE BUS TIMING

When the 82370 is in the Master Mode, it will be in one of six bus states. Figure 2-5 shows the complete bus state diagram of the Master Mode, including pipelined address states. As seen in the figure, the 82370 state diagram is very similar to that of the 80376. The major difference is that in the 82370, there is no Hold state. Also, in the 82370, the conditions for some state transitions depend upon whether it is the end of a DMA process.

NOTE:
The term 'end of a DMA process' is loosely defined here. It depends on the DMA modes of operation as well as the state of the EOP# and DREQ inputs. This is expained in detail in section 3—DMA Controller.

The 82370 will enter the idle state, Ti, upon RESET and whenever the internal address is not available at the end of a DMA cycle or at the end of a DMA process. When address pipelining is not used (NA# is not asserted), a new bus cycle always begins with state T1. During T1, address and bus cycle definition signals will be driven on the bus. T1 is always followed by T2.

If a bus cycle is not acknowledged (with READY#) during T2 and NA# is negated, T2 will be repeated. When the end of the bus cycle is acknowledged during T2, the following state will be T1 of the next bus cycle (if the internal address latch is loaded and if this is not the end of the DMA process). Otherwise, the Ti state will be entered. Therefore, if the memory or peripheral accessed is fast enough to respond within the first T2, the fastest non-pipelined cycle will take one T1 and one T2 state.

Use of the address pipelining feature allows the 82370 to enter three additional bus states: T1P, T2P and T2i. T1P is the first bus state of a pipelined bus cycle. T2P follows T1P (or T2) if NA# is asserted when sampled. The 82370 will drive the bus with the address and bus cycle definition signals of the next cycle during T2P. From the state diagram, it can be seen that after an idle state Ti, the first bus cycle must begin with T1, and is therefore a non-pipelined bus cycle. The next bus cycle can be pipelined if

NA# is asserted and the previous bus cycle ended in a T2P state. Once the 82370 is in a pipelined cycle and provided that NA# is asserted in subsequent cycles, the 82370 will be switching between T1P and T2P states. If the end of the current bus cycle is not acknowledged by the READY# input, the 82370 will extend the cycle by adding T2P states. The fastest pipelined cycle will consist of one T1P and one T2P state.

The 82370 will enter state T2i when NA# is asserted and when one of the following two conditions occurs. The first condition is when the 82370 is in state T2. T2i will be entered if READY# is not asserted and there is no next address available. This situation is similar to a wait state. The 82370 will stay in T2i for as long as this condition exists. The second condition which will cause the 82370 to enter T2i is when the 82370 is in state T1P. Before going to state T2P, the 82370 needs to wait in state T2i until the next address is available. Also, in both cases, if the DMA process is complete, the 82370 will enter the T2i state in order to finish the current DMA cycle.

Figure 2-6 is a timing diagram showing non-pipelined bus accesses in the Master Mode. Figure 2-7 shows the timing of pipelined accesses in the Master Mode.

2.3.3 SLAVE MODE BUS TIMING

Figure 2-8 shows the Slave Mode bus timing in both pipelined and non-pipelined cycles when the 82370 is being accessed. Recall that during Slave Mode, the 82370 will constantly monitor the ADS# and READY# signals to determine if the next cycle is pipelined. In Figure 2-8, the first cycle is non-pipelined and the second cycle is pipelined. In the pipelined cycle, the 82370 will start decoding the address and bus cycle signals one bus state earlier than in a non-pipelined cycle.

The READY# input signal is sampled by the 80376 host processor to determine the completion of a bus cycle. This occurs during the end of every T2, T2i and T2P state. Normally, the output of the 82370 Wait State Generator, READYO#, is directly connected to the READY# input of the 80376 host processor and the 82370. In such case, READYO# and READY# will be identical (see Wait State Generator).

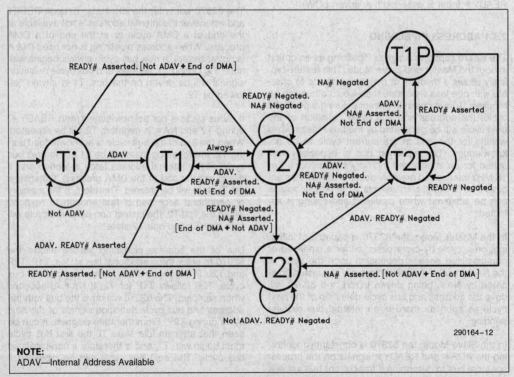

NOTE:
ADAV—Internal Address Available

290164–12

Figure 2-5. Master Mode State Diagram

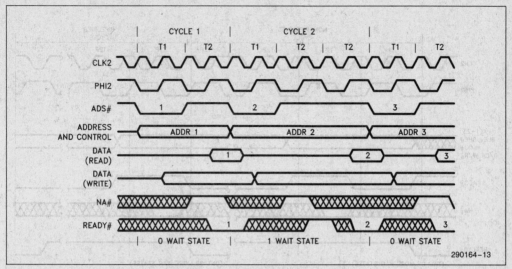

Figure 2-6. Non-Pipelined Bus Cycles

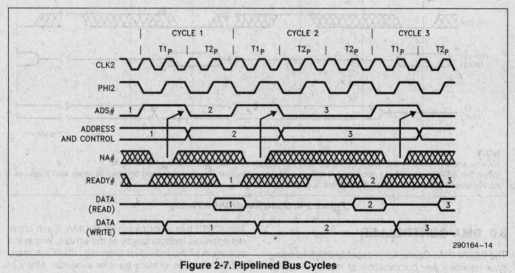

Figure 2-7. Pipelined Bus Cycles

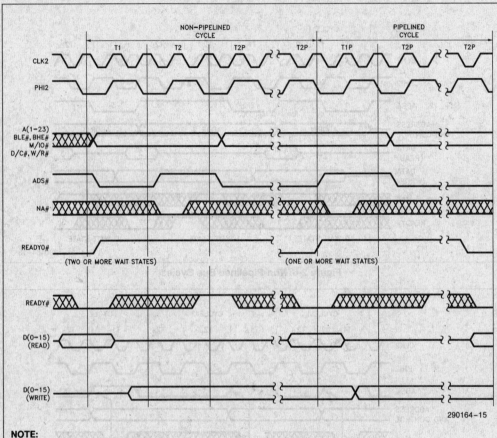

NOTE:
NA# is shown here only for timing reference. It is not sampled by the 82370 during Slave Mode.
When the 82370 registers are accessed, it will take one or more wait states in pipelined and two or more wait states in non-pipelined cycle to complete the internal access.

Figure 2-8. Slave Read/Write Timing

3.0 DMA CONTROLLER

The 82370 DMA Controller is capable of transferring data between any combination of memory and/or I/O, with any combination of data path widths. The 82370 DMA Controller can be programmed to accommodate 8- or 16-bit devices. With its 16-bit external data path, it can transfer data in units of byte or a word. Bus bandwidth is optimized through the use of an internal temporary register which can disassemble or assemble data to or from either an aligned or non-aligned destination or source. Figure 3-1 is a block diagram of the 82370 DMA Controller.

The 82370 has eight channels of DMA. Each channel operates independently of the others. Within the operation of the individual channels, there are many different modes of data transfer available. Many of the operating modes can be intermixed to provide a very versatile DMA controller.

3.1 Functional Description

In describing the operation of the 82370's DMA Controller, close attention to terminology is required. Be-

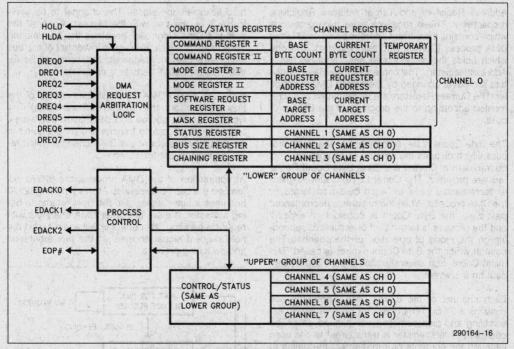

Figure 3-1. 82370 DMA Controller Block Diagram

fore entering the discussion of the function of the 82370 DMA Controller, the following explanations of some of the terminology used herein may be of benefit. First, a few terms for clarification:

DMA PROCESS—A DMA process is the execution of a programmed DMA task from beginning to end. Each DMA process requires intitial programming by the host 80376 microprocessor.

BUFFER—A contiguous block of data.

BUFFER TRANSFER—The action required by the DMA to transfer an entire buffer.

DATA TRANSFER—The DMA action in which a group of bytes or words are moved between devices by the DMA Controller. A data transfer operation may involve movement of one or many bytes.

BUS CYCLE—Access by the DMA to a single byte or word.

Each DMA channel consists of three major components. These components are identified by the contents of programmable registers which define the memory or I/O devices being serviced by the DMA. They are the Target, the Requester, and the Byte Count. They will be defined generically here and in greater detail in the DMA register definition section.

The Requester is the device which requires service by the 82370 DMA Controller, and makes the request for service. All of the control signals which the DMA monitors or generates for specific channels are logically related to the Requester. Only the Requester is considered capable of initiating or terminating a DMA process.

The Target is the device with which the Requester wishes to communicate. As far as the DMA process is concerned, the Target is a slave which is incapable of control over the process.

The direction of data transfer can be either from Requester to Target or from Target to Requester; i.e. each can be either a source or a destination.

The Requester and Target may each be either I/O or memory. Each has an address associated with it that can be incremented, decremented, or held constant. The addresses are stored in the Requester

Address Registers and Target Address Registers, respectively. These registers have two parts: one which contains the current address being used in the DMA process (Current Address Register), and one which holds the programmed base address (Base Address Register). The contents of the Base Registers are never changed by the 82370 DMA Controller. The Current Registers are incremented or decremented according to the progress of the DMA process.

The Byte Count is the component of the DMA process which dictates the amount of data which must be transferred. Current and Base Byte Count Registers are provided. The Current Byte Count Register is decremented once for each byte transferred by the DMA process. When the register is decremented past zero, the Byte Count is considered 'expired' and the process is terminated or restarted, depending on the mode of operation of the channel. The point at which the Byte Count expires is called 'Terminal Count' and several status signals are dependent on this event.

Each channel of the 82370 DMA Controller also contains a 32-bit Temporary Register for use in assembling and disassembling non-aligned data. The operation of this register is transparent to the user, although the contents of it may affect the timing of some DMA handshake sequences. Since there is data storage available for each channel, the DMA Controller can be interrupted without loss of data.

To avoid unexpected results, care should be taken in programming the byte count correctly when assembling and disassembling non-aligned data. For example:

Words to Bytes:
Transferring two words to bytes, but setting the byte count to three, will result in three bytes transferred and the final byte flushed.

Bytes to Words:
Transferring six bytes to three words, but setting the byte count to five, will result in the sixth byte transferred being undefined.

The 82370 DMA Controller is a slave on the bus until a request for DMA service is received via either a software request command or a hardware request signal. The host processor may access any of the control/status or channel registers at any time the 82370 is a bus slave. Figure 3-2 shows the flow of operations that the DMA Controller performs.

At the time a DMA service request is received, the DMA Controller issues a bus hold request to the host processor. The 82370 becomes the bus master when the host relinquishes the bus by asserting a hold acknowledge signal. The channel to be serviced will be the one with the highest priority at the time the DMA Controller becomes the bus master. The DMA Controller will remain in control of the bus until the hold acknowledge signal is removed, or until the current DMA transfer is complete.

While the 82370 DMA Controller has control of the bus, it will perform the required data transfer(s). The type of transfer, source and destination addresses, and amount of data to transfer are programmed in the control registers of the DMA channel which received the request for service.

At completion of the DMA process, the 82370 will remove the bus hold request. At this time the 82370 becomes a slave again, and the host returns to being a master. If there are other DMA channels with requests pending, the controller will again assert the hold request signal and restart the bus arbitration and switching process.

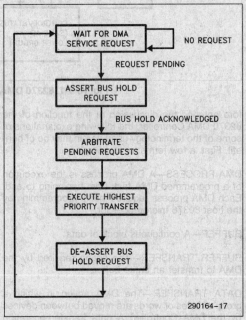

Figure 3-2. Flow of DMA Controller Operation

3.2 Interface Signals

There are fourteen control signals dedicated to the DMA process. They include eight DMA Channel Requests (DREQn), three Encoded DMA Acknowledge signals (EDACKn), Processor Hold and Hold Ac-

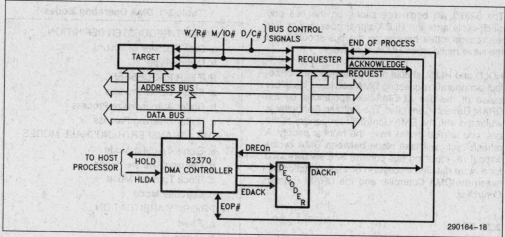

Figure 3-3. Requester, Target and DMA Controller Interconnection

knowledge (HOLD, HLDA), and End-of-Process (EOP#). The DREQn inputs and EDACK (0–2) outputs are handshake signals to the devices requiring DMA service. The HOLD output and HLDA input are handshake signals to the host processor. Figure 3-3 shows these signals and how they interconnect between the 82370 DMA Controller, and the Requester and Target devices.

3.2.1 DREQn and EDACK (0–2)

These signals are the handshake signals between the peripheral and the 82370. When the peripheral requires DMA service, it asserts the DREQn signal of the channel which is programmed to perform the service. The 82370 arbitrates the DREQn against other pending requests and begins the DMA process after finishing other higher priority processes.

When the DMA service for the requested channel is in progress, the EDACK (0–2) signals represent the DMA channel which is accessing the Requester. The 3-bit code on the EDACK (0–2) lines indicates the number of the channel presently being serviced. Table 3-2 shows the encoding of these signals. Note that Channel 4 does not have a corresponding hardware acknowledge.

The DMA acknowledge (EDACK) signals indicate the active channel only during DMA accesses to the Requester. During accesses to the Target, EDACK (0–2) has the idle code (100). EDACK (0–2) can thus be used to select a Requester device during a transfer.

DREQn can be programmed as either an Asynchronous or Synchronous input. See section 3.4.1 for details on synchronous versus asynchronous operation of these pins.

**Table 3-2. EDACK Encoding
During a DMA Transfer**

EDACK2	EDACK1	EDACK0	Active Channel
0	0	0	0
0	0	1	1
0	1	0	2
0	1	1	3
1	0	0	Target Access
1	0	1	5
1	1	0	6
1	1	1	7

The EDACKn signals are always active. They either indicate 'no acknowledge' or they indicate a bus access to the requester. The acknowledge code is either 100, for an idle DMA or during a DMA access to the Target, or 'n' during a Requester access, where n is the binary value representing the channel. A simple 3-line to 8-line decoder can be used to provide discrete acknowledge signals for the peripherals.

3.2.2 HOLD AND HLDA

The Hold Request (HOLD) and Hold Acknowledge (HLDA) signals are the handshake signals between the DMA Controller and the host processor. HOLD is an output from the 82370 and HLDA is an input. HOLD is asserted by the DMA Controller when there is a pending DMA request, thus requesting the processor to give up control of the bus so the DMA process can take place. The 80376 responds by asserting HLDA when it is ready to relinquish control of the bus.

The 82370 will begin operations on the bus one clock cycle after the HLDA signal goes active. For this reason, other devices on the bus should be in the slave mode when HLDA is active.

HOLD and HLDA should not be used to gate or select peripherals requesting DMA service. This is because of the use of DMA-like operations by the DRAM Refresh Controller. The Refresh Controller is arbitrated with the DMA Controller for control of the bus, and refresh cycles have the highest priority. A refresh cycle will take place between DMA cycles without relinquishing bus control. See section 3.4.3 for a more detailed discussion of the interaction between the DMA Controller and the DRAM Refresh Controller.

3.2.3 EOP#

EOP# is a bi-directional signal used to indicate the end of a DMA process. The 82370 activates this as an output during the T2 states of the last Requester bus cycle for which a channel is programmed to execute. The Requester should respond by either withdrawing its DMA request, or interrupting the host processor to indicate that the channel needs to be programmed with a new buffer. As an input, this signal is used to tell the DMA Controller that the peripheral being serviced does not require any more data to be transferred. This indicates that the current buffer is to be terminated.

EOP# can be programmed as either an Asynchronous or a Synchronous input. See section 3.4.1 for details on synchronous versus asynchronous operation of this pin.

3.3 Modes of Operation

The 82370 DMA Controller has many independent operating functions. When designing peripheral interfaces for the 82370 DMA Controller, all of the functions or modes must be considered. All of the channels are independent of each other (except in priority of operation) and can operate in any of the modes. Many of the operating modes, though independently programmable, affect the operation of other modes. Because of the large number of combinations possible, each programmable mode is discussed here with its affects on the operation of other modes. The entire list of possible combinations will not be presented.

Table 3-1 shows the categories of DMA features available in the 82370. Each of the five major categories is independent of the others. The sub-categories are the available modes within the major func-

Table 3-1. DMA Operating Modes

I. TARGET/REQUESTER DEFINITION
   a. Data Transfer Direction
   b. Device Type

II. BUFFER PROCESSES
   a. Single Buffer Process
   b. Buffer Auto-Initialize Process
   c. Buffer Chaining Process

III. DATA TRANSFER/HANDSHAKE MODES
   a. Single Transfer Mode
   b. Demand Transfer Mode
   c. Block Transfer Mode
   d. Cascade Mode

IV. PRIORITY ARBITRATION
   a. Fixed
   b. Rotating
   c. Programmable Fixed

V. BUS OPERATION
   a. Fly-By (Single-Cycle)/Two-Cycle
   b. Data Path Width
   c. Read, Write, or Verify Cycles

tion or mode category. The following sections explain each mode or function and its relation to other features.

3.3.1 TARGET/REQUESTER DEFINITION

All DMA transfers involve three devices: the DMA Controller, the Requester, and the Target. Since the devices to be accessed by the DMA Controller vary widely, the operating characteristics of the DMA Controller must be tailored to the Requester and Target devices.

The Requester can be defined as either the source or the destination of the data to be transferred. This is done by specifying a Write or a Read transfer, respectively. In a Read transfer, the Target is the data source and the Requester is the destination for the data. In a Write transfer, the Requester is the source and the Target is the destination.

The Requester and Target addresses can each be independently programmed to be incremented, decremented, or held constant. As an example, the 82370 is capable of reversing a string of data by having the Requester address increment and the Target address decrement in a memory-to-memory transfer.

3.3.2 BUFFER TRANSFER PROCESSES

The 82370 DMA Controller allows three programmable Buffer Transfer Processes. These processes define the logical way in which a buffer of data is accessed by the DMA.

The three Buffer Transfer Processes include the Single Buffer Process, the Buffer Auto-Initialize Process, and the Buffer Chaining Process. These processes require special programming considerations. See the DMA Programming section for more details on setting up the Buffer Transfer Processes.

Single Buffer Process

The Single Buffer Process allows the DMA channel to transfer only one buffer of data. When the buffer has been completely transferred (Current Byte Count decremented past zero or EOP# input active), the DMA process ends and the channel becomes idle. In order for that channel to be used again, it must be reprogrammed.

The Single Buffer Process is usually used when the amount of data to be transferred is known exactly, and it is also known that there is not likely to be any data to follow before the operating system can reprogram the channel.

Buffer Auto-Initialize Process

The Buffer Auto-Initialize Process allows multiple groups of data to be transferred to or from a single buffer. This process does not require reprogramming. The Current Registers are automatically reprogrammed from the Base Registers when the current process is terminated, either by an expired Byte Count or by an external EOP# signal. The data transferred will always be between the same Target and Requester.

The auto-initialization/process-execution cycle is repeated until the channel is either disabled or re-programmed.

Buffer Chaining Process

The Buffer Chaining Process is useful for transferring large quantities of data into non-contiguous buffer areas. In this process, a single channel is used to process data from several buffers, while having to program the channel only once. Each new buffer is programmed in a pipelined operation that provides the new buffer information while the old buffer is being processed. The chain is created by loading new buffer information while the 82370 DMA Controller is processing the Current Buffer. When the Current Buffer expires, the 82370 DMA Controller automatically restarts the channel using the new buffer information.

Loading the new buffer information is done by an interrupt routine which is requested by the 82370. Interrupt Request 1 (IRQ1) is tied internally to the 82370 DMA Controller for this purpose. IRQ1 is generated by the 82370 when the new buffer information is loaded into the channel's Current Registers, leaving the Base Registers 'empty'. The interrupt service routine loads new buffer information into the Base Registers. The host processor is required to load the information for another buffer before the current Byte Count expires. The process repeats until the host programs the channel back to single buffer operation, or until the channel runs out of buffers.

The channel runs out of buffers when the Current Buffer expires and the Base Registers have not yet been loaded with new buffer information. When this occurs, the channel must be reprogrammed.

If an external EOP# is encountered while executing a Buffer Chaining Process, the current buffer is considered expired and the new buffer information is loaded into the Current Registers. If the Base Registers are 'empty', the chain is terminated.

The channel uses the Base Target Address Register as an indicator of whether or not the Base Registers are full. When the most significant byte of the Base Target Register is loaded, the channel considers all of the Base Registers loaded, and removes the interrupt request. This requires that the other Base Registers (Base Requester Address, Base Byte Count) must be loaded before the Base Target Address Register. The reason for implementing the reloading process this way is that, for most applications, the Byte Count and the Requester will not change from one buffer to the next, and therefore do not need to be reprogrammed. The details of programming the channel for the Buffer Chaining Process can be found in the section on DMA programming.

3.3.3 DATA TRANSFER MODES

Three Data Transfer modes are available in the 82370 DMA Controller. They are the Single Transfer, Block Transfer, and Demand Transfer Modes. These transfer modes can be used in conjunction with any one of three Buffer Transfer modes: Single Buffer, Auto-Initialized Buffer and Buffer Chaining. Any Data Transfer Mode can be used under any of the Buffer Transfer Modes. These modes are independently available for all DMA channels.

Different devices being serviced by the DMA Controller require different handshaking sequences for data transfers to take place. Three handshaking modes are available on the 82370, giving the designer the opportunity to use the DMA Controller as efficiently as possible. The speed at which data can be presented or read by a device can affect the way a DMA Controller uses the host's bus, thereby affecting not only data throughput during the DMA process, but also affecting the host's performance by limiting its access to the bus.

Single Transfer Mode

In the Single Transfer Mode, one data transfer to or from the Requester is performed by the DMA Controller at a time. The DREQn input is arbitrated and the HOLD/HLDA sequence is executed for each transfer. Transfers continue in this manner until the Byte Count expires, or until EOP# is sampled active. If the DREQn input is held active continuously, the entire DREQ-HOLD-HLDA-DACK sequence is repeated over and over until the programmed number of bytes has been transferred. Bus control is released to the host between each transfer. Figure 3-4 shows the logical flow of events which make up a buffer transfer using the Single Transfer Mode. Refer to section 3.4 for an explanation of the bus control arbitration procedure.

The Single Transfer Mode is used for devices which require complete handshake cycles with each data access. Data is transferred to or from the Requester only when the Requester is ready to perform the transfer. Each transfer requires the entire DREQ-

HOLD-HLDA-DACK handshake cycle. Figure 3-5 shows the timing of the Single Transfer Mode cycle.

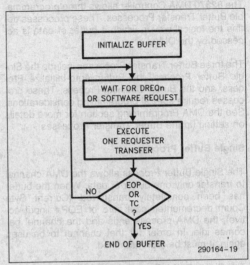

Figure 3-4. Buffer Transfer in Single Transfer Mode

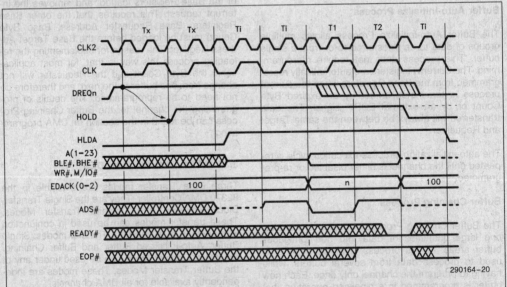

NOTE:
The Single Transfer Mode is more efficient (15%–20%) in the case where the source is the Target. Because of the internal pipeline of the 82370 DMA Controller, two idle states are added at the end of a transfer in the case where the source is the Requester.

Figure 3-5. DMA Single Transfer Mode

Block Transfer Mode

In the Block Transfer Mode, the DMA process is initiated by a DMA request and continues unti the Byte Count expires, or until EOP # is activated by the Requester. The DREQn signal need only be held active until the first Requester access. Only a refresh cycle will interrupt the block transfer process.

Figure 3-6 illustrates the operation of the DMA during the Block Transfer Mode. Figure 3-7 shows the timing of the handshake signals during Block Mode Transfers.

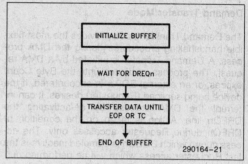

Figure 3-6. Buffer Transfer in Block Transfer Mode

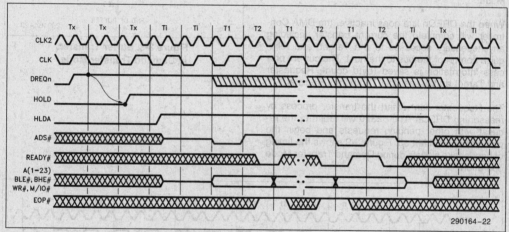

290164–22

Figure 3-7. Block Mode Transfers

Demand Transfer Mode

The Demand Transfer Mode provides the most flexible handshaking procedures during the DMA process. A Demand Transfer is initiated by a DMA request. The process continues until the Byte Count expires, or an external EOP# is encountered. If the device being serviced (Requester) desires, it can interrupt the DMA process by de-activating the DREQn line. Action is taken on the condition of DREQn during Requester accesses only. The access during which DREQn is sampled inactive is the last Requester access which will be performed during the current transfer. Figure 3-8 shows the flow of events during the transfer of a buffer in the Demand Mode.

When the DREQn line goes inactive, the DMA Controller will complete the current transfer, including any necessary accesses to the Target, and relinquish control of the bus to the host. The current process information is saved (byte count, Requester and Target addresses, and Temporary Register).

The Requester can restart the transfer process by reasserting DREQn. The 82370 will arbitrate the request with other pending requests and begin the process where it left off. Figure 3-9 shows the timing of handshake signals during Demand Transfer Mode operation.

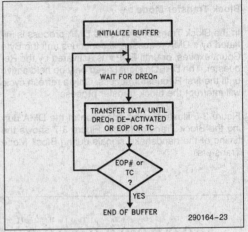

Figure 3-8. Buffer Transfer in Demand Transfer Mode

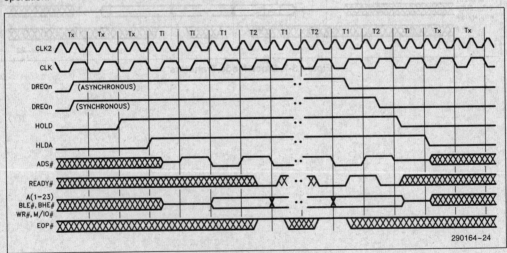

290164-24

Figure 3-9. Demand Mode Transfers

Using the Demand Transfer Mode allows peripherals to access memory in small, irregular bursts without wasting bus control time. The 82370 is designed to give the best possible bus control latency in the Demand Transfer Mode. Bus control latency is defined here as the time form the last active bus cycle of the previous bus master to the first active bus cycle of the new bus master. The 82370 DMA Controller will perform its first bus access cycle two bus states after HLDA goes active. In the typical configuration, bus control is returned to the host one bus state after the DREQn goes inactive.

There are two cases where there may be more than one bus state of bus control latency at the end of a transfer. The first is at the end of an Auto-Initialize process, and the second is at the end of a process where the source is the Requester and Two-Cycle transfers are used.

When a Buffer Auto-Initialize Porcess is complete, the 82370 requires seven bus states to reload the Current Registers from the Base Registers of the Auto-Initialized channel. The reloading is done while the 82370 is still the bus master so that it is prepared to service the channel immediately after relinquishing the bus, if necessary.

In the case where the Requester is the source, and Two-Cycle transfers are being used, there are two extra idle states at the end of the transfer process. This occurs due to the housekeeping in the DMA's internal pipeline. These two idle states are present only after the very last Requester access, before the DMA Controller de-activates the HOLD signal.

3.3.4 CHANNEL PRIORITY ARBITRATION

DMA channel priority can be programmed into one of two arbitration methods: Fixed or Rotating. The four lower DMA channels and the four upper DMA channels operate as if they were two separate DMA controllers operating in cascade. The lower group of four channels (0–3) is always prioritized between channels 7 and 4 of the upper group of channels (4–7). Figure 3-10 shows a pictorial representation of the priority grouping.

The priority can thus be set up as rotating for one group of channels and fixed for the other, or any other combination. While in Fixed Priority, the programmer can also specify which channel has the lowest priority.

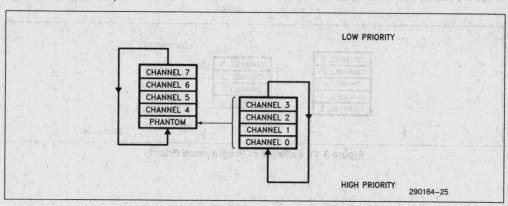

Figure 3-10. DMA Priority Grouping

The 82370 DMA Controller defaults to Fixed Priority. Channel 0 has the highest priority, then 1, 2, 3, 4, 5, 6, 7. Channel 7 has the lowest priority. Any time the DMA Controller arbitrates DMA requests, the requesting channel with the highest priority will be serviced next.

Fixed Priority can be entered into at any time by a software command. The priority levels in effect after the mode switch are determined by the current setting of the Programmable Priority.

Programmable Priority is available for fixing the priority of the DMA channels within a group to levels other than the default. Through a software command, the channel to have the lowest priority in a group can be specified. Each of the two groups of four channels can have the priority fixed in this way. The other channels in the group will follow the natural Fixed Priority sequence. This mode affects only the priority levels while operating with Fixed Priority.

For example, if channel 2 is programmed to have the lowest priority in its group, channel 3 has the highest priority. In descending order, the other channels would have the following priority: (3,0,1,2),4,5,6,7 (channel 2 lowest, channel 3 highest). If the upper

group were programmed to have channel 5 as the lowest priority channel, the priority would be (again, highest to lowest): 6,7, (3,0,1,2), 4,5. Figure 3-11 shows this example pictorially. The lower group is always prioritized as a fifth channel of the upper group (between channels 4 and 7).

The DMA Controller will only accept Programmable Priority commands while the addressed group is operating in Fixed Priority. Switching from Fixed to Rotating Priority preserves the current priority levels. Switching from Rotating to Fixed Priority returns the priority levels to those which were last programmed by use of Programmable Priority.

Rotating Priority allows the devices using DMA to share the system bus more evenly. An individual channel does not retain highest priority after being serviced, priority is passed to the next highest priority channel in the group. The channel which was most recently serviced inherits the lowest priority. This rotation occurs each time a channel is serviced. Figure 3-12 shows the sequence of events as priority is passed between channels. Note that the lower group rotates within the upper group, and that servicing a channel within the lower group causes rotation within the group as well as rotation of the upper group.

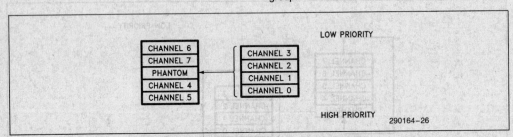

Figure 3-11. Example of Programmed Priority

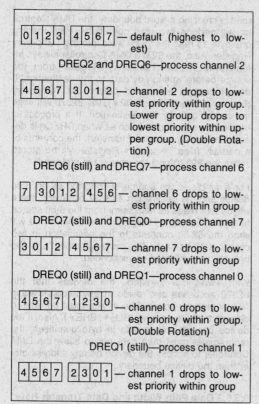

0	1	2	3	4	5	6	7	— default (highest to lowest)

DREQ2 and DREQ6—process channel 2

| 4 | 5 | 6 | 7 | 3 | 0 | 1 | 2 | — channel 2 drops to lowest priority within group. Lower group drops to lowest priority within upper group. (Double Rotation) |

DREQ6 (still) and DREQ7—process channel 6

| 7 | 3 | 0 | 1 | 2 | 4 | 5 | 6 | — channel 6 drops to lowest priority within group |

DREQ7 (still) and DREQ0—process channel 7

| 3 | 0 | 1 | 2 | 4 | 5 | 6 | 7 | — channel 7 drops to lowest priority within group |

DREQ0 (still) and DREQ1—process channel 0

| 4 | 5 | 6 | 7 | 1 | 2 | 3 | 0 | — channel 0 drops to lowest priority within group. (Double Rotation) |

DREQ1 (still)—process channel 1

| 4 | 5 | 6 | 7 | 2 | 3 | 0 | 1 | — channel 1 drops to lowest priority within group |

**Figure 3-12. Rotating Channel Priority.
Lower and upper groups are programmed
for the Rotating Priority Mode.**

3.3.5 COMBINING PRIORITY MODES

Since the DMA Controller operates as two four-channel controllers in cascade, the overall priority scheme of all eight channels can take on a variety of forms. There are four possible combinations of priority modes between the two groups of channels: Fixed Priority only (default), Fixed Priority upper group/Rotating Priority lower group, Rotating Priority upper group/Fixed Priority lower group, and Rotating Priority only. Figure 3-13 illustrates the operation of the two combined priority methods.

**Case 1—
0–3 Fixed Priority, 4–7 Rotating Priority**

	High						Low	
Default priority	0	1	2	3	4	5	6	7
After servicing channel 2	4	5	6	7	0	1	2	3
After servicing channel 6	7	0	1	2	3	4	5	6
After servicing channel 1	4	5	6	7	0	1	2	3

**Case 2—
0–3 Rotating Priority, 4–7 Fixed Priority**

	High						Low	
Default priority	0	1	2	3	4	5	6	7
After servicing channel 2	3	0	1	2	4	5	6	7
After servicing channel 6	3	0	1	2	4	5	6	7
After servicing channel 1	2	3	0	1	4	5	6	7

Figure 3-13. Combining Priority Modes

3.3.6 BUS OPERATION

Data may be transferred by the DMA Controller using two different bus cycle operations: Fly-By (one-cycle) and Two-Cycle. These bus handshake methods are selectable independently for each channel through a command register. Device data path widths are independently programmable for both Target and Requester. Also selectable through software is the direction of data transfer. All of these parameters affect the operation of the 82370 on a bus-cycle by bus-cycle basis.

3.3.6.1 Fly-By Transfers

The Fly-By Transfer Mode is the fastest and most efficient way to use the 82370 DMA Controller to transfer data. In this method of transfer, the data is written to the destination device at the same time it is read from the source. Only one bus cycle is used to accomplish the transfer.

In the Fly-By Mode, the DMA acknowledge signal is used to select the Requester. The DMA Controller simultaneously places the address of the Target on the address bus. The state of M/IO# and W/R# during the Fly-By transfer cycle indicate the type of Target and whether the Target is being written to or read from. The Target's Bus Size is used as an incrementer for the Byte Count. The Requester address registers are ignored during Fly-By transfers.

Note that memory-to-memory transfers cannot be done using the Fly-By Mode. Only one memory of I/O address is generated by the DMA Controller at a time during Fly-By transfers. Only one of the devices being accessed can be selected by an address. Also, the Fly-By method of data transfer limits the hardware to accesses of devices with the same data bus width. The Temporary Registers are not affected in the Fly-By Mode.

Fly-By transfers also require that the data paths of the Target and Requester be directly connected. This requires that successive Fly-By access be to word boundaries, or that the Requester be capable of switching its connections to the data bus.

3.3.6.2. Two-Cycle Transfers

Two-Cycle transfers can also be performed by the 82370 DMA Controller. These transfers require at least two bus cycles to execute. The data being transferred is read into the DMA Controller's Temporary Register during the first bus cycle(s). The second bus cycle is used to write the data from the Temporary Register to the destination.

If the addresses of the data being transferred are not word aligned, the 82370 will recognize the situation and read and write the data in groups of bytes, placing them always at the proper destination. This process of collecting the desired bytes and putting them together is called "byte assembly". The reverse process (reading from aligned locations and writing to non-aligned locations) is called "byte disassembly".

The assembly/disassembly process takes place transparent to the software, but can only be done while using the Two-Cycle transfer method. The 82370 will always perform the assembly/disassembly process as necessary for the current data transfer. Any data path widths for either the Requester or Target can be used in the Two-Cycle Mode. This is very convenient for interfacing existing 8- and 16-bit peripherals to the 80376's 16-bit bus.

The 82370 DMA Controller always reads and write data within the word boundaries; i.e. if a word to be read is crossing a word boundary, the DMA Controller will perform two read operations, each reading one byte, to read the 16-bit word into the Temporary Register. Also, the 82370 DMA Controller always attempts to fill the Temporary Register from the source before writing any data to the destination. If the process is terminated before the Temporary Register is filled (TC or EOP#), the 82370 will write the partial data to the destination. If a process is temporarily suspended (such as when DREQn is deactivated during a demand transfer), the contents of a partially filled Temporary Register will be stored within the 82370 until the process is restarted.

For example, if the source is specified as an 8-bit device and the destination as a 32-bit device, there will be four reads as necessary from the 8-bit source to fill the Temporary Register. Then the 82370 will write the 32-bit contents to the destination in two cycles of 16-bit each. This cycle will repeat until the process is terminated or suspended.

With Two-Cycle transfers, the devices that the 82370 accesses can reside at any address within I/O or memory space. The device must be able to decode the byte-enables (BLE#, BHE#). Also, if the device cannot accept data in byte quantities, the programmer must take care not to allow the DMA Controller to access the device on any address other than the device boundary.

3.3.6.3 Data Path Width and Data Transfer Rate Considerations

The number of bus cycles used to transfer a single "word" of data is affected by whether the Two-Cycle or the Fly-By (Single-Cycle) transfer method is used.

The number of bus cycles used to transfer data directly affects the data transfer rate. Inefficient use of bus cycles will decrease the effective data transfer rate that can be obtained. Generally, the data transfer rate is halved by using Two-Cycle transfers instead of Fly-By transfers.

The choice of data path widths of both Target and Requester affects the data transfer rate also. During each bus cycle, the largest pieces of data possible should be transferred.

The data path width of the devices to be accessed must be programmed into the DMA controller. The 82370 defaults after reset to 8-bit-to-8-bit data transfers, but the Target and Requester can have different data path widths, independent of each other and independent of the other channels. Since this is a software programmable function, more discussion of the uses of this feature are found in the section on programming.

3.3.6.4 Read, Write and Verify Cycles

Three different bus cycles types may be used in a data transfer. They are the Read, Write and Verify cycles. These cycle types dictate the way in which the 82370 operates on the data to be transferred.

A Read Cycle transfers data from the Target to the Requester. A Write Cycle transfers data from the Requester to the target. In a Fly-By transfer, the address and bus status signals indicate the access (read of write) to the Target; the access to the Requester is assumed to be the opposite.

The Verify Cycle is used to perform a data read only. No write access is indicated or assumed in a Verify Cycle. The Verify Cycle is useful for validating block fill operations. An external comparator must be provided to do any comparisons on the data read.

3.4 Bus Arbitration and Handshaking

Figure 3-14 shows the flow of events in the DMA request arbitration process. The arbitration sequence starts when the Requester asserts a DREQn (or DMA service is requested by software). Figure 3-15 shows the timing of the sequence of events following a DMA request. This sequence is executed for each channel that is activated. The DREQn signal can be replaced by a software DMA channel request with no change in the sequence.

After the Requester asserts the service request, the 82370 will request control of the bus via the HOLD signal. The 82370 will always assert the HOLD signal one bus state after the service request is asserted. The 80376 responds by asserting the HLDA signal, thus releasing control of the bus to the 82370 DMA Controller.

Priority of pending DMA service requests is arbitrated during the first state after HLDA is asserted by the 80376. The next state will be the beginning of the first transfer access of the highest priority process.

When the 82370 DMA Controller is finished with its current bus activity, it returns control of the bus to the host processor. This is done by driving the HOLD signal inactive. The 82370 does not drive any address or data bus signals after HOLD goes low. It enters the Slave Mode until another DMA process is requested. The processor acknowledges that it has regained control of the bus by forcing the HLDA signal inactive. Note that the 82370's DMA Controller will not re-request control of the bus until the entire HOLD/HLDA handshake sequence is complete.

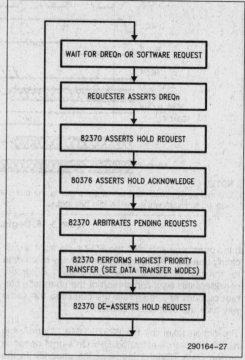

290164-27

Figure 3-14. Bus Arbitration and DMA Sequence

The 82370 DMA Controller will terminate a current DMA process for one of three reasons: expired byte count, end-of-process command (EOP# activated) from a peripheral, or deactivated DMA request signal. In each case, the controller will de-assert HOLD immediately after completing the data transfer in progress. These three methods of process termination are illustrated in Figures 3-16, 3-19 and 3-18, respectively.

An expired byte count indicates that the current process is complete as programmed and the channel has no further transfers to process. The channel must be restarted according to the currently programmed Buffer Transfer Mode, or reprogrammed completely, including a new Buffer Transfer Mode.

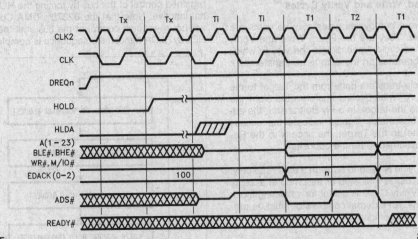

NOTE:
Channel priority resolution takes place during the bus state before HOLDA is asserted, allowing the DMA Controller to respond to HLDA without extra idle bus states.

290164-28

Figure 3-15. Beginning of a DMA process

If the peripheral activates the EOP# signal, it is indicating that it will not accept or deliver any more data for the current buffer. The 82370 DMA Controller considers this as a completion of the channel's current process and interprets the condition the same way as if the byte count expired.

The action taken by the 82370 DMA Controller in response to a de-activated DREQn signal depends on the Data Transfer Mode of the channel. In the Demand Mode, data transfers will take place as long as the DREQn is active and the byte count has not expired. In the Block Mode, the controller will complete the entire block transfer without relinquishing the bus, even if DREQn goes inactive before the transfer is complete. In the Single Mode, the controller will execute single data transfers, relinquishing the bus between each transfer, as long as DREQn is active.

Normal termination of a DMA process due to expiration of the byte count (Terminal Count—TC) is shown if Figure 3-16. The condition of DREQn is ignored until after the process is terminated. If the channel is programmed to auto-initialize, HOLD will be held active for an additional seven clock cycles while the auto-initialization takes place.

Table 3-3 shows the DMA channel activity due to EOP# or Byte Count expiring (Terminal Count).

Table 3-3. DMA Channel Activity Due to Terminal Count or External EOP#

Buffer Process	Single or Chaining-Base Empty		Auto-Initialize		Chaining-Base Loaded	
EVENT						
Terminal Count	True	X	True	X	True	X
EOP#	X	0	X	0	X	0
RESULTS						
Current Registers			Load	Load	Load	Load
Channel Mask	Set	Set				
EOP# Output	0	X	0	X	1	X
Terminal Count Status	Set	Set	Set	Set		
Software Request	CLR	CLR	CLR	CLR		

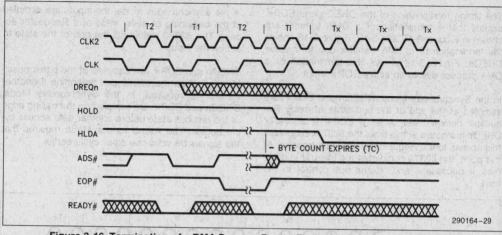

Figure 3-16. Termination of a DMA Process Due to Expiration of Current Byte Count

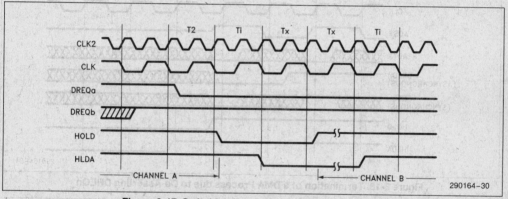

Figure 3-17. Switching between Active DMA Channels

The 82370 always relinquishes control of the bus between channel services. This allows the hardware designer the flexibility to externally arbitrate bus hold requests, if desired. If another DMA request is pending when a higher priority channel service is completed, the 82370 will relinquish the bus until the hold acknowledge is inactive. One bus state after the HLDA signal goes inactive, the 82370 will assert HOLD again. This is illustrated in Figure 3-17.

3.4.1 SYNCHRONOUS AND ASYNCHRONOUS SAMPLING OF DREQn AND EOP#

As an indicator that a DMA service is to be started, DREQn is always sampled asynchronous. It is sam-

pled at the beginning of a bus state and acted upon at the end of the state. Figure 3-15 illustrates the start of a DMA process due to a DREQn input.

The DREQn and EOP# inputs can be programmed to be sampled either synchronously or asynchronously to signal the end of a transfer.

The synchronous mode affords the Requester one bus state of extra time to react to an access. This means the Requester can terminate a process on the current access, without losing any data. The asynchronous mode requires that the input signal be presented prior to the beginning of the last state of the Requester access.

The timing relationships of the DREQn and EOP# signals to the termination of a DMA transfer are shown in Figures 3-18 and 3-19. Figure 3-18 shows the termination of a DMA transfer due to inactive DREQn. Figure 3-19 shows the termination of a DMA process due to an active EOP# input.

In the Synchronous Mode, DREQn and EOP# are sampled at the end of the last state of every Requester data transfer cycle. If EOP# is active or DREQn is inactive at this time, the 82370 recognizes this access to the Requester as the last transfer. At this point, the 82370 completes the transfer in progress, if necessary, and returns bus control to the host.

In the asynchronous mode, the inputs are sampled at the beginning of every state of a Requester access. The 82370 waits until the end of the state to act on the input.

DREQn and EOP# are sampled at the latest possible time when the 82370 can determine if another transfer is required. In the Synchronous Mode, DREQn and EOP# are sampled on the trailing edge of the last bus state before another data access cycle begins. The Asynchronous Mode requires that the signals be valid one clock cycle earlier.

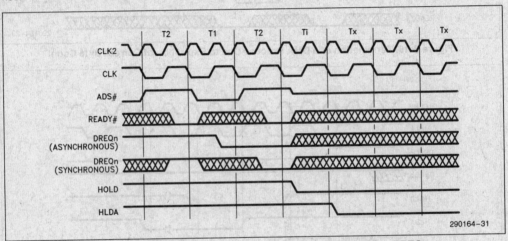

Figure 3-18. Termination of a DMA Process due to De-Asserting DREQn

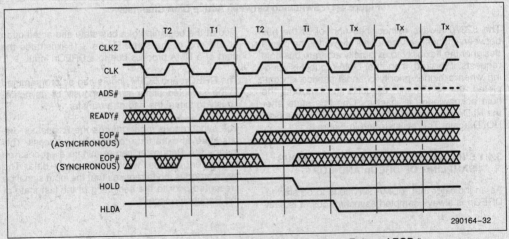

Figure 3-19. Termination of a DMA Process due to an External EOP#

While in the Pipeline Mode, if the NA# signal is sampled active during a transfer, the end of the state where NA# was sampled active is when the 82370 decides whether to commit to another transfer. The device must de-assert DREQn or assert EOP# before NA# is asserted, otherwise the 82370 will commit to another, possibly undesired, transfer.

Synchronous DREQn and EOP# sampling allows the peripheral to prevent the next transfer from occurring by de-activating DREQn or asserting EOP# during the current Requester access, before the 82370 DMA Controller commits itself to another transfer. The DMA Controller will not perform the next transfer if it has not already begun the bus cycle. Asynchronous sampling allows less stringent timing requirements than the Synchronous Mode, but requires that the DREQn signal be valid at the beginning of the next to last bus state of the current Requester access.

Using the Asynchronous Mode with zero wait states can be very difficult. Since the addresses and control signals are driven by the 82370 near half-way through the first bus state of a transfer, and the Asynchronous Mode requires that DREQn be inactive before the end of the state, the peripheral being accessed is required to present DREQn only a few nanoseconds after the control information is available. This means that the peripheral's control logic must be extremely fast (practically non-causal). An alternative is the Synchronous Mode.

3.4.2 ARBITRATION OF CASCADED MASTER REQUESTS

The Cascade Mode allows another DMA-type device to share the bus by arbitrating its bus accesses with the 82370's. Seven of the eight DMA channels (0–3 and 5–7) can be connected to a cascaded device. The cascaded device requests bus control through the DREQn line of the channel which is programmed to operate in Cascade Mode. Bus hold acknowledge is signalled to the cascaded device through the EDACK lines. When the EDACK lines are active with the code for the requested cascade channel, the bus is available to the cascaded master device.

A cascade cycle begins the same way a regular DMA cycle begins. The requesting bus master asserts the DREQn line on the 82370. This bus control request is arbitrated as any other DMA request would be. If any channel receives a DMA request, the 82370 requests control of the bus. When the host acknowledges that it has released bus control, the 82370 acknowledges to the requesting master that it may access the bus. The 82370 enters an idle state until the new master relinquishes control.

A cascade cycle will be terminated by one of two events: DREQn going inactive, or HLDA going inactive. The normal way to terminate the cascade cycle

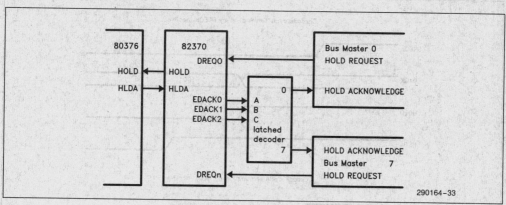

Figure 3-20. Cascaded Bus Master

is for the cascaded master to drop the DREQn signal. Figure 3-21 shows the two cascade cycle termination sequences.

The Refresh Controller may interrupt the cascaded master to perform a refresh cycle. If this occurs, the 82370 DMA Controller will de-assert the EDACK signal (hold acknowledge to cascaded master) and wait for the cascaded master to remove its hold request. When the 82370 regains bus control, it will perform the refresh cycle in its normal fashion. After the refresh cycle has been completed, and if the cascaded device has re-asserted its request, the 82370 will return control to the cascaded master which was interrupted.

The 82370 assumes that it is the only device monitoring the HLDA signal. If the system designer wishes to place other devices on the bus as bus masters, the HLDA from the processor must be intercepted before presenting it to the 82370. Using the Cascade capabililty of the 82370 DMA Controller offers a much better solution.

3.4.3 ARBITRATION OF REFRESH REQUESTS

The arbitration of refresh requests by the DRAM Refresh Controller is slightly different from normal DMA channel request arbitration. The 82370 DRAM Refresh Controller always has the highest priority of any DMA process. It also can interrupt a process in progress. Two types of processes in progress may be encountered: normal DMA, and bus master cascade.

In the event of a refresh request during a normal DMA process, the DMA Controller will complete the data transfer in progress and then execute the refresh cycle before continuing with the current DMA process. The priority of the interrupted process is not lost. If the data transfer cycle interrupted by the Refresh Controller is the last of a DMA process, the refresh cycle will always be executed before control of the bus is transferred back to the host.

When the Refresh Controller request occurs during a cascade cycle, the Refresh Controller must be assured that the cascaded master device has relinquished control of the bus before it can execute the refresh cycle. To do this, the DMA Controller drops the EDACK signal to the cascaded master and waits for the corresponding DREQn input to go inactive. By dropping the DREQn signal, the cascaded master relinquishes the bus. The Refresh Controller then performs the refresh cycle. Control of the bus is returned to the cascaded master if DREQn returns to an active state before the end of the refresh cycle, otherwise control is passed to the processor and the cascaded master loses its priority.

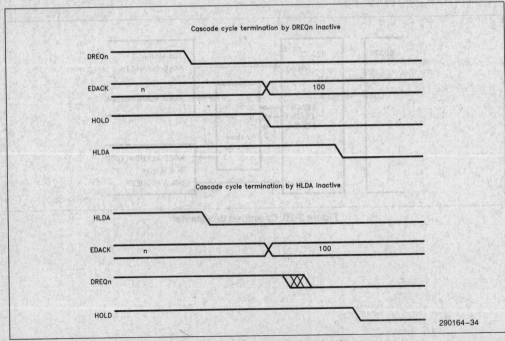

Figure 3-21. Cascade Cycle Termination

3.5 DMA Controller Register Overview

The 82370 DMA Controller contains 44 registers which are accessable to the host processor. Twenty-four of these registers contain the device addresses and data counts for the individual DMA channels (three per channel). The remaining registers are control and status registers for initiating and monitoring the operation of the 82370 DMA Controller. Table 3-4 lists the DMA Controller's registers and their accessability.

Table 3-4. DMA Controller Registers

Register Name	Access
Control/Status Registers—one each per group	
Command Register I	write only
Command Register II	write only
Mode Register I	write only
Mode Register II	write only
Software Request Register	read/write
Mask Set-Reset Register	write only
Mask Read-Write Register	read/write
Status Register	read only
Bus Size Register	write only
Chaining Register	read/write
Channel Registers—one each per channel	
Base Target Address	write only
Current Target Address	read only
Base Requester Address	write only
Current Requester Address	read only
Base Byte Count	write only
Current Byte Count	read only

3.5.1 CONTROL/STATUS REGISTERS

The following registers are available to the host processor for programming the 82370 DMA Controller into its various modes and for checking the operating status of the DMA processes. Each set of four DMA channels has one of each of these registers associated with it.

Command Register I

Enables or disables the DMA channel as a group. Sets the Priority Mode (Fixed or Rotating) of the group. This write-only register is cleared by a hardware reset, defaulting to all channels enabled and Fixed Priority Mode.

Command Register II

Sets the sampling mode of the DREQn and EOP# inputs. Also sets the lowest priority channel for the group in the Fixed Priority Mode. The functions programmed through Command Register II default after

a hardware reset to: asynchronous DREQn and EOP#, and channels 3 and 7 lowest priority.

Mode Registers I

Mode Register I is identical in function to the Mode register of the 8237A. It programs the following functions for an individually selected channel:

Type of Transfer—read, write, verify
Auto-Initialize—enable or disable
Target Address Count—increment or decrement
Data Transfer Mode—demand, single, block, cascade

Mode Register I functions default to the following after reset: verify transfer, Auto-Initialize disabled, Increment Target address, Demand Mode.

Mode Register II

Programs the following functions for an individually selected channel:

Target Address Hold—enable or disable
Requester Address Count—increment or decrement
Requester Address Hold—enable or disable
Target Device Type—I/O or Memory
Requester Device Type—I/O or Memory
Transfer Cycles—Two-Cycle or Fly-By

Mode Register II functions are defined as follows after a hardware reset: Disable Target Address Hold, Increment Requester Address, Target (and Requester) in memory, Fly-By Transfer Cycles. Note: Requester Device Type ignored in Fly-By Transfers.

Software Request Register

The DMA Controller can respond to service requests which are initiated by software. Each channel has an internal request status bit associated with it. The host processor can write to this register to set or reset the request bit of a selected channel.

The status of a group's software DMA service requests can be read from this register as well. Each status bit is cleared upon Terminal Count or external EOP#.

The software DMA requests are non-maskable and subject to priority arbitration with all other software and hardware requests. The entire register is cleared by a hardware reset.

Mask Registers

Each channel has associated with it a mask bit which can be set/reset to disable/enable that channel. Two methods are available for setting and clearing the mask bits. The Mask Set/Reset Register is a write-only register which allows the host to select an individual channel and either set or reset the mask bit for that channel only. The Mask Read/Write Register is available for reading the mask bit status and for writing mask bits in groups of four.

The mask bits of a group may be cleared in one step by executing the Clear Mask Command. See the DMA Programming section for details. A hardware reset sets all of the channel mask bits, disabling all channels.

Status Register

The Status register is a read-only register which contains the Terminal Count (TC) and Service Request status for a group. Four bits indicate the TC status and four bits indicate the hardware request status for the four channels in the group. The TC bits are set when the Byte Count expires, or when and external EOP# is asserted. These bits are cleared by reading from the Status Register. The Service Request bit for a channel indicates when there is a hardware DMA request (DREQn) asserted for that channel. When the request has been removed, the bit is cleared.

Bus Size Register

This write-only register is used to define the bus size of the Target and Requester of a selected channel. The bus sizes programmed will be used to dictate the sizes of the data paths accessed when the DMA channel is active. The values programmed into this register affect the operation of the Temporary Register. When 32-bit bus width is programmed, the 82370 DMA Controller will access the device twice through its 16-bit external Data Bus to perform a 32-bit data transfer. Any byte-assembly required to make the transfers using the specified data path widths will be done in the Temporary Register. The Bus Size register of the Target is used as an increment/decrement value for the Byte Counter and Target Address when in the Fly-By Mode. Upon reset, all channels default to 8-bit Targets and 8-bit Requesters.

Chaining Register

As a command or write register, the Chaining register is used to enable or disable the Chaining Mode for a selected channel. Chaining can either be disabled or enabled for an individual channel, independently of the Chaining Mode status of other channels. After a hardware reset, all channels default to Chaining disabled.

When read by the host, the Chaining Register provides the status of the Chaining Interrupt of each of the channels. These interrupt status bits are cleared when the new buffer information has been loaded.

3.5.2 CHANNEL REGISTERS

Each channel has three individually programmable registers necessary for the DMA process; they are the Base Byte Count, Base Target Address, and Base Requester Address registers. The 24-bit Base Byte Count register contains the number of bytes to be transferred by the channel. The 24-bit Base Target Address Register contains the beginning address (memory or I/O) of the Target device. The 24-bit Base Requester Address register contains the base address (memory or I/O) of the device which is to request DMA service.

Three more registers for each DMA channel exist within the DMA Controller which are directly related to the registers mentioned above. These registers contain the current status of the DMA process. They are the Current Byte Count register, the Current Target Address, and the Current Requester Address. It is these registers which are manipulated (incremented, decremented, or held constant) by the 82370 DMA Controller during the DMA process. The Current registers are loaded from the Base registers at the beginning of a DMA process.

The Base registers are loaded when the host processor writes to the respective channel register addresses. Depending on the mode in which the channel is operating, the Current registers are typically loaded in the same operation. Reading from the channel register addresses yields the contents of the corresponding Current register.

To maintain compatibility with software which accesses an 8237A, a Byte Pointer Flip-Flop is used to control access to the upper and lower bytes of some words of the Channel Registers. These words are accessed as byte pairs at single port addresses. The Byte Pointer Flip-Flop acts as a one-bit pointer which is toggled each time a qualifying Channel Register byte is accessed.

It always points to the next logical byte to be accessed of a pair of bytes.

The Channel registers are arranged as pairs of words, each pair with its own port address. Addressing the port with the Byte Pointer Flip-Flop reset accesses the least significant byte of the pair. The most significant byte is accessed when the Byte Pointer is set.

For compatibility with existing 8237A designs, there is one exception to the above statements about the Byte Pointer Flip-Flop. The third byte (bits 16-23) of the Target Address is accessed through its own port address. The Byte Pointer Flip-Flop is not affected by any accesses to this byte.

The upper eight bits of the Byte Count Register are cleared when the least significant byte of the register is loaded. This provides compatibility with software which accesses an 8237A. The 8237A has 16-bit Byte Count Registers.

NOTE:

The 82370 is a subset of the Intel 82380 32-bit DMA Controller with Integrated System Peripherals.

Although the 82370 has 24 address bits externally, the programming model is actually a full 32 bits wide. For this reason, there are some "hidden" DMA registers in the 82370 register set. These hidden registers correspond to what would be A24–A31 in a 32-bit system.

Think of the 82370 addresses as though they were 32 bits wide, with only the lower 24 bits available externally.

This should be of concern in two areas:

1. Understanding the Byte Pointer Flip Flop
2. Removing the IRQ1 Chaining Interrupt

The byte pointer flip flop will behave as though the hidden upper address bits were accessible.

The IRQ1 Chaining Interrupt will be removed only when the hidden upper address bits are programmed. You will note that since the hidden upper address bits are not available externally, the **value** you program into the registers is not important. The **act** of programming the hidden register is critical in removing the IRQ1 Chaining interrupt for a DMA channel.

The port assignments for these hidden upper address bits come directly from the port assignments of the Intel 82380. For your convenience, those port definitions have been included in this data sheet in section 3.7.

3.5.3 TEMPORARY REGISTERS

Each channel has a 32-bit Temporary Register used for temporary data storage during two-cycle DMA transfers. It is this register in which any necessary byte assembly and disassembly of non-aligned data is performed. Figure 3-22 shows how a block of data will be moved between memory locations with different boundaries. Note that the order of the data does not change.

If the destination is the Requester and an early process termination has been indicated by the EOP# signal or DREQn inactive in the Demand Mode, the Temporary Register is not affected. If data remains in the Temporary Register due to differences in data path widths of the Target and Requester, it will not

Source		Destination	
20H	A	50H	
21H	B	51H	
22H	C	52H	
23H	D	53H	A
24H	E	54H	B
25H	F	55H	C
26H	G	56H	D
27H		57H	E
		58H	F
		59H	G
		5AH	

Target = source = 00000020H
Requester = destination = 00000053H
Byte Count = 000007H

Figure 3-22. Transfer of data between memory locations with different boundaries. This will be the result, independent of data path width.

be transferred or otherwise lost, but will be stored for later transfer.

If the destination is the Target and the EOP# signal is sensed active during the Requester access of a transfer, the DMA Controller will complete the transfer by sending to the Target whatever information is in the Temporary Register at the time of process termination. This implies that the Target could be accessed with partial data in two accesses. For this reason it is advisable to have an I/O device designated as a Requester, unless it is capable of handling partial data transfers.

3.6 DMA Controller Programming

Programming a DMA Channel to perform a needed DMA function is in general a four step process. First the global attributes of the DMA Controller are programmed via the two Command Registers. These global attributes include: priority levels, channel group enables, priority mode, and DREQn/EOP# input sampling.

The second step involves setting the operating modes of the particular channel. The Mode Registers are used to define the type of transfer and the handshaking modes. The Bus Size Register and Chaining Register may also need to be programmed in this step.

The third step in setting up the channel is to load the Base Registers in accordance with the needs of the operating modes chosen in step two. The Current Registers are automatically loaded from the Base Registers, if required by the Buffer Transfer Mode in effect. The information loaded and the order in which it is loaded depends on the operating mode. A channel used for cascading, for example, needs no buffer information and this step can be skipped entirely.

The last step is to enable the newly programmed channel using one of the Mask Registers. The channel is then available to perform the desired data transfer. The status of the channel can be observed at any time through the Status Register, Mask Register, Chaining Register, and Software Request register.

Once the channel is programmed and enabled, the DMA process may be initiated in one of two ways, either by a hardware DMA request (DREQn) or a software request (Software Request Register).

Once programmed to a particular Process/Mode configuration, the channel will operate in that configuration until programmed otherwise. For this reason, restarting a channel after the current buffer expires does not require complete reprogramming of the channel. Only those parameters which have changed need to be reprogrammed. The Byte Count Register is always changed and must be reprogrammed. A Target or Requester Address Register which is incremented or decremented should be reprogrammed also.

3.6.1 BUFFER PROCESSES

The Buffer Process is determined by the Auto-Initialize bit of Mode Register I and the Chaining Register. If Auto-Initialize is enabled, Chaining should not be used.

3.6.1.1 Single Buffer Process

The Single Buffer Process is programmed by disabling Chaining via the Chaining Register and programming Mode Register I for non-Auto-Initialize.

3.6.1.2 Buffer Auto-Initialize Process

Setting the Auto-Initialize bit in Mode Register I is all that is necessary to place the channel in this mode. Buffer Auto-Initialize must not be enabled simultaneous to enabling the Buffer Chaining Mode as this will have unpredictable results.

Once the Base Registers are loaded, the channel is ready to be enabled. The channel will reload its Current Registers from the Base Registers each time the Current Buffer expires, either by an expired Byte Count or an external EOP#.

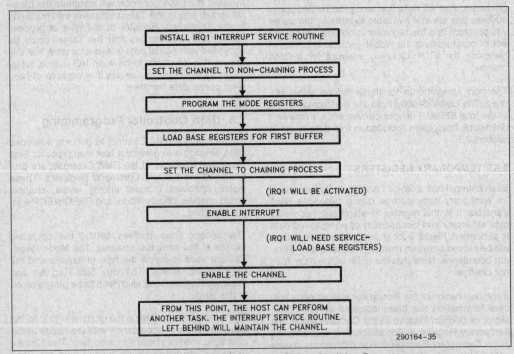

Figure 3-23. Flow of Events in the Buffer Chaining Process

3.6.1.3 Buffer Chaining Process

The Buffer Chaining Process is entered into from the Single Buffer Process. The Mode Registers should be programmed first, with all of the Transfer Modes defined as if the channel were to operate in the Single Buffer Process. The channel's Base Registers are then loaded. When the channel has been set up in this way, and the chaining interrupt service routine is in place, the Chaining Process can be entered by programming the Chaining Register. Figure 3-23 illustrates the Buffer Chaining Process.

An interrupt (IRQ1) will be generated immediately after the Chaining Process is entered, as the channel then perceives the Base Registers as empty and in need of reloading. It is important to have the interrupt service routine in place at the time the Chaining Process is entered into. The interrupt request is removed when the most significant byte of the Base Target Address is loaded.

The interrupt will occur again when the first buffer expires and the Current Registers are loaded from the Base Registers. The cycle continues until the Chaining Process is disabled, or the host fails to respond to IRQ1 before the Current Buffer expires.

Exiting the Chaining Process can be done by resetting the Chaining Mode Register. If an interrupt is pending for the channel when the Chaining Register is reset, the interrupt request will be removed. The Chaining Process can be temporarily disabled by setting the channel's Mask bit in the Mask Register.

The interrupt service routine for IRQ1 has the responsibility of reloading the Base Registers as necessary. It should check the status of the channel to determine the cause of channel expiration, etc. It should also have access to operating system information regarding the channel, if any exists. The IRQ1 service routine should be capable of determining whether the chain should be continued or terminated and act on that information.

3.6.2 DATA TRANSFER MODES

The Data Transfer Modes are selected via Mode Register I. The Demand, Single, and Block Modes are selected by bits D6 and D7. The individual transfer type (Fly-By vs Two-Cycle, Read-Write-Verify, and I/O vs Memory) is programmed through both of the Mode registers.

3.6.3 CASCADED BUS MASTERS

The Cascade Mode is set by writing ones to D7 and D6 of Mode Register I. When a channel is programmed to operate in the Cascade Mode, all of the other modes associated with Mode Registers I and II are ignored. The priority and DREQn/EOP# definitions of the Command Registers will have the same effect on the channel's operation as any other mode.

3.6.4 SOFTWARE COMMANDS

There are five port addresses which, when written to, command certain operations to be performed by the 82370 DMA Controller. The data written to these locations is not of consequence, writing to the location is all that is necessary to command the 82370 to perform the indicated function. Following are descriptions of the command functions.

Clear Byte Pointer Flip-Flop—Location 000CH

Resets the Byte Pointer Flip-Flop. This command should be performed at the beginning of any access to the channel registers in order to be assured of beginning at a predictable place in the register programming sequence.

Master Clear—Location 000DH

All DMA functions are set to their default states. This command is the equivalent of a hardware reset to the DMA Controller. Functions other than those in the DMA Controller section of the 82370 are not affected by this command.

Clear Mask Register— Channels 0–3
— Location 000EH

Channels 4–7
— Location 00CEH

This command simultaneously clears the Mask Bits of all channels in the addressed group, enabling all of the channels in the group.

Clear TC Interrupt Request—Location 001EH

This command resets the Terminal Count Interrupt Request Flip-Flop. It is provided to allow the program which made a software DMA request to acknowledge that it has responded to the expiration of the requested channel(s).

3.7 Register Definitions

The following diagrams outline the bit definitions and functions of the 82370 DMA Controller's Status and Control Registers. The function and programming of the registers is covered in the previous section on DMA Controller Programming. An entry of "X" as a bit value indicates "don't care."

Channel Registers (read Current, write Base)

Channel	Register Name	Address (hex)	Byte Pointer	Bits Accessed
Channel 0	Target Address	00	0	0–7
			1	8–15
		87	x	16–23
		10	0	24–31(*)
	Byte Count	01	0	0–7
			1	8–15
		11	0	16–23
	Requester Address	90	0	0–7
			1	8–15
		91	0	16–23
			1	24–31(*)
Channel 1	Target Address	02	0	0–7
			1	8–15
		83	x	16–23
		12	0	24–31(*)
	Byte Count	03	0	0–7
			1	8–15
		13	0	16–23
	Requester Address	92	0	0–7
			1	8–15
		93	0	16–23
			1	24–31(*)
Channel 2	Target Address	04	0	0–7
			1	8–15
		81	x	16–23
		14	0	24–31(*)
	Byte Count	05	0	0–7
			1	8–15
		15	0	16–23
	Requester Address	94	0	0–7
			1	8–15
		95	0	16–23
			1	24–31(*)
Channel 3	Target Address	06	0	0–7
			1	8–15
		82	x	16–23
		16	0	24–31(*)
	Byte Count	07	0	0–7
			1	8–15
		17	0	16–23
	Requester Address	96	0	0–7
			1	8–15
		97	0	16–23
			1	24–31(*)

Channel Registers (read Current, write Base) (Continued)

Channel	Register Name	Address (hex)	Byte Pointer	Bits Accessed
Channel 4	Target Address	C0	0	0–7
			1	8–15
		8F	x	16–23
		D0	0	24–31(*)
	Byte Count	C1	0	0–7
			1	8–15
		D1	0	16–23
	Requester Address	98	0	0–7
			1	8–15
		99	0	16–23
			1	24–31(*)
Channel 5	Target Address	C2	0	0–7
			1	8–15
		8B	x	16–23
		D2	0	24–31(*)
	Byte Count	C3	0	0–7
			1	8–15
		D3	0	16–23
	Requester Address	9A	0	0–7
			1	8–15
		9B	0	16–23
			1	24–31(*)
Channel 6	Target Address	C4	0	0–7
			1	8–15
		89	x	16–23
		D4	0	24–31(*)
	Byte Count	C5	0	0–7
			1	8–15
		D5	0	16–23
	Requester Address	9C	0	0–7
			1	8–15
		9D	0	16–23
			1	24–31(*)
Channel 7	Target Address	C6	0	0–7
			1	8–15
		8A	x	16–23
		D6	0	24–31(*)
	Byte Count	C7	0	0–7
			1	8–15
		D7	0	16–23
	Requester Address	9E	0	0–7
			1	8–15
		9F	0	16–23
			1	24–31(*)

NOTE:
(*)These bits are not available externally. You need to be aware of their existence for chaining and Byte Pointer Flip-Flop operations. Please see section 3.5.2 for further details.

Command Register I (write only)

Port Addresses— Channels 0–3—0008H
Channels 4–7—00C8H

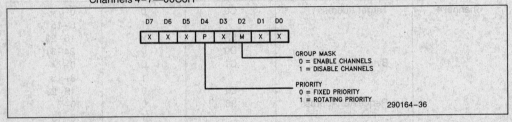

Command Register II (write only)

Port Addresses— Channels 0–3—001AH
Channels 4–7—00DAH

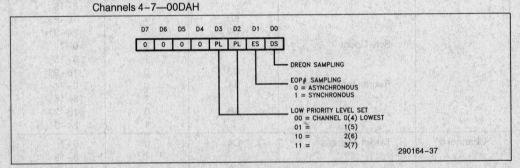

Mode Register I (write only)

Port Addresses— Channels 0–3—000BH
Channels 4–7—00CBH

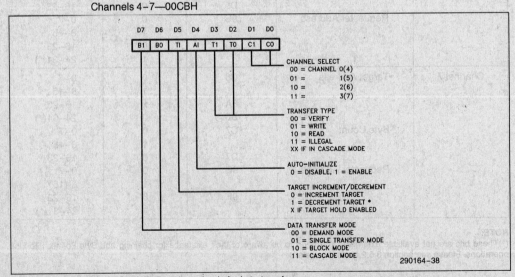

*Target and Requester DECREMENT is allowed only for byte transfers.

Mode Register II (write only)

Port Addresses— Channels 0–3—001BH
Channels 4–7—00DBH

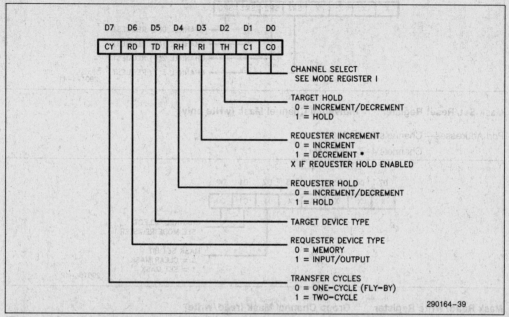

```
        D7   D6   D5   D4   D3   D2   D1   D0
       ┌────┬────┬────┬────┬────┬────┬────┬────┐
       │ CY │ RD │ TD │ RH │ RI │ TH │ C1 │ C0 │
       └────┴────┴────┴────┴────┴────┴────┴────┘
```

CHANNEL SELECT
SEE MODE REGISTER I

TARGET HOLD
0 = INCREMENT/DECREMENT
1 = HOLD

REQUESTER INCREMENT
0 = INCREMENT
1 = DECREMENT *
X IF REQUESTER HOLD ENABLED

REQUESTER HOLD
0 = INCREMENT/DECREMENT
1 = HOLD

TARGET DEVICE TYPE

REQUESTER DEVICE TYPE
0 = MEMORY
1 = INPUT/OUTPUT

TRANSFER CYCLES
0 = ONE–CYCLE (FLY–BY)
1 = TWO–CYCLE

290164–39

*Target and Requester DECREMENT is allowed only for byte transfers.

Software Request Register (read/write)

Port Addresses— Channels 0–3—0009H
Channels 4–7—00C9H

Write Format: Software DMA Service Request

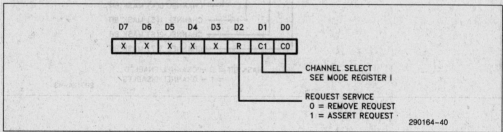

```
        D7   D6   D5   D4   D3   D2   D1   D0
       ┌────┬────┬────┬────┬────┬────┬────┬────┐
       │ X  │ X  │ X  │ X  │ X  │ R  │ C1 │ C0 │
       └────┴────┴────┴────┴────┴────┴────┴────┘
```

CHANNEL SELECT
SEE MODE REGISTER I

REQUEST SERVICE
0 = REMOVE REQUEST
1 = ASSERT REQUEST

290164–40

Read Format: Software Requests Pending

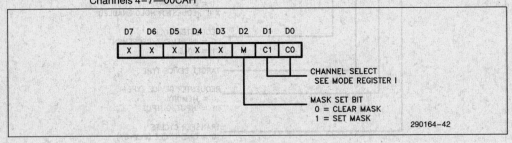

290164-41

Mask Set/Reset Register   Individual Channel Mask (write only)

Port Addresses— Channels 0–3—000AH

Channels 4–7—00CAH

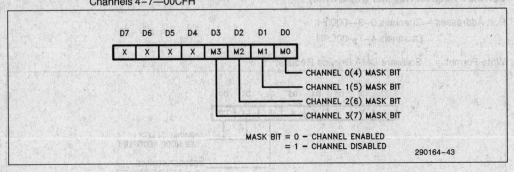

290164-42

Mask Read/Write Register   Group Channel Mask (read/write)

Port Addresses— Channels 0–3—000FH

Channels 4–7—00CFH

290164-43

Status Register   Channel Process Status (read only)

Port Addresses— Channels 0–3—0008H
Channels 4–7—00C8H

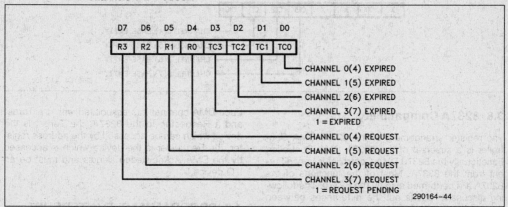

Bus Size Register   Set Data Path Width (write only)

Port Addresses— Channels 0–3—0018H
Channels 4–7—00D8H

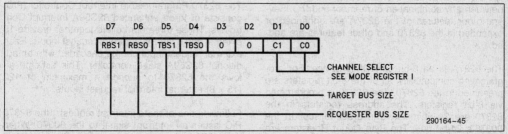

Bus Size Encoding:
  00 = Reserved by Intel   10 = 16-bit Bus
  01 = 32-bit Bus*   11 = 8-bit Bus
*If programmed as 32-bit bus width, the corresponding device will be accessed in two 16-bit cycles provided that the data is aligned within word boundary.

Chaining Register (read/write)

Port Addresses— Channels 0–3—0019H
Channels 4–7—00D9H

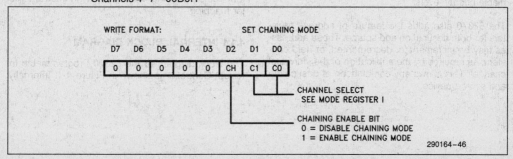

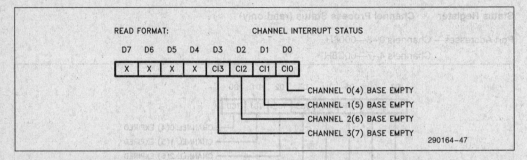

READ FORMAT: CHANNEL INTERRUPT STATUS

D7 D6 D5 D4 D3 D2 D1 D0

| X | X | X | X | CI3 | CI2 | CI1 | CI0 |

CHANNEL 0(4) BASE EMPTY
CHANNEL 1(5) BASE EMPTY
CHANNEL 2(6) BASE EMPTY
CHANNEL 3(7) BASE EMPTY

290164–47

3.8 8237A Compatibility

The register arrangement of the 82370 DMA Controller is a superset of the 8237A DMA Controller. Functionally the 82370 DMA Controller is very different from the 8237A. Most of the functions of the 8237A are performed also by the 82370. The following discussion points out the differences between the 8237A and the 82370.

The 8237A is limited to transfers between I/O and memory only (except in one special case, where two channels can be used to perform memory-to-memory transfers). The 82370 DMA Controller can transfer between any combination of memory and I/O. Several other features of the 8237A are enhanced or expanded in the 82370 and other features are added.

The 8237A is an 8-bit only DMA device. For programming compatibility, all of the 8-bit registers are preserved in the 82370. The 82370 is programmed via 8-bit registers. The address registers in the 82370 are 24-bit registers in order to support the 80376's 24-bit bus. The Byte Count Registers are 24-bit registers, allowing support of larger data blocks than possible with the 8237A.

All of the 8237A's operating modes are supported by the 82370 (except the cumbersome two-channel memory-to-memory transfer). The 82370 performs memory-to-memory transfers using only one channel. The 82370 has the added features of buffer pipelining (Buffer Chaining Process) and programmable priority levels.

The 82370 also adds the feature of address registers for both destination and source. These addresses may be incremented, decremented, or held constant, as required by the application of the individual channel. This allows any combination of destination and source device.

Each DMA channel has associated with it a Target and a Requester. In the 8237A, the Target is the device which can be accessed by the address register, the Requester is the device which is accessed by the DMA Acknowledge signals and must be an I/O device.

4.0 PROGRAMMABLE INTERRUPT CONTROLLER (PIC)

4.1 Functional Description

The 82370 Programmable Interrupt Controller (PIC) consists of three enhanced 82C59A Interrupt Controllers. These three controllers together provide 15 external and 5 internal interrupt request inputs. Each external request input can be cascaded with an additional 82C59A slave controller. This scheme allows the 82370 to support a maximum of 120 (15 x 8) external interrupt request inputs.

Following one or more interrupt requests, the 82370 PIC issues an interrupt signal to the 80376. When the 80376 host processor responds with an interrupt acknowledge signal, the PIC will arbitrate between the pending interrupt requests and place the interrupt vector associated with the highest priority pending request on the data bus.

The major enhancement in the 82370 PIC over the 82C59A is that each of the interrupt request inputs can be individually programmed with its own interrupt vector, allowing more flexibility in interrupt vector mapping.

4.1.1 INTERNAL BLOCK DIAGRAM

The block diagram of the 82370 Programmable Interrupt Controller is shown in Figure 4-1. Internally, the PIC consists of three 82C59A banks: A, B and C. The three banks are cascaded to one another: C is cascaded to B, B is cascaded to A. The INT output of Bank A is used externally to interrupt the 80376.

Bank A has nine interrupt request inputs (two are unused), and Banks B and C have eight interrupt request inputs. Of the fifteen external interrupt request inputs, two are shared by other functions. Specifically, the Interrupt Request 3 input (IRQ3#) can be used as the Timer 2 output (TOUT2#). This pin can be used in three different ways: IRQ3# input only, TOUT2# output only, or using TOUT2# to generate an IRQ3# interrupt request. Also, the Interrupt Request 9 input (IRQ9#) can be used as DMA Request 4 input (DREQ 4). Typically, only IRQ9# or DREQ4 can be used at a time.

4.1.2 INTERRUPT CONTROLLER BANKS

All three banks are identical, with the exception of the IRQ1.5 on Bank A. Therefore, only one bank will be discussed. In the 82370 PIC, all external requests can be cascaded into and each interrupt controller bank behaves like a master. As compared to the 82C59A, the enhancements in the banks are:

— All interrupt vectors are individually programmable. (In the 82C59A, the vectors must be programmed in eight consecutive interrupt vector locations.)

— The cascade address is provided on the Data Bus (D0-D7). (In the 82C59A, three dedicated control signals (CAS0, CAS1, CAS2) are used for master/slave cascading.)

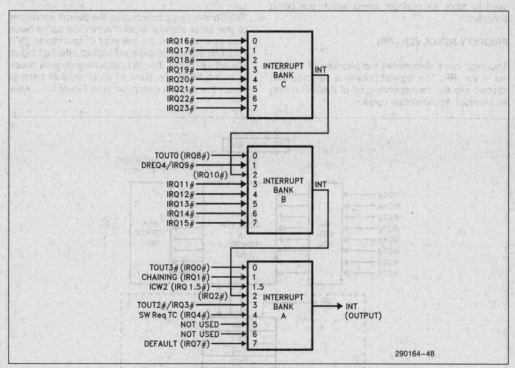

Figure 4-1. Interrupt Controller Block Diagram

The block diagram of a bank is shown in Figure 4-2. As can be seen from this figure, the bank consists of six major blocks: the Interrupt Request Register (IRR), the In-Service Register (ISR), the Interrupt Mask Register (IMR), the Priority Resolver (PR), the Vector Registers (VR), and the Control Logic. The functional description of each block is included below.

INTERRUPT REQUEST (IRR) AND
IN-SERVICE REGISTER (ISR)

The interrupts at the Interrupt Request (IRQ) input lines are handled by two registers in cascade, the Interrupt Request Register (IRR) and the In-Service Register (ISR). The IRR is used to store all interrupt levels which are requesting service; and the ISR is used to store all interrupt levels which are being serviced.

PRIORITY RESOLVER (PR)

This logic block determines the priorities of the bits set in the IRR. The highest priority is selected and strobed into the corresponding bit of the ISR during an Interrupt Acknowledge cycle.

INTERRUPT MASK REGISTER (IMR)

The IMR stores the bits which mask the interrupt lines to be masked (disabled). The IMR operates on the IRR. Masking of a higher priority input will not affect the interrupt request lines of lower priority.

VECTOR REGISTERS (VR)

This block contains a set of Vector Registers, one for each interrupt request line, to store the pre-programmed interrupt vector number. The corresponding vector number will be driven onto the Data Bus of the 82370 during the Interrupt Acknowledge cycle.

CONTROL LOGIC

The Control Logic coordinates the overall operations of the other internal blocks within the same bank. This logic will drive the Interrupt Output signal (INT) HIGH when one or more unmasked interrupt inputs are active (LOW). The INT output signal goes directly to the 80376 (in bank A) or to another bank to which this bank is cascaded (see Figure 4-1). Also,

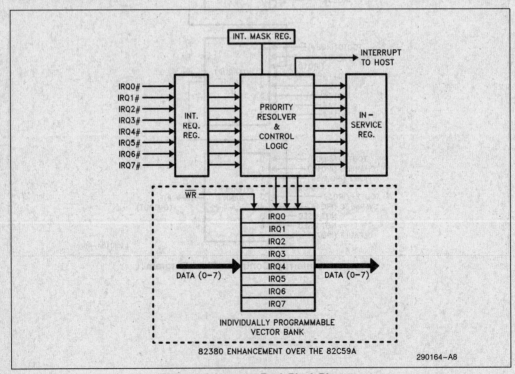

Figure 4-2. Interrupt Bank Block Diagram

this logic will recognize an Interrupt Acknowledge cycle (via M/IO#, D/C# and W/R# signals). During this bus cycle, the Control Logic will enable the corresponding Vector Register to drive the interrupt vector onto the Data Bus.

In bank A, the Control Logic is also responsible for handling the special ICW2 interrupt request input (IRQ1.5).

4.2 Interface Signals

4.2.1 INTERRUPT INPUTS

There are 15 external Interrupt Request inputs and 5 internal Interrupt Requests. The external request inputs are: IRQ3#, IRQ9#, IRQ11# to IRQ23#. They are shown in bold arrows in Figure 4-1. All IRQ inputs are active LOW and they can be programmed (via a control bit in the Initialization Command Word 1 (ICW1)) to be either edge-triggered or level-triggered. In order to be recognized as a valid interrupt request, the interrupt input must be active (LOW) until the first INTA cycle (see Bus Functional Description). Note that all 15 external Interrupt Request inputs have weak internal pull-up resistors.

As mentioned earlier, an 82C59A can be cascaded to each external interrupt input to expand the interrupt capacity to a maximum of 120 levels. Also, two of the interrupt inputs are dual functions: IRQ3# can be used as Timer 2 output (TOUT2#) and IRQ9# can be used as DREQ4 input. IRQ3# is a bidirectional dual function pin. This interrupt request input is wired-OR with the output of Timer 2 (TOUT2#). If only IRQ3# function is to be used, Timer 2 should be programmed so that OUT2 is LOW. Note that TOUT2# can also be used to generate an interrupt request to IRQ3# input.

The five internal interrupt requests serve special system functions. They are shown in Table 4-1. The following paragraphs describe these interrupts.

Table 4-1. 82370 Internal Interrupt Requests

Interrupt Request	Interrupt Source
IRQ0#	Timer 3 Output (TOUT3)
IRQ8#	Timer 0 Output (TOUT0)
IRQ1#	DMA Chaining Request
IRQ4#	DMA Terminal Count
IRQ1.5#	ICW2 Written

TIMER 0 AND TIMER 3 INTERRUPT REQUESTS

IRQ8# and IRQ0# interrupt requests are initiated by the output of Timers 0 and 3, respectively. Each of these requests is generated by an edge-detector flip-flop.

The flip-flops are activated by the following conditions:

Set — Rising edge of timer output (TOUT);

Clear — Interrupt acknowledge for this request; OR Request is masked (disabled); OR Hardware Reset.

CHAINING AND TERMINAL COUNT INTERRUPTS

These interrupt requests are generated by the 82370 DMA Controller. The chaining request (IRQ1#) indicates that the DMA Base Register is not loaded. The Terminal Count request (IRQ4#) indicates that a software DMA request was cleared.

ICW2 INTERRUPT REQUEST

Whenever an Initialization Control Word 2 (ICW2) is written to a Bank, a special ICW2 interrupt request is generated. The interrupt will be cleared when the newly programmed ICW2 Register is read. This interrupt request is in Bank A at level 1.5. This interrupt request is internally ORed with the Cascaded Request from Bank B and is always assigned a higher priority than the Cascaded Request.

This special interrupt is provided to support compatibility with the original 82C59A. A detailed description of this interrupt is discussed in the Programming section.

DEFAULT INTERRUPT (IRQ7#)

During an Interrupt Acknowledge cycle, if there is no active pending request, the PIC will automatically generate a default vector. This vector corresponds to the IRQ7# vector in bank A.

4.2.2 INTERRUPT OUTPUT (INT)

The INT output pin is taken directly from bank A. This signal should be tied to the Maskable Interrupt Request (INTR) of the 80376. When this signal is active (HIGH), it indicates that one or more internal/external interrupt requests are pending. The 80376 is expected to respond with an interrupt acknowledge cycle.

4.3 Bus Functional Description

The INT output of bank A will be activated as a result of any unmasked interrupt request. This may be a non-cascaded or cascaded request. After the PIC has driven the INT signal HIGH, the 80376 will respond by performing two interrupt acknowledge cycles. The timing diagram in Figure 4-3 shows a typical interrupt acknowledge process between the 82370 and the 80376 CPU.

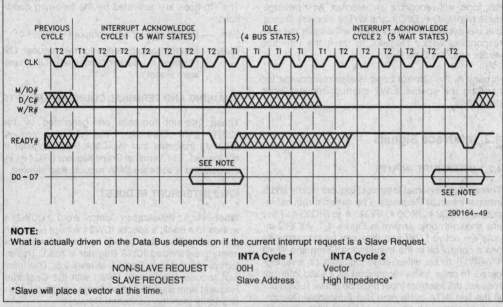

PREVIOUS CYCLE | INTERRUPT ACKNOWLEDGE CYCLE 1 (5 WAIT STATES) | IDLE (4 BUS STATES) | INTERRUPT ACKNOWLEDGE CYCLE 2 (5 WAIT STATES)

290164-49

NOTE:
What is actually driven on the Data Bus depends on if the current interrupt request is a Slave Request.

	INTA Cycle 1	INTA Cycle 2
NON-SLAVE REQUEST	00H	Vector
SLAVE REQUEST	Slave Address	High Impedence*

*Slave will place a vector at this time.

Figure 4-3. Interrupt Acknowledge Cycle

After activating the INT signal, the 82370 monitors the status lines (M/IO#, D/C#, W/R#) and waits for the 80376 to initiate the first interrupt acknowledge cycle. In the 80376 environment, two successive interrupt acknowledge cycles (INTA) marked by M/IO# = LOW, D/C# = LOW, and W/R# = LOW are performed. During the first INTA cycle, the PIC will determine the highest priority request. Assuming this interrupt input has no external Slave Controller cascaded to it, the 82370 will drive the Data Bus with 00H in the first INTA cycle. During the second INTA cycle, the 82370 PIC will drive the Data Bus with the corresponding pre-programmed interrupt vector.

If the PIC determines (from the ICW3) that this interrupt input has an external Slave Controller cascaded to it, it will drive the Data Bus with the specific Slave Cascade Address (instead of 00H) during the first INTA cycle. This Slave Cascade Address is the pre-programmed content in the corresponding Vector Register. This means that no Slave Address should be chosen to be 00H. Note that the Slave Address and Interrupt Vector are different interpretations of the same thing. They are both the contents of the programmable Vector Register. During the second INTA cycle, the Data Bus will be floated so that the external Slave Controller can drive its interrupt vector on the bus. Since the Slave Interrupt Controller resides on the system bus, bus transceiver enable and direction control logic must take this into consideration.

In order to have a successful interrupt service, the interrupt request input must be held valid (LOW) until the beginning of the first interrupt acknowledge cycle. If there is no pending interrupt request when the first INTA cycle is generated, the PIC will generate a default vector, which is the IRQ7 vector (Bank A, level 7).

According to the Bus Cycle definition of the 80376, there will be four Bus Idle States between the two interrupt acknowledge cycles. These idle bus cycles will be initiated by the 80376. Also, during each interrupt acknowledge cycle, the internal Wait State Generator of the 82370 will automatically generate the required number of wait states for internal delays.

4.4 Modes of Operation

A variety of modes and commands are available for controlling the 82370 PIC. All of them are programmable; that is, they may be changed dynamically under software control. In fact, each bank can be programmed individually to operate in different modes. With these modes and commands, many possible configurations are conceivable, giving the user enough versatility for almost any interrupt controlled application.

This section is not intended to show how the 82370 PIC can be programmed. Rather, it describes the operation in different modes.

4.4.1 END-OF-INTERRUPT

Upon completion of an interrupt service routine, the interrupted bank needs to be notified so its ISR can be updated. This allows the PIC to keep track of which interrupt levels are in the process of being serviced and their relative priorities. Three different End-Of-Interrupt (EOI) formats are available. They are: Non-Specific EOI Command, Specific EOI Command, and Automatic EOI Mode. Selection of which EOI to use is dependent upon the interrupt operations the user wishes to perform.

If the 82370 is NOT programmed in the Automatic EOI Mode, an EOI command must be issued by the 80376 to the specific 82370 PIC Controller Bank. Also, if this controller bank is cascaded to another internal bank, an EOI command must also be sent to the bank to which this bank is cascaded. For example, if an interrupt request of Bank C in the 82370 PIC is serviced, an EOI should be written into Bank C, Bank B and Bank A. If the request comes from an external interrupt controller cascaded to Bank C, then an EOI should be written into the external controller as well.

NON-SPECIFIC EOI COMMAND

A Non-Specific EOI command sent from the 80376 lets the 82370 PIC bank know when a service routine has been completed, without specification of its exact interrupt level. The respective interrupt bank automatically determines the interrupt level and resets the correct bit in the ISR.

To take advantage of the Non-Specific EOI, the interrupt bank must be in a mode of operation in which it can predetermine its in-service routine levels. For this reason, the Non-Specific EOI command should only be used when the most recent level acknowledged and serviced is always the highest priority level (i.e. in the Fully Nested Mode structure to be described below). When the interrupt bank receives a Non-Specific EOI command, it simply resets the highest priority ISR bit to indicate that the highest priority routine in service is finished.

Special consideration should be taken when deciding to use the Non-Specific EOI command. Here are two operating conditions in which it is best NOT used since the Fully Nested Mode structure will be destroyed:

— Using the Set Priority command within an interrupt service routine.

— Using a Special Mask Mode.

These conditions are covered in more detail in their own sections, but are listed here for reference.

SPECIFIC EOI COMMAND

Unlike a Non-Specific EOI command which automatically resets the highest priority ISR bit, a Specific EOI command specifies an exact ISR bit to be reset. Any one of the IRQ levels of an interrupt bank can be specified in the command.

The Specific EOI command is needed to reset the ISR bit of a completed service routine whenever the interrupt bank is not able to automatically determine it. The Specific EOI command can be used in all conditions of operation, including those that prohibit Non-Specific EOI command usage mentioned above.

AUTOMATIC EOI MODE

When programmed in the Automatic EOI Mode, the 80376 no longer needs to issue a command to notify the interrupt bank it has completed an interrupt routine. The interrupt bank accomplishes this by performing a Non-Specific EOI automatically at the end of the second INTA cycle.

Special consideration should be taken when deciding to use the Automatic EOI Mode because it may disturb the Fully Nested Mode structure. In the Automatic EOI Mode, the ISR bit of a routine in service is reset right after it is acknowledged, thus leaving no designation in the ISR that a service routine is being executed. If any interrupt request within the same bank occurs during this time and interrupts are enabled, it will get serviced regardless of its priority. Therefore, when using this mode, the 80376 should keep its interrupt request input disabled during execution of a service routine. By doing this, higher priority interrupt levels will be serviced only after the completion of a routine in service. This guideline restores the Fully Nested Mode structure. However, in this scheme, a routine in service cannot be interrupted since the host's interrupt request input is disabled.

4.4.2 INTERRUPT PRIORITIES

The 82370 PIC provides various methods for arranging the interrupt priorities of the interrupt request inputs to suit different applications. The following subsections explain these methods in detail.

4.4.2.1 Fully Nested Mode

The Fully Nested Mode of operation is a general purpose priority mode. This mode supports a multi-level interrupt structure in which all of the Interrupt Request (IRQ) inputs within one bank are arranged from highest to lowest.

Unless otherwise programmed, the Fully Nested Mode is entered by default upon initialization. At this time, IRQ0# is assigned the highest priority (priority = 0) and IRQ7# the lowest (priority = 7). This default priority can be changed, as will be explained later in the Rotating Priority Mode.

When an interrupt is acknowledged, the highest priority request is determined from the Interrupt Request Register (IRR) and its vector is placed on the bus. In addition, the corresponding bit in the In-Service Register (ISR) is set to designate the routine in service. This ISR bit will remain set until the 80376 issues an End Of Interrupt (EOI) command immediately before returning from the service routine; or alternately, if the Automatic End Of Interrupt (AEOI) bit is set, the ISR bit will be reset at the end of the second INTA cycle.

While the ISR bit is set, all further interrupts of the same or lower priority are inhibited. Higher level interrupts can still generate an interrupt, which will be acknowledged only if the 80376 internal interrupt enable flip-flop has been reenabled (through software inside the current service routine).

4.4.2.2 Automatic Rotation–Equal Priority Devices

Automatic rotation of priorities serves in applications where the interrupting devices are of equal priority within an interrupt bank. In this kind of environment, once a device is serviced, all other equal priority peripherals should be given a chance to be serviced before the original device is serviced again. This is accomplished by automatically assigning a device the lowest priority after being serviced. Thus, in the worst case, the device would have to wait until all other peripherals connected to the same bank are serviced before it is serviced again.

There are two methods of accomplishing automatic rotation. One is used in conjunction with the Non-Specific EOI command and the other is used with the Automatic EOI mode. These two methods are discussed below.

ROTATE ON NON-SPECIFIC EOI COMMAND

When the Rotate On Non-Specific EOI command is issued, the highest ISR bit is reset as in a normal Non-Specific EOI command. However, after it is reset, the corresponding Interrupt Request (IRQ) level is assigned the lowest priority. Other IRQ priorities rotate to conform to the Fully Nested Mode based on the newly assigned low priority.

Figure 4-4 shows how the Rotate On Non-Specific EOI command affects the interrupt priorities. Assume the IRQ priorities were assigned with IRQ0 the highest and IRQ7 the lowest. IRQ6 and IRQ4 are

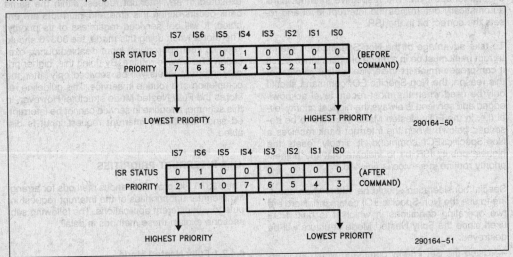

Figure 4-4. Rotate On Non-Specific EOI Command

8-148

already in service but neither is completed. Being the higher priority routine, IRQ4 is necessarily the routine being executed. During the IRQ4 routine, a rotate on Non-Specific EOI command is executed. When this happens, Bit 4 in the ISR is reset. IRQ4 then becomes the lowest priority and IRQ5 becomes the highest.

ROTATE ON AUTOMATIC EOI MODE

The Rotate On Automatic EOI Mode works much like the Rotate On Non-Specific EOI Command. The main difference is that priority rotation is done automatically after the second INTA cycle of an interrupt request. To enter or exit this mode, a Rotate-On-Automatic-EOI Set Command and Rotate-On-Automatic-EOI Clear Command is provided. After this mode is entered, no other commands are needed as in the normal Automatic EOI Mode. However, it must be noted again that when using any form of the Automatic EOI Mode, special consideration should be taken. The guideline presented in the Automatic EOI Mode also applies here.

4.4.2.3 Specific Rotation–Specific Priority

Specific rotation gives the user versatile capabilities in interrupt controlled operations. It serves in those applications in which a specific device's interrupt priority must be altered. As opposed to Automatic Rotation which will automatically set priorities after each interrupt request is serviced, specific rotation is completely user controlled. That is, the user selects which interrupt level is to receive the lowest or the highest priority. This can be done during the main program or within interrupt routines. Two specific ro-

tation commands are available to the user: Set Priority Command and Rotate On Specific EOI Command.

SET PRIORITY COMMAND

The Set Priority Command allows the programmer to assign an IRQ level the lowest priority. All other interrupt levels will conform to the Fully Nested Mode based on the newly assigned low priority.

ROTATE ON SPECIFIC EOI COMMAND

The Rotate On Specific EOI Command is literally a combination of the Set Priority Command and the Specific EOI Command. Like the Set Priority Command, a specified IRQ level is assigned lowest priority. Like the Specific EOI Command, a specified level will be reset in the ISR. Thus, this command accomplishes both tasks in one single command.

4.4.2.4 Interrupt Priority Mode Summary

In order to simplify understanding the many modes of interrupt priority, Table 4-2 is provided to bring out their summary of operations.

4.4.3 INTERRUPT MASKING

VIA INTERRUPT MASK REGISTER

Each bank in the 82370 PIC has an Interrupt Mask Register (IMR) which enhances interrupt control ca-

Table 4-2. Interrupt Priority Mode Summary

Interrupt Priority Mode	Operation Summary	Effect On Priority After EOI	
		Non-Specific/Automatic	Specific
Fully-Nested Mode	IRQ0# - Highest Priority IRQ7# - Lowest Priority	No change in priority. Highest ISR bit is reset.	Not Applicable.
Automatic Rotation (Equal Priority Devices)	Interrupt level just serviced is the lowest priority. Other priorities rotate to conform to Fully-Nested Mode.	Highest ISR bit is reset and the corresponding level becomes the lowest priority.	Not Applicable.
Specific Rotation (Specific Priority Devices)	User specifies the lowest priority level. Other priorities rotate to conform to Fully-Nested Mode.	Not Applicable.	As described under "Operation Summary".

pabilities. This IMR allows individual IRQ masking. When an IRQ is masked, its interrupt request is disabled until it is unmasked. Each bit in the 8-bit IMR disables one interrupt channel if it is set (HIGH). Bit 0 masks IRQ0, Bit 1 masks IRQ1 and so forth. Masking an IRQ channel will only disable the corresponding channel and does not affect the others' operations.

The IMR acts only on the output of the IRR. That is, if an interrupt occurs while its IMR bit is set, this request is not "forgotten". Even with an IRQ input masked, it is still possible to set the IRR. Therefore, when the IMR bit is reset, an interrupt request to the 80376 will then be generated, providing that the IRQ request remains active. If the IRQ request is removed before the IMR is reset, the Default Interrupt Vector (Bank A, level 7) will be generated during the interrupt acknowledge cycle.

SPECIAL MASK MODE

In the Fully Nested Mode, all IRQ levels of lower priority than the routine in service are inhibited. However, in some applications, it may be desirable to let a lower priority interrupt request to interrupt the routine in service. One method to achieve this is by using the Special Mask Mode. Working in conjunction with the IMR, the Special Mask Mode enables interrupts from all levels except the level in service. This is usually done inside an interrupt service routine by masking the level that is in service and then issuing the Special Mask Mode Command. Once the Special Mask Mode is enabled, it remains in effect until it is disabled.

4.4.4 EDGE OR LEVEL INTERRUPT TRIGGERING

Each bank in the 82370 PIC can be programmed independently for either edge or level sensing for the interrupt request signals. Recall that all IRQ inputs are active LOW. Therefore, in the edge triggered mode, an active edge is defined as an input transition from an inactive (HIGH) to active (LOW) state. The interrupt input may remain active without generating another interrupt. During level triggered mode, an interrupt request will be recognized by an active (LOW) input, and there is no need for edge detection. However, the interrupt request must be removed before the EOI Command is issued, or the 80376 must be disabled to prevent a second false interrupt from occurring.

In either modes, the interrupt request input must be active (LOW) during the first INTA cycle in order to be recognized. Otherwise, the Default Interrupt Vector will be generated at level 7 of Bank A.

4.4.5 INTERRUPT CASCADING

As mentioned previously, the 82370 allows for external Slave interrupt controllers to be cascaded to any of its external interrupt request pins. The 82370 PIC indicates that an external Slave Controller is to be serviced by putting the contents of the Vector Register associated with the particular request on the 80376 Data Bus during the first INTA cycle (instead of 00H during a non-slave service). The external logic should latch the vector on the Data Bus using the INTA status signals and use it to select the external Slave Controller to be serviced (see Figure 4-5). The selected Slave will then respond to the second INTA cycle and place its vector on the Data Bus. This method requires that if external Slave Controllers are used in the system, no vector should be programmed to 00H.

Since the external Slave Cascade Address is provided on the Data Bus during INTA cycle 1, an external latch is required to capture this address for the Slave Controller. A simple scheme is depicted in Figure 4-5 below.

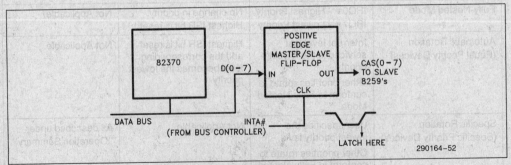

Figure 4-5. Slave Cascade Address Capturing

4.4.5.1 Special Fully Nested Mode

This mode will be used where cascading is employed and the priority is to be conserved within each Slave Controller. The Special Fully Nested Mode is similar to the "regular" Fully Nested Mode with the following exceptions:

— When an interrupt request from a Slave Controller is in service, this Slave Controller is not locked out from the Master's priority logic. Further interrupt requests from the higher priority logic within the Slave Controller will be recognized by the 82370 PIC and will initiate interrupts to the 80376. In comparing to the "regular" Fully Nested Mode, the Slave Controller is masked out when its request is in service and no higher requests from the same Slave Controller can be serviced.

— Before exiting the interrupt service routine, the software has to check whether the interrupt serviced was the only request from the Slave Controller. This is done by sending a Non-Specific EOI Command to the Slave Controller and then reading its In Service Register. If there are no requests in the Slave Controller, a Non-Specific EOI can be sent to the corresponding 82370 PIC bank also. Otherwise, no EOI should be sent.

4.4.6 READING INTERRUPT STATUS

The 82370 PIC provides several ways to read different status of each interrupt bank for more flexible interrupt control operations. These include polling the highest priority pending interrupt request and reading the contents of different interrupt status registers.

4.4.6.1 Poll Command

The 82370 PIC supports status polling operations with the Poll Command. In a Poll Command, the pending interrupt request with the highest priority can be determined. To use this command, the INT output is not used, or the 80376 interrupt is disabled. Service to devices is achieved by software using the Poll Command.

This mode is useful if there is a routine command common to several levels so that the INTA sequence is not needed. Another application is to use the Poll Command to expand the number of priority levels.

Notice that the ICW2 mechanism is not supported for the Poll Command. However, if the Poll Command is used, the programmable Vector Registers are of no concern since no INTA cycle will be generated.

4.4.6.2 Reading Interrupt Registers

The contents of each interrupt register (IRR, ISR, and IMR) can be read to update the user's program on the present status of the 82370 PIC. This can be a versatile tool in the decision making process of a service routine, giving the user more control over interrupt operations.

The reading of the IRR and ISR contents can be performed via the Operation Control Word 3 by using a Read Status Register Command and the content of IMR can be read via a simple read operation of the register itself.

4.5 Register Set Overview

Each bank of the 82370 PIC consists of a set of 8-bit registers to control its operations. The address map of all the registers is shown in Table 4-3 below. Since all three register sets are identical in functions, only one set will be described.

Functionally, each register set can be divided into five groups. They are: the four Initialization Command Words (ICW's), the three Operation Control Words (OCW's), the Poll/Interrupt Request/In-Service Register, the Interrupt Mask Register, and the Vector Registers. A description of each group follows.

Table 4-3. Interrupt Controller Register Address Map

Port Address	Access	Register Description
20H	Write	Bank B ICW1, OCW2, or OCW3
	Read	Bank B Poll, Request or In-Service Status Register
21H	Write	Bank B ICW2, ICW3, ICW4, OCW1
	Read	Bank B Mask Register
22H	Read	Bank B ICW2
28H	Read/Write	IRQ8 Vector Register
29H	Read/Write	IRQ9 Vector Register
2AH	Read/Write	Reserved
2BH	Read/Write	IRQ11 Vector Register
2CH	Read/Write	IRQ12 Vector Register
2DH	Read/Write	IRQ13 Vector Register
2EH	Read/Write	IRQ14 Vector Register
2FH	Read/Write	IRQ15 Vector Register
A0H	Write	Bank C ICW1, OCW2, or OCW3
	Read	Bank C Poll, Request or In-Service Status Register
A1H	Write	Bank C ICW2, ICW3, ICW4, OCW1
	Read	Bank C Mask Register
A2H	Read	Bank C ICW2
A8H	Read/Write	IRQ16 Vector Register
A9H	Read/Write	IRQ17 Vector Register
AAH	Read/Write	IRQ18 Vector Register
ABH	Read/Write	IRQ19 Vector Register
ACH	Read/Write	IRQ20 Vector Register
ADH	Read/Write	IRQ21 Vector Register
AEH	Read/Write	IRQ22 Vector Register
AFH	Read/Write	IRQ23 Vector Register
30H	Write	Bank A ICW1, OCW2, or OCW3
	Read	Bank A Poll, Request or In-Service Status Register
31H	Write	Bank A ICW2, ICW3, ICW4, OCW1
	Read	Bank A Mask Register
32H	Read	Bank ICW2
38H	Read/Write	IRQ0 Vector Register
39H	Read/Write	IRQ1 Vector Register
3AH	Read/Write	IRQ1.5 Vector Register
3BH	Read/Write	IRQ3 Vector Register
3CH	Read/Write	IRQ4 Vector Register
3DH	Read/Write	Reserved
3EH	Read/Write	Reserved
3FH	Read/Write	IRQ7 Vector Register

4.5.1 INITIALIZATION COMMAND WORDS (ICW)

Before normal operation can begin, the 82370 PIC must be brought to a known state. There are four 8-bit Initialization Command Words in each interrupt bank to setup the necessary conditions and modes for proper operation. Except for the second command word (ICW2) which is a read/write register, the other three are write-only registers. Without going into detail of the bit definitions of the command words, the following subsections give a brief description of what functions each command word controls.

ICW1

The ICW1 has three major functions. They are:

- To select between the two IRQ input triggering modes (edge- or level-triggered);

- To designate whether or not the interrupt bank is to be used alone or in the cascade mode. If the cascade mode is desired, the interrupt bank will accept ICW3 for further cascade mode programming. Otherwise, no ICW3 will be accepted;

- To determine whether or not ICW4 will be issued; that is, if any of the ICW4 operations are to be used.

ICW2

ICW2 is provided for compatibility with the 82C59A only. Its contents do not affect the operation of the interrupt bank in any way. Whenever the ICW2 of any of the three banks is written into, an interrupt is generated from bank A at level 1.5. The interrupt request will be cleared after the ICW2 register has been read by the 80376. The user is expected to program the corresponding vector register or to use it as an indicator that an attempt was made to alter the contents. Note that each ICW2 register has different addresses for read and write operations.

ICW3

The interrupt bank will only accept an ICW3 if programmed in the external cascade mode (as indicated in ICW1). ICW3 is used for specific programming within the cascade mode. The bits in ICW3 indicate which interrupt request inputs have a Slave cascaded to them. This will subsequently affect the interrupt vector generation during the interrupt acknowledge cycles as described previously.

ICW4

The ICW4 is accepted only if it was selected in ICW1. This command word register serves two functions:

- To select either the Automatic EOI mode or software EOI mode;

- To select if the Special Nested mode is to be used in conjunction with the cascade mode.

4.5.2 OPERATION CONTROL WORDS (OCW)

Once initialized by the ICW's, the interrupt banks will be operating in the Fully Nested Mode by default and they are ready to accept interrupt requests. However, the operations of each interrupt bank can be further controlled or modified by the use of OCW's. Three OCW's are available for programming various modes and commands. Note that all OCW's are 8-bit write-only registers.

The modes and operations controlled by the OCW's are:

- Fully Nested Mode;
- Rotating Priority Mode;
- Special Mask Mode;
- Poll Mode;
- EOI Commands;
- Read Status Commands.

OCW1

OCW1 is used solely for masking operations. It provides a direct link to the Internal Mask Register (IMR). The 80376 can write to this OCW register to enable or disable the interrupt inputs. Reading the pre-programmed mask can be done via the Interrupt Mask Register which will be discussed shortly.

OCW2

OCW2 is used to select End-Of-Interrupt, Automatic Priority Rotation, and Specific Priority Rotation operations. Associated commands and modes of these operations are selected using the different combinations of bits in OCW2.

Specifically, the OCW2 is used to:

- Designate an interrupt level (0–7) to be used to reset a specific ISR bit or to set a specific priority. This function can be enabled or disabled;

- Select which software EOI command (if any) is to be executed (i.e. Non-Specific or Specific EOI);

- Enable one of the priority rotation operations (i.e. Rotate On Non-Specific EOI, Rotate On Automatic EOI, or Rotate On Specific EOI).

OCW3

There are three main categories of operation that OCW3 controls. They are summarized as follows:

— To select and execute the Read Status Register Commands, either reading the Interrupt Request Register (IRR) or the In-Service Register (ISR);

— To issue the Poll Command. The Poll Command will override a Read Register Command if both functions are enabled simultaneously;

— To set or reset the Special Mask Mode.

4.5.3 POLL/INTERRUPT REQUEST/IN-SERVICE STATUS REGISTER

As the name implies, this 8-bit read-only register has multiple functions. Depending on the command issued in the OCW3, the content of this register reflects the result of the command executed. For a Poll Command, the register read contains the binary code of the highest priority level requesting service (if any). For a Read IRR Command, the register content will show the current pending interrupt request(s). Finally, for a Read ISR Command, this register will specify all interrupt levels which are being serviced.

4.5.4 INTERRUPT MASK REGISTER (IMR)

This is a read-only 8-bit register which, when read, will specify all interrupt levels within the same bank that are masked.

4.5.5 VECTOR REGISTERS (VR)

Each interrupt request input has an 8-bit read/write programmable vector register associated with it. The registers should be programmed to contain the interrupt vector for the corresponding request. The contents of the Vector Register will be placed on the Data Bus during the INTA cycles as described previously.

4.6 Programming

Programming the 82370 PIC is accomplished by using two types of command words: ICW's and OCW's. All modes and commands explained in the previous sections are programmable using the ICW's and OCW's. The ICW's are issued from the 80376 in a sequential format and are used to setup the banks in the 82370 PIC in an initial state of operation. The OCW's are issued as needed to vary and control the 82370 PIC's operations.

Both ICW's and OCW's are sent by the 80376 to the interrupt banks via the Data Bus. Each bank distinguishes between the different ICW's and OCW's by the I/O address map, the sequence they are issued (ICW's only), and by some dedicated bits among the ICW's and OCW's.

An example of programming the 82370 interrupt controllers is given in Appendix C (Programming the 82370 Interrupt Controllers).

All three interrupt banks are programmed in a similar way. Therefore, only a single bank will be described in the following sections.

4.6.1 INITIALIZATION (ICW)

Before normal operation can begin, each bank must be initialized by programming a sequence of two to four bytes written into the ICW's.

Figure 4-6 shows the initialization flow for an interrupt bank. Both ICW1 and ICW2 must be issued for any form of operation. However, ICW3 and ICW4 are used only if designated in ICW1. Once initialized, if any programming changes within the ICW's are to be made, the entire ICW sequence must be reprogrammed, not just an individual ICW.

Note that although the ICW2's in the 82370 PIC do not effect the Bank's operation, they still must be programmed in order to preserve the compatibility with the 82C59A. The contents programmed are not relevant to the overall operations of the interrupt banks. Also, whenever one of the three ICW2's is programmed, an interrupt level 1.5 in Bank A will be generated. This interrupt request will be cleared upon reading of the ICW2 registers. Since the three ICW2's share the same interrupt level and the system may not know the origin of the interrupt, all three ICW2's must be read.

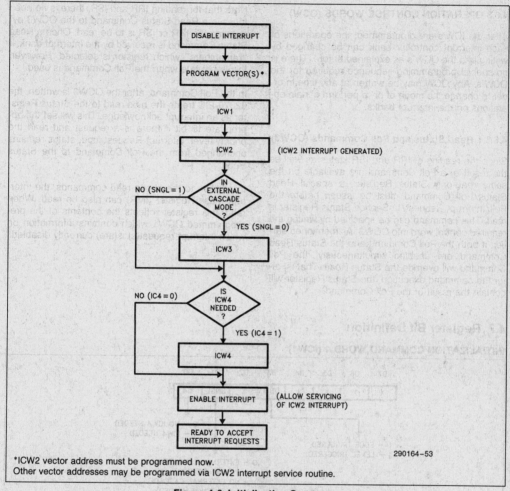

*ICW2 vector address must be programmed now.
Other vector addresses may be programmed via ICW2 interrupt service routine.

290164–53

Figure 4-6. Initialization Sequence

Certain internal setup conditions occur automatically within the interrupt bank after the first ICW (ICW1) has been issued. These are:

— The edge sensitive circuit is reset, which means that following initialization, an interrupt request input must make a HIGH-to-LOW transition to generate an interrupt;

— The Interrupt Mask Register (IMR) is cleared; that is, all interrupt inputs are enabled;

— IRQ7 input of each bank is assigned priority 7 (lowest);

— Special Mask Mode is cleared and Status Read is set to IRR;

— If no ICW4 is needed, then no Automatic-EOI is selected.

4.6.2 VECTOR REGISTERS (VR)

Each interrupt request input has a separate Vector Register. These Vector Registers are used to store the pre-programmed vector number corresponding to their interrupt sources. In order to guarantee proper interrupt handling, all Vector Registers must be programmed with the predefined vector numbers. Since an interrupt request will be generated whenever an ICW2 is written during the initialization sequence, it is important that the Vector Register of IRQ1.5 in Bank A should be initialized and the interrupt service routine of this vector is set up before the ICW's are written.

4.6.3 OPERATION CONTROL WORDS (OCW)

After the ICW's are programmed, the operations of each interrupt controller bank can be changed by writing into the OCW's as explained before. There is no special programming sequence required for the OCW's. Any OCW may be written at any time in order to change the mode of or to perform certain operations on the interrupt banks.

4.6.3.1 Read Status and Poll Commands (OCW3)

Since the reading of IRR and ISR status as well as the result of a Poll Command are available on the same read-only Status Register, a special Read Status/Poll Command must be issued before the Poll/Interrupt Request/In-Service Status Register is read. This command can be specified by writing the required control word into OCW3. As mentioned earlier, if both the Poll Command and the Status Read Command are enabled simultaneously, the Poll Command will override the Status Read. That is, after the command execution, the Status Register will contain the result of the Poll Command.

Note that for reading IRR and ISR, there is no need to issue a Read Status Command to the OCW3 every time the IRR or ISR is to be read. Once a Read Status Command is received by the interrupt bank, it "remembers" which register is selected. However, this is not true when the Poll Command is used.

In the Poll Command, after the OCW3 is written, the 82370 PIC treats the next read to the Status Register as an interrupt acknowledge. This will set the appropriate IS bit if there is a request and read the priority level. Interrupt Request input status remains unchanged from the Poll Command to the Status Read.

In addition to the above read commands, the Interrupt Mask Register (IMR) can also be read. When read, this register reflects the contents of the preprogrammed OCW1 which contains information on which interrupt request(s) is(are) currently disabled.

4.7 Register Bit Definition

INITIALIZATION COMMAND WORD 1 (ICW1)

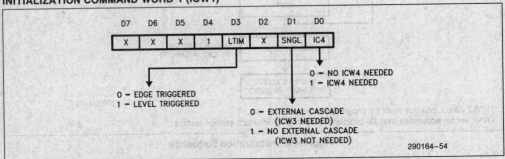

INITIALIZATION COMMAND WORD 2 (ICW2)

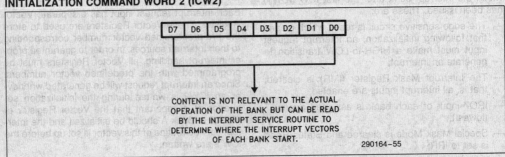

INITIALIZATION COMMAND WORD 3 (ICW3)

ICW3 for Bank A:

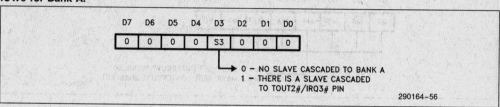

```
      D7   D6   D5   D4   D3   D2   D1   D0
       0    0    0    0   S3    0    0    0
```

0 – NO SLAVE CASCADED TO BANK A
1 – THERE IS A SLAVE CASCADED
      TO TOUT2#/IRQ3# PIN

290164–56

ICW3 for Bank B:

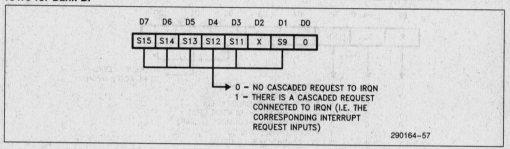

```
      D7    D6    D5    D4    D3    D2    D1    D0
     S15   S14   S13   S12   S11    X     S9    0
```

0 – NO CASCADED REQUEST TO IRQN
1 – THERE IS A CASCADED REQUEST
      CONNECTED TO IRQN (I.E. THE
      CORRESPONDING INTERRUPT
      REQUEST INPUTS)

290164–57

ICW3 for Bank C:

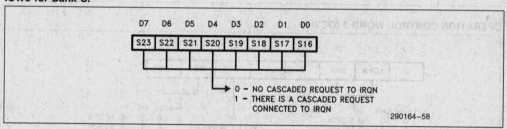

```
      D7    D6    D5    D4    D3    D2    D1    D0
     S23   S22   S21   S20   S19   S18   S17   S16
```

0 – NO CASCADED REQUEST TO IRQN
1 – THERE IS A CASCADED REQUEST
      CONNECTED TO IRQN

290164–58

INITIALIZATION COMMAND WORD 4 (ICW4)

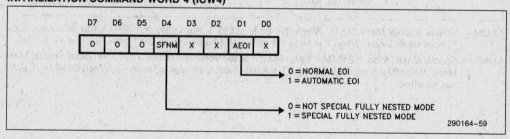

```
      D7   D6   D5   D4    D3   D2   D1    D0
       0    0    0   SFNM   X    X   AEOI   X
```

0 = NORMAL EOI
1 = AUTOMATIC EOI

0 = NOT SPECIAL FULLY NESTED MODE
1 = SPECIAL FULLY NESTED MODE

290164–59

OPERATION CONTROL WORD 1 (OCW1)

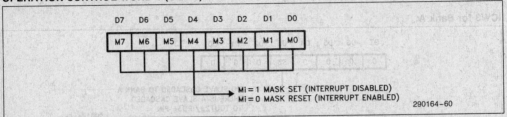

290164-60

OPERATION CONTROL WORD 2 (OCW2)

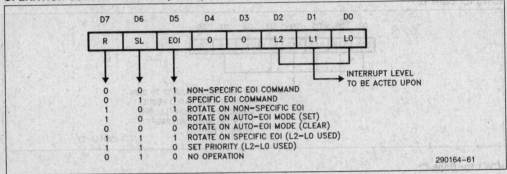

290164-61

OPERATION CONTROL WORD 3 (OCW3)

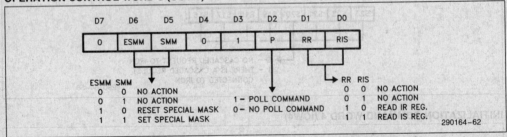

290164-62

ESMM — Enable Special Mask Mode. When this bit is set to 1, it enables the SMM bit to set or reset the Special Mask Mode. When this bit is set to 0, SMM bit becomes don't care.

SMM — Special Mask Mode. If ESMM = 1 and SMM = 1, the interrupt controller bank will enter Special Mask Mode. If ESMM = 1 and SMM = 0, the bank will revert to normal mask mode. When ESMM = 0, SMM has no effect.

POLL/INTERRUPT REQUEST/IN-SERVICE STATUS REGISTER

Poll Command Status

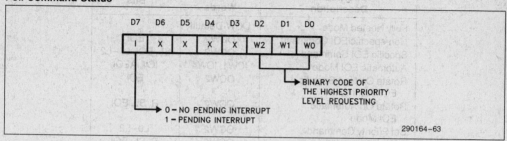

Interrupt Request Status

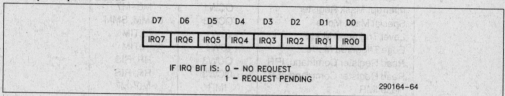

NOTE:
Although all Interrupt Request inputs are active LOW, the internal logical will invert the state of the pins so that when there is a pending interrupt request at the input, the corresponding IRQ bit will be set to HIGH in the Interrupt Request Status register.

In-Service Status

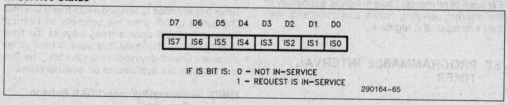

VECTOR REGISTER (VR)

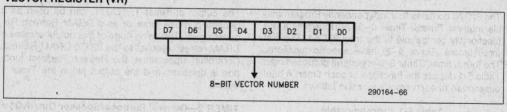

Table 4-4. Register Operational Summary

Operational Description	Command Words	Bits
Fully Nested Mode	OCW-Default	
Non-specific EOI Command	OCW2	EOI
Specific EOI Command	OCW2	SL, EOI, L0–L2
Automatic EOI Mode	ICW1, ICW4	IC4, AEOI
Rotate On Non-Specific EOI Command	OCW2	EOI
Rotate On Automatic EOI Mode	OCW2	R, SL, EOI
Set Priority Command	OCW2	L0–L2
Rotate On Specific EOI Command	OCW2	R, SL, EOI
Interrupt Mask Register	OCW1	M0–M7
Special Mask Mode	OCW3	ESMM, SMM
Level Triggered Mode	ICW1	LTIM
Edge Triggered Mode	ICW1	LTIM
Read Register Command, IRR	OCW3	RR, RIS
Read Register Command, ISR	OCW3	RR, RIS
Read IMR	IMR	M0–M7
Poll Command	OCW3	P
Special Fully Nested Mode	ICW1, ICW4	IC4, SFNM

4.8 Register Operational Summary

For ease of reference, Table 4-4 gives a summary of the different operating modes and commands with their corresponding registers.

5.0 PROGRAMMABLE INTERVAL TIMER

5.1 Functional Description

The 82370 contains four independently Programmable Interval Timers: Timer 0–3. All four timers are functionally compatible to the Intel 82C54. The first three timers (Timer 0–2) have specific functions. The fourth timer, Timer 3, is a general purpose timer. Table 5-1 depicts the functions of each timer. A brief description of each timer's function follows.

Table 5-1. Programmable Interval Timer Functions

Timer	Output	Function
0	IRQ8	Event Based IRQ8 Generator
1	TOUT1/REF#	Gen. Purpose/DRAM Refresh Req.
2	TOUT2/IRQ3#	Gen. Purpose/Speaker Out/IRQ3#
3	TOUT3#	Gen. Purpose/IRQ0 Generator

TIMER 0—Event Based Interrupt Request 8 Generator

Timer 0 is intended to be used as an Event Counter. The output of this timer will generate an Interrupt Request 8 (IRQ8) upon a rising edge of the timer output (TOUT0). Normally, this timer is used to implement a time-of-day clock or system tick. The Timer 0 output is not available as an external signal.

TIMER 1—General Purpose/DRAM Refresh Request

The output of Timer 1, TOUT1, can be used as a general purpose timer or as a DRAM Refresh Request signal. The rising edge of this output creates a DRAM refresh request to the 82370 DRAM Refresh Controller. Upon reset, the Refresh Request function is disabled, and the output pin is the Timer 1 output.

TIMER 2—General Purpose/Speaker Out/IRQ3#

The Timer 2 output, TOUT2#, could be used to support tone generation to an external speaker. This pin is a bidirectional signal. When used as an input, a logic LOW asserted at this pin will generate an Interrupt Request 3 (IRQ3#) (see Programmable Interrupt Controller).

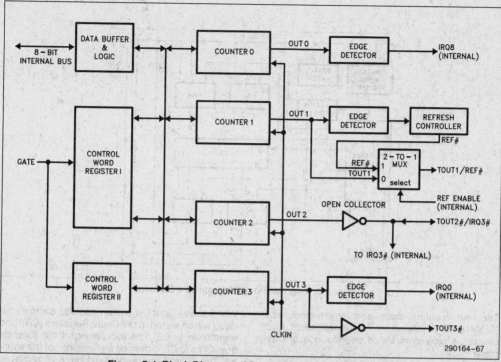

Figure 5-1. Block Diagram of Programmable Interval Timer

TIMER 3—General Purpose/Interrupt Request 0 Generator

The output of Timer 3 is fed to an edge detector and generates an Interrupt Request 0 (IRQ0) in the 82370. The inverted output of this timer (TOUT3#) is also available as an external signal for general purpose use.

5.1.1 INTERNAL ARCHITECTURE

The functional block diagram of the Programmable Interval Timer section is shown in Figure 5-1. Following is a description of each block.

DATA BUFFER & READ/WRITE LOGIC

This part of the Programmable Interval Timer is used to interface the four timers to the 82370 internal bus. The Data Buffer is for transferring commands and data between the 8-bit internal bus and the timers.

The Read/Write Logic accepts inputs from the internal bus and generates signals to control other functional blocks within the timer section.

CONTROL WORD REGISTERS I & II

The Control Word Registers are write-only registers. They are used to control the operating modes of the timers. Control Word Register I controls Timers 0, 1 and 2, and Control Word Register II controls Timer 3. Detailed description of the Control Word Registers will be included in the Register Set Overview section.

COUNTER 0, COUNTER 1, COUNTER 2, COUNTER 3

Counters 0, 1, 2, and 3 are the major parts of Timers 0, 1, 2, and 3, respectively. These four functional blocks are identical in operation, so only a single counter will be described. The internal block diagram of one counter is shown in Figure 5-2.

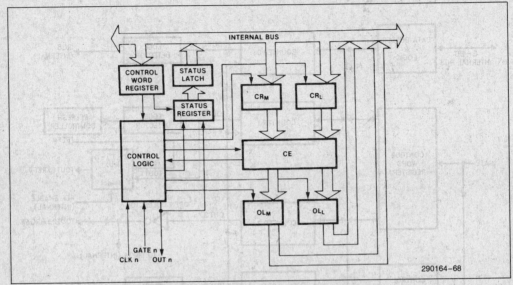

Figure 5-2. Internal Block Diagram of a Counter

The four counters share a common clock input (CLKIN), but otherwise are fully independent. Each counter is programmable to operate in a different mode.

Although the Control Word Register is shown in the figure, it is not part of the counter itself. Its programmed contents are used to control the operations of the counters.

The Status Register, when latched, contains the current contents of the Control Word Register and status of the output and Null Count Flag (see Read Back Command).

The Counting Element (CE) is the actual counter. It is a 16-bit presettable synchronous down counter.

The Output Latches (OL) contain two 8-bit latches (OLM and OLL). Normally, these latches "follow" the content of the CE. OLM contains the most significant byte of the counter and OLL contains the least significant byte. If the Counter Latch Command is sent to the counter, OL will latch the present count until read by the 80376 and then return to follow the CE. One latch at a time is enabled by the timer's Control Logic to drive the internal bus. This is how the 16-bit Counter communicates over the 8-bit internal bus. Note that CE cannot be read. Whenever the count is read, it is one of the OL's that is being read.

When a new count is written into the counter, the value will be stored in the Count Registers (CR), and transferred to CE. The transferring of the contents from CR's to CE is defined as "loading" of the counter. The Count Register contains two 8-bit registers: CRM (which contains the most significant byte) and CRL (which contains the least significant byte). Similar to the OL's, the Control Logic allows one register at a time to be loaded from the 8-bit internal bus. However, both bytes are transferred from the CR's to the CE simultaneously. Both CR's are cleared when the Counter is programmed. This way, if the Counter has been programmed for one byte count (either the most significant or the least significant byte only), the other byte will be zero. Note that CE cannot be written into directly. Whenever a count is written, it is the CR that is being written.

As shown in the diagram, the Control Logic consists of three signals: CLKIN, GATE, and OUT. CLKIN and GATE will be discussed in detail in the section that follows. OUT is the internal output of the counter. The external outputs of some timers (TOUT) are the inverted version of OUT (see TOUT1, TOUT2#, TOUT3#). The state of OUT depends on the mode of operation of the timer.

5.2 Interface Signals

5.2.1 CLKIN

CLKIN is an input signal used by all four timers for internal timing reference. This signal can be independent of the 82370 system clock, CLK2. In the following discussion, each "CLK Pulse" is defined as the time period between a rising edge and a falling edge, in that order, of CLKIN.

During the rising edge of CLKIN, the state of GATE is sampled. All new counts are loaded and counters are decremented on the falling edge of CLKIN.

5.2.2 TOUT1, TOUT2#, TOUT3#

TOUT1, TOUT2# and TOUT3# are the external output signals of Timer 1, Timer 2 and Timer 3, respectively. TOUT2# and TOUT3# are the inverted signals of their respective counter outputs, OUT. There is no external output for Timer 0.

If Timer 2 is to be used as a tone generator of a speaker, external buffering must be used to provide sufficient drive capability.

The Outputs of Timer 2 and 3 are dual function pins. The output pin of Timer 2 (TOUT2#/IRQ3#), which is a bidirectional open-collector signal, can also be used as interrupt request input. When the interrupt function is enabled (through the Programmable Interrupt Controller), a LOW on this input will generate an Interrupt Request 3# to the 82370 Programmable Interrupt Controller. This pin has a weak internal pull-up resistor. To use the IRQ3# function, Timer 2 should be programmed so that OUT2 is LOW. Additionally, OUT3 of Timer 3 is connected to an edge detector which will generate an Interrupt Request 0 (IRQ0) to the 82370 after the rising edge of OUT3 (see Figure 5-1).

5.2.3 GATE

GATE is not an externally controllable signal. Rather, it can be software controlled with the Internal Control Port. The state of GATE is always sampled on the rising edge of CLKIN. Depending on the mode of operation, GATE is used to enable/disable counting or trigger the start of an operation.

For Timer 0 and 1, GATE is always enabled (HIGH). For Timer 2 and 3, GATE is connected to Bit 0 and 6, respectively, of an Internal Control Port (at address 61H) of the 82370. After a hardware reset, the state of GATE of Timer 2 and 3 is disabled (LOW).

5.3 Modes of Operation

Each timer can be independently programmed to operate in one of six different modes. Timers are programmed by writing a Control Word into the Control Word Register followed by an Initial Count (see Programming).

The following are defined for use in describing the different modes of operation.

CLK Pulse— A rising edge, then a falling edge, in that order, of CLKIN.

Trigger— A rising edge of a timer's GATE input.

Timer/Counter Loading— The transfer of a count from Count Register (CR) to Count Element (CE).

5.3.1 MODE 0–INTERRUPT ON TERMINAL COUNT

Mode 0 is typically used for event counting. After the Control Word is written, OUT is initially LOW, and will remain LOW until the counter reaches zero. OUT then goes HIGH and remains HIGH until a new count or a new Mode 0 Control Word is written into the counter.

In this mode, GATE=HIGH enables counting; GATE = LOW disables counting. However, GATE has no effect on OUT.

After the Control Word and initial count are written to a timer, the initial count will be loaded on the next CLK pulse. This CLK pulse does not decrement the count, so for an initial count of N, OUT does not go HIGH until N+1 CLK pulses after the initial count is written.

If a new count is written to the timer, it will be loaded on the next CLK pulse and counting will continue from the new count. If a two-byte count is written, the following happens:

1. Writing the first byte disables counting, OUT is set LOW immediately (i.e. no CLK pulse required).

2. Writing the second byte allows the new count to be loaded on the next CLK pulse.

This allows the counting sequence to be synchronized by software. Again, OUT does not go HIGH until N+1 CLK pulses after the new count of N is written.

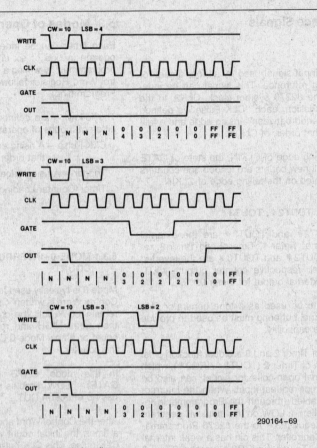

290164−69

NOTES:
The following conventions apply to all mode timing diagrams.
1. Counters are programmed for binary (not BCD) counting and for reading/writing least significant byte (LSB) only.
2. The counter is always selected (CS # always low).
3. CW stands for "Control Word"; CW = 10 means a control word of 10, Hex is written to the counter.
4. LSB stands for "Least significant byte" of count.
5. Numbers below diagrams are count values.
The lower number is the least significant byte.
The upper number is the most significant byte. Since the counter is programmed to read/write LSB only, the most significant byte cannot be read.
N stands for an undefined count.
Vertical lines show transitions between count values.

Figure 5-3. Mode 0

If an initial count is written while GATE is LOW, the counter will be loaded on the next CLK pulse. When GATE goes HIGH, OUT will go HIGH N CLK pulses later; no CLK pulse is needed to load the counter as this has already been done.

5.3.2 MODE 1−GATE RETRIGGERABLE ONE-SHOT

In this mode, OUT will be initially HIGH. OUT will go LOW on the CLK pulse following a trigger to start the one-shot operation. The OUT signal will then remain LOW until the timer reaches zero. At this point, OUT will stay HIGH until the next trigger comes in. Since the state of GATE signals of Timer 0 and 1 are internally set to HIGH.

After writing the Control Word and initial count, the timer is considered "armed". A trigger results in loading the timer and setting OUT LOW on the next CLK pulse. Therefore, an initial count of N will result in a one-shot pulse width of N CLK cycles. Note

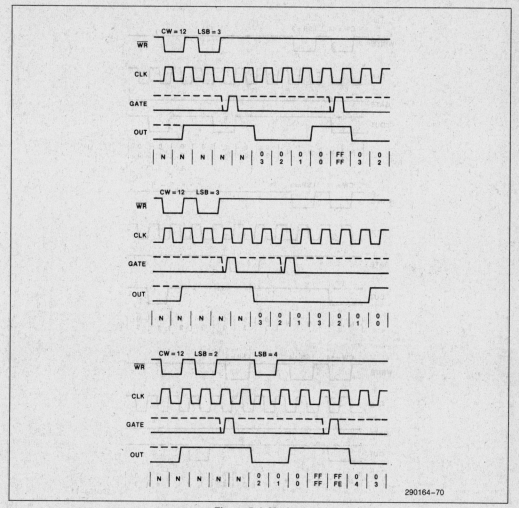

Figure 5-4. Mode 1

that this one-shot operation is retriggerable; i.e. OUT will remain LOW for N CLK pulses after every trigger. The one-shot operation can be repeated without re-writing the same count into the timer.

If a new count is written to the timer during a one-shot operation, the current one-shot pulse width will not be affected until the timer is retriggered. This is because loading of the new count to CE will occur only when the one-shot is triggered.

5.3.3 MODE 2-RATE GENERATOR

This mode is a divide-by-N counter. It is typically used to generate a Real Time Clock interrupt. OUT will initially be HIGH. When the initial count has dec-remented to 1, OUT goes LOW for one CLK pulse, then OUT goes HIGH again. Then the timer reloads the initial count and the process is repeated. In other words, this mode is periodic since the same sequence is repeated itself indefinitely. For an initial count of N, the sequence repeats every N CLK cycles.

Similar to Mode 0, GATE = HIGH enables counting, where GATE = LOW disables counting. If GATE goes LOW during an output pulse (LOW), OUT is set HIGH immediately. A trigger (rising edge on GATE) will reload the timer with the initial count on the next CLK pulse. Then, OUT will go LOW (for one CLK pulse) N CLK pulses after the new trigger. Thus, GATE can be used to synchronize the timer.

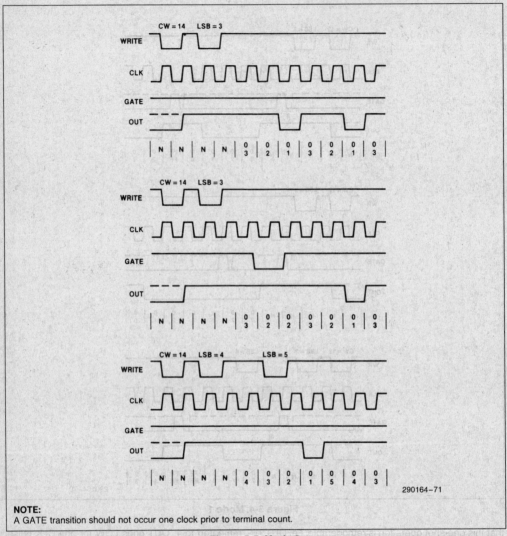

NOTE:
A GATE transition should not occur one clock prior to terminal count.

Figure 5-5. Mode 2

After writing a Control Word and initial count, the timer will be loaded on the next CLK pulse. OUT goes LOW (for one CLK pulse) N CLK pulses after the initial count is written. This is another way the timer may be synchronized by software.

Writing a new count while counting does not affect the current counting sequence because the new count will not be loaded until the end of the current counting cycle. If a trigger is received after writing a new count but before the end of the current period, the timer will be loaded with the new count on the next CLK pulse after the trigger, and counting will continue with the new count.

5.3.4 MODE 3—SQUARE WAVE GENERATOR

Mode 3 is typically used for Baud Rate generation. Functionally, this mode is similar to Mode 2 except for the duty cycle of OUT. In this mode, OUT will be initially HIGH. When half of the initial count has expired, OUT goes low for the remainder of the count. The counting sequence will be repeated, thus this mode is also periodic. Note that an initial count of N results in a square wave with a period of N CLK pulses.

The GATE input can be used to synchronize the timer. GATE = HIGH enables counting; GATE = LOW disables counting. If GATE goes LOW while OUT is LOW, OUT is set HIGH immediately (i.e. no CLK pulse is required). A trigger reloads the timer with the initial count on the next CLK pulse.

After writing a Control Word and initial count, the timer will be loaded on the next CLK pulse. This allows the timer to be synchronized by software.

Writing a new count while counting does not affect the current counting sequence. If a trigger is received after writing a new count but before the end of the current half-cycle of the square wave, the timer will be loaded with the new count on the next CLK pulse and counting will continue from the new count. Otherwise, the new count will be loaded at the end of the current half-cycle.

There is a slight difference in operation depending on whether the initial count is EVEN or ODD. The following description is to show exactly how this mode is implemented.

EVEN COUNTS:

OUT is initially HIGH. The initial count is loaded on one CLK pulse and is decremented by two on succeeding CLK pulses. When the count expires (decremented to 2), OUT changes to LOW and the timer is reloaded with the initial count. The above process is repeated indefinitely.

ODD COUNTS:

OUT is initially HIGH. The initial count minus one (which is an even number) is loaded on one CLK pulse and is decremented by two on succeeding CLK pulses. One CLK pulse after the count expires (decremented to 2), OUT goes LOW and the timer is loaded with the initial count minus one again. Succeeding CLK pulses decrement the count by two. When the count expires, OUT goes HIGH immediately and the timer is reloaded with the initial count minus one. The above process is repeated indefinitely. So for ODD counts, OUT will HIGH or (N + 1)/2 counts and LOW for (N − 1)/2 counts.

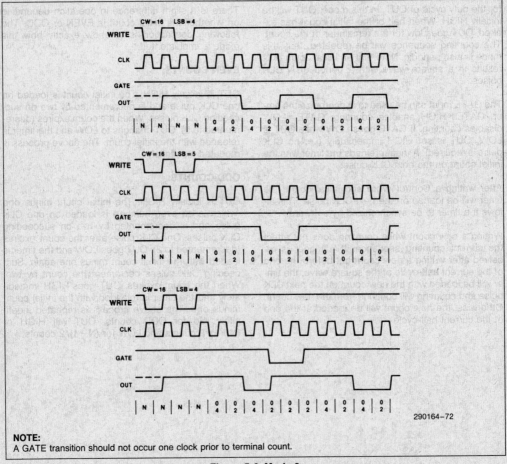

NOTE:
A GATE transition should not occur one clock prior to terminal count.

Figure 5-6. Mode 3

5.3.5 MODE 4-INITIAL COUNT TRIGGERED STROBE

This mode allows a strobe pulse to be generated by writing an initial count to the timer. Initially, OUT will be HIGH. When a new initial count is written into the timer, the counting sequence will begin. When the initial count expires (decremented to 1), OUT will go LOW for one CLK pulse and then go HIGH again.

Again, GATE=HIGH enables counting while GATE = LOW disables counting. GATE has no effect on OUT.

After writing the Control Word and initial count, the timer will be loaded on the next CLK pulse. This CLK pulse does not decrement the count, so for an initial count of N, OUT does not strobe LOW until N+1 CLK pulses after initial count is written.

If a new count is written during counting, it will be loaded in the next CLK pulse and counting will continue from the new count.

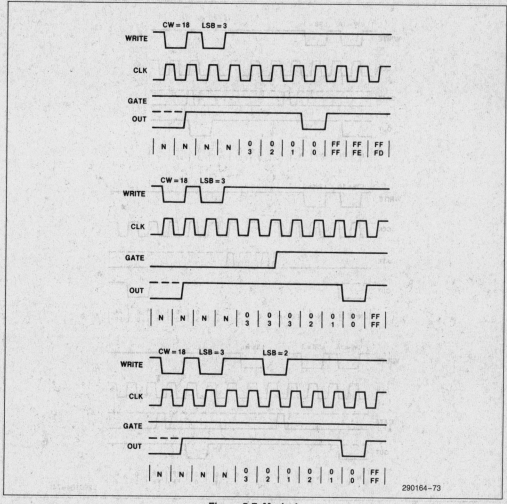

Figure 5-7. Mode 4

If a two-byte count is written, the following will occur:

1. Writing the first byte has no effect on counting.

2. Writing the second byte allows the new count to be loaded on the next CLK pulse.

OUT will strobe LOW N+1 CLK pulses after the new count of N is written. Therefore, when the strobe pulse will occur after a trigger depends on the value of the initial count loaded.

5.3.6 MODE 5—GATE RETRIGGERABLE STROBE

Mode 5 is very similar to Mode 4 except the count sequence is triggered by the gate signal instead of

by writing an initial count. Initially, OUT will be HIGH. Counting is triggered by a rising edge of GATE. When the initial count has expired (decremented to 1), OUT will go LOW for one CLK pulse and then go HIGH again.

After loading the Control Word and initial count, the Count Element will not be loaded until the CLK pulse after a trigger. This CLK pulse does not decrement the count. Therefore, for an initial count of N, OUT does not strobe LOW until N+1 CLK pulses after a trigger.

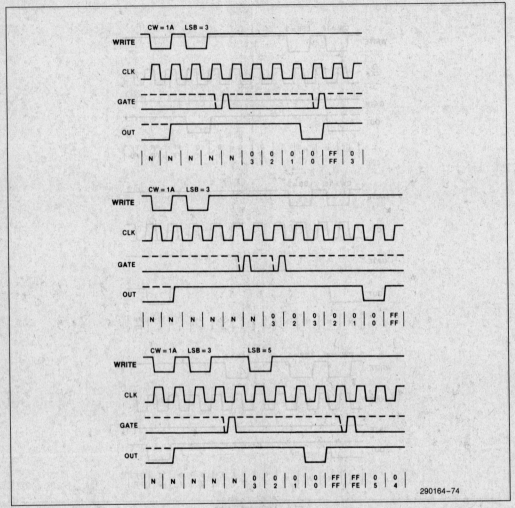

Figure 5-8. Mode 5

The counting sequence is retriggerable. Every trigger will result in the timer being loaded with the initial count on the next CLK pulse.

If the new count is written during counting, the current counting sequence will not be affected. If a trigger occurs after the new count is written but before the current count expires, the timer will be loaded with the new count on the next CLK pulse and a new count sequence will start from there.

5.3.7 OPERATION COMMON TO ALL MODES

5.3.7.1 GATE

The GATE input is always sampled on the rising edge of CLKIN. In Modes 0, 2, 3 and 4, the GATE input is level sensitive. The logic level is sampled on the rising edge of CLKIN. In Modes 1, 2, 3 and 5, the GATE input is rising edge sensitive. In these modes,

Summary of Gate Operations

Mode	GATE LOW or Going LOW	GATE Rising	HIGH
0	Disable count	No Effect	Enable count
1	No Effect	1. Initiate count 2. Reset output after next clock	No Effect
2	1. Disable count 2. Sets output HIGH immediately	Initiate count	Enable count
3	1. Disable count 2. Sets output HIGH immediately	Initiate count	Enable count
4	Disable count	No Effect	Enable count
5	No Effect	Initiate count	No Effect

a rising edge of GATE (trigger) sets an edge sensitive flip-flop in the timer. The flip-flop is reset immediately after it is sampled. This way, a trigger will be detected no matter when it occurs; i.e. a HIGH logic level does not have to be maintained until the next rising edge of CLKIN. Note that in Modes 2 and 3, the GATE input is both edge and level sensitive.

5.3.7.2 Counter

New counts are loaded and counters are decremented on the falling edge of CLKIN. The largest possible initial count is 0. This is equivalent to 2**16 for binary counting and 10**4 for BCD counting.

Note that the counter does not stop when it reaches zero. In Modes 0, 1, 4 and 5, the counter 'wraps around' to the highest count: either FFFF Hex for binary counting or 9999 for BCD counting, and continues counting. Modes 2 and 3 are periodic. The counter reloads itself with the initial count and continues counting from there.

The minimum and maximum initial count in each counter depends on the mode of operation. They are summarized below.

Mode	Min	Max
0	1	0
1	1	0
2	2	0
3	2	0
4	1	0
5	1	0

5.4 Register Set Overview

The Programmable Interval Timer module of the 82370 contains a set of six registers. The port address map of these registers is shown in Table 5-2.

Table 5-2. Timer Register Port Address Map

Port Address	Description
40H	Counter 0 Register (read/write)
41H	Counter 1 Register (read/write)
42H	Counter 2 Register (read/write)
43H	Control Word Register I (Counter 0, 1 & 2) (write-only)
44H	Counter 3 Register (read/write)
45H	Reserved
46H	Reserved
47H	Control Word Register II (Counter 3) (write-only)

5.4.1 COUNTER 0, 1, 2, 3 REGISTER

These four 8-bit registers are functionally identical. They are used to write the initial count value into the respective timer. Also, they can be used to read the latched count value of a timer. Since they are 8-bit registers, reading and writing of the 16-bit initial count must follow the count format specified in the Control Word Registers; i.e. least significant byte only, most significant byte only, or least significant byte then most significant byte (see Programming).

5.4.2 CONTROL WORD REGISTER I & II

There are two Control Word Registers associated with the Timer section. One of the two registers (Control Word Register I) is used to control the operations of Counters 0, 1 and 2 and the other (Control Word Register II) is for Counter 3. The major functions of both Control Word Registers are listed below:

— Select the timer to be programmed.

— Define which mode the selected timer is to operate in.

— Define the count sequence; i.e. if the selected timer is to count as a Binary Counter or a Binary Coded Decimal (BCD) Counter.

— Select the byte access sequence during timer read/write operations; i.e. least significant byte only, most significant only, or least significant byte first, then most significant byte.

Also, the Control Word Registers can be programmed to perform a Counter Latch Command or a Read Back Command which will be described later.

5.5 Programming

5.5.1 INITIALIZATION

Upon power-up or reset, the state of all timers is undefined. The mode, count value, and output of all timers are random. From this point on, how each timer operates is determined solely by how it is programmed. Each timer must be programmed before it can be used. Since the outputs of some timers can generate interrupt signals to the 82370, all timers should be initialized to a known state.

Counters are programmed by writing a Control Word into their respective Control Word Registers. Then, an Initial Count can be written into the corresponding Count Register. In general, the programming procedure is very flexible. Only two conventions need to be remembered:

1. For each timer, the Control Word must be written before the initial count is written.

2. The 16-bit initial count must follow the count format specified in the Control Word (least significant byte only, most significant byte only, or least significant byte first, followed by most significant byte).

Since the two Control Word Registers and the four Counter Registers have separate addresses, and each timer can be individually selected by the appropriate Control Word Register, no special instruction sequence is required. Any programming sequence that follows the conventions above is acceptable.

A new initial count may be written to a timer at any time without affecting the timer's programmed mode in any way. Count sequence will be affected as described in the Modes of Operation section. Note that the new count must follow the programmed count format.

If a timer is previously programmed to read/write two-byte counts, the following precaution applies. A program must not transfer control between writing the first and second byte to another routine which also writes into the same timer. Otherwise, the read/write will result in incorrect count.

Whenever a Control Word is written to a timer, all control logic for that timer(s) is immediately reset (i.e. no CLK pulse is required). Also, the corresponding output in, TOUT#, goes to a known initial state.

5.5.2 READ OPERATION

Three methods are available to read the current count as well as the status of each timer. They are: Read Counter Registers, Counter Latch Command and Read Back Command. Below is a description of these methods.

READ COUNTER REGISTERS

The current count of a timer can be read by performing a read operation on the corresponding Counter Register. The only restriction of this read operation is that the CLKIN of the timers must be inhibited by using external logic. Otherwise, the count may be in the process of changing when it is read, giving an undefined result. Note that since all four timers are sharing the same CLKIN signal, inhibiting CLKIN to read a timer will unavoidably disable the other timers also. This may prove to be impractical. Therefore, it is suggested that either the Counter Latch Command or the Read Back Command can be used to read the current count of a timer.

Another alternative is to temporarily disable a timer before reading its Counter Register by using the GATE input. Depending on the mode of operation, GATE=LOW will disable the counting operation. However, this option is available on Timer 2 and 3 only, since the GATE signals of the other two timers are internally enabled all the time.

COUNTER LATCH COMMAND

A Counter Latch Command will be executed whenever a special Control Word is written into a Control Word Register. Two bits written into the Control Word Register distinguish this command from a 'regular' Control Word (see Register Bit Definition). Also, two other bits in the Control Word will select which counter is to be latched.

Upon execution of this command, the selected counter's Output Latch (OL) latches the count at the time the Counter Latch Command is received. This count is held in the latch until it is read by the 80376, or until the timer is reprogrammed. The count is then unlatched automatically and the OL returns to "following" the Counting Element (CE). This allows reading the contents of the counters "on the fly" without affecting counting in progress. Multiple Counter Latch Commands may be used to latch more than one counter. Each latched count is held until it is read. Counter Latch Commands do not affect the programmed mode of the timer in any way.

If a counter is latched, and at some time later, it is latched again before the prior latched count is read, the second Counter Latch Command is ignored. The count read will then be the count at the time the first command was issued.

In any event, the latched count must be read according to the programmed format. Specifically, if the timer is programmed for two-byte counts, two bytes must be read. However, the two bytes do not have to be read right after the other. Read/write or programming operations of other timers may be performed between them.

Another feature of this Counter Latch Command is that read and write operations of the same timer may be interleaved. For example, if the timer is programmed for two-byte counts, the following sequence is valid.

1. Read least significant byte.
2. Write new least significant byte.
3. Read most significant byte.
4. Write new most significant byte.

If a timer is programmed to read/write two-byte counts, the following precaution applies. A program must not transfer control between reading the first and second byte to another routine which also reads from that same timer. Otherwise, an incorrect count will be read.

READ BACK COMMAND

The Read Back Command is another special Command Word operation which allows the user to read the current count value and/or the status of the selected timer(s). Like the Counter Latch Command, two bits in the Command Word identify this as a Read Back Command (see Register Bit Definition).

The Read Back Command may be used to latch multiple counter Output Latches (OL's) by selecting more than one timer within a Command Word. This single command is functionally equivalent to several Counter Latch Commands, one for each counter to

be latched. Each counter's latched count will be held until it is read by the 80376 or until the timer is reprogrammed. The counter is automatically unlatched when read, but other counters remain latched until they are read. If multiple Read Back commands are issued to the same timer without reading the count, all but the first are ignored; i.e. the count read will correspond to the very first Read Back Command issued.

As mentioned previously, the Read Back Command may also be used to latch status information of the selected timer(s). When this function is enabled, the status of a timer can be read from the Counter Register after the Read Back Command is issued. The status information of a timer includes the following:

1. Mode of timer:

   This allows the user to check the mode of operation of the timer last programmed.

2. State of TOUT pin of the timer:

   This allows the user to monitor the counter's output pin via software, possibly eliminating some hardware from a system.

3. Null Count/Count available:

   The Null Count Bit in the status byte indicates if the last count written to the Count Register (CR) has been loaded into the Counting Element (CE). The exact time this happens depends on the mode of the timer and is described in the Programming section. Until the count is loaded into the Counting Element (CE), it cannot be read from the timer. If the count is latched or read before this occurs, the count value will not reflect the new count just written.

If multiple status latch operations of the timer(s) are performed without reading the status, all but the first command are ignored; i.e. the status read in will correspond to the first Read Back Command issued.

Both the current count and status of the selected timer(s) may be latched simultaneously by enabling both functions in a single Read Back Command. This is functionally the same as issuing two separate Read Back Commands at once. Once again, if multiple read commands are issued to latch both the count and status of a timer, all but the first command will be ignored.

If both count and status of a timer are latched, the first read operation of that timer will return the latched status, regardless of which was latched first. The next one or two (if two count bytes are to be read) read operations return the latched count. Note that subsequent read operations on the Counter Register will return the unlatched count (like the first read method discussed).

5.6 Register Bit Definitions

COUNTER 0, 1, 2, 3 REGISTER (READ/WRITE)

Port Address	Description
40H	Counter 0 Register (read/write)
41H	Counter 1 Register (read/write)
42H	Counter 2 Register (read/write)
44H	Counter 3 Register (read/write)
45H	Reserved
46H	Reserved

Note that these 8-bit registers are for writing and reading of one byte of the 16-bit count value, either the most significant or the least significant byte.

CONTROL WORD REGISTER I & II (WRITE-ONLY)

Port Address	Description
43H	Control Word Register I (Counter 0, 1, 2 (write-only)
47H	Control Word Register II (Counter 3) (write-only)

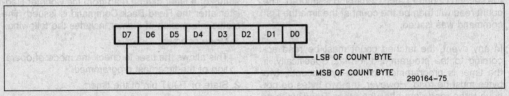

290164–75

Control Word Register I

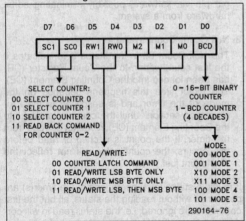

290164–76

Control Word Register II

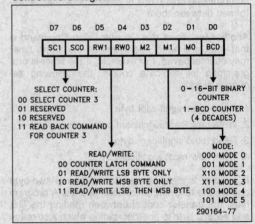

290164–77

COUNTER LATCH COMMAND FORMAT

(Write to Control Word Register)

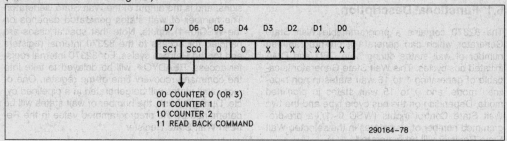

D7	D6	D5	D4	D3	D2	D1	D0
SC1	SC0	0	0	X	X	X	X

00 COUNTER 0 (OR 3)
01 COUNTER 1
10 COUNTER 2
11 READ BACK COMMAND

290164-78

READ BACK COMMAND FORMAT

(Write to Control Word Register)

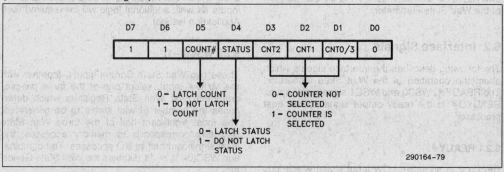

D7	D6	D5	D4	D3	D2	D1	D0
1	1	COUNT#	STATUS	CNT2	CNT1	CNT0/3	0

0 — LATCH COUNT
1 — DO NOT LATCH COUNT

0 — LATCH STATUS
1 — DO NOT LATCH STATUS

0 — COUNTER NOT SELECTED
1 — COUNTER IS SELECTED

290164-79

STATUS FORMAT

(Returned from Read Back Command)

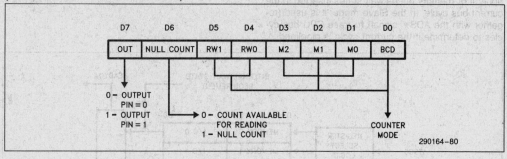

D7	D6	D5	D4	D3	D2	D1	D0
OUT	NULL COUNT	RW1	RW0	M2	M1	M0	BCD

0 — OUTPUT PIN = 0
1 — OUTPUT PIN = 1

0 — COUNT AVAILABLE FOR READING
1 — NULL COUNT

COUNTER MODE

290164-80

6.0 WAIT STATE GENERATOR

6.1 Functional Description

The 82370 contains a programmable Wait State Generator which can generate a pre-programmed number of wait states during both CPU and DMA initiated bus cycles. This Wait State Generator is capable of generating 1 to 16 wait states in non-pipelined mode, and 0 to 15 wait states in pipelined mode. Depending on the bus cycle type and the two Wait State Control inputs (WSC 0-1), a pre-programmed number of wait states in the selected Wait State Register will be generated.

The Wait State Generator can also be disabled to allow the use of devices capable of generating their own READY# signals. Figure 6-1 is a block diagram of the Wait State Generator.

6.2 Interface Signals

The following describes the interface signals which affect the operation of the Wait State Generator. The READY#, WSC0 and WSC1 signals are inputs. READYO# is the ready output signal to the host processor.

6.2.1 READY#

READY# is an active LOW input signal which indicates to the 82370 the completion of a bus cycle. In the Master mode (e.g. 82370 initiated DMA transfer), this signal is monitored to determine whether a peripheral or memory needs wait states inserted in the current bus cycle. In the Slave mode, it is used (together with the ADS# signal) to trace CPU bus cycles to determine if the current cycle is pipelined.

6.2.2 READYO#

READYO# (Ready Out#) is an active LOW output signal and is the output of the Wait State Generator. The number of wait states generated depends on the WSC(0-1) inputs. Note that special cases are handled for access to the 82370 internal registers and for the Refresh cycles. For 82370 internal register access, READYO# will be delayed to take into the command recovery time of the register. One or more wait states will be generated in a pipelined cycle. During refresh, the number of wait states will be determined by the preprogrammed value in the Refresh Wait State Register.

In the simplest configuration, READYO# can be connected to the READY# input of the 82370 and the 80376 CPU. This is, however, not always the case. If external circuitry is to control the READY# inputs as well, additional logic will be required (see Application Issues).

6.2.3 WSC(0-1)

These two Wait State Control inputs, together with the M/IO# input, select one of the three pre-programmed 8-bit Wait State Registers which determines the number of wait states to be generated. The most significant half of the three Wait State Registers corresponds to memory accesses, the least significant half to I/O accesses. The combination WSC(0-1) = 11 disables the Wait State Generator.

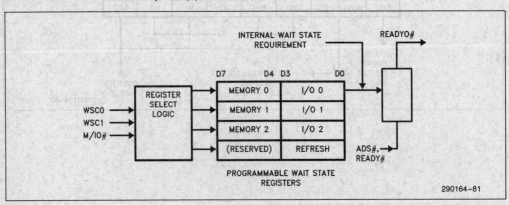

Figure 6-1. Wait State Generator Block Diagram

6.3 Bus Function

6.3.1 WAIT STATES IN NON-PIPELINED CYCLE

The timing diagram of two typical non-pipelined cycles with 82370 generated wait states is shown in Figure 6-2. In this diagram, it is assumed that the internal registers of the 82370 are not addressed. During the first T2 state of each bus cycle, the Wait State Control and the M/IO# inputs are sampled to determine which Wait State Register (if any) is selected. If the WSC inputs are active (i.e. not both are driven HIGH), the pre-programmed number of wait states corresponding to the selected Wait State Register will be requested. This is done by driving the READYO# output HIGH during the end of each T2 state.

The WSC (0–1) inputs need only be valid during the very first T2 state of each non-pipelined cycle. As a general rule, the WSC inputs are sampled on the rising edge of the next clock (82384 CLK) after the last state when ADS# (Address Status) is asserted.

The number of wait states generated depends on the type of bus cycle, and the number of wait states requested. The various combinations are discussed below.

1. Access the 82370 internal registers: 2 to 5 wait states, depending upon the specific register addressed. Some back-to-back sequences to the Interrupt Controller will require 7 wait states.

2. Interrupt Acknowledge to the 82370: 5 wait states.

3. Refresh: As programmed in the Refresh Wait State Register (see Register Set Overview). Note that if WCS (0–1) = 11, READYO# will stay inactive.

4. Other bus cycles: Depending on WCS (0–1) and M/IO# inputs, these inputs select a Wait State Register in which the number of wait states will be equal to the pre-programmed wait state count in the register plus 1. The Wait State Register selection is defined as follows (Table 6-1).

Table 6-1. Wait State Register Selection

M/IO#	WSC(0–1)	Register Selected
0	00	WAIT REG 0 (I/O half)
0	01	WAIT REG 1 (I/O half)
0	10	WAIT REG 2 (I/O half)
1	00	WAIT REG 0 (MEM half)
1	01	WAIT REG 1 (MEM half)
1	10	WAIT REG 2 (MEM half)
X	11	Wait State Gen. Disabled

The Wait State Control signals, WSC (0–1), can be generated with the address decode and the Read/Write control signals as shown in Figure 6-3.

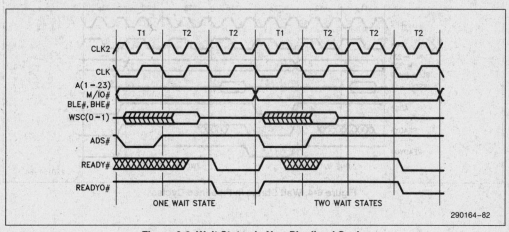

Figure 6-2. Wait States in Non-Pipelined Cycles

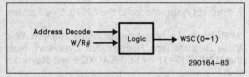

Figure 6-3. WSC (0–1) Generation

Note that during HALT and SHUTDOWN, the number of wait states will depend on the WSC (0–1) inputs, which will select the memory half of one of the Wait State Registers (see CPU Reset and Shutdown Detect).

6.3.2 WAIT STATES IN PIPELINED CYCLES

The timing diagram of two typical pipelined cycles with 82370 generated wait states is shown in Figure 6-4. Again, in this diagram, it is assumed that the 82370 internal registers are not addressed. As defined in the timing of the 80376 processor, the Address (A1–23), Byte Enable (BHE#, BLE#), and other control signals (M/IO#, ADS#) are asserted one T-state earlier than in a non-pipelined cycle; i.e. they are asserted at T2P. Similar to the non-pipelined case, the Wait State Control (WSC) inputs are sampled in the middle of the state after the last state the ADS# signal is asserted. Therefore, the WSC inputs should be asserted during the T1P state of each pipelined cycle (which is one T-state earlier than in the non-pipelined cycle).

The number of wait states generated in a pipelined cycle is selected in a similar manner as in the non-pipelined case discussed in the previous section. The only difference here is that the actual number of wait states generated will be one less than that of the non-pipelined cycle. This is done automatically by the Wait State Generator.

6.3.3 EXTENDING AND EARLY TERMINATING BUS CYCLE

The 82370 allows external logic to either add wait states or cause early termination of a bus cycle by controlling the READY# input to the 82370 and the host processor. A possible configuration is shown in Figure 6-5.

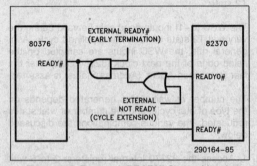

Figure 6-5. External 'READY' Control Logic

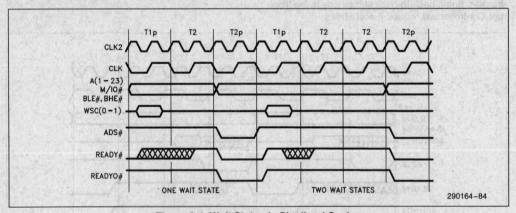

Figure 6-4. Wait States in Pipelined Cycles

The EXT. RDY# (External Ready) signal of Figure 6-5 allows external devices to cause early termination of a bus cycle. When this signal is asserted LOW, the output of the circuit will also go LOW (even though the READYO# of the 82370 may still be HIGH). This output is fed to the READY# input of the 80376 and the 82370 to indicate the completion of the current bus cycle.

Similarly, the EXT. NOT READY (External Not Ready) signal is used to delay the READY# input of the processor and the 82370. As long as this signal is driven HIGH, the output of the circuit will drive the READY# input HIGH. This will effectively extend the duration of a bus cycle. However, it is important to note that if the two-level logic is not fast enough to satisfy the READY# setup time, the OR gate should be eliminated. Instead, the 82370 Wait State Generator can be disabled by driving both WSC (0-1) HIGH. In this case, the addressed memory or I/O device should activate the external READY# input whenever it is ready to terminate the current bus cycle.

Figures 6-6 and 6-7 show the timing relationships of the ready signals for the early termination and extension of the bus cycles. Section 6-7, Application Issues, contains a detailed timing analysis of the external circuit.

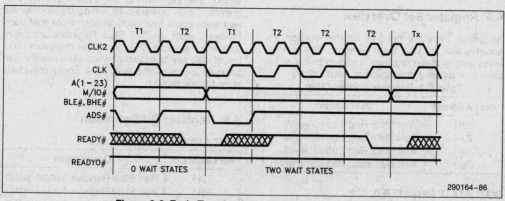

Figure 6-6. Early Termination of Bus Cycle By 'READY#'

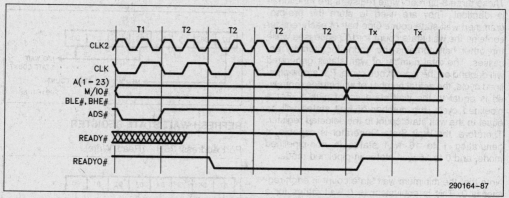

Figure 6-7. Extending Bus Cycle by 'READY#'

Due to the following implications, it should be noted that early termination of bus cycles in which 82370 internal registers are accessed is not recommended.

1. Erroneous data may be read from or written into the addressed register.

2. The 82370 must be allowed to recover either before HLDA (Hold Acknowledge) is asserted or before another bus cycle into an 82370 internal register is initiated.

The recovery time, in clock periods, equals the remaining wait states that were avoided plus 4.

6.4 Register Set Overview

Altogether, there are four 8-bit internal registers associated with the Wait State Genertor. The port address map of these registers is shown below in Table 6-2. A detailed description of each follows.

Table 6-2. Register Address Map

Port Address	Description
72H	Wait State Reg 0 (read/write)
73H	Wait State Reg 1 (read/write)
74H	Wait State Reg 2 (read/write)
75H	Ref. Wait State Reg (read/write)

WAIT STATE REGISTER 0, 1, 2

These three 8-bit read/write registers are functionally identical. They are used to store the pre-programmed wait state count. One half of each register contains the wait state count for I/O accesses while the other half contains the count for memory accesses. The total number of wait states generated will depend on the type of bus cycle. For a non-pipelined cycle, the actual number of wait states requested is equal to the wait state count plus 1. For a pipelined cycle, the number of wait states will be equal to the wait state count in the selected register. Therefore, the Wait State Generator is capable of generating 1 to 16 wait states in non-pipelined mode, and 0 to 15 wait states in pipelined mode.

Note that the minimum wait state count in each register is 0. This is equivalent to 0 wait states for a pipelined cycle and 1 wait state for a non-pipelined cycle.

REFRESH WAIT STATE REGISTER

Similar to the Wait State Registers discussed above, this 4-bit register is used to store the number of wait states to be generated during a DRAM refresh cycle.

Note that the Refresh Wait State Register is not selected by the WSC inputs. It will automatically be chosen whenever a DRAM refresh cycle occurs. If the Wait State Generator is disabled during the refresh cycle (WSC (0–1) = 11), READYO# will stay inactive and the Refresh Wait State Register is ignored.

6.5 Programming

Using the Wait State Generator is relatively straightforward. No special programming sequence is required. In order to ensure the expected number of wait states will be generated when a register is selected, the registers to be used must be programmed after power-up by writing the appropriate wait state count into each register. Note that upon hardware reset, all Wait State Registers are initialized with the value FFH, giving the maximum number of wait states possible. Also, each register can be read to check the wait state count previously stored in the register.

6.6 Register Bit Definition

WAIT STATE REGISTER 0, 1, 2

Port Address	Description
72H	Wait State Register 0 (read/write)
73H	Wait State Register 1 (read/write)
74H	Wait State Register 2 (read/write)

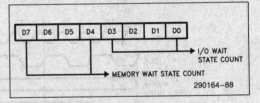

REFRESH WAIT STATE REGISTER

Port Address: 75H   (Read/Write)

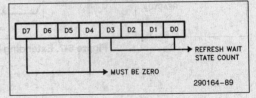

6.7 Application Issues

6.7.1 EXTERNAL 'READY' CONTROL LOGIC

As mentioned in section 6.3.3, wait state cycles generated by the 82370 can be terminated early or extended longer by means of additional external logic (see Figure 6-5). In order to ensure that the READY# input timing requirement of the 80376 and the 82370 is satisfied, special care must be taken when designing this external control logic. This section addresses the design requirements.

A simplified block diagram of the external logic along with the READY# timing diagram is shown in Figure 6-8. The purpose is to determine the maximum delay

time allowed in the external control logic in order to satisfy the READY# setup time.

First, it will be assumed that the 80376 is running at 16 MHz (i.e. CLK2 is 32 MHz). Therefore, one bus state (two CLK2 periods) will be equivalent to 62.5 ns. According to the AC specifications of the 82370, the maximum delay time for valid READYO# signal is 31 ns after the rising edge of CLK2 in the beginning of T2 (for non-pipelined cycle) or T2P (for pipelined cycle). Also, the minimum READY# setup time of the 80376 and the 82370 should be 19 ns before the rising edge of CLK2 at the beginning of the next bus state. This limits the total delay time for the external READY# control logic to be 12.5 ns (62.5−31−19) in order to meet the READY# setup timing requirement.

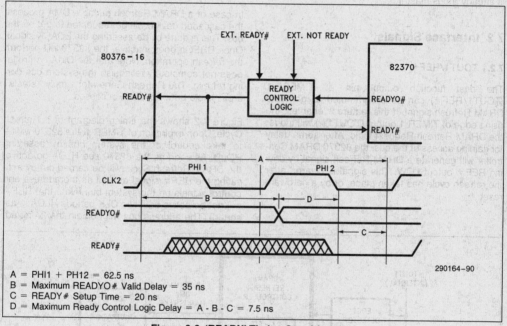

A = PHI1 + PH12 = 62.5 ns
B = Maximum READYO# Valid Delay = 35 ns
C = READY# Setup Time = 20 ns
D = Maximum Ready Control Logic Delay = A - B - C = 7.5 ns

290164-90

Figure 6-8. 'READY' Timing Consideration

7.0 DRAM REFRESH CONTROLLER

7.1 Functional Description

The 82370 DRAM Refresh Controller consists of a 24-bit Refresh Address Counter and Refresh Request logic for DRAM refresh operations (see Figure 7-1). TIMER 1 can be used as a trigger signal to the DRAM Refresh Request logic. The Refresh Bus Size can be programmed to be 8- or 16-bit wide. Depending on the Refresh Bus Size, the Refresh Address Counter will be incremented with the appropriate value after every refresh cycle. The internal logic of the 82370 will give the Refresh operation the highest priority in the bus control arbitration process. Bus control is not released and re-requested if the 82370 is already a bus master.

7.2 Interface Signals

7.2.1 TOUT1/REF#

The dual function output pin of TIMER 1 (TOUT1/REF#) can be programmed to generate DRAM Refresh signal. If this feature is enabled, the rising edge of TIMER 1 output (TOUT1#) will trigger the DRAM Refresh Request logic. After some delay for gaining access of the bus, the 82370 DRAM Controller will generate a DRAM Refresh signal by driving REF# output LOW. This signal is cleared after the refresh cycle has taken place, or by a hardware reset.

If the DRAM Refresh feature is disabled, the TOUT1/REF# output pin is simply the TIMER 1 output. Detailed information of how TIMER 1 operates is discussed in section 6—Programmable Interval Timer, and will not be repeated here.

7.3 Bus Function

7.3.1 ARBITRATION

In order to ensure data integrity of the DRAMs, the 82370 gives the DRAM Refresh signal the highest priority in the arbitration logic. It allows DRAM Refresh to interrupt DMA in progress in order to perform the DRAM Refresh cycle. The DMA service will be resumed after the refresh is done.

In case of a DRAM Refresh during a DMA process, the cascaded device will be requested to get off the bus. This is done by de-asserting the EDACK signal. Once DREQn goes inactive, the 82370 will perform the refresh operation. Note that the DMA controller does not completely relinquish the system bus during refresh. The Refresh Generator simply "steals" a bus cycle between DMA accesses.

Figure 7-2 shows the timing diagram of a Refresh Cycle. Upon expiration of TIMER 1, the 82370 will try to take control of the system bus by asserting HOLD. As soon as the 82370 see HLDA go active, the DRAM Refresh Cycle will be carried out by activating the REF# signal as well as the address and control signals on the system bus (Note that REF# will not be active until two CLK periods HLDA is asserted). The address bus will contain the 24-bit ad-

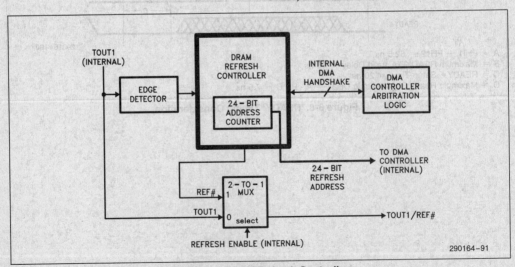

Figure 7-1. DRAM Refresh Controller

dress currently in the Refresh Address Counter. The control signals are driven the same way as in a Memory Read cycle. This "read" operation is complete when the READY# signal is driven LOW. Then, the 82370 will relinquish the bus by de-asserting HOLD. Typically, a Refresh Cycle without wait states will take five bus states to execute. If "n" wait states are added, the Refresh Cycle will last for five plus "n" bus states.

How often the Refresh Generator will initiate a refresh cycle depends on the frequency of CLKIN as will as TIMER 1's programmed mode of operation. For this specific application, TIMER 1 should be programmed to operate in Mode 2 to generate a constant clock rate. See section 6—Programmable Interval Timer for more information on programming the timer. One DRAM Refresh Cycle will be generated each time TIMER 1 expires (when TOUT1 changes from LOW to HIGH).

The Wait State Generator can be used to insert wait states during a refresh cycle. The 82370 will automatically insert the desired number of wait states as programmed in the Refresh Wait State Register (see Wait State Generator).

7.4 Modes of Operation

7.4.1 WORD SIZE AND REFRESH ADDRESS COUNTER

The 82370 supports 8- and 16-bit refresh cycle. The bus width during a refresh cycle is programmable (see Programming). The bus size can be programmed via the Refresh Control Register (see Register Overview). If the DRAM bus size is 8- or 16-bits, the Refresh Address Counter will be incremented by 1 or 2, respectively.

The Refresh Address Counter is cleared by a hardware reset.

7.5 Register Set Overview

The Refresh Generator has two internal registers to control its operation. They are the Refresh Control Register and the Refresh Wait State Register. Their port address map is shown in Table 7-1 below.

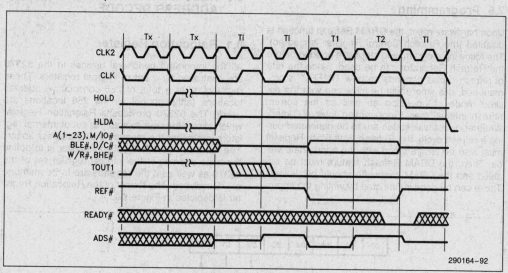

Figure 7-2. 82370 Refresh Cycle

290164-92

Table 7-1. Register Address Map

Port Address	Description
1CH	Refresh Control Reg. (read/write)
75H	Ref. Wait State Reg. (read/write)

The Refresh Wait State Register is not part of the Refresh Generator. It is only used to program the number of wait states to be inserted during a refresh cycle. This register is discussed in detailed in section 7 (Wait State Generator) and will not be repeated here.

REFRESH CONTROL REGISTER

This 2-bit register serves two functions. First, it is used to enable/disable the DRAM Refresh function output. If disabled, the output of TIMER 1 is simply used as a general purpose timer. The second function of this register is to program the DRAM bus size for the refresh operation. The programmed bus size also determines how the Refresh Address Counter will be incremented after each refresh operation.

7.6 Programming

Upon hardware reset, the DRAM Refresh function is disabled (the Refresh Control Register is cleared). The following programming steps are needed before the Refresh Generator can be used. Since the rate of refresh cycles depends on how TIMER 1 is programmed, this timer must be initialized with the desired mode of operation as well as the correct refresh interval (see Programming Interval Timer). Whether or not wait states are to be generated during a refresh cycle, the Refresh Wait State Register must also be programmed with the appropriate value. Then, the DRAM Refresh feature must be enabled and the DRAM bus width should be defined. These can be done in one step by writing the appro-

priate control word into the Refresh Control Register (see Register Bit Definition). After these steps are done, the refresh operation will automatically be invoked by the Refresh Generator upon expiration of Timer 1.

In addition to the above programming steps, it should be noted that after reset, although the TOUT1/REF# becomes the Time 1 output, the state of this pin in undefined. This is because the Timer module has not been initialized yet. Therefore, if this output is used as a DRAM Refresh signal, this pin should be disqualified by external logic until the Refresh function is enabled. One simple solution is to logically AND this output with HLDA, since HLDA should not be active after reset.

7.7 Register Bit Definition

REFRESH CONTROL REGISTER

Port Address: 1CH   (Read/Write)

8.0 RELOCATION REGISTER AND ADDRESS DECODE

8.1 Relocation Register

All the integrated peripheral devices in the 82370 are controlled by a set of internal registers. These registers span a total of 256 consecutive address locations (although not all the 256 locations are used). The 82370 provides a Relocation Register which allows the user to map this set of internal registers into either the memory or I/O address space. The function of the Relocation Register is to define the base address of the internal register set of the 82370 as well as if the registers are to be memory- or I/O-mapped. The format of the Relocation Register is depicted in Figure 9-1.

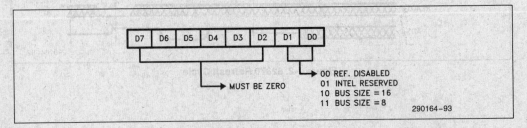

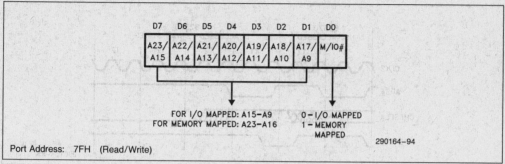

Port Address: 7FH (Read/Write)

290164-94

Figure 8-1. Relocation Register

Note that the Relocation Register is part of the internal register set of the 82370. It has a port address of 7FH. Therefore, any time the content of the Relocation Register is changed, the physical location of this register will also be moved. Upon reset of the 82370, the content of the Relocation Register will be cleared. This implies that the 82370 will respond to its I/O addresses in the range of 0000H to 00FFH.

8.1.1 I/O-MAPPED 82370

As shown in the figure, Bit 0 of the Relocation Register determines whether the 82370 registers are to be memory-mapped or I/O mapped. When Bit 0 is set to '0', the 82370 will respond to I/O Addresses. Address signals BHE#, BLE#, A1–A7 will be used to select one of the internal registers to be accessed. Bit 1 to Bit 7 of the Relocation Register will correspond to A9 to A15 of the Address bus, respectively. Together with A8 implied to be '0', A15 to A8 will be fully decoded by the 82370. The following shows how the 82370 is mapped into the I/O address space.

Example

Relocation Register = 11001110 (0CEH)

82370 will respond to I/O address range from 0CE00H to 0CEFFH.

Therefore, this I/O mapping mechanism allows the 82370 internal registers to be located on any even, contiguous, 256 byte boundary of the system I/O space.

8.1.2 MEMORY-MAPPED 82370

When Bit 0 of the Relocation Register is set to '1', the 82370 will respond to memory addresses. Again,

Address signals BHE#, BLE#, A1–A7 will be used to select one of the internal registers to be accessed. Bit 1 to Bit 7 of the Relocation Register will correspond to A17–A23, respectively. A16 is assumed to be '0', and A8–A15 are ignored. Consider the following example.

Example

Relocation Register = 10100111 (0A7H)

The 82370 will respond to memory addresses in the range of A6XX00H to A60XXFFH (where 'X' is don't care).

This scheme implies that the internal registers can be located in any even, contiguous, 2**16 byte page of the memory space.

8.2 Address Decoding

As mentioned previously, the 82370 internal registers do not occupy the entire contiguous 256 address locations. Some of the locations are 'unoccupied'. The 82370 always decodes the lower 8 address signals (BHE#, BLE#, A1–A7) to determine if any one of its registers is being accessed. If the address does not correspond to any of its registers, the 82370 will not respond. This allows external devices to be located within the 'holes' in the 82370 address space. Note that there are several unused addresses reserved for future Intel peripheral devices.

8.3 Chip-Select (CHPSEL#)

The Chip-Select signal (CHPSEL#) will go active when the 82370 is addressed in a Slave bus

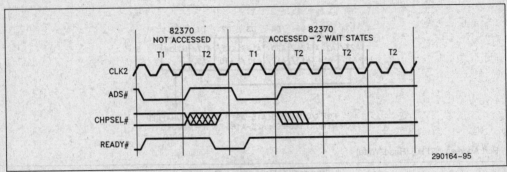

Figure 8-2. CHPSEL# Timing

cycle (either read or write), or in an interrupt acknowledge cycle in which the 82370 will drive the Data Bus. For a given bus cycle, CHPSEL# becomes active and valid in the first T2 (in a non-pipelined cycle) or in T1P (in a pipelined cycle). It will stay valid until the cycle is terminated by READY# driven active. As CHPSEL# becomes valid well before the 82370 drives the Data Bus, it can be used to control the transceivers that connect the local CPU bus to the system bus. The timing diagram of CHPSEL# is shown in Figure 8-2.

9.0 CPU RESET AND SHUTDOWN DETECT

The 82370 will activate the CPURST signal to reset the host processor when one of the following conditions occurs:

— 82370 RESET is active;

— 82370 detects a 80376 Shutdown cycle (this feature can be disabled);

— CPURST software command is issued to 80376.

Whenever the CPURST signal is activated, the 82370 will reset its own internal Slave-Bus state machine.

9.1 Hardware Reset

Following a hardware reset, the 82370 will assert its CPURST output to reset the host processor. This output will stay active for as long as the RESET input is active. During a hardware reset, the 82370 internal registers will be initialized as defined in the corresponding functional descriptions.

9.2 Software Reset

CPURST can be generated by writing the following bit pattern into 82370 register location 64H.

$$D7 \quad . \quad . \quad . \quad D0$$
$$1 \; 1 \; 1 \; 1 \; X \; X \; X \; 0$$

The Write operation into this port is considered as an 82370 access and the internal Wait State Generator will automatically determine the required number of wait states. The CPURST will be active following the completion of the Write cycle to this port. This signal will last for 62 CLK2 periods. The 82370 should not be accessed until the CPURST is deactivated.

This internal port is Write-Only and the 82370 will not respond to a Read operation to this location. Also, during a software reset command, the 82370 will reset its Slave-Bus state machine. However, its internal registers remain unchanged. This allows the operating system to distinguish a 'warm' reset by reading any 82370 internal register previously programmed for a non-default value. The Diagnostic registers can be used for this purpose (see Internal Control and Diagnostic Ports).

9.3 Shutdown Detect

The 82370 is constantly monitoring the Bus Cycle Definition signals (M/IO#, D/C#, W/R#) and is able to detect when the 80376 is in a Shutdown bus cycle. Upon detection of a processor shutdown, the 82370 will activate the CPURST output for 62 CLK2 periods to reset the host processor. This signal is generated after the Shutdown cycle is terminated by the READY# signal.

Although the 82370 Wait State Generator will not automatically respond to a Shutdown (or Halt) cycle, the Wait State Control inputs (WSC0, WSC1) can be used to determine the number of wait states in the same manner as other non-82370 bus cycles.

This Shutdown Detect feature can be enabled or disabled by writing a control bit in the Internal Control Port at address 61H (see Internal Control and Diagnostic Ports). This feature is disabled upon a hardware reset of the 82370. As in the case of Software Reset, the 82370 will reset its Slave-Bus state machine but will not change any of its internal register contents.

10.0 INTERNAL CONTROL AND DIAGNOSTIC PORTS

10.1 Internal Control Port

The format of the Internal Control Port of the 82370 is shown in Figure 10-1. This Control Port is used to enable/disable the Processor Shutdown Detect mechanism as well as controlling the Gate inputs of the Timer 2 and 3. Note that this is a Write-Only port. Therefore, the 82370 will not respond to a read operation to this port. Upon hardware reset, this port will be cleared; i.e., the Shutdown Detect feature and the Gate inputs of Timer 2 and 3 are disabled.

Port Address: 61H (Write only)

10.2 Diagnostic Ports

Two 8-bit read/write Diagnostic Ports are provided in the 82370. These are two storage registers and have no effect on the operation of the 82370. They can be used to store checkpoint data or error codes in the power-on sequence and in the diagnostic service routines. As mentioned in the CPU RESET AND SHUTDOWN DETECT section, these Diagnostic Ports can be used to distinguish between 'cold' and 'warm' reset. Upon hardware reset, both Diagnostic Ports are cleared. The address map of these Diagnostic Ports is shown in Figure 10-2.

Port		Address
Diagnostic Port 1	(Read/Write)	80H
Diagnostic Port 2	(Read/Write)	88H

Figure 10-2. Address Map of Diagnostic Ports

11.0 INTEL RESERVED I/O PORTS

There are nineteen I/O ports in the 82370 address space which are reserved for Intel future peripheral device use only. Their address locations are: 10H, 12H, 14H, 16H, 2AH, 3DH, 3EH, 45H, 46H, 76H, 77H, 7DH, 7EH, CCH, CDH, D0H, D2H, D4H, and D6H. These addresses should not be used in the system since the 82370 will respond to read/write operations to these locations and bus contention may occur if any peripheral is assigned to the same address location.

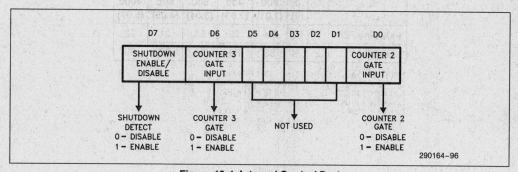

Figure 10-1. Internal Control Port

82370

12.0 PACKAGE THERMAL SPECIFICATIONS

The intel 82370 Integrated System Peripheral is specified for operation when case temperature is within the range of 0°C to 78°C for the ceramic 132-pin PGA package, and 68°C for the 100-pin plastic package. The case temperature may be measured in any environment, to determine whether the 82370 is within specified operating range. The case temperature should be measured at the center of the top surface opposite the pins.

The ambient temperature is guaranteed as long as T_C is not violated. The ambient temperature can be calculated from the θ_{jc} and θ_{ja} from the following equations:

$$T_J = T_c + P^*\theta_{jc}$$
$$T_A = T_j - P^*\theta_{ja}$$
$$T_C = T_a + P^*[\theta_{ja} - \theta_{jc}]$$

Values for θ_{ja} and θ_{jc} are given in Table 12.1 for the 100-lead fine pitch. θ_{ja} is given at various airflows. Table 12.2 shows the maximum T_a allowable (without exceeding T_C) at various airflows. Note that T_a can be improved further by attaching "fins" or a "heat sink" to the package. P is calculated using the maximum **hot** I_{cc}.

Table 12.1 82370 Package Thermal Characteristics
Thermal Resistances (°C/Watt) θ_{jc} and θ_{ja}

Package	θ_{jc}	θ_{ja} Versus Airflow-ft^3/min (m^3/sec)					
		0 (0)	200 (1.01)	400 (2.03)	600 (3.04)	800 (4.06)	1000 (5.07)
100L Fine Pitch	7	33	27	24	21	18	17
132L PGA	2	21	17	14	12	11	10

Table 12.2 82370 Maximum Allowable Ambient
Temperature at Various Airflows

Package	θ_{jc}	T_a(c) Versus Airflow-ft^3/min (m^3/sec)					
		0 (0)	200 (1.01)	400 (2.03)	600 (3.04)	800 (4.06)	1000 (5.07)
100L Fine Pitch	7	63	74	79	85	91	92
132L PGA	2	74	83	88	93	97	99

100L PQFP Pkg:
$T_c = T_a + P^*(\theta_{ja} - \theta_{jc})$
$T_c = 63 + 1.21(33 - 7)$
$T_c = 63 + 1.21(26)$
$T_c = 63 + 31.46$
$T_c = 94\,°C$

132L PGA Pkg:
$T_c = T_a + P^*(\theta_{ja} - \theta_{jc})$
$T_c = 74 + 1.21(21 - 2)$
$T_c = 74 + 1.21(19)$
$T_c = 74 + 22.99$
$T_c = 96\,°C$

13.0 ELECTRICAL SPECIFICATIONS

82370 D.C. Specifications Functional Operating Range:

$V_{CC} = 5.0V \pm 10\%$; $T_{CASE} = 0°C$ to $96°C$ for 132-pin PGA, $0°C$ to $94°C$ for 100-pin plastic

Symbol	Parameter Description	Min	Max	Units	Notes
V_{IL}	Input Low Voltage	−0.3	0.8	V	(Note 1)
V_{IH}	Input High Voltage	2.0	$V_{CC} + 0.3$	V	
V_{ILC}	CLK2 Input Low Voltage	−0.3	0.8	V	(Note 1)
V_{IHC}	CLK2 Input High Voltage	$V_{CC} - 0.8$	$V_{CC} + 0.3$	V	
V_{OL}	Output Low Voltage $I_{OL} = 4$ mA: $\quad A_{1-23}, D_{0-15}, BHE\#, BLE\#$ $I_{OL} = 5$ mA: $\quad$ All Others		0.45 0.45	V V	
V_{OH}	Output High Voltage				
$I_{OH} = -1$ mA	$A_{23}-A_1, D_{15}-D_0, BHE\#, BLE\#$	2.4		V	(Note 5)
$I_{OH} = -0.2$ mA	$A_{23}-A_1, D_{15}-D_0, BHE\#, BLE\#$	$V_{CC} - 0.5$		V	(Note 5)
$I_{OH} = -0.9$ mA	All Others	2.4		V	(Note 5)
$I_{OH} = -0.18$ mA	All Others	$V_{CC} - 0.5$		V	(Note 5)
I_{LI}	Input Leakage Current All Inputs Except: $\quad IRQ11\#-IRQ23\#$ $\quad EOP\#, TOUT2/IRQ3\#$ $\quad DREQ4/IRQ9\#$		±15	μA	
I_{LI1}	Input Leakage Current Inputs: $\quad IRQ11\#-IRQ23\#$ $\quad EOP\#, TOUT2/IRQ3$ $\quad DREQ4/IRQ9$	10	−300	μA	$0 < V_{IN} < V_{CC}$ (Note 3)
I_{LO}	Output Leakage Current		±15	μA	$0 < V_{IN} < V_{CC}$
I_{CC}	Supply Current (CLK2 = 32 MHz)		220	mA	(Note 4)
C_I	Input Capacitance		12	pF	(Note 2)
C_{CLK}	CLK2 Input Capacitance		20	pF	(Note 2)

NOTES:
1. Minimum value is not 100% tested.
2. $f_C = 1$ MHz; sampled only.
3. These pins have weak internal pullups. They sould not be left floating.
4. I_{CC} is specified with inputs driven to CMOS levels, and outputs driving CMOS loads. I_{CC} may be higher if inputs are driven to TTL levels, or if outputs are driving TTL loads.
5. Tested at the minimum operating frequency of the part.

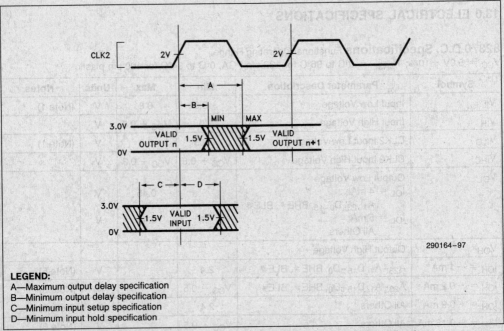

LEGEND:
A—Maximum output delay specification
B—Minimum output delay specification
C—Minimum input setup specification
D—Minimum input hold specification

290164-97

Figure 13-1. Drive Levels and Measurement Points for A.C. Specification

82370 A.C. Specifications

These A.C. timings are tested at 1.5V thresholds, except as noted.
Functional Operating Range: $V_{CC} = 5.0V \pm 10\%$; $T_{CASE} = 0°C$ to $96°C$ for 132-pin PGA, $0°C$ to $94°C$ for 100-pin plastic

Symbol	Parameter Description	Min	Max	Units	Notes
	Operating Frequency 1/(t1a × 2)	4	16	MHz	
t1	CLK2 Period	31	125	ns	
t2a	CLK2 High Time	9		ns	At 2.0V
t2b	CLK2 High Time	5		ns	At V_{CC} − 0.8V
t3a	CLK2 Low Time	9		ns	At 2.0V
t3b	CLK2 Low Time	7		ns	At 0.8V
t4	CLK2 Fall Time		7	ns	V_{CC} − 0.8V to 0.8V
t5	CLK2 Rise Time		7	ns	0.8V to V_{CC} − 0.8V
t6	A1–A23, BHE#, BLE# EDACK0–EDACK2 Valid Delay	4	36	ns	$C_L = 120$ pF
t7	A1–A23, BHE#, BLE# EDACK0–EDACK3 Float Delay	4	40	ns	(Note 1)
t8	A1–A23, BHE#, BLE# Setup Time	6		ns	
t9	A1–A23, BHE#, BLE# Hold Time	4		ns	
t10	W/R#, M/IO#, D/C# Valid Delay	4	33	ns	$C_L = 75$ pF
t11	W/R#, M/IO#, D/C# Float Delay	4	35	ns	(Note 1)

82370

82370 A.C. Specifications

These A.C. timings are tested at 1.5V thresholds, except as noted. Functional Operating Range: $V_{CC} = 5.0V \pm 10\%$; $T_{CASE} = 0°C$ to $96°C$ for 132-pin PGA, $0°C$ to $94°C$ for 100-pin plastic (Continued)

Symbol	Parameter Description	Min	Max	Units	Notes
t12	W/R#, M/IO#, D/C# Setup Time	6		ns	
t13	W/R#, M/IO#, D/C# Hold Time	4		ns	
t14	ADS# Valid Delay	6	33	ns	CL = 50 pF
t15	ADS# Float Delay	4	35	ns	(Note 1)
t16	ADS# Setup Time	21		ns	
t17	ADS# Hold Time	4		ns	
t18	Slave Mode D0–D15 Read Valid	3	46	ns	$C_L = 120$ pF
t19	Slave Mode D0–D15 Read Float	6	35	ns	(Note 1)
t20	Slave Mode D0–D15 Write Setup	31		ns	
t21	Slave Mode D0–D15 Write Hold	26		ns	
t22	Master Mode D0–D15 Write Valid	4	40	ns	$C_L = 120$ pF
t23	Master Mode D0–D15 Write Float	4	35	ns	(Note 1)
t24	Master Mode D0–D15 Read Setup	8		ns	
t25	Master Mode D0–D15 Read Hold	6		ns	
t26	READY# Setup Time	19		ns	
t27	READY# Hold Time	4		ns	
t28	WSC0–WSC1 Setup Time	6		ns	
t29	WSC0–WSC1 Hold Time	21		ns	
t30	RESET Setup Time	13		ns	
t31	RESET Hold Time	4		ns	
t32	READYO# Valid Delay	4	31	ns	$C_L = 25$ pF
t33	CPURST Valid Delay (Falling Edge Only)	2	18	ns	$C_L = 50$ pF
t34	HOLD Valid Delay	5	33	ns	$C_L = 100$ pF
t35	HLDA Setup Time	21		ns	
t36	HLDA Hold Time	6		ns	
t37a	EOP# Setup (Synchronous)	21		ns	
t38a	EOP# Hold (Synchronous)	6		ns	
t37b	EOP# Setup (Asynchronous)	11		ns	
t38b	EOP# Hold (Asynchronous)	11		ns	
t39	EOP# Valid Delay (Falling Edge Only)	5	38	ns	$C_L = 100$ pF
t40	EOP# Float Delay	5	40	ns	(Note 1)
t41a	DREQ Setup (Synchronous)	21		ns	
t42a	DREQ Hold (Synchronous)	4		ns	
t41b	DREQ Setup (Asynchronous)	11		ns	
t42b	DREQ Hold (Asynchronous)	11		ns	
t43	INT Valid Delay from IRQn		500	ns	
t44	NA# Setup Time	5		ns	
t45	NA# Hold Time	15		ns	

82370 A.C. Specifications
These A.C. timings are tested at 1.5V thresholds, except as noted.
Functional Operating Range: $V_{CC} = 5.0V \pm 10\%$; $T_{CASE} = 0°C$ to $96°C$ for 132-pin PGA, $0°C$ to $94°C$ for 100-pin plastic (Continued)

Symbol	Parameter Description	Min	Max	Units	Notes
t46	CLKIN Frequency	DC	10	MHz	
t47	CLKIN High Time	30		ns	2.0V
t48	CLKIN Low Time	50		ns	0.8V
t49	CLKIN Rise Time		10	ns	0.8V to 3.7V
t50	CLKIN Fall Time		10	ns	3.7V to 0.8V
t51	TOUT1#/REF# Valid Delay from CLK2 (Refresh)	4	36	ns	$C_L = 120$ pF
t52	from CLKIN (Timer)	3	93	ns	$C_L = 120$ pF
t53	TOUT2# Valid Delay (from CLKIN, Falling Edge Only)	3	93	ns	$C_L = 120$ pf
t54	TOUT2# Float Delay	3	36	ns	(Note 1)
t55	TOUT3# Valid Delay (from CLKIN)	3	93	ns	$C_L = 120$ pF
t56	CHPSEL# Valid Delay	1	35	ns	$C_L = 25$ pF

NOTE:
1. Float condition occurs when the maximum output current becomes less than I_{LO} in magnitude. Float delay is not tested. For testing purposes, the float condition occurs when the dynamic output driven voltage changes with current loads.

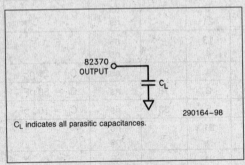

Figure 13-2. A.C. Test Load

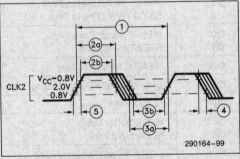

Figure 13-3

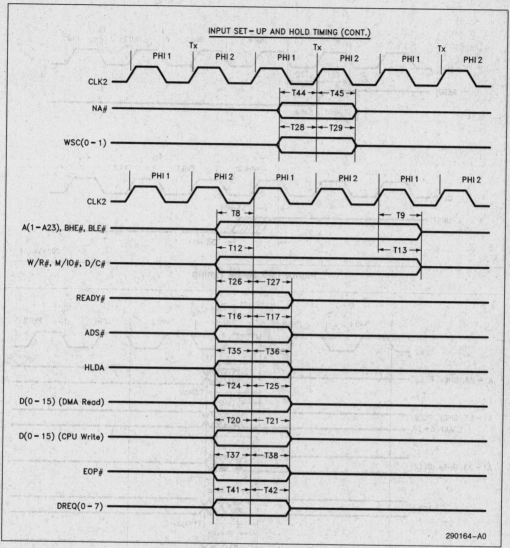

INPUT SET – UP AND HOLD TIMING (CONT.)

290164–A0

Figure 13-4. Input Setup and Hold Timing

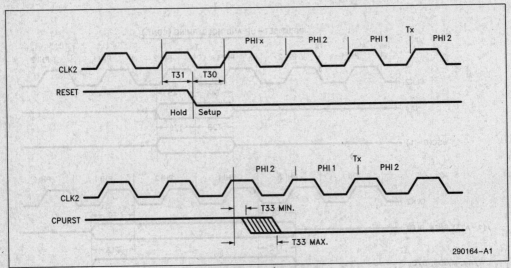

Figure 13-5. Reset Timing

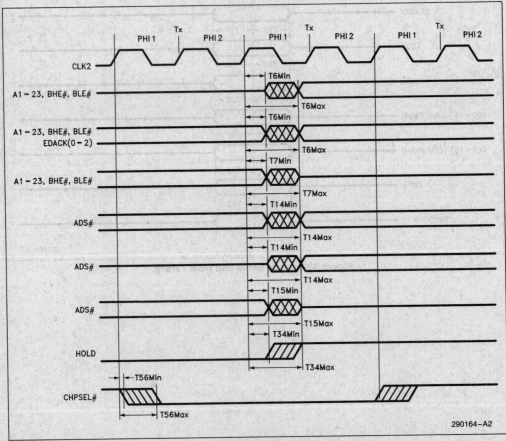

Figure 13-6. Address Output Delays

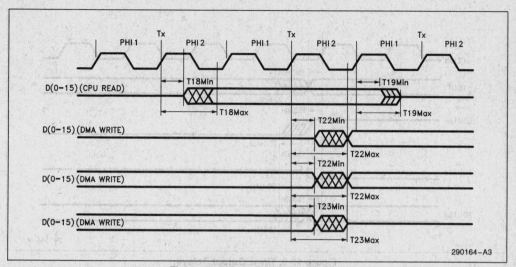

Figure 13-7. Data Bus Output Delays

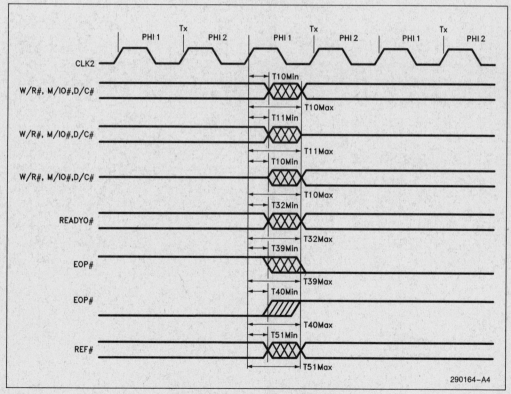

Figure 13-8. Control Output Delays

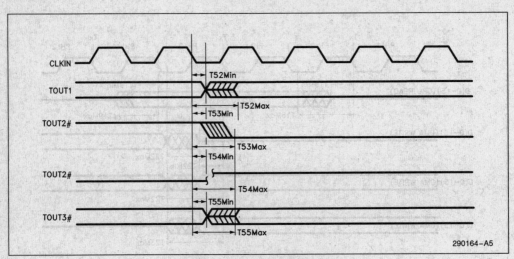

290164-A5

Figure 13-9. Timer Output Delays

APPENDIX A
PORTS LISTED BY ADDRESS

Port Address (HEX)	Description
00	Read/Write DMA Channel 0 Target Address, A0–A15
01	Read/Write DMA Channel 0 Byte Count, B0–B15
02	Read/Write DMA Channel 1 Target Address, A0–A15
03	Read/Write DMA Channel 1 Byte Count, B0–B15
04	Read/Write DMA Channel 2 Target Address, A0–A15
05	Read/Write DMA Channel 2 Byte Count, B0–B15
06	Read/Write DMA Channel 3 Target Address, A0–A15
07	Read/Write DMA Channel 3 Byte Count, B0–B15
08	Read/Write DMA Channel 0–3 Status/Command I Register
09	Read/Write DMA Channel 0–3 Software Request Register
0A	Write DMA Channel 0–3 Set-Reset Mask Register
0B	Write DMA Channel 0–3 Mode Register I
0C	Write Clear Byte-Pointer FF
0D	Write DMA Master-Clear
0E	Write DMA Channel 0–3 Clear Mask Register
0F	Read/Write DMA Channel 0–3 Mask Register
10	Intel Reserved
11	Read/Write DMA Channel 0 Byte Count, B16–B23
12	Intel Reserved
13	Read/Write DMA Channel 1 Byte Count, B16–B23
14	Intel Reserved
15	Read/Write DMA Channel 2 Byte Count, B16–B23
16	Intel Reserved
17	Read/Write DMA Channel 3 Byte Count, B16–B23
18	Write DMA Channel 0–3 Bus Size Register
19	Read/Write DMA Channel 0–3 Chaining Register
1A	Write DMA Channel 0–3 Command Register II
1B	Write DMA Channel 0–3 Mode Register II
1C	Read/Write Refresh Control Register
1E	Reset Software Request Interrupt
20	Write Bank B ICW1, OCW2 or OCW3 Read Bank B Poll, Interrupt Request or In-Service Status Register
21	Write Bank B ICW2, ICW3, ICW4 or OCW1 Read Bank B Interrupt Mask Register
22	Read Bank B ICW2
28	Read/Write IRQ8 Vector Register
29	Read/Write IRQ9 Vector Register
2A	Reserved

Port Address (HEX)	Description
2B	Read/Write IRQ11 Vector Register
2C	Read/Write IRQ12 Vector Register
2D	Read/Write IRQ13 Vector Register
2E	Read/Write IRQ14 Vector Register
2F	Read/Write IRQ15 Vector Register
30	Write Bank A ICW1, OCW2 or OCW3
	Read Bank A Poll, Interrupt Request or In-Service Status Register
31	Write Bank A ICW2, ICW3, ICW4 or OCW1
	Read Bank A Interrupt Mask Register
32	Read Bank A ICW2
38	Read/Write IRQ0 Vector Register
39	Read/Write IRQ1 Vector Register
3A	Read/Write IRQ1.5 Vector Register
3B	Read/Write IRQ3 Vector Register
3C	Read/Write IRQ4 Vector Register
3D	Reserved
3E	Reserved
3F	Read/Write IRQ7 Vector Register
40	Read/Write Counter 0 Register
41	Read/Write Counter 1 Register
42	Read/Write Counter 2 Register
43	Write Control Word Register I—Counter 0, 1, 2
44	Read/Write Counter 3 Register
45	Reserved
46	Reserved
47	Write Word Register II—Counter 3
61	Write Internal Control Port
64	Write CPU Reset Register (Data—1111XXX0H)
72	Read/Write Wait State Register 0
73	Read/Write Wait State Register 1
74	Read/Write Wait State Register 2
75	Read/Write Refresh Wait State Register
76	Reserved
77	Reserved
7D	Reserved
7E	Reserved
7F	Read/Write Relocation Register
80	Read/Write Internal Diagnostic Port 0
81	Read/Write DMA Channel 2 Target Address, A16–A23
82	Read/Write DMA Channel 3 Target Address, A16–A23
83	Read/Write DMA Channel 1 Target Address, A16–A23
87	Read/Write DMA Channel 0 Target Address, A16–A23
88	Read/Write Internal Diagnostic Port 1
89	Read/Write DMA Channel 6 Target Address, A16–A23
8A	Read/Write DMA Channel 7 Target Address, A16–A23
8B	Read/Write DMA Channel 5 Target Address, A16–A23
8F	Read/Write DMA Channel 4 Target Address, A16–A23

Port Address (HEX)	Description
90	Read/Write DMA Channel 0 Requester Address, A0–A15
91	Read/Write DMA Channel 0 Requester Address, A16–A23
92	Read/Write DMA Channel 1 Requester Address, A0–A15
93	Read/Write DMA Channel 1 Requester Address, A16–A23
94	Read/Write DMA Channel 2 Requester Address, A0–A15
95	Read/Write DMA Channel 2 Requester Address, A16–A23
96	Read/Write DMA Channel 3 Requester Address, A0–A15
97	Read/Write DMA Channel 3 Requester Address, A16–A23
98	Read/Write DMA Channel 4 Requester Address, A0–A15
99	Read/Write DMA Channel 4 Requester Address, A16–A23
9A	Read/Write DMA Channel 5 Requester Address, A0–A15
9B	Read/Write DMA Channel 5 Requester Address, A16–A23
9C	Read/Write DMA Channel 6 Requester Address, A0–A15
9D	Read/Write DMA Channel 6 Requester Address, A16–A23
9E	Read/Write DMA Channel 7 Requester Address, A0–A15
9F	Read/Write DMA Channel 7 Requester Address, A16–A23
A0	Write Bank C ICW1, OCW2 or OCW3 Read Bank C Poll, Interrupt Request or In-Service Status Register
A1	Write Bank C ICW2, ICW3, ICW4 or OCW1 Read Bank C Interrupt Mask Register
A2	Read Bank C ICW2
A8	Read/Write IRQ16 Vector Register
A9	Read/Write IRQ17 Vector Register
AA	Read/Write IRQ18 Vector Register
AB	Read/Write IRQ19 Vector Register
AC	Read/Write IRQ20 Vector Register
AD	Read/Write IRQ21 Vector Register
AE	Read/Write IRQ22 Vector Register
AF	Read/Write IRQ23 Vector Register
C0	Read/Write DMA Channel 4 Target Address, A0–A15
C1	Read/Write DMA Channel 4 Byte Count, B0–B15
C2	Read/Write DMA Channel 5 Target Address, A0–A15
C3	Read/Write DMA Channel 5 Byte Count, B0–B15
C4	Read/Write DMA Channel 6 Target Address, A0–A15
C5	Read/Write DMA Channel 6 Byte Count, B0–B15
C6	Read/Write DMA Channel 7 Target Address, A0–A15
C7	Read/Write DMA Channel 7 Byte Count, B0–B15
C8	Read DMA Channel 4–7 Status/Command I Register
C9	Read/Write DMA Channel 4–7 Software Request Register
CA	Write DMA Channel 4–7 Set-Reset Mask Register
CB	Write DMA Channel 4–7 Mode Register I
CC	Reserved
CD	Reserved
CE	Write DMA Channel 4–7 Clear Mask Register
CF	Read/Write DMA Channel 4–7 Mask Register
D0	Intel Reserved
D1	Read/Write DMA Channel 4 Byte Count, B16–B23
D2	Intel Reserved
D3	Read/Write DMA Channel 5 Byte Count, B16–B23

Port Address (HEX)	Description
D4	Intel Reserved
D5	Read/Write DMA Channel 6 Byte Count, B16–B23
D6	Intel Reserved
D7	Read/Write DMA Channel 7 Byte Count, B16–B23
D8	Write DMA Channel 4–7 Bus Size Register
D9	Read/Write DMA Channel 4–7 Chaining Register
DA	Write DMA Channel 4–7 Command Register II
DB	Write DMA Channel 4–7 Mode Register II

APPENDIX B
PORTS LISTED BY FUNCTION

Port Address (HEX)	Description
DMA CONTROLLER	
0D	Write DMA Master-Clear
0C	Write DMA Clear Byte-Pointer FF
08	Read/Write DMA Channel 0–3 Status/Command I Register
C8	Read/Write DMA Channel 4–7 Status/Command I Register
1A	Write DMA Channel 0–3 Command Register II
DA	Write DMA Channel 4–7 Command Register II
0B	Write DMA Channel 0–3 Mode Register I
CB	Write DMA Channel 4–7 Mode Register I
1B	Write DMA Channel 0–3 Mode Register II
DB	Write DMA Channel 4–7 Mode Register II
09	Read/Write DMA Channel 0–3 Software Request Register
C9	Read/Write DMA Channel 4–7 Software Request Register
1E	Reset Software Request Interrupt
0E	Write DMA Channel 0–3 Clear Mask Register
CE	Write DMA Channel 4–7 Clear Mask Register
0F	Read/Write DMA Channel 0–3 Mask Register
CF	Read/Write DMA Channel 4–7 Mask Register
0A	Write DMA Channel 0–3 Set-Reset Mask Register
CA	Write DMA Channel 4–7 Set-Reset Mask Register
18	Write DMA Channel 0–3 Bus Size Register
D8	Write DMA Channel 4–7 Bus Size Register
19	Read/Write DMA Channel 0–3 Chaining Register
D9	Read/Write DMA Channel 4–7 Chaining Register
00	Read/Write DMA Channel 0 Target Address, A0–A15
87	Read/Write DMA Channel 0 Target Address, A16–A23
01	Read/Write DMA Channel 0 Byte Count, B0–B15
11	Read/Write DMA Channel 0 Byte Count, B16–B23
90	Read/Write DMA Channel 0 Requester Address, A0–A15
91	Read/Write DMA Channel 0 Requester Address, A16–A23

Port Address (HEX)	Description
DMA CONTROLLER (Continued)	
02	Read/Write DMA Channel 1 Target Address, A0–A15
83	Read/Write DMA Channel 1 Target Address, A16–A23
03	Read/Write DMA Channel 1 Byte Count, B0–B15
13	Read/Write DMA Channel 1 Byte Count, B16–B23
92	Read/Write DMA Channel 1 Requester Address, A0–A15
93	Read/Write DMA Channel 1 Requester Address, A16–A23
04	Read/Write DMA Channel 2 Target Address, A0–A15
81	Read/Write DMA Channel 2 Target Address, A16–A23
05	Read/Write DMA Channel 2 Byte Count, B0–B15
15	Read/Write DMA Channel 2 Byte Count, B16–B23
94	Read/Write DMA Channel 2 Requester Address, A0–A15
95	Read/Write DMA Channel 2 Requester Address, A16–A23
06	Read/Write DMA Channel 3 Target Address, A0–A15
82	Read/Write DMA Channel 3 Target Address, A16–A23
07	Read/Write DMA Channel 3 Byte Count, B0–B15
17	Read/Write DMA Channel 3 Byte Count, B16–B23
96	Read/Write DMA Channel 3 Requester Address, A0–A15
97	Read/Write DMA Channel 3 Requester Address, A16–A23
C0	Read/Write DMA Channel 4 Target Address, A0–A15
8F	Read/Write DMA Channel 4 Target Address, A16–A23
C1	Read/Write DMA Channel 4 Byte Count, B0–B15
D1	Read/Write DMA Channel 4 Byte Count, B16–B23
98	Read/Write DMA Channel 4 Requester Address, A0–A15
99	Read/Write DMA Channel 4 Requester Address, A16–A23
C2	Read/Write DMA Channel 5 Target Address, A0–A15
8B	Read/Write DMA Channel 5 Target Address, A16–A23
C3	Read/Write DMA Channel 5 Byte Count, B0–B15
D3	Read/Write DMA Channel 5 Byte Count, B16–B23
9A	Read/Write DMA Channel 5 Requester Address, A0–A15
9B	Read/Write DMA Channel 5 Requester Address, A16–A23
C4	Read/Write DMA Channel 6 Target Address, A0–A15
89	Read/Write DMA Channel 6 Target Address, A16–A23
C5	Read/Write DMA Channel 6 Byte Count, B0–B15
D5	Read/Write DMA Channel 6 Byte Count, B16–B23
9C	Read/Write DMA Channel 6 Requester Address, A0–A15
9D	Read/Write DMA Channel 6 Requester Address, A16–A23
C6	Read/Write DMA Channel 7 Target Address, A0–A15
8A	Read/Write DMA Channel 7 Target Address, A16–A23
C7	Read/Write DMA Channel 7 Byte Count, B0–B15
D7	Read/Write DMA Channel 7 Byte Count, B16–B23
9E	Read/Write DMA Channel 7 Requester Address, A0–A15
9F	Read/Write DMA Channel 7 Requester Address, A16–A23

Port Address (HEX)	Description
INTERRUPT CONTROLLER	
20	Write Bank B ICW1, OCW2 or OCW3
	Read Bank B Poll, Interrupt Request or In-Service Status Register
21	Write Bank B ICW2, ICW3, ICW4 or OCW1
	Read Bank B Interrupt Mask Register
22	Read Bank B ICW2
28	Read/Write IRQ8 Vector Register
29	Read/Write IRQ9 Vector Register
2A	Reserved
2B	Read/Write IRQ11 Vector Register
2C	Read/Write IRQ12 Vector Register
2D	Read/Write IRQ13 Vector Register
2E	Read/Write IRQ14 Vector Register
2F	Read/Write IRQ15 Vector Register
A0	Write Bank C ICW1, OCW2 or OCW3
	Read Bank C Poll, Interrupt Request or In-Service Status Register
A1	Write Bank C ICW2, ICW3, ICW4 or OCW1
	Read Bank C Interrupt Mask Register
A2	Read Bank C ICW2
A8	Read/Write IRQ16 Vector Register
A9	Read/Write IRQ17 Vector Register
AA	Read/Write IRQ18 Vector Register
AB	Read/Write IRQ19 Vector Register
AC	Read/Write IRQ20 Vector Register
AD	Read/Write IRQ21 Vector Register
AE	Read/Write IRQ22 Vector Register
AF	Read/Write IRQ23 Vector Register
30	Write Bank A ICW1, OCW2 or OCW3
	Read Bank A Poll, Interrupt Request or In-Service Status Register
31	Write Bank A ICW2, ICW3, ICW4 or OCW1
	Read Bank A Interrupt Mask Register
32	Read Bank A ICW2
38	Read/Write IRQ0 Vector Register
39	Read/Write IRQ1 Vector Register
3A	Read/Write IRQ1.5 Vector Register
3B	Read/Write IRQ3 Vector Register
3C	Read/Write IRQ4 Vector Register
3D	Reserved
3E	Reserved
3F	Read/Write IRQ7 Vector Register

82370

Port Address (HEX)	Description
PROGRAMMABLE INTERVAL TIMER	
40	Read/Write Counter 0 Register
41	Read/Write Counter 1 Register
42	Read/Write Counter 2 Register
43	Write Control Word Register I—Counter 0, 1, 2
44	Read/Write Counter 3 Register
47	Write Word Register II—Counter 3
CPU RESET	
64	Write CPU Reset Register (Data—1111XXX0H)
WAIT STATE GENERATOR	
72	Read/Write Wait State Register 0
73	Read/Write Wait State Register 1
74	Read/Write Wait State Register 2
75	Read/Write Refresh Wait State Register
DRAM REFRESH CONTROLLER	
1C	Read/Write Refresh Control Register
INTERNAL CONTROL AND DIAGNOSTIC PORTS	
61	Write Internal Control Port
80	Read/Write Internal Diagnostic Port 0
88	Read/Write Internal Diagnostic Port 1
RELOCATION REGISTER	
7F	Read/Write Relocation Register
INTEL RESERVED PORTS	
10	Reserved
12	Reserved
14	Reserved
16	Reserved
2A	Reserved
3D	Reserved
3E	Reserved
45	Reserved
46	Reserved
76	Reserved
77	Reserved
7D	Reserved
7E	Reserved
CC	Reserved
CD	Reserved
D0	Reserved
D2	Reserved
D4	Reserved
D6	Reserved

APPENDIX C
PROGRAMMING THE 82370 INTERRUPT CONTROLLERS

This Appendix describes two methods of programming and initializing the Interrupt Controllers of the 82370. A simple interrupt service routine is also shown which provides compatibility with the 82C59 Interrupt Controller.

The two methods of programming the 82370 Interrupt Controllers are needed to provide simple initialization procedures in different software environments. For new applications, a simple initialization and programming sequence can be used. For PC-DOS or other applications which expect 8259s, an interrupt handler for initialization traps must be provided. Once the handler is in place, all three 82370 Interrupt Controller banks can be programmed or initialized in the same manner as an 8259.

The ICW2 interrupt is generated by the 82370 when writing the ICW2 command to any of the interrupt controller banks. This interrupt is supplied to provide compatibility to existing code that expects to be programming 82C59s. The ICW2 value is stored in the ICW2 register of the associated bank, but is ignored by the controller. It is the responsibility of the ICW2 interrupt handler to read the ICW2 register and use its value to program the individual vector registers accordingly.

NEW APPLICATIONS

New applications do not generally require compatibility with previous code, or at least the code is usually easily modifiable. If the application fits this description, then the ICW2 interrupt can be ignored. This is done by initializing the interrupt controller as necessary, and before enabling CPU interrupts, removing the ICW2 interrupt request by reading the ICW2 register. Listing 1 shows the code for doing this for bank A. The same procedure can be used for the other banks.

Listing 1.
Initialization of an 82370 Interrupt Controller Bank
Without ICW2 Interrupts

```
INIT_BANK_A     proc near

    cli                     ;disable all interrupts

;initialize controller logic
    mov al,ICW1             ;begin sequence
    out 30h,al
    mov al,ICW2             ;send dummy ICW2
    out 31h,al
    mov al,ICW3             ;send ICW3 if necessary
    out 31h,al
    mov al,ICW4             ;send ICW4
    out 31h,al

    mov al,BANK_A_MASK      ;write to mask register (OCW1)
    out 31h,al

;program vector registers

    mov al,ICW2             ;IRQ0
    out 38h,al
    mov al,ICW2+1           ;IRQ1
    out 39h,al
    mov al,ICW2_VECTOR      ;IRQ1.5 (probably never used in
    out 3Ah,al             ;         this system)
    mov al,ICW2+3           ;IRQ3
    out 3Bh,al
    mov al,ICW2+4           ;IRQ4
    out 3Ch,al
    mov al,ICW2+7           ;IRQ7
    out 3Fh,al

;remove ICW2 interrupt request

    in  al,31h              ;read mask register to work around
                            ; A-step errata

    in  al,32h              ;read ICW2 register to clear
                            ; interrupt request

;return to calling program

    sti                     ;re-enable interrupts
    ret

INIT_BANK_A     endp
```

OLD APPLICATIONS

In applications where 8259 compatibility is required, the ICW2 interrupt handler must be invoked whenever an interrupt controller is initialized (ICW1–ICW2–ICWn sequence). The handler's purpose is to read the ICW2 value from the ICW2 read register and write the appropriate sequence of vectors to the vector registers. Listing 2 shows the typical initialization sequence (this is not changed from the 8259), and the required initialization for operation of the ICW2 interrupt handler. Listing 2 shows the ICW2 interrupt handler.

```
                     Listing 2.
         Initialization of Bank A for ICW2 Interrupts

    cli                 ;disable all interrupts

;initialize controller logic

    mov  al,ICW1        ;begin sequence
    out  30h,al
    mov  al,ICW2        ;send dummy ICW2
    out  31h,al

;*******
    mov  al,ICW3        ;send ICW3 if necessary
    out  31h,al         ; note that using ICW3 for
                        ; cascading bank B is not required
                        ; and will affect the way EOIs are
                        ; required for nesting. It is
                        ; advised that ICW3 not be used.
;*******

    mov  al,ICW4        ;send ICW4
    out  ;31h,al

    mov  al,Bank_A_Mask ;write to mask register (OCW1=7Bh)
    out  31h,al         ;don't mask off IRQ1.5 or Default
                        ; interrupt (IRQ7)

;program necessary vector registers

    mov  al,ICW2_VECTOR ;IRQ1.5
    out  3Ah,al

    mov  al,IRQ7_DEFAULT_VECTOR
    out  3Fh,al

;remove ICW2 interrupt request for bank A

    in   al,31h         ;read mask register to work around
                        ; A-step errata

    in   al.32h         ;read ICW2 register to clear
                        ; interrupt request

;at this point install interrupt call vector for ICW2, if
;not already done somewhere else in the code

    sti                 ;re-enable interrupts
```

Listing 3.
ICW2 Interrupt Service Routine

```
ICW2_INT_HANDLER        proc near

    push ax                 ;save registers
    push cx
    push dx

; service bank B

    in   al,21h             ;read mask register for A-step errata

    in   al,22h             ;read ICW2
    mov  cx,8               ;count vectors
    mov  dx,28h             ;point to vectors

BANK_B_LOOP;

    out  dx,al             ;write vector
    inc  al                ;next vector
    inc  dx                ;next vector I/O address
    loop BANK_B_LOOP

;service bank C

    in   al,0A1h            ;read mask register for A-step errata

    in   al,0A2h            ;read ICW2
    mov  cx,8               ;count vectors
    mov  dx,0A8h            ;point to vectors

BANK_C_LOOP:

    out  dx,al             ;write vector
    inc  al                ;next vector
    inc  dx                ;next vector i/o address
    loop BANK_C_LOOP

    pop  dx                ;restore registers
    pop  cx
    pop  ax
    iret                   ;return

ICW2_INT_HANDLER        endp
```

Table 1. Interrupt Controller Registers

Bank A:

30H	write	ICW1, OCW2, OCW3
	read	Poll, IRR, ISR
31H	write	ICW2, ICW3, ICW4, OCW1
	read	IMR
32H	read	ICW2 read register
38H	read/write	IRQ0 vector
39H	read/write	IRQ1 vector
3AH	read/write	IRQ1.5 vector
3BH	read/write	IRQ3 vector
3CH	read/write	IRQ4 vector
3DH		RESERVED
3EH		RESERVED
3FH	read/write	IRQ7 vector

Bank B:

20H	write	ICW1, OCW2, OCW3
	read	Poll, IRR, ISR
21H	write	ICW2, ICW3, ICW4, OCW1
	read	IMR
22H	read	ICW2 read register
28H	read/write	IRQ8 vector
29H	read/write	IRQ9 vector
2AH		RESERVED
2BH	read/write	IRQ11 vector
2CH	read/write	IRQ12 vector
2DH	read/write	IRQ13 vector
2EH	read/write	IRQ14 vector
2FH	read/write	IRQ15 vector

Bank C:

A0H	write	ICW1, OCW2, OCW3
	read	Poll, IRR, ISR
A1H	write	ICW2, ICW3, ICW4, OCW1
	read	IMR
A2H	read	ICW2 read register
A8H	read/write	IRQ16 vector
A9H	read/write	IRQ17 vector
AAH	read/write	IRQ18 vector
ABH	read/write	IRQ19 vector
ACH	read/write	IRQ20 vector
ADH	read/write	IRQ21 vector
AEH	read/write	IRQ22 vector
AFH	read/write	IRQ23 vector

APPENDIX D
SYSTEM NOTES

1. BHE# IN MASTER MODE.

In Master Mode, BHE# will be activated during DMA to/from 8-bit devices residing at even locations when the remaining byte count is greater than 1.

For example, if an 8-bit device is located at 00000000 Hex and the number of bytes to be transferred is > 1, the first address/BHE# combination will be 00000000/0. In some systems this will cause the bus controller to perform two 8-bit accesses, the first to 0000000 Hex and the second to 00000001 Hex. However, the 82370's DMA will only read/write one byte. This may or may not cause a problem in the system depending on what is located at 00000001 Hex.

Solution:

There are two solutions if BH# active is unacceptable. Of the two, number 2 is the cleanest and most recommended.

1. If there is an 8-bit device that uses DMA located at an even address, do not use that address + 1. The limitation of this solution is that the user must have complete control over what addresses will be used in the end system.

2. Do not allow the Bus Controller to split cycles for the DMA.

2. RESET OUTPUT OF 82370:

The 80376 requires its RESET line to be active for 80 clock cycles. The 82370 generates holds the RESET line active for 62 clock cycles.

The following design example shows how the user can extend the active high of the RESET line to 80 clock cycles.

Extending the RESET Output of the 82370

This section describes a hardware solution for using the 82370's CPURST output and the software reset command to cause the 80376 to enter into a self-test.

The 80376 requires two simultaneous events in order to initiate the self-test sequence. The RESET input of the processor must be held active for at least 80 CLK2 periods and the BUSY# input must be low 8 CLK2 periods prior to and 8 CLK2 periods subsequent to RESET going inactive.

A system which does not have an 80387SX will simply have the BUSY# input to the 80376 tied low. A system which contains the 80387SX will require extra logic between the BUSY# output of the 80387SX and the BUSY# input of the 80376 in order to force self-test on reset. The extra BUSY# logic required will not be described here.

The 82370 CPURST output is intended to be retimed with faster TTL components in order to meet the RESET input setup time requirements of the 80376 and 80387SX. This requires a 74F379 (quad flip-flop with enable) or equivalent. The flip-flops required are described in TECHBIT (Ed Grochowski, April 10, 1987).

The 82370 does not meet the RESET pulse duration requirements for causing self-test of the 80376 when a software reset command is issued to the 82370. The 82370 provides a RESET pulse width of 62 CLK2 periods, the 80376 requires 80 CLK2 periods as mentioned earlier.

In order to cause the 80376 to do a self-test after a software reset, the CPURST output pulse of the 82370 must be lengthened. Figure 1 shows a circuit which will do this.

Note that the CPURST output is the OR of the 82370 RESET input and the output of the software reset command logic, and thus will have the same duration as the RESET input during power-on.

The additional circuitry required consists of an OR gate, a one-shot, a capacitor, and a resistor more than is found in a system without the 82370. The one-shot (74121) is inserted between the CPURST output of the 82370 and the input of the retiming flip-flops (74F379). The period of the one-shot should be long enough to guarantee the 80 CLK2 periods that the 80376 requires.

The OR gate (74F32) is required to guarantee that the 80376 is held in a RESET state while the 82370 is being reset. This is done to be sure that BE3# is held low when the RESET input to the 82370 goes inactive. BE3# is used during the reset to determine whether it is necessary to enter a special factory test mode. It must be low when the RESET input goes inactive, and the 80376 drives it low during reset.

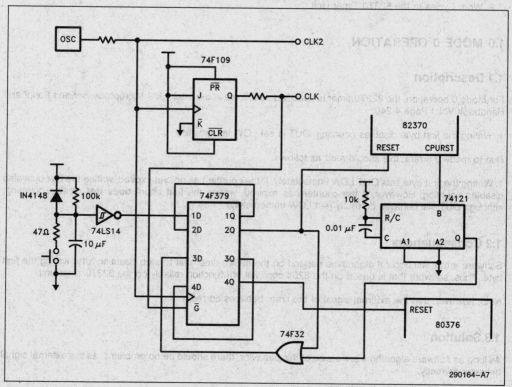

Figure D-1. Extending 82370 Reset Output

82370 TIMER UNIT NOTES

The 82370 DMA Controller with Integrated System Peripherals is functionally inconsistent with the data sheet. This document explains the behavior of the 82370 Timer Unit and outlines subsequent limitations of the timer unit. This document also provides recommended workarounds.

Overview:

There are two areas in which the 82370 timer unit exhibits non-specified behavior:

1. Mode 0 operation

2. Write Cycles to the 82370 Timer Unit

1.0 MODE 0 OPERATION

1.1 Description

For Mode 0 operation, the 82370 timer is specified as follows in the Intel 1989 Microprocessor and Peripheral Handbook Vol. I Page 4-240:

1. Writing the first byte disables counting, OUT is set LOW immediately ...

Due to mode 0 errata, this should read as follows:

1. Writing the first byte sets OUT LOW immediately. If the counter has not yet expired, writing the first byte also disables counting. However, if the counter has expired, writing the first count **does not** disable counting, although OUT still behaves correctly (set LOW immediately).

1.2 Consequences

Software errors will occur if algorithms depend on the 82370 timer unit to stop counting after writing the first byte. Thus, software that is based on the 8254 core will not function reliably on the 82370 timer unit.

Note, however, that the external signal of the timer behaves correctly.

1.3 Solution

As long as software algorithms are aware of this behavior, there should be no problems, as the external signal behaves correctly.

1.4 Long Term Plans

Currently, Intel has no plans to fix this behavior of the 82370 timer unit.

2.0 WRITE CYCLES TO THE 82370 TIMER UNIT:

This errata applies only to SLAVE WRITE cycles to the 82370 timer unit. During these cycles, the data being written into the 82370 timer unit may be corrupted if CLKIN is not inhibited during a certain "window" of the write cycle.

2.1 Description

Please refer to Figure D-2.

During write cycles to the 82370 timer unit, the 82370 translates the 80376 interface signals such as #ADS, #W/R, #M/IO, and #D/C into several internal signals that control the operation of the internal sub-blocks (e.g. Timer Unit).

The 82370 timer uint is controlled by such internal signals. These internal signals are generated and sampled with respect to two separate clock signals: CLK2 (the system clock) and CLKIN (the 82370 timer unit clock).

Since the CLKIN and CLK2 clock signals are used internally to generate control signals for the interface to the timer unit, some timing parameters must be met in order for the interface logic to function properly.

Those timing parameters are met by inhibiting the CLKIN signal for a specific window during Write Cycles to the 82370 Timer Unit.

The CLKIN signal must be inhibited using external logic, as the GATE function of the 82370 timer unit is not guaranteed to totally inhibit CLKIN.

2.2 Consequences

This CLKIN inhibits circuitry guarantees proper write cycles to the 82370 timer unit.

Without this solution, write cycles to the 82370 timer unit could place corrupted data into the timer unit registers. This, in turn, could yield inaccurate results and improper timer operation.

The proposed solution would involve a hardware modification for existing systems.

2.3 Solution

A timing waveform (Figure D-3) shows the specific window during which CLKIN must be inhibited. Please note that CLKIN must only be inhibited during the window shown in Figure D-3. This window is defined by two AC timing parameters:

t_a = 9 ns

t_b = 28 ns

The proposed solution provides a certain amount of system "guardband" to make sure that this window is avoided.

PAL equations for a suggested workaround are also included. Please refer to the comments in the PAL codes for stated assumptions of this particular workaround. A state diagram (Figure D-4) is provided to help clarify how this PAL is designed.

Figure D-5 shows how this PAL would fit into a system workaround. In order to show the effect of this workaround on the CLKIN signal, Figure D-6 shows how CLKIN is inhibited. Note that you must still meet the CLKIN AC timing parameters (e.g. t_{47} (min), t_{48} (min)) in order for the timer unit to function properly.

Please note that this workaround has not been tested. It is provided as a suggested solution. Actual solutions will vary from system to system.

2.4 Long Term Plans

Intel has no plans to fix this behavior in the 82370 timer unit.

```
module Timer_82370_Fix
flag '-r2', '-q2', '-f1', '-t4', '-w1,3,6,5,4,16,7,12,17,18,15,14'
title '82370 Timer Unit CLKIN
      INHIBIT signal PAL Solution '
Timer_Unit_Fix device 'P16R6';


"This PAL inhibits the CLKIN signal (that comes from an oscillator)
"during Slave Writes to the 82370 Timer unit.
"
"ASSUMPTION:    This PAL assumes that an external system address
"              decoder provides a signal to indicate that an 82370
"              Timer Unit access is taking place. This input
"              signal is called TMR in this PAL. This PAL also
"              assumes that this TMR signal occurs during a
"              specific T-State. Please see Figure 2 of this
"              document to see when this signal is expected to
"              be active by this PAL.
"
"
"NOTE:         This PAL does not support pipelined 82370 SLAVE
"              cycles.
"
"(c) Intel Corporation 1989. This PAL is provided as a proposed
"method of solving a certain 82370 Timer Unit problem. This PAL
"has not been tested or validated. Please validate this solution
"for your system and application.
"
"Input Pins"



CLK2           pin       1; "System Clock
RESET          pin       2; "Microprocessor RESET signal
TMR            pin       3; "Input from Address Decoder, indicating
                             "an access to the timer unit of the
                             "82370.
!RDY           pin       4; "End of Cycle indicator
!ADS           pin       5; "Address and control strobe
CLK            pin       6; "PHI2 clock
W_R            pin       7; "Write/Read Signal"
nc1            pin       8; "No Connect 0"
nc3            pin       9; "No Connect 1"
GNDa           pin      10; "Tied to ground, documentation only
GNDb           pin      11; "Output enable, documentation only
CLKIN_IN       pin      12; "Input-CLKIN directly from oscillator

"Output Pins"
Q_0            pin      18; "Internal signal only, fed back to
                             "PAL logic"
CLKIN_OUT      pin      17; "CLKIN signal fed to 82370 Timer Unit
INHIBIT        pin      16; "CLKIN Inhibit signal
S0             pin      15; "Unused State Indicator Pin
S1             pin      14; "Unused State Indicator Pin

"Declarations"
```

```
Valid_ADS = ADS & CLK    ; "#ADS sampled in PHI1 of 80376 T-State
Valid_RDY = RDY & CLK    ; "#RDY sampled in PHI1 of 80376 T-State
Timer_Acc = TMR & CLK    ; "Timer Unit Access, as provided by
                            "external Address Decoder"


State_Diagram [INHIBIT, S1, S0]

state 000:      if RESET then 000
                else if Valid_ADS & W_R then 001
                else 000;

state 001:      if RESET then 000
                else if Timer_Acc then 010
                else if !Timer_Acc then 000
                else 001;

state 010:      if RESET then 000
                else if CLK then 110
                else 010;

state 110:      if RESET then 000
                else if CLK then 111
                else 110;

state 111:      if RESET then 000
                else if CLK then 011
                else 111;

state 011:      if RESET then 000
                else if Valid_RDY then 000
                else 011;

state 100:      if RESET then 000
                else 000;

state 101:      if RESET then 000
                else 000;

EQUATIONS
Q_0 := CLKIN_IN; "Latched incoming clock. This signal is used
                    "internally to feed into the MUX-ing logic"


CLKIN_OUT := (INHIBIT & CLKIN_OUT & !RESET)
            +(!INHIBIT & Q_0 & !RESET);


                    "Equation for CLKIN_OUT. This
                    "feeds directly to the 82370 Timer Unit."


END
```

82370 Timer Unit CLKIN
    INHIBIT signal PAL Solution
Equations for Module Timer__82370__Fix

Device Timer__Unit__Fix

—Reduced Equations:

    !!INHIBIT := (!CLK & !!INHIBIT # CLK & S0 # RESET # !S1);

    !S1 := (RESET
        # INHIBIT & !S1
        # CLK & !!INHIBIT & !~RDY & S0 & S1
        # !CLK & !S1
        # !S1 & !TMR
        # !S0 & !S1);

    !S0 := (RESET
        # INHIBIT & !S1
        # CLK & !!INHIBIT & !~RDY & S1
        #!!INHIBIT & !S0 & S1
        # !CLK & !S0
        # !INHIBIT & !S0 & S1
        # S0 & !S1
        # !S1 & !W__R
        # ~ADS & !S̄1);

    !Q__0 := (!CLKIN__IN);

    !CLKIN__OUT := (RESET # !CLKIN__OUT & INHIBIT # !!INHIBIT & !Q__0);

82370 Timer Unit CLKIN
  INHIBIT signal PAL Solution
Chip diagram for Module Timer__82370__Fix

Device Timer__Unit__Fix

P16R6

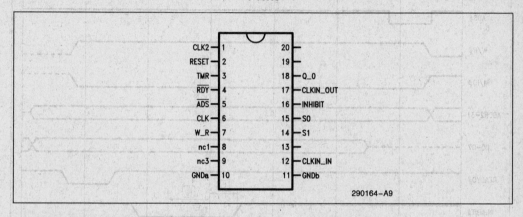

CLK2	1	20
RESET	2	19
TMR	3	18 — Q_0
RDY̅	4	17 — CLKIN_OUT
A̅D̅S̅	5	16 — INHIBIT
CLK	6	15 — S0
W_R	7	14 — S1
nc1	8	13
nc3	9	12 — CLKIN_IN
GNDa	10	11 — GNDb

290164–A9

end of module Timer__82370__Fix

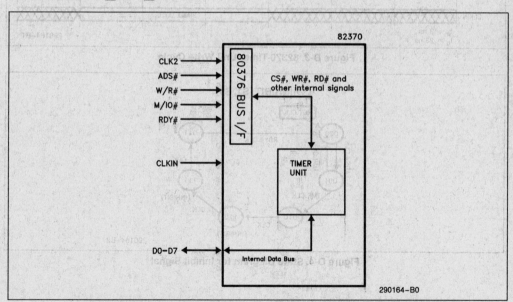

Figure D-2. Translation of 80376 Signals to Internal 82370 Timer Unit Signals

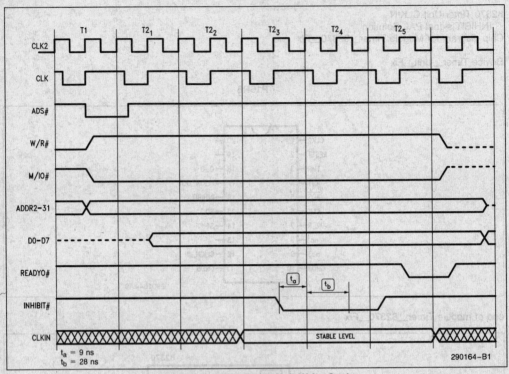

t_a = 9 ns
t_b = 28 ns

290164-B1

Figure D-3. 82370 Timer Unit Write Cycle

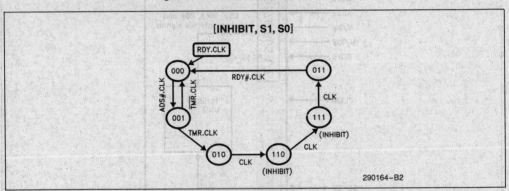

[INHIBIT, S1, S0]

290164-B2

Figure D-4. State Diagram for Inhibit Signal

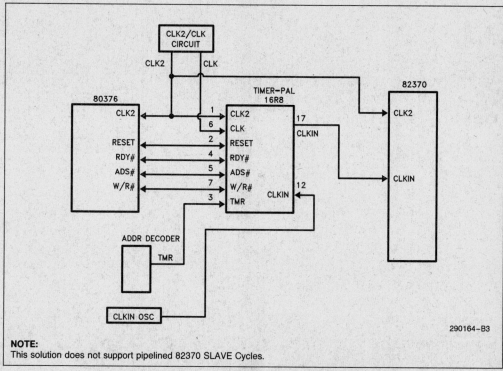

NOTE:
This solution does not support pipelined 82370 SLAVE Cycles.

Figure D-5. System with 82370 Timer Unit "INHIBIT" Circuitry

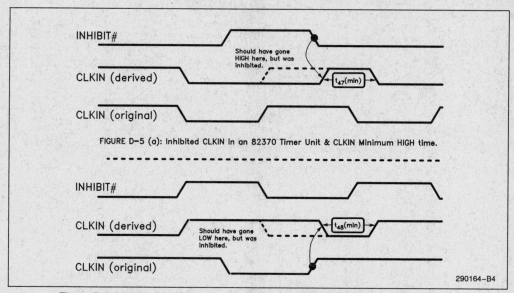

FIGURE D-5 (a): Inhibited CLKIN in an 82370 Timer Unit & CLKIN Minimum HIGH time.

Figure D-6. Inhibited CLKIN in an 82370 Timer Unit and CLKIN Minimum LOW Time

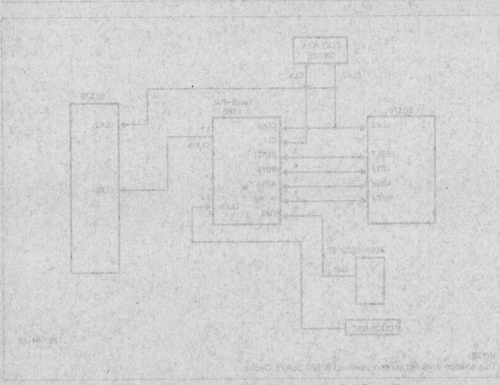

NOTE:
This solution does not support pipelined 82370 SLAVE Cycles.

Figure D-6. System with 82370 Timer Unit "INHIBIT" Circuitry

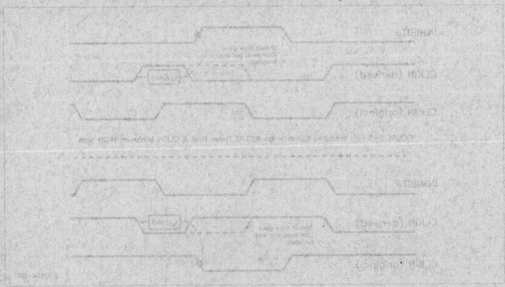

FIGURE D-5 (a). Inhibited CLKIN in the 82370 Timer Unit & CLKIN Minimum HIGH Time

Figure D-5. Inhibited CLKIN in an 82370 Timer Unit and CLKIN Minimum LOW Time

376™ Development Support Tools

9

COMPREHENSIVE DEVELOPMENT SUPPORT FOR THE INTEL386™ FAMILY OF MICROPROCESSORS

The perfect complement to the Intel386™ Family of microprocessors is the optimum development solution. From a single source, Intel, comes a complete, synergistic hardware and software development toolset, delivering full access to the power of the Intel386 architecture in a way that only Intel can.

Intel development tools are easy to use, yet powerful, with contemporary user interface techniques and productivity boosting features such as symbolic debugging. And you'll find Intel first to market with the tools needed to start development, and with lasting product quality and comprehensive support to keep development on-track.

If what interests you is getting the best product to market in as little time as possible, Intel is the choice.

FEATURES

- Comprehensive support for the full 32 bit Intel386 architecture, including protected mode and 4 gigabyte physical memory addressing
- Source display and symbolics allow debugging in the context of the original program
- Architectural extensions in Intel high-level languages provides for manipulating hardware directly without assembly language routines

- A common object code format (OMF-386™) supports the intermixing of modules written in various languages
- ROM-able code is output directly from the language tools, significantly reducing the effort necessary to integrate software into the final target system
- Support for the 80387 numeric coprocessor
- Operation in DOS and VAX*/VMS* environments

© Intel Corporation 1989

February, 1989
Order Number: 280808-002

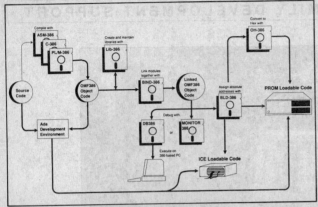

Figure 1. Intel Microprocessor Development Environment

ASM-386™ MACRO ASSEMBLER

ASM-386™ is a "high-level" macro assembler for the Intel386 Family. ASM-386 offers many features normally found only in high-level languages. The macro facility in ASM-386 saves development time by allowing common program sequences to be coded only once. The assembly language is strongly typed, performing extensive checks on the usage of variables and labels.

Other ASM-386 features include:

- "High-level" assembler mnemonics to simplify the language
- Structures and records for data representation
- Upward compatibility with ASM-286

PL/M-386™ COMPILER

PL/M-386™ is a structured high-level system implementation language for the Intel386 Family. PL/M-386 supports the implementation of protected operating system software by providing built-in procedures and variables to access the Intel386 architecture.

For efficient code generation, PL/M-386 features four levels of optimization, a virtual symbol table, and four models of program size and memory usage.

Other PL/M-386 features include:

- The ability to define a procedure as an interrupt handler as well as facilities for generating interrupts
- Direct support of byte, half-word, and word input and output from microprocessor ports
- Upward compatibility with PL/M-286 and PL/M-86 source code

PL/M-386 combines the benefits of a high-level language with the ability to access the Intel386 architecture. For the development of systems software, PL/M-386 is a cost-effective alternative to assembly language programming.

C-386™ COMPILER

C-386™ brings the C language to the Intel386 Family. For code efficiency, C-386 features two levels of optimization, three models of program size and memory usage, and an extremely efficient register allocator. The C-386 compiler eliminates common code, eliminates redundant loads and stores, and resolves span dependencies (shortens branches) within a program.

C-386 allows full access to the Intel386 architecture through control of bit fields, pointers, addresses, and register allocations.

Other C-386 features include:

- An interrupt directive defining a function as an interrupt function
- Built-in functions allow direct access to the microprocessor through the inline insertion of machine code
- Structure assignments, functions taking structure arguments, and returning structures, and the void and enum data types

The C-386 runtime library is implemented in layers. The upper layers include the standard I/O library (STDIO), memory management routines, conversion routines, and string manipulation routines. The lowest layer, operating system interface routines, is documented for adaptation to the target environment.

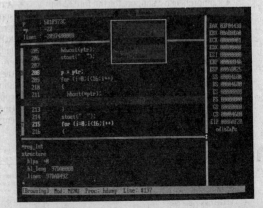

RLL-386™ RELOCATION, LINKAGE, AND LIBRARY TOOLS

The RLL-386™ relocation, linkage, and library tools are a cohesive set of utilities featuring comprehensive support of the full Intel386 architecture. RLL-386 provides for a variety of functions—from linking separate modules, building an object library, or linking in 80387 support, to building a task to execute under protected mode or the multi-tasking, memory protected system software itself.

The RLL-386 relocation, linkage, and library tools package includes a program binder for linking ASM, PL/M, and C modules together, a system builder for configuring protected, multi-task systems, a cross reference mapper, a program librarian, an 80387 numeric coprocessor support library, and a conversion utility for outputing hex format code for PROM programming.

Ada-386™ CROSS COMPILATION PACKAGE

The Ada-386™ Cross-Compilation Package is a complete development environment for embedded real-time Ada applications for the 386™ microprocessor. The Ada cross compiler, which runs under VAX/VMS, generates code highly optimized for the 80386. The Ada-386 Cross-Compilation Package also features a VMS hosted and targeted compiler and tools to support software debugging before the target system is available. Sophisticated code generation tools, such as the Global Optimizer, help make the target code smaller and more efficient.

Ada-386 includes a source level symbolic debugger working in unison with a small debug monitor supplied in PROM. Code can also be downloaded and debugged using Intel's ICE™-386 In-Circuit Emulator.

Other Ada-386 features include:

- The ability to directly call Intel's iRMK real-time kernel
- An object module importer allows program modules written in other Intel386 Family languages to be linked with Ada modules
- Built in support for the 386, including machine code insertion and full representation specifications
- Highly optimized interrupt handling—fast execution of interrupt handlers without requiring a context switch

INTEL386™ FAMILY IN-CIRCUIT EMULATORS

Intel386 Family in-circuit emulators embody exclusive technology that gives the emulator access to internal processor states that are accessible in no other way. Intel386 microprocessors fetch and execute instructions in parallel; fetched instructions are not necessarily executed. Because of this, an emulator without this access to internal processor states is prone to error in determining what actually occurred inside the microprocessor. With Intel's exclusive technology, Intel386 Family emulators are one hundred percent accurate.

Other features of Intel386 Family in-circuit emulators include:

- Unparalleled support of the Intel386 architecture, notably the native protected mode
- Emulation at clock speeds to 25MHz and full-featured trigger and trace capabilities
- Non-intrusive operation
- Convertible to support any Intel386 microprocessor

With symbolic debugging, memory locations can be examined or modified using symbolic references to the original program, such as a procedure or a variable name, line number, or program label. Source code associated with a given line number can be displayed, as can the type information of variables, such as byte, word, record, or array. Microprocessor data structures, such as registers, descriptor tables, and page tables, can also be examined and modified using symbolic names. The symbolic debugging information for use with Intel development tools is produced only by Intel languages.

DOS-RESIDENT SOFTWARE DEBUGGER

DB386™ is an on-host software execution environment with source-level symbolic debug capabilities for object modules produced by Intel's ASM-386, iC-386, and PL/M-386 translators. This software debug environment allows 386 code to be executed and debugged directly on a 386 or 386SX-™microprocessor based PC, without any additional target hardware required. With Intel's standard windowed human interface, users can focus their efforts on finding bugs rather than spending time learning and manipulating the debug environment.

- **Supports key features of the 386™ architecture.** A run-time interface allows protected-mode 386 programs to be executed directly on a 386- or 386SX-based PC.
- **Ease of learning.** Drop-down menus make the tool easy to learn for new or casual users. A command line interface is also provided for more complex problems.
- **Extensive debug modes.** Watch windows (display user-specified variables), trace points, and breakpoints (including fixed, temporary, and conditional) can be set and modified as needed, even during a debug session.
- **See into the 386 application.** The user can browse source and call stacks, observe processor registers, and access watch window variables by either the pull down menu or by a single keystroke using the function keys. An easy-to-use disassembler and single-line assembler can also speed the debug process.

DOS-RESIDENT SOFTWARE DEBUGGER (continued)

- **Full debug symbolics for maximum productivity.** The user need not know whether a variable is an unsigned integer, a real, or a structure. The debugger utilizes the wealth of typing information available in Intel languages to display program variables in their respective type formats.

MONITOR-386™ SOFTWARE DEBUGGER

MONITOR-386™ is a software debugger primarily for non-PC 386 and 386SX microprocessor based target systems. The monitor allows 386 software applications to be downloaded and symbolically debugged on virtually any target system using the 386 architecture. MONITOR-386, used in conjunction with Intel single board computers iSBC® 386/22 and iSBC 386/116, can debug software before a functional prototype of the target system is available.

- **Breakpoints.** Both hardware and software breakpoints can be set at symbolic addresses.
- **Program Execution.** Users can single-step through assembly or high-level language applications.
- **Debug Procedures.** MONITOR-386 command sequences can be defined as macros, significantly reducing the amount of repetitive information which needs to be entered.
- **Disassembler/Single Line Assembler.** Users can display and patch memory with 80386/80387 mnemonics.

iPAT-386™ PERFORMANCE ANALYSIS TOOL

iPAT-386™ performance analysis tool provides analysis of real-time software executing on a 386-based target system. With iPAT-386, it is possible to speed-tune applications, optimize use of operating systems, determine response characteristics, and identify code execution coverage.

By examining iPAT-386 histogram and tabular information about procedure usage (with the option of including interaction with other procedures, hardware, the operating system, or interrupt service routines) for critical functions, performance bottlenecks can be identified. With iPAT-386 code execution coverage information, the completeness of testing can be confirmed. iPAT-386 can be used in conjunction with Intel's ICE-386™ in-circuit emulator to control test conditions.

iPAT-386 provides real-time analysis up to 20MHz, performance profiles of up to 125 partitions, and code execution coverage analysis over 252K.

Intel386, 386, 386SX, 376, ICE, and iSBC are trademarks of Intel Corporation. VAX and VMS are registered trademarks of Digital Equipment Corporation.

SERVICE, SUPPORT, AND TRAINING

To augment its development tools, Intel offers a full array of seminars, classes, and workshops, field application engineering expertise, hotline technical support, and on-site service.

PRODUCT SUPPORT MATRIX

Product	Component			Host	
	386	386sx	376	DOS	VAX/VMS
ASM-386 Macro Assembler	✓	✓	✓	✓	✓
PL/M-386 Compiler	✓	✓	✓	✓	✓
C-386 Compiler	✓	✓	✓	✓	✓
RLL-386 Relocation, Linkage, and Library tools	✓	✓	✓	✓	✓
Ada-386 Cross Compilation Package	✓				✓
Intel386 Family In-Circuit Emulators	✓	✓	✓	✓	
Windowed Software Debugger	✓	✓		✓	
Monitor-386 Software Debugger	✓	✓		✓	
iPAT-386 Performance Analysis Tool	✓			✓	

ORDERING INFORMATION

For direct information on Intel's Development Tools, or for the number of your nearest sales office or distributor, call 800-874-6835 (U.S.). For information or literature on additional Intel products, call 800-548-4725 (U.S. and Canada).

UNITED STATES, Intel Corporation
3065 Bowers Ave., Santa Clara, CA 95051
Tel: (408) 765-8080

JAPAN, Intel Japan K.K.
5-6 Tokodai, Tsukuba-shi,
Ibaraki, 300-26
Tel: 029747-8511

FRANCE, Intel Corporation S.A.R.L.
1, Rue Edison, BP 303,
78054 Saint-Quentin-en-Yvelines Cedex
Tel: (33) 1-30 57 70 00

UNITED KINGDOM, Intel Corporation (U.K.) Ltd.
Pipers Way, Swindon, Wiltshire, England SN3 1RJ
Tel: (0793) 696000

WEST GERMANY, Intel Semiconductor GmbH
Dornacher Strasse 1, 8016 Feldkirchen bei Muenchen
Tel: 089/90 99 20

HONG KONG, Intel Semiconductor Ltd.
10/F East Tower, Bond Center,
Queensway, Central
Tel: (5) 8444-555

CANADA, Intel Semiconductor of Canada, Ltd.
190 Attwell Drive, Suite 500
Rexdale, Ontario M9W 6H8
Tel. (416) 675-2105

ACCURATE AND SOPHISTICATED EMULATION FOR THE INTEL386™ FAMILY OF MICROPROCESSORS

Intel386™ In-Circuit Emulators are the cornerstone of the optimum development solution for the Intel386 family of microprocessors. From the inventor of the microprocessor comes a development tool that delivers absolute access to the sophistication of the architecture in a way that only Intel can.

Productivity boosting features such as symbolic debugging make Intel386 emulators easy to use and powerful. Intel product quality and world class technical support and service minimizes the "downtime" incurred in resolving problems. And your investment in development tools is protected via interchangeable probes for the 386™, 386SX™, and 376™ processors.

Maximize your productivity with Intel development tools. Reduced time to market and increased market acceptance for your microprocessor-based product are the benefits when Intel is the choice.

FEATURES

- Exclusive technology giving access to internal processor states provides absolutely accurate emulation history
- Unparalleled support of all of the Intel386 operating modes opens the door to the full potential of the Intel386 architecture
- Non-intrusive emulation to processor speeds of 25MHz
- Versatile event recognition makes short work of uncovering complex bugs

- Dynamic trace display of bus and execution information during emulation
- A comprehensive software development system creates the most complete development environment available from a single vendor
- A companion performance analysis tool provides analysis of software for optimized performance and reliability

© Intel Corporation 1989

October, 1989
Order Number: 280850-001

ABSOLUTELY ACCURATE EMULATION

Intel386 Family in-circuit emulators embody exclusive technology that accesses internal processor states that are otherwise invisible. Intel386 microprocessors fetch and execute instructions in parallel; fetched instructions are not necessarily executed. Because of this, an emulator without this capability is prone to error in determining what actually occurred inside the microprocessor. With Intel's exclusive technology, an Intel386 emulator displays execution history with one hundred percent accuracy.

OPENING THE DOOR TO PROTECTED MODE

Intel386 emulators open the door to the full potential of the architecture with unparalleled support of protected mode. Not only does the emulator display and modify task state segments and global, local, and interrupt descriptor tables (with symbolic access to all descriptor components like privilege level and segment type), but emulator functions are sensitive to the operating mode of the processor, greatly improving ease of use.

Intel386 emulators support all aspects of protected mode addressing, including paged virtual memory. Processor tables are used to automatically translate virtual addresses to linear and physical addresses. Physical addresses can be translated to symbolic references to indicate the module, procedure, or data segment accessed. And when debugging a memory management system, components of the page table and directory can be displayed and modified.

FLEXIBLE AND VERSATILE EVENT RECOGNITION

Flexibility and versatility in event recognition makes short work of uncovering the most complex bugs. Bus event recognition circuitry may be used to trigger on specific or masked data input, output, read, written, or fetched at a physical address or range of addresses. Or on-chip debug registers may be used to trigger on virtual, linear, or symbolic addresses being executed, accessed, or written.

Versatility shows in other triggering options—upon a task switch, an external signal from another emulator or a logic analyzer, multiple occurrences of an event, a full trace buffer, halt or shutdown cycles, or interrupt acknowledge. And up to four sequential event triggers can be combined with a high-level construct.

Intel386 emulators continuously capture all bus activity, and optionally execution information, into a trace buffer of 4096 frames with PRE, POST, and CENTERED collection modes. The contents of the trace buffer can be displayed during full speed emulation in either execution cycle or machine-level instruction formats. Symbolic information can optionally be included in the trace display. A third trace display, the current chain of procedure calls, can be displayed when emulating high-level language programs.

SPEEDING DEVELOPMENT WITH SYMBOLICS

Intel386 processor data structures, such as registers, descriptor tables, and page tables, can be examined and modified using symbolic names. And with the symbolic debugging information that is a feature of Intel languages, memory locations can be accessed using symbolic references to the source program (such as a procedure and variable names, line numbers, or program labels) rather than via cumbersome virtual, linear, or physical addresses. The type information of variables (such as byte, word, record, or array) can also be displayed.

ACCESSING THE POWER

The power of the Intel386 emulator is reflected in the sophisticated user interface. Refined for ease of use, the command line interface contains many features to boost productivity and customize functionality.

On-line help, a syntax menu, command line editing, command history, and error message query promote ease of learning and use. I/O redirection and the ability to escape to the host operating system provide versatility for the power user. Customized procedures with variables and literal definitions can be created to assist in debugging or for manufacturing test or field service applications.

SYSTEM CONNECTIVITY AND CONFIGURATION

The Intel386 emulator can be combined with a variety of devices. I/O lines synchronize emulation starts and triggers with external tools such as a logic analyzer or another emulator. An optional time tag board synchronizes multiple Intel386 emulators and records timestamp information in the trace buffer with 20 nanosecond resolution. An optional clips pod supplements two general purpose input lines with eight data lines captured and displayed in the trace. The bus isolation board buffers the emulation processor from faults in an untested target. And with the stand-alone/self-test board the emulator can be used to debug software before the target system is functional, as well as execute confidence tests.

THE INVESTMENT PICTURE

As designs move from one Intel386 Family processor to another, the reinvestment cost is limited to probes that adapt the emulator base to the specific processor. Beside cost savings, migration from one processor to another is accomplished with minimum disruption in the engineering environment, as the same command language applies to the entire emulator family.

FEATURES

SOFTWARE COMPLETES THE SYSTEM

Intel wraps a comprehensive software development system around the emulator to deliver the most complete development environment available from a single vendor. Like the emulator, Intel's software development system supports every aspect of the Intel386 architecture.

Overlooked at times is that a significant part of developing a system is making sure the code works. Intel languages integrate seamlessly with the Intel386 emulator and provide the symbolics so important for efficient debugging. Only by using Intel languages with the Intel386 emulator can the full power of Intel development solution be utilized.

The software development system offers a broad choice of languages with object code compatibility so performance can be maximized by using different languages for specialized, performance critical modules. Architectural extensions in the high-level languages allows hardware features such as interrupts, input/output, or flags to be controlled directly, avoiding the tediousness of coding assembly language routines.

Intel's software portfolio includes a unique, sophisticated, and very powerful system builder, simplifying the generation of protected mode systems. To further reduce the effort necessary to integrate software into the final target configuration, Intel tools produce ROM-able code directly from the development system.

OPTIMIZING PERFORMANCE AND RELIABILITY

A companion performance analysis tool, iPAT™-386, provides analysis of real-time software executing on 80386-based target systems. With iPAT-386, it is possible to speed-tune applications, optimize use of operating systems, determine response characteristics, and identify code execution coverage. And iPAT-386 can be used in conjunction with an Intel386 in-circuit emulator to control test conditions.

WORLD CLASS, WORLDWIDE SERVICES

Augmenting the Intel386 Family development tools is a full array of seminars, classes and workshops; on-site consulting services; field application engineering expertise; telephone hotline support; and software and hardware maintenance contracts.

No one can match Intel's motivation to supply you with the absolute best in microprocessor development tools. When the heart of your design is an Intel microprocessor, Intel development tools help to insure we both enjoy continued success.

ORDERING INFORMATION

ICE376D	In-circuit emulator for 80376 component. Operates to 16MHz. Includes control unit, power supply, 376 processor module with PQFP adaptor, stand-alone self-test board, isolation board, and DOS host software and interface cable.
ICE376DAB	Identical to ICE376D with PC/AT® compatible 2MB Above Board.
ICE386SXD	In-circuit emulator for 80386SX component. Operates to 16MHz. Includes control unit, power supply, 386SX processor module with PQFP adaptor, stand-alone self-test board, isolation board, and DOS host software and interface cable.
ICE386SXDAB	Identical to ICE386SXD with PC/AT compatible 2MB Above Board.

ICE38625D	In-circuit emulator for 80386 component. Operates to 25MHz. Includes control unit, power supply, 386 processor module with 132 pin PGA adaptor, stand-alone self-test board, isolation board, and DOS host software and interface cable.
ICE38625DAB	Identical to ICE38625D with PC/AT compatible 2MB Above Board.
ICE376TO386SXD	Conversion kit to adapt ICE376D to support the 80386SX component. Operates to 16MHz. Includes 386SX processor module and DOS host software.
ICE376TO386D	Conversion kit to adapt ICE376D to support the 80386 component. Operates to 25MHz. Includes 386 processor module and DOS host software.

ICE386SXTO376D   Conversion kit to adapt ICE386SXD to support the 80376 component. Operates to 16MHz. Includes 376 processor module and DOS host software.

ICE386SXTO386D   Conversion kit to adapt ICE386SXD to support the 80386 component. Operates to 25MHz. Includes 386 processor module and DOS host software.

ICE386TO376D   Conversion kit to adapt ICE38625D to support the 80376 component. Operates to 16MHz. Includes 376 processor module and DOS host software.

ICE386TO386SXD   Conversion kit to adapt ICE38625D to support the 80386SX component. Operates to 16MHz. Includes 386SX processor module and DOS host software.

88PGAADAPT   Adaptor for ICE376D to support 88 pin PGA component packaging.

ICE3XXCPO   Clips Pod Option for ICE376D, ICE386SXD, and ICE38625D.

ICE3XXTTB   Time Tag Board Option for ICE376D, ICE386SXD, and ICE38625D.

For more information on Intel's Development Tools, or for the number of your nearest sales office or distributor, call 800-874-6835 (U.S.). For information or literature on additional Intel products, call 800-548-4725 (U.S. and Canada).

HOST SYSTEM REQUIREMENTS

The user supplied host system can be either an IBM® PC/AT® or Personal System/2® Model 60. Host system requirements to run the emulator include the following:

- DOS version 3.2
- 640K bytes of RAM in conventional memory
- An Above™ board with 1 megabyte of RAM configured in expanded memory mode, EMM.SYS software version 3.2
- A 20 MB hard disk

- A serial port or the National Instruments GPIB-PCII™, GPIB-PCIIA™, or MC-GPIB™ board
- A math coprocessor if either the optional time tag board is used or if a math coprocessor resides on the target system

ELECTRICAL CHARACTERISTICS

100-120V or 220-240V selectable
50-60 Hz
2 amps (AC max) @ 120V
1 amp (AC max) @ 240V

ENVIRONMENTAL CHARACTERISTICS

Operating temperature: +10 C to +40 C
(50 to 104 F)
Operating Humidity: Maximum of 85% relative humidity, non-condensing

The Emulator's Physical Characteristics

Unit	Width		Height		Length	
	inches	cm	inches	cm	inches	cm
Base Unit	13.4	34.0	4.6	11.7	11.0	27.9
Processor Module	3.8	9.7	0.7	1.8	4.4	11.2
Optional Isolation Board	3.8	9.7	0.5	1.3	4.4	11.2
Power Supply	7.7	19.6	4.1	10.4	11.0	27.9
User Cable	1.9	4.8			17.3	43.9
100-Pin Target-Adapter Cable	2.3	5.3	0.5	1.3	5.1	13.0
88-Pin Target-Adapter Cable	2.3	5.3	0.5	1.3	5.8	14.7
Serial Cable					144	366
Optional Clips Pod	3.3	8.4	0.8	2.0	6.0	15.2

The Processor Module and BIB Dimensions

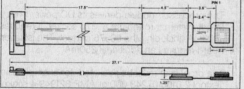
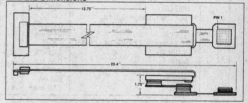

ELECTRICAL SPECIFICATIONS

The synchronization input lines must be valid for at least four CLK2 cycles as they are only sampled on every other cycle. These input lines are standard TTL inputs. The synchronization output lines are driven by TTL open

collector outputs that have 4.7K-ohm pull-up resistors. The synchronization input and output signals on the optional clips pod are standard TTL input and outputs.

AC Specifications With the Bus Isolation Board Installed.

Symbol	Parameter	Minimum	Maximum	Notes
t1	CLK2 period	50 nS	t1 Max	
t2a	CLK2 high time	t2a Min + 2 nS		@ 2V
t3b	CLK2 low time	t3b Min + 2 nS		@ 0.8v
t6	A1-A23 valid delay	t6 Min + 3.5 nS	t6 Max + 24.6 nS	CL = 120 pF
t7	A1-A23 float delay	t14 Min + 5.5 nS	t14 Max + 37.6 nS	
t8	BLE#, BHE# LOCK# valid delay	t8 Min + 3.5 nS	t8 Max + 24.6	CL = 75pF
t9	BLE#, BHE# LOCK# float delay	t14 Min + 5.5 nS	t14 Max + 37.6	
t10	W/R#, M/IO#, D/C#, ADS# valid delay	t10 Min + 3.5 nS	t10 Min + 24.6	CL = 75 pF
t11	W/R#, M/IO#, D/C#, ADS# float delay	t14 Min + 5.5 nS	t14 Max + 37.6	
t12	D0-D15 write data valid delay	t12 Min + 4.5 nS	t12 Max + 20.6	CL = 120 pF
t13	D0-D15 write data float delay	7.5 nS	45.6 nS	
t14	HLDA valid delay	t14 Min = 3 nS	t14 Max + 21.2 nS	
t16	NA# hold time	t16 Min + 10.6 nS		
t20	READY# hold time	t20 Min + 10.6 nS		
t21	D0-D15 read setup time	t21 Min + 8.5 nS		
t22	D0-D15 read hold time	t22 Min + 7.6 nS		
t24	HOLD hold time	t24 Min + 10.6 nS		
t25	RESET setup time	t25 Min + 2.1 nS		
t26	RESET hold time	t26 Min + 2.1 nS		
t28	NMI, INTR hold time	t28 Min + 10.6 nS		
t30	PEREQ, ERROR#, BUSY# hold time	t30 Min + 10.6 nS		

SPECIFICATIONS

Emulator Capacitance Specifications
With Target-Adapter Cable Installed

Symbol	Description	Typical (Note 1)
C_{IN}	Input Capacitance	
	CLK2	55pF
	READY#, ERROR#	35pF
	HOLD, BUSY#, PEREQ, NA#,	
	INTR, NMI	20pF
	RESET	30pF
C_{OUT}	Output or I/O Capacitance	
	D15-D0	50pF
	A15-A1, BLE#	40pF
	A23-A16, BHE#, D/C#	30pF
	HLDA, W/R#	55pF
	ADS#, M/IO#, LOCK#	35pF

Note 1: Not tested. These specifications include the 80376 component and all additional emulator loading.

Emulator DC Specifications
Without the BIB Installed

Item	Description	Max.	Notes
PM-I_{CC}	Processor Module Supply Current	376-I_{CC} + 940 mA	
I_{IH}	Input High Leakage Current		
	A23-A1, BLE#, BHE#, D/C#, HLDA	0.02 mA	1
	D15-D0	0.06 mA	1
	ADS#, M/IO#, LOCK#, READY#,		
	ERROR#	0.01 mA	1
	W/R#	0.03 mA	1
	CLK2	0.04 mA	1
	RESET	0.06 mA	2
I_{IL}	Input Low Leakage Current		
	A23-A1, BLE#, BHE#, D/C#	0.6 mA	1
	D15-D0	0.06 mA	1
	ADS#, M/IO#, LOCK#, READY#,		
	ERROR#	0.01 mA	1
	W/R#	0.51 mA	1
	CLK2	0.62 mA	1
	RESET	0.6 mA	2
	HLDA	0.02 mA	1

Note 1: This specification is the DC input loading of the emulator circuitry only and does not include any 80376 leakage current.

Note 2: This specification replaces the 80376 specification for this signal.

Emulator DC Specifications
With the BIB Installed

Item	Description	Min.	Max.
BIB-I_{CC}	BIB Supply Current		PM-I_{CC} + 350 mA
V_{OL}	Output Low Voltage (I_{OL} = 48 mA)		
	A23-A1, BLE#, BHE#, D/C#, ADS#		0.5 v
	D15-D0, M/IO#, LOCK#, W/R#		0.5 v
	HLDA (I_{OL} = 24 mA)		0.44 v
V_{OH}	Output High Voltage (I_{OH} = 3 mA)		
	A23-A1, BLE#, BHE#, D/C#, ADS#	2.4 v	
	D15-D0, M/IO#, LOCK#, W/R#	2.4 v	
	HLDA (I_{OH} = 24 mA)	3.8 v	
I_{IH}	Input High Current		
	CLK2, RESET		1.0 μA
	READY#		25 μA
I_{IL}	Input Low Current		
	CLK2, RESET		1.0 μA
	READY#		250 μA
I_{IO}	Output Leakage Current		
	A23-A1, BLE#, BHE#, D/C#, ADS#		± 20 μA
	D15-D0, M/IO#, LOCK#, W/R#		± 20 μA

PROCESSOR MODULE INTERFACE CONSIDERATIONS

With the processor module directly attached to the target system without using the bus isolation board (BIB), the target system must meet the following requirements:

- The user bus controller must only drive the data bus during a valid read cycle of the emulator processor or while the emulator processor is in a hold state (the emulator processor uses the data bus to communicate with the emulator hardware).
- Before driving the address bus, the user must gain control by asserting HOLD and receiving HLDA.
- The user reset signal is disabled during the interrogation mode. It is enabled in emulation, but is delayed by 2 or 4 CLK2 cycles.
- The user system must be able to drive one additional TTL load on all signals that go to the emulation processor.

When the target system does not satisfy the first two restrictions, the bus isolation board is used to isolate the emulation processor from the target system. With the isolation board installed, the processor CLK2 is restricted to running at 20 MHz.

The processor module derives its DC power from the target system through the 80376 socket. It requires 1400mA, including the 80376 current. The isolation board requires an additional 350mA.

The processor must be socketed, for example using Textool 2-0100-07243-000 or AMP 821949-4 sockets.

The printed circuit board design should locate the processor socket at the physical ends of the printed circuit board traces that connect the processor to the other logic of the target system. This reduces transmission line noise. Additionally, if the target system is enclosed in a box, pin one of the processor socket should be oriented away from the target system's box opening to make connecting the target-adapter cable easier.

For direct information on Intel's Development Tools, or for the number of your nearest sales office or distributor, call 800-874-6835 (U.S.). For information or literature on additional Intel products, call 800-548-4725 (U.S. and Canada).

DOMESTIC SALES OFFICES

ALABAMA

†Intel Corp.
5015 Bradford Dr., #2
Huntsville 35805
Tel: (205) 830-4010
FAX: (205) 837-2640

ARIZONA

†Intel Corp.
11225 N. 28th Dr.
Suite D-214
Phoenix 85029
Tel: (602) 869-4980
FAX: (602) 869-4294

Intel Corp.
1161 N. El Dorado Place
Suite 301
Tucson 85715
Tel: (602) 299-6815
FAX: (602) 296-8234

CALIFORNIA

†Intel Corp.
21515 Vanowen Street
Suite 116
Canoga Park 91303
Tel: (818) 704-8500
FAX: (818) 340-1144

†Intel Corp.
2250 E. Imperial Highway
Suite 218
El Segundo 90245
Tel: (213) 640-6040
FAX: (213) 640-7133

Intel Corp.
1510 Arden Way
Suite 101
Sacramento 95815
Tel: (916) 920-8096
FAX: (916) 920-8253

†Intel Corp.
9665 Chesapeake Dr.
Suite 325
San Diego 95123
Tel: (619) 292-8086
FAX: (619) 292-0628

†Intel Corp.*
400 N. Tustin Avenue
Suite 450
Santa Ana 92705
Tel: (714) 835-9642
TWX: 910-595-1114
FAX: (714) 541-9157

†Intel Corp.
San Tomas 4
2700 San Tomas Expressway
2nd Floor
Santa Clara 95051
Tel: (408) 986-8086
TWX: 910-338-0255
FAX: (408) 727-2620

COLORADO

Intel Corp.
4445 Northpark Drive
Suite 100
Colorado Springs 80907
Tel: (719) 594-6622
FAX: (303) 594-0720

†Intel Corp.*
650 S. Cherry St.
Suite 915
Denver 80222
Tel: (303) 321-8086
TWX: 910-931-2289
FAX: (303) 322-8670

CONNECTICUT

†Intel Corp.
301 Lee Farm Corporate Park
83 Wooster Heights Rd.
Danbury 06810
Tel: (203) 748-3130
FAX: (203) 794-0339

FLORIDA

†Intel Corp.
6363 N.W. 6th Way
Suite 100
Ft. Lauderdale 33309
Tel: (305) 771-0600
TWX: 510-956-9407
FAX: (305) 772-8193

†Intel Corp.
5850 T.G. Lee Blvd.
Suite 340
Orlando 32822
Tel: (407) 240-8000
FAX: (407) 240-8097

Intel Corp.
11300 4th Street North
Suite 170
St. Petersburg 33716
Tel: (813) 577-2413
FAX: (813) 578-1607

GEORGIA

Intel Corp.
20 Technology Parkway, N.W.
Suite 150
Norcross 30092
Tel: (404) 449-0541
FAX: (404) 605-9762

ILLINOIS

†Intel Corp.*
300 N. Martingale Road
Suite 400
Schaumburg 60173
Tel: (312) 605-8031
FAX: (312) 706-9762

INDIANA

†Intel Corp.
8777 Purdue Road
Suite 125
Indianapolis 46268
Tel: (317) 875-0623
FAX: (317) 875-8938

IOWA

Intel Corp.
1930 St. Andrews Drive N.E.
2nd Floor
Cedar Rapids 52402
Tel: (319) 393-1294

KANSAS

†Intel Corp.
10985 Cody St.
Suite 140, Bldg. D
Overland Park 66210
Tel: (913) 345-2727
FAX: (913) 345-2076

MARYLAND

†Intel Corp.*
10010 Junction Dr.
Suite 200
Annapolis Junction 20701
Tel: (301) 206-2860
FAX: (301) 206-3677
(301) 206-3678

MASSACHUSETTS

†Intel Corp.*
Westford Corp. Center
3 Carlisle Road
2nd Floor
Westford 01886
Tel: (508) 692-3222
TWX: 710-343-6333
FAX: (508) 692-7867

MICHIGAN

†Intel Corp.
7071 Orchard Lake Road
Suite 100
West Bloomfield 48322
Tel: (313) 851-8096
FAX: (313) 851-8770

MINNESOTA

†Intel Corp.
3500 W. 80th St.
Suite 360
Bloomington 55431
Tel: (612) 835-6722
TWX: 910-576-2867
FAX: (612) 831-6497

MISSOURI

†Intel Corp.
4203 Earth City Expressway
Suite 131
Earth City 63045
Tel: (314) 291-1990
FAX: (314) 291-4341

NEW JERSEY

†Intel Corp.*
Parkway 109 Office Center
328 Newman Springs Road
Red Bank 07701
Tel: (201) 747-2233
FAX: (201) 747-0983

†Intel Corp.
280 Corporate Center
75 Livingston Avenue
First Floor
Roseland 07068
Tel: (201) 740-0111
FAX: (201) 740-0626

NEW YORK

Intel Corp.*
850 Cross Keys Office Park
Fairport 14450
Tel: (716) 425-2750
TWX: 510-253-7391
FAX: (716) 223-2561

†Intel Corp.*
2950 Expressway Dr., South
Suite 130
Islandia 11722
Tel: (516) 231-3300
TWX: 510-227-6236
FAX: (516) 348-7939

†Intel Corp.
Westage Business Center
Bldg. 300, Route 9
Fishkill 12524
Tel: (914) 897-3860
FAX: (914) 897-3125

NORTH CAROLINA

†Intel Corp.
5800 Executive Center Dr.
Suite 105
Charlotte 28212
Tel: (704) 568-8966
FAX: (704) 535-2236

Intel Corp.
5540 Centerview Dr.
Suite 215
Raleigh 27606
Tel: (919) 851-9537
FAX: (919) 851-8974

OHIO

†Intel Corp.*
3401 Park Center Drive
Suite 220
Dayton 45414
Tel: (513) 890-5350
TWX: 810-450-2528
FAX: (513) 890-8658

†Intel Corp.*
25700 Science Park Dr.
Suite 100
Beachwood 44122
Tel: (216) 464-2736
TWX: 810-427-9298
FAX: (804) 282-0673

OKLAHOMA

Intel Corp.
6801 N. Broadway
Suite 115
Oklahoma City 73162
Tel: (405) 848-8086
FAX: (405) 840-9819

OREGON

†Intel Corp.
15254 N.W. Greenbrier Parkway
Building B
Beaverton 97005
Tel: (503) 645-8051
TWX: 910-467-8741
FAX: (503) 645-8181

PENNSYLVANIA

†Intel Corp.*
455 Pennsylvania Avenue
Suite 230
Fort Washington 19034
Tel: (215) 641-1000
TWX: 510-661-2077
FAX: (215) 641-0785

†Intel Corp.*
400 Penn Center Blvd.
Suite 610
Pittsburgh 15235
Tel: (412) 823-4970
FAX: (412) 829-7578

PUERTO RICO

†Intel Corp.
South Industrial Park
P.O. Box 910
Las Piedras 00671
Tel: (809) 733-8616

TEXAS

Intel Corp.
8911 Capital of Texas Hwy.
Austin 78759
Tel: (512) 794-8086
FAX: (512) 338-9335

†Intel Corp.*
12000 Ford Road
Suite 400
Dallas 75234
Tel: (214) 241-8087
FAX: (214) 484-1180

†Intel Corp.*
7322 S.W. Freeway
Suite 1490
Houston 77074
Tel: (713) 988-8086
TWX: 910-881-2490
FAX: (713) 988-3660

UTAH

†Intel Corp.
428 East 6400 South
Suite 104
Murray 84107
Tel: (801) 263-8051
FAX: (801) 268-1457

VIRGINIA

†Intel Corp.
1504 Santa Rosa Road
Suite 108
Richmond 23288
Tel: (804) 282-5668
FAX: (216) 464-2270

WASHINGTON

†Intel Corp.
155 108th Avenue N.E.
Suite 386
Bellevue 98004
Tel: (206) 453-8086
TWX: 910-443-3002
FAX: (206) 451-9556

Intel Corp.
408 N. Mullan Road
Suite 102
Spokane 99206
Tel: (509) 928-8086
FAX: (509) 928-9467

WISCONSIN

Intel Corp.
330 S. Executive Dr.
Suite 102
Brookfield 53005
Tel: (414) 784-8087
FAX: (414) 796-2115

CANADA

BRITISH COLUMBIA

Intel Semiconductor of
Canada, Ltd.
4585 Canada Way
Suite 202
Burnaby V5G 4L6
Tel: (604) 298-0387
FAX: (604) 298-8234

ONTARIO

†Intel Semiconductor of
Canada, Ltd.
2650 Queensview Drive
Suite 250
Ottawa K2B 8H6
Tel: (613) 829-9714
FAX: (613) 820-5936

†Intel Semiconductor of
Canada, Ltd.
190 Attwell Drive
Suite 500
Rexdale M9W 6H8
Tel: (416) 675-2105
FAX: (416) 675-2438

QUEBEC

Intel Semiconductor of
Canada, Ltd.
620 St. Jean Boulevard
Pointe Claire H9R 3K2
Tel: (514) 694-9130
FAX: 514-694-0064

†Sales and Service Office
*Field Application Location